CRIMINAL PROCEDURE
Eighth Edition

LexisNexis Law School Publishing Advisory Board

CRIMINAL PROCEDURE

Eighth Edition

JOSEPH G. COOK
Williford Gragg Professor of Law
University of Tennessee

PAUL MARCUS
Haynes Professor of Law
College of William and Mary

MELANIE D. WILSON
Associate Dean for Academic Affairs and
Professor of Law
University of Kansas

ISBN: 978–1–6304–3531–8 (casebook)
ISBN: 978–1–6304–3533–2 (looseleaf)
ISBN: 978–1–6304–3532–5 (eBook)

Library of Congress Cataloging-in-Publication Data

Cook, Joseph G., 1939- author.
Criminal procedure / Joseph G. Cook, Williford Gragg Professor of Law, University of Tennessee; Paul Marcus , Haynes Professor of Law, College of William and Mary; Melanie D. Wilson, Associate Dean for Academic Affairs and Professor of Law, University of Kansas. -- Eighth Edition.
p. cm.
Includes index.
ISBN 978-1-63043-531-8
1. Criminal procedure--United States. I. Marcus, Paul, author. II. Wilson, Melanie D., author. III. Title.
KF9618.C665 2014
345.73'05--dc23

2014012000

NOTE TO USERS
To ensure that you are using the latest materials available in this area, please be sure to periodically check the LexisNexis Law School web site for downloadable updates and supplements at www.lexisnexis.com/lawschool.

Editorial Offices
121 Chanlon Rd., New Providence, NJ 07974 (908) 464-6800
201 Mission St., San Francisco, CA 94105-1831 (415) 908-3200
www.lexisnexis.com

MATTHEW BENDER

(2014–Pub.669)

Dedication

This book is dedicated to:
Norma Cox Cook,
Becca Nimmer Marcus, and
L.M. Reeves.

Preface

Our purpose in this latest edition, as previously, has been to produce a classroom casebook of manageable length that stresses the interplay of constitutional principles and the practical considerations that confront both prosecution and defense attorneys. Lengthy Supreme Court decisions have been substantially edited, although hopefully the "flavor" of the constitutional views of the various Justices has been retained. The insertion of sample forms is intended to illustrate the manner in which Supreme Court edict has filtered down to work-a-day law enforcement and prosecution. Problems, for the most part extracted from lower court decisions, serve to demonstrate the vague parameters of Supreme Court pronouncements.

To achieve the result we sought, the major sacrifice has been scope of coverage. Our emphasis has been upon three major subject areas: Arrest, Search and Seizure; Right to Counsel; and Confessions. Numerous other areas are touched upon throughout the book, but we believe a basic course in criminal procedure is best taught by exploring these areas in depth. Finally, the book is designed to promote a high quality classroom experience. It is not a research tool; it does not mention every "major" case. It is our hope, above all else, that it is a highly teachable book.

Joseph G. Cook
Knoxville, Tennessee

Paul Marcus
Williamsburg, Virginia

Melanie D. Wilson
Lawrence, Kansas

January, 2014

Table of Contents

Chapter 1

INTRODUCTION

§ 1.01 OVERVIEW OF THE CRIMINAL JUSTICE SYSTEM

The criminal justice system in the United States is the product of centuries of gradual development in England combined with modern constitutional theory and interpretation. Despite its unified heritage, the criminal justice process in this country is not perfectly uniform. A major urban center and a rural town share the same Constitution; yet, their operations and handling of criminal cases may vary considerably. Differences may exist among states, between a state and the federal system, and even between localities within a single state.

Some of these differences reflect a basic philosophical dilemma underlying our system of justice. Is our primary goal to punish the criminal offender? To rehabilitate him? To deter others from criminal conduct? To protect society? Society has failed to clearly define its expectations of justice. These fundamental questions affect public opinion about crime and law enforcement, as well as the functioning of the system itself. As long as this controversy remains unresolved, it will continue to contribute to many of the conflicting and contradictory forces within the system.

In addition to the philosophical differences that result in variations in the way states and other governmental units apply their criminal laws, the American criminal justice system provides numerous opportunities for police, prosecutors, and judges to exercise discretion throughout the process. Police exercise discretion in deciding what crimes to investigate, the methods they will use to conduct investigations, whom they will arrest, and with what crime they will initially charge the suspect. The prosecutor maintains discretion over whether to prosecute, whether to increase or decrease the initial charge, and whether to entertain plea negotiations. Similarly, the judge exercises discretion in managing the trial and in sentencing convicted defendants. Even the definition of a crime can create opportunities for discretion. For example, laws regarding "disorderly conduct" or "disturbing the peace" are necessarily ambiguous because the condition of public order is a matter open to debate.

Some stages of the criminal justice process require discretion and flexibility. For instance, police departments could not feasibly "fully enforce" all laws at all times because they would be unable to consider the human or mitigating factors of a particular situation. Full enforcement would also require a greater budget than the average department is allotted, and politically such a stance would almost certainly be unpopular. Thus, the police officer is necessarily endowed with considerable discretion. But too much discretion can be equally harmful to an effective system of justice. For example, justice will suffer if police exercise their discretion in arbitrary or discriminatory ways, such as singling out African Americans or other distinct groups for disproportionate scrutiny.

It is not only police discretion that is controversial. Consider plea bargaining. Procedures allowing a defendant to plead guilty in exchange for a lesser charge, or for dropping certain of several charges, may seem unfair or capricious. Thus, some scholars and commentators have argued for abolition of plea bargains. *See, e.g.*, Stephen J. Schulhofer, *Plea Bargaining as Disaster*, 101 Yale L.J. 1979, 1979 (1992) (arguing for abolition of plea bargaining to "serve both justice and efficiency"). Others contend that extensive reforms are needed. *See* Robert E. Scott & William J. Stuntz, *Plea Bargaining as Contract*, 101 Yale L.J. 1909, 1910 (1992) (asking why plea bargaining is "at once so widely condemned and so widely tolerated," and proposing reforms, not abolition, of the process); Ronald F. Wright, *Trial Distortion and the End of Innocence in Federal Criminal Justice*, 154 U. Pa. L. Rev. 79, 82–3 (2005) (arguing that plea bargains are so entrenched in the American criminal courtroom that "no one will abolish" them; therefore, reform is needed, and advocating a "trial distortion" theory of reform, which would seek to replicate, through guilty pleas, the same pattern that would have emerged from trial outcomes); Stephanos Bibas, *Incompetent Pleas Bargaining and Extrajudicial Reforms*, 126 Harv. L. Rev. 150, 174 (2012) (contending that to make the Sixth Amendment right to counsel meaningful in a world dominated by guilty pleas, courts must spur other actors, like prosecutors, to reform the system).

Police and prosecutors also exercise discretion when deciding whether to use cooperating (sometimes referred to as "snitch") witnesses. Should the government rely on criminals for information to solve other crimes? Some scholars argue that such witnesses pose too great a risk for wrongful convictions. *See, e.g.*, Myrna S. Raeder, *See No Evil: Wrongful Convictions and the Prosecutorial Ethics of Offering Testimony by Jailhouse Informants and Dishonest Experts*, 76 Fordham L. Rev. 1413 (2007); *but see* Melanie D. Wilson, *Prosecutors "Doing Justice" Through Osmosis — Reminders to Encourage a Culture of Cooperation*, 45 Am. Crim. L. Rev. 67 (2008) (arguing that the "value of untapped cooperation is immeasurable" and that prosecutors should more diligently pursue and reward such cooperating witnesses).

Cognizant of the realities of the American criminal justice system, and some of its limitations, let us examine its various stages.

[A] Investigation

Investigation includes inquiry into crimes observed by, or reported to, the police. Crimes vary greatly in complexity. Some are easily observed, for example an exchange of drugs for money on an urban street corner. Others, such as wire fraud and money laundering, often require extensive review of subtle and complex paper trails, not easily, quickly, or publicly detected. Because crimes vary, police enforcement, of necessity, includes administrative policy determinations about whether and how to curtail criminal behavior. In pursuit of a criminal investigation, officers may interview witnesses and gather tangible items thought to be associated with the crime. They may conduct undercover operations, surreptitiously recording phone calls or other conversations. They may rely on secret grand jury proceedings to obtain statements, handwriting exemplars, or documents. Or they may obtain and execute search warrants to search private places for suspected contraband or evidence. They may even surreptitiously obtain hair, saliva, skin, or other biological evidence unwittingly left behind in a public place by a suspect.

[B] Arrest

Arrest is the taking of a person into custody to charge with a crime. Most arrests are "on-view arrests." A police officer sees someone committing a crime or believes a person has just done so and, therefore, has reasonable grounds for taking that person into custody. The critical feature for such arrests, which proceed without a warrant, is the reasonable grounds requirement. An officer must have observed a crime or reasonably believe that a crime was committed by this particular suspect.

Alternatively, the officer may issue a "notice to appear." This device is typically used in connection with minor offenses, such as traffic violations. If the accused fails to appear in court as directed by the notice, the court may issue a summons or bench warrant.

As a third variation of arrest, a court, acting upon a sworn complaint of a citizen, a police officer, or a prosecutor, may issue a summons or warrant. A summons commands the accused to appear in court at a specified time. In contrast, an arrest warrant commands a peace officer to arrest the accused.

For persons arrested on a criminal charge, the next step is generally "booking." Booking is simply a clerical procedure involving entry on police records of the suspect's name, offense, time of arrest, and, in some cases, photographing, fingerprinting and, more recently, the swabbing of the suspect's cheek to obtain DNA. Depending on the circumstances (the severity of the charge, the amount of evidence, the existence of pre-trial diversion programs, which take offenders out of the criminal justice system and place them under civil control), and the practice of the local jurisdiction, some form of pre-trial screening may then take place. These screening decisions are made during the period between arrest and the beginning of the court procedures, usually by a senior police officer or a prosecuting attorney. These decisions are necessary to ensure that the events giving rise to the charge actually constitute a crime. If it is decided that the case should be prosecuted, the prosecutor will prepare a "complaint," officially charging the suspect with a crime.

[C] Presentment or Initial Judicial Appearance

In this stage, the defendant is brought before a judge who informs the defendant of the charges against him, the right to counsel, the privilege against compelled self-incrimination, and the right to trial by jury. A defendant is entitled to counsel at the first appearance, even if the appearance is an informal one with no prosecutor present for the government.

If the defendant is charged with a misdemeanor, the defendant enters a plea of guilty or not guilty. In general, if he pleads guilty, he may be sentenced, especially if the crime is a relatively minor misdemeanor (such as a traffic infraction or public drunkenness), or sentencing may be delayed for a presentence report, a written document outlining the defendant's personal circumstances and past criminal conduct, if any. If the defendant pleads not guilty, the court will set the case for trial.

If the charge is a felony, or a misdemeanor which has not been resolved with a plea of guilty, the magistrate judge decides whether bail is appropriate. Bail often involves the defendant posting ten percent of the amount set by the judge to ensure the defendant's presence at the next court appearance. In some jurisdictions, the amount of bail is a routine matter prescribed by a schedule listing bail amounts for each specified offense. In other jurisdictions, for example in federal court, the magistrate judge makes an individual assessment as to whether the defendant should be detained or released on bail and, if released, the amount appropriate for bail. In these jurisdictions, the judge evaluates the individual characteristics of the particular defendant (does the defendant have a criminal history and, if so, for what crimes; does the defendant have a history of flight from prosecution; does the defendant have strong ties to the community) and the nature of the crime (how serious and dangerous is the current charge), rather than relying on a set schedule. The bond system has been criticized on the grounds that it, in effect, grants power to impose a fine regardless of whether the accused is ultimately found guilty, and confines those too indigent to raise money for the bondsman's premium. Perhaps for these reasons, courts sometimes release defendants on their own recognizance (sometimes called "ROR bonds"), particularly if the accused has a substantial connection to the community. An ROR bond does not require the defendant to post money to guarantee his appearance at trial. Rather, it involves a formal agreement that he will not leave the jurisdiction, will return to court as instructed, and that he comply with other conditions (such as maintaining employment, avoiding possession of weapons, surrendering any passport).

[D] Preliminary Hearing or Examination

The preliminary hearing or examination is designed to determine whether there is sufficient evidence to justify a trial. This procedure is used in more than half of the states and is usually an alternative to the grand jury. In federal court, a defendant is entitled to both a preliminary hearing and indictment by the grand jury for felony crimes. During a preliminary hearing, the prosecution must produce sufficient evidence to convince the judge that there is probable cause to believe that the defendant is guilty of the crime charged. It is not necessary, however, for the prosecution to show that the defendant is guilty beyond a reasonable doubt. The defendant is entitled to be present at the preliminary hearing, to be represented by counsel, to cross-examine the prosecution's witnesses, and to introduce evidence.

In most jurisdictions the defendant can waive, or voluntarily relinquish, the preliminary hearing, although the judge and prosecution usually must agree. Defendants sometimes waive this procedure to speed up the process or avoid publicity. Sometimes the defendant waives the preliminary hearing as a bargaining chip for release on bail. But defendants should not waive these hearings lightly.

The preliminary examination can result in the case's dismissal for lack of evidence, and the hearing is often useful as a discovery tool, giving the defense the opportunity to preview at least some of the prosecution's case and cross-examine its witnesses.[1]

If the magistrate judge finds that probable cause does not exist, the complaint is dismissed. However, this dismissal does not prevent the prosecution from bringing another charge. The preliminary hearing is not a trial, so there is no "double jeopardy." If the magistrate does find probable cause for the charge(s), the defendant will be "bound over" for trial. After the probable cause determination, the official accusation against the defendant is presented in the form of an "information" or an "indictment."

[E] Grand Jury

Although issued by different parties, the formal documents of accusation — the information and the indictment — are functionally similar. An information is a written accusation signed by the prosecution that charges the defendant with a criminal offense. An indictment is also a document formally charging the defendant with a crime. Both documents lead to the same steps in the criminal justice system, but a grand jury, not a prosecutor, issues an indictment.

The grand jury is composed of a relatively large group of ordinary citizens — up to two dozen in some jurisdictions — who receive evidence from the prosecution in closed proceedings and then decide whether to prosecute. Unanimity is not needed; most state statutes require a two-thirds or three-quarters majority decision to indict. The grand jury can initiate investigations and compel the attendance of, and grant immunity to, witnesses. But typically the grand jury receives the prosecution's evidence and accedes to its recommendation to go forward with a prosecution in which case the grand jury issues its indictment. If the grand jury finds that probable cause is lacking for a charge, the grand jury issues a "no bill" and the case is dismissed.

There are key differences between the grand jury proceeding and the preliminary hearing. The defendant has the right to participate in the preliminary hearing, to present evidence, to question witnesses, and to object to the prosecution's evidence or testimony. He has no similar rights in the grand jury. It is a closed proceeding in most jurisdictions. Only the prosecution, a court reporter, and the grand jurors are permitted during the presentation of evidence. The grand jury then deliberates in secret with only its members present.

[F] Arraignment

At the arraignment the defendant is informed of the charge(s) in the information or indictment and of the pleas available to her (guilty or not guilty). It is at this stage that the defendant formally pleads to the charge(s). If the defendant

[1] Fed. R. Crim. P. 16 exemplifies the modern trend in increasing the defense's opportunities for criminal discovery, though criminal discovery remains far more limited than discovery in the civil litigation process.

pleads guilty, she waives her right to require the prosecution to prove her guilt beyond a reasonable doubt and her right to trial by jury. Therefore, certain safeguards are required, namely that the accused understand the charge and the potential penalties, and that the plea be free from coercion and not unfairly obtained. In addition, the judge must feel assured that there is a reasonable factual basis for the plea. In most cases, this involves the prosecution summarizing the evidence it expects to present should a trial be necessary. If these conditions are fulfilled, and the judge accepts the defendant's plea, no trial is held. The next stage in the process is sentencing.

The use of the guilty plea has been the subject of heated controversy throughout the years. Depending on the jurisdiction, between seventy-five and ninety-seven percent of defendants plead guilty, the majority doing so as a result of plea bargaining. *See Southern Union Co. v. United States*, 132 S. Ct. 2344, 2371 (2012) (Breyer, J.) (dissenting) (noting that ninety-seven percent of federal convictions and ninety-four percent of all state convictions result from guilty pleas). Supporters of plea bargains argue that the practice is necessary to accommodate the enormous number of defendants passing through the system.

As stated by former Chief Justice Burger in *Santobello v. New York*, 404 U.S. 257, 260 (1971):

> The disposition of criminal charges by agreement between the prosecutor and the accused, sometimes loosely called "plea bargaining," is an essential component of the administration of justice. Properly administered, it is to be encouraged. If every criminal charge were subjected to a full-scale trial, the States and the Federal Government would need to multiply by many times the number of judges and court facilities. Disposition of charges after plea discussions is not only an essential part of the process but a highly desirable part for many reasons. It leads to prompt and largely final disposition of most criminal cases; it avoids much of the corrosive impact of enforced idleness during pre-trial confinement for those who are denied release pending trial; it protects the public from those accused persons who are prone to continue criminal conduct even while on pretrial release; and, by shortening the time between charge and disposition, it enhances whatever may be the rehabilitative prospects of the guilty when they are ultimately imprisoned.

In short, plea bargaining is said to benefit the system by reducing the financial costs of prosecuting a case, improving the courts' administrative efficiency, enabling the prosecution and the courts to devote more attention to crimes of greater severity or significance, and reducing both defendants' pre-trial detention and sentence. Nonetheless, some critics of plea bargains contend that plea agreements are overly coercive and that they ultimately deprive the criminal defendant of the most fundamental of Constitutional protections—the jury trial. Moreover, there is now proof that factually innocent people plead guilty despite their innocence. *See, e.g.*, The Innocence Project, www.innocenceproject.com (documenting that some of those convicted by a plea of guilty were later exonerated by DNA evidence). At present, plea bargaining remains a necessary, controversial aspect of the criminal justice system.

The plea of *nolo contendere* (literally, "I will not contest it") is essentially the same as the guilty plea and has the same consequences. However, it is less commonly used. The key difference between the guilty plea and that of *nolo contendere* is that the latter cannot be used later as an admission of guilt in a civil lawsuit (because the defendant has not admitted guilt). The plea is acceptable in about half of the states and is used most frequently in cases in which the defendant is also subject to a civil suit for damages and in some political cases. In federal cases, the Department of Justice demands that its prosecutors oppose *nolo contendere* pleas as a matter of policy.

If the defendant pleads not guilty, or if she stands mute, refusing to enter a plea, the court enters a not guilty plea, and the case goes to trial. The "not guilty" plea means that the accused denies every material allegation contained in the government's accusation and requires the government to establish these allegations beyond a reasonable doubt.

[G] Pretrial Motions

Motions are requests that the judge rule on particular legal issues and can be made by either the defense or the prosecution. Many important issues are resolved, and cases are both lost and won, on the outcome of a motion. For instance, if the judge excludes key evidence from the trial of the case, the prosecution often dismisses the entire case because it cannot prove guilt beyond a reasonable doubt. Likewise, if the judge denies a motion to suppress key evidence, the defendant often agrees to plead guilty, recognizing that with the key evidence, he is likely to be convicted.

The timing of motions is often important. Some must be made before the plea (*e.g.*, attacks on the preliminary hearing, or motions based on the statute of limitations or a speedy trial statute), while others can be made after the plea. The significance of the various motions varies with the facts of each individual case and the local practice. Among the most important and most frequently encountered motions are motions to discharge or dismiss the case and the motion to suppress or quash evidence. Common examples of the motion to dismiss include: an improperly selected grand jury; defects in the indictment or information; immunity; and a fundamental denial of a defendant's rights. The motion to suppress evidence, arguing that evidence was illegally obtained in violation of a defendant's rights, is typically based on an illegal search and seizure or a challenge to the validity of a defendant's confession.

Other relatively common motions may also impact the case's outcome. Included among these are motions for a continuance, change of judge, the appointment of expert witnesses, the joinder of related prosecutions, the severance of joint prosecutions, and change of venue.[2] Ultimately these issues are resolved by the judge, and the case may then proceed to trial.

---

[2] Venue refers to the "locus of the trial," and a motion for its change is frequently used to minimize the effects of adverse pre-trial publicity.

[H] Trial

Trial is the adversary process by which the facts of the case and the guilt of the accused are decided. The prosecution must prove beyond a reasonable doubt that the defendant committed the crime charged. This proof is offered to the trier of fact — the jury when a jury is used or the judge when the case is tried to the bench. The standard of proof is significantly more rigorous than the burden on a plaintiff in a civil proceeding, where the standard is merely proof by a preponderance of the evidence. Nevertheless, the acquittal rate in cases that actually go to trial is low, presumably because of extensive screening as well as opportunities for negotiation and dismissal.

The presence of a jury as trier of fact is governed by the Sixth and Fourteenth Amendments. Jurors are selected by a process known as "voir dire," which involves the questioning of prospective jurors to determine their biases and their suitability to the case. Both the prosecution and the defense can exclude an unlimited number of jurors "for cause"; that is, when jurors are biased, have already formed an opinion, or are unable to perform the duties of a juror fairly. Each side of the case is also permitted to exercise a certain number of "peremptory challenges" to exclude prospective jurors without articulating any cause or objection. The number of peremptory challenges available varies from jurisdiction to jurisdiction.

A criminal trial is similar in many respects to a civil trial. The prosecution begins the trial with its opening statement, after which the defense usually does the same. The prosecution presents its case first by calling and directly examining its witnesses. The defense can then cross-examine the prosecution's witnesses. In some instances, the prosecution then engages in re-direct examination of its witness, in which case the defense can re-cross-examine the witnesses. When the prosecution has presented all of its witnesses and evidence, the defense is given its turn to present its case by introducing and directly examining witnesses, whom the prosecution may cross-examine. Although the defendant has this opportunity, in a criminal case, the defendant is under no obligation to present evidence. He may sit quietly and demand that the prosecution carry its burden of proof.

After each side presents its case, each side is allowed to make closing arguments, summarizing the evidence presented and urging conviction or acquittal respectively.

The next important stage of the trial is the charge conference, during which the judge decides how to instruct the jury about the applicable law. Both the prosecution and defense submit to the judge their formulation of instructions, and the judge chooses the instructions that best fit the law and particular facts presented during trial. Incorrect instructions can be the basis for subsequent appeal and reversal. As a result, many jurisdictions have standard, approved instructions for concepts that reoccur in trials. For instance, there is typically a standard instruction on the burden of proof, the effect of inconsistent statements by witnesses, and the defendant's right to refrain from testifying, among others. Once the instructions are finalized, the judge generally reads the instructions to the jurors. After receiving the instructions, the jury retires and deliberates on a verdict.

In the overwhelming majority of cases, the jury arrives at a verdict. Although federal courts require both, neither jury unanimity nor twelve-person juries are constitutionally required. *Apodaca v. Oregon*, 406 U.S. 404 (1971); *Williams v. Florida*, 399 U.S. 78 (1970). If the verdict is "not guilty," the defendant is acquitted. This verdict does not necessarily mean that the defendant is innocent but rather may mean that the prosecution was unable to establish guilt by the required standard of proof. Where the defense of insanity has been asserted in the case, the jury sometimes returns the specialized verdict of "not guilty by reason of insanity," which may lead to the defendant's placement in a facility for the mentally ill, rather than his return to freedom. The last verdict available, of course, is that the defendant is guilty.

[I] Post-Trial Motions

Following a guilty verdict, the defense may make several key motions. Arguing that the jury instructions were improper or that evidence was improperly admitted, for example, the defense may move for a new trial. If this motion is successful, the accused will be given a new trial; she is not acquitted. In addition to motions for new trial, the defense may make a motion n.o.v., a motion notwithstanding the verdict. This motion asks the judge to rule that no reasonable jury could have concluded that the defendant was guilty beyond a reasonable doubt based on the evidence presented, and therefore the defendant must be declared not guilty.

[J] Sentencing

Traditionally, sentencing has been the province of the judge. Nevertheless, many states require presentence reports. These reports are typically prepared by probation officers and focus on the offense, the offender, and her background. The presentence report serves four main purposes: (1) aiding the court to determine the appropriate sentence; (2) aiding the probation officer in the rehabilitative efforts during probation; (3) assisting the Department of Corrections in classification, treatment, and release planning; and (4) furnishing the parole board with information relevant to its later consideration of parole. In some states, the judge has discretion to order or forego a presentence report, but when one is ordered, most judges follow the probation officers' recommendations.

In general, depending on the crime, the judge decides whether to impose a fine, incarceration, probation (release subject to conditions without being confined to a penal or correctional institution), commitment to a state mental hospital (if the defendant was found not guilty by reason of insanity), and/or restitution. The amount of discretion the judge has in imposing a sentence depends on the jurisdiction's sentencing statutes. Many states provide "guidelines" to curb some of the judge's discretion at sentencing,[3] but some statutes provide for

[3] Such guidelines must be carefully tailored so as not to infringe on a defendant's Sixth Amendment rights to trial by jury and proof beyond a reasonable doubt. *See* United States v. Booker, 543 U.S. 220 (2005) (holding that mandatory-nature of federal sentencing guidelines made guidelines unconstitutional), and discussion *infra* § 7.01.

"indeterminate" sentencing, leaving the judge with wide authority to select a sentence she thinks appropriate for the particular defendant and crime. Also, many states (and the federal law) have some criminal statutes that specify minimum mandatory sentences for certain crimes. Additionally, many states have enacted "habitual offender" statutes, which increase the period of imprisonment for someone convicted of two or more crimes.

[K] Post-Conviction Remedies

Even conviction and sentencing are not always final. Decisions can be modified or reversed through three major avenues: appeal, collateral attack, or executive review.

Appeal involves the review by a higher court of a lower court's proceedings. Appeals are restricted to the paper record and focus on questions of law, not of fact. An appeal does not involve retrying the facts of the case. Most appeals are based on disputes over the quantum of evidence and the procedures applied in the case that may have impacted the finder of facts, usually the jury.

To obtain appellate review, the defense must give the trial court notice of its intent to do so within a specified time, request a transcript of the trial proceedings, and compile the requisite records. Through objections made at trial, the defense lawyer preserves these questions as issues for review. The defense must then file its petition with the appellate court, specifying those errors and issues upon which the appeal is based. Errors not objected to at trial are considered waived and will not be reviewed at the appellate level, except for seriously prejudicial defects in the proceedings below, *i.e.*, plain errors.

Both the prosecution and the defense prepare written briefs arguing their positions. Sometimes they also present oral arguments before the appeals court. The court renders its decision in the form of a written opinion. If the appellate court finds an error, it can order that the prosecution be dismissed or strike the conviction and remand for a new trial, giving the government another opportunity to win a conviction. If the losing party in the appeal wishes further review, the state supreme court — and sometimes the United States Supreme Court — may then be asked to consider the case.

A second major avenue for obtaining a post-conviction remedy is collateral attack. A decision by a state supreme court, or by an intermediate court with a denial of further review, is usually the final disposition of a case. However, the defendant may seek further review by filing a petition for a writ of *habeas corpus*.

Habeas corpus, which means "you have the body," provides a procedure for a convicted defendant to show that his detention is illegal.

Some states restrict the writ of habeas corpus by providing that it cannot be used as a means to raise issues that should have been raised on appeal. In these jurisdictions, the writ may be used only to show that the court lacked jurisdiction to impose a sentence, the statute was previously held unconstitutional, the sentence imposed was in excess of the statute, or the indictment or information failed to adequately allege the commission of a crime.

In most states, when the writ is granted, the prisoner is brought to court and the attorney general or local prosecutor is notified to appear and establish cause for the detention. Usually there is a strong presumption as to the legality of the detention, so the prisoner has a heavy burden of showing the defects.

After fully pursuing or "exhausting" any state procedures for collateral attack, the prisoner may turn to federal habeas corpus if the case involves a violation of the United States Constitution or federal laws. However, the utility of the writ for challenges asserting a search or seizure in violation of the Fourth Amendment was sharply limited by a Supreme Court decision, *Stone v. Powell*, 428 U.S. 465 (1976), which held that a state prisoner cannot be granted federal habeas corpus relief where the state has provided an opportunity for full and fair litigation of such a claim. The writ's effectiveness has been further limited by Congress. The Antiterrorism and Effective Death Penalty Act (AEDPA), Pub. L. No 104–132, (codified in various sections of 28 U.S.C.), makes it more difficult to make successive claims, and it contains a provision applying a one-year statute of limitation to applications for such a writ. 28 U.S.C. § 2244(a) and (d)(1)(D) (2000).

Executive review, the final post-conviction avenue, is similar to collateral attacks in that both are frequently used but rarely successful. The governor of a state or the President of the United States can pardon, commute to a lower sentence, or reprieve (delay execution). A pardon relieves the defendant of guilt and prevents retrial. Commuting a sentence merely means it is reduced to one of lesser duration or severity. Commutation often involves reducing a death sentence to life imprisonment. Some states have placed the matter of executive review in the hands of a clemency board, which administers the many requests for executive review and makes recommendations to the chief executive.

One or more of these post-conviction remedies may be pursued when newly discovered, scientific evidence casts doubt on a conviction. For instance, DNA evidence has resulted in the reversal of more than 210 convictions. When DNA casts doubt on the integrity of a conviction, the defendant typically files a motion to bring the new-found evidence to the attention of the court and prosecutor.

ADDITIONAL READINGS

ABA Standards for Criminal Justice: Pretrial Release (3d. ed. 2007).

Stephanos Bibas, *Plea Bargaining Outside the Shadow of Trial*, 117 Harv. L. Rev. 2463 (2004).

Gabriel J. Chin & Richard W. Holmes, *Effective Assistance of Counsel and the Consequences of Guilty Pleas*, 87 Cornell L. Rev. 697 (2002).

Robert O. Dawson, *Sentencing: The Decision as to Type, Length and Conditions of Sentence* (1969).

Michael Gottfredson and Travis Hirshi, *A General Theory of Crime* (1990).

Kyle Graham, *Crimes, Widgets, and Plea Bargaining: An Analysis of Charge Content, Pleas, and Trials*, 100 Cal. L. Rev. 1573 (2012).

Benard E. Harcourt, *Introduction: Guns, Crime, and Punishment in America*, 43 Ariz. L. Rev. 261 (2001).

David B. Mustard, *Racial, Ethnic, and Gender Disparities in Sentencing: Evidence From the U.S. Federal Courts*, 44 J. L. & Econ. 285 (2001).

Arthur I. Rosett and Donald Ray Cressy, *Justice By Consent: Plea Bargains in the American Courthouse* (1976).

Stephen J. Schulhofer, *Is Plea Bargaining Inevitable?*, 97 Harv. L. Rev. 1037 (1984).

Christopher Slobogin, *Deceit, Pretext, and Trickery: Investigative Lies by the Police*, 76 Or. L. Rev. 755 (1997).

The Innocence Project, www.innocenceproject.org

§ 1.02 THE CONSTITUTION IN CRIMINAL PROSECUTIONS

At one level, the study of criminal procedure is an analogue to the study of civil procedure — it is a study of the rules and practices associated with the use of the judicial system to resolve a dispute between two parties. One of the parties is the federal, state, or local government; the other is a private party charged with violating the criminal law. The procedures followed vary considerably from jurisdiction to jurisdiction, although certain patterns emerge, as described in the preceding section.

At another level, criminal procedure is the study of a specialized area of federal constitutional law. That is the primary focus of this book. Cases, which originally were tried in either federal or state courts, are heard on appeal by the United States Supreme Court. While the Court on occasion exercises non-constitutional supervisory power over the federal judicial system, and the interpretation of federal statutes is an unavoidable responsibility, in most cases, the Court is concerned with whether the conduct of officials — legislative, executive, or judicial — comports with the minimal requirements established by the federal Constitution.

The propriety of such rulings in the context of federal prosecutions has been a topic of little controversy. But the imposition of federal constitutional standards in state criminal prosecutions has been a different matter. Although today much of the substance of the recognized rights is derived from the Bill of Rights, these provisions were added to the Constitution prior to its ratification and were intended to impose explicit restrictions on the power of the federal government. In the beginning, there was no intimation that the Bill of Rights would apply to abuses by state governments. *See Barron v. City of Baltimore*, 32 U.S. 243 (1833). While most state constitutions contained bills of rights strikingly similar to the federal provisions, the fact remained that protections provided by those provisions were purely matters of state law. Thus, the interpretation of state bills of rights by state courts, however antithetical to the purposes the bills of rights were designed to serve, was essentially non-reviewable in federal courts.

The application of federal constitutional standards to protect against the actions of state officials became a question of significant importance upon the adoption of the Fourteenth Amendment in 1868. That amendment provides in pertinent part, "[N]or shall any State deprive any person of life, liberty, or property, without due process of law." The meaning of the Fourteenth Amendment Due Process Clause has been a perennial source of disagreement among the justices of the Supreme Court. If the Fourteenth Amendment incorporates all of the Bill of Rights, then federal actors and state actors would be restricted to the same degree. If none of the rights guaranteed by the first nine amendments is incorporated, state actors would be free from the limits of the federal Bill of Rights. In this section, we examine four theories of incorporation: The independent content approach; the total incorporation approach; the selective incorporation approach; and the neo-incorporation approach.

The independent content approach. Hurtado v. California, 110 U.S. 516 (1884), was the Court's first look at the meaning of the Fourteenth Amendment's Due Process Clause. There, the accused claimed a right to an indictment by a grand jury as a prerequisite to a state prosecution. The Court rejected the argument on both analytical and historical grounds. First, it observed that the right to due process appears in both the Fifth and the Fourteenth Amendments. Unlike the Fourteenth, "[the Fifth Amendment] makes specific and express provision for perpetuating the institution of the grand jury, so far as relates to prosecutions for the more aggravated crimes under the laws of the United States." Following the Fifth Amendment's express reference to the grand jury, it "then immediately adds" the due process language. The Court explained that absent evidence to the contrary, the Due Process clause in the Fifth and Fourteenth has the same meaning in both instances. Thus, concluded the Court, the Due Process clause of the Fifth Amendment does not encompass the right to a grand jury indictment. Reading the Fifth Amendment otherwise, the Court said, would make the specific reference to the grand jury superfluous. Ergo, the Due Process Clause of the Fourteenth Amendment contains no such protection. The Court held:

> The conclusion is . . . irresistible, that when the same phrase was employed in the fourteenth amendment to restrain the action of the states, it was used in the same sense and with no greater extent; and that if in the adoption of that amendment it had been part of its purpose to perpetuate the institution of the grand jury in all the states, it would have embodied, as did the fifth amendment, express declaration to that effect.

Id. at 534–35.

Historically, the argument fared no better. The Court said:

> Due process of law, in spite of the absolutism of continental governments, is not alien to that Code which survived the Roman empire as the foundation of modern civilization in Europe, and which has given us that fundamental maxim of distributive justice, *sum cuique tribuere*. There is nothing in Magna Charta, rightly construed as a broad charter of public right and law, which ought to exclude the best ideas of all systems and of every age; and as it was the characteristic principle of the common law to draw its inspiration from every fountain of justice, we are not to assume that the sources of its supply have been exhausted. On the contrary, we

should expect that the new and various experiences of our own situation and system will mould and shape it into new and not less useful forms.

Id. at 531.

The total incorporation approach. The total incorporation approach maintains that all of the protections of the first nine amendments were made applicable to the states by virtue of the ratification of the Fourteenth Amendment. This view has never commanded the support of a majority of the justices. Its staunchest advocate was Justice Black, usually joined by Justice Douglas.

Justice Black was convinced that the theory of total incorporation was consistent with the intent of the drafters of the Fourteenth Amendment. In his dissenting opinion in *Adamson v. California*, 332 U.S. 46 (1947), Justice Black explained:

> My study of the historical events that culminated in the Fourteenth Amendment, and the expressions of those who sponsored and favored, as well as those who opposed its submission and passage, persuades me that one of the chief objects that the provisions of the Amendment's first section, separately, and as a whole, were intended to accomplish was to make the Bill of Rights, applicable to the states.

Id. at 71–72.

The selective incorporation approach. While a majority of the justices of the Supreme Court has never accepted the total incorporation approach, certain protections of the Bill of Rights have been viewed as so fundamental that they have been generally acknowledged as essential to the concept of due process of law. What emerged over the years was the selective incorporation of the Bill of Rights into the Fourteenth Amendment. Under the selective incorporation approach, the task of the Court is to determine which of the specific protections do and which do not extend to state action. The process began with *Gitlow v. New York*, 268 U.S. 652 (1925), in which the Court applied the First Amendment protections of free speech and press to the states.

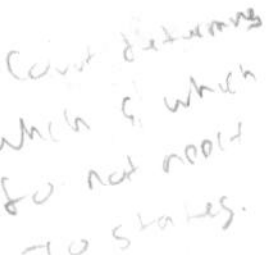

Typical of this approach is the majority opinion in *Palko v. Connecticut*, 302 U.S. 319 (1937), the substance of which has since been overruled. In *Palko*, the Court was confronted with a state statute granting the prosecution a right of appeal in criminal cases, which was coextensive with the appellate rights of the defense. The prosecution had been dissatisfied with a conviction of second degree murder with punishment set at life imprisonment and had successfully appealed certain trial errors prejudicial to the state. On retrial the accused was convicted of first degree murder and received the death penalty. The accused appealed, contending that the conviction of the greater offense on retrial had violated the Fifth Amendment protection against double jeopardy.

Justice Cardozo, speaking for the Court, explained that certain provisions of the Bill of Rights had been extended to the states, although others had not. The test, the Court declared, was whether the right in question was among the "fundamental principles of liberty and justice which lie at the base of all our civil and political institutions." The Court concluded that the right involved in the case was not fundamental.

Later, in *Adamson v. California*, 332 U.S. 46 (1947), Justice Black contended that this selective incorporation approach was too subjective because the Court took it upon itself to pick and choose among an array of constitutional protections with no contextual indication that some were more fundamental than others. Justice Black maintained that as a matter of judicial restraint, either all the protections should be extended to state prosecutions or none should.

In support of the selective incorporation approach, justices have from time to time suggested sources the Court might turn to in deciding which provisions of the Bill of Rights are so fundamental as to require their incorporation into the Due Process Clause, including: (1) The Court may look to the implicit views of society. In *Betts v. Brady*, 316 U.S. 455 (1942), a right to counsel case, the Court, in searching for fundamental principles of fairness, turned to "the common understanding of those who have lived under the Anglo-American system of law." (2) The Court may attempt to determine the intent of the Framers or ratifiers of the Constitution, a method which seems inevitably inconclusive. (3) The Court may look to the practices of the individual states to determine if a particular right has been viewed as fundamental. In *Snyder v. Massachusetts*, 291 U.S. 97 (1934), for example, the Court found that the right of the accused to be present at his trial had been virtually universally accepted as fundamental and, thus, could be deemed a requisite of due process. (4) The Court may rely upon judicial decisions of state and lower federal courts. In *Powell v. Alabama*, 287 U.S. 45 (1932), the Court found that lower courts "invariably recognize the right to the aid of counsel as fundamental in character" in capital cases. (5) The Court may look to foreign jurisdictions, particularly the British Commonwealth, to determine whether a particular procedural right has been viewed as fundamental. This technique was employed in *Wolf v. Colorado*, 338 U.S. 25 (1949), in which the Court observed that most of the English-speaking world did not regard as vital the exclusion from trial of evidence which had been illegally seized.

The neo-incorporation approach. An implicit assumption in the total incorporation and selective incorporation theories has been the notion that, once incorporated, a right is enforced in state proceedings coextensively as it would be in a federal proceeding. The remaining approach takes the view that a particular provision of the Bill of Rights may be interpreted differently depending upon whether the action challenged is an action of the federal government versus one of a state governmental actor.

The first decision in which a majority of the justices accepted the neo-incorporation approach was *Williams v. Florida*, 399 U.S. 78 (1970), in which Justice White, speaking for six justices, held that while the right to trial by jury, which is protected by the Sixth Amendment, applies to the states, the twelve-person jury used in federal prosecutions, *see* Fed. R. Crim. P. 23, is not constitutionally essential in state prosecutions.

For further discussion of the meaning of the Fourteenth Amendment in the context of state criminal prosecutions, the following articles, among many more, may be helpful. James A. Gardner, *Whose Constitution Is It? Why Federalism and Constitutional Positivism Don't Mix*, 46 Wm. & Mary L. Rev. 1245 (2005); Robert Fairchild Cushman, *Incorporation: Due Process and the Bill of Rights*, 51 Cornell

L.Q. 467 (1966); Alex B. Lacy, Jr., *The Bill of Rights and the Fourteenth Amendment: The Evolution of the Absorption Doctrine*, 23 WASH. & LEE L. REV. 37 (1966); Louis Henkin, *"Selective Incorporation" in the Fourteenth Amendment*, 73 Yale L.J. 74 (1963).

§ 1.03 EXTENDING PROTECTION THROUGH STATE CONSTITUTIONS

The constitutions of most states contain bills of rights that substantially parallel the Bill of Rights in the federal Constitution. In most jurisdictions, these provisions remained largely dormant for a century or more, leaving the protection of rights and liberties the near-exclusive domain of the United States Supreme Court. In recent years, however, the retrenchment of the Supreme Court on Bill of Rights issues has been accompanied by increasing concern in state courts.

State courts are bound by the decisions of the United States Supreme Court in matters of federal constitutional law. Not only may they not construe a federal constitutional right more narrowly than mandated by the Supreme Court, but they also may not construe their own law, constitutional or otherwise, in a manner inconsistent with federal constitutional standards. States are not precluded, however, from interpreting their own law in a manner that recognizes a broader protection than that minimally mandated for federal constitutional purposes. Such rulings would fall beyond the reach of federal review under the independent state ground doctrine. *See generally* David Schuman, *Using State Constitutions to Find and Enforce Civil Liberties*, 15 LEWIS & CLARK L. REV. 783 (2011); Paul Marcus, *State Constitutional Protection for Defendants in Criminal Prosecutions*, 20 ARIZ. ST. L.J. 151 (1988); Shirley S. Abrahamson, *Criminal Law and State Constitutions: The Emergence of State Constitutional Law*, 63 Tex. L. Rev. 1141 (1985); William Brennan, Jr., *State Constitutions and the Protection of Individual Rights*, 90 Harv. L. Rev. 489 (1977). *See also* Symposium: *Dual Enforcement of State Constitutional Law*, 45 Wm. & Mary L. Rev. 1231 (2005); Symposium: *Independent State Grounds: Should State Courts Depart From the Fourth Amendment in Construing Their Own Constitutions, and if so, on What Basis Beyond Simple Disagreement With the United States Supreme Court's Result?*, 77 Miss. L. J. 265 (2007); *and see* State v. Harris, 98 So. 3d 903 (La. Ct. App. 2012) (interpreting Louisiana Constitution to protect suspects from seizures of the person beyond what the federal Constitution protects); *Commonwealth v. Simon*, 923 N.E.2d 58 (Mass. 2010) (giving suspects more protection under Massachusetts Constitution than Fifth Amendment gives against self-incrimination); *State v. Eckel*, 888 A.2d 1266 (N.J. 2006) (applying the New Jersey Constitution to avoid application of the Supreme Court's decision in *New York v. Belton*, which allows officers to search a car incident to a lawful arrest of a recent occupant of the car, explaining: "We decline to adopt *Belton* and its progeny because to do so would require us to accept a theoretically rootless doctrine that would erode the rights guaranteed to our own citizens by Article I, Paragraph 7 of our constitution"); *Yebra v. State*, 915 S.W.2d 492 (Tex. Crim. App. 1996) (interpreting the Texas Constitution to provide more protection against racially discriminatory use of peremptory challenges than does the U.S. Constitution); *Autran v. State*, 887 S.W.2d 31 (Tex. Crim. App. 1994) (relying on the Texas

Constitution to provide more privacy protection for items found in closed containers inside a vehicle as a result of an inventory search).

§ 1.04 THE CONSTITUTION AND PRIVATE ACTION

Whatever the constitutional limits on the activities of officers of federal and state governments may be, similar restraints are not imposed upon private parties. If, for example, a private individual physically attacks a public speaker, he may be criminally prosecuted for assault; he may be liable for civil damages in tort; but he has not deprived the victim of a First Amendment or other constitutional right. *See, e.g., Minneci v. Pollard*, 132 S. Ct. 617 (2012) (holding in the context of a civil rights suit that a prisoner may not sue an employee of a privately operated federal prison for violation of the prisoner's Eighth Amendment rights).

Nevertheless, the Supreme Court has sometimes attributed state action to private parties. The varied permutations of state action theory are beyond the scope of our present concern, and therefore an example must suffice. In most jurisdictions, bail bonding — the practice of posting security for the release of a person charged with a crime — remains a practice largely carried out by private parties. Suppose, however, as is sometimes the case, a state by statute gives persons licensed to post bonds extraordinary powers of arrest to ensure the presence of bonded parties in court at designated times. In exercising such power, should the private parties be required to satisfy the same constitutional standards required of governmental officials making arrests? Some courts have concluded that they should. *See, e.g., Hill v. Toll*, 320 F. Supp. 185 (E.D. Pa. 1970). Others have held that bounty hunters are not state actors subject to the Fourth Amendment. *See United States v. Poe*, 556 F.3d 1113 (10th Cir. 2009).

If a constitutional protection is designed to reach private action, then no further inquiry is needed. Such is the case with the Thirteenth Amendment, which abolished the institution of slavery. The amendment has been construed to prohibit various "badges of slavery" as well. Finally, actions which would be constitutionally prohibited if engaged in by the government may be precluded in the private sector by means of statutory sanctions. Thus, for example, it may be impermissible to discriminate on the basis of race in housing (42 U.S.C. § 3601 *et seq.*), in activities affecting interstate commerce (42 U.S.C. § 2000a), or the making of contracts (42 U.S.C. § 1981). Such statutory prohibitions may themselves raise serious constitutional questions when the party charged with the wrongful act, in turn, asserts a constitutional right (*e.g.*, freedom of religion, association, or property rights) in defense.

Chapter 2

THE FOURTH AMENDMENT AND THE DEPRIVATION OF LIBERTY

§ 2.01 THE SEIZURE REQUIREMENT

CALIFORNIA v. HODARI D.

United States Supreme Court
499 U.S. 621 (1991)

Justice Scalia delivered the opinion of the Court.

Late one evening in April 1988, Officers Brian McColgin and Jerry Pertoso were on patrol in a high-crime area of Oakland, California. They were dressed in street clothes but wearing jackets with "Police" embossed on both front and back. Their unmarked car proceeded west on Foothill Boulevard, and turned south onto 63rd Avenue. As they rounded the corner, they saw four or five youths huddled around a small red car parked at the curb. When the youths saw the officers' car approaching they apparently panicked, and took flight. The respondent here, Hodari D., and one companion ran west through an alley; the others fled south. The red car also headed south, at a high rate of speed.

The officers were suspicious and gave chase. McColgin remained in the car and continued south on 63rd Avenue; Pertoso left the car, ran back north along 63rd, then west on Foothill Boulevard, and turned south on 62nd Avenue. Hodari, meanwhile, emerged from the alley onto 62nd and ran north. Looking behind as he ran, he did not turn and see Pertoso until the officer was almost upon him, whereupon he tossed away what appeared to be a small rock. A moment later, Pertoso tackled Hodari, handcuffed him, and radioed for assistance. Hodari was found to be carrying $130 in cash and a pager; and the rock he had discarded was found to be crack cocaine.

In the juvenile proceeding brought against him, Hodari moved to suppress the evidence relating to the cocaine. The court denied the motion without opinion. The California Court of Appeal reversed, holding that Hodari had been "seized" when he saw Officer Pertoso running towards him, that this seizure was unreasonable under the Fourth Amendment, and that the evidence of cocaine had to be suppressed as the fruit of that illegal seizure. The California Supreme Court denied the State's application for review. . . . As this case comes to us, the only issue presented is whether, at the time he dropped the drugs, Hodari had been "seized" within the meaning of the Fourth Amendment.[1] If so, respondent argues, the drugs were the fruit of that seizure and the evidence concerning them was properly excluded. If not, the drugs were abandoned by Hodari and lawfully recovered by the police, and the evidence should have been admitted. . . .

We have long understood that the Fourth Amendment's protection against "unreasonable . . . seizures" includes seizures of the person. . . . From the time of the founding to the present, the word "seizure" has meant a "taking possession," 2 N. Webster, *An American Dictionary of the English Language* 67 (1828); 2 J. Bouvier, *A Law Dictionary* 510 (6th ed. 1856); *Webster's Third New International Dictionary* 2057 (1981). For most purposes at common law, the word connoted not merely grasping, or applying physical force to, the animate or inanimate object in question, but actually bringing it within physical control. A ship still fleeing, even though under attack, would not be considered to have been seized as a war prize. Cf. *The Josefa Segunda*, 10 Wheat. 312, 325–326 (1825). A *res* capable of manual delivery was not seized until "tak[en] into custody." *Pelham v. Rose*, 9 Wall. 103, 106 (1870). To constitute an arrest, however — the quintessential "seizure of the person" under our Fourth Amendment jurisprudence — the mere grasping or application of physical force with lawful authority, whether or not it succeeded in subduing the arrestee, was sufficient. . . .

To say that an arrest is effected by the slightest application of physical force, despite the arrestee's escape, is not to say that for Fourth Amendment purposes there is a *continuing* arrest during the period of fugitivity. If, for example, Pertoso had laid his hands upon Hodari to arrest him, but Hodari had broken away and had *then* cast away the cocaine, it would hardly be realistic to say that disclosure had been made during the course of an arrest. Cf. *Thompson v. Whitman*, 18 Wall. 457, 471 (1874) ("A seizure is a single act, and not a continuous fact"). The present case, however, is even one step further removed. It does not involve the application of any physical force; Hodari was untouched by Officer Pertoso at the time he discarded the cocaine. His defense relies instead upon the proposition that a seizure occurs "when the officer, by means of physical force *or show of authority*, has in some way restrained the liberty of a citizen." *Terry v. Ohio* . . . (emphasis added). Hodari contends (and we accept as true for purposes of this decision) that Pertoso's pursuit qualified as a "show of authority" calling upon Hodari to halt. The narrow question before us is whether, with respect to a show of authority as with respect to application of physical force, a seizure occurs even though the subject does not yield. We hold that it does not.

The language of the Fourth Amendment, of course, cannot sustain respondent's contention. The word "seizure" readily bears the meaning of a laying on of hands or application of physical force to restrain movement, even when it is ultimately unsuccessful. ("She seized the purse-snatcher, but he broke her grasp.") It does not remotely apply, however, to the prospect of a policeman yelling "Stop, in the name

[1] [1] California conceded below that Officer Pertoso did not have the "reasonable suspicion" required to justify stopping Hodari, see *Terry v. Ohio*. . . . That it would be unreasonable to stop, for brief inquiry, young men who scatter in panic upon the mere sighting of the police is not self-evident, and arguably contradicts proverbial common sense. See Proverbs 28:1 ("the wicked flee when no man pursueth"). We do not decide that point here, but rely entirely upon the State's concession.

of the law!" at a fleeing form that continues to flee. That is not a seizure.[2] Nor can the result respondent wishes to achieve be produced — indirectly, as it were — by suggesting that Pertoso's uncomplied-with show of authority was a common-law arrest, and then appealing to the principle that all common-law arrests are seizures. An arrest requires *either* physical force (as described above) *or*, where that is absent, *submission* to the assertion of authority.

. . .

We do not think it desirable, even as a policy matter, to stretch the Fourth Amendment beyond its words and beyond the meaning of arrest, as respondent urges.[3] Street pursuits always place the public at some risk, and compliance with police orders to stop should therefore be encouraged. Only a few of those orders, we presume, will be without adequate basis, and since the addressee has no ready means of identifying the deficient ones it almost invariably is the reasonable course to comply. Unlawful orders will not be deterred, moreover, by sanctioning through the exclusionary rule those of them that are *not* obeyed. Since policemen do not command "Stop!" expecting to be ignored, or give chase hoping to be outrun, it fully suffices to apply the deterrent to their genuine, successful seizures.

. . .

In sum, assuming that Pertoso's pursuit in the present case constituted a "show of authority" enjoining Hodari to halt, since Hodari did not comply with that injunction he was not seized until he was tackled. The cocaine abandoned while he was running was in this case not the fruit of a seizure, and his motion to exclude evidence of it was properly denied.

JUSTICE STEVENS, with whom JUSTICE MARSHALL joins, dissenting.

. . . Prior to *Terry*, the Fourth Amendment proscribed any seizure of the person that was not supported by the same probable cause showing that would justify a custodial arrest. . . . Given the fact that street encounters between citizens and police officers "are incredibly rich in diversity," . . . the Court recognized the need for flexibility and held that "reasonable" suspicion — a quantum of proof less demanding than probable cause — was adequate to justify a stop for investigatory purposes. . . . As a corollary to the lesser justification for the stop, the Court necessarily encompasses official restraints on individual freedom that fall short of a common-law arrest. Thus, *Terry* broadened the range of encounters between the

---

[2] [2] For this simple reason — which involved neither "logic-chopping," . . . nor any arcane knowledge of legal history — it is irrelevant that English law proscribed "an unlawful *attempt* to take a presumptively innocent person into custody." . . . We have consulted the common-law to explain the meaning of seizure — and, contrary to the dissent's portrayal, to expand rather than contract that meaning (since one would not normally think that the mere touching of a person would suffice). But neither usage nor common-law tradition makes an *attempted* seizure a seizure. The common-law may have made an attempted seizure unlawful in certain circumstances; but it made many things unlawful, very few of which were elevated to constitutional proscriptions.

[3] [3] Nor have we ever done so. The dissent is wrong in saying that *Terry v. Ohio* . . . "broadened the range of encounters . . . encompassed within the term 'seizure' ". . . . *Terry* unquestionably involved conduct that would constitute a common-law seizure; its novelty (if any) was in expanding the acceptable *justification* for such a seizure, beyond probable cause. . . .

police and the citizen encompassed within the term "seizure," while at the same time, lowering the standard of proof necessary to justify a "stop" in the newly expanded category of seizures now covered by the Fourth Amendment. The Court explained:

> . . . It is quite plain that the Fourth Amendment governs "seizures" of the person which do not eventuate in a trip to the station house any prosecution for crime — "arrests" in traditional terminology. It must be recognized that whenever a police officer accosts an individual and restrains his freedom to walk away, he has "seized" that person. . . .
>
> The distinctions of classical "stop-and-frisk" theory thus serve to divert attention from the central inquiry under the Fourth Amendment — the reasonableness in all the circumstances of the particular governmental invasion of a citizen's personal security. "Search" and "seizure" are not talismans. We therefore reject the notions that the Fourth Amendment does not come into play at all as a limitation upon police conduct if the officers stop short of something called a "technical arrest" or a "full-blown search." . . .

. . . [I]n *Terry*, the court abandoned its traditional view that a seizure under the Fourth Amendment required probable cause. Thus, the major premise underpinning the majority's entire analysis today — that the common law of arrest should define the term "seizure" for Fourth Amendment purposes . . . — is seriously flawed. . . .

Because the facts of this case are somewhat unusual, it is appropriate to note that the same issue would arise if the show of force took the form of a command to "freeze," a warning shot, or the sound of sirens accompanied by a patrol car's flashing lights. In any of these situations, there may be a significant time interval between the initiation of the officer's show of force and the complete submission by the citizen. At least on the facts of this case, the Court concludes that the timing of the seizure is governed by the citizen's reaction, rather than by the officer's conduct. . . . One consequence of this conclusion is that the point at which the interaction between citizen and police officer becomes a seizure occurs, not when a reasonable citizen believes he or she is no longer free to go, but rather, only after the officer exercises control over the citizen.

. . . In the present case, if Officer Pertoso had succeeded in tackling respondent before he dropped the rock of cocaine, the rock unquestionably would have been excluded as the fruit of the officer's unlawful seizure. Instead, under the Court's logic-chopping analysis, the exclusionary rule has no application because an attempt to make an unconstitutional seizure is beyond the coverage of the Fourth Amendment no matter how outrageous or unreasonable the officer's conduct may be.

NOTES AND QUESTIONS

(1) *The Precursors. Hodari D.* is best understood when read in context with two prior decisions which it closely follows. In *Michigan v. Chesternut*, 486 U.S. 567 (1988), the facts were substantially similar to *Hodari D.* (patrolling officers

suspected a drug transaction) but rather than chasing the suspect, the officers drove alongside the suspect for a short distance, in reaction to which the suspect discarded a packet of narcotics. The Court, without dissent, held that the suspect had not been seized. In a concurring opinion, Justice Kennedy, joined by Justice Scalia, interpreted the opinion of the Court as holding that the police had engaged in no improper conduct. The concurring justices would have gone further to hold that "neither 'chase' nor 'investigative pursuit' need be included in the lexicon of the Fourth Amendment."

Brower v. Inyo County, 489 U.S. 593 (1989), was an action for damages under 42 U.S.C. § 1983 claiming a violation of the Fourth Amendment in the use of excessive force. In an effort to apprehend the driver of a stolen car who had been pursued by the police for some twenty miles, officials had placed an 18-wheel truck completely across the highway. The Court, once again without dissent, held that the collision of the deceased with the barrier was a seizure for Fourth Amendment purposes. The Court remanded the case to determine whether the use of the roadblock was reasonable.

The upshot of the three decisions appears thus: Insofar as it protects individuals, as opposed to property, the Fourth Amendment is inapplicable unless and until a seizure of the person occurs, either by virtue of the acquiescence of the individual, or because of some force applied to the person. If a seizure has occurred, then the question becomes whether the official conduct was reasonable for purposes of the Fourth Amendment.

(2) *The Rationale.* Justice Scalia's opinion in *Hodari D.* has a "let's decide this issue once-and-for-all" air about it. Is the reasoning, analytical and historical, persuasive? The pertinent language of the Fourth Amendment provides: "The right of the people to be secure in their persons . . . against unreasonable searches and seizures, shall not be violated. . . . " Has the Court focused on "seizures" while ignoring "searches"? Might one argue plausibly that the right "to be secure" in one's person is implicated when one is being chased as well as when one is caught? As to the historical justification, Justice Scalia makes no "framers' intent" argument, but he does cite several nineteenth century decisions on the meaning of a seizure, none of which entailed the application of the Fourth Amendment or, indeed, were even criminal cases.

(3) *The Implications.* The outcome of cases such as *Hodari D.* would appear to be controlled by fortuities which have little to do with the values secured by the Fourth Amendment. If Hodari D. had either (1) stopped or (2) been tackled by Pertoso *before* he discarded the rock, the evidence would be excluded unless the government convinced the court that the decision to detain was reasonable. On the other hand, so long as Hodari D. neither stopped of his own volition nor was physically impeded, apparently no conduct of the officers would violate the Fourth Amendment. So, for example, if under similar circumstances a pursuing officer shoots at the suspect and misses, evidence abandoned in the continued flight would be admissible. If, however, the officer hits the suspect, a finding of a violation of the Fourth Amendment would be likely. See *Tennessee v. Garner*, 471 U.S. 1 (1985). See also *Clark v. State*, 648 So. 2d 848 (Fla. App. 1995), in which a suspect, riding a bicycle, passed a parked police car. The officer opened the door causing the suspect

to collide with it and fall to the pavement. The court held that a detention had occurred for purposes of the Fourth Amendment.

Consistent with *Hordari D.*, in *County of Sacramento v. Lewis*, 523 U.S. 833 (1998), the Supreme Court observed that "[a]ttempted seizures of a person are beyond the scope of the Fourth Amendment." But any physical contact between the officer and suspect may be sufficient to constitute a seizure. For example, in *United States v. Eustaquio*, 198 F.3d 1068 (8th Cir. 1999), the act of the officer in touching the individual's midsection was enough. Indeed, a suspect may be seized without any physical contact at all. In *Commonwealth v. Ramos*, 430 Mass. 545, 549, 721 N.E.2d 923, 927 (2000), the court held that the defendant had been seized "when the police notified her that they would not leave until she came out of the apartment and that if she continued to refuse, they would have the fire department break down the door." Many state courts have held that a seizure occurs when the emergency lights on a police vehicle are activated. *See, e.g.*, *Blake v. State*, 939 So. 2d 192 (Fla. Dist. Ct. App. 2006); *State v. Williams*, 185 S.W.3d 311 (Tenn. 2006). *But see United States v. Carr*, 674 F.3d 570, 573 (6th Cir. 2012) ("The officers' use of blue lights was not sufficiently coercive to transfer this encounter into a compulsory stop. An encounter does not become compulsory merely because a person identified himself as a police officer.").

Should the giving of a *Miranda* warning be sufficient in itself to make a confrontation a seizure? The Florida Supreme Court has held that it does not. *Caldwell v. State*, 41 So. 3d 188 (Fla. 2010). The court acknowledged that "courts that have considered the application of *Miranda* in the context of an on-the-street police encounter have generally found it to be at least a factor in determining whether an individual has been subjected to an illegal investigatory stop under the Fourth Amendment," but "the proper test is whether, based on the totality of the circumstances, a reasonable person would feel free to end the encounter and depart."

(4) *The Unpersuaded.* A few courts have declined to follow Hodari D.'s bright line rule. In *Greeno v. State*, 861 N.E.2d 1232, 1237 (Ind. App. 2007), the court reasoned that "[w]hen [the officer] began chasing Greeno, Greeno obviously was no longer 'free to . . . walk away.' Therefore, contrary to the State's assertion, when [the officer] yelled stop and began chasing Greeno, the Fourth Amendment was implicated." Similarly, the Tennessee Supreme Court held that "[w]hether a person has been physically restrained or has stopped or yielded to the show of authority is not dispositive of whether there has been a seizure." The question, it concluded, was whether under all the circumstances "a reasonable person would have believed he or she was not free to leave." *State v. Randolph*, 74 S.W.3d 330, 337 (Tenn. 2002).

(5) *Vehicle Stops.* When a vehicle is the target of a traffic stop, clearly the driver has been detained. Is this also true of a passenger in the vehicle? This question was raised in *Brendlin v. California*, 551 U.S. 249 (2007). After stopping a car without justification (a point conceded by the State), the officer recognized the passenger in the vehicle as a parole violator and arrested him. Incriminating evidence was recovered in an incident search. The State argued that Brendlin had not been seized and hence could not claim that the evidence was tainted. Speaking for a unanimous Court, Justice Souter held that "Brendlin was seized from the moment [the] car

came to a halt on the side of the road." Implicitly, if the stop of the vehicle is constitutional, the seizure of the passengers is reasonable, notwithstanding the absence of any suspicion associated with them at the moment of the seizure. What if, while a citation is being issued to the driver, a passenger attempts to get out of the car and leave?

(6) *The Breakaway Detainee.* If a suspect abandons incriminating evidence while being illegally detained, the object will likely be inadmissible as the fruit of the illegality. Suppose, however, a suspect breaks free from an illegal detention and thereafter abandons the object. Is this case indistinguishable from *Hodari D.*, or does the intervening illegal detention change the outcome? Some courts find the seizure lawful. *See State v. Zuniga*, 146 P.3d 697 (Idaho Ct. App. 2006); *State v. Lisenbee*, 13 P.3d 947 (Nev. 2000); *People v. Henderson*, 989 N.E.2d 192, 203 (Ill. 2013) ("Although defendant's flight did not 'wipe the slate clean, as if the illegal seizure never took place,' it did interrupt the causal connection between the two events."). *But see State v. Ramsey*, 224 P.3d 977, 980 (Ariz. Ct. App. 2010) ("[I]f a defendant briefly stops after a show of authority and then subsequently flees, a seizure occurs at the time the defendant is first stopped, and not when he is ultimately apprehended.").

Assuming that there was insufficient suspicion to justify the initial detention, would a breakaway provide the suspicion to sustain a subsequent detention? *People v. Thomas*, 734 N.E.2d 1015, 1022 (Ill. App. Ct. 2000), *judgment aff'd*, 198 Ill. 2d 103, 259 Ill. Dec. 838, 759 N.E.2d 899 (2001), held that it did. "It simply does not serve a legitimate purpose to suppress evidence where an unlawful show of authority was not submitted to, and, instead, precipitated headlong flight indicative of criminal activity."

PROBLEM A
THE OBLIVIOUS DETAINEE

An officer observed the defendant's car at 4:35 AM with the driver's window down and the engine running. Other cars were parked on either side and in front of the vehicle. The officer pulled his cruiser up behind the defendant, thereby preventing any significant movement of the vehicle. Efforts to arouse the defendant from sleep were initially unsuccessful, but eventually the officer detected the presence of alcohol and arrested the defendant for driving while intoxicated. Is the arrest legal? *See Tate v. People*, 290 P.3d 1268 (Colo. 2012).

UNITED STATES v. DRAYTON
United States Supreme Court
536 U.S. 194 (2002)

JUSTICE KENNEDY delivered the opinion of the Court.

The Fourth Amendment permits police officers to approach bus passengers at random to ask questions and to request their consent to searches, provided a reasonable person would understand that he or she is free to refuse. *Florida v. Bostick*, 501 U.S. 429 (1991). This case requires us to determine whether officers must advise bus passengers during these encounters of their right *not* to cooperate.

I

On February 4, 1999, respondents Christopher Drayton and Clifton Brown, Jr., were traveling on a Greyhound bus in route from Ft. Lauderdale, Florida, to Detroit, Michigan. The bus made a scheduled stop in Tallahassee, Florida. The passengers were required to disembark so the bus could be refueled and cleaned. As the passengers reboarded, the driver checked their tickets and then left to complete paperwork inside the terminal. As he left, the driver allowed three members of the Tallahassee Police Department to board the bus as part of a routine drug and weapons interdiction effort. The officers were dressed in plain clothes and carried concealed weapons and visible badges.

Once onboard Officer Hoover knelt on the driver's seat and faced the rear of the bus. He could observe the passengers and ensure the safety of the two other officers without blocking the aisle or otherwise obstructing the bus exit. Officers Lang and Blackburn went to the rear of the bus. Blackburn remained stationed there, facing forward. Lang worked his way toward the front of the bus, speaking with the individual passengers as he went. He asked the passengers about their travel plans and sought to match passengers with luggage in the overhead racks. To avoid blocking the aisle, Lang stood next to or just behind each passenger with whom he spoke.

According to Lang's testimony, passengers who declined to cooperate with him or who chose to exit the bus at any time would have been allowed to do so without argument. In Lang's experience, however, most people are willing to cooperate. Some passengers go so far as to commend the police for their efforts to ensure the safety of their travel. Lang could recall five to six instances in the previous year in which passengers had declined to have their luggage searched. It also was common for passengers to leave the bus for a cigarette or a snack while the officers were on board. Lang sometimes informed passengers of their right to refuse to cooperate. On the day in question, however, he did not.

Respondents were seated next to each other on the bus. Drayton was in the aisle seat, Brown in the seat next to the window. Lang approached respondents from the rear and leaned over Drayton's shoulder. He held up his badge long enough for respondents to identify him as a police officer. With his face 12-to-18 inches away from Drayton's, Lang spoke in a voice just loud enough for respondent to hear:

> "I'm Investigator Lang with the Tallahassee Police Department. We're conducting bus interdiction [sic], attempting to deter drugs and illegal weapons being transported on this bus. Do you have any bags on the bus?"

. . .

Both respondents pointed to a single green bag in the overhead luggage rack. Lang asked, "Do you mind if I check it?" and Brown responded, "Go ahead". . . . Lang handed the bag to Officer Blackburn to check. The bag contained no contraband.

Officer Lang noticed that both respondents were wearing heavy jackets and baggy pants despite the warm weather. In Lang's experience drug traffickers often use baggy clothing to conceal weapons or narcotics. The officer thus asked Brown if he had any weapons or drugs in his possession. And he asked Brown: "Do you mind if I check your person?" Brown answered, "Sure," and cooperated by leaning up in his seat, pulling a cell phone out of his pocket, and opening up his jacket. . . . Lang reached across Drayton and patted down Brown's jacket and pockets, including his waist areas, sides, and upper thighs. In both thigh areas, Lang detected hard objects similar to drug packages detected on other occasions. Lang arrested and handcuffed Brown. Officer Hoover escorted Brown from the bus.

Lang then asked Drayton, "Mind if I check you?" . . . Drayton responded by lifting his hands about eight inches from his legs. Lang conducted a pat-down of Drayton's thighs and detected hard objects similar to those found on Brown. He arrested Drayton and escorted him from the bus. A further search revealed that respondents had duct-taped plastic bundles of powder cocaine between several pairs of their boxer shorts. Brown possessed three bundles containing 483 grams of cocaine. Drayton possessed two bundles containing 295 grams of cocaine.

[The Court of Appeals for the Eleventh Circuit held that the evidence should have been suppressed because, relying upon its own precedent, "bus passengers do not feel free to disregard police officers' requests to search absent 'some positive indication that consent could have been refused.' "]

We granted certiorari. . . . The respondents, we conclude, were not seized and their consent to the search was voluntary; and we reverse.

II

. . .

The Court has addressed on a previous occasion the specific question of drug interdiction efforts on buses. In *Bostick*, two police officers requested a bus passenger's consent to a search of his luggage. The passenger agreed, and the resulting search revealed cocaine in his suitcase. The Florida Supreme Court suppressed the cocaine. In doing so it adopted a *per se* rule that due to the cramped confines onboard a bus the act of questioning would deprive a person of his or her freedom of movement and so constitute a seizure under the Fourth Amendment.

This Court reversed. *Bostick* first made it clear that for the most part per se rules are inappropriate in the Fourth Amendment context. The proper inquiry necessitates a consideration of "all the circumstances surrounding the encounter." . . . The Court noted next that the traditional rule, which states that a seizure does not occur so long as a reasonable person would feel free "to disregard the police and go about his business," *California v. Hodari D.*, . . . is not an accurate measure of the coercive effect of a bus encounter. A passenger may not want to get off a bus if there is a risk it will depart before the opportunity to reboard. . . . A bus rider's movements are confined in this sense, but this is the natural result of choosing to take the bus; it says nothing about whether the police conduct is coercive. . . . The proper inquiry "is whether a reasonable person would feel free to decline the officers' requests or otherwise terminate the encounter." . . . Finally, the Court rejected Bostick's argument that he must have been seized because no reasonable person would consent to a search of luggage containing drugs. The reasonable person test, the Court explained, is objective and "presupposes an *innocent* person." . . .

In light of the limited record, *Bostick* refrained from deciding whether a seizure occurred. . . . The Court, however, identified two factors "particularly worth noting" on remand. . . . First, although it was obvious that an officer was armed, he did not remove the gun from its pouch or use it in a threatening way. Second, the officer advised the passenger that he could refuse consent to the search. . . .

Applying the *Bostick* framework to the facts of this particular case, we conclude that the police did not seize respondents when they boarded the bus and began questioning passengers. The officers gave the passengers no reason to believe that they were required to answer the officers' questions. When Officer Lang approached respondents, he did not brandish a weapon or make any intimidating movements. He left the aisle free so that respondents could exit. He spoke to passengers one by one and in a polite, quiet voice. Nothing he said would suggest to a reasonable person that he or she was barred from leaving the bus or otherwise terminating the encounter.

There were ample grounds for the District Court to conclude that "everything that took place between Officer Land and [respondents] suggests that it was cooperative" and that there "was nothing coercive [or] confrontational" about the encounter. . . . There was no application of force, no intimidating movement, no overwhelming show of force, no brandishing of weapons, no blocking exits, no threat, no command, not even an authoritative tone of voice. It is beyond question that had this encounter occurred on the street, it would be constitutional. The fact that an encounter takes place on a bus does not on its own transform standard police questioning of citizens into an illegal seizure. See *Bostick*, ... Indeed, because many fellow passengers are present to witness officers' conduct, a reasonable person may feel even more secure in his or her decision not to cooperate with police on a bus than in other circumstances.

. . .

Drayton contends that even if Brown's cooperation with the officers was consensual, Drayton was seized because no reasonable person would feel free to terminate the encounter with the officers after Brown had been arrested. The Court of Appeals did not address this claim; and in any event the argument fails. The arrest of one person does not mean that everyone around him has been seized by police. If anything, Brown's arrest should have put Drayton on notice of the consequences of continuing the encounter by answering the officers' questions. Even after arresting Brown, Lang addressed Drayton in a polite manner and provided him with no indication that he was required to answer Lang's questions.

[The portion of the opinion of the Court addressing the consent to search issue, as well as the dissenting opinion, will be found in § 3.04[G], *infra.*]

QUESTIONS

(1) The Court cites with approval the statement in *Bostick* that the reasonable person test "presupposes an innocent person." Is an individual's awareness of his wrongdoing irrelevant? One court has maintained that "the particular personal traits or subjective state of mind of the defendant are irrelevant to the objective 'reasonable person' test set out in *Bostick*." *United States v. Hill*, 199 F.3d 1143, 1149 (10th Cir. 1999), *cert. denied*, 531 U.S. 830 (2000).

(2) Lower courts are likely to find a detention occurred if an officer has retained identification papers or transportation tickets. *See, e.g.*, *United States v. Lambert*, 46 F.3d 1064 (10th Cir. 1995); *Finger v. State*, 799 N.E.2d 528 (Ind. 2003).

(3) For a discussion of the issues raised by drug interdiction programs, see Janice Nadler, *No Need to Shout: Bus Sweeps and the Psychology of Coercion*, 2002 Sup. Ct. Rev. 153.

§ 2.02 THE SLIDING SCALE OF SUSPICION

[A] The Random Stop

DELAWARE v. PROUSE

United States Supreme Court
440 U.S. 648 (1979)

MR. JUSTICE WHITE delivered the opinion of the Court.

The question is whether it is an unreasonable seizure under the Fourth and Fourteenth Amendments to stop an automobile, being driven on a public highway, for the purpose of checking the driving license of the operator and the registration of the car, where there is neither probable cause to believe nor reasonable suspicion that the car is being driven contrary to the laws governing the operation of motor vehicles or that either the car or any of its occupants is subject to seizure or detention in connection with the violation of any other applicable law.

At 7:20 p.m. on November 30, 1976, a New Castle County, Del. patrolman in a police cruiser stopped the automobile occupied by respondent. The patrolman smelled marihuana smoke as he was walking toward the stopped vehicle, and he seized marihuana in plain view on the car floor. Respondent was subsequently indicted for illegal possession of a controlled substance. At a hearing on respondent's motion to suppress the marihuana seized as a result of the stop, the patrolman testified that prior to stopping the vehicle he had observed neither traffic nor equipment violations nor any suspicious activity, and that he made the stop only in order to check the driver's license and registration. The patrolman was not acting pursuant to any standards, guidelines, or procedures pertaining to document spot checks, promulgated by either his department or the State Attorney General. Characterizing the stop as "routine," the patrolman explained, "I saw the car in the area and was not answering any complaints so I decided to pull them off." . . . The trial court granted the motion to suppress, finding the stop and detention to have been wholly capricious and therefore violative of the Fourth Amendment.

The Delaware Supreme Court affirmed, noting first that "the issue of the legal validity of systematic, roadblock-type stops of a number of vehicles for license and vehicle registration check is *not* now before the Court," 332 A.2d 1359, 1362 (1978) (emphasis in original). The court held that "a random stop of a motorist in the absence of specific articulable facts which justify the stop by indicating a reasonable suspicion that a violation of the law has occurred is constitutionally impermissible and violative of the Fourth and Fourteenth Amendments to the Constitution." 382 A.2d, at 1364. We granted certiorari to resolve the conflict between this decision, which is in accord with decisions in five other jurisdictions, and the contrary determination in six jurisdictions that the Fourth Amendment does not prohibit the kind of automobile stop that occurred here.

The Fourth and Fourteenth Amendments are implicated in this case because stopping an automobile and detaining its occupants constitute a "seizure" within the meaning of those Amendments, even though the purpose of the stop is limited and the resulting detention quite brief. . . . The essential purpose of the proscriptions in the Fourth Amendment is to impose a standard of "reasonableness" upon the exercise of discretion by government officials, including law-enforcement agents, in order "to safeguard the privacy and security of individuals against arbitrary invasion. . . ." Thus, the permissibility of a particular law-enforcement practice is judged by balancing its intrusion on the individual's Fourth Amendment interests against its promotion of legitimate governmental interests. Implemented in this manner, the reasonableness standard usually requires, at a minimum, that the facts upon which an intrusion is based be capable of measurement against "an objective standard," whether this be probable cause or a less stringent test.

But the State of Delaware urges that these stops are reasonable under the Fourth Amendment because the State's interest in the practice as a means of promoting public safety upon its roads more than outweighs the intrusion entailed. Although the record discloses no statistics concerning the extent of the problem of lack of highway safety, in Delaware or in the Nation as a whole, we are aware of the danger to life and property posed by vehicular traffic and of the difficulties that even a cautious and an experienced driver may encounter. We agree that the States have a vital interest in ensuring that only those qualified to do so are permitted to operate motor vehicles, that these vehicles are fit for safe operation, and hence that licensing, registration, and vehicle inspection requirements are being observed. Automobile licenses are issued periodically to evidence that the drivers holding them are sufficiently familiar with the rules of the road and are physically qualified to operate a motor vehicle. The registration requirement and, more pointedly, the related annual inspection requirement in Delaware are designed to keep dangerous automobiles off the road. Unquestionably, these provisions, properly administered, are essential elements in a highway safety program. Furthermore, we note that the State of Delaware requires a minimum amount of insurance coverage as a condition to automobile registration, implementing its legitimate interest in seeing to it that its citizens have protection when involved in a motor vehicle accident.

The question remains, however, whether in the service of these important ends the discretionary spot check is a sufficiently productive mechanism to justify the intrusion upon Fourth Amendment interests which such stops entail. On the record before us, that question must be answered in the negative. Given the alternative mechanisms available, both those in use and those that might be adopted, we are unconvinced that the incremental contribution to highway safety of the random spot check justifies the practice under the Fourth Amendment.

The foremost method of enforcing traffic and vehicle safety regulations, it must be recalled, is acting upon observed violations. Vehicle stops for traffic violations occur countless times each day; and on these occasions, licenses and registration papers are subject to inspection and drivers without them will be ascertained. Furthermore, drivers without licenses are presumably the less safe drivers whose propensities may well exhibit themselves. Absent some empirical data to the contrary, it must be assumed that finding an unlicensed driver among those who commit traffic violations is a much more likely event than finding an unlicensed driver by choosing randomly from the entire universe of drivers. If this were not so, licensing of drivers would hardly be an effective means of promoting roadway safety. It seems common sense that the percentage of all drivers on the road who are driving without a license is very small and that the number of licensed drivers who will be stopped in order to find one unlicensed operator will be large indeed. The contribution to highway safety made by discretionary stops selected from among drivers generally will therefore be marginal at best. Furthermore, and again absent something more than mere assertion to the contrary, we find it difficult to believe that the unlicensed driver would not be deterred by the possibility of being involved in a traffic violation or having some other experience calling for proof of his entitlement to drive but that he would be deterred by the possibility that he would be one of those chosen for a spot check. In terms of actually discovering unlicensed drivers or deterring them from driving, the spot check does not appear sufficiently productive to qualify as a reasonable law-enforcement practice under the Fourth Amendment.

Much the same can be said about the safety aspects of automobiles as distinguished from drivers. Many violations of minimum vehicle safety requirements are observable, and something can be done about them by the observing officer, directly and immediately. Furthermore, in Delaware, as elsewhere, vehicles must carry and display current license plates, which themselves evidence that the vehicle is properly registered; and, under Delaware law, to qualify for annual registration a vehicle must pass the annual safety inspection and be properly insured. It does not appear, therefore, that a stop of a Delaware-registered vehicle is necessary in order to ascertain compliance with the State's registration requirements; and because there is nothing to show that a significant percentage of automobiles from other States do not also require license plates indicating current registration, there is no basis for concluding that stopping even out-of-state cars for document checks substantially promotes the State's interest.

The marginal contribution to roadway safety possibly resulting from a system of spot checks cannot justify subjecting every occupant of every vehicle on the roads to a seizure limited in magnitude compared to other intrusions but nonetheless constitutionally cognizable at the unbridled discretion of law-enforcement officials. To insist upon neither an appropriate factual basis for suspicion directed at a particular automobile nor upon some other substantial and objective standard or rule to govern the exercise of discretion "would invite intrusions upon constitutionally guaranteed rights based on nothing more substantial than inarticulate hunches." *Terry v. Ohio, supra*, at 22. By hypothesis, stopping apparently safe drivers is necessary only because the danger presented by some drivers is not observable at the time of the stop. When there is not probable cause to believe that a driver is violating any one of the multitude of applicable traffic and equipment regulations nor other articulable basis amounting to reasonable suspicion that the driver is unlicensed or his vehicle unregistered we cannot conceive of any legitimate basis upon which a patrolman could decide that stopping a particular driver for a spot check would be more productive than stopping any other driver. This kind of standardless and unconstrained discretion is the evil the Court has discerned when in previous cases it has insisted that the discretion of the official in the field be circumscribed, at least to some extent.

Accordingly, we hold that except in those situations in which there is at least articulable and reasonable suspicion that a motorist is unlicensed or that an automobile is not registered, or that either the vehicle or an occupant is otherwise subject to seizure for violation of law, stopping an automobile and detaining the driver in order to check his driver's license and the registration of the automobile are unreasonable under the Fourth Amendment. This holding does not preclude the State of Delaware or other States from developing methods for spot checks that involve less intrusion or that do not involve the unconstrained exercise of discretion. Questioning of all oncoming traffic at roadblock-type stops is one possible alternative. We hold only that persons in automobiles on public roadways may not for that reason alone have their travel and privacy interfered with at the unbridled discretion of police officers. The judgment below is affirmed.

So ordered.

MR. JUSTICE BLACKMUN, with whom MR. JUSTICE POWELL joins, concurring.

The Court carefully protects from the reach of its decision other less intrusive spot checks "that do not involve the unconstrained exercise of discretion." The roadblock stop for all traffic is given as an example. I necessarily assume that the Court's reservation also includes other not purely random stops (such as every 10th car to pass a given point) that equate with, but are less intrusive than, a 100% roadblock stop. And I would not regard the present case as a precedent that throws any constitutional shadow upon the necessarily somewhat individualized and perhaps largely random examinations by game wardens in the performance of their duties. In a situation of that type, it seems to me, the Court's balancing process, and the value factors under consideration, would be quite different.

With this understanding, I join the Court's opinion and its judgment.

MR. JUSTICE REHNQUIST, dissenting.

The Court holds, in successive sentences, that absent an articulable, reasonable suspicion of unlawful conduct, a motorist may not be subjected to a random license check, but that the States are free to develop "methods for spot checks that do not involve the unconstrained exercise of discretion," such as "questioning all on-coming

conduct will not withstand constitutional scrutiny. Thus, courts have invalidated searches of all persons attending Klan rallies, *Wilkinson v. Forst*, 639 F. Supp. 518 (D. Conn. 1986), *aff'd in part, rev'd in part*, 832 F.2d 1330 (2d Cir. 1987), *cert. denied*, 485 U.S. 1034 (1988), and rock concerts, *State v. Carter*, 267 N.W.2d 385 (Iowa 1978); *Jacobsen v. City of Seattle*, 98 Wash. 2d 668, 658 P.2d 653 (1983) (injunction issued).

(5) *The Use of Profiles.* In recent years, law enforcement personnel have placed increasing reliance on "profiles" to aid in the identification of suspects — particularly airplane hijackers and drug couriers. Because such devices inevitably entail stereotyping, and thus many perfectly innocent individuals may be singled out for investigation because of their age, gender, race, national origin, physical appearance, luggage, point of departure or destination, method of ticket purchase, or some combination of these, the practice has been subjected to constitutional challenge. (A widely-publicized example of such screening, albeit in the private sector, surfaced during the 1991 Persian Gulf Conflict when at least one airline refused to accept Iraqis on its flights.) Nevertheless, the Supreme Court rendered the use of a drug courier profile a non-issue in *United States v. Sokolow*, 409 U.S. 1(1989). In sustaining the airport detention of an individual known to have (1) paid cash for his tickets, (2) traveled under a name that did not match his telephone directory listing, (3) flown from Miami, (4) stayed in Miami only 48 hours following a 20-hour flight from Hawaii, (5) appeared nervous, and (6) checked no baggage, the Court said:

> We do not agree with respondent that our analysis is somehow changed by the agents' belief that his behavior was consistent with one of the DEA's "drug courier profiles." . . . A court sitting to determine the existence of reasonable suspicion must require the agent to articulate the factors leading to that conclusion, but the fact that these factors may be set forth in a "profile" does not somehow detract from their evidentiary significance as seen by the trained agent.

Justice Marshall, joined by Justice Brennan, dissenting, observed:

> Reflexive reliance on a profile of drug courier characteristics runs a far greater risk than does ordinary, case-by-case police work, of subjecting innocent individuals to unwarranted police harassment and detention. This risk is enhanced by the profile's "chameleon-like way of adapting to any particular set of observations."

Judge Norris, speaking for the Court of Appeals for the Ninth Circuit in *Sokolow*, had observed: "Certainly no one can doubt that the police cannot, even in part, justify an investigatory stop of a person suspected of insider trading because that person wears a pin-striped suit and a gold Cartier watch." *United States v. Sokolow*, 808 F.2d 1366, 1370 (9th Cir. 1987).

[B] The Pervasive Roadblock

MICHIGAN DEPARTMENT OF STATE POLICE v. SITZ

United States Supreme Court
496 U.S. 444 (1990)

CHIEF JUSTICE REHNQUIST delivered the opinion of the Court.

This case poses the question whether a State's use of highway sobriety checkpoints violates the Fourth and Fourteenth Amendments to the United States Constitution. We hold that it does not and therefore reverse the contrary holding of the Court of Appeals of Michigan.

Petitioners, the Michigan Department of State Police and its director, established a sobriety checkpoint pilot program in early 1986. The director appointed a Sobriety Checkpoint Advisory Committee comprising representatives of the State Police force, local police forces, state prosecutors, and the University of Michigan Transportation Research Institute. Pursuant to its charge, the advisory committee created guidelines setting forth procedures governing checkpoint operations, site selection, and publicity.

Under the guidelines, checkpoints would be set up at selected sites along state roads. All vehicles passing through a checkpoint would be stopped and their drivers briefly examined for signs of intoxication. In cases where a checkpoint officer detected signs of intoxication, the motorist would be directed to a location out of the traffic flow where an officer would check the motorist's driver's license and car registration and, if warranted, conduct further sobriety tests. Should the field tests and the officer's observations suggest that the driver was intoxicated, an arrest would be made. All other drivers would be permitted to resume their journey immediately.

The first — and to date the only — sobriety checkpoint operated under the program was conducted in Saginaw County with the assistance of the Saginaw County Sheriff's Department. During the [75-minute] duration of the checkpoint's operation, 126 vehicles passed through the checkpoint. The average delay for each vehicle was approximately 25 seconds. Two drivers were detained for field sobriety testing, and one of the two was arrested for driving under the influence of alcohol. A third driver who drove through without stopping was pulled over by an officer in an observation vehicle and arrested for driving under the influence.

On the day before the operation of the Saginaw County checkpoint, respondents filed a complaint in the Circuit Court of Wayne County seeking declaratory and injunctive relief from potential subjection to the checkpoints. Each of the respondents "is a licensed driver in the State of Michigan . . . who regularly travels throughout the State in his automobile." . . . During pretrial proceedings, petitioners agreed to delay further implementation of the checkpoint program pending the outcome of this litigation.

After the trial, at which the court heard extensive testimony concerning, *inter alia*, the "effectiveness" of highway sobriety checkpoint programs, the court ruled that the Michigan program violated the Fourth Amendment and Art. 1, § 11 of the Michigan Constitution. . . . On appeal, the Michigan Court of Appeals affirmed the holding that the program violated the Fourth Amendment and, for that reason, did not consider whether the program violated the Michigan Constitution. . . . After the Michigan Supreme Court denied petitioners' application for leave to appeal, we granted certiorari. . . .

In *Delaware v. Prouse* . . . we disapproved random stops made by Delaware Highway Patrol officers in an effort to apprehend unlicensed drivers and unsafe vehicles. We observed that no empirical evidence indicated that such stops would be an effective means of promoting roadway safety and said that "it seems common sense that the percentage of all drivers on the road who are driving without a license is very small and that the number of licensed drivers who will be stopped in order to find one unlicensed operator will be large indeed." . . . We observed that the random stops involved the "kind of standardless and unconstrained discretion [which] is the evil the Court has discerned when in previous cases it has insisted that the discretion of the official in the field be circumscribed, at least to some extent." . . . We went on to state that our holding did not "cast doubt on the permissibility of roadside truck weigh-stations and inspection checkpoints, at which some vehicles may be subject to further detention for safety and regulatory inspection than are others." . . .

Unlike *Prouse*, this case involves neither a complete absence of empirical data nor a challenge to random highway stops. During the operation of the Saginaw County checkpoint, the detention of each of the 126 vehicles that entered the checkpoint resulted in the arrest of two drunken drivers. Stated as a percentage, approximately 1.5 percent of the drivers passing through the checkpoint were arrested for alcohol impairment. In addition, an expert witness testified at the trial that experience in other States demonstrated that, on the whole, sobriety checkpoints resulted in drunken driving arrests of around 1 percent of all motorists stopped. . . .

In sum, the balance of the State's interest in preventing drunken driving, the extent to which this system can reasonably be said to advance that interest, and the degree of intrusion upon individual motorists who are briefly stopped, weighs in favor of the state program. We therefore hold that it is consistent with the Fourth Amendment. The judgment of the Michigan Court of Appeals is accordingly reversed, and the cause is remanded for further proceedings not inconsistent with this opinion.

[Justice Blackmun concurred in the judgment; Justice Brennan, joined by Justice Marshall, dissented; Justice Stevens, joined by Justices Brennan and Marshall, dissented.]

NOTES AND QUESTIONS

(1) The Court took note of the success rate of the drunk driving checkpoint in the county (1.5 percent of drivers stopped were arrested), and the success rate nationally (1 percent). Does this settle the matter for the foreseeable future, or is the reasonableness of a particular checkpoint fact specific. Suppose the defendant

has proof that the success rate in the county in which he was arrested was less than 0.25 percent. Does it matter? What if the defendant can show that there are more effective (and less intrusive) ways to deter drunk driving? In *Commonwealth v. Beaman*, 583 Pa. 636, 880 A.2d 578 (2005), the appellant offered statistical evidence that roving patrols were a more efficient use of law enforcement resources than fixed checkpoints. The court did not question the accuracy of the appellant's data, but found the statistical difference "not overwhelming," and deferred to the judgment of law enforcement officials. It also noted that the deterrent effect of highly visible checkpoints was difficult to quantify.

(2) Suppose a driver is observed by officers maneuvering his vehicle in a legal manner so as to avoid being detained in a roadblock. Would such behavior standing alone provide the suspicion which would justify stopping the vehicle? Most courts have held that it does not. *See United States v. Carpenter*, 462 F.3d 981 (8th Cir. 2006); *United States v. Neff*, 681 F.3d 1134 (10th Cir. 2012). *But see State v. Anaya*, 217 P.3d 586, 589 (N.M. 2009) ("Evading a marked DWI checkpoint is a specific and articulable fact that is sufficient to predicate reasonable suspicion for an investigatory stop.") Might a state make it an offense to intentionally avoid a checkpoint?

CITY OF INDIANAPOLIS v. EDMOND

United States Supreme Court
531 U.S. 32 (2000)

JUSTICE O'CONNOR delivered the opinion of the Court.

In *Michigan Dept. of State Police v. Sitz* . . . and *United States v. Martinez-Fuerte* . . . we held that brief, suspicionless seizures at highway checkpoints for the purposes of combating drunk driving and intercepting illegal immigrants were constitutional. We now consider the constitutionality of a highway checkpoint program whose primary purpose is the discovery and interdiction of illegal narcotics.

I

In August 1998, the city of Indianapolis began to operate vehicle checkpoints on Indianapolis roads in an effort to interdict unlawful drugs. The city conducted six such roadblocks between August and November that year, stopping 1,161 vehicles and arresting 104 motorists. Fifty-five arrests were for drug-related crimes, while 49 were for offenses unrelated to drugs. . . . The overall "hit rate" of the program was thus approximately nine percent.

The parties stipulated to the facts concerning the operation of the checkpoints by the Indianapolis Police Department (IPD) for purposes of the preliminary injunction proceedings instituted below. At each checkpoint location, the police stop a predetermined number of vehicles. Approximately 30 officers are stationed at the checkpoint. Pursuant to written directives issued by the chief of police, at least one officer approaches the vehicle, advises the driver that he or she is being stopped briefly at a drug checkpoint, and asks the driver to produce a license and registration. The officer also looks for signs of impairment and conducts an open-view examination of the vehicle from the outside. A narcotics-detection dog walks around the outside of each stopped vehicle.

The directives instruct the officers that they may conduct a search only by consent or based on the appropriate quantum of particularized suspicion. The officers must conduct each stop in the same manner until particularized suspicion develops, and the officers have no discretion to stop any vehicle out of sequence. The city agreed in the stipulation to operate the checkpoints in such a way as to ensure that the total duration of each stop, absent reasonable suspicion or probable cause, would be five minutes or less.

The affidavit of Indianapolis Police Sergeant Marshall DePew, although it is technically outside the parties' stipulation, provides further insight concerning the operation of the checkpoints. According to Sergeant DePew, checkpoint locations are selected weeks in advance based on such considerations as area crime statistics and traffic flow. The checkpoints are generally operated during daylight hours and are identified with lighted signs reading, "NARCOTICS CHECKPOINT [__] MILE AHEAD, NARCOTICS K-9 IN USE, BE PREPARED TO STOP." . . . Once a group of cars has been stopped, other traffic proceeds without interruption until all the stopped cars have been processed or diverted for further processing. Sergeant DePew also stated that the average stop for a vehicle not subject to further processing lasts two to three minutes or less.

Respondents James Edmond and Joell Palmer were each stopped at a narcotics checkpoint in late September 1998. Respondents then filed a lawsuit on behalf of themselves and the class of all motorists who had been stopped or were subject to being stopped in the future at the Indianapolis drug checkpoints. Respondents claimed that the roadblocks violated the Fourth Amendment of the United States Constitution and the search and seizure provision of the Indiana Constitution. Respondents requested declaratory and injunctive relief for the class, as well as damages and attorney's fees for themselves.

Respondents then moved for a preliminary injunction. Although respondents alleged that the officers who stopped them did not follow the written directives, they agreed to the stipulation concerning the operation of the checkpoints for purposes of the preliminary injunction proceedings. The parties also stipulated to certification of the plaintiff class. The United States District Court for the Southern District of Indiana agreed to class certification and denied the motion for a preliminary injunction, holding that the checkpoint program did not violate the Fourth Amendment. . . . A divided panel of the United States Court of Appeals for the Seventh Circuit reversed, holding that the checkpoints contravened the Fourth Amendment. . . . We granted certiorari, . . . and now affirm.

III

. . .

We have never approved a checkpoint program whose primary purpose was to detect evidence of ordinary criminal wrongdoing. Rather, our checkpoint cases have recognized only limited exceptions to the general rule that a seizure must be accompanied by some measure of individualized suspicion. We suggested in *Prouse* that we would not credit the "general interest in crime control" as justification for a regime of suspicionless stops. . . . Consistent with this suggestion, each of the checkpoint programs that we have approved was designed primarily to serve purposes closely related to the problems of policing the border or the necessity of ensuring roadway safety. Because the primary purpose of the Indianapolis narcotics checkpoint program is to uncover evidence of ordinary criminal wrongdoing, the program contravenes the Fourth Amendment.

Petitioners propose several ways in which the narcotics-detection purpose of the instant checkpoint program may instead resemble the primary purposes of the checkpoints in *Sitz* and *Martinez-Fuerte*. Petitioners state that the checkpoints in those cases had the same ultimate purpose of arresting those suspected of committing crimes. . . . Securing the border and apprehending drunk drivers are, of course, law enforcement activities, and law enforcement officers employ arrests and criminal prosecutions in pursuit of these goals. . . . If we were to rest the case at this high level of generality, there would be little check on the ability of the authorities to construct roadblocks for almost any conceivable law enforcement purpose. Without drawing the line at roadblocks designed primarily to serve the general interest in crime control, the Fourth Amendment would do little to prevent such intrusions from becoming a routine part of American life.

Petitioners also emphasize the severe and intractable nature of the drug problem as justification for the checkpoint program. . . . There is no doubt that traffic in illegal narcotics creates social harms of the first magnitude. . . . The law enforcement problems that the drug trade creates likewise remain daunting and complex, particularly in light of the myriad forms of spin-off crime that it spawns. . . . The same can be said of various other illegal activities, if only to a lesser degree. But the gravity of the threat alone cannot be dispositive of questions concerning what means law enforcement officers may employ to pursue a given purpose. Rather, in determining whether individualized suspicion is required, we must consider the nature of the interests threatened and their connection to the particular law enforcement practices at issue. We are particularly reluctant to recognize exceptions to the general rule of individualized suspicion where governmental authorities primarily pursue their general crime control ends.

Nor can the narcotics-interdiction purpose of the checkpoints be rationalized in terms of a highway safety concern similar to that present in *Sitz*. The detection and punishment of almost any criminal offense serves broadly the safety of the community, and our streets would no doubt be safer but for the scourge of illegal drugs. Only with respect to a smaller class of offenses, however, is society confronted with the type of immediate, vehicle-bound threat to life and limb that the sobriety checkpoint in *Sitz* was designed to eliminate.

. . .

The primary purpose of the Indianapolis narcotics checkpoints is in the end to advance "the general interest in crime control." . . . We decline to suspend the usual requirement of individualized suspicion where the police seek to employ a checkpoint primarily for the ordinary enterprise of investigating crimes. We cannot sanction stops justified only by the generalized and ever-present possibility that interrogation and inspection may reveal that any given motorist has committed some crime.

Of course, there are circumstances that may justify a law enforcement checkpoint where the primary purpose would otherwise, but for some emergency, relate to ordinary crime control. For example, as the Court of Appeals noted, the Fourth Amendment would almost certainly permit an appropriately tailored roadblock set up to thwart an imminent terrorist attack or to catch a dangerous criminal who is likely to flee by way of a particular route. . . . The exigencies created by these scenarios are far removed from the circumstances under which authorities might simply stop cars as a matter of course to see if there just happens to be a felon leaving the jurisdiction. While we do not limit the purposes that may justify a checkpoint program to any rigid set of categories, we decline to approve a program whose primary purpose is ultimately indistinguishable from the general interest in crime control.[4]

. . .

Because the primary purpose of the Indianapolis checkpoint program is ultimately indistinguishable from the general interest in crime control, the checkpoints violate the Fourth Amendment. The judgment of the Court of Appeals is accordingly affirmed.

Chief Justice Rehnquist, with whom Justice Thomas joins, and with whom Justice Scalia joins as to Part I, dissenting.

The State's use of a drug-sniffing dog, according to the Court's holding, annuls what is otherwise plainly constitutional under our Fourth Amendment jurisprudence: brief, standardized, discretionless, roadblock seizures of automobiles, seizures which effectively serve a weighty state interest with only minimal intrusion on the privacy of their occupants. Because these seizures serve the State's accepted and significant interests of preventing drunken driving and checking for driver's licenses and vehicle registrations, and because there is nothing in the record to indicate that the addition of the dog sniff lengthens these otherwise legitimate seizures, I dissent.

I

. . .

This case follows naturally from *Martinez-Fuerte* and *Sitz*. Petitioners acknowledge that the "primary purpose" of these roadblocks is to interdict illegal drugs, but

---

[4] [4] The Chief Justice's dissent erroneously characterizes our opinion as resting on the application of a "non-law-enforcement primary purpose test." . . . Our opinion nowhere describes the purposes of the *Sitz* and *Martinez-Fuerte* checkpoints as being "not primarily related to criminal law enforcement." . . . Rather, our judgment turns on the fact that the primary purpose of the Indianapolis checkpoints is to advance the general interest in crime control. The Chief Justice's dissent also erroneously characterizes our opinion as holding that the "use of a drug-sniffing dog . . . annuls what is otherwise plainly constitutional under our Fourth Amendment jurisprudence." . . . Again, the constitutional defect of the program is that its primary purpose is to advance the general interest in crime control.

this fact should not be controlling. Even accepting the Court's conclusion that the checkpoints at issue in *Martinez-Fuerte* and *Sitz* were not primarily related to criminal law enforcement, the question whether a law enforcement purpose could support a roadblock seizure is not presented in this case. The district court found that another "purpose of the checkpoints is to check driver's licenses and vehicle registrations," . . . and the written directives state that the police officers are to "[l]ook for signs of impairment." . . . The use of roadblocks to look for signs of impairment was validated by *Sitz*, and the use of roadblocks to check for driver's licenses and vehicle registrations was expressly recognized in *Delaware v. Prouse*. . . . That the roadblocks serve these legitimate state interests cannot be seriously disputed, as the 49 people arrested for offenses unrelated to drugs can attest. . . . And it would be speculative to conclude — given the District Court's findings, the written directives, and the actual arrests — that petitioners would not have operated these roadblocks but for the State's interest in interdicting drugs.

Because of the valid reasons for conducting these roadblock seizures, it is constitutionally irrelevant that petitioners also hoped to interdict drugs. In *Whren v. United States*, . . . we held that an officer's subjective intent would not invalidate an otherwise objectively justifiable stop of an automobile. The reasonableness of an officer's discretionary decision to stop an automobile, at issue in *Whren*, turns on whether there is probable cause to believe that a traffic violation has occurred. The reasonableness of highway checkpoints, at issue here, turns on whether they effectively serve a significant state interest with minimal intrusion on motorists. The stop in *Whren* was objectively reasonable because the police officers had witnessed traffic violations; so too the roadblocks here are objectively reasonable because they serve the substantial interests of preventing drunken driving and checking for driver's licenses and vehicle registrations with minimal intrusion on motorists.

NOTE

Edmond was distinguished in *Illinois v. Lidster*, 540 U.S. 419 (2004), where police set up a highway checkpoint to gather information about a hit-and-run accident which had occurred at the same location a week earlier and resulted in a fatality. Speaking for a unanimous Court, Justice Breyer held that here, unlike in *Edmond*, "[t]he stop's primary law enforcement purpose was *not* to determine whether a vehicle's occupants were committing a crime, but to ask vehicle occupants, as members of the public, for their help in providing information about a crime in all likelihood committed by others." Lidster had been arrested for driving under the influence of alcohol. See also *Underwood v. State*, 252 P.3d 221, 233 (Okla. Crim. App. 2011), *cert. denied*, 132 S. Ct. 1019 (2012), a case similar to *Lidster*, "the obvious difference being that the person challenging the roadblock was actually implicated in the crime that prompted the roadblock in the first place. That difference, however, is of no constitutional significance, since the legality of a search or seizure is not dependent on the kind of evidence it produces."

PROBLEM B
THE SUCKER ROADBLOCK

Law enforcement officials post signs on a limited access highway indicating a drug interdiction roadblock ahead. There is in fact no such roadblock, but vehicles taking the next exit ramp discover a roadblock at the end of the ramp. Does the possibility that drivers are attempting to evade the roadblock provide the suspicion sufficient to distinguish *Edmond*? *Compare United States v. Yousif*, 308 F.3d 820, 827 (8th Cir. 2002), with *State v. Mack*, 66 S.W.3d 706 (Mo. 2002).

[C] A Modicum of Suspicion

NORWELL v. CINCINNATI
United States Supreme Court
414 U.S. 14 (1973)

Per Curiam.

Petitioner Edward Norwell, on a plea of not guilty, was convicted of a violation of Cincinnati's disorderly conduct ordinance. The charge was that petitioner "did unlawfully and wilfully conduct himself in a disorderly manner, with intent to annoy some person." The judgment of conviction was affirmed by the Ohio Court of Appeals. Further appeal to the Supreme Court of Ohio was dismissed by that court sua sponte "for the reason that no substantial constitutional question exists herein."

We are persuaded that the ordinance, as applied to this petitioner on the facts of his case, operated to punish his constitutionally protected speech. We therefore grant certiorari and reverse.

The ordinance, 901-D4 of the city's Municipal Code, reads: "No person shall wilfully conduct himself or herself in a noisy, boisterous, rude, insulting or other disorderly manner, with the intent to abuse or annoy any person." Petitioner, 69 years of age and an immigrant 20 years ago, is employed by his son who manages and is part owner of a "pony keg," a small package liquor store. Petitioner works at the pony keg every evening and helps his son "because it is very dangerous." There have been break-ins at the store on several occasions and a former owner was killed there. On Christmas night, 1971, the pony keg closed about 10:30. The son drove home, but petitioner "wanted to take a walk and get home at 11:00 to hear the news." Down the street, he was approached by Officer Johnson, who had been notified that a "suspicious man" was in the neighborhood of the pony keg. Officer Johnson testified that he approached petitioner and asked him if he lived in the area. Petitioner looked at him, "and then he turned around and walked away." The officer twice attempted to stop him, but each time petitioner threw off his arm and protested, "I don't tell you people anything." He did not run. Petitioner then was placed under arrest for disorderly conduct. Officer Johnson said he had to "push the man approximately half a block to get him into the police car. He didn't understand why he was being arrested." Petitioner testified that he "was far from the pony keg" when the officer drove up in his car and called out something which petitioner did not understand.

> He told me something, but I couldn't understand . . . I said — I asked him, "What do you want from me?" He said, "Why are you on the street?" I said, "I am walking on the street." After then, he said, "Where are you going?" I said, "I go home." After then, he didn't ask me anything. He was in a car. I continued to walk.

The officer pursued petitioner and grabbed him. Petitioner testified, "I didn't resist because I was concerned about my health and my life."

There is no indication in the record that it was the physical act of pushing off the officer's arm that precipitated the arrest or supported the conviction. Had this been so, one could argue, perhaps, that Mr. Norwell might have been properly charged for disorderly conduct or under a statute or ordinance that made it illegal to interfere with a police officer in the performance of his duty. That, however, is not this case. Officer Johnson testified that he "didn't charge the man with resisting because I didn't think it was a warranted cause," but that he arrested petitioner for "being loud and boisterous," and "he was annoying me." The municipal judge found that petitioner was "hostile" to the officer. "I'm sure the officer had no feeling against this man, but this man had a feeling against him, at this time, and was not at a liberty to say." The court proceeded to find Mr. Norwell "guilty of disorderly conduct with the intent to annoy" and fined him $10 and costs "for being so noisy."

Upon this record, we are convinced that petitioner was arrested and convicted merely because he verbally and negatively protested Officer Johnson's treatment of him. Surely, one is not to be punished for nonprovocatively voicing his objection to what he obviously felt was a highly questionable detention by a police officer. Regardless of what the motivation may have been behind the expression in this case, it is clear that there was no abusive language or fighting words. If there had been, we would have a different case. See *Chaplinsky v. New Hampshire*, 315 U.S. 568 (1942).

The petition for certiorari is granted. The judgment is reversed.

NOTES AND QUESTIONS

(1) Should the Court be understood to say that the arrest would have been sustained had the officer testified "that it was the physical act of pushing off the officer's arm that precipitated the arrest"?

(2) Would it have been constitutionally permissible for the officer to make inquiries of Norwell had it been 2 AM instead of 10:30 PM? If so, would Norwell be obligated to stop? To speak?

(3) In *Kramer v. State*, 15 So. 3d 790, 792 (Fla. Dist. Ct. App. 2009), the court held that the suspect's "mere act of 'actively chewing,' while walking late at night in a high-crime area, did not give [the officer] a reasonable suspicion to believe that Kramer was engaged in criminal activity.").

(4) Many courts now recognize a "community caretaking function" for law enforcement officers. The notion is defended not so much as an exception to the Fourth Amendment protection but as a responsibility outside the ambit of law enforcement. Given the open-ended nature of the rationale, courts have sought to

impose limitations on its use. The concept may not be used as a subterfuge to pursue a criminal investigation, and to rely on the community caretaking rationale the officer must be primarily motivated by it. The Delaware Supreme Court has articulated a typical explanation:

> The community caretaking doctrine has three elements. First, if there are objective, specific and articulable facts from which an experienced officer would suspect that a citizen is in apparent peril, distress or need of assistance, the police officer may stop and investigate for the purpose of assisting the person. Second, if the citizen is in need of aid, then the officer may take appropriate action to render assistance or mitigate the peril. Third, once, however, the officer is assured that the citizen is not in peril, is no longer in need of assistance, or that the peril has been mitigated, the caretaking function is over and any further detention constitutes an unreasonable seizure unless the officer has a warrant, or some exception to the warrant requirement applies.

Williams v. State, 962 A.2d 210, 219 (Del. 2008).

BROWN v. TEXAS

United States Supreme Court
443 U.S. 47 (1979)

MR. CHIEF JUSTICE BURGER delivered the opinion of the Court.

This appeal presents the question whether appellant was validly convicted for refusing to comply with a policeman's demand that he identify himself pursuant to a provision of the Texas Penal Code which makes it a crime to refuse such identification on request.

I

At 12:45 on the afternoon of December 9, 1977, officers Venegas and Sotelo of the El Paso Police Department were cruising in a patrol car. They observed appellant and another man walking opposite directions away from one another in an alley. Although the two men were a few feet apart when they first were seen, officer Venegas later testified that both officers believed the two had been together or were about to meet until the patrol car appeared.

The car entered the alley, and officer Venegas got out and asked appellant to identify himself and explain what he was doing there. The other man was not questioned or detained. The officer testified that he stopped appellant because the situation "looked suspicious and we had never seen that subject in that area before." The area of El Paso where appellant was stopped has a high incidence of drug traffic. However, the officers did not claim to suspect appellant of any specific misconduct; nor did they have any reason to believe that he was armed.

Appellant refused to identify himself and angrily asserted that the officers had no right to stop him. Officer Venegas replied that he was in a "high drug problem area"; officer Sotelo then "frisked" appellant, but found nothing.

When appellant continued to refuse to identify himself, he was arrested for violation of Texas Penal Code Ann. 38.02(a), which makes it a criminal act for a person to refuse to give his name and address to an officer "who has lawfully stopped him and requested the information."[5] Following the arrest the officers searched appellant; nothing untoward was found.

While being taken to the El Paso County Jail appellant identified himself. Nonetheless, he was held in custody and charged with violating 38.02(a). When he was booked he was routinely searched a third time. Appellant was convicted in the El Paso Municipal Court and fined $20 plus court costs for violation of 38.02. He then exercised his right under Texas law to a trial de novo in the El Paso County Court. There, he moved to set aside the information on the ground that 38.02(a) of the Texas Penal Code violated the First, Fourth, and Fifth Amendments and was unconstitutionally vague in violation of the Fourteenth Amendment. The motion was denied. Appellant waived jury, and the court convicted him and imposed a fine of $45 plus court costs.

. . . We reverse.

II

. . .

The State does not contend that appellant was stopped pursuant to a practice embodying neutral criteria, but rather maintains that the officers were justified in stopping appellant because they had a "reasonable, articulable suspicion that a crime had just been, was being, or was about to be committed." We have recognized that in some circumstances an officer may detain a suspect briefly for questioning although he does not have "probable cause" to believe that the suspect is involved in criminal activity as is required for a traditional arrest. . . . However, we have required the officers to have a reasonable suspicion, based on objective facts, that the individual is involved in criminal activity. *Delaware v. Prouse*. . . .

The flaw in the State's case is that none of the circumstances preceding the officers' detention of appellant justified a reasonable suspicion that he was involved in criminal conduct. Officer Venegas testified at appellant's trial that the situation in the alley "looked suspicious," but he was unable to point to any facts supporting that conclusion. There is no indication in the record that it was unusual for people to be in the alley. The fact that appellant was in a neighborhood frequented by drug users, standing alone, is not a basis for concluding that appellant himself was engaged in criminal conduct. In short, the appellant's activity was no different from the activity of other pedestrians in that neighborhood. When pressed, officer Venegas acknowledged that the only reason he stopped appellant was to ascertain his identity. The record suggests an understandable desire to assert a police presence; however that purpose does not negate Fourth Amendment guarantees.

---

5 [5] The entire section reads as follows:

"§ 38.02 FAILURE TO IDENTIFY AS WITNESS

(a) person commits an offense if he intentionally refuses to report or gives a false report of his name and residence address to a peace officer who has lawfully stopped him and requested the information."

In the absence of any basis for suspecting appellant of misconduct, the balance between the public interest and appellant's right to personal security and privacy tilts in favor of freedom from police interference. The Texas statute under which appellant was stopped and required to identify himself is designed to advance a weighty social objective in large metropolitan centers: prevention of crime. But even assuming that purpose is served to some degree by stopping and demanding identification from an individual without any specific basis for believing he is involved in criminal activity, the guarantees of the Fourth Amendment do not allow it. When such a stop is not based on objective criteria, the risk of arbitrary and abusive police practices exceeds tolerable limits. *See Delaware v. Prouse*. . . .

The application of Texas Penal Code Ann. 38.02 to detain appellant and require him to identify himself violated the Fourth Amendment because the officers lacked any reasonable suspicion to believe appellant was engaged or had engaged in criminal conduct. Accordingly, appellant may not be punished for refusing to identify himself, and the conviction is reversed.

Reversed.

NOTES AND QUESTIONS

(1) In an Appendix to the Opinion, the Court included the following excerpt from the trial transcript:

THE COURT: What do you think about if you stop a person lawfully, and then if he doesn't want to talk to you, you put him in jail for committing a crime.

MR. PATTON [Prosecutor]: Well first of all, I would question the Defendant's statement in his motion that the First Amendment gives an individual the right to silence.

THE COURT: I'm asking you why should the State put you in jail because you don't want to say anything.

MR. PATTON: Well, I think there's certain interests that have to be viewed.

THE COURT: Okay, I'd like you to tell me what those are.

MR. PATTON: Well, the Governmental interest to maintain the safety and security of the society and the citizens to live in the society, and there are certainly strong Governmental interests in that direction and because of that, these interests outweigh the interests of an individual for a certain amount of intrusion upon his personal liberty. I think these Governmental interests outweigh the individual's interests in this respect, as far as simply asking an individual for his name and address under the proper circumstances.

THE COURT: But why should it be a crime not to answer?

MR. PATTON: Again, I can only contend that if an answer is not given, it tends to disrupt.

THE COURT: What does it disrupt?

MR. PATTON: I think it tends to disrupt the goal of this society to maintain security over its citizens to make sure they are secure in their gains and their homes.

THE COURT: How does that secure anybody by forcing them, under penalty of being prosecuted, to giving their name and address, even though they are lawfully stopped?

MR. PATTON: Well I, you know, under the circumstances in which some individuals would be lawfully stopped, it's presumed that perhaps this individual is up to something, and the officer is doing his duty simply to find out the individual's name and address, and to determine what exactly is going on.

THE COURT: I'm not questioning, I'm not asking whether the officer shouldn't ask questions. I'm sure they should ask everything they possibly could find out. *What I'm asking is what's the State's interest in putting a man in jail because he doesn't want to answer something.* I realize lots of times an officer will give a defendant a Miranda warning which means a defendant doesn't have to make a statement. Lots of defendants go ahead and confess, which is fine if they want to do that. But if they don't confess, you can't put them in jail, can you, for refusing to confess to a crime?

App. 15–17 (emphasis added).

(2) Is the Court concerned about the officers' tactics or the subject of the prosecution? The primary focus of the Court is upon the statute under which the defendant was arrested, which might be typified as an alternative to now-judicially condemned vagrancy ordinances, at one time the catch-all crime. *See Papachristou v. City of Jacksonville*, 405 U.S. 156 (1972). Suppose the frisk had divulged a pistol, for the possession of which the suspect had been arrested, and a search of his person uncovered narcotics. Would the case have come out the same way? Should it?

(3) In 1972, New York City police establish the Taxi-Livery Task Force as a response to the high incidence of violent crimes against cab drivers. As described by the Court of Appeals of New York in *In re Muhammad F.*, 94 N.Y.2d 136, 700 N.Y.S.2d 77 (1999):

> The taxi program targeted certain neighborhoods, especially between 6:00 P.M. and 2:00 A.M. Special attention was given to cabs with passengers. Members of the Task Force would stop a taxi, hand the driver a pamphlet with safety tips and question the cab driver as to his safety, while at the same time watching the reaction of the passengers in the cab. Generally, such a safety check would involve asking the passenger to "step out briefly" or "telling passengers to get out" while the officers search around and under the seats.

In the two cases under review in *Muhammad F.*, searches of taxis revealed narcotics, for the possession of which the passengers were arrested. The Court of

Appeals held that the procedure was constitutionally impermissible under the holdings in *Prouse* and *Brown v. Texas.*

The Boston police Taxi Inspection Program for Safety (TIPS) differed in that it was a voluntary program for taxi owners. Cabs participating bore a decal in the passenger compartment reading: "THIS VEHICLE MAY BE STOPPED AND VISUALLY INSPECTED BY THE BOSTON POLICE AT ANY TIME TO ENSURE DRIVER'S SAFETY." The procedure followed was similar to that in New York, as described by the Court of Appeals for the First Circuit in *United States v. Woodrum*, 202 F.3d 1 (1st Cir.), *cert. denied*, 531 U.S. 1035 (2000):

> Stops should be conducted when and wherever necessary, particularly during the evening and early morning hours. Attention will be given to isolated and high crime areas. Taxi drivers are not to be detained longer than is necessary to check on the welfare of the operator. Passengers in occupied taxi are to be given a brief explanation of the purpose of the stop: **Operator Safety.** A Taxi Inspection Program for Safety form . . . shall be completed at the time of the stop.

In *Woodrum*, officers had stopped a taxi following the report of a shooting in the vicinity, when they noticed the passenger slouch down upon seeing the officers. The subject was found to be in possession of a gun, crack cocaine, a pipe, a pager, and some cash. He was eventually charged with federal offenses for firearms possession and possession of cocaine base with intent to distribute. The court sustained the search on the ground that the owner of the taxi had consented to the search, and the consent extended to the passenger as well.

HIIBEL v. SIXTH JUDICIAL COURT OF NEVADA

United States Supreme Court
542 U.S. 177 (2004)

Justice Kennedy delivered the opinion of the Court.

The petitioner was arrested and convicted for refusing to identify himself during a stop allowed by *Terry v. Ohio*, ... He challenges his conviction under the Fourth and Fifth Amendments to the United States Constitution, applicable to the States through the Fourteenth Amendment.

I

The sheriff's department in Humboldt County, Nevada, received an afternoon telephone call reporting an assault. The caller reported seeing a man assault a woman in a red and silver GMC truck on Grass Valley Road. Deputy Sheriff Lee Dove was dispatched to investigate. When the officer arrived at the scene, he found the truck parked on the side of the road. A man was standing by the truck, and a young woman was sitting inside it. The officer observed skid marks in the gravel behind the vehicle, leading him to believe it had come to a sudden stop.

The officer approached the man and explained that he was investigating a report of a fight. The man appeared to be intoxicated. The officer asked him if he had "any identification on [him]," which we understand as a request to produce a driver's license or some other form of written identification. The man refused and asked why the officer wanted to see identification. The officer responded that he was conducting an investigation and needed to see some identification. The unidentified man became agitated and insisted he had done nothing wrong. The officer explained that he wanted to find out who the man was and what he was doing there. After continued refusals to comply with the officer's request for identification, the man began to taunt the officer by placing his hands behind his back and telling the officer to arrest him and take him to jail. This routine kept up for several minutes: the officer asked for identification 11 times and was refused each time. After warning the man that he would be arrested if he continued to refuse to comply, the officer placed him under arrest.

We now know that the man arrested on Grass Valley Road is Larry Dudley Hiibel. Hiibel was charged with "willfully resist[ing], delay[ing], or obstruct[ing] a public officer in discharging or attempting to discharge any legal duty of his office" in violation of Nev.Rev.Stat. (NRS) § 199.280 (2003). The government reasoned that Hiibel had obstructed the officer in carrying out his duties under § 171.123, a Nevada statute that defines the legal rights and duties of a police officer in the context of an investigative stop. Section 171.123 provides in relevant part:

> "1. Any peace officer may detain any person whom the officer encounters under circumstances which reasonably indicate that the person has committed, is committing or is about to commit a crime.
>
> . . .
>
> "3. The officer may detain the person pursuant to this section only to ascertain his identity and the suspicious circumstances surrounding his presence abroad. Any person so detained shall identify himself, but may not be compelled to answer any other inquiry of any peace officer."

Hiibel was tried in the Justice Court of Union Township. The court agreed that Hiibel's refusal to identify himself as required by § 171.123 "obstructed and delayed Dove as a public officer in attempting to discharge his duty" in violation of § 199.280. . . . Hiibel was convicted and fined $250. The Sixth Judicial District Court affirmed, rejecting Hiibel's argument that the application of § 171.123 to his case violated the Fourth and Fifth Amendments. On review the Supreme Court of Nevada rejected the Fourth Amendment challenge in a divided opinion. . . . Hiibel petitioned for rehearing, seeking explicit resolution of his Fifth Amendment challenge. The petition was denied without opinion. We granted certiorari. . . .

II

. . .

Stop and identify statutes often combine elements of traditional vagrancy laws with provisions intended to regulate police behavior in the course of investigatory stops. The statutes vary from State to State, but all permit an officer to ask or require a suspect to disclose his identity. . . .

Stop and identify statutes have their roots in early English vagrancy laws that required suspected vagrants to face arrest unless they gave "a good Account of themselves." 15 Geo. 2, ch. 5, § 2 (1744), a power that itself reflected common-law rights of private persons to "arrest any suspicious night-walker, and detain him till he give a good account of himself. . . ." 2 W. Hawkins, *Pleas of the Crown*, ch. 13, § 6, p. 130 (6th ed. 1787). In recent decades, the Court has found constitutional infirmity in traditional vagrancy laws. In *Papachristou v. Jacksonville*, . . . the Court held that a traditional vagrancy law was void for vagueness. Its broad scope and imprecise terms denied proper notice to potential offenders and permitted police officers to exercise unfettered discretion in the enforcement of the law. . . .

The Court has recognized similar constitutional limitations on the scope and operation of stop and identify statutes. [*Brown v. Texas; Kolender v. Lawson*]. . . .

The present case begins where our prior cases left off. Here there is no question that the initial stop was based on reasonable suspicion satisfying the Fourth Amendment requirements noted in *Brown*. Further, the petitioner has not alleged that the statute is unconstitutionally vague, as in *Kolender*. . . .

III

Hiibel argues that his conviction cannot stand because the officer's conduct violated his Fourth Amendment rights. We disagree.

. . .

Although it is well established that an officer may ask a suspect to identify himself in the course of a *Terry* stop, it has been an open question whether the suspect can be arrested and prosecuted for refusal to answer. . . . Petitioner draws our attention to statements in prior opinions that, according to him, answer the question in his favor. In *Terry*, Justice White stated in a concurring opinion that a person detained in an investigative stop can be questioned but is "not obliged to answer, answers may not be compelled, and refusal to answer furnishes no basis for an arrest." . . . The Court cited this opinion in dicta in *Berkemer v. McCarty*, . . . a decision holding that a routine traffic stop is not a custodial stop requiring the protections of *Miranda*. . . . In the course of explaining why *Terry* stops have not been subject to *Miranda*, the Court suggested reasons why *Terry* stops have a "nonthreatening character," among them the fact that a suspect detained during a *Terry* stop "is not obliged to respond" to questions. . . . According to petitioner, these statements establish a right to refuse to answer questions during a *Terry* stop.

We do not read these statements as controlling. The passages recognize that the Fourth Amendment does not impose obligations on the citizen but instead provides rights against the government. As a result, the Fourth Amendment itself cannot require a suspect to answer questions. This case concerns a different issue, however. Here, the source of the legal obligation arises from Nevada state law, not the Fourth Amendment. Further, the statutory obligation does not go beyond answering an officer's request to disclose a name. . . . As a result, we cannot view the dicta in *Berkemer* or Justice White's concurrence in *Terry* as answering the question whether a State can compel a suspect to disclose his name during a *Terry* stop.

The principles of *Terry* permit a State to require a suspect to disclose his name in the course of a *Terry* stop. The reasonableness of a seizure under the Fourth Amendment is determined "by balancing the intrusion on the individual's Fourth Amendment interests against its promotion of legitimate government interests." *Delaware v. Prouse*, ... The Nevada statute satisfies that standard. The request for identity has an immediate relation to the purpose, rationale, and practical demands of a *Terry* stop. The threat of criminal sanction helps ensure that the request for identity does not become a legal nullity. On the other hand, the Nevada statute does not alter the nature of the stop itself: it does not change its duration, *Place*, . . . or its location, *Dunaway*. . . . A state law requiring a suspect to disclose his name in the course of a valid *Terry* stop is consistent with Fourth Amendment prohibitions against unreasonable searches and seizures.

Petitioner argues that the Nevada statute circumvents the probable cause requirement, in effect allowing an officer to arrest a person for being suspicious. According to petitioner, this creates a risk of arbitrary police conduct that the Fourth Amendment does not permit. . . . These are familiar concerns; they were central to the opinion in *Papachristou*, and also to the decisions limiting the operation of stop and identify statutes in *Kolender* and *Brown*. Petitioner's concerns are met by the requirement that a *Terry* stop must be justified at its inception and "reasonably related in scope to the circumstances which justified" the initial stop. . . . Under these principles, an officer may not arrest a suspect for failure to identify himself if the request for identification is not reasonably related to the circumstances justifying the stop. . . .

[In the remainder of the Opinion, the Court rejected the contention that requiring an individual to identify himself violated the Fifth Amendment prohibition against self-incrimination, holding that "petitioner's challenge must fail because in this case disclosure of his name presented no reasonable danger of incrimination."]

[JUSTICE STEVENS dissented, concluding that the statutory requirement for identification violated the privilege against self-incrimination.]

JUSTICE BREYER, with whom JUSTICE SOUTER and JUSTICE GINSBURG join, dissenting.

. . . [T]he Court's statement in *Berkemer*, while technically dicta, is the kind of strong dicta that the legal community typically takes as a statement of the law. And that law has remained undisturbed for more than 20 years.

There is no good reason now to reject this generation-old statement of the law. There are sound reasons rooted in Fifth Amendment considerations for adhering to this Fourth Amendment legal condition circumscribing police authority to stop an individual against his will. . . . Administrative considerations also militate against change. Can a State, in addition to requiring a stopped individual to answer "What's your name?" also require an answer to "What's your license number?" or "Where do you live?" Can a police officer, who must know how to make a *Terry* stop, keep track of the constitutional answers? After all, answers to any of these questions may, or may not, incriminate, depending upon the circumstances.

Indeed, as the majority points out, a name itself — even if it is not "Killer Bill" or "Rough 'em up Harry" — will sometimes provide the police with "a link in the chain of evidence needed to convict the individual of a separate offense." . . . The majority reserves judgment about whether compulsion is permissible in such instances. . . . How then is a police officer in the midst of a *Terry* stop to distinguish between the majority's ordinary case and this special case where the majority reserves judgment?

. . .

NOTES AND QUESTIONS

Brown v. Texas (*see supra*) also involved a mandatory identification statute but the Court avoided the question of constitutionality, finding that there was an insufficient basis for detaining Brown. Here the Court finds the detention reasonable and hence the statute applies. Whether a particular detention is constitutionally reasonable is always an after-the-fact determination. The suspect, of course, may not be sufficiently versed in constitutional law to know if the detention is reasonable. In light of *Hiibel*, does he act at his peril if he declines to identify himself? Should it be incumbent upon the officer to at least inform the suspect of the reason for the stop? Constitutionally required? Is the statutory requirement that one "identify himself" satisfied if the suspect states his name and nothing more? *See generally* Loewy, *The Cowboy and the Cop: The Sage of Dudley Hiibel, 9/11, and the Vanishing Fourth Amendment*, 109 Pa. St. L. Rev. 929 (2005).

[D] Reasonable Suspicion

TERRY v. OHIO

United States Supreme Court
392 U.S. 1 (1968)

Mr. Chief Justice Warren delivered the opinion of the Court.

This case presents serious questions concerning the role of the Fourth Amendment in the confrontation on the street between the citizen and the policeman investigating suspicious circumstances.

Petitioner Terry was convicted of carrying a concealed weapon and sentenced to the statutorily prescribed term of one to three years in the penitentiary. Following the denial of a pretrial motion to suppress, the prosecution introduced in evidence two revolvers and a number of bullets seized from Terry and a codefendant, Richard Chilton, by Cleveland Police Detective Martin McFadden. At the hearing on the motion to suppress this evidence, Officer McFaden testified that while he was patrolling in plain clothes in downtown Cleveland at approximately 2:30 in the afternoon of October 31, 1963, his attention was attracted by two men, Chilton and Terry, standing on the corner of Huron Road and Euclid Avenue. He had never seen the two men before, and he was unable to say precisely what first drew his eye to them. However, he testified that he had been a policeman for 39 years and a detective for 35 and that he had been assigned to patrol this vicinity of downtown Cleveland for shoplifters and pickpockets for 30 years. He explained that he had developed routine habits of observation over the years and that he would "stand and watch people or walk and watch people at many intervals of the day." He added: "Now, in this case when I looked over they didn't look right to me at the time."

His interest aroused, Officer McFadden took up a post of observation in the entrance to a store 300 to 400 feet away from the two men. "I get more purpose to watch them when I seen their movements," he testified. He saw one of the men leave the other one and walk southwest on Huron Road, past some stores. The man paused for a moment and looked in a store window, then walked on a short distance, turned around and walked back toward the corner, pausing once again to look in the same store window. He rejoined his companion at the corner, and the two conferred briefly. Then the second man went through the same series of motions, strolling down Huron Road, looking in the same window, walking on a short distance, turning back, peering in the store window again, and returning to confer with the first man at the corner. The two men repeated this ritual alternately between five and six times apiece in all, roughly a dozen trips. At one point, while the two were standing together on the corner, a third man approached them and engaged them briefly in conversation. This man then left the two others and walked west on Euclid Avenue. Chilton and Terry resumed their measured pacing, peering, and conferring. After this had gone on for 10 to 12 minutes, the two men walked off together, heading west on Euclid Avenue, following the path taken earlier by the third man.

By this time Officer McFadden had become thoroughly suspicious. He testified that after observing their elaborately casual and oft-repeated reconnaissance of the store window on Huron Road, he suspected the two men of "casing a job; a stick-up," and that he considered it his duty as a police officer to investigate further. He added that he feared "they may have a gun." Thus, Officer McFadden followed Chilton and Terry and saw them stop in front of Zucker's store to talk to the same man who had conferred with them earlier on the street corner. Deciding that the situation was ripe for direct action, Officer McFadden approached the three men, identified himself as a police officer and asked for their names. At this point his knowledge was confined to what he had observed. He was not acquainted with any of the three men by name or by sight, and he had received no information concerning them from any other source. When the men "mumbled something" in response to his inquiries, Officer McFadden grabbed petitioner Terry, spun him around so that they were facing the other two, with Terry between McFadden and the others, and patted down the outside of his clothing. In the left breast pocket of Terry's overcoat Officer McFadden felt a pistol. He reached inside the overcoat pocket, but was unable to remove the gun. At this point, keeping Terry between himself and the others, the officer ordered all three men to enter Zucker's store. As they went in, he removed Terry's overcoat completely, removed a.38-caliber revolver from the pocket and ordered all three men to face the wall with their hands raised. Officer McFadden proceeded to pat down the outer clothing of Chilton and the third man, Katz. He discovered another revolver in the outer pocket of Chilton's overcoat, but no weapons were found on Katz. The officer testified that he only patted the men down to see whether they had weapons, and that he did not put his hands beneath the outer garments of either Terry or Chilton until he felt their guns. So far as appears from the record, he never placed his hands beneath Katz' outer garments. Officer McFadden seized Chilton's gun, asked the proprietor of the store to call a police wagon, and took all three men to the station, where Chilton and Terry were formally charged with carrying concealed weapons.

On the motion to suppress the guns the prosecution took the position that they had been seized following a search incident to a lawful arrest. The trial court rejected this theory, stating that it "would be stretching the facts beyond reasonable comprehension" to find that Officer McFadden had had probable cause to arrest the men before he patted them down for weapons. However, the court denied the defendants' motion on the ground that Officer McFadden, on the basis of his experience, "had reasonable cause to believe that the defendants were conducting themselves suspiciously, and some interrogation should be made of their action." Purely for his own protection, the court held, the officer had the right to pat down the outer clothing of these men, who he had reasonable cause to believe might be armed. The court distinguished between an investigatory "stop" and an arrest, and between a "frisk" of the outer clothing for weapons and a full-blown search for evidence of crime. The frisk, it held, was essential to the proper performance of the officer's investigatory duties, for without it "the answer to the police officer may be a bullet, and a loaded pistol discovered during the frisk is admissible."

After the court denied their motion to suppress, Chilton and Terry waived jury trial and pleaded not guilty. The court adjudged them guilty, and the Court of Appeals for the Eighth Judicial District, Cuyahoga County, affirmed. . . . We affirm the conviction.

I

We would be less than candid if we did not acknowledge that this question thrusts to the fore difficult and troublesome issues regarding a sensitive area of police activity issues which have never before been squarely presented to this Court. Reflective of the tensions involved are the practical and constitutional arguments pressed with great vigor on both sides of the public debate over the power of the police to "stop and frisk," as it is sometimes euphemistically termed, suspicious persons.

On the one hand, it is frequently argued that in dealing with the rapidly unfolding and often dangerous situations on city streets the police are in need of an escalating set of flexible responses, graduated in relation to the amount of information they possess. For this purpose it is urged that distinctions should be made between a "stop" and an "arrest" (or a "seizure" of a person), and between a "frisk" and a "search." Thus, it is argued, the police should be allowed to "stop" a person and detain him briefly for questioning upon suspicion that he may be connected with criminal activity. Upon suspicion that the person may be armed, the police should have the power to "frisk" him for weapons. If the "stop" and the "frisk" give rise to probable cause to believe that the suspect has committed a crime, then the police should be empowered to make a formal "arrest," and a full incident "search" of the person. This scheme is justified in part upon the notion that a "stop" and a "frisk" amount to a mere "minor inconvenience and petty indignity;" which can properly be imposed upon the citizen in the interest of effective law enforcement on the basis of a police officer's suspicion.

On the other side the argument is made that the authority of the police must be strictly circumscribed by the law of arrest and search as it has developed to date in the traditional jurisprudence of the Fourth Amendment. It is contended with some force that there is not and cannot be a variety of police activity which does not depend solely upon the voluntary cooperation of the citizen and yet which stops short of an arrest based upon probable cause to make such an arrest. The heart of the Fourth Amendment, the argument runs, is a severe requirement of specific justification for any intrusion upon protected personal security; coupled with a highly developed system of judicial controls to enforce upon the agents of the State the commands of the Constitution. Acquiescence by the courts in the compulsion inherent in the field interrogation practices at issue here, it is urged, would constitute an abdication of judicial control over, and indeed an encouragement of, substantial interference with liberty and personal security by police officers whose judgment is necessarily colored by their primary involvement in "the often competitive enterprise of ferreting out crime." *Johnson v. United States*, 333 U.S. 10, 14 (1948). This, it is argued, can only serve to exacerbate police-community tensions in the crowded centers of our Nation's cities.

Proper adjudication of cases in which the exclusionary rule is invoked demands a constant awareness of these limitations. The wholesale harassment by certain elements of the police community, of which minority groups, particularly Negroes, frequently complain, will not be stopped by the exclusion of any evidence from any criminal trial. Yet a rigid and unthinking application of the exclusionary rule, in futile protest against practices which it can never be used effectively to control, may exact a high toll in human injury and frustration of efforts to prevent crime. No judicial opinion can comprehend the protean variety of the street encounter, and we can only judge the facts of the case before us. Nothing we say today is to be taken as indicating approval of police conduct outside the legitimate investigative sphere. Under our decision, courts still retain their traditional responsibility to guard against police conduct which is overbearing or harassing, or which trenches upon personal security without the objective evidentiary justification which the Constitution requires. When such conduct is identified, it must be condemned by the judiciary and its fruits must be excluded from evidence in criminal trials. And, of course, our approval of legitimate and restrained investigative conduct undertaken on the basis of ample factual justification should in no way discourage the employment of other remedies than the exclusionary rule to curtail abuses for which that sanction may prove inappropriate.

Having thus roughly sketched the perimeters of the constitutional debate over the limits on police investigative conduct in general and the background against which this case presents itself, we turn our attention to the quite narrow question posed by the facts before us: whether it is always unreasonable for a policeman to seize a person and subject him to a limited search for weapons unless there is probable cause for an arrest. Given the narrowness of this question, we have no occasion to canvass in detail the constitutional limitations upon the scope of a policeman's power when he confronts a citizen without probable cause to arrest him.

II

Our first task is to establish at what point in this encounter the Fourth Amendment becomes relevant. That is, we must decide whether and when Officer McFadden "seized" Terry and whether and when he conducted a "search." There is some suggestion in the use of such terms as "stop" and "frisk" that such police conduct is outside the purview of the Fourth Amendment because neither action rises to the level of a "search" or "seizure" within the meaning of the Constitution. We emphatically reject this notion. It is quite plain that the Fourth Amendment governs "seizures" of the person which do not eventuate in a trip to the station house and prosecution for crime "arrests" in traditional terminology. It must be recognized that whenever a police officer accosts an individual and restrains his freedom to walk away, he has "seized" that person. And it is nothing less than sheer torture of the English language to suggest that a careful exploration of the outer surfaces of a person's clothing all over his or her body in an attempt to find weapons is not a "search." Moreover, it is simply fantastic to urge that such a procedure performed in public by a policeman while the citizen stands helpless, perhaps facing a wall with his hands raised, is a "petty indignity."[6] It is a serious intrusion upon the sanctity of the person, which may inflict great indignity and arouse strong resentment, and it is not to be undertaken lightly.

. . .

The distinctions of classical "stop-and-frisk" theory thus serve to divert attention from the central inquiry under the Fourth Amendment the reasonableness in all the circumstances of the particular governmental invasion of a citizen's personal security. "Search" and "seizure" are not talismans. We therefore reject the notions that the Fourth Amendment does not come into play at all as a limitation upon police conduct if the officers stop short of something called a "technical arrest" or a "full-blown search."

In this case there can be no question, then, that Officer McFadden "seized" petitioner and subjected him to a "search" when he took hold of him and patted down the outer surfaces of his clothing. We must decide whether at that point it was reasonable for Officer McFadden to have interfered with petitioner's personal security as he did.[7] And in determining whether the seizure and search were "unreasonable" our inquiry is a dual one whether the officer's action was justified at

---

[6] [6] Consider the following apt description:

"The officer must feel with sensitive fingers every portion of the prisoner's body. A thorough search must be made of the prisoner's arms and armpits, waistline, and back, the groin and area about the testicles, and entire surface of the legs down to the feet." Priar & Martin, *Searching and Disarming Criminals*, 45 J. Crim. L.C. & P.S. 481 (1954).

[7] [7] We thus decide nothing today concerning the constitutional propriety of an investigative "seizure" upon less than probable cause for purposes of "detention" and/or interrogation. Obviously, not all personal intercourse between policemen and citizens involves "seizures" of persons. Only when the officer, by means of physical force or show of authority, has in some way restrained the liberty of a citizen may we conclude that a "seizure" has occurred. We cannot tell with any certainty upon this record whether any such "seizure" took place here prior to Officer McFadden's initiation of physical contact for purposes of searching Terry for weapons, and we thus may assume that up to that point no intrusion upon constitutionally protected rights had occurred.

its inception, and whether it was reasonably related in scope to the circumstances which justified the interference in the first place.

. . .

IV

We must now examine the conduct of Officer McFadden in this case to determine whether his search and seizure of petitioner were reasonable, both at their inception and as conducted. He had observed Terry, together with Chilton and another man, acting in a manner he took to be preface to a "stick-up." We think on the facts and circumstances Officer McFadden detailed before the trial judge a reasonably prudent man would have been warranted in believing petitioner was armed and thus presented a threat to the officer's safety while he was investigating his suspicious behavior. The actions of Terry and Chilton were consistent with McFadden's hypothesis that these men were contemplating a daylight robbery which, it is reasonable to assume, would be likely to involve the use of weapons and nothing in their conduct from the time he first noticed them until the time he confronted them and identified himself as a police officer gave him sufficient reason to negate that hypothesis. Although the trio had departed the original scene, there was nothing to indicate abandonment of an intent to commit a robbery at some point. Thus, when Officer McFadden approached the three men gathered before the display window at Zucker's store he had observed enough to make it quite reasonable to fear that they were armed; and nothing in their response to his hailing them, identifying himself as a police officer, and asking their names served to dispel that reasonable belief. We cannot say his decision at that point to seize Terry and pat his clothing for weapons was the product of a volatile or inventive imagination, or was undertaken simply as an act of harassment; the record evidences the tempered act of a policeman who in the course of an investigation had to make a quick decision as to how to protect himself and limited steps to do so.

Officer McFadden patted down the outer clothing of petitioner and his two companions. He did not place his hands in their pockets or under the outer surface of their garments until he had felt weapons, and then he merely reached for and removed the guns. He never did invade Katz' person beyond the outer surfaces of his clothes; since he discovered nothing in his pat-down which might have been a weapon, Officer McFadden confined his search strictly to what was minimally necessary to learn whether the men were armed and to disarm them once he discovered the weapons. He did not conduct a general exploratory search for whatever evidence of criminal activity he might find.

V

We conclude that the revolver seized from Terry was properly admitted in evidence against him. At the time he seized petitioner and searched him for weapons, Officer McFadden had reasonable grounds to believe that petitioner was armed and dangerous, and it was necessary for the protection of himself and others to take swift measures to discover the true facts and neutralize the threat of harm if it materialized. The policeman carefully restricted his search to what was appropriate to the discovery of the particular items which he sought. Each case of this sort will, of course, have to be decided on its own facts. We merely hold today that where a police officer observes unusual conduct which leads him reasonably to conclude in light of his experience that criminal activity may be afoot and that the persons with whom he is dealing may be armed and presently dangerous, where in the course of investigating this behavior he identifies himself as a policeman and makes reasonable inquiries, and where nothing in the initial stages of the encounter serves to dispel his reasonable fear for his own or others' safety, he is entitled for the protection of himself and others in the area to conduct a carefully limited search of the outer clothing of such persons in an attempt to discover weapons which might be used to assault him. Such a search is a reasonable search under the Fourth Amendment, and any weapons seized may properly be introduced in evidence against the person from whom they were taken.

Affirmed.

MR. JUSTICE HARLAN, concurring.

While I unreservedly agree with the Court's ultimate holding in this case, I am constrained to fill in a few gaps, as I see them, in its opinion. I do this because what is said by this Court today will serve as initial guidelines for law enforcement authorities and courts throughout the land as this important new field of law develops.

The holding has, however, two logical corollaries that I do not think the Court has fully expressed.

In the first place, if the frisk is justified in order to protect the officer during an encounter with a citizen, the officer must first have constitutional grounds to insist on an encounter, to make a *forcible* stop. Any person, including a policeman, is at liberty to avoid a person he considers dangerous. If and when a policeman has a right instead to disarm such a person for his own protection, he must first have a right not to avoid him but to be in his presence. That right must be more than the liberty (again, possessed by every citizen) to address questions to other persons, for ordinarily the person addressed has an equal right to ignore his interrogator and walk away; he certainly need not submit to a frisk for the questioner's protection. I would make it perfectly clear that the right to frisk in this case depends upon the reasonableness of a forcible stop to investigate a suspected crime.

Where such a stop is reasonable, however, the right to frisk must be immediate and automatic if the reason for the stop is, as here, an articulable suspicion of a crime of violence. Just as a full search incident to a lawful arrest requires no additional justification, a limited frisk incident to a lawful stop must often be rapid and routine. There is no reason why an officer, rightfully but forcible confronting a person suspected of a serious crime, should have to ask one question and take the risk that the answer might be a bullet.

MR. JUSTICE WHITE, concurring.

Although the Court puts the matter aside in the context of this case, I think an additional word is in order concerning the matter of interrogation during an investigative stop. There is nothing in the Constitution which prevents a policeman from addressing questions to anyone on the streets. Absent special circumstances, the person approached may not be detained or frisked but may refuse to cooperate and go on his way. However, given the proper circumstances, such as those in this case, it seems to me the person may be briefly detained against his will while pertinent questions are directed to him. Of course, the person stopped is not obliged to answer, and refusal to answer furnishes no basis for an arrest, although it may alert the officer to the need for continued observation.

MR. JUSTICE DOUGLAS, dissenting.

The infringement on personal liberty of any "seizure" of a person can only be "reasonable" under the Fourth Amendment if we require the police to possess "probable cause" before they seize him. Only that line draws a meaningful distinction between an officer's mere inkling and the presence of facts within the officer's personal knowledge which would convince a reasonable man that the person seized has committed, is committing, or is about to commit a particular crime.

NOTES AND QUESTIONS

(1) In footnote 7 of the opinion, the Court notes that it does not address the propriety of a detention without a frisk. Is this true? Unless the Court is saying that detaining Terry and his companions raises no Fourth Amendment issue (a possibility repudiated in *Brown*, if not before), is it not saying that the detention of the suspects under the circumstances was constitutionally reasonable?

(2) Why did Chief Justice Warren feel compelled to write such a lengthy opinion for a relatively simple question?

(3) Justice Harlan adds two caveats which go beyond the facts in *Terry*. First, he maintains that the power to stop implies the power to forcibly stop if necessary. Is this an inevitable implication of the holding in *Terry*? If so, what distinguishes a forcible detention from an arrest, for which the level of suspicion would have to reach probable cause? *Compare Edwards v. United States*, 364 A.2d 1209 (App. D.C. 1976), with *In re D.J.*, 532 A.2d 138 (App. D.C. 1987). Second, Justice Harlan submits that in circumstances such as those presented in *Terry*, "the right to frisk must be immediate and automatic." Would Chief Justice Warren have reached the same result had Officer McFadden immediately frisked Terry without a preliminary inquiry? *Cf. Adams v. Williams*, 407 U.S 143 (1972).

(4) The decision in *Terry*, and the subject of field detentions, received extensive analysis in a double issue of the St. John's Law Review. *See* Charles Bobis, Terry v. Ohio *30 Years Later: A Symposium on the Fourth Amendment, Law Enforcement and Police-Citizen Encounters*, 72 St. John's L. Rev. 721 (1998).

(5) The prerogative of an officer to draw conclusions based on his experience is not without limits. In *State v. Betow*, 593 N.W.2d 499 (Wis. 1999), the accused was stopped for speeding, and when he produced his driver's license, the officer noticed the picture of a mushroom sewn on it. The officer did not issue a speeding citation but inquired about the mushroom, to which the accused responded that he thought "it looked neat." The officer said that based on his experience mushrooms were symbols of drug use. When the accused declined to consent to a search of the vehicle, the officer detained him and summoned a drug-sniffing dog. Based on the dog's cues, the car was searched and a packet of marijuana recovered. The appellate court held that the evidence should have been suppressed, because the officer's knowledge that some people regarded a mushroom as a symbol for use of hallucinogens was insufficient to support the detention.

SIBRON v. NEW YORK

United States Supreme Court
392 U.S. 40 (1968)

MR. CHIEF JUSTICE WARREN delivered the opinion of the Court.

These are companion cases to No. 67, *Terry v. Ohio*, . . . decided today. They present related questions under the Fourth and Fourteenth Amendments, but the cases arise in the context of New York's "stop-and-frisk" law, N.Y. Code Crim. Proc. 180-a. This statute provides:

> 1. A police officer may stop any person abroad in a public place whom he reasonably suspects is committing, has committed or is about to commit a felony or any of the offenses specified in section five hundred fifty-two of this chapter, and may demand of him his name, address and an explanation of his actions.
>
> 2. When a police officer has stopped a person for questioning pursuant to this section and reasonably suspects that he is in danger of life or limb, he may search such person for a dangerous weapon. If the police officer finds such a weapon or any other thing the possession of which may constitute a crime, he may take and keep it until the completion of the questioning, at which time he shall either return it, if lawfully possessed, or arrest such person.

The appellants, Sibron and Peters, were both convicted of crimes in New York state courts on the basis of evidence seized from their persons by police officers. The Court of Appeals of New York held that the evidence was properly admitted, on the ground that the searches which uncovered it were authorized by the statute. . . .

The facts in these cases may be stated briefly. Sibron, the appellant in No. 63, was convicted of the unlawful possession of heroin. He moved before trial to suppress the heroin seized from his person by the arresting officer, Brooklyn Patrolman Anthony Martin. After the trial court denied his motion, Sibron pleaded guilty to the charge, preserving his right to appeal the evidentiary ruling. At the hearing on the motion to suppress, Officer Martin testified that while he was patrolling his beat in uniform on March 9, 1965, he observed Sibron "continually from the hours of 4:00 p.m. to 12:00, midnight in the vicinity of 742 Broadway." He stated that during this period of time he saw Sibron in conversation with six or eight persons whom he (Patrolman Martin) knew from past experience to be narcotics addicts. The officer testified that he did not overhear any of these conversations, and that he did not see anything pass between Sibron and any of the others. Late in the evening Sibron entered a restaurant. Patrolman Martin saw Sibron speak with three more known addicts inside the restaurant. Once again, nothing was overheard and nothing was seen to pass between Sibron and the addicts. Sibron sat down and ordered pie and coffee, and, as he was eating, Patrolman Martin approached him and told him to come outside. Once outside, the officer said to Sibron, "You know what I am after." According to the officer, Sibron "mumbled something and reached into his pocket." Simultaneously, Patrolman Martin thrust his hand into the same pocket, discovering several glassine envelopes, which, it turned out, contained heroin.

The State has had some difficulty in settling upon a theory for the admissibility of these envelopes of heroin. In his sworn complaint Patrolman Martin stated:

> As the officer approached the defendant, the latter being in the direction of the officer and seeing him, he did put his hand in his left jacket pocket and pulled out a tinfoil envelope and did attempt to throw same to the ground. The officer never losing sight of the said envelope seized it from the defendant's left hand, examined it and found it to contain ten glascine [sic] envelopes with a white substance alleged to be Heroin.

This version of the encounter, however, bears very little resemblance to Patrolman Martin's testimony at the hearing on the motion to suppress. In fact, he discarded the abandonment theory at the hearing.[8] Nor did the officer ever seriously suggest that he was in fear of bodily harm and that he searched Sibron in self-protection to find weapons.

Peters, the appellant in No. 74, was convicted of possessing burglary tools under circumstances evincing an intent to employ them in the commission of a crime. The tools were seized from his person at the time of his arrest, and like Sibron he made a pretrial motion to suppress them. When the trial court denied the motion, he too pleaded guilty, preserving his right to appeal. Officer Samuel Lasky of the New York City Police Department testified at the hearing on the motion that he was at

---

[8] [8] Patrolman Martin stated several times that he put his hand into Sibron's pocket and seized the heroin before Sibron had any opportunity to remove his own hand from the pocket. The trial court questioned him on this point:

> Q. Would you say at that time that he reached into his pocket and handed the packets to you? Is that what he did or did he drop the packets?
>
> A. He did not drop them. *I do not know what his intentions were.* He pushed his hand into his pocket.
>
> Mr. Joseph [Prosecutor]: You intercepted it; didn't you, Officer?
>
> The Witness: Yes.
>
> (Emphasis added.)

It is of course highly unlikely that Sibron, facing the officer at such close quarters, would have tried to remove the heroin from his pocket and throw it to the ground in the hope that he could escape responsibility for it.

home in his apartment in Mount Vernon, New York, at about 1 p.m. on July 10, 1964. He had just finished taking a shower and was drying himself when he heard a noise at his door. His attempt to investigate was interrupted by a telephone call, but when he returned and looked through the peephole into the hall, Officer Lasky saw "two men tiptoeing out of the alcove toward the stairway." He immediately called the police, put on some civilian clothes and armed himself with his service revolver. Returning to the peephole, he saw "a tall man tiptoeing away from the alcove and followed by this shorter man, Mr. Peters, toward the stairway." Officer Lasky testified that he had lived in the 120-unit building for 12 years and that he did not recognize either of the men as tenants. Believing that he had happened upon the two men in the course of an attempted burglary, Officer Lasky opened his door, entered the hallway and slammed the door loudly behind him. This precipitated a flight down the stairs on the part of the two men, and Officer Lasky gave chase. His apartment was located on the sixth floor, and he apprehended Peters between the fourth and fifth floors. Grabbing Peters by the collar, he continued down another flight in unsuccessful pursuit of the other man. Peters explained his presence in the building to Officer Lasky by saying that he was visiting a girlfriend. However, he declined to reveal the girlfriend's name, on the ground that she was a married woman. Officer Lasky patted Peters down for weapons, and discovered a hard object in his pocket. He stated at the hearing that the object did not feel like a gun, but that it might have been a knife. He removed the object from Peters' pocket. It was an opaque plastic envelope, containing burglar's tools.

The trial court explicitly refused to credit Peters' testimony that he was merely in the building to visit his girlfriend. It found that Officer Lasky had the requisite "reasonable suspicion" of Peters under 180-a to stop him and question him. It also found that Peters' response was "clearly unsatisfactory," and that "under the circumstances Lasky's action in frisking Peters for a dangerous weapon was reasonable, even though Lasky was himself armed." It held that the hallway of the apartment building was a "public place" within the meaning of the statute. The Appellate Division of the Supreme Court affirmed without opinion. The Court of Appeals also affirmed, essentially adopting the reasoning of the trial judge, with Judges Fuld and Van Voorhis dissenting separately.

IV

Turning to the facts of Sibron's case, it is clear that the heroin was inadmissible in evidence against him. The prosecution has quite properly abandoned the notion that there was probable cause to arrest Sibron for any crime at the time Patrolman Martin accosted him in the restaurant, took him outside and searched him. The officer was not acquainted with Sibron and had no information concerning him. He merely saw Sibron talking to a number of known narcotics addicts over a period of eight hours. It must be emphasized that Patrolman Martin was completely ignorant regarding the content of these conversations, and that he saw nothing pass between Sibron and the addicts. So far as he knew, they might indeed "have been talking about the World Series." The inference that persons who talk to narcotics addicts are engaged in the criminal traffic in narcotics is simply not the sort of reasonable inference required to support an intrusion by the police upon an individual's personal security. Nothing resembling probable cause existed until after the search had turned up the envelopes of heroin. It is axiomatic that an incident search may not precede an arrest and serve as part of its justification. E.g. *Henry v. United States*, 361 U.S. 98 (1959); *Johnson v. United States*, 333 U.S. 10, 16,17 (1948). Thus the search cannot be justified as incident to a lawful arrest.

If Patrolman Martin lacked probable cause for an arrest, however, his seizure and search of Sibron might still have been justified at the outset if he had reasonable grounds to believe that Sibron was armed and dangerous. *Terry v. Ohio*, . . . The police officer is not entitled to seize and search every person whom he sees on the street or of whom he makes inquiries. Before he places a hand on the person of a citizen in search of anything, he must have constitutionally adequate, reasonable grounds for doing so. In the case of the self-protective search for weapons, he must be able to point to particular facts from which he reasonably inferred that the individual was armed and dangerous. *Terry v. Ohio, supra.* Patrolman Martin's testimony reveals no such facts. The suspect's mere act of talking with a number of known narcotics addicts over an eight-hour period no more gives rise to reasonable fear of life or limb on the part of the police officer than it justifies an arrest for committing a crime. Nor did Patrolman Martin urge that when Sibron put his hand in his pocket, he feared that he was going for a weapon and acted in self-defense. His opening statement to Sibron "You know what I am after" made it abundantly clear that he sought narcotics, and his testimony at the hearing left no doubt that he thought there were narcotics in Sibron's pocket.

Even assuming *arguendo* that there were adequate grounds to search Sibron for weapons, the nature and scope of the search conducted by Patrolman Martin were so clearly unrelated to that justification as to render the heroin inadmissible. The search for weapons approved in *Terry* consisted solely of a limited patting of the outer clothing of the suspect for concealed objects which might be used as instruments of assault. Only when he discovered such objects did the officer in *Terry* place his hands in the pockets of the men he searched. In this case, with no attempt at an initial limited exploration for arms, Patrolman Martin thrust his hand into Sibron's pocket and took from him envelopes of heroin. His testimony shows that he was looking for narcotics, and he found them. The search was not reasonably limited in scope to the accomplishment of the only goal which might conceivably have justified its inception the protection of the officer by disarming a potentially dangerous man. Such a search violates the guarantee of the Fourth Amendment, which protects the sanctity of the person against unreasonable intrusions on the part of all government agents.

V

We think it is equally clear that the search in Peter's case was wholly reasonable under the Constitution. The Court of Appeals of New York held that the search was made legal by 180-a, since Peters was "abroad in a public place," and since Officer Lasky was reasonably suspicious of his activities and, once he had stopped Peters, reasonably suspected that he was in danger of life or limb, even though he held Peters at gun point. This may be the justification for the search under state law. We think, however, that for purposes of the Fourth Amendment the search was properly incident to a lawful arrest. By the time Officer Lasky caught up with

Peters on the stairway between the fourth and fifth floors of the apartment building, he had probable cause to arrest him for attempted burglary. The officer heard strange noises at his door which apparently led him to believe that someone sought to force entry. When he investigated these noises he saw two men, whom he had never seen before in his 12 years in the building, tiptoeing furtively about the hallway. They were still engaged in these maneuvers after he called the police and dressed hurriedly. And when Officer Lasky entered the hallway, the men fled down the stairs. It is difficult to conceive of stronger grounds for an arrest, short of actual eyewitness observation of criminal activity. As the trial court explicitly recognized, deliberately furtive actions and flight at the approach of strangers or law officers are strong indicia of *mens rea*, and when coupled with specific knowledge on the part of the officer relating the suspect to the evidence of crime, they are proper factors to be considered in the decision to make an arrest.

Mr. Justice Harlan concurring in the result.

I fully agree with the results the Court has reached in these cases. They are, I think, consonant with and dictated by the decision in *Terry v. Ohio.* For reasons I do not understand, however, the Court has declined to rest the judgments here upon the principles of *Terry.* In doing so it has, in at least one particular, made serious inroads upon the protection afforded by the Fourth and Fourteenth Amendments.

The forcible encounter between Officer Martin and Sibron did not meet the *Terry* reasonableness standard. In the first place, although association with known criminals may, I think, properly be a factor contributing to the suspiciousness of circumstances, it does not, entirely by itself, create suspicion adequate to support a stop. There must be something at least in the activities of the person being observed or in his surroundings that affirmatively suggests particular criminal activity, completed, current, or intended. That was the case in *Terry*, but it palpably was not the case here. For eight continuous hours, up to the point when he interrupted Sibron eating a piece of pie, Officer Martin apparently observed not a single suspicious action and heard not a single suspicious word on the part of Sibron himself or any person with whom he associated. If anything, that period of surveillance pointed away from suspicion.

Furthermore, in *Terry*, the police officer judged that his suspect was about to commit a violent crime and that he had to assert himself in order to prevent it. Here there was no reason for Officer Martin to think that an incipient crime, or flight, or the destruction of evidence would occur if he stayed his hand; indeed, there was no more reason for him to intrude upon Sibron at the moment when he did than there had been four hours earlier, and no reason to think the situation would have changed four hours later. While no hard-and-fast rule can be drawn, I would suggest that one important factor, missing here, that should be taken into account in determining whether there are reasonable grounds for a forcible intrusion is whether there is any need for immediate action.

For these reasons I would hold that Officer Martin lacked reasonable grounds to intrude forcibly upon Sibron. In consequence, the essential premise for the right to conduct a self-protective frisk was lacking. See my concurring opinion in *Terry.* I therefore find it unnecessary to reach two further troublesome questions. First, although I think that, as in *Terry*, the right to frisk is automatic when an officer lawfully stops a person suspected of a crime whose nature creates a substantial likelihood that he is armed, it is not clear that suspected possession of narcotics falls into this category. If the nature of the suspected offense creates no reasonable apprehension for the officer's safety, I would not permit him to frisk unless other circumstances did so. Second, I agree with the Court that even where a self-protective frisk is proper, its scope should be limited to what is adequate for its purposes. I see no need here to resolve the question whether this frisk exceeded those bounds.

Turning now to No. 74, *Peters*, I agree that the conviction should be upheld, but here I would differ strongly and fundamentally with the Court's approach. The Court holds that the burglar's tools were recovered from Peters in a search incident to a lawful arrest. I do not think that Officer Lasky had anything close to probable cause to arrest Peters before he recovered the burglar's tools. Indeed, if probable cause existed here, I find it difficult to see why a different rationale was necessary to support the stop and frisk in *Terry* and why States such as New York have had to devote so much thought to the constitutional problems of field interrogation. This case will be the latest in an exceedingly small number of cases in this Court indicating what suffices for probable cause. While, as the Court noted in *Terry*, the influence of this Court on police tactics "in the field" is necessarily limited, the influence of a decision here on hundreds of courts and magistrates who have to decide whether there is probable cause for a real arrest or a full search will be large.

Officer Lasky testified that at 1 o'clock in the afternoon he heard a noise at the door to his apartment. He did not testify, nor did any state court conclude, that this "led him to believe that someone sought to force entry." He looked out into the public hallway and saw two men whom he did not recognize, surely not a strange occurrence in a large apartment building. One of them appeared to be tip-toeing. Lasky did not testify that the other man was tip-toeing or that either of them was behaving "furtively." Lasky left his apartment and ran to them, gun in hand. He did not testify that there was any "flight," though flight at the approach of a gun-carrying stranger (Lasky was apparently not in uniform) is hardly indicative of *mens rea*.

Probable cause to arrest means evidence that would warrant a prudent and reasonable man (such as a magistrate, actual or hypothetical) in believing that a particular person has committed or is committing a crime. Officer Lasky had no extrinsic reason to think that a crime had been or was being committed, so whether it would have been proper to issue a warrant depends entirely on his statements of his observations of the men. Apart from his conclusory statement that he thought the men were burglars, he offered very little specific evidence. I find it hard to believe that if Peters had made good his escape and there were no report of a burglary in the neighborhood, this Court would hold it proper for a prudent neutral magistrate to issue a warrant for his arrest.

[JUSTICES WHITE, FORTAS and DOUGLAS concurred in both judgments; JUSTICE BLACK concurred in the affirmance in *Peters* but dissented from the reversal in *Sibron*.]

NOTES AND QUESTIONS

(1) Would the government have prevailed in *Sibron* if (1) the officer had waited until Sibron emerged on the street before confronting him; (2) while reaching into his pocket, Sibron had said, "You've got me this time"; (3) the officer had testified that he feared for his safety when Sibron reached in his pocket; (4) the officer had grabbed Sibron's wrist to prevent his withdrawing his hand from his pocket, then felt the pocket, then arrested Sibron and removed the heroin?

(2) If Officer Lasky had probable cause to arrest Peters, did not Officer McFadden have probable cause to arrest Terry? Justice Harlan contended that the facts in *Peters* are *weaker* than the facts in *Terry.* Are the decisions deeply inconsistent? Why did not the Court, as Justice Harlan suggested, apply the *Terry* analysis in *Peters* and come out with the same result?

(3) After this decision, what is the status of the New York stop-and-frisk law? Note that the stop and frisk power is constitutionally approved in *Terry*, without the support of an authorizing statute. Is the power to engage in field detentions in New York now greater, less or the same as the power in Ohio?

(4) Of the three cases, the only judicially approved frisk occurred in *Terry*, in which case Officer McFadden had anticipated the possibility of arms, and he felt what indeed seemed to be a firearm. Suppose the officer detects coins, keys or a cigarette lighter. Can such items be removed? Compare *People v. Bueno*, 173 Colo. 69, 475 P.2d 702 (1970), with *Taylor v. Superior Court*, 275 Cal. App. 2d 146, 79 Cal. Rptr. 677 (Cal. App. 4th Dist. 1969). Should courts take judicial notice of the fact that virtually anything could conceivably be used as a weapon? The California Court of Appeals once mused that even a soft object might turn out to be "a rubber water pistol loaded with carbolic acid or some other liquid, which if used by a suspect could permanently blind an officer." *People v. Armenta*, 268 Cal. App. 2d 248, 251, 73 Cal. Rptr. 819, 821 (Cal. App. 2d Dist. 1968). Subsequently, however, the California Supreme Court concluded that it could not "condone fanciful speculations such as that indulged in by Armenta. . . ." *People v. Collins*, 1 Cal. 3d 658, 663, 83 Cal. Rptr. 179, 183, 463 P.2d 403, 407 (1970). *See generally* Cook, *The Art of Frisking*, 40 Ford. L. Rev. 789 (1972).

(5) A Massachusetts court has held that it is inappropriate for the trial judge to re-enact the frisk in court to determine the credibility of the officer's assertion that he suspected a weapon. "The question to be decided was whether the search for a weapon was reasonable in the circumstances confronting the officer in the field, . . . not those facing the judge in the tranquility of the courtroom." *Commonwealth v. Dedomenicis*, 42 Mass. App. 76, 674 N.E.2d 1099 (1997).

PROBLEM C
CIVILITY IN THE SUBWAY

Two officers of the Massachusetts Bay Transportation Authority, assigned to a MBTA station used by large numbers of high school students, "observed two young males acting in a disorderly manner. . . . [T]hey were banging on the train windows and giving the other students the middle finger and they were becoming quite loud . . . pounding against the windows. . . . There were obscenities." One of the individuals, defendant Villaneuva, was wearing a hooded sweatshirt just over the belt and a goose down type coat hanging below his knees, clothing which could conceal a weapon. The officers had "decided to talk to the two gentlemen to let them know that their behavior was extremely disorderly and we didn't expect that from them." When Villaneuva reached the top of the escalator rising from the platform, one of the officers told him that he wanted to speak to him. At that point, the officer testified that Villaneuva appeared "extremely nervous," whereupon the officer patted his outside clothing around the waist, immediately feeling a gun. Villaneuva sought to flee, but was restrained. Was the seizure of the weapon constitutional? *See United States v. Villaneuva*, 15 F.3d 197 (1st Cir. Mass. 1994).

ALABAMA v. WHITE

United States Supreme Court
496 U.S. 325 (1990)

JUSTICE WHITE delivered the opinion of the Court.

Based on an anonymous telephone tip, police stopped respondent's vehicle. A consensual search of the car revealed drugs. The issue is whether the tip, as corroborated by independent police work, exhibited sufficient indica of reliability to provide reasonable suspicion to make the investigatory stop. We hold that it did.

On April 22, 1987, at approximately 3 p.m., Corporal B.H. Davis of the Montgomery Police Department received a telephone call from an anonymous person, stating that Vanessa White would be leaving 235-C Lynwood Terrace Apartments at a particular time in a brown Plymouth station wagon with the right taillight lens broken, that she would be going to Dobey's Motel, and that she would be in possession of about an ounce of cocaine inside a brown attache case. Corporal Davis and his partner, Corporal P.A. Reynolds, proceeded to the Lynwood Terrace Apartments. The officers saw a brown Plymouth station wagon with a broken right taillight in the parking lot in front of the 235 building. The officers observed respondent leave the 235 building, carrying nothing in her hands, and enter the station wagon. They followed the vehicle as it drove the most direct route to Dobey's Motel. When the vehicle reached the Mobile Highway, on which Dobey's Motel is located, Corporal Reynolds requested a patrol unit to stop the vehicle. The vehicle was stopped at approximately 4:18 p.m., just short of Dobey's Motel. Corporal Davis asked respondent to step to the rear of her car, where he informed her that she had been stopped because she was suspected of carrying cocaine in the vehicle. He asked if they could look for cocaine, and respondent said they could look. The officers found marijuana in the attache case and placed respondent under arrest. During the processing at the station, the officers found three milligrams of cocaine in respondent's purse.

Respondent was charged in Montgomery County Court with possession of marijuana and possession of cocaine. The trial court denied respondent's motion to suppress, and she pleaded guilty to the charges, reserving the right to appeal the denial of her suppression motion. The Court of Criminal Appeals of Alabama held that the officers did not have the reasonable suspicion necessary under *Terry v. Ohio* . . . to justify the investigatory stop of respondent's car, and that the marijuana and cocaine were fruits of respondent's unconstitutional detention. The court concluded that respondent's motion to dismiss should have been granted and reversed her conviction. . . . The Supreme Court of Alabama denied the State's petition for writ of certiorari, two justices dissenting. . . . Because of differing views in the state and federal courts over whether an anonymous tip may furnish reasonable suspicion for a stop, we granted the State's petition for certiorari,. . . . We now reverse.

Adams v. Williams, 407 U.S. 143 (1972), sustained a *Terry* stop and frisk undertaken on the basis of a tip given in person by a known informant who had provided information in the past. We concluded that, while the unverified tip may have been insufficient to support an arrest or search warrant, the information carried sufficient "indicia of reliability" to justify a forcible stop. . . .

Reasonable suspicion is a less demanding standard than probable cause not only in the sense that reasonable suspicion can be established with information that is different in quantity or content than that required to establish probable cause, but also in the sense that reasonable suspicion can arise from information that is less reliable than that required to show probable cause. *Adams v. Williams* . . . demonstrates as much. We there assumed that the unverified tip from the known informant might not have been reliable enough to establish probable cause, but nevertheless found it sufficiently reliable to justify a *Terry* stop. . . . Reasonable suspicion, like probable cause, is dependent upon both the content of information possessed by police and its degree of reliability. Both factors — quantity and quality — are considered in the "totality of the circumstances — the whole picture," *United States v. Cortez*, 449 U.S. 411(1981), that must be taken into account when evaluating whether there is reasonable suspicion. Thus, if a tip has a relatively low degree of reliability, more information will be requiretablish the requisite quantum of suspicion than would be required if the tip were more reliable. . . . Contrary to the court below, we conclude that when the officers stopped respondent, the anonymous tip had been sufficiently corroborated to furnish reasonable suspicion that respondent was engaged in criminal activity and that the investigative stop therefore did not violate the Fourth Amendment.

It is true that not every detail mentioned by the tipster was verified, such as the name of the woman leaving the building or the precise apartment from which she left; but the officers did corroborate that a woman left the 235 building and got into the particular vehicle that was described by the caller. With respect to the time of departure predicted by the informant, Corporal Davis testified that the caller gave a particular time when the woman would be leaving, . . . but he did not state what that time was. He did testify that, after the call, he and his partner proceeded to the Lynwood Terrace Apartments to put the 235 building under surveillance,. . . . Given the fact that the officers proceeded to the indicated address immediately after the call and that respondent emerged not too long thereafter, it appears from the record before us that respondent's departure from the building was within the timeframe predicted by the caller. As for the caller's prediction of respondent's destination, it is true that the officers stopped her just short of Dobey's Motel and did not know whether she would have pulled in or continued past it. But given that the 4-mile route driven by respondent was the most direct route possible to Dobey's Motel, . . . but nevertheless involved several turns, . . . we think respondent's destination was significantly corroborated.

. . . What was important was the caller's ability to predict respondent's *future behavior*, because it demonstrated inside information — a special familiarity with respondent's affairs. The general public would have had no way of knowing that respondent would shortly leave the building, get in the described car, and drive the most direct route to Dobey's Motel. Because only a small number of people are generally privy to an individual's itinerary, it is reasonable for police to believe that a person with access to such information is likely to also have access to reliable information about that individual's illegal activities. . . . When significant aspects of the caller's predictions were verified, there was reason to believe not only that the caller was honest but also that he was well informed, at least well enough to justify the stop.

Although it is a close case, we conclude that under the totality of the circumstances the anonymous tip, as corroborated, exhibited sufficient indicia of reliability to justify the investigatory stop of respondent's car. We therefore reverse the judgment of the Court of Criminal Appeals of Alabama and remand the case for further proceedings not inconsistent with this opinion.

JUSTICE STEVENS, with whom JUSTICE BRENNAN and JUSTICE MARSHALL join, dissenting.

Millions of people leave their apartments at about the same time every day carrying an attache case and heading for a destination known to their neighbors. Usually, however, the neighbors do not know what the briefcase contains. An anonymous neighbor's prediction about somebody's time of departure and probable destination is anything but a reliable basis for assuming that the commuter is in possession of an illegal substance — particularly when the person is not even carrying the attache case described by the tipster.

The record in this case does not tell us how often respondent drove from the Lynwood Terrace Apartments to Dobey's Motel; for all we know, she may have been a room clerk or telephone operator working the evening shift. It does not tell us whether Officer Davis made an effort to ascertain the informer's identity, his reason for calling, or the basis of his prediction about respondent's destination. Indeed, for all that this record tells us, the tipster may well have been another police officer who had a "hunch" that respondent might have cocaine in her attache case.

Anybody with enough knowledge about a given person to make her the target of a prank, or to harbor a grudge against her, will certainly be able to formulate a tip about her like the one predicting Vanessa White's excursion. In addition, under the Court's holding, every citizen is subject to being seized and questioned by any officer who is prepared to testify that the warrantless stop was based on an anonymous tip predicting whatever conduct the officer just observed. Fortunately, the vast majority of those in our law enforcement community would not adopt such a practice. But the Fourth Amendment was intended to protect the citizens from the overzealous and unscrupulous officer as well as from those who are conscientious and truthful. This decision makes a mockery of that protection.

I respectfully dissent.

NOTES AND QUESTIONS

(1) In the case cited by the Court, *Adams v. Williams*, "[a]t approximately 2:15 a.m. a person known to Sgt. Connolly approached his cruiser and informed him that an individual seated in a nearby vehicle was carrying narcotics and had a gun at his waist." The officer approached the vehicle in which the defendant was seated with the windows rolled up, tapped on the window, and when it was rolled down, immediately reached in and removed a loaded revolver from the defendant's waistband. The only confirmation of the tip in this case was the observation of a parked car with an unknown individual seated within; there was no observation of predicted behavior comparable to that in *White.* Nevertheless, the Court found the tip adequate to support a *Terry* stop. In addressing the reasonableness of the officer's reliance on the tip, in *Adams*, the Court said that "[t]he informant was known to him personally and had provided him with information in the past." This characterization of the *Adams* tip was reiterated in *White.* Only by reading Justice Marshall's dissenting opinion in *Adams* does one learn that while it was true that the informant "had provided him with information in the past," the information provided had proved to be worthless. At a hearing on the motion to suppress the evidence, the officer referred to a single prior incident in which he had received information from the informant. On that occasion he told the officer of homosexual activity in a local railroad station, but the officer had found "no substantiating evidence," and no arrests were made.

(2) *Terry, Sibron, Peters, Adams*, and *White* all concern efforts to interrupt or prevent the occurrence of a crime. Does the rationale for field detentions apply as well to apprehensions for prior offenses? In *United States v. Hensley*, 469 U.S. 221 (1985), the Court sustained the detention of a person believed to be the subject of a "wanted flyer" for the time required to determine an arrest warrant had been issued. Speaking for the Court, Justice O'Connor held that "if police have a reasonable suspicion, grounded on specific and articulable facts, that a person they encounter was involved in or is wanted in connection with a completed felony, then a *Terry* stop may be made to investigate the suspicion." Some courts suggest that *Hensley* may be applicable when the prior offense is a misdemeanor. *United States v. Grigg*, 498 F.3d 1070, 1081 (9th Cir. 2007); *United States v. Moran*, 503 F.3d 1135 (10th Cir. 2007), *cert. denied*, 128 S. Ct. 2424 (2008).

(3) Should the reputation of a neighborhood for criminal activity and the flight of an individual upon seeing the police be enough to justify a *Terry* stop? In *Illinois v. Wardlow*, 528 U.S. 119 (2000), officers were patrolling an area known for heavy narcotics trafficking. Wardlow, who was standing next to a building holding an opaque bag, fled when he saw the patrol car. The officers pursued and detained him and immediately conducted a frisk. Detecting a heavy and hard object in the bag Wardlow was carrying, the officer opened it an discovered a loaded handgun, for the possession of which he was arrested. The state courts concluded that there was insufficient suspicion to justify the detention. The Supreme Court reversed. Chief Justice Rehnquist, speaking for a 5-4 majority, acknowledged that "presence in an area of expected criminal activity, standing alone, is not enough to support a reasonable, particularized suspicion that the person is committing a crime," but held nonetheless that "officers are not required to ignore the relevant characteristics of a location in determining whether the circumstances are sufficiently suspicious to

warrant further investigation." Similarly, he observed, "[h]eadlong flight . . . is not necessarily indicative of wrongdoing, but it is certainly suggestive of such." Hence the combination of facts supported the *Terry* stop and frisk. Justice Stevens, speaking for the dissenters, agreed that the totality of the circumstances was to be assessed, but maintained that "even in a high crime neighborhood unprovoked flight does not invariably lead to reasonable suspicion."

PROBLEM D
THE APOLOGETIC OFFICER

One summer night, Trooper Williams was following a Mazda that he observed did not have a visible license tag, and determined to make a traffic stop. As he was pulling the car to the side of the road, the trooper realized he was mistaken. While there was no permanent license plate, his spotlight on the rear window revealed a valid temporary registration tag properly displayed. The trooper nonetheless continued the detention, and in the process determined that the driver was under the influence of alcohol, and an arrest followed. A subsequent search of the car disclosed drugs and drug paraphernalia. On appeal, the state conceded that any justification for the detention had been dispelled before the trooper reached the car but that it was reasonable for the officer to offer an explanation to the driver and tell him he was free to go. Was the evidence legitimately seized? *See State v. Morris*, 259 P.3d 116, 124 (Utah 2011).

FLORIDA v. J.L.

United States Supreme Court
529 U.S. 266 (2000)

JUSTICE GINSBURG delivered the opinion of the Court.

The question presented in this case is whether an anonymous tip that a person is carrying a gun is, without more, sufficient to justify a police officer's stop and frisk of that person. We hold that it is not.

I.

On October 13, 1995, an anonymous caller reported to the Miami-Dade Police that a young black male standing at a particular bus stop and wearing a plaid shirt was carrying a gun. . . . So far as the record reveals, there is no audio recording of the tip, and nothing is known about the informant. Sometime after the police received the tip — the record does not say how long — two officers were instructed to respond. They arrived at the bus stop about six minutes later and saw three black males "just hanging out [there]." . . . One of the three, respondent J.L., was wearing a plaid shirt. . . . Apart from the tip, the officers had no reason to suspect any of the three of illegal conduct. The officers did not see a firearm, and J.L. made no threatening or otherwise unusual movements. . . . One of the officers approached J.L., told him to put his hands up on the bus stop, frisked him, and seized a gun from J.L.'s pocket. The second officer frisked the other two individuals, against whom no allegations had been made, and found nothing.

J.L., who was at the time of the frisk "10 days shy of his 16th birth[day]," . . . was charged under state law with carrying a concealed firearm without a license and possessing a firearm while under the age of 18. He moved to suppress the gun as the fruit of an unlawful search and the trial court granted his motion. The intermediate appellate court reversed, but the Supreme Court of Florida quashed that decision and held the search invalid under the Fourth Amendment.

. . .

Anonymous tips, the Florida Supreme Court stated, are generally less reliable than tips from known informants and can form the basis for reasonable suspicion only if accompanied by specific indicia of reliability, for example, the correct forecast of a subject's " 'not easily predicted' " movements. . . . The tip leading to the frisk of J.L., the court observed, provided no such predictions, nor did it contain any other qualifying indicia of reliability. . . .

. . . We granted certiorari, . . . and now affirm the judgment of the Florida Supreme Court.

. . .

The tip in the instant case lacked the moderate indicia of reliability present in *White* and essential to the Court's decision in that case. The anonymous call concerning J.L. provided no predictive information and therefore left the police without means to test the informant's knowledge or credibility. That the allegation about the gun turned out to be correct does not suggest that the officers, prior to the frisks, had a reasonable basis for suspecting J.L. of engaging in unlawful conduct: The reasonableness of official suspicion must be measured by what the officers knew before they conducted their search. All the police had to go on in this case was the bare report of an unknown, unaccountable informant who neither explained how he knew about the gun or supplied any basis for believing he had inside information about J.L. If *White* was a close case on the reliability of anonymous tips, this one surely falls on the other side of the line.

Florida contends that the tip was reliable because its description of the suspect's visible attributes proved accurate: There really was a young black male wearing a plaid shirt at the bus stop. . . . The United States as *amicus curiae* makes a similar argument, proposing that a stop and frisk should be permitted "when (1) an anonymous tip provides a description of a particular person at a particular location illegally carrying a concealed firearm, (2) police promptly verify the pertinent details of the tip except the existence of the firearm, and (3) there are no factors that cast doubt on the reliability of the tip. . . ." . . . These contentions misapprehend the reliability needed for a tip to justify a *Terry* stop.

An accurate description of a subject's readily observable location and appearance is of course reliable in this limited sense: It will help the police correctly identify the person whom the tipster means to accuse. Such a tip, however, does not show that the tipster has knowledge of concealed criminal activity. The reasonable suspicion here at issue requires that a tip be reliable in its assertion of illegality, not just in its tendency to identify a determinate person. . . .

A second major argument advanced by Florida and the United States as *amicus* is, in essence, that the standard *Terry* analysis should be modified to license a "firearm exception." Under such an exception, a tip alleging an illegal gun would justify a stop and frisk even if the accusation would fail standard pre-search reliability testing. We decline to adopt this position.

Firearms are dangerous, and extraordinary dangers sometimes justify unusual precautions. Our decisions recognize the serious threat that armed criminals pose to public safety; *Terry*'s rule, which permits protective police searches on the basis of reasonable suspicion rather than demanding that officers meet the higher standard of probable cause, responds to this concern. . . . But an automatic firearm exception to our established reliability analysis would rove too far. Such an exception would enable any person seeking to harass another to set in motion an intrusive, embarrassing police search of the targeted person simply by placing an anonymous call falsely reporting the target's unlawful carriage of a gun. Nor could one securely confine such an exception to allegations involving firearms. Several Courts of Appeals have held it *per se* foreseeable for people carrying significant amounts of illegal drugs to be carrying guns was well. . . . If police officers may properly conduct *Terry* frisks on the basis of bare-boned tips about guns, it would be reasonable to maintain under the above-cited decisions that the police should similarly have discretion to frisk based on bare-boned tips about narcotics. As we clarified when we made indicia of reliability critical in *Adams* and *White*, the Fourth Amendment is not so easily satisfied. . . .

The facts of this case do not require us to speculate about the circumstances under which the danger alleged in an anonymous tip might be so great as to justify a search even without a showing of reliability. We do not say, for example, that a report of a person carrying a bomb need bear the indicia of reliability we demand for a report of a person carrying a firearm before the police can constitutionally conduct a frisk. Nor do we hold that public safety officials in quarters where the reasonable expectation of Fourth Amendment privacy is diminished, such as airports, . . . cannot conduct protective searches on the basis of information insufficient to justify searches elsewhere.

Finally, the requirement that an anonymous tip bear standard indicia of reliability in order to justify a stop in no way diminishes a police officer's prerogative, in accord with *Terry*, . . . to conduct a protective search of a person who has already been legitimately stopped. We speak in today's decision only of cases in which the officer's authority to make the initial stop is at issue. In that context, we hold that an anonymous tip lacking indicia of reliability of the kind contemplated in *Adams* and *White* does not justify a stop and frisk whenever and however it alleges the illegal possession of a firearm.

The judgment of the Florida Supreme Court is affirmed.

JUSTICE KENNEDY, with whom the CHIEF JUSTICE joins, concurring.

. . .

It seems appropriate to observe that a tip might be anonymous in some sense yet have certain other features, either supporting reliability or narrowing the likely class of informants, so that the tip does provide the lawful basis for some police action. One such feature, as the Court recognizes, is that the tip predicts future conduct of the alleged criminal. There may be others. For example, if an unnamed caller with a voice which sounds the same each time tells police on two successive nights about criminal activity which in fact occurs each night, a similar call on the third night ought not to be treated automatically like the tip in the case now before us. In the instance supposed, there would be a plausible argument that experience cures some of the uncertainty surrounding the anonymity. In today's case, however, the State provides us with no data about the reliability of anonymous tips. Nor do we know whether the dispatcher or arresting officer had any objective reason to believe that this tip had some particular indicia of reliability.

If an informant places his anonymity at risk, a court can consider this factor in weighing the reliability of the tip. An instance where a tip might be considered anonymous but nevertheless sufficiently reliable to justify a proportionate police response may be when an unnamed person driving a car the police officer later describes stops for a moment and, face to face, informs the police that criminal activity is occurring. This too seems to be different from the tip in the present case. . . .

Instant caller identification is widely available to police, and, if anonymous tips are proving unreliable and distracting to police, squad cars can be sent within seconds to the location of the telephone used by the informant. Voice recording of telephone tips might, in appropriate cases, be used by police to locate the caller. It is unlawful to make false reports to the police, . . . and the ability of the police to trace the identity of anonymous telephone informants may be a factor which lends reliability to what, years earlier, might have been considered unreliable anonymous tips.

NOTES

(1) *A potential danger.* The anonymous caller in *J.L.* said only that the suspect was carrying a gun. While potentially dangerous, the possession of a weapon is not necessarily illegal and might be constitutionally protected. Justice Ginsburg noted that a different result might be reached should the report be that the individual was carrying a bomb, suggesting that the magnitude of the risk may be taken into account. *United States v. Simmons*, 560 F.3d 98 (2d Cir.), *cert. denied*, 558 U.S. 1008 (2009). Concern for public safety would also appear paramount in cases in which the anonymous tip concerns impaired or reckless driving. *See, e.g.*, *United States v. Wheat*, 278 F.3d 722 (8th Cir. 2001), *cert. denied*, 537 U.S. 850 (2002); *State v. Hanning*, 296 S.W.3d 44 (Tenn. 2009).

(2) *A manifest danger. J.L.* is sometimes distinguished in cases in which the anonymous informant articulates an immediate danger. *See People v. Dolly*, 150 P.3d 693, *cert. denied*, 552 U.S. 828 (2007) (anonymous caller said that an individual had pointed a revolver at him).

(3) *The credibility of the tipster.* A face-to-face encounter with the tipster may satisfy the reliability concerns. *United States v. Sanchez*, 519 F.3d 1208 (10th Cir.), *cert. denied*, 555 U.S. 870 (2008). Multiple corroborating tips may be relied on. *United States v. Hampton*, 585 F.3d 1033, 1038 (7th Cir. 2009).

(4) *Race or ethnicity of the suspect.* For obvious constitutional reasons, courts frequently admonish law enforcement personnel that the race or ethnicity of the suspect is not to be taken into account in evaluating suspicious circumstances. Adhering to this principle is today a greater challenge. In *United States v. Ramos*, 629 F.3d 60 (1st Cir. 2010), *cert. denied*, 131 S. Ct. 3045 (2011), the court recognized that Middle Eastern ethnicity was a legitimate consideration in addressing the matter of terrorist attacks in public transportation. The court acknowledged that "[w]hile in other situations there may be merit in the argument that a description of ethnic appearance is irrelevant and nothing more than impermissible profiling, the argument fails on the facts here. . . . Not just the recent history of Middle East-originated terrorism, but also the explicit warnings, issued some eleven weeks before, of future strikes by the same groups in the United States, meant it was material for the officers to consider, among other facts, the risk of terrorist attacks on transit stations in major urban centers and that the persons they were investigating had a Middle Eastern appearance."

[E] The Problem of Pretext

WHREN v. UNITED STATES

United States Supreme Court
517 U.S. 806 (1996)

JUSTICE SCALIA delivered the opinion of the Court.

In this case we decide whether the temporary detention of a motorist who the police have probable cause to believe has committed a civil traffic violation is inconsistent with the Fourth Amendment's prohibition against unreasonable seizures unless a reasonable officer would have been motivated to stop the car by a desire to enforce the traffic laws.

I

On the evening of June 10, 1993, plainclothes vice-squad officers of the District of Columbia Metropolitan Police Department were patrolling a "high drug area" of the city in an unmarked car. Their suspicions were aroused when they passed a dark Pathfinder truck with temporary license plates and youthful occupants waiting at a stop sign, the driver looking down into the lap of the passenger at his right. The truck remained stopped at the intersection for what seemed an unusually long time — more than 20 seconds. When the police car executed a U-turn in order to head back toward the truck, the Pathfinder turned suddenly to its right, without signaling, and sped off at an "unreasonable" speed. The policemen followed, and in a short while overtook the Pathfinder when it stopped behind other traffic at a red light. They pulled up alongside, and Officer Ephraim Soto stepped out and approached the driver's door, identifying himself as a police officer and directing the driver, petitioner Brown, to put the vehicle in park. When Soto drew up to the driver's window, he immediately observed two large plastic bags of what appeared to be crack cocaine in petitioner Whren's hands. Petitioners were arrested, and quantities of several types of illegal drugs were retrieved from the vehicle.

Petitioners were charged in a four-count indictment with violating various federal drug laws. . . . At a pretrial suppression hearing, they challenged the legality of the stop and the resulting seizure of the drugs. They argued that the stop had not been justified by probable cause to believe, or even reasonable suspicion, that petitioners were engaged in illegal drug-dealing activity; and that Officer Soto's asserted ground for approaching the vehicle — to give the driver a warning concerning traffic violations — was pretextual. The District Court denied the suppression motion, concluding that "the facts of the stop were not controverted," and "there was nothing to really demonstrate that the actions of the officers were contrary to a normal traffic stop." . . .

Petitioners were convicted of the counts at issue here. The Court of Appeals affirmed the convictions, holding with respect to the suppression issue that, "regardless of whether a police officer subjectively believes that the occupants of an automobile may be engaging in some other illegal behavior, a traffic stop is permissible as long as a reasonable officer in the same circumstances *could have* stopped the car for the suspected traffic violation." . . . We granted certiorari. . . .

II

. . .

Petitioners accept that Officer Soto had probable cause to believe that various provisions of the District of Columbia traffic code had been violated. . . . They argue, however, that "in the unique context of civil traffic regulations" probable cause is not enough. Since, they contend, the use of automobiles is so heavily and minutely regulated that total compliance with traffic and safety rules is nearly impossible, a police officer will almost invariably be able to catch any given motorist in a technical violation. This creates the temptation to use traffic stops as a means of investigating other law violations, as to which no probable cause or even articulable suspicion exists. Petitioners, who are both black, further contend that police officers might decide which motorists to stop based on decidedly impermissible factors, such as the race of the car's occupants. To avoid this danger, they say, the Fourth Amendment test for traffic stops should be, not the normal one (applied by the Court of Appeals) of whether probable cause existed to justify the stop; but rather, whether a police officer, acting reasonably, would have made the stop for the reason given.

A

. . . We of course agree with petitioners that the Constitution prohibits selective enforcement of the law based on considerations such as race. But the constitutional basis for objecting to intentionally discriminatory application of laws is the Equal Protection Clause, not the Fourth Amendment. Subjective intentions play no role in ordinary probable-cause Fourth Amendment analysis.

. . .

III

In what would appear to be an elaboration on the "reasonable officer" test, petitioners argue that the balancing inherent in any Fourth Amendment inquiry requires us to weigh the governmental and individual interest implicated in a traffic stop such as we have here. That balancing, petitioners claim, does not support investigation of minor traffic infractions by plainclothes police in unmarked vehicles; such investigation only minimally advances the government's interest in traffic safety, and may indeed retard it by producing motorist confusion and alarm — a view said to be supported by the Metropolitan Police Department's own regulations generally prohibiting this practice. And as for the Fourth Amendment interests of the individuals concerned, petitioners point out that our cases acknowledge that even ordinary traffic stops entail "a possibly unsettling show of authority"; that they at best "interfere with freedom of movement, are inconvenient, and consume time" and at worst "may create substantial anxiety," *Prouse*. . . . That anxiety is likely to be even more pronounced when the stop is conducted by plainclothes officers in unmarked cars.

It is of course true that in principle every Fourth Amendment case, since it turns upon a "reasonableness" determination, involves a balancing of all relevant factors. With rare exceptions not applicable here, however, the result of that balancing is not in doubt where the search or seizure is based upon probable cause. That is why petitioners must rely upon cases like *Prouse* to provide examples of actual "balancing" analysis. There, the police action in question was a random traffic stop for the purpose of checking a motorist's license and vehicle registration, a practice that — like the practices at issue in the inventory search and administrative inspection cases upon which petitioners rely in making their "pretext" claim — involves police intrusion *without the probable cause that is its traditional justification.* Our opinion in *Prouse* expressly distinguished the case from a stop based on precisely what is at issue here: "probable cause to believe that a driver is violating any one of the multitude of applicable traffic and equipment regulations." . . .

Petitioners urge as an extraordinary factor in this case that the "multitude of applicable traffic and equipment regulations" is so large and so difficult to obey perfectly that virtually everyone is guilty of violation, permitting the police to single out almost whomever they wish for a stop. But we are aware of no principle that would allow us to decide at what point a code of law becomes so expansive and so commonly violated that infraction itself can no longer be the ordinary measure of the lawfulness of enforcement. And even if we could identify such exorbitant codes, we do not know by what standard (or what right) we would decide, as petitioners would have us do, which particular provisions are sufficiently important to merit enforcement.

For the run-of-the-mine case, which this surely is, we think there is no realistic alternative to the traditional common-law rule that probable cause justifies a search and seizure.

. . .

[Judgment affirmed.]

NOTE

The holding in *Whren* was reaffirmed by the Supreme Court in *Devenpeck v. Alford*, 543 U.S. 146 (2004), a case not involving a purported pretext arrest but rather an arrest for what turned out to be no offense at all, notwithstanding the good faith of the arresting officer. There were, however, other unrelated crimes for which the suspect might have been arrested legitimately, and the Court held that such probable cause would sustain the constitutionality of the action. It said, "Our cases make clear that an arresting officer's state of mind (except for the facts that he knows) is irrelevant to the existence of probable cause," citing *Whren. And see* Lawton, *The Road to* Whren *and Beyond: Does the "Would Have" Test Work?*, 57 DePaul L. Rev. 917 (2008).

[F] The Scope of the Frisk

MICHIGAN v. LONG
United States Supreme Court
463 U.S. 1032 (1983)

Justice O'Connor delivered the opinion of the Court.

In *Terry v. Ohio*, we upheld the validity of a protective search for weapons in the absence of probable cause to arrest because it is unreasonable to deny a police officer the right "to neutralize the threat of physical harm," when he possesses an articulable suspicion that an individual is armed and dangerous. We did not, however, expressly address whether such a protective search for weapons could extend to an area beyond the person in the absence of probable cause to arrest. In the present case, respondent David Long was convicted for possession of marijuana found by police in the passenger compartment and trunk of the automobile that he was driving. The police searched the passenger compartment because they had reason to believe that the vehicle contained weapons potentially dangerous to the officers. We hold that the protective search of the passenger compartment was reasonable under the principles articulated in *Terry* and other decisions of this Court.

Deputies Howell and Lewis were on patrol in a rural area one evening when, shortly after midnight, they observed a car traveling erratically and at excessive speed. The officers observed the car turning down a side road, where it swerved off into a shallow ditch. The officers stopped to investigate. Long, the only occupant of the automobile, met the deputies at the rear of the car, which was protruding from the ditch onto the road. The door on the driver's side of the vehicle was left open.

Deputy Howell requested Long to produce his operator's license, but he did not respond. After the request was repeated, Long produced his license. Long again failed to respond when Howell requested him to produce the vehicle registration. After another repeated request, Long, whom Howell through "appeared to be under the influence of something," turned from the officers and began walking toward the open door of the vehicle. The officers followed Long and both observed a large hunting knife on the floorboard of the driver's side of the car. The officers then stopped Long's progress and subjected him to a *Terry* protective pat-down, which revealed no weapons.

Long and Deputy Lewis then stood by the rear of the vehicle while Deputy Howell shined his flashlight into the interior of the vehicle, but did not actually enter it. The purpose of Howell's action was to search for other weapons. The officer noticed that something was protruding from under the armrest on the front seat. He knelt in the vehicle and lifted the armrest. He saw an open pouch on the front seat, and upon flashing his light on the pouch, determined that it contained what appeared to be marijuana. After Deputy Howell showed the pouch and its contents to Deputy Lewis, Long was arrested for possession of marijuana. A further search of the interior of the vehicle, including the glovebox, revealed neither more contraband nor the vehicle registration. The officers decided to impound the vehicle. Deputy Howell opened the trunk, which did not have a lock, and discovered inside it approximately 75 pounds of marijuana.

The Barry County Circuit Court denied Long's motion to suppress the marijuana taken from both the interior of the car and its trunk. He was subsequently convicted of possession of marijuana.

The court below held, and respondent Long contends, that Deputy Howell's entry into the vehicle cannot be justified under the principles set forth in *Terry* because "*Terry* authorized only a limited pat-down search of a person suspected of criminal activity" rather than a search of an area. Although *Terry* did involve the protective frisk of a person, we believe that the police action in this case is justified by the principles that we have already established in *Terry* and other cases.

In *Terry*, the Court examined the validity of a "stop and frisk" in the absence of probable cause and a warrant. The police officer in *Terry* detained several suspects to ascertain their identities after the officer had observed the suspects for a brief period of time and formed the conclusion that they were about to engage in criminal activity. Because the officer feared that the suspects were armed, he patted down the outside of the suspects' clothing and discovered two revolvers.

Examining the reasonableness of the officer's conduct in *Terry*, we held that there is " 'no ready test for determining reasonableness other than by balancing the need to search or seize against the invasion which the search or seizure entails.' " 392 U.S., at 21 (quoting *Camara v. Municipal Court*, 387 U.S. 523, 536, 537 (1967)). Although the conduct of the officer in *Terry* involved a "severe, though brief, intrusion upon cherished personal security," 392 U.S., at 24–25, we found that the conduct was reasonable when we weighed the interest of the individual against the legitimate interest in "crime prevention and detection," *id.*, at 22, and the "need for law enforcement officers to protect themselves and prospective victims of violence in situations where they lack probable cause for an arrest," *id.*, at 24. When the officer has a reasonable belief "that the individual whose suspicious behavior he is investigating at close range is armed and presently dangerous to the officer or to others, it would appear to be clearly unreasonable to deny the officer the power to take necessary measures to determine whether the person is in fact carrying a weapon and to neutralize the threat of physical harm." (*Ibid.*)

Although *Terry* itself involved the stop and subsequent pat-down search of a person, we were careful to note that "we need not develop at length in this case, however, the limitations which the Fourth Amendment places upon a protective search and seizure for weapons. These limitations will have to be developed in the concrete factual circumstances of individual cases." *Id.*, at 29. Contrary to Long's view, *Terry* need not be read as restricting the preventative search to the person of the detained suspect.

Our past cases indicate then that protection of police and others can justify protective searches when police have a reasonable belief that the suspect poses a danger, that roadside encounters between police and suspects are especially hazardous, and that danger may arise from the possible presence of weapons in the area surrounding a suspect. These principles compel our conclusion that the search of the passenger compartment of an automobile, limited to those areas in which a weapon may be placed or hidden, is permissible if the police officer possesses a reasonable belief based on "specific and articulable facts which, taken together with the rational inferences from those facts, reasonably warrant" the officers in believing that the suspect is dangerous and the suspect may gain immediate control of weapons.[9]

The circumstances of this case clearly justified Deputies Howell and Lewis in their reasonable belief that Long posed a danger if he were permitted to reenter his vehicle. The hour was late and the area rural. Long was driving his automobile at excessive speed, and his car swerved into a ditch. The officers had to repeat their questions to Long, who appeared to be "under the influence" of some intoxicant. Long was not frisked until the officers observed that there was a large knife in the interior of the car into which Long was about to reenter. The subsequent search of the car was restricted to those areas to which Long would generally have immediate control, and that could contain a weapon. The trial court determined that the leather pouch containing marijuana could have contained a weapon. It is clear that the intrusion was "strictly circumscribed by the exigencies which justifi[ed] its initiation."

---

[9] [12] We stress that our decision does not mean that the police may conduct automobile searches *whenever* they conduct an investigative stop, although the "bright line"that we drew in [*New York v.*] *Belton*, [453 U.S. 454 (1981)], clearly authorizes such a search whenever officers effect a custodial arrest. An additional interest exists in the arrest context, *i.e.*, preservation of evidence, and this justifies an "automatic" search. However, that additional interest does not exist in the *Terry* context. A *Terry* search, "unlike a search without a warrant incident to a lawful arrest, is not justified by any need to prevent the disappearance or destruction of evidence of crime. . . . The sole justification of the search . . . is the protection of police officers and others nearby. . . ." 392 U.S., at 29. What we borrow now from *Chimel v. California*, 395 U.S. 752 (1969) and *Belton* is merely the recognition that part of the reason to allow area searches incident to an arrest is that the arrestee, who may not himself be armed, may be able to gain access to weapons to injure officers or others nearby, or otherwise to hinder legitimate police activity. This recognition applies as well in the *Terry* context. However, because the interest in collecting and preserving evidence is not present in the *Terry* context, we require that officers who conduct area searches during investigative detentions must do so only when they have the level of suspicion identified in *Terry*.

JUSTICE BRENNAN, with whom JUSTICE MARSHALL joins, dissenting.

It is clear that *Terry* authorized only limited searches of the person for weapons. In light of what *Terry* said, relevant portions of which the Court neglects to quote, the Court's suggestion that "*Terry* need not be read as restricting the preventive search to the person of the detained suspect," can only be described as disingenuous. Nothing in *Terry* authorized police officers to search a suspect's car based on reasonable suspicion. The Court confirmed this very term in *United States v. Place*, where it described the search authorized by *Terry* as a "limited search for weapons, or " 'frisk'. . . ."

The search at issue in this case is a far cry from a "frisk" and certainly was not "limited."

The Court's reliance on *Chimel v. California*, and *New York v. Belton*, as support for its new "area search" rule within the context of *Terry* stop is misplaced. In *Chimel*, the Court addressed the scope of a search incident to a lawful arrest, and held invalid the search at issue there because it "went far beyond the petitioner's persons and the area from within which he might have obtained a weapon or something that would have been used as evidence against him." *Chimel* stressed the need to limit the scope of searches incident to arrest and overruled two prior decisions of this Court validating overly broad searches.

In *Belton*, the Court considered the scope of a search incident to the lawful custodial arrest of an occupant of an automobile. In this "particular and problematic context," the Court held that "when a policeman has made a lawful custodial arrest of the occupant of an automobile, he may, as a contemporaneous incident of that arrest, search the passenger compartment of that automobile."

The critical distinction between this case and *Terry* on the one hand, and *Chimel* and *Belton* on the other, is that the latter two cases arose within the context of lawful custodial arrests supported by probable cause. The Court in *Terry* expressly recognized the difference between a search incident to arrest and the "limited search for weapons," involved in that case.

NOTES AND QUESTIONS

(1) Does the presence of a hunting knife on the floorboard of an automobile give rise to a reasonable suspicion that weapons other than the knife may be found on the person of the suspect or within the vehicle? On the authority of *Long*, once suspicion is aroused, are officers free to examine anything "protruding from under the armrest," or for that matter anything which is not part of the car itself? An article of clothing? A sack of groceries?

(2) Had Long already been arrested, it is clear from the *Belton* decision cited by the Court (*see* note 9) that a search of the interior of the vehicle would have been reasonable. As Justice Brennan argued in dissent, the present case does not involve a search incident to an arrest, and therefore it is the *Terry* rationale which must support the result. After studying the search incident to arrest cases, consider whether the dissent is correct that reliance upon *Chimel* and *Belton* is "misplaced."

(3) Not all courts have limited a *Long* "frisk" to items in plain view. "[A] valid *Long* search extends to closed containers, such as the pouch, that are found within the vehicle's passenger compartment. Because the heart of [*Terry*] and [*Long*] is the safety of the officers (and others), an officer may search a container found in a vehicle when that container might hold a weapon." *United States v. Shranklen*, 315 F.3d 959, 963 (8th Cir.), *cert. denied*, 538 U.S. 971 (2003).

MINNESOTA v. DICKERSON

United States Supreme Court
508 U.S. 366 (1993)

Justice White delivered the opinion of the Court.

In this case, we consider whether the Fourth Amendment permits the seizure of contraband detected through a police officer's sense of touch during a protective pat-down search.

On the evening of November 9, 1989, two Minneapolis police officers were patrolling an area in the city's north side in a marked squad car. At about 8:15 p.m., one of the officers observed respondent leaving a 12-unit apartment building on Morgan Avenue North. The officer, having previously responded to complaints of drug sales in the building's hallways and having executed several search warrants on the premises, considered the building to be a notorious "crack house." According to testimony credited by the trial court, respondent began walking toward the police but, upon spotting the squad car and making eye contact with one of the officers, abruptly halted and began walking in the opposite direction. His suspicion aroused, this officer watched as respondent turned and entered an alley on the other side of the apartment building. Based upon respondent's seemingly evasive actions and the fact that he had just left a building known for cocaine traffic, the officers decided to stop respondent and investigate further.

The officers pulled their squad car into the alley and ordered respondent to stop and submit to a pat-down search. The search revealed no weapons, but the officer conducting the search did take an interest in a small lump in respondent's nylon jacket. The officer later testified:

> [A]s I pat-searched the front of his body, I felt a lump, a small lump, in the front pocket. I examined it with my fingers and it slid and it felt to be a lump of crack cocaine in cellophane.

The officer then reached into respondent's pocket and retrieved a small plastic bag containing one fifth of one gram of crack cocaine. Respondent was arrested and charged in Hennepin County District Court with possession of a controlled substance.

Before trial, respondent moved to suppress the cocaine. The trial court first concluded that the officers were justified under *Terry* . . . in stopping respondent to investigate whether he might be engaged in criminal activity. The court further found that the officers were justified in frisking respondent to ensure that he was not carrying a weapon. Finally, analogizing to the "plain-view" doctrine, under which officers may make a warrantless seizure of contraband found in plain view during a lawful search for other items, the trial court ruled that the officers' seizure of the cocaine did not violate the Fourth Amendment:

> To this Court there is no distinction as to which sensory perception the officer uses to conclude that the material is contraband. An experienced officer may rely upon his sense of smell in DWI stops or in recognizing the smell of burning marijuana in an automobile. The sound of a shotgun being racked would clearly support certain reactions by an officer. The sense of touch, grounded in experience and training, is as reliable as perceptions drawn from other senses. "Plain feel," therefore, is no different than plain view and will equally support the seizure here. . . .

His suppression motion having failed, respondent proceeded to trial and was found guilty.

[The Minnesota Court of Appeals reversed, declining to adopt the plain feel exception. The Minnesota Supreme Court affirmed.]

We granted certiorari . . . to resolve a conflict among the state and federal courts over whether contraband detected through the sense of touch during a pat-down search may be admitted into evidence. We now affirm.

The Minnesota Supreme Court rejected an analogy to the plain-view doctrine on two grounds: first, its belief that "the sense of touch is inherently less immediate and less reliable than the sense of sight," and second, that "the sense of touch is far more intrusive into the personal privacy that is the core of the [F]ourth [A]mendment." . . . We have a somewhat different view. First, *Terry* itself demonstrates that the sense of touch is capable of revealing the nature of an object with sufficient reliability to support a seizure. The very premise of *Terry*, after all, is that officers will be able to detect the presence of weapons through the sense of touch and *Terry* upheld precisely such a seizure. Even if it were true that the sense of touch is generally less reliable than the sense of sight, that only suggests that officers will less often be able to justify seizures of unseen contraband. Regardless of whether the officer detects the contraband by sight or by touch, however, the Fourth Amendment's requirement that the officer have probable cause to believe that the item is contraband before seizing it ensures against excessively speculative seizures. The court's second concern — that touch is more intrusive into privacy than sight — is inapposite in light of the fact that the intrusion the court fears has already been authorized by the lawful search for weapons. The seizure of an item whose identity is already known occasions no further invasion of privacy. . . . Accordingly, the suspect's privacy interests are not advanced by a categorical rule barring the seizure of contraband plainly detected through the sense of touch.

The Minnesota Supreme Court, after "a close examination of the record," held that the officer's own testimony "belies any notion" that he "immediately" recognize the lump as crack cocaine. . . . Rather, the court concluded, the officer determined that the lump was contraband only after "squeezing, sliding and otherwise manipulating the contents of the defendant's pocket" — a pocket which the officer already knew contained no weapon.

Under the State Supreme Court's interpretation of the record before it, it is clear that the court was correct in holding that the police officer in this case overstepped the bounds of the "strictly circumscribed" search for weapons allowed under *Terry*. . . . Here, the officer's continued exploration of respondent's pocket after having concluded that it contained no weapon was unrelated to "[t]he sole justification of the search [under *Terry*:] . . . the protection of the police officer and others nearby." . . .

Although the officer was lawfully in a position to feel the lump in respondent's pocket, because *Terry* entitled him to place his hands upon respondent's jacket, the court below determined that the incriminating character of the object was not immediately apparent to him. Rather, the officer determined that the item was contraband only after conducting a further search, one not authorized by *Terry* or by any other exception to the warrant requirement. Because this further search of respondent's pocket was constitutionally invalid, the seizure of the cocaine that followed is likewise unconstitutional. . . .

Justice Scalia, concurring.

I take it to be a fundamental principle of constitutional adjudication that the terms in the Constitution must be given the meaning ascribed to them at the time of their ratification. Thus, when the Fourth Amendment provides that "[t]he right of the people to be secure in their persons, houses, papers, and effects, against *unreasonable searches and seizures*, shall not be violated" (emphasis added), it "is to be construed in the light of what was deemed an unreasonable search and seizure when it was adopted". . . . The purpose of the provision, in other words, is to preserve that degree of respect for the privacy of persons and the inviolability of their property that existed when the provision was adopted, even if a later, less virtuous age should become accustomed to considering all sorts of intrusions "reasonable."

My problem with the present case is that I am not entirely sure that the physical search — the "frisk" — that produced the evidence at issue here complied with that standard. The decision of ours that gave approval to such searches, *Terry v. Ohio*, made no serious attempt to determine compliance with traditional standards, but rather, according to the style of this Court at the time, simply adjudged that such a search was "reasonable" by current estimations. . . .

There is good evidence, I think, that the "stop" portion of the *Terry* "stop-and-frisk" holding accords with the common law — that it had long been considered reasonable to detain suspicious persons for the purpose of demanding that they give an account of themselves. . . .

I am unaware, however, of any precedent for a physical search of a person thus temporarily detained for questioning. Sometimes, of course, the temporary detention of a suspicious character would be elevated to a full custodial arrest on probable cause — as, for instance, when a suspect was unable to provide a sufficient accounting of himself. At that point, it is clear that the common law would permit not just a protective "frisk," but a physical search incident to the arrest. When, however, the detention did not rise to the level of a full-blown arrest (and was not supported by the degree of cause needful for that purpose), there appears to be no clear support at common law for physically searching the suspect. . . .

I frankly doubt, moreover, whether the fiercely proud men who adopted our Fourth Amendment would have allowed themselves to be subjected, on mere suspicion of being armed and dangerous, to such indignity — which is described as follows in a police manual:

> "Check the subject's neck and collar. A check should be made under the subject's arm. Next a check should be made of the upper back. The lower back should also be checked.
>
> "A check should be made of the upper part of the man's chest and lower region around the stomach. The belt, a favorite concealment spot, should be checked. The inside thigh and crotch area also should be searched. The legs should be checked for possible weapons. The last items to be checked are the shoes and cuffs of the subject." J. Mohnahan, *Police Searching Procedures* 7 (1963) (citations omitted).

On the other hand, even if a "frisk" prior to arrest would have been considered impermissible in 1791, perhaps it was considered permissible by 1868, when the Fourteenth Amendment (the basis for applying the Fourth Amendment to the States) was adopted. Or perhaps it is only since that time that concealed weapons capable of harming the interrogator quickly and from beyond arm's reach have become common — which might alter the judgment of what is "reasonable" under the original standard. But technological changes were no more discussed in *Terry* than was the original state of the law.

If I were of the view that *Terry* was (insofar as the power to "frisk" is concerned) incorrectly decided, I might — even if I felt bound to adhere to that case — vote to exclude the evidence incidentally discovered, on the theory that half a constitutional guarantee is better than none. I might also vote to exclude it if I agreed with the original-meaning-is-irrelevant, good-policy-is-constitutional-law school of jurisprudence that the *Terry* opinion represents. As a policy matter, it may be desirable to permit "frisks" for weapons, but not to encourage "frisks" for drugs by admitting evidence other than weapons.

I adhere to original meaning, however. And though I do not favor the mode of analysis in *Terry*, I cannot say that its result was wrong. Constitutionality of the "frisk" in the present case was neither challenged nor argued. Assuming, therefore, that the search was lawful, I agree with the Court's premise that any evidence incidentally discovered in the course of it would be admissible, and join the Court's opinion in its entirety.

CHIEF JUSTICE REHNQUIST with whom JUSTICE BLACKMUN and JUSTICE THOMAS join, concurring in part and dissenting in part.

The Court, correctly in my view, states that "the dispositive question before this Court is whether the officer who conducted the search was acting within the lawful bounds marked by *Terry* . . . at the time he gained probable cause to believe that the lump in the respondent's jacket was contraband." . . . The Court then goes on to point out that the state trial court did not make precise findings on this point, but accepts the appellate findings made by the Supreme Court of Minnesota. I believe that these findings, like those of the trial court, are imprecise and not directed expressly to the question of the officer's probable cause to believe that the lump was contraband. Because the Supreme Court of Minnesota employed a Fourth Amendment analysis which differs significantly from that now adopted by this Court, I would vacate its judgment and remand the case for further proceedings there in light of this Court's opinion.

NOTES AND QUESTIONS

(1) Justice White seeks to downplay the significance of the issue by observing that *Terry* itself was a "plain feel" case. *Terry*, of course, held only that the officer's tactile sense could be used to determine whether or not the suspect was armed. On first glance, *Dickerson* may appear to expand the frisking power significantly. The holding may be seen, however, as nothing more than a special case of the general principle that an officer, otherwise engaged in a legitimate activity, may act on probable cause that comes within her knowledge fortuitously. There is, of course, always the danger that an officer may be overly imaginative in the conclusions drawn. It should not be overlooked, however, that the defendant in *Dickerson* prevailed. Clearly, the plausibility of the officer's claim is open to challenge.

(2) In his concurring opinion, Justice Scalia takes exception to the "mode of analysis" of the *Terry* decision, and more broadly, to the "good-policy-is-constitutional-law school of jurisprudence" that it represents. Is Justice Scalia contending that the Warren Court gave law enforcement officers a power to which they are not entitled under the Fourth Amendment? If so, why the disclaimer, "I cannot say that its [*Terry*'s] result was wrong"? How would Justice Scalia have decided *Terry*?

(3) In *State v. Craven*, 253 Neb. 601, 571 N.W.2d 612 (1997), in the course of a frisk, an officer detected what he believed to be a pipe used to smoke marijuana. The object, which was at the bottom of the pocket, turned out to be a spark plug. In the process of removing it, however, the officer discovered a quantity of crack cocaine. In sustaining the seizure, the court reasoned that the innocuousness of the spark plug was irrelevant so long as the officer had probable cause to believe the suspect was harboring contraband.

(4) The resort to a "plain hear" exception may prove too speculative. In *United States v. Thomas*, 211 F.3d 1186 (9th Cir. 2000), in an effort to establish suspicion sufficient for a *Terry* stop, an officer testified to hearing three or four thumps from within a garage, which he identified as the sound of packages of marijuana being dropped into the bed of a pickup truck. The court dismissed this as "mere conjecture," noting that the sound "could have been generated by dropped 12- or 13-pound bags or bales of potting soil, cut grass, bird seed, dog food — anything."

PROBLEM E
THE CASUALLY SQUEEZING BORDER PATROL AGENT

A border patrol agent boarded a Greyhound bus in Sierra Blanca, Texas, to determine the immigration status of passengers. After walking the length of the bus and concluding that no illegal immigrants were on board, he began walking toward the front of the bus, and while doing so, squeezed the soft luggage located in the overhead storage rack. Sensing a "brick-like" object in a canvas bag, the agent inquired of passenger Bond, who acknowledged that the bag was his and allowed the agent to open it. Within the bag, the agent found a brick of methamphetamine, for the possession of which Bond was convicted. Was the seizure constitutional? Consider the implications of both *Dickerson* and *Florida v. Bostick, supra. See Bond v. United States*, 529 U.S. 324 (2000).

PROBLEM F
THE UBIQUITOUS PILL BOTTLE

Officer Blackwell was told by an informant of established reliability that Bridges "was selling crack cocaine 'right then' at a club called 'Preacher's.' " Thirty minutes later, Blackwell "found Bridges sitting at a table inside Preacher's engaged in conversation. Aware that Bridges previously had been convicted of felony assault and recently had been involved in an armed altercation with police, Officer Blackwell identified himself and ordered Bridges to stand against the wall. Officer Blackwell then patted down the outside of Bridges clothing to ensure he was not carrying weapons. During the pat-down, Officer Blackwell felt a small object 'in the shape of a pill bottle' in the defendant's right jacket pocket and, recognized it as 'the kind that a lot of other crack dealers will use to keep their crack in.' Officer Blackwell seized the bottle, and upon inspection, determined that it contained crack cocaine, and he also found a knife in the defendant's right pants pocket. As a result, Bridges was arrested, and a further search was conducted of the defendant's person, during which Officer Blackwell discovered a plastic bag of cocaine 'in the same pocket' from which the pill box had been removed." Assuming probable cause to arrest was lacking prior to the pat-down, are the seizures legal? *See State v. Bridges*, 963 S.W.2d 487 (Tenn. 1997). *Cf. Ball v. United States*, 803 A.2d 971 (D.C. App. 2002).

[G] The Duration of the Detention

ILLINOIS v. CABALLES
United States Supreme Court
543 U.S. 405 (2005)

JUSTICE STEVENS delivered the opinion of the Court.

Illinois State Trooper Daniel Gillette stopped respondent for speeding on an interstate highway. When Gillette radioed the police dispatcher to report the stop, a second trooper, Craig Graham, a member of the Illinois State Police Drug Interdiction Team, overheard the transmission and immediately headed for the scene with his narcotics-detection dog. When they arrived, respondent's car was on the shoulder of the road and respondent was in Gillette's vehicle. While Gillette was in the process of writing a warning ticket, Graham walked his dog around respondent's car. The dog alerted at the trunk. Based on that alert, the officers searched the trunk, found marijuana, and arrested respondent. The entire incident lasted less than 10 minutes.

Respondent was convicted of a narcotics offense and sentenced to 12 years' imprisonment and a $256,136 fine. The trial judge denied his motion to suppress the seized evidence and to quash his arrest. He held that the officers had not unnecessarily prolonged the stop and that the dog alert was sufficiently reliable to provide probable cause to conduct the search. Although the Appellate Court affirmed, the Illinois Supreme Court reversed, concluding that because the canine sniff was performed without any " 'specific and articulable facts' " to suggest drug activity, the use of the dog "unjustifiably enlarg[ed] the scope of a routine traffic stop into a drug investigation." . . .

The question on which we granted certiorari . . . is narrow: "Whether the Fourth Amendment requires reasonable, articulable suspicion to justify using a drug-detection dog to sniff a vehicle during a legitimate traffic stop." . . . Thus, we proceed on the assumption that the officer conducting the dog sniff had no information about respondent except that he had been stopped for speeding; accordingly, we have omitted any reference to facts about respondent that might have triggered a modicum of suspicion.

Here, the initial seizure of respondent when he was stopped on the highway was based on probable cause, and was concededly lawful. It is nevertheless clear that a seizure that is lawful at its inception can violate the Fourth Amendment if its manner of execution unreasonably infringes interests protected by the Constitution. . . . A seizure that is justified solely by the interest in issuing a warning ticket to the driver can become unlawful if it is prolonged beyond the time reasonably required to complete that mission. In an earlier case involving a dog sniff that occurred during an unreasonably prolonged traffic stop, the Illinois Supreme Court held that use of the dog and the subsequent discovery of contraband were the product of an unconstitutional seizure. *People v. Cox*, 202 Ill. 2d 462, 782 N.E.2d 275 (2002). We may assume that a similar result would be warranted in this case if the dog sniff had been conducted while respondent was being unlawfully detained.

In the state-court proceedings, however, the judges carefully reviewed the details of Officer Gillette's conversations with respondent and the precise timing of his radio transmissions to the dispatcher to determine whether he had improperly extended the duration of the stop to enable the dog sniff to occur. We have not recounted those details because we accept the state court's conclusion that the duration of the stop in this case was entirely justified by the traffic offense and the ordinary inquiries incident to such a stop.

Despite this conclusion, the Illinois Supreme Court held that the initially lawful traffic stop became an unlawful seizure solely as a result of the canine sniff that occurred outside respondent's stopped car. That is, the court characterized the dog sniff as the cause rather than the consequence of a constitutional violation. In its view, the use of the dog converted the citizen-police encounter from a lawful traffic stop into a drug investigation, and because the shift in purpose was not supported by any reasonable suspicion that respondent possessed narcotics, it was unlawful. In our view, conducting a dog sniff would not change the character of a traffic stop that is lawful at its inception and otherwise executed in a reasonable manner, unless the dog sniff itself infringed respondent's constitutionally protected interest in privacy. Our cases hold that it did not.

NOTES AND QUESTIONS

(1) The *Caballes* decision also addressed the constitutionality of the use of narcotics-detecting canines to determine probable cause. This aspect of the case will be examined subsequently in § 3.03[D], *infra*.

(2) The Court appears to nimbly sidestep the question of whether the detention was excessively prolonged, awaiting the arrival of the dog, noting simply that "[t]he entire incident lasted less than 10 minutes." It is, of course, possible that the speeding ticket could have been issued in five minutes. We do know that the dog was not on the scene at the time of the stop but was brought there by another officer. As a general rule, courts hold that a detention may continue no longer than necessary to accomplish its purpose (assuming no justification for continuing the stop arises), and a detention which exceeds reasonable limits is a violation of the Fourth Amendment. The *Caballes* Court must be understood to hold that the reasonable time for issuing the traffic citation had not expired when the dog signaled the presence of drugs.

(3) The legitimate duration of a *Terry* stop was a more prominent question in *United States v. Sharpe*, 470 U.S. 675 (1985). In that case, a federal drug enforcement officer observed a pickup truck with an attached camper shell and an automobile apparently traveling in tandem at 6:30 a.m. in a rural area suspected of drug trafficking. Eventually, three different law enforcement agencies were involved in the detention of the two vehicles, which occurred about a half mile apart because of the evasive action taken by one of the suspects. A twenty minute detention before probable cause was established was found not unreasonable. While conceding that "if an investigative stop continues indefinitely, at some point it can no longer be justified as an investigative stop," the Court concluded that there could be "no rigid time limitation on *Terry* stops."

(4) Time constraints are of little significance when individuals entering the United States at international borders are concerned. In *United States v. Montoya de Hernandez*, 473 U.S. 531 (1985), the Court sustained the 16-hour detention of an international traveler suspected of having narcotics secreted in her alimentary canal, awaiting a bowel movement. The suspect had declined to leave the country or submit to an x-ray. Ultimately the authorities recovered 88 cocaine-filled balloons. In *United States v. Flores-Montano*, 541 U.S. 149 (2004), the Court upheld the seizure of 37 kilograms of marijuana discovered by disassembling the gasoline tank of a station wagon, detained for a customs inspection at an international border. Without dissent, the Court dismissed the respondent's claim of invasion of privacy, observing that any expectation in this regard was diminished because a border search was involved. It found nothing extraordinary about the procedure employed, noting that "in fiscal year 2003, 348 gas tank searches along the southern border were negative (*i.e.*, no contraband was found), the gas tanks were reassembled, and the vehicles continued their entry into the United States without incident."

ARIZONA v. UNITED STATES

United States Supreme Court
132 S. Ct. 2492 (2012)

[The Court, in a 5-3 decision, held that federal law had preempted in large part a state law, the purpose of which was to "discourage and deter the unlawful entry and presence of aliens and economic activity by persons unlawfully present in the United States." The following portion of the opinion addressed the only portion of the law not deemed to be preempted.]

JUSTICE KENNEDY delivered the opinion of the Court.

. . .

IV

D

Section 2(B)

Section 2(B) of S.B. 1070 requires state officers to make a "reasonable attempt . . . to determine the immigration status" of any person they stop, detain, or arrest on some other legitimate basis if "reasonable suspicion exists that the person is an alien and is unlawfully present in the United States." . . . The law also provides that "[a]ny person who is arrested shall have the person's immigration status determined before the person is released." . . . The accepted way to perform these status checks is to contact ICE [Immigration and Customs Enforcement], which maintains a database of immigration records.

Three limits are built into the state provision. First, a detainee is presumed not to be an alien unlawfully present in the United States if he or she provides a valid Arizona driver's license or similar identification. Second, officers "may not consider race, color or national origin . . . except to the extent permitted by the United States [and] Arizona Constitution[s]." . . . Third, the provisions must be "implemented in a manner consistent with federal law regulating immigration, protecting the civil rights of all persons and respecting the privileges and immunities of United States citizens." . . .

The United States and its *amici* contend that, even with these limits, the State's verification requirements pose an obstacle to the framework Congress put in place. The first concern is the mandatory nature of the status checks. The second is the possibility of prolonged detention while the checks are being performed.

1

. . . It is true that § 2(B) does not allow state officers to consider federal enforcement priorities in deciding whether to consult ICE about someone they have detained . . . . In other words, the officers must make an inquiry even in cases where it seems unlikely that the Attorney General would have the alien removed. This might be the case, for example, when the alien is an elderly veteran with significant and longstanding ties to the community . . . .

Congress has done nothing to suggest it is inappropriate to communicate with ICE in these situations, however. Indeed, it has encouraged the sharing of information about possible immigration violations . . . . A federal statute regulating the public benefits provided to qualified aliens in fact instructs that "no State or local government entity may be prohibited, or in any way restricted, from sending to or receiving from [ICE] information regarding the immigration status, lawful or unlawful, or an alien in the United States." . . . The federal scheme thus leaves room for a policy requiring state officials to contact ICE as a routine matter. . . .

2

Some who support the challenge to § 2(B) argue that, in practice, state officers will be required to delay the release of some detainees for no reason other than to verify their immigration status. . . . Detaining individuals solely to verify their immigration status would raise constitutional concerns. See, . . . *Illinois v. Caballes*, 543 U.S. 405, 407 (2005) ("A seizure that is justified solely by the interest in issuing a warning ticket to the driver can become unlawful if it is prolonged beyond the time reasonably required to complete that mission"). And it would disrupt the federal framework to put state officers in the position of holding aliens in custody for possible unlawful presence without federal direction and supervision. Cf. Part IV-C, *supra* (concluding that Arizona may not authorize warrantless arrests on the basis of removability). The program put in place by Congress does not allow state or local officers to adopt this enforcement mechanism.

But § 2(B) could be read to avoid these concerns. To take one example, a person might be stopped for jaywalking in Tucson and be unable to produce identification. The first sentence of § 2(B) instructs officers to make a "reasonable" attempt to verify his immigration status with ICE if there is reasonable suspicion that his presence in the United States is unlawful. The state courts may conclude that, unless the person continues to be suspected of some crime for which he may be detained by state officers, it would not be reasonable to prolong the stop for the immigration inquiry. . . .

To take another example, a person might be held pending release on a charge of driving under the influence of alcohol. As this goes beyond a mere stop, the arrestee (unlike the jaywalker) would appear to be subject to the categorical requirement in the second sentence of § 2(B) that "[a]ny person who is arrested shall have the person's immigration status determined before [he] is released." State courts may read this as an instruction to initiate a status check every time someone is arrested, or in some subset of those cases, rather than as a command to hold the person until the check is complete no matter the circumstances. Even if the law is read as an instruction to complete a check while the person is in custody, moreover, it is not clear at this stage and on this record that the verification process would result in prolonged detention.

However the law is interpreted, if § 2(B) only requires state officers to conduct a status check during the course of an authorized, lawful detention or after a detainee has been released, the provision likely would survive preemption-at least absent some showing that it has other consequences that are adverse to federal law and its objectives. There is no need in this case to address whether reasonable suspicion of illegal entry or another immigration crime would be a legitimate basis for prolonging a detention, or whether this too would be preempted by federal law. . . .

The nature and timing of this case counsel caution in evaluating the validity of § 2(B). The Federal Government has brought suit against a sovereign State to challenge the provision even before the law has gone into effect. There is a basic uncertainty about what the law means and how it will be enforced. At this stage, without the benefit of a definitive interpretation from the state courts, it would be inappropriate to assume § 2(B) will be construed in a way that creates a conflict with federal law. . . . This opinion does not foreclose other preemption and constitutional challenges to the law as interpreted and applied after it goes into effect.

Justice Scalia, concurring in part and dissenting in part.

. . . The Government has conceded that "even before Section 2 was enacted, state and local officers had state-law authority to inquire of DHS [the Department of Homeland Security] about a suspect's unlawful status and otherwise cooperate with federal immigration officers." . . . The concession, in my view, obviates the need for further inquiry.

. . . Of course, any investigatory detention, including one under § 2(B), may become an "unreasonable . . . seizure," U.S. Const., Amdt. IV, if it lasts too long. See *Illinois v. Caballes*. . . . But that has nothing to do with this case, in which the Government claims that § 2(B) is preempted by federal immigration law, not that anyone's Fourth Amendment rights have been violated. And I know of no reason why a protracted detention that does not violate the Fourth Amendment would contradict or conflict with any federal immigration law.

Justice Alito, concurring in part and dissenting in part.

. . . The United States does not deny that officers may, *at their own discretion*, inquire about the immigration status of persons whom they lawfully detain. Instead, the United States argues that § 2(B) is pre-empted because it impedes federal-state cooperation by *mandating* that officers verify the immigration status of every detained person if there is reason to believe that the person is unlawfully present in the country. The United States claims that § 2(B)'s mandate runs contrary to federal law in that it "precludes officers from taking [the Federal Government's] priorities and discretion into account." . . .

The underlying premise of the United States' argument seems to be that state and local officers, when left to their own devices, generally take federal enforcement priorities into account. But there is no reason to think that this premise is true. And even if it were, it would not follow that § 2(B)'s blanket mandate is at odds with federal law. Nothing in the relevant federal statutes *requires* state and local officers to consider the Federal Government's priorities before requesting verification of a person's immigration status. . . .

The United States' attack on § 2(B) is quite remarkable. The United States suggests that a state law may be preempted, not because it conflicts with a federal statute or regulation, but because it is inconsistent with a federal agency's current enforcement priorities. Those priorities, however, are not law. They are nothing more than agency policy. I am aware of no decision of this Court recognizing that mere policy can have pre-emptive force. . . . If § 2(B) were pre-empted at the present time because it is out of sync with the Federal Government's current priorities, would it be unpreempted at some time in the future if the agency's priorities changed?

. . .

If properly implemented, § 2(B) should not lead to federal constitutional violations, but there is no denying that enforcement of § 2(B) will multiply the occasions on which sensitive Fourth Amendment issues will crop up. These civil-liberty concerns, I take it, are at the heart of most objections to § 2(B). Close and difficult questions will inevitably arise as to whether an officer had reasonable suspicion to believe that a person who is stopped for some other reason entered the country illegally, and there is a risk that citizens, lawful permanent residents, and others who are lawfully present in the country will be detained. To mitigate this risk, Arizona could issue guidance to officers detailing the circumstances that typically give rise to reasonable suspicion of unlawful presence. And in the spirit of the federal-state cooperation that the United States champions, the Federal Government could share its own guidelines. Arizona could also provide officers with a nonexclusive list containing forms of identification sufficient under § 2(B) to dispel any suspicion of unlawful presence. If Arizona accepts licenses from most States as proof of legal status, the problem of roadside detentions will be greatly mitigated.

[H] The Site of the Detention

DUNAWAY v. NEW YORK

United States Supreme Court
442 U.S. 200 (1979)

MR. JUSTICE BRENNAN delivered the opinion of the Court.

We decide in this case the question reserved 10 years ago in *Morales v. New York*, 396 U.S. 102 (1969), namely, "the question of the legality of custodial questioning on less than probable cause for a full-fledged arrest." *Id.*, at 106.

I

On March 26, 1971, the proprietor of a pizza parlor in Rochester, N.Y. was killed during an attempted robbery. On August 10, 1971, Detective Anthony Fantigrossi of the Rochester Police was told by another officer that an informant had supplied a possible lead implicating petitioner in the crime. Fantigrossi questioned the supposed source of the lead — a jail inmate awaiting trial for burglary but learned nothing that supplied "enough information to get a warrant" for petitioner's arrest. App., at 60. Nevertheless, Fantigrossi ordered other detectives to "pick up" petitioner and "bring him in." *Id.*, at 54. Three detectives located petitioner at a neighbor's house on the morning of August 11. Petitioner was taken into custody; although he was not told he was under arrest, he would have been physically restrained if he had attempted to leave. *People v. Dunaway*, Monroe Cty. Ct., App. 116, 117 (Mar. 11, 1977). He was driven to police headquarters in a police car and placed in an interrogation room, where he was questioned by officers after being given the warnings required by *Miranda v. Arizona*, 384 U.S. 436 (1966). Petitioner waived counsel and eventually made statements and drew sketches that incriminated him in the crime.

. . .

In contrast to the brief and narrowly circumscribed intrusions involved in those cases, the detention of petitioner was in important respects indistinguishable from a traditional arrest. Petitioner was not questioned briefly where he was found. Instead, he was taken from a neighbor's home to a police car, transported to a police station, and placed in an interrogation room. He was never informed that he was "free to go"; indeed, he would have been physically restrained if he had refused to accompany the officers or had tried to escape their custody. The application of the Fourth Amendment's requirement of probable cause does not depend on whether an intrusion of this magnitude is termed an "arrest" under state law. The mere facts that petitioner was not told he was under arrest, was not "booked," and would not have had an arrest record if the interrogation had proved fruitless, while not insignificant for all purposes, see *Cupp v. Murphy*, 412 U.S. 291 (1973), obviously do not make petitioner's seizure even roughly analogous to the narrowly defined intrusions involved in *Terry* and its progeny. Indeed, any "exception" that could cover a seizure as intrusive as that in this case would threaten to swallow the general rule that Fourth Amendment seizures are "reasonable" only if based on probable cause.

The central importance of the probable cause requirement to the protection of a citizen's privacy afforded by the Fourth Amendment's guarantees cannot be compromised in this fashion. "The requirement of probable cause has roots that are deep in our history." *Henry v. United States*, 361 U.S. 98, 100 (1959). Hostility to seizures based on mere suspicion was a prime motivation for the adoption of the Fourth Amendment, and decisions immediately after its adoption affirmed that "common rumor or report, suspicion, or even 'strong reason to suspect' was not adequate to support a warrant for arrest." *Ibid.* (footnotes omitted). The familiar threshold standard of probable cause for Fourth Amendment seizures reflects the benefit of extensive experience accommodating the factors relevant to the "reasonableness" requirement of the Fourth Amendment, and provides the relative simplicity and clarity necessary to the implementation of a workable rule. . . .

In effect, respondents urge us to adopt a multifactor balancing test of "reasonable police conduct under the circumstances" to cover all seizures that do not amount to technical arrests. But the protections intended by the Framers could all too easily disappear in the consideration and balancing of the multifarious circumstances presented by different cases, especially when that balancing may be done in the first instance by police officers engaged in the "often competitive enterprise of ferreting out crime." *Johnson v. United States*, 333 U.S. 10, 14 (1948). A single, familiar standard is essential to guide police officers, who have only limited time and expertise to reflect on and balance the social and individual interests involved in the specific circumstances they confront. Indeed, our recognition of these dangers, and our consequent reluctance to depart from the proven protections afforded by the general rule, is reflected in the narrow limitations emphasized in the cases employing the balancing test. For all but those narrowly defined intrusions, the requisite "balancing" has been performed in centuries of precedent and is embodied in the principle that seizures are "reasonable" only if supported by probable cause.

MR. JUSTICE REHNQUIST, with whom the CHIEF JUSTICE joins, dissenting.

If the Court did no more in this case than it announced in the opening sentence of its opinion "decide . . . the question reserved 10 years ago in *Morales v. New York*, 396 U.S. 102 (1969), namely 'the question of the legality of custodial questioning on less than probable cause for a full fledged arrest' " I would have little difficulty joining its opinion. The decision of this question, however, does not, contrary to the implication in the Court's opening sentence, decide this case. For the Court goes on to conclude that petitioner Dunaway was in fact "seized" within the meaning of the Fourth Amendment, and that the connection between Dunaway's purported detention and the evidence obtained therefrom was not sufficiently attenuated as to dissipate the taint of the alleged unlawful police conduct. I cannot agree with either conclusion, and accordingly, I dissent.

There is obviously nothing in the Fourth Amendment that prohibits police from calling from their vehicle to a particular individual on the street and asking him to come over and talk with them; nor is there anything in the Fourth Amendment that prevents the police from knocking on the door of a person's house and when the person answers the door, inquiring whether he is willing to answer questions that they wish to put to him. "Obviously, not all personal intercourse between policemen and citizens involves 'seizures' of persons." *Terry v. Ohio*, 392 U.S., at 19 n. 16. Voluntary questioning not involving any "seizure" for Fourth Amendment purposes may take place under any number of varying circumstances. And the occasions will not be few when a particular individual agrees voluntarily to answer questions that the police wish to put to him either on the street, at the station, or in his house, and later regrets his willingness to answer those questions. However, such morning-after regrets do not render involuntary responses that were voluntary at the time they were made. In my view, this is a case where the defendant voluntarily accompanied the police to the station to answer their questions.

. . .

NOTES AND QUESTIONS

(1) Is Justice Brennan correct in stating that *Terry* substituted a balancing test for probable cause in regard to field detentions? Don't both situations call for balancing? Or, alternatively, differing levels of probable cause? In short, has Justice

Brennan drawn a meaningful distinction?

(2) What does Justice Rehnquist mean when he says, "There is obviously nothing in the Fourth Amendment that prohibits police from calling from their vehicle to a particular individual on the street . . ."? Was there anything "in" the Fourth Amendment which made the seizure of Sibron's heroin impermissible?

(3) As Justice Brennan noted, the Court had avoided the issue raised in *Dunaway* ten years earlier in *Morales v. New York*, 396 U.S. 102 (1969), by remanding the case in hope that the state court would find (1) probable cause, (2) consent or (3) that the confessions were not the product of the illegal detention. Dutifully, the court found that the accused had consented to the police detention but at the same time adhered to its previous holding that a brief stationhouse detention was constitutionally permissible. *People v. Morales*, 42 N.Y.2d 129, 397 N.Y.S.2d 587, 366 N.E.2d 248 (1977).

(4) The real source of dispute between the majority and dissent concerns the proper interpretation of the facts. Justice Brennan: "Petitioner was taken into custody; although he was not told he was under arrest, he would have been physically restrained if he had attempted to leave." Justice Rehnquist: "In my view, this is a case where the defendant voluntarily accompanied the police to the station to answer their questions." Once a judgment has been reached on this factual issue, the result reached — in both opinions — is inevitable. After *Dunaway*, under what circumstances might an accused be found to have voluntarily submitted to stationhouse interrogation?

BAILEY v. UNITED STATES

United States Supreme Court
133 S. Ct. 1031 (2013)

Justice Kennedy delivered the opinion of the Court.

The Fourth Amendment guarantees the right to be free from unreasonable searches and seizures. A search may be of a person, a thing, or a place. So too a seizure may be of a person, a thing, or a place. A search or a seizure may occur singly or in combination, and in differing sequence. In some cases the validity of one determines the validity of the other. The instant case involves the search of a place (an apartment dwelling) and the seizure of a person. But here, though it is acknowledged that the search was lawful, it does not follow that the seizure was lawful as well. The seizure of the person is quite in question. The issue to be resolved is whether the seizure of the person was reasonable when he was stopped and detained at some distance away from the premises to be searched when the only justification for the detention was to ensure the safety and efficacy of the search.

I

A

At 8:45 p.m. on July 28, 2005, local police obtained a warrant to search a residence for a .380-caliber handgun. The residence was a basement apartment at 103 Lake Drive, in Wyandanch, New York. A confidential informant had told police he observed the gun when he was at the apartment to purchase drugs from "a heavy set black male with short hair" known as "Polo." . . . As the search unit began preparations for executing the warrant, two officers, Detectives Richard Sneider and Richard Gorbecki, were conducting surveillance in an unmarked car outside the residence. About 9:56 p.m., Sneider and Gorbecki observed two men — later identified as petitioner Chunon Bailey and Bryant Middleton — leave the gated area above the basement apartment and enter a car parked in the driveway. Both matched the general physical description of "Polo" provided by the informant. There was no indication that the men were aware of the officers' presence or had any knowledge of the impending search. The detectives watched the car leave the driveway. They waited for it to go a few hundred yards down the street and followed. The detectives informed the search team of their intent to follow and detain the departing occupants. The search team then executed the search warrant at the apartment.

Detectives Sneider and Gorbecki tailed Bailey's car for about a mile — and for about five minutes — before pulling the vehicle over in a parking lot by a fire station. They ordered Bailey and Middleton out of the car and did a patdown search of both men. The officers found no weapons but discovered a ring of keys in Bailey' pocket. Bailey identified himself and said he was coming from his home at 103 Lake Drive. His driver's license, however, showed his address as Bayshore, New York, the town where the confidential informant told the police the suspect, "Polo," used to live. . . . Bailey's passenger, Middleton, said Bailey was giving him a ride home and confirmed they were coming from Bailey's residence at 103 Lake Drive. The officers put both men in handcuffs. When Bailey asked why, Gorbecki stated that they were being detained incident to the execution of a search warrant at 103 Lake Drive. Bailey responded: "I don't live there. Anything you find there ain't mine, and I'm not cooperating with your investigation." . . .

The detectives called for a patrol car to take Bailey and Middleton back to the Lake Drive apartment. Detective Sneider drove the unmarked car back, while Detective Gorbecki used Bailey's set of keys to drive Bailey's car back to the search scene. By the time the group returned to 103 Lake Drive, the search team had discovered a gun and drugs in plain view inside the apartment. Bailey and Middleton were placed under arrest, and Bailey's keys were seized incident to the arrest. Officers later discovered that one of Bailey's keys opened the door of the basement apartment.

B

Bailey was charged with three federal offenses: possession of cocaine with intent to distribute, . . . possession of a firearm by a felon, . . . and possession of a firearm in furtherance of a drug trafficking offense. . . . At trial Bailey moved to suppress the apartment key and the statements he made when stopped by Detectives Sneider and Gorbecki. That evidence, Bailey argued, derived from an unreasonable seizure. After an evidentiary hearing the United States District Court for the Eastern District of New York denied the motion to suppress. The District Court held that Bailey's detention was permissible under *Michigan v. Summers*, . . . as a detention incident to the execution of a search warrant. In the alternative, it held that Bailey's detention was lawful as an investigatory detention supported by reasonable suspicion under *Terry v. Ohio*, . . . After a trial the jury found Bailey guilty on all three counts.

The Court of Appeals for the Second Circuit ruled that Bailey's detention was proper and affirmed denial of the suppression motion. It interpreted the Court's decision in *Summers* to "authorize[e] law enforcement to detain the occupant of premises subject to a valid search warrant when that person is seen leaving those premises and the detention is effected *as soon as reasonably practicable*." . . . Having found Bailey's detention justified under *Summers*, the Court of Appeals did not address the District Court's alternative holding that the stop was permitted under *Terry*.

The Federal Courts of Appeals have reached differing conclusions as to whether *Michigan v. Summers* justifies the detention of occupants beyond the immediate vicinity of the premises covered by a search warrant. This Court granted certiorari to address the question. . . .

. . .

II

In *Summers* and later cases the occupants detained were found within or immediately outside a residence at the moment the police officers executed the search warrant. In *Summers*, the defendant was detained on a walk leading down from the front steps of the house. . . . Here, however, petitioner left the apartment before the search began; and the police officers waited to detain him until he was almost a mile away. The issue is whether the reasoning in *Summers* can justify detentions beyond the immediate vicinity of the premises being searched. An exception to the Fourth Amendment rule prohibiting detention absent probable cause must not diverge from its purpose and rationale. . . . It is necessary, then, to discuss the reasons for the rule explained in *Summers* to determine if its rationale extends to a detention like the one here.

A

In *Summers*, the Court recognized three important law enforcement interests that, taken together, justify the detention of an occupant who is on the premises during the execution of a search warrant: officer safety, facilitating the completion of the search, and preventing flight. . . .

1

The first interest identified in *Summers* was "the interest in minimizing the risk of harm to the officers." . . . There the Court held that "the execution of a warrant to search for narcotics is the kind of transaction that may give rise to sudden violence or frantic efforts to conceal or destroy evidence," and "[t]he risk of harm to both the police and the occupants is minimized if the officers routinely exercise unquestioned command of the situation." . . .

When law enforcement officers execute a search warrant, safety considerations require that they secure the premises, which may include detaining current occupants. By taking "unquestioned command of the situation," . . . the officers can search without fear that occupants, who are on the premises and able to observe the course of the search, will become disruptive, dangerous, or otherwise frustrate the search.

After *Summers*, this Court decided *Muehler v. Mena*. The reasoning and conclusions in *Muehler* in applying the *Summers* rule go quite far in allowing seizure and detention of persons to accommodate the necessities of a search. There, the person detained and held in handcuffs was not suspected of the criminal activity being investigated; but, the Court held, she could be detained nonetheless, to secure the premises while the search was underway. The "safety risk inherent in executing a search warrant for weapons was sufficient to justify the use of handcuffs, [and] the need to detain multiple occupants made the use of handcuffs all the more reasonable." . . . While the Court in *Muehler* did remand for consideration of whether the detention there — alleged to have been two or three hours — was necessary in light of all the circumstances, the fact that so prolonged a detention indeed might have been permitted illustrates the far-reaching authority the police have when the detention is made at the scene of the search. This in turn counsels caution before extending the power to detain persons stopped or apprehended away from the premises where the search is being conducted.

It is likely, indeed almost inevitable in the case of a resident, that an occupant will return to the premises at some point; and this might occur when the officers are still conducting the search. Officers can and do mitigate that risk, however, by taking routine precautions, for instance by erecting barricades or posting someone on the perimeter or at the door. In the instant case Bailey had left the premises, apparently without knowledge of the search. He posed little risk to the officers at the scene. If Bailey had rushed back to his apartment, the police could have apprehended and detained him under *Summers*. There is no established principle, however, that allows the arrest of anyone away from the premises who is likely to return. . . .

. . .

2

The second law enforcement interest relied on in *Summers* was that "the orderly completion of the search may be facilitated if the occupants of the premises are present." 452 U.S., at 703. This interest in efficiency derives from distinct, but related, concerns.

If occupants are permitted to wander around the premises, there is the potential for interference with the execution of the search warrant. They can hide or destroy evidence, seek to distract the officers, or simply get in the way. Those risks are not presented by an occupant who departs beforehand. So, in this case, after Bailey drove away from the Lake Drive apartment, he was not a threat to the proper execution of the search. Had he returned, officers would have been free to detain him at that point. A general interest in avoiding obstruction of a search, however, cannot justify detention beyond the vicinity of the premises to be searched.

. . .

3

The third law enforcement interest addressed in *Summers* was "the legitimate law enforcement interest in preventing flight in the event that incriminating evidence is found." . . . The proper interpretation of this language, in the context of *Summers* and in the broader context of the reasonableness standard that must govern and inform the detention incident to a search, is that the police can prohibit an occupant from leaving the scene of the search. As with the other interests identified in *Summers*, this justification serves to preserve the integrity of the search by controlling those persons who are on the scene. If police officers are concerned about flight, and have to keep close supervision of occupants who are not restrained, they might rush the search, causing unnecessary damage to property or compromising its careful execution. Allowing officers to secure the scene by detaining those present also prevents the search from being impeded by occupants leaving with the evidence being sought or the means to find it.

The concern over flight is not because of the danger of flight itself but because of the damage that potential flight can cause to the integrity of the search. This interest does not independently justify detention of an occupant beyond the immediate vicinity of the premises to be searched. The need to prevent flight, if unbounded, might be used to argue for detention, while a search is underway, of any regular occupant regardless of his or her location at the time of the search. If not circumscribed, the rationale of preventing flight would justify, for instance, detaining a suspect who is 10 miles away, ready to board a plane. The interest in preventing escape from police cannot extend this far without undermining the usual rules for arrest based on probable cause or a brief stop for questioning under standards derived from *Terry*. . . .

In sum, of the three law enforcement interests identified to justify the detention in *Summers*, none applies with the same or similar force to the detention of recent occupants beyond the immediate vicinity of the premises to be searched. Any of the individual interests is also insufficient, on its own, to justify an expansion of the rule in *Summers* to permit the detention of a former occupant, wherever he may be found away from the scene of the search. This would give officers too much discretion. The categorical authority to detain incident to the execution of a search warrant must be limited to the immediate vicinity of the premises to be searched.

. . .

The judgment of the Court of Appeals is reversed, and the case is remanded for further proceedings consistent with this opinion. . . .

JUSTICE SCALIA, with whom JUSTICE GINSBURG and JUSTICE KAGAN join, concurring.

I join the Court's opinion. I write separately to emphasize why the Court of Appeals' interest-balancing approach to this case — endorsed by the dissent — is incompatible with the categorical rule set forth in *Michigan v. Summers*, . . .

. . .

The Court of Appeals' mistake, echoed by the dissent, was to replace that straightforward, binary inquiry with open-ended balancing. Weighing the equities-Bailey "posed a risk of harm to the officers," his detention "was not unreasonably prolonged," and so forth-the Court of Appeals proclaimed the officers' conduct, "in the circumstances presented, reasonable and prudent." . . . That may be so, but it is irrelevant to whether *Summers* authorized the officers to seize Bailey without probable cause. To resolve that issue, a court need ask only one question: Was the person seized within "the immediate vicinity of the premises to be searched"? . . .

. . .

It bears repeating that the "general rule" is "that Fourth Amendment seizures are 'reasonable' only if based on probable cause." . . . Summers embodies a categorical judgment that *in one narrow circumstance* — the pressure of occupants during the execution of a search warrant — seizures are reasonable despite the absence of probable cause. *Summers* itself foresaw that without clear limits its exception could swallow the general rule. If a "multifactor balancing test of 'reasonable police conduct under the circumstances' " were extended "to cover all seizures that do not amount to technical arrests," it recognized, the "protections intended by the Framers could all too easily disappear in the consideration and balancing of the multifarious circumstances presented by different cases.' "

. . .

JUSTICE BREYER, with whom JUSTICE THOMAS and JUSTICE ALITO join, dissenting.

Did the police act reasonably when they followed (for 0.7 miles), and then detained, two men who left a basement apartment as the police were about to enter to execute a search warrant for a gun? The Court of Appeals for the Second Circuit found that the police action was reasonable because (1) the "premises [were] subject to a valid search warrant," (2) the detained persons were "seen leaving those premises," and (3) "the detention [was] effected *as soon as reasonably practicable.*" . . . In light of the risks of flight, of evidence destruction, and of human injury present in this and similar cases, I would follow the approach of the Court of Appeals and uphold its determination.

. . .

NOTE

Where the *Summers* criteria are satisfied, individuals other than those resident on the premises may be detained. *See, e.g., United States v. Sanchez*, 555 F.3d 910 (10th Cir. 2009); *State v. Wilburn*, 93 So. 3d 1115 (Fla. Dist. Ct. App. 2012). But there must be a connection between the party detained and the purpose of the search. *See Commonwealth v. Gray*, 896 A.2d 601 (2006) (defendant a bona fide customer at an auto parts store caught up in mid-day drug raid).

§ 2.03 ARREST

[A] The Presence of Probable Cause

DRAPER v. UNITED STATES

United States Supreme Court
358 U.S. 307 (1959)

Mr. Justice Whittaker delivered the opinion of the Court.

Petitioner was convicted of knowingly concealing and transporting narcotic drugs in Denver, Colorado, in violation of 35 Stat. 614, as amended, 21 U.S.C. § 174. His conviction was based in part on the use in evidence against him of two "envelopes containing 865 grams of heroin" and a hypodermic syringe that had been taken from his person, following his arrest, by the arresting officer. Before the trial, he moved to suppress that evidence as having been secured through an unlawful search and seizure. After the hearing, the District Court found that the arresting officer had probable cause to arrest petitioner without a warrant and that the subsequent search and seizure were therefore incident to a lawful arrest, and overruled the motion to suppress. 146 F. Supp. 689. At the subsequent trial, that evidence was offered and, over petitioner's renewed objection, was received in evidence, and the trial resulted, as we have said, in petitioner's conviction. The Court of Appeals affirmed the conviction, 248 F. 2d 295, and certiorari was sought on the sole ground that the search and seizure violated the Fourth Amendment and therefore the use of the heroin in evidence vitiated the conviction. We granted the writ to determine that question. 357 U.S. 935.

The evidence offered at the hearing on the motion to suppress was not substantially disputed. It established that one Marsh, a federal narcotic agent with 29 years' experience, was stationed at Denver; that one Hereford had been engaged as a "special employee" of the Bureau of Narcotics at Denver for about six months, and from time to time gave information to Marsh regarding violations of the narcotics laws, for which Hereford was paid small sums of money, and that Marsh had always found the information given by Hereford to be accurate and reliable. On September 3, 1956, Hereford told Marsh that James Draper (petitioner) recently had taken up abode at a stated address in Denver and "was peddling narcotics to several addicts" in that city. Four days later, on September 7, Hereford told Marsh "that Draper had gone to Chicago the day before [September 6] by train and that he was going to bring back three ounces of heroin [and] that he would return to

Denver either on the morning of the 8th of September or the morning of the 9th of September also by train." Hereford also gave Marsh a detailed physical description of Draper and of the clothing he was wearing,[10] and said that he would be carrying "a tan zipper bag," and that he habitually "walked real fast."

On the morning of September 8, Marsh and a Denver police officer went to the Denver Union Station and kept watch over all incoming trains from Chicago, but they did not see anyone fitting the description that Hereford had given. Repeating the process on the morning of September 9, they saw a person, having the exact physical attributes and wearing the precise clothing described by Hereford, alight from an incoming Chicago train and start walking "fast" toward the exit. He was carrying a tan zipper bag in his right hand and the left was thrust in his raincoat pocket. Marsh, accompanied by the police officer, overtook, stopped and arrested him. They then searched him and found the two "envelopes containing heroin" clutched in his left hand in his raincoat pocket, and found the syringe in the tan zipper bag. Marsh then took him (petitioner) into custody. Hereford died four days after the arrest and therefore did not testify at the hearing on the motion.

The crucial question for us then is whether knowledge of the related facts and circumstances gave Marsh "probable cause" within the meaning of the Fourth Amendment to believe that petitioner had committed or was committing a violation of the narcotic laws. If it did, the arrest, though without a warrant, was lawful and the subsequent search of petitioner's person and the seizure of the found heroin were validly made incident to a lawful arrest, and therefore the motion to suppress was properly overruled and the heroin was competently received in evidence at the trial. . . .

Petitioner does not dispute this analysis of the question for decision. Rather, he contends (1) that the information given by Hereford to Marsh was "hearsay" and, because hearsay is not legally competent evidence in a criminal trial, could not legally have been considered, but should have been put out of mind, by Marsh in assessing whether he had "probable cause" and "reasonable grounds" to arrest petitioner without a warrant, and (2) that, even if hearsay could lawfully have been considered, Marsh's information should be held insufficient to show "probable cause" and "reasonable grounds" to believe that petitioner had violated or was violating the narcotic laws and to justify his arrest without a warrant.

Considering the first contention, we find petitioner entirely in error. *Brinegar v. United States*, 338 U.S. 160, 172–173, has settled the question the other way. There, in a similar situation, the convict contended "that the factors relating to inadmissibility of the evidence [for] *purposes of proving guilt at the trial*, deprive[d] the evidence as a whole of sufficiency to show probable cause for the search . . ." *Id.* at 172. (Emphasis added.) But this Court, rejecting that contention, said:

> [The] so-called distinction places a wholly unwarranted emphasis upon the criterion of admissibility in evidence; to prove the accused's guilt, of the facts relied upon to show probable cause. That emphasis, we think, goes

---

10 [13] Hereford told Marsh that Draper was a Negro of light brown complexion, 27 years of age, 5 feet 8 inches tall, weighed about 160 pounds, and that he was wearing a light colored raincoat, brown slacks and black shoes.

> much too far in confusing and disregarding the difference between what is required to prove guilt in a criminal case and what is required to show probable cause for arrest or search. It approaches requiring (if it does not in practical effect require) proof sufficient to establish guilt in order to substantiate the existence of probable cause. There is a large difference between the two things to be proved [guilt and probable cause], as well as between the tribunals which determine them, and therefore a like difference in the *quanta* and modes of proof required to establish them.

338 U.S., at 172–173.

Nor can we agree with petitioner's second contention that Marsh's information was insufficient to show probable cause and reasonable grounds to believe that petitioner had violated or was violated the narcotic laws and to justify his arrest without a warrant. The information given to narcotic agent Marsh by "special employee" Hereford may have been hearsay to Marsh, but coming from one employed for that purpose and whose information had always been found accurate and reliable, it is clear that Marsh would have been derelict in his duties had he not pursued it. And when, in pursuing that information, he saw a man, having the exact physical attributes and wearing the precise clothing and carrying the tan zipper bag that Hereford had described, alight from one of the very trains from the very place stated by Hereford and start to walk at a "fast" pace toward the station exit, Marsh had personally verified every facet of the information given him by Hereford except whether petitioner had accomplished his mission and had the three ounces of heroin on his person or in his bag. And surely, with every other bit of Hereford's information being thus personally verified, Marsh had "reasonable grounds" to believe that the remaining unverified bit of Hereford's information — that Draper would have the heroin with him — was likewise true.

"In dealing with probable cause . . . as the very name implies, we deal with probabilities. These are not technical; they are the factual and practical considerations of everyday life on which reasonable and prudent men, not legal technicians, act." *Brinegar v. United States, supra*, at 175. Probable cause exists where "the facts and circumstances within [the arresting officers'] knowledge and of which they had reasonably trustworthy information [are] sufficient in themselves to warrant a man of reasonable caution in the belief that" an offense has been or is being committed. . . .

We believe that, under the facts and circumstances here, Marsh had probable cause and reasonable grounds to believe that petitioner was committing a violation of the laws of the United States relating to narcotic drugs at the time he arrested him. The arrest was therefore lawful, and the subsequent search and seizure, having been made incident to that lawful arrest, were likewise valid. It follows that petitioner's motion to suppress was properly denied and that the seized heroin was competent evidence lawfully received at the trial.

Affirmed.

MR. JUSTICE DOUGLAS, dissenting.

Here the officers had no evidence — apart from the mere word of an informer — that petitioner was committing a crime. The fact that petitioner walked fast and carried a tan zipper bag was not evidence of any crime. The officers knew nothing except what they had been told by the informer. If they went to a magistrate to get a warrant of arrest and relied solely on the report of the informer, it is not conceivable to me that one would be granted. See *Giordenello v. United States*, 357 U.S. 480, 486. For they could not present to the magistrate any of the facts which the informer may have had. They could swear only to the fact that the informer had made the accusation. They could swear to no evidence that lay in their own knowledge. They could present, on information and belief, no facts which the informer disclosed. No magistrate could issue a warrant on the mere word of an officer, without more. See *Giordenello v. United States, supra.* We are not justified in lowering the standard when an arrest is made without a warrant and allowing the officers more leeway than we grant the magistrate.

With all deference I think we break with tradition when we sustain this arrest. We said in *United States v. Di Re*, ". . . a search is not to be made legal by what it turns up. In law it is good or bad when it starts and does not change character from its success." In this case it was only after the arrest and search were made that there was a shred of evidence known to the officers that a crime was in the process of being committed.

NOTES AND QUESTIONS

(1) Suppose Agent Marsh had incorporated everything told him by Hereford on September 3 into an affidavit which he had taken to an appropriate magistrate and requested a warrant for Draper's arrest. Should the warrant issue? If so, are Agent Marsh's observations immaterial? If not, did Agent Marsh's observations increase the probability that Draper was committing a crime?

(2) Most people engage in behavior which is habitual, and therefore predictable by anyone who knows them very well. There is nothing extraordinary in Draper's appearance or behavior. Is the Court holding that because the informant was accurate as to nonincriminatory matters, it may be concluded that he is correct as to the nonobserved criminal matters? *See* Joseph Cook, *Probable Cause to Arrest*, 24 Vand. L. Rev. 317, 332 (1971).

(3) *Distinctive odors.* An officer may rely upon olfactory as well as visual data in determining probable cause to arrest. The most frequent resort to this principle is the detection of the odor of marijuana. The exceptional ability of canines to identify narcotics may establish probable cause. *See* § 3.03[D], *infra*.

(4) *Furtive actions and flight.* Recall *Peters v. New York* (discussed in *Sibron*, § 2.02[D], *supra*), in which the flight of the suspect upon seeing an off-duty police officer emerge from his apartment was critical to the finding of probable cause. Is this result sound? Compare *Wong Sun v. United States* (*see* § 6.03[A], *infra*) in which officers went to a laundry at six in the morning, and when they identified themselves, the accused slammed the door and ran to the living quarters in the rear

of the building. The Court held that the accused's "refusal to admit officers and his flight down the hallway thus signified a guilty knowledge no more clearly than it did a natural desire to repel an apparently unauthorized intrusion. . . . A contrary holding here would mean that a vague suspicion could be transformed into probable cause for arrest by reason of ambiguous conduct which the arresting officers themselves provoked." Is *Peters* distinguishable?

(5) While the prosecution must be able to demonstrate that probable cause to arrest was objectively present at the time the arrest was made, it is not essential that the officer making the arrest have personal knowledge of its justification. Thus, an officer instructed by radio bulletin to arrest a particular individual may do so legitimately without further explanation. Conversely, if the prosecution cannot establish the probable cause for the arrest, the fact that the arresting officer acted in good faith reliance upon the bulletin will not insulate it from constitutional challenge. See *Whiteley v. Warden*, 401 U.S. 560 (1971).

[B] The Significance of a Good Faith Error

HILL v. CALIFORNIA

United States Supreme Court
401 U.S. 797 (1971)

Mr. Justice White delivered the opinion of the Court.

On June 4, 1966, four armed men robbed a residence in Studio City, California. On June 5, Alfred Baum and Richard Bader were arrested for possession of narcotics; at the time of their arrest, they were driving petitioner Hill's car, and a search of the car produced property stolen in the Studio City robbery the day before. Bader and Baum both admitted taking part in the June 4 robbery, and both implicated Hill. Bader told the police that he was sharing an apartment with Hill at 9311 Sepulveda Boulevard. He also stated that the guns used in the robbery and other stolen property were in the apartment. On June 6, Baum and Bader again told the police that Hill had been involved in the June 4 robbery.

One of the investigating officers then checked official records on Hill, verifying his prior association with Bader, his age and physical description, his address, and the make of his car. The information the officer uncovered corresponded with the general descriptions by the robbery victims and the statements made by Baum and Bader.

Hill concedes that this information gave the police probable cause to arrest him, and the police undertook to do so on June 6. Four officers went to the Sepulveda Boulevard apartment, verified the address, and knocked. One of the officers testified: "The door was opened and a person who fit the description exactly of Archie Hill, as I had received it from both the cards and from Baum and Bader, answered the door. . . . We placed him under arrest for robbery."

The police had neither an arrest nor a search warrant. After arresting the man who answered the door, they asked him whether he was Hill and where the guns and stolen goods were. The arrestee replied that he was not Hill, that his name was

Miller, that it was Hill's apartment and that he was waiting for Hill. He also claimed that he knew nothing about any stolen property or guns, although the police testified that an automatic pistol and a clip of ammunition were lying in plain view on a coffee table in the living room where the arrest took place. The arrestee then produced identification indicating that he was in fact Miller, but the police were unimpressed and proceeded to search the apartment — living room, bedroom; kitchen area, and bath — for a period which one officer described as "a couple of hours."

During the course of the search, the police seized several items: rent receipts and personal correspondence bearing Hill's name from a dresser drawer in the bedroom; a starter pistol, two switchblade knives, a camera and case stolen in the Studio City robbery, and two hoodmasks made from white T-shirts, all from the bedroom; a.22-caliber revolver from under the living room sofa; and two pages of petitioner Hill's diary from a bedroom dresser drawer.

Based on our own examination of the record, we find no reason to disturb either the findings of the California courts that the police had probable cause to arrest Hill and that the arresting officers had a reasonable, good-faith belief that the arrestee Miller was in fact Hill, or the conclusion that "[w]hen the police have probable cause to arrest one party, and when they reasonably mistake a second party for the first party, then the arrest of the second party is a valid arrest." 69 Cal. 2d, at 553, 446 P.2d, at 523. The police unquestionably had probable cause to arrest Hill; they also had his address and a verified description. The mailbox at the indicated address listed Hill as the occupant of the apartment. Upon gaining entry to the apartment, they were confronted with one who fit the description of Hill received from various sources. That person claimed he was Miller, not Hill. But aliases and false identifications are not uncommon. Moreover, there was a lock on the door and Miller's explanation for his mode of entry was not convincing. He also denied knowledge of firearms in the apartment although a pistol and loaded ammunition clip were in plain view in the room. The upshot was that the officers in good faith believed Miller was Hill and arrested him. They were quite wrong as it turned out, and subjective good-faith belief would not in itself justify either the arrest or the subsequent search. But sufficient probability, not certainty, is the touchstone of reasonableness under the Fourth Amendment and on the record before us the officers' mistake was understandable and the arrest a reasonable response to the situation facing them at the time.

Nor can we agree with petitioner that however valid the arrest of Miller, the subsequent search violated the Fourth Amendment. It is true that Miller was not Hill; nor did Miller have authority or control over the premises, although at the very least he was Hill's guest. But the question is not what evidence would have been admissible against Hill (or against Miller for that matter) if the police, with probable cause to arrest Miller, had arrested him in Hill's apartment and then carried out the search at issue. Here there was probable cause to arrest Hill and the police arrested Miller in Hill's apartment, reasonably believing him to be Hill. In these circumstances the police were entitled to do what the law would have allowed them to do if Miller had in fact been Hill, that is, to search incident to arrest and to seize evidence of the crime the police had probable cause to believe Hill had committed. When judged in accordance with "the factual and practical considerations of everyday life on which reasonable and prudent men, not legal technicians, act," *Brinegar v. United States*, 338 U.S. 160, 175 (1949), the arrest and subsequent search were reasonable and valid under the Fourth Amendment.

[JUSTICE BLACK concurred in the result; JUSTICE DOUGLAS took no part in the decision; JUSTICE HARLAN, joined by JUSTICE MARSHALL, concurred in part and dissented in part.]

NOTES AND QUESTIONS

(1) The scope of the search in this case would now be impermissible in light of *Chimel v. California* (*see* § 3.02[A], *infra*). The impact of the decision is otherwise undiminished. For a case in which the mistaken identify resulted from the arrestee and the wanted party having the same name, see *People v. Campos*, 184 Cal. App. 2d 489, 7 Cal. Rptr. 513 (1960).

(2) *Mistake regarding probable cause.* A more likely occurrence is a good faith error as to the existence of probable cause. Courts consistently sustain arrests under such circumstances. "If the officer acts with probable cause, he is protected even though it turns out that the citizen is innocent." *Henry v. United States*, 361 U.S. 98 (1959). A similar result has been reached when the initial arrest was made for the wrong offense. *See, e.g., Pennington v. Commonwealth*, 429 S.W.2d 364 (Ky. App. 1967).

(3) *Bad faith.* How should courts respond to situations in which probable cause is objectively present, but the arresting officer did not believe it to be present at the time of the arrest? Cases are not in accord, and the position of the Supreme Court, albeit in dictum, is ambivalent. In *Carroll v. United States*, 267 U.S. 132 (1925), the Court observed that "[T]he usual rule is that a police officer may arrest without warrant one believed by the officer upon reasonable cause to have been guilty of a felony. . . ." This has been construed by some lower courts to mean that not only must probable cause be objectively present, but the officer must have acted in good faith. *See Winkle v. Kropp*, 279 F. Supp. 532 (E.D. Mich. 1968), *cert. denied*, 394 U.S. 1003; *Moss v. Cox*, 311 F. Supp. 1245 (E.D. Va. 1970). On the other hand, in *Terry v. Ohio* (*see* § 2.02[D] *supra*), the Court said, "It is imperative that the facts be judged against an objective standard: would the facts available to the officer at the moment of the seizure or the search 'warrant a man of reasonable caution in the belief' that the action taken was appropriate." This passage has been interpreted by some courts to mean that the officer's subjective evaluation of the fact is immaterial. *See Klingler v. United States*, 409 F.2d 299 (8th Cir.), *cert. denied* 396 U.S. 859 (1969); *People v. Smith*, 62 Misc. 2d 473, 308 N.Y.S.2d 909 (Sup. Ct. 1970). Such results would appear consistent with *Whren v. United States*, § 2.03[D], *infra*.

MICHIGAN v. DE FILLIPPO

United States Supreme Court

443 U.S. 31 (1979)

MR. CHIEF JUSTICE BURGER delivered the opinion of the Court.

The question presented by this case is whether an arrest made in good-faith reliance on an ordinance, which at the time had not been declared unconstitutional, is valid regardless of a subsequent judicial determination of its unconstitutionality.

I

At approximately 10:00 p.m. on September 14, 1976, Detroit police officers on duty in a patrol car received a radio call to investigate two persons reportedly appearing to be intoxicated in an alley. When they arrived at the alley, they found respondent and a young woman. The woman was in the process of lowering her slacks. One of the officers asked what they were doing, and the woman replied that she was about to relieve herself. The officer then asked respondent for identification; respondent asserted that he was Sergeant Mash, of the Detroit Police Department; he also purported to give his badge number, but the officer was unable to hear it. When respondent again was asked for identification, he changed his answer and said either that he worked for or that he knew Sergeant Mash. Respondent did not appear to be intoxicated.

Section 39-1-52.3 of the Code of the City of Detroit provides that a police officer may stop and question an individual if he has reasonable cause to believe that the individual's behavior warrants further investigation for criminal activity. In 1976 the Detroit Common Council amended § 39-1-52.3 to provide that it should be unlawful for any person stopped pursuant thereto to refuse to identify himself and produce evidence of his identify.[11]

When he failed to identify himself, respondent was taken into custody for violation of § 39-1-52.3; he was searched by one of the officers who found a package of marihuana in one of respondent's shirt pockets, and a tinfoil packet secreted inside a cigarette package in the other. The tinfoil packet subsequently was opened at the station; an analysis established that it contained phencyclidine, another controlled substance.

---

[11] [14] As amended, Code of the City of Detroit § 39-1-52.3 provided:

When a police officer has reasonable cause to believe that the behavior of an individual warrants further investigation for criminal activity, the officer may stop and question such person. It shall be unlawful for any person stopped pursuant to this section to refuse to identify himself, and to produce verifiable documents or other evidence of such identification. In the event that such person is unable to provide reasonable evidence of his true identity, the police officer may transport him to the nearest precinct in order to ascertain his identity.

While holding the ordinance unconstitutional the Michigan Court of Appeals construed the ordinance to make refusal to identify oneself a crime meriting arrest. People v. DeFillippo, 80 Mich. App. 197, 201 n. 1, 262 N.W.2d 921, 923 n. 1 (1977).

The preamble to the amendment indicates that it was enacted in response to an emergency caused by a marked increase in crime, particularly street crime by gangs of juveniles.

Respondent was charged with possession of the controlled substance phencyclidine. At the preliminary examination, he moved to suppress the evidence obtained in the search following the arrest; the trial court denied the motion. The Michigan Court of Appeals allowed an interlocutory appeal and reversed. It held that the Detroit ordinance, § 39-1-52.3, was unconstitutionally vague and concluded that since respondent had been arrested pursuant to that ordinance, both the arrest and the search were invalid.

The court expressly rejected the contention that an arrest made in good-faith reliance on a presumptively valid ordinance is valid regardless of whether the ordinance subsequently is declared unconstitutional. . . .

The Michigan Supreme Court denied leave to appeal. . . .

II

Respondent was not charged with or tried for violation of the Detroit ordinance. The State contends that because of the violation of the ordinance, *i.e.*, refusal to identify himself, which respondent committed in the presence of the officers, respondent was subject to a valid arrest. The search that followed being incidental to that arrest, the State argues that it was equally valid and the drugs found should not have been suppressed. Respondent contends that since the ordinance which he was arrested for violating has been found unconstitutionally vague on its face, the arrest and search were invalid as violative of his rights under the Fourth and Fourteenth Amendments. Accordingly, he contends the drugs found in the search were correctly suppressed.

III

When the officer arrested respondent, he had abundant probable cause to believe that respondent's conduct violated the terms of the ordinance. The ordinance provides that a person commits an offense if (a) an officer has reasonable cause to believe that given behavior warrants further investigation, (b) the officer stops him, and (c) the suspect refuses to identify himself. The offense is then complete.

Respondent's presence with a woman in the circumstances described in an alley at 10:00 p.m. was clearly, in the words of the ordinance, "behavior warranting further investigation." Respondent's inconsistent and evasive responses to the officer's request that he identify himself, stating first that he was Sergeant Mash of the Detroit Police Department and then that he worked for or knew Sergeant Mash, constituted a refusal by respondent to identify himself as the ordinance required. Assuming, arguendo, that a person may not constitutionally be required to answer questions put by an officer in some circumstances, the false identification violated the plain language of the Detroit ordinance.

The remaining question, then, is whether, in these circumstances, it can be said that the officer lacked probable cause to believe that the conduct he observed and the words spoken constituted a violation of law simply because he should have known the ordinance was invalid and would be judicially declared unconstitutional. The answer is clearly negative.

This Court repeatedly has explained that "probable cause" to justify an arrest means facts and circumstances within the officer's knowledge that are sufficient to warrant a prudent person, or one of reasonable caution, in believing in the circumstances shown, that the suspect has committed, is committing, or is about to commit an offense.

On this record there was abundant probable cause to satisfy the constitutional prerequisite for an arrest. At that time, of course, there was no controlling precedent that this ordinance was or was not constitutional, and hence the conduct observed violated a presumptively valid ordinance. A prudent officer, in the course of determining whether respondent had committed an offense under all the circumstances shown by this record, should not have been required to anticipate that a court would later hold the ordinance unconstitutional.

Police are charged to enforce laws until and unless they are declared unconstitutional. The enactment of a law forecloses speculation by enforcement officers concerning its constitutionality — with the possible exception of a law so grossly and flagrantly unconstitutional that any person of reasonable prudence would be bound to see its flaws. Society would be ill served if its police officers took it upon themselves to determine which laws are and which are not constitutionally entitled to enforcement.

In *Pierson v. Ray*, 386 U.S. 547, 555 (1967), persons who had been arrested for violating a statute later declared unconstitutional by this Court sought damages for false arrest under state law and for violation of the Fourteenth Amendment under 42 U.S.C. § 1983. Mr. Chief Justice Warren speaking for the Court, in holding that police action based on a presumptively valid law was subject to a valid defense of good faith, observed: "[a] policeman's lot is not so unhappy that he must choose between being charged with dereliction of duty if he does not arrest when he has probable cause, and being mulcted in damages if he does." The Court held that "the defense of good faith and probable cause, which the Court of Appeals found to be available to the officers in the commonlaw action for false arrest and imprisonment, is also available to them in the action under § 1983." *Id.*, at 557. Here, the police were not required to risk "being charged with dereliction of duty if they did not arrest when they had probable cause" on the basis of the conduct observed.[12]

IV

We have held that the exclusionary rule required suppression of evidence obtained in searches carried out pursuant to statutes, not previously declared unconstitutional, which purported to authorize the searches in question without probable cause and without a valid warrant. . . . Our holding today is not inconsistent with these decisions; the statutes involved in those cases bore a

[12] [15] The purpose of the Exclusionary Rule is to deter unlawful police action. No conceivable purpose of deterrence would be served by suppressing evidence which, at the time it was found on the person of the respondent, was the product of a lawful arrest and a lawful search. To deter police from enforcing a presumptively valid statute was never remotely in the contemplation of even the most zealous advocate of the Exclusionary Rule.

different relationship to the challenged searches than did the Detroit ordinance to respondent's arrest and search.

Those decisions involved statutes which, by their own terms, authorized searches under circumstances which did not satisfy the traditional warrant and probable cause requirements of the Fourth Amendment. For example, in *Almeida-Sanchez v. United States*, . . . we held invalid a search pursuant to a federal statute which authorized the Border Patrol to search any vehicle within a "reasonable distance" of the border, without a warrant or probable cause. The Attorney General, by regulation, fixed 100 miles as a "reasonable distance" from the border. 413 U.S., at 268. We held a search so distant from the point of entry was unreasonable under the Constitution. In *Berger v. New York*, . . . we struck down a statute authorizing searches under warrants which did not "particularly describe the place to be searched and the persons or things to be seized," as required by the Fourth and Fourteenth Amendments. 388 U.S., at 55–56.

In contrast, the ordinance here declared it a misdemeanor for one stopped for "investigation" to "refuse to identify himself"; it did not directly authorize the arrest or search. Once respondent refused to identify himself as the presumptively valid ordinance required, the officer had probable cause to believe respondent was committing an offense in his presence and Michigan's general arrest statute, Mich. Comp. Laws Ann. § 764.15, authorized the arrest of respondent, independent of the ordinance. The search which followed was valid because it was incidental to that arrest. The ordinance is relevant to the validity of the arrest and search only as it pertains to the "facts and circumstances" we hold constituted probable cause for arrest.

The subsequently determined invalidity of the Detroit ordinance on vagueness grounds does not undermine the validity of the arrest made for violation of that ordinance and the evidence discovered in the search of respondent should not have been suppressed. Accordingly, the case is remanded for further proceedings not inconsistent with this opinion.

Reversed and remanded.

Mr. Justice Blackmun, concurring.

I join the Court's opinion, but add a few words about the concern so evident in Mr. Justice Brennan's dissenting opinion that today's decision will allow States and municipalities to circumvent the probable cause requirement of the Fourth Amendment. There is some danger, I acknowledge, that the police will use a Stop and Identify ordinance to arrest persons for improper identification; that they will then conduct a search pursuant to the arrest; that if they discover contraband or other evidence of crime, the arrestee will be charged with some other offense; and that if they do not discover contraband or other evidence of crime, the arrestee will be released. In this manner, if the arrest for violation of the Stop and Identify ordinance is not open to challenge, the ordinance itself could perpetually evade constitutional review.

There is no evidence in this case, however, that the Detroit ordinance is being used in such a pretextual manner. See Tr. of Oral Arg. 8. If a defendant in a proper case showed that the police habitually arrest, but do not prosecute, under a Stop and Identify ordinance, then I think this would suffice to rebut any claim that the police were acting in reasonable, good-faith reliance on the constitutionality of the ordinance. The arrestee could then challenge the validity of the ordinance, and, if the court concluded it was unconstitutional, could have the evidence obtained in the search incident to the arrest suppressed.

MR. JUSTICE BRENNAN, with whom MR. JUSTICE MARSHALL and MR. JUSTICE STEVENS join, dissenting.

The Court errs, in my view, in focusing on the good faith of the arresting officers and on whether they were entitled to rely upon the validity of the Detroit ordinance. For the dispute in this case is not between the arresting officers and respondent. Cf. *Pierson v. Ray*, 386 U.S. 547 (1967). The dispute is between respondent and the State of Michigan. The ultimate issue is whether the State gathered evidence against respondent through unconstitutional means. Since the State is responsible for the actions of its legislative bodies as well as for the actions of its police, the State can hardly defend against this charge of unconstitutional conduct by arguing that the constitutional defect was the product of legislative action and that the police were merely executing the laws in good faith. See *Torres v. Puerto Rico*, 442 U.S. 465 (1979); *Almeida-Sanchez v. United States*, 413 U.S. 266 (1973); *Berger v. New York*, 388 U.S. 41 (1967). States "may not . . . authorize police conduct which trenches upon Fourth Amendment rights, regardless of the labels which it attaches to such conduct." The question in this Court upon review of a state-approved search or seizure "is not whether the search or seizure was authorized by state law. The question is rather whether the search [or seizure] was reasonable under the Fourth Amendment." *Sibron v. New York*, 392 U.S. 40, 61 (1968), quoting in part from *Cooper v. California*, 386 U.S. 58, 61 (1967).

If the Court's inquiry were so directed and had not asked whether the arresting officers faithfully applied state law, invalidation of respondent's arrest and search would have been inescapable. For the Court's assumption that the Detroit ordinance is unconstitutional is well founded; the ordinance is indeed unconstitutional and patently so. And if the reasons for that constitutional infirmity had only been explored, rather than simply assumed, it would have been obvious that the application of the ordinance to respondent by Detroit police in this case trenched upon respondent's Fourth Amendment rights and resulted in an unreasonable search and seizure.

A major constitutional defect of the ordinance is that it forces individuals accosted by police solely on the basis of suspicion to choose between foregoing their right to remain silent and foregoing their right not to be searched if they choose to remain silent. Clearly, a constitutional prohibition merely against prosecutions under the ordinance and not against arrests under the ordinance as well would not solve this dilemma. For the fact would remain that individuals who chose to remain silent would be forced to relinquish their right not to be searched (and indeed would risk conviction on the basis of any evidence seized from them), while those who chose not to be searched would be forced to forego their constitutional right to remain silent. This Hobson's choice can be avoided only by invalidating such police intrusions whether or not authorized by ordinance and holding fast to the rule of *Terry* and its progeny: that police acting on less than probable cause may not search, compel answers or search those who refuse to answer their questions.

NOTES AND QUESTIONS

(1) What is the strongest argument to be made on behalf of the government for sustaining this conviction? For the defense for a reversal?

(2) Should the Court be influenced by the fact that the conviction was for a narcotics offense, not for failing to identify? Does the result give rise to an opportunity for abusive use of stop and identify statutes?

(3) Suppose the Michigan Court of Appeals had not declared § 39-1-52.3 unconstitutional. Would the Supreme Court have addressed the issue? Assuming it did so, what would be the likely result?

(4) If there was no statute involved in the case and the officer's conduct was evaluated in terms of *Terry, et al.*, what result?

[C] The Presence or Absence of an Arrest Warrant

GERSTEIN v. PUGH

United States Supreme Court
420 U.S. 103 (1975)

Mr. Justice Powell delivered the opinion of the Court.

. . .

II

As framed by the proceedings below, this case presents two issues: whether a person arrested and held for trial on an information is entitled to a judicial determination of probable cause for detention, and if so, whether the adversary hearing ordered by the District Court and approved by the Court of Appeals is required by the Constitution.

A

Maximum protection of individual rights could be assured by requiring a magistrate's review of the factual justification prior to any arrest, but such a requirement would constitute an intolerable handicap for legitimate law enforcement. Thus, while the Court has expressed a preference for the use of arrest warrants when feasible, . . . it has never invalidated an arrest supported by probable cause solely because the officers failed to secure a warrant. . . .

Under this practical compromise, a policeman's on-the-scene assessment of probable cause provides legal justification for arresting a person suspected of crime, and for a brief period of detention to take the administrative steps incident to arrest. Once the suspect is in custody, however, the reasons that justify dispensing with the magistrate's neutral judgment evaporate. There no longer is any danger that the suspect will escape or commit further crimes while the police submit their evidence to a magistrate. And, while the State's reasons for taking summary action subside, the suspect's need for a neutral determination of probable cause increases significantly. The consequences of prolonged detention may be more serious than the interference occasioned by arrest. Pretrial confinement may imperil the suspect's job, interrupt his source of income, and impair his family relationships. See R. Goldfarb, *Ransom* 32–91 (1965); L. Katz, *Justice Is the Crime* 51–62 (1972). Even pretrial release may be accompanied by burdensome conditions that effect a significant restraint of liberty. See, e.g., 18 U.S.C. §§ 3146(a)(2), (5). When the stakes are this high, the detached judgment of a neutral magistrate is essential if the Fourth Amendment is to furnish meaningful protection from unfounded interference with liberty. Accordingly, we hold that the Fourth Amendment requires a judicial determination of probable cause as a prerequisite to extended restraint of liberty following arrest.

B

Under the Florida procedures challenged here, a person arrested without a warrant and charged by information may be jailed or subjected to other restraints pending trial without any opportunity for a probable cause determination. Petitioner defends this practice on the ground that the prosecutor's decision to file an information is itself a determination of probable cause that furnishes sufficient reason to detain a defendant pending trial. Although a conscientious decision that the evidence warrants prosecution affords a measure of protection against unfounded detention, we do not think prosecutorial judgment standing alone meets the requirements of the Fourth Amendment. Indeed, we think the Court's previous decisions compel disapproval of the Florida procedure. In *Albrecht v. United States*, 273 U.S. 1, 5 (1927), the Court held that an arrest warrant issued solely upon a United States Attorney's information was invalid because the accompanying affidavits were defective. Although the Court's opinion did not explicitly state that the prosecutor's official oath could not furnish probable cause, that conclusion was implicit in the judgment that the arrest was illegal under the Fourth Amendment. More recently, in *Coolidge v. New Hampshire*, 403 U.S. 443, 449–453 (1971), the Court held that a prosecutor's responsibility to law enforcement is inconsistent with the constitutional role of a neutral and detached magistrate. We reaffirmed that principle in *Shadwick v. City of Tampa*, 407 U.S. 345 (1972), and held that probable cause for the issuance of an arrest warrant must be determined by someone independent of police and prosecution. . . . The reason for this separation of functions was expressed by Mr. Justice Frankfurter in a similar context:

> A democratic society, in which respect for the dignity of all men is central, naturally guards against the misuse of the law enforcement process. Zeal in tracking down crime is not in itself an assurance of soberness of judgment. Disinterestedness in law enforcement does not alone prevent disregard of cherished liberties. Experience has therefore counseled that safeguards must be provided against the dangers of the overzealous as well as the

> despotic. The awful instruments of the criminal law cannot be entrusted to a single functionary. The complicated process of criminal justice is therefore divided into different parts, responsibility for which is separately vested in the various participants upon whom the criminal law relies for its vindication.

McNabb v. United States, 318 U.S. 332, 343 (1943).

In holding that the prosecutor's assessment of probable cause is not sufficient alone to justify restraint of liberty pending trial, we do not imply that the accused is entitled to judicial oversight or review of the decision to prosecute. Instead, we adhere to the Court's prior holding that a judicial hearing is not prerequisite to prosecution by information. . . . Nor do we retreat from the established rule that illegal arrest or detention does not void a subsequent conviction. . . . Thus, as the Court of Appeals noted below, although a suspect who is presently detained may challenge the probable cause for that confinement, a conviction will not be vacated on the ground that the defendant was detained pending trial without a determination of probable cause. 483 F.2d, at 786–787. . . .

III

Both the District Court and the Court of Appeals held that the determination of probable cause must be accompanied by the full panoply of adversary safeguards-counsel, confrontation, cross-examination, and compulsory process for witnesses. A full preliminary hearing of this sort is modeled after the procedure used in many States to determine whether the evidence justifies going to trial under an information or presenting the case to a grand jury. . . . The standard of proof required of the prosecution is usually referred to as "probable cause," but in some jurisdictions it may approach a prima facie case of guilt. ALI, Model Code of Prearraignment Procedure, Commentary on Art. 330, pp. 90–91 (Tent. Draft No. 5, 1972). When the hearing takes this form, adversary procedures are customarily employed. The importance of the issue to both the State and the accused justifies the presentation of witnesses and full exploration of their testimony on cross-examination. This kind of hearing also requires appointment of counsel for indigent defendants. *Coleman v. Alabama, supra.* And, as the hearing assumes increased importance and the procedures become more complex, the likelihood that it can be held promptly after arrest diminishes. See ALI, Model Code of Prearraignment Procedure, *supra*, at 33–34.

These adversary safeguards are not essential for the probable cause determination required by the Fourth Amendment. The sole issue is whether there is probable cause for detaining the arrested person pending further proceedings. This issue can be determined reliably without an adversary hearing. The standard is the same as that for arrest. That standard — probable cause to believe the suspect has committed a crime — traditionally has been decided by a magistrate in a nonadversary proceeding on hearsay and written testimony, and the Court has approved these informal modes of proof.

MR. JUSTICE STEWART, with whom MR. JUSTICE DOUGLAS, MR. JUSTICE MARSHALL join, concurring.

I concur in Parts I and II of the Court's opinion, since the Constitution clearly requires at least a timely judicial determination of probable cause as a prerequisite to pretrial detention. Because Florida does not provide all defendants in custody pending trial with a fair and reliable determination of probable cause for their detention, the respondents and the members of the class they represent are entitled to declaratory and injunctive relief.

Having determined that Florida's current pretrial detention procedures are constitutionally inadequate, I think it is unnecessary to go further by way of dicta. In particular, I would not, in the abstract, attempt to specify those procedural protections that constitutionally need *not* be accorded incarcerated suspects awaiting trial.

It is the prerogative of each State in the first instance to develop pretrial procedures that provide defendants in pretrial custody with the fair and reliable determination of probable cause for detention required by the Constitution, Cf. *Morrissey v. Brewer*, 408 U.S. 471, 488. The constitutionality of any particular method for determining probable cause can be properly decided only by evaluating a State's pretrial procedures as a whole, not by isolating a particular part of its total system. As the Court recognizes, great diversity exists among the procedures employed by the States in this aspect of their criminal justice system.

There will be adequate opportunity to evaluate in an appropriate future case the constitutionality of any new procedures that may be adopted by Florida in response to the Court's judgment today holding that Florida's present procedures are constitutionally inadequate.

NOTES AND QUESTIONS

(1) The Court here imposes a requirement of consistency between the constitutional standards for warrant and warrantless arrests. An individual arrested pursuant to a warrant has received a prior judicial appraisal of the legitimacy of his arrest. Surely one arrested without the use of a warrant should receive the equivalent judicial oversight, albeit after the fact. But, just as the Court has held consistently that an illegal arrest, without more, is not reversible error, *see Frisbie v. Collins*, 342 U.S. 519 (1952), so it holds in *Gerstein* that "a conviction will not be vacated on the ground that the defendant was detained pending trial without a determination of probable cause." In both instances, the implicit rationale would appear to be that, once the accused has been convicted, any doubts regarding probable cause to arrest have been resolved. Hence, assuming *arguendo* that a portion of the pretrial detention of the accused was not supported by probable cause, the violation was harmless error.

(2) The failure to accord an accused a *Gerstein* hearing might be of significance if the accused could point to fruits of that denial which adversely affected his trial. Suppose, for example, that in the wake of a *Gerstein* violation the accused had been subjected to interrogation and confessed. (The question could only arise if (a) the accused was not in fact under illegal arrest and (b) the accused had been accorded

the protections of the privilege against self-incrimination and the right to counsel; if these conditions were not satisfied, then the confession would be inadmissible for independent reasons.) Would the denial of a *Gerstein* hearing, without more, render the confession inadmissible? Notably, the *Gerstein* Court did not address this question, nor has it been raised in any subsequent case to reach the Court. The Supreme Court of Tennessee has held that the exclusionary rule does apply when the evidence was obtained by exploitation of the illegality. *State v. Huddleston*, 924 S.W.2d 666 (Tenn. 1996). *See also Black v. State*, 871 P.2d 35 (Okla. Crim. App. 1994) (photograph and confession obtained during illegal detention were inadmissible, but error was harmless). *But see Lawhorn v. Allen*, 519 F.3d 1272 (11th Cir. 2008) (suppression of confession inappropriate where product of accused's free will).

(3) While the *Gerstein* decision mandated a judicial hearing on the issue of probable cause, it contained no indication of how prompt such a hearing must be. In *County of Riverside v. McLaughlin*, 500 U.S. 44 (1991), the Court held that "a jurisdiction that provides judicial determinations of probable cause within 48 hours of arrest will, as a general matter, comply with the promptness requirement of *Gerstein.*" After 48 hours, the burden shifts to the government to demonstrate that there were extraordinary circumstances justifying the delay. Moreover, the Court held, even a hearing within 48 hours may be constitutionally unreasonable "if the arrested individual can prove that his or her probable cause determination was delayed unreasonably. Examples of unreasonable delay are delays for the purpose of gathering additional evidence to justify the arrest, a delay motivated by ill will against the arrested individual, or delay for delay's sake." In a dissenting opinion, Justice Scalia maintained that a prompt hearing on probable cause was mandated by the constitution, and that there was no basis for the presumption that 48 hours was reasonable.

[D] The Method of Accomplishing the Arrest

PAYTON v. NEW YORK

United States Supreme Court
445 U.S. 573 (1980)

Mr. Justice Stevens delivered the opinion of the Court.

These appeals challenge the constitutionality of New York statutes that authorize police officers to enter a private residence without a warrant and with force, if necessary, to make a routine felony arrest.

The important constitutional question presented by this challenge has been expressly left open in a number of our prior opinions.

On January 14, 1970, after two days of intensive investigation, New York detectives had assembled evidence sufficient to establish probable cause to believe that Theodore Payton had murdered the manager of a gas station two days earlier. At about 7:30 a.m. on January 15, six officers went to Payton's apartment in the Bronx, intending to arrest him. They had not obtained a warrant. Although light and music emanated from the apartment, there was no response to their knock on the metal door. They summoned emergency assistance and, about 30 minutes later, used crowbars to break open the door and enter the apartment. No one was there. In plain view, however, was a.30-caliber shell casing that was seized and later admitted into evidence at Payton's murder trial.

In due course Payton surrendered to the police, was indicted for murder, and moved to suppress the evidence taken from his apartment. The trial judge held that the warrantless and forcible entry was authorized by the New York Code of Criminal Procedure, and that the evidence in plain view was properly seized. He found that exigent circumstances justified the officers' failure to announce their purpose before entering the apartment as required by the statute. He had no occasion, however, to decide whether those circumstances also would have justified the failure to obtain a warrant, because he concluded that the warrantless entry was adequately supported by the statute without regard to the circumstances. The Appellate Division, First Department, summarily affirmed.

On March 14, 1974, Obie Riddick was arrested for the commission of two armed robberies that had occurred in 1971. He had been identified by the victims in June of 1973 and in January 1974 the police had learned his address. They did not obtain a warrant for his arrest. At about noon on March 14, a detective, accompanied by three other officers, knocked on the door of the Queens house where Riddick was living. When his young son opened the door, they could see Riddick sitting in bed covered by a sheet. They entered the house and placed him under arrest. Before permitting him to dress, they opened a chest of drawers two feet from the bed in search of weapons and found narcotics and related paraphernalia. Riddick was subsequently indicted on narcotics charges. At a suppression hearing, the trial judge held that the warrantless entry into his home was authorized by the revised New York statute, and that the search of the immediate area was reasonable under *Chimel v. California*, 395 U.S. 752. The Appellate Division, Second Department, affirmed the denial of the suppression motion.

The New York Court of Appeals, in a single opinion, affirmed the convictions of both Payton and Riddick. The court recognized that the question whether and under what circumstances an officer may enter a suspect's home to make a warrantless arrest had not been settled either by that court or by this Court. In answering that question, the majority of four judges relied primarily on its perception that there is a

> . . . substantial difference between the intrusion which attends an entry for the purpose of searching the premises and that which results from an entry for the purpose of making an arrest, and on the significant difference in the governmental interest in achieving the objective of the intrusion in the two instances.

45 N.Y. 2d, at 310, 380 N.E. 2d, at 228–229. The majority supported its holding by noting the "apparent historical acceptance" of warrantless entries to make felony arrests, both in the English common law and in the practice of many American States.

Before addressing the narrow question presented by these appeals, we put to one side other related problems that are *not* presented today. Although it is arguable that the warrantless entry to effect Payton's arrest might have been justified by exigent circumstances, none of the New York courts relied on any such justification. The Court of Appeals majority treated both Payton's and Riddick's cases as involving routine arrests in which there was ample time to obtain a warrant, and we will do the same. Accordingly, we have no occasion to consider the sort of emergency or dangerous situation, described in our cases as "exigent circumstances," that would justify a warrantless entry into a home for the purpose of either arrest or search.

Nor do these cases raise any question concerning the authority of the police, without either a search or arrest warrant, to enter a third party's home to arrest a suspect. The police broke into Payton's apartment intending to arrest Payton and they arrested Riddick in his own dwelling. We also note that in neither case is it argued that the police lacked probable cause to believe that the suspect was at home when they entered. Finally, in both cases we are dealing with entries into homes made without the consent of any occupant. In *Payton*, the police used crowbars to break down the door and in *Riddick*, although his three-year-old son answered the door, the police entered before Riddick had an opportunity either to object or to consent.

Without contending that *United States v. Watson* decided the question presented by these appeals, New York argues that the reasons that support the *Watson* holding require a similar result here. In *Watson* the Court relied on (a) the well-settled common-law rule that a warrantless arrest in a public place is valid if the arresting officer had probable cause to believe the suspect is a felon; (b) the clear consensus among the States adhering to that well settled common-law rule; and (c) the expression of the judgment of Congress that such an arrest is "reasonable." We consider each of these reasons as it applies to a warrantless entry into a home for the purpose of making a routine felony arrest.

A.

[O]ur study of the relevant common law does not provide the same guidance that was present in *Watson*. Whereas the rule concerning the validity of an arrest in a public place was supported by cases directly in point and by the unanimous views of the commentators, we have found no direct authority supporting forcible entries into a home to make a routine arrest and the weight of the scholarly opinion is somewhat to the contrary. Indeed, the absence of any Seventeenth or Eighteenth Century English cases directly in point, together with the unequivocal endorsement of the tenet that "a man's house is his castle," strongly suggests that the prevailing practice was not to make such arrests except in hot pursuit or when authorized by a warrant. Cf. *Agnello v. United States*, 269 U.S. 20, 33. In all events, the issue is not one that can be said to have been definitively settled by the common law at the time the Fourth Amendment was adopted.

B.

A majority of the States that have taken a position on the question permit warrantless entry into the home to arrest even in the absence of exigent circumstances. At this time, 24 States permit such warrantless entries; 15 States clearly prohibit them, though three States do so on federal constitutional grounds alone; and 11 States have apparently taken no position on the question.

But these current figures reflect a significant decline during the last decade in the number of States permitting warrantless entries for arrest. Recent dicta in this Court raising questions about the practice . . . , and Federal Courts of Appeals' decisions on point . . . , have led state courts to focus on the issue. Virtually all of the state courts that have had to confront the constitutional issue directly have held warrantless entries into the home to arrest to be invalid in the absence of exigent circumstances. Three state courts have relied on Fourth Amendment grounds alone, while seven have squarely placed their decisions on both federal and state constitutional grounds. A number of other state courts, though not having had to confront the issue directly, have recognized the serious nature of the constitutional question. Apparently, only the Supreme Court of Florida and the New York Court of Appeals in this case have expressly upheld warrantless entries to arrest in the face of a constitutional challenge.

A long-standing, widespread practice is not immune from constitutional scrutiny. But neither is it to be lightly brushed aside. This is particularly so when the constitutional standard is as amorphous as the word "reasonable," and when custom and contemporary norms necessarily play such a large role in the constitutional analysis. In this case, although the weight of state-law authority is clear, there is by no means the kind of virtual unanimity on this question that was present in *United States v. Watson*, with regard to warrantless arrests in public places. See 423 U.S., at 422–423. Only 24 of the 50 States currently sanction warrantless entries into the home to arrest . . . , and there is an obvious declining trend. Further, the strength of the trend is greater than the numbers alone indicate. Seven state courts have recently held that warrantless home arrests violate their respective *state* constitutions. That is significant because by invoking a state constitutional provision, a state court immunizes its decision from review by this Court. This heightened degree of immutability underscores the depth of the principle underlying the result.

C.

No congressional determination that warrantless entries into the home are "reasonable" has been called to our attention. None of the federal statutes cited in the *Watson* opinion reflects any such legislative judgment. Thus, that support for the *Watson* holding finds no counterpart in this case.

MR. JUSTICE POWELL, concurring in *United States v. Watson, supra*, 423 U.S., at 429, stated:

> But logic sometimes must defer to history and experience. The Court's opinion emphasizes the historical sanction accorded warrantless felony arrests [in public places].

In this case, however, neither history nor this Nation's experience requires us to disregard the overriding respect for the sanctity of the home that has been embedded in our traditions since the origins of the Republic.

Finally, we note the State's suggestion that only a search warrant based on probable cause to believe the suspect is at home at a given time can adequately protect the privacy interests at stake, and since such a warrant requirement is manifestly impractical, there need be no warrant of any kind. We find this ingenious argument unpersuasive. It is true that an arrest warrant requirement may afford less protection than a search warrant requirement; but it will suffice to interpose the magistrate's determination of probable cause between the zealous officer and the citizen. If there is sufficient evidence of a citizen's participation in a felony to persuade a judicial officer that his arrest is justified, it is constitutionally reasonable to require him to open his doors to the officers of the law. Thus, for Fourth Amendment purposes, an arrest warrant founded on probable cause implicitly carries with it the limited authority to enter a dwelling in which the suspect lives when there is reason to believe the suspect is within.

NOTES AND QUESTIONS

(1) Does *Payton* prevent an officer, with probable cause to arrest, from knocking on the door to a residence and making the arrest when the target opens the door? Lower courts have sustained such arrests, even when an element of subterfuge is present. In *People v. Colt*, 118 Cal. App. 4th 1404, 1409–10, 13 Cal. Rptr. 3d 852, 854–55 (2004), the officer "simply knocked on the door and stepped out of sight for officer safety. It was not unreasonable for the officers to take precautionary self-defense measures, *i.e.*, concealing themselves, when seeking an interview with a suspected methamphetamine seller. . . . A simple knock, standing alone, does not violate the Fourth Amendment." *Compare United States v. Reeves*, 524 F.3d 1161, 1169 (10th Cir. 2008): "A reasonable person faced with several police officers consistently knocking and yelling at their door for twenty minutes in the early morning hours would not feel free to ignore the officers' implicit command to open the door."

(2) In *Kirk v. Louisiana*, 536 U.S. 635 (2002), the Court unanimously reaffirmed the holding in *Payton* that absent exigent circumstances, a warrantless arrest within a residence is constitutionally impermissible. Additionally, officers executing an arrest warrant must have probable cause to believe the subject will be found on the premises. *United States v. Gorman*, 314 F.3d 1105 (9th Cir. 2002).

(3) Consistent with the holding in *Whren v. United States*, 517 U.S. 806 (1996), if officers have an arrest warrant, it is immaterial that their primary motivation in getting it was the possible discovery of seizable evidence in the course of making the arrest. *United States v. Clayton*, 210 F.3d 841 (8th Cir. 2000).

PROBLEM G
THE FLUSHED QUARRY

With probable cause to believe illegal narcotics sales were being made from the home of the accused, but without obtaining a search or an arrest warrant, an officer made an anonymous telephone call to the home, warning the accused that the police were on their way to the house with a search warrant. Officers surveilling the premises watched the lights in the house go off, followed by a great deal of activity for three or four minutes. Then the lights came back on. The accused came out of the house and departed in an automobile. Shortly thereafter, another suspect entered the premises, remained for a brief period, and departed in a van. The occupants of both vehicles were detained a short distance from the location, narcotics and narcotics paraphernalia were observed in plain view in both vehicles, and all were arrested. Are the arrests legal? *See State v. Hendrix*, 782 S.W.2d 833 (Tenn. 1989).

PROBLEM H
THE ARRESTED GUEST

Federal agents had probable cause to believe that Ricky Lyons, a fugitive wanted on narcotics charges, was hiding in the home of Gary Steagald. They entered the Steagald residence with an arrest warrant for Lyons, but he was not to be found. During the search for Lyons, however, officers observed what they believed to be cocaine. Ultimately, 43 pounds of cocaine were seized from the house on the authority of search warrants. Is this evidence admissible against Steagald? *See Steagald v. United States*, 451 U.S. 204 (1981).

If Lyons had been on the premises, would his arrest have been legal? Would it have been legal if the police had neither an arrest warrant for him nor a search warrant for the Steagald residence? Does it make a difference whether he is a casual visitor or an overnight guest? *See Minnesota v. Olson*, 495 U.S. 91 (1990).

WELSH v. WISCONSIN

Supreme Court of the United States
466 U.S. 740 (1984)

JUSTICE BRENNAN delivered the opinion of the Court.

Payton v. New York, . . . held that, absent probable cause and exigent circumstances, warrantless arrests in the home are prohibited by the Fourth Amendment. But the Court in that case explicitly refused "to consider the sort of emergency or dangerous situation, described in our cases as 'exigent circumstances,' that would justify a warrantless entry into a home for the purpose of either arrest or search." *Id.*, at 583. Certiorari was granted in this case to decide at least one aspect of the unresolved question: whether, and if so under what circumstances, the Fourth Amendment prohibits the police from making a warrantless night entry of a person's home in order to arrest him for violation of a nonjailable traffic offense.

I

A.

Shortly before 9:00 p.m. on the rainy night of April 24, 1978, a lone witness, Randy Jablonic, observed a car being driven erratically. After changing speeds and veering from side to side, the car eventually swerved off the road and came to a stop in an open field. No damage to any person or property occurred. Concerned about the driver and fearing that the car would get back on the highway, Jablonic drove his truck up behind the car so as to block it from returning to the road. Another passerby also stopped at the scene, and Jablonic asked her to call the police. Before the police arrived, however, the driver of the car emerged from his vehicle, approached Jablonic's truck, and asked Jablonic for a ride home. Jablonic instead suggested that they wait for assistance in removing or repairing the car. Ignoring Jablonic's suggestion, the driver walked away from the scene.

A few minutes later, the police arrived and questioned Jablonic. He told one officer what he had seen, specifically noting that the driver was either very inebriated or very sick. The officer checked the motor vehicle registration of the abandoned car and learned that it was registered to the petitioner, Edward G. Welsh. In addition, the officer noted that the petitioner's residence was a short distance from the scene, and therefore easily within walking distance.

Without securing any type of warrant, the police proceeded to the petitioner's home, arriving about 9:00 p.m. When the petitioner's stepdaughter answered the door, the police gained entry into the house. Proceeding upstairs to the petitioner's bedroom, they found him lying naked in bed. At this point, the petitioner was placed under arrest for driving or operating a motor vehicle while under the influence of an intoxicant, in violation of Wis. Stat. § 346.63(1) (1977). The petitioner was taken to the police station, where he refused to submit to a Breathalyzer test.

. . .

II

It is axiomatic that "the physical entry of the home is the chief evil against which the wording of the Fourth Amendment is directed." *United States v. United States District Court*, 407 U.S. 297, 313 (1972). And a principal protection against unnecessary intrusions into private dwellings is the warrant requirement imposed by the Fourth Amendment on agents of the government who seek to enter the home for purposes of search or arrest. See *Johnson v. United States*, 333 U.S. 10, 13–14 (1948). It is not surprising, therefore, that the Court has recognized, as "a 'basic principle of Fourth Amendment law[,]' that searches and seizures inside a home without a warrant are presumptively unreasonable." *Payton v. New York*.

Our hesitation in finding exigent circumstances, especially when warrantless arrests in the home are at issue, is especially appropriate when the underlying offense for which there is probable cause to arrest is relatively minor. Before agents of the government may invade the sanctity of the home, the burden is on the government to demonstrate exigent circumstances that overcome the presumption of unreasonableness that attaches to all warrantless home entries. See *Payton v. New York*, [445 U.S. 573,] at 586. When the government's interest is only to arrest for a minor offense, that presumption of unreasonableness is difficult to rebut, and the government usually should be allowed to make such arrests only with a warrant issued upon probable cause by a neutral and detached magistrate.

. . .

Consistently with this approach, the lower courts have looked to the nature of the underlying offense as an important factor to be considered in the exigent-circumstances calculus. . . .

We therefore conclude that the common sense approach utilized by most lower courts is required by the Fourth Amendment prohibition on "unreasonable searches and seizures," and hold that an important factor to be considered when determining whether any exigency exists is the gravity of the underlying offense for which the arrest is being made. Moreover, although no exigency is created simply because there is probable cause to believe that a serious crime has been committed, see *Payton, supra,* application of the exigent-circumstances exception in the context of a home entry should rarely be sanctioned when there is probable cause to believe that only a minor offense, such as the kind at issue in this case, has been committed.

Application of this principle to the facts of the present case is relatively straightforward. The petitioner was arrested in the privacy of his own bedroom for a noncriminal, traffic offense. The State attempts to justify the arrest by relying on the hot-pursuit doctrine, on the threat to public safety, and on the need to preserve evidence of the petitioner's blood-alcohol level. On the facts of this case, however, the claim of hot pursuit is unconvincing because there was no immediate or continuous pursuit of the petitioner from the scene of a crime. Moreover, because the petitioner had already arrived home, and had abandoned his car at the scene of the accident, there was little remaining threat to the public safety. Hence, the only potential emergency claimed by the State was the need to ascertain the petitioner's blood-alcohol level.

Even assuming, however, that the underlying facts would support a finding of this exigent circumstance, mere similarity to other cases involving the imminent destruction of evidence is not sufficient. The State of Wisconsin has chosen to classify the first offense for driving while intoxicated as a noncriminal, civil forfeiture offense for which no imprisonment is possible. See Wis. Stat. § 346.65(2) (1975); *id.*, § 346.65(2)(a) (1981-82); *supra,* at 5. This is the best indication of the state's interest in precipitating an arrest, and is one that can be easily identified both by the courts and by officers faced with a decision to arrest. . . . Given this expression of the state's interest, a warrantless home arrest cannot be upheld simply because evidence of the petitioner's blood-alcohol level might have dissipated while the police obtained a warrant. To allow a warrantless home entry on these facts would be to approve unreasonable police behavior that the principles of the Fourth Amendment will not sanction.

. . .

JUSTICE WHITE, with whom JUSTICE REHNQUIST joins, dissenting.

. . .

A warrantless home entry to arrest is no more intrusive when the crime is "minor" than when the suspect is sought in connection with a serious felony. The variable factor, if there is one, is the governmental interest that will be served by the warrantless entry. Wisconsin's Legislature and its Supreme Court have both concluded that warrantless in-home arrests under circumstances like those present here promote valid and substantial state interests. In determining whether the challenged governmental conduct was reasonable, we are not bound by these determinations. But nothing in our previous decisions suggests that the fact that a State has defined an offense as a misdemeanor for a variety of social, cultural, and political reasons necessarily requires the conclusion that warrantless in-home arrests designed to prevent the imminent destruction or removal of evidence of that offense are always impermissible. . . .

[T]he fact that Wisconsin has chosen to punish the first offense for driving under the influence with a fine rather than a prison term does not demand the conclusion that the State's interest in punishing first offenders is insufficiently substantial to justify warrantless in-home arrests under exigent circumstances. As the Supreme Court of Wisconsin observed, "[t]his is a model case demonstrating the urgency involved in arresting the suspect in order to preserve evidence of the statutory violation." 108 Wis. 2d, at 338,321 N.W.2d, at 255. We have previously recognized that "the percentage of alcohol in the blood begins to diminish shortly after drinking stops, as the body functions to eliminate it from the system." *Schmerber v. California*, 384 U.S. 757, 770 (1966). Moreover, a suspect could cast substantial doubt on the validity of a blood or breath test by consuming additional alcohol upon arriving at his home. In light of the promptness with which the officers reached Welsh's house, therefore, I would hold that the need to prevent the imminent and ongoing destruction of evidence of a serious violation of Wisconsin's traffic laws provided an exigent circumstance justifying the warrantless in-home arrest.

NOTES AND QUESTIONS

(1) At the outset Justice Brennan describes the subject of the investigation as "a nonjailable traffic offense." Later he refers to it as "a minor offense." Does the outcome on this case turn on the fortuity that Welsh's car "came to a stop in an open field"? Presumably the warrantless entry would have been permissible had the car come to a stop when it hit a farm worker. What if it had hit a cow? Is the Fourth Amendment protection governed by the way the state chooses to classify the crime? A number of lower courts had held that the odor of burning marijuana emanating from a residence will not justify a warrantless entry under the reasoning of *Welsh*. *See, e.g., State v. Holland*, 328 N.J. Super. 1, 744 A.2d 656 (2000).

(2) Since Welsh had sufficient time to walk home, take off his clothes and go to bed, obviously he had time to consume additional alcohol. Does this undercut the reasoning of the dissent?

(3) In what has come to be known as the "soccer mom case," the Supreme Court held in *Atwater v. City of Lago Vista*, 532 U.S. 318 (2001), that with probable cause, an officer could make a custodial arrest (as opposed to merely issuing a citation) for a misdemeanor that did not involve a breach of the peace. The plaintiff (the issue was raised in a civil rights action for damages) had been stopped for violating a statute punishable only by fine which required drivers and small children riding in the front seat to wear seat belts. A police officer, observing the seat belt violations, pulled Atwater over, verbally berated her, handcuffed her, placed her in his squad car, and drove her to the local police station, where she was made to remove her shoes, jewelry, and eyeglasses, and empty her pockets. "Officers took [her] 'mug shot' and placed her, alone, in a jail cell for about one hour, after which she was

taken before a magistrate and released on $310 bond." In a 6-3 holding, the Supreme Court sustained the actions of the police, observing that "[t]he arrest and booking were inconvenient and embarrassing to Atwater, but not so extraordinary as to violate the Fourth Amendment."

(4) *Welsh* was distinguished by the Supreme Court in *Illinois v. McArthur*, 531 U.S. 326, 336 (2001), in which the defendant was only permitted to enter his residence if he was accompanied by an officer while a warrant to search the premises was being obtained. The Court noted that in *McArthur*, the subject of the investigation was "jailable" offenses. Additionally, it noted, "[t]emporarily keeping a person from entering his home, a consequence whenever police stop a person on the street, is considerably less intrusive than police entry into the home itself in order to make a warrantless arrest or conduct a search."

RICHARDS v. WISCONSIN

United States Supreme Court
520 U.S. 385 (1997)

JUSTICE STEVENS delivered the opinion of the Court.

In *Wilson v. Arkansas*, 514 U.S. 927 (1995), we held that the Fourth Amendment incorporates the common law requirement that police officers entering a dwelling must knock on the door and announce their identity and purpose before attempting forcible entry. At the same time, we recognized that the "flexible requirement of reasonableness should not be read to mandate a rigid rule of announcement that ignores countervailing law enforcement interests," . . . and left "to the lower courts the task of determining the circumstances under which an unannounced entry is reasonable under the Fourth Amendment." . . .

In this case, the Wisconsin Supreme Court concluded that police officers are *never* required to knock and announce their presence when executing a search warrant in a felony drug investigation. In so doing, it reaffirmed a pre-*Wilson* holding and concluded that *Wilson* did not preclude this *per se* rule. We disagree with the court's conclusion that the Fourth Amendment permits a blanket exception to the knock-and-announce requirement for this entire category of criminal activity. But because the evidence presented to support the officers' actions in this case establishes that the decision not to knock and announce was a reasonable one under the circumstances, we affirm the judgment of the Wisconsin court.

I

On December 31, 1991, police officers in Madison, Wisconsin obtained a warrant to search Steiney Richards' hotel room for drugs and related paraphernalia. The search warrant was the culmination of an investigation that had uncovered substantial evidence that Richards was one of several individuals dealing drugs out of hotel rooms in Madison. The police requested a warrant that would have given advance authorization for a "no-knock" entry into the hotel room, but the magistrate explicitly deleted those portions of the warrant. . . .

The officers arrived at the hotel room at 3:40 a.m. Officer Pharo, dressed as a maintenance man, led the team. With him were several plainclothes officers and at least one man in uniform. Officer Pharo knocked on Richards' door and, responding to the query from inside the room, stated that he was a maintenance man. With the chain still on the door, Richards cracked it open. Although there is some dispute as to what occurred next, Richards acknowledges that when he opened the door he saw the man in uniform standing behind Officer Pharo. . . . He quickly slammed the door closed and, after waiting two or three seconds, the officers began kicking and ramming the door to gain entry to the locked room. At trial, the officers testified that they identified themselves as police while they were kicking the door in. . . . When they finally did break into the room, the officers caught Richards trying to escape through the window. They also found cash and cocaine hidden in plastic bags above the bathroom ceiling tiles.

Richards sought to have the evidence from his hotel room suppressed on the ground that the officers had failed to knock and announce their presence prior to forcing entry into the room. The trial court denied the motion, concluding that the officers could gather from Richards' strange behavior when they first sought entry that he knew they were police officers and that he might try to destroy evidence or to escape. . . . The judge emphasized that the easily disposable nature of the drugs the police were searching for further justified their decision to identify themselves as they crossed the threshold instead of announcing their presence before seeking entry. . . . Richards appealed the decision to the Wisconsin Supreme Court and that court affirmed. . . .

[T]he Wisconsin court found it reasonable — after considering criminal conduct surveys, newspaper articles, and other judicial opinions — to assume that all felony drug crimes will involve "an extremely high risk of serious if not deadly injury to the police as well as the potential for the disposal of drugs by the occupants prior to entry by the police." . . . Notwithstanding its acknowledgment that in "some cases, police officers will undoubtedly decide that their safety, the safety of others, and the effective execution of the warrant dictate that they knock and announce," . . . the court concluded that exigent circumstances justifying a no-knock entry are always present in felony drug cases. Further, the court reasoned that the violation of privacy that occurs when officers who have a search warrant forcibly enter is minimal, given that the residents would ultimately be without authority to refuse the police entry. The principal intrusion on individual privacy interests in such a situation, the court concluded, comes from the issuance of the search warrant, not the manner in which it is executed. . . . Accordingly, the court determined that police in Wisconsin do not need specific information about dangerousness, or the possible destruction of drugs in a particular case, in order to dispense with the knock-and-announce requirement in felony drug cases.

. . .

II

We recognized in *Wilson* that the knock-and-announce requirement could give way "under circumstances presenting a threat of physical violence," or "where police officers have reason to believe that evidence would likely be destroyed if advance notice were given." . . . It is indisputable that felony drug investigations may frequently involve both of these circumstances. The question we must resolve is whether this fact justifies dispensing with case-by-case evaluation of the manner in which a search was executed.

The Wisconsin court explained its blanket exception as necessitated by the special circumstances of today's drug culture . . . and the State asserted at oral argument that the blanket exception was reasonable in "felony drug cases because of the convergence in a violent and dangerous form of commerce of weapons and the destruction of drugs." . . . But creating exceptions to the knock-and-announce rule based on the "culture" surrounding a general category of criminal behavior presents at least two serious concerns.[13]

First, the exception contains considerable overgeneralization. For example, while drug investigation frequently does pose special risks to officer safety and the preservation of evidence, not every drug investigation will pose these risks to a substantial degree. For example, a search could be conducted at a time when the only individuals present in a residence have no connection with the drug activity and thus will be unlikely to threaten officers or destroy evidence. Or the police could know that the drugs being searched for were of a type or in a location that make them impossible to destroy quickly. In those situations, the asserted governmental interests in preserving evidence and maintaining safety may not outweigh the individual privacy interests intruded upon by a no-knock entry.[14] Wisconsin's blanket rule impermissibly insulates these cases from judicial review.

A second difficulty with permitting a criminal-category exception to the knock-and-announce requirement is that the reasons for creating an exception in one category can, relatively easily, be applied to others. Armed bank robbers, for example, are, by definition, likely to have weapons, and the fruits of their crime may be destroyed without too much difficulty. If a *per se* exception were allowed for each category of criminal investigation that included a considerable — albeit hypothetical — risk of danger to officers or destruction of evidence, the knock-and-announce

---

[13] [16] It is always somewhat dangerous to ground exceptions to constitutional protections in the social norms of a given historical moment. The purpose of the Fourth Amendment's requirement of reasonableness "is to preserve that degree of respect for the privacy of persons and the inviolability of their property that existed when the provision was adopted — even if a later, less virtuous age should become accustomed to considering all sorts of intrusion "reasonable." *Minnesota v. Dickerson.*

[14] [17] The State asserts that the intrusion on individual interests effectuated by a no-knock entry is minimal because the execution of the warrant itself constitutes the primary intrusion on individual privacy and that the individual privacy interest cannot outweigh the generalized governmental interest in effective and safe law enforcement. . . . While it is true that a no-knock entry is less intrusive than, for example, a warrantless search, the individual interests implicated by an unannounced, forcible entry should not be unduly minimized. As we observed in *Wilson v. Arkansas*, . . . the common law recognized that individuals should have an opportunity to themselves comply with the law and to avoid the destruction of property occasioned by a forcible entry. These interests are not inconsequential.

Additionally, when police enter a residence without announcing their presence, the residents are not given any opportunity to prepare themselves for such an entry. The State pointed out at oral argument that, in Wisconsin, most search warrants are executed during the late night and early morning hours. . . . The brief interlude between announcement and entry with a warrant may be the opportunity that an individual has to pull on clothes or get out of bed.

element of the Fourth Amendment's reasonableness requirement would be meaningless.

Thus, the fact that felony drug investigations may frequently present circumstances warranting a no-knock entry cannot remove from the neutral scrutiny of a reviewing court the reasonableness of the police decision not to knock and announce in a particular case. Instead, in each case, it is the duty of a court confronted with the question to determine whether the facts and circumstances of the particular entry justified dispensing with the knock-and-announce requirement.

In order to justify a "no-knock" entry, the police must have a reasonable suspicion that knocking and announcing their presence, under the particular circumstances, would be dangerous or futile, or that it would inhibit the effective investigation of the crime by, for example, allowing the destruction of evidence. This standard — as opposed to a probable cause requirement — strikes the appropriate balance between the legitimate law enforcement concerns at issue in the execution of search warrants and the individual privacy interests affected by no-knock entries. . . . This showing is not high, but the police should be required to make it whenever the reasonableness of a no-knock entry is challenged.

III

Although we reject the Wisconsin court's blanket exception to the knock-and-announce requirement, we conclude that the officers' no-knock entry into Richards' hotel room did not violate the Fourth Amendment. We agree with the trial court . . . that the circumstances in this case show that the officers had a reasonable suspicion that Richards might destroy evidence if given further opportunity to do so.

The judge who heard testimony at Richards' suppression hearing concluded that it was reasonable for the officers executing the warrant to believe that Richards knew, after opening the door to his hotel room the first time, that the men seeking entry to his room were the police. . . . Once the officers reasonably believed that Richards knew who they were, the court concluded, it was reasonable for them to force entry immediately given the disposable nature of the drugs. . . .

In arguing that the officers' entry was unreasonable, Richards places great emphasis on the fact that the magistrate who signed the search warrant for his hotel room deleted the portions of the proposed warrant that would have given the officers permission to execute a no-knock entry. But this fact does not alter the reasonableness of the officers' decision, which must be evaluated as of the time they entered the hotel room. At the time the officers obtained the warrant, they did not have evidence sufficient, in the judgment of the magistrate, to justify a no-knock warrant. Of course, the magistrate could not have anticipated in every particular the circumstances that would confront the officers which they arrived at Richards' hotel room.[15] These actual circumstances — petitioner's apparent recognition of the

[15] [18] A number of States give magistrate judges the authority to issue a "no-knock" warrant if the officers demonstrate ahead of time a reasonable suspicion that entry without prior announcement will be appropriate in a particular context.

officers combined with the easily disposable nature of the drugs — justified the officers' ultimate decision to enter without first announcing their presence and authority.

Accordingly, although we reject the blanket exception to the knock-and-announce requirement for felony drug investigations, the judgment of the Wisconsin Supreme Court is affirmed.

NOTES AND QUESTIONS

(1) *Richards* is a rare case in which a single opinion reflects the view of a unanimous Court. If a particularized justification for a no-knock entry is always required, why doesn't it follow that advance judicial authorization for a no-knock entry is impermissible? Since the Court holds that such an entry may be reasonable, as in this case, notwithstanding the refusal of a magistrate to authorize it — and implicitly, a no-knock entry may be unreasonable, even when judicially authorized — is any purpose served by giving such authority to magistrates?

(2) The *Wilson* requirement of notice before entry has been found inapplicable if an undercover agent has gained entrance to the premises and with probable cause signals back-up officers to enter to effect the arrest. In *United States v. Pollard*, 215 F.3d 643 (6th Cir.), *cert. denied*, 531 U.S. 999 (2000), the court described this exception as the doctrine of "consent once removed."

(3) In *United States v. Banks*, 540 U.S. 31 (2003), a case involving the execution of a search warrant for cocaine, a unanimous Court sustained the use of a battering ram to break open the front door of the residence when officers received no response after a wait of 15 to 20 seconds. The Court made clear that the reasonableness of such an entry required a fact-specific inquiry.

(4) *In Tennessee v. Garner*, 471 U.S. 1 (1985), an action for damages under a federal civil rights statute, the Court rejected a *per se* rule, derived from the common law, that deadly force could be used to apprehend a fleeing felon. Such force could be used, it concluded, only "[w]here the officer has probable cause to believe that the suspect poses a threat of serious physical harm, either to the officer or to others."

The practice of allowing magistrates to issue no-knock warrants seems entirely reasonable when sufficient cause to do so can be demonstrated ahead of time. But, as the facts of this case demonstrate, a magistrate's decision not to authorize a no-knock entry should not be interpreted to remove the officers' authority to exercise independent judgment concerning the wisdom of a no-knock entry at the time the warrant is being executed.

Chapter 3

THE FOURTH AMENDMENT AND THE SEIZURE OF EVIDENCE

§ 3.01 THE CONSTITUTIONAL CHOICE: TRESPASS V. PRIVACY

OLMSTEAD v. UNITED STATES

United States Supreme Court
277 U.S. 438 (1928)

Mr. Chief Justice Taft delivered the opinion of the Court.

The petitioners were convicted in the District Court for the Western District of Washington of a conspiracy to violate the National Prohibition Act . . . by unlawfully possessing, transporting and importing intoxicating liquors and maintaining nuisances, and by selling intoxicating liquors. Seventy-two others, in addition to the petitioners, were indicted. Some were not apprehended, some were acquitted, and others pleaded guilty.

The evidence in the records discloses a conspiracy of amazing magnitude to import, possess, and sell liquor unlawfully. It involved the employment of not less than 50 persons, of two sea-going vessels for the transportation of liquor to British Columbia, of smaller vessels for coastwise transportation in the state of Washington, the purchase and use of a branch beyond the suburban limits of Seattle, with a large underground cache for storage and a number of smaller caches in that city, the maintenance of a central office manned with operators, and the employment of executives, salesmen, deliverymen dispatchers, scouts, bookkeepers, collectors, and an attorney. In a bad month sales amounted to $176,000; the aggregate for a year must have exceeded $2,000,000.

. . .

The information which led to the discovery of the conspiracy and its nature and extent was largely obtained by intercepting messages on the telephones of the conspirators by four federal prohibition officers. Small wires were inserted along the ordinary telephone wires from the residences of four of the petitioners and those leading from the chief office. The insertions were made without any trespass upon any property of the defendants. They were made in the basement of the large office building. The taps from house lines were made in the streets near the houses.

The gathering of evidence continued for many months. Conversations of the conspirators, of which refreshing stenographic notes were currently made, were testified to by the government witnesses. They revealed to large business transactions of the partners and their subordinates. Men at the wires heard orders given for liquor by customers and the acceptances; they became auditors of the conversations between the partners. All this disclosed the conspiracy charged in the indictment.

. . .

The [Fourth] Amendment itself shows that the search is to be of material things — the person, the house, the papers, or his effects. The description of the warrant necessary to make the proceedings lawful is that it must specify the place to be searched and the person or things to be seized.

. . . The amendment does not forbid what was done here. There was no searching. There was no seizure. The evidence was secured by the use of the sense of hearing and that only. There was no entry of the houses or offices of the defendants.

By the invention of the telephone 50 years ago, and its application for the purpose of extending communications, one can talk with another at a far distant place.

The language of the amendment cannot be extended and expanded to include telephone wires, reaching to the whole world from the defendant's house or office. The intervening wires are not part of his house or office, any more than are the highways along which they are stretched. . . .

Neither the cases we have cited nor any of the many federal decisions brought to our attention hold the Fourth Amendment to have been violated as against a defendant, unless there has been an official search and seizure of his person or such a seizure of his papers or his tangible material effects or an actual physical invasion of his house "or curtilage" for the purpose of making a seizure.

We think, therefore, that the wire tapping here disclosed did not amount to a search or seizure within the meaning of the Fourth Amendment.

MR. JUSTICE BRANDEIS (dissenting).

. . .

When the Fourth and Fifth Amendments were adopted, "the form that evil had heretofore taken" had been necessarily simple. Force and violence were then the only means known to man by which a government could directly effect self-incrimination. It could compel the individual to testify — a compulsion effected, if need be, by torture. It could secure possession of his papers and other articles incident to his private life — a seizure effected, if need be, by breaking and entry. Protection against such invasion of "the sanctities of a man's home and the privacies of life" was provided in the Fourth and Fifth Amendments by specific language . . . But "time works changes, brings into existence new conditions and purposes." Subtler and more far-reaching means of invading privacy have become available to the government. Discovery and invention have made it possible for the government, by means far more effective than stretching upon the rack, to obtain disclosure in court of what is whispered in the closet.

Moreover, "in the application of a Constitution, our contemplation cannot be only what has been, but of what may be." The progress of science in furnishing the government with means of espionage is not likely to stop with wiretapping. Ways may someday be developed by which the government, without removing papers from secret drawers, can reproduce them in court, and by which it will be enabled to expose to a jury the most intimate occurrences of the home. Advances in the psychic and related sciences may bring means of exploring unexpressed beliefs, thoughts and emotions. . . .

. . . Whenever a telephone line is tapped, the privacy of the persons at both ends of the line is invaded, and all conversations between them upon any subject, and although proper, confidential, and privileged, may be overheard. Moreover, the tapping of one man's telephone line involves the tapping of the telephone of every other person whom he may call, or who may call him. As a means of espionage, writs of assistance and general warrants are but puny instruments of tyranny and oppression when compared to wiretapping.

. . . It is, of course, immaterial where the physical connection with the telephone wire leading into the defendants' premises was made. And it is also immaterial that the intrusion was in aid of law enforcement. Experience should teach us to be most on our guard to protect liberty when the government's purposes are beneficent. Men born to freedom are naturally alert to repel invasion of their liberty by evil-minded rulers. The greatest dangers to liberty lurk in insidious encroachment by men of zeal, well-meaning but without understanding.

KATZ v. UNITED STATES

United States Supreme Court
389 U.S. 347 (1967)

Mr. Justice Stewart delivered the opinion of the Court.

The petitioner was convicted in the District Court for the Southern District of California under an eight-count indictment charging him with transmitting wagering information by telephone from Los Angeles to Miami and Boston, in violation of a federal statute. At trial the Government was permitted, over the petitioner's objection, to introduce evidence of the petitioner's end of telephone conversations, overheard by FBI agents who had attached an electronic listening and recording device to the outside of the public telephone booth from which he had placed his calls. In affirming his conviction, the Court of Appeals rejected the contention that the recordings had been obtained in violation of the Fourth Amendment, because "[t]here was no physical entrance into the area occupied by [the petitioner]." We granted certiorari in order to consider the constitutional questions thus presented.

The petitioner has phrased those questions as follows:

> A. Whether a public telephone booth is a constitutionally protected area so that evidence obtained by attaching an electronic listening recording device

to the top of such a booth is obtained in violation of the right to privacy of the user of the booth.

B. Whether physical penetration of a constitutionally protected area is necessary before a search and seizure can be said to be violative of the Fourth Amendment to the United States Constitution.

We decline to adopt this formulation of the issues. In the first place, the correct solution of Fourth Amendment problems is not necessarily promoted by incantation of the phrase "constitutionally protected area." Secondly, the Fourth Amendment cannot be translated into a general constitutional "right to privacy." That Amendment protects individual privacy against certain kinds of governmental intrusion, but its protections go further, and often have nothing to do with privacy at all. Other provisions of the Constitution protect personal privacy from other forms of governmental invasion. But the protection of a person's *general* right to privacy — his right to be let alone by other people — is, like the protection of his property and of his very life, left largely to the law of the individual States.

Because of the misleading way the issues have been formulated, the parties have attached great significance to the characterization of the telephone booth from which the petitioner placed his calls. The petitioner has strenuously argued that the booth was a "constitutionally protected area." The Government has maintained with equal vigor that it was not. But this effort to decide whether or not a given "area," viewed in the abstract, is "constitutionally protected" deflects attention from the problem presented by this case. For the Fourth Amendment protects people, not places. What a person knowingly exposes to the public, even in his own home or office, is not a subject of Fourth Amendment protection. See *Lewis v. United States*, 385 U.S. 206, 210; *United States v. Lee*, 274 U.S. 559, 563, Treas. Dec. 42252. But what he seeks to preserve as private, even in an area accessible to the public, may be constitutionally protected. See *Rios v. United States*, 364 U.S. 253; *Ex parte Jackson*, 96 U.S. 727, 733.

The Government stresses the fact that the telephone booth from which the petitioner made his calls was constructed partly of glass, so that he was as visible after he entered it as he would have been if he had remained outside. But what he sought to exclude when he entered the booth was not the intruding eye — it was the uninvited ear. He did not shed his right to do so simply because he made his calls from a place where he might be seen. No less than an individual in a business office, in a friend's apartment, or in a taxicab, a person in a telephone booth may rely upon the protection of the Fourth Amendment. One who occupies it, shuts the door behind him, and pays the toll that permits him to place a call is surely entitled to assume that the words he utters into the mouthpiece will not be broadcast to the world. To read the Constitution more narrowly is to ignore the vital role that the public telephone has come to play in private communication.

The Government contends, however, that the activities of its agents in this case should not be tested by Fourth Amendment requirements, for the surveillance technique they employed involved no physical penetration of the telephone booth from which the petitioner placed his calls. It is true that the absence of such penetration was at one time thought to foreclose further Fourth Amendment inquiry, *Olmstead v. United States*, 277 U.S. 438, 457, 464, 466; *Goldman v. United*

States, 316 U.S. 129, 134–136, for that Amendment was thought to limit only searches and seizures of tangible property. But "[t]he premise that property interests control the right of the Government to search and seize has been discredited." *Warden v. Hayden*, 387 U.S. 294, 304. Thus, although a closely divided Court supposed in *Olmstead* that surveillance without any trespass and without the seizure of any material object fell outside the ambit of the Constitution, we have since departed from the narrow view on which that decision rested. Indeed, we have expressly held that the Fourth Amendment governs not only the seizure of tangible items, but extends as well to the recording of oral statements, overheard without any "technical trespass under local property law." *Silverman v. United States*, 365 U.S. 505, 511. Once this much is acknowledged, and once it is recognized that the Fourth Amendment protects people — and not simply "areas" — against unreasonable searches and seizures, it becomes clear that the reach of that Amendment cannot turn upon the presence or absence of a physical intrusion into any given enclosure.

We conclude that the underpinnings of *Olmstead* and *Goldman* have been so eroded by our subsequent decisions that the "trespass" doctrine there enunciated can no longer be regarded as controlling. The Government's activities in electronically listening to and recording the petitioner's words violated the privacy upon which he justifiably relied while using the telephone booth and thus constituted a "search and seizure" within the meaning of the Fourth Amendment. The fact that the electronic device employed to achieve that end did not happen to penetrate the wall of the booth can have no constitutional significance.

The question remaining for decision, then, is whether the search and seizure conducted in this case complied with constitutional standards. In that regard, the Government's position is that its agents acted in an entirely defensible manner: They did not begin their electronic surveillance until investigation of the petitioner's activities had established a strong probability that he was using the telephone in question to transmit gambling information to persons in other States, in violation of federal law. Moreover, the surveillance was limited, both in scope and in duration, to the specific purpose of establishing the contents of the petitioner's unlawful telephonic communications. The agents confined their surveillance to the brief periods during which he used the telephone booth, and they took great care to overhear only the conversations of the petitioner himself.

Accepting this account of the Government's actions as accurate, it is clear that this surveillance was so narrowly circumscribed that a duly authorized magistrate, properly notified of the need for such investigation, specifically informed of the basis on which it was to proceed, and clearly apprised of the precise intrusion it would entail, could constitutionally have authorized, with appropriate safeguards, the very limited search and seizure that the Government asserts in fact took place.

Wherever a man may be, he is entitled to know that he will remain free from unreasonable searches and seizures. The government agents here ignored "the procedure of antecedent justification . . . that is central to the Fourth Amendment," a procedure that we hold to be a constitutional precondition of the kind of electronic surveillance involved in this case. Because the surveillance here failed to meet that condition, and because it led to the petitioner's conviction, the judgment must be reversed.

MR. JUSTICE HARLAN, concurring.

I join the opinion of the Court, which I read to hold only (a) that an enclosed telephone booth is an area where, like a home, . . . a person has a constitutionally protected reasonable expectation of privacy; (b) that electronic as well as physical intrusion into a place that is in this sense private may constitute a violation of the Fourth Amendment; and (c) that the invasion of a constitutionally protected area by federal authorities is, as the Court has long held, presumptively unreasonable in the absence of a search warrant.

As the Court's opinion states, "the Fourth Amendment protects people, not places." The question, however, is what protection it affords to those people. Generally, as here, the answer to that question requires reference to a "place." My understanding of the rule that has emerged from prior decisions is that there is a twofold requirement, first that a person have exhibited an actual (subjective) expectation of privacy and, second, that the expectation be one that society is prepared to recognize as "reasonable." Thus a man's home is, for most purposes, a place where he expects privacy, but objects, activities, or statements that he exposes to the "plain view" of outsiders are not "protected" because no intention to keep them to himself has been exhibited. On the other hand, conversations in the open would not be protected against being overheard, for the expectation of privacy under the circumstances would be unreasonable.

The critical fact in this case is that "[o]ne who occupies it, [a telephone booth] shuts the door behind him, and pays the toll that permits him to place a call is surely entitled to assume" that his conversation is not being intercepted. . . . The point is not that the booth is "accessible to the public" at other times, . . . but that it is a temporarily private place whose momentary occupants' expectations of freedom from intrusion are recognized as reasonable.

MR. JUSTICE BLACK, dissenting.

If I could agree with the Court that eavesdropping carried on by electronic means (equivalent to wiretapping) constitutes a "search" or "seizure," I would be happy to join the Court's opinion.

My basic objection is twofold: (1) I do not believe that the words of the Amendment will bear the meaning given them by today's decision, and (2) I do not believe that it is the proper role of this Court to rewrite the Amendment in order "to bring it into harmony with the times" and thus reach a result that many people believe to be desirable.

While I realize that an argument based on the meaning of words lacks the scope, and no doubt the appeal, of broad policy discussions and philosophical discourses on such nebulous subjects as privacy, for me the language of the Amendment is the crucial place to look in construing a written document such as our Constitution. The Fourth Amendment says that

> The right of the people to be secure in their persons, houses, papers, and effects, against unreasonable searches and seizures, shall not be violated, and no Warrants shall issue, but upon probable cause, supported by Oath or affirmation, and particularly describing the place to be searched, and the persons or things to be seized.

The first clause protects "persons, houses, papers, and effects, against unreasonable searches and seizures. . . ." These words connote the idea of tangible things with size, form, and weight, things capable of being searched, seized, or both. The second clause of the Amendment still further establishes its Framers' purpose to limit its protection to tangible things by providing that no warrants shall issue but those "particularly describing the place to be searched, and the persons or things to be seized." A conversation overheard by eavesdropping, whether by plain snooping or wiretapping, is not tangible and, under the normally accepted meanings of the words, can neither be searched nor seized. In addition the language of the second clause indicates that the Amendment refers not only to something tangible so it can be seized but to something already in existence so it can be described. Yet the Court's interpretation would have the Amendment apply to overhearing future conversations which by their very nature are nonexistent until they take place. How can one "describe" a future conversation, and, if one cannot, how can a magistrate issue a warrant to eavesdrop one in the future? It is argued that information showing what is expected to be said is sufficient to limit the boundaries of what later can be admitted into evidence; but does such general information really meet the specific language of the Amendment which says "particularly describing"? Rather than using language in a completely artificial way, I must conclude that the Fourth Amendment simply does not apply to eavesdropping. Tapping telephone wires, of course, was an unknown possibility at the time the Fourth Amendment was adopted. But eavesdropping (and wire-tapping is nothing more than eavesdropping by telephone) was, as even the majority opinion in *Berger* . . . recognized "an ancient practice which at common law was condemned as a nuisance. 4 Blackstone, Commentaries 168. In those days the eavesdropper listened by naked ear under the eaves of houses or their windows, or beyond their walls seeking out private discourse." 388 U.S., at 45. There can be no doubt that the Framers were aware of this practice, and if they had desired to outlaw or restrict the use of evidence obtained by eavesdropping, I believe that they would have used the appropriate language to do so in the Fourth Amendment. They certainly would not have left such a task to the ingenuity of language-stretching judges. No one, it seems to me, can read the debates on the Bill of Rights without reaching the conclusion that its Framers and critics well knew the meaning of the words they used, what they would be understood to mean by others, their scope and their limitations. Under these circumstances it strikes me as a charge against their scholarship, their common sense and their candor to give to the Fourth Amendment's language the eavesdropping meaning the Court imputes to it today.

Since I see no way in which the words of the Fourth Amendment can be construed to apply to eavesdropping, that closes the matter for me. In interpreting the Bill of Rights, I willingly go as far as a liberal construction of the language takes me, but I simply cannot in good conscience give a meaning to words which they have never before been thought to have and which they certainly do not have in common ordinary usage. I will not distort the words of the Amendment in order to "keep the Constitution up to date" or "to bring it into harmony with the times." It was never meant that this Court have such power, which in effect would make us a continuously functioning constitutional convention.

With this decision the Court has completed, I hope, its rewriting of the Fourth Amendment, which started only recently when the Court began referring incessantly to the Fourth Amendment not so much as a law against *unreasonable* searches and seizures as one to protect an individual's privacy. By clever word juggling the Court finds it plausible to argue that language aimed specifically at searches and seizures of things that can be searched and seized may, to protect privacy, be applied to eavesdropped evidence of conversations that can neither be searched nor seized. Few things happen to an individual that do not affect his privacy in one way or another. Thus, by arbitrarily substituting the Court's language, designed to protect privacy, for the Constitution's language, designed to protect against unreasonable searches and seizures, the Court has made the Fourth Amendment its vehicle for holding all laws violative of the Constitution which offend the Court's broadest concept of privacy. As I said in *Griswold v. Connecticut*, 381 U.S. 479, "The Court talks about a constitutional 'right of privacy' as though there is some constitutional provision or provisions forbidding any law ever to be passed which might abridge the 'privacy' of individuals. But there is not." (Dissenting opinion, at 508.) I made clear in that dissent my fear of the dangers involved when this Court uses the "broad, abstract and ambiguous concept" of "privacy" as a "comprehensive substitute for the Fourth Amendment's guarantee against 'unreasonable searches and seizures.' " (See generally, dissenting opinion, at 507–527.)

The Fourth Amendment protects privacy only to the extent that it prohibits unreasonable searches and seizures of "persons, houses, papers, and effects." No general right is created by the Amendment so as to give this Court the unlimited power to hold unconstitutional everything which affects privacy. Certainly the Framers, well acquainted as they were with the excesses of governmental power, did not intend to grant this Court such omnipotent lawmaking authority as that. The history of governments proves that it is dangerous to freedom to repose such powers in courts.

[JUSTICE DOUGLAS, joined by JUSTICE BRENNAN, concurred; JUSTICE WHITE concurred separately; JUSTICE MARSHALL took no part in the decision.]

NOTES AND QUESTIONS

(1) Does the *Katz* Court hold that the interception of telephone messages was constitutionally impermissible? Or does it hold merely that a court order was required? If a court order had been sought, should it issue?

(2) Is the observation that "the Fourth Amendment protects people, not places" — a frequently quoted passage from the *Katz* opinion — illuminating? Isn't the place the interception occurs *still* of paramount significance in determining whether the individual has knowingly exposed his conversation to the public?

(3) Suppose that while making his telephone call, Katz had smoked a marijuana cigarette, and this activity was observed by the officer listening to his conversation.

Could the officer testify as to what he saw? Just as Katz had not excluded "the intruding eye" by entering the telephone booth, so the Court of Appeal for Utah held in *State v. Holden*, 964 P.2d 318 (Utah Ct. App. 1998), the *Katz* decision afforded no protection against the videotaping of activities occurring in the accused's front yard, obtained from the vantage point of a neighbor's property.

(4) In *Cowles v. State*, 23 P.3d 1168 (Alaska 2001), *cert. denied*, 534 U.S. 1131 (2002), campus police received information from the University of Alaska box office manager that an employee was stealing cash from ticket sales. Without obtaining a judicial order, they installed a hidden video camera and recorded the employee taking money from the University cash bag, transferring it to her desk, and then to her purse. In finding the videotaping not to be an illegal search, the court took note of the public nature of the office — visible to members of the public through the ticket window and to fellow employees continuously within the office — and cited *Katz* for the principle that which is knowingly exposed to the public is not subject to Fourth Amendment protection.

UNITED STATES v. JONES

United States Supreme Court
132 S. Ct. 945 (2012)

Justice Scalia delivered the opinion of the Court.

We decide whether the attachment of a Global-Positioning-System (GPS) tracking device to an individual's vehicle, and subsequent use of that device to monitor the vehicle's movements on public streets, constitutes a search or seizure within the meaning of the Fourth Amendment.

I

In 2004 respondent Antoine Jones, owner and operator of a nightclub in the District of Columbia, came under suspicion of trafficking in narcotics and was made the target of an investigation by a joint FBI and Metropolitan Police Department task force. Officers employed various investigative techniques, including visual surveillance of the nightclub, installation of a camera focused on the front door of the club, and a pen register and wiretap covering Jones's cellular phone.

Based in part on information gathered from these sources, in 2005 the Government applied to the United States District Court for the District of Columbia for a warrant authorizing the use of an electronic tracking device on the Jeep Grand Cherokee registered to Jones' wife. A warrant issued authorizing installation of the device in the District of Columbia and within 10 days.

On the 11th day, and not in the District of Columbia but in Maryland, agents installed a GPS tracking device on the undercarriage of the Jeep while it was parked in a public parking lot. Over the next 28 days, the Government used the device to track the vehicle's movements, and once had to replace the device's battery when the vehicle was parked in a different public lot in Maryland. By means of signals from multiple satellites, the device established the vehicle's location within

50 to 100 feet, and communicated that location by cellular phone to a Government computer. It relayed more than 2,000 pages of data over the 4-week period.

The Government ultimately obtained a multiple-count indictment charging Jones and several co-conspirators with, as relevant here, conspiracy to distribute and possess with intent to distribute five kilograms or more of cocaine and 50 grams or more of cocaine base. . . . Before trial, Jones filed a motion to suppress evidence obtained through the GPS device. The District Court granted the motion only in part, suppressing the data obtained while the vehicle was parked in the garage adjoining Jones's residence. . . . It held the remaining data admissible, because "[a] person traveling in an automobile on public thoroughfares has no reasonable expectation of privacy in his movements from one place to another." (quoting *United States v. Knotts*) . . .

[Following a conviction in a second trial, [t]he United States Court of Appeals for the District of Columbia Circuit reversed the conviction because of admission of evidence obtained by warrantless use of the GPS device which, it said, violated the Fourth Amendment. . . .

II

A

. . .

It is important to be clear about what occurred in this case. The Government physically occupied private property for the purpose of obtaining information. We have no doubt that such a physical intrusion would have been considered a "search" within the meaning of the Fourth Amendment when it was adopted. *Entick v. Carrington*, 95 Eng. Rep. 807 (C.P. 1765) is a "case we have described as a 'monument of English freedom' undoubtedly familiar to 'every American statesman' at the time the Constitution was adopted, and considered to be 'the true and ultimate expression of constitutional law' " with regard to search and seizure. . . . In that case, Lord Camden expressed in plain terms the significance of property rights in search-and-seizure analysis:

> "[O]ur law holds the property of every man so sacred, that no man can set his foot upon his neighbor's close without his leave; if he does he is a trespasser, though he does no damage at all; if he will tread upon his neighbour's ground, he must justify it by law."

The text of the Fourth Amendment reflects the close connection to property, since otherwise it would have referred simply to "the right of the people to be secure against unreasonable searches and seizures"; the phrase "in their persons, houses, papers and effects" would have been superfluous.

Consistent with this understanding of the Fourth Amendment jurisprudence was tied to common-law trespass, at least until the latter half of the 20th century. . . . Thus, in *Olmstead v. United States*, 277 U.S. 438 (1928), we held that wiretaps attached to telephone wires on the public streets did not constitute a Fourth

Amendment search because "[t]here was no entry of the houses or offices of the defendants," . . .

Our later cases, of course, have deviated from that exclusively property-based approach. In *Katz v. United States* . . . , we said that "the Fourth Amendment protects people, no places," and found a violation in attachment of an eavesdropping device to a public telephone booth. Our later cases have applied the analysis of Justice Harlan's concurrence in that case, which said that a violation occurs when government officers violate a person's "reasonable expectation of privacy." . . .

The Government contends that the Harlan standard shows that no search occurred here, since Jones had no "reasonable expectation of privacy" in the area of the Jeep accessed by the Government agents (its underbody) and in the locations of the Jeep on the public roads, which were visible to all. But we need not address the Government's contentions, because Jones's Fourth Amendment rights do not rise or fall with the *Katz* formulation. At bottom, we must "assur[e] preservation of that degree of privacy that existed when the Fourth Amendment was adopted." . . .

The Government contends that several of our post-*Katz* cases foreclose the conclusion that what occurred here constituted a search. It relies principally on two cases in which we rejected Fourth Amendment challenges to "beepers," electronic tracking devices that represent another form of electronic monitoring. The first case, *Knotts*, upheld against Fourth Amendment challenge the use of a "beeper" that had been placed in a container of chloroform, allowing law enforcement to monitor the location of the container. . . . We said that there had been no infringement of Knotts' reasonable expectation of privacy since the information obtained — the location of the automobile carrying the container on public roads, and the location of the off-loaded container in open fields near Knotts' cabin — had been voluntarily conveyed to the public. . . . But as we have discussed, the *Katz* reasonable-expectation-of-privacy test has been *added to*, not *substituted for*, the common-law trespassory test. The holding in *Knotts* addressed only the former, since the latter was not at issue. The beeper had been placed in the container before it came into Knotts' possession, with the consent of the then-owner. . . . Knotts did not challenge that installation, and we specifically declined to consider its effect on the Fourth Amendment analysis. . . .

The second "beeper" case, *United States v. Karo*, . . . does not suggest a different conclusion. There we addressed the question left open by *Knotts*, whether the installation of a beeper in a container amounted to a search and seizure. . . . As in *Knotts*, at the time the beeper was installed the container belonged to a third party, and it did not come into possession of the defendant until later. . . . Thus, the specific question we considered was whether the installation "*with the consent of the original owner* constitute[d] a search or seizure . . . when the container is delivered to a buyer having no knowledge of the presence of the beeper." . . . We held not. The Government, we said, came into physical contact with the container only before it belonged to the defendant Karo, and the transfer of the container with the unmonitored beeper inside it did not convey any information and thus did not invade Karo's privacy. . . .

The Government also points to our exposition in *New York v. Class*, . . . that "[t]he exterior of a car . . . is thrust into the public eye, and thus to examine it does not constitute a 'search.' " . . . That statement is of marginal relevance here since, as the Government acknowledges, "the officers in this case did *more* than conduct a visual inspection of respondent's vehicle." . . . By attaching the device to the Jeep, officers encroached on a protected area. In *Class* itself we suggested that this would make a difference, for we concluded that an officer's momentary reaching into the interior of a vehicle did constitute a search. . . .

B

The concurrence begins by accusing us of applying "18th-century tort law." . . . That is a distortion. What we apply is an 18th-century guarantee against unreasonable searches, which we believe must provide *at a minimum* the degree of protection it afforded when it was adopted. The concurrence does not share that belief. It would apply *exclusively Katz's* reasonable-expectation-of-privacy test, even when that eliminates rights that previously existed.

The concurrence faults our approach for "present[ing] particularly vexing problems" in cases that do not involve physical contact, such as those that involve the transmission of electronic signals. . . . We entirely fail to understand that point. For unlike the concurrence, which would make *Katz* the *exclusive* test, we do not make trespass the exclusive test. Situations involving merely the transmission of electronic signals without trespass would *remain* subject to *Katz* analysis.

. . .

The judgment of the Court of Appeals for the D.C. Circuit is affirmed.

Justice SOTOMAYOR, concurring.

I join the Court's opinion because I agree that a search within the meaning of the Fourth Amendment occurs, at a minimum, "[w]here, as here, the Government obtains information by physically intruding on a constitutionally protected area." . . .

Of course, the Fourth Amendment is not concerned only with trespassory intrusions on property. See, e.g., *Kyllo v. United States*. . . . Rather, even in the absence of a trespass, "a Fourth Amendment search occurs when the government violates a subjective expectation of privacy that society recognizes as reasonable." . . . In *Katz*, this Court enlarged its then-prevailing focus on property rights by announcing that the reach of the Fourth Amendment does not "turn upon the presence or absence of a physical intrusion." . . . Justice ALITO's approach, which discounts altogether the constitutional relevance of the Government's physical intrusion on Jones' Jeep, erodes that longstanding protection for privacy expectations inherent in items of majority's opinion reflects an irreducible constitutional minimum: When the Government physically invades personal property to gather information, a search occurs. The reaffirmation of that principle suffices to decide this case.

Justice ALITO, with whom Justice GINSBURG, Justice BREYER, and Justice KAGAN join, concurring in the judgment.

I would analyze the question presented in this case by asking whether respondent's reasonable expectations of privacy were violated by the long-term monitoring of the vehicle he drove.

I

B

The Court's reasoning in this case is very similar to that in the Court's early decisions involving wiretapping and electronic eavesdropping, namely, that a technical trespass followed by the gathering of evidence constitutes a search. In the early electronic surveillance cases, the Court concluded that a Fourth Amendment search occurred when private conversations were monitored as a result of an "unauthorized physical penetration into the premises occupied" by the defendant. . . .

The trespass-based rule was repeatedly criticized. In *Olmstead [v. United States*, 277 U.S. 438 (1928)], Justice Brandeis wrote that it was "immaterial where the physical connection with the telephone wires was made." . . . Although a private conversation transmitted by wire did not fall within the literal words of the Fourth Amendment, he argued, the Amendment should be understood as prohibiting "every unjustifiable intrusion by the government upon the privacy of the individual." [dissenting opinion] . . .

Katz . . . finally did away with the old approach, holding that a trespass was not required for a Fourth Amendment violation. Katz involved the use of a listening device that was attached to the outside of a public telephone booth and that allowed police officers to eavesdrop on one end of the target's phone conversation. This procedure "did not physically intrude on the area occupied by the target, but the Katz Court, "repudiate[d]" the old doctrine, . . . and held that "[t]he fact that the electronic device employed . . . did not happen to penetrate the wall of the booth can have no constitutional significance." . . .

III

Disharmony with a substantial body of existing case law is only one of the problems with the Court's approach in this case.

I will briefly note four others. First, the Court's reasoning largely disregards what is really important (the *use* of a GPS for the purpose of long-term tracking) and instead attaches great significance to something that most would view as relatively minor (attaching to the bottom of a car a small, light object that does not interfere in any way with the car's operation). Attaching such an object is generally regarded as so trivial that it does not provide a basis for recovery under modern tort law. . . . But under the Court's reasoning, this conduct may violate the Fourth Amendment. By contrast, if long-term monitoring can be accomplished without committing a technical trespass — suppose, for example, that the Federal

Government required or persuaded auto manufacturers to include a GPS tracking device in every car — the Court's theory would provide no protection.

Second, the Court's approach leads to incongruous results. If the police attach a GPS device to a car and use the device to follow the car for even a brief time, under the Court's theory, the Fourth Amendment applies. But if the police follow the same car for a much longer period using unmarked cars and aerial assistance, this tracking is not subject to any Fourth Amendment constraints. . . .

Third, under the Court's theory, the coverage of the Fourth Amendment may vary from State to State. If the events at issue here had occurred in a community property State or a State that has adopted the Uniform Marital Property Act respondent would likely be an owner of the vehicle, and it would not matter whether the GPS was installed before or after his wife turned over the keys. In non-community-property States, on the other hand, the registration of the vehicle in the name of respondent's wife would generally be regarded as presumptive evidence that she was the sole owner. . . .

Fourth, the Court's reliance on the law of trespass will present particularly vexing problems in cases involving surveillance that is carried out by making electronic, as opposed to physical, contact with the item to be tracked. For example, suppose that the officers in the present case had followed respondent by surreptitiously activating a stolen vehicle detection system that came with the car when it was purchased. Would the sending of a radio signal to activate this system constitute a trespass to chattels? Trespass to chattels has traditionally required a physical touching of the property. . . . In recent years, courts have wrestled with the application of this old tort in cases involving unwanted electronic contact with computer systems, and some have held that even the transmission of electrons that occur when a communication is sent from one computer to another is enough. . . . But may such decisions be followed in applying the Court's trespass theory? Assuming that what matters under the Court's theory is the law of trespass as it existed at the time of the adoption of the Fourth Amendment, do these recent decisions represent a change in the law or simply the application of the old tort law to new situations?

NOTES

(1) After 1967, most courts addressed Fourth Amendment issues with the assumption that the *Katz* privacy approach had essentially supplemented the trespass theory of the *Olmstead* decision. The occurrence of a trespass remained relevant in determining whether there was an encroachment on privacy. Just as *Katz* would have led to the opposite result in *Olmstead*, the constitutional protection was broadened on occasion. At the same time, if trespass was no longer a dispositive factor, convincing a court might become more difficult. Thus, for example, a seizure from a so-called open field might be permitted, even though the property belonged to the defendant. *See* § 3.04[C],*infra.* And if officials removed evidence from the defendant's garbage can, whether he harbored a reasonable expectation of privacy might be a close question. *See* § 3.04[F], *infra.*

(2) The return of *Olmstead* to prominence would appear largely engineered by the efforts of Justice Scalia who, one suspects, would prefer to do away with the *Katz* and privacy protection under the Fourth Amendment. Short of that, he cobbles a solution, tolerable to a majority of the Court, which retains viability for both theories.

§ 3.02 OBTAINING SEARCH WARRANTS

[A] The Requisite Particularity

The language of the Fourth Amendment has lent itself to a flexible standard of constitutional reasonableness. In one respect, however, the mandate is quite precise: If authorization for the official action is to be in the form of a warrant, the warrant must particularly describe "the place to be searched, and the persons or things to be seized."[1] The particularity requirement was prompted by a fear of "general warrants" which gave the bearer an unlimited authority to search and seize.[2]

The Place to Be Searched

In *Steele v. United States,*[3] the earliest Supreme Court decision concerning the sufficiency of the description of the place to be searched, Chief Justice Taft held that it was "enough if the description is such that the officer with a search warrant can with a reasonable effort ascertain and identify the place intended."[4] Normally, this specification will be included in the warrant itself, but it may be provided in the supporting affidavit. An error in the number of the address will not render the warrant void if from the totality of the description there is no ambiguity regarding the identity of the premises. Nor is it essential that the owner or occupant of the premises be identified.

When a warrant is sought to search a multi-dwelling or multi-office building, unless there is probable cause to search the entire premises,[5] the particular premises must be identified. This requirement may, however, be excused. In *Maryland v. Garrison,*[6] officers had obtained a warrant to search a third floor apartment, unaware of the fact that the floor was divided into two apartments. Only after the evidence had been seized was the error discovered. Included in the seizure was contraband belonging to the respondent, in respect to whom the officers had no probable cause. While acknowledging that "if the officers had known or even if they should have known, that there were two separate dwelling units on the third floor . . . , they would have been obligated to exclude respondent's

---

[1] U.S. Const. amend. IV.

[2] *See* Boyd v. United States, 116 U.S. 616 (1886); Olmstead v. United States, 361 U.S. 98 (1959). *See generally* Barrett, *Personal Rights, Property Rights and the Fourth Amendment*, 1960 Sup. Ct. Rev. 46.

[3] 267 U.S. 498.

[4] *Id.* at 503.

[5] *See, e.g.*, People v. Coulson, 273 Cal. App. 2d 148, 78 Cal. Rptr. 95 (1969).

[6] 480 U.S. 79.

apartment from the scope of the requested warrant," *id.* at 85, the Court concluded that the case was analogous to *Hill v. California* (*see* § 2.03[B], *supra*). Because "the officers' failure to realize the overbreadth of the warrant was objectively understandable and reasonable," the evidence was lawfully seized.

A warrant to search a person must likewise adequately identify the individual. Such a warrant will authorize the search of containers carried by the person described,[7] but will not authorize bodily intrusions.[8] Lower courts have traditionally taken the view that a warrant to search designated premises does not authorize the search of individuals found on the premises.[9] If, however, there is an effort on the part of someone present to frustrate the search a personal search may be reasonable.[10]

Alternatively, an officer may obtain a warrant that by its terms authorizes the search of all persons found on designated premises. In such a case, the dispositive question becomes whether probable cause exists to believe that all those on the premises will be in possession of seizable evidence.[11]

In many cases, warrants fail because of inept drafting, and as a result, the premises described are not those, or are in excess of those, for which probable cause has been established. Nevertheless, in executing the warrant, officers may have searched only those places for which they had probable cause. Some courts take the view that a warrant which inaccurately describes the premises is void, and therefore any evidence seized under it is inadmissible. In such cases, an accused, eligible for a legal search, is the incidental beneficiary of the enforcement of a constitutional standard designed to prevent the use of general warrants to the detriment of innocent parties.[12] More often, however, courts have concluded that evidence seized within the lawful parameters of the warrant is admissible even though other evidence, improperly seized, is not.[13]

Items to Be Seized

The constitutional standard for the specification of items to be seized was stated in *Marron v. United States*:[14]

> The requirement that warrants shall particularly describe the things to be seized makes general searches under them impossible and prevents the seizure of one thing under a warrant describing another. As to what is to be taken, nothing is left to the discretion of the officer executing the warrant.

---

[7] United States v. Graham, 638 F.2d 111 (7th Cir.), *cert. denied*, 450 U.S. 1034 (1981).

[8] People v. Bracamonte, 15 Cal. 3d 394, 124 Cal. Rptr. 528, 540 P.2d 624 (1975).

[9] *See Ybarra v. Illinois, infra*, which provides some support for this conclusion.

[10] *See, e.g.*, State v. Sais, 106 Ariz. 352, 476 P.2d 515 (1970).

[11] *See, e.g.*, Commonwealth v. Smith, 348 N.E.2d 101 (Mass.), *cert. denied*, 429 U.S. 944 (1976).

[12] *See, e.g.*, United States v. Hinton, 219 F.2d 324 (7th Cir. 1955).

[13] *See, e.g.*, People v. Hansen, 38 N.Y.2d 17, 377 N.Y.S.2d 461, 339 N.E.2d 873 (1975).

[14] 275 U.S. 192, Treas. Dec. 42528 (1927).

The enumeration of the items to be seized should be included in the warrant itself. Alternatively, it may appear in the affidavit upon which the warrant is issued, but only if the warrant expressly incorporates the affidavit.[15]

Courts have not demanded a high degree of specificity in the description of the items to be seized. In *Steele v. United States*,[16] for example, the Supreme Court found "cases of whiskey" to be adequate, and in *Andresen v. Maryland*[17] the phrase "other fruits, instruments and evidence of crime at this time unknown" appearing "at the end of a sentence containing a lengthy list of specified and particular items to be seized," was found acceptable. The affidavit must contain allegations of probable cause that each of the enumerated items will be found at the described premises. Even when a warrant contains an impermissibly vague description of items or specifications unsupported by probable cause, it may nevertheless be sustained insofar as the specifically enumerated items are concerned.

Seizing Items Not Specified

Notwithstanding the constitutional requirement that a search warrant specifically enumerate the items to be seized, nonenumerated objects otherwise seizable discovered in the lawful execution of a search warrant may also be seized.[18] Frequently the objects in question are of the same generic quality as those enumerated or related to the criminal endeavor under investigation, but the principle is equally applicable when evidence of wholly unrelated crimes is discovered. Such seizures are viewed as an application of the plain view doctrine.[19]

FEDERAL RULES OF CRIMINAL PROCEDURE

Rule 41. Search and Seizure

(a) **Scope and Definitions.**

(1) **Scope.** This rule does not modify any statute regulating search and seizure, or the issuance and execution of a search warrant in special circumstances.

(2) **Definitions.** The following definitions apply under this rule:

(A) "Property" includes documents, books, paper, any other tangible objects, and information.

(B) "Daytime" means the hours between 6:00 a.m. and 10:00 p.m. according to local time.

(C) "Federal law enforcement officer" means a government agent (other than an attorney for the government) who is engaged in enforcing the criminal

---

[15] *See* Groh v. Ramirez, 540 U.S. 551 (2004).

[16] 267 U.S. 498, 504 (1925).

[17] 427 U.S. 463 (1976).

[18] *See* Adams v. New York, 192 U.S. 585 (1904).

[19] *See* § 3.04[B], *infra*.

laws and is within any category of officers authorized by the Attorney General to request a search warrant.

(b) **Authority to Issue a Warrant.** At the request of a federal law enforcement officer or an attorney for the government:

(1) a magistrate judge with authority in the district — or if none is reasonably available, a judge of a state court of record in the district — has authority to issue a warrant to search and seize a person or property located within the district;

(2) a magistrate judge with authority in the district has authority to issue a warrant for a person or property outside the district if the person or property is located within the district when the warrant is issued but might move or be moved outside the district before the warrant is executed; and

(3) a magistrate judge — in an investigation of domestic terrorism or international terrorism (as defined in 18 U.S.C. § 2331) — having authority in any district in which activities related to the terrorism may have occurred, may issue a warrant for a person or property within or outside that district.

(c) **Persons or Property Subject to Search or Seizure.** A warrant may be issued for any of the following:

(1) evidence of a crime;

(2) contraband, fruits of crime, or other items illegally possessed;

(3) property designed for use, intended for use, or used in committing a crime; or

(4) a person to be arrested or a person who is unlawfully restrained.

(d) **Obtaining a Warrant.**

(1) **Probable Cause.** After receiving an affidavit or other information, a magistrate judge or a judge of a state court of record must issue the warrant if there is probably cause to search for and seize a person or property under rule 41(c).

(2) **Requesting a Warrant in the Presence of a Judge.**

(A) **Warrant on an Affidavit.** When a federal law enforcement officer or an attorney for the government presents an affidavit in support of a warrant, the judge may require the affiant to appear personally and may examine under oath the affiant and witness the affiant produces.

(B) **Warrant on Sworn Testimony.** The judge may wholly or partially dispense with a written affidavit and base a warrant on sworn testimony if doing so is reasonable under the circumstances.

(C) **Recording Testimony.** Testimony taken in support of a warrant must be recorded by a court reporter or by a suitable recording device, and the judge must file the transcript or recording with the clerk, along with the affidavit.

(3) **Requesting a Warrant by Telephonic or Other Means.**

(A) **In General.** A magistrate judge may issue a warrant based on information communicated by telephone or other appropriate means, including facsimile transmission.

(B) **Recording Testimony.** Upon learning that an applicant is requesting a warrant, a magistrate judge must:

(i) place under oath the applicant and any person on whose testimony the application is based; and

(ii) make a verbatim record of the conversation with a suitable recording device, if available, or by a court reporter, or in writing.

(C) **Certifying Testimony.** The magistrate judge must have any recording or court reporter's notes transcribed, certify the transcription's accuracy, and file a copy of the record and the transcription with the clerk. Any written verbatim record must be signed by the magistrate judge and filed with the clerk.

(D) **Suppression Limited.** Absent a finding of bad faith, evidence obtained from a warrant issued under Rule 41(d)(3)(A) is not subject to suppression on the ground that issuing the warrant in that manner was unreasonable under the circumstances.

(e) **Issuing the Warrant.**

(1) **In General.** The magistrate judge or a judge of a state court of record must issue the warrant to an officer authorized to execute it.

(2) **Contents of a Warrant.** The warrant must identify the person or property to be searched, identify any person or property to be seized, and designate the magistrate judge to whom it must be returned. The warrant must command the officer to:

(A) execute the warrant within a specified time no longer than 10 days;

(B) execute the warrant during the daytime, unless the judge for good cause expressly authorizes execution at another time; and

(C) return the warrant to the magistrate judge designated in the warrant.

(3) **Warrant by Telephonic or Other Means.** If a magistrate judge decides to proceed under Rule 41(d)(3)(A), the following additional procedures apply:

(A) **Preparing a Proposed Duplicate Original Warrant.** The applicant must prepare a "proposed duplicate original warrant" and must read or otherwise transmit the contents of that document verbatim to the magistrate judge.

(B) **Preparing an Original Warrant.** The magistrate judge must enter the contents of the proposed duplicate original warrant into an original warrant.

(C) **Modifications.** The magistrate judge may direct the applicant to modify the proposed duplicate original warrant. In that case, the judge may also modify the original warrant.

(D) **Signing the Original Warrant and the Duplicate Original Warrant.**

Upon determining to issue the warrant, the magistrate judge must immediately sign the original warrant, enter on its face the exact time it is issued, and direct the applicant to sign the judge's name on the duplicate original warrant.

(f) **Executing and Returning the Warrant.**

(1) **Noting the Time.** The officer executing the warrant must enter on its face the exact date and time it is executed.

(2) **Inventory.** An officer present during the execution of the warrant must prepare and verify an inventory of any property seized. The officer must do so in the presence of another officer and the person from whom, or from whose premises, the property was taken. If either one is not present, the officer must prepare and verify the inventory in the presence of at least one other credible person.

(3) **Receipt.** The officer executing the warrant must:

(A) give a copy of the warrant and a receipt for the property taken to the person from whom, or from whose premises, the property was taken; or

(B) leave a copy of the warrant and receipt at the place where the officer took the property.

(4) **Return.** The officer executing the warrant must promptly return it — together with a copy of the inventory — to the magistrate judge designated on the warrant. The judge must, on request, give a copy of the inventory to the person from whom, or from whose premises, the property was taken and to the applicant of the warrant.

(g) **Motion to Return Property.** A person aggrieved by an unlawful search and seizure of property or by the deprivation of property may move for the property's return. The motion must be filed in the district where the property was seized. The court must receive evidence of any factual issue necessary to decide the motion. If it grants the motion, the court must return the property to the movant, but may impose reasonable conditions to protect access to the property and its use in later proceedings.

(h) **Motion to Suppress.** A defendant may move to suppress evidence in the court where the trial will occur, as Rule 12 provides.

(i) **Forwarding Papers to the Clerk.** The magistrate judge to whom the warrant is returned must attach to the warrant a copy of the return, of the inventory, and of all other related papers and must deliver them to the clerk in the district where the property was seized.

SEARCH WARRANT PROCEDURE

FORM 3-1 (Chicago Police Departmental Order—Search Warrant)

DEPARTMENT SPECIAL ORDER	DATE OF ISSUE	EFFECTIVE DATE	NO.
	5 December 1975	5 December 1975	75-46

SUBJECT	DISTRIBUTION	AMENDS
SEARCH WARRANTS	8	

RELATED DIRECTIVES	RESCINDS
Chapter 38, Sec. 108 IRS General Order 73-10 Department Special Order 74-6	Department Special Order 75-41

I. PURPOSE

This order:

A. outlines procedures for preparing complaints for Search Warrants.

B. outlines procedures for obtaining, executing and returning Search Warrants.

C. prescribes a review of Complaints for Search Warrants (CCMC-1-219 New) by unit or watch commanders before they are brought to the State's Attorney.

II. OBTAINING SEARCH WARRANTS

A. A member of the Department seeking to obtain a Search Warrant will:

1. prepare four copies of the Complaint for Search Warrant and five copies of the Search Warrant.

2. ensure that both the Complaint for Search Warrant and the Search Warrant accurately and specifically describe the person and/or premises to be searched, and the instruments and/or articles to be seized.

3. ensure that the unit/watch commander has entered his initials and star number on the reverse side of the complaint and warrant to acknowledge that his review has been made.

4. have the Complaint for Search Warrant and the Search Warrant examined by an assistant state's attorney:

a. at any one of the Area Headquarters or,

b. if one is not available, then at the Office of the State's Attorney located at 2600 South California Avenue or 1121 South State Street, Room 702, between the hours of 0900 and 1700 on regular court days.

5. ensure that the assistant state's attorney who examines the complaint:

a. affixes his signature to both the Complaint for Search Warrant and to the Search Warrant, and

b. enters the Search Warrant number on both the Complaint for Search Warrant and the Search Warrant. The signature and warrant number must appear on the original copy of the Search Warrant and Complaint for Search Warrant.

6. present the Complaint for Search Warrant and the Search Warrant to a judge for his signature.

7. enter the name of the approving judge and state's attorney on all duplicate file copies.

B. The Watch Commander will:

1. study both the Complaint for Search Warrant and the Search Warrant in light of the statutory and constitutional requirements.

2. determine:

a. that the contents of the complaint are reliable and credible. (IF BASED UPON INFORMATION OF AN INFORMER AND NOT UPON INFORMATION OF A NAMED CITIZEN, A REVIEW WILL BE MADE OF DOCUMENTARY EVIDENCE WHICH MUST EITHER SUBSTANTIATE THE ACCURACY OF AN ASSERTION OF PRIOR USE OF THE PARTICULAR INFORMER OR CLEARLY INDICATE THAT AN INVESTIGATION UNDERTAKEN AS A RESULT OF THE INFORMATION VALIDATES PROBABLE CAUSE.)

b. that all facts alleged in the complaint were properly obtained.

c. that the investigation leading up to the request for the Search Warrant is thorough. (If additional investigation appears necessary, he will return the complaint to the member and direct that appropriate action be taken.)

d. that the information concerning the place and/or persons to be searched is specifically and accurately described in both the Complaint for Search Warrant and the Search Warrant.

e. that the things to be seized are described with particularity.

f. that the technical aspects of both the Complaint for Search Warrant and Search Warrant are correct, e.g., dates, times, spelling of names, etc.

g. that probable cause for the issuance of the Search Warrant is presented in the Complaint for Search Warrant. (Reasonable grounds for suspicion, supported by circumstances sufficiently strong in themselves to warrant a cautious man to believe that a crime has been committed and the matter sought to be seized is located at the place or on the person named constitutes Probable Cause. People v. Fiorito, 19 Ill. 2d. 246 (1960).)

3. interview the officer requesting the Search Warrant, if necessary, for clarification or verification.

4. indicate his approval of both the Complaint for Search Warrant and the Search Warrant by placing his initials, time and date on each document.

III. EXECUTION OF SEARCH WARRANTS

A. Upon obtaining a Search Warrant, the officers assigned to execute the warrant will:

1. enter the Search Warrant number on all copies.

2. immediately prior to execution, notify the district station in which the warrant is to be executed, and the Communication Operations Section of the impending execution.

3. prior to entering any building, part of a building, or vehicle to execute the warrant, verify that the premises are in fact those described in the warrant.

4. during execution of the warrant, be ever mindful of the rights of those involved, use the minimum amount of force necessary, and make every effort to leave the premises in the same order in which they were found.

B. Upon completion of the execution of the Search Warrant, the watch commander of the executing unit will notify Operations Command, PAX 301, of the:

1. location.

2. nature of the raid.

3. nature of the property seized, if any.

4. number of persons arrested, if any.

IV. RETURNING SEARCH WARRANTS

A. When a Search Warrant is executed, the original Search Warrant and Complaint for Search Warrant will be attached to the court complaint and listed below the arrestee's name and charges on the next unshaded line of the Court Complaint Transmittal Listing (CPD-11.551). If property is seized and no arrest consummated, the executed Search Warrant, complaint and the court copy (pink) of the property inventory, will be returned to the proper court using the Court Complaint Transmittal Listing. The returned warrant will be identified on the transmittal listing by entering the address of execution and the State's Attorney's Search Warrant number (*i.e.*, 2500 East Madison Street, Search Warrant number). A copy of both the Search Warrant and Complaint for Search Warrant should be kept by the investigating officer.

B. When the warrant is executed, the duplicate copy of the warrant will be left with any person from whom any instruments, articles or things are seized; or if no person is available, the copy shall be left at the place from which the instruments, articles or things were seized.

C. When property has been seized, the seizing officer will at the first scheduled court appearance seek a court order to:

1. return the seized property to its legal owner; or

2. have the seized property impounded by the court and turned over to the court clerk for safekeeping until disposed of by the court having jurisdiction; or

3. authorize the seized property to be retained by the Department for the purposes of investigation or scientific analysis; or

4. dispose of the seized property.

D. When a Search Warrant is executed the officer who obtained the warrant will submit either a case report or supplementary report if a case report has already been submitted regardless of whether or not the executed Search Warrant resulted in the seizure of any property, contraband, etc. The report will state that a Search Warrant was obtained and executed. Facts, evidence, or testimony used to obtain the Search Warrant and stated in the Complaint for Search Warrant will not be reiterated in the report.

E. When a Search Warrant is not executed within 96 hours after the time of issuance, the Search Warrant will be endorsed by the returning officer and listed on the Court Complaint Transmittal Listing and returned to the Clerk of the Court of origin within twenty days. The Search Warrant will be identified by entering both the State's Attorney's Search Warrant number and the address of the location for which the Search Warrant was issued in the space provided for the defendant's name on the Court Complaint Transmittal Listing.

V. UNIT SEARCH WARRANT FILE

A. Upon execution or return of a Search Warrant the officer will:

1. enter the R.D. number and, if appropriate, the Raid number, if executed.
2. forward a copy of both the Complaint for Search Warrant and the Search Warrant to his unit commander. After reviewing the documents the unit commander will forward them to the watch commander. A file of a copy of both the Complaint for Search Warrant and the Search Warrant will be maintained in the watch commander's office of the unit to which the member who obtained the Search Warrant is assigned. This file will be referred to by the watch commander when reviewing and approving subsequent requests for Search Warrants.
3. forward a copy of both the Complaint for Search Warrant and the Search Warrant to:
    a. the Narcotics Unit, VCD, if the matter relates to narcotics,
    b. the Gambling Unit, VCD, if the matter relates to gambling, or
    c. the appropriate Section of the Criminal Investigation Division when the matter relates to some other crime.

B. Retention of the above copies will be for one year.

Authenticated by: J.Z.
Indicates new or changed item.
James M. Rochford
Superintendent of Police

SEARCH WARRANT

MORGAN M. FINLEY
Clerk of Court

CMCC 1-220

STATE OF ILLINOIS } ss.
COUNTY OF COOK }

THE CIRCUIT COURT OF COOK COUNTY

The People of the State of Illinois to all peace officers of the state

SEARCH WARRANT

On this day ______________________________ Complainant has subscribed and sworn to a complaint for search warrant before me. Upon examination of the complaint, I find that it states facts sufficient to show probable cause.

I therefore command that you search ______________________________
(PERSON)

and ______________________________
(PREMISES) (CITY AND STATE)

and seize ______________________________
INSTRUMENTS ARTICLES AND THINGS

____

which have been used in the commission of or which constitutes evidence of the offense of ______________________________

I further command that a return of anything so seized shall be made without necessary delay before me or before Judge ______________ ______________ or before any court of competent jurisdiction.

____
Judge

Time and date of issuance ______________________________

CMCC 1-220

Returned Not Executed

I did not execute this warrant within 96 hours from the time of issuance and is hereby returned to the court as void and not executed.

____
Officer

Date

COMPLAINT FOR SEARCH WARRANT

CCMC-1-219 REV
MORGAN M. FINLEY, CLERK OF THE CIRCUIT COURT OF COOK COUNTY

__________ __________
(Court Branch) (Court Date)

STATE OF ILLINOIS)
COUNTY OF COOK) ss. THE CIRCUIT COURT OF COOK COUNTY

COMPLAINT FOR SEARCH WARRANT

______________________________ complainant now appears before the undersigned judge of the Circuit Court of Cook County and requests the issuance of a search warrant to search (the person of ____________
____ and
____
(Premises, City and State)

and seize the following instruments, articles and things: ____________________

which have been used in the commission of, or which constitute evidence of the offense of ______________________________

Complainant says that he has probable cause to believe, based upon the following facts, that the above listed things to be seized are now located upon the (person and) premises set forth above:

____
Complainant

Subscribed and sworn to before me on ____________________ 19___

____
Judge

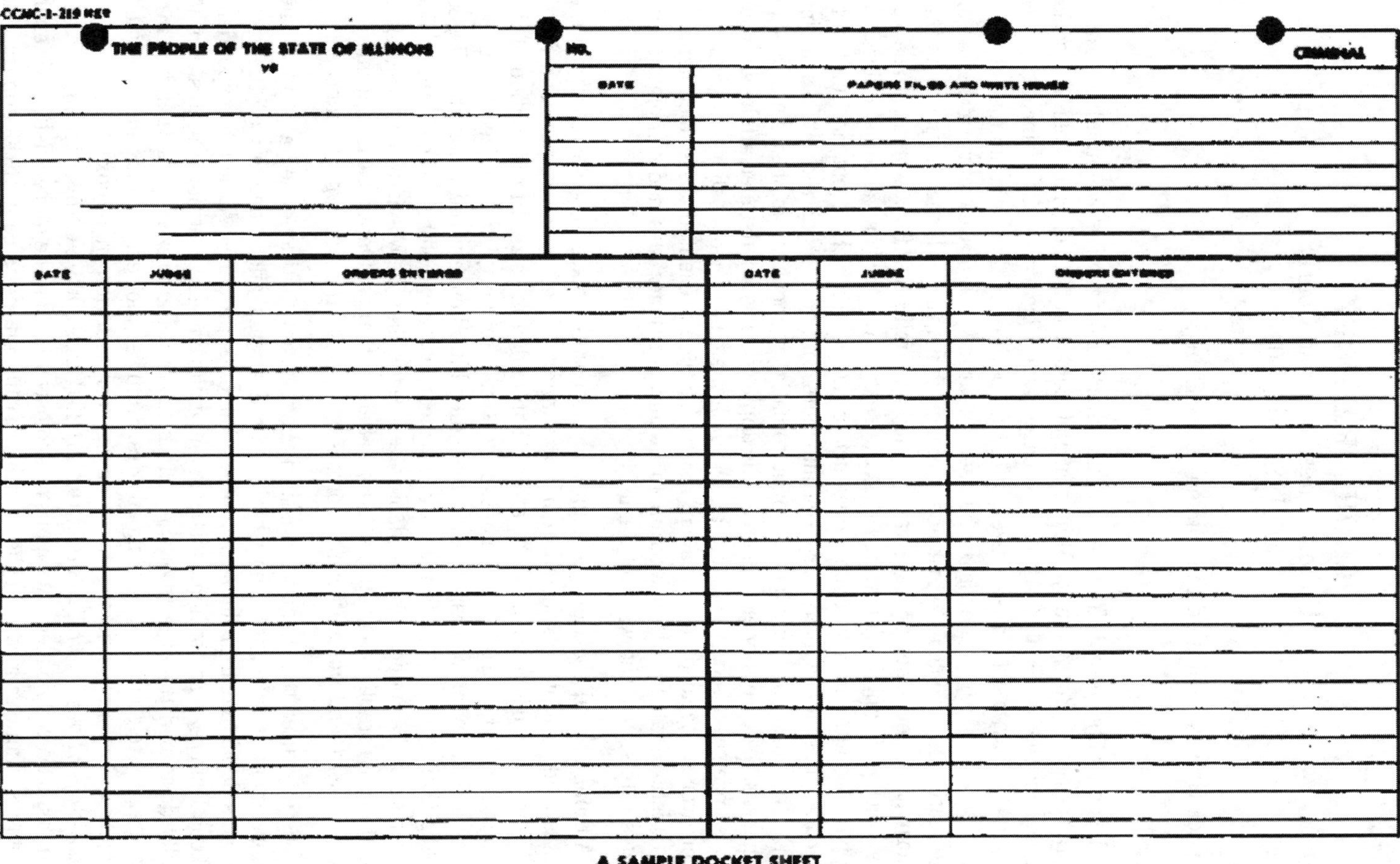

CCMC-1-219 REV

THE PEOPLE OF THE STATE OF ILLINOIS
vs

NR.

CRIMINAL

DATE	PAPERS FILED AND WRITS ISSUED

DATE	JUDGE	ORDERS ENTERED	DATE	JUDGE	ORDERS ENTERED

A SAMPLE DOCKET SHEET

[B] Method of Execution

GROH v. RAMIREZ
United States Supreme Court
540 U.S. 551 (2004)

JUSTICE STEVENS delivered the opinion of the Court.

. . .

Respondents, Joseph Ramirez and members of his family, live on a large ranch in Butte-Silver Bow County, Montana. Petitioner, Jeff Groh, has been a Special Agent for the Bureau of Alcohol, Tobacco and Firearms (ATF) since 1989. In February 1997, a concerned citizen informed petitioner that on a number of visits to respondents' ranch the visitor had seen a large stock of weaponry, including an automatic rifle, grenades, a grenade launcher, and a rocket launcher. Based on that information, petitioner prepared and signed an application for a warrant to search the ranch. The application stated that the search was for "any automatic firearms or parts to automatic weapons, destructive devices to include but not limited to grenades, grenade launchers, rocket launchers, and any and all receipts pertaining to the purchase or manufacture of automatic weapons or explosive devices or launchers." . . . Petitioner supported the application with a detailed affidavit, which he also prepared and executed, that set forth the basis for his belief that the listed items were concealed on the ranch. Petitioner then presented these documents to a Magistrate, along with a warrant form that petitioner also had completed. The Magistrate signed the warrant form.

Although the application particularly described the place to be searched and the contraband petitioner expected to find, the warrant itself was less specific; it failed to identify any of the items that petitioner intended to seize. In the portion of the form that called for a description of the "person or property" to be seized, petitioner typed a description of respondents' two-story blue house rather than the alleged stockpile of firearms. The warrant did not incorporate by reference the itemized list contained in the application. It did, however, recite that the Magistrate was satisfied the affidavit established probable cause to believe that contraband was concealed on the premises, and that sufficient grounds existed for the warrant's issuance.

The day after the Magistrate issued the warrant, petitioner led a team of law enforcement officers, including both federal agents and members of the local sheriff's department, in the search of respondents' premises. Although respondent Joseph Ramirez was not home, his wife and children were. Petitioner states that he orally described the objects of the search to Mrs. Ramirez in person and to Mr. Ramirez by telephone. According to Mrs. Ramirez, however, petitioner explained only that he was searching for " 'an explosive device in a box.' " *Ramirez v. Butte-Silver Bow County*, 298 F.3d 1022, 1026 (C.A.9 2002). At any rate, the officers' search uncovered no illegal weapons or explosives. When the officers left, petitioner gave Mrs. Ramirez a copy of the search warrant, but not a copy of the application, which had been sealed. The following day, in response to a request from respondents' attorney, petitioner faxed the attorney a copy of the page of the application that listed the items to be seized. No charges were filed against the Ramirezes.

Respondents sued petitioner and the other officers under *Bivens v. Six Unknown Fed. Narcotics Agents*, 403 U.S. 388, and Rev. Stat. § 1979, 42 U.S.C. § 1983, raising eight claims, including violation of the Fourth Amendment. . . . The District Court entered summary judgment for all defendants. The court found no Fourth Amendment violation, because it considered the case comparable to one in which the warrant contained an inaccurate address, and in such a case, the court reasoned, the warrant is sufficiently detailed if the executing officers can locate the correct house. . . . The court added that even if a constitutional violation occurred, the defendants were entitled to qualified immunity because the failure of the warrant to describe the objects of the search amounted to a mere "typographical error." . . .

The Court of Appeals affirmed the judgment with respect to all defendants and all claims, with the exception of respondents' Fourth Amendment claim against petitioner. . . . On that claim, the court held that the warrant was invalid because it did not "describe with particularly the place to be searched and the items to be seized," and that oral statements by petitioner during or after the search could not cure the omission. . . . The court observed that the warrant's facial defect "increased the likelihood and degree of confrontation between the Ramirezes and the police" and deprived respondents of the means "to challenge officers who might have exceeded the limits imposed by the magistrate." . . . The court also expressed concern that "permitting officers to expand the scope of the warrant by oral statements would broaden the area of dispute between the parties in subsequent litigation." . . .

II

The warrant was plainly invalid. The Fourth Amendment states unambiguously that "no Warrants shall issue, but upon probable cause, supported by Oath or affirmation, and *particularly describing* the place to be searched, and *the persons or things to be seized.*" (Emphasis added.) The warrant in this case complied with the first three of these requirements: It was based on probable cause and supported by a sworn affidavit, and it described particularly the place of the search. On the fourth requirement, however, the warrant failed altogether. Indeed, petitioner concedes that "the warrant . . . was deficient in particularity because it provided no description of the type of evidence sought." . . .

The fact that the *application* adequately described the "things to be seized" does not save the *warrant* from its facial invalidity. The Fourth Amendment by its terms requires particularity in the warrant, not in the supporting documents. . . . We do not say that the Fourth Amendment prohibits a warrant from cross-referencing other documents. Indeed, most Courts of Appeals have held that a court may construe a warrant with reference to a supporting application or affidavit if the warrant uses appropriate words of incorporation, and if the supporting document accompanies the warrant. . . . But in this case the warrant did not incorporate other documents by reference, nor did either the affidavit or the application (which had been placed under seal) accompany the warrant. Hence, we need not further explore the matter of incorporation.

. . .

Petitioner asks us to hold that a search conducted pursuant to a warrant lacking particularity should be exempt from the presumption of unreasonableness if the goals served by the particularity requirement are otherwise satisfied. He maintains that the search in this case satisfied those goals — which he says are "to prevent general searches, to prevent the seizure of one thing under a warrant describing another, and to prevent warrants from being issued on vague or dubious information," Brief for Petitioner 16 — because the scope of the search did not exceed the limits set forth in the application. But unless the particular items described in the affidavit are also set forth in the warrant itself (or at least incorporated by reference, and the affidavit present at the search), there can be no written assurance that the Magistrate actually found probable cause to search for, and to seize, every item mentioned in the affidavit. . . .

We have long held, moreover, that the purpose of the particularity requirement is not limited to the prevention of general searches. See *Garrison*, 480 U.S., at 84. A particular warrant also "assures the individual whose property is searched or seized of the lawful authority of the executing officer, his need to search, and the limits of his power to search." . . .

. . .

It is incumbent on the officer executing a search warrant to ensure the search is lawfully authorized and lawfully conducted. Because petitioner did not have in his possession a warrant particularly describing the things he intended to seize, proceeding with the search was clearly "unreasonable" under the Fourth Amendment. . . .

. . .

YBARRA v. ILLINOIS

United States Supreme Court
444 U.S. 85 (1979)

MR. JUSTICE STEWART delivered the opinion of the Court.

An Illinois statute authorizes law enforcement officers to detain and search any person found on premises being searched pursuant to a search warrant, to protect themselves from attack or to prevent the disposal or concealment of anything described in the warrant. The question before us is whether the application of this statute to the facts of the present case violated the Fourth and Fourteenth Amendments.

I

On March 1, 1976, a special agent of the Illinois Bureau of Investigation presented a "Complaint for Search Warrant" to a judge of an Illinois Circuit Court. The Complaint recited that the Agent had spoken with an informant known to the police to be reliable and:

. . .

> "3. The informant related . . . that over the weekend of 28 and 29 February he was in the Aurora Tap Tavern, located in the city of Aurora, Ill., and observed fifteen to twenty-five tin-foil packets on the person of the bartender 'Greg' and behind the bar. He also has been in the tavern on at least ten other occasions and has observed tin-foil packets on 'Greg' and in a drawer behind the bar. The informant has used heroin in the past and knows that tin-foil packets are a common method of packaging heroin.
>
> "4. The informant advised that over the weekend of 28 and 29 February he had a conversation with 'Greg' and was advised that 'Greg' would have heroin for sale on Monday, March 1, 1976. This conversation took place in the tavern described."

On the strength of this Complaint, the judge issued a warrant authorizing the search of "the following person or place: . . . [t]he Aurora Tap Tavern. . . . Also the person of 'Greg,' the bartender, a male white with blondish hair appx. 25 years." The warrant authorized the police to search for: "evidence of the offense of possession of a controlled substance," to wit, "[h]eroin, contraband, other controlled substances, money, instrumentalities and narcotics, paraphernalia used in the manufacture, processing and distribution of controlled substances."

In the late afternoon of that day, seven or eight officers proceeded to the tavern. Upon entering it, the officers announced their purpose and advised all those present that they were going to conduct a "cursory search for weapons." One of the officers then proceeded to pat down each of the 9 to 13 customers present in the tavern, while the remaining officers engaged in an extensive search of the premises.

The police officer who frisked the patrons found the appellant, Ventura Ybarra, in front of the bar standing by a pinball machine. In his first pat-down of Ybarra, the officer felt what he described as "a cigarette pack with objects in it." He did not remove this pack from Ybarra's pocket. Instead, he moved on and proceeded to pat down other customers. After completing this process the officer returned to Ybarra and frisked him once again. This second search of Ybarra took place approximately 2 to 10 minutes after the first. The officer relocated and retrieved the cigarette pack from Ybarra's pants pocket. Inside the pack he found six tinfoil packets containing a brown powdery substance which later turned out to be heroin.

II

There is no reason to suppose that, when the search warrant was issued on March 1, 1976, the authorities had probable cause to believe that any person found on the premises of the Aurora Tap Tavern, aside from "Greg," would be violating the law. The search warrant complaint did not allege that the bar was frequented by persons illegally purchasing drugs. It did not state that the informant had ever seen a patron of the tavern purchase drugs from "Greg" or from any other person. Nowhere, in fact, did the complaint even mention the patrons of the Aurora Tap Tavern.

Not only was probable cause to search Ybarra absent at the time the warrant was issued; it was still absent when the police executed the warrant. Upon entering the tavern, the police did not recognize Ybarra and had no reason to believe that he had committed, was committing or was about to commit, any offense under state or federal law. Ybarra made no gestures indicative of criminal conduct, made no movements that might suggest an attempt to conceal contraband, and said nothing of a suspicious nature to the police officers. In short, the agents knew nothing in particular about Ybarra, except that he was present, along with several other customers, in a public tavern at a time when the police had reason to believe that the bartender would have heroin for sale.

It is true that the police possessed a warrant based on probable cause to search the tavern in which Ybarra happened to be at the time the warrant was executed. But, a person's mere propinquity to others independently suspected of criminal activity does not, without more, give rise to probable cause to search that person. *Sibron v. New York*. . . . Where the standard is probable cause, a search or seizure of a person must be supported by probable cause particularized with respect to that person. This requirement cannot be undercut or avoided by simply pointing to the fact that coincidentally there exists probable cause to search or seize another or to search the premises where the person may happen to be. The Fourth and Fourteenth Amendments protect the "legitimate expectations of privacy" of persons, not places. See *Rakas v. Illinois*, . . . *Katz v. United States.*

Each patron who walked into the Aurora Tap Tavern on March 1, 1976, was clothed with constitutional protection against an unreasonable search or an unreasonable seizure. That individualized protection was separate and distinct from the Fourth and Fourteenth Amendment protection possessed by the proprietor of the tavern or by "Greg." Although the search warrant, issued upon probable cause, gave the officers authority to search the premises and to search "Greg," it gave them no authority whatever to invade the constitutional protections possessed individually by the tavern's customers.[20]

Notwithstanding the absence of probable cause to search Ybarra, the State argues that the action of the police in searching him and seizing what was found in his pocket was nonetheless constitutionally permissible. We are asked to find that the first pat down search of Ybarra constituted a reasonable frisk for weapons under the doctrine of *Terry v. Ohio*. . . . If this finding is made, it is then possible to conclude, the State argues, that the second search of Ybarra was constitutionally justified. The argument is that the pat down yielded probable cause to believe that Ybarra was carrying narcotics, and that this probable cause constitutionally supported the second search, no warrant being required in light of the exigencies of

---

[20] The Fourth Amendment directs that "no Warrants shall issue, but upon probable cause . . . and particularly describing the place to be searched, and the persons or things to be seized." Thus, "open-ended" or "general" warrants are constitutionally prohibited. See Lo-Ji Sales, Inc. New York, 442 U.S. 319; Marshall v. Barlow's Inc., 436 U.S. 307, 311; United States v. Chadwick, 433 U.S. 1, 7–8; Stanford v. Texas, 379 U.S. 476, 480–482. It follows that a warrant to search a place cannot normally be construed to authorize a search of each individual in that place. The warrant for the Aurora Tap Tavern provided no basis for departing from this general rule. Consequently, we need not consider situations where the warrant itself authorizes the search of unnamed persons in a place and is supported by probable cause to believe that persons who will be in the place at the time of the search will be in possession of illegal drugs.

the situation coupled with the ease with which Ybarra could have disposed of the illegal substance.

We are unable to take even the first step required by this argument. The initial frisk of Ybarra was simply not supported by a reasonable belief that he was armed and presently dangerous, a belief which this Court has invariably held must form the predicate to a pat down of a person for weapons. *Adams v. Williams*, . . . *Terry v. Ohio*. . . . When the police entered the Aurora Tap Tavern on March 1, 1976, the lighting was sufficient for them to observe the customers. Upon seeing Ybarra, they neither recognized him as a person with a criminal history nor had any particular reason to believe that he might be inclined to assault them. Moreover, as police agent Johnson later testified, Ybarra, whose hands were empty, gave no indication of possessing a weapon, made no gestures or other actions indicative of an intent to commit an assault, and acted generally in a manner that was not threatening. At the suppression hearing, the most agent Johnson could point to was that Ybarra was wearing a 3/4-length lumber jacket, clothing which the State admits could be expected on almost any tavern patron in Illinois in early March. In short, the State is unable to articulate any specific fact that would have justified a police officer at the scene in even suspecting that Ybarra was armed and dangerous.

What has been said largely disposes of the State's second and alternative argument in this case. Emphasizing the important governmental interest "in effectively controlling traffic in dangerous, hard drugs" and the ease with which the evidence of narcotics possession may be concealed or moved around from person to person, the State contends that the *Terry* "reasonable belief or suspicion" standard should be made applicable to aid the evidence-gathering function of the search warrant. More precisely, we are asked to construe the Fourth and Fourteenth Amendments to permit evidence searches of persons who, at the commencement of the search, are on "compact" premises subject to a search warrant, at least where the police have a "reasonable belief" that such persons "are connected with" drug trafficking and "may be concealing or carrying away the contraband."

Over 30 years ago, the Court rejected a similar argument in *United States v. Di Re*, 332 U.S. 581, 583–587. . . . In that case, a federal investigator had been told by an informant that a transaction in counterfeit gasoline ration coupons was going to occur at a particular place. The investigator went to that location at the appointed time and saw the car of one of the suspected parties to the illegal transaction. The investigator went over to the car and observed a man in the driver's seat, another man (Di Re) in the passenger's seat, and the informant in the back. The informant told the investigator that the person in the driver's seat had given him counterfeit coupons. Thereupon, all three men were arrested and searched. Among the arguments unsuccessfully advanced by the Government to support the constitutionality of the search of Di Re was the contention that the investigator could lawfully have searched the car, since he had reasonable cause to believe that it contained contraband, and correspondingly could have searched any occupant of the car because the contraband sought was of the sort "which could easily be concealed on the person." Not deciding whether or not under the Fourth Amendment the car could have been searched, the Court held that it was "not convinced that a person, by mere presence in a suspected car, loses immunities from search of his person to which he would otherwise be entitled."

The *Di Re* case does not, of course, completely control the case at hand. There the Government investigator was proceeding without a search warrant, and here the police possessed a warrant authorizing the search of the Aurora Tap Tavern. Moreover, in *Di Re* the Government conceded that its officers could not search all the persons in a house being searched pursuant to a search warrant. The State makes no such concession in this case. Yet the governing principle in both cases is basically the same, and we follow that principle today. The "long prevailing" constitutional standard of probable cause embodies " 'the best compromise that has been found for accommodating [the] often opposing interests' in 'safeguard[ing] citizens from rash and unreasonable interferences with privacy' and in 'seek[ing] to give fair leeway for enforcing the law in the community's protection.' "

For these reasons, we conclude that the searches of Ybarra and the seizure of what was in his pocket contravened the Fourth and Fourteenth Amendments. Accordingly, the judgment is reversed and the case is remanded to the Appellate Court of Illinois, Second District, for further proceedings not inconsistent with this opinion.

It is so ordered.

MR. CHIEF JUSTICE BURGER, with whom MR. JUSTICE BLACKMUN and MR. JUSTICE REHNQUIST join, dissenting.

I join MR. JUSTICE REHNQUIST's dissent since I cannot subscribe to the Court's unjustifiable narrowing of the rule of *Terry v. Ohio*. . . . The Court would require a particularized and individualized suspicion that a person is armed and dangerous as a condition to a *Terry* search. This goes beyond the rationale of *Terry* and overlooks the practicalities of a situation which no doubt often confronts officers executing a valid search warrant. The Court's holding is but another manifestation of the practical poverty of the judge-made exclusionary rule. "The suppression of truth is a grievous necessity at best, more especially when as here the inquiry concerns the public interest; it can be justified at all only when the opposed private interest is supreme." *McMann v. SEC*, 87 F.2d 377, 378 (CA2 1937) (L. Hand, J.). Here, the Court's holding operates as but a further hindrance on the already difficult effort to police the narcotics traffic which takes such a terrible toll on human beings.

These officers had validly obtained a warrant to search a named person and a rather small, one-room tavern for narcotics. Upon arrival, they found the room occupied by 12 persons. Were they to ignore these individuals and assume that all were unarmed and uninvolved? Given the setting and the reputation of those who trade in narcotics, it does not go too far to suggest that they might pay for such an easy assumption with their lives. The law does not require that those executing a search warrant must be so foolhardy. That is precisely what Mr. Chief Justice Warren's opinion in *Terry* stands for. Indeed, the *Terry* Court recognized that a balance must be struck between the privacy interest of individuals and the safety of police officers in performing their duty. I would hold that when police execute a search warrant for narcotics in a place of known narcotics activity they may protect themselves by conducting a *Terry* search. They are not required to assume that they will not be harmed by patrons of the kind of establishment shown here, something quite different from a ballroom at the Waldorf. "The officer need not be absolutely certain that the individual is armed; the issue is whether a reasonably prudent man in the circumstances would be warranted in the belief that his safety or that of others was in danger." *Terry v. Ohio*. . . .

I do not find it controlling that the heroin was not actually retrieved from appellant until the officer returned after completing the first search. The "cigarette pack with objects in it" was noticed in the first search. In the "second search," the officer did no more than return to the appellant and retrieve the pack he had already discovered. That there was a delay of minutes between the search and the seizure is not dispositive in this context, where the searching officer made the on-the-spot judgment that he need not seize the suspicious package immediately. He could first reasonably make sure that none of the patrons was armed before returning to appellant. Thus I would treat the second search and its fruits just as I would had the officer taken the pack immediately upon noticing it, which plainly would have been permissible.

Under this analysis I need not reach the validity of the Illinois statute under which the Illinois court sustained the search. Parenthetically, I find the Court's failure to pass on the Illinois statute puzzling in light of the Court's holding that the searches were not authorized by *Terry*.

Mr. Justice Rehnquist, with whom the Chief Justice and Mr. Justice Blackmun join, dissenting.

I believe it error to analyze this case as if the police were under an obligation to act within one of the narrow exceptions to the warrant requirement, yet this is precisely what Ybarra would have us do. Whereas in *Terry* the warrant requirement was inapposite, here the warrant requirement has been fully satisfied. In either case we should give full scope to the reasonableness requirement of the first clause of the Fourth Amendment. Thus, in judging the reasonableness of a search pursuant to a warrant, which search extends to persons present on the named premises, this Court should consider the scope of the intrusion as well as its justification.

Viewed sequentially, the actions of the police in this case satisfy the scope/justification test of reasonableness established by the first clause of the Fourth Amendment as interpreted in *Terry*. The police entered the Aurora Tap pursuant to the warrant and found themselves confronting a dozen people, all standing or sitting at the bar, the suspected location of the contraband. Because the police were aware that heroin was being offered for sale in the tavern, it was quite reasonable to assume that any one or more of the persons at the bar could have been involved in drug trafficking. This assumption, by itself, might not have justified a full-scale search of all the individuals in the tavern. Nevertheless, the police also were quite conscious of the possibility that one or more of the patrons could be armed in preparation for just such an intrusion. In the narcotics business, "firearms are as much 'tools of the trade' as are most commonly recognized articles of narcotics paraphernalia." *United States v. Oates*, 560 F.2d 45, 62 (CA2 1977). The potential danger to the police executing the warrant and to innocent individuals in this dimly lit tavern cannot be minimized. By conducting an immediate frisk of those persons at the bar, the police eliminated this danger and "froze" the area in preparation for the search of the premises.

Ybarra contends that *Terry* requires an "individualized" suspicion that a particular person is armed and dangerous. While this factor may be important in the case of an on-the-street stop, where the officer must articulate some reason for singling the person out of the general population, there are at least two reasons why it has less significance in the present situation, where execution of a valid warrant had thrust the police into a confrontation with a small, but potentially dangerous, group of people. First, in place of the requirement of "individualized suspicion" as a guard against arbitrary exercise of authority, we have here the determination of a neutral and detached magistrate that a search was necessary. As this Court noted in *Fisher v. United States*, 425 U.S. 391, 400 (1976), the Framers of the Fourth Amendment "struck a balance so that when the State's reason to believe incriminating evidence will be found becomes sufficiently great, the invasion of privacy becomes justified and a warrant to search and seize will issue." The question then becomes whether, given the initial decision to intrude, the scope of the intrusion is reasonable.

In addition, the task performed by the officers executing a search warrant is inherently more perilous than is a momentary encounter on the street. The danger is greater "not only because the suspect and the officer will be in close proximity for a longer period of time, but also . . . because the officer's investigative responsibilities under the warrant require him to direct his attention to the premises rather than the person." W. LaFave, Search & Seizure § 4.9, at 150–151 (1978). To hold a police officer in such a situation to the same standard of "individualized suspicion" as might be required in the case of an on-the-street stop would defeat the purpose of gauging reasonableness in terms of all the circumstances surrounding an encounter.

Measured against the purpose for the initial search is the scope of that search. I do not doubt that a pat-down for weapons is a substantial intrusion into one's privacy. See *Terry v. Ohio*. . . . Nevertheless, such an intrusion was more than justified, under the circumstances here, by the potential threat to the lives of the searching officers and innocent bystanders. In the rubric of *Terry* itself, a "man of reasonable caution" would have been warranted in the belief that it was appropriate to frisk the 12 or so persons in the vicinity of the bar for weapons. . . . Thus, the initial frisk of Ybarra was legitimate.

During this initial pat-down, Officer Johnson felt something suspicious: a cigarette package with objects in it. The record below is not entirely clear as to the shape or texture of the objects, but it is clear that Officer Johnson had at least a subjective suspicion that the objects were packets of heroin like those described in the warrant. He testified, for example, that after patting down the other persons at the bar, he returned directly to Ybarra to search him "for controlled substances." . . . At this point, he reached into Ybarra's pants pocket, removed the cigarette package, and confirmed his suspicion.

While the test of reasonableness under the Fourth Amendment is necessarily objective as opposed to subjective, see *Terry v. Ohio* . . . , Officer Johnson's subjective suspicions help fill out his cryptic description of the "objects" that he felt in Ybarra's pocket. The objects clearly did not feel like cigarettes. In this case we need not decide whether, as a general rule, an officer conducting an on-the-street frisk under *Terry* can carry his search into the pockets of a suspect to examine material that he suspects to be contraband. We are dealing here with a case where the police had obtained a warrant to search for precisely the item that Officer Johnson suspected was present in Ybarra's pocket. Whether Officer Johnson's level of certainty could be labeled "probable cause," "reasonable suspicion," or some indeterminate, intermediate level of cognition, the limited pursuit of his suspicions by extracting the item from Ybarra's pocket was reasonable. The justification for the intrusion was linked closely to the terms of the search warrant; the intrusion itself was carefully tailored to conform to its justification.

NOTES AND QUESTIONS

(1) In footnote 20, *Ybarra* leaves open the possibility of a warrant authorizing a search of persons found on designated premises, provided probable cause to believe such individuals possess seizable evidence is established. *See, e.g., State v. De Simone*, 288 A.2d 849 (N.J. 1972).

(2) Justice Stewart observes that the complaint did not allege that persons who frequented the bar were purchasers of narcotics. Is not such a conclusion a reasonable inference from the complaint? How critical is this conclusion to the outcome of the case?

(3) Viewed as a stop-and-frisk case, is *Ybarra* consistent with *Terry* and its progeny? Chief Justice Burger maintains that, "[g]iven the setting and the reputation of those who trade in narcotics, it does not go too far to suggest that they might pay for such an easy assumption with their lives." Would the acceptance of this justification substantially broaden the *Terry* power?

(4) If it were concluded that under the circumstances presented a frisk of Ybarra was reasonable, would the seizure of the cigarette pack be constitutional? *Compare Sibron v. New York, supra.*

(5) Consider the validity of the following provisions of the Illinois Code of Criminal Procedure:

> **§ 108-6. Execution of Search Warrants**. The warrant shall be executed within 96 hours from the time of issuance. If the warrant is executed the duplicate copy shall be left with any person from whom any instruments, articles or things are seized or if no person is available the copy shall be left at the place from which the instruments, articles or things were seized. Any warrant not executed within such time shall be void and shall be returned to the court of the judge issuing the same as "not executed."
>
> **§ 108-8.** Use of Force in Execution of Search Warrant. All necessary and reasonable force may be used to effect an entry into any building or property or part thereof to execute a search warrant.
>
> **§ 108-13.** When Warrant may be Executed. The warrant may be executed at any time of any day or night.

§ 108-14. No Warrant Quashed for Technicality. No warrant shall be quashed nor evidence suppressed because of technical irregularities not affecting the substantial rights of the accused.

MARYLAND v. PRINGLE

United States Supreme Court
540 U.S. 366 (2003)

CHIEF JUSTICE REHNQUIST delivered the opinion of the Court.

[Ed. Note: This is not a search warrant case. It is included at this point because of the reliance of the defendant upon *Ybarra.*]

. . .

In this case, Pringle was one of three men riding in a Nissan Maxima at 3:16 a.m. There was $763 of rolled-up cash in the glove compartment directly in front of Pringle. Five plastic glassine baggies of cocaine were behind the back-seat armrest and accessible to all three men. Upon questioning, the three men failed to offer any information with respect to the ownership of the cocaine or the money.

We think it is an entirely reasonable inference from these facts that any or all three of the occupants had knowledge of, and exercised dominion and control over, the cocaine. Thus a reasonable officer could conclude that there was probable cause to believe Pringle committed the crime of possession of cocaine, either solely or jointly.

Pringle's attempt to characterize this as a guilt-by-association case is unavailing. His reliance on *Ybarra v. Illinois*, . . . and *United States v. Di Re*, 332 U.S. 581 . . . (1948), is misplaced. . . .

This case is quite different from *Ybarra.* Pringle and his two companions were in a relatively small automobile, not a public tavern. In *Wyoming v. Houghton*, 526 U.S. 295 . . . (1999), we noted that "a car passenger — unlike the unwitting tavern patron in *Ybarra* — will often be engaged in a common enterprise with the driver, and have the same interest in concealing the fruits of the evidence of their wrongdoing." . . . Here we think it was reasonable for the officer to infer a common enterprise among the three men. The quantity of drugs and cash in the car indicated the likelihood of drug dealing, an enterprise to which a dealer would be unlikely to admit an innocent person with the potential to furnish evidence against him.

In *Di Re*, a federal investigator had been told by an informant, Reed, that he was to receive counterfeit gasoline ration coupons from a certain Buttitta at a particular place. The investigator went to the appointed place and saw Reed, the sole occupant of the rear seat of the car, holding gasoline ration coupons. There were two other occupants in the car: Buttitta in the driver's seat and Di Re in the front passenger's seat. Reed informed the investigator that Buttitta had given him counterfeit coupons. Thereupon, all three men were arrested and searched. After noting that the officers had no information implicating Di Re and no information pointing to Di Re's possession of coupons, unless presence in the car warranted that inference, we concluded that the officer lacked probable cause to believe that Di Re was involved in the crime. . . . We said "[a]ny inference that everyone on the scene of a crime is a party to it must disappear if the Government informer singles out the guilty person." . . . No such singling out occurred in this case; none of the three men provided information with respect to the ownership of the cocaine or money.

We hold that the officer had probable cause to believe that Pringle had committed the crime of possession of a controlled substance. Pringle's arrest therefore did not contravene the Fourth and Fourteenth Amendments.

NOTES

(1) If one of the occupants of the vehicle had acknowledged that the cocaine was his, presumably there would be no probable cause to arrest the other two. But because none of them so confessed, and there was no basis for the officer to choose between them, there was probable cause to arrest them all, or so the Court holds. Is this troubling? Or is the alternative — that no lawful arrest is possible because particularized responsibility cannot be attributed — more so? Of course, Pringle's associates can later raise ignorance or absence of intent as a defense, but this would not render their arrests invalid, nor bar the admission of other evidence revealed at the time of the arrests.

(2) Lower courts have found *Pringle* to be a useful precedent. *See, e.g., United States v. Romero*, 452 F.3d 610, 617–18 (6th Cir. 2006) ("Like the enclosed space of the automobile in which the individuals were arrested in *Pringle*, the relatively small and confined space of the hotel room supports the conclusion that it was reasonable for the officers to infer from the facts known to them at the time of the arrest that [the defendant] was involved in a common illegal-drug enterprise."); *United States v. Cowan*, 674 F.3d 947, 954 (8th Cir. 2012) ("As with the car in *Pringle* and the hotel room in *Romero*, the officers had probable cause to believe Cowan, who was present in the apartment, was engaged in a common drug trafficking enterprise with the apartment's occupants. Cowan was unlike "the unwitting tavern patrons' in *Ybarra*, whose reasons for being at the public tavern during the search probably were not connected to any illegal activity taking place at the tavern.").

(3) The Hawaii supreme court, however, would appear to have rejected the rationale of *Pringle*: "To the extent that the [lower court] relied upon the 'common enterprise' rationale of *Maryland v. Pringle*, . . . to circumvent the requirements of probable cause, we reject such reliance, as 'common enterprise' is not a substitute for the mandate in our jurisdiction that probable cause based on specific 'facts leading sensibly to their conclusions of probability' . . . [that] must be established in each case." *State v. Maganis*, 123 P.3d 679, 684 (Haw. 2005).

[C] Anticipatory Search Warrants

UNITED STATES v. GRUBBS

United States Supreme Court
547 U.S. 90 (2006)

Justice Scalia delivered the opinion of the Court.

Federal law enforcement officers obtained a search warrant for respondent's house on the basis of an affidavit explaining that the warrant would be executed only after a controlled delivery of contraband to that location. We address two challenges to the constitutionality of this anticipatory warrant.

I

Respondent Jeffrey Grubbs purchased a videotape containing child pornography from a Web site operated by an undercover postal inspector. Officers from the Postal Inspection Service arranged a controlled delivery of a package containing the videotape to Grubbs' residence. A postal inspector submitted a search warrant application to a Magistrate Judge for the Eastern District of California, accompanied by an affidavit describing the proposed operation in detail. The affidavit stated:

> "Execution of this search warrant will not occur unless and until the parcel has been received by a person(s) and has been physically taken into the residence . . . At that time, and not before, this search warrant will be executed by me and other United States Postal inspectors, with appropriate assistance from other law enforcement officers in accordance with this warrant's command." . . .

In addition to describing this triggering condition, the affidavit referred to two attachments, which described Grubbs' residence and the items officers would seize. These attachments, but not the body of the affidavit, were incorporated into the requested warrant. The affidavit concluded:

> "Based upon the foregoing facts, I respectfully submit there exists probable cause to believe that the items set forth in Attachment B to this affidavit and the search warrant, will be found [at Grubbs' residence], which residence is further described at Attachment A." . . .

The Magistrate Judge issued the warrant as requested. Two days later, an undercover postal inspector delivered the package. Grubbs' wife signed for it and took the unopened package inside. The inspectors detained Grubbs as he left his home a few minutes later, then entered the house and commenced the search. Roughly 30 minutes into the search, Grubbs was provided with a copy of the warrant, which included both attachments but not the supporting affidavit that explained when the warrant would be executed. Grubbs consented to interrogation by the postal inspectors and admitted ordering the videotape. He was placed under arrest, and various items were seized, including the videotape.

A grand jury for the Eastern District of California indicted Grubbs on one count of receiving a visual depiction of a minor engaged in sexually explicit conduct. . . . He moved to suppress the evidence seized during the search of his residence, arguing as relevant here that the warrant was invalid because it failed to list the triggering condition. After an evidentiary hearing, the District Court denied the motion. Grubbs pleaded guilty, but reserved his right to appeal the denial of his motion to suppress.

The Court of Appeals for the Ninth Circuit reversed. 377 F.3d 1072, amended, 389 F.3d 1306 (9th Cir. 2004). Relying on Circuit precedent, it held that "the particularity requirement of the Fourth Amendment applies with full force to the conditions precedent to an anticipatory search warrant." 377 F.3d, at 1077–1078 (citing *United States v. Hotal*, 143 F.3d 1223, 1226 (9th Cir. 1988)). An anticipatory warrant defective for that reason may be "cur[ed]" if the conditions precedent are set forth in an affidavit that is incorporated in the warrant and "presented to the person whose property is being searched." 377 F.3d, at 1079. Because the postal inspectors "failed to present the affidavit — the only document in which the triggering conditions were listed" — to Grubbs or his wife, the "warrant was . . . inoperative, and the search was illegal." *Ibid.* We granted certiorari. . . .

II

Before turning to the Ninth Circuit's conclusion that the warrant at issue here ran afoul of the Fourth Amendment's particularity requirement, we address the antecedent question whether anticipatory search warrants are categorically unconstitutional. An anticipatory warrant is "a warrant based upon an affidavit showing probable cause that at some future time (but not presently) certain evidence of crime will be located at a specified place." . . . Most anticipatory warrants subject their execution to some condition precedent other than the mere passage of time — a so-called "triggering condition." The affidavit at issue here, for instance, explained that "[e]xecution of th[e] search warrant will not occur unless and until the parcel [containing child pornography] has been received by a person(s) and has been physically taken into the residence." . . . If the government were to execute an anticipatory warrant before the triggering condition occurred, there would be no reason to believe the item described in the warrant could be found at the searched location; by definition, the triggering condition which establishes probable cause has not yet been satisfied when the warrant is issued. Grubbs argues that for this reason anticipatory warrant contravene the Fourth Amendment's provision that "no Warrant shall issue, but upon probable cause."

We reject this view, as has every Court of Appeals to confront the issue, . . . because the probable-cause requirement looks to whether evidence will be found *when the search is conducted*, all warrants are, in a sense, "anticipatory." In the typical case where the police seek permission to search a house for an item they believe is already located there, the magistrate's determination that there is probable cause for the search amounts to a prediction that the item will still be there when the warrant is executed. . . .

Anticipatory warrants are, therefore, no different in principle from ordinary warrants. They require the magistrate to determine (1) that it is *now probable* that (2) contraband, evidence of a crime, or a fugitive *will be* on the described premises

(3) when the warrant is executed. It should be noted, however, that where the anticipatory warrant places a condition (other than the mere passage of time) upon its execution, the first of these determinations goes not merely to what will probably be found *if* the condition is met. (If that were the extent of the probability determination, an anticipatory warrant could be issued for every house in the country, authorizing search and seizure *if* contraband should be delivered — though for any single location there is no likelihood that contraband will be delivered.) Rather, the probability determination for a conditioned anticipatory warrant looks also to the likelihood that the condition will occur, and thus that a proper object of seizure will be on the described premises. In other words, for a conditioned anticipatory warrant to comply with the Fourth Amendment's requirement of probable cause, two prerequisites of probability must be satisfied. It must be true not only that *if* the triggering condition occurs "there is a fair probability that contraband or evidence of a crime will be found in a particular place," . . . but also that there is probable cause to believe that the triggering condition *will occur*. The supporting affidavit must provide the magistrate with sufficient information to evaluate both aspects of the probable-cause determination. . . .

In this case, the occurrence of the triggering condition — successful delivery of the videotape to Grubbs' residence — would plainly establish probable cause for the search. In addition, the affidavit established probable cause to believe the triggering condition would be satisfied. Although it is possible that Grubbs could have refused delivery of the videotape he had ordered, that was unlikely. The Magistrate therefore "had a 'substantial basis for . . . conclud[ing]' that probable cause existed." . . .

III

The Ninth Circuit invalidated the anticipatory search warrant at issue here because the warrant failed to specify the triggering condition. The Fourth Amendment's particularity requirement, it held, "applies with full force to the conditions precedent to an anticipatory search warrant." . . .

The Fourth Amendment, however, does not set forth some general "particularity requirement." It specified only two matters that must be "particularly describ[ed]" in the warrant: "the place to be searched" and "the person or things to be seized." . . .

* * *

Because the Fourth Amendment does not require that the triggering condition for an anticipatory search warrant be set forth in the warrant itself, the Court of Appeals erred in invalidating the warrant at issue here. The judgment of the Court of Appeals is reversed, and the case is remanded for further proceedings consistent with this opinion.

[JUSTICE ALITO took no part in the consideration or the decision of the case. JUSTICE SOUTER, joined by JUSTICE STEVENS and JUSTICE GINSBURG, concurred, but expressed concern that a warrant which failed to include the condition could mislead an officer who lacked knowledge of the condition. He also observed that the target of the search could be misinformed as to its authority.]

[D] Allegations of Probable Cause

AGUILAR v. TEXAS

United States Supreme Court
378 U.S. 108 (1964)

MR. JUSTICE GOLDBERG delivered the opinion of the Court.

This case presents questions concerning the constitutional requirements for obtaining a state search warrant.

Two Houston police officers applied to a local Justice of the Peace for a warrant to search for narcotics in petitioner's home. In support of their application, the officers submitted an affidavit which, in relevant part, recited that:

> Affiants have received reliable information from a credible person and do believe that heroin, marijuana, barbiturates and other narcotics and narcotic paraphernalia are being kept at the above described premises for the purpose of sale and use contrary to the provisions of the law.

The search warrant was issued.

In *Nathanson v. United States*, 290 U.S. 41, a warrant was issued upon the sworn allegation that the affiant "has cause to suspect and does believe" that certain merchandise was in a specified location. *Id.*, at 44. The Court, noting that the affidavit "went upon a mere affirmation of suspicion and belief *without any statement of adequate supporting facts*," *id.*, at 46 (emphasis added), announced the following rule:

> Under the Fourth Amendment, an officer may not properly issue a warrant to search a private dwelling unless he can find probable cause therefore from *facts or circumstances* presented to him under oath or affirmation. Mere affirmance of belief or suspicion is not enough.

Id., at 47. (Emphasis added.)

The Court, in *Giordenello v. United States*, 357 U.S. 480, applied this rule to an affidavit similar to that relied upon here. Affiant in that case swore that petitioner "did receive, conceal, etc., narcotic drugs . . . with knowledge of unlawful importation. . . ." *Id.*, at 481. The Court announced the guiding principles to be:

> that the inferences from the facts which lead to the complaint "[must] be drawn by a neutral and detached magistrate instead of being judged by the officer engaged in the often competitive enterprise of ferreting out crime." *Johnson v. United States*, 333 U.S. 10, 14. The purpose of the complaint, then, is to enable the appropriate magistrate . . . to determine whether the "probable cause" required to support a warrant exists. The Commissioner must judge for himself the persuasiveness of the facts relied on by a complaining officer to show probable cause. He should not accept without question the complainant's mere conclusion. . . .

357 U.S., at 486.

The Court, applying these principles to the complaint in that case, stated that:

> it is clear that it does not pass muster because it does not provide any basis for the Commissioner's determination . . . that probable cause existed. The complaint contains no affirmative allegation that the affiant spoke with personal knowledge of the matters contained therein; it does not indicate any sources for the complainant's belief; and it does not set forth any other sufficient basis upon which a finding of probable cause could be made.

Ibid.

The vice in the present affidavit is at least as great as in *Nathanson* and *Giordenello.* Here the "mere conclusion" that petitioner possessed narcotics was not even that of the affiant himself; it was that of an unidentified informant. The affidavit here not only "contains no affirmative allegation that the affiant spoke with personal knowledge of the matters contained therein," it does not even contain an "affirmative allegation" that the affiant's unidentified source "spoke with personal knowledge." For all that appears, the source here merely suspected, believed or concluded that there were narcotics in petitioner's possession. The magistrate here certainly could not "judge for himself the persuasiveness of the facts relied on . . . to show probable cause." He necessarily accepted "without question" the informant's "suspicion," "belief" or "mere conclusion."

Although an affidavit may be based on hearsay information and need not reflect the direct personal observations of the affiant, *Jones v. United States*, 362 U.S. 257, the magistrate must be informed of some of the underlying circumstances from which the informant concluded that the narcotics were where he claimed they were, and some of the underlying circumstances from which the officer concluded that the informant, whose identity need not be disclosed, see *Rugendorf v. United States*, 376 U.S. 528, was "credible" or his information "reliable." Otherwise, "the inferences from the facts which lead to the complaint" will be drawn not "by a neutral and detached magistrate," as the Constitution requires, but instead, by a police officer "engaged in the often competitive enterprise of ferreting out crime," *Giordenello v. United States*, *supra*, at 486; *Johnson v. United States*, *supra*, at 14, or, as in this case, by an unidentified informant.

We conclude, therefore, that the search warrant should not have been issued because the affidavit did not provide a sufficient basis for a finding of probable cause and that the evidence obtained as a result of the search warrant was inadmissible in petitioner's trial.

[JUSTICE HARLAN concurred; JUSTICE CLARK, joined by JUSTICES BLACK and STEWART, dissented.]

NOTES AND QUESTIONS

(1) The use of warrants is preferred, because such a procedure permits a determination of the constitutional legitimacy of searches by "a neutral and detached magistrate," *Johnson v. United States*, 333 U.S. 10 (1948), prior to the governmental intrusion. The benefit is effectively neutralized if the magistrate acts

as no more than a rubber stamp on warrants. Such would be the result if a warrant were issued on the conclusory assertions in the affidavit.

(2) The requirement of "a neutral and detached magistrate" precludes the issuance of warrants by prosecutors and law enforcement officers. *See Coolidge v. New Hampshire*, 403 U.S. 443 (1971). In *Connally v. Georgia*, 429 U.S. 245 (1977), the Court held that the requirement was compromised by a state statute under which justices of the peace were compensated on a fee basis for the issuance of search warrants but were paid nothing when a request for a warrant was denied.

THE *SPINELLI* AFFIDAVIT

I, Robert L. Bender, being duly sworn, depose and say that I am a Special Agent of the Federal Bureau of Investigation, and as such am authorized to make searches and seizures.

That on August 6, 1965, at approximately 11:44 a.m., William Spinelli was observed by an Agent of the Federal Bureau of Investigation driving a 1964 Ford convertible, Missouri license HC3-649, onto the Eastern approach of the Veterans Bridge leading from East St. Louis, Illinois, to St. Louis, Missouri.

That on August 11, 1965, at approximately 11:16 a.m., William Spinelli was observed by an Agent of the Federal Bureau of Investigation driving a 1964 Ford convertible, Missouri license HC3-649, onto the Eastern approach of the Eads Bridge leading from East St. Louis, Illinois, to St. Louis, Missouri.

Further, at approximately 11:18 a.m. on August 11, 1965, I observed William Spinelli driving the aforesaid Ford convertible from the Western approach of the Eads Bridge into St. Louis, Missouri.

Further, at approximately 4:40 p.m. on August 11, 1965, I observed the aforesaid Ford convertible, bearing Missouri license HC3-649, parked in a parking lot used by residents of The Chieftain Manor Apartments, approximately one block east of 1108 Indian Circle Drive.

On August 12, 1965, at approximately 12:07 p.m., William Spinelli was observed by an Agent of the Federal Bureau of Investigation driving the aforesaid 1964 Ford convertible onto the Eastern approach of the Veterans Bridge from East St. Louis, Illinois, in the direction of St. Louis, Missouri.

Further, on August 12, 1965, at approximately 3:46 p.m., I observed William Spinelli driving the aforesaid 1964 Ford convertible onto the parking lot used by the residents of The Chieftain Manor Apartments approximately one block east of 1108 Indian Circle Drive.

Further, on August 12, 1965, at approximately 3:49 p.m., William Spinelli was observed by an Agent of the Federal Bureau of Investigation entering the front entrance of the two-story apartment building located at 1108 Indian Circle Drive, this building being one of The Chieftain Manor Apartments.

On August 13, 1965, at approximately 11:08 a.m., William Spinelli was observed by an Agent of the Federal Bureau of Investigation driving the aforesaid Ford convertible onto the Eastern approach of the Eads Bridge from East St. Louis, Illinois, heading towards St. Louis, Missouri.

Further, on August 13, 1965, at approximately 11:11 a.m., I observed William Spinelli driving the aforesaid Ford convertible from the Western approach of the Eads Bridge into St. Louis, Missouri.

Further, on August 13, 1965, at approximately 3:45 p.m., I observed William Spinelli driving the aforesaid 1964 Ford convertible onto the parking area used by residents of The Chieftain Manor Apartments, said parking area being approximately one block from 1108 Indian Circle Drive.

Further, on August 13, 1965, at approximately 3:55 p.m., William Spinelli was observed by an Agent of the Federal Bureau of Investigation entering the corner apartment located on the second floor in the southwest corner, known as Apartment F, of the two-story apartment building known and numbered as 1108 Indian Circle Drive.

On August 16, 1965, at approximately 3:22 p.m., I observed William Spinelli driving the aforesaid Ford convertible onto the parking lot used by the residents of The Chieftain Manor Apartments approximately one block east of 1108 Indian Circle Drive.

Further, an Agent of the FBI observed William Spinelli alight from the aforesaid Ford convertible and walk toward the apartment building located at 1108 Indian Circle Drive.

The records of the Southwestern Bell Telephone Company reflect that there are two telephones located in the southwest corner apartment on the second floor of the apartment building located at 1108 Indian Circle Drive under the name of Grace P. Hagen.The numbers listed in the Southwestern Bell Telephone Company records for the aforesaid telephones are WYdown 4-0029 and WYdown 4-0136.

William Spinelli is known to this affiant and to federal law enforcement agents and local law enforcement agents as a bookmaker, an associate of bookmakers, a gambler, and an associate of gamblers.

The Federal Bureau of Investigation has been informed by a confidential reliable informant that William Spinelli is operating a handbook and accepting wagers and disseminating wagering information by means of the telephones which have been assigned the numbers WYdown 4-0029 and WYdown 4-0136.

/s/ Robert L. Bender,

Special Agent, Federal Bureau of Investigation.

Subscribed and sworn to before me this 18th day of August, 1965, at St. Louis, Missouri.

/s/ William R. O'Toole.

SPINELLI v. UNITED STATES

United States Supreme Court
393 U.S. 410 (1969)

Mr. Justice Harlan delivered the opinion of the Court.

William Spinelli was convicted under 18 U.S.C. § 1952 of traveling to St. Louis, Missouri, from a nearby Illinois suburb with the intention of conducting gambling activities proscribed by Missouri law. See Mo. Rev. Stat. § 563.360 (1959). At every appropriate stage in the proceedings in the lower courts, the petitioner challenged the constitutionality of the warrant which authorized the FBI search that uncovered the evidence necessary for his conviction. At each stage, Spinelli's challenge was treated in a different way. At a pretrial suppression hearing the United States District Court for the Eastern District of Missouri held that Spinelli lacked standing to raise a Fourth Amendment objection. A unanimous panel of the Court of Appeals for the Eighth Circuit rejected the District Court's ground, a majority holding further that the warrant was issued without probable cause. After an *en banc* rehearing, the Court of Appeals sustained the warrant and affirmed the conviction by a vote of six to two. 382 F.2d 871. Both the majority and dissenting *en banc* opinions reflect a most conscientious effort to apply the principles we announced in *Aguilar v. Texas*, 378 U.S. 108 (1964), to a factual situation whose basic characteristics have not been at all uncommon in recent search warrant cases. Believing it desirable that the principles of *Aguilar* should be further explicated, we granted certiorari, 390 U.S. 942, our writ being later limited to the question of the constitutional validity of the search and seizure. 391 U.S. 933. For reasons that follow we reverse.

. . .

In essence, . . . the affidavit contained the following allegations:

1. The FBI had kept track of Spinelli's movements on five days during the month of August 1965. On four of these occasions, Spinelli was seen crossing one of two bridges leading from Illinois into St. Louis, Missouri, between 11 a.m. and 12:15 p.m. On four of the five days, Spinelli was also seen parking his car in a lot used by residents of an apartment house at 1108 Indian Circle Drive in St. Louis, between 3:30 p.m. and 4:45 p.m. On one day, Spinelli was followed further and seen to enter a particular apartment in the building.

2. An FBI check with the telephone company revealed that this apartment contained two telephones listed under the name of Grace P. Hagen, and carrying the numbers WYdown 4-0029 and WYdown 4-0136.

3. The application stated that "William Spinelli is known to this affiant and to federal law enforcement agents and local law enforcement agents as a bookmaker, an associate of bookmakers, a gambler, and an associate of gamblers."

4. Finally, it was stated that the FBI "has been informed by a confidential reliable informant that William Spinelli is operating a handbook and accepting wagers and disseminating wagering information by means of the telephones which have been assigned the numbers WYdown 4-0029 and WYdown 4-0136."

There can be no question that the last item mentioned, detailing the informant's tip, has a fundamental place in this warrant application. Without it, probable cause could not be established. The first two items reflect only innocent-seeming activity and data. Spinelli's travels to and from the apartment building and his entry into a particular apartment on one occasion could hardly be taken as bespeaking gambling activity; and there is surely nothing unusual about an apartment containing two separate telephones. Many a householder indulges himself in this petty luxury. Finally, the allegation that Spinelli was "known" to the affiant and to other federal and local law enforcement officers as a gambler and an associate of gamblers is but a bald and unilluminating assertion of suspicion that is entitled to no weight in appraising the magistrate's decision. . . .

So much indeed the Government does not deny. Rather, following the reasoning of the Court of Appeals, the Government claims that the informant's tip gives a suspicious color to the FBI's reports detailing Spinelli's innocent-seeming conduct and that, conversely, the FBI's surveillance corroborates the informant's tip, thereby entitling it to more weight. It is true, of course, that the magistrate is obligated to render a judgment based upon a common-sense reading of the entire affidavit. . . . We believe, however, that the "totality of circumstances" approach taken by the Court of Appeals paints with too broad a brush. Where, as here, the informer's tip is a necessary element in a finding of probable cause, its proper weight must be determined by a more precise analysis.

The informer's report must first be measured against *Aguilar*'s standards so that its probative value can be assessed. If the tip is found inadequate under *Aguilar*, the other allegations which corroborate the information contained in the hearsay report should then be considered. At this stage as well, however, the standards enunciated in *Aguilar* must inform the magistrate's decision. He must ask: Can it fairly be said that the tip, even when certain parts of it have been corroborated by independent sources, is as trustworthy as a tip which would pass *Aguilar's* tests without independent corroboration? *Aguilar* is relevant at this stage of the inquiry as well because the tests it establishes were designed to implement the long-standing principle that probable cause must be determined by a "neutral and detached magistrate," and not by "the officer engaged in the often competitive enterprise of ferreting out crime." *Johnson v. United States*, 333 U.S. 10, 14 (1948). A magistrate cannot be said to have properly discharged his constitutional duty if he relies on an informer's tip which — even when partially corroborated — is not as reliable as one which passes *Aguilar*'s requirements when standing alone.

Applying these principles to the present case, we first consider the weight to be given the informer's tip when it is considered apart from the rest of the affidavit. It is clear that a Commissioner could not credit it without abdicating his constitutional function. Though the affiant swore that his confidant was "reliable," he offered the magistrate no reason in support of this conclusion. Perhaps even more important is the fact that *Aguilar*'s other test has not been satisfied. The tip does not contain a sufficient statement of underlying circumstances from which the informer concluded that Spinelli was running a bookmaking operation. We are not told how the FBI's source received his information; it is not alleged that the informant personally observed Spinelli at work or that he had ever placed a bet with him. Moreover, if the informant came by the information indirectly, he did not explain why his sources were reliable. . . . In the absence of a statement detailing the manner in which the information was gathered, it is especially important that the tip describe the accused's criminal activity in sufficient detail that the magistrate may know that he is relying on something more substantial than a casual rumor circulating in the underworld or an accusation based merely on an individual's general reputation.

The detail provided by the informant in *Draper v. United States* . . . provides a suitable benchmark. While Hereford, the Government's informer in that case, did not state the way in which he had obtained his information, he reported that Draper had gone to Chicago the day before by train and that he would return to Denver by train with three ounces of heroin on one of two specified mornings. Moreover, Hereford went on to describe, with minute particularity, the clothes that Draper would be wearing upon his arrival at the Denver station. A magistrate, when confronted with such detail, could reasonably infer that the informant had gained his information in a reliable way. Such an inference cannot be made in the present case. Here, the only facts supplied were that Spinelli was using two specified telephones and that these phones were being used in gambling operations. This meager report could easily have been obtained from an offhand remark heard at a neighborhood bar.

Nor do we believe that the patent doubts *Aguilar* raises as to the report's reliability are adequately resolved by a consideration of the allegations detailing the FBI's independent investigative efforts. At most, these allegations indicated that Spinelli could have used the telephones specified by the informant for some purpose. This cannot by itself be said to support both the inference that the informer was generally trustworthy and that he had made his charge against Spinelli on the basis of information obtained in a reliable way. Once again, *Draper* provides a relevant comparison. Independent police work in that case corroborated much more than one small detail that had been provided by the informant. There, the police, upon meeting the inbound Denver train on the second morning specified by informer Hereford, saw a man whose dress corresponded precisely to Hereford's detailed description. It was then apparent that the informant had not been fabricating his report out of whole cloth; since the report was of the sort which in common experience may be recognized as having been obtained in a reliable way, it was perfectly clear that probable cause had been established.

We conclude, then, that in the present case the informant's tip — even when corroborated to the extent indicated — was not sufficient to provide the basis for a finding of probable cause. This is not to say that the tip was so insubstantial that it could not properly have counted in the magistrate's determination. Rather, it needed some further support. When we look to the other parts of the application, however, we find nothing alleged which would permit the suspicions engendered by the informant's report to ripen into a judgment that a crime was probably being committed. As we have already seen, the allegations detailing the FBI's surveillance of Spinelli and its investigation of the telephone company records contain no suggestion of criminal conduct when taken by themselves — and they are not endowed with an aura of suspicion by virtue of the informer's tip. Nor do we find that the FBI's reports take on a sinister color when read in light of common knowledge that bookmaking is often carried on over the telephone and from premises ostensibly used by others for perfectly normal purposes. Such an argument would carry weight in a situation in which the premises contain an unusual number of telephones or abnormal activity is observed, cf. *McCray v. Illinois*, 386 U.S. 300, 302 (1967), but it does not fit this case where neither of these factors is present. All that remains to be considered is the flat statement that Spinelli was "known" to the FBI and others as a gambler. But just as a simple assertion of police suspicion is not itself a sufficient basis for a magistrate's finding of probable cause, we do not believe it may be used to give additional weight to allegations that would otherwise be insufficient.

The affidavit, then, falls short of the standards set forth in *Aguilar*, *Draper*, and our other decisions that give content to the notion of probable cause.

The judgment of the Court of Appeals is reversed and the case is remanded to that court for further proceedings consistent with this opinion.

[JUSTICE WHITE concurred.]

MR. JUSTICE BLACK, dissenting.

In my view, this Court's decision in *Aguilar v. Texas* . . . was bad enough. That decision went very far toward elevating the magistrate's hearing for issuance of a search warrant to a full-fledged trial, where witnesses must be brought forward to attest personally to all the facts alleged. But not content with this, the Court today expands *Aguilar* to almost unbelievable proportions. Of course, it would strengthen the probable-cause presentation if eyewitnesses could testify that they saw the defendant commit the crime. It would be stronger still if these witnesses could explain in detail the nature of the sensual perceptions on which they based their "conclusion" that the person they had seen was the defendant and that he was responsible for the events they observed. Nothing in our Constitution, however, requires that the facts be established with that degree of certainty and with such elaborate specificity before a policeman can be authorized by a disinterested magistrate to conduct a carefully limited search.

The Fourth Amendment provides that "no Warrants shall issue, but upon probable cause, supported by Oath or affirmation, and particularly describing the place to be searched, and the persons or things to be seized." In this case a search warrant was issued supported by an oath and particularly describing the place to be searched and the things to be seized. The supporting oath was three printed pages and the full text of it is included in an Appendix to the Court's opinion. The magistrate, I think properly, held the information set forth sufficient facts to show "probable cause" that the defendant was violating the law. Six members of the Court of Appeals also agreed that the affidavit was sufficient to show probable cause. A majority of this Court today holds, however, that the magistrate and all of these judges were wrong. In doing so, they substitute their own opinion for that of the local magistrate and the circuit judges, and reject the *en banc* factual conclusion of the Eighth Circuit and reverse the judgment based upon that factual conclusion. I cannot join in any such disposition of an issue so vital to the administration of justice, and dissent as vigorously as I can.

I repeat my belief that the affidavit given the magistrate was more than ample to show probable cause of the petitioner's guilt. The affidavit meticulously set out facts sufficient to show the following:

1. The petitioner had been shown going to and coming from a room in an apartment which contained two telephones listed under the name of another person. Nothing in the record indicates that the apartment was of that large and luxurious type which could only be occupied by a person to whom it would be a "petty luxury" to have two separate telephones, with different numbers, both listed under the name of a person who did not live there.

2. The petitioner's car had been observed parked in the apartment's parking lot. This fact was, of course, highly relevant in showing that the petitioner was extremely interested in some enterprise which was located in the apartment.

3. The FBI had been informed by a reliable informant that the petitioner was accepting wagering information by telephones — the particular telephones located in the apartment the defendant had been repeatedly visiting. Unless the Court, going beyond the requirements of the Fourth Amendment, wishes to require magistrates to hold trials before issuing warrants, it is not necessary — as the Court holds — to have the affiant explain "the underlying circumstances from which the informer concluded that Spinelli was running a bookmaking operation." *Ante*, at 416.

4. The petitioner was known by federal and local law enforcement agents as a bookmaker and an associate of gamblers. I cannot agree with the Court that this knowledge was only a "bald and unilluminating assertion of suspicion that is entitled to no weight in appraising the magistrate's decision." *Ante*, at 414. Although the statement is hearsay that might not be admissible in a regular trial, everyone knows, unless he shuts his eyes to the realities of life, that this is a relevant fact which, together with other circumstances, might indicate a factual probability that gambling is taking place.

The foregoing facts should be enough to constitute probable cause for anyone who does not believe that the only way to obtain a search warrant is to prove beyond a reasonable doubt that a defendant is guilty. Even *Aguilar*, on which the Court relies, cannot support the contrary result, at least as that decision was written before today's massive escalation of it.

[Justices Fortas and Stewart also dissented; Justice Marshall took no part in the decision.]

NOTES AND QUESTIONS

(1) It would appear beyond dispute that the informant's tip in this case is no more illuminating or less conclusory than the informant's tip in *Aguilar*. Here, however, there is more than just a tip, and Justice Harlan poses the following question: "Can it fairly be said that the tip, even when certain parts of its have been corroborated by independent sources, is as trustworthy as a tip which would pass *Aguilar*'s test without independent corroboration?" Is this a meaningful standard? *See generally* Moylan, *Hearsay and Probable Cause: An* Aguilar *and* Spinelli *Primer*, 25 Mercer L. Rev. 741 (1974).

(2) Justice Harlan contrasts the allegations in this affidavit with the facts known to the officer in *Draper.* Because *Draper* involved a warrantless arrest, the Court is comparing its summation of the facts in *Draper* with an officer's affidavit for a search warrant in *Spinelli.* From this, it might be concluded that *Spinelli* places too great a premium on drafting affidavits. The mistake, however, is not so much that of Agent Bender as it is the magistrate who erroneously issued the warrant. Not only is it the responsibility of an issuing magistrate to decline the issuance of warrants when probable cause is not alleged, it is equally important that the affiant be advised of the shortcomings in the affidavit. In many cases, probable cause may be present, but the affiant has failed to articulate the facts known with adequate specificity. There is nothing improper in the magistrate questioning the affiant as to the information in his or her possession and incorporating additional facts in the affidavit. *See State v. Haron,* 220 N.W.2d 829 (S.D. 1974).

(3) More troublesome are cases in which the affidavit has been supplemented by oral testimony. Many courts have indicated that only information submitted to the magistrate in writing can be considered in determining probable cause. The strongest argument for this position is that without such a record it will likely be impossible for an appellate court to review a determination of probable cause. Furthermore, since warrants are initially issued in ex parte proceedings, the defendant may be effectively denied an opportunity to challenge the validity of the warrant without a record of the basis for its issuance. *See* Justice Brennan, joined by Justice Marshall, dissenting from a denial of certiorari in *Christofferson v. Washington,* 393 U.S. 1090, 1091(1969):

> The substantive right created by the requirement of probable cause is hardly accorded full sweep without an effective procedural means of assuring meaningful review of a determination by the issuing magistrate of the existence of probable cause. Reliance on a record prepared after the fact involves a hazard of impairment of that right.

Justice Brennan quoted *Glodowski v. State,* 196 Wis. 265, 271–272, 220 N.W. 227, 230 (1928):

> It is an anomaly in judicial procedure to attempt to review the judicial act of a magistrate issuing a search warrant upon a record made up wholly or partially by oral testimony taken in the reviewing court long after the search warrant was issued. Judicial action must be reviewed upon the record made at or before the time that the judicial act was performed. The validity of a judicial action cannot be made to depend upon the facts recalled by a fallible human memory at a time somewhat removed from that when the judicial determination was made.

The consideration of information not contained in the affidavit for the purpose of establishing probable cause has never come before the Supreme Court, although a footnote in *Aguilar* leaves open the possibility:

> The record does not reveal, nor is it claimed, that any other information was brought to the attention of the Justice of the Peace. It is elementary that in passing on the validity of a warrant, the reviewing court may consider *only* information brought to the magistrate's attention.

In some jurisdictions, the issuance of warrants pursuant to oral affidavits given to the magistrate over the telephone has been sustained. *See* Marek, *Telephonic Search Warrants: A New Equation for Exigent Circumstances*, 27 Clev. St. L. Rev. 35 (1978).

ILLINOIS v. GATES

United States Supreme Court
462 U.S. 213 (1983)

JUSTICE REHNQUIST delivered the opinion of the Court.

Respondents Lance and Susan Gates were indicted for violation of state drug laws after police officers, executing a search warrant, discovered marijuana and other contraband in their automobile and home. Prior to trial the Gates' moved to suppress evidence seized during this search. The Illinois Supreme Court affirmed the decisions of lower state courts granting the motion. It held that the affidavit submitted in support of the State's application for a warrant to search the Gates' property was inadequate under this Court's decision in *Aguilar v. Texas*, and *Spinelli v. United States*.

Bloomingdale, Ill., is a suburb of Chicago located in DuPage County. On May 3, 1978, the Bloomingdale Police Department received by mail an anonymous handwritten letter which read as follows:

> This letter is to inform you that you have a couple in your town who strictly make their living on selling drugs. They are Sue and Lance Gates, they live on Greenway, off Bloomingdale Rd. in the condominiums. Most of their buys are done in Florida. Sue his wife drives their car to Florida, where she leaves it to be loaded up with drugs, then Lance flys [sic] down and drives it back. Sue flys [sic] back after she drops the car off in Florida. May 3 she is driving down there again and Lance will be flying down in a few days to drive it back. At the time Lance drives the car back he has the trunk loaded with over $100,000.00 in drugs. Presently they have over $100,000.00 worth of drugs in their basement.
>
> They brag about the fact they never have to work, and make their entire living on pushers.
>
> I guarantee if you watch them carefully you will make a big catch. They are friends with some big drugs dealers, who visit their house often.
>
> Lance & Susan Gates Greenway in Condominiums

The letter was referred by the Chief of Police of the Bloomingdale Police Department to Detective Mader, who decided to pursue the tip. Mader learned, from the office of the Illinois Secretary of State, that an Illinois driver's license had been issued to one Lance Gates, residing at a stated address in Bloomingdale. He contacted a confidential informant, whose examination of certain financial records revealed a more recent address for the Gates, and he also learned from a police officer assigned to O'Hare Airport that "L. Gates" had made a reservation on

Eastern Airlines flight 245 to West Palm Beach, Fla., scheduled to depart from Chicago on May 5 at 4:15 p.m.

Mader then made arrangements with an agent of the Drug Enforcement Administration for surveillance of the May 5 Eastern Airlines flight. The agent later reported to Mader that Gates had boarded the flight, and that federal agents in Florida had observed him arrive in West Palm Beach and take a taxi to the nearby Holiday Inn. They also reported that Gates went to a room registered to one Susan Gates and that, at 7:00 a.m. the next morning, Gates and an unidentified woman left the motel in a Mercury bearing Illinois license plates and drove northbound on an interstate frequently used by travelers to the Chicago area. In addition, the DEA agent informed Mader that the license plate number on the Mercury was registered to a Hornet station wagon owned by Gates. The agent also advised Mader that the driving time between West Palm Beach and Bloomingdale was approximately 22 to 24 hours.

Mader signed an affidavit setting forth the foregoing facts, and submitted it to a judge of the Circuit Court of DuPage County, together with a copy of the anonymous letter. The judge of that court thereupon issued a search warrant for the Gates' residence and for their automobile. The judge, in deciding to issue the warrant, could have determined that the *modus operandi* of the Gates had been substantially corroborated. As the anonymous letter predicted, Lance Gates had flown from Chicago to West Palm Beach late in the afternoon of May 5th, had checked into a hotel room registered in the name of his wife, and, at 7:00 a.m. the following morning, had headed north, accompanied by an unidentified woman, out of West Palm Beach on an interstate highway used by travelers from South Florida to Chicago in an automobile bearing a license plate issued to him.

At 5:15 a.m. on May 7th, only 36 hours after he had flown out of Chicago, Lance Gates, and his wife, returned to their home in Bloomingdale, driving the car in which they had left West Palm Beach some 22 hours earlier. The Bloomingdale police were awaiting them, searched the trunk of the Mercury, and uncovered approximately 350 pounds of marijuana. A search of the Gates' home revealed marijuana, weapons, and other contraband. The Illinois Circuit Court ordered suppression of all these items, on the ground that the affidavit submitted to the Circuit Judge failed to support the necessary determination of probable cause to believe that the Gates' automobile and home contained the contraband in question. This decision was affirmed in turn by the Illinois Appellate Court and by a divided vote of the Supreme Court of Illinois.

The Illinois Supreme Court concluded — and we are inclined to agree — that, standing alone, the anonymous letter sent to the Bloomingdale Police Department would not provide the basis for a magistrate's determination that there was probable cause to believe contraband would be found in the Gates' car and home. The letter provides virtually nothing from which one might conclude that its author is either honest or his information reliable; likewise, the letter gives absolutely no indication of the basis for the writer's predictions regarding the Gates' criminal activities. Something more was required, then, before a magistrate could conclude that there was probable cause to believe that contraband would be found in the Gates' home and car.

The Illinois Supreme Court also properly recognized that Detective Mader's affidavit might be capable of supplementing the anonymous letter with information sufficient to permit a determination of probable cause. See *Whitely v. Warden*. In holding that the affidavit in fact did not contain sufficient additional information to sustain a determination of probable cause, the Illinois court applied a "two-pronged test," derived from our decision in *Spinelli v. United States*.

We agree with the Illinois Supreme Court that an informant's "veracity," "reliability" and "basis of knowledge" are all highly relevant in determining the value of his report. We do not agree, however, that these elements should be understood as entirely separate and independent requirements to be rigidly exacted in every case, which the opinion of the Supreme Court of Illinois would imply. Rather, as detailed below, they should be understood simply as closely intertwined issues that may usefully illuminate the common-sense, practical question whether there is "probable cause" to believe that contraband or evidence is located in a particular place.

This totality of the circumstances approach is far more consistent with our prior treatment of probable cause than is any rigid demand that specific "tests" be satisfied by every informant's tip. . . .

[T]he "two-pronged test" directs analysis into two largely independent channels — the informant's "veracity" or "reliability" and his "basis of knowledge." There are persuasive arguments against according these two elements such independent status. Instead, they are better understood as relevant considerations in the totality of circumstances analysis that traditionally has guided probable cause determinations: a deficiency in one may be compensated for, in determining the overall reliability of a tip, by a strong showing as to the other, or by some other indicia of reliability.

If, for example, a particular informant is known for the unusual reliability of his predictions of certain types of criminal activities in a locality, his failure, in a particular case, to thoroughly set forth the basis of his knowledge surely should not serve as an absolute bar to a finding of probable cause based on his tip. Likewise, if an unquestionably honest citizen comes forward with a report of criminal activity — which if fabricated would subject him to criminal liability — we have found rigorous scrutiny of the basis of his knowledge unnecessary. *Adams v. Williams*. Conversely, even if we entertain some doubt as to an informant's motives, his explicit and detailed description of alleged wrongdoing, along with a statement that the event was observed first hand, entitles his tip to greater weight than might otherwise be the case. Unlike a totality of circumstances analysis, which permits a balanced assessment of the relative weights of all the various indicia of reliability (and unreliability) attending an informant's tip, the "two-pronged test" has encouraged an excessively technical dissection of informant's tips, with undue attention being focused on isolated issues that cannot sensibly be divorced from the other facts presented to the magistrate.

We also have recognized that affidavits "are normally drafted by non-lawyers in the midst and haste of a criminal investigation. Technical requirements of elaborate specificity once enacted under common law pleading have no proper place in this area. . . ." Likewise, search and arrest warrants long have been issued by persons who are neither lawyers nor judges, and who certainly do not remain abreast of each judicial refinement of the nature of "probable cause." See *Shadwick v. City of Tampa*, 407 U.S. 345, 348–350 (1972). The rigorous inquiry into the *Spinelli* prongs and the complex superstructure of evidentiary and analytical rules that some have seen implicit in our *Spinelli* decision, cannot be reconciled with the fact that many warrants are — quite properly, *ibid.* — issued on the basis of nontechnical, common-sense judgments of laymen applying a standard less demanding than those used in more formal legal proceedings. Likewise, given the informal, often hurried context in which it must be applied, the "built-in subtleties," *Stanley v. State*, 313 A.2d 847, 860 (Md. App. 1974), of the "two-pronged test" are particularly unlikely to assist magistrates in determining probable cause.

Finally, the direction taken by decisions following *Spinelli* poorly serves "the most basic function of any government": "to provide for the security of the individual and of his property." *Miranda v. Arizona*, 384 U.S. 436, 539 (1966) (White, J., dissenting). The strictures that inevitably accompany the "two-pronged test" cannot avoid seriously impeding the task of law enforcement. If, as the Illinois Supreme Court apparently thought, that test must be rigorously applied in every case, anonymous tips seldom would be of greatly diminished value in police work. Ordinary citizens, like ordinary witnesses, see Federal Rules of Evidence 701, Advisory Committee Note (1976), generally do not provide extensive recitations of the basis of their everyday observations. Likewise, as the Illinois Supreme Court observed in this case, the veracity of persons supplying anonymous tips is by hypothesis largely unknown, and unknowable. As a result, anonymous tips seldom could survive a rigorous application of either of the *Spinelli* prongs. Yet, such tips, particularly when supplemented by independent police investigation, frequently contribute to the solution of otherwise "perfect crimes." While a conscientious assessment of the basis for crediting such tips is required by the Fourth Amendment, a standard that leaves virtually no place for anonymous citizen informants is not.

For all these reasons, we conclude that it is wiser to abandon the "two-pronged test" established by our decisions in *Aguilar* and *Spinelli*.[21] In its place we reaffirm the totality of the circumstances analysis that traditionally has informed probable cause determinations. . . . The task of the issuing magistrate is simply to make a practical, common-sense decision whether, given all the circumstances set forth in the affidavit before him, including the "veracity" and "basis of knowledge" of persons supplying hearsay information, there is a fair probability that contraband or evidence of a crime will be found in a particular place. And the duty of a reviewing

---

[21] [11] The Court's decision in *Spinelli* has been the subject of considerable criticism, both by members of this Court and others. Justice Blackmun, concurring in United States v. Harris, 403 U.S. 573, 585–586 (1971), noted his long-held view "that *Spinelli* . . . was wrongly decided" by this Court. Justice Black similarly would have overruled that decision. *Ibid.*

Whether the allegations submitted to the magistrate in *Spinelli* would, under the view we now take, have supported a finding of probable cause, we think it would not be profitable to decide. There are so many variables in the probable cause equation that one determination will seldom be a useful "precedent" for another. Suffice it to say that while we in no way abandon *Spinelli*'s concern for the trustworthiness of informers and for the principle that it is the magistrate who must ultimately make a finding of probable cause, we reject the rigid categorization suggested by some of its language.

court is simply to ensure that the magistrate had a "substantial basis for conclud[ing]" that probable cause existed. *Jones v. United States*, 362 U.S., at 271. We are convinced that this flexible, easily applied standard will better achieve the accommodation of public and private interests that the Fourth Amendment requires than does the approach that has developed from *Aguilar* and *Spinelli.*

Our earlier cases illustrate the limits beyond which a magistrate may not venture in issuing a warrant. A sworn statement of an affiant that "he has cause to suspect and does believe that" liquor illegally brought into the United States is located on certain premises will not do. *Nathanson v. United States*, 290 U.S. 41 (1933). An affidavit must provide the magistrate with a substantial basis for determining the existence of probable cause, and the wholly conclusory statement at issue in *Nathanson* failed to meet this requirement. An officer's statement that "affiants have received reliable information from a credible person and believe" that heroin is stored in a home, is likewise inadequate. *Aguilar.* As in *Nathanson*, this is a mere conclusory statement that gives the magistrate virtually no basis at all for making a judgment regarding probable cause. Sufficient information must be presented to the magistrate to allow that official to determine probable cause; his action cannot be a mere ratification of the bare conclusions of others. In order to ensure that such an abdication of the magistrate's duty does not occur, courts must continue to conscientiously review the sufficiency of affidavits on which warrants are issued. But when we move beyond the "bare bones" affidavits present in cases such as *Nathanson* and *Aguilar*, this area simply does not lend itself to a prescribed set of rules, like that which had developed from *Spinelli.* Instead, the flexible, common-sense standard articulated in *Jones, Ventresca*, and *Brinegar* better serves the purposes of the Fourth Amendment's probable cause requirement.

Our decision in *Draper*, however, is the classic case on the value of corroborative efforts of police officials. There, an informant named Hereford reported that Draper would arrive in Denver on a train from Chicago on one of two days, and that he would be carrying a quantity of heroin. The informant also supplied a fairly detailed physical description of Draper, and predicted that he would be wearing a light colored raincoat, brown slacks and black shoes, and would be walking "real fast." Hereford gave no indication of the basis for his information.[22]

On one of the stated dates police officers observed a man matching this description exit a train arriving from Chicago; his attire and luggage matched Hereford's report and he was walking rapidly. We explained in *Draper* that, by this point in his investigation, the arresting officer "had personally verified every facet of the information given him by Hereford except whether petitioner had accomplished his mission and had the three ounces of heroin on his person or in his bag. And surely, with every other bit of Hereford's information being thus personally verified, [the officer] had 'reasonable grounds' to believe that the remaining

[22] [12] The tip in *Draper* might well not have survived the rigid application of the "two-pronged test" that developed following *Spinelli.* The only reference to Hereford's reliability was that he had "been engaged as a 'special employee' of the Bureau of Narcotics at Denver for about six months, and from time to time gave information to [the police] for small sums of money, and that [the officer] had always found the information given by Hereford to be accurate and reliable." 358 U.S., at 309. Likewise, the tip gave no indication of how Hereford came by his information. At most, the detailed and accurate predictions in the tip indicated that, however Hereford obtained the information, it was reliable.

unverified bit of Hereford's information that Draper would have the heroin with him was likewise true." *Id.*, at 313.

The showing of probable cause in the present case was fully as compelling as that in *Draper*. Even standing alone, the facts obtained through the independent investigation of Mader and the DEA at least suggested that the Gates were involved in drug trafficking. In addition to being a popular vacation site, Florida is well-known as a source of narcotics and other illegal drugs. Lance Gates' flight to Palm Beach, his brief, overnight stay in a motel, and apparent immediate return north to Chicago in the family car, conveniently awaiting him in West Palm Beach, is as suggestive of a pre-arranged drug run, as it is of an ordinary vacation trip.

In addition, the magistrate could rely on the anonymous letter, which had been corroborated in major part by Mader's efforts just as had occurred in *Draper*.[23] The Supreme Court of Illinois reasoned that *Draper* involved an informant who had given reliable information on previous occasions, while the honesty and reliability of the anonymous informant in this case were unknown to the Bloomingdale police. While this distinction might be an apt one at the time the police department received the anonymous letter, it became far less significant after Mader's independent investigative work occurred. The corroboration of the letter's predictions that the Gates' car would be in Florida, that Lance Gates would fly to Florida in the next day or so, and that he would drive the car north toward Bloomingdale all indicated, albeit not with certainty, that the informant's other assertions also were true. "Because an informant is right about some things, he is more probably right about other facts," *Spinelli, supra*, 393 U.S., at 427 (White, J., concurring) — including the claim regarding the Gates' illegal activity. This may well not be the type of "reliability" or "veracity" necessary to satisfy some views of the "veracity prong" of *Spinelli*, but we think it suffices for the practical, common-sense judgment called for in making a probable cause determination. It is enough, for purposes of assessing probable cause, that "corroboration through other sources of information reduced the chances of a reckless or prevaricating tale," thus providing "a substantial basis for crediting the hearsay."

Finally, the anonymous letter contained a range of details relating not just to easily obtained facts and conditions existing at the time of the tip, but to future

---

[23] [13] The Illinois Supreme Court thought that the verification of details contained in the anonymous letter in this case amounted to "the corroboration of innocent activity," and that this was insufficient to support a finding of probable cause. We are inclined to agree, however, with the observation of Justice Moran in his dissenting opinion that "In this case, just as in *Draper*, seemingly innocent activity became suspicious in the light of the initial tip." And it bears noting that *all* of the corroborating detail established in *Draper, supra*, was of entirely innocent activity — a fact later pointed out by the Court of both *Jones v. United States*, 362 U.S. 257, 269–270 (1960), and *Ker v. California*, 374 U.S. 23, 36 (1963).

This is perfectly reasonable. As discussed previously, probable cause requires only a probability or substantial chance of criminal activity, not an actual showing of such activity. By hypothesis, therefore, innocent behavior frequently will provide the basis for a showing of probable cause; to require otherwise would be to *sub silentio* impose a drastically more rigorous definition of probable cause than the security of our citizens demands. We think the Illinois court attempted a too rigid classification of the types of conduct that may be relied upon in seeking to demonstrate probable cause. See Brown v. Texas, 443 U.S. 47, 52, n. 2 (1979). In making a determination of probable cause the relevant inquiry is not whether particular conduct is "innocent" or "guilty," but the degree of suspicion that attaches to particular types of non-criminal acts.

actions of third parties ordinarily not easily predicted. The letter writer's accurate information as to the travel plans of each of the Gates was of a character likely obtained only from the Gates themselves, or from someone familiar with their not entirely ordinary travel plans. If the informant had access to accurate information of this type a magistrate could properly conclude that it was not unlikely that he also had access to reliable information of the Gates' alleged illegal activities. Of course, the Gates' travel plans might have been learned from a talkative neighbor or travel agent; under the "two-pronged test" developed from *Spinelli*, the character of the details in the anonymous letter might well not permit a sufficiently clear inference regarding the letter writer's "basis of knowledge." But, as discussed previously, . . . probable cause does not demand the certainty we associate with formal trials. It is enough that there was a fair probability that the writer of the anonymous letter had obtained his entire story either from the Gates or someone they trusted. And corroboration of major portions of the letter's predictions provides just this probability. It is apparent, therefore, that the judge issuing the warrant had a "substantial basis for . . . conclud[ing]" that probable cause to search the Gates' home and car existed. The judgment of the Supreme Court of Illinois therefore must be

Reversed.

[JUSTICE WHITE, concurring, was convinced that probable cause could be found under the *Aguilar-Spinelli* test.]

JUSTICE BRENNAN, with whom JUSTICE MARSHALL joins, dissenting.

Findings of probable cause, and attendant intrusions, should not be authorized unless there is some assurance that the information on which they are based has been obtained in a reliable way by an honest or credible person. As applied to police officers, the rules focus on the way in which the information was acquired. As applied to informants, the rules focus both on the honesty or credibility of the informant and on the reliability of the way in which the information was acquired. Insofar as it is more complicated, an evaluation of affidavits based on hearsay involves a more difficult inquiry. This suggests a need to structure the inquiry in an effort to insure greater accuracy. The standards announced in *Aguilar*, as refined by *Spinelli*, fulfill that need. The standards inform the police of what information they have to provide and magistrates of what information they should demand. The standards also inform magistrates of the subsidiary findings they must make in order to arrive at an ultimate finding of probable cause. *Spinelli*, properly understood, directs the magistrate's attention to the possibility that the presence of self-verifying detail might satisfy *Aguilar*'s basis of knowledge prong and that corroboration of the details of a tip might satisfy *Aguilar*'s veracity prong. By requiring police to provide certain crucial information to magistrates and by structuring magistrates' probable cause inquiries, *Aguilar* and *Spinelli* assure the magistrate's role as an independent arbiter of probable cause, insure greater accuracy in probable cause determinations, and advance the substantive value identified above. . . .

To suggest that anonymous informant's tips are subject to the tests established by *Aguilar* and *Spinelli* is not to suggest that they can never provide a basis for a finding of probable cause. It is conceivable that police corroboration of the details of the tip might establish the reliability of the informant under *Aguilar*'s veracity prong, as refined in *Spinelli*, and that the details in the tip might be sufficient to qualify under the "self-verifying detail" test established by *Spinelli* as a means of satisfying *Aguilar*'s basis of knowledge prong. The *Aguilar* and *Spinelli* tests must be applied to anonymous informants' tips, however, if we are to continue to insure that findings of probable cause, and attendant intrusions, are based on information provided by an honest or credible person who has acquired the information in a reliable way. . . .

By replacing *Aguilar* and *Spinelli* with a test that provides no assurance that magistrates, rather than the police, or informants, will make determinations of probable cause; imposes no structure on magistrates' probable cause inquiries; and invites the possibility that intrusions may be justified on less than reliable information from an honest or credible person, today's decision threatens to "obliterate one of the most fundamental distinctions between our form of government, where officers are under the law, and the police-state where they are the law." *Johnson v. United States*, 333 U.S. 10, 17 (1948).

[JUSTICE STEVENS, joined by JUSTICE BRENNAN, dissenting, concluded that probable cause was absent even under the test adopted by the majority. In his view, the fact that the informant had been incorrect in predicting that Sue would fly home after delivering the automobile undermined the conclusion that there was a substantial cache of drugs in the house.]

NOTES AND QUESTIONS

(1) Was it necessary to repudiate *Aguilar* and *Spinelli* if the search warrant in *Gates* was sustained? Granted, an anonymous tip can not on its own provide probable cause, but *Spinelli* said that "[i]f the tip is found inadequate under *Aguilar*, the other allegations which corroborate the information contained in the hearsay report should then be considered," and the judgment made on the aggregate information. Were the corroborating observations in *Gates* more compelling than those in *Spinelli* or *Draper*?

(2) Might it be said that Justice Rehnquist's analysis is needlessly hostile to the precedent? What does the Court achieve by saying more than necessary to resolve the merits of the case? For a penetrating analysis of *Gates*, see Kamisar, Gates, *"Probable Cause," "Good Faith," and Beyond*, 69 Iowa L. Rev. 551 (1984).

(3) The fact that an anonymous tip was the precipitating event which led to a valid search warrant in *Gates* makes the use of such tips for *Terry* stops all the more palatable. In *Alabama v. White, supra*, the Court acknowledged the bootstrapping which may result from innocuous corroboration:

> The Court's opinion in *Gates* gave credit to the proposition that because an informant is shown to be right about some things, he is probably right about other facts that he has alleged, including the claim that the object of the tip is engaged in criminal activity. . . . Thus, it is not unreasonable to conclude in this case that the independent corroboration by the police of

significant aspects of the informer's predictions imparted some degree of reliability to the other allegations made by the caller.

We think it is also important that, as in *Gates*, "the anonymous [tip] contained a range of details relating not just to easily obtained facts and conditions existing at the time of the tip, but to future actions of third parties ordinarily not easily predicted." . . . The fact that the officers found a car precisely matching the caller's description in front of the 235 building is an example of the former. Anyone could have "predicted" that fact because it was a condition presumably existing at the time of the call. What was important was the caller's ability to predict respondent's *future behavior*, because it demonstrated inside information — a special familiarity with respondent's affairs. The general public would have had no way of knowing that respondent would shortly leave the building, get in the described car, and drive the most direct route to Dobey's Motel. Because only a small number of people are generally privy to an individual's itinerary, it is reasonable for police to believe that a person with access to such information is likely to also have access to reliable information about the individual's illegal activities.

The *White* dissenters, all of whom had dissented in *Gates*, made no reference to that decision.

(4) The deference extended by *Gates* to probable cause determinations in warrant issuance does not extend to warrantless searches. In *Ornelas v. United States*, 134 L. Ed. 2d 911 (1996), Chief Justice Rehnquist, speaking for the Court, held that trial court rulings on reasonable suspicion and probable cause in cases not involving a warrant were subject to de novo review on appeal. Justice Scalia was the lone dissenter. The Court adhered to the *Ornelas* holding in *United States v. Arvizu*, 534 U.S. 266 (2002), but reversed the judgment of the Court of Appeals for failing to give sufficient deference to the totality of the circumstances determination of reasonable suspicion made by the district court.

(5) In *State v. Profit*, 778 So. 2d 1127 (La. 2001), in the course of a chase the defendant threw a bag out of the window of an automobile, which when retrieved was found to contain three pounds of marijuana. Upon being apprehended, the defendant first gave a false address for his residence, which was corrected by a passenger and confirmed from the defendant's driver's license. A computer check revealed that the defendant had twice been arrested for the possession of marijuana, convicted once, and was currently on probation for that offense. Is there probable cause to support a search warrant for defendant's residence? The court, citing *Gates*, held that there was.

FRANKS v. DELAWARE

United States Supreme Court
438 U.S. 154 (1978)

MR. JUSTICE BLACKMUN delivered the opinion of the Court.

This case presents an important and long-standing issue of Fourth Amendment law. Does a defendant in a criminal proceeding ever have the right, under the Fourth and Fourteenth Amendments, subsequent to the *ex parte* issuance of a search warrant, to challenge the truthfulness of factual statements made in an affidavit supporting the warrant?

In the present case the Supreme Court of Delaware held, as a matter of first impression for it, that a defendant under *no* circumstances may so challenge the veracity of a sworn statement used by police to procure a search warrant. We reverse, and we hold that, where the defendant makes a substantial preliminary showing that a false statement knowingly and intentionally, or with reckless disregard for the truth, was included by the affiant in the warrant affidavit, and if the allegedly false statement is necessary to the finding of probable cause, the Fourth Amendment requires that a hearing be held at the defendant's request. In the event that at that hearing the allegation of perjury or reckless disregard is established by the defendant by a preponderance of the evidence, and, with the affidavit's false material set to one side, the affidavit's remaining content is insufficient to establish probable cause, the search warrant must be voided and the fruits of the search excluded to the same extent as if probable cause was lacking on the face of the affidavit.

I

The controversy over the veracity of the search warrant affidavit in this case arose in connection with petitioner Jerome Franks' state conviction for rape, kidnaping, and burglary. On Friday, March 5, 1976, Mrs. Cynthia Bailey told police in Dover, Delaware, that she had been confronted in her home earlier that morning by a man with a knife, and that he had sexually assaulted her. She described her assailant's age, race, height, build, and facial hair, and gave a detailed description of his clothing as consisting of a white thermal undershirt, black pants with a silver or gold buckle, a brown leather three-quarter length coat, and a dark knit cap that he wore pulled down around his eyes.

That same day, petitioner Franks coincidentally was taken into custody for an assault involving a 15-year-old girl, Brenda B. —, six days earlier. After his formal arrest, and while awaiting a bail hearing in Family Court, petitioner allegedly stated to Robert McClements, the youth officer accompanying him, that he was surprised the bail hearing was "about Brenda B. —. I know her. I thought you said Bailey. I don't know her." Trial Tr. 175, 186. At the time of this statement, the police allegedly had not yet recited to petitioner his rights under *Miranda v. Arizona*, 384 U.S. 436 (1966).

On the following Monday, March 8, officer McClements happened to mention the courthouse incident to a detective, Ronald R. Brooks, who was working on the Bailey case. Trial Tr. 186, 190–191. On March 9, detective Brooks and detective Larry D. Gray submitted a sworn affidavit to a justice of the peace in Dover, in support of a warrant to search petitioner's apartment. In paragraph 8 of the affidavit's "probable cause page" mention was made of petitioner's statement to McClements. In paragraph 10, it was noted that the description of the assailant given to the police by Mrs. Bailey included the above-mentioned clothing. Finally, the affidavit also described the attempt made by police to confirm that petitioner's typical outfit matched that of the assailant. Paragraph 15 recited: "On Tuesday, 3/9/76, your affiant contacted Mr. James Williams and Mr. Wesley Lucas of the Delaware Youth Center where Jerome Franks is employed and did have personal conversation with both these people." Paragraphs 16 and 17 respectively stated: "Mr. James Williams revealed to your affiant that the normal dress of Jerome Franks does consist of a white knit thermal undershirt and a brown leather jacket," and "Mr. Wesley Lucas revealed to your affiant that in addition to the thermal undershirt and jacket, Jerome Franks often wears a large green knit hat."

The warrant was issued on the basis of this affidavit. App. 9, Pursuant to the warrant, police searched petitioner's apartment and found a white thermal undershirt, a knit hat, dark pants, and a leather jacket, and, on petitioner's kitchen table, a single-blade knife. All these ultimately were introduced in evidence at trial.

Prior to the trial, however, petitioner's counsel filed a written motion to suppress the clothing and the knife found in the search; this motion alleged that the warrant on its face did not show probable cause and that the search and seizure were in violation of the Fourth and Fourteenth Amendments. *Id.*, at 11–12. At the hearing on the motion to suppress, defense counsel orally amended the challenge to include an attack on the veracity of the warrant affidavit; he also specifically requested the right to call as witnesses detective Brooks, Wesley Lucas of the Youth Center, and James D. Morrison, formerly of the Youth Center. *Id.*, at 14–17. Counsel asserted that Lucas and Morrison would testify that neither had been personally interviewed by the warrant affiants, and that, although they might have talked to another police officer, any information given by them to that officer was "somewhat different" from what was recited in the affidavit. *Id.*, at 16. Defense counsel charged that the misstatements were included in the affidavit not inadvertently, but in "bad faith." *Id.*, at 25. Counsel also sought permission to call officer McClements and petitioner as witnesses, to seek to establish that petitioner's courthouse statement to police had been obtained in violation of petitioner's *Miranda* rights, and that the search warrant was thereby tainted as the fruit of an illegally obtained confession. *Id.*, at 17, 27.

In rebuttal, the State's attorney argued in detail, App. 15–24, (a) that Del. Code Ann., Tit. 11, §§ 2306 and 2307 (1974), contemplated that any challenge to a search warrant was to be limited to questions of sufficiency based on the face of the affidavit; (b) that, purportedly, a majority of the States whose practice was not dictated by statute observed such a rule; and (c) that federal cases on the issue were to be distinguished because of Fed. Rule Crim. Proc. 41(e). He also noted that this Court had reserved the general issue of subfacial challenge to veracity in *Rugendorf v. United States*, 376 U.S. 528, 531–532 (1964), when it disposed of that case on the ground that, even if a veracity challenge were permitted, the alleged factual inaccuracies in that case's affidavit "were of only peripheral relevancy to the showing of probable cause, and, not being within the personal knowledge of the affiant, did not go to the integrity of the affidavit." *Id.*, at 532. The State objected to petitioner's "going behind [the warrant affidavit] in any way" and argued that the court must decide petitioner's motion "on the four corners" of the affidavit. App. 21.

The trial court sustained the State's objection to petitioner's proposed evidence. *Id.*, at 25, 27. The motion to suppress was denied; and the clothing and knife were admitted as evidence at the ensuing trial. Trial Tr. 192–196. Petitioner was convicted. In a written Motion for Judgment of Acquittal and/or New Trial, Record Document No. 23, petitioner repeated his objection to the admission of the evidence, stating that he "should have been allowed to impeach the Affidavit used in the Search Warrant to show purposeful misrepresentation of information contained therein." *Id.*, at 2. The motion was denied, and petitioner was sentenced to two consecutive terms of 25 years each and an additional consecutive life sentence.

On appeal, the Supreme Court of Delaware affirmed. 373 A.2d 578 (1977). It agreed with what it deemed to be the "majority rule" that no attack upon the veracity of a warrant affidavit could be made:

> We agree with the majority rule for two reasons. First, it is the function of the issuing magistrate to determine the reliability of information and credibility of affiants in deciding whether the requirement of probable cause has been met. There has been no need demonstrated for interfering with this function. Second, neither the probable cause nor suppression hearings are adjudications of guilt or innocence; the matters asserted by defendant are more properly considered in a trial on the merits.

Id., at 580.

III

Whether the Fourth and Fourteenth Amendments, and the derivative exclusionary rule made applicable to the States under *Mapp v. Ohio*, 367 U.S. 643 (1961), ever mandate that a defendant be permitted to attack the veracity of a warrant affidavit after the warrant has been issued and executed, is a question that encounters conflicting values. The bulwark of Fourth Amendment protection, of course, is the Warrant Clause, requiring that, absent certain exceptions, police obtain a warrant from a neutral and disinterested magistrate before embarking upon a search. In deciding today that, in certain circumstances, a challenge to a warrant's veracity must be permitted, we derive our ground from language of the Warrant Clause itself, which surely takes the affiant's good faith as its premise: "[N]o warrants shall issue, but upon probable cause, supported by Oath or affirmation. . . ." Judge Frankel, in *United States v. Halsey*, 257 F. Supp. 1002, 1005 (S.D.N.Y. 1966), aff'd No. 31369 (CA2 1967) (unreported), put the matter simply: "[W]hen the Fourth Amendment demands a factual showing sufficient to comprise 'probable cause,' the obvious assumption is that there will be a *truthful* showing" (emphasis in original). This does not mean "truthful" in the sense that every fact recited in the warrant affidavit is necessarily correct, for probable cause may be founded upon hearsay and upon information received from informants, as well as upon information within the affiant's own knowledge that sometimes must be garnered hastily. But surely it is to be "truthful" in the sense that the information put forth is believed or appropriately accepted by the affiant as true. It is established law . . . that a warrant affidavit must set forth particular facts and circumstances underlying the existence of probable cause, so as to allow the magistrate to make an independent evaluation of the matter. If an informant's tip is the source of information, the affidavit must recite "some of the underlying circumstances from which the informant concluded" that relevant evidence might be discovered, and "some of the underlying circumstances from which the officer concluded that the informant, whose identity need not be disclosed, . . . was 'credible' or his information 'reliable.' " . . . Because it is the magistrate who must determine independently whether there is probable cause, . . . it would be an unthinkable imposition upon his authority if a warrant affidavit, revealed after the fact to contain a deliberately or recklessly false statement, were to stand beyond impeachment.

In saying this, however, one must give cognizance to competing values that lead us to impose limitations. They perhaps can best be addressed by noting the arguments of respondent and others against allowing veracity challenges. The arguments are several:

First, respondent argues that the exclusionary rule, created in *Weeks v. United States*, 232 U.S. 383 (1914), is not a personal constitutional right, but only a judicially created remedy extended where its benefit as a deterrent promises to outweigh the societal cost of its use; that the Court has declined to apply the exclusionary rule when illegally seized evidence is used to impeach the credibility of a defendant's testimony, *Walder v. United States*, 347 U.S. 62 (1954), is used in a grand jury proceeding, *United States v. Calandra*, 414 U.S. 338 (1974), or is used in a civil trial, *United States v. Janis*, 428 U.S. 433 (1976); and that the Court similarly has restricted application of the Fourth Amendment exclusionary rule in federal habeas corpus review of a state conviction. See *Stone v. Powell*, 428 U.S. 465 (1976). Respondent argues that applying the exclusionary rule to another situation — the deterrence of deliberate or reckless untruthfulness in a warrant affidavit — is not justified for many of the same reasons that led to the above restrictions; interfering with a criminal conviction in order to deter official misconduct is a burden too great to impose on society.

Second, respondent argues that a citizen's privacy interests are adequately protected by a requirement that applicants for a warrant submit a sworn affidavit and by the magistrate's independent determination of sufficiency based on the face of the affidavit. Applying the exclusionary rule to attacks upon veracity would weed out a minimal number of perjurious government statements, says respondent, but would overlap unnecessarily with existing penalties against perjury, including criminal prosecutions, departmental discipline for misconduct, contempt of court, and civil actions.

Third, it is argued that the magistrate already is equipped to conduct a fairly vigorous inquiry into the accuracy of the factual affidavit supporting a warrant application. He may question the affiant, or summon other persons to give testimony at the warrant proceeding. The incremental gain from a post-search adversary proceeding, it is said, would not be great.

Fourth, it is argued that it would unwisely diminish the solemnity and moment of the magistrate's proceeding to make his inquiry into probable cause reviewable in regard to veracity. The less final, and less deference paid to, the magistrate's determination of veracity, the less initiative will he use in that task. Denigration of the magistrate's function would be imprudent insofar as his scrutiny is the last bulwark preventing any particular invasion of privacy before it happens.

Fifth, it is argued that permitting a post-search evidentiary hearing on issues of veracity would confuse the pressing issue of guilt or innocence with the collateral question as to whether there had been official misconduct in the drafting of the affidavit. The weight of criminal dockets, and the need to prevent diversion of attention from the main issue of guilt or innocence, militate against such an added burden on the trial courts. And if such hearings were conducted routinely, it is said, they would be misused by defendants as a convenient source of discovery. Defendants might even use the hearings in an attempt to force revelation of the identity of informants.

Sixth and finally, it is argued that a post-search veracity challenge is inappropriate because the accuracy of an affidavit in large part is beyond the control of the affiant. An affidavit may properly be based on hearsay, on fleeting observations, and on tips received from unnamed informants whose identity often will be properly protected from revelation under *McCray v. Illinois*, 386 U.S. 300 (1967).

None of these considerations is trivial. Indeed, because of them, the rule announced today has a limited scope, both in regard to when exclusion of the seized evidence is mandated, and when a hearing on allegations of misstatements must be accorded. But neither do the considerations cited by respondent and others have a fully controlling weight; we conclude that they are insufficient to justify an *absolute* ban on post-search impeachment of veracity. On this side of the balance, also, there are pressing considerations:

First, a flat ban on impeachment of veracity could denude the probable cause requirement of all real meaning. The requirement that a warrant not issue "but upon probable cause, supported by Oath or affirmation," would be reduced to a nullity if a police officer was able to use deliberately falsified allegations to demonstrate probable cause, and, having misled the magistrate, then was able to remain confident that the ploy was worthwhile. It is this specter of intentional falsification that, we think, has evoked such widespread opposition to the flat nonimpeachment rule from the commentators, from the American Law Institute in its Model Code of Pre-Arraignment Procedure, § SS290.3(1), from the federal courts of appeals, and from state courts. On occasion, of course, an instance of deliberate falsity will be exposed and confirmed without a special inquiry either at trial, see *United States ex rel. Petillo v. New Jersey*, 400 F. Supp. 1152, 1171–1172 (NJ 1975), vacated and remanded by order *sub nom, Albanese v. Yeager*, 541 F.2d 275 (CA3 1976), or at a hearing on the sufficiency of the affidavit, cf. *United States v. Upshaw*, 448 F.2d 1218, 1221–1222 (CA5 1971), *cert. denied*, 405 U.S. 934 (1972). A flat nonimpeachment rule would bar re-examination of the warrant even in these cases.

Second, the hearing before the magistrate not always will suffice to discourage lawless or reckless misconduct. The pre-search proceeding is necessarily *ex parte*, since the subject of the search cannot be tipped off to the application for a warrant lest he destroy or remove evidence. The usual reliance of our legal system on adversary proceedings itself should be an indication that an *ex parte* inquiry is likely to be less vigorous. The magistrate has no acquaintance with the information that may contradict the good faith and reasonable basis of the affiant's allegations. The pre-search proceeding will frequently be marked by haste, because of the understandable desire to act before the evidence disappears; this urgency will not always permit the magistrate to make an extended independent examination of the affiant or other witnesses.

Third, the alternative sanctions of a perjury prosecution, administrative discipline, contempt, or a civil suit are not likely to fill the gap. *Mapp v. Ohio*, implicitly rejected the adequacy of these alternatives. Mr. Justice Douglas noted this in his concurrence in *Mapp*, 367 U.S., at 670, where he quoted from *Wolf v. Colorado*, 338 U.S. 25, 42 (1949): " 'Self-scrutiny is a lofty ideal, but its exaltation reaches new heights if we expect a District Attorney to prosecute himself or his associates for well-meaning violations of the search and seizure clause during a raid the District Attorney or his associates have ordered.' "

Fourth, allowing an evidentiary hearing, after a suitable preliminary proffer of material falsity, would not diminish the importance and solemnity of the warrant-issuing process. It is the *ex parte* nature of the initial hearing, rather than the magistrate's capacity, that is the reason for the review. A magistrate's determination is presently subject to review before trial as to *sufficiency* without any undue interference with the dignity of the magistrate's function. Our reluctance today to extend the rule of exclusion beyond instances of deliberate misstatements, and those of reckless disregard, leaves a broad field where the magistrate is the sole protection of a citizen's Fourth Amendment rights, namely, in instances where police have been merely negligent in checking or recording the facts relevant to a probable cause determination.

Fifth, the claim that a post-search hearing will confuse the issue of the defendant's guilt with the issue of the State's possible misbehavior is footless. The hearing will not be in the presence of the jury. An issue extraneous to guilt already is examined in any probable cause determination or review of probable cause. Nor, if a sensible threshold showing is required and sensible substantive requirements for suppression are maintained, need there be any new large-scale commitment of judicial resources; many claims will wash out at an early stage, and the more substantial ones in any event would require judicial resources for vindication if the suggested alternative sanctions were truly to be effective. The requirement of a substantial preliminary showing should suffice to prevent the misuse of a veracity hearing for purposes of discovery or obstruction. And because we are faced today with only the question of the integrity of the affiant's representations as to his own activities, we need not decide, and we in no way predetermine, the difficult question whether a reviewing court must ever require the revelation of the identity of an informant once a substantial preliminary showing of falsity has been made. *McCray v. Illinois*, 386 U.S. 300 (1967), the Court's earlier disquisition in this area, concluded only that the Due Process Clause of the Fourteenth Amendment did not require the State to expose an informant's identity routinely, upon a defendant's mere demand, when there was ample evidence in the probable cause hearing to show that the informant was reliable and his information credible.

Sixth and finally, as to the argument that the exclusionary rule should not be extended to a "new" area, we cannot regard any such extension really to be at issue here. Despite the deep skepticism of Members of this Court as to the wisdom of extending the exclusionary rule to collateral areas, such as civil or grand jury proceedings, the Court has not questioned, in the absence of a more efficacious sanction, the continued application of the rule to suppress evidence from the State's case where a Fourth Amendment violation has been substantial and deliberate. See *Brewer v. Williams*, 430 U.S. 387, 422 (1977) (dissenting opinion); *Stone v. Powell*, 428 U.S. 465, 538 (1976) (dissenting opinion). We see no principled basis for distinguishing between the question of the sufficiency of an affidavit, which also is subject to a post-search reexamination, and the question of its integrity.

IV

In sum, and to repeat with some embellishment what we stated at the beginning of this opinion: There is, of course, a presumption of validity with respect to the affidavit supporting the search warrant. To mandate an evidentiary hearing, the challenger's attack must be more than conclusory and must be supported by more than a mere desire to cross-examine. There must be allegations of deliberate falsehood or of reckless disregard for the truth, and those allegations must be accompanied by an offer of proof. They should point out specifically the portion of the warrant affidavit that is claimed to be false; and they should be accompanied by a statement of supporting reasons. Affidavits or sworn or otherwise reliable statements of witnesses should be furnished, or their absence satisfactorily explained. Allegations of negligence or innocent mistake are insufficient. The deliberate falsity or reckless disregard whose impeachment is permitted today is only that of the affiant, not of any nongovernmental informant. Finally, if these requirements are met, and if, when material that is the subject of the alleged falsity or reckless disregard is set to one side, there remains sufficient content in the warrant affidavit to support a finding of probable cause, no hearing is required. On the other hand, if the remaining content is insufficient, the defendant is entitled, under the Fourth Amendment, to his hearing. Whether he will prevail at that hearing is, of course, another issue.

Because of Delaware's absolute rule, its courts did not have occasion to consider the proffer put forward by petitioner Franks. Since the framing of suitable rules to govern proffers is a matter properly left to the States, we decline ourselves to pass on petitioner's proffer. The judgment of the Supreme Court of Delaware is reversed, and the case is remanded for further proceedings not inconsistent with this opinion.

MR. JUSTICE REHNQUIST, with whom the CHIEF JUSTICE joins, dissenting.

If the function of the warrant requirement is to obtain the determination of a neutral magistrate as to whether sufficient grounds have been urged to support the issuance of a warrant, that function is fulfilled at the time the magistrate concludes that the requirement has been met. Like any other determination of a magistrate, of a court, or of countless other factfinding tribunals, the decision may be incorrect as a matter of law. Even if correct, some inaccurate or falsified information may have gone into the making of the determination. But unless we are to exalt as the *ne plus ultra* of our system of criminal justice the absolute correctness of every factual determination made along the tortuous route from the filing of the complaint or the issuance of an indictment to the final determination that a judgment of conviction was properly obtained, we shall lose perspective as to the purposes of the system as well as of the warrant requirement of the Fourth and Fourteenth Amendments.

I am quite confident that if our system of justice were not administered by judges who were once lawyers, it might well be less satisfactory than it now is. But I am equally confident that one improvement which would manifest itself as a result of such a change would be a willingness, reflected in almost all callings in our society except lawyers, to refrain from constant relitigation, whether in the form of collateral attack, appeal, retrial, or whatever, of issues that have originally been decided by a competent authority.

NOTES AND QUESTIONS

(1) How can a defendant make "a substantial preliminary showing that a false statement" was included *before* getting a hearing? Is this no more than a pleading requirement?

(2) If the defendant is able to prove perjury, does not the purpose of the exclusionary rule compel the invalidation of the warrant, irrespective of materiality? Compare *State v. Little*, 560 S.W.2d 403 (Tenn. 1978), when the court held that a warrant would fail if the affidavit contained ". . . (1) a false statement made with intent to deceive the Court, whether material or immaterial to the issue of probable cause. . . ." The court had placed primary reliance upon *United States v. Luna*, 525 F.2d 4 (6th Cir. 1975), *cert. denied*, 424 U.S. 965 (1976). After the *Franks* decision, the Court of Appeals for the Sixth Circuit modified its rule for federal courts to coincide with *Franks*. *United States v. Barone*, 584 F.2d 118 (6th Cir. 1978), *cert. denied*, 439 U.S. 1115 (1979). The Tennessee Supreme Court, however, has not backed off from the more stringent standard. *See also People v. Cook*, 583 P.2d 130 (Cal. 1978).

(3) If the false statement is material to the showing of probable cause, why shouldn't negligence be sufficient to justify impeachment? *Compare United States v. Smith*, 588 F.2d 737 (9th Cir. 1978), *cert. denied*, 440 U.S. 939 (1979), *with United States v. Astroff*, 556 F.2d 1369 (5th Cir. 1977), *vacated*, 578 F.2d 133 (5th Cir. 1978). Or even an innocent mistake?

(4) Would *Franks* support a challenge that an informant cited in an affidavit did not exist? *See People v. Pointdexter*, 282 N.W.2d 411 (Mich. Ct. App. 1979).

(5) In *Commonwealth v. Ramirez*, 416 Mass. 41, 617 N.E.2d 983 (1993), eight months after the defendant's conviction, in an opinion in an unrelated case, the Supreme Judicial Court of Massachusetts had "detailed egregious instances of perjurious and fraudulent conduct by officers of the drug control unit of the Boston police department, including the fabrication of a confidential informant as a means of obtaining search warrants in ostensible compliance with constitutional require-

ments." Counsel for the defendant had "uncovered suspiciously frequent reliance on a single informant throughout the city by a member of the drug control unit. The defendant also has shown discomforting similarities among the applications relying on this informant and an apparent conflict between these applications and [the arresting officer's] testimony." The court concluded that the defendant was entitled to a *Franks* hearing.

PROBLEM A
CHALLENGING THE VERACITY OF THE AFFIDAVIT

A search warrant was issued on the basis of the following affidavit:

> Your affiant [Eric Dureton] states that on January 25, 1995 he received information from investigator Sam C. Cureton of the Greenville County Sheriff's Office pertaining to Victor Wyatt Missouri. The information that was relayed to your affiant that Missouri was involved in the manufacture and distribution of crack cocaine. The following is a chronological chain of events leading to your affiants [sic] belief that Victor Wyatt Missouri, and others not yet identified, are manufacturing and distributing crack cocaine. . . .
>
> The confidential source of information, who from here forward will be referred to as CSI, stated that for the past two months he has purchased a total of two kilograms of cocaine from Victor Missouri. He would receive this in half kilo quantities every two weeks.
>
> On January 31, 1995, CSI stated that he had talked with Missouri and another subject who is only known as "Hot Sauce." During this conversation Missouri and "Hot Sauce" stated that they were going to Atlanta, Georgia on February 1, 1995 and obtain four kilos of powder cocaine. This cocaine would then be delivered to Greenville, South Carolina and cooked into crack cocaine. On February 1, 1995 this same CSI went by "Hot Sauce's" apartment at 400 Summit Drive apartment 5-D, Summit Place Apartments. During a conversation with "Hot Sauce" CSI was told that he had not been able to leave for the trip to Atlanta, that they had some things to get together beforehand. During this same conversation CSI told "Hot Sauce" that he wanted to purchase from him a half of a kilo. "Hot Sauce" told CSI that it would cost him around $13,000.00 for the half kilo. CSI told "Hot Sauce" to call him when he left for Atlanta.
>
> On February 2, 1995 at 4:00 in the afternoon, CSI went to Missouri's residence at 126 Sycamore Drive in the City of Greenville, South Carolina. At the residence was Missouri and "Hot Sauce." "Hot Sauce" told CSI that he was leaving for Atlanta around 4:30 and would return around midnight that same night. "Hot Sauce" told CSI that he would page him as soon as he got back in town.
>
> On February 3, 1995, at 4:00 in the morning, Missouri called CSI and told him that "Hot Sauce" was back and they needed somewhere to cook the crack. He said he couldn't cook it at his (Missouri) house because he had relatives there. CSI told him he would give him an answer later and he

> ultimately told him no. Around 9:00 this same morning CSI paged "Hot Sauce" via his digital pager. "Hot Sauce" returned the call and told CSI they were still trying to get it together. At 10:15 another page was made to "Hot Sauce" with the same results. At 2:00 in the afternoon the CSI drove to "Hot Sauce's" apartment at 400 Summit Drive and went in to inquire about his portion of the cocaine. Your affiant wired the CSI with a body transmitter that would enable your affiant to monitor the conversations he had while inside this apartment. Your affiant, while monitoring the audio transmitter, heard a male voice, whom CSI later stated was "Hot Sauce", question CSI about the phone that had been used earlier trying to set the transaction up. This male appeared to be somewhat reserved about talking with CSI about the cocaine. CSI told your affiant that "Hot Sauce" did appear to be nervous about the deal they were trying to make. "Hot Sauce" told CSI that he had the crack but he would call him when it was right.
>
> While officers of the Vice and Narcotics Bureau were surveilling 400 Summit Drive, Apartment 5-D on February 3, 1995, it was determined that Missouri, "Hot Sauce" and others who have not been identified, were in the apartment. Around 5:00 a black male and black female left the apartment in a white dodge van. . . . The van then traveled to Parkersway Foods at Worley Road and Rutherford Road. The female again went inside. After the female left Detective Sergeant T.D. Christy interviewed the clerk and the clerk stated that the black female had purchased 5 boxes of Arm & Hammer baking soda. The van then traveled back to apartment 5-D and the female took a grocery bag into the apartment. She returned to the van and they left again. The surveillance on the van was terminated at this time.
>
> Your affiant, through training, experience and working with other experienced investigators, believes that Victor Wyatt Missouri, "Hot Sauce" and others yet unknown are manufacturing crack cocaine inside of apartment 5-D Summit Place Apartments, 400 Summit Drive in the City of Greenville, South Carolina.
>
> When the warrant was executed, Missouri was discovered standing over the kitchen sink which contained a quantity of cooked, crack cocaine.

At the suppression hearing, Officer Cureton conceded that the statement " 'Hot Sauce' told CSI that he had the crack but he would call him when it was right," was false. He testified further that at no time had "Hot Sauce" told CSI that there was crack in his apartment. Furthermore, "Hot Sauce" had told CSI that he did not want to cook the cocaine at his apartment because his wife was trying to go straight, and CSI had been within the apartment and failed to observe any cocaine. Should the evidence be suppressed? *See State v. Missouri*, 524 S.E.2d 394 (S.C. 1999).

§ 3.03 SPECIAL CONSIDERATIONS

[A] Physical Integrity

[1] The "Shocks the Conscience" Test

ROCHIN v. CALIFORNIA
United States Supreme Court
342 U.S. 165 (1952)

MR. JUSTICE FRANKFURTER delivered the opinion of the Court.

Having "some information that [the petitioner here] was selling narcotics," three deputy sheriffs of the County of Los Angeles, on the morning of July 1, 1949, made for the two-story dwelling house in which Rochin lived with his mother, common-law wife, brothers and sisters. Finding the outside door open, they entered and then forced open the door to Rochin's room on the second floor. Inside they found petitioner sitting partly dressed on the side of the bed, upon which his wife was lying. On a "night stand" beside the bed the deputies spied two capsules. When asked "Whose stuff is this?" Rochin seized the capsules and put them in his mouth. A struggle ensued, in the course of which the three officers "jumped upon him" and attempted to extract the capsules. The force they applied proved unavailing against Rochin's resistance. He was handcuffed and taken to a hospital. At the direction of one of the officers a doctor forced an emetic solution through a tube into Rochin's stomach against his will. This "stomach pumping" produced vomiting. In the vomited matter were found two capsules which proved to contain morphine.

Rochin was brought to trial before a California Superior Court, sitting without a jury, on the charge of possessing "a preparation of morphine" in violation of the California Health and Safety Code, 1947, § 11, 500. Rochin was convicted and sentenced to sixty days' imprisonment. The chief evidence against him was the two capsules. They were admitted over petitioner's objection, although the means of obtaining them was frankly set forth in the testimony by one of the deputies, substantially as here narrated.

Regard for the requirements of the Due Process Clause "inescapably imposes upon this Court an exercise of judgment upon the whole course of the proceedings resulting in a conviction in order to ascertain whether they offend those canons of decency and fairness which express the notions of justice of English-speaking peoples even toward those charged with the most heinous offenses." . . . These standards of justice are not authoritatively formulated anywhere as though they were specifics. Due process of law is a summarized constitutional guarantee of respect for those personal immunities which, as Mr. Justice Cardozo twice wrote for the Court, are "so rooted in the traditions and conscience of our people as to be ranked as fundamental," *Snyder v. Massachusetts*, 291 U.S. 97, 105, or are "implicit in the concept of ordered liberty." *Palko v. Connecticut*, 302 U.S. 319, 325.

The vague contours of the Due Process Clause do not leave judges at large. We may not draw on our merely personal and private notions and disregard the limits that bind judges in their judicial function. Even though the concept of due process of law is not final and fixed, these limits are derived from considerations that are fused in the whole nature of our judicial process. See Cardozo, *The Nature of the Judicial Process; The Growth of the Law; The Paradoxes of Legal Science*. These are considerations deeply rooted in reason and in the compelling traditions of the legal profession. The Due Process Clause places upon this Court the duty of exercising a judgment, within the narrow confines of judicial power in reviewing State convictions, upon interests of society pushing in opposite directions.

Due process of law thus conceived is not to be derided as resort to a revival of "natural law." To believe that this judicial exercise of judgment could be avoided by freezing "due process of law" at some fixed stage of time or thought is to suggest that the most important aspect of constitutional adjudication is a function for inanimate machines and not for judges, for whom the independence safeguarded by Article III of the Constitution was designed and who are presumably guided by established standards of judicial behavior. Even cybernetics has not yet made that haughty claim. To practice the requisite detachment and to achieve sufficient objectivity no doubt demands of judges the habit of self-discipline and self-criticism, incertitude that one's own views are incontestable and alert tolerance toward views not shared. But these are precisely the presuppositions of our judicial process. They are precisely the qualities society has a right to expect from those entrusted with ultimate judicial power.

Restraints on our jurisdiction are self-imposed only in the sense that there is from our decisions no immediate appeal short of impeachment or constitutional amendment. But that does not make due process of law a matter of judicial caprice. The faculties of the Due Process Clause may be indefinite and vague, but the mode of their ascertainment is not self-willed. In each case "due process of law" requires an evaluation based on a disinterested inquiry pursued in the spirit of science, on a balanced order of facts exactly and fairly stated, on the detached consideration of conflicting claims, . . . on a judgment not *ad hoc* and episodic but duly mindful of reconciling the needs both of continuity and of change in a progressive society.

Applying these general considerations to the circumstances of the present case, we are compelled to conclude that the proceedings by which this conviction was obtained do more than offend some fastidious squeamishness or private sentimentalism about combatting crime too energetically. This is conduct that shocks the conscience. Illegally breaking into the privacy of the petitioner, the struggle to open his mouth and remove what was there, the forcible extraction of his stomach's contents — this course of proceeding by agents of government to obtain evidence is bound to offend even hardened sensibilities. They are methods too close to the rack and the screw to permit of constitutional differentiation.

We are not unmindful that hypothetical situations can be conjured up, shading imperceptibly from the circumstances of this case and by gradations producing practical differences despite seemingly logical extensions. But the Constitution is "intended to preserve practical and substantial rights, not to maintain theories." . . .

On the facts of this case the conviction of the petitioner has been obtained by methods that offend the Due Process Clause. The judgment below must be

Reversed.

MR. JUSTICE BLACK, concurring.

What the majority hold is that the Due Process Clause empowers this Court to nullify any state law if its application "shocks the conscience," offends "a sense of justice" or runs counter to the "decencies of civilized conduct." The majority emphasize that these statements do not refer to their own consciences or to their senses of justice and decency. For we are told that "we may not draw on our merely personal and private notions"; our judgment must be grounded on "considerations deeply rooted in reason and in the compelling traditions of the legal profession." We are further admonished to measure the validity of state practices, not by our reason, or by the traditions of the legal profession, but by "the community's sense of fair play and decency"; by the "traditions and conscience of our people"; or by "those canons of decency and fairness which express the notions of justice of English-speaking peoples." These canons are made necessary, it is said, because of "interests of society pushing in opposite directions."

If the Due Process Clause does vest this court with such unlimited power to invalidate laws, I am still in doubt as to why we should consider only the notions of English-speaking peoples to determine what are immutable and fundamental principles of justice. Moreover, one may well ask what avenues of investigation are open to discover "canons" of conduct so universally favored that this Court should write them into the Constitution? All we are told is that the discovery must be made by an "evaluation based on a disinterested inquiry pursued in the spirit of science, on a balanced order of facts."

Some constitutional provisions are stated in absolute and unqualified language such, for illustration, as the First Amendment stating that no law shall be passed prohibiting the free exercise of religion or abridging the freedom of speech or press. Other constitutional provisions do require courts to choose between competing policies, such as the Fourth Amendment which, by its terms, necessitates a judicial decision as to what is an "unreasonable" search or seizure. There is, however, no express constitutional language granting judicial power to invalidate *every* state law of *every* kind deemed "unreasonable" or contrary to the Court's notion of civilized decencies; yet the constitutional philosophy used by the majority has, in the past, been used to deny a state the right to fix the price of gasoline, *Williams v. Standard Oil Co.*, 278 U.S. 235; and even the right to prevent bakers from palming off smaller for larger loaves of bread, *Jay Burns Baking Co. v. Bryan*, 264 U.S. 504. These cases, and others, show the extent to which the evanescent standards of the majority's philosophy have been used to nullify state legislative programs passed to suppress evil economic practices. What paralyzing role this same philosophy will play in the future economic affairs of this country is impossible to predict. Of even graver concern, however, is the use of the philosophy to nullify the Bill of Rights. I long ago concluded that the accordion-like qualities of this philosophy must inevitably imperil all the individual liberty safeguards specifically enumerated in the Bill of Rights. Reflection and recent decisions of this Court sanctioning abridgment of the freedom of speech and press have strengthened this conclusion.

[JUSTICE DOUGLAS also concurred.]

NOTES AND QUESTIONS

(1) In *Adamson v. California*, 332 U.S. 46 (1947), Justice Frankfurter had maintained in a concurring opinion that the Fourteenth Amendment had its own "independent potency," a notion which he was able to employ to decide *Rochin*. What are the strengths and weaknesses of the Frankfurter approach as compared to the Black approach?

(2) In *Irvine v. California*, 347 U.S. 128 (1954), police, suspecting gambling violations and without obtaining a warrant, duplicated the defendant's house key and surreptitiously placed microphones in several rooms. Evidence so obtained led to a conviction. In a five-four decision, containing five different opinions, the Supreme Court held the evidence admissible. Two prior decisions were considered by the Court: *Wolf v. Colorado*, 338 U.S. 25 (1949), which held that illegally obtained evidence was admissible in state courts, and *Rochin*. Frankfurter had authored both majority opinions. Justice Jackson, speaking for the majority in *Irvine*, held that the Court was bound by *Wolf*. Justice Frankfurter, dissenting, maintained that *Rochin* controlled.

(3) Consider the application of *Rochin* in the following cases:

(a) During a narcotics arrest, defendant put an object in his mouth, and the officer immediately used a judo choke. After a minute, the defendant spit out the object. At trial, the officer testified that the tactic "stops the person from swallowing or eventually it stops the blood flow to the head, then he passes out." *See People v. Sanders*, 268 Cal. App. 2d 802, 74 Cal. Rptr. 350 (1969).

(b) In the process of an arrest, the officer forced open the mouth of the defendant and removed particles of marijuana from his teeth with the cap of a ball point pen. See *State ex rel. Flournoy v. Wren*, 108 Ariz. 356, 498 P.2d 444 (1972). *See also Foxall v. State*, 157 Ind. App. 19, 298 N.E. 2d 470 (1973).

(c) Defendant, accused of child molestation, was judicially ordered to submit to an involuntary ejaculation to determine if he was infected with trichomoniasis, from which the purported victim of the crime suffered. *See People v. Scott*, 21 Cal. 3d 284, 145 Cal. Rptr. 876, 578 P.2d 123 (1978).

(4) 725 Ill. Comp. Stat. Ann. 5/103.1 (2004):

(c) No person arrested for a traffic, regulatory or misdemeanor offense, except in cases involving weapons or a controlled substance, shall be strip searched unless there is reasonable belief that the individual is concealing a weapon or controlled substance.

(d) "Strip search" means having an arrested person remove or arrange some or all of his or her clothing so as to permit a visual inspection of the genitals, buttocks, anus, female breasts or undergarments of such person.

(e) All strip searches conducted under this Section shall be performed by persons of the same sex as the arrested person and on premises where the search cannot be observed by persons not physically conducting the search.

(f) Every peace officer or employee of a police department conducting a strip search shall:

(1) Obtain the written permission of the police commander or an agent thereof designated for the purposes of authorizing a strip search in accordance with this Section.

(2) Prepare a report of the strip search. The report shall include the written authorization required by subsection (e)(1); the name of the person subjected to the search; (2) the name of the persons conducting the search; and (3) the time, date and place of the search. A copy of the report shall be provided to the person subject to the search.

(g) No search of any body cavity other than the mouth shall be conducted without a duly executed search warrant; any warrant authorizing a body cavity search shall specify that the search must be performed under sanitary conditions and conducted either by or under the supervision of a physician licensed to practice medicine in all of its branches in this State.

(h) Any peace officer or employee who knowingly or intentionally fails to comply with any provision of this Section is guilty of official misconduct as provided in Section 103-8; provided however, that nothing contained in this Section shall preclude prosecution of a peace officer or employee under another section of this Code.

What purposes does such a statute serve? Are arrestees in Illinois protected to a greater extent than arrestees in states without such a provision?

[2] Taking Bodily Fluids

MISSOURI v. McNEELY

United States Supreme Court
133 S. Ct. 1552 (2013)

Justice Sotomayor announced the judgment of the Court and delivered the opinion of the Court with respect to Parts I, II-A, II-B, and IV, and an opinion with respect to Parts II-C and III, in which Justice Scalia, Justice Ginsburg, and Justice Kagan join.

In *Schmerber v. California*, . . . this Court upheld a warrantless blood test of an individual arrested for driving under the influence of alcohol because the officer "might reasonably have believed that he was confronted with an emergency, in which the delay necessary to obtain a warrant, under the circumstances, threatened the destruction of evidence." . . . The question presented here is whether the natural metabolization of alcohol in the bloodstream presents a *per se* exigency that justifies an exception to the Fourth Amendment's warrant requirement for nonconsensual blood testing in all drunk-driving cases. We conclude that it does not, and we hold, consistent with general Fourth Amendment principles, that exigency in this context must be determined case by case based on the totality of the circumstances.

I

While on highway patrol at approximately 2:08 a.m., a Missouri police officer stopped Tyler McNeely's truck after observing it exceed the posted speed limit and repeatedly cross the centerline. The officer noticed several signs that McNeely was intoxicated, including McNeely's bloodshot eyes, his slurred speech, and the smell of alcohol on his breath. McNeely acknowledged to the officer that he had consumed "a couple of beers" at a bar, . . . and he appeared unsteady on his feet when he exited the truck. After McNeely performed poorly on a battery of field-sobriety tests and declined to use a portable breath-test device to measure his blood alcohol concentration (BAC), the officer placed him under arrest.

The officer began to transport McNeely to the station house. But when McNeely indicated that he would again refuse to provide a breath sample, the officer changed course and took McNeely to a nearby hospital for blood testing. The officer did not attempt to secure a warrant. Upon arrival at the hospital, the officer asked McNeely whether he would consent to a blood test. Reading from a standard implied consent form, the officer explained to McNeely that under state law refusal to submit voluntarily to the test would lead to the immediate revocation of his driver's license for one year and could be used against him in a future prosecution. . . . McNeely nonetheless refused. The officer then directed a hospital lab technician to take a blood sample, and the sample was secured at approximately 2:35 a.m. Subsequent laboratory testing measured McNeely's BAC at 0.154 percent, which was well above the legal limit of 0.08 percent. . . .

McNeely was charged with driving while intoxicated (DWI), . . . He moved to suppress the results of the blood test, arguing in relevant part that, under the circumstances, taking his blood for chemical testing without first obtaining a search warrant violated his rights under the Fourth Amendment. The trial court agreed. It concluded that the exigency exception to the warrant requirement did not apply because, apart from the fact that "[a]s in all cases involving intoxication, [McNeely's] blood alcohol was being metabolized by his liver," there were no circumstances suggesting the officer faced an emergency in which he could not practicably obtain a warrant. . . .

The Missouri Supreme Court affirmed.

. . .

We granted certiorari to resolve a split of authority on the question whether the natural dissipation of alcohol in the bloodstream establishes a *per se* exigency that suffices on its own to justify an exception to the warrant requirement for nonconsensual blood testing in drunk-driving investigations. . . . We now affirm.

II

A

. . .

To determine whether a law enforcement officer faced an emergency that justified acting without a warrant, this Court looks to the totality of circumstances.

. . .

Our decision in *Schmerber* applied this totality of the circumstances approach.

. . .

B

The State properly recognizes that the reasonableness of a warrantless search under the exigency exception to the warrant requirement must be evaluated based on the totality of the circumstances. . . . But the State nevertheless seeks a *per se* rule for blood testing in drunk-driving cases. The State contends that whenever an officer has probable cause to believe an individual has been driving under the influence of alcohol, exigent circumstances will necessarily exist because BAC evidence is inherently evanescent. As a result, the State claims that so long as the officer has probable cause and the blood test is conducted in a reasonable manner, it is categorically reasonable for law enforcement to obtain the blood sample without a warrant.

It is true that as a result of the human body's natural metabolic processes, the alcohol level in a person's blood begins to dissipate once the alcohol is fully absorbed and continues to decline until the alcohol is eliminated. . . . Testimony before the trial court in this case indicated that the percentage of alcohol in an individual's blood typically decreases by approximately 0.015 percent to 0.02 percent per hour once the alcohol has been fully absorbed. . . . More precise calculations of the rate at which alcohol dissipates depend on various individual characteristics (such as weight, gender, and alcohol tolerance) and the circumstances in which the alcohol was consumed. . . . Regardless of the exact elimination rate, it is sufficient for our purposes to note that because an individual's alcohol level gradually declines soon after he stops drinking, a significant delay in testing will negatively affect the probative value of the results. This fact was essential to our holding in *Schmerber*, as we recognized that, under the circumstances, further delay in order to secure a warrant after the time spent investigating the scene of the accident and transporting the injured suspect to the hospital to receive treatment would have threatened the destruction of evidence. . . .

But it does not follow that we should depart from careful case-by-case assessment of exigency and adopt the categorical rule proposed by the State and its amici. In those drunk-driving investigations where police officers can reasonably obtain a warrant before a blood sample can be drawn without significantly undermining the efficacy of the search, the Fourth Amendment mandates that they do so.

. . .

The State's proposed *per se* rule . . . fails to account for advances in the 47 years since *Schmerber* was decided that allow for the more expeditious processing of warrant applications, particularly in contexts like drunk-driving investigations where the evidence offered to establish probable cause is simple. The Federal Rules of Criminal Procedure were amended in 1977 to permit federal magistrate judges to issue a warrant based on sworn testimony communicated by telephone. See 91 Stat. 319. As amended, the law now allows a federal magistrate judge to consider "information communicated by telephone or other reliable electronic means." Fed. Rule Crim. Proc. 4.1. States have also innovated. Well over a majority of States allow police officers or prosecutors to apply for search warrants remotely through various means, including telephonic or radio communication, electronic communication such as e-mail, and video conferencing. And in addition to technology-based developments, jurisdictions have found other ways to streamline the warrant process, such as by using standard-form warrant applications for drunk-driving investigations.

. . .

C

In an opinion concurring in part and dissenting in part, The Chief Justice agrees that the State's proposed *per se* rule is overbroad because "[f]or exigent circumstances to justify a warrantless search . . . there must . . . be 'no time to secure a warrant.' " . . . But The Chief Justice then goes on to suggest his own categorical rule under which a warrantless blood draw is permissible if the officer could not secure a warrant (or reasonably believed he could not secure a warrant) in the time it takes to transport the suspect to a hospital or similar facility and obtain medical assistance. . . . Although we agree that delay inherent to the blood-testing process is relevant to evaluating exigency, . . . we decline to substitute The Chief Justice's modified per se rule for our traditional totality of the circumstances analysis.

For one thing, making exigency completely dependent on the window of time between an arrest and a blood test produces odd consequences. Under The Chief Justice's rule, if a police officer serendipitously stops a suspect near an emergency room, the officer may conduct a nonconsensual warrantless blood draw even if all agree that a warrant could be obtained with very little delay under the circumstances (perhaps with far less delay than an average ride to the hospital in the jurisdiction). The rule would also distort law enforcement incentives. As with the State's *per se* rule, The Chief Justice's rule might discourage efforts to expedite the warrant process because it categorically authorizes warrantless blood draws so long as it takes more time to secure a warrant than to obtain medical assistance. On the flip side, making the requirement of independent judicial oversight turn exclusively on the amount of time that elapses between an arrest and BAC testing could induce police departments and individual officers to minimize testing delay to the detriment of other values. The Chief Justice correctly observes that "[t]his case involves medical personnel drawing blood at a medical facility, not police officers doing so by the side of the road." . . . But The Chief Justice does not say that roadside blood draws are necessarily unreasonable, and if we accepted The Chief Justice's approach, they would become a more attractive option for the police.

. . .

While the desire for a bright-line rule is understandable, the Fourth Amendment will not tolerate adoption of an overly broad categorical approach that would dilute the warrant requirement in a context where significant privacy interests are at stake. Moreover, a case-by-case approach is hardly unique within our Fourth Amendment jurisprudence. Numerous police actions are judged based on fact-intensive, totality of the circumstances analyses rather than according to categorical rules, including in situations that are more likely to require police officers to make difficult split-second judgments.

. . .

As to the nature of a blood test conducted in a medical setting by trained personnel, it is concededly less intrusive than other bodily invasions we have found unreasonable. See *Winston*, 470 U.S., at 759–766, 105 S. Ct. 1611 . . . For that reason, we have held that medically drawn blood tests are reasonable in appropriate circumstances. . . . We have never retreated, however, from our recognition that any compelled intrusion into the human body implicates significant, constitutionally protected privacy interests.

. . .

IV

. . .

Because this case was argued on the broad proposition that drunk-driving cases present a *per se* exigency, the arguments and the record do not provide the Court with an adequate analytic framework for a detailed discussion of all the relevant factors that can be taken into account in determining the reasonableness of acting without a warrant. It suffices to say that the metabolization of alcohol in the bloodstream and the ensuing loss of evidence are among the factors that must be considered in deciding whether a warrant is required. No doubt, given the large number of arrests for this offense in different jurisdictions nationwide, cases will arise when anticipated delays in obtaining a warrant will justify a blood test without judicial authorization, for in every case the law must be concerned that evidence is being destroyed. But that inquiry ought not to be pursued here where the question is not properly before this Court. Having rejected the sole argument presented to us challenging the Missouri Supreme Court's decision, we affirm its judgment.

* * *

We hold that in drunk-driving investigations, the natural dissipation of alcohol in the bloodstream does not constitute an exigency in every case sufficient to justify conducting a blood test without a warrant.

The judgment of the Missouri Supreme Court is affirmed.

. . .

Chief Justice Roberts, with whom Justice Breyer and Justice Alito join, concurring in part and dissenting in part.

A police officer reading this Court's opinion would have no idea — no idea — what the Fourth Amendment requires of him, once he decides to obtain a blood sample from a drunk-driving suspect who has refused a breathalyzer test. I have no quarrel with the Court's "totality of the circumstances" approach as a general matter; that is what our cases require. But the circumstances in drunk driving cases are often typical, and the Court should be able to offer guidance on how police should handle cases like the one before us.

In my view, the proper rule is straightforward. Our cases establish that there is an exigent circumstances exception to the warrant requirement. That exception applies when there is a compelling need to prevent the imminent destruction of important evidence, and there is no time to obtain a warrant. The natural dissipation of alcohol in the bloodstream constitutes not only the imminent but ongoing destruction of critical evidence. That would qualify as an exigent circumstance, except that there may be time to secure a warrant before blood can be drawn. If there is, an officer must seek a warrant. If an officer could reasonably conclude that there is not, the exigent circumstances exception applies by its terms, and the blood may be drawn without a warrant.

. . .

Justice Thomas, dissenting.

This case requires the Court to decide whether the Fourth Amendment prohibits an officer from obtaining a blood sample without a warrant when there is probable cause to believe that a suspect has been driving under the influence of alcohol. Because the body's natural metabolization of alcohol inevitably destroys evidence of the crime, it constitutes an exigent circumstance. As a result, I would hold that a warrantless blood draw does not violate the Fourth Amendment.

PROBLEM B
THE INVISIBLE ASSAULT

Bryan Barlow was marching at the head of the San Francisco Gay Freedom Day Marching Band and Twirling Corp in a Gay Pride Parade in San Diego. He became involved in a scuffle with police monitoring the event. During the struggle, he bit one of the officers on the right shoulder puncturing the skin and leaving a drop of blood. Barlow bit another officer on the right knuckle breaking the skin and drawing blood.

Barlow was arrested. To treat his injuries sustained in the struggle, he was taken to the hospital. There, before *Miranda* warnings had been given, an officer, concerned for his colleagues' well-being, asked Barlow if he was a homosexual and if he had AIDS. Barlow replied he was a homosexual and "You better take it that I do have AIDS for the officers' sake." Responsive to that statement, Barlow was taken to the central police station where, without a warrant and over his objection, blood samples for AIDS analysis were taken.

> Barlow was charged with two counts of battery against a police officer . . . and one count of resisting arrest. . . . At arraignment, the People sought and the municipal court issued a search warrant authorizing the taking but not the testing of a blood sample from Barlow. The People then moved to test the warrant-approved blood sample for AIDS antibodies and to release the results to the prosecution, the victims and their physicians.

Was the warrantless taking of the blood sample constitutionally valid? Should the warrant authorizing a blood test be issued? *See Barlow v. Superior Court*, 190 Cal. App. 3d 1652 (Cal. Ct. App. 1987).

MARYLAND v. KING

United States Supreme Court
133 S. Ct. 1958 (2013)

JUSTICE KENNEDY delivered the opinion of the Court.

In 2003 a man concealing his face and armed with a gun broke into a woman's home in Salisbury, Maryland. He raped her. The police were unable to identify or apprehend the assailant based on any detailed description or other evidence they then had, but they did obtain from the victim a sample of the perpetrator's DNA.

In 2009 Alonzo King was arrested in Wicomico County, Maryland, and charged with first- and second-degree assault for menacing a group of people with a shotgun. As part of a routine booking procedure for serious offenses, his DNA sample was taken by applying a cotton swab or filter paper — known as a buccal swab — to the inside of his cheeks. The DNA was found to match the DNA taken from the Salisbury rape victim. King was tried and convicted for the rape. Additional DNA samples were taken from him and used in the rape trial, but there seems to be no doubt that it was the DNA from the cheek sample taken at the time he was booked in 2009 that led to his first having been linked to the rape and charged with its commission.

The Court of Appeals of Maryland, on review of King's rape conviction, ruled that the DNA taken when King was booked for the 2009 charge was an unlawful seizure because obtaining and using the cheek swab was an unreasonable search of the person. It set the rape conviction aside. This Court granted certiorari and now reverses the judgment of the Maryland court.

I

When King was arrested on April 10, 2009, for menacing a group of people with a shotgun and charged in state court with both first- and second-degree assault, he was processed for detention in custody at the Wicomico County Central Booking facility. Booking personnel used a cheek swab to take the DNA sample from him pursuant to provisions of the Maryland DNA Collection Act (or Act).

On July 13, 2009, King's DNA record was uploaded to the Maryland DNA database, and three weeks later, on August 4, 2009, his DNA profile was matched to the DNA sample collected in the unsolved 2003 rape case. Once the DNA was matched to King, detectives presented the forensic evidence to a grand jury, which indicted him for the rape. Detectives obtained a search warrant and took a second sample of DNA from King, which again matched the evidence from the rape. He moved to suppress the DNA match on the grounds that Maryland's DNA collection law violated the Fourth Amendment. The Circuit Court Judge upheld the statute as constitutional. King pleaded not guilty to the rape charges but was convicted and sentenced to life in prison without the possibility of parole.

In a divided opinion, the Maryland Court of Appeals struck down the portions of the Act authorizing collection of DNA from felony arrestees as unconstitutional. The majority concluded that a DNA swab was an unreasonable search in violation of the Fourth Amendment because King's "expectation of privacy is greater than the State's purported interest in using King's DNA to identify him." . . . In reaching that conclusion the Maryland Court relied on the decisions of various other courts that have concluded that DNA identification of arrestees is impermissible.

Both federal and state courts have reached differing conclusions as to whether the Fourth Amendment prohibits the collection and analysis of a DNA sample from persons arrested, but not yet convicted, on felony charges. This Court granted certiorari, . . . to address the question. King is the respondent here.

II

The advent of DNA technology is one of the most significant scientific advancements of our era. The full potential for use of genetic markers in medicine and science is still being explored, but the utility of DNA identification in the criminal justice system is already undisputed. Since the first use of forensic DNA analysis to catch a rapist and murderer in England in 1986, see J. Butler, Fundamentals of Forensic DNA Typing 5 (2009) (hereinafter Butler), law enforcement, the defense bar, and courts have acknowledged DNA testing's "unparalleled ability both to exonerate the wrongly convicted and to identify the guilty. It has the potential to significantly improve both the criminal justice system and police investigative practices." *District Attorney's Office for Third Judicial Dist. v. Osborne*, 557 U.S. 52, 55 (2009).

. . .

III

A

Although the DNA swab procedure used here presents a question the Court has not yet addressed, the framework for deciding the issue is well established. The Fourth Amendment, binding on the States by the Fourteenth Amendment provides that "[t]he right of the people to be secure in their persons, houses, papers, and effects, against unreasonable searches and seizures, shall not be violated." It can be agreed that using a buccal swab on the inner tissues of a person's cheek in order to obtain DNA samples is a search. Virtually any "intrusio[n] into the human body," *Schmerber v. California*, . . . will work an invasion of "'cherished personal security' that is subject to constitutional scrutiny," . . .

. . .

A buccal swab is a far more gentle process than a venipuncture to draw blood. It involves but a light touch on the inside of the cheek; and although it can be deemed a search within the body of the arrestee, it requires no "surgical intrusions beneath the skin." *Winston*, . . . The fact that an intrusion is negligible is of central relevance to determining reasonableness, although it is still a search as the law defines that term.

B

To say that the Fourth Amendment applies here is the beginning point, not the end of the analysis. "[T]he Fourth Amendment's proper function is to constrain, not against all intrusions as such, but against intrusions which are not justified in the circumstances, or which are made in an improper manner." *Schmerber*, . . . "As the test of the Fourth Amendment indicates, the ultimate measure of the constitutionality of a governmental search is 'reasonableness.'" *Vernonia School Dist. 47J v. Acton*, . . . In giving content to the inquiry whether an intrusion is reasonable, the Court has preferred "some quantum of individualized suspicion . . . [as] a prerequisite to a constitutional search or seizure. But the Fourth Amendment imposes no irreducible requirement of such suspicion." *United States v. Martinez-Fuerte*, 428 U.S. 543, 560–61 (1976) . . . .

. . .

The Maryland DNA Collection Act provides that, in order to obtain a DNA sample, all arrestees charged with serious crimes must furnish the sample on a buccal swab applied, as noted, to the inside of the cheeks. The arrestee is already in valid police custody for a serious offense supported by probable cause. The DNA collection is not subject to the judgment in 'the often competitive enterprise of ferreting out crime.'" *Terry*, . . . As noted by this Court in a different but still instructive context involving blood testing, "[b]oth the circumstances justifying toxicological testing and the permissible limits of such intrusions are defined narrowly and specifically in the regulations that authorize them. . . . Indeed, in light of the standardized nature of the tests and the minimal discretion vested in those charged with administering the program, there are virtually no facts for a neutral magistrate to evaluate." . . . Here, the search effected by the buccal swab of respondent falls within the category of cases this Court has analyzed by reference to the proposition that the "touchstone of the Fourth Amendment is reasonableness, not individualized suspicion." . . .

Even if a warrant is not required, a search is not beyond Fourth Amendment scrutiny; for it must be reasonable in its scope and manner of execution. Urgent government interests are not a license for indiscriminate police behavior. To say that no warrant is required is merely to acknowledge that "rather than employing a *per se* rule of unreasonableness, we balance the privacy-related and law enforcement-related concerns to determine if the intrusion was reasonable." . . . This application of "traditional standards of reasonableness" requires a court to weigh "the promotion of legitimate governmental interests" against "the degree to which [the search] intrudes upon an individual's privacy." . . . An assessment of reasonableness to determine the lawfulness of requiring this class of arrestees to provide a DNA sample is central to the instant case.

IV

A

The legitimate government interest served by the Maryland DNA Collection Act is one that is well established: the need for law enforcement officers is a safe and accurate way to process and identify the persons and possessions they must take into custody. It is beyond dispute that "probable cause provides legal justification for arresting a person suspected of crime, and for a brief period of detention to take the administrative steps incident to arrest." *Gerstein v. Pugh*, . . . Also uncontested is the "right on the part of the Government, always recognized under English and American law, to search the person of the accused when legally arrested." . . . "The validity of the search of a person incident to a lawful arrest has been regarded as settled from its first enunciation, and has remained virtually unchallenged." *United States v. Robinson*, . . . Even in that context, the Court has been clear that individual suspicion is not necessary, because "[t]he constitutionality of a search incident to an arrest does not depend on whether there is any indication that the person arrested possesses weapons or evidence. The fact of a lawful arrest, standing alone, authorizes a search." *Michigan v. DeFillippo*, . . .

The "routine administrative procedure[s] at a police station house incident to booking and jailing the suspect" derive from different origins and have different constitutional justifications than, say, the search of a place, *Illinois v. Lafayette*, . . . ; for the search of a place not incident to an arrest depends on the "fair probability that contraband or evidence of a crime will be found in a particular place," *Illinois v. Gates*, . . . The interests are further different when an individual is formally processed into police custody. Then "the law is in the act of subjecting the body of the accused to its physical dominion." *People v. Chiagles*, 237 N.Y. 193, 197, 142 N.E. 583, 584 (1923) (Cardozo, J.). When probable cause exists to remove an individual from the normal channels of society and hold him in legal custody, DNA identification plays a critical role in serving those interests.

First, "[i]n every criminal case, it is known and must be known who has been arrested and who is being tried." *Hibel v. Sixth Judicial Dist. Court of Nev., Humboldt Cty.*, . . . An individual's identity is more than just his name or Social Security number, and the government's interest in identification goes beyond ensuring that the proper name is typed on the indictment. Identity has never been considered limited to the name on the arrestee's birth certificate. In fact, a name is of little value compared to the real interest in identification at stake when an individual is brought into custody. "It is a well recognized aspect of criminal conduct that the perpetrator will take unusual steps to conceal not only his conduct, but also his identity.

. . .

A suspect's criminal history is a critical part of his identity that officers should know when processing him for detention. It is a common occurrence that "[p]eople detained for minor offenses can turn out to be the most devious and dangerous criminals. Hours after the Oklahoma [p]eople detained for minor offenses can turn out to be the most devious and dangerous criminals. Hours after the Oklahoma City bombing. Timothy McVeigh was stopped by a state trooper who noticed he was driving without a license plate. Police stopped serial killer Joel Rifkin for the same reason. One of the terrorists involved in the September 11 attacks was stopped and ticketed for speeding just two days before hijacking Flight 92." . . . Police already seek this crucial identifying information. They use routine and accepted means as varied as comparing the suspect's booking photograph to sketch artists' depictions of persons of interest, showing his mugshot to potential witnesses, and of course making a computerized comparison to the arrestee's fingerprints against electronic databases of known criminal and unsolved crimes. In this respect the only difference between DNA analysis and the accepted use of fingerprint databases is the unparalleled accuracy DNA provides.

. . .

Second, law enforcement officers bear a responsibility for ensuring that the custody of an arrestee does not create inordinate "risks for facility staff, for the existing detainee population, and for a new detainee." . . . DNA identification can provide untainted information to those charged with detaining suspects and detaining the property of any felon. For these purposes officers must know the type of person whom they are detaining, and DNA allows them to make critical choices about how to proceed.

. . .

Third, looking forward to future stages of criminal prosecution, "the Government has a substantial interest in ensuring that persons accused of crimes are available for trials." . . . A person who is arrested for one offense but knows that he has yet to answer for some past crime may be more inclined to flee the instant charges, lest continued contact with the criminal justice system expose one or more other serious offenses. For example, a defendant who had committed a prior sexual assault might be inclined to flee on a burglary charge, knowing that in every State a DNA sample would be taken from him after his conviction on the burglary charge that would tie him to the more serious charge of rape. In addition to subverting the administration of justice with respect to the crime of arrest, this ties back to the interest in safety; for a detainee who absconds from custody presents a risk to law enforcement officers, other detainees, victims of previous crimes, witnesses, and society at large.

Fourth, an arrestee's past conduct is essential to an assessment of the danger he poses to the public, and this will inform a court's determination whether the individual should be released on bail. . . . DNA identification of a suspect in a violent crime provides critical information to the police and judicial officials in making a determination of the arrestee's future dangerousness. . . . Knowing that the defendant is wanted for a previous violent crime based on DNA identification is especially probative of the court's consideration of "the danger of the defendant to the alleged victim, another person, or the community." . . .

. . .

B

DNA identification represents an important advance in the techniques used by law enforcement to serve legitimate police concerns for as long as there have been arrests, concerns the courts have acknowledged and approved for more than a century. Law enforcement agencies routinely have used scientific advancements in their standard procedures for the identification of arrestees. . . .

. . .

DNA identification is an advanced technique superior to fingerprinting in many ways, so much so that to insist on fingerprints as the norm would make little sense to either the forensic expert or a layperson. The additional intrusion upon the arrestee's privacy beyond that associated with fingerprinting is not significant, . . . and DNA is a markedly more accurate form of identifying arrestees. A suspect who has changed his facial features to evade photographic identification or even one who has undertaken the more arduous task of altering his fingerprints cannot escape the revealing power of his DNA.

. . .

V

A

By comparison to this substantial government interest and the unique effectiveness of DNA identification, the intrusion of a cheek swab to obtain a DNA sample is a minimal one. True, a significant government interest does not alone suffice to justify a search. The government interest must outweigh the degree to which the search invades an individual's legitimate expectations of privacy. In considering those expectations in this case, however, the necessary predicate of a valid arrest for a serious offense is fundamental. . . .

. . .

In this critical respect, the search here at issue differs from the sort of programmatic searches of either the public at large or a particular class of regulated but otherwise law-abiding citizens that the Court has previously labeled as "'special needs' " searches. . . .

. . .

In light of the context of a valid arrest supported by probable cause respondent's expectations of privacy were not offended by the minor intrusion of a brief swab of his cheeks. By contrast, that same context of arrest gives rise to significant state interests in identifying respondent not only so that the proper name can be attached to his charges but also so that the criminal justice system can make informed decisions concerning pretrial custody. Upon these considerations the Court concludes that DNA identification of arrestees is a reasonable search that can be considered part of a routine booking procedure. When officers make an arrest supported by probable cause to hold for a serious offense and they bring the suspect to the station to be detained in custody, taking and analyzing a cheek swab of the arrestee's DNA is, like fingerprinting and photographing, a legitimate police booking procedure that is reasonable under the Fourth Amendment.

The judgment of the Court of Appeals of Maryland is reversed. . . .

JUSTICE SCALIA, with whom JUSTICE GINSBURG, JUSTICE SOTOMAYOR, and JUSTICE KAGAN join, dissenting.

The Fourth Amendment forbids searching a person for evidence of a crime when there is no basis for believing the person is guilty of the crime or is in possession of incriminating evidence. That prohibition is categorical and without exception; it lies at the very heart of the Fourth Amendment. Whenever this Court has allowed a suspicionless search, it has insisted upon a justifying motive apart from the investigation of crime.

It is obvious that no such noninvestigative motive exists in this case. The Court's assertion that DNA is being taken, not to solve crimes, but to *identify* those in the State's custody, taxes the credulity of the credulous. And the Court's comparison of Maryland's DNA searches to other techniques, such a fingerprinting, can seem apt only to those who know no more than today's opinion has chosen to tell them about how those DNA searches actually work.

I

. . .

B

The Court alludes at several points . . . to the fact that King was an arrestee, and arrestees may be validly searched incident to their arrest. But the Court does not really *rest* on this principle, and for good reason: The objects of a search incident to arrest must be either (1) weapons or evidence that might easily be destroyed, or (2) evidence relevant to the crime of arrest. See *Arizona v. Gant*, . . . Neither is the object of the search at issue here.

. . .

No matter the degree of invasiveness, suspicionless searches are *never* allowed if their principal end is ordinary crime-solving. A search incident to arrest either serves other ends (such as officer safety, in a search for weapons) or is not suspicionless (as when there is reason to believe the arrestee possesses evidence relevant to the crime of arrest).

Sensing (correctly) that it needs more, the Court elaborates at length the ways that the search here served the special purpose of "identifying" King. But that seems to me quite wrong — unless what one means by "identifying" someone is "searching for evidence that he has committed crimes unrelated to the crime of his arrest." At points the Court does appear to use "identifying" in that peculiar sense — claiming, for example, that knowing "an arrestee's past conduct is essential to an assessment of the danger he poses." . . . If identifying someone means finding out what unsolved crimes he has committed, then identification is indistinguishable from the ordinary law-enforcement aims that have never been though to justify a suspicionless search. Searching every lawfully stopped car, for example, might turn up information about unsolved crimes the driver had committed, but no one would say that such a search was aimed at "identifying" him, and no court would hold such a search lawful. I will therefore assume that the Court means that the DNA search at issue here was useful to "identify" King in the normal sense of that word — in the sense that would identify the author of Introduction to the Principles of Morals and Legislation as Jeremy Bentham.

. . .

If one wanted to identify someone in custody using his DNA, the logical thing to do would be to compare that DNA against the Convict and Arrestee Collection: to search, in other words, the collection that could be used (by checking back with the submitting state agency) to identify people, rather than the collection of evidence from unsolved crimes, whose perpetrators are by definition unknown. But that is not what was done. And this is because this search had nothing to do with identification.

In fact, if anything was "identified" as the moment that the DNA database returned a match, it was not King — his identity was already known. (The docket for the original criminal charges lists his full name, his race, his sex, his height, his weight, his date of birth, and his address.) Rather, what the August 4 match "identified" was *the previously-taken sample from the earlier crime.* That sample was genuinely mysterious to Maryland: the State knew that it had probably been left by the victim's attacker, but nothing else. King was not identified by his association with the sample; rather, the sample was identified by its association with King. The Court effectively destroys its own "identification" theory when it acknowledges that the object of this search was "to see what [was] already known about [King}." King was who he was, and volumes of his biography could not make him any more or any less King. No minimally competent speaker of English would say, upon noticing a known arrestee's similarity "to a wanted poster of a previously unidentified suspect," . . . that the *arrestee* had thereby been identified. It was the previously unidentified suspect who had been identified — just as, here, it was the previously unidentified rapist.

. . .

The Court disguises the vast (and scary) scope of its holding by promising a limitation it cannot deliver. The Court repeatedly says that DNA testing, and entry into a national DNA registry, will not befall thee and me, dear reader, but only those arrested for "serious offense[s]." . . . I cannot imagine what principle could possibly justify this limitation, and the Court does not attempt to suggest any. If one believes that DNA will "identify" someone arrested for assault, he must believe that it will "identify" someone arrested for a traffic offense. This Court does not base its judgments on senseless distinctions. At the end of the day, *logic will out.* When there comes before us the taking of DNA from an arrestee for a traffic violation, the Court will predictably (and quite rightly) say, "We can find no significant difference between this case and *King.*" Make no mistake about it: As an entirely predictable consequence of today's decision, your DNA can be taken and entered into a national DNA database if you are ever arrested, rightly or wrongly, and for whatever reason.

The most regrettable aspect of the suspicionless search that occurred here is that it proved to be quite unnecessary. All parties concede that it would have been entirely permissible, as far as the Fourth Amendment is concerned, for Maryland to take a sample of King's DNA as a consequence of his conviction for second-degree assault. So the ironic result of the Court's error is this: The only arrestees to whom the outcome here will ever make a difference are those who *have been acquitted* of the crime of arrest (so that their DNA could not have been taken upon conviction). In other words, this Act manages to burden uniquely the sole group for whom the Fourth Amendment's protections ought to be most jealously guarded: people who are innocent of the State's accusations.

Today's judgment will, to be sure, have the beneficial effect of solving more crimes; then again, so would the taking of DNA samples from anyone who flies on an airplane (surely the Transportation Security Administration needs to know the "identity" of the flying public), applies for a driver's license, or attends a public school. Perhaps the construction of such a genetic panopticon is wise. But I doubt that the proud men who wrote the charter of our liberties would have been so eager to open their mouths for royal inspection.

[3] Surgical Procedures

WINSTON v. LEE

United States Supreme Court
470 U.S. 753 (1985)

JUSTICE BRENNAN delivered the opinion of the Court.

In this case, the Commonwealth of Virginia seeks to compel the respondent Rudolph Lee, who is suspected of attempting to commit armed robbery, to undergo a surgical procedure under a general anesthetic for removal of a bullet lodged in his chest. Petitioners allege that the bullet will provide evidence of respondent's guilt or innocence. We conclude that the procedure sought here is an example of the "more substantial intrusion" cautioned against in *Schmerber*, and hold that to permit the procedure would violate respondent's right to be secure in his person guaranteed by the Fourth Amendment.

I

A

At approximately 1 a.m. on July 18, 1982, Ralph E. Watkinson was closing his shop for the night. As he was locking the door, he observed someone armed with a gun coming toward him from across the street. Watkinson was also armed and when he drew his gun, the other person told him to freeze. Watkinson then fired at the other person, who returned his fire. Watkinson was hit in the legs, while the other individual, who appeared to be wounded in his left side, ran from the scene. The police arrived on the scene shortly thereafter, and Watkinson was taken by ambulance to the emergency room of the Medical College of Virginia (MCV) Hospital.

Approximately 20 minutes later, police officers responding to another call found respondent eight blocks from where the earlier shooting occurred. Respondent was suffering from a gunshot wound to his left chest area and told the police that he had been shot when two individuals attempted to rob him. An ambulance took respondent to the MCV Hospital. Watkinson was still in the MCV emergency room and, when respondent entered that room, said "[t]hat's the man that shot me." After an investigation, the police decided that respondent's story of having been himself the victim of a robbery was untrue and charged respondent with attempted robbery, malicious wounding, and two counts of using a firearm in the commission of a felony.

B

The Commonwealth shortly thereafter moved in state court for an order directing respondent to undergo surgery to remove an object thought to be a bullet lodged under his left collarbone. The court conducted several evidentiary hearings on the motion. At the first hearing, the Commonwealth's expert testified that the surgical procedure would take 45 minutes and would involve a three to four percent chance of temporary nerve damage, one per cent chance of permanent nerve damage, and a one-tenth of one percent chance of death. At the second hearing, the expert testified that on re-examination of respondent, he discovered that the bullet was not "back inside close to the nerves and arteries," as he originally had thought. Instead, he now believed the bullet to be located "just beneath the skin." He testified that the surgery would require an incision of only one and one-half centimeters (slightly more than one-half inch) could be performed under local anesthesia, and would result in "no danger on the basis that there's no general anesthesia employed."

The state trial judge granted the motion to compel the surgery. Respondent petitioned the Virginia Supreme Court for a writ of prohibition and/or writ of habeas corpus, both of which were denied. Respondent then brought an action in the United States District Court for the Eastern District of Virginia to enjoin the pending operation on Fourth Amendment grounds. The court refused to issue a preliminary injunction, holding that respondent's cause had little likelihood of success on the merits.

On October 18, 1982, just before the surgery was scheduled, the surgeon ordered that X rays be taken of respondent's chest. The X rays revealed that the bullet was in fact lodged two and one-half to three centimeters (approximately one inch) deep in muscular tissue in respondent's chest, substantially deeper than had been thought when the state court granted the motion to compel surgery. The surgeon now believed that a general anesthetic would be desirable for medical reasons.

Respondent moved the state trial court for a rehearing based on the new evidence. After holding an evidentiary hearing, the state trial court denied the rehearing and the Virginia Supreme Court affirmed. Respondent then returned to federal court, where he moved to alter or amend the judgment previously entered against him. After an evidentiary hearing, the District Court enjoined the threatened surgery. A divided panel of the Court of Appeals for the Fourth Circuit affirmed.

II

The Fourth Amendment protects "expectations of privacy," see *Katz* — the individual's legitimate expectations that in certain places and at certain times he has "the right to be let alone — the most comprehensive of rights and the right most valued by civilized men." Putting to one side the procedural protections of the warrant requirement, the Fourth Amendment generally protects the "security" of "persons, houses, papers, and effects" against official intrusions up to the point where the community's need for evidence surmounts a specified standard, ordinarily "probable cause." Beyond this point, it is ordinarily justifiable for the community to demand that the individual give up some part of his interest in privacy and security to advance the community's vital interests in law enforcement; such a search is generally "reasonable" in the Amendment's terms.

A compelled surgical intrusion into an individual's body for evidence, however, implicates expectations of privacy and security of such magnitude that the intrusion may be "unreasonable" even if likely to produce evidence of a crime.

The reasonableness of surgical intrusions beneath the skin depends on a case-by-case approach, in which the individual's interest in privacy and security are weighed against society's interests in conducting the procedure. In a given case, the question whether the community's need for evidence outweighs the substantial privacy interests at stake is a delicate one admitting of few categorical answers. We believe that *Schmerber*, however, provides the appropriate framework of analysis for such cases.

III

Applying the *Schmerber* balancing test in this case, we believe that the Court of Appeals reached the correct result. The Commonwealth plainly had probable cause to conduct the search. In addition, all parties apparently agree that respondent has had a full measure of procedural protections and has been able fully to litigate the difficult medical and legal questions necessarily involved in analyzing the reasonableness of a surgical incision of this magnitude. Our inquiry therefore must focus on the extent of the intrusion on respondent's privacy interests and on the State's need for the evidence.

Both lower courts in this case believed that the proposed surgery, which for purely medical reasons required the use of a general anesthetic, would be an "extensive" intrusion on respondent's personal privacy and bodily integrity. When conducted with the consent of the patient, surgery requiring general anesthesia is not necessarily demeaning or intrusive. In such a case, the surgeon is carrying out the patient's own will concerning the patient's body and the patient's right to privacy is therefore preserved. In this case, however, the Court of Appeals noted that the Commonwealth proposes to take control of respondent's body, to "drug this citizen — not yet convicted of a criminal offense — with narcotics and barbiturates into a state of unconsciousness," and then to search beneath his skin for evidence of a crime. This kind of surgery involves a virtually total divestment of respondent's ordinary control over surgical probing beneath his skin.

The other part of the balance concerns the Commonwealth's need to intrude into respondent's body to retrieve the bullet. The Commonwealth claims to need the bullet to demonstrate that it was fired from Watkinson's gun, which in turn would show that respondent was the robber who confronted Watkinson. However, although we recognize the difficulty of making determinations in advance as to the strength of the case against respondent, petitioners' assertions of a compelling need for the bullet are hardly persuasive. The very circumstances relied on in this case to demonstrate probable cause to believe that evidence will be found tend to vitiate the Commonwealth's need to compel respondent to undergo surgery. The Commonwealth has available substantial additional evidence that respondent was the individual who accosted Watkinson on the night of the robbery. No party in this case suggests that Watkinson's entirely spontaneous identification of respondent at the hospital would be inadmissible. In addition, petitioners can no doubt prove that Watkinson was found a few blocks from Watkinson's store shortly after the incident took place. And petitioners can certainly show that the location of the bullet (under respondent's left collarbone) seems to correlate with Watkinson's report that the robber "jerked" to the left. . . . The fact that the Commonwealth has available such substantial evidence of the origin of the bullet restricts the need for the Commonwealth to compel respondent to undergo the contemplated surgery.

In weighing the various factors in this case, we therefore reach the same conclusion as the courts below. The operation sought will intrude substantially on respondent's protected interests. The medical risks of the operation, although apparently not extremely severe, are a subject of considerable dispute; the very undertaking militates against finding the operation to be "reasonable." In addition, the intrusion on respondent's privacy interests entailed by the operation can only be characterized as severe. On the other hand, although the bullet may turn out to be useful to the Commonwealth in prosecuting respondent, the Commonwealth has failed to demonstrate a compelling need for it. We believe that in these circumstances the Commonwealth has failed to demonstrate that it would be "reasonable" under the terms of the Fourth Amendment to search for evidence of this crime by means of the contemplated surgery.

NOTES AND QUESTIONS

(1) At the beginning of the opinion, Justice Brennan says, "[w]e conclude that the procedure sought here is an example of the 'more substantial intrusion' cautioned against in *Schmerber*," which suggests that the surgical procedure is inherently objectionable. By the end of the opinion, however, he says that "the Commonwealth has failed to demonstrate a compelling need" for the bullet, thus capping off what in retrospect is a balancing test. The result is that every case contemplating surgical procedures must be examined in terms of the relative interests of the parties, a process certainly *not* required for blood tests. Is the resulting constitutional standard too amorphous, or is this all the Court can do? Would a *Rochin* analysis produce the same result?

(2) In *State v. Payano-Roman*, 290 Wis. 2d 548, 714 N.W.2d 548, *cert. denied*, 549 U.S. 935 (2006), officers and medical personnel sought to speed the passage of a baggy of illegal narcotics through the accused's digestive system by administering a laxative. Applying the factors discussed in *Winston*, the court noted that the procedure employed was medically indicated and did not threaten the safety or health of the accused. It acknowledged that the use of the laxative resulted in "a significant intrusion on [the accused's] dignitary interests," but that this was offset by the potential danger had the baggy ruptured. It was undisputed that the procedure would produce evidence of a crime, and it was not insignificant that the "situation was self-created" by the accused, who had swallowed the evidence for the purpose of concealment.

PROBLEM C
THE CLOSED-MOUTH SUSPECT

The defendant was arrested for selling drugs and was observed to have something in his mouth, which he refused to disgorge. Officers had begun the process for obtaining a search warrant. The court describes what happened next:

> While awaiting the warrant, the police noticed that the defendant was beginning to twitch and sweat as if experiencing a seizure. The defendant was then transported by ambulance to Saint John's Hospital. An officer accompanied the defendant to ensure that he did not dispose of anything in his mouth. On the way to the hospital, an emergency medical technician administered an I.V. to counteract the effect of any drugs the defendant might have swallowed.
>
> At approximately 11:00 p.m., an Illinois associate circuit judge issued a warrant to search "[t]he body of Eunice Husband" for "illegal drugs, weapons, or contraband." The issuance of the warrant occurred at about the same time the defendant was received in the emergency room. At the hospital, and before the police knew that a warrant had been issued, the police informed the attending doctor that they were attempting to obtain a warrant to search the defendant's mouth. The defendant was repeatedly asked to open his mouth voluntarily and was later informed that a warrant had been issued and that he should open his mouth. In addition, a brief attempt was made to pry open the defendant's mouth with a ceramic spoon. None of these attempts was successful. The doctor finally informed the defendant that a drug would be administered through an I.V. that would enable the police to recover the items in his mouth if he refused to comply with the warrant voluntarily. The defendant was administered 40 mg. of Amidate through an I.V. at approximately 11:22 p.m. According to the attending doctor, this general anesthetic was administered both for the purposes of treating a possible drug overdose and in order to comply with the warrant. Within three minutes of the administration of the drug, the defendant fell unconscious. Three small plastic bags were subsequently recovered from the defendant's mouth. The bags contained a total of 20.3 grams of cocaine base.

Is the evidence admissible? *See United States v. Husband*, 226 F.3d 626 (7th Cir. 2000).

[B] Detention for Identification

DAVIS v. MISSISSIPPI

United States Supreme Court
394 U.S. 721 (1969)

MR. JUSTICE BRENNAN delivered the opinion of the Court.

Petitioner was convicted of rape and sentenced to life imprisonment by a jury in the Circuit Court of Lauderdale County, Mississippi. The only issue before us is whether fingerprints obtained from petitioner should have been excluded from evidence as the product of a detention which was illegal under the Fourth and Fourteenth Amendments.

The rape occurred on the evening of December 2, 1965, at the victim's home in Meridian, Mississippi. The victim could give no better description of her assailant than that he was a Negro youth. Finger and palm prints found on the sill and borders of the window through which the assailant apparently entered the victim's home constituted the only other lead available at the outset of the police investigation. Beginning on December 3, and for a period of about 10 days, the Meridian police, without warrants, took at least 24 Negro youths to police headquarters where they were questioned briefly, fingerprinted, and then released without charge. The police also interrogated 40 or 50 other Negro youths either at police headquarters, at school, or on the street. Petitioner, a 14-year-old youth who had occasionally worked for the victim as a yardboy, was brought in on December 3 and released after being fingerprinted and routinely questioned. Between December 3 and December 7, he was interrogated by the police on several occasions — sometimes in his home or in a car, other times at police headquarters. This questioning apparently related primarily to investigation of other potential suspects. Several times during this same period petitioner was exhibited to the victim in her hospital room. A police officer testified that these confrontations were for the purpose of sharpening the victim's description of her assailant by providing "a gauge to go by on size and color." The victim did not identify petitioner as her assailant at any of these confrontations.

On December 12, the police drove petitioner 90 miles to the city of Jackson and confined him overnight in the Jackson jail. The State conceded on oral argument in this Court that there was neither a warrant nor probable cause for this arrest. The next day, petitioner, who had not yet been afforded counsel, took a lie detector test and signed a statement. He was then returned to and confined in the Meridian jail. On December 14, while so confined, petitioner was fingerprinted a second time. That same day, these December 14 prints, together with the fingerprints of 23 other Negro youths apparently still under suspicion, were sent to the Federal Bureau of Investigation in Washington, D.C., for comparison with the latent prints taken from the window of the victim's house. The FBI reported that petitioner's prints matched those taken from the window. Petitioner was subsequently indicted and tried for the rape, and the fingerprint evidence was admitted in evidence at trial over petitioner's timely objections that the fingerprints should be excluded as the product of an unlawful detention. The Mississippi Supreme Court sustained the admission of the fingerprint evidence and affirmed the conviction. . . . We reverse.

At the outset, we find no merit in the suggestion in the Mississippi Supreme Court's opinion that fingerprint evidence, because of its trustworthiness, is not subject to the proscriptions of the Fourth and Fourteenth Amendments. Our decisions recognize no exception to the rule that illegally seized evidence is inadmissible at trial, however relevant and trustworthy the seized evidence may be as an item of proof. The exclusionary rule was fashioned as a sanction to redress and deter overreaching governmental conduct prohibited by the Fourth Amendment. To make an exception for illegally seized evidence which is trustworthy would fatally undermine these purposes. Thus, in *Mapp v. Ohio*, . . . we held that "*all* evidence obtained by searches and seizures in violation of the Constitution is, by that same authority, inadmissible in a state court." (Italics supplied.) Fingerprint evidence is no exception to this comprehensive rule. We agree with and adopt the conclusion of the Court of Appeals for the District of Columbia Circuit in *Bynum v. United States*, 262 F. 2d 465, 467, 104 U.S. App. D.C. 368, 370 (1958):

> True, fingerprints can be distinguished from statements given during detention. They can also be distinguished from articles taken from a prisoner's possession. Both similarities and differences of each type of evidence to and from the others are apparent. But all three have the decisive common characteristic of being something of evidentiary value which the public authorities have caused an arrested person to yield to them during illegal detention. If one such product of illegal detention is proscribed, by the same token all should be proscribed.

We turn then to the question whether the detention of petitioner during which the fingerprints used at trial were taken constituted an unreasonable seizure of his person in violation of the Fourth Amendment. The opinion of the Mississippi Supreme Court proceeded on the mistaken premise that petitioner's prints introduced at trial were taken during his brief detention on December 3. In fact, as both parties before us agree, the fingerprint evidence used at trial was obtained on December 14, while petitioner was still in detention following his December 12 arrest. The legality of his arrest was not determined by the Mississippi Supreme Court. However, on oral argument here, the State conceded that the arrest on December 12 and the ensuing detention through December 14 were based on neither a warrant nor probable cause and were therefore constitutionally invalid. The State argues, nevertheless, that this invalidity should not prevent us from affirming petitioner's conviction. The December 3 prints were validly obtained, it is argued, and "it should make no difference in the practical or legal sense which fingerprint card was sent to the F.B.I. for comparison." It may be that it does make a difference in light of the objectives of the exclusionary rule, see *Bynum v. United States*, . . . but we need not decide the question since we have concluded that the prints of December 3 were not validly obtained.

The State makes no claim that petitioner voluntarily accompanied the police officers to headquarters on December 3 and willingly submitted to fingerprinting.

The State's brief also candidly admits that "[a]ll that the Meridian Police could possibly have known about petitioner at the time . . . would not amount to probable cause for his arrest. . . ." The State argues, however, that the December 3 detention was of a type which does not require probable cause. Two rationales for this position are suggested. First, it is argued that the detention occurred during the investigatory rather than accusatory stage and thus was not a seizure requiring probable cause. The second and related argument is that, at the least, detention for the sole purpose of obtaining fingerprints does not require probable cause.

It is true that at the time of the December 3 detention the police had no intention of charging petitioner with the crime and were far from making him the primary focus of their investigation. But to argue that the Fourth Amendment does not apply to the investigatory stage is fundamentally to misconceive the purposes of the Fourth Amendment. Investigatory seizures would subject unlimited numbers of innocent persons to the harassment and ignominy incident to involuntary detention. Nothing is more clear than that the Fourth Amendment was meant to prevent wholesale intrusions upon the personal security of our citizenry, whether these intrusions be termed "arrests" or "investigatory detentions." We made this explicit only last Term in *Terry v. Ohio* . . . when we rejected "the notions that the Fourth Amendment does not come into play at all as a limitation upon police conduct if the officers stop short of something called a 'technical arrest' or a 'full-blown search.' "

Detentions for the sole purpose of obtaining fingerprints are no less subject to the constraints of the Fourth Amendment. It is arguable, however, that, because of the unique nature of the fingerprinting process, such detentions might, under narrowly defined circumstances, be found to comply with the Fourth Amendment even though there is no probable cause in the traditional sense. See *Camara v. Municipal Court*. . . . Detention for fingerprinting may constitute a much less serious intrusion upon personal security than other types of police searches and detentions. Fingerprinting involves none of the probing into an individual's private life and thoughts that marks an interrogation or search. Nor can fingerprint detention be employed repeatedly to harass any individual, since the police need only one set of each person's prints. Furthermore, fingerprinting is an inherently more reliable and effective crime-solving tool than eyewitness identifications or confessions and is not subject to such abuses as the improper line-up and the "third degree." Finally, because there is no danger of destruction of fingerprints, the limited detention need not come unexpectedly or at an inconvenient time. For this same reason, the general requirement that the authorization of a judicial officer be obtained in advance of detention would seem not to admit of any exception in the fingerprinting context.

We have no occasion in this case, however, to determine whether the requirements of the Fourth Amendment could be met by narrowly circumscribed procedures for obtaining, during the course of a criminal investigation, the fingerprints of individuals for whom there is no probable cause to arrest. For it is clear that no attempt was made here to employ procedures which might comply with the requirements of the Fourth Amendment: the detention at police headquarters of petitioner and the other young Negroes was not authorized by a judicial officer; petitioner was unnecessarily required to undergo two fingerprinting sessions; and petitioner was not merely fingerprinted during the December 3 detention but also subjected to interrogation. The judgment of the Mississippi Supreme Court is therefore

Reversed.

MR. JUSTICE FORTAS took no part in the consideration or decision of this case.

MR. JUSTICE HARLAN, concurring.

I join the opinion of the Court, with one reservation. The Court states in dictum that, because fingerprinting may be scheduled for a time convenient to the citizen, "the general requirement that the authorization of a judicial officer be obtained in advance of detention would seem not to admit of any exception in the fingerprinting context." I cannot concur in so sweeping a proposition. There may be circumstances, falling short of the "dragnet" procedures employed in this case, where compelled submission to fingerprinting would not amount to a violation of the Fourth Amendment even in the absence of a warrant, and I would leave that question open.

MR. JUSTICE BLACK, dissenting.

The petitioner here was convicted of a brutal rape of a woman, committed in her own home. Fingerprints of the petitioner, left on the window sill of her home, were the clinching evidence bringing about petitioner's conviction. The Court, by once more expanding the reach of the judicially declared exclusionary rule, ostensibly resting on the Fourth Amendment, holds the fingerprint evidence constitutionally inadmissible and thereby reverses petitioner's conviction. The rape occurred on December 2, 1965, and, as was their duty, the police authorities began to make a searching investigation the morning of December 3. The raped woman was originally able to describe the rapist only as a young Negro male. With this evidence the police proceeded to interrogate a number of young Negroes on the streets, at their homes, or at the police station, and then permitted them to go on their way. The petitioner was among those so interrogated on December 3, at which time his fingerprints were made. The fingerprints were again taken on December 14. The record does not show that petitioner or any other young man who was questioned and fingerprinted ever made the slightest objection. Apparently all of them cooperated with the police in efforts to find out who had committed the rape. This case is but one more in an ever-expanding list of cases in which this Court has been so widely blowing up the Fourth Amendment's scope that its original authors would be hard put to recognize their creation. For this most unnecessary expansion of the Amendment, the Court is compelled to put its chief reliance on a Court of Appeals decision. I think it is high time this Court, in the interest of the administration of criminal justice made a new appraisal of the language and history of the Fourth Amendment and cut it down to its intended size. Such a judicial action would, I believe, make our cities a safer place for men, women, and children to live.

I dissent from this reversal.

Mr. Justice Stewart, dissenting.

I do not disagree with the Court's conclusion that the petitioner was arrested and detained without probable cause. But it does not follow that his fingerprints were inadmissible at the trial.

Fingerprints are not "evidence" in the conventional sense that weapons or stolen goods might be. Like the color of a man's eyes, his height, or his very physiognomy, the tips of his fingers are an inherent and unchanging characteristic of the man. And physical impressions of his fingertips can be exactly and endlessly reproduced.

We do not deal here with a confession wrongfully obtained or with property wrongfully seized-so tainted as to be forever inadmissible as evidence against a defendant. We deal, instead, with "evidence" that can be identically reproduced and lawfully used at any subsequent trial.

I cannot believe that the doctrine of *Mapp v. Ohio* . . . requires so useless a gesture as the reversal of this conviction.

NOTES AND QUESTIONS

(1) On its face, *Davis* would appear an inevitable and undistinguished holding: a suspect was arrested without probable cause. Fingerprints were obtained as a fruit of the illegal detention. Under the *Mapp* exclusionary rule, evidence so obtained is inadmissible. What is extraordinary in *Davis* is the dictum:

> It is arguable . . . that, because of the unique nature of the fingerprinting process, such detentions might, under narrowly defined circumstances, be found to comply with the Fourth Amendment even though there is no probable cause in the traditional sense. See *Camara v. Municipal Court.* . . .

The implication appears clear: the dragnet fingerprinting of all black youth in Meridian is not constitutionally offensive in itself; it is the failure to obtain a prior judicial authorization — as in *Camara* — that is objectionable.

Camara v. Municipal Court, 387 U.S. 523 (1967), is a non-criminal case involving a Department of Public Health housing inspector inspecting an apartment building for code violations. The issue before the Court was whether a warrant was required when an occupant refused entry for the inspection. The Court concluded that the Fourth Amendment precluded warrantless inspections without the consent of the occupant. The Court then softened the blow of its decision by holding that the normal probable cause standard would not apply. Rather,

> "probable cause" to issue a warrant to inspect must exist if reasonable legislative or administrative standards for conducting an area inspection are satisfied with respect to a particular dwelling. Such standards, which will vary with the municipal program being enforced, may be based upon the passage of time, the nature of the building (e.g., a multi-family apartment house), or the condition of the entire area, but they will not necessarily depend upon specific knowledge of the condition of the particular building.

(2) Thus encouraged, Arizona enacted the following statute in 1971:

§ 13-3905. Detention for obtaining evidence of identifying physical characteristics

A. A peace officer who is engaged, within the scope of his authority, in the investigation of an alleged criminal offense punishable by at least one year in the state prison, may make written application upon oath or affirmation to a magistrate for an order authorizing the temporary detention, for the purpose of obtaining evidence of identifying physical characteristics, of an identified or particularly described individual residing in or found in the jurisdiction over which the magistrate presides. The order shall require the presence of the identified or particularly described individual at such time and place as the court shall direct for obtaining the identifying physical characteristic evidence. Such order may be issued by the magistrate upon a showing of all of the following:

1. Reasonable cause for belief that a specifically described criminal offense punishable by at least one year in the state prison has been committed.

2. Procurement of evidence of identifying physical characteristics from an identified or particularly described individual may contribute to the identification of the individual who committed such offense.

3. Such evidence cannot otherwise be obtained by the investigating officer from either the law enforcement agency employing the affiant or the criminal identification division of the Arizona Department of Public Safety.

B. Any order issued pursuant to the provisions of this section shall specify the following:

1. The alleged criminal offense which is the subject of the application.

2. The specific type of identifying physical characteristic evidence which is sought.

3. The relevance of such evidence to the particular investigation.

4. The identity or description of the individual who may be detained for obtaining such evidence.

5. The name and official status of the investigative officer authorized to effectuate such detention and obtain such evidence.

6. The place at which the obtaining of such evidence shall be effectuated.

7. The time that such evidence shall be taken except that no person may be detained for a period of more than three hours for the purpose of taking such evidence.

8. The period of time, not exceeding fifteen days, during which the order shall continue in force and effect. If the order is not executed within fifteen days, a new order may be issued, pursuant to the provisions of this section.

C. The order issued pursuant to this section shall be returned to the court not later than thirty days after its date of issuance and shall be accompanied by a sworn statement indicating the type of evidence taken. The court shall give to the person from whom such evidence was taken a copy of the order and a copy of the sworn statement indicating what type of evidence was taken, if any.

D. For the purposes of this section, "identifying physical characteristics" includes, but is not limited to, the fingerprints, palm prints, footprints, measurements, handwriting, handprinting, sound of voice, blood-samples, urine samples, saliva samples, hair samples, comparative personal appearance, or photographs of an individual.

The statute was held constitutional in *State v. Grijalva*, 111 Ariz. 476, 533 P.2d 533 (1975), *cert. denied*, 423 U.S. 873.

(3) Statutory authorization has not, however, been a prerequisite to legitimize identification screening.

(a) *Biehunik v. Felicitta*, 441 F.2d 228 (2d Cir.), *cert. denied*, 403 U.S. 932 (1971). An order was issued by the police commissioner for some 62 officers to appear in a lineup in connection with numerous incidents of alleged police brutality. The district court granted the officers an injunction against the lineup, but the court of appeals reversed on the authority of *Davis.*

(b) *In re Fingerprinting of M.B.*, 125 N.J. Super. 115, 309 A.2d 3 (1973). A ring of the 1973 graduating class of the Martin Luther King, Junior Elementary School in Newark was found forty-five feet from the body of a homicide victim, and unidentified fingerprints were found in the victim's automobile. A court order directed the male members of the 1973 eighth grade class to submit to fingerprinting during a six day period. The individuals could be accompanied by a parent, guardian or attorney. The fingerprints were only to be used for the investigation of this homicide and then were to be destroyed. The appellate court held that *Davis* provided authority to sustain the order.

(4) In *In re Nontestimonial Identification Order Directed to R.H.*, 171 Vt. 227, 762 A.2d 1239 (2000), *Davis* was cited in support of a judicial order for DNA testing of an individual for comparison to that found on the body of a homicide victim.

HAYES v. FLORIDA

United States Supreme Court
470 U.S. 811 (1985)

JUSTICE WHITE delivered the opinion of the Court.

The issue before us in this case is whether the Fourth Amendment to the Constitution of the United States, applicable to the States by virtue of the Fourteenth Amendment, was properly applied by the Court of Appeal of Florida, Second District, to allow police to transport a suspect to the station house for fingerprinting, without his consent and without probable cause or prior judicial authorization.

A series of burglary-rapes occurred in Punta Gorda, Florida, in 1980. Police found latent fingerprints on the doorknob of the bedroom of one of the victims, fingerprints they believed belonged to the assailant. The police also found a herringbone pattern tennis shoe print near the victim's front porch. Although they had little specific information to tie petitioner Hayes to the crime, after police interviewed him along with 30 to 40 other men who generally fit the description of the assailant, the investigators came to consider petitioner a principal suspect. They decided to visit petitioner's home to obtain his fingerprints or, if he was uncooperative, to arrest him. They did not seek a warrant authorizing this procedure.

Arriving at petitioner's house, the officers spoke to petitioner on his front porch. When he expressed reluctance voluntarily to accompany them to the station for fingerprinting, one of the investigators explained that they would therefore arrest him. Petitioner, in the words of the investigator, then "blurted out" that he would rather go with the officers to the station than be arrested. While the officers were on the front porch, they also seized a pair of herringbone pattern tennis shoes in plain view.

Petitioner was then taken to the station house, where he was fingerprinted. When police determined that his prints matched those left at the scene of the crime, petitioner was placed under formal arrest. Before trial, petitioner moved to suppress the fingerprint evidence, claiming it was the fruit of an illegal detention. The trial court denied the motion and admitted the evidence without expressing a reason. Petitioner was convicted of the burglary and sexual battery committed at the scene where the latent fingerprints were found.

We agree with petitioner that *Davis v. Mississippi* requires reversal of the judgment below.

None of our later cases have undercut the holding in *Davis* that transportation to and investigative detention at the station house without probable cause or judicial authorization together violate the Fourth Amendment. Indeed, some 10 years later, in *Dunaway v. New York*, we refused to extend *Terry* to authorize investigative interrogations at police stations on less than probable cause, even though proper warnings under *Miranda* had been given.

Nor are we inclined to forswear *Davis*. There is no doubt that at some point in the investigative process, police procedures can qualitatively and quantitatively be so intrusive with respect to a suspect's freedom of movement and privacy interests as to trigger the full protection of the Fourth and Fourteenth Amendments. And our view continues to be that the line is crossed when the police, without probable cause or a warrant, forcibly remove a person from his home or other place in which he is entitled to be and transport him to the police station, where he is detained, although briefly, for investigative purposes. We adhere to the view that such seizures, at least where not under judicial supervision, are sufficiently like arrests to invoke the traditional rule that arrests may constitutionally be made only on probable cause.

None of the foregoing implies that a brief detention in the field for the purpose of fingerprinting, where there is only reasonable suspicion not amounting to probable cause, is necessarily impermissible under the Fourth Amendment. In addressing the reach of a *Terry* stop in *Adams v. Williams*, we observed that "[a] brief stop of a suspicious individual, in order to determine his identity or maintain the status quo momentarily while obtaining more information, may be most reasonable in light of the facts known to the officer at the time." Also, just this Term, we concluded that if there are articulable facts supporting a reasonable suspicion that a person has committed a criminal offense, that person may be stopped in order to identify him, to question him briefly, or to detain him briefly while attempting to obtain additional information. *United States v. Hensley*. There is thus support in our cases for the view that the Fourth Amendment would permit seizures for the purpose of fingerprinting, if there is reasonable suspicion that the suspect has committed a criminal act, if there is a reasonable basis for believing that fingerprinting will establish or negate the suspect's connection with that crime, and if the procedure is carried out with dispatch. Of course, neither reasonable suspicion nor probable cause would suffice to permit the officers to make a warrantless entry into a person's house for the purpose of obtaining fingerprint identification. *Payton v. New York*.

We also do not abandon the suggestion in *Davis* that under circumscribed procedures, the Fourth Amendment might permit the judiciary to authorize the seizure of a person on less than probable cause and his removal to the police station for the purpose of fingerprinting. We do not, of course, have such a case before us. We do note, however, that some States, in reliance on the suggestion in *Davis*, have enacted procedures for judicially authorized seizures for the purpose of fingerprinting. The state courts are not in accord on the validity of these efforts to insulate investigative seizures from Fourth Amendment invalidation.

Justice Brennan, with whom Justice Marshall joins, concurring in the judgment.

[T]he Court today — after tidily disposing of the case before it — returns to its regrettable assault on the Fourth Amendment by reaching beyond any issue properly before us virtually to hold that on-site fingerprinting without probable cause or a warrant is constitutionally reasonable. . . .

If the police wanted to detain an individual for on-site fingerprinting, the intrusion would have to be measured by the standards of *Terry* and our other Fourth Amendment cases. Yet the record here contains no information useful in applying *Terry* to this hypothetical police practice. It would seem that on-site fingerprinting (apparently undertaken in full view of any passerby) would involve a singular intrusion on the suspect's privacy, an intrusion that would not be justifiable (as was the pat-down in *Terry*) as necessary for the officer's protection. How much time would elapse before the individual would be free to go? Could the police hold the individual until the fingerprints could be compared with others? The parties did not brief or argue these questions, the record contains nothing that is useful in their resolution, and (naturally enough) the courts below did not address them.

Ordinarily — outside the Fourth Amendment context, at any rate — we wait for a case to arise before addressing the application of a legal standard to a set of facts. I disagree with the Court's apparent attempt to render an advisory opinion concerning the Fourth Amendment implications of a police practice that, as far as we know, has never been attempted by the police in this or any other case.

PROBLEM D
PASSERS-BY FINGERPRINTED IN HUNT FOR KILLER OF FIVE

The Associated Press reported that, following apparent homicides of five college students in Gainesville, Florida, police commenced fingerprinting and questioning people passing through the neighborhood in which the crimes occurred. Because the assailant was believed to have ridden a bicycle to at least one of the crime scenes, police had focused on individuals using bicycles, mopeds, and motorcycles, as well as pedestrians. A police spokesman told a local newspaper, "We're stopping people in the area if there are any questions why they're there. This is not being done in an accusatory way." *New York Times*, Oct. 30, 1990. Are such procedures constitutionally legitimate?

[C] Technological Devices

[1] Wiretapping and Electronic Eavesdropping

The Supreme Court's refusal to recognize constitutional protection against wiretapping in *Olmstead v. United States (see supra* § 3.01) remained the law for nearly forty years until the decision in *Katz v. United States (see supra* § 3.01). In the absence of judicial sympathy, Congress provided a limited protection against wiretapping in § 605 of the Federal Communications Act of 1934:

> [N]o person not being authorized by the sender shall intercept any communication and divulge or publish the existence, contents, substance, purport, effect, or meaning of such intercepted communication to any person.

In *Nardone v. United States*, 302 U.S. 379 (1937), the Act was held to extend to federal officers as well as private citizens, and in *Benanti v. United States*, 355 U.S. 96 (1957), it was extended to state officials.

But the protection of § 605 was largely circumscribed by two limitations: (1) Only a party to the conversation could object to its admissibility, and (2) the statute was inapplicable if one of the parties to the conversation had given consent to the interception. Moreover, because the Federal Communications Act applied only to the interception of a telephone, telegraph, or radio telegraph conversation, it was no bar for more sophisticated means of electronic eavesdropping. In such cases, the rationale of *Olmstead* continued to apply; the target of an interception would likely prevail only if a trespass could be shown.

For example, in *Goldman v. United States*, 316 U.S. 129 (1942), officials had first placed a hidden microphone inside the office of the defendant, but it failed to work. Then, from an adjacent office, they placed the device against the wall and listened while not on the property of the defendant. The Court held (1) the interception did not fall within the federal statute as the means of interception did not come within the definition of the Act, and (2) it did not trigger the protection of the Fourth Amendment because there was no trespass.

In *Silverman v. United States*, 365 U.S. 505 (1961), the facts were materially distinguishable from *Goldman* only in that the listening device pierced the wall and made contact with the heating system, through which sound was conducted. The Court excluded the evidence.

> Here . . . the officers overheard the petitioner's conversations only by usurping part of the petitioners' house or office — a heating system which was an integral part of the premises occupied by the petitioners, a usurpation that was effected without their knowledge or without their consent. In these circumstances we need not pause to consider whether or not there was a technical trespass under the local property law relating to party walls.

Id. at 511. Anticipating the decision in *Katz*, Justice Douglas, in a concurring opinion, maintained that the Court's "concern should not be with the trivialities of the local law of trespass, as the opinion of the Court indicates. Rather our sole concern should be with whether the privacy of the home was invaded."

While the *Katz* decision eliminated the need to scrutinize the presence or absence of a trespass, by requiring that the eavesdropping would normally require a prior judicial authorization — to wit, a search warrant — new questions arose. Could such an order be narrowly tailored to comport with the Fourth Amendment requirement of "particularly describing . . . the person or things to be seized," when the "target" of the search was a future conversation? In this respect, the *Katz* case was perhaps too easy: the interception could be limited to telephone communications in which Katz was a participant, and there was a fair probability that he was using the particular telephone in conjunction with his gambling activities.

When the Supreme Court confronted the problem, the difficulties became clear. In *Berger v. New York*, 388 U.S. 41 (1967), the Court held that a New York statute authorizing electronic eavesdropping could not be reconciled with the Fourth Amendment. The Court was concerned, first, with the absence of a particularity requirement regarding the crime which had been or was being committed, and the items to be seized. Second, the Court said that the permitted sixty-day order was "the equivalent of a series of intrusions, searches, and seizures pursuant to a single showing of probable cause." Third, the statute did not require termination of the eavesdropping once the conversation sough had been obtained. Finally, the statute contained no requirement of notice comparable to that typical in the case of conventional search warrants.

Congress responded to the *Berger* decision in Title III of the Omnibus Crime Control and Safe Streets Act of 1968, which largely tracked the guidelines established by the Court for constitutionally permissible electronic surveillance. Many provisions of Title III have been interpreted by the Supreme Court, but no broad-based constitutional challenge has succeeded.

In *Dalia v. United States*, 441 U.S. 238 (1979), the Supreme Court held that when electronic eavesdropping is permissible under Title III, officers may make covert entry on private premises to install the listening device. Moreover, such authority would be implicit in any electronic eavesdropping order; the government would not be required to obtain explicit authorization for covert entry.

PROBLEM E
THE ACCIDENTAL EAVESDROP

Federal agents intercepted a telephone conversation pursuant to a Title III authorization for a wiretap. At the conclusion of the conversation, the target of the wiretap neglected to replace the receiver firmly in its cradle, as a result of which the line remained open and the agents were able to hear conversations within the target's residence. Approximately fifty minutes of conversation between the defendants relating to drug trafficking was recorded. Should the prosecution be permitted to use this evidence? *See United States v. Baranek*, 903 F.2d 1068 (6th Cir. 1990).

PROBLEM F
THE LOQUACIOUS PAGER

> While defendant was being booked on charges of possession of cocaine for sale and possession of marijuana for sale . . . his pager audibly signalled on at least 20 occasions that it had received messages. Following each signal, the booking officer pushed a button on the pager which caused the calling party's telephone number or code to be displayed on a screen. When the officer returned the calls, several persons who answered requested the delivery of rock cocaine.

Is this evidence admissible against the defendant? *See People v. Bullock*, 226 Cal. App. 3d 380 (Cal. Ct. App. 1990). *See also United States v. De La Paz*, 43 F. Supp. 2d 370 (S.D.N.Y. 1999) (officers answered calls received on cellular telephone seized at time of arrest).

PROBLEM G
THE BIONIC EARS

Deputy Miller was conducting a surveillance of suspected illegal drug activity at nighttime at a distance of fifty to seventy-five feet, using light-enhancing binoculars and "bionic ears," the powers of which were not described by the court. "Using the 'bionic ears,' Miller overheard one of the men tell an occupant in the vehicle, 'I've got better shit then he does,' apparently referring to the other man who approached the van . . . and pulled out what looked like United States currency." The van departed and thereafter was stopped for investigation. After a consent to search the vehicle was obtained, a trained canine detected narcotics in the vehicle. Was the evidence lawfully obtained? *See Stevenson v. State*, 667 So. 2d 410 (Fla. Dist. Ct. App. 1996).

[2] Electronic Tracking

UNITED STATES v. KNOTTS

United States Supreme Court
460 U.S. 276 (1983)

JUSTICE REHNQUIST delivered the opinion of the Court.

A beeper is a radio transmitter, usually battery operated, which emits periodic signals that can be picked up by a radio receiver. In this case, a beeper was placed in a five gallon drum containing chloroform purchased by one of respondent's codefendants. By monitoring the progress of a car carrying the chloroform Minnesota law enforcement agents were able to trace the can of chloroform from its place of purchase in Minneapolis, Minnesota to respondent's secluded cabin near Shell Lake, Wisconsin. The issue presented by the case is whether such use of a beeper violated respondent's rights secured by the Fourth Amendment to the United States Constitution.

I

Respondent and two codefendants were charged in the United States District Court for the District of Minnesota with conspiracy to manufacture controlled substances, including but not limited to methamphetamine, in violation of 21 U.S.C. § 846 (1976). One of the codefendants, Darryl Petschen, was tried jointly with respondent; the other codefendant, Tristan Armstrong, pleaded guilty and testified for the government at trial.

Suspicion attached to this trio when the 3M Company, which manufactures chemicals in St. Paul, notified a narcotics investigator for the Minnesota Bureau of Criminal Apprehension that Armstrong, a former 3M employee, had been stealing chemicals which could be used in manufacturing illicit drugs. Visual surveillance of Armstrong revealed that after leaving the employ of 3M Company, he had been purchasing similar chemicals from the Hawkins Chemical Company in Minneapolis. The Minnesota narcotics officers observed that after Armstrong had made a purchase, he would deliver the chemicals to codefendant Petschen.

With the consent of the Hawkins Chemical Company, officers installed a beeper inside a five gallon container of chloroform, one of the so-called "precursor" chemicals used to manufacture illicit drugs. Hawkins agreed that when Armstrong next purchased chloroform, the chloroform would be placed in this particular container. When Armstrong made the purchase, officers followed the car in which the chloroform had been placed, maintaining contact by using both visual surveillance and a monitor which received the signals sent from the beeper.

Armstrong proceeded to Petschen's house, where the container was transferred to Petschen's automobile. Officers then followed that vehicle eastward towards the state line, across the St. Croix River, and into Wisconsin. During the latter part of this journey, Petschen began making evasive maneuvers, and the pursuing agents ended their visual surveillance. At about the same time officers lost the signal from the beeper, but with the assistance of a monitoring device located in a helicopter the approximate location of the signal was picked up again about one hour later. The signal now was stationary and the location identified was a cabin occupied by respondent near Shell Lake, Wisconsin. The record before us does not reveal that the beeper was used after the location in the area of the cabin had been initially determined.

Relying on the location of the chloroform derived through the use of the beeper and additional information obtained during three days of intermittent visual surveillance of respondent's cabin, officers secured a search warrant. During execution of the warrant, officers discovered a fully operable, clandestine drug laboratory in the cabin. In the laboratory area officers found formulas for amphetamine and methamphetamine, over $10,000 worth of laboratory equipment, and chemicals in quantities sufficient to produce 14 pounds of pure amphetamine. Under a barrel outside the cabin, officers located the five gallon container of chloroform.

After his motion to suppress evidence based on the warrantless monitoring of the beeper was denied, respondent was convicted for conspiring to manufacture controlled substances in violation of 21 U.S.C. § 846 (1976). He was sentenced to five years imprisonment. A divided panel of the United States Court of Appeals for the Eighth Circuit reversed the conviction, finding that the monitoring of the beeper was prohibited by the Fourth Amendment because its use had violated respondent's reasonable expectation of privacy, and that all information derived after the location of the cabin was a fruit of the illegal beeper monitoring. We granted certiorari, and we now reverse the judgment of the Court of Appeals. . . .

The governmental surveillance conducted by means of the beeper in this case amounted principally to the following of an automobile on public streets and highways. We have commented more than once on the diminished expectation of privacy in an automobile:

> One has a lesser expectation of privacy in a motor vehicle because its function is transportation and it seldom serves as one's residence or as the repository of personal effects. A car has little capacity for escaping public scrutiny. It travels public thoroughfares where both its occupants and its contents are in plain view.

Cardwell v. Lewis, 417 U.S. 583, 590 (1974) (plurality). . . .

A person travelling in an automobile on public thoroughfares has no reasonable expectation of privacy in his movements from one place to another. When Petschen travelled over the public streets he voluntarily conveyed to anyone who wanted to look the fact that he was travelling over particular roads in a particular direction, the fact of whatever stops he made, and the fact of his final destination when he exited from public roads onto private property.

Respondent Knotts, as the owner of the cabin and surrounding premises to which Petschen drove, undoubtedly had the traditional expectation of privacy within a dwelling place insofar as the cabin was concerned:

> Crime, even in the privacy of one's own quarters, is, of course, of grave concern to society, and the law allows such crime to be reached on proper showing. The right of officers to thrust themselves into a home is also of grave concern, not only to the individual, but to a society which chooses to dwell in reasonable security and freedom from surveillance. When the right of privacy must reasonably yield to the right of search is, as a rule, to be decided by a judicial officer, not by a policeman or government enforcement agent.

Johnson v. United States, 333 U.S. 10, 13–14 (1948) (footnote omitted), quoted with approval in *Payton v. New York*, 445 U.S. 573, 586 (1980). But no such expectation of privacy extended to the visual observation of Petschen's automobile arriving on his premises after leaving a public highway, nor to movements of objects such as the drum of chloroform outside the cabin in the "open fields." *Hester v. United States*, 265 U.S. 57 (1924).

Visual surveillance from public places along Petschen's route or adjoining Knotts' premises would have sufficed to reveal all of these facts to the police. The fact that the officers in this case relied not only on visual surveillance, but on the use of the beeper to signal the presence of Petschen's automobile to the police receiver, does not alter the situation. Nothing in the Fourth Amendment prohibited the police from augmenting the sensory faculties bestowed upon them at birth with such enhancement as science and technology afforded them in this case. . . .

. . .

We have recently had occasion to deal with another claim which was to some extent a factual counterpart of respondent's assertions here. In *Smith v. Maryland* . . . , we said:

> This analysis dictates that [Smith] can claim no legitimate expectation of privacy here. When he used this phone, [Smith] voluntarily conveyed numerical information to the telephone company and "exposed" that information to its equipment in the ordinary course of business. In so doing, [Smith] assumed the risk that the company would reveal to police the numbers he dialed. The switching equipment that processed those numbers is merely the modern counterpart of the operator who, in an earlier day, personally completed calls for the subscriber. [Smith] concedes that if he had placed his calls through an operator, he could claim no legitimate expectation of privacy. [Citation omitted.] We are not inclined to hold that a different constitutional result is required because the telephone company has decided to automate.

442 U.S., at 744–745.

Respondent does not actually quarrel with this analysis, though he expresses the generalized view that the result of the holding sought by the government would be that "twenty-four hour surveillance of any citizen of this country will be possible, without judicial knowledge or supervision." Br. for Resp., at 9 (footnote omitted). But the fact is that the "reality hardly suggests abuse," *Zurcher v. Stanford Daily*,

436 U.S. 547, 566 (1978); if such dragnet type law enforcement practices as respondent envisions should eventually occur, there will be time enough then to determine whether different constitutional principles may be applicable. *Ibid.* Insofar as respondent's complaint appears to be simply that scientific devices such as the beeper enabled the police to be more effective in detecting crime, it simply has no constitutional foundation. We have never equated police efficiency with unconstitutionality, and we decline to do so now.

Respondent specifically attacks the use of the beeper insofar as it was used to determine that the can of chloroform had come to rest on his property at Shell Lake, Wisconsin. He repeatedly challenges the "use of the beeper to determine the location of the chemical drum at Respondent's premises," Br. for Resp., at 26; he states that "[t]he government thus overlooks the fact that this case involves the sanctity of Respondent's residence, which is accorded the greatest protection available under the Fourth Amendment." *Ibid.* The Court of Appeals appears to have rested its decision on this ground:

> As noted above, a principal rationale for allowing warrantless tracking of beepers, particularly beepers in or on an auto, is that beepers are merely a more effective means of observing what is already public. But people pass daily from public to private spheres. When police agents track bugged personal property without first obtaining a warrant, they must do so at the risk that this enhanced surveillance, intrusive at best, might push fortuitously and unreasonably into the private sphere protected by the Fourth Amendment.

Det., at 6a.

We think that respondent's contentions, and the above quoted language from the opinion of the Court of Appeals, to some extent lose sight of the limited use which the government made of the signals from this particular beeper. As we have noted, nothing in this record indicates that the beeper signal was received or relied upon after it had indicated that the drum containing the chloroform had ended its automotive journey at rest on respondent's premises in rural Wisconsin. Admittedly, because of the failure of the visual surveillance, the beeper enabled the law enforcement officials in this case to ascertain the ultimate resting place of the chloroform when they would not have been able to do so had they relied solely on their naked eyes. But scientific enhancement of this sort raises no constitutional issues which visual surveillance would not also raise. A police car following Petschen at a distance throughout his journey could have observed him leaving the public highway and arriving at the cabin owned by respondent, with the drum of chloroform still in the car. This fact, along with others, was used by the government in obtaining a search warrant which led to the discovery of the clandestine drug laboratory. But there is no indication that the beeper was used in any way to reveal information as to the movement of the drum within the cabin, or in any way that would not have been visible to the naked eye from outside the cabin. Just as notions of physical trespass based on the law of real property were not dispositive in *Katz* . . . , neither were they dispositive in *Hester v. United States*, 265 U.S. 57 (1924).

We thus return to the question posed at the beginning of our inquiry in discussing *Katz* . . . ; did monitoring the beeper signals complained of by respondent invade any legitimate expectation of privacy on his part? For the reasons previously stated, we hold they did not. Since they did not, there was neither a "search" nor a "seizure" within the contemplation of the Fourth Amendment. The judgment of the Court of Appeals is therefore

Reversed.

JUSTICE BRENNAN, with whom JUSTICE MARSHALL joins, concurring in the judgment.

I join JUSTICE BLACKMUN'S and JUSTICE STEVENS' opinions concurring in the judgment. I should add, however, that I think this would have been a much more difficult case if respondent had challenged, not merely certain aspects of the monitoring of the beeper installed in the chloroform container purchased by respondent's compatriot, but also its original installation. I am not at all sure that, for purposes of the Fourth Amendment, there is a constitutionally significant difference between planting a beeper in an object in the possession of a criminal suspect and purposefully arranging that he be sold an object that, unknown to him, already has a beeper installed inside it.

Respondent claimed at oral argument that, under this Court's cases, he would not have standing to challenge the original installation of the beeper in the chloroform drum because the drum was sold, not to him, but to one of his compatriots. . . . If respondent is correct, that would only confirm for me the formalism and confusion in this Court's recent attempts to redefine Fourth Amendment standing. . . .

JUSTICE BLACKMUN, with whom JUSTICE BRENNAN, JUSTICE MARSHALL, and JUSTICE STEVENS join, concurring in the judgment.

The Court's opinion gratuitously refers to the "open fields" doctrine and twice cites *Hester v. United States*, 265 U.S. 57 (1924). For me, the present case does not concern the open fields doctrine, and I regard these references and citations as unnecessary for the Court's decision.

JUSTICE STEVENS, with whom JUSTICE BRENNAN, and JUSTICE MARSHALL join, concurring in the judgment.

The Court suggests that the Fourth Amendment does not inhibit "the police from augmenting the sensory faculties bestowed upon them at birth with such enhancement as science and technology afforded them." But the Court held to the contrary in *Katz v. United States*, 389 U.S. 347 (1967). Although the augmentation in this case was unobjectionable, it by no means follows that the use of electronic detection techniques does not implicate especially sensitive concerns.

UNITED STATES v. KARO

United States Supreme Court
468 U.S. 705 (1984)

JUSTICE WHITE delivered the opinion of the Court.

In *United States v. Knotts*, 460 U.S. 276 (1983), we held that the warrantless monitoring of an electronic tracking device ("beeper") inside a container of chemicals did not violate the Fourth Amendment when it revealed no information that could not have been obtained through visual surveillance. In this case, we are called upon to address two questions left unresolved in *Knotts*: (1) whether installation of a beeper in a container of chemicals with the consent of the original owner constitutes a search or seizure within the meaning of the Fourth Amendment when the container is delivered to a buyer having no knowledge of the presence of the beeper, and (2) whether monitoring of a beeper falls within the ambit of the Fourth Amendment when it reveals information that could not have been obtained through visual surveillance.

I

In August 1980, Agent Rottinger of the Drug Enforcement Administration (DEA) learned that respondents James Karo, Richard Horton, and William Harley had ordered 50 gallons of ether from government informant Carl Muehlenweg of Graphic Photo Design in Albuquerque, New Mexico. Muehlenweg told Rottinger that the ether was to be used to extract cocaine from clothing that had been imported into the United States. The Government obtained a court order authorizing the installation and monitoring of a beeper in one of the cans of ether. With Muehlenweg's consent, agents substituted their own can containing a beeper for one of the cans in the shipment and then had all 10 cans painted to give them a uniform appearance.

On September 20, 1980, agents saw Karo pick up the ether from Muehlenweg. They then followed Karo to his house using visual and beeper surveillance. At one point later that day, agents determined by using the beeper that the ether was still inside the house, but they later determined that it had been moved undetected to Horton's house, where they located it using the beeper. Agent Rottinger could smell the ether from the public sidewalk near Horton's residence. Two days later, agents discovered that the ether had once again been moved, and, using the beeper, they located it at the residence of Horton's father. The next day, the beeper was no longer transmitting from Horton's father's house, and agents traced the beeper to a commercial storage facility.

Because the beeper equipment was not sensitive enough to allow agents to learn precisely which locker the ether was in, agents obtained a subpoena for the records of the storage company and learned that locker 143 had been rented by Horton. Using the beeper, agents confirmed that the ether was indeed in one of the lockers in the row containing locker 143, and using their noses they detected the odor of ether emanating from locker 143. On October 8 agents obtained an order authorizing installation of an entry tone alarm into the door jamb of the locker so they would be able to tell when the door was opened. While installing the alarm, agents observed that the cans containing ether were still inside. Agents ceased visual and beeper surveillance, relying instead on the entry tone alarm. However, on October 16 Horton retrieved the contents from the locker without sounding the alarm. Agents did not learn of the entry until the manager of the storage facility notified them that Horton had been there.

Using the beeper, agents traced the beeper can to another self-storage facility three days later. Agents detected the smell of ether coming from locker 15 and learned from the manager that Horton and Harley had rented that locker using an alias the same day that the ether had been removed from the first storage facility. The agents obtained an order authorizing the installation of an entry tone alarm in locker 15, but instead of installing that alarm, they obtained consent from the manager of the facility to install a closed-circuit video camera in a locker that had a view of locker 15. On February 6, 1981, agents observed, by means of the video camera, Gene Rhodes and an unidentified woman removing the cans from the locker and loading them into the rear bed of Horton's pickup truck. Using both visual and beeper surveillance, agents tracked the truck to Rhodes' residence where it was parked in the driveway. Agents then observed Rhodes and a woman bringing boxes and other items from inside the house and loading the items into the trunk of an automobile. Agents did not see any cans being transferred from the pickup.

At about 6:00 p.m. on February 6, the car and the pickup left the driveway and travelled along public highways to Taos. During the trip, the two vehicles were under both physical and electronic surveillance. When the vehicles arrived at a house in Taos rented by Horton, Harley, and Michael Steele, the agents did not maintain tight surveillance for fear of detection. When the vehicles left the Taos residence, agents determined using the beeper monitor that the beeper can was still inside the house. Again on February 7, the beeper revealed that the ether can was still on the premises. At one point, agents noticed that the windows of the house were wide open on a cold windy day, leading them to suspect that the ether was being used. On February 8, the agents applied for and obtained a warrant to search the Taos residence based in part on information derived through use of the beeper. The warrant was executed on February 10, 1981, and Horton, Harley, Steele, and Evan Roth were arrested, and cocaine and laboratory equipment were seized.

Respondents Karo, Horton, Harley, Steele and Roth were indicted for conspiring to possess cocaine with intent to distribute and with the underlying offense. 21 U.S.C. §§ 841(a)(1) and 846. Respondent Rhodes was indicted only for conspiracy to possess. The District Court granted respondents' pre-trial motion to suppress the evidence seized from the Taos residence on the grounds that the initial warrant to install the beeper was invalid and that the Taos seizure was the tainted fruit of an unauthorized installation and monitoring of that beeper. The United States appealed but did not challenge the invalidation of the initial warrant. The Court of Appeals affirmed, except with respect to Rhodes, holding that a warrant was required to install the beeper in one of the 10 cans of ether and to monitor it in private dwellings and storage lockers. The warrant for the search in Taos and the resulting seizure were tainted by the prior illegal conduct of the Government. The evidence was therefore properly suppressed with respect to respondents Horton, Harley, Steele and Roth, who were held to have protectable interests in the privacy of the Taos dwelling, and with respect to respondent Karo because the beeper had been installed without a warrant and had been monitored while its ether-can host was in his house. We granted the Government's petition for certiorari, which raised the question whether a warrant was required to authorize either the installation of the beeper or its subsequent monitoring. We deal with each contention in turn.

II

Because the judgment below in favor of Karo rested in major part on the conclusion that the installation violated his Fourth Amendment rights and that any information obtained from monitoring the beeper was tainted by the initial illegality, we must deal with the legality of the warrantless installation. It is clear that the actual placement of the beeper into the can violated no one's Fourth Amendment rights. The can into which the beeper was placed belonged at the time to the DEA, and by no stretch of the imagination could it be said that respondents then had any legitimate expectation of privacy in it. The ether and the original 10 cans, on the other hand, belonged to, and were in the possession of, Muehlenweg, who had given his consent to any invasion of those items that occurred. Thus, even if there had been no substitution of cans and the agents had placed the beeper into one of the original 10 cans, Muehlenweg's consent was sufficient to validate the placement of the beeper in the can. See *United States v. Matlock*, 415 U.S. 164 (1974); *Frazier v. Cupp*, 394 U.S. 731 (1969).

The Court of Appeals acknowledged that before Karo took control of the ether "the DEA and Muehlenweg presumably could do with the can and ether whatever they liked without violating Karo's rights." 710 F.2d at 1438. It did not hold that the actual placement of the beeper into the ether can violated the Fourth Amendment. Instead, it held that the violation occurred at the time the beeper-laden can was transferred to Karo. The court stated:

> All individuals have a legitimate expectation of privacy that objects coming into their rightful ownership do not have electronic devices attached to them, devices that would give law enforcement agents the opportunity to monitor the location of the objects at all times and in every place that the objects are taken, including inside private residences and other areas where the right to be free from warrantless governmental intrusion is unquestioned.

Ibid.

Not surprisingly, the Court of Appeals did not describe the transfer as either a "search" or a "seizure," for plainly it is neither. A "search" occurs "when an expectation of privacy that society is prepared to consider reasonable is infringed." *United States v. Jacobsen*, 466 U.S. 109 (1984). The mere transfer to Karo of a can containing an unmonitored beeper infringed no privacy interest. It conveyed no information that Karo wished to keep private, for it conveyed no information at all. To be sure, it created a *potential* for an invasion of privacy, but we have never held that potential, as opposed to actual, invasions of privacy constitute searches for purposes of the Fourth Amendment. A holding to that effect would mean that a policeman walking down the street carrying a parabolic microphone capable of picking up conversations in nearby homes would be engaging in a search even if the microphone were not turned on. It is the exploitation of technological advances that implicates the Fourth Amendment, not their mere existence.

We likewise do not believe that the transfer of the container constituted a seizure. A "seizure" of property occurs when "there is some meaningful interference with an individual's possessory interests in that property." *Ibid.* Although the can may have contained an unknown and unwanted foreign object, it cannot be said that anyone's possessory interest was interfered with in a meaningful way. At most, there was a technical trespass on the space occupied by the beeper. The existence of a physical trespass is only marginally relevant to the question of whether the Fourth Amendment has been violated, however, for an actual trespass is neither necessary nor sufficient to establish a constitutional violation. Compare *Katz v. United States*, 389 U.S. 347 (1967) (no trespass, but Fourth Amendment violation), with *Oliver v. United States*, 464 U.S. 170 (1984) (trespass, but no Fourth Amendment violation). Of course, if the presence of a beeper in the can constituted a seizure merely because of its occupation of space, it would follow that the presence of any object, regardless of its nature, would violate the Fourth Amendment.

We conclude that no Fourth Amendment interest of Karo or of any other respondent was infringed by the installation of the beeper. Rather, any impairment of their privacy interests that may have occurred was occasioned by the monitoring of the beeper.

III

In this case, had a DEA agent thought it useful to enter the Taos residence to verify that the ether was actually in the house and had he done so surreptitiously and without a warrant, there is little doubt that he would have engaged in an unreasonable search within the meaning of the Fourth Amendment. For purposes of the Amendment, the result is the same where, without a warrant, the Government surreptitiously employs an electronic device to obtain information that it could not have obtained by observation from outside the curtilage of the house. The beeper tells the agent that a particular article is actually located at a particular time in the private residence and is in the possession of the person or persons whose residence is being surveilled. Even if visual surveillance has revealed that the article to which the beeper is attached has entered the house, the later monitoring not only verifies the officers' observations but also establishes that the article remains on the premises. Here, for example, the beeper was monitored for a significant period after the arrival of the ether in Taos and before the application for a warrant to search.

The monitoring of an electronic device such as a beeper is, of course, less intrusive than a full-scale search, but it does reveal a critical fact about the interior of the premises that the Government is extremely interested in knowing and that it could not have otherwise obtained without a warrant. The case is thus not like *Knotts*, for there the beeper told the authorities nothing about the interior of Knotts' cabin. The information obtained in *Knotts* was "voluntarily conveyed to anyone who wanted to look. . . ." . . . Here, as we have said, the monitoring indicated that the beeper was inside the house, a fact that could not have been visually verified.

We cannot accept the Government's contention that it should be completely free from the constraints of the Fourth Amendment to determine by means of an electronic device, without a warrant and without probable cause or reasonable suspicion, whether a particular article — or a person, for that matter — is in an individual's home at a particular time. Indiscriminate monitoring of property that has been withdrawn from public view would present far too serious a threat to privacy interests in the home to escape entirely some sort of Fourth Amendment oversight.

IV

As we have said, by maintaining the beeper the agents verified that the ether was actually located in the Taos house and that it remained there while the warrant was sought. This information was obtained without a warrant and would therefore be inadmissible at trial against those with privacy interests in the house — Horton, Harley, Steele, and Roth. That information, which was included in the warrant affidavit, would also invalidate the warrant for the search of the house if it proved to be critical to establishing probable cause for the issuance of the warrant. However, if sufficient untainted evidence was presented in the warrant affidavit to establish probable cause, the warrant was nevertheless valid. . . .

It requires only a casual examination of the warrant affidavit, which in relevant respects consists of undisputed factual assertions, to conclude that the officers could have secured the warrant without relying on the beeper to locate the ether in the house sought to be searched. The affidavit recounted the months-long tracking of the evidence, including the visual and beeper surveillance of Horton's pickup on its trip from Albuquerque to the immediate vicinity of the Taos residence; its departure a short time later without the ether; its later return to the residence; and the visual observation of the residence with its window open on a cold night.

That leaves the question whether any part of this additional information contained in the warrant was itself the fruit of a Fourth Amendment violation to which any of the occupants of the house could object. As far as the present record reveals, two of the four respondents who had standing to object to the search of the residence — Steele and Roth — had no interest in any of the arguably private places in which the beeper was monitored prior to its arrival in Taos. The evidence seized in the house would be admissible against them.

The question as to Horton and Harley is somewhat more complicated. On the initial leg of its journey, the ether came to rest in Karo's house where it was monitored; it then moved in succession to two other houses, including Horton's, before it was moved first to a locker in one public warehouse and then to a locker in another. Both lockers were rented jointly by Horton and Harley. On September 6, the ether was removed from the second storage facility and transported to Taos.

Assuming for present purposes that prior to its arrival at the second warehouse the beeper was illegally used to locate the ether in a house or other place in which Horton or Harley had a justifiable claim to privacy, we are confident that such use of the beeper does not taint its later use in locating the ether and tracking it to Taos. The movement of the ether from the first warehouse was undetected, but by monitoring the beeper the agents discovered that it had been moved to the second storage facility. No prior monitoring of the beeper contributed to this discovery; using the beeper for this purpose was thus untainted by any possible prior illegality. Furthermore, the beeper informed the agents only that the ether was somewhere in the warehouse; it did not identify the specific locker in which the ether was located. Monitoring the beeper revealed nothing about the contents of the locker that Horton and Harley had rented and hence was not a search of that locker. The locker was identified only when agents traversing the public part of the facility found that the smell of ether was coming from a specific locker.

The agents set up visual surveillance of that locker and on September 6, they observed Rhodes and a female remove the ether and load it into Horton's pickup truck. The truck moved over the public streets and was tracked by beeper to Rhodes' house, where it was temporarily parked. At about 6:00 p.m. the truck was observed departing and was tracked visually and by beeper to the vicinity of the house in Taos. Because locating the ether in the warehouse was not an illegal search — and because the ether was seen being loaded into Horton's truck, which then travelled the public highways — it is evident that under *Knotts* there was no violation of the Fourth Amendment as to anyone with or without standing to complain about monitoring the beeper while it was located in Horton's truck. Under these circumstances, it is clear that the warrant affidavit, after striking the facts about monitoring the beeper while it was in the Taos residence, contained sufficient untainted information to furnish probable cause for the issuance of the search warrant. The evidence seized in the house should not have been suppressed with respect to any of the respondents.

The judgment of the Court of Appeals is accordingly

Reversed.

NOTES

(1) *Knotts* and *Karo* both involved the use of a tracking device in an on-going investigation of an identified suspect. In *United States v. Levine*, 80 F.2d 129 (5th Cir. 1996), the question before the court was whether such a device could provide probable cause for an arrest. The defendant had robbed a bank, and an electronic transmitter had been included in the packets of money taken. The transmitter was part of a joint effort of the police and financial institutions to apprehend bank robbers. "The tracking system included a network of remote tower antennae, mobile tracking units in police vehicles, and hand-held detectors. . . . After an alert was picked up by a tower, approximately thirty patrol units were assigned to search for the signal." The court held that an officer who intercepted a vehicle from which the signal was emanating had probable cause to arrest the driver, analogizing the case to an arrest made on the basis of a dog sniff.

(2) Critical to the outcome in *Knotts* and *Karo* was the determination whether the tracking device revealed information from within a constitutionally protected area. In *People v. Stanley*, 72 Cal. App. 4th 1547, 86 Cal. Rptr. 2d 89 (1999), the accused submitted that a device attached to a utility pole which measured the amount of electricity received at his house was impermissible under this standard.

The court disagreed, distinguishing *Karo* with the observation that "[t]he technology used here did not peer inside Stanley's house or otherwise penetrate its inner sanctum."

PROBLEM H
THE PHONY PHOTO ALBUM

A package shipped from Peru and addressed to King Kelly . . . arrived at the Honolulu International Airport mail room on September 9, 1983. The package was subjected to a dog sniff. The trained dog indicated a potential contraband substance in the package. Customs Officer Jerome Tomaino opened the package and found a photo album that had bulges in the front and back cover. He inserted a knife in the back cover and a white powdery substance adhered to the blade. The substance was subsequently tested and positively identified as cocaine. . . .

Ten days after the package was confiscated by Tomaino, DEA agents cut open the back cover of the album and removed four out of five packets of cocaine. The agents replaced the four packets of cocaine with four packets of fake cocaine. Also inserted in the back cover of the album was a beeper which would enable the agents to monitor the location of the package and to learn when the back cover of the album was being opened. The agents made a "controlled delivery" of the package on the same day to Kelly at the University of Hawaii School of Business. Kelly signed for the package and went upstairs to a conference room. He then exited from the building carrying a knapsack which emitted signals from the beeper.

The officers followed Kelly to his residence, commenced surveillance of the house, and monitored the beeper signals. After five to seven minutes, the signals from the beeper changed to a droning tone indicating that the back cover of the album had been opened.

Following two unsuccessful efforts to speak to Kelly at the door, officers forcibly entered the premises, arrested Kelly and seized the album which he was holding.

What result under *Knotts* and *Karo*? *See State v. Kelly*, 708 P.2d 820 (1985).

[3] Global Positioning Systems

UNITED STATES v. JONES
United States Supreme Court
132 S. Ct. 945 (2012)

[*See* § 3.01, *supra.*]

[4] Thermal Imaging

KYLLO v. UNITED STATES

United States Supreme Court
533 U.S. 27 (2001)

Justice Scalia delivered the opinion of the Court.

This case presents the question whether the use of a thermal-imaging device aimed at a private home from a public street to detect relative amounts of heat within the home constitutes a "search" within the meaning of the Fourth Amendment.

I

In 1991 Agent William Elliott of the United States Department of the Interior came to suspect that marijuana was being grown in the home belonging to petitioner Danny Kyllo, part of a triplex on Rhododendron Drive in Florence, Oregon. Indoor marijuana growth typically requires high-intensity lamps. In order to determine whether an amount of heat was emanating from petitioner's home consistent with the use of such lamps, at 3:20 a.m. on January 16, 1992, Agent Elliott and Dan Haas used an Agema Thermovision 210 thermal imager to scan the triplex. Thermal imagers detect infrared radiation, which virtually all objects emit but which is not visible to the naked eye. The imager converts radiation into images based on relative warmth — black is cool, white is hot, shades of gray connote relative differences; in that respect, it operates somewhat like a video camera showing heat images. The scan of Kyllo's home took only a few minutes and was performed from the passenger seat of Agent Elliott's vehicle across the street from the front of the house and also from the street in back of the house. The scan showed that the roof over the garage and a side wall of petitioner's home were relatively hot compared to the rest of the home and substantially warmer than neighboring homes in the triplex. Agent Elliott concluded that petitioner was using halide lights to grow marijuana in his house, which indeed he was. Based on tips from informants, utility bills, and the thermal imaging, a Federal Magistrate Judge issued a warrant authorizing a search of petitioner's home, and the agents found an indoor growing operation involving more than 100 plants. Petitioner was indicted on one count of manufacturing marijuana, in violation of 21 U.S.C. § 841(a)(1). He unsuccessfully moved to suppress the evidence seized form his home and then entered a conditional guilty plea.

The Court of Appeals for the Ninth Circuit remanded the case for an evidentiary hearing regarding the intrusiveness of thermal imaging. On remand the District Court found that the Agema 210 "is a non-intrusive device which emits no rays or beams and shows a crude visual image of the heat being radiated from the outside of the house"; it "did not show any people or activity within the walls of the structure"; "[t]he device used cannot penetrate walls or windows to reveal conversations or human activities"; and "[n]o intimate details of the home were observed." . . . Based on these findings, the District Court upheld the validity of the warrant that relied in part upon the thermal imaging, and reaffirmed the denial of the motion to suppress. A divided Court of Appeals initially reversed, 140 F.3d 1249 (1998)), but that opinion was withdrawn and the panel (after a change in composition) affirmed, 190 F.3d 1041 (1999), with Judge Noonan dissenting. The court held that petitioner had shown no subjective expectation of privacy because he had made no attempt to conceal the heat escaping from his home, . . . and even if he had, there was no objectively reasonable expectation of privacy because the imager "did not expose any intimate details of Kyllo's life," only "amorphous 'hot spots' on the roof and exterior wall,". . . . We granted certiorari.

. . .

III

It would be foolish to contend that the degree of privacy secured to citizens by the Fourth Amendment has been entirely unaffected by the advance of technology. For example, . . . the technology enabling human flight has exposed to public view (and hence, we have said, to official observation) uncovered portions of the house and its curtilage that once were private. See *Ciraolo*. . . . The question we confront today is what limits there are upon this power of technology to shrink the realm of guaranteed privacy.

The *Katz* test — whether the individual has an expectation of privacy that society is prepared to recognize as reasonable — has often been criticized as circular, and hence subjective and unpredictable. . . . While it may be difficult to refine *Katz* when the search of areas such as telephone booths, automobiles, or even the curtilage and uncovered portions of residences are at issue, in the case of the search of the interior of homes — the prototypical and hence most commonly litigated area of protected privacy — there is a ready criterion, with roots deep in the common law, of the minimal expectation of privacy that *exists*, and that is acknowledged to be *reasonable*. To withdraw protection of this minimum expectation would be to permit police technology to erode the privacy guaranteed by the Fourth Amendment. We think that obtaining by sense-enhancing technology any information regarding the interior of the home that could not otherwise have been obtained without physical "intrusion into a constitutionally protected area," . . . constitutes a search — at least where (as here) the technology in question is not in general public use. This assures preservation of that degree of privacy against government that existed when the Fourth Amendment was adopted. On the basis of this criterion, the information obtained by the thermal imager in this case was the product of a search.[24]

---

[24] The dissent's repeated assertion that the thermal imaging did not obtain information regarding the interior of the home . . . is simply inaccurate. A thermal imager reveals the relative heat of various rooms in the home. The dissent may not find that information particularly private or important, . . . but there is no basis for saying it is not information regarding the interior of the home. The dissent's comparison of the thermal imaging to various circumstances in which outside observers might be able to perceive, without technology, the heat of the home — for example, by observing snow melt on the roof, . . . — is quite irrelevant. The fact that equivalent information could sometimes be obtained by other means does not make lawful the use of means that violate the Fourth Amendment. The police might, for example, learn how many people are in a particular house by setting up year-round surveillance; but that

The Government maintains, however, that the thermal imaging must be upheld because it detected "only heat radiating from the external surface of the house". . . . The dissent makes this its leading point, . . . contending that there is a fundamental difference between what it calls "off-the-wall" observations and "through-the-wall" observations and "through-the-wall surveillance." But just as a thermal imager captures only heat emanating from a house, so also a powerful directional microphone picks up only sound emanating from a house — and a satellite capable of scanning from many miles away would pick up only visible light emanating from a house. We rejected such a mechanical interpretation of the Fourth Amendment in *Katz*, where the eavesdropping device picked up only sound waves that reached the exterior of the phone booth. Reversing that approach would leave the homeowner at the mercy of advancing technology — including imaging technology that could discern all human activity in the home. While the technology used in the present case was relatively crude, the rule we adopt must take account of more sophisticated systems that are already in use or in development.[25] The dissent's reliance on the distinction between "off-the-wall" and "through-the-wall" observation is entirely incompatible with the dissent's belief, which we discuss below, that thermal-imaging observations of the intimate details of a home are impermissible. The most sophisticated thermal imaging devices continue to measure heat "off-the-wall" rather than "through-the-wall"; the dissent's disapproval of those more sophisticated thermal-imaging devices . . . is an acknowledgment that there is no substance to this distinction. As for the dissent's extraordinary assertion that anything learned through "an inference" cannot be a search, . . . that would validate even the "through-the-wall" technologies that the dissent purports to disapprove. Surely the dissent does not believe that the through-the-wall radar or ultrasound technology produces an 8-by-10 Kodak glossy that needs no analysis (*i.e.*, the making of inferences). And, of course, the novel proposition that inference insulates a search is blatantly contrary to *United States v. Karo*, . . . where the police "inferred" from the activation of a beeper that a certain can of ether was in the home. The police activity was held to be a search, and the search was held unlawful.

. . . Where, as here, the Government uses a device that is not in general public use, to explore details of the home that would previously have been unknowable without physical intrusion, the surveillance is a "search" and is presumptively unreasonable without a warrant.

Since we hold the Thermovision imaging to have been an unlawful search, it will remain for the District Court to determine whether, without the evidence it

---

does not make breaking and entering to find out the same information lawful. In any event, on the night of January 16, 1992, no outside observer could have discerned the relative heat of Kyllo's home without thermal imaging.

[25] The ability to "see" through walls and other opaque barriers is a clear, and scientifically feasible, goal of law enforcement research and development. The National Law Enforcement and Corrections Technology Center, a program within the United States Department of Justice, features on its Internet Website projects that include a "Radar-Based Through-the-Wall Surveillance System," "Handheld Ultrasound Through the Wall Surveillance," and a "Radar Flashlight" that "will enable law officers to detect individuals through interior building walls." www.nlectc.org/techproj/ (visited May 3, 2001). Some devices may emit low levels of radiation that travel "through-the-wall," but others, such as more sophisticated thermal imaging devices, are entirely passive, or "off-the-wall" as the dissent puts it.

provided, the search warrant issued in this case was supported by probable cause — and if not, whether there is any other basis for supporting admission of the evidence that the search pursuant to the warrant produced.

JUSTICE STEVENS, with whom the CHIEF JUSTICE, JUSTICE O'CONNOR, and JUSTICE KENNEDY join, dissenting.

There is, in my judgment, a distinction of constitutional magnitude between "through-the-wall surveillance" that gives the observer or listener direct access to information in a private area, on the one hand, and the thought processes used to draw inferences from information in the public domain, on the other hand. The Court has crafted a rule that purports to deal with direct observations of the inside of the home, but the case before us merely involves indirect deductions from "off-the-wall" surveillance, that is, observations of the exterior of the home. Those observations were made with a fairly primitive thermal imager that gathered data exposed on the outside of petitioner's home but did not invade any constitutionally protected interest in privacy. Moreover, I believe that the supposedly "bright-line" rule the Court has created in response to its concerns about future technological developments is unnecessary, unwise, and inconsistent with the Fourth Amendment.

. . .

The two reasons advanced by the Court as justifications for the adoption of its new rule are both unpersuasive. First, the Court suggests that its rule is compelled by our holding in *Katz*, because in that case, as in this, the surveillance consisted of nothing more than the monitoring of waves emanating from a private area into the public domain. . . . Yet there are critical differences between the cases. In *Katz*, the electronic listening device attached to the outside of the phone booth allowed the officers to pick up the content of the conversation inside the booth, making them the functional equivalent of intruders because they gathered information that was otherwise available only to someone inside the private area; it would be as if, in this case, the thermal imager presented a view of the heat-generating activity inside petitioner's home. By contrast, the thermal imager here disclosed only the relative amounts of heat radiating from the house; it would be as if, in *Katz*, the listening device disclosed only the relative volume of sound leaving the booth, which presumably was discernible in the public domain. Surely, there is a significant difference between the general and well-settled expectation that strangers will not have direct access to the contents of private communications, on the one hand, and the rather theoretical expectation that an occasional homeowner would even care if anybody noticed the relative amounts of heat emanating from the walls of his house, on the other. It is pure hyperbole for the Court to suggest that refusing to extend the holding of *Katz* to this case would leave the homeowner at the mercy of "technology that could discern all human activity in the home." . . .

Second, the Court argues that the permissibility of "through-the-wall surveillance" cannot depend on a distinction between observing "intimate details" such as "the lady of the house [taking] her daily sauna and bath," and noticing only "the nonintimate rug on the vestibule floor" or "objects no smaller than 36 by 36 inches." . . . This entire argument assumes, of course, that the thermal imager in this case could or did perform "through-the-wall surveillance" that could identify any detail "that would previously have been unknowable without physical intrusion." . . . In fact, the device could not, . . . and did not, . . . enable its user to identify either the lady of the house, the rug on the vestibule floor, or anything else inside the house, whether smaller or larger than 36 by 36 inches. Indeed, the vague thermal images of petitioner's home . . . were submitted by him to the District Court as part of an expert report raising the question whether the device could even take "accurate, consistent infrared images" of the *outside* of his house. . . . But even if the device could reliably show extraordinary differences in the amounts of heat leaving his home, drawing the inference that there was something suspicious occurring inside the residence — a conclusion that officers far less gifted than Sherlock Holmes would readily draw — does not qualify as "through-the-wall surveillance," much less a Fourth Amendment violation.

NOTE

The *Kyllo* decision has generated much commentary. *See* Seamon, Kyllo v. United States *and the Partial Ascendance of Justice Scalia's Fourth Amendment,* 79 Wash. U. L.Q. 1013 (2001); Simmons, *From* Katz *to* Kyllo: *A Blueprint for Adapting the Fourth Amendment to Twenty-first Century Technologies,* 53 Hast. L.J. 1303 (2002); Symposium, *Searching for the Meaning of Fourth Amendment Privacy after* Kyllo v. United States, 86 Minn. L. Rev. 1325 (2002); Symposium, *The Effect of Technology on Fourth Amendment Analysis and Individual Rights,* 72 Miss. L.J. 1 (2002).

[D] Narcotics Detecting Canines

ILLINOIS v. CABALLES

United States Supreme Court
543 U.S. 405 (2005)

Justice Stevens delivered the opinion of the Court.

. . .

. . . In *United States v. Place,* 462 U.S. 696 . . . (1983), we treated a canine sniff by a well-trained narcotics-detection dog as "sui generis" because it "discloses only the presence or absence of narcotics, a contraband item." . . . [S]ee also *Indianapolis v. Edmond,* 531 U.S. 32, 40 . . . (2000). Respondent likewise concedes that "drug sniffs are designed, and if properly conducted are generally likely, to reveal only the presence of contraband." . . . Although respondent argues that the error rates, particularly the existence of false positives, call into question the premise that drug-detection dogs alert only to contraband, the record contains no evidence or findings that support his argument. Moreover, respondent does not suggest that an erroneous alert, in and of itself, reveals any legitimate private information, and, in this case, the trial judge found that the dog sniff was sufficiently reliable to establish probable cause to conduct a full-blown search of the trunk.

Accordingly, the use of a well-trained narcotics-detection dog — one that "does not expose noncontraband items that otherwise would remain hidden from public view," . . . — during a lawful traffic stop, generally does not implicate legitimate privacy interests. In this case, the dog sniff was performed on the exterior of respondent's car while he was lawfully seized for a traffic violation. Any intrusion on respondent's privacy expectations does not rise to the level of a constitutionally cognizable infringement.

This conclusion is entirely consistent with our recent decision that the use of a thermal-imaging device to detect the growth of marijuana in a home constituted an unlawful search. *Kyllo v. United States*, 533 U.S. 27 . . . (2001). Critical to that decision was the fact that the device was capable of detecting lawful activity — in that case, intimate details in a home, such as "at what hour each night the lady of the house takes her daily sauna and bath." . . . The legitimate expectation that information about perfectly lawful activity will remain private is categorically distinguishable from respondent's hopes or expectations concerning the nondetection of contraband in the trunk of his car. A dog sniff conducted during a concededly lawful traffic stop that reveals no information other than the location of a substance that no individual has any right to possess does not violate the Fourth Amendment.

The judgment of the Illinois Supreme Court is vacated, and the case is remanded for further proceedings not inconsistent with this opinion.

It is so ordered.

The Chief Justice took no part in the decision of this case.

JUSTICE SOUTER, dissenting.

I would hold that using the dog for the purposes of determining the presence of marijuana in the car's trunk was a search unauthorized as an incident of the speeding stop and unjustified on any other ground. I would accordingly affirm the judgment of the Supreme Court of Illinois, and I respectfully dissent.

In *United States v. Place*, . . . we categorized the sniff of the narcotics-seeking dog as "sui generis" under the Fourth Amendment and held it was not a search. . . . The classification rests not only upon the limited nature of the intrusion, but on a further premise that experience has shown to be untenable, the assumption that trained sniffing dogs do not err. What we have learned about the fallibility of dogs in the years since *Place* was decided would itself be reason to call for reconsidering *Place*'s decision against treating the intentional use of a trained dog as a search. The portent of this very case, however, adds insistence to the call, for an uncritical adherence to *Place* would render the Fourth Amendment indifferent to suspicionless and indiscriminate sweeps of cars in parking garages and pedestrians on sidewalks; if a sniff is not preceded by a seizure subject to Fourth Amendment notice, it escapes Fourth Amendment review entirely unless it is treated as a search. We should not wait for these developments to occur before rethinking *Place*'s analysis, which invites such untoward consequences.

. . .

JUSTICE GINSBURG, with whom JUSTICE SOUTER joins, dissenting.

. . .

In *Terry v. Ohio*, the Court upheld the stop and subsequent frisk of an individual based on an officer's observation of suspicious behavior and his reasonable belief that the suspect was armed. . . . In a *Terry*-type investigatory stop, "the officer's action [must be] justified at its inception, and . . . reasonably related in scope to the circumstances which justified the interference in the first place." . . . In applying *Terry*, the Court has several times indicated that the limitation on "scope" is not confined to the duration of the seizure; it also encompasses the manner in which the seizure is conducted. See, e.g., *Hiibel v. Sixth Judicial Dist. Court*, . . . (an officer's request that an individual identify himself "has an immediate relation to the purpose, rationale, and practical demands of a *Terry* stop"); *United States v. Hensley*, . . . (examining, under *Terry*, both "the length and intrusiveness of the stop and detention"); *Florida v. Royer*, . . . ("[A]n investigative detention must be temporary and last no longer than is necessary to effectuate the purpose of the stop [and] . . . the investigative methods employed should be the least intrusive means reasonably available to verify or dispel the officer's suspicion. . . .").

. . .

It is hardly dispositive that the dog sniff in this case may not have lengthened the duration of the stop. . . . *Terry*, it merits repetition, instructs that any investigation must be "reasonably related in *scope* to the circumstances which justified the interference in the first place." 392 U.S., at 20 . . . (emphasis added). The unwarranted and nonconsensual expansion of the seizure here from a routine traffic stop to a drug investigation broadened the scope of the investigation in a manner that, in my judgment, runs afoul of the Fourth Amendment. . . .

Today's decision also undermines this Court's situation-sensitive balancing of Fourth Amendment interests in other contexts. For example, in *Bond v. United States*, 529 U.S. 334, 338–339 (2000), the Court held that a bus passenger had an expectation of privacy in a bag placed in an overhead bin and that a police officer's physical manipulation of the bag constituted an illegal search. If canine drug sniffs are entirely exempt from Fourth Amendment inspection, a sniff could substitute for an officer's request to a bus passenger for permission to search his bag, with this significant difference: The passenger would not have the option to say "No."

. . .

NOTES AND QUESTIONS

(1) The Court distinguished the *Kyllo* decision on the ground that the heat-sensing device would detect wholly innocent as well as suspicious activity, whereas the narcotics-detecting dog would only signal the presence of contraband. Justice Souter contended in dissent that empirical data demonstrated that the dogs are fallible. Assuming this to be correct, does it undermine the rationale for the Court's decision? Or is it sufficient for the government to show that whenever a properly trained dog signals it is probable that narcotics are present?

(2) *Caballes* involved a vehicle which had been stopped for independent reasons. Does this decision support the use of narcotics-detecting canines absent a detention? For example, could officers station a dog at the entrance to a rock concert and detain individuals in the crowd flow when the presence of marijuana is indicated? Could a dog be walked through a parking garage in an effort to identify suspect vehicles?

FLORIDA v. HARRIS

United States Supreme Court
133 S. Ct. 1050 (2013)

JUSTICE KAGAN delivered the opinion of the court.

In this case, we consider how a court should determine if the "alert" of a drug-detection dog during a traffic-stop provides probable cause to search a vehicle. The Florida Supreme Court held that the State must in every case present an exhaustive set of records, including a log of the dog's performance in the field, to establish the dog's reliability. . . . We think that demand inconsistent with the "flexible, common-sense standard" of probable cause. *Illinois v. Gates*, . . .

I

William Wheetley is a K-9 Officer in the Liberty County, Florida Sheriff's Office. On June 24, 2006, he was on a routine patrol with Aldo, a German shepherd trained to detect certain narcotics (methamphetamine, marijuana, cocaine, heroin, and ecstasy). Wheetley pulled over respondent Clayton Harris's truck because it had an expired license plate. On approaching the driver's-side door, Wheetley saw that Harris was "visibly nervous," unable to sit still, shaking, and breathing rapidly. Wheetley also noticed an open can of beer in the truck's cup holder. . . . Wheetley asked Harris for consent to search the truck, but Harris refused. At that point, Wheetley retrieved Aldo from the patrol car and walked him around Harris's truck for a "free air sniff." . . . Aldo alerted at the driver's-side door handle — signaling, through a distinctive set of behaviors, that he smelled drugs there.

Wheetley concluded, based principally on Aldo's alert, that he had probable cause to search the truck. His search did not turn up any of the drugs Aldo was trained to detect. But it did reveal 200 loose pseudoephedrine pills, 8,000 matches, a bottle of hydrochloric acid, two containers of antifreeze, and a coffee filter full of iodine crystals — all ingredients for making methamphetamine. Wheetley accordingly arrested Harris, who admitted after proper *Miranda* warnings that he routinely "cooked" methamphetamine at his house and could not go "more than a few days without using" it. . . . The State charged Harris with possessing pseudoephedrine for use in manufacturing methamphetamine.

Harris moved to suppress the evidence found in his truck on the ground that Aldo's alert had not given Wheetley probable cause for a search. At the hearing on that motion, Wheetley testified about both his and Aldo's training in drug detection. . . . In 2004, Wheetley (and a different dog) completed a 160-hour course in narcotics detection offered by the Dothan, Alabama Police Department, while Aldo (and a different handler) completed a similar, 120-hour course given by the Apopka, Florida Police Department. That same year, Aldo received a one-year certification from Drug Beat, a private company that specializes in testing and certifying K-9 dogs. Wheetley and Aldo teamed up in 2005 and went through another, 40-hour refresher course in Dothan together. They also did four hours of training exercises each week to maintain their skills. Wheetley would hide drugs in certain vehicles or buildings while leaving others "blank" to determine whether Aldo alerted at the right places. . . . According to Wheetley, Aldo's performance in those exercises was "really good." . . . The State introduced "Monthly Canine Detection Training Logs" consistent with that testimony: They showed that Aldo always found hidden drugs and that he performed "satisfactorily" (the higher of two possible assessments) on each day of training. . . .

The trial court concluded that Wheetley had probable cause to search Harris's truck and so denied the motion to suppress. Harris then entered a no-contest plea while reserving the right to appeal the trial court's ruling. An intermediate state court summarily affirmed. . . .

The Florida Supreme Court reversed, holding that Wheetley lacked probable cause to search Harris' vehicle under the Fourth Amendment. "[W]hen a dog alerts," the court wrote, "the fact that the dog has been trained and certified is simply not enough to establish probable cause." . . . To demonstrate a dog's reliability, the State needed to produce a wider array of evidence:

> "[T]he State must present . . . the dog's training and certification records, an explanation of the meaning of the particular training and certification, field performance records (including any unverified alerts), and evidence concerning the experience and training of the officer handling the dog, as well as any other objective evidence known to the officer about the dog's reliability." . . .

The court particularly stressed the need for "evidence of the dog's performance history," including records showing "how often the dog has alerted in the field without illegal contraband having been found." . . . That data, the court stated, could help to expose such problems as a handler's tendency (conscious or not) to "cue [a] dog to alert" and "a dog's inability to distinguish between residual odors and actual dogs." . . . Accordingly, an officer like Wheetley who did not keep full records of his dog's field performance could never have the requisite cause to think "that the dog is a reliable indicator of drugs." . . .

Judge Canady dissented, maintaining that the majority's "elaborate and inflexible evidentiary requirements" went beyond the demands of probable cause. *Id.*, at 775. He would have affirmed the trial court's ruling on the strength of Aldo's training history and Harris's "fail[ure] to present any evidence challenging" it. *Id.*, at 776.

We granted certiorari, . . . and now reverse.

II

A police officer has probable cause to conduct a search when "the facts available to [him] would 'warrant a [person] of reasonable caution in the belief" that contraband or evidence of a crime is present. *Texas v. Brown*, 460 U.S. 730, 742 (1983) (plurality opinion) . . . The test for probable cause is not reducible to "precise definition or quantification." *Maryland v. Pringle*, . . . "Finely tuned standards such as proof beyond a reasonable doubt or by a preponderance of the evidence . . . have no place in the [probable-cause] decision." *Gates*, . . . All we have required is the kind of "fair probability" on which "reasonable and prudent [people,] not legal technicians act." . . .

In evaluating whether the State has met this practical and common-sensical standard, we have consistently looked to the totality of the circumstances. See, *e.g.*, *Pringle*, . . . ; *Gates*, . . . We have rejected rigid rules, bright-line tests, and mechanistic inquiries in favor of a more flexible, all-things-considered approach. In *Gates*, for example, we abandoned our old test for assessing the reliability of informants' tips because it had devolved into a "complex superstructure of evidentiary and analytical rules," any one of which, if not complied with, would derail a finding of probable cause. . . . We lamented the development of a list of "inflexible, independent requirements applicable in every case." . . . Probable cause, we emphasized, is "a fluid concept — turning on the assessment of probabilities in particular factual contexts — not readily, or even usefully, reduced to a neat set of legal rules." . . .

The Florida Supreme Court flouted this established approach to determining probable cause. To assess the reliability of a drug-detection dog, the court created a strict evidentiary checklist, whose every item the State must tick off. Most prominently, an alert cannot establish probable cause under the Florida court's decision of the dog's prior "hits" and "misses" in the field. (One wonders how the court would apply its test to a rookie dog.) No matter how much other proof the State offers of the dog's reliability, the absent field performance records will preclude a finding of probable cause. That is the antithesis of a totality-of-the-circumstances analysis. It is indeed the very thing we criticized in *Gates* when we overhauled our method for assessing the trustworthiness of an informant's tip. A gap as to any one matter, we explained, should not sink the State's case; rather, that "deficiency . . . may be compensated for, in determining the overall reliability of a tip, by a strong showing as to . . . other indicia of reliability." . . . So too here, a finding of a drug-detection dog's reliability cannot depend on the State's satisfaction in multiple, independent evidentiary requirements. No more for dogs than for human informants is such an inflexible checklist the way to prove reliability, and thus establish probable cause.

Making matters worse, the decision below treats records of a dog's field performance as the gold standard in evidence, when in most cases they have relatively limited import. Errors may abound in such records. If a dog on patrol fails to alert to a car containing drugs, the mistake usually will go undetected because the officer will not initiate a search. Field data thus may not capture a dog's false negatives. Conversely (and more relevant here), if the dog alerts to a car in which the officer finds no narcotics, the dog may not have made a mistake at all. The dog may have detected substances that were too well hidden or present in quantities too small for the officer to locate. Or the dog may have smelled the residual odor of drugs previously in the vehicle or on the driver's person. Field data thus may markedly overstate a dog's real false positives. By contrast, those inaccuracies — in either direction — do not taint records of a dog's performance in standard training and certification settings. There, the designers of an assessment know where drugs are hidden and where they are not — and so where a dog should alert and where he should not. The better measure of a dog's reliability thus comes away from the field, in controlled testing environments.

For that reason, evidence of a dog's satisfactory performance in a certification or training program can itself provide sufficient reason to trust his alert. If a bona fide organization has certified a dog after testing his reliability in a controlled setting, a court can presume (subject to any conflicting evidence offered) that the dog's alert provides probable cause to search. The same is true, even in the absence of formal certification, if the dog has recently and successfully completed a training program that evaluated his proficiency in locating drugs. After all, law enforcement units have their own strong incentive to use effective training and certification programs, because only accurate drug-detection dogs enable officers to locate contraband without incurring unnecessary risks or wasting limited time and resources.

. . .

In short, a probable-cause hearing focusing on a dog's alert should proceed much like any other. The court should allow the parties to make their best case, consistent with the usual rules of criminal procedure. And the court should then evaluate the proffered evidence to decide what all circumstances demonstrate. If the State has produced proof from controlled settings that a dog performs reliably in detecting drugs, and the defendant has not contested that showing, then the court should find probable cause. If, in contrast, the defendant has challenged the State's case (by disputing the reliability of the dog overall or of a particular alert), then the court should weigh the competing evidence. In all events, the court should not prescribe, as the Florida Supreme Court did, an inflexible set of evidentiary requirements. The question — similar to every inquiry into probable cause — is whether all the facts surrounding a dog's alert, viewed through the lens of common sense, would make a reasonably prudent person think that a search would reveal contraband or evidence of a crime. A sniff is up to snuff when it meets that test.

And here, Aldo's did. The record in this case amply supported the trial court's determination that Aldo's alert gave Wheetley probable cause to search Harris's truck.

. . .

Because training records established Aldo's reliability in detecting drugs and Harris failed to undermine that showing, we agree with the trial court that Wheetley had probable cause to search Harris's truck. We accordingly reverse the judgment of the Florida Supreme Court. . . .

NOTE

Illinois v. Gates was a search warrant case and in sustaining the search, repudiated the prevailing standard in search warrant cases established in *Aguilar* and *Spinelli. Florida v. Harris* concerns a warrantless search falling within the vehicle exception to the warrant requirement. Yet in the first paragraph of the opinion for a unanimous Court, Justice Kagan cites the *Gates* decision as the controlling precedent. *Harris* thus indicates that in all cases in which the issue is the presence of probable cause, the "flexible, common-sense standard" of *Gates* is controlling.

FLORIDA v. JARDINES

United States Supreme Court
133 S. Ct. 1409 (2013)

Justice SCALIA delivered the opinion of the Court.

We consider whether using a drug-sniffing dog on a homeowner's porch to investigate the contents of the home is a "search" within the meaning of the Fourth Amendment.

I

In 2006, Detective William Pedraja of the Miami-Dade Police Department received an unverified tip that marijuana was being grown in the home of respondent Joelis Jardines. One month later, the Department and the Drug Enforcement Administration sent a joint surveillance team to Jardines' home. Detective Pedraja was part of that team. He watched the home for fifteen minutes and saw no vehicles in the driveway or activity around the home, and could not see inside because the blinds were drawn. Detective Pedraja then approached Jardines' home accompanied by Detective Douglas Bartelt, a trained canine handler who had just arrived at the scene with his drug-sniffing dog. The dog was trained to detect the scent of marijuana, cocaine, heroin, and several other drugs, indicating the presence of any of these substances through particular behavioral changes recognizable by his handler.

Detective Bartelt had the dog on a six-foot leash, owing in part to the dog's "wild" nature, . . . and tendency to dart around erratically while searching. As the dog approached Jardines' front porch, he apparently sensed one of the odors he had been trained to detect, and began energetically exploring the area for the strongest point source of that odor. As Detective Bartelt explained, the dog "began tracking that airborne odor by . . . tracking back and forth," engaging in what is called "bracketing," back and forth, back and forth." . . . Detective Bartelt gave the dog "the full six feet of the leash plus whatever safe distance [he could] give him" to do this-he testified that he needed to give the dog "as much distance as I can." . . . And Detective Pedraja stood back while this was occurring, so that he would not "get knocked over" when the dog was "spinning around trying to find" the source. . . .

After sniffing the base of the front door, the dog sat, which is the trained behavior upon discovering the odor's strongest point. Detective Bartelt then pulled the dog away from the door and returned to his vehicle. He left the scene after informing Detective Pedraja that there had been a positive alert for narcotics.

On the basis of what he had learned at the home, Detective Pedraja applied for and received a warrant to search the residence. When the warrant was executed later that day, Jardines attempted to flee and was arrested; the search revealed marijuana plants, and he was charged with trafficking in cannabis.

At trial, Jardines moved to suppress the marijuana plants on the ground that the canine investigation was an unreasonable search. The trial court granted the motion, and the Florida Third District Court of Appeal reversed. On a petition for discretionary review, the Florida Supreme Court quashed the decision to suppress, holding (as relevant here) that the use of the trained narcotics dog to investigate Jardines' home was a Fourth Amendment search unsupported by probable cause, rendering invalid the warrant based upon information gathered in that search. . . .

We granted certiorari, limited to the question of whether the officers' behavior was a search within the meaning of the Fourth Amendment. . . .

II

The Fourth Amendment provides in relevant part that the "right of the people to be secure in their persons, houses, papers, and effects, against unreasonable searches and seizures, shall not be violated." The Amendment establishes a simple baseline, one that for much of our history formed the exclusive basis for its protections: When "the Government obtains information by physically intruding" on persons, houses, papers, or effects, "a 'search' within the original meaning of the Fourth Amendment" has "undoubtedly occurred." *United States v. Jones*, . . . (2012). By reason of our decision in *Katz v. United States*, . . . property rights "are not the sole measure of Fourth Amendment violations," . . . but though *Katz* may add to the baseline, it does not subtract anything from the Amendment's protections "when the Government does engage in [a] physical intrusion of a constitutionally protected area," *United States v. Knotts*, . . . (Brennan, J., concurring in the judgment).

That principle renders this case a straightforward one. The officers were gathering information in an area belonging to Jardines and immediately surrounding his house — in the curtilage of the house, which we have held enjoys protection as part of the home itself. And they gathered that information by physically entering and occupying the area to engage in conduct not explicitly or implicitly permitted by the homeowner.

. . .

At the Amendment's "very core" stands "the right of a man to retreat into his own home and there be free from unreasonable governmental intrusion." . . . This right would be of little practical value if the State's agents could stand in a home's porch or side garden and trawl for evidence with impunity; the right to retreat would be significantly diminished if the police could enter a man's property to observe his repose from just outside the front window.

We therefore regard the area "immediately surrounding and associated with the home" — what our cases call the curtilage — as "part of the home itself for Fourth Amendment purposes." *Oliver*, . . .

. . .

The front porch is the classic exemplar of an area adjacent to the home and "to which the activity of home life extends." . . .

. . .

"A license may be implied from the habits of the country," notwithstanding the "strict rule of the English common law as to entry upon a close." . . . We have accordingly recognized the "the knocker on the front door is treated as an invitation or license to attempt an entry, justifying ingress to the home by solicitors, hawkers and peddlers of all kinds." . . . This implicit license typically permits the visitor to approach the home by the front path, knock promptly, wait briefly to be received, and then (absent invitation to linger longer) leave. Complying with the terms of that traditional invitation does not require fine-grained legal knowledge; it is generally managed without incident by the Nation's Girl Scouts and trick-or-treaters. Thus a police officer not armed with a warrant may approach a home and knock, precisely because that is "no more than any private citizen might do." *Kentucky v. King*, . . .

But introducing a trained police dog to explore the area around the home in hopes of discovering incriminating evidence is something else. There is no customary invitation to do *that*. An invitation to engage in canine forensic investigation assuredly does not inhere in the very act of hanging a knocker.[26] To find a visitor knocking on the door is routine (even if sometimes unwelcome); to spot that same visitor exploring the front path with a metal detector, or marching his bloodhound into the garden before saying hello and asking permission, would inspire most of us to — well, call the police. The scope of a license — express or implied — is limited not only to a particular area but also to a specific purpose. Consent at a traffic stop to an officer's checking out an anonymous tip that there is a body in the trunk does not permit the officer to rummage through the trunk for narcotics. Here, the background social norms that invite a visitor to the front door do not invite him there to conduct a search.[27]

---

[26] [2] The dissent insists that our argument must rest upon "the particular instrument that Detective Bartelt used to detect the odor of marijuana" — the dog. . . . It is not the dog that is the problem, but the behavior that here involved use of the dog. We think a typical person would find it " 'a cause for great alarm' " (the kind of reaction the dissent quite rightly relies upon to justify its no-night-visits rule, . . .) to find a stranger snooping about his front porch *with or without* a dog. The dissent would let the police do whatever they want by way of gathering evidence so long as they stay on the base-path, to use a baseball analogy — so long as they "stick to the path that is typically used to approach a front door, such as a paved walkway." . . . From that vantage point they can presumably peer into the house through binoculars with impunity. That is not the law, as even the State concedes. . . .

[27] [3] The dissent argues, *citing King*, that "gathering evidence — even damning evidence — is a lawful activity that falls within the scope of the license to approach." . . . That is a false generalization. What *King* establishes is that it is not a Fourth Amendment search to approach the home in order to speak with the occupant, *because all are invited to do that*. The mere "purpose of discovering information," . . . in the course of engaging in that permitted conduct does not cause it to violate the Fourth Amendment. But no one is impliedly invited to enter the protected premises of the home in order to do nothing but conduct a search.

The State points to our decisions holding that the subjective intent of the officer is irrelevant. See *Whren v. United States*, . . . But those cases merely hold that a stop or search *that is objectively reasonable* is not vitiated by the fact that the officer's real reason for making the stop or search has nothing to do with the validating reason. Thus, the defendant will not be heard to complain that although he was speeding the officer's real reason for the stop was racial harassment. . . . Here, however, the question before the court is precisely whether the officer's conduct was an objectively reasonable search. As we have described, that depends upon whether the officers had an implied license to enter the porch, which in turn depends upon the purpose for which they entered. Here, their behavior objectively reveals a purpose to conduct a search, which is not what anyone would think he had license to do.

III

The State argues that investigation by a forensic narcotics dog by definition cannot implicate any legitimate privacy interest. The State cites for authority our decisions in *United States v. Place*, . . . *United States v. Jacobsen*, . . . and *Illinois v. Caballes*, . . . which held, respectively, that canine inspection of luggage in an airport, chemical testing of a substance that had fallen from a parcel in transit, and canine inspection of an automobile during a lawful traffic stop, do not violate the "reasonable expectation of privacy" described in *Katz*.

Just last Term, we considered an argument much like this. *Jones* held that tracking an automobile's whereabouts using a physically-mounted GPS receiver is a Fourth Amendment search. The Government argued that the *Katz* standard "show[ed] that no search occurred," as the defendant had "no 'reasonable expectation of privacy'" in his whereabouts on the public roads — a proposition with at least as much support in our case law as the one the State marshals here. . . . But because the GPS receiver had been physically mounted on the defendant's automobile (thus intruding on his "effects"), we held that tracking the vehicle's movements was a search: a person's "Fourth Amendment right do not rise or fall with the *Katz* formulation," *Jones, supra*, . . . The *Katz* reasonable-expectations test "has been *added to*, not *substituted for*," the traditional property-based understanding of the Fourth Amendment, and so is unnecessary to consider when the government gains evidence by physically intruding on constitutionally protected areas. . . .

Thus, we need not decide whether the officers' investigation of Jardines' home violated his expectation of privacy under *Katz*. One virtue of the Fourth Amendment's property-rights baseline is that it keeps easy cases easy. That the officers learned what they learned only by physically intruding on Jardines' property to gather evidence is enough to establish that a search occurred.

For a related reason we find irrelevant the State's argument (echoed by the dissent) that forensic dogs have been commonly used by police for centuries. This argument is apparently directed to our holding in *Kyllo v. United States*, 533 U.S. 27, 121 S. Ct. 2038, 150 L. Ed. 2d 94 (2001), that surveillance of the home is a search where "the Government uses a device that is not in general public use" to "explore details of the home that would previously have been unknowable *without physical intrusion.*" . . . But the implication of that statement (*inclusio unius est exclusio alterius*) is that when the government uses a physical intrusion to explore details of the home (including its curtilage), the antiquity of the tools that they bring along is irrelevant.

* * *

The government's use of trained police dogs to investigate the home and its immediate surroundings is a "search" within the meaning of the Fourth Amendment. The judgment of the Supreme Court of Florida is therefore affirmed. . . .

JUSTICE KAGAN, with whom JUSTICE GINSBURG and JUSTICE SOTOMAYOR join, concurring.

For me, a simple analogy clinches this case — and does so on privacy as well as property grounds. A stranger come to the front door of your home carrying super-high-powered binoculars. . . . He doesn't knock or say hello. Instead, he stands on the porch and uses the binoculars to peer through your windows, into your home's furthest corners. It doesn't take long (the binoculars are really very fine): In just a couple of minutes, his uncommon behavior allows him to learn details of your life you disclose to no one. Has your "visitor" trespassed on your property, exceeding the license you have granted to members of the public to, say, drop off the mail or distribute campaign flyers? Yes, he has. And has he also invaded your "reasonable expectation of privacy," by nosing into intimacies you sensibly thought protected from disclosure? . . . Yes, of course, he had done that too.

That case is this case in the very way that matters. Here, police officers came to Joelis Jardines' door with a super-sensitive instrument, which they deployed to detect things inside that they could not perceive unassisted. The equipment they used was animal, not mineral. But contra the dissent, see *post*, at 1420 (opinion of ALITO, J.) (noting the ubiquity of dogs in American households), that is of no significance in determining whether a search occurred. Detective Bartelt's dog was not your neighbor's pet, come to your porch on a leisurely stroll. As this Court discussed earlier this Term, drug-detection dogs are highly trained tools of law enforcement, geared to respond in distinctive ways to specific scents so as to convey clear and reliable information to their human partners. See *Florida v. Harris*, . . . They are to the poodle down the street as high-powered binoculars are to a piece of plain glass. Like the binoculars, a drug-detection dog is a specialized device for discovering objects not in plain view (or plain smell). And as in the hypothetical above, that device was aimed here at a home — the most private and inviolate (or so we expect) of all the places and things the Fourth Amendment protects. Was this activity a trespass? Yes, as the Court holds today. Was it also an invasion of privacy? Yes, that as well.

. . .

Justice Alito, with whom the Chief Justice, Justice Kennedy, and Justice Breyer join, dissenting.

The Court's decision in this important Fourth Amendment case is based on a putative rule of trespass law that is nowhere to be found in the annals of Anglo-American jurisprudence.

The law of trespass generally gives members of the public a license to use a walkway to approach the front door of a house and to remain there for a brief time. This license is not limited to persons who intend to speak to an occupant or who actually do so. (Mail carriers and persons delivering packages and flyers are examples of individuals who may lawfully approach a front door without intending to converse.) Nor is the license restricted to categories of visitors whom an occupant of the dwelling is likely to welcome; as the Court acknowledges, this license applies even to "solicitors, hawkers and peddlers of all kinds." . . . And the license even extends to police officers who wish to gather evidence against an occupant (by asking potentially incriminating questions).

According to the Court, however, the police officer in this case, Detective Bartelt, committed a trespass because he was accompanied during his otherwise lawful visit to the front door of respondent's house by his dog, Franky. Where is the authority evidencing such a rule? Dogs have been domesticated for about 12,000 years; they were ubiquitous in both this country and Britain at the time of the adoption of the Fourth Amendment; and their acute sense of smell has been used in law enforcement for centuries. Yet the Court has been unable to find a single case — from the United States or any other common-law nation — that supports the rule on which its decision is based. Thus trespass law provides no support for the Court's holding today.

The Court's decision is also inconsistent with the reasonable-expectations-of-privacy test that the Court adopted in *Katz v. United States*, . . . A reasonable person understands that odors emanating from a house may be detected from locations that are open to the public, and a reasonable person will not count on the strength of those odors remaining within the range that, while detectible by a dog, cannot be smelled by a human.

For these reasons, I would hold that no search within the meaning of the Fourth Amendment took place in this case, and I would reverse the decision below.

[E] Misplaced Confidence[28] — The Misplaced Confidence Exception

Just as the reasonable expectation of privacy does not extend to utterances lawfully overheard by an officer, so too an accused will not be heard to complain if a party with whom he engages in conversation repeats his statements or permits law enforcement officers to overhear and/or record the conversation. Indeed, in *Katz v. United States*, *supra*, the government could have called as a witness the other participant in the telephone conversation and asked him to repeat Katz's

[28] From J. Cook, Constitutional Rights of the Accused § 4:8 (3d ed. 1996). Copyright © 1996 by Thomson Reuters. Modified with footnotes omitted. Reprinted with permission.

portion of the conversation. Or, had a third party waiting in line to use the telephone booth been able to understand Katz's utterances, most courts would permit that witness to testify as to what she heard. In both cases, Katz would be found not to harbor a reasonable expectation of privacy in his spoken words insofar as those to whom he has communicated them or those in a position to overhear them. Courts have held routinely that no right of the accused is violated when a party to a telephone conversation permits a government agent to listen or record the conversation.

The same principle is applicable in a face-to-face conversation which is overheard by means of a microphone hidden on one of the participants. In *On Lee v. United States*, 343 U.S. 747 (1952), an undercover agent entered a laundry operated by the accused and elicited incriminating statements from him. The accused was unaware of the conversant's status as a government agent, nor was he aware that the conversation was being broadcasted to a second agent situated outside of the laundry. The second agent gave testimony regarding the substance of the conversation. The Supreme Court sustained the admission of the testimony because the accused had consented to the entry and thereby assumed the risk of divulgence.

Similarly, in *Lopez v. United States*, 373 U.S. 427 (1963), an internal revenue agent advised the petitioner that his place of business might be subject to a cabaret tax. The petitioner urged the agent to drop the case and gave him a sum of money, indicating there would be more in the future. The agent advised his superiors of the incident and was instructed to "play along with the scheme." On his next visit he recorded the conversation with the petitioner, without the knowledge of the latter. This recording was admitted into evidence. The Court found no violation of the petitioner's Fourth Amendment rights. "[T]he device was used only to obtain the most reliable evidence possible of a conversation in which the Government's own agent was a participant and which that agent was fully entitled to disclose." A like result was reached in *Lewis v. United States*, 385 U.S. 206 (1966), in which the accused invited a party, not known by him to be a narcotics agent, into his home to consummate a narcotics sale.

Finally, in *Hoffa v. United States*, 385 U.S. 293 (1966), the accused, while being tried on an unrelated matter, was visited by a government agent in his hotel suite and elsewhere. The agent reported to federal agents and later testified at another trial of the accused for attempting to bribe jurors. In affirming the conviction, the Supreme Court observed that "[n]either this Court nor any member of it has ever expressed the view that the Fourth Amendment protects a wrongdoer's misplaced belief that a person to whom he voluntarily confides his wrongdoing will not reveal it."

In *United States v. White*, 401 U.S. 745 (1971), the Court was called upon to determine whether the misplaced confidence decisions had been implicitly overruled or modified by *Katz*. Eight separate conversations between the accused and a government informant were transmitted through radio equipment concealed on the person of the informant to officers located nearby. The government was unable to produce the agent who had participated in the conversations, but it was permitted to introduce the testimony of the officers who conducted the electronic surveillance. The Court of Appeals for the Seventh Circuit had concluded that *Katz* had overruled the *On Lee* decision.

A four-Justice plurality of the Supreme Court found the cases distinguishable. The question, in terms of the *Katz* standard, was not whether a particular suspect had relied on the discretion of his companions but rather what expectations of privacy were constitutionally justifiable. If nothing in the Constitution protected an individual from the decision of a confidant to testify respecting statements made by the accused,

> for constitutional purposes, no different result is required if the agent instead of immediately reporting and transcribing his conversations with the defendant, either (1) simultaneously records them with electronic equipment which he is carrying on his person . . . ; (2) or carries radio equipment which simultaneously transmits the conversations either to recording equipment located elsewhere or to other agents monitoring the transmitting frequency.

Nor, submitted the Court, should the unavailability at the trial of the agent who participated in the conversation have any bearing on the scope of the protection of the Fourth Amendment.

An equal number of Justices, however, believed that *Katz* had altered the misplaced confidence rule. Three Justices expressed such a view in dissent, while a fourth concurred in the outcome only because he believed *Katz* should not be given retroactive application. The ninth Justice, Justice Black, concurred separately, relying on his dissent in *Katz* which denied application of the Fourth Amendment to oral conversations. Notwithstanding the absence of a majority view, most lower courts have read *White* to reaffirm the misplaced confidence rule.

PROBLEM I
THE CASE OF THE OPEN HOUSE

A fraternity at the University of Maine at Orono distributed flyers, which were labeled "invitations," announcing that a party would be held at the fraternity house on the evening of February 24, 1979. Because these circulars also announced that mixed drinks and beer would be available at the function, university police gave one of the widely disseminated invitations to the state bureau of liquor enforcement. Two undercover enforcement inspectors were assigned to attend the party to determine whether liquor would be sold without a license. On the night of the event, these inspectors, with invitation in hand, joined a line of persons awaiting entrance outside the fraternity house. At the door, the two men were asked whether they were liquor inspectors. They responded in the negative and proceeded into the house, noting a posted sign which read: "No pets or Liquor Inspectors Allowed." Each inspector then purchased a mixed drink from the defendant, who was selling liquor from behind a bar.

Have any Fourth Amendment rights been violated? *See State v. Carey*, 417 A.2d 979 (Me. 1980).

[F] First Amendment Interests

ZURCHER v. STANFORD DAILY

United States Supreme Court
436 U.S. 547 (1978)

MR. JUSTICE WHITE delivered the opinion of the Court.

I

Late in the day on Friday, April 9, 1971, officers of the Palo Alto Police Department and of the Santa Clara County Sheriff's Department responded to a call from the director of the Stanford University Hospital requesting the removal of a large group of demonstrators who had seized the hospital's administrative offices and occupied them since the previous afternoon. After several futile efforts to persuade the demonstrators to leave peacefully, more drastic measures were employed. The demonstrators had barricaded the doors at both ends of a hall adjacent to the administrative offices. The police chose to force their way in at the west end of the corridor. As they did so, a group of demonstrators emerged through the doors at the east end and, armed with sticks and clubs, attacked the group of nine police officers stationed there. One officer was knocked to the floor and struck repeatedly on the head; another suffered a broken shoulder. All nine were injured. There were no police photographers at the east doors, and most bystanders and reporters were on the west side. The officers themselves were able to identify only two of their assailants, but one of them did see at least one person photographing the assault at the east doors.

On Sunday, April 11, a special edition of the Stanford Daily (Daily), a student newspaper published at Stanford University, carried articles and photographs devoted to the hospital protest and the violent clash between demonstrators and police. The photographs carried the byline of a Daily staff member and indicated that he had been at the east end of the hospital hallway where he could have photographed the assault on the nine officers. The next day, the Santa Clara County District Attorney's Office secured a warrant from the municipal court for an immediate search of the Daily's offices for negatives, film and pictures showing the events and occurrences at the hospital on the evening of April 9. The warrant issued on a finding of "just, probable and reasonable cause for believing that: Negatives and photographs and films, evidence material and relevant to the identification of the perpetrators of felonies, to wit, Battery on a Peace Officer, and Assault with a Deadly Weapon, will be located [on the premises of the Daily]." App. 31–32. The warrant affidavit contained no allegation or indication that members of the Daily staff were in any way involved in unlawful acts at the hospital.

The search pursuant to the warrant was conducted later that day by four police officers and took place in the presence of some members of the Daily staff. The Daily's photographic laboratories, filing cabinets, desks, and waste paper baskets were searched. Locked drawers and rooms were not opened. The officers apparently had opportunity to read notes and correspondence during the search; but contrary to claims of the staff, the officers denied that they had exceeded the limits of the warrant. They had not been advised by the staff that the areas they were searching contained confidential materials. The search revealed only the photographs that had already been published on April 11, and no materials were removed from the Daily's office.

A month later the Daily and various members of its staff, respondents here, brought a civil action in the United States District Court for the Northern District of California seeking declaratory and injunctive relief under 42 U.S.C. § 1983 against the police officers who conducted the search, the chief of police, the district attorney and one of his deputies, and the judge who had issued the warrant. The complaint alleged that the search of the Daily's office had deprived respondents under color of state law of rights secured to them by the First, Fourth, and Fourteenth Amendments of the United States Constitution.

The District Court denied the request for an injunction but on respondents' motion for summary judgment, granted declaratory relief. *Stanford Daily v. Zurcher*, 353 F. Supp. 124 (ND Cal. 1972). The court did not question the existence of probable cause to believe that a crime had been committed and to believe that relevant evidence would be found on the Daily's premises. It held, however, that the Fourth and Fourteenth Amendments forbade the issuance of a warrant to search for materials in possession of one not suspected of crime unless there is probable cause to believe, based on facts presented in a sworn affidavit, that a subpoena *duces tecum* would be impracticable. Moreover, the failure to honor a subpoena would not alone justify a warrant; it must also appear that the possessor of the objects sought would disregard a court order not to remove or destroy them. The District Court further held that where the innocent object of the search is a newspaper, First Amendment interests are also involved and that such a search is constitutionally permissible "only in the rare circumstance where there is a *clear showing* that (1) important materials will be destroyed or removed from the jurisdiction; *and* (2) a restraining order would be futile." *Id.*, at 135. Since these preconditions to a valid warrant had not been satisfied here, the search of the Daily's offices was declared to have been illegal. The Court of Appeals affirmed *per curiam*, adopting the opinion of the District Court. F.2d 464 (CA9 1977). We issued the writs of certiorari requested by petitioners. 434 U.S. 816 (1977). We reverse.

II

The issue here is how the Fourth Amendment is to be construed and applied to the "third party" search, the recurring situation where state authorities have probable cause to believe that fruits, instrumentalities, or other evidence of crime is located on identified property but do not then have probable cause to believe that the owner or possessor of the property is himself implicated in the crime that has occurred or is occurring. Because under the District Court's rule impracticability can be shown only by furnishing facts demonstrating that the third party will not only disobey the subpoena but will also ignore a restraining order not to move or destroy the property, it is apparent that only in unusual situations could the State satisfy such a severe burden and that for all practical purposes the effect of the rule is that fruits, instrumentalities, and evidence of crime may be recovered from third parties only by subpoena, not by search warrant. At least, we assume that the District Court did not intend its rule to be toothless and anticipated that only subpoenas would be available in many cases where without the rule a search warrant would issue.

It is an understatement to say that there is no direct authority in this or any other federal court for the District Court's sweeping revision of the Fourth Amendment. Under existing law, valid warrants may be issued to search *any* property, whether or not occupied by a third party, at which there is probable cause to believe that fruits, instrumentalities, or evidence of a crime will be found. Nothing on the face of the Amendment suggests that a third-party search warrant should not normally issue. The warrant clause speaks of search warrants issued on "probable cause" and "particularly describing the place to be searched and the persons or things to be seized." In situations where the State does not seek to seize "persons" but only those "things" which there is probable cause to believe are located on the place to be searched, there is no apparent basis in the language of the Amendment for also imposing the requirements for a valid arrest-probable cause to believe that the third party is implicated in the crime.

III

In any event, the reasons presented by the District Court and adopted by the Court of Appeals for arriving at its remarkable conclusion do not withstand analysis. First, as we have said, it is apparent that whether the third-party occupant is suspect or not, the State's interest in enforcing the criminal law and recovering the evidence remains the same; and it is the seeming innocence of the property owner that the District Court relied on to foreclose the warrant to search. But as respondents themselves now concede, if the third party knows that contraband or other illegal materials are on his property, he is sufficiently culpable to justify the issuance of a search warrant. Similarly, if his ethical stance is the determining factor, it seems to us that whether or not he knows that the sought-after articles are secreted on his property and whether or not he knows that the articles are in fact the fruits, instrumentalities, or evidence of crime, he will be so informed when the search warrant is served, and it is doubtful that he should then be permitted to object to the search, to withhold, if it is there, the evidence of crime reasonably believed to be possessed by him or secreted on his property, and to forbid the search and insist that the officers serve him with a subpoena *duces tecum*.

Second, we are unpersuaded that the District Court's new rule denying search warrants against third parties and insisting on subpoenas would substantially further privacy interests without seriously undermining law enforcement efforts. Because of the fundamental public interest in implementing the criminal law, the search warrant, a heretofore effective and constitutionally acceptable enforcement tool, should not be suppressed on the basis of surmise and without solid evidence supporting the change. As the District Court understands it, denying third-party search warrants would not have substantial adverse effects on criminal investigations because the nonsuspect third party, once served with a subpoena, will preserve the evidence and ultimately lawfully respond. The difficulty with this assumption is that search warrants are often employed early in an investigation, perhaps before the identity of any likely criminal and certainly before all the perpetrators are or could be known. The seemingly blameless third party in possession of the fruits or evidence may not be innocent at all; and if he is, he may nevertheless be so related to or so sympathetic with the culpable that he cannot be relied upon to retain and preserve the articles that may implicate his friends, or at least not to notify those who would be damaged by the evidence that the authorities are aware of its location. In any event, it is likely that the real culprits will have access to the property, and the delay involved in employing the subpoena *duces tecum*, offering as it does the opportunity to litigate its validity, could easily result in the disappearance of the evidence, whatever the good faith of the third party.

IV

The District Court held, and respondents assert here, that whatever may be true of third-party searches generally, where the third party is a newspaper, there are additional factors derived from the First Amendment that justify a nearly *per se* rule forbidding the search warrant and permitting only the subpoena *duces tecum*. The general submission is that searches of newspaper offices for evidence of crime reasonably believed to be on the premises will seriously threaten the ability of the press to gather, analyze, and disseminate news. This is said to be true for several reasons: first, searches will be physically disruptive to such an extent that timely publication will be impeded. Second, confidential sources of information will dry up, and the press will also lose opportunities to cover various events because of fears of the participants that press files will be readily available to the authorities. Third, reporters will be deterred from recording and preserving their recollections for future use if such information is subject to seizure. Fourth, the processing of news and its dissemination will be chilled by the prospects that searches will disclose internal editorial deliberations. Fifth, the press will resort to self-censorship to conceal its possession of information of potential interest to the police. . . .

Neither the Fourth Amendment nor the cases requiring consideration of First Amendment values in issuing search warrants, however, call for imposing the regime ordered by the District Court. Aware of the long struggle between Crown and press and desiring to curb unjustified official intrusions, the Framers took the enormously important step of subjecting searches to the test of reasonableness and to the general rule requiring search warrants issued by neutral magistrates. They nevertheless did not forbid warrants where the press was involved, did not require special showings that subpoenas would be impractical, and did not insist that the owner of the place to be searched, if connected with the press, must be shown to be implicated in the offense being investigated. Further, the prior cases do no more than insist that the courts apply the warrant requirements with particular exactitude when First Amendment interests would be endangered by the search. As we see it, no more than this is required where the warrant requested is for the seizure of criminal evidence reasonably believed to be on the premises occupied by a newspaper. Properly administered, the preconditions for a warrant — probable cause, specificity with respect to the place to be searched and the things to be seized, and overall reasonableness — should afford sufficient protection against the harms that are assertedly threatened by warrants for searching newspaper offices.

There is no reason to believe, for example, that magistrates cannot guard against searches of the type, scope, and intrusiveness that would actually interfere with the timely publication of a newspaper. Nor, if the requirements of specificity and reasonableness are properly applied, policed, and observed, will there be any occasion or opportunity for officers to rummage at large in newspaper files or to intrude into or to deter normal editorial and publication decisions. The warrant issued in this case authorized nothing of this sort. Nor are we convinced, anymore than we were in *Branzburg v. Hayes*, 408 U.S. 665 (1972), that confidential sources will disappear and that the press will suppress news because of fears of warranted searches. Whatever incremental effect there may be in this regard if search warrants, as well as subpoenas, are permissible in proper circumstances, it does not make a constitutional difference in our judgment.

[JUSTICE POWELL concurred.]

MR. JUSTICE STEWART, with whom MR. JUSTICE MARSHALL joins, dissenting.

It seems to me self-evident that police searches of newspaper offices burden the freedom of the press. The most immediate and obvious First Amendment injury caused by such a visitation by the police is physical disruption of the operation of the newspaper. Policemen occupying a newsroom and searching it thoroughly for what may be an extended period of time will inevitably interrupt its normal operations and thus impair or even temporarily prevent the processes of news-gathering, writing, editing, and publishing. By contrast a subpoena would afford the newspaper itself an opportunity to locate whatever material might be requested and produce it.

But there is another and more serious burden on a free press imposed by an unannounced police search of a newspaper office; the possibility of disclosure of information received from confidential sources, or of the identity of the sources themselves. Protection of those sources is necessary to ensure that the press can fulfill its constitutionally designated function of informing the public, because important information can often be obtained only by an assurance that the source will not be revealed. *Branzburg v. Hayes*, 408 U.S. 665, 725–736 (dissenting opinion). And the Court has recognized that "without some protection for seeking out the news, freedom of the press could be eviscerated." *Pell v. Procunier*, 417 U.S. 817, 833s.

Today the Court does not question the existence of this constitutional protection, but says only that it is not "convinced . . . that confidential sources will disappear and that the press will suppress news because of fears of warranted searches." . . . This facile conclusion seems to me to ignore common experience. It requires no blind leap of faith to understand that a person who gives information to a journalist only on condition that his identity will not be revealed will be less likely to give that information if he knows that, despite the journalist's assurance, his identity may in fact be disclosed. And it cannot be denied that confidential information may be exposed to the eyes of police officers who execute a search warrant by rummaging through the files, cabinets, desks and wastebaskets of a newsroom. Since the indisputable effect of such searches will thus be to prevent a newsman from being able to promise confidentiality to his potential sources, it seems obvious to me that a journalist's access to information, and thus the public's, will thereby be impaired.

A search warrant allows police officers to ransack the files of a newspaper, reading each and every document until they have found the one named in the warrant, while a subpoena would permit the newspaper itself to produce only the specific documents requested. A search, unlike a subpoena, will therefore lead to the needless exposure of confidential information completely unrelated to the purpose of the investigation. The knowledge that police officers can make an unannounced raid on a newsroom is thus bound to have a deterrent effect on the availability of confidential news sources. The end result, wholly inimical to the First Amendment, will be diminishing flow of potentially important information to the public.

[Justice Stevens also dissented.]

NOTES AND QUESTIONS

(1) Was there probable cause to believe that evidence of crime would be found at the offices of the *Stanford Daily*?

(2) Conceding that nothing in the Fourth Amendment precludes searching premises though the occupant is not inculpated, should not this be a factor considered in the determination of constitutional reasonableness? Suppose, after this search proved unsuccessful, the police then obtained a warrant for the search of the apartment of the photographer. No additional photographs were discovered, but a quantity of marijuana was seized from his desk drawer and used as evidence against him. Would (should) the Court reach the same result?

(3) Does the statement, "the prior cases do no more than insist that the courts apply the warrant requirements with particular exactitude when First Amendment interest would be endangered by the search" say anything? Is the Court condoning sloppiness when First Amendment rights are not implicated?

(4) Is the Court remarkably insensitive to the threat to the free press posed by government intrusions of this sort? Or is the Court merely holding that the designation of press membership does not afford an exemption from the operation of the law?

(5) 38 Ill. Comp. Stat. Ann. 5/108-3 (2004) now provides:

> (a) Except as provided in subsection (b), upon the written complaint of any person under oath or affirmation which states facts sufficient to show probable cause and which particularly describes the place or person, or both, to be searched and the things to be seized, any judge may issue a search warrant.
>
> (b) When the things to be seized are the work product of, or used in the ordinary course of business, and in the possession, custody, or control of any person known to be engaged in the gathering or dissemination of news for the print or broadcast media, no judge may issue a search warrant unless the requirements set forth in subsection (a) are satisfied and there is probable cause to believe that:

(1) such person has committed or is committing a criminal offense; or

(2) the things to be seized will be destroyed or removed from the State if the search warrant is not issued.

(6) Is *Zurcher* pertinent if evidence in possession of the news media is sought by the defense?

[G] Fifth Amendment Interests

ANDRESEN v. MARYLAND

United States Supreme Court
427 U.S. 463 (1976)

MR. JUSTICE BLACKMUN delivered the opinion of the Court.

This case presents the issue whether the introduction into evidence of a person's business records, seized during a search of his offices, violates the Fifth Amendment's command that "[n]o person . . . shall be compelled in any criminal case to be a witness against himself."

Petitioner contends that "the Fifth Amendment prohibition against compulsory self-incrimination applies as well to personal business papers seized from his offices as it does to the same papers being required to be produced under a subpoena." Brief for Petitioner 9. He bases his argument, naturally, on dicta in a number of cases which imply, or state, that the search for and seizure of a person's private papers violate the privilege against self-incrimination. Thus, in *Boyd v. United States*, 116 U.S. 616, 633 (1886), the Court said: "[W]e have been unable to perceive that the seizure of a man's private books and papers to be used in evidence against him is substantially different from compelling him to be a witness against himself." And in *Hale v. Henkel*, 201 U.S. 43, 76 (1906), it was observed that "the substance of the offense is the compulsory production of private papers, whether under a search warrant or a *subpoena duces tecum*, against which the person . . . is entitled to protection."

We do not agree, however, that these broad statements compel suppression of this petitioner's business records as a violation of the Fifth Amendment. In the very recent case of *Fisher v. United States*, 425 U.S. 391 (1976), the Court held that an attorney's production, pursuant to a lawful summons, of his client's tax records in his hands did not violate the Fifth Amendment privilege of the taxpayer "because enforcement against a taxpayer's lawyer would not 'compel' the taxpayer to do anything — and certainly would not compel him to be a 'witness' against himself." *Id.*, at 397 (slip op. 5). We recognized that the continued validity of the broad statements contained in some of the Court's earlier cases had been discredited by later opinions. *Id.*, at 407–409 (slip op. 15–17). In those earlier cases, the legal predicate for the inadmissibility of the evidence seized was a violation of the Fourth Amendment; the unlawfulness of the search and seizure was thought to supply the compulsion of the accused necessary to invoke the Fifth Amendment. Compulsion of the accused was also absent in *Couch v. United States*, 409 U.S. 322 (1973), where the Court held that a summons served on a taxpayer's accountant requiring him to produce the taxpayer's personal business records in his possession did not violate the taxpayer's Fifth Amendment rights.

Similarly, in this case, petitioner was not asked to say or to do anything. The records seized contained statements that petitioner had voluntarily committed to writing. The search for and seizure of these records were conducted by law enforcement personnel. Finally, when these records were introduced at trial, they were authenticated by a handwriting expert, not by petitioner. Any compulsion of petitioner to speak, other than the inherent psychological pressure to respond at trial to unfavorable evidence, was not present.

This case thus falls within the principle stated by Mr. Justice Holmes: "A party is privileged from producing the evidence but not from its production." *Johnson v. United States*, 228 U.S. 457, 458 (1913). This principle recognizes that the protection afforded by the self-incrimination clause of the Fifth Amendment "adheres basically to the person, not to information that may incriminate him." *Couch v. United States*, 409 U.S., at 328. Thus, although the Fifth Amendment may protect an individual from complying with a subpoena for the production of his personal records in his possession because the very act of production may constitute a compulsory authentication of incriminating information, see *Fisher v. United States*, *supra*, a seizure of the same materials by law enforcement officers differs in a crucial respect — the individual against whom the search is directed is not required to aid in the discovery, production, or authentication of incriminating evidence.

A contrary determination that the seizure of a person's business records and their introduction into evidence at a criminal trial violates the Fifth Amendment, would undermine the principles announced in earlier cases. Nearly a half century ago, in *Marron v. United States*, 275 U.S. 192, Treas. Dec. 42528 (1927), the Court upheld, against both Fourth and Fifth Amendment claims, the admission into evidence of business records seized during a search of the accused's illegal liquor business. And in *Abel v. United States*, 362 U.S. 217 (1960), the Court again upheld, against both Fourth and Fifth Amendment claims, the introduction into evidence at an espionage trial of false identity papers and a coded message seized during a search of the accused's hotel room. These cases recognize a general rule: "There is no special sanctity in papers, as distinguished from other forms of property, to render them immune from search and seizure, if only they fall within the scope of the principles of the cases in which other property may be seized, and if they be adequately described in the affidavit and warrant." *Gouled v. United States*, 255 U.S. 298, 309 (1921).

Moreover, a contrary determination would prohibit the admission of evidence traditionally used in criminal cases and traditionally admissible despite the Fifth Amendment. For example, it would bar the admission of an accused's gambling records in a prosecution for gambling; a note given temporarily to a bank teller during a robbery and subsequently seized in the accused's automobile or home in a prosecution for bank robbery; and incriminating notes prepared, but not sent, by an accused in a kidnapping or blackmail prosecution.

. . .

In this case, petitioner, at the time he recorded his communication, at the time of the search, and at the time the records were admitted at trial, was not subjected to "the cruel trilemma of self-accusation, perjury or contempt." *Ibid.* Indeed, he was never required to say or to do anything under penalty of sanction. Similarly, permitting the admission of the records in question does not convert our accusatorial system of justice into an inquisitorial system. "The requirement of specific charges, their proof beyond a reasonable doubt, the protection of the accused from confessions extorted through whatever form of police pressures, the right to a prompt hearing before a magistrate, the right to assistance of counsel, to be supplied by government when circumstances make it necessary, the duty to advise the accused of his constitutional rights — these are all characteristics of the accusatorial system and manifestations of its demands." *Watts v. Indiana*, 338 U.S. 49, 54 (1949). None of these attributes is endangered by the introduction of business records "independently secured through skillful investigation." *Ibid.* Further, the search for and seizure of business records pose no danger greater than that inherent in every search that evidence will be "elicited by inhumane treatment and abuses." 378 U.S., at 55. In this case, the statements seized were voluntarily committed to paper before the police arrived to search for them, and petitioner was not treated discourteously during the search. Also, the "good cause" to "disturb," *ibid.*, petitioner was independently determined by the judge who issued the warrants; and the State bore the burden of executing them. Finally, there is no chance, in this case, of petitioner's statements being self-deprecatory and untrustworthy because they were extracted from him — they were already in existence and had been made voluntarily.

We recognize, of course, that the Fifth Amendment protects privacy to some extent. However, "the Court has never suggested that every invasion of privacy violates the privilege." . . . Indeed, we recently held that unless incriminating testimony is "compelled," any invasion of privacy is outside the scope of the Fifth Amendment's protection, saying that "the Fifth Amendment protects against 'compelled self-incrimination not [the disclosure of] private information.' " . . . Here, as we have already noted, petitioner was not compelled to testify in any manner.

Accordingly, we hold that the search of an individual's office for business records, their seizure, and subsequent introduction into evidence does not offend the Fifth Amendment's prescription that "[n]o person . . . shall be compelled in any criminal case to be a witness against himself."

[JUSTICES BRENNAN and MARSHALL separately dissented.]

QUESTIONS

Suppose in the course of executing a search warrant for a murder weapon in the residence of the suspect, officers come upon an open diary in which the suspect confesses to the crime, which they take. Is the diary admissible in evidence against the accused? Would the result be different if instead a subpoena had been issued ordering the suspect to deliver the diary to the authorities?

[H] Sixth Amendment Interests

O'CONNOR v. JOHNSON

Minnesota Supreme Court
287 N.W.2d 400 (1979)

WAHL, JUSTICE.

This case arose from an investigation into certain liquor establishments by the St. Paul Police Department. Believing that false written statements had been made in the applications for liquor licenses for Patrick's Lounge, the police applied for a search warrant to obtain the business records of Patrick's Lounge. When the warrant was executed on July 24, 1978, the accountant indicated that the business records of the former owners were in the possession of attorney David O'Connor, petitioner in this case. The police then obtained a warrant to search petitioner's office for these records.

On July 25, 1978, when three police officers appeared at petitioner's office to execute the warrant, petitioner refused to permit the search and indicated that all his records concerning Patrick's Lounge were contained in a box and his work product file. Petitioner accompanied the police officers to respondent's chambers to move to quash the warrant. Respondent permitted petitioner to retain his work product file but ordered him to leave the box of records in the court's custody. On August 4, 1978, respondent held the box of records not privileged and the search warrant valid. He ordered that the box be turned over to the St. Paul Police Department and that a representative of the Ramsey County Attorney's Office obtain all documents pertaining to Patrick's Lounge from petitioner's work product file after determining that the documents were not protected by the attorney-client privilege or the work product doctrine. After petitioner applied to this court for a writ of prohibition to quash the search warrant, respondent amended his order so that the court, rather than a representative of the county attorney's office, would determine which documents were protected by the attorney-client privilege or the work product doctrine. Only those documents which are not so protected would be given to the police department.

In his application for a writ of prohibition petitioner challenges only that portion of the court's order requiring him to turn over his work product file to the court for this determination. He has apparently abandoned his claim to the box of records. Because the attorney was present so that his office was not searched as the officers had a right to do in executing the warrant, and because the officers were willing to allow the attorney to bring the file and box of records before the court to make a determination of privilege before a seizure was made, it would be relatively easy to find on this record no violation of constitutional rights, the attorney-client privilege, or the work product doctrine, and thus to approve a hybrid procedure — part warrant, part subpoena. This we decline to do. We must instead examine the validity of the search warrant upon which the court's order was based to determine the propriety of that order. The case thus presents us with the very difficult and delicate issue of the reasonableness of searching an attorney's office for documents and files of a particular client to find evidence of criminal wrongdoing. We have here no claim of wrongdoing by the attorney, as in *Andresen v. Maryland*, 427 U.S. 463 (1976), nor have we taxpayers urging a Fifth Amendment claim where their attorneys are directed by summons, not by warrant, to produce documents for the I.R.S., as in *Couch v. United States*, 409 U.S. 322 (1973), and *Fisher v. United States*, 425 U.S. 391 (1976).

Even the most particular warrant cannot adequately safeguard client confidentiality, the attorney-client privilege, the attorney's work product, and the criminal defendant's constitutional right to counsel of all of the attorney's clients. It is unreasonable, in any case, to permit law enforcement officers to peruse miscellaneous documents in an attorney's office while attempting to locate documents listed in a search warrant. Even if it were possible to meet the particularity requirement regarding the place to be searched, the file would still contain some confidential information that is immune from seizure under the attorney-client privilege or the work product doctrine. Once that information is revealed to the police, the privileges are lost, and the information cannot be erased from the minds of the police. . . .

It will not unreasonably burden prosecutors' offices and effective law enforcement to require officers to proceed by subpoena duces tecum in seeking documents held by an attorney. Attorneys are required by statute, the Code of Professional Responsibility, and the oath of admission to the bar to preserve and protect the judicial process. Thus, attorneys must respond faithfully and promptly, while still being allowed the opportunity to assert applicable privileges by a motion to quash. The very dearth of reported cases from other jurisdictions regarding the seizure by warrant of clients' files from an attorney's office indicates to us that the subpoena procedure is used elsewhere with satisfactory results. Subpoenas may be issued in conjunction with a grand jury proceeding or a hearing or trial before the court. Rules 22.01, 22.02, Rules of Criminal Procedure. Though this may be seen as limiting the ability of the police to obtain information in the early stages of an investigation, we find this measure necessary to protect the overriding interest of our society in preserving the attorney-client privilege, client confidentiality, the work product doctrine, and the constitutional right to counsel.

We are aware that the United States Supreme Court has held that a rule denying a search warrant for the premises of a third party and requiring a subpoena duces tecum was not constitutionally mandated. *Zurcher v. Stanford Daily*. . . . That case is distinguishable from the present case because the newspaper had announced a policy of destroying any evidence that might aid in the prosecution of protestors, while an attorney has an ethical obligation to the legal system and would be subject to discipline if he destroyed documents which had been subpoenaed. Moreover, there is no indication that the attorney in this case would have attempted to destroy the documents. A more important distinction between this case and *Zurcher* is that our decision rests not only on the Fourth Amendment of the United States Constitution, but also on Article I, section 10 of the Minnesota Constitution. The states may, as the United States Supreme Court has often recognized, afford their citizens greater protection than the safeguards guaranteed in the Federal Constitution.

NOTE

Cases involving the search of an attorney's office may be of three types: (1) those in which the attorney is suspected of criminal activity but no clients are implicated in the investigation; (2) those in which evidence is sought incriminating a client, but the attorney is not implicated; and (3) those in which the attorney is implicated in the criminal activity of a client.

The first category normally will present no unique problems. Attorneys as criminal suspects are no different from others, and no Sixth Amendment interests are implicated merely because the subject of the investigation is a lawyer. If, however, the wrongdoing of the attorney relates to the affairs of a client, an intrusion into the protected interests of the client may be unavoidable. In *Burrows v. Superior Court*, 13 Cal. 3d 238, 118 Cal. Rptr. 166, 529 P.2d 590 (1974), the California Supreme Court held a warrant to seize "any file or documents" relating to a client of an attorney who was suspected of misappropriating the client's funds too broad to satisfy constitutional requirements.

O'Connor is illustrative of the second variety of cases. The search of an attorney's office for evidence implicating a client gives rise to Sixth as well as Fourth Amendment implications. The potential for a "fishing expedition" as well as invading the constitutional rights of persons other than the subject of the investigation is apparent, and therefore a subpoena duces tecum would appear a more desirable alternative.

The third category of cases is illustrated by *National City Trading Corporation v. United States*, 635 F.2d 1020 (2d Cir. 1980). There the warrant authorized the search of a business suite, including an attorney's office, upon a showing of probable cause to believe that illegal "boiler room" sales of commodity options were taking place therein. Twenty-five FBI agents were assigned to participate in the search, and they received cautionary instructions from an Assistant United States Attorney advising them of the unique problems presented. The agents did not enter the attorney's personal office except in his presence and did not search any closed file cabinets. They saw one file in an open drawer bearing the name of an NCTC salesman, which the attorney handed over, and they asked the attorney to produce the NCTC legal records, in response to which the attorney handed them another file. The Court of Appeals for the Second Circuit found cases such as *O'Connor* distinguishable, because "here the lawyer actually permitted the allegedly criminal business operation to take place at his office." Under these circumstances, the court found "nothing more sacred" about a law office than the Supreme Court had found in *Zurcher* about the premises of a newspaper.

[I] Public School Searches

NEW JERSEY v. T.L.O.

United States Supreme Court
469 U.S. 325 (1985)

Justice White delivered the opinion of the Court.

We granted certiorari in this case to examine the appropriateness of the exclusionary rule as a remedy for searches carried out in violation of the Fourth Amendment by public school authorities. Our consideration of the proper application of the Fourth Amendment to the public schools, however, has led us to conclude that the search that gave rise to the case now before us did not violate the Fourth Amendment. Accordingly, we here address only the questions of the proper standard for assessing the legality of searches conducted by public school officials and the application of that standard to the facts of this case.

I

On March 7, 1980, a teacher at Piscataway High School in Middlesex County, N.J., discovered two girls smoking in a lavatory. One of the two girls was the respondent T.L.O., who at that time was a 14-year-old high school freshman. Because smoking in the lavatory was a violation of a school rule, the teacher took the two girls to the Principal's office, where they met with Assistant Vice Principal Theodore Choplick. In response to questioning by Mr. Choplick, T.L.O.'s companion admitted that she had violated the rule. T.L.O., however, denied that she had been smoking in the lavatory and claimed that she did not smoke at all.

Mr. Choplick asked T.L.O. to come into his private office and demanded to see her purse. Opening the purse, he found a pack of cigarettes, which he removed from the purse and held before T.L.O. as he accused her of having lied to him. As he reached into the purse for the cigarettes, Mr. Choplick also noticed a package of cigarette rolling papers. In his experience, possession of rolling papers by high school students was closely associated with the use of marihuana. Suspecting that a closer examination of the purse might yield further evidence of drug use, Mr. Choplick proceeded to search the purse thoroughly. The search revealed a small amount of marihuana, a pipe, a number of empty plastic bags, a substantial quantity of money in one-dollar bills, an index card that appeared to be a list of students who owed T.L.O. money, and two letters that implicated T.L.O. in marihuana dealing.

Mr. Choplick notified T.L.O.'s mother and the police and turned the evidence of drug dealing over to the police. At the request of the police, T.L.O.'s mother took her daughter to police headquarters, where T.L.O. confessed that she had been selling marihuana at the high school. On the basis of the confession and the evidence seized by Mr. Choplick, the State brought delinquency charges against T.L.O. in the Juvenile and Domestic Relations Court of Middlesex County. Contending that Mr. Choplick's search of her purse violated the Fourth Amendment, T.L.O. moved to suppress the evidence found in her purse as well as her confession, which, she argued, was tainted by the allegedly unlawful search. The Juvenile Court denied the motion to suppress.

With respect to the question of the legality of the search before it, the [New Jersey Supreme Court] agreed with the Juvenile Court that a warrantless search by a school official does not violate the Fourth Amendment so long as the official "has reasonable grounds to believe that a student possesses evidence of illegal activity or activity that would interfere with school discipline and order." . . . However the court, with two justices dissenting, sharply disagreed with the Juvenile Court's conclusion that the search of the purse was reasonable. According to the majority, the contents of T.L.O.'s purse had no bearing on the accusation against T.L.O., for possession of cigarettes (as opposed to smoking them in the lavatory) did not violate school rules, and a mere desire for evidence that would impeach T.L.O.'s claim that she did not smoke cigarettes could not justify the search. Moreover, even if a reasonable suspicion that T.L.O. had cigarettes in her purse would justify a search, Mr. Choplick had no such suspicion, as no one had furnished him with any specific information that there were cigarettes in the purse. Finally, leaving aside the question whether Mr. Choplick was justified in opening the purse, the court held that the evidence of drug use that he saw inside did not justify the extensive "rummaging" through T.L.O.'s papers and effects that followed.

II

We have held school officials subject to the commands of the First Amendment and the Due Process Clause of the Fourteenth Amendment. If school authorities are state actors for purposes of the constitutional guarantees of freedom of expression and due process, it is difficult to understand why they should be deemed to be exercising parental rather than public authority when conducting searches of their students. In carrying out searches and other disciplinary functions pursuant to such policies, school officials act as representatives of the State, not merely as surrogates for the parents, and they cannot claim the parents' immunity from the strictures of the Fourth Amendment.

III

To hold that the Fourth Amendment applies to searches conducted by school authorities is only to begin the inquiry into the standards governing such searches. Although the underlying command of the Fourth Amendment is always that searches and seizures be reasonable, what is reasonable depends on the context within which a search takes place.

The State of New Jersey has argued that because of the pervasive supervision to which children in the schools are necessarily subject, a child has virtually no legitimate expectation of privacy in articles of personal property "unnecessarily" carried into a school. This argument has two factual premises: (1) the fundamental incompatibility of expectations of privacy with the maintenance of a sound educational environment; and (2) the minimal interest of the child in bringing any items of personal property into the school. Both premises are severely flawed.

Although this Court may take notice of the difficulty of maintaining discipline in the public schools today, the situation is not so dire that students in the schools may claim no legitimate expectations of privacy.

Nor does the State's suggestion that children have no legitimate need to bring personal property into the schools seem well anchored in reality. Students at a minimum must bring to school not only the supplies needed for their studies, but also keys, money, and the necessaries of personal hygiene and grooming. In addition, students may carry on their persons or in purses or wallets such nondisruptive yet highly personal items as photographs, letters, and diaries. Finally, students may have perfectly legitimate reasons to carry with them articles of property needed in connection with extracurricular or recreational activities. In short, schoolchildren may find it necessary to carry with them a variety of legitimate, noncontraband items, and there is no reason to conclude that they have necessarily waived all rights to privacy in such items merely by bringing them onto school grounds.

Against the child's interest in privacy must be set the substantial interest of teachers and administrators in maintaining discipline in the classroom and on school grounds. Maintaining order in the classroom has never been easy, but in recent years, school disorder has often taken particularly ugly forms: drug use and violent crime in the schools have become major social problems. . . . Even in schools that have been spared the most severe disciplinary problems, the preservation of order and a proper educational environment requires close supervision of schoolchildren, as well as the enforcement of rules against conduct that would be perfectly permissible if undertaken by an adult.

How, then, should we strike the balance between the schoolchild's legitimate expectation of privacy and the school's equally legitimate need to maintain an environment in which learning can take place? It is evident that the school setting requires some easing of the restrictions to which searches by public authorities are ordinarily subject. The warrant requirement, in particular, is unsuited to the school environment: requiring a teacher to obtain a warrant before searching a child suspected of an infraction of school rules (or of the criminal law) would unduly interfere with the maintenance of the swift and informal disciplinary procedures needed in the schools.

The school setting also requires some modification of the level of suspicion of illicit activity needed to justify a search. Ordinarily, a search — even one that may permissibly be carried out without a warrant — must be based upon "probable cause" to believe that a violation of the law has occurred. However, "probable cause" is not an irreducible requirement of a valid search. Where a careful balancing of governmental and private interests suggests that the public interest is best served by a Fourth Amendment standard of reasonableness that stops short of probable cause, we have not hesitated to adopt such a standard.

We join the majority of courts that have examined this issue in concluding that the accommodation of the privacy interests of schoolchildren with the substantial need of teachers and administrators for freedom to maintain order in the schools does not require strict adherence to the requirement that searches be based on probable cause to believe that the subject of the search has violated or is violating the law. Rather, the legality of a search of a student should depend simply on the reasonableness, under all the circumstances, of the search. Determining the reasonableness of any search involves a twofold inquiry: first, one must consider "whether the action was justified at its inception," *Terry v. Ohio* . . . ; second, one must determine whether the search as actually conducted "was reasonably related in scope to the circumstances which justified the interference in the first place," *ibid.* Under ordinary circumstances, a search of a student by a teacher or other school official will be "justified at its inception" when there are reasonable grounds for suspecting that the search will turn up evidence that the student has violated or is violating either the law or the rules of the school. Such a search will be permissible in its scope when the measures adopted are reasonably intrusive in light of the age and sex of the student and the nature of the infraction.

IV

There remains the question of the legality of the search in this case. We recognize that the "reasonable grounds" standard applied by the New Jersey Supreme Court in its consideration of this question is not substantially different from the standard that we have adopted today. Nonetheless, we believe that the New Jersey court's application of that standard to strike down the search of T.L.O.'s purse reflects a somewhat crabbed notion of reasonableness. . . .

T.L.O. had been accused of smoking, and had denied the accusation in the strongest possible terms when she stated that she did not smoke at all. Surely it cannot be said that under these circumstances, T.L.O.'s possession of cigarettes would be irrelevant to the charges against her or to her response to these charges. T.L.O.'s possession of cigarettes, once it was discovered, would both corroborate the report that she had been smoking and undermine the credibility of her defense to the charge of smoking. To be sure, the discovery of the cigarettes would not prove that T.L.O. had been smoking in the lavatory; nor would it, strictly speaking, necessarily be inconsistent with her claim that she did not smoke at all. But it is universally recognized that evidence, to be relevant to an inquiry, need not conclusively prove the ultimate fact in issue, but only have "any tendency to make the existence of any fact that is of consequence to the determination of the action more probable or less probable than it would be without the evidence." Fed. Rule Evid. 401. The relevance of T.L.O.'s possession of cigarettes to the question whether she had been smoking and to the credibility of her denial that she smoked supplied the necessary "nexus" between the item searched for and the infraction under investigation. Thus, if Mr. Choplick in fact had a reasonable suspicion that T.L.O. had cigarettes in her purse, the search was justified despite the fact that the cigarettes, if found, would constitute "mere evidence" of a violation.

Of course, the New Jersey Supreme Court also held that Mr. Choplick had no reasonable suspicion that the purse would contain cigarettes. This conclusion is puzzling. A teacher had reported that T.L.O. was smoking in the lavatory. Certainly this report gave Mr. Choplick reason to suspect that T.L.O. was carrying cigarettes with her; and if she did have cigarettes, her purse was the obvious place in which to find them. Mr. Choplick's suspicion that there were cigarettes in the purse was not an "inchoate and unparticularized suspicion or 'hunch,' " rather, it was the sort of "common-sense conclusio[n] about human behavior" upon which "practical people" — including government officials — are entitled to rely. . . . Of course, even if the teacher's report were true, T.L.O. *might* not have had a pack of cigarettes with her; she might have borrowed a cigarette from someone else or have been sharing a cigarette with another student. But the requirement of reasonable suspicion is not a requirement of absolute certainty.

Our conclusion that Mr. Choplick's decision to open T.L.O.'s purse was reasonable brings us to the question of the further search for marihuana once the pack of cigarettes was located. The suspicion upon which the search for marihuana was founded was provided when Mr. Choplick observed a package of rolling papers in the purse as he removed the pack of cigarettes. Although T.L.O. does not dispute the reasonableness of Mr. Choplick's belief that the rolling papers indicated the presence of marihuana, she does contend that the scope of the search Mr. Choplick conducted exceeded permissible bounds when he seized and read certain letters that implicated T.L.O. in drug dealing. This argument, too, is unpersuasive. The discovery of the rolling papers concededly gave rise to a reasonable suspicion that T.L.O. was carrying marihuana as well as cigarettes in her purse. This suspicion justified further exploration of T.L.O.'s purse, which turned up more evidence of drug-related activities: a pipe, a number of plastic bags of the type commonly used to store marihuana, a small quantity of marihuana, and a fairly substantial amount of money. Under these circumstances, it was not unreasonable to extend the search to a separate zippered compartment of the purse; and when a search of that compartment revealed an index card containing a list of "people who owe me money" as well as two letters, an inference that T.L.O. was involved in marihuana trafficking was substantial enough to justify Mr. Choplick in examining the letters to determine whether they contained any further evidence. In short, we cannot conclude that the search for marihuana was unreasonable in any respect.

Because the search resulting in the discovery of the evidence of marihuana dealing by T.L.O. was reasonable, the New Jersey Supreme Court's decision to exclude that evidence from T.L.O.'s juvenile delinquency proceedings on Fourth Amendment grounds was erroneous. Accordingly, the judgment of the Supreme Court of New Jersey is

Reversed.

JUSTICE BRENNAN, with whom JUSTICE MARSHALL joins, concurring in part and dissenting in part.

I fully agree with Part II of the Court's opinion. Teachers, like all other government officials, must conform their conduct to the Fourth Amendment's protections of personal privacy and personal security.

I do not, however, otherwise join the Court's opinion. Today's decision sanctions school officials to conduct full-scale searches on a "reasonableness" standard whose only definite content is that it is not the same test as the "probable cause" standard found in the text of the Fourth Amendment. In adopting this unclear, unprecedented, and unnecessary departure from generally applicable Fourth Amendment standards, the Court carves out a broad exception to standards that this Court has developed over years of considering Fourth Amendment problems. In the past several Terms, this Court has produced a succession of Fourth Amendment opinions in which "balancing tests" have been applied to resolve various questions concerning the proper scope of official searches.

All of these "balancing tests" amount to brief nods by the Court in the direction of a neutral utilitarian calculus while the Court in fact engages in an unanalyzed exercise of judicial will. Perhaps this doctrinally destructive nihilism is merely a convenient umbrella under which a majority that cannot agree on a genuine rationale can conceal its differences. And it may be that real force underlying today's decision is the belief that the Court purports to reject — the belief that the unique role served by the schools justifies an exception to the Fourth Amendment on their behalf. If so, the methodology of today's decision may turn out to have as little influence in future cases as will its result, and the Court's departure from traditional Fourth Amendment doctrine will be confined to the schools.

[JUSTICE STEVENS also concurred in part and dissented in part, in an opinion joined by JUSTICE MARSHALL and JUSTICE BRENNAN in part.]

NOTES AND QUESTIONS

(1) Is Justice Brennan correct in contending that the Court has provided no guidance other than that probable cause is not required? Are there compelling reasons for requiring less than probable cause for public school searches?

(2) A critical factor in school detentions and searches is the government official responsible. (No Fourth Amendment standards are applicable to the conduct of administrators in private schools.) Where, as in *T.L.O.*, the search is conducted exclusively by a school official, the relaxed standards of that decision control. *See People v. Dilworth*, 661 N.E.2d 310 (Ill.), *cert. denied*, 517 U.S. 1197 (1996). The same result may be reached when the search is initiated by a school official who subsequently engages the assistance of a law enforcement officer. *See, e.g., J.A.R. v. State*, 689 So. 2d 1242, 1244 (Fla. Dist. Ct. App. 1997) ("If a school official has a reasonable suspicion that a student is carrying a dangerous weapon on his or her person, that official may request any police officer to perform a pat-down for weapons without fear that the involvement of police will somehow violate the student's Fourth Amendment rights or require probable cause for such a search."). But if the search is initiated by a law enforcement officer, the more stringent probable cause standard will apply. *See, e.g., State v. Tywayne H.*, 933 P.2d 251 (N.M. Ct. App.), *cert. denied*, 123 N.M. 83, 934 P.2d 277 (1997); *In Interest of Angelia D.B.*, 564 N.W.2d 682 (Wis. 1997). *See generally* Pinard, *From the Classroom to the Courtroom: Reassessing Fourth Amendment Standards and Public School Searches Involving Law Enforcement Authorities*, 45 ARIZ. L. REV. 1067 (2003).

(3) In *In re Randy G.*, 28 P.3d 239 (2001), a public high school security officer observed two students in an area in which students were not permitted to congregate, and instructed them to go to class. She followed the two students, one of whom she believed was acting "very paranoid and nervous." She and another security officer called the student out of class and asked if he had anything on him,

to which he replied, "no." He consented to a pat-down search, which revealed a knife, the possession of which led to his being declared a ward of the court and placed on probation. The intermediate appellate court found that a reasonable suspicion standard had been satisfied. The California Supreme Court concluded that it was unnecessary to address this issue because, under the authority of *T.L.O.*, "[T]he broad authority of school administrators over student behavior, school safety, and the learning environment requires that school officials have the power to stop a minor student in order to ask questions or conduct an investigation even in the absence of reasonable suspicion, so long as such authority is not exercised in an arbitrary, capricious, or harassing manner." *Cf. D.I.R. v. State*, 683 N.E.2d 251 (Ind. Ct. App. 1997), holding that *T.L.O.* did not support the search of a student for no reason other than her late arrival for class.

(4) Lower courts have disagreed on whether public school students harbor a reasonable expectation of privacy in their school lockers. Among the decisions finding a reasonable expectation of privacy are the following: *State v. Jones*, 666 N.W.2d 142 (Iowa 2003) (but a cleanout of all lockers for health and safety purposes was reasonable); *S.C. v. State*, 583 So. 2d 188 (Miss. 1991); *In re Adam*, 697 N.E.2d 1100 (Ohio Ct. App. 1997). Cases in which no reasonable expectation of privacy was found include the following: *In re Patrick Y.*, 746 A.2d 405 (Md. 2000); *Shoemaker v. State*, 971 S.W.2d 178 (Tex. App. 1998); *In re Isiah B.*, 500 N.W.2d 637, *cert. denied*, 510 U.S. 884 (1993).

(5) Does *T.L.O.* have any relevance to institutions of higher education? For example, could school officials inspect state-owned dormitory rooms for the illicit possession of liquor or narcotics? Would *Camara* support such inspections? Courts are generally agreed that when police are involved in the search of a college dormitory room, absent consent or exigent circumstances, a warrant supported by probable cause is required. *See, e.g., Commonwealth v. Neilson*, 666 N.E.2d 984 (Mass. 1996). *See generally* Stanley, *The Fourth Amendment and Dormitory Searches — A New Truce*, 65 U. Chi. L. Rev. 1403 (1998).

SAFFORD UNIFIED SCHOOL DISTRICT #1 v. REDDING

United States Supreme Court
557 U.S. 364 (2009)

Justice Souter delivered the opinion of the Court.

The issue here is whether a 13-year-old student's Fourth Amendment right was violated when she was subjected to a search of her bra and underpants by school officials acting on reasonable suspicion that she had brought forbidden prescription and over-the-counter drugs to school. Because there were no reasons to suspect the drugs presented a danger or were concealed in her underwear, we hold that the search did violate the Constitution, but because there is reason to question the clarity with which the right was established, the official who ordered the unconstitutional search is entitled to qualified immunity from liability.

I

The event immediately prior to the search in question began in 13 year-old Savana Redding's math class at Safford Middle School one October day in 2003. The assistant principal of the school, Kerry Wilson, came into the room and asked Savana to go to his office. There, he showed her a day planner, unzipped and open flat on his desk, in which there were several knives, lighters, a permanent marker, and a cigarette. Wilson asked Savana whether the planner was hers; she said it was, but that a few days before she had lent it to her friend, Marissa Glines. Savana stated that none of the items in the planner belonged to her.

Wilson then showed Savana four white prescription-strength ibuprofen 400-mg pills, and one over-the-counter blue naproxen 200-mg pill, all used for pain and inflammation but banned under school rules without advance permission. He asked Savana if she knew anything about the pills, Savana answered that she did not. Wilson then told Savana that he had received a report that she was giving these pills to fellow students; Savana denied it and agreed to let Wilson search her belongings. Helen Romero, an administrative assistant, came into the office, and together with Wilson they searched Savana's backpack, finding nothing.

At that point, Wilson instructed Romero to take Savana to the school nurse's office to search her clothes for pills. Romero and the nurse, Peggy Schwallier, asked Savana to remove her jacket, socks, and shoes, leaving her in stretch pants and a T-shirt (both without pockets), which she was then asked to remove. Finally, Savana was told to pull her bra out and to the side and shake it, and to pull out the elastic on her underpants, thus exposing her breasts and pelvic area to some degree. No pills were found.

Savana's mother filed suit against Safford Unified School District #1, Wilson, Romero, and Schwallier for conducting a strip search in violation of Savana's Fourth Amendment rights. The individuals, (hereinafter petitioners) moved for summary judgment, raising a defense of qualified immunity. The District Court for the District of Arizona granted the motion on ground that there was no Fourth Amendment violation, and a panel of the Ninth Circuit affirmed. . . .

A closely divided Circuit sitting en banc, however, reversed. . . . [T]he Ninth Circuit held that the strip search was unjustified under the Fourth Amendment test for searches of children by school officials set out in *New Jersey v. T.L.O.* . . .

II

. . . In T.L.O., we recognized that the school setting "requires some modification of the level of suspicion of illicit activity needed to justify a search," . . . and held that for searches by school officials "a careful balancing of governmental and private interests suggests that the public interest is best served by a Fourth Amendment standard of reasonableness that stops short of probable cause," . . . We have thus applied a standard of reasonable suspicion to determine the legality of a school administrator's search of a student, . . . and have held that a school search "will be permissible in its scope when the measures adopted are reasonably related to the objectives of the search and not excessively intrusive in light of the age and sex of the student and the nature of the infraction." . . .

Perhaps the best that can be said generally about the required knowledge component of probable cause for a law enforcement officer's evidence search is that it raises a "fair probability," . . . or a "substantial chance," . . . of discovering evidence of criminal activity. The lesser standard for school searches could as readily be described as a moderate chance of finding evidence of wrongdoing.

III

A

In this case, the school's policies strictly prohibit the nonmedical use, possession, or sale of any drug on school grounds, including "[a]ny prescription or over-the-counter drug, except those for which permission to use in school has been granted pursuant to Board policy." . . .[29] [A] week before Savana was searched, another student, Jordan Romero (no relation of the school's administrative assistant), told the principal and Assistant Principal Wilson that "certain students were bringing drugs and weapons on campus," and that he had been sick after taking some pills that "he got from a classmate." . . . On the morning of October 8, the same boy handed Wilson a white pill that he said Marissa Glines had given him. He told Wilson that students were planning to take the pills at lunch.

Wilson learned from Peggy Schwallier, the school nurse, that the pill was Ibuprofen 400 mg, available only by prescription. Wilson then called Marissa out of class. Outside the classroom, Marissa's teacher handed Wilson the day planner, found within Marissa's reach, containing various contraband items. Wilson escorted Marissa back to his office.

In the presence of Helen Romero, Wilson requested Marissa to turn out her pockets and open her wallet. Marissa produced a blue pill, several white ones, and a razor blade. Wilson asked where the blue pill came from, and Marissa answered, " 'I guess it slipped in when she gave me the IBU 400s.' " . . . When Wilson asked whom she meant, Marissa replied " 'Savana Redding.' " . . . Wilson then inquired about the day planner and its contents; Marissa denied knowing anything about them. Wilson did not ask Marissa any follow up questions to determine whether there was any likelihood that Savana presently had pills: neither asking when Marissa received the pills from Savana nor where Savana might be hiding them.

Schwallier did not immediately recognize the blue pill, but information provided by a poison control hotline indicated that the pill was a 200-mg dose of an

---

[29] [4] When the object of a school search is the enforcement of a school rule, a valid search assumes, of course, the rule's legitimacy. But the legitimacy of the rule usually goes without saying as it does here. The Court said plainly in *New Jersey v. T.L.O.* . . . , that standards of conduct for schools are for school administrators to determine without second-guessing by courts lacking the experience to appreciate what may be needed. Except in patently arbitrary instances, Fourth Amendment analysis takes the rule as a given, as it obviously should do in this case. There is no need here either to explain the imperative of keeping drugs out of schools, or to explain the reasons for the school's rule banning all drugs, no matter how benign, without advance permission. Teachers are not pharmacologists trained to identify pills and powders, and an effective drug ban has to be enforceable fast. The plenary ban makes sense, and there is no basis to claim that the search was unreasonable owing to some defect or shortcoming of the rule it was aimed at enforcing.

anti-inflammatory drug, generically called naproxen, available over the counter. At Wilson's direction, Marissa was then subjected to a search of her bra and underpants by Romero and Schwallier, as Savana was later on. The search revealed no additional pills.

It was at this juncture that Wilson called Savana into his officer and showed her the day planner. Their conversation established that Savana and Marissa were on friendly terms: while she denied knowledge of the contraband, Savana admitted that the day planner was hers and that she had lent it to Marissa. Wilson had other reports of their friendship from staff members, who had identified Savana and Marissa as part of an unusually rowdy group at the school's opening dance in August, during which alcohol and cigarettes were found in the girls' bathroom. Wilson had reason to connect the girls with this contraband, for Wilson knew that Jordan Romero had told the principal that before the dance, he had been at a party at Savana's house where alcohol was served. Marissa's statement that the pills came from Savana was thus sufficiently plausible to warrant suspicion that Savana was involved in pill distribution.

This suspicion of Wilson's was enough to justify a search of Savana's backpack and outer clothing.[30] If a student is reasonably suspected of giving out contraband pills, she is reasonably suspected of carrying them on her person and in the carryall that has become an item of student uniform in most places today. If Wilson's reasonable suspicion of pill distribution were not understood to support searches of outer clothes and backpack, it would not justify any search worth making. And the look into Savana's bag, in her presence and in the relative privacy of Wilson's office, was not excessively intrusive, any more than Romero's subsequent search of her outer clothing.

B

Here it is that the parties part company, with Savana's claim that extending the search at Wilson's behest to the point of making her pull out her underwear was constitutionally unreasonable. The exact label for this final step in the intrusion is not important, though strip search is a fair way to speak of it. Romero and Schwallier directed Savana to remove her clothes down to her underwear, and then "pull out" her bra and the elastic band on her underpants. . . . Although Romero and Schwallier stated that they did not see anything when Savana followed their instructions, . . . we would not define strip search and its Fourth Amendment consequences in a way that would guarantee litigation about who was looking and how much was seen. The very fact of Savana's pulling her underwear away from her body in the presence of the two officials who were able to see her necessarily exposed breasts and pelvic area to some degree, and both subjective and reasonable societal expectations of personal privacy support the treatment of such a search as categorically distinct, requiring distinct elements of justification on the part of

---

30 [3] There is no question here that justification for the school officials' search was required in accordance with the *T.L.O.* standard of reasonable suspicion, for it is common ground that Savana had a reasonable expectation of privacy covering the personal things she chose to carry in her backpack, . . . and that Wilson's decision to look through it was a "search" within the meaning of the Fourth Amendment.

school authorities for getting beyond a search of outer clothing and belongings.

Savana's subjective expectation of privacy against such a search is inherent in her account of it as embarrassing, frightening, and humiliating. The reasonableness of her expectation (required by the Fourth Amendment standard) is indicated by the consistent experiences of other young people similarly searched, whose adolescent vulnerability intensifies the patent intrusiveness of the exposure. . . .

The indignity of the search does not, of course, outlaw it, but it does implicate the rule of reasonableness as stated in T.L.O, that "the search as actually conducted [be] reasonably related in scope to the circumstances which justified the interference in the first place." . . . The scope will be permissible, that is, when it is "not excessively intrusive in light of the age and sex of the student and the nature of the infraction." . . .

Here, the content of the suspicion failed to match the degree of intrusion. Wilson knew beforehand that the pills were prescription-strength ibuprofen and over-the-counter naproxen, common pain relievers equivalent to two Advil, or one Aleve. He must have been aware of the nature and limited threat of the specific drugs he was searching for, and while just about anything can be taken in quantities that will do real harm, Wilson had no reason to suspect that large amounts of the drugs were being passed around, or that individual students were receiving great numbers of pills.

Nor could Wilson have suspected that Savana was hiding common painkillers in her underwear. Petitioners suggest, as a truth universally acknowledged, that "students . . . hid[e] contraband in or under their clothing," . . . and cite a smattering of cases of students with contraband in their underwear. . . . But when the categorically extreme intrusiveness of a search down to the body of an adolescent requires some justification in suspected facts, general background possibilities fall short; a reasonable search that extensive calls for suspicion that it will pay off. But nondangerous school contraband does not raise the specter of stashes in intimate places, and there is no evidence in the record of any general practice among Safford Middle School students of hiding that sort of thing in underwear; neither Jordan nor Marissa suggested to Wilson that Savana was doing that, and the preceding search of Marissa that Wilson ordered yielded nothing. Wilson never even determined when Marissa had received the pills from Savana if it had been a few days before, that would weigh heavily against any reasonable conclusion that Savana presently had the pills on her person, much less in her underwear.

In sum, what was missing from the suspected facts that pointed to Savana was any indication of danger to the students from the power of the drugs or their quantity, and any reason to suppose that Savana was carrying pills in her underwear. We think that the combination of these deficiencies was fatal to finding the search reasonable.

In so holding, we mean to cast no ill reflection on the assistant principal, for the record raises no doubt that his motive throughout was to eliminate drugs from his school and protect students from what Jordan Romero had gone through. Parents are known to overreact to protect their children from danger, and a school official with responsibility for safety may tend to do the same. The difference is that the Fourth Amendment places limits on the official, even with the high degree of deference that courts must pay to the educator's professional judgment.

We do mean, though, to make it clear that the T.L.O. concern to limit a school search to reasonable scope requires the support of reasonable suspicion of danger or of resort to underwear for hiding evidence of wrongdoing before a search can reasonably make the quantum leap from outer clothes and backpacks to exposure of intimate parts. The meaning of such a search, and the degradation its subject may reasonably feel, place a search that intrusive in a category of its own demanding its own specific suspicions.

[In the remainder of the opinion, the Court held that because the law regarding the strip searching of students had not been clearly established, the school officials were entitled to qualified immunity.]

[In separate opinions, Justices Stevens and Ginsburg concurred on the Fourth Amendment issue, but dissented on the question of qualified immunity.]

Justice THOMAS, concurring in the judgment in part and dissenting in part.

I agree with the Court that the judgment against the school officials with respect to qualified immunity should be reversed. . . . Unlike the majority, however, I would hold that the search of Savana Redding did not violate the Fourth Amendment. The majority imposes a vague and amorphous standard on school administrators. It also grants judges sweeping authority to second-guess the measures that these officials take to maintain discipline in their schools and ensure the health and safety of the students in their charge. This deep intrusion into the administration of public school exemplifies why the Court should return to the common-law doctrine of in loco parentis under which "the judiciary was reluctant to interfere in the routine business of school administration, allowing schools and teachers to set and enforce rules and to maintain order." . . . But even under the prevailing Fourth Amendment test established by New Jersey v. T.L.O., . . . all petitioners, including the school district, are entitled to judgment as a matter of law in their favor.

. . . [I]n the majority's view, although the school officials had reasonable suspicion to believe that Redding had the pills on her person, . . . they needed some grater level of particularized suspicion to conduct this "strip search." There is no support for this contortion of the Fourth Amendment.

The Court has generally held that the reasonableness of a search's scope depends only on whether it is limited to the area that is capable of concealing the object of the search. . . .

In keeping with this longstanding rule, the "nature of the infraction" referenced in T.L.O. delineates the proper scope of a search of students in a way that is identical to that permitted for searches outside the school — *i.e.*, the search must be limited to the areas where the object of that infraction could be concealed. . . . The reasonable suspicion that Redding possessed the pills for distribution purposes did not dissipate simply because the search of her backpack turned up nothing. It was eminently reasonable to conclude that the backpack was empty because

Redding was secreting the pills in a place she thought no one would look. . . .

The majority compounds its error by reading the "nature of the infraction" aspect of the T.L.O. test as a license to limit searches based on a judge's assessment of a particular school policy. According to the majority, the scope of the search was impermissible because the school official "must have been aware of the nature and limited threat of the specific drugs he was searching for" and because he "had no reason to suspect that large amounts of the drugs were being passed around, or that individual students were receiving great numbers of pills." . . . Thus, in order to locate a rationale for finding a Fourth Amendment violation in this case, the majority retreats from its observation that the school's firm no-drug policy "makes sense, and there is no basis to claim that the search was unreasonable owing to some defect or shortcoming of the rule it was aimed at enforcing." . . .

Even accepting the majority's assurances that it is not attacking the rule's reasonableness, it certainly is attacking the rule's importance. This approach directly conflicts with T.L.O. in which the Court was "unwilling to adopt a standard under which the legality of a search is dependent upon a judge's evaluation of the relative importance of school rules." . . . Indeed, the Court in T.L.O expressly rejected the proposition that the majority seemingly endorses-that "some rules regarding student conduct are by nature too 'trivial' to justify a search based upon reasonable suspicion." . . .

The majority has placed school officials in this "impossible spot" by questioning whether possession of Ibuprofen and Naproxen causes a severe enough threat to warrant investigation. Had the suspected infraction involved a street drug, the majority implies that it would have approved the scope of the search. . . . In effect, then, the majority has replaced a school rule that draws no distinction among drugs with a new one that does. As a result, a full search of a student's person for prohibited drugs will be permitted only if the Court agrees that the drug in question was sufficiently dangerous. Such a test is unworkable and unsound. School officials cannot be expected to halt searches based on the possibility that a court might later find that the particular infraction at issue is not severe enough to warrant an intrusive investigation.

§ 3.04 WARRANTLESS SEARCHES

[A] Incident to Arrest

CHIMEL v. CALIFORNIA

United States Supreme Court
395 U.S. 752 (1969)

MR. JUSTICE STEWART delivered the opinion of the Court.

This case raises basic questions concerning the permissible scope under the Fourth Amendment of a search incident to a lawful arrest.

The relevant facts are essentially undisputed. Late in the afternoon of September 13, 1965, three police officers arrived at the Santa Ana, California, home of the petitioner with a warrant authorizing his arrest for the burglary of a coin shop. The officers knocked on the door, identified themselves to the petitioner's wife, and asked if they might come inside. She ushered them into the house, where they waited 10 or 15 minutes until the petitioner returned home from work. When the petitioner entered the house, one of the officers handed him the arrest warrant and asked for permission to "look around." The petitioner objected, but was advised that "on the basis of the lawful arrest," the officers would nonetheless conduct a search. No search warrant had been issued.

Accompanied by the petitioner's wife, the officers then looked through the entire three-bedroom house, including the attic, the garage, and a small workshop. In some rooms the search was relatively cursory. In the master bedroom and sewing room, however, the officers directed the petitioner's wife to open drawers and "to physically move contents of the drawers from side to side so that [they] might view any items that would have come from [the] burglary." After completing the search, they seized numerous items primarily coins, but also several medals, tokens, and a few other objects. The entire search took between 45 minutes and an hour.

[*In Harris v. United States*, 331 U.S. 145 (1947)] officers had obtained a warrant for Harris' arrest on the basis of his alleged involvement with the cashing and interstate transportation of a forged check. He was arrested in the living room of his four-room apartment, and in an attempt to recover two concealed checks thought to have been used in effecting the forgery, the officers undertook a thorough search of the entire apartment. Inside a desk drawer they found a sealed envelope marked "George Harris, personal papers." The envelope, which was then torn open, was found to contain altered Selective Service documents, and those documents were used to secure Harris' conviction for violating the Selective Training and Service Act of 1940. The Court rejected Harris' Fourth Amendment claim, sustaining the search as "incident to arrest." *Id.*, at 151.

Only a year after *Harris*, however, the pendulum swung again. In *Trupiano v. United States*, 334 U.S. 699, agents raided the site of an illicit distillery, saw one of several conspirators operating the still, and arrested him, contemporaneously "seiz[ing] the illicit distillery." *Id.*, at 702. The Court held that the arrest and others made subsequently had been valid, but that the unexplained failure of the agents to procure a search warrant — in spite of the fact that they had had more than enough time before the raid to do so — rendered the search unlawful. The opinion stated:

> It is a cardinal rule that, in seizing goods and articles, law enforcement agents must secure and use search warrants wherever reasonably practicable. . . . This rule rests upon the desirability of having magistrates rather than police officers determine when searches and seizures are permissible and what limitations should be placed upon such activities. . . . To provide the necessary security against unreasonable intrusions upon the private lives of individuals, the framers of the Fourth Amendment required adherence to judicial processes wherever possible. And subsequent history has confirmed the wisdom of that requirement.
>
> . . .

> A search or seizure without a warrant as an incident to a lawful arrest has always been considered to be a strictly limited right. It grows out of the inherent necessities of the situation at the time of the arrest. But there must be something more in the way of necessity than merely a lawful arrest.

Id., at 705, 708.

In 1950, two years after *Trupiano*, came *United States v. Rabinowitz*, 339 U.S. 56, the decision upon which California primarily relies in the case now before us. In *Rabinowitz*, federal authorities had been informed that the defendant was dealing in stamps bearing forged overprints. On the basis of that information they secured a warrant for his arrest, which they executed at his one-room business office. At the time of the arrest, the officers "searched the desk, safe, and file cabinets in the office for about an hour and a half," *id.*, at 59, and seized 573 stamps with forged overprints. The stamps were admitted into evidence at the defendant's trial, and this Court affirmed his conviction, rejecting the contention that the warrantless search had been unlawful. The Court held that the search in its entirety fell within the principle giving law enforcement authorities "[t]he right to search the place where the arrest is made in order to find and seize things connected with the crime. . . .' " *Id.*, at 61. *Harris* was regarded as "ample authority" for that conclusion. *Id.*, at 63. The opinion rejected the rule of *Trupiano* that "in seizing goods and articles, law enforcement agents must secure and use search warrants wherever reasonably practicable." The test, said the Court, "is not whether it is reasonable to procure a search warrant, but whether the search was reasonable." *Id.*, at 66.

Rabinowitz has come to stand for the proposition, *inter alia*, that a warrantless search "incident to a lawful arrest" may generally extend to the area that is considered to be in the "possession" or under the "control" of the person arrested. And it was on the basis of that proposition that the California courts upheld the search of the petitioner's entire house in this case. That doctrine, however, at least in the broad sense in which it was applied by the California courts in this case, can withstand neither historical nor rational analysis.

Only last Term in *Terry v. Ohio* . . . we emphasized that "the police must, whenever practicable, obtain advance judicial approval of searches and seizures through the warrant procedure," . . . and that "[t]he scope of [a] search must be 'strictly tied to and justified by' the circumstances which rendered its initiation permissible." . . . The search undertaken by the officer in that "stop and frisk" case was sustained under that test, because it was no more than a "protective . . . search for weapons." . . . But in a companion case, *Sibron v. New York* . . . we applied the same standard to another set of facts and reached a contrary result, holding that a policeman's action in thrusting his hand into a suspect's pocket had been neither motivated by nor limited to the objective of protection. Rather, the search had been made to order to find narcotics, which were in fact found.

A similar analysis underlies the "search incident to arrest" principle, and marks its proper extent. When an arrest is made, it is reasonable for the arresting officer to search the person arrested in order to remove any weapons that the latter might seek to use in order to resist arrest or effect his escape. Otherwise, the officer's safety might well be endangered, and the arrest itself frustrated. In addition, it is entirely reasonable for the arresting officer to search for and seize any evidence on the arrestee's person in order to prevent its concealment or destruction. And the area into which an arrestee might reach in order to grab a weapon or evidentiary items must, of course, be governed by a like rule. A gun on a table or in a drawer in front of one who is arrested can be as dangerous to the arresting officer as one concealed in the clothing of the person arrested. There is ample justification, therefore, for a search of the arrestee's person and the area "within his immediate control" — construing that phrase to mean the area from within which he might gain possession of a weapon or destructible evidence.

There is no comparable justification, however, for routinely searching any room other than that in which an arrest occurs — or, for that matter, for searching through all the desk drawers or other closed or concealed areas in that room itself. Such searches, in the absence of well-recognized exceptions, may be made only under the authority of a search warrant. The "adherence to judicial processes" mandated by the Fourth Amendment requires no less.

[Justice Harlan concurred; Justice White, joined by Justice Black, dissented.]

NOTE

Pre-Chimel Standard. The *Chimel* decision is a substantial retrenchment from a judicial tolerance which had culminated in the incident to arrest exception to the warrant requirement virtually swallowing the rule. The two decisions explicitly overruled — *Harris* and *Rabinowitz* — were recognized as authority for the notion that incident to an arrest within a home, the entire home or apartment could be searched without a warrant. Nor was this simply a question of whether any harm resulted from the failure to obtain a warrant, for in the typical situation a warrant could not have been obtained, either because probable cause was lacking, or because the particular item seized could not have been enumerated prior to the discovery, or both. The search incident to arrest exception was therefore carte blanche for a fishing expedition throughout the premises within the control of the arrestee at the time of the arrest.

There were outer limits of spatial and temporal proximity. Arrests made away from the premises would not support a search, *Agnello v. United States*, 269 U.S. 20 (1925), (arrestee in home of another); *Stoner v. California*, 376 U.S. 483 (1964), (arrest in Nevada, search in California), nor would an arrest in front of the residence justify entering to search. *Shipley v. California*, 395 U.S. 818 (1969); *Vale v. Louisiana*, 399 U.S. 30 (1970). On the other hand, there was little to discourage the police from waiting until the suspect was in a location which raised the most lucrative possibilities for a search before they made the arrest. Occasionally, a lower court would find a search illegal on the theory that in reality the arrest was incident to the search rather than vice versa.

Typically a search incident to arrest follows shortly thereafter. An extended delay may render the search indefensible, as, for example, in *Preston v. United States*, 376 U.S. 364 (1964), in which the arrest occurred while the suspects were sitting in an automobile, but the search of the vehicle took place after they were in the police station and it was in a garage. The Court found the search unreasonable both as incident to an arrest and under the automobile exception.

Occasionally a search which briefly precedes an arrest will be sustained under the incident to arrest exception. In such cases, the dispositive question is whether the police had probable cause to arrest *before* the search. If so, the order of events is inconsequential. If not, circularity results — the arrest is being justified by the search, and the search is being justified by the arrest. This principle has survived the *Chimel* decision.

PROBLEM J
VARIATIONS ON THE THEME

What result under *Chimel* in the following cases:

(a) D is arrested for income tax evasion. He is seated at his desk at the time of the arrest. The arresting officer has him stand and handcuffs him. The officer takes his wallet from his hip pocket, looks inside and extracts a counterfeit twenty dollar bill.

(b) D is carrying a tan zipper bag when arrested at the train station. The officer takes the zipper bag away from D, puts D in back of the squad car and transports him to the station. D is booked and locked up. The officer then opens the bag and finds narcotics.

(c) D does not have the tan zipper bag when arrested, but he does have a key to a rental locker at the railroad station. D is taken into custody by one officer while the other goes and retrieves the bag from the locker.

(d) D is arrested in his living room and indicates he needs to get his coat from a closet. The officer follows him into an adjoining room, and sees narcotics on the chest of drawers.

(e) Before D goes into the closet, the officer precedes him, and discovers a pistol in a shoe box.

(f) D is arrested in his living room for armed robbery shortly after the crime. The officer says, "where's the gun?" D responds, "it's in that drawer," pointing to a closed drawer in a table twenty feet away. The officer walks across the room, opens the drawer, and seizes a pistol.

(g) D is arrested in his living room for a crime involving additional suspects. The police lack probable cause to believe that other might be on the premises but nonetheless make a "protective sweep," finding no one but in the process coming upon evidence in plain view which they seize. *See Maryland v. Buie*, 494 U.S. 325 (1990).

PROBLEM K
THE PERSONAL SEARCH DELAYED

Defendant Edwards was lawfully arrested late at night on suspicion of burglary. An investigation at the scene indicated that an attempt had been made to pry open a window of a post office, in the process of which paint chips had been left on the window sill and screen. Defendant was immediately incarcerated, and the following day he was provided with substitute clothing. The clothing he had been wearing was then examined, and paint chips matching those found at the scene of the crime were discovered and introduced at his trial. Was the seizure legal? *See United States v. Edwards*, 415 U.S. 800 (1974).

PROBLEM L
THE SEARCH INCIDENT TO A NON-ARREST

If an arrest *could* have been made, is it essential that it *was* made in order to sustain a search incident to an arrest? In *Cupp v. Murphy*, 412 U.S. 291(1973), following the murder of his wife, the defendant went to the police station on his own initiative. While there police observed something under his fingernail which they thought might be dried blood. Defendant would not consent to the taking of a scraping, where upon the sample was taken over his protest. Thereafter, defendant was allowed to leave and was not formally arrested for another month. The sample contained traces of skin and blood and was included in the evidence used to convict him of second degree murder. Should the seizure be sustained?

UNITED STATES v. ROBINSON
United States Supreme Court
414 U.S. 218 (1973)

Mr. Justice Rehnquist delivered the opinion of the Court.

On April 23, 1968, at approximately 11 p.m., Officer Richard Jenks, a 15-year veteran of the District of Columbia Metropolitan Police Department, observed the respondent driving a 1965 Cadillac near the intersection of 8th and C Streets, N. E., in the District of Columbia. Jenks, as a result of previous investigation following a check of respondent's operator's permit four days earlier, determined there was reason to believe that respondent was operating a motor vehicle after the revocation of his operator's permit. This is an offense defined by statute in the District of Columbia which carries a mandatory minimum jail term, a mandatory minimum fine, or both. D.C. Code Ann. § 40-302(d) (1967).

Jenks signaled respondent to stop the automobile, which respondent did, and all three of the occupants emerged from the car. At that point Jenks informed respondent that he was under arrest for "operating after revocation and obtaining a permit by misrepresentation." It was assumed by the Court of Appeals, and is conceded by the respondent here, that Jenks had probable cause to arrest respondent, and that he effected a full-custody arrest.

In accordance with procedures prescribed in police department instructions, Jenks then began to search respondent. He explained at a subsequent hearing that he was "face-to-face" with the respondent, and "placed [his] hands on [the respondent], my right-hand to his left breast like this (demonstrating) and proceeded to pat him down thus [with the right hand]." During this pat-down, Jenks felt an object in the left breast pocket of the heavy coat respondent was wearing, but testified that he "couldn't tell what it was" and also that he "couldn't actually tell the size of it." Jenks then reached into the pocket and pulled out the object, which turned out to be a "crumpled up cigarette package." Jenks testified that at this point he still did not know what was in the package:

> As I felt the package I could feel objects in the package but I couldn't tell what they were. . . . I knew they weren't cigarettes.

The officer then opened the cigarette pack and found 14 gelatin capsules of white powder which he thought to be, and which later analysis proved to be, heroin. Jenks then continued his search of respondent to completion, feeling around his waist and trouser legs, and examining the remaining pockets. The heroin seized from the respondent was admitted into evidence at the trial which resulted in his conviction in the District Court.

The opinion for the plurality judges of the Court of Appeals, written by Judge Wright, the concurring opinion of Chief Judge Bazelon, and the dissenting opinion of Judge Wilkey, concurred in by three judges, gave careful and comprehensive treatment to the authority of a police officer to search the person of one who has been validly arrested and taken into custody. We conclude that the search conducted by Jenks in this case did not offend the limits imposed by the Fourth Amendment, and we therefore reverse the judgment of the Court of Appeals.

The Court of Appeals in effect determined that the *only* reason supporting the authority for a *full* search incident to lawful arrest was the possibility of discovery of evidence or fruits. Concluding that there could be no evidence or fruits in the case of an offense such as that with which respondent was charged, it held that any protective search would have to be limited by the conditions laid down in *Terry* for a search upon less than probable cause to arrest. Quite apart from the fact that *Terry* clearly recognized the distinction between the two types of searches, and that a different rule governed one than governed the other, we find additional reason to disagree with the Court of Appeals.

The justification or reason for the authority to search incident to a lawful arrest rests quite as much on the need to disarm the suspect in order to take him into custody as it does on the need to preserve evidence on his person for later use at trial. *Agnello v. United States*, 269 U.S. 20 (1925); *Abel v. United States*, 362 U.S. 217 (1960). The standards traditionally governing a search incident to lawful arrest are not, therefore, commuted to the stricter *Terry* standards by the absence of probable fruits or further evidence of the particular crime for which the arrest is made.

Nor are we inclined, on the basis of what seems to us to be a rather speculative judgment, to qualify the breadth of the general authority to search incident to a lawful custodial arrest on an assumption that persons arrested for the offense of driving while their licenses have been revoked are less likely to possess dangerous weapons than are those arrested for other crimes. It is scarcely open to doubt that the danger to an officer is far greater in the case of the extended exposure which follows the taking of a suspect into custody and transporting him to the police station than in the case of the relatively fleeting contact resulting from the typical *Terry*-type stop. This is an adequate basis for treating all custodial arrests alike for purposes of search justification.

But quite apart from these distinctions, our more fundamental disagreement with the Court of Appeals arises from its suggestion that there must be litigated in each case the issue of whether or not there was present one of the reasons supporting the authority for a search of the person incident to a lawful arrest. We do not think the long line of authorities of this Court dating back to *Weeks*, or what we can glean from the history of practice in this country and in England, requires such a case-by-case adjudication. A police officer's determination as to how and where to search the person of a suspect whom he has arrested is necessarily a quick *ad hoc* judgment which the Fourth Amendment does not require to be broken down in each instance into an analysis of each step in the search. The authority to search the person incident to a lawful custodial arrest, while based upon the need to disarm and to discover evidence, does not depend on what a court may later decide was the probability in a particular arrest situation that weapons or evidence would in fact be found upon the person of the suspect. A custodial arrest of a suspect based on probable cause is a reasonable intrusion under the Fourth Amendment; that intrusion being lawful, a search incident to the arrest requires no additional justification. It is the fact of the lawful arrest which establishes the authority to search, and we hold that in the case of a lawful custodial arrest a full search of the person is not only an exception to the warrant requirement of the Fourth Amendment, but is also a "reasonable" search under that Amendment.

The search of respondent's person conducted by Officer Jenks in this case and the seizure from him of the heroin, were permissible under established Fourth Amendment law. While thorough, the search partook of none of the extreme or patently abusive characteristics which were held to violate the Due Process Clause of the Fourteenth Amendment in *Rochin v. California*. . . . Since it is the fact of custodial arrest which gives rise to the authority to search, it is of no moment that Jenks did not indicate any subjective fear of the respondent or that he did not himself suspect that respondent was armed. Having in the course of a lawful search come upon the crumpled package of cigarettes, he was entitled to inspect it; and when his inspection revealed the heroin capsules, he was entitled to seize them as "fruits, instrumentalities, or contraband" probative of criminal conduct. . . .

MR. JUSTICE MARSHALL, with whom MR. JUSTICE DOUGLAS and MR. JUSTICE BRENNAN join, dissenting.

As I view the matter, the search in this case divides into three distinct phases: the pat-down of respondent's coat pocket; the removal of the unknown object from the pocket; and the opening of the crumpled-up cigarette package.

A

No question is raised here concerning the lawfulness of the pat-down of respondent's coat pocket.

B

With respect to the removal of the unknown object from the coat pocket, the first issue presented is whether that aspect of the search can be sustained as part of the limited frisk for weapons. The weapons search approved by the Court of Appeals was modeled upon the narrowly drawn protective search for weapons authorized in

Terry, which consists "of a limited patting of the outer clothing of the suspect for concealed objects which might be used as instruments of assault." . . .

It appears to have been conceded by the Government below that the removal of the object from respondent's coat pocket exceeded the scope of a *Terry* frisk for weapons, since, under *Terry*, an officer may not remove an object from the suspect's pockets unless he has reason to believe it to be a dangerous weapon. . . .

In the present case, however, Officer Jenks had no reason to believe and did not in fact believe that the object in respondent's coat pocket was a weapon. He admitted later that the object did not feel like a gun. . . . In fact, he did not really have any thought one way or another about what was in the pocket. As Jenks himself testified, "I just searched him. I didn't think about what I was looking for. I just searched him." Since the removal of the object from the pocket cannot be justified as part of a limited *Terry* weapons frisk, the question arises whether it is reasonable for a police officer, when effecting an in-custody arrest of a traffic offender, to make a fuller search of the person than is permitted pursuant to *Terry*.

Nor was there any particular reason in this case to believe that respondent was dangerous. He had not attempted to evade arrest, but had quickly complied with the police both in bringing his car to a stop after being signaled to do so and in producing the documents Officer Jenks requested. In fact, Jenks admitted that he searched respondent face to face rather than in spread-eagle fashion because he had no reason to believe respondent would be violent.

C

The majority opinion fails to recognize that the search conducted by Officer Jenks did not merely involve a search of respondent's person. It also included a separate search of effects found on his person. And even were we to assume, *arguendo*, that it was reasonable for Jenks to remove the object he felt in respondent's pocket, clearly there was no justification consistent with the Fourth Amendment which would authorize his opening the package and looking inside.

To begin with, after Jenks had the cigarette package in his hands, there is no indication that he had reason to believe or did in fact believe that the package contained a weapon. More importantly, even if the crumpled-up cigarette package had in fact contained some sort of small weapon, it would have been impossible for respondent to have used it once the package was in the officer's hands. Opening the package, therefore, did not further the protective purpose of the search.

NOTES AND QUESTIONS

(1) A companion case, *Gustafson v. Florida*, 414 U.S. 260 (1973), involved a state prosecution with remarkably similar facts. An officer had stopped an automobile driven by the accused after observing it weaving on the road. When the accused was unable to produce a driver's license he was arrested and searched, in the process of which the officer extracted a Benson and Hedges cigarette box which he opened and observed what appeared to be marijuana cigarettes. The accused sought to distinguish *Robinson* by the trivial nature of the arrest. The Court held

that the officer had the authority to make a custodial arrest and had done so, and the search of the box was lawful.

(2) *Robinson* and *Gustafson* would appear to substantially compromise the notion that the *Chimel* test is purposive, because in both instances an article had been removed from the person of the arrestee, thereby preventing its use or destruction, and the Court sustained the authority of the officer to more intensively examine the article to determine whether it contained incriminating evidence. For a decision reflecting this conclusion, see *State v. Dubay*, 313 A.2d 908 (Me. 1974).

(3) A new term emerges in *Robinson* and *Gustafson*: "Custodial arrest." What does it mean? Is it critical to the results in the cases?

(4) Relying on the California Constitution, in *People v. Brisendine*, 13 Cal. 3d 528, 119 Cal. Rptr. 315, 531 P.2d 1099 (1975), the Supreme Court of that state rejected the *Robinson-Gustafson* holding:

> We cannot accept the *Robinson* implication that "an individual lawfully subjected to a custodial arrest retains no significant Fourth Amendment interest in the privacy of his person." Whatever may be the merit of that view when an individual is ultimately to be booked and incarcerated — a question not presented here — we find it inappropriate in the context of an arrestee who will never be subjected to that process.

Other courts have also repudiated *Robinson* and *Gustafson*: *Reeves v. State*, 599 P.2d 727 (Alaska 1979); *State v. Kaluna*, 55 Haw. 361, 520 P.2d 51 (1974); *State v. Williams*, 17 Or. App. 513, 522 P.2d 1213 (1974).

(5) *Robinson and the Cell Phone.* The Court of Appeals for the Seventh Circuit has noted the similarity between the crumpled cigarette pack in *Robinson* and a cell phone found with increasing frequency during the search of an arrestee. While both are "containers" capable of harboring incriminating evidence, the court remained skeptical of a literal application of *Robinson*. *United States v. Flores-Lopez*, 670 F.3d 803 (7th Cir. 2012). *See also Smallwood v. State*, 113 So. 3d 724 (Fla. 2013) (*Robinson* would not support cell phone search). Courts are sensitive to the prodigious amount of information potentially accessible through a cell phone or similar device. A possible limitation would permit the search of the contents of a cell phone, but limit the seizure to information related to the crime for which the individual was arrested. *United States v. Flores-Lopez*, *supra* (dicta); *Hawkins v. State*, 723 S.E.2d 924 (Ga. 2012). The inevitable inter-mingling of relevant and irrelevant data will give rise to serious invasion of privacy concerns. *State v. Barajas*, 817 N.W.2d 204, 216–17 (Minn. Ct. App.), *review denied*, 2012 Minn. LEXIS 568 (Oct. 16, 2012). A cell phone search may be sustained based on exigent circumstances because of the potential for evidence destruction. *United States v. Parada*, 289 F. Supp. 2d 1291 (D. Kan. 2003); *United States v. Santillan*, 571 F. Supp. 2d 1093 (D. Ariz. 2008).

KNOWLES v. IOWA

United States Supreme Court
525 U.S. 113 (1977)

CHIEF JUSTICE REHNQUIST delivered the opinion of the Court.

An Iowa police officer stopped petitioner Knowles for speeding, but issued him a citation rather than arresting him. The question presented is whether such a procedure authorizes the officer, consistently with the Fourth Amendment, to conduct a full search of the car. We answer this question "no."

Knowles was stopped in Newton, Iowa, after having been clocked driving 43 miles per hour on a road where the speed limit was 25 miles per hour. The police officer issued a citation to Knowles, although under Iowa law he might have arrested him. The officer then conducted a full search of the car, and under the driver's seat he found a bag of marijuana and a "pot pipe." Knowles was then arrested and charged with violation of state laws dealing with controlled substances.

Before trial, Knowles moved to suppress the evidence so obtained. He argued that the search could not be sustained under the "search incident to arrest" exception recognized in *United States v. Robinson*, . . . because he had not been placed under arrest. At the hearing on the motion to suppress, the police officer conceded that he had neither Knowles' consent nor probable cause to conduct the search. He relied on Iowa law dealing with such searches.

Iowa Code Ann. § 321.485(1)(a) (1997) provides that Iowa peace officers having cause to believe that a person has violated any traffic or motor vehicle equipment law may arrest the person and immediately take the person before a magistrate. Iowa law also authorizes the far more usual practice of issuing a citation in lieu of arrest or in lieu of continued custody after an initial arrest. See Iowa Code Ann. § 805.1(1) (Supp. 1997). Section 805.1(4) provides that the issuance of a citation in lieu of an arrest "does not affect the officer's authority to conduct an otherwise lawful search." The Iowa Supreme Court has interpreted this provision as providing authority to officers to conduct a full-blown search of an automobile and driver in those cases where police elect not to make a custodial arrest and instead issue a citation — that is, a search incident to citation. . . .

Based on this authority, the trial court denied the motion to suppress and found Knowles guilty. The Supreme Court of Iowa, sitting in banc, affirmed by a divided vote [upholding] the constitutionality of the search under a bright-line "search incident to citation" exception to the Fourth Amendment's warrant requirement, reasoning that so long as the arresting officer had probable cause to make a custodial arrest, there need not in fact have been a custodial arrest. We granted certiorari . . . and we now reverse.

In *Robinson*, . . . we noted the two historical rationales for the "search incident to arrest" exception: (1) the need to disarm the suspect in order to take him into custody, and (2) the need to preserve evidence for later use at trial. . . . But neither of these underlying rationales for the search incident to arrest exception is sufficient to justify the search in the present case. . . .

We have recognized that the first rationale — officer safety — is " 'both legitimate and weighty,' " . . . The threat to officer safety from issuing a traffic citation, however, is a good deal less than in the case of a custodial arrest. In *Robinson*, we stated that a custodial arrest involves "danger to an officer" because of "the extended exposure which follows the taking of a suspect into custody and transporting him to the police station." . . . We recognized that "[t]he danger to the police officer flows from the fact of the arrest, and its attendant proximity, stress, and uncertainty, and not from the grounds for the arrest." . . . A routine traffic stop, on the other hand, is a relatively brief encounter and "is more analogous to a so-called '*Terry* stop' . . . than to a formal arrest." . . .

This is not to say that the concern for officer safety is absent in the case of a routine traffic stop. It plainly is not. . . . But while the concern for officer safety in this context may justify the "minimal" additional intrusion of ordering a driver and passenger out of the car, it does not by itself justify the often considerably greater intrusion attending a full field-type search. Even without the search authority Iowa urges, officers have other, independent bases to search for weapons and protect themselves from danger. For example, they may order out of a vehicle both the driver, *Mimms*, . . . and any passengers, *Wilson* . . . ; perform a "pat-down" of a driver and any passengers upon reasonable suspicion that they may be armed and dangerous, *Terry* . . . ; conduct a "*Terry* pat-down" of the passenger compartment of a vehicle upon reasonable suspicion that an occupant is dangerous and may gain immediate control of a weapon, *Michigan v. Long*, . . . ; and even conduct a full search of the passenger compartment, including any containers therein, pursuant to a custodial arrest, *New York v. Belton*. . . .

Nor has Iowa shown the second justification for the authority to search incident to arrest — the need to discover and preserve evidence. Once Knowles was stopped for speeding and issued a citation, all the evidence necessary to prosecute that offense had been obtained. No further evidence of excessive speed was going to be found either on the person of the offender or in the passenger compartment of the car.

Iowa nevertheless argues that a "search incident to citation" is justified because a suspect who is subject to a routine traffic stop may attempt to hide or destroy evidence related to his identity (e.g., a driver's license or vehicle registration), or destroy evidence of another, as yet undetected crime. As for the destruction of evidence relating to identity, if a police officer is not satisfied with the identification furnished by the driver, this may be a basis for arresting him rather than merely issuing a citation. As for destroying evidence of other crimes, the possibility that an officer would stumble onto evidence wholly unrelated to the speeding offense seems remote.

In *Robinson*, we held that the authority to conduct a full field search as incident to an arrest was a "bright-line rule," which was based on the concern for officer safety and destruction or loss of evidence, but which did not depend in every case upon the existence of either concern. Here we are asked to extend that "bright-line rule" to a situation where the concern for officer safety is not present to the same extent and the concern for destruction of evidence is not present at all. We decline to do so. The judgment of the Supreme Court of Iowa is reversed, and the cause remanded for further proceedings not inconsistent with this opinion.

NOTES AND QUESTIONS

(1) While the *rationale* for the search incident to arrest is the protection of safety and the prevention of the destruction of evidence, the Court has never required a particularized showing of these concerns. To this extent, the search incident to arrest exception has been a bright line rule. *Compare New York v. Belton, infra.* Does this decision challenge that assumption, or is its application limited to traffic citations?

(2) The Iowa statute authorized the officer to make an arrest in this case. Had he elected to do so, the safety rationale would have entitled him to search the arrestee. Does this decision encourage officers to make arrests in order to validate an ensuing search? Is any purpose served in this case by invalidating the search? *Compare Washington v. Chrisman*, § 3.04[B], *infra*. An officer's action in opening a car door rather than orally directing the occupant to do so has been held no more intrusive. *State v. Irwin*, 143 Idaho 102, 137 P.3d 1024, 1027-28 (App. 2006).

See also United States v. Meredith, 480 F.3d 366, 370 (5th Cir.), *cert. denied*, 127 S. Ct. 2928 (2007) ("[T]he most reasonable way to serve the officer-safety purpose of *Mimms* and *Wilson* under the circumstances like these is to extend the Court's reasoning to include a minimally necessary visual inspection of a non-exiting occupant while he is still seated in the car. This solution adds the additional benefit of ensuring equal treatment of handicapped and non-handicapped occupants alike.").

(3) When an arrest is illegal under state law, but absent such law would not be constitutionally objectionable, the Fourth Amendment exclusionary rule does not apply. Such was the conclusion of the Supreme Court in *Virginia v. Moore*, 128 S. Ct. 1598 (U.S. 2008). Moore had been arrested for driving on a suspended license. The arrest was supported by probable cause, but Virginia law required the issuance of a summons in such cases. Incident to the arrest, crack cocaine was seized, and Moore was convicted on drug charges. The Virginia Supreme Court reversed the conviction, finding that the seizure violated the Fourth Amendment. A unanimous Supreme Court reversed. While not questioning the power of the state to establish higher standards for legitimate searches, and indeed to exclude evidence gained in violation of those standards, such results were not mandated by the Fourth Amendment.

PENNSYLVANIA v. MIMMS

United States Supreme Court
434 U.S. 106 (1977)

PER CURIAM.

The facts are not in dispute. While on routine patrol, two Philadelphia police officers observed respondent Harry Mimms driving an automobile with an expired license plate. The officers stopped the vehicle for the purpose of issuing a traffic summons. One of the officers approached and asked respondent to step out of the car and produce his owner's card and operator's license. Respondent alighted, whereupon the officer noticed a large bulge under respondent's sports jacket. Fearing that the bulge might be a weapon, the officer frisked respondent and discovered in his waistband a. 38-caliber revolver loaded with five rounds of ammunition. The other occupant of the car was also carrying a. 32-caliber revolver. Respondent was immediately arrested and subsequently indicted for carrying a firearm without a license. His motion to suppress the revolver was denied, and after a trial at which the revolver was introduced into evidence, respondent was convicted on both counts.

The Supreme Court of Pennsylvania reversed respondent's conviction, however, holding that the revolver should have been suppressed because it was seized contrary to the guarantees contained in the Fourth and Fourteenth Amendments to the United States Constitution. The Pennsylvania court did not doubt that the officers acted reasonably in stopping the car. It was also willing to assume, arguendo, that the limited search for weapons was proper once the officer observed the bulge under respondent's coat. But the court nonetheless thought the search constitutionally infirm because the officer's order to respondent to get out of the car was an impermissible "seizure." This was so because the officer could not point to "objective observable facts to support a suspicion that criminal activity was afoot or that the occupants of the vehicle posed a threat to police safety." Since this unconstitutional intrusion led directly to observance of the bulge and to the subsequent "pat-down," the revolver was the fruit of an unconstitutional search, and, in the view of the Supreme Court of Pennsylvania, should have been suppressed.

We do not agree with this conclusion. The touchstone of our analysis under the Fourth Amendment is always "the reasonableness in all the circumstances of the particular governmental invasion of a citizen's personal security." *Terry v. Ohio*. . . . Reasonableness, of course, depends "on a balance between the public interest, and the individual's right to personal security free from arbitrary interference by law officers." *United States v. Brignoni-Ponce*, 422 U.S. 873, 878 (1975).

In this case, unlike *Terry v. Ohio*, there is no question about the propriety of the initial restrictions on respondent's freedom of movement. Respondent was driving an automobile with expired license tags in violation of the Pennsylvania Motor Vehicle Code. Deferring for a moment the legality of the "frisk" once the bulge had been observed, we need presently deal only with the narrow question of whether the order to get out of the car, issued after the driver was lawfully detained, was reasonable and thus permissible under the Fourth Amendment. This inquiry must therefore focus not on the intrusion resulting from the request to stop the vehicle or from the later "pat-down," but on the incremental intrusion resulting from the request to get out of the car once the vehicle was lawfully stopped.

Placing the question in this narrowed frame, we look first to that side of the balance which bears the officer's interest in taking the action that he did. The State freely concedes the officer had no reason to suspect foul play from the particular driver at the time of the stop, there having been nothing unusual or suspicious about his behavior. It was apparently his practice to order all drivers out of their vehicles as a matter of course whenever they had been stopped for a traffic violation. The State argues that this practice was adopted as a precautionary measure to afford a degree of protection to the officer and that it may be justified on that ground. Establishing a face-to-face confrontation diminishes the possibility, otherwise substantial, that the driver can make unobserved movements; this, in turn, reduces the likelihood that the officer will be the victim of an assault.

We think it too plain for argument that the State's proffered justification — the safety of the officer — is both legitimate and weighty. "Certainly it would be unreasonable to require that police officers take unnecessary risks in the performance of their duties." *Terry v. Ohio*. . . . And we have specifically recognized the inordinate risk confronting an officer as he approaches a person seated in an automobile. " 'According to one study, approximately 30% of police shootings occurred when a police officer approached a suspect seated in an automobile.' Bristow, 'Police Officer Shootings — A Tactical Evaluation,' 54 Crim. L. C. & P. S. 93 (1963)." *Adams v. Williams*, 407 U.S. 143, 148 n. 3 (1972). We are aware that not all these assaults occur when issuing traffic summons, but we have before expressly declined to accept the argument that traffic violations necessarily involve less danger to officers than other types of confrontations. *United States v. Robinson*, 414 U.S. 218, 234 (1973). Indeed, it appears "that a significant percentage of murders of police officers occurs when the officers are making traffic stops." *Id.*, at 234 n. 5.

The hazard of accidental injury from passing traffic to an officer standing on the driver's side of the vehicle may also be appreciable in some situations. Rather than conversing while standing exposed to moving traffic, the officer prudently may prefer to ask the driver of the vehicle to step out of the car and off onto the shoulder of the road where the inquiry may be pursued with greater safety to both.

Against this important interest we are asked to weigh the intrusion into the driver's personal liberty occasioned not by the initial stop of the vehicle, which was admittedly justified, but by the order to get out of the car. We think this additional intrusion can only be described as de minimis. The driver is being asked to expose to view very little more of his person than is already exposed. The police have already lawfully decided that the driver shall be briefly detained; the only question is whether he shall spend that period sitting in the driver's seat of his car or standing alongside it. Not only is the insistence of the police on the latter choice not a "serious intrusion upon the sanctity of the person," but it hardly rises to the level of a "petty indignity." *Terry v. Ohio*. . . . What is at most a mere inconvenience cannot prevail when balanced against legitimate concerns for the officer's safety.

There remains the second question of the propriety of the search once the bulge in the jacket was observed. We have as little doubt on this point as on the first; the answer is controlled by *Terry v. Ohio*. . . . In that case we thought the officer justified in conducting a limited search for weapons once he had reasonably concluded that the person whom he had legitimately stopped might be armed and presently dangerous. Under the standard enunciated in that case — whether "the facts available to the officer at the moment of the seizure or the search 'warrant a man of reasonable caution in the belief' that the action taken was appropriate" — there is little question the officer was justified. The bulge in the jacket permitted the officer to conclude that Mimms was armed and thus posed a serious and present danger to the safety of the officer. In these circumstances, any man of "reasonable caution" would likely have conducted the "pat-down."

Mr. Justice Marshall, dissenting.

The Court cannot seriously believe that the risk to the arresting officer is so universal that his safety is always a reasonable justification for ordering a driver out of his car. The commuter on his way home to dinner, the parent driving children to school, the tourist circling the Capitol, or the family on a Sunday afternoon outing hardly pose the same threat as a driver curbed after a high speed chase through a high-crime area late at night. Nor is it universally true that the driver's interest in remaining in the car is negligible. A woman stopped at night may fear for her safety; a person in poor health may object to standing in the cold or rain; another who left home in haste to drive children or spouse to school or to the train may not be fully dressed; an elderly driver who presents no possible threat of violence may regard the police command as nothing more than an arrogant and unnecessary display of authority. Whether viewed from the standpoint of the officer's interest in his own safety, or of the citizen's interest in not being required to obey an arbitrary command, it is perfectly obvious that the millions of traffic stops that occur every year are not fungible.

Until today the law applicable to seizures of a person has required individualized inquiry into the reason for each intrusion, or some comparable guarantee against arbitrary harassment. A factual demonstration of probable cause is required to justify an arrest; an articulable reason to suspect criminal activity and possible violence is needed to justify a stop and frisk. But to eliminate any requirement that an officer be able to explain the reasons for his actions signals an abandonment of effective judicial supervision of this kind of seizure and leaves police discretion utterly without limits. Some citizens will be subjected to this minor indignity while others — perhaps those with more expensive cars, or different bumper stickers, or different-colored skin — may escape it entirely.

NOTES AND QUESTIONS

(1) Unquestionably the officers had probable cause to arrest Mimms for a traffic violation which occurred in their presence. This is not, therefore, a *Terry* case, insofar as finding a sufficient basis for the initiation of the confrontation. Is the issue, absent unique circumstances, whether a traffic arrestee: (a) Can be required to get out of the car? (b) Can be routinely frisked? (c) Can be frisked upon the observation of a bulge? (d) Can be searched incident to the arrest?

(2) In *Maryland v. Wilson*, 519 U.S. 408 (1997), Chief Justice Rehnquist, speaking for a 7-2 majority, held that "as a matter of course" a police officer may order passengers as well as the driver to exit a stopped vehicle. Justice Stevens, joined by Justice Kennedy, dissented. They objected to the breadth of the rule which applied "equally to stops in which there is not even a scintilla of evidence of any potential risk to the police officer."

Lower courts have interpreted *Wilson* to permit an officer to require a passenger to stay within the vehicle as well. *See United States v. Moorefield*, 111 F.3d 10 (3d

Cir. 1997); *Carter v. State*, 229 Ga. App. 417, 494 S.E.2d 108 (1997); *People v. Gonzalez*, 184 Ill. 2d 402, 704 N.E.2d 375 (1998), *cert. denied*, 528 U.S. 825 (1999).

(3) The reaction of state courts to *Mimms* has not been entirely enthusiastic. Consider, for example, *People v. Satchell*, 81 Cal. App. 3d 347, 146 Cal. Rptr. 307 (1978):

> First, *Mimms* . . . certainly did not decide that a routine traffic stop authorizes a pat-down of the occupants of the vehicle. . . . Second, at this point we simply do not know whether *Mimms* will be held to accord with " article I, section 13, of the California Constitution, which requires a more exacting standard for cases arising within this state."

UNITED STATES v. CHADWICK

United States Supreme Court
433 U.S. 1 (1977)

MR. CHIEF JUSTICE BURGER delivered the opinion of the Court.

We granted certiorari in this case to decide whether a search warrant is required before federal agents may open a locked footlocker which they have lawfully seized at the time of the arrest of its owners, when there is probable cause to believe the footlocker contains contraband.

(1)

On May 8, 1973, Amtrak railroad officials in San Diego observed respondents Gregory Machado and Bridget Leary load a brown footlocker onto a train bound for Boston. Their suspicions were aroused when they noticed that the trunk was unusually heavy for its size, and that it was leaking talcum powder, a substance often used to mask the odor of marihuana or hashish. Because Machado matched a profile used to spot drug traffickers, the railroad officials reported these circumstances to federal agents in San Diego, who in turn relayed the information, together with detailed descriptions of Machado and the footlocker, to their counterparts in Boston.

When the train arrived in Boston two days later, federal narcotics agents were on hand. Though the officers had not obtained an arrest or search warrant, they had with them a police dog trained to detect marihuana. The agents identified Machado and Leary and kept them under surveillance as they claimed their suitcases and the footlocker, which had been transported by baggage cart from the train to the departure area. Machado and Leary lifted the footlocker from the baggage cart, placed it on the floor and sat down on it.

The agents then released the dog near the footlocker. Without alerting respondents, the dog signaled the presence of a controlled substance inside. Respondent Chadwick then joined Machado and Leary, and they engaged an attendant to move the footlocker outside to Chadwick's waiting automobile. Machado, Chadwick and the attendant together lifted the 200-pound footlocker into the trunk of the car, while Leary waited in the front seat. At that point, while the trunk of the car was still open and before the car engine had been started, the officers arrested all three. A search disclosed no weapons, but the keys to the footlocker were apparently taken from Machado.

Respondents were taken to the federal building in Boston; the agents followed with Chadwick's car and the footlocker. As the Government concedes, from the moment of respondents' arrests at about 9 p.m., the footlocker remained under the exclusive control of law enforcement officers at all times. The footlocker and luggage were placed in the federal building, where, as one of the agents later testified, "there was no risk that whatever was contained in the footlocker trunk would be removed by the defendants or their associates." The agents had no reason to believe that the footlocker contained explosives or other inherently dangerous items, or that it contained evidence which would lose its value unless the footlocker were opened at once. Facilities were readily available in which the footlocker could have been stored securely; it is not contended that there was any exigency calling for an immediate search.

At the federal building an hour and a half after the arrests, the agents opened the footlocker and luggage. They did not obtain respondents' consent; they did not secure a search warrant. The footlocker was locked with a padlock and a regular trunk lock. It is unclear whether it was opened with the keys taken from respondent Machado, or by other means. Large amounts of marihuana were found in the footlocker.

In this case, important Fourth Amendment privacy interests were at stake. By placing personal effects inside a double-locked footlocker, respondents manifested an expectation that the contents would remain free from public examination. No less than one who locks the doors of his home against intruders, one who safeguards his personal possessions in this manner is due the protection of the Fourth Amendment Warrant Clause. There being no exigency, it was unreasonable for the Government to conduct this search without the safeguards a judicial warrant provides.

. . .

(4)

The Government does not contend that the footlocker's brief contact with Chadwick's car makes this an automobile search, but it is argued that the rationale of our automobile search cases demonstrates the reasonableness of permitting warrantless searches of luggage; the Government views such luggage as analogous to motor vehicles for Fourth Amendment purposes. It is true that, like the footlocker in issue here, automobiles are "effects" under the Fourth Amendment, and searches and seizures of automobiles are therefore subject to the constitutional standard of reasonableness. But this Court has recognized significant differences between motor vehicles and other property which permit warrantless searches of automobiles in circumstances in which warrantless searches would not be reasonable in other contexts. . . .

. . .

The answer lies in the diminished expectation of privacy which surrounds the automobile: "One has a lesser expectation of privacy in a motor vehicle because its function is transportation and it seldom serves as one's residence or as the repository of personal effects. . . . It travels public thoroughfares where both its occupants and its contents are in plain view.". . .

The factors which diminish the privacy aspects of an automobile do not apply to respondents' footlocker. Luggage contents are not open to public view, except as a condition to a border entry or common carrier travel; nor is luggage subject to regular inspections and official scrutiny on a continuing basis. Unlike an automobile, whose primary function is transportation, luggage is intended as a repository of personal effects. In sum, a person's expectations of privacy in personal luggage are substantially greater than in an automobile.

Nor does the footlocker's mobility justify dispensing with the added protections of the Warrant Clause. Once the federal agents had seized it at the railroad station and had safely transferred it to the Boston federal building under their exclusive control, there was not the slightest danger that the footlocker or its contents could have been removed before a valid search warrant could be obtained. The initial seizure and detention of the footlocker, the validity of which respondents do not contest, were sufficient to guard against any risk that evidence might be lost. With the footlocker safely immobilized, it was unreasonable to undertake the additional and greater intrusion of a search without a warrant.[31]

Finally, the Government urges that the Constitution permits the warrantless search of any property in the possession of a person arrested in public, so long as there is probable cause to believe that the property contains contraband or evidence of crime. Although recognizing that the footlocker was not within respondents' immediate control, the Government insists that the search was reasonable because the footlocker was seized contemporaneously with respondents' arrests and was searched as soon thereafter as was practicable. The reasons justifying search in a custodial arrest are quite different. When a custodial arrest is made, there is always some danger that the person arrested may seek to use a weapon, or that evidence may be concealed or destroyed. To safeguard himself and others, and to prevent the loss of evidence, it has been held reasonable for the arresting officer to conduct a prompt, warrantless "search of the arrestee's person and the area within his 'immediate control'— construing that phrase to mean the area from within which he might gain possession of a weapon or destructible evidence." *Chimel v. California*. . . . See also *Terry v. Ohio*. . . .

Such searches may be conducted without a warrant, and they may also be made

---

[31] [8] Respondents' principal privacy interest in the footlocker was of course not in the container itself, which was exposed to public view, but in its contents. A search of the interior was therefore a far greater intrusion into Fourth Amendment values than the impoundment of the footlocker. Though surely a substantial infringement with respondent's use and possession, the seizure did not diminish respondents' legitimate expectation that the footlocker's contents would remain private.

It was the greatly reduced expectation of privacy in the automobile, coupled with the transportation function of the vehicle, which made the Court in *Chambers* unwilling to decide whether an immediate search of an automobile, or its seizure and indefinite immobilization, constituted a greater interference with the rights of the owner. This is clearly not the case with locked luggage.

whether or not there is probable cause to believe that the person arrested may have a weapon or is about to destroy evidence. The potential dangers lurking in all custodial arrests make warrantless searches of items within the "immediate control" area reasonable without requiring the arresting officer to calculate the probability that weapons or destructible evidence may be involved. *United States v. Robinson* . . . ; *Terry v. Ohio*. . . . However, warrantless searches of luggage or other property seized at the time of an arrest cannot be justified as incident to that arrest either if the "search is remote in time or place from the arrest," . . . or no exigency exists. Once law enforcement officers have reduced luggage or other personal property not immediately associated with the person of the arrestee to their exclusive control, and there is no longer any danger that the arrestee might gain access to the property to seize a weapon or destroy evidence, a search of that property is no longer an incident of the arrest.[32]

Here the search was conducted more than an hour after federal agents had gained exclusive control of the footlocker and long after respondents were securely in custody; the search therefore cannot be viewed as incidental to the arrest or as justified by any other exigency. Even though on this record the issuance of a warrant by a judicial officer was reasonably predictable, a line must be drawn. In our view, when no exigency is shown to support the need for an immediate search, the Warrant Clause places the line at the point where the property to be searched comes under the exclusive dominion of police authority. Respondents were therefore entitled to the protection of the Warrant Clause with the evaluation of a neutral magistrate, before their privacy interest in the contents of the footlocker were invaded.[33]

Mr. Justice Blackmun, with whom Mr. Justice Rehnquist joins, dissenting.

The approach taken by the Court has the perverse result of allowing fortuitous circumstances to control the outcome of the present case. The agents probably could have avoided having the footlocker search held unconstitutional either by delaying the arrest for a few minutes or by conducting the search on the spot rather than back at their office. Probable cause for the arrest was present from the time respondents Machado and Leary were seated on the footlocker inside Boston's South Station and the agents' dog signalled the presence of marihuana. Rather than make an arrest at this moment, the agents commendably sought to determine the possible involvement of others in the illegal scheme. They waited a short time until respondent Chadwick arrived and the footlocker had been loaded into the trunk of his car, and then made the arrest. But if the agents had postponed the arrest just a few minutes longer until the respondents started to drive away, then the car could

---

32 [9] Of course, there may be other justifications for a warrantless search of luggage taken from a suspect at the time of his arrest: for example, if officers have reason to believe that luggage contains some immediately dangerous instrumentality, such as explosives, it would be foolhardy to transport it to the station house without opening the luggage and disarming the weapon. See, e.g., United States v. Johnson, 467 F.2d 630, 639 (CA2 1972).

33 [10] Unlike searches of the person, *United States v. Robinson*, 414 U.S. 218 (1973); *United States v. Edwards*, 415 U.S. 800 (1974), searches of possessions within an arrestee's immediate control cannot be justified by any reduced expectations of privacy caused by the arrest. Respondents' privacy interest in the contents of the footlocker was not eliminated simply because they were under arrest.

have been seized, taken to the agents' office, and all its contents — including the footlocker — searched without a warrant.

Alternatively, the agents could have made a search of the footlocker at the time and place of the arrests. Machado and Leary were standing next to an open automobile trunk containing the footlocker, and thus it was within the area of their "immediate control." And certainly the footlocker would have been properly subject to search at the time if the arrest had occurred a few minutes earlier while Machado and Leary were seated on it.

NOTES AND QUESTIONS

(1) Is the dissent correct in its assumption that the seizure would have been sustained had the search occurred either coincidental with the arrest, or after the automobile was in motion? As to the latter possibility, see *Arkansas v. Sanders*, 442 U.S. 753 (1979).

(2) Should *Chadwick* preclude the warrantless search of a brief case? a purse? a tool box? a paper bag? a cigarette pack?

(3) In *Illinois v. Lafayette*, 462 U.S. 640 (1983), at the time of his arrest for disturbing the peace, the defendant had been carrying a shoulder bag. At the police station an officer removed the contents and found illegal amphetamines inside a cigarette case. The Court held that it was "entirely proper for police to remove and list or inventory property found on the person or in possession of an arrested person who is to be jailed," and the inspection was properly extended to "every item carried on or by a person who has lawfully been taken into custody." The *Chadwick* decision was not referred to in the majority opinion. Is the implication of this decision that the search in *Chadwick* would have been reasonable if done as part of an inventory? Or is the distinction to be found in the privacy expectation in an accessible shoulder bag as compared to a padlocked footlocker?

ARIZONA v. GANT

United States Supreme Court
556 U.S. 332 (2009)

JUSTICE STEVENS delivered the opinion of the Court.

After Rodney Gant was arrested for driving with a suspended license, handcuffed, and locked in the back of a patrol car, police officers searched his car and discovered cocaine in the pocket of a jacket on the backseat. Because Gant could not have accessed his car to retrieve weapons or evidence at the time of the search, the Arizona Supreme Court held that the search-incident-to-arrest exception to the Fourth Amendment's warrant requirement, as defined in *Chimel* . . . , and applied to vehicle searches in *New York v. Belton* . . . , did not justify the search in this case. We agree with that conclusion.

Under *Chimel*, police may search incident to arrest only the space within an arrestee's " 'immediate control,' " meaning "the area from within which he might gain possession of a weapon or destructible evidence." . . . The safety and evidentiary justifications underlying *Chimel*'s reaching-distance rule determine *Belton*'s scope. Accordingly, we hold that *Belton* does not authorize a vehicle search incident to a recent occupant's arrest after the arrestee has been secured and cannot access the interior of the vehicle. Consistent with the holding in *Thornton v. United States*, . . . and following the suggestion in Justice Scalia's opinion concurring in the judgment in that case, . . . we also conclude that circumstances unique to the automobile context justify a search incident to arrest when it is reasonable to believe that evidence of the offense of arrest might be found in the vehicle.

I

On August 25, 1999, acting on an anonymous tip that the residence at 2524 North Walnut Avenue was being used to sell drugs, Tucson police officers Griffith and Reed knocked on the front door and asked to speak to the owner. Gant answered the door and, after identifying himself, stated that he expected the owner to return later. The officers left the residence and conducted a records check, which revealed that Gant's driver's license had been suspended and there was an outstanding warrant for his arrest for driving with a suspended license.

When the officers returned to the house that evening, they found a man near the back of the house and a woman in a car parked in front of it. After a third officer arrived, they arrested the man for providing a false name and the woman for possessing drug paraphernalia. Both arrestees were handcuffed and secured in separate patrol cars when Gant arrived. The officers recognized his car as it entered the driveway, and Officer Griffith confirmed that Gant was the driver by shining a flashlight into the car as it drove by him. Gant parked at the end of the driveway, got out of his car, and shut the door. Griffith, who was about 30 feet away, called to Gant, and they approached each other, meeting 10-to-12 feet from Gant's car. Griffith immediately arrested Gant and handcuffed him.

Because the other arrestees were secured in the only patrol cars at the scene, Griffith called for backup. When two more officers arrived, they locked Gant in the backseat of their vehicle. After Gant had been handcuffed and placed in the back of a patrol car, two officers searched his car: One of them found a gun, and the other discovered a bag of cocaine in the pocket of a jacket on the backseat.

Gant was charged with two offenses — possession of a narcotic drug for sale and possession of drug paraphernalia (*i.e.*, the plastic bag in which the cocaine was found). He moved to suppress the evidence seized from his car on the ground that the warrantless search violated the Fourth Amendment. Among other things, Gant argued that *Belton* did not authorize the search of his vehicle because he posed no threat to the officers after he was handcuffed in the patrol car and because he was arrested for a traffic offense for which no evidence could be found in his vehicle. When asked at the suppression hearing why the search was conducted, Officer Griffith responded: "Because the law says we can do it." . . .

The trial court rejected the State's contention that the officers had probable cause to search Gant's car for contraband when the search began, . . . but it denied the motion to suppress. Relying on the fact that the police saw Gant commit the crime of driving without a license and apprehended him only shortly after he exited his car, the court held that the search was permissible as a search incident to arrest. . . . A jury found Gant guilty on both drug counts, and he was sentenced to a 3-year term of imprisonment.

After protracted state-court proceedings, the Arizona Supreme Court concluded that the search of Gant's car was unreasonable within the meaning of the Fourth Amendment. . . . The court distinguished *Belton* as a case concerning the permissible scope of a vehicle search incident to arrest and concluded that it did not answer "the threshold question whether the police may conduct a search incident to arrest at all once the scene is secure." . . . Relying on our earlier decision in *Chimel*, the court observed that the search-incident-to-arrest exception to the warrant requirement is justified by interests in officer safety and evidence preservation. . . . When "the justifications underlying *Chimel* no longer exist because the scene is secure and the arrestee is handcuffed, secured in the back of a patrol car, and under the supervision of an officer," the court concluded, a "warrantless search of the arrestee's car cannot be justified as necessary to protect the officers at the scene or prevent the destruction of evidence." . . . Accordingly, the court held that the search of Gant's car was unreasonable. . . .

. . .

In [*New York v.*] *Belton* [,453 U.S. 454 (1981)], we considered *Chimel*'s application to the automobile context. A lone police officer in that case stopped a speeding car in which Belton was one of four occupants. While asking for the driver's license and registration, the officer smelled burnt marijuana and observed an envelope on the car floor marked "Supergold"-a name he associated with marijuana. Thus having probable cause to believe the occupants had committed a drug offense, the officer ordered them out of the vehicle, placed them under arrest, and patted them down. Without handcuffing the arrestees, the officer " 'split them up into four separate areas of the Thruway . . . so they would not be in physical touching area of each other' " and searched the vehicle, including the pocket of a jacket on the backseat, in which he found cocaine. . . .

The New York Court of Appeals found the search unconstitutional, concluding that after the occupants were arrested, the vehicle and its contents were "safely within the exclusive custody and control of the police." . . . The State asked this Court to consider whether the exception recognized in *Chimel* permits an officer to search "a jacket found inside the automobile while the automobile's four occupants, all under arrest, are standing unsecured around the vehicle." . . . We granted certiorari because "courts [ha[d] found no workable definition of 'the area within the immediate control of the arrestee' when that area arguably includes the interior of an automobile." . . .

[W]e held that when an officer lawfully arrests "the occupant of an automobile, he may, as a contemporaneous incident of that arrest, search the passenger compartment of the automobile" and any containers therein. . . . That holding was based in large part on our assumption "that articles inside the relatively narrow compass of the passenger compartment of an automobile are in fact generally, even if not inevitably, within 'the area into which an arrestee might reach.'" . . .

The Arizona Supreme Court read our decision in *Belton* as merely delineating "the proper scope of a search of the interior of an automobile" incident to an arrest. . . . That is, *when* the passenger compartment is within an arrestee's reaching distance, *Belton* supplies the generalization that the entire compartment and any containers therein may be reached. On that view of *Belton*, the state court concluded that the search of Gant's car was unreasonable because Gant clearly could not have accessed his car at the time of the search. It also found that no other exception to the warrant requirement applied in this case.

Gant now urges us to adopt the reading of *Belton* followed by the Arizona Supreme Court.

III

Despite the textual and evidentiary support for the Arizona Supreme Court's reading on *Belton*, our opinion has been widely understood to allow a vehicle search incident to the arrest of a recent occupant even if there is no possibility the arrestee could gain access to the vehicle at the time of the search. . . .

Under this broad reading of *Belton*, a vehicle search would be authorized incident to every arrest of a recent occupant notwithstanding that in most cases the vehicle's passenger compartment will not be with the arrestee's reach at the time of the search. To read *Belton* as authorizing a vehicle search incident to every recent occupant's arrest would thus untether the rule from the justifications underlying the *Chimel* exception — a result clearly incompatible with our statement in *Belton* that it "in no way alters the fundamental principles established in the *Chimel* case regarding the basic scope of searches incident to lawful custodial arrests." . . . Accordingly, we reject this reading of *Belton* and hold that the *Chimel* rationale authorizes police to search a vehicle incident to a recent occupant's arrest only when the arrestee is unsecured and within reaching distance of the passenger compartment at the time of the search.

Although it does not follow from *Chimel*, we also conclude that circumstances unique to the vehicle context justify a search incident to a lawful arrest when it is "reasonable to believe evidence relevant to the crime of arrest might be found in the vehicle." *Thornton* [*v. United States*, 541 U.S. 615, 632 (2004)] . . . (Scalia, J., concurring in judgment). In many cases, as when a recent occupant is arrested for a traffic violation, there will be no reasonable basis to believe the vehicle contains relevant evidence. See, e.g., . . . *Knowles v. Iowa*. . . . But in others, including *Belton* and *Thornton*, the offense of arrest will supply a basis for searching the passenger compartment of an arrestee's vehicle and any containers therein.

Neither the possibility of access nor the likelihood of discovering offense-related evidence authorized the search in this case. Unlike in *Belton*, which involved a single officer confronted with four unsecured arrestees, the five officers in this case outnumbered the three arrestees, all of whom had been handcuffed and secured in separate patrol cars before the officers searched Gant's car. Under those circumstances, Gant clearly was not within reaching distance of his car at the time of the search. An evidentiary basis for the search was also lacking in this case. Whereas Belton and Thornton were arrested for drug offenses, Gant was arrested for driving with a suspended license — an offense for which police could not expect to find evidence in the passenger compartment of Gant's car. Cf. *Knowles*,. . . . Because police could not reasonably have believed either that Gant could have accessed his car at the time of the search or that evidence of the offense for which he was arrested might have been found therein, the search in this case was unreasonable.

IV

The State does not seriously disagree with the Arizona Supreme Court's conclusion that Gant could not have accessed his vehicle at the time of the search, but it nevertheless asks us to uphold the search of his vehicle under the broad reading of *Belton* discussed above. The State argues that *Belton* searches are reasonable regardless of the possibility of access in a given case because that expansive rule correctly balances law enforcement interests, including the interest in a bright-line rule, with an arrestee's limited privacy interest in this vehicle.

For several reasons, we reject the State's argument. First, the State seriously undervalues the privacy interests at stake. Although we have recognized that a motorist's privacy interest in his vehicle is less substantial than in his home, . . . the former interest is nevertheless important and deserving of constitutional protection,. . . . It is particularly significant that *Belton* searches authorize police officers to search not just the passenger compartment but every purse, briefcase, or other container within that space. A rule that gives police the power to conduct such a search whenever an individual is caught committing a traffic offense, when there is no basis for believing evidence of the offense might be found in the vehicle, creates a serious and recurring threat to privacy of countless individuals. Indeed, the character of that threat implicates the central concern underlying the Fourth Amendment — the concern about giving police officers unbridled discretion to rummage at will among a person's private effects.

At the same time as it undervalues these privacy concerns, the State exaggerates the clarity that its reading of *Belton* provides. Courts that have read *Belton* expansively are at odds regarding how close in time to the arrest and how proximate to the arrestee's vehicle an officer's first contact with the arrestee must be to bring the encounter within *Belton*'s purview and whether a search is reasonable when it commences or continues after the arrestee has been removed from the scene. The rule has thus generated a great deal of uncertainty, particularly for a rule touted as providing a "bright line."

Contrary to the State's suggestion, a broad reading of *Belton* is also unnecessary to protect law enforcement safety and evidentiary interests. Under our view, *Belton* and *Thornton* permit an officer to conduct a vehicle search when an arrestee is within reaching distance of the vehicle or it is reasonable to believe the vehicle contains evidence of the offense of arrest. Other established exceptions to the warrant requirement authorize a vehicle search under additional circumstances when safety or evidentiary concerns demand. For instance, *Michigan v. Long*, . . . permits an officer to search a vehicle's passenger compartment when he has reasonable suspicion that an individual, whether or not the arrestee, is "dangerous" and might access the vehicle to "gain immediate control of weapons." . . .

. . . Construing *Belton* broadly to allow vehicle searches incident to any arrest would serve no purpose except to provide a police entitlement, and it is anathema to the Fourth Amendment to permit a warrantless search on that basis. For these reasons, we are unpersuaded by the State's arguments that a broad reading of *Belton* would meaningfully further law enforcement interests and justify a substantial intrusion on individuals' privacy.

. . .

VI

Police may search a vehicle incident to a recent occupant's arrest only if the arrestee is within reaching distance of the passenger compartment at the time of the search or it is reasonable to believe the vehicle contains evidence of the offense of arrest. When these justifications are absent, a search of an arrestee's vehicle will be unreasonable unless police obtain a warrant or show that another exception to the warrant requirement applies. The Arizona Supreme Court correctly held that this case involve an unreasonable search. Accordingly the judgment of the State Supreme Court is affirmed.

Justice Scalia, concurring.

To determine what is an "unreasonable" search within the meaning of the Fourth Amendment, we look first to the historical practices the Framers sought to preserve; if those provide inadequate guidance, we apply traditional standards of reasonableness. . . . Since the historical scope of officers' authority to search vehicles incident to arrest is uncertain, . . . traditional standards of reasonableness govern. It is abundantly clear that those standards do not justify what I take to be the rule set forth in *New York v. Belton*, . . . and *Thornton*: that arresting officers may always search an arrestee's vehicle in order to protect themselves from hidden weapons. When an arrest is made in connection with a roadside stop, police virtually always have a less intrusive and more effective means of ensuring their safety — and a means that is virtually always employed: ordering the arrestee away from the vehicle, patting him down in the open, handcuffing him, and placing him in the squad car. . . .

Justice Stevens acknowledges that an officer-safety rationale cannot justify all vehicle searches incident to arrest, but asserts that that is not the rule *Belton* and *Thornton* adopted. (As described above, I read those cases differently.) Justice Stevens would therefore retain the application of *Chimel* . . . in the car-search context but would apply in the future what he believes our cases held in the past: that officers making a roadside stop may search the vehicle so long as the "arrestee is within reaching distance of the passenger compartment at the time of the search." . . . I believe that this standard fails to provide the needed guidance to arresting officers and also leaves much room for manipulation, inviting officers to leave the scene unsecured (at least where dangerous suspects are not involved) in order to conduct a vehicle search. In my view we should simply abandon the *Belton-Thornton* charade of officer safety and overrule those cases. I would hold that a vehicle search incident to arrest is *ipso facto* "reasonable" only when the object of the search is evidence of the crime for which the arrest was made, or of another crime that the officer has probable cause to believe occurred. Because respondent was arrested for driving without a license (a crime for which no evidence could be expected to be found in the vehicle), I would hold in the present case that the search was unlawful. . . .

No other Justice, however, shares my view that application of *Chimel* in this context should be entirely abandoned. It seems to me unacceptable for the Court to come forth with a 4-to-1-to-4 opinion that leaves the governing rule uncertain. I am therefore confronted with the choice of either leaving the current understanding of *Belton* and *Thornton* in effect, or acceding to what seems to me the artificial narrowing of these cases adopted by Justice Stevens. The latter, as I have said, does not provide the degree of certainty I think desirable in this field; but the former opens the field to what I think are plainly unconstitutional searches — which is the greater evil. I therefore join the opinion of the Court.

[JUSTICE BREYER dissented separately.]

JUSTICE ALITO, with whom THE CHIEF JUSTICE and JUSTICE KENNEDY join, and with whom JUSTICE BREYER joins except as to Part II-E, dissenting.

Twenty-eight years ago, in *New York v. Belton*, . . . this Court held that "when a policeman has made a lawful custodial arrest of the occupant of an automobile, he may, as a contemporaneous incident of that arrest, search the passenger compartment of that automobile." . . . Five years ago, in *Thornton v. United States*, . . . — a case involving a situation not materially distinguishable from the situation here — the Court not only reaffirmed but extended the holding of *Belton*, making it applicable to recent occupants. Today's decision effectively overrules those important decisions, even though respondent Gant has not asked us to do so.

To take the place of the overruled precedents, the Court adopts a new two-part rule under which a police officer who arrests a vehicle occupant or recent occupant may search the passenger compartment if (1) the arrestee is within reaching distance of the vehicle at the time of the search or (2) the officer has reason to believe that the vehicle contains evidence of the offense of arrest. . . . The first part of this new rule may endanger arresting officers and is truly endorsed by only four Justices; Justice Scalia joins solely for the purpose of avoiding a "4-to-1-to-4 opinion." . . . The second part of the new rule is taken from Justice Scalia's separate opinion in *Thornton* without any independent explanation of its origin or justification and is virtually certain to confuse law enforcement officers and judges for some time to come. The Court's decision will cause the suppression of evidence gathered in many searches carried out in good-faith reliance on well-settled case law, and although the Court purports to base its analysis on the landmark decision in *Chimel v. California*, . . . the Court's reasoning undermines *Chimel*. I would follow *Belton*, and I therefore respectfully dissent.

I

Although the Court refuses to acknowledge that it is overruling *Belton* and *Thornton*, there can be no doubt that it does so. . . .

The precise holding in *Belton* could hardly be clearer. The Court stated unequivocally: "[W]e hold that when a policeman has made a lawful custodial arrest of the occupant of an automobile, he may, as a contemporaneous incident of that arrest, search the passenger compartment of that automobile." . . .

Despite this explicit statement, the opinion of the Court in the present case curiously suggests that *Belton* may reasonably be read as adopting a holding that is narrower than the one explicitly set out in the *Belton* opinion, namely, that an officer arresting a vehicle occupant may search the passenger compartment "*when* the passenger compartment is within an arrestee's reaching distance." . . .

II

Because the Court has substantially overruled *Belton* and *Thornton*, the Court must explain why its departure from the usual rule of *stare decisis* is justified. . . .

C

Workability. The *Belton* rule has not proved to be unworkable. On the contrary, the rule was adopted for the express purpose of providing a test that would be relatively easy for police officers and judges to apply. The Court correctly notes that even the *Belton* rule is not perfectly clear in all situations. Specifically, it is sometimes debatable whether a search is or is not contemporaneous with an arrest, but that problem is small in comparison with the problems that the Court's new two-part rule will produce.

The first part of the Court's new rule — which permits the search of a vehicle's passenger compartment if it is within an arrestee's reach at the time of the search — reintroduces the same sort of case-by-case, fact-specific decisionmaking that the *Belton* rule was adopted to avoid. As the situation in *Belton* illustrated, there are cases in which it is unclear whether an arrestee could retrieve a weapon or evidence in the passenger compartment of a car.

Even more serious problems will also result from the second part of the Court's rule, which requires officers making roadside arrests to determine whether there is reason to believe that the vehicle contains evidence of the crime of the arrest. What this rule permits in a variety of situation is entirely unclear. . . .

E

Bad reasoning. The Court is harshly critical of *Belton*'s reasoning, but the problem that the Court perceives cannot be remedied simply by overruling *Belton. Belton* represented only a modest — and quite defensible — extension of *Chimel*, as I understand that decision.

Prior to *Chimel*, the Court's precedents permitted an arresting officer to search the area within an arrestee's "possession" and "control" for the purpose of gathering evidence. . . . Based on this "abstract doctrine," . . . the Court had sustained searches that extended far beyond an arrestee's grabbing area. . . .

The *Chimel* Court, in an opinion written by Justice Stewart, overruled these cases. Concluding that there are only two justifications for a warrantless search incident to arrest — officer safety and the preservation of evidence — the Court stated that such a search must be confined to "the arrestee's person" and "the area from within which he might gain possession of a weapon or destructible evidence." . . .

Unfortunately, *Chimel* did not say whether "the area from within which [an arrestee] might gain possession of a weapon or destructible evidence" is to be measured at the time of the arrest or at the time of the search, but unless the *Chimel* rule was meant to be a specialty rule, applicable to only a few unusual cases, the Court must have intended for this area to be measured at the time of arrest.

This is so because the Court can hardly have failed to appreciate the following two facts. First, in the great majority of cases, an officer making an arrest is able to handcuff the arrestee and remove him to a secure place before conducting a search incident to the arrest. . . . Second, because it is safer for an arresting officer to secure an arrestee before searching, it is likely that this is what arresting officers do in the great majority of cases. (And it appears, not surprisingly, that this is in fact the prevailing practice.) Thus, if the area within an arrestee's reach were assessed, not at the time of arrest, but at the time of the search, the *Chimel* rule would rarely come into play. . . .

F

The Court, however, does not reexamine *Chimel* and thus leaves the law relating to searches incident to arrest in a confused and unstable state. The first part of the Court's new two-part rule — which permits an arresting officer to search the area within an arrestee's reach at the time of the search — applies, at least for now, only to vehicle occupants and recent occupants, but there is no logical reason why the same rule should not apply to all arrestees.

The second part of the Court's new rule, which the Court takes uncritically from Justice Scalia's separate opinion in *Thornton*, raises doctrinal and practical problems that the Court makes no effort to address. Why, for example, is the standard for this type of evidence-gathering search "reason to believe" rather than probable cause? And why is this type of search restricted to evidence of the offense of arrest? It is true that an arrestee's vehicle is probably more likely to contain evidence of the crime of arrest than of some other crime, but if reason-to-believe is the governing standard for an evidence-gathering search incident to arrest, it is not easy to see why an officer should not be able to search when the officer has reason to believe that the vehicle in question possesses evidence of a crime other than the crime of arrest.

Nor is it easy to see why an evidence-gathering search incident to arrest should be restricted to the passenger compartment. The *Belton* rule was limited in this way because the passenger compartment was considered to be the area that vehicle occupants can generally reach, . . . but since the second part of the new rule is not based on officer safety or the preservation of evidence, the ground for this limitation is obscure.

NOTES AND QUESTIONS

(1) With *Gant*, the *Belton/Thornton* rule concerning searches incident to arrests in, or in the proximity of, vehicles becomes two rules. First, the Court holds that the mere arrest of the recent occupant of a vehicle does not support a search of the vehicle "after the arrestee has been secured and cannot access the interior of the vehicle." In *Belton*, the Court had held "that when a policeman has made a lawful custodial arrest of the occupant of an automobile, he may, as contemporaneous incident of that arrest, search the passenger compartment of that automobile." In *Thornton*, it held, in the interest of a "clear rule" that "[o]nce an officer determines that there is probable cause to make an arrest, it is reasonable to allow officers to ensure their safety and to preserve evidence by searching the entire passenger compartment." The *Gant* Court submits that in this regard its decision is consistent with *Belton* and *Thornton*. Is it?

(2) The second rule from *Gant* is completely independent of the first. "[C]ircumstances unique to the automobile context justify a search incident to arrest when it is reasonable to believe that evidence of the offense of arrest might be found in the vehicle." Later, the Court limits this authority to the passenger compartment of the arrestee's vehicle. Justice Alito, dissenting, finds this rule puzzling in two respects: First, because this authority is not tethered to the security rationale of *Belton*, nor is it confined to evidence in plain view, why shouldn't the trunk of the vehicle be searchable as well? Second, the search incident to the arrest is no longer automatic, as it appeared to be under *Belton*. At the same time, it does not require probable cause. Instead, the Court employs a previously unused test — reason to believe that evidence of the offense for which the arrest was made may be found in the vehicle. What is to be made of this? Does it lie somewhere between suspicion and probable cause?

(3) Vehicle searches, to be examined later, are an exception to the warrant requirement but normally require probable cause. *Gant* leads to the anomalous result that incident to an arrest, the interior of the vehicle, may be searched with reason to believe, but the trunk can only be searched with probable cause. Could a "reason to believe" search produce evidence within the car which then would provide "probable cause" to search the trunk for more?

(4) It would appear that the standard for vehicle arrest incident searches and arrest incident searches generally (*i.e.*, *Chimel* searches) are also now inconsistent. Should the *Chimel* rule be revised to limit its application only to cases in which the arrestee is not under police control, or is Justice Alito's interpretation of *Chimel* correct, that implicitly the Court must have been defining the search area at the time of the arrest, not at the time of the search? More importantly, should *Chimel* searches beyond security concerns only be legitimate when the arresting officers have reason to believe that evidence of the crime for which the arrest was made will be discovered? *Compare United States v. Shakir*, 616 F.3d 315, 319–20 (3d Cir.), *cert. denied*, 131 S. Ct. 841 (2010) ("The *Gant* Court expressly stated its desire to keep the rule of *Belton* tethered to 'the justifications underlying the *Chimel* exception,'. . . and *Chimel* did not involve a car search."), *with People v. Coates*, 266 P.3d 397, 399 (Colo. 2011) ("Although the Court in *Gant* clarified the bases for and scope of a search incident in the vehicle context, it did not purport to alter the

search-incident-to-arrest doctrine outside that context.").

(5) Justice Scalia's position is ambivalent in that he would prefer to overrule *Belton* and *Thornton*, but finds no support from any of the other justices for this solution. He therefore signs onto the majority opinion, finding it "unacceptable" to "leave[] the governing rule uncertain." Is this position defensible, if in fact he finds the holding of the majority unprincipled? Justice Alito suggests that, notwithstanding Justice Scalia's candor, the fact remains that this is a 4-1-4 decision.

(6) The majority opinion chides *Belton* for not being the "bright line" holding that it is purported to be. In fact, there have been few rules of search and seizure easier to apply than the broadly understood interpretation of *Belton*, that if an individual is arrested in a car, the interior of car can be searched. The only significant ambiguity appeared to be effectively dealt with in *Thornton*. Will the *Gant* standard be more or less difficult in application than the standard it replaced?

[B] Plain View

ARIZONA v. HICKS

United States Supreme Court
480 U.S. 321 (1987)

JUSTICE SCALIA delivered the opinion of the Court.

In *Coolidge v. New Hampshire*, 403 U.S. 443 (1971), we said that in certain circumstances a warrantless seizure by police of an item that comes within plain view during their lawful search of a private area may be reasonable under the Fourth Amendment. . . . We granted certiorari . . . in the present case to decide whether this "plain view" doctrine may be invoked when the police have less than probable cause to believe that the item in question is evidence of a crime or is contraband.

On April 18, 1984, a bullet was fired through the floor of respondent's apartment, striking and injuring a man in the apartment below. Police officers arrived and entered respondent's apartment to search for the shooter, for other victims, and for weapons. They found and seized three weapons, including a sawed-off rifle, and in the course of their search also discovered a stocking-cap mask.

One of the policemen, Officer Nelson, noticed two sets of expensive stereo components, which seemed out of place in the squalid and otherwise ill-appointed four-room apartment. Suspecting that they were stolen, he read and recorded their serial numbers — moving some of the components, including a Bang and Olufsen turnable, in order to do so — which he then reported by phone to his headquarters. On being advised that the turntable had been taken in an armed robbery, he seized it immediately. It was later determined that some of the other serial numbers matched those on other stereo equipment taken in the same armed robbery, and a warrant was obtained and executed to seize that equipment as well. Respondent was subsequently indicted for the robbery.

The state trial court granted respondent's motion to suppress the evidence that had been seized. The Court of Appeals of Arizona affirmed. It was conceded that the initial entry and search, although warrantless, were justified by the exigent circumstance of the shooting. The Court of Appeals viewed the obtaining of the serial numbers, however, as an additional search, unrelated to that exigency. . . . The Arizona Supreme Court denied review, and the State filed this petition.

II

As an initial matter, the State argues that Officer Nelson's actions constituted neither a "search" nor a "seizure" within the meaning of the Fourth Amendment. We agree that the mere recording of the serial numbers did not constitute a seizure. To be sure, that was the first step in a process by which respondent was eventually deprived of the stereo equipment. In and of itself, however, it did not "meaningfully interfere" with respondent's possessory interest in either the serial numbers or the equipment, and therefore did not amount to a seizure. . . .

Officer Nelson's moving of the equipment, however, did constitute a "search" separate and apart from the search for the shooter, victims, and weapons that was the lawful objective of his entry into the apartment. Merely inspecting those parts of the turntable that came into view during the latter search would not have constituted an independent search, because it would have produced no additional invasion of respondent's privacy interest. . . . But taking action, unrelated to the objectives of the authorized intrusion, which exposed to view concealed portions of the apartment or its contents, did produce a new invasion of respondent's privacy unjustified by the exigent circumstance that validated the entry. This is why, contrary to Justice Powell's suggestion, the "distinction between 'looking' at a suspicious object in plain view and 'moving' it even a few inches" is much more than trivial for purposes of the Fourth Amendment. It matters not that the search uncovered nothing of any great personal value to the respondent — serial numbers rather than (what might conceivably have been hidden behind or under the equipment) letters or photographs. A search is a search, even if it happens to disclose nothing but the bottom of a turntable.

III

The remaining question is whether the search was "reasonable" under the Fourth Amendment. . . .

. . . It would be absurd to say that an object could lawfully be seized and taken from the premises, but could not be moved for closer examination. It is clear, therefore, that the search here was valid if the "plain view" doctrine would have sustained a seizure of the equipment.

There is no doubt it would have done so if Officer Nelson had probable cause to believe that the equipment was stolen. The State has conceded, however, that he had only a "reasonable suspicion," by which it means something less than probable cause. . . . We have not ruled on the question whether probable cause is required in order to invoke the "plain view" doctrine. . . .

We now hold that probable cause is required. To say otherwise would be to cut the "plain view" doctrine loose from its theoretical and practical moorings. . . . Dispensing with the need for a warrant is worlds apart from permitting a lesser standard of *cause* for the seizure than a warrant would require, *i.e.*, the standard of probable cause. No reason is apparent why an object should routinely be seizable on lesser grounds, during an unrelated search and seizure, than would have been needed to obtain a warrant for that same object if it had been known to be on the premises.

The same considerations preclude us from holding that, even though probable cause would have been necessary for a *seizure*, the *search* of objects in plain view that occurred here could be sustained on lesser grounds. A dwelling-place search, no less than a dwelling-place seizure, requires probable cause, and there is no reason in theory or practicality why application of the plain-view doctrine would supplant that requirement. Although the interest protected by the Fourth Amendment injunction against unreasonable searches is quite different from that protected by its injunction against unreasonable seizures, . . . neither the one nor the other is of inferior worth or necessarily requires only lesser protection. We have not elsewhere drawn a categorical distinction between the two insofar as concerns the degree of justification needed to establish the reasonableness of police action, and we see no reason for a distinction in the particular circumstances before us here. . . .

For the reasons stated, the judgment of the Court of Appeals of Arizona is affirmed.

JUSTICE O'CONNOR with whom THE CHIEF JUSTICE and JUSTICE POWELL join, dissenting.

. . . I agree with the Court that even under the plain view doctrine, probable cause is required before the police seize an item, or conduct a full-blown search of evidence in plain view. . . . Such a requirement of probable cause will prevent the plain view doctrine from authorizing general searches. This is not to say, however, that even a mere inspection of a suspicious item must be supported by probable cause. When a police officer makes a cursory inspection of a suspicious item in plain view in order to determine whether it is indeed evidence of a crime, there is no "exploratory rummaging." Only those items that the police officer "reasonably suspects" as evidence of a crime may be inspected, and perhaps more importantly the scope of such an inspection is quite limited. In short, if police officers have a reasonable, articulable suspicion that an object they come across during the course of a lawful search is evidence of crime, in my view they may make a cursory examination of the object to verify their suspicion. If the officers wish to go beyond such a cursory examination of the object, however, they must have probable cause.

NOTES AND QUESTIONS

(1) Why is Justice Scalia so concerned about what is certainly a *de minimis* invasion of the privacy of the defendant?

(2) Should it matter that the stereo components were physically moved? Any effort on the part of the officer to ascertain the serial numbers will be "action,

unrelated to the objectives of the authorized intrusion." If the officer had used a mirror (his own) to read the serial numbers, without moving the components, would the Court have sustained the search? Photographing evidence has been held not to "meaningfully interfere" with any possessory interest. *United States v. Mancari*, 463 F.3d 590 (7th Cir. 2006), but moving items in order to photograph them is impermissible. *State v. Pender*, 748 N.W.2d 471 (Wis. App. 2008).

"[U]sing a mouse and/or keyboard to shuffle between files that are not plainly visible on an active computer screen is just as much of a search as opening and looking through Appellant's filing cabinets or desk drawers." *State v. Sachs*, 372 S.W.3d 56, 61 (Mo. Ct. App. 2012). Similarly, using a computer mouse to deactivate a screen saver or change from sleep mode has been held a search under the authority of *Hicks*. *United States v. Payton*, 573 F.3d 859 (9th Cir. 2009); *United States v. Hill*, 795 F. Supp. 2d 1304 (M.D. Fla. 2011).

(3) Suppose an item comes within plain view by virtue of a legitimate act of an officer. In *Maddox v. United States*, 745 A.2d 284, 291 (D.C. App. 2000), officers stopped a vehicle matching a description received of the perpetrators of a robbery and the vehicle in which they were traveling. In the course of a *Terry* frisk, encompassing the vehicle under the authority of *Long*, one of the officers removed a purse from the glove compartment to check for weapons possibly hidden behind it. Rather than returning the purse to the glove compartment, the officer left it resting on the seat, and thereafter another officer observed in plain view (the purse being open) an identification card bearing the name of one of the victims of the robbery. This observation, critical to the identification of the culprit, was found constitutionally reasonable, the court noting, "[w]hile it is true that if the searching officer had promptly replaced the purse in the glove compartment, 'plain view' would have disappeared, we do not think that the validity of the seizure can turn upon such details of an officer's tidiness in conducting a search so that she had a constitutional duty to return the item to where it was originally found."

(4) In *Bond v. United States*, 529 U.S. 334 (2000), the Supreme Court held that the action of a law enforcement officer in squeezing a bus passenger's carry-on luggage, as a result of which he detected what proved to be a "brick" of methamphetamine, violated the Fourth Amendment. Is this result inevitable after *Hicks*? Justice Scalia joined Justice Breyer's dissenting opinion which argued otherwise. They maintained that anyone using an overhead luggage rack on a bus should hardly be surprised to see their belongings tossed about. While conceding that the purpose of the officer's manipulation was to detect the presence of contraband, in determining whether a reasonable expectation of privacy had been invaded, it was the effect of the action, not its purpose, that should be controlling.

PROBLEM M
THE PRUDENT ARREST

Jerome Maple was lawfully arrested while in his automobile and, following standard procedure, rather than impounding the vehicle, it was moved to a safe nearby parking space. While in the process of locking the passenger seat door, the officer observed a cell phone on the floor. Concerned that this could prompt a break-in of the vehicle, he opened the console between the bucket seats to secrete the cell phone. Within the console, he found a pistol. Is it seizable? *See United States v. Maple*, 334 F.3d 15 (D.C. Cir.), *vacated in part on rehearing*, 348 F.3d 260 (D.C. Cir. 2003).

PROBLEM N
THE ALMOST-PRIVATE CRAP GAME

On May 2, 1975, in the late evening, members of the vice squad of the Honolulu Police Department went to investigate certain violations of the gambling laws. The investigating officer testified that he had received numerous telephone calls alleging that gambling activity was taking place at a specific location. At approximately 8:30 PM, he observed the lights to be on and heard sounds resembling the pounding of a dice cup. One of the windows of the building at that address was covered by drawn drapes and closed venetian blinds, but at the top of the window the drapes were sagging and there appeared to be a small hole in the blinds. Consequently, there was about a one-inch aperture in the top of the window through which one could look into the building; however, the hole was high enough off the ground that, by merely standing on the sidewalk, it would have been impossible to look through.

Upon their arrival, one of the officers stacked a crate upon a bench that was against the side of the building. By standing on the crate, he was able to peer through the one-inch hole into the building. The officer saw appellees engaged in the alleged gambling activities. The officers then entered the premises and arrested appellees.

See State v. Kaaheena, 575 P.2d 462 (Haw. 1978). Are the arrests legal?

WASHINGTON v. CHRISMAN

United States Supreme Court
455 U.S. 1 (1982)

CHIEF JUSTICE BURGER delivered the opinion of the Court.

We granted certiorari to consider whether a police officer may, consistent with the Fourth Amendment, accompany an arrested person into his residence and seize contraband discovered there in plain view.

I

On the evening of January 21, 1978, Officer Daugherty of the Washington State University police department observed Carl Overdahl, a student at the University, leave a student dormitory carrying a half-gallon bottle of gin. Because Washington law forbids possession of alcoholic beverages by persons under 21, Wash. Rev. Code § 66.44.270, and Overdahl appeared to be under age, the officer stopped him and asked for identification. Overdahl said that his identification was in his dormitory room and asked if the officer would wait while he went to retrieve it. The officer answered that under the circumstances he would have to accompany Overdahl, to which Overdahl replied "O.K."

Overdahl's room was approximately 11 by 17 feet and located on the 11th floor of the dormitory. Respondent Chrisman, Overdahl's roommate, was in the room when the officer and Overdahl entered. The officer remained in the open doorway, leaning against the doorjamb while watching Chrisman and Overdahl. He observed that Chrisman, who was in the process of placing a small box in the room's medicine cabinet, became nervous at the sight of an officer.

Within 30 to 45 seconds after Overdahl entered the room, the officer noticed seeds and a small pipe lying on a desk 8 to 10 feet from where he was standing. From his training and experience, the officer believed the seeds were marihuana and the pipe was of a type used to smoke marihuana. He entered the room and examined the pipe and seeds, confirming that the seeds were marihuana and observing that the pipe smelled of marihuana.

The officer informed Overdahl and Chrisman of their rights under *Miranda v. Arizona*, . . . each acknowledged that he understood his rights and indicated that he was willing to waive them. Officer Daugherty then asked whether the students had any other drugs in the room. The respondent handed Daugherty the box he had been carrying earlier, which contained three small plastic bags filled with marihuana and $112 in cash. At that point, Officer Daugherty called by radio for a second officer; on his arrival, the two students were told that a search of the room would be necessary. The officers explained to Overdahl and Chrisman that they had an absolute right to insist that the officers first obtain a search warrant, but that they could voluntarily consent to the search. Following this explanation, which was given in considerable detail, the two students conferred in whispers for several minutes before announcing their consent; they also signed written forms consenting to the search of the room. The search yielded more marihuana and a quantity of lysergic acid diethylamide (LSD), both controlled substances.

Respondent was charged with one count of possessing more than 40 grams of marihuana and one count of possessing LSD, both felonies under Wash. Rev. Code § 69.50.401(c) (current version at Wash. Rev. Code § 69.50.401(d) (Supp. 1981)). A pretrial motion to suppress the evidence seized in the room was denied; respondent was convicted of both counts. On appeal, the Washington Court of Appeals affirmed the convictions, upholding the validity of the search. . . .

The Supreme Court of Washington reversed. . . . It held that, although Overdahl had been placed under lawful arrest and "there was nothing to prevent Officer Daugherty from accompanying Overdahl to his room," the officer had no right to enter the room and either examine or seize contraband without a warrant. The court reasoned there was no indication that Overdahl might obtain a weapon or destroy evidence, and, with the officer blocking the only exit from the room, his presence inside the room was not necessary to prevent escape. Because the officer's entry into the room and his observations of its interior were not justified by "exigent circumstances," the seizure of the seeds and pipe were held not to fall within the plain view exception to the Fourth Amendment's warrant requirement. The court went on to hold that because the students' consent to the subsequent search of the room was the fruit of the officer's initial entry, the contraband found during that search should also have been suppressed.

Three Justices dissented. They concluded it was reasonable for a police officer to keep an arrested person in sight at all times; accordingly, the officer had a legitimate reason for being in the place where he discovered the contraband, and was entitled, under the plain view doctrine, to seize it.

. . .

II

A

The "plain view" exception to the Fourth Amendment warrant requirement permits a law enforcement officer to seize what clearly is incriminating evidence or contraband when it is discovered in a place where the officer has a right to be. Here, the officer had placed Overdahl under lawful arrest, and therefore was authorized to accompany him to his room for the purpose of obtaining identification. The officer had a right to remain literally at Overdahl's elbow at all times; nothing in the Fourth Amendment is to the contrary.

The central premise of the opinion of the Supreme Court of Washington is that Officer Daugherty was not entitled to accompany Overdahl from the public corridor of the dormitory into his room, absent a showing that such "intervention" was required by "exigent circumstances." We disagree with this novel reading of the Fourth Amendment. The absence of an affirmative indication that an arrested person might have a weapon available or might attempt to escape does not diminish the arresting officer's authority to maintain custody over the arrested person. Nor is that authority altered by the nature of the offense for which the arrest was made.

Every arrest must be presumed to present a risk of danger to the arresting officer. There is no way for an officer to predict reliably how a particular subject will react to arrest or the degree of the potential danger. Moreover, the possibility that an arrested person will attempt to escape if not properly supervised is obvious. Although the Supreme Court of Washington found little likelihood that Overdahl could escape from his dormitory room, an arresting officer's custodial authority over an arrested person does not depend upon a reviewing court's after-the-fact assessment of the particular arrest situation.

We hold, therefore, that it is not "unreasonable" under the Fourth Amendment for a police officer, as a matter of routine, to monitor the movements of an arrested person, as his judgment dictates, following the arrest. The officer's need to ensure his own safety — as well as the integrity of the arrest — is compelling. Such surveillance is not an impermissible invasion of the privacy or personal liberty of an individual who has been arrested.

It follows that Officer Daugherty properly accompanied Overdahl into his room, and that his presence in the room was lawful. With restraint, the officer remained in the doorway momentarily, entering no farther than was necessary to keep the arrested person in his view. It was only by chance that, while in the doorway, the officer observed in plain view what he recognized to be contraband. Had he exercised his undoubted right to remain at Overdahl's side, he might well have observed the contraband sooner.

B

Respondent nevertheless contends that the officer lacked authority to seize the contraband, even though in plain view, because he was "outside" the room at the time he made his observations. The Supreme Court of Washington noted that "[t]he record is in conflict as to whether Officer Daugherty stood in the doorway and then entered the room or whether, while in the doorway, he was in fact in the room." It concluded, however, that it "need not . . . let the result be determined by such niceties," and assumed for purposes of its decision that the officer "was in the room at the time he observed the seeds and pipe." We agree that on this record "such niceties" are not relevant. It is of no legal significance whether the officer was in the room, on the threshold, or in the hallway, since he had a right to be in any of these places as an incident of a valid arrest.

Respondent's argument appears to be that, even if the officer could have stationed himself "inside" the room had he done so immediately upon Overdahl's entry, his 30- to 45 second hesitation was fatal; and that having chosen to remain in the doorway, the officer was precluded from proceeding further to seize the contraband. We reject this contention. Respondent's argument, if accepted, would have the perverse effect of penalizing the officer for exercising more restraint than was required under the circumstances. Moreover, it ignores the fundamental premise that the Fourth Amendment protects only against unreasonable intrusions into an individual's privacy.

The "intrusion" in this case occurred when the officer, quite properly, followed Overdahl into a private area to a point from which he had unimpeded view of an access to the area's contents and its occupants. His right to custodial control did not evaporate with his choice to hesitate briefly in the doorway rather than at some other vantage point inside the room. It cannot be gainsaid that the officer would have had unrestricted access to the room at the first indication that he was in danger, or that evidence might be destroyed — or even upon reassessment of the wisdom of permitting a distance between himself and Overdahl.

We therefore conclude that, regardless of where the officer was positioned with respect to the threshold, he did not abandon his right to be in the room whenever he considered it essential. Accordingly, he had the right to act as soon as he observed the seeds and pipe.[34] This is a classic instance of incriminating evidence found in plain view when a police officer, for unrelated but entirely legitimate reasons, obtains lawful access to an individual's area of privacy. The Fourth Amendment does not prohibit seizure of evidence of criminal conduct found in these circumstances.

---

[34] [5] The circumstances of this case distinguish it significantly from one in which an officer, who happens to pass by chance an open doorway to a residence, observes what he believes to be contraband inside. See, e.g., Payton v. New York, 445 U.S. 573, 585–589 (1980); Johnson v. United States, 333 U.S. 10, 14–15 (1948).

JUSTICE WHITE with whom JUSTICE BRENNAN and JUSTICE MARSHALL join, dissenting.

The record in this case is clear, however, that Daugherty did not leave the doorway and enter the room in order to protect himself or maintain control over respondent. Daugherty's uncontradicted testimony was that he entered the room solely to confirm his suspicion that the seeds and the seashell he had observed from the doorway were marijuana seeds and a seashell pipe that had been used to smoke marijuana. Daugherty made no claim that he entered the room as a necessary incident to the permission given Overdahl to secure his identification. Rather, he claimed that the entry was justified because of what was in plain view on the desk inside the room.

If a police officer passing by an open door of a home sees incriminating evidence within the house, his observation may provide probable cause for the issuance of a search warrant. Yet the officer may not enter the home without a warrant unless an exception to the warrant requirement applies. This rule is fully supported by *Coolidge v. New Hampshire* . . . and the cases cited in the Court's opinion in that case. Any contrary rule would severely undercut the protection afforded by the Fourth Amendment, for it is the physical entry of the home that is the chief evil against which the Amendment is directed.

NOTES

(1) On remand, the Supreme Court of Washington relied on the state constitution in again holding that the warrantless entry into the dormitory room was impermissible. *State v. Chrisman*, 676 P.2d 419 (Wash. 1984).

(2) Officer Daugherty's conduct would appear tempered and reasonable at every step. A different result will likely follow if the officer has manipulated the individual in an effort to create opportunities for plain view seizures. *See United States v. Hill*, 730 F.2d 1163 (8th Cir.), *cert. denied*, 469 U.S. 884 (1984).

UNITED STATES v. JACOBSEN

United States Supreme Court
466 U.S. 109 (1984)

JUSTICE STEVENS delivered the opinion of the Court.

During their examination of a damaged package, the employees of a private freight carrier observed a white powdery substance, originally concealed within eight layers of wrappings. They summoned a federal agent, who removed a trace of the powder, subjected it to a chemical test and determined that it was cocaine. The question presented is whether the Fourth Amendment required the agent to obtain a warrant before he did so.

The relevant facts are not in dispute. Early in the morning of May 1, 1981, a supervisor at the Minneapolis-St. Paul airport Federal Express office asked the office manager to look at a package that had been damaged and torn by a forklift. They then opened the package in order to examine its contents pursuant to a written company policy regarding insurance claims.

The container was an ordinary cardboard box wrapped in brown paper. Inside the box five or six pieces of crumpled newspaper covered a tube about 10 inches long; the tube was made of the silver tape used on basement ducts. The supervisor and office manager cut open the tube, and found a series of four zip-lock plastic bags, the outermost enclosing the other three and the innermost containing about six and a half ounces of white powder. When they observed the white powder in the innermost bag, they notified the Drug Enforcement Administration. Before the first DEA agent arrived, they replaced the plastic bags in the tube and put the tube and the newspapers back into the box.

When the first federal agent arrived, the box, still wrapped in brown paper, but with a hole punched in its side and the top open, was placed on a desk. The agent saw that one end of the tube had been slit open; he removed the four plastic bags from the tube and saw the white powder. He then opened each of the four bags and removed a trace of the white substance with a knife blade. A field test made on the spot identified the substance as cocaine.

In due course, other agents arrived, made a second field test, rewrapped the package, obtained a warrant to search the place to which it was addressed, executed the warrant, and arrested respondents. After they were indicted for the crime of possessing an illegal substance with intent to distribute, their motion to suppress the evidence on the ground that the warrant was the product of an illegal search and seizure was denied; they were tried and convicted, and appealed. The Court of Appeals reversed. It held that the validity of the search warrant depended on the validity of the agents' warrantless test of the white powder, that the testing constituted a significant expansion of the earlier private search, and that a warrant was required. . . .

The initial invasions of respondents' package were occasioned by private action. Those invasions revealed that the package contained only one significant item, a suspicious looking tape tube. Cutting the end of the tube and extracting its contents revealed a suspicious looking plastic bag of white powder. Whether those invasions were accidental or deliberate, and whether they were reasonable or unreasonable, they did not violate the Fourth Amendment because of their private character.

The additional invasions of respondents' privacy by the government agent must be tested by the degree to which they exceeded the scope of the private search.

This standard follows from the analysis applicable when private parties reveal other kinds of private information to the authorities. It is well-settled that when an individual reveals private information to another, he assumes the risk that his confidant will reveal that information to the authorities, and if that occurs the Fourth Amendment does not prohibit governmental use of that information. Once frustration of the original expectation of privacy occurs, the Fourth Amendment does not prohibit governmental use of the now-nonprivate information.

When the first federal agent on the scene initially saw the package, he knew it contained nothing of significance except a tube containing plastic bags and, ultimately, white powder. It is not entirely clear that the powder was visible to him before he removed the tube from the box.[35] Even if the white powder was not itself in "plain view" because it was still enclosed in so many containers and covered with papers, there was a virtual certainty that nothing else of significance was in the package and that a manual inspection of the tube and its contents would not tell him anything more than he already had been told. Respondents do not dispute that the Government could utilize the Federal Express employees' testimony concerning the contents of the package. If that is the case, it hardly infringed respondents' privacy for the agents to reexamine the contents of the open package by brushing aside a crumpled newspaper and picking up the tube. The advantage the Government gained thereby was merely avoiding the risk of a flaw in the employees' recollection, rather than in further infringing respondents' privacy. Protecting the risk of misdescription hardly enhances any legitimate privacy interest, and is not protected by the Fourth Amendment. Respondents could have no privacy interest in the contents of the package, since it remained unsealed and since the Federal Express employees had just examined the package and had, of their own accord, invited the federal agent to their offices for the express purpose of viewing its contents. The agent's viewing of what a private party had freely made available for his inspection did not violate the Fourth Amendment. See *Coolidge*.

Similarly, the removal of the plastic bags from the tube and the agent's visual inspection of their contents enabled the agent to learn nothing that had not previously been learned during the private search.[36] It infringed no legitimate

---

[35] [15] Daniel Stegemoller, the Federal Express office manager, testified at the suppression hearing that the white substance was not visible without reentering the package at the time the first agent arrived. App. 42–43; 58. As Justice White points out, the magistrate found that the "tube was in plain view in the box and the bags of white powder were visible from the end of the tube." App. to Pet. for Cert. 18a. The bags were, however, only visible if one picked up the tube and peered inside through a small aperture; even then, what was visible was only the translucent bag that contained the white powder. The powder itself was barely visible, and surely was not so plainly in view that the agents did "no more than fail to avert their eyes," . . . . In any event, respondents filed objections to the magistrate's report with the District Court. The District Court declined to resolve respondents' objection, ruling that fact immaterial and assuming for purposes of its decision "that the newspaper in the box covered the gray tube and that neither the gray tube nor the contraband could be seen when the box was turned over to the DEA agents." App. to Pet. for Cert. 12a-13a. At trial, the federal agent first on the scene testified that the powder was not visible until after he pulled the plastic bags out of the tube. App. 71-72. Respondents continue to argue this case on the assumption that the Magistrate's report is incorrect. Brief for Respondents 2-3. As our discussion will make clear, we agree with the District Court that it does not matter whether the loose piece of newspaper covered the tube at the time the agent first saw the box.

[36] [17] We reject Justice White's suggestion that this case is indistinguishable from one in which the police simply learn from a private party that a container contains contraband, seize it from its owner, and conduct a warrantless search which, as Justice White properly observes, would be unconstitutional. Here, the Federal Express employees who were lawfully in possession of the package invited the agent to examine its contents; the governmental conduct was made possible only because private parties had compromised the integrity of this container. Justice White would have this case turn on the fortuity of whether the Federal Express agents placed the tube back into the box. But in the context of their previous examination of the package, their communication of what they had learned to the agent, and their offer to have the agent inspect it, that act surely could not create any privacy interest with respect to the package that would not otherwise exist. See Illinois v. Andreas, 463 U.S. 765, (1983). Thus the precise character of the white powder's visibility to the naked eye is far less significant than the facts that the container could no longer support any expectation of privacy, and that it was virtually certain that it contained nothing but contraband. Contrary to Justice White's suggestion, we do not "sanction warrantless searches of closed or covered containers or packages whenever probable cause exists as a

expectation of privacy and hence was not a "search" within the meaning of the Fourth Amendment.

While the agents' assertion of dominion and control over the package and its contents did constitute a "seizure," that seizure was not unreasonable. The fact that, prior to the field test, respondents' privacy interest in the contents of the package had been largely compromised, is highly relevant to the reasonableness of the agents' conduct in this respect. The agents had already learned a great deal about the contents of the package from the Federal Express employees, all of which was consistent with what they could see. The package itself, which had previously been opened, remained unsealed, and the Federal Express employees had invited the agents to examine its contents. Under these circumstances, the package could no longer support any expectation of privacy; it was just like a balloon "the distinctive character [of which] spoke volumes as to its contents, particularly to the trained eye of the officer," *Texas v. Brown*, 460 U.S. 730, (1983) (plurality opinion); see also *id.*, at — (Powell, J., concurring in the judgment); or the hypothetical gun case in *Arkansas v. Sanders*, 442 U.S. 753, 764–765, n. 13 (1979). Such containers may be seized, at least temporarily, without a warrant. Accordingly, since it was apparent that the tube and plastic bags contained contraband and little else, this warrantless seizure was reasonable, for it is well-settled that it is constitutionally reasonable for law enforcement officials to seize "effects" that cannot support a justifiable expectation of privacy without a warrant, based on probable cause to believe they contain contraband.

The question remains whether the additional intrusion occasioned by the field test, which had not been conducted by the Federal Express agents and therefore exceeded the scope of the private search, was an unlawful "search" or "seizure" within the meaning of the Fourth Amendment.

The field test at issue could disclose only one fact previously unknown to the agent — whether or not a suspicious white powder was cocaine. It could tell him nothing more, not even whether the substance was sugar or talcum powder. We must first determine whether this can be considered a "search" subject to the Fourth Amendment — did it infringe an expectation of privacy that society is prepared to consider reasonable?

The concept of an interest in privacy that society is prepared to recognize as reasonable is, by its very nature, critically different from the mere expectation, however well justified, that certain facts will not come to the attention of the authorities. Indeed, this distinction underlies the rule that Government may utilize information voluntarily disclosed to a governmental informant, despite the criminal's reasonable expectation that his associates would not disclose confidential information to the authorities. See *United States v. White*.

A chemical test that merely discloses whether or not a particular substance is cocaine does not compromise any legitimate interest in privacy. This conclusion is

result of a prior private search." A container which can support a reasonable expectation of privacy may not be searched, even on probable cause, without a warrant. See United States v. Ross, 456 U.S. 798, 809–812 (1982); Robbins v. California, 453 U.S. 420, 426–427 (1981) (plurality opinion); Arkansas v. Sanders, 442 U.S. 753, 764–765 (1979); United States v. Chadwick, 433 U.S. 1 (1977).

not dependent on the result of any particular test. It is probably safe to assume that virtually all of the tests conducted under circumstances comparable to those disclosed by this record would result in a positive finding; in such cases, no legitimate interest has been compromised. But even if the results are negative — merely disclosing that the substance is something other than cocaine — such a result reveals nothing of special interest. Congress has decided — and there is no question about its power to do so — to treat the interest in "privately" possessing cocaine as illegitimate; thus governmental conduct that can reveal whether a substance is cocaine, and no other arguably "private" fact, compromises no legitimate privacy interest.

[W]e conclude that the destruction of the powder during the course of the field test was reasonable. The law enforcement interests justifying the procedure were substantial; the suspicious nature of the material made it virtually certain that the substance tested was in fact contraband. Conversely, because only a trace amount of material was involved, the loss of which appears to have gone unnoticed by respondents, and since the property had already been lawfully detained, the "seizure" could, at most, have only a *de minimis* impact on any protected property interest.

In sum, the federal agents did not infringe any constitutionally protected privacy interest that had not already been frustrated as the result of private conduct. To the extent that a protected possessory interest was infringed, the infringement was *de minimis* and constitutionally reasonable. The judgment of the Court of Appeals is

Reversed.

JUSTICE WHITE concurring in part and concurring in the judgment.

It is relatively easy for me to concur in the judgment in this case, since in my view the case should be judged on the basis of the Magistrate's finding that, when the first DEA agent arrived, the "tube was in plain view in the box and the bags of white powder were visible from the end of the tube."

[I]f this case must be judged on the basis that the plastic bags and their contents were concealed when the first agent arrived, I disagree with the Court's conclusion that the agent could, without a warrant, uncover or unwrap the tube and remove its contents simply because a private party had previously done so.

If government agents are unwilling or unable to rely on information or testimony provided by a private party concerning the results of a private search and that search has not left incriminating evidence in plain view, the agents may wish to duplicate the private search to observe first-hand what the private party has related to them or to examine and seize the suspected contraband the existence of which has been reported. The information provided by the private party clearly would give the agents probable cause to secure a warrant authorizing such actions. Nothing in our previous cases suggests, however, that the agents may proceed to conduct their own search of the same or lesser scope as the private search without first obtaining a warrant. . . .

[JUSTICE BRENNAN, joined by JUSTICE MARSHALL, dissented, agreeing with JUSTICE

White on the dispositive question, and concluding that the case should be remanded for further fact finding "[b]ecause the record in this case is unclear on the question whether the contents of respondents' package were plainly visible when the Federal Express employee showed the package to the DEA officer." The dissent, however, found nothing constitutionally objectionable in the chemical field test, assuming the sample was properly taken.]

In this case, the chemical field test was used to determine whether certain white powder was cocaine. Upon visual inspection of the powder in isolation, one could not identify it as cocaine. In the abstract, therefore, it is possible that an individual could keep the powder in such a way as to preserve a reasonable expectation of privacy in its identity. For instance, it might be kept in a transparent pharmaceutical vial and disguised as legitimate medicine. Under those circumstances, the use of a chemical field test would constitute a search. However, in this case the context in which the powder was found could not support a reasonable expectation of privacy. In particular, the substance was found in four plastic bags, which had been inside a tube wrapped with tape and sent to respondents via Federal Express. It was essentially inconceivable that a legal substance would be packaged in this manner for transport by a common carrier. Thus, viewing the powder as they did at the offices of Federal Express, the DEA agent could identify it with "virtual certainty"; it was essentially as though the chemical identity of the powder was plainly visible. See *Texas v. Brown*. . . . (Stevens, J., concurring in the judgment). Under these circumstances, therefore, respondents had no reasonable expectation of privacy in the identity of the powder, and the use of the chemical field test did not constitute a "search" violative of the Fourth Amendment.

QUESTIONS

(1) Is the outcome of this case controlled by the fortuity of the package being damaged by the forklift? Suppose under its contract with the shipper, the carrier reserves the right to open parcels, ostensibly to determine that prohibited items are not included. Would it be of significance that the DEA had instructed the private carrier on spotting parcels containing narcotics, or individuals likely to be making such shipments?

(2) Is the conclusion that the DEA agents went no further than the Federal Express agents in invading the privacy of the accused convincing? If powder had leaked from the package and the carrier's agent had called the federal authorities without opening it, would a warrant be required?

(3) Why is the case that "[a] chemical test that merely discloses whether or not a particular substance is cocaine does not compromise any legitimate interest in privacy"? Does the presence or absence of a reasonable expectation or privacy turn on what the search reveals?

[C] Open Fields

OLIVER v. UNITED STATES

United States Supreme Court
466 U.S. 170 (1984)

JUSTICE POWELL delivered the opinion of the Court.

The "open fields" doctrine, first enunciated by this Court in *Hester v. United States*, 265 U.S. 57 (1924), permits police officers to enter and search a field without a warrant. We granted certiorari in these cases to clarify confusion that has arisen as to the continued vitality of the doctrine.

I

No. 82-15. Acting on reports that marijuana was being raised on the farm of petitioner Oliver, two narcotics agents of the Kentucky State Police went to the farm to investigate. Arriving at the farm, they drove past petitioner's house to a locked gate with a "No Trespassing" sign. A foot-path led around one side of the gate. The agents walked around the gate and along the road for several hundred yards, passing a barn and a parked camper. At that point, someone standing in front of the camper shouted, "No hunting is allowed, come back here." The officers shouted back that they were Kentucky State Police officers, but found no one when they returned to the camper. The officers resumed their investigation of the farm and found a field of marijuana over a mile from petitioner's home.

Petitioner was arrested and indicted for "manufacturing" a "controlled substance." 21 U.S.C. § 841(a)(1). After a pretrial hearing, the District Court suppressed evidence of the discovery of the marijuana fields. Applying *Katz v. United States*, . . . the court found that petitioner had a reasonable expectation that the fields would remain private because petitioner "had done all that could be expected of him to assert his privacy in the area of farm that was searched." He had posted no trespassing signs at regular intervals and had locked the gate at the entrance to the center of the farm. Further, the court noted that the fields themselves are highly secluded: they are bounded on all sides by woods, fences and embankments and cannot be seen from any point of public access. The court concluded that this was not an "open" field that invited casual intrusion.

The Court of Appeals for the Sixth Circuit, sitting *en banc*, reversed the district court. . . . The court concluded that *Katz*, upon which the District Court relied, had not impaired the vitality of the open fields doctrine of *Hester*. Rather, the open fields doctrine was entirely compatible with *Katz*'s emphasis on privacy. The court reasoned that the "human relations that create the need for privacy do not ordinarily take place" in open fields, and that the property owner's common law right to exclude trespassers is insufficiently linked to privacy to warrant the Fourth Amendment's protection.

No. 82-1273. After receiving an anonymous tip that marijuana was being grown in the woods behind respondent Thornton's residence, two police officers entered the woods by a path between his residence and a neighboring house. They followed a footpath through the woods until they reached two marijuana patches fenced with chicken wire. Later, the officers determined that the patches were on the property of respondent, obtained a warrant to search the property and seized the marijuana. On the basis of this evidence, respondent was arrested and indicted.

The trial court granted respondent's motion to suppress the fruits of the second search. The warrant for this search was premised on information that the police had obtained during their previous warrantless search, that the court found to be unreasonable. "No Trespassing" signs and the secluded location of the marijuana patches evinced a reasonable expectation of privacy. Therefore, the court held, the "open fields" doctrine did not apply.

The Maine Supreme Judicial Court affirmed. . . . It agreed with the trial court that the correct question was whether the search "is a violation of privacy on which the individual justifiably relied," *id*. . . . , and that the search violated respondent's privacy. The court also agreed that the "open fields" doctrine did not justify the search. That doctrine applies, according to the court, only when officers are lawfully present on property and observe "open and patent" activity. . . . In this case, the officers had trespassed upon defendant's property, and the respondent had made every effort to conceal his activity.

II

The rule announced in *Hester v. United States* was founded upon the explicit language of the Fourth Amendment. That Amendment indicates with some precision the places and things encompassed by its protections. As Justice Holmes explained for the Court in his characteristically laconic style: "[T]he special protection accorded by the Fourth Amendment to the people in their 'persons, houses, papers, and effects,' is not extended to the open fields. The distinction between the latter and the house is as old as the common law." . . .

Nor are the open fields' "effects" within the meaning of the Fourth Amendment. In this respect, it is suggestive that James Madison's proposed draft of what became the Fourth Amendment preserves "[t]he rights of the people to be secure in their persons, their houses, their papers, and their other property, from all unreasonable searches and seizures." See N. Lasson, *The History and Development of the Fourth Amendment to the United States Constitution* 100, n. 77 (1937). Although Congress' revisions of Madison's proposal broadened the scope of the Amendment in some respects, *id.*, at 100–103, the term "effects" is less inclusive than "property" and cannot be said to encompass open fields. We conclude, as did the Court in deciding *Hester v. United States*, that the government's intrusion upon the open fields is not one of those "unreasonable searches" proscribed by the text of the Fourth Amendment.

III

This interpretation of the Fourth Amendment's language is consistent with the understanding of the right to privacy expressed in our Fourth Amendment jurisprudence. Since *Katz v. United States*, . . . the touchstone of Fourth Amendment analysis has been the question whether a person has a "constitutionally protected reasonable expectation of privacy." 389 U.S., at 360. The Amendment does not protect the merely subjective expectation of privacy, but only "those expectations that society is prepared to recognize as 'reasonable.'" *Id.* . . .

[T]he rule of *Hester v. United States* . . . , that we reaffirm today, may be understood as providing that an individual may not legitimately demand privacy for activities conducted out of doors in fields, except in the area immediately surrounding the home. . . . This rule is true to the conception of the right to privacy embodied in the Fourth Amendment. The Amendment reflects the recognition of the Founders that certain enclaves should be free from arbitrary government interference. For example, the Court since the enactment of the Fourth Amendment has stressed "the overriding respect for the sanctity of the home that has been embedded in our traditions since the origins of the Republic." *Payton v. New York.*

In contrast, open fields do not provide the setting for those intimate activities that the Amendment is intended to shelter from government interference or surveillance. There is no societal interest in protecting the privacy of those activities, such as the cultivation of crops, that occur in open fields. Moreover, as a practical matter these lands usually are accessible to the public and the police in ways that a home, an office or commercial structure would not be. It is not generally true that fences or no trespassing signs effectively bar the public from viewing open fields in rural areas. And both petitioner Oliver and respondent Thornton concede that the public and police lawfully may survey lands from the air. For these reasons, the asserted expectation of privacy in open fields is not an expectation that "society recognizes as reasonable."

The historical underpinnings of the "open fields" doctrine also demonstrate that the doctrine is consistent with respect for "reasonable expectations of privacy." As Justice Holmes, writing for the Court, observed in *Hester*, 265 U.S., at 57, the common law distinguished "open fields" from the "curtilage," the land immediately surrounding and associated with the home. See 4 Blackstone, Commentaries 225. The distinction implies that only the curtilage, not the neighboring open fields, warrants the Fourth Amendment protections that attach to the home. At common law, the curtilage is the area to which extends the intimate activity associated with the "sanctity of a man's home and the privacies of life," *Boyd v. United States*, 116 U.S. 616, 630 (1886), and therefore has been considered part of home itself for Fourth Amendment purposes. Thus, courts have extended Fourth Amendment protection to the curtilage; and they have defined the curtilage, as did the common law, by reference to the factors that determine whether an individual reasonably may expect that an area immediately adjacent to the home will remain private.

We conclude, from the text of the Fourth Amendment and from the historical and contemporary understanding of its purposes, that an individual has no legitimate expectation that open fields will remain free from warrantless intrusion by government officers.

JUSTICE MARSHALL, with whom JUSTICE BRENNAN and JUSTICE STEVENS join, dissenting.

The Court's inability to reconcile its parsimonious reading of the phrase "persons, houses, papers, and effects" with our prior decisions or even its own holding is a symptom of a more fundamental infirmity in the Court's reasoning. The Fourth Amendment, like the other central provisions of the Bill of Rights that loom large in our modern jurisprudence, was designed, not to prescribe with "precision" permissible and impermissible activities, but to identify a fundamental human liberty that should be shielded forever from government intrusion. We do not construe constitutional provisions of this sort the way we do statutes, whose drafters can be expected to indicate with some comprehensiveness and exactitude the conduct they wish to forbid or control and to change those prescriptions when they become obsolete. Rather, we strive, when interpreting these seminal constitutional provisions to effectuate their purposes — to lend them meanings that ensure that the liberties the Framers sought to protect are not undermined by the changing activities of government officials.

Certain spaces are so presumptively private that signals of this sort are unnecessary; a homeowner need not post a "do not enter" sign on his door in order to deny entrance to uninvited guests. Privacy interests in other spaces are more ambiguous, and the taking of precautions is consequently more important; placing a lock on one's footlocker strengthens one's claim that an examination of its contents is impermissible. See *United States v. Chadwick*. . . . Still other spaces are, by positive law and social convention, presumed accessible to members of the public unless the owner manifests his intention to exclude them.

. . .

. . . Private land marked in a fashion sufficient to render entry thereon a criminal trespass under the law of the state in which the land lies is protected by the Fourth Amendment's proscription of unreasonable searches and seizures. One of the advantages of the foregoing rule is that it draws upon a doctrine already familiar to both citizens and government officials. In each jurisdiction, a substantial body of statutory and case law defines the precautions a landowner must take in order to avail himself of the sanctions of the criminal law. The police know that body of law, because they are entrusted with responsibility for enforcing it against the public; it therefore would not be difficult for the police to abide by it themselves.

By contrast, the doctrine announced by the Court today is incapable of determinate application. Police officers, making warrantless entries upon private land, will be obliged in the future to make on-the-spot judgments as to how far the curtilage extends, and to stay outside that zone. In addition, we may expect to see a spate of litigation over the question of how much improvement is necessary to remove private land from the category of "unoccupied or undeveloped area" to which the "open fields exception" is not deemed applicable.

NOTES AND QUESTIONS

(1) Certainly the posting of "No Trespassing" signs by both defendants removed any ambiguity as to their intention of securing privacy on their property.

Is there any way they could have succeeded in making entry upon the land a violation of the Fourth Amendment? Or is the Court saying that no matter how well enclosed, an open field is not protected?

(2) For a dissenting view, see *Morse v. State*, 655 S.E.2d 217 (2007):

> [T]here is something odious about the government in a free country intruding upon privately owned property without a warrant, consent, or exigent circumstances. But in *Oliver v. United States*, the Supreme Court concluded that "an individual has no legitimate expectation that open fields will remain free from warrantless intrusion by government officers." According to the *Oliver* majority, this is true even if the landowner takes steps to protect his privacy, such as posting 'No Trespassing" signs or erecting a fence. Although bound by the *Oliver* holding, we — like the *Oliver* dissenters — see "no reason why a government official should not be obliged to respect [these] unequivocal and universally understood manifestations of a landowner's desire for privacy." And we question how the *Oliver* majority could have concluded that an expectation of privacy in such property is unreasonable.

(3) Given the renewed interest by the Supreme Court in trespass as a basis for finding Fourth Amendment violations (*see United States v. Jones, supra* § 3.01), should the Court reconsider the open fields exception?

[D] Curtilage

UNITED STATES v. DUNN

United States Supreme Court

480 U.S. 294 (1987)

JUSTICE WHITE delivered the opinion of the Court.

We granted the Government's petition for certiorari to decide whether the area near a barn, located approximately 50 yards from a fence surrounding a ranch house, is, for Fourth Amendment purposes, within the curtilage of the house. . . .

I

Respondent Ronald Dale Dunn and a codefendant, Robert Lyle Carpenter, were convicted by jury of conspiring to manufacture phenylacetone and amphetamine, and to possess amphetamine with intent to distribute, in violation of 21 U.S.C. § 846. Respondent was also convicted of manufacturing these two controlled substances and possessing amphetamine with intent to distribute. The events giving rise to respondent's apprehension and conviction began in 1980 when agents from the Drug Enforcement Administration (DEA) discovered that Carpenter had purchased large quantities of chemicals and equipment used in the manufacture of amphetamine and phenylacetone. DEA agents obtained warrants from a Texas state judge authorizing installation of miniature electronic transmitter tracking devices, or "beepers," in an electric hot plate stirrer, a drum of acetic anhydride, and a container holding phenylacetic acid, a processor to phenylacetone. All of these items had been ordered by Carpenter. On September 3, 1980, Carpenter took possession of the electric hot plate stirrer, but the agents lost the signal from the "beeper" in the container of chemicals, however, from October 27, 1980, until November 5, 1980, on which date Carpenter's pickup truck, which was carrying the container, arrived at respondent's ranch. Aerial photographs of the ranch property showed Carpenter's truck backed up to a barn behind the ranch house. The agents also began receiving transmission signals from the "beeper" in the hot plate stirrer that they had lost in early September and determined that the stirrer was on respondent's ranch property.

Respondent's ranch comprised approximately 198 acres and was completely encircled by a perimeter fence. The property also contained several interior fences, constructed mainly of posts and multiple strands of barbed wire. The ranch residence was situated one-half mile from a public road. A fence encircled the residence and a nearby small greenhouse. Two barns were located approximately 50 yards from this fence. The front of the larger of the two barns was enclosed by a wooden fence and had an open overhang. Locked, waist-high gates barred entry into the barn proper, and netting material stretched from the ceiling to the top of the wood gates.

On the evening of November 5, 1980, law enforcement officials made a warrantless entry onto respondent's ranch property. A DEA agent accompanied by an officer from the Houston Police Department crossed over the perimeter fence and one interior fence. Standing approximately midway between the residence and the barns, the DEA agent smelled what he believed to be phenylacetic acid, the odor coming from the direction of the barns. The officers approached the smaller of the barns — crossing over a barbed wire fence — and, looking into the barn, observed only empty boxes. The officers walked under the barn's overhang to the locked wooden gates and, shining a flashlight through the netting on top of the gates, peered into the barn. They observed what the DEA agent thought to be a phenylacetone laboratory. The officers did not enter the barn. At this point the officers departed from respondent's property, but entered it twice more on November 6 to confirm the presence of the phenylacetone laboratory.

On November 6, 1980, at 8:30 p.m., a federal magistrate issued a warrant authorizing search of respondent's ranch. DEA agents and state law enforcement officials executed the warrant on November 8, 1980. The officers arrested respondent and seized chemicals and equipment, as well as bags of amphetamines they discovered in a closet in the ranch house.

[The Court of Appeals for the Fifth Circuit reversed the conviction holding that the barn was within the curtilage of the residence and thus protected by the Fourth Amendment.]

II

. . .

Drawing upon the court's own cases and the cumulative experience of the lower courts that have grappled with the task of defining the extent of a home's curtilage, we believe that curtilage questions should be resolved with particular reference to four factors: the proximity of the area claimed to be curtilage to the home, whether the area is included within an enclosure surrounding the home, the nature of the uses to which the area is put, and the steps taken by the resident to protect the area from observation by people passing by. . . . We do not suggest that combining these factors produces a finely tuned formula that, when mechanically applied, yields a "correct" answer to all extent-of-curtilage questions. Rather, these factors are useful analytical tools only to the degree that, in any given case, they bear upon the centrally relevant consideration — whether the area in question is so intimately tied to the home itself that it should be placed under the home's "umbrella" of Fourth Amendment protection. Applying these factors to respondent's barn and to the area immediately surrounding it, we have little difficulty in concluding that this area lay outside the curtilage of the ranch house.

First. The record discloses that the barn was located 50 yards from the fence surrounding the house, and 60 yards from the house itself. . . . Standing in isolation, this substantial distance supports no inference that the barn should be treated as an adjunct of the house.

Second. It is also significant that respondent's barn did not lie within the area surrounding the house that was enclosed by a fence. We noted in *Oliver* . . . that "for most homes, the boundaries of the curtilage will be clearly marked; and the conception defining the curtilage — as the area around the home to which the activity of home life extends — is a familiar one easily understood from our daily experience." . . . Viewing the physical layout of respondent's ranch in its entirety . . . it is plain that the fence surrounding the residence serves to mark a specific area of land immediately adjacent to the house that is readily identifiable as part and parcel of the house. Conversely, the barn — the front portion itself enclosed by a fence — and the area immediately surrounding it, stands out as a distant portion of respondent's ranch, quite separate from the residence.

Third. It is especially significant that the law enforcement possessed objective data indicating that the barn was not being used for intimate activities of the home. The aerial photographs showed that the truck Carpenter had been driving that contained the container of phenylacetic acid was backed up to the barn, "apparently," in the words of the Court of Appeals, "for the unloading of its contents." . . . When on respondent's property, the officers' suspicion was further directed toward the barn because of "a very strong odor" of phenylacetic acid. . . . As the DEA agent approached the barn, he "could hear a motor running, like a pump motor of some sort. . . . " . . . Furthermore, the officers detected an "extremely strong" odor of phenylacetic acid coming from a small crack in the wall of the barn. . . . Finally, as the officers were standing in front of the barn, immediately prior to looking into its interior through the netting material, "the smell was very, very strong . . . [and the officers] could hear the motor running very loudly." . . . When considered together, the above facts indicated to the officers that the use to which the barn was being put could not fairly be characterized as so associated with the activities and privacies of domestic life that the officers should have deemed the barn as part of respondent's home.

Fourth. Respondent did little to protect the barn area from observation by those standing in the open field. Nothing in the record suggests that the various interior fences on respondent's property had any function other than that of the typical ranch fence; the fences were designed and constructed to corral livestock, not to prevent persons from observing what lay inside the enclosed areas.

III

Respondent submits an alternative basis for affirming the judgment below, one that was presented to but ultimately not relied upon by the Court of Appeals. Respondent asserts that he possessed an expectation of privacy, independent from his home's curtilage, in the barn and its contents, because the barn is an essential part of his business. . . .

We may accept, for the sake of argument, respondent's submission that the barn enjoyed Fourth Amendment protection and could not be entered and its contents seized without a warrant. But it does not follow on the record before us that the officers' conduct and the ensuing search and seizure violates the Constitution. *Oliver* reaffirmed the precept, established in *Hester*, that an open field is neither a "house" nor an "effect," and, therefore, "the government's intrusion upon the open fields is not one of those 'unreasonable searches' proscribed by the text of the Fourth Amendment." . . . The Court expressly rejected the argument that the erection of fences on an open field — at least of the variety involved in those cases and in the present case — creates a constitutionally protected privacy interest. . . . It follows that no constitutional violation occurred here when the officers crossed over respondent's ranch-style perimeter fence, and over several similarly constructed interior fences, prior to stopping at the locked front gate of the barn. As previously mentioned, the officers never entered the barn, nor did they enter any other structure on respondent's premises. Once at their vantage point, they merely stood, outside the curtilage of the house and in the open fields, upon which the barn was constructed, and peered into the barn's open front. And, standing as they were in the open fields, the Constitution did not forbid them to observe the phenylacetone laboratory located in respondent's barn. This conclusion flows naturally from our previous decisions.

Under *Oliver* and *Hester*, there is no constitutional difference between police observations conducted while in a public place and while standing in the open fields. Similarly, the fact that the objects observed by the officers lay within an area that we have assumed, but not decided, was protected by the Fourth Amendment does not affect our conclusion. . . .

The officers lawfully viewed the interior of respondent's barn, and their observations were properly considered by the magistrate in issuing a search warrant for respondent's premises. Accordingly, the judgment of the Court of Appeals is reversed.

[JUSTICE BRENNAN, joined by JUSTICE MARSHALL, dissented.]

QUESTIONS

Because the Court concludes that the barn was neither part of the dwelling nor within the curtilage of the dwelling, could the officers have carried out the seizure forthwith? Or is the interior of the barn protected from warrantless entry? If so, why? Is there yet another classification between open fields and curtilage?

[E] Aerial Surveillance

CALIFORNIA v. CIRAOLO

United States Supreme Court
476 U.S. 207 (1986)

CHIEF JUSTICE BURGER delivered the opinion of the Court.

We granted certiorari to determine whether the Fourth Amendment is violated by aerial observation without a warrant from an altitude of 1,000 feet of fenced-in backyard within the curtilage of a home.

I

On September 2, 1982, Santa Clara Police received an anonymous telephone tip that marijuana was growing in respondent's backyard. Police were unable to observe the contents of a respondent's yard from ground level because of a 6-foot outer fence and a 10-foot inner fence completely enclosing the yard. Later that day, Officer Shutz, who was assigned to investigate, secured a private plane and flew over respondent's house at an altitude of 1,000 feet, within navigable airspace; he was accompanied by Officer Rodriquez. Both officers were trained in marijuana identification. From the overflight, the officers readily identified marijuana plants 8 feet to 10 feet in height growing in a 15-by-25 foot plot in respondent's yard; they photographed the area with a standard 35mm camera.

On September 8, 1982, Officer Shutz obtained a search warrant on the basis of an affidavit describing the anonymous tip and their observations; a photograph depicting respondent's house, the backyard, and neighboring homes was attached to the affidavit as an exhibit. The warrant was executed the next day and 73 plants were seized; it is not disputed that these were marijuana.

After the trial court denied respondent's motion to suppress the evidence of the search, respondent pleaded guilty to a charge of cultivation of marijuana. The California Court of Appeal reversed, however, on the ground that the warrantless aerial *observation* of respondent's yard which led to the issuance of the warrant violated the Fourth Amendment. . . . The court held first that respondent's backyard marijuana garden was within the "curtilage" of his home, under *Oliver v. United States*. . . . The court emphasized that the height and existence of the two fences constituted "objective criteria from which we may conclude he manifested a reasonable expectation of privacy by any standard." . . .

Examining the particular method of surveillance undertaken, the court then found it "significant" that the flyover "was not the result of a routine patrol conducted for any other legitimate law enforcement or public safety objective, but was undertaken for the specific purpose of observing this particular enclosure within [respondent's] curtilage." . . . It held this focused observation was "a direct and unauthorized intrusion into the sanctity of the home" which violates respondent's reasonable expectation of privacy. . . . The California Supreme Court denied the State's petition for review.

We granted the State's petition for certiorari. . . . We reverse. . . .

II

The touchstone of Fourth Amendment analysis is whether a person has a "constitutionally protected reasonable expectation of privacy." . . . *Katz* posits a two-part inquiry: first, has the individual manifested a subjective expectation of privacy in the object of the challenged search? Second, is society willing to recognize that expectation as reasonable? . . .

Clearly — and understandably — respondent has met the test of manifesting his own subjective intent and desire to maintain privacy as to his unlawful agricultural pursuits. . . . It can reasonably be assumed that the 10-foot fence was placed to conceal the marijuana crop from at least street level views. So far as the normal sidewalk traffic was concerned, this fence served that purpose, because respondent "took normal precautions to maintain his privacy. . . . "

Yet a 10-foot fence might not shield these plants from the eyes of a citizen or a policeman perched on the top of a truck or a 2-level bus. Whether respondent therefore manifested a subjective expectation of privacy from all observations of his backyard, or whether instead he manifested merely a hope that no one would observe his unlawful gardening pursuits, is not entirely clear in these circumstances. Respondent appears to challenge the authority of the government to observe his activity from any vantage point or place if the viewing is motivated by a law enforcement purpose, and not the result of a casual, accidental observation.

We turn, therefore, to the second inquiry under *Katz, i.e.*, whether that expectation is reasonable.

That the area is within the curtilage does not itself bar all police observation. The Fourth Amendment protection of the home has never been extended to require law enforcement officers to shield their eyes when passing by a home on public thoroughfares. Nor does the mere fact that an individual has taken measures to restrict some view of his activities preclude an officer's observations from a public vantage point where he has a right to be and which renders the activities clearly visible. . . .

The observations by Officers Shutz and Rodriquez in this case took place within public navigable airspace, . . . in physically nonintrusive manner; from this point they were able to observe plants readily discernible to the naked eye as marijuana. That the observation from aircraft was directed at identifying the plants and the officers were trained to recognize marijuana is irrelevant. Such observation is precisely what a judicial officer needs to provide a basis for a warrant. Any member of the public flying in this airspace who glanced down could have seen everything that these officers observed. On this record, we readily conclude that respondent's expectation that his garden was protected from such observation is unreasonable and is not an expectation that society is prepared to honor.

[*Reversed.*]

JUSTICE POWELL, with whom JUSTICE BRENNAN, JUSTICE MARSHALL, and JUSTICE BLACKMUN join, dissenting.

The Court's holding . . . must rest solely on the fact that members of the public fly in planes and may look down at homes as they fly over them. . . . The Court does not explain why it finds this fact to be significant. One may assume that the Court believes that citizens bear the risk that air travelers will observe activities occurring within backyards that are open to the sun and air. This risk, the Court appears to hold, nullifies expectations of privacy in those yards even as to purport police surveillance from the air. . . .

This line of reasoning is flawed. First, the actual risk to privacy from commercial or pleasure aircraft is virtually nonexistent. Travelers on commercial flights, as well as private planes used for business or personal reasons, normally obtain at most a fleeting, anonymous, and non-discriminating glimpse of the landscape and buildings over which they pass. The risk that a passenger on such a plane might observe private activities, and might connect those activities with particular people, is simply too trivial to protect against. It is no accident that, as a matter of common experience, many people build fences around their residential areas, but few build roofs over their backyards.

NOTE

In *Florida v. Riley*, 488 U.S. 445 (1989), the Court followed *Ciraolo* in sustaining surveillance by use of a helicopter hovering some 400 feet above the property of the accused.

[F] Abandoned Property

CALIFORNIA v. GREENWOOD

United States Supreme Court

486 U.S. 35 (1988)

JUSTICE WHITE delivered the opinion of the Court.

The issue here is whether the Fourth Amendment prohibits the warrantless search and seizure of garbage left for collection outside the curtilage of a home. We conclude, in accordance with the vast majority of lower courts that have addressed the issue, that it does not.

I.

In early 1984, Investigator Jenny Stracner of the Laguna Beach Police Department received information indicating that respondent Greenwood might be engaged in narcotics trafficking. Stracner learned that a criminal suspect had informed a federal drug-enforcement agent in February 1984 that a truck filled with illegal drugs was en route to the Laguna Beach address at which Greenwood resided. In addition, a neighbor complained of heavy vehicular traffic late at night in front of Greenwood's single-family home. The neighbor reported that the vehicles remained at Greenwood's house for only a few minutes.

Stracner sought to investigate this information by conducting a surveillance of Greenwood's home. She observed several vehicles make brief stops at the house during the late-night and early-morning hours, and she followed a truck from the house to a residence that had previously been under investigation as a narcotics trafficking location.

On April 6, 1984, Stracner asked the neighborhood's regular trash collector to pick up the plastic garbage bags that Greenwood had left on the curb in front of his house and to turn the bags over to her without mixing their contents with garbage from other houses. The trash collector cleaned his truck bin of other refuse, collected the garbage bags from the street in front of Greenwood's house, and turned the bags over to Stracner. The officer searched through the rubbish and found items indicative of narcotics use. She recited the information that she had gleaned from the trash search in an affidavit in support of a warrant to search Greenwood's home. . . .

II

The warrantless search and seizure of the garbage bags left at the curb outside the Greenwood house would violate the Fourth Amendment only if respondents manifested a subjective expectation of privacy in their garbage that society accepts as objectively reasonable. . . . Respondents do not disagree with this standard.

They assert, however, that they had, and exhibited, an expectation of privacy with respect to the trash that was searched by the police: The trash, which was placed on the street for collection at a fixed time, was contained in opaque plastic bags, which the garbage collector was expected to pick up, mingle with the trash of others, and deposit at the garbage dump. The trash was only temporarily on the street, and there was little likelihood that it would be inspected by anyone.

It may well be that respondents did not expect that the contents of their garbage bags would become known to the police or other members of the public. An expectation of privacy does not give rise to Fourth Amendment protection, however, unless society is prepared to accept that expectation as objectively reasonable.

Here, we conclude that respondents exposed their garbage to the public sufficiently to defeat their claim to Fourth Amendment protection. It is common knowledge that plastic garbage bags left on or at the side of a public street are readily accessible to animals, children, scavengers,[37] snoops,[38] and other members of the public. Moreover, respondents placed their refuse at the curb for the express purpose of conveying it to a third party, the trash collector, who might himself have sorted through respondents' trash or permitted others, such as the police, to do so. Accordingly, having deposited their garbage "in an area particularly suited for public inspection and, in a manner of speaking, public consumption, for the express purpose of having strangers take it," . . . respondents could have no reasonable expectation of privacy in the inculpatory items that they discarded.

Our conclusion that society would not accept as reasonable respondents' claim to an expectation of privacy in trash left for collection in an area accessible to the public is reinforced by the unanimous rejection of similar claims by the Federal Courts of Appeal. . . . In addition, of those state appellate courts that have considered the issue, the vast majority have held that the police may conduct warrantless searches and seizures of garbage discarded in public areas. . . .[39]

JUSTICE BRENNAN, with whom JUSTICE MARSHALL joints, dissenting.

. . .

Scrutiny of another's trash is contrary to commonly accepted notions of civilized behavior. I suspect, therefore, that members of our society will be shocked to learn that the Court, the ultimate guarantor of liberty, deems unreasonable our expectation that the aspects of our private lives that are concealed safely in a trash bag will not become public.

. . . In evaluating the reasonableness of Greenwood's expectation that his trash bags would not be invaded, the Court has held that we must look to "understandings that are recognized and permitted by society." Most of us, I believe, would be incensed to discover a meddler — whether a neighbor, a reporter, or a detective — scrutinizing our sealed trash containers to discover some detail of our personal lives. . . . That was, quite naturally, the reaction to the sole incident on which the Court bases its conclusion that "snoops" and the like defeat the expectation of privacy in trash. . . .

---

[37] [3] It is not only the homeless of the Nation's cities who make use of others' refuse. For example, a nationally syndicated consumer columnist has suggested that apartment dwellers obtain cents-off coupons by "mak[ing] friends with the fellow who handles the trash" in their buildings, and has recounted the tale of "the Rich lady" from Westmont who once a week puts on rubber gloves and hip boots and wades into the town garbage dump looking for labels and other proofs of purchase "needed to obtain manufacturers" refunds. M. Sloane, *The Supermarket Shopper's 1980 Guide to Coupons and Refunds* 74, 161 (1980).

[38] [4] Even the refuse of prominent Americans has not been invulnerable. In 1975, for example, a reporter for a weekly tabloid seized five bags of garbage from the sidewalk outside the home of Secretary of State Henry Kissinger. Washington Post, July 8, 1975, p. Al, col. 8. A newspaper editorial criticizing this journalistic "trashpicking" observed that "[e]vidently . . . 'everybody does it.' " Washington Post, July 10, 1975, p. A18, col. 1. We of course do not, as the dissent implies, "bas[e] [our] conclusion" that individuals have no reasonable expectation of privacy in their garbage on this "sole incident." . . . Post, at 1634.

[39] [5] Given that the dissenters are among the tiny minority of judges whose views are contrary to ours, we are distinctly unimpressed with the dissent's prediction that "society will be shocked to learn" of today's decision. . . .

Had Greenwood flaunted his intimate activity by strewing his trash all over the curb for all to see, or had some nongovernmental intruder invaded his privacy and done the same, I could accept the Court's conclusion that an expectation of privacy would have been unreasonable. Similarly, had police searching the city dump run across incriminating evidence that, despite commingling with the trash of others, still retained its identity as Greenwood's, we would have a different case. But all that Greenwood "exposed . . . to the public" . . . were the exteriors of several opaque, sealed containers. Until the bags were opened by police, they hid their contents from the public's view every bit as much as did Chadwick's double-locked footlocker and Robbin's green plastic wrapping. . . .

The mere *possibility* that unwelcome meddlers *might* open and rummage through the containers does not negate the expectation of privacy in their contents any more than the possibility of a burglary negates an expectation of privacy in the home; or the possibility of a private intrusion negates an expectation of privacy in an unopened package; or the possibility that an operator will listen in on a telephone conversation negates an expectation of privacy in the words spoken on the telephone.

NOTES AND QUESTIONS

(1) Is it of significance that "the neighborhood's regular trash collector" picked up the plastic garbage bags and turned them over to the officer at her request? Would the case come out differently if the officer had simply removed the garbage bags herself? Note that according to the Court, Greenwood had left the garbage for collection outside the curtilage of his home, more particularly at the curb in front of his house. Suppose the normal procedure had been for the trash collector to come on the property of the resident and empty the garbage cans appurtenant to the house. Would turning the bags over to an officer be illegitimate under those circumstances? What about the direct removal of the bags by the officer? Is it a sufficient answer that the individual has consented to the garbage pick-up? *See Sampson v. State*, 130 Md. App. 79, 744 A.2d 588 (2000), holding that the consent is limited to garbage collectors. The Supreme Court of Kentucky, noting that the recent *Jones* decision proclaims that "Fourth Amendment rights do not rise or fall with the *Katz* formulation," held that trash containers will be protected if they are located within the curtilage of a house. *Commonwealth v. Ousley*, 393 S.W.3d 15 (Ky. 2013).

(2) The reasonableness of the warrantless seizure of abandoned property is sustained typically in circumstances far more prosaic than those in *Greenwood*. In *Hester v. United States*, 265 U.S. 57 (1924), for example, officers were chasing two suspected bootleggers, both of whom dropped containers of liquor as they fled. In the absence of any suggestion that the pursuit had been illegal, the Court held that the evidence was seized legally. It does not follow that any brief relinquishment of possession or control constitutes an abandonment. In *Rios v. United States*, 364 U.S. 253 (1960), the Court observed that "a passenger who lets a package drop to the floor of the taxi cab in which he is riding can hardly be said to have 'abandoned' it." In any event, if the abandonment is the result of *unlawful* police activity, then the seizure will not be sustained.

(3) A separate line of cases concerns the abandonment of premises by an accused, thereby relinquishing any reasonable expectation of privacy therein. In *Abel v. United States*, 362 U.S. 217 (1960), the petitioner was arrested in his hotel room by immigration authorities. Thereafter FBI agents secured the consent of the hotel management to search the room, in the process of which incriminating items were found in the waste paper basket. The Court held that the property had been abandoned. The reasoning in Abel has been criticized on the ground that the purported abandonment was the product of the petitioner's arrest — hardly a voluntary act on his part. *See, e.g., United States v. Robinson*, 430 F.2d 1141 (6th Cir. 1970). Nevertheless, the general principle — that an accused can claim no Fourth Amendment protection in an area which he has abandoned — is widely followed.

(4) One court has relied on *Greenwood* in holding that an industrial company had no reasonable expectation of privacy in the wastewater located in its sewer connection. *People v. Electronic Plating Co.*, 291 Ill. App. 3d 328, 225 Ill. Dec. 297, 683 N.E.2d 465 (1997).

(5) In *State v. Reed*, 182 N.C. App. 109, 641 S.E.2d 320 (2007), the court held that a cigarette butt, flicked into a pile of trash at the corner of a concrete patio, could not be seized as abandoned property. The butt had been surreptitiously retrieved by an officer during the course of an interview at the defendant's apartment. DNA evidence thereby obtained was introduced against him. The court reasoned that "the uncontroverted evidence is that tenants are responsible for bringing their own trash to dumpsters provided by the apartment complex." Hence, the cigarette butt had not, or perhaps more accurately could not, be abandoned.

A different result is likely if the act of abandonment occurs in a public area. In *Commonwealth v. Cabral*, 69 Mass. App. Ct. 68, 866 N.E.2d 429 (2007), the court held that a party who "expectorates onto a public street" has voluntarily abandoned any constitutional protection and "assumed the risk of the public witnessing his action and thereafter taking possession of his bodily fluids."

PROBLEM O
THE UNSUCCESSFUL ATTEMPT TO ABANDON EVIDENCE

John Jackson murdered his paramour, and checked into a hotel under an assumed name. Later in the day, he jumped out of the hotel window in an attempt to kill himself, but instead landed on a roof three floors below, and survived, only breaking both legs and an arm. Ultimately, Jackson was charged with and convicted of the murder. On appeal, he challenged the failure of the trial court to suppress evidence seized from the hotel room from which he attempted the suicide. Was the evidence legitimately seized? *See State v. Jackson*, 40 A.3d 290 (Conn. 2012).

PROBLEM P
THE SHREDDED DOCUMENTS

Appellee was suspected by the Internal Revenue Service ("IRS") of involvement in a scheme to defraud the United States through the filing of false income tax returns. IRS agents systematically seized and combed

> through garbage bags left for collection in front of appellee's house. Their search revealed numerous shredded documents reduced to 5/32 inch strips which, when painstakingly pieced together, produced incriminating evidence. The agents then used this evidence as the basis for establishing probable cause to request various search warrants. The search warrants were issued and executed, and the searches garnered additional evidence used to secure appellee's 47 count indictment. . . . Appellee moved to suppress the reconstructed documents as well as the evidence seized pursuant to the search warrants.

Should this evidence be admitted? *See United States v. Scott*, 975 F.2d 927 (1st Cir. 1992), *cert. denied*, 507 U.S. 1042 (1993).

[G] Consent

BUMPER v. NORTH CAROLINA

United States Supreme Court
391 U.S. 543 (1962)

MR. JUSTICE STEWART delivered the opinion of the Court.

The petitioner was brought to trial in a North Carolina court upon a charge of rape, an offense punishable in that State by death unless the jury recommends life imprisonment. Among the items of evidence introduced by the prosecution at the trial was a.22-caliber rifle allegedly used in the commission of the crime. The jury found the petitioner guilty, but recommended a sentence of life imprisonment.

The petitioner lived with his grandmother, Mrs. Hattie Leath, a 66-year-old Negro widow, in a house located in a rural area at the end of an isolated mile-long dirt road. Two days after the alleged offense but prior to the petitioner's arrest, four white law enforcement officers — the county sheriff, two of his deputies, and a state investigator — went to this house and found Mrs. Leath there with some young children. She met the officers at the front door. One of them announced, "I have a search warrant to search your house." Mrs. Leath responded, "Go ahead," and opened the door. In the kitchen the officers found the rifle that was later introduced in evidence at the petitioner's trial after a motion to suppress had been denied.

At the hearing on this motion, the prosecutor informed the court that he did not rely upon a warrant to justify the search, but upon the consent of Mrs. Leath. She testified at the hearing, stating, among other things:

> Four of them came. I was busy about my work, and they walked into the house and one of them walked up and said, "I have a search warrant to search your house," and I walked out and told them to come on in. . . . He just come on in and said he had a warrant to search the house, and he didn't read it to me or nothing. So, I just told him to come on in and go ahead and search, and I went on about my work. I wasn't concerned what he was about. I was just satisfied. He just told me he had a search warrant, but he didn't read it to me. He did tell me he had a search warrant.

. . .

> . . . He said he was the law and had a search warrant to search the house, why I thought he could go ahead. I believed he had a search warrant. I took him at his word. . . . I just seen them out there in the yard. They got through the door when I opened it. At that time, I did not know my grandson had been charged with crime. Nobody told me anything. They didn't tell me anything, just picked it up like that. They didn't tell me nothing about my grandson.

Upon the basis of Mrs. Leath's testimony, the trial court found that she had given her consent to the search, and denied the motion to suppress. The Supreme Court of North Carolina approved the admission of the evidence on the same basis.

The issue thus presented is whether a search can be justified as lawful on the basis of consent when that "consent" has been given only after the official conducting the search has asserted that he possesses a warrant. We hold that there can be no consent under such circumstances.

When a prosecutor seeks to rely upon consent to justify the lawfulness of a search, he has the burden of proving that the consent was, in fact, freely and voluntarily given. This burden cannot be discharged by showing no more than acquiescence to a claim of lawful authority. A search conducted in reliance upon a warrant cannot later be justified on the basis of consent if it turns out that the warrant was invalid. The result can be no different when it turns out that the State does not even attempt to rely upon the validity of the warrant, or fails to show that there was, in fact, any warrant at all.

When a law enforcement officer claims authority to search a home under a warrant, he announces in effect that the occupant has no right to resist the search. The situation is instinct with coercion — albeit colorably lawful coercion. Where there is coercion there cannot be consent.

We hold that Mrs. Leath did not consent to the search, and that it was constitutional error to admit the rifle in evidence against the petitioner.

[JUSTICES HARLAN and DOUGLAS concurred separately; JUSTICES BLACK and WHITE dissented separately.]

NOTES AND QUESTIONS

(1) It is not clear in *Bumper* whether the officers did not have a search warrant or had one which later proved to be invalid. Should it make a difference?

(2) Because consent is an exception to the warrant requirement, the authority to search is no greater than that given by the consenting party, both as to scope and time. Suppose a suspect in custody consents to a search of his home "in his presence." The police take him to the premises, and during the course of the search he escapes, but the search continues. Should items seized subsequent to his departure be admissible? *See Herron v. State*, 456 S.W.2d 873 (Tenn. Crim. App. 1970) (officers could continue search). *But see Pierre v. State*, 732 So. 2d 376 (Fla. Dist. Ct. App. 1999) (consent to search vehicle withdrawn when suspect fled).

PROBLEM Q
CONSENT EXTENDED TO CYBERSPACE

At 2:00 A.M., Daniel Turner reported an assault in his neighbor's apartment. When officers arrived, he said that he had been seated at his computer when he observed the intruder fleeing. The victim had cut her hands when she grabbed the knife of the assailant. The following morning, investigators returned to the crime scene and noticed that window screens on both Turner's and the victim's apartments were ajar, and that the sill on Turner's window was smeared with blood. Surmising that the assailant had entered both apartments, the officers obtained consent from Turner to "look around." When a knife and blood stains were found around the apartment, including in the computer room, the officers began to suspect Turner. They obtained his written consent to search "the premises," "his vehicle," and "personal property." In the course of a 90-minute search,

> Detective Gould . . . noticed that Turner's computer monitor screen suddenly turned on, and the Windows "desktop" disclosed a photograph of a nude woman with "light-colored hair," which Gould concluded was "similar" to [that of the victim].
>
> At that point, Gould seated himself at the computer and engaged the "mouse" to access the "Documents" index from the Windows 95 task bar, which itemized titles of files most recently accessed by Turner. Gould noticed several indexed files with the suffix ".jpg," denoting a file containing a photograph. After clicking on these file names, he located photographs of nude blonde women in bondage. Further into the "Documents" listing, he noted several text files bearing titles which suggested rape and/or bondage. After calling the district attorney's office for guidance, Gould copied the adult-pornography files onto a floppy disk.

A further search of the hard drive revealed files which the officer believed to be child pornography. Gould thereupon closed down and seized the computer.

Turner was charged with possessing child pornography. Are the computer files admissible? *See United States v. Turner*, 169 F.3d 84 (1st Cir. 1999).

OHIO v. ROBINETTE
United States Supreme Court
519 U.S. 33 (1996)

CHIEF JUSTICE REHNQUIST delivered the opinion of the Court.

We are here presented with the question whether the Fourth Amendment requires that a lawfully seized defendant must be advised that he is "free to go" before his consent to search will be recognized as voluntary. We hold that it does not.

This case arose on a stretch of Interstate 70 north of Dayton, Ohio, where the posted speed limit was 45 miles per hour because of construction. Respondent Robert D. Robinette was clocked at 69 miles per hour as he drove his car along this stretch of road, and was stopped by Deputy Roger Newsome of the Montgomery

County Sheriff's office. Newsome asked for and was handed Robinette's driver's license, and he ran a computer check which indicated that Robinette had no previous violations. Newsome then asked Robinette to step out of his car, turned on his mounted video camera, issued a verbal warning to Robinette, and returned his license.

At this point, Newsome asked, "One question before you get gone: [A]re you carrying any illegal contraband in your car? Any weapons of any kind, drugs, anything like that?" . . . Robinette answered "no" to these questions, after which Deputy Newsome asked if he could search the car. Robinette consented. In the car, Deputy Newsome discovered a small amount of marijuana and, in a film container, a pill which was later determined to be methylenedioxymethamphetamine (MDMA). Robinette was then arrested and charged with knowing possession of a controlled substance, MDMA, in violation of Ohio Rev. Code Ann. § 2925.11(A) (1993).

Before trial, Robinette unsuccessfully sought to suppress this evidence. He then pleaded "no contest," and was found guilty. On appeal, the Ohio Court of Appeals reversed, ruling that the search resulted from an unlawful detention. The Supreme Court of Ohio, by a divided vote, affirmed. . . . In its opinion, that court established a bright-line prerequisite for consensual interrogation under these circumstances:

> "The right, guaranteed by the federal and Ohio Constitutions, to be secure in one's person and property requires that citizens stopped for traffic offenses be clearly informed by the detaining officer when they are free to go after a valid detention, before an officer attempts to engage in a consensual interrogation. Any attempt at consensual interrogation must be preceded by the phrase 'At this time you legally are free to go' or by words of similar import."

We granted certiorari . . . to review this *per se* rule, and we now reverse.

. . .

We think that under our recent decision in *Whren v. United States* . . . (decided after the Supreme Court of Ohio decided the present case), the subjective intentions of the officer did not make the continued detention of respondent illegal under the Fourth Amendment. As we made clear in *Whren*, " 'the fact that [an] officer does not have the state of mind which is hypothecated by the reasons which provide the legal justification for the officer's action does not invalidate the action taken as long as the circumstances, viewed objectively, justify that action.' . . . Subjective intentions play no role in ordinary, probable-cause Fourth Amendment analysis." . . . And there is no question that, in light of the admitted probable cause to stop Robinette for speeding, Deputy Newsome was objectively justified in asking Robinette to get out of the car, subjective thoughts notwithstanding. See *Pennsylvania v. Mimms*.

We have previously rejected a *per se* rule very similar to that adopted by the Supreme Court of Ohio in determining the validity of a consent to search. In *Schneckloth v. Bustamonte*, 412 U.S. 218 (1973), it was argued that such a consent could not be valid unless the defendant knew that he had a right to refuse the request. We rejected this argument: "While knowledge of the right to refuse consent is one factor to be taken into account, the government need not establish such knowledge as the *sine qua non* of an effective consent." . . . And just as it "would be thoroughly impractical to impose on the normal consent search the detailed requirements of an effective warning," . . . so too would it be unrealistic to require police officers to always inform detainees that they are free to go before a consent to search may be deemed voluntary.

The Fourth Amendment test for a valid consent to search is that the consent be voluntary, and "[v]oluntariness is a question of fact to be determined from all the circumstances,". . . . The Supreme Court of Ohio having held otherwise, its judgment is reversed, and the case is remanded for further proceedings not inconsistent with this opinion.

[Justice Ginsburg concurred in the judgment, but doubted that the Ohio Supreme Court had understood its ruling to be compelled by the United States Constitution. If such was the case, she submitted that the state court acted within its authority in imposing a higher standard for consent searches in Ohio.]

[Justice Stevens dissented, contending that the prolonged detention was unreasonable under *United States v. Sharpe, supra*, and that the consent to search was the fruit of that illegality. While agreeing with the majority that the United States Constitution did not mandate telling the detainee he was free to go before seeking consent to search, he viewed that point as immaterial to the resolution of the case.]

NOTES AND QUESTIONS

(1) Suppose that the party is in custody (as that term is used in *Miranda* analysis, see *infra*) at the time a consent to search is sought. Should he first be advised of his rights under the Fourth Amendment? In *United States v. Watson*, 423 U.S. 411 (1976), the consent to search obtained without prior advisement of a right of refusal was sustained by the Supreme Court. The accused had received *Miranda* warnings, but this factor, while relevant, was not dispositive. Some courts have held that once an accused has requested the assistance of counsel, consent to search may not be sought. *See Larkin v. State*, 393 N.E.2d 180 (Ind. 1979); *People v. Johnson*, 48 N.Y.2d 565, 423 N.Y.S.2d 905, 399 N.E.2d 936 (1979).

(2) The Supreme Court of New Jersey has elected to impose a higher standard than that mandated by the Fourth Amendment under its state constitution:

> [W]here the State seeks to justify a search on the basis of consent it has the burden of showing that the consent was voluntary, an essential element of which is knowledge of the right to refuse consent.
>
> Many persons, perhaps most, would view the request of a police officer to make a search as having the force of law. Unless it is shown by the State that the person involved knew that he had the right to refuse to accede to such a request, his assenting to the search is not meaningful. One cannot be held to have waived a right if he was unaware of its existence.

State v. Johnson, 68 N.J. 349, 353–354, 346 A.2d 66, 68 (1975).

(3) The application of the container doctrine to consent searches was addressed in *Florida v. Jimeno*, 500 U.S. 248 (1991). The Court held (7-2) that the search of a

closed paper bag in the course of a consensual search of an automobile was reasonable in light of the fact that the party was suspected of drug dealing, Chief Justice Rehnquist observing that "[a] reasonable person may be expected to know that narcotics are generally carried in some form of a container." At the same time, the Court did not declare open season on *all* containers: "It is very likely unreasonable to think that a suspect, by consenting to the search of his trunk, has agreed to the breaking open of a locked briefcase within the trunk, but it is otherwise with respect to a closed paper bag." Is it disconcerting that narcotics carried in a locked attache case enjoy greater constitutional protection than those in a paper bag? Does the statement of the Court suggest a different result if the attache case is not locked?

(4) The Court of Appeals of New York has held that a general consent to search a car does not acquiesce in the impairment of "the structural integrity of a vehicle." "A reasonable person would not have understood the officer's request to search to include prying open a hole in the floorboard and gas tank with a crowbar." *People v. Gomez,* 5 N.Y.3d 416, 805 N.Y.S.2d 24, 26, 838 N.E.2d 1271 (2005).

UNITED STATES v. DRAYTON

United States Supreme Court
536 U.S. 194 (2002)

JUSTICE KENNEDY delivered the opinion of the Court.

[For the facts of the case and the Court's consideration of the detention issue, see § 2.01, *supra.*]

. . .

We turn now from the question whether respondents were seized to whether they were subjected to an unreasonable search, *i.e.*, whether their consent for the suspicionless search was involuntary. In circumstances such as these, where the question of voluntariness pervades both the search and seizure inquiries, the respective analyses turn on very similar facts. And, as the facts above suggest, respondents' consent to the search of their luggage and their persons was voluntary. Nothing Officer Lang said indicated a command to consent to the search. Rather, when respondents informed Lang that they had a bag on the bus, he asked for their permission to check it. And when Lang requested to search Brown and Drayton's persons, he asked first if they objected, thus indicating to a reasonable person that he or she was free to refuse. Even after arresting Brown, Lang provided Drayton with no indication that he was required to consent to a search. To the contrary, Lang asked for Drayton's permission to search him ("Mind if I check you?"), and Drayton agreed.

The Court has rejected in specific terms the suggestion that police officers must always inform citizens of their right to refuse when seeking permission to conduct a warrantless consent search. See, e.g., *Ohio v. Robinette*. . . . Nor do this Court's decisions suggest that even though there are no per se rules, a presumption of invalidity attaches if a citizen consented without explicit notification that he or she was free to refuse to cooperate. Instead, the Court has repeated that the totality of the circumstances must control, without giving extra weight to the absence of this type of warning. . . . Although Officer Lang did not inform respondents of their right to refuse the search, he did request permission to search, and the totality of the circumstances indicates that their consent was voluntary, so the searches were reasonable.

In a society based on law, the concept of agreement and consent should be given a weight and dignity of its own. Police officers act in full accord with the law when they ask citizens for consent. It reinforces the rule of law for the citizen to advise the police of his or her wishes and for the police to act in reliance on that understanding. When this exchange takes place, it dispels inferences of coercion.

Justice Souter, with whom Justice Stevens and Justice Ginsburg join, dissenting.

[F]or reasons unexplained, the driver with the tickets entitling the passengers to travel had yielded his custody of the bus and its seated travelers to three police officers, whose authority apparently superseded the driver's own. The officers took control of the entire passenger compartment, one stationed at the door keeping surveillance of all the occupants, the others working forward from the back. With one officer right behind him and the other one forward, a third officer accosted each passenger at quarters extremely close and so cramped that as many as half the passengers could not even have stood to face the speaker. None was asked whether he was willing to converse with the police or to take part in the enquiry. Instead the officer said the police were "conducting an interdiction," in the course of which they "would like . . . cooperation." . . . The reasonable inference was that the "interdiction" was not a consensual exercise, but one the police would carry out whatever the circumstances; that they would prefer "cooperation" but would not let the lack of it stand in their way. There was no contrary indication that day, since no passenger had refused the cooperation requested, and there was no reason for any passenger to believe that the driver would return and the trip resume until the police were satisfied. The scene was set and an atmosphere of obligatory participation was established by this introduction. Later requests to search prefaced with "Do you mind . . ." would naturally have been understood in the terms with which the encounter began.

It is very hard to imagine that either Brown or Drayton would have believed that he stood to lose nothing if he refused to cooperate with the police, or that he had any free choice to ignore the police altogether. No reasonable passenger could have believed that, only an uncomprehending one. It is neither here nor there that the interdiction was conducted by three officers, not one, as a safety precaution. . . . The fact was that there were three, and when Brown and Drayton were called upon to respond, each one was presumably conscious of an officer in front watching, one at his side questioning him, and one behind for cover, in case he became unruly, perhaps, or "cooperation" was not forthcoming. The situation is much like the one in the alley, with civilians in close quarters, unable to move effectively, being told their cooperation is expected. While I am not prepared to say that no bus interrogation and search can pass the *Bostick* test without a warning that passengers are free to say no, the facts here surely required more from the officers than a quiet tone of voice. A police officer who is certain to get his way has no need to shout.

GEORGIA v. RANDOLPH

United States Supreme Court
547 U.S. 103 (2006)

JUSTICE SOUTER delivered the opinion of the Court.

The Fourth Amendment recognizes as valid warrantless entry and search of premises when police obtain the voluntary consent of an occupant who shares, or is reasonably believed to share, authority over the area common with a co-occupant who later objects to the use of evidence so obtained. *Illinois v. Rodriguez*, 497 U.S. 177; *United States v. Matlock*, 415 U.S. 164. The question here is whether such an evidentiary seizure is likewise lawful with the permission of one occupant when the other who later seeks to suppress the evidence, is present at the scene and expressly refuses to consent. We hold that, in the circumstances here at issue, a physically present co-occupant's stated refusal to permit entry prevails, rendering the warrantless search unreasonable and invalid as to him.

I

Respondent Scott Randolph and his wife Janet, separated in late May 2001, when she left the marital residence in Americus, Georgia, and went to stay with her parents in Canada, taking their son and some belongings. In July, she returned to the Americus house with the child, though the record does not reveal whether her object was reconciliation or retrieval of remaining possessions.

On the morning of July 6, she complained to the police that after a domestic dispute her husband took their son away, and when officers reached the house she told them that her husband was a cocaine user whose habit had caused financial troubles. She mentioned the marital problems and said that she and their son had only recently returned after a stay of several weeks with her parents. Shortly after the police arrived, Scott Randolph returned and explained that he had removed the child to a neighbor's house out of concern that his wife might take the boy out of the country again; he denied cocaine use, and countered that it was in fact his wife who abused drugs and alcohol.

One of the officers, Sergeant Murray, went with Janet Randolph to reclaim the child, and when they returned she not only renewed her complaints about her husband's drug use, but also volunteered that there were " 'items of drug evidence' " in the house. . . . Sergeant Murray asked Scott Randolph for permission to search the house, which he unequivocally refused.

The sergeant turned to Janet Randolph for consent to search, which she readily gave. She led the officer upstairs to a bedroom that she identified as Scott's, where the sergeant noticed a section of a drinking straw with a powdery residue he suspected was cocaine. He then left the house to get an evidence bag from his car and to call the district attorney's office, which instructed him to stop the search and apply for a warrant. When Sergeant Murray returned to the house, Janet Randolph withdrew her consent. The police took the straw to the police station, along with the Randolphs. After getting a search warrant, they returned to the house and seized further evidence of drug use, on the basis of which Scott Randolph was indicted for possession of cocaine.

He moved to suppress the evidence, as products of a warrantless search of his house unauthorized by his wife's consent over his express refusal. The trial court denied the motion, ruling that Janet Randolph had common authority to consent to the search.

The Court of Appeals of Georgia reversed, . . . and was itself sustained by the State Supreme Court, principally on the ground that "the consent to conduct a warrantless search of a residence given by one occupant is not valid in the face of the refusal of another occupant who is physically present at the scene to permit a warrantless search." . . . The Supreme Court of Georgia acknowledged this Court's holding in *Matlock*, . . . that "the consent of one who possesses common authority over premises or effects is valid as against the absent, nonconsenting person with whom that authority is shared," . . . and found *Matlock* distinguishable just because Scott Randolph was not "absent" from the colloquy on which the police relied for consent to make the search. The State Supreme Court stressed that the officers in *Matlock* had not been "faced with the physical presence of joint occupants, with one consenting to the search and the other objecting." . . . It held that an individual who chooses to live with another assumes a risk no greater than " 'an inability to control access to the premises during [his] absence,' " . . . and does not contemplate that his objection to a request to search commonly shared premises, if made, will be overlooked.

We granted certiorari to resolve a split of authority on whether one occupant may give law enforcement effective consent to search shared premises, as against a co-tenant who is present and states a refusal to permit the search. . . . We now affirm.

II

. . .

D

Since the co-tenant wishing to open the door to a third party has no recognized authority in law or social practice to prevail over a present and objecting co-tenant, his disputed invitation, without more, give a police officer no better claim to reasonableness in entering than the officer would have in the absence of any consent at all. Accordingly, in the balancing of competing individual and governmental interests entailed by the bar to unreasonable searches, . . . the cooperative occupant's invitation adds nothing to the government's side to counter the force of an objecting individual's claim to security against the government's intrusion into his dwelling place. . . .

This case has no bearing on the capacity of the police to protect domestic victims.

The dissent's argument rests on the failure to distinguish two different issues: when the police may enter without committing a trespass, and when the police may enter to search for evidence. No question has been raised, or reasonably could be, about the authority of the police to enter a dwelling to protect a resident from domestic violence; so long as they have good reason to believe such a threat exists, it would be silly to suggest that the police would commit a tort by entering, say, to give a complaining tenant the opportunity to collect belongings and get out safely, or to determine whether violence (or threat of violence) has just occurred or is about to (or soon will) occur, however much a spouse or other co-tenant objected. (And since the police would then be lawfully in the premises, there is no question that they could seize any evidence in plain view or take further action supported by any consequent probable cause),. . . .

E

There are two loose ends, the first being the explanation given in *Matlock* for the constitutional sufficiency of a co-tenant's consent to enter and search: it "rests . . . on the mutual use of the property by persons generally having joint access or control for most purposes, so that it is reasonable to recognize that any of the co-inhabitants has the right to permit the inspection in his own right. . . ." If *Matlock's* co-tenant is giving permission "in his own right," how can his "own right" be eliminated by another tenant's objection? The answer appears in the very footnote from which the quoted statement is taken: the "right" to admit the police to which *Matlock* refers is not an enduring and enforceable ownership right as understood by the private law of property, but is instead the authority recognized by customary and social usage as having a substantial bearing on Fourth Amendment reasonableness in specific circumstances. Thus, to ask whether the consenting tenant has the right to admit the police when a physically present fellow tenant objects is not to question whether some property right may be divested by the mere objection of another. It is, rather, the question whether customary social understanding accords the consenting tenant authority powerful enough to prevail over the co-tenant's objection. The *Matlock* Court did not purport to answer this question, a point made clear by another statement (which the dissent does not quote): the Court described the co-tenant's consent as good against "the absent, nonconsenting resident." . . .

The second loose end is the significance of *Matlock* and *Rodriguez* after today's decision. Although the *Matlock* defendant was not present with the opportunity to object, he was in a squad car not far away; the *Rodriguez* defendant was actually asleep in the apartment, and the police might have roused him with a knock on the door before they entered with only the consent of an apparent co-tenant. If those cases are not to be undercut by today's holding, we have to admit that we are drawing a fine line; if a potential defendant with self-interest in objecting is in fact at the door and objects, the co-tenant's permission does not suffice for a reasonable search, whereas the potential objector, nearby but not invited to take part in the threshold colloquy, loses out.

This is the line we draw, and we think the formalism is justified. So long as there is no evidence that the police have removed the potentially objecting tenant from the entrance for the sake of avoiding a possible objection, there is practical value in the simple clarity of complementary rules, one recognizing the co-tenant's permission when there is no fellow occupant on hand, the other according dispositive weight of the fellow occupant's contrary indication when he expresses it. For the very reason that *Rodriguez* held it would be unjustifiably impractical to require the police to take affirmative steps to confirm the actual authority of a consenting individual whose authority was apparent, we think it would needlessly limit the capacity of the police to respond to ostensibly legitimate opportunities in the field if we were to hold that reasonableness required the police to take affirmative steps to find a potentially objecting co-tenant before acting on the permission they had already received. There is no ready reason to believe that efforts to invite a refusal would make a difference in many cases, whereas every co-tenant consent case would turn into a test about the adequacy of the police's efforts to consult with a potential objector. Better to accept the formalism of distinguishing *Matlock* from this case than to impose a requirement, time-consuming in the field and in the courtroom, with no apparent systemic justification. The pragmatic decision to accept the simplicity of this line is, moreover, supported by the substantial number of instances in which suspects who are asked for permission to search actually consent, albeit imprudently, a fact that undercuts any argument that the police should try to locate a suspected inhabitant because his denial of consent would be a foregone conclusion.

III

This case invites a straightforward application of the rule that a physically present inhabitant's express refusal of consent to a police search is dispositive as to him, regardless of the consent of a fellow occupant. Scott Randolph's refusal is clear, and nothing in the record justifies the search on grounds independent of Janet Randolph's consent. The State does not argue that she gave any indication to the police of a need for protection inside the house that might have justified entry into the portion of the premises where the police found the powdery straw (which, if lawfully seized, could have been used when attempting to establish probable cause for the warrant issued later). Nor does the State claim that the entry and search should be upheld under the rubric of exigent circumstances, owing to some apprehension by the police officers that Scott Randolph would destroy evidence of drug use before any warrant could be obtained.

The judgment of the Supreme Court of Georgia is therefore affirmed. . . .

[Justice Alito took no part in the consideration or decision of the case. Justice Stevens and Justice Breyer concurred in separate opinions.]

Chief Justice Roberts, with whom Justice Scalia joins, dissenting.

The Court creates constitutional law by surmising what is typical when a social guest encounters an entirely atypical situation. The rule the majority fashions does not implement the high office of the Fourth Amendment to protect privacy, but instead provides protection on a random and happenstance basis, protecting, for example, a co-occupant who happens to be at the front door when the other occupant consents to a search, but not one napping or watching television in the next room. And the cost of affording such random protection is great, as demonstrated by the recurring cases in which abused spouses seek to authorize police entry into a home they share with a nonconsenting abuser.

The correct approach to the question presented is clearly mapped out in our precedents: The Fourth Amendment protects privacy. If an individual shares information, papers, or *places* with another, he assumes the risk that the other person will in turn share access to that information or those papers or places with the government. And just as an individual who has shared illegal plans or incriminating documents with another cannot interpose an objection when that other person turns the information over to the government, just because the individual happens to be present at the time, so too someone who shares a place with another cannot interpose an objection when that person decides to grant access to the police, simply because the objecting individual happens to be present.

A warrantless search is reasonable if police obtain the voluntary consent of a person authorized to give it. Co-occupants have "assumed the risk that one of their number might permit [a] common area to be searched." *United States v. Matlock* . . . Just as Mrs. Randolph could walk upstairs, come down, and turn her husband's cocaine straw over to the police, she can consent to police entry and search of what is, after all, her home, too. . . .

III

. . .

Just as the source of the majority's rule is not privacy, so too the interest it protects cannot reasonably be described as such. That interest is not protected if a co-owner happens to be absent when the police arrive, in the backyard gardening, asleep in the next room, or listening to music through earphones so that only his co-occupant hears the knock on the door. That the rule is so random in its application confirms that it bears no real relation to the privacy protected by the Fourth Amendment. What the majority's rule protects is not so much privacy as the good luck of a co-owner who just happens to be present at the door when the police arrive. . . .

Rather than draw such random and happenstance lines — and pretend that the Constitution decreed them — the more reasonable approach is to adopt a rule acknowledging that shared living space entails a limited yielding of privacy to others, and that the law historically permits those to whom we have yielded our privacy to in turn cooperate with the government. Such a rule flows more naturally from our cases concerning Fourth Amendment reasonableness and is logically grounded in the concept of privacy underlying that Amendment.

[JUSTICE SCALIA and JUSTICE THOMAS dissented in separate opinions.]

NOTES AND QUESTIONS

(1) In what Justice Stevens, concurring, referred to as "an odd flyspeck of a case," a unanimous Supreme Court held in *Brigham City v. Stuart*, 547 U.S. 398 (2006), that "police may enter a home without a warrant when they have an objectively reasonable basis for believing that an occupant is seriously injured or

imminently threatened with such injury." Police had responded to a call regarding a loud party at a residence at 3 AM and observed an altercation through a screen door and kitchen windows. The officers entered the premises and restored order and subsequently made arrests for contributing to the delinquency of a minor, disorderly conduct, and intoxication. Chief Justice Roberts, speaking for the Court, held that the officers might reasonably have concluded that one of the parties observed required medical aid, and that the affray was still in its early stages. Because the intervention was objectively reasonable, the actual motivation of the officers was of no consequence.

In light of this decision and innumerable lower court cases sustaining warrantless entries to aid parties in distress, is the suggestion of the *Randolph* dissenters that this decision jeopardizes the safety of victims of spousal abuse a bogus argument?

(2) In *United States v. Murphy*, 516 F.3d 1117 (9th Cir. 2008), the prosecution sought to distinguish *Randolph* on two grounds. First, the area searched was a storage locker, which the defendant shared but for which he did not pay rent. Second, the defendant had refused consent before being arrested and removed from the scene, and two hours later the co-occupant gave consent. The court held that *Randolph* still controlled the case. *But see United States v. Hudspeth*, 518 F.3d 94, 960 (8th Cir. 2008) (The "rationale for the narrow holding of *Randolph*, which repeatedly referenced the defendant's physical presence and immediate objection, is inapplicable here."). A co-occupant who remains silent behind a locked bedroom door after an effective consent to search by his spouse has not countermanded the consent. *People v. Fuerst*, 302 P.3d 253, 257 (Colo. 2013) ("Fuerst was more like an absent co-tenant who, even if nearby when his co-tenant consents to a police search, 'loses out' on his opportunity to refuse consent.").

(3) Implicit in the third party consent cases is the assumption that the consenting party has a superior or at least a roughly equivalent right to occupy the premises. The Supreme Court has held that a landlord cannot effectively consent to the search of the premises of a tenant, *Chapman v. United States*, 365 U.S. 610 (1961), nor can an innkeeper consent to the search of the room of a guest *Stoner v. California*, 376 U.S. 483 (1964), at least so long as the tenancy is in effect.

(4) In *United States v. Johnson*, 22 F.3d 674 (6th Cir. 1994), the court found it unreasonable for officers to believe that a kidnap victim had authority to consent to a search of the premises on which he was held captive. While exigent circumstances supported an entry to rescue the victim, the seizure of firearms from a closet could not be sustained.

[H] Vehicles

[1] With Probable Cause

CHAMBERS v. MARONEY

United States Supreme Court
399 U.S. 42 (1970)

MR. JUSTICE WHITE delivered the opinion of the Court.

The principle question in this case concerns the admissibility of evidence seized from an automobile, in which petitioner was riding at the time of his arrest, after the automobile was taken to a police station and was there thoroughly searched without a warrant. The Court of Appeals for the Third Circuit found no violation of petitioner's Fourth Amendment rights. We affirm.

I

During the night of May 20, 1963, a Gulf service station in North Braddock, Pennsylvania, was robbed by two men, each of whom carried and displayed a gun. The robbers took the currency from the cash register; the service station attendant, one Stephen Kovacich, was directed to place the coins in his right-hand glove, which was then taken by the robbers. Two teenagers, who had earlier noticed a blue compact station wagon circling the block in the vicinity of Gulf station, then saw the station wagon speed away from a parking lot close to the Gulf station. About the same time, they learned that the Gulf station had been robbed. They reported to police, who arrived immediately, that four men were in the station wagon and one was wearing a green sweater. Kovacich told the police that one of the men who robbed him was wearing a green sweater and the other was wearing a trench coat. A description of the car and the two robbers was broadcast over the police radio. Within an hour, a light blue compact station wagon answering the description and carrying four men was stopped by the police about two miles from the Gulf station. Petitioner was one of the men in the station wagon. He was wearing a green sweater and there was a trench coat in the car. The occupants were arrested and the car was driven to the police station. In the course of a thorough search of the car at the station, the police found concealed in a compartment under the dashboard two.38-caliber revolvers (one loaded with dumdum bullets), a right-handed glove containing small change, and certain cards bearing the name of Raymond Havicon, the attendant at a Boron service station in McKeesport, Pennsylvania, who had been robbed at gunpoint on May 13, 1963. In the course of a warrant-authorized search of petitioner's home the day after petitioner's arrest, police found and seized certain.38-caliber ammunition, including some dumdum bullets similar to those found in one of the guns taken from the station wagon.

In terms of the circumstances justifying a warrantless search, the court has long distinguished between an automobile and a home or office. In *Carroll v. United States*, 267 U.S. 132 (1925), the issue was the admissibility in evidence of contraband liquor seized in a warrantless search of a car on the highway. After surveying the law from the time of the adoption of the Fourth Amendment onward, the Court held that automobiles and other conveyances may be searched without a warrant in circumstances that would not justify the search without a warrant of a house or an office, provided that there is probable cause to believe that the car contains articles that the officers are entitled to seize. The Court expressed its holdings as follows:

> We have made a somewhat extended reference to these statutes to show that the guaranty of freedom from unreasonable searches and seizures by the Fourth Amendment has been construed, practically since the beginning of the Government, as recognizing a necessary difference between a search of a store, dwelling house or other structure in respect of which a proper official warrant readily may be obtained, and a search of a ship, motor boat, wagon or automobile, for contraband goods, where it is not practical to secure a warrant because the vehicle can be quickly moved out of the locality or jurisdiction in which the warrant must be sought.
>
> Having thus established that contraband goods concealed and illegally transported in an automobile or other vehicle may be searched for without a warrant, we come now to consider under what circumstances such search may be made. . . . [T]hose lawfully within the country, entitled to use the public highways, have a right to free passage without interruption or search unless there is known to a competent official authorized to search, probable cause for believing that their vehicles are carrying contraband or illegal merchandise.
>
> . . .
>
> The measure of legality of such a seizure is, therefore, that the seizing officer shall have reasonable or probable cause for believing that the automobile which he stops and seizes has contraband liquor therein which is being illegally transported.

267 U.S., at 153–154, 155–156. The Court also noted that the search of an auto on probable cause proceeds on a theory wholly different from that justifying the search incident to an arrest:

> The right to search and the validity of the seizure are not dependent on the right to arrest. They are dependent on the reasonable cause the seizing officer has for belief that the contents of the automobile offend against the law.

267 U.S., at 158–159. Finding that there was probable cause for the search and seizure at issue before it, the Court affirmed the convictions.

Neither *Carroll, supra*, nor other cases in this Court require or suggest that in every conceivable circumstance the search of an auto even with probable cause may be made without the extra protection for privacy that a warrant affords. But the circumstances that furnish probable cause to search a particular auto for particular articles are most often unforeseeable; moreover, the opportunity to search is fleeting since a car is readily movable. Where this is true, as in *Carroll* and the case before us now, if an effective search is to be made at any time, either the search must be made immediately without a warrant or the car itself must be seized and held without a warrant for whatever period is necessary to obtain a warrant for the search.

In enforcing the Fourth Amendment's prohibition against unreasonable searches and seizures, the Court has insisted upon probable cause as a minimum requirement for a reasonable search permitted by the Constitution. As a general rule, it has also required the judgment of a magistrate on the probable-cause issue and the issuance of a warrant before a search is made. Only in exigent circumstances will the judgment of the police as to probable cause serve as a sufficient authorization for a search. *Carroll, supra,* holds a search warrant unnecessary where there is probable cause to search an automobile stopped on the highway; the car is movable, the occupants are alerted, and the car's contents may never be found again if a warrant must be obtained. Hence an immediate search is constitutionally permissible.

Arguably, because of the preference for a magistrate's judgment, only the immobilization of the car should be permitted until a search warrant is obtained; arguably, only the "lesser" intrusion is permissible until the magistrate authorizes the "greater." But which is the "greater" and which the "lesser" intrusion is itself a debatable question and the answer may depend on a variety of circumstances. For constitutional purposes, we see no difference between on the one hand seizing and holding a car before presenting the probable cause issue to a magistrate and on the other hand carrying out an immediate search without a warrant. Given probable cause to search, either course is reasonable under the Fourth Amendment.

On the facts before us, the blue station wagon could have been searched on the spot when it was stopped since there was probable cause to search and it was a fleeting target for a search. The probable-cause factor still obtained at the station house and so did the mobility of the car and the denial of its use to anyone until a warrant is secured. In that event there is little to choose in terms of practical consequences between an immediate search without a warrant and the car's immobilization until a warrant is obtained. The same consequences may not follow where there is unforeseeable cause to search a house. Compare *Vale v. Louisiana.* . . . But as *Carroll, supra,* held, for the purposes of the Fourth Amendment, there is a constitutional difference between houses and cars.

[JUSTICES STEWART and HARLAN concurred separately.]

NOTES AND QUESTIONS

(1) Does the Court hold that there is a lesser expectation of privacy in an automobile than a home because that is a fact, or is it a fact because the Court so holds?

(2) Justice White concludes, "[f]or constitutional purposes, we see no difference between on the one hand seizing and holding a car before presenting the probable cause issue to a magistrate and on the other hand carrying out an immediate search without a warrant." Does this miss the issue?

(3) It must, of course, be shown that there was probable cause to search the vehicle for the *Carroll-Chambers* rule to apply. In *Preston v. United States,* 376 U.S.

364 (1964), officers investigated a complaint received at three in the morning that three men in a parked car in a business district were "acting suspiciously." Upon failing to explain their presence to the satisfaction of the officers, they were arrested for vagrancy. The automobile was towed to a garage, and some time later two loaded revolvers were found in the glove compartment and burglary paraphernalia was discovered in the trunk. The Court held that the search could not be sustained either as incident to the arrest or under the *Carroll* rationale. In *Chambers*, the Court identified as the crucial factor in *Preston* that the occupants of the vehicle had been taken into custody, and there was no probable cause to believe the vehicle contained seizable property. *See also Dyke v. Taylor Implement Mfg. Co.*, 391 U.S. 216 (1968).

CALIFORNIA v. CARNEY

United States Supreme Court
471 U.S. 386 (1985)

Chief Justice Burger delivered the opinion of the Court.

We granted certiorari to decide whether law enforcement agents violated the Fourth Amendment when they conducted a warrantless search, based on probable cause, of a fully mobile "motor home" located in a public place.

I

On May 31, 1979, Drug Enforcement Agency Agent Robert Williams watched respondent, Charles Carney, approach a youth in downtown San Diego. The youth accompanied Carney to a Dodge Mini Motor Home parked in a nearby lot. Carney and the youth closed the window shades in the motor home, including one across the front window. Agent Williams had previously received uncorroborated information that the same motor home was used by another person who was exchanging marijuana for sex. Williams, with assistance from other agents, kept the motor home under surveillance for the entire one and one-quarter hours that Carney and the youth remained inside. When the youth left the motor home, the agents followed and stopped him. The youth told the agents that he had received marijuana in return for allowing Carney sexual contacts.

At the officer's request, the youth returned to the motor home and knocked on its door; Carney stepped out. The agents identified themselves as law enforcement officers. Without a warrant or consent, one agent entered the motor home and observed marijuana, plastic bags, and a scale of the kind used for weighing drugs on a table. Agent Williams took Carney into custody and took possession of the motor home. A subsequent search of the motor home at the police station revealed additional marijuana in the cupboards and refrigerator.

The California Supreme Court reversed the conviction. . . . The California Supreme Court held that the expectations of privacy in a motor home are more like those in a dwelling than in an automobile because the primary function of motor homes is not to provide transportation but to "provide the occupant with living quarters."

While it is true that respondent's vehicle possessed some, if not many of the attributes of a home, it is equally clear that the vehicle falls clearly within the scope of the exception laid down in *Carroll* and applied in succeeding cases. Like the automobile in *Carroll*, respondent's motor home was readily mobile. Absent the prompt search and seizure, it could readily have been moved beyond the reach of the police. Furthermore, the vehicle was licensed to "operate on public streets; [was] serviced in public places; and [was] subject to extensive regulation and inspection." And the vehicle was so situated that an objective observer would conclude that it was being used not as a residence, but as a vehicle.

Respondent urges us to distinguish his vehicle from other vehicles within the exception because it was *capable of functioning as a home*. In our increasingly mobile society, many vehicles used for transportation can be and are being used not only for transportation but for shelter, *i.e.*, as a "home" or "residence." To distinguish between respondent's motor home and an ordinary sedan for purposes of the vehicle exception would require that we apply the exception depending upon the size of the vehicle and the quality of its appointments. Moreover, to fail to apply the exception to vehicles such as a motor home ignores the fact that a motor home lends itself easily to use as an instrument of illicit drug traffic and other illegal activity.

Our application of the vehicle exception has never turned on the other uses to which a vehicle might be put. The exception has historically turned on the ready mobility of the vehicle, and on the presence of the vehicle in a setting that objectively indicates that the vehicle is being used for transportation. These two requirements for application of the exception ensure that law enforcement officials are not unnecessarily hamstrung in their efforts to detect and prosecute criminal activity, and that the legitimate privacy interests of the public are protected.

The judgment of the California Supreme Court is reversed, and the case is remanded for further proceedings not inconsistent with this opinion.

JUSTICE STEVENS, with whom JUSTICE BRENNAN and JUSTICE MARSHALL join, dissenting.

[S]earches of places that regularly accommodate a wide range of private human activity are fundamentally different from searches of automobiles which primarily serve a public transportation function. Although it may not be a castle, a motor home is usually the functional equivalent of a hotel room, a vacation and retirement home, or a hunting and fishing cabin. These places may be as spartan as a humble cottage when compared to the most majestic mansion, but the highest and most legitimate expectations of privacy associated with these abodes should command the respect of this Court.

QUESTION

Suppose late at night a park ranger has probable cause to believe that marijuana is being smoked in a camper which is parked at a location designated for overnight use. The camper is occupied by a man, a woman and two children, all of whom are asleep at the time the search is instigated. Does *Carney* cover that case?

UNITED STATES v. ROSS

United States Supreme Court
456 U.S. 798 (1982)

JUSTICE STEVENS delivered the opinion of the Court.

In *Carroll v. United States* . . . the Court held that a warrantless search of an automobile stopped by police officers who had probable cause to believe the vehicle contained contraband was not unreasonable within the meaning of the Fourth Amendment. The Court in *Carroll* did not explicitly address the scope of the search that is permissible. In this case, we consider the extent to which police officers — who have legitimately stopped an automobile and who have probable cause to believe that contraband is concealed somewhere within it — may conduct a probing search of compartments and containers within the vehicle whose contents are not in plain view. We hold that they may conduct a search of the vehicle that is as thorough as a magistrate could authorize in a warrant "particularly describing the place to be searched."

I

In the evening of November 27, 1978, an informant who had previously proved to be reliable telephoned Detective Marcum of the District of Columbia Police Department and told him that an individual known as "Bandit" was selling narcotics kept in the trunk of a car parked at 439 Ridge Street. The informant stated that he had just observed "Bandit" complete a sale and that "Bandit" had told him that additional narcotics were in the trunk. The informant gave Marcum a detailed description of "Bandit" and stated that the car was a "purplish maroon" Chevrolet Malibu with District of Columbia license plates.

Accompanied by Detective Cassidy and Sergeant Gonzales, Marcum immediately drove to the area and found a maroon Malibu parked in front of 439 Ridge Street. A license check disclosed that the car was registered to Albert Ross; a computer check on Ross revealed that he fit the informant's description and used the alias "Bandit." In two passes through the neighborhood the officers did not observe anyone matching the informant's description. To avoid alerting persons on the street, they left the area.

The officers returned five minutes later and observed the maroon Malibu turning off Ridge Street onto Fourth Street. They pulled alongside the Malibu, noticed that the driver matched the informant's description, and stopped the car. Marcum and Cassidy told the driver — later identified as Albert Ross, the respondent in this action — to get out of the vehicle. While they searched Ross, Sergeant Gonzales discovered a bullet on the car's front seat. He searched the interior of the car and found a pistol in the glove compartment. Ross then was arrested and handcuffed. Detective Cassidy took Ross' keys and opened the trunk, where he found a closed brown paper bag. He opened the bag and discovered a number of glassine bags containing a white powder. Cassidy replaced the bag, closed the trunk, and drove the car to Headquarters.

At the police station Cassidy thoroughly searched the car. In addition to the "lunch-type" brown paper bag, Cassidy found in the trunk a zippered red leather pouch. He unzipped the pouch and discovered $3,200 in cash. The police laboratory later determined that the powder in the paper bag was heroin. No warrant was obtained.

Ross was charged with possession of heroin with intent to distribute, in violation of 21 U.S.C. § 841(a). Prior to trial, he moved to suppress the heroin found in the paper bag and the currency found in the leather pouch. After an evidentiary hearing, the District Court denied the motion to suppress. The heroin and currency were introduced in evidence at trial and Ross was convicted. . . .

. . .

III

The rationale justifying a warrantless search of an automobile that is believed to be transporting contraband arguably applies with equal force to any movable container that is believed to be carrying an illicit substance. That argument, however, was squarely rejected in *United States v. Chadwick*. . . .

The facts in *Arkansas v. Sanders*, 411 U.S. 753 . . . were similar to those in *Chadwick*. In *Sanders*, a Little Rock police officer received information from a reliable informant that Sanders would arrive at the local airport on a specified flight that afternoon carrying a green suitcase containing marijuana. The officer went to the airport. Sanders arrived on schedule and retrieved a green suitcase from the airline baggage service. Sanders gave the suitcase to a waiting companion who placed it in the trunk of a taxi. Sanders and his companion drove off in the cab; police officers followed and stopped the taxi several blocks from the airport. The officers opened the trunk, seized the suitcase, and searched it on the scene without a warrant. As predicted, the suitcase contained marijuana.

. . . In rejecting the State's argument that the warrantless search of the suitcase was justified on the ground that it had been taken from an automobile lawfully stopped on the street, the Court broadly suggested that a warrantless search of a container found in an automobile could never be sustained as part of a warrantless search of the automobile itself. The Court did not suggest that it mattered whether probable cause existed to search the entire vehicle. It is clear, however, that in neither *Chadwick* nor *Sanders* did the police have probable cause to search the vehicle or anything within it except the footlocker in the former case and the green suitcase in the latter.

. . . Unlike *Chadwick* and *Sanders*, in this case police officers had probable cause to search respondent's entire vehicle. . . .

IV

In *Carroll* itself, the whiskey that the prohibition agents seized was not in plain view. It was discovered only after an officer opened the rumble seat and tore open the upholstery of the lazyback. The Court did not find the scope of the search unreasonable. Having stopped Carroll and Kiro on a public road and subjected them to the indignity of a vehicle search — which the Court found to be a reasonable intrusion on their privacy because it was based on probable cause that their vehicle was transporting contraband — prohibition agents were entitled to tear open a portion of the roadster itself. The scope of the search was no greater than a magistrate could have authorized by issuing a warrant based on the probable cause that justified the search. Since such a warrant could have authorized the agents to open the rear portion of the roadster and to rip the upholstery in their search for concealed whiskey the search was constitutionally permissible.

In *Chambers v. Maroney*, the police found weapons and stolen property "concealed in a compartment under the dashboard." . . . No suggestion was made that the scope of the search was impermissible. It would be illogical to assume that the outcome of *Chambers* — or the outcome of *Carroll* itself — would have been different if the police had found the secreted contraband enclosed within a secondary container and had opened that container without a warrant. If it was reasonable for prohibition agents to rip open the upholstery in *Carroll*, it certainly would have been reasonable for them to look into a burlap sack stashed inside; if it was reasonable to open the concealed compartment in *Chambers*, it would have been equally reasonable to open a paper bag crumpled within it. A contrary rule could produce absurd results inconsistent with the decision in *Carroll* itself.

[T]he decision in *Carroll* was based on the Court's appraisal of practical considerations viewed in the perspective of history. It is therefore significant that the practical consequences of the *Carroll* decision would be largely nullified if the permissible scope of a warrantless search of an automobile did not include containers and packages found inside the vehicle. Contraband goods rarely are strewn across the trunk or floor of a car; since by their very nature such goods must be withheld from public view, they rarely can be placed in an automobile unless they are enclosed within some form of container. The Court in *Carroll* held that "contraband goods concealed and illegally transported in an automobile or other vehicle may be searched for without a warrant." . . .

A lawful search of fixed premises generally extends to the entire area in which the object of the search may be found and is not limited by the possibility that separate acts of entry or opening may be required to complete the search. Thus, a warrant that authorizes an officer to search a home for illegal weapons also provides authority to open closets, chest, drawers, and containers in which the weapon might be found. A warrant to open a footlocker to search for marijuana would also authorize the opening of packages found inside. A warrant to search a vehicle would support a search of every part of the vehicle that might contain the object of the search. When a legitimate search is under way, and when its purpose and its limits have been precisely defined, nice distinctions between closets, drawers and containers, in the case of a home, or between glove compartments, upholstered seats, trunks, and wrapped packages, in the case of a vehicle, must give way to the interest in the prompt and efficient completion of the task at hand.

This rule applies equally to all containers, as indeed we believe it must. One point on which the Court was in virtually unanimous agreement in *Robbins* was that a constitutional distinction between "worthy" and "unworthy" containers would be improper. Even though such a distinction perhaps could evolve in a series of cases in which paper bags, locked trunks, lunch buckets, and orange crates were placed on one side of the line or the other, the central purpose of the Fourth Amendment forecloses such a distinction. For just as the most frail cottage in the kingdom is absolutely entitled to the same guarantees of privacy as the most majestic mansion, so also may a traveler who carries a toothbrush and a few articles of clothing in a paper bag or knotted scarf claim an equal right to conceal his possessions from official inspection as the sophisticated executive with the locked attaché case.

As Justice Stewart stated in *Robbins*, the Fourth Amendment provides protection to the owner of every container that conceals its contents from plain view (plurality opinion). But the protection afforded by the Amendment varies in different settings. The luggage carried by a traveler entering the country may be searched at random by a customs officer; the luggage may be searched no matter how great the traveler's desire to conceal the contents may be. A container carried at the time of arrest often may be searched without a warrant and even without any specific suspicion concerning its contents. A container that may conceal the object of a search authorized by a warrant may be opened immediately; the individual's interest in privacy must give way to the magistrate's official determination of probable cause.

In the same manner, an individual's expectation of privacy in a vehicle and its contents may not survive if probable cause is given to believe that the vehicle is transporting contraband. Certainly the privacy interests in a car's trunk or glove compartment may be no less than those in a movable container. An individual undoubtedly has a significant interest that the upholstery of his automobile will not be ripped or a hidden compartment within it opened. These interests must yield to the authority of a search, however, which — in light of *Carroll* — does not itself require the prior approval of a magistrate. The scope of a warrantless search based on probable cause is no narrower — and no broader — than the scope of a search authorized by a warrant supported by probable cause. Only the prior approval of the magistrate is waived; the search otherwise is as the magistrate could authorize.

The scope of a warrantless search of an automobile thus is not defined by the nature of the container in which the contraband is secreted. Rather, it is defined by the object of the search and the places in which there is probable cause to believe that it may be found. Just as probable cause to believe that a stolen lawnmower may be found in a garage will not support a warrant to search an upstairs bedroom, probable cause to believe that undocumented aliens are being transported in a van will not justify a warrantless search of a suitcase. Probable cause to believe that a container placed in the trunk of a taxi contains contraband or evidence does not justify a search of the entire cab.

[JUSTICES BLACKMUN and POWELL concurred; JUSTICES WHITE, MARSHALL and BRENNAN dissented.]

WYOMING v. HOUGHTON

United States Supreme Court
526 U.S. 295 (1999)

JUSTICE SCALIA delivered the opinion of the Court.

This case presents the question whether police officers violate the Fourth Amendment when they search a passenger's personal belongings inside an automobile that they have probable cause to believe contains contraband.

I

In the early morning hours of July 23, 1995, a Wyoming Highway Patrol officer stopped an automobile for speeding and driving with a faulty brake light. There were three passengers in the front seat of the car: David Young (the driver), his girlfriend, and respondent. While questioning Young, the officer noticed a hypodermic syringe in Young's shirt pocket. He left the occupants under the supervision of two backup officers as he went to get gloves from his patrol car. Upon his return, he instructed Young to step out of the car and place the syringe on the hood. The officers then asked Young why he had a syringe; with refreshing candor, Young replied that he used it to take drugs.

At this point, the backup officers ordered the two female passengers out of the car and asked them for identification. Respondent falsely identified herself as "Sandra James" and stated that she did not have any identification. Meanwhile, in light of Young's admission, the officer searched the passenger compartment of the car for contraband. On the back seat, he found a purse, which respondent claimed as hers. He removed from the purse a wallet containing respondent's driver's license, identifying her property as Sandra K. Houghton. When the officer asked her why she had lied about her name, she replied: "In case things went bad."

Continuing his search of the purse, the officer found a brown pouch and a black wallet-type container. Respondent denied that the former was hers, and claimed ignorance of how it came to be there; it was found to contain drug paraphernalia and a syringe with 60 ccs of methamphetamine. Respondent admitted ownership of the black container, which was also found to contain drug paraphernalia, and a syringe (which respondent acknowledged was hers) with 10 ccs of methamphetamine — an amount insufficient to support the felony conviction at issue in this case. The officer also found fresh needle-track marks on respondent's arms. He placed her under arrest.

The State of Wyoming charged respondent with felony possession of methamphetamine in a liquid amount greater than three-tenths of a gram. . . . After a hearing, the trial court denied her motion to suppress all evidence obtained from the purse as the fruit of a violation of the Fourth and Fourteenth Amendments. The court held that the officer had probable cause to search the car for contraband, and, by extension, any containers therein that could hold such contraband. A jury convicted respondent as charged.

The Wyoming Supreme Court, by divided vote, reversed the conviction and announced the following rule:

> "Generally, once probable cause is established to search a vehicle, an officer is entitled to search all containers therein which contain the object of the search. However, if the officer knows or should know that a container is the personal effect of a passenger who is not suspected of criminal activity, then the container is outside the scope of the search unless someone had the opportunity to conceal the contraband within the personal effect to avoid detection." 956 P.2d 363, 372 (1998).

The court held that the search of respondent's purse violated the Fourth and Fourteenth Amendments because the officer "knew or should have known that the purse did not belong to the driver, but to one of the passengers," and because "there was no probable cause to search the passengers' personal effects and no reason to believe that contraband had been placed within the purse." *Ibid.*

II

. . . In *Ross*, . . . we upheld as reasonable the warrantless search of a paper bag and leather pouch found in the trunk of the defendant's car by officers who had probable cause to believe that the trunk contained drugs. . . .

To be sure, there was no passenger in *Ross*, and it was not claimed that the package in the trunk belonged to anyone other than the driver. Even so, if the rule of law that *Ross* announced were limited to contents belonging to the driver, or contents other than those belonging to passengers, one would have expected that substantial limitation to be expressed. And, more importantly one would have expected that limitation to be apparent in the historical evidence that formed the basis for *Ross*'s holding. In fact, however, nothing in the statutes *Ross* relied upon, or in the practice under those statutes, would except from authorized warrantless search packages belonging to passengers on the suspect ship, horse-drawn carriage, or automobile.

Finally, we must observe that the analytical principle underlying the rule announced in *Ross* is fully consistent — as respondent's proposal is not — with the balance of our Fourth Amendment jurisprudence. *Ross* concluded from the historical evidence that the permissible scope of a warrantless car search "is defined by the object of the search and the places in which there is probable cause to believe that it may be found." . . . The same principle is reflected in an earlier case involving the constitutionality of a search warrant directed at premises belonging to one who is not suspected of any crime: "The critical element in a reasonable search is not that the owner of the property is suspected of crime but that there is reasonable cause to believe that the specific 'things' to be searched for and seized are located on the property to which entry is sought." *Zurcher v. Stanford Daily*. . . .

In sum, neither *Ross* itself nor the historical evidence it relied upon admits of a distinction among packages or containers based on ownership. When there is probable cause to search for contraband in a car, it is reasonable for police officers — like customs officials in the Founding era — to examine packages and containers without a showing of individualized probable cause for each one. A passenger's personal belongings, just like the driver's belongings or containers attached to the car like a glove compartment, are "in" the car, and the officer has probable cause to search for contraband *in* the car.

Even if the historical evidence, as described in *Ross*, were thought to be equivocal, we would find that the balancing of the relative interests weighs decidedly in favor of allowing searches of a passenger's belongings. Passengers, no less than drivers, possess a reduced expectation of privacy with regard to the property that they transport in cars, which "trave[l] public thoroughfares," *Cardwell v. Lewis* . . . , "seldom serv[e] as . . . the repository of personal effects," *ibid.*, are subjected to police stop and examination to enforce "pervasive" governmental controls "[a]s an everyday occurrence," *South Dakota v. Opperman*, . . . and, finally, are exposed to traffic accidents that may render all their contents open to public scrutiny.

. . . We hold that police officers with probable cause to search a car may inspect passengers' belongings found in the car that are capable of concealing the object of the search. The judgment of the Wyoming Supreme Court is reversed.

Justice Breyer, concurring.

. . . [T]he container here at issue, a woman's purse, was found at a considerable distance from its owner, who did not claim ownership until the officer discovered her identification while looking through it. Purses are special containers. They are repositories of especially personal items that people generally like to keep with them at all times. So I am tempted to say that a search of a purse involves an intrusion so similar to a search of one's person that the same rule should govern both. However, given this Court's prior cases, I cannot argue that the fact that the container was a purse *automatically* makes a legal difference, for the Court has warned against trying to make that kind of distinction. *United States v. Ross*, ... But I can say that it would matter if a woman's purse, like a man's billfold, were attached to her person. It might then amount to a kind of "outer clothing," *Terry v. Ohio* . . . which under the Court's cases would properly receive increased protection. . . . In this case, the purse was separate from the person, and no one has claimed that, under those circumstances, the type of container makes a difference. For that reason, I join the Court's opinion.

Justice Stevens, with whom Justice Souter and Justice Ginsburg join, dissenting.

. . . [I am not] persuaded that the mere spatial association between a passenger and a driver provides an acceptable basis for presuming that they are partners in crime or for ignoring privacy interests in a purse. Whether or not the Fourth Amendment required a warrant to search Houghton's purse, . . . at the very least the trooper in this case had to have probable cause to believe that her purse contained contraband. The Wyoming Supreme Court concluded that he did not.

. . . Instead of applying ordinary Fourth Amendment principles to this case, the majority extends the automobile warrant exception to allow searches of passenger belongings based on the driver's misconduct. Thankfully, the Court's automobile-centered analysis limits the scope of its holding. But it does not justify the outcome in this case.

NOTES AND QUESTIONS

(1) Arguably, two passengers on the front seat with a driver possessing narcotics paraphernalia in plain view are implicated in his illegal drug use. This, however, is not the rationale for the Court's holding. Rather, the syringe gives rise to probable cause that the vehicle contains narcotics and/or narcotics paraphernalia. This is all the officer needs, and the person associated with the particular item is irrelevant. Should (will) the Court reach the same result in the case of an arms' length relationship between the parties? Suppose the vehicle is a taxi. Would the driver's possession of a syringe support a search of the purse of a fare?

(2) In *State v. Boyd*, 275 Kan. 271, 64 P.3d 419 (2003), the court held that if a vehicle passenger seeks to take her purse with her when she exits, the purse may not be searched under the vehicle search rationale. "If we hold an officer can lawfully order a passenger to leave her purse in the car and thereby make it subject to search, then what prevents the officer from ordering the passenger to remain in the car, thus subjecting her to be subsequently searched along with the car."

CALIFORNIA v. ACEVEDO

United States Supreme Court
500 U.S. 565 (1991)

JUSTICE BLACKMUN delivered the opinion of the Court.

This case requires us once again to consider the so-called "automobile exception" to the warrant requirement of the Fourth Amendment and its application to the search of a closed container in the trunk of a car.

I

On October 28, 1987, Officer Coleman of the Santa Ana, Cal., Police Department received a telephone call from a federal drug enforcement agent in Hawaii. The agent informed Coleman that he had seized a package containing marijuana which was to have been addressed to J.R. Daza at 805 West Stevens Avenue in that city. The agent arranged to send the package to Coleman instead. Coleman then was to take the package to the Federal Express office and arrest the person who arrived to claim it.

Coleman received the package on October 29, verified its contents, and took it to the Senior Operations Manager at the Federal Express office. At about 10:00 a.m. on October 30, a man, who identified himself as Jamie Daza, arrived to claim the package. He accepted it and drove to his apartment on West Stevens. He carried the package into the apartment.

At 11:45 a.m., officers observed Daza leave the apartment and drop the box and paper that had contained the marijuana into a trash bin. Coleman at that point left the scene to get a search warrant. About 12:05 p.m., the officers saw Richard St. George leave the apartment carrying a blue knapsack which appeared to be half full. The officers stopped him as he was driving off, searched the knapsack, and found 1 1/2 pounds of marijuana.

At 12:30 p.m., respondent Charles Steven Acevedo arrived. He entered Daza's apartment, stayed for about 10 minutes, and reappeared carrying a brown paper bag that looked full. The officers noticed that the bag was the size of one of the wrapped marijuana packages sent from Hawaii. Acevedo walked to a silver Honda in the parking lot. He placed the bag in the trunk of the car and started to drive away. Fearing the loss of evidence, officers in a marked police car stopped him. They opened the trunk and the bag, and found marijuana.

. . .

The California Court of Appeal, Fourth District, concluded that the marijuana found in the paper bag in the car's trunk should have been suppressed. . . . The court concluded that the officers had probable cause to believe that the paper bag contained drugs but lacked probable cause to suspect that Acevedo's car, itself, otherwise contained contraband. Because the officers' probable cause was directed specifically at the bag, the court held that the case was controlled by *United States v. Chadwick* . . . , rather than by *United States v. Ross*. . . .

II

. . .

In *United States v. Ross*, 456 U.S. 798, decided in 1982, we held that a warrantless search of an automobile under the *Carroll* doctrine could include a search of a container or package found inside the car when such a search was supported by probable cause. The warrantless search of Ross' car occurred after an informant told the police that he had seen Ross complete a drug transaction using drugs stored in the trunk of his car. The police stopped the car, searched it, and discovered in the trunk a brown paper bag containing drugs. We decided that the search of Ross' car was not unreasonable under the Fourth Amendment: "The scope of a warrantless search based on probable cause is no narrower — and no broader — than the scope of a search authorized by a warrant supported by probable cause." . . . Thus, "[i]f probable cause justifies the search of a lawfully stopped vehicle, it justifies the search of every part of the vehicle and its contents that may conceal the object of the search." . . . In *Ross*, therefore, we clarified the scope of the *Carroll* doctrine as properly including a "probing search" of compartments and containers within the automobile so long as the search is supported by probable cause. . . .

In *Arkansas v. Sanders* . . . , the Court extended *Chadwick's* rule to apply to a suitcase actually being transported in the trunk of a car. In *Sanders*, the police had probable cause to believe a suitcase contained marijuana. They watched as the defendant placed the suitcase in the trunk of a taxi and was driven away. The police pursued the taxi for several blocks, stopped it, found the suitcase in the trunk, and searched it. Although the Court had applied the *Carroll* doctrine to searches of integral parts of the automobile itself, (indeed, in *Carroll*, contraband whiskey was in the upholstery of the seats . . .), it did not extend the doctrine to the warrantless search of personal luggage "merely because it was located in an automobile lawfully stopped by the police." . . . Again, the *Sanders* majority stressed the heightened privacy expectation in personal luggage and concluded that the presence of luggage in an automobile did not diminish the owner's expectation of privacy in his personal items. . . .

In *Ross*, the Court endeavored to distinguish between *Carroll*, which governed the *Ross* automobile search, and *Chadwick*, which governed the *Sanders* automobile search. It held that the *Carroll* doctrine covered searches of automobiles when the police had probable cause to search an entire vehicle, but that the *Chadwick* doctrine governed searches of luggage when the officers had probable cause to search only a container within a vehicle. Thus, in a *Ross* situation, the police could conduct a reasonable search under the Fourth Amendment without obtaining a warrant, whereas in a *Sanders* situation, the police had to obtain a warrant before they searched. . . .

IV

Dissenters in *Ross* asked why the suitcase in *Sanders* was "more private, less difficult for police to seize and store, or in any other relevant respect more properly subject to the warrant requirement, than a container that police discover in a probable-cause search of an entire automobile?" . . . We now agree that a container found after a general search of the automobile and a container found in a car after a limited search for the container are equally easy for the police to store and for the suspect to hide or destroy. In fact, we see no principled distinction in terms of either the privacy expectation or the exigent circumstances between the paper bag found by the police in *Ross* and the paper bag found by the police here. Furthermore, by attempting to distinguish between a container for which the police are specifically searching and a container which they come across in a car, we have provided only minimal protection for privacy and have impeded effective law enforcement.

The line between probable cause to search a vehicle and probable cause to search a package in that vehicle is not always clear, and separate rules that govern the two objects to be searched may enable the police to broaden their power to make warrantless searches and disserve privacy interests. . . . At the moment when the officers stop an automobile, it may be less than clear whether they suspect with a high degree of certainty that the vehicle contains drugs in a bag or simply contains drugs. If the police know they may open a bag only if they are actually searching the entire car, they may search more extensively than they otherwise would in order to establish the general probable cause required by *Ross*.

Such a situation is not far fetched. In *United States v. Johns*, 469 U.S. 478 (1985), customs agents saw two trucks drive to a private airstrip and approach two small planes. The agents drew near the trucks, smelled marijuana, and then saw in the backs of the trucks packages wrapped in a manner that marijuana smugglers customarily employed. The agents took the trucks to headquarters and searched the packages without a warrant. . . . Relying on *Chadwick*, the defendants argued that the search was unlawful. . . . The defendants contended that *Ross* was inapplicable because the agents lacked probable cause to search anything but the package themselves and supported this contention by noting that a search of the entire vehicle never occurred. . . . We rejected that argument and found *Chadwick* and *Sanders* inapposite because the agents had probable cause to search the entire body of each truck, although they had chosen not to do so. . . . We cannot see the benefit of a rule that requires law enforcement officers to conduct a more intrusive search in order to justify a less intrusive one.

. . .

Finally, the search of a paper bag intrudes far less on individual privacy than does the incursion sanctioned long ago in *Carroll.* In that case, prohibition agents slashed the upholstery of the automobile. This Court nonetheless found their search to be reasonable under the Fourth Amendment. If destroying the interior of an automobile is not unreasonable, we cannot conclude that looking inside a closed container is. In light of the minimal protection to privacy afforded by the *Chadwick-Sanders* rule, and our serious doubt whether that rule substantially serves privacy interests, we now hold that the Fourth Amendment does not compel separate treatment for an automobile search that extends only to a container within the vehicle.

V

. . .

Although we have recognized firmly that the doctrine of *stare decisis* served profoundly important purposes in our legal system, this Court has overruled a prior case on the comparatively rare occasion when it has bred confusion or been derelict or led to anomalous results . . . *Sanders* was explicitly undermined in *Ross*, . . . and the existence of the dual regimes for automobile searches that uncover containers has proved as confusing as the *Chadwick* and *Sanders* dissenters predicted. We conclude that it is better to adopt one clear-cut rule to govern automobile searches and eliminate the warrant requirement for closed containers set forth in *Sanders*.

VI

The interpretation of the *Carroll* doctrine set forth in *Ross* now applies to all searches of containers found in an automobile. In other words, the police may search without a warrant if their search is supported by probable cause. . . . In the case before us, the police had probable cause to believe that the paper bag in the automobile's trunk contained marijuana. That probable cause now allows a warrantless search of the paper bag. The facts in the record reveal that the police did not have probable cause to believe that contraband was hidden in any other part of the automobile and a search of the entire vehicle would have been without probable cause and unreasonable under the Fourth Amendment.

. . .

Until today, this Court has drawn a curious line between the search of an automobile that coincidentally turns up a container and the search of a container that coincidentally turns up in an automobile. The protections of the Fourth Amendment must not turn on such coincidences. We therefore interpret *Carroll* as providing one rule to govern all automobile searches. The police may search an automobile and the containers within it where they have probable cause to believe contraband or evidence is contained.

JUSTICE SCALIA, concurring in the judgment.

I agree with the dissent that it is anomalous for a briefcase to be protected by the "general requirement" of a prior warrant when it is being carried along the street, but for that same briefcase to become unprotected as soon as it is carried into an automobile. On the other hand, I agree with the Court that it would be anomalous for a locked compartment in an automobile to be unprotected by the "general requirement" of a prior warrant, but for an unlocked briefcase within the automobile to be protected. I join in the judgment of the Court because I think its holding is more faithful to the text and tradition of the Fourth Amendment, and if these anomalies in our jurisprudence are ever to be eliminated that is the direction in which we should travel.

. . .

I would reverse the judgment in the present case, not because a closed container carried inside a car becomes subject to the "automobile" exception to the general warrant requirement, but because the search of a closed container, outside a privately owned building, with probable cause to believe that the container contains contraband, and when it in fact does contain contraband, is not one of these searches whose Fourth Amendment reasonableness depends upon a warrant.

JUSTICE STEVENS, with whom JUSTICE MARSHALL joins, dissenting.

. . .

In its opinion today, the Court recognizes that the police did not have probable cause to search respondent's vehicle and that a search of anything but the paper bag that respondent had carried from Daza's apartment and placed in the trunk of his car would have been unconstitutional. . . . Moreover, as I read the opinion, the Court assumes that the police could not have made a warrantless inspection of the bag before it was placed in the car. . . . Finally, the Court also does not question the fact that, under our prior cases, it would have been lawful for the police to seize the container and detain it (and respondent) until they obtained a search warrant. . . . Thus, all of the relevant facts that governed our decisions in *Chadwick* and *Sanders* are present here whereas the relevant fact that justified the vehicle search in *Ross* is not present.

The Court does not attempt to identify any exigent circumstances that would justify its refusal to apply the general rule against warrantless searches. Instead, it advances these three arguments: First, the rules . . . are confusing and anomalous. . . . Second, the rules do not protect any significant interest in privacy. . . . And, third, the rules impede effective law enforcement. . . . None of these arguments withstands scrutiny.

The "Confusion"

. . .

The decided cases . . . provide no support for the Court's concern about "confusion." The Court instead relies primarily on predictions that were made by Justice Blackmun in his dissenting opinions in *Chadwick* and *Sanders*. The Court, however, cites no evidence that these predictions have in fact materialized or that anyone else has been unable to understand the "inherent opaqueness" . . . of this uncomplicated issue. . . .

The Court summarizes the alleged "anomaly" created by the coexistence of *Ross, Chadwick,* and *Sanders* with the statement that "the more likely the police are to discover drugs in a container, the less authority they have to search it." . . . This juxtaposition is only anomalous, however, if one accepts the flawed premise that the degree to which the police are likely to discover contraband is correlated with their authority to search *without a warrant*. Yet even proof beyond a reasonable doubt will not justify a warrantless search that is not supported by one of the exceptions to the warrant requirement. And even when the police have a warrant or an exception applies, once the police possess probable cause, the extent to which they are more or less certain of the contents of a container has no bearing on their authority to search it.

To the extent there was an "anomaly" in our prior jurisprudence, the Court has "cured" it at the expense of creating a more serious paradox. For, surely it is anomalous to prohibit a search of a briefcase while the owner is carrying it exposed on a public street yet to permit a search once the owner has placed the briefcase in the locked trunk of his car. One's privacy interest in one's luggage can certainly not be diminished by one's removing it from a public thoroughfare and place it — out of sight — in a privately owned vehicle. Nor is the danger that evidence will escape increased if the luggage is in a car rather than on the street. In either location, if the police have probable cause, they are authorized to seize the luggage and to detain it until they obtain judicial approval for a search. Any line demarking an exception to the warrant requirement will appear blurred at the edges, but the Court has certainly erred if it believes that, by erasing one line and drawing another, it has drawn a clearer boundary.

The Privacy Argument

. . .

Under the Court's holding today, the privacy interest that protects the contents of a suitcase or a briefcase from a warrantless search when it is in public view simply vanishes when its owner climbs into a taxicab. Unquestionably the rejection of the *Sanders* line of cases by today's decision will result in a significant loss of individual privacy.

To support its argument that today's holding works only a minimal intrusion on privacy, the Court suggests that "[i]f the police know that they may open a bag only if they are actually searching the entire car, they may search more extensively than they otherwise would in order to establish the general probable cause required by *Ross*." . . . [T]his fear is unexplained and inexplicable. Neither evidence uncovered in the course of a search nor the scope of the search conducted can be used to provide *post hoc* justification for a search unsupported by probable cause at its inception.

. . .

The Burden on Law Enforcement

The Court's suggestion that *Chadwick* and *Sanders* have created a significant burden on effective law enforcement is unsupported, inaccurate, and, in any event, an insufficient reason for creating a new exception to the warrant requirement.

Despite repeated claims that *Chadwick* and *Sanders* have "impeded effective law enforcement," . . . the Court cites no authority for its contentions. Moreover, all evidence that does exist points to the contrary conclusion. In the years since *Ross* was decided, the Court has heard argument in 30 Fourth Amendment cases involving narcotics. In all but one, the government was the petitioner. All save two involved a search or seizure without a warrant or with a defective warrant. And, in all except three, the Court upheld the constitutionality of the search or seizure.

In the meantime, the flow of narcotics cases through the courts has steadily and dramatically increased. . . . No impartial observer could criticize this Court for hindering the progress of the war on drugs. On the contrary, decisions like the one the Court makes today will support the conclusion that this Court has become a loyal foot soldier in the Executive's fight against crime.

Even if the warrant requirement does inconvenience the police to some extent, the fact does not distinguish this constitutional requirement from any other procedural protection secured by the Bill of Rights. It is merely a part of the price that our society must pay in order to preserve its freedom. . . .

It is too early to know how much freedom America has lost today. The magnitude of the loss is, however, not nearly as significant as the Court's willingness to inflict it without even a colorable basis for its rejection of prior law.

QUESTION

Both Justice Scalia in his concurring opinion and Justice Stevens in his dissenting opinion call attention to the new anomaly created by this decision. Does this portend the demise of *Chadwick* as well as *Sanders*?

[2] The Inventory Rationale

CADY v. DOMBROWSKI

United States Supreme Court
413 U.S. 433 (1973)

Opinion of the Court by Mr. Justice Rehnquist, announced by Mr. Justice Blackmun.

I

On September 9, 1969, respondent was a member of the Chicago, Illinois, police force and either owned or possessed a 1960 Dodge automobile. That day he drove from Chicago to West Bend, Wisconsin, the county seat of Washington County located some hundred-odd miles northwest of Chicago. He was identified as having been in two taverns in the small town of Kewaskum, Wisconsin, seven miles north of West Bend, during the late evening of September 9th and the early morning of September 10th. At some time before noon on the 10th, respondent's automobile became disabled, and he had it towed to a farm owned by his brother in Fond du Lac County, which adjoins Washington County on the north. He then drove back to Chicago early that afternoon with his brother in the latter's car.

Just before midnight of the same day, respondent rented a maroon 1967 Ford Thunderbird at O'Hare Field outside of Chicago, and apparently drove back to Wisconsin early the next morning. A tenant on his brother's farm saw a car answering the description of the rented car pull alongside the disabled 1960 Dodge at approximately 4 a.m. At approximately 9:30 a.m. on September 11th, respondent purchased two towels, one light brown and the other blue, from a department store in Kewaskum.

From 7 to 10:15 p.m. on the 11th respondent was in a steak house or tavern in West Bend. He ate dinner and also drank, apparently quite heavily. He left the tavern and drove the 1967 Thunderbird in a direction away from West Bend toward his brother's farm. On the way, respondent had an accident, with the Thunderbird breaking through a guard rail and crashing into a bridge abutment. A passing motorist drove him into Kewaskum, and, after being let off in Kewaskum, respondent telephoned the police. Two police officers picked him up at a tavern and drove to the scene of the accident. On the way, the officers noticed that respondent appeared to be drunk; he offered three conflicting versions of how the accident occurred.

At the scene, the police observed the 1967 Thunderbird and took various measurements relevant to the accident. Respondent was, in the opinion of the officers, drunk. He had informed them that he was a Chicago police officer. The Wisconsin policemen believed that Chicago police officers were required by regulation to carry their service revolvers at all times. After calling a towtruck to remove the disabled Thunderbird, and not finding the revolver on respondent's person, one of the officers looked into the front seat and glove compartment of that car for respondent's service revolver. No revolver was found. The wrecker arrived and the Thunderbird was towed to a privately owned service station in Kewaskum, approximately seven miles from the West Bend police station. It was left outside by the wrecker, and no police guard was posted. At 11:33 p.m. on the 11th respondent was taken directly to the West Bend police station from the accident scene, and, after being interviewed by an assistant district attorney, to whom respondent again stated he was a Chicago policeman, respondent was formally arrested for drunken driving. Respondent was "in a drunken condition" and "incoherent at times." Because of his injuries sustained in the accident, the same two officers took respondent to a local hospital. He lapsed into an unexplained coma, and a doctor, fearing the possibility of complications, had respondent hospitalized overnight for observation. One of the policemen remained at the hospital as a guard, and the other, Officer Weiss, drove at some time after 2 a.m. on the 12th to the garage to which the 1967 Thunderbird had been towed after the accident.

The purpose for going to the Thunderbird, as developed on the motion to suppress, was to look for respondent's service revolver. Weiss testified that respondent did not have a revolver when he was arrested, and that the West Bend authorities were under the impression that Chicago police officers were required to carry their service revolvers at all times. He stated that the effort to find the revolver was "standard procedure in our department."

Weiss opened the door of the Thunderbird and found, on the floor of the car, a book of Chicago police regulations and, between the two front seats, a flashlight which appeared to have "a few spots of blood on it." He then opened the trunk of the car, which had been locked, and saw various items covered with what was later determined to be type O blood. These included a pair of police uniform trousers, a pair of gray trousers, a nightstick with the name "Dombrowski" stamped on it, a raincoat, a portion of a car floor mat, and a towel. The blood on the car mat was moist. The officer removed these items to the police station.

When, later that day, respondent was confronted with the condition of the items discovered in the trunk, he requested the presence of counsel before making any statement. After conferring with respondent, a lawyer told the police that respondent "authorized me to state he believed there was a body lying near the family picnic area in the north end of his brother's farm."

Fond du Lac County police went to the farm and found, in a dump, the body of a male, later identified as the decedent McKinney, clad only in a sportshirt. The deceased's head was bloody; a white sock was found near the body. In observing the area, one officer looked through the window of the disabled 1960 Dodge, located not far from where the body was found, and saw a pillowcase, backseat, and briefcase covered with blood. Police officials obtained, on the evening of the 12th, returnable within 48 hours, warrants to search the 1960 Dodge and the 1967 Thunderbird, as well as orders to impound both automobiles. The 1960 Dodge was examined at the farm on the 12th and then towed to the police garage where it was held as evidence. On the 13th, criminologists came from the Wisconsin Crime Laboratory in Madison and searched the Dodge; they seized the back and front seats, a white sock covered with blood, a part of a bloody rear floor mat, a briefcase, and a front floor mat. A return of the search warrant was filed in the county court on the 14th, but it did not recite that the sock and floor mat had been seized. At a hearing held on the 14th, the sheriff who executed the warrant did not specifically state that these two items had been seized.

At the trial, the State introduced testimony tending to establish that the deceased was first hit over the head and then shot with a .38 caliber gun, dying approximately an hour after the gunshot wound was inflicted; that death occurred at approximately 7 a.m. on the 11th, with a six hour margin of error either way; that respondent owned two .38 caliber guns; that respondent had type A blood; that the deceased had type O blood and that the blood stains found in the 1960 Dodge and on the items found in the two cars were type O.

The prosecution introduced the nightstick discovered in the 1967 Thunderbird and testimony that it had traces of type O blood on it; the portion of the floor mat found in the 1967 car with testimony that it matched the portion of the floor mat found in the 1960 Dodge; the bloody towel found in the 1967 car with testimony that it was identical to one of the towels purchased by respondent on the 11th; the police uniform trousers; the sock found in the 1960 Dodge with testimony that it was identical in composition and stitching to that found near the body of the deceased.

The State's case was based wholly on circumstantial evidence. The Supreme Court of Wisconsin, in reviewing the conviction on direct appeal, stated that "even though the evidence that led to his conviction was circumstantial, we have seldom seen a stronger collection of such evidence assembled as presented by the prosecution." . . .

II

Here we must decide whether a "search" of the trunk of the 1967 Ford was unreasonable solely because the local officer had not previously obtained a warrant. And, if that be answered in the negative, we must then determine whether the warrantless search was unreasonable within the meaning of the Fourth and Fourteenth Amendments. In answering these questions, two factual considerations deserve emphasis. First, the police had exercised a form of custody or control over the 1967 Thunderbird. Respondent's vehicle was disabled as a result of the accident, and constituted a nuisance along the highway. Respondent, being intoxicated (and later comatose), could not make arrangements to have the vehicle towed and stored. At the direction of the police, and for elemental reasons of safety, the automobile was towed to a private garage. Second, both the state courts and the district courts found as a fact that the search of the trunk to retrieve the revolver was "standard procedure in [that police] department," to protect the public from the possibility that a revolver would fall into untrained or perhaps malicious hands. Although the trunk was unlocked, the car was left outside, in a lot seven miles from the police station to which respondent had been taken, and no guard was posted over it. For reasons not apparent from the opinion of the Court of Appeals, that court concluded that as "no further evidence was needed to sustain" the drunk driving charge, "[t]he search must therefore have been for incriminating evidence of other offenses." While the court was obligated to exercise its independent judgment on the underlying constitutional issue presented by the facts of this case, it was not free on this record to disregard these findings of fact. Particularly in non-metropolitan jurisdictions such as those involved here, enforcement of the traffic laws and supervision of vehicle traffic may be a large part of a police officer's job. We believe that the Court of Appeals should have expected, as did the state court and the District Court, and the findings with respect to Officer Weiss' specific motivation and the fact that the procedure he followed was "standard."

. . . We believe that the instant case is controlled by principles that may be extrapolated from *Harris v. United States*, [390 U.S. 234 (1968)], and *Cooper v. California*, [348 U.S. 58 (1967)].

In *Harris*, petitioner was arrested for robbery. As petitioner's car had been identified leaving the site of the robbery, it was impounded as evidence. A regulation of the District of Columbia Police Department required that an impounded vehicle be searched, that all valuables be removed, and that a tag detailing certain information be placed on the vehicle. In compliance with this regulation, and without a warrant, an officer searched the car and, while opening one of the doors, spotted an automobile registration card, belonging to the victim, lying face up on the metal door stripping. This item was introduced into evidence at petitioner's trial for robbery. In rejecting the contention that the evidence was inadmissible, the Court stated:

> The admissibility of evidence found as a result of a search under the police regulation is not presented by this case. The precise and detailed findings of the District Court, accepted by the Court of Appeals, were to the effect that the discovery of the card was not the result of a search of the car, but of a measure taken to protect the car while it was in police custody. Nothing in the Fourth Amendment requires the police to obtain a warrant in these narrow circumstances.
>
> Once the door had been lawfully opened, the registration card . . . was plainly visible. It has long been settled that objects falling in the plain view of an officer who has a right to be in the position to have that view are subject to seizing and may be introduced in evidence.

390 U.S., at 236.

In *Cooper*, the petitioner was arrested for selling heroin, and his car impounded pending forfeiture proceedings. A week later, a police officer searched the car and found, in the glove compartment, incriminating evidence subsequently admitted at petitioner's trial. This Court upheld the validity of the warrantless search and seizure with the following language:

> This case is not *Preston*, nor is it controlled by it. Here the officers seized petitioner's car because they were required to do so by state law. They seized it because of the crime for which they arrested petitioner. They seized it to impound it and they had to keep it until forfeiture proceedings were concluded. Their subsequent search of the car — whether the State had "legal title" to it or not — was closely related to the reason petitioner had been arrested, the reason the car had been impounded, and the reason it was being retained. The forfeiture of petitioner's car did not take place until over four months after it was lawfully seized. It would be unreasonable to hold that the police, having to retain the car in their custody for such a length of time, had no right, even for their own protection, to search it.

386 U.S., at 61–62

These decisions, while not on all fours with the instant case, lead us to conclude that the intrusion into the trunk of 1967 Thunderbird at the garage was not unreasonable within the meaning of the Fourth and Fourteenth Amendments solely because a warrant had not been obtained by Officer Weiss after he left the hospital. The police did not have actual, physical custody of the vehicles as in *Harris* and *Cooper*, but the vehicle had been towed there — the officers' directions. These officers in a rural area were simply reacting to the effects of an accident — one of the recurring practical situations that results from the operation of motor vehicles and with which local police officers must deal every day. The Thunderbird was not parked adjacent to the dwelling place of the owner as in *Coolidge*, nor simply momentarily unoccupied on a street. Rather, like an obviously abandoned vehicle, it represented a nuisance, and there is no suggestion in the record that the officers' action in exercising control over it by having it towed away was unwarranted either in terms of state law or sound police procedure.

In *Harris* the justification for the initial intrusion into the vehicle was to safeguard the owner's property, and in *Cooper* it was to guarantee the safety of the custodians. Here the justification, while different, was as immediate and constitutionally reasonable as those in *Harris* and *Cooper*: concern for the safety of the general public who might be endangered if an intruder removed a revolver from the trunk of the vehicle. The record contains uncontradicted testimony to support the findings of the state courts and District Court. Furthermore, although there is no record basis for discrediting such testimony, it was corroborated by the circumstantial fact that at the time the search was conducted Officer Weiss was ignorant of the fact that a murder, or any other crime, had been committed. While perhaps in a metropolitan area the responsibility to the general public might have been discharged by the posting of a police guard during the night, what might be normal police procedure in such an area may be neither normal nor possible in Kewaskum, Wisconsin. The fact that the protection of the public might, in the abstract, have been accomplished by "less intrusive" means does not, by itself, render the search unreasonable. Cf. *Chambers v. Maroney*. . . .

The Court's previous recognition of the distinction between motor vehicles and dwelling places leads us to conclude that the type of caretaking "search" conducted here of a vehicle that was neither in the custody nor on the premises of its owner, and that had been placed where it was by virtue of lawful police action, was not unreasonable solely because a warrant had not been obtained. The Framers of the Fourth Amendment have given us only the general standard of "unreasonableness" as a guide in determining whether searches and seizures meet the standard of that Amendment in those cases where a warrant is not required. Very little that has been said in our previous decisions, see *Cooper, supra, Harris, supra, Chambers, supra*, and very little that we might say here can usefully refine the language of the Amendment itself in order to evolve some detailed formula for judging cases such as this. Where, as here, the trunk of an automobile, which the officer reasonably believed to contain a gun, was vulnerable to intrusion by vandals, we hold that the search was not "unreasonable" within the meaning of the Fourth and Fourteenth Amendments.

[JUSTICE BRENNAN, joined by JUSTICES DOUGLAS, STEWART and MARSHALL, dissented.]

NOTES AND QUESTIONS

(1) Cady and the two decisions discussed therein, *Cooper* and *Harris*, indicate that a vehicle search without probable cause will be reasonable at least when (1) the police have lawful custody of a vehicle subject to forfeiture (*Cooper*), (2) the vehicle is itself evidence of the crime (*Harris*), or (3) the presence of the vehicle poses a threat to public safety, the party in interest is incapable of making arrangements for its removal, and there is reason to believe (but not probable cause) that a weapon may be within (*Cady*). Note that in *Cady*, unlike the other cases, the vehicle was not in official custody, but the Court views this all the more reason to permit the search. Would the result in *Cady* have been different if the defendant had not been intoxicated and following his arrest for reckless driving offered to make arrangements for the removal of the vehicle, but police "routinely" took care of the matter themselves? *See, e.g.*, *Drinkard v. State*, 584 S.W.2d 650 (Tenn. 1979).

(2) In *Florida v. White*, 526 U.S. 559 (1999), the Supreme Court held (7-2), that officers with probable cause to believe that a vehicle was subject to forfeiture under state law — in this instance because it was an instrumentality of drug trafficking — could seize the vehicle (and having seized it, search it) without first obtaining a search warrant. The Court rejected the distinction drawn by the Florida Supreme Court between searching a vehicle with probable cause to believe it contained contraband, and seizing the vehicle itself. Speaking for the majority, Justice Thomas held that "[r]ecognition of the need to seize readily movable contraband before it is spirited away undoubtedly underlies the early federal laws relied upon in *Carroll*. . . . This need is equally weighty when the *automobile*, as opposed to its contents, is the contraband that the police seek to secure." Curiously, the Court does not cite *Cooper v. California* (discussed in *Cady v. Dombrowski*) which would appear to provide ample support for its conclusion. Justice Stevens, joined by Justice Ginsburg, dissented, contending that while exigent circumstances might support the search of a vehicle believed to contain contraband, the same could not be said as to the seizure of a vehicle, itself presumptively innocuous.

(3) In *Cardwell v. Lewis*, 417 U.S. 583 (1974), the defendant had been requested to appear at the police station in regard to a homicide investigation. By the time of his arrival, an arrest warrant had been obtained, and the police had probable cause to believe that his automobile had been used in the perpetration of the crime, although no search warrant had been sought. It was thought that an automobile had pushed another automobile occupied by the victim over an embankment, causing his death. Casts of tire tracks and paint scrapings, both left by the supposed assaulting vehicle, had been taken at the scene of the offense. The defendant parked his automobile in a commercial lot a short distance from the station. Upon his arrest he surrendered his car keys and the parking lot claim check. Thereafter, the vehicle was removed by officers to the police impoundment lot. The following day a positive identification was made of the tire tread, and paint samples were taken which were found to match those that were left on the automobile used by the victim. The Supreme Court sustained the search, although splitting four-four on the substantive

issue. The prevailing justices reasoned that

> [o]ne has a lesser expectation of privacy in a motor vehicle because its function is transportation and it seldom serves as one's residence or as the repository of personal effects. A car has little capacity for escaping public scrutiny. It travels public thoroughfares where its occupants and its contents are in plain view.

Moreover, the search did not intrude within the vehicle. Given the conceded probable cause to carry out the search, the Justices "fail[ed] to comprehend what expectation of privacy was infringed."

The plurality opinion then turned to the question of impoundment of the automobile without a warrant, a procedure which was not necessary to obtain the identification evidence. This contention suggested two possibilities: The police could have obtained a warrant for the seizure of the vehicle and postponed the examination for evidence until their possession was with judicial authorization, or the police could have obtained the identification evidence at the commercial parking lot, without moving the vehicle. Either alternative would have been less constitutionally intrusive than the course followed. The inherent mobility argument is far less persuasive when, as here, the party controlling the vehicle is incarcerated. Nevertheless, the Justices concluded that the manner of the search was constitutionally reasonable, relying upon the passage in *Chambers* which saw no constitutional distinction "between on the one hand seizing and holding a car before presenting the probable cause issue to a magistrate and on the other hand carrying out an immediate search without a warrant."

The four dissenting Justices contended that, in the absence of any argument that the vehicle would or could be moved, the justification for the vehicle exception was simply not present. Therefore the presumption favoring the use of a warrant whenever possible should have been honored.

PROBLEM R
THE OBSCURED VIN

Beningo Class was stopped and issued traffic citations for driving with a cracked windshield and speeding. While Class was outside of the vehicle, the officer sought to check the Vehicle Identification Number (VIN), first by opening the door to look at the door jamb, and not finding it there, then brushing aside some papers which obscured the area on the dashboard where the VIN is located in late-model cars. In the process, the officer observed a gun protruding about an inch from underneath the driver's seat, which he seized. Is the seizure valid? *See New York v. Class*, 475 U.S. 106 (1986). Should it make a difference if it was necessary to remove an opaque cover from the vehicle before examining the VIN? *See United States v. $277,000.00 U.S. Currency*, 941 F.2d 898 (9th Cir. 1991).

COLORADO v. BERTINE

United States Supreme Court
479 U.S. 367 (1987)

CHIEF JUSTICE REHNQUIST delivered the opinion of the Court.

On February 10, 1984, a police officer in Boulder, Colorado, arrested respondent Steven Lee Bertine for driving while under the influence of alcohol. After Bertine was taken into custody and before the arrival of a tow truck to take Bertine's van to an impoundment lot, a backup officer inventoried the contents of the van. The officer opened a closed backpack in which he found controlled substances, cocaine paraphernalia, and a large amount of cash. Bertine was subsequently charged with driving while under the influence of alcohol, unlawful possession of cocaine with intent to dispense, sell, and distribute, and unlawful possession of methaqualone. We are asked to decide whether the Fourth Amendment prohibits the State from proving these charges with the evidence discovered during the inventory of Bertine's van. We hold that it does not.

The backup officer inventoried the van in accordance with local police procedures, which require a detailed inspection and inventory of impounded vehicles. He found the backpack directly behind the frontseat of the van. Inside the pack, the officer observed a nylon bag containing metal canisters. Opening the canisters, the officer discovered that they contained cocaine, methaqualone tablets, cocaine paraphernalia, and $700 in cash. In an outside zippered pouch of the backpack, he also found $210 in cash in a sealed envelope. After completing the inventory of the van, the officer had the van towed to an impound lot and brought the backpack, money, and contraband to the police station.

After Bertine was charged with the offenses described above, he moved to suppress the evidence found during the inventory search on the ground, *inter alia*, that the search of the closed backpack and containers exceeded the permissible scope of such a search under the Fourth Amendment. The Colorado trial court ruled that probable cause supported Bertine's arrest and that the police officers had made the decision to impound the vehicle and to conduct a thorough inventory search in good faith. Although noting that the inventory of the vehicle was performed in a "somewhat slipshod" manner, the District Court concluded that "the search of the backpack was done for the purpose of protecting the owner's property, protection of the police from subsequent claims of loss or stolen property, and the protection of the police from dangerous instrumentalities." . . . The court observed that the standard procedures for impounding vehicles mandated a "detailed inventory involving the opening of containers and the listing of [their] contents." . . . Based on these findings, the court determined that the inventory search did not violate Bertine's right under the Fourth Amendment of the United States Constitution. . . . The court, nevertheless, granted Bertine's motion to suppress, holding that the inventory search violated the Colorado Constitution.

On the State's interlocutory appeal, the Supreme Court of Colorado affirmed. . . . In contrast to the District Court, however, the Colorado Supreme Court premised its ruling on the United States Constitution. The court recognized that in

South Dakota v. Opperman, 428 U.S. 364 (1976), we had held inventory searches of automobiles to be consistent with the Fourth Amendment, and that in *Illinois v. Lafayette*, 462 U.S. 640 (1983), we had held that the inventory search of personal effects of an arrestee at a police station was also permissible under that Amendment. The Supreme Court of Colorado felt, however, that our decisions in *Arkansas v. Sanders*, 442 U.S. 753 (1979), and *United States v. Chadwick*, 433 U.S. 1 (1977), holding searches of closed trunks and suitcases to violate the Fourth Amendment, meant that *Opperman* and *Lafayette* did not govern this case.

We granted certiorari to consider the important and recurring question of federal law decided by the Colorado Supreme Court. . . . As that court recognized, inventory searches are now a well-defined exception to the warrant requirement of the Fourth Amendment. . . . The policies behind the warrant requirement are not implicated in an inventory search, *Opperman*, 428 U.S., at 370, n. 5, . . . nor is the related concept of probable cause:

> "The standard of probable cause is peculiarly related to criminal investigations, not routine, noncriminal procedures. . . . The probable-cause approach is unhelpful when analysis centers upon the reasonableness of routine administrative caretaking functions, particularly when no claim is made that the protective procedures are a subterfuge for criminal investigations." *Ibid.*

. . . For these reasons, the Colorado Supreme Court's reliance on *Arkansas v. Sanders*, . . . and *United States v. Chadwick*, . . . was incorrect. Both of these cases concerned searches solely for the purpose of investigating criminal conduct, with the validity of the searches therefore dependent on the application of the probable-cause and warrant requirements of the Fourth Amendment.

By contrast, an inventory search may be "reasonable" under the Fourth Amendment even though it is not conducted pursuant to a warrant based upon probable cause. In *Opperman*, this Court assessed the reasonableness of an inventory search of the glove compartment in an abandoned automobile impounded by the police. We found that inventory procedures serve to protect an owner's property while it is in the custody of the police, to insure against claims of lost, stolen, or vandalized property, and to guard the police from danger. In light of these strong governmental interests and the diminished expectation of privacy in an automobile, we upheld the search. In reaching this decision, we observed that our cases accorded deference to police caretaking procedures designed to secure and protect vehicles and their contents within police custody. . . .

In our more recent decision, *Lafayette*, a police officer conducted an inventory search of the contents of a shoulder bag in the possession of an individual being taken into custody. In deciding whether this search was reasonable, we recognized that the search served legitimate governmental interests similar to those identified in *Opperman*. We determined that those interests outweighed the individual's Fourth Amendment interests and upheld the search.

In the present case, as in *Opperman* and *Lafayette*, there was no showing that the police, who were following standardized procedures, acted in bad faith or for the sole purpose of investigation. In addition, the governmental interests justifying the inventory searches in *Opperman* and *Lafayette* are nearly the same as those which obtain here. In each case, the police were potentially responsible for the property taken into their custody. By securing the property, the police protected the property from unauthorized interference. Knowledge of the precise nature of the property helped guard against claims of theft, vandalism, or negligence. Such knowledge also helped to avert any danger to police or others that may have been posed by the property.

. . .

While both *Opperman* and *Lafayette* are distinguishable from the present case on their facts, we think that the principles enunciated in those cases govern the present one. The judgment of the Supreme Court of Colorado is therefore

Reversed.

JUSTICE BLACKMUN, with whom JUSTICE POWELL and JUSTICE O'CONNOR join, concurring.

The Court today holds that police officers may open closed containers while conducting a routine inventory search of an impounded vehicle. I join the Court's opinion, but write separately to underscore the importance of having such inventories conducted only pursuant to standardized police procedures. The underlying rationale for allowing an inventory exception to the Fourth Amendment warrant rule is that police officers are not vested with discretion to determine the scope of the inventory search. . . . This absence of discretion ensures that inventory searches will not be used as a purposeful and general means of discovering evidence of crime. . . .

JUSTICE MARSHALL, with whom JUSTICE BRENNAN joins, dissenting.

. . .

As the Court acknowledges, . . . inventory searches are reasonable only if conducted according to standardized procedures. In both *Opperman* and *Lafayette*, the Court relied on the absence of police discretion in determining that the inventory searches in question were reasonable. . . .

The Court today attempts to evade these clear prohibitions on unfettered police discretion by declaring that "the discretion afforded the Boulder police was exercised in light of standardized criteria, related to the feasibility and appropriateness of parking and locking a vehicle rather than impounding it." . . . This vital assertion is flatly contradicted by the record in this case. The officer who conducted the inventory, Officer Reichenbach, testified at the suppression hearing that the decision not to "park and lock" respondent's vehicle was his "own individual discretionary decision." . . . Indeed, application of these supposedly standardized "criteria" upon which the Court so heavily relies would have yielded a different result in this case. Since there was ample public parking adjacent to the intersection where respondent was stopped, consideration of "feasibility" would certainly have militated in favor of the "park and lock" option, not against it. I do not comprehend how consideration of "appropriateness" serves to channel a field officer's discretion;

nonetheless, the "park and lock" option would seem particularly appropriate in this case, where respondent was stopped for a traffic offense and was not likely to be in custody for a significant length of time.

Indeed, the record indicates that *no* standardized criteria limit a Boulder police officer's discretion. According to a departmental directive, after placing a driver under arrest, an officer has three options for disposing of the vehicle. First, he can allow a third party to take custody. Second, the officer or the driver (depending on the nature of the arrest) may take the car to the nearest public parking facility, lock it, and take the keys. Finally, the officer can do what was done in this case: impound the vehicle, and search and inventory its contents, including closed containers.

Under the first option, the police have no occasion to search the automobile. Under the "park and lock" option, "[c]losed containers that give no indication of containing either valuables or a weapon *may not be opened and the contents searched* (*i.e.* inventoried.)" . . . (emphasis added). Only if the police choose the third option are they entitled to search closed containers in the vehicle. Where the vehicle is not itself evidence of a crime, as in the case, the police apparently have totally unbridled discretion as to which procedure to use. . . .

. . . [T]o invalidate a search that is conducted without established procedures, it is not necessary to establish that the police actually acted in bad faith, or that the inventory was in fact a "pretext." By allowing the police unfettered discretion, Boulder's discretionary scheme, like the random spot check in *Delaware v. Prouse*, is unreasonable because of the " 'grave danger' of abuse of discretion."

NOTE

Notwithstanding the emphasis placed in *Bertine* on limiting officer discretion, in *Florida v. Wells*, 495 U.S. 1 (1990), the Court held that "[a] police officer may be allowed sufficient latitude to determine whether a particular container should or should not be opened in light of the nature of the search and characteristics of the container itself." While the standardized procedure could require opening and inventorying the contents of all containers found in vehicles, "it would be equally permissible . . . to allow the opening of closed containers whose contents officers determine they are unable to ascertain from examining the containers' exteriors. The allowance of the exercise of judgment based on concerns related to the purposes of an inventory search does not violate the Fourth Amendment."

[I] Exigent Circumstances

WARDEN v. HAYDEN
United States Supreme Court
387 U.S. 294 (1967)

MR. JUSTICE BRENNAN delivered the opinion of the Court.

I

About 8 a.m. on March 17, 1962, an armed robber entered the business premises of the Diamond Cab Company in Baltimore, Maryland. He took some $363 and ran. Two cab drivers in the vicinity, attracted by shouts of "Holdup," followed the man to 2111 Cocoa Lane. One driver notified the company dispatcher by radio that the man was a Negro about 5' 8" tall, wearing a light cap and dark jacket, and that he had entered the house on Cocoa Lane. The dispatcher relayed the information to police who were proceeding to the scene of the robbery. Within minutes, police arrived at the house in a number of patrol cars. An officer knocked and announced their presence. Mrs. Hayden answered, and the officers told her they believed that a robber had entered the house, and asked to search the house. She offered no objection.

The officers spread out through the first and second floors and the cellar in search of the robber. Hayden was found in an upstairs bedroom feigning sleep. He was arrested when the officers on the first floor and in the cellar reported that no other man was in the house. Meanwhile an officer was attracted to an adjoining bathroom by the noise of running water, and discovered a shotgun and a pistol in a flush tank; another officer who, according to the District Court, "was searching the cellar for a man or the money" found in a washing machine a jacket and trousers of the type the fleeing man was said to have worn. A clip of ammunition for the pistol and a cap were found under the mattress of Hayden's bed, and ammunition for the shotgun was found in a bureau drawer in Hayden's room. All these items of evidence were introduced against respondent at his trial.

II

We agree with the Court of Appeals that neither the entry without warrant to search for the robber, nor the search for him without warrant was invalid. Under the circumstances of this case, "the exigencies of the situation made that course imperative." . . . The police were informed that an armed robbery had taken place, and that the suspect had entered 2111 Cocoa Lane less than five minutes before they reached it. They acted reasonably when they entered the house and began to search for a man of the description they had been given and for weapons which he had used in the robbery or might use against them. The Fourth Amendment does not require police officers to delay in the course of an investigation if to do so would gravely endanger their lives or the lives of others. Speed here was essential, and only a thorough search of the house for persons and weapons could have insured that Hayden was the only man present and that the police had control of all weapons which could be used against them or to effect an escape.

. . .

It is argued that, while the weapons, ammunition, and cap may have been seized in the course of a search for weapons, the officer who seized the clothing was searching neither for the suspect nor for weapons when he looked into the washing machine in which he found the clothing. But even if we assume, although we do not decide, that the exigent circumstances in this case made lawful a search without warrant only for the suspect or his weapons, it cannot be said on this record that the officer who found the clothes in the washing machine was not searching for weapons. He testified that he was searching for the man or the money, but his failure to state explicitly that he was searching for weapons, in the absence of a specific question to that effect, can hardly be accorded controlling weight. He knew that the robber was armed and he did not know that some weapons had been found at the time he opened the machine. In these circumstances the inference that he was in fact also looking for weapons is fully justified.

[JUSTICE BLACK concurred; JUSTICE FORTAS, joined by CHIEF JUSTICE WARREN, concurred; JUSTICE DOUGLAS dissented.]

NOTES AND QUESTIONS

(1) Viewed as a search incident to arrest case, *Hayden* has been superseded by *Chimel*, but is it that? If there is probable cause to believe that Hayden is within the house, would the case come out any differently should it turn out he is not? *See People v. Sprovieri*, 43 Ill. 2d 223, 252 N.E.2d 531 (1969). *Cf. Hill v. California*, *supra*. *See also* Pringle & Garfield, *The Expanding Power of Police to Search and Seize: Effect of Recent U.S. Supreme Court Decisions on Criminal Investigation*, 40 U. Colo. L. Rev. 491, 495 (1968).

(2) In addition to the apprehending of a fleeing felon, exigent circumstances have been found to justify the warrantless entry of residential premises when officers have received a report of serious illness or injury, an unattended child, a bomb, etc.

(3) In *Mincey v. Arizona*, 437 U.S. 385 (1978), the prosecution had relied on a "murder scene" exception to the warrant requirement, which had been recognized by the Arizona Supreme Court. The Supreme Court rejected the notion that an exigency could be based on the magnitude of the crime under investigation. "[T]he warrantless search of Mincey's apartment was not constitutionally permissible simply because a homicide had recently occurred there."

(4) On the morning following the assassination of Senator Robert Kennedy in the Ambassador Hotel in Los Angeles, a warrantless search was carried out in the residence of Sirhan B. Sirhan, in the course of which evidence was seized which was used to convict him of first degree murder. On appeal, "[t]he Attorney General asserted that there was a pressing emergency to ascertain the existence of a possible conspiracy to assassinate presidential candidates or high governmental officials, and he relied on the emergency exception to the warrant requirement." In

sustaining the search, the Supreme Court of California said:

> Their beliefs were entirely reasonable. The crime was one of enormous gravity, and the "gravity of the offense" is an appropriate factor to take into consideration. . . . The victim was a major presidential candidate, and a crime of violence had already been committed against him. The crime thus involved far more than possibly idle threats. Although the officers did not have reasonable cause to believe that the house contained evidence of a conspiracy to assassinate prominent political leaders, we believe that the mere possibility that there might be such evidence in the house fully warranted the officers' actions. It is not difficult to envisage what would have been the effect on this nation if several more political assassinations had followed that of Senator Kennedy. Today, when assassinations of persons of prominence have repeatedly been committed in this country, it is essential that law enforcement officers be allowed to take fast action in their endeavors to combat such crimes.

People v. Sirhan, 497 P.2d 1121, 1140 (1972), *cert. denied*, 410 U.S. 947 (1973).

MICHIGAN v. FISHER

United States Supreme Court
558 U.S. 45 (2009)

PER CURIAM.

Police officers responded to a complaint of a disturbance near Allen Road in Brownstown, Michigan. Officer Christopher Goolsby later testified that, as he and his partner approached the area, a couple directed them to a residence where a man was "going crazy." . . . Upon their arrival, the officers found a household in considerable chaos: a pickup truck in the driveway with its front smashed, damaged fence posts along the side of the property, and three broken house windows, the glass still on the ground outside. The officers also noticed blood on the hood of the pickup and on clothes inside of it, as well as one of the doors to the house. (It is disputed whether they noticed this immediately upon reaching the house, but undisputed that they noticed it before the allegedly unconstitutional entry.) Through a window, the officers could see respondent, Jeremy Fisher, inside the house, screaming and throwing things. The back door was locked, and a couch had been placed to block the front door.

The officers knocked, but Fisher refused to answer. They saw that Fisher had a cut on his hand, and they asked him whether he needed medical attention. Fisher ignored these questions and demanded, with accompanying profanity, that the officers go to get a search warrant. Officer Goolsby then pushed the front door partway open and ventured into the house. Through the window of the open door he saw Fisher pointing a long gun at him. Officer Goolsby withdrew.

Fisher was charged under Michigan law with assault with a dangerous weapon and possession of a firearm during the commission of a felony. The trial court concluded that Officer Goolsby violated the Fourth Amendment when he entered Fisher's house, and granted Fisher's motion to suppress the evidence obtained as a result-that is, Officer Goolsby's statement that Fisher pointed a rifle at him.

[The Michigan Court of Appeals sustained the ruling of the trial court, and the Michigan Supreme Court denied leave to appeal.] Because the decision of the Michigan Court of Appeals is indeed contrary to our Fourth Amendment case law, particularly Brigham City v. Stuart, 547 U.S. 398 (2006), we grant the State's petition for certiorari and reverse. . .

[L]aw enforcement officers "may enter a home without a warrant to render emergency assistance to an injured occupant or to protect an occupant from imminent injury." . . . This "emergency aid exception" does not depend on the officers' subjective intent or the seriousness of any crime they are investigating when the emergency arises. . . . It requires only "an objectively reasonable basis for believing," . . . that "a person within [the house] is in need of immediate aid." . . .

Brigham City illustrates the application of this standard. There, police officers responded to a noise complaint in the early hours of the morning. "As they approached the house, they could hear from within an altercation occurring, some kind of fight." . . . Following the tumult to the back of the house whence it came, the officers saw juveniles drinking beer in the backyard and a fight unfolding in the kitchen. They watched through the window as a juvenile broke free from the adults restraining him and punched another adult in the face, who recoiled to the sink, spitting blood. . . . Under these circumstances, we found it "plainly reasonable" for the officers to enter the house and quell the violence, for they had "an objectively reasonable basis for believing both that the injured adult might need help and that the violence in the kitchen was just beginning." . . .

A straightforward application of the emergency aid exception, as in Brigham City, dictates that the officer's entry was reasonable. Just as in Brigham City, the police officers here were responding to a report of a disturbance. Just as in Brigham City, when they arrived on the scene they encountered a tumultuous situation in the house — and here they also found signs of a recent injury, perhaps from a car accident, outside. And just as in Brigham City, the officers could see violent behavior inside. Although Officer Goolsby and his partner did not see punches thrown, as did the officers in Brigham City, they did see Fisher screaming and throwing things. It would be objectively reasonable to believe that Fisher's projectiles might have a human target (perhaps a spouse or a child), or that Fisher would hurt himself in the course of his rage. In short, we find it as plain here as we did in Brigham City that the officer's entry was reasonable under the Fourth Amendment. . . .

Justice Stevens, with whom Justice Sotomayor joins, dissenting.

. . . Today, without having heard Officer Goolsby's testimony, this Court decides that the trial judge got it wrong. I am not persuaded that he did, but even if we made that assumption, it is hard to see how the Court is justified in micromanaging the day-to-day business of state tribunals making fact-intensive decisions of this kind. We ought not usurp the role of the factfinder when faced with a close question of the reasonableness of an officer's actions, particularly in a case tried in a state court. I therefore respectfully dissent.

KENTUCKY v. KING

United States Supreme Court
131 S. Ct. 1849 (2011)

JUSTICE ALITO delivered the opinion of the Court.

It is well established that "exigent circumstances," including the need to prevent the destruction of evidence, permit police officers to conduct an otherwise permissible search without first obtaining a warrant. In this case, we consider whether this rule applies when police, by knocking on the door of a residence and announcing their presence, cause the occupants to attempt to destroy evidence. The Kentucky Supreme Court held that the exigent circumstances rule does not apply in the case at hand because the police should have foreseen that their conduct would prompt the occupants to attempt to destroy evidence. We reject this interpretation of the exigent circumstances rule. The conduct of the police prior to their entry into the apartment was entirely lawful. They did not violate the Fourth Amendment or threaten to do so. In such a situation, the exigent circumstances rule applies.

I

A

This case concerns the search of an apartment in Lexington, Kentucky. Police officers set up a controlled buy of crack cocaine outside an apartment complex. Undercover Officer Gibbons watched the deal take place from an unmarked car in a nearby parking lot. After the deal occurred, Gibbons radioed uniformed officers to move in on the suspect. He told the officers that the suspect was moving quickly toward the breezeway of an apartment building, and he urged them to "hurry up and get there" before the suspect entered an apartment. . . .

In response to the radio alert, the uniformed officers drove into the nearby parking lot, left their vehicles, and ran to the breezeway. Just as they entered the breezeway, they heard a door shut and detected a very strong odor of burnt marijuana. As the end of the breezeway, the officers saw two apartments, one on the left and one on the right, and they did not know which apartment the suspect had entered. Gibbons had radioed that the suspect was running into the apartment on the right, but the officers did not hear this statement because they had already left their vehicles. Because they smelled marijuana smoke emanating from the apartment on the left, they approached the door of that apartment.

Officer Steven Cobb, one of the uniformed officers who approached the door, testified that the officers banged on the left apartment door "as loud as [they] could" and announced, " 'This is the police' " or " 'Police, police, police.' " . . . Cobb said that "[a]s soon as [the officers] started banging on the door," they "could hear people inside moving," and "[i]t sounded as [though] things were being moved inside the apartment." . . . These noises, Cobb testified, led the officers to believe that drug-related evidence was about to be destroyed.

At that point, the officers announced that they "were going to make entry inside the apartment." . . . Cobb then kicked in the door, the officers entered the apartment, and they found three people in the front room: respondent Hollis King, respondent's girlfriend, and a guest who was smoking marijuana. The officers performed a protective sweep of the apartment during which they saw marijuana and powder cocaine in plain view. In a subsequent search, they also discovered crack cocaine, cash, and drug paraphernalia.

Police eventually entered the apartment on the right. Inside, they found the suspected drug dealer who was the initial target of the investigation.

B

In the Fayette County Circuit Court, a grand jury charged respondent with trafficking in marijuana, first degree trafficking in a controlled substance, and second-degree persistent felony offender status. Respondent filed a motion to suppress the evidence from the warrantless search, but the Circuit Court denied the motion. The Circuit Court concluded that the officers had probable cause to investigate the marijuana odor and that the officers "properly conducted [the investigation] by initially knocking on the door of the apartment unit and awaiting the response or consensual entry." . . . Exigent circumstances justified the warrantless entry, the court held, because "there was no response at all to the knocking," and because "Officer Cobb heard movement in the apartment which he reasonably concluded were persons in the act of destroying evidence, particularly narcotics because of the smell." . . . Respondent then entered a conditional guilty plea, reserving his right to appeal the denial of the suppression motion. The court sentenced respondent to 11 years' imprisonment.

The Kentucky Court of Appeals affirmed. It held that exigent circumstances justified the warrantless entry because the police reasonably believed that evidence would be destroyed. The police did not impermissibly create the exigency, the court explained, because they did not deliberately evade the warrant requirement.

The Supreme Court of Kentucky reversed. . . As a preliminary matter, the court observed that there was "certainly some question as to whether the sound of persons moving [inside the apartment] was sufficient to establish that evidence was being destroyed." . . . But the court did not answer that question. Instead, it "assume[d] for the purpose of argument that exigent circumstances existed." . . .

To determine whether police impermissibly created the exigency, the Supreme Court of Kentucky announced a two-part test. First, the court held, police cannot "deliberately creat[e] the exigent circumstances with the bad faith intent to avoid the warrant requirement." . . . Second, even absent bad faith, the court concluded, police may not rely on exigent circumstances if "it was reasonably foreseeable that the investigative tactics employed by the police would create the exigent circumstances." . . . Although the court found no evidence of bad faith, it held that exigent circumstances could not justify the search because it was reasonably foreseeable that the occupants would destroy evidence when the police knocked on the door and announced their presence. . . .

We granted certiorari. . . .

II

. . .

B

Over the years, lower courts have developed an exception to the exigent circumstances rule, the so-called "police-created exigency" doctrine. Under this doctrine, police may not rely on the need to prevent destruction of evidence when that exigency was "created" or "manufactured" by the conduct of the police. . . .

In applying this exception for the "creation" or "manufacturing" of an exigency by the police, courts require something more than mere proof that fear of detection by the police caused the destruction of evidence. An additional showing is obviously needed because, as the Eighth Circuit has recognized, "in some sense the police always create the exigent circumstances." *United States v. Duchi*, 906 F.2d 1278, 1284 (CA8 1990). That is to say, in the vast majority of cases in which evidence is destroyed by persons who are engaged in illegal conduct, the reason for the destruction is fear that the evidence will fall into the hands of law enforcement. Destruction of evidence issues probably occur most frequently in drug cases because drugs may be easily destroyed by flushing them down a toilet or rinsing them down a drain. Persons in possession of valuable drugs are unlikely to destroy them unless they fear discovery by the police. Consequently, a rule that precludes the police from making a warrantless entry to prevent the destruction of evidence whenever their conduct causes the exigency would unreasonably shrink the reach of this well-established exception to the warrant requirement.

Presumably for the purpose of avoiding such a result, the lower courts have held that the police-created exigency doctrine requires more than simple causation, but the lower courts have not agreed on the test to be applied. Indeed, the petition in this case maintains that "[t]here are currently five different tests being used by the United States Courts of Appeals," . . . and some state courts have crafted additional tests. . . .

III

A

Despite the welter of tests devised by the lower courts, the answer to the question presented in this case follows directly and clearly from the principle that permits warrantless searches in the first place. As previously noted, warrantless searches are allowed when the circumstances make it reasonable, within the meaning of the Fourth Amendment, to dispense with the warrant requirement. Therefore the answer to the question before us is that the exigent circumstances rule justifies a warrantless search when the conduct of the police preceding the exigency is reasonable in the same sense. Where, as here, the police did not create the exigency by engaging or threatening to engage in conduct that violates the Fourth Amendment, warrantless entry to prevent the destruction of evidence is reasonable and thus allowed.[40]

. . .

B

Some lower courts have adopted a rule that is similar to the one we recognize today. . . . But others, including the Kentucky Supreme Court, have imposed additional requirements that are unsound and that we now reject.

Bad faith. Some courts, including the Kentucky Supreme Court, ask whether law enforcement officers " 'deliberately created the exigent circumstances with the bad faith intent to avoid the warrant requirement.' " . . .

This approach is fundamentally inconsistent with our Fourth Amendment jurisprudence. "Our cases have repeatedly rejected" a subjective approach, asking only whether "the circumstances, viewed objectively, justify the action." . . .

Reasonable foreseeability. Some courts, again including the Kentucky Supreme Court, hold that police may not rely on an exigency if "'it was reasonably foreseeable that the investigative tactics employed by the police would create the exigent circumstances.' " . . .

Contrary to this reasoning, however, we have rejected the notion that police may seize evidence without a warrant only when they come across the evidence by happenstance. In *Horton* . . . we held that the police may seize evidence in plain view even though the officers may be "interested in an item of evidence and fully expec[t] to find it in the course of a search." . . .

Adoption of a reasonable foreseeability test would also introduce an unacceptable degree of unpredictability. For example, whenever law enforcement officers knock on the door of premises occupied by a person who may be involved in the drug trade, there is some possibility that the occupants may possess drugs and may seek to destroy them. Under a reasonable foreseeability test, it would be necessary to quantify the degree of predictability that must be reached before the police-created exigency doctrine comes into play.

. . .

Probable cause and time to secure a warrant. Some courts, in applying the police-created exigency doctrine, fault law enforcement officers if, after acquiring evidence that is sufficient to establish probable cause to search particular premises, the officers do not seek a warrant but instead knock on the door and seek either to

---

[40] [4] There is a strong argument to be made that, at least in most circumstances, the exigent circumstances rule should not apply where the police, without a warrant or any legally sound basis for a warrantless entry, threaten that they will enter without permission unless admitted. In this case, however, no such actual threat was made, and therefore we have no need to reach that question.

speak with an occupant or to obtain consent to search. . . .

This approach unjustifiably interferes with legitimate law enforcement strategies. There are many entirely proper reasons why police may not want to seek a search warrant as soon as the bare minimum of evidence needed to establish probable cause is acquired. Without attempting to provide a comprehensive list of these reasons, we note a few.

First, the police may wish to speak with the occupants of a dwelling before deciding whether it is worthwhile to seek authorization for a search. They may think that a short and simple conversation may obviate the need to apply for and execute a warrant. . . . Second, the police may want to ask an occupant of the premises for consent to search because doing so is simpler, faster, and less burdensome than applying for a warrant. A consensual search also "may result in considerably less inconvenience" and embarrassment to the occupants than a search conducted pursuant to a warrant. . . . Third, law enforcement officers may wish to obtain more evidence before submitting what might otherwise be considered a marginal warrant application. Fourth, prosecutors may wish to wait until they acquire evidence that can justify a search that is broader in scope than the search that a judicial officer is likely to authorize based on the evidence then available. And finally, in many cases, law enforcement may not want to execute a search that will disclose the existence of an investigation because doing so may interfere with the acquisition of additional evidence against those already under suspicion or evidence about additional but as yet unknown participants in a criminal scheme.

We have said that "[l]aw enforcement officers are under no constitutional duty to call a halt to a criminal investigation the moment they have the minimum evidence to establish probable cause." *Hoffa v. United States*. . . . Faulting the police for failing to apply for a search warrant at the earliest possible time after obtaining probable cause imposes a duty that is nowhere to be found in the Constitution.

Standard of good investigative tactics. Finally, some lower court cases suggest that law enforcement officers may be found to have created or manufactured an exigency if the court concludes that the course of their investigation was "contrary to standard or good law enforcement practices (or to the policies or practices of their jurisdictions)." . . . This approach fails to provide clear guidance for law enforcement officers and authorizes courts to make judgments on matters that are the province of those who are responsible for federal and state law enforcement agencies.

C

Respondent argues for a rule that differs from those discussed above, but his rule is also flawed. Respondent contends that law enforcement officers impermissibly create an exigency when they "engage in conduct that would cause a reasonable person to believe that entry is imminent and inevitable." . . . In respondent's view, relevant factors include the officers' tone of voice in announcing their presence and the forcefulness of their knocks. But the ability of law enforcement officers to respond to an exigency cannot turn on such subtleties.

Police officers may have a very good reason to announce their presence loudly and to knock on the door with some force. A forceful knock may be necessary to alert the occupants that someone is at the door . . . Furthermore, unless police officers identify themselves loudly enough, occupants may not know who is at their doorstep. Officers are permitted-indeed, encouraged-to identify themselves to citizens, and 'in many circumstances this is a cause for assurance, not discomfort." . . . Citizens who are startled by an unexpected knock on the door or by the sight of unknown persons in plain clothes on their doorstep may be relieved to learn that these persons are police officers. Others may appreciate the opportunity to make an informed decision about whether to answer the door to the police.

If respondent's test were adopted, it would be extremely difficult for police officers to know how loudly they may announce their presence or how forcefully they may knock on a door without running afoul of the police-created exigency rule. And in most cases, it would be nearly impossible for a court to determine whether that threshold had been passed. The Fourth Amendment does not require the nebulous and impractical test that respondent proposes.

D

For these reasons, we conclude that the exigent circumstances rule applies when the police do not gain entry to premises by means of an actual or threatened violation of the Fourth Amendment. This holding provides ample protection for the privacy rights that the Amendment protects.

When law enforcement officers who are not armed with a warrant knock on a door, they do no more than any private citizen might do. And whether the person who knocks on the door and requests the opportunity to speak is a police officer or a private citizen, the occupant has no obligation to open the door or to speak. . . . And even if an occupant chooses to open the door and speak with the officers, the occupant need not allow the officers to enter the premises and may refuse to answer any questions at any time.

Occupants who choose not to stand on their constitutional rights but instead elect to attempt to destroy evidence have only themselves to blame for the warrantless exigent circumstances search that may ensue.

IV

We now apply our interpretation of the police-created exigency doctrine to the facts of this case.

A

We need not decide whether exigent circumstances existed in this case. Any warrantless entry based on exigent circumstances must, of course, be supported by a genuine exigency. . . . The trial court and the Kentucky Court of Appeals found that there was a real exigency in this case, but the Kentucky Supreme Court expressed doubt on this issue, observing that there was "certainly some question as to whether the sound of persons moving [inside the apartment] was sufficient to establish that evidence was being destroyed." . . . The Kentucky Supreme Court "assum[ed] for the purpose of argument that exigent circumstances existed," . . . and it held that the police had impermissibly manufactured the exigency.

We, too, assume for purposes of argument that an exigency existed. We decide only the question on which the Kentucky Supreme Court ruled and on which we granted certiorari. Under what circumstances do police impermissibly create an exigency? Any question about whether an exigency actually existed is better addressed by the Kentucky Supreme Court on remand. . . .

B

In this case, we see no evidence that the officers either violated the Fourth Amendment or threatened to do so prior to the point when they entered the apartment. Officer Cobb testified without contradiction that the officers "banged on the door as loud as [they] could" and announced either " 'Police, police, police' " or " 'This is the police.' " . . . This conduct was entirely consistent with the Fourth Amendment, and we are aware of no other evidence that might show that the officers either violated the Fourth Amendment or threatened to do so (for example, by announcing that they would break down the door if the occupants did not open the door voluntarily).

Respondent argues that the officers "demanded" entry to the apartment, but he has not pointed to any evidence in the record that supports this assertion. He relies on a passing statement made by the trial court in its opinion denying respondent's motion to suppress. . . . In recounting the events that preceded the search, the judge wrote that the officers "banged on the door of the apartment on the back left of the breezeway identifying themselves as police officers and demanding that the door be opened by the persons inside." . . . However, at a later point in the opinion, the judge stated that the officers "initially knock[ed] on the door of the apartment unit and await[ed] the response or consensual entry." . . . This latter statement is consistent with the testimony at the suppression hearing and with the finding of the state appellate courts. . . . There is no evidence of a "demand" of any sort, much less a demand that amounts to a threat to violate the Fourth Amendment. If there is contradictory evidence that has not been brought to our attention, the state court may elect to address that matter on remand.

Finally, respondent claims that the officers "explained to [the occupants that the officers] were going to make entry inside the apartment," . . . but the record is clear that the officers did not make this statement until after the exigency arose. As Officer Cobb testified, the officers "knew that there was possibly something that was going to be destroyed inside the apartment," and "[a]t *that point*, . . . [they] explained [that they] were going to make entry." . . . (emphasis added). Given that this announcement was made after the exigency arose, it could not have created the exigency.

. . .

The judgment of the Kentucky Supreme Court is reversed, and the case is remanded for further proceedings not inconsistent with this opinion.

Justice Ginsburg, dissenting.

The Court today arms the police with a way routinely to dishonor the Fourth Amendment's warrant requirement in drug cases. In lieu of presenting their evidence to a neutral magistrate, police officers may now knock, listen, then break the door down, never mind that they had ample time to obtain a warrant. I dissent from the Court's reduction of the Fourth Amendment's force.

. . . The question presented: May police, who could pause to gain the approval of a neutral magistrate, dispense with the need to get a warrant by themselves creating exigent circumstances? I would answer no, as did the Kentucky Supreme Court. The urgency must exist, I would rule, when the police come on the scene, not subsequent to their arrival, prompted by their own conduct.

I

Two pillars of our Fourth Amendment jurisprudence should have controlled the Court's ruling: First, "whenever practical, [the police must] obtain advance judicial approval of searches and seizures through the warrant procedure." *Terry v. Ohio* . . . ; second, unwarranted "searches and seizures inside a home" bear heightened scrutiny, *Payton v. New York*. . . . "[T]he police bear a heavy burden," the Court has cautioned, "when attempting to demonstrate an urgent need that might justify warrantless searches." *Welsh v. Wisconsin* . . .

The heavy burden has not been carried here. There was little risk that drug-related evidence would have been destroyed had the police delayed the search pending a magistrate's authorization. As the Court recognizes, "[p]ersons in possession of valuable drugs are unlikely to destroy them unless they fear discovery by the police." . . . Nothing in the record shows that, prior to the knock at the apartment door, the occupants were apprehensive about police proximity . . . .

II

. . . Under an appropriately reined-in "emergency" or "exigent circumstances" exception, the result in this case should not be in doubt. The target of the investigation's entry into the building, and the smell of marijuana seeping under the apartment door into the hallway, the Kentucky Supreme Court rightly determined, gave the police "probable cause . . . sufficient . . . to obtain a warrant to search . . . the apartment. . . ." As the court observed, nothing made it impracticable for the police to post officers on the premises while proceeding to obtain a warrant authorizing their entry.

NOTES AND QUESTIONS

(1) It would appear undisputed that the exigent circumstances justifying the warrantless entry resulted from the police activity within the apartment building. It is equally obvious that the offense preceding the search was initiated by the police who had "set up a controlled buy." Is the exigency for the search more dubious because, but for official inducement, the particular crime would not have occurred

at all?

(2) The officers entered the wrong apartment, a fact the Court notes but apparently considers insignificant. Do you agree? The only facts implicating the occupants of the entered apartment (one of whom is the respondent in this prosecution) was an odor of burning of marijuana and noises which "led the officers to believe that drug-related evidence was about to be destroyed." Should that be enough? What if marijuana use is not a crime?

The drug dealer targeted by the police presumably was inside one of the two apartments. Once the police discover they have the wrong one, would they be justified in making a warrantless entry into the other one, notwithstanding the absence of any suspicious odors or sounds?

(3) Justice Ginsburg observes that exceptions to the search warrant requirement are indeed *exceptions*, and warrants are presumed to be the rule. She also notes that this is particularly the case when residential premises are the target of the search. The idea that warrants are needed when officers have both probable cause and time to secure a warrant is dismissed by the majority with the explanation, "[t]his approach unjustifiably interferes with legitimate law enforcement strategies." Is it possible that any requirement that a warrant must be obtained may be seen by officers to interfere with "legitimate law enforcement strategies"? Does the present case suggest that the Court will stand ready to legitimize such strategies?

(4) The *King* decision appears to focus solely on narcotics investigations. The dissent seems to assume that the holding is relevant only to drug cases. Can you envision any other situation in which the decision would validate a warrantless search which otherwise would not come within the exigent circumstances exception?

(5) *King* was distinguished in *State v. Campbell*, 300 P.3d 72 (Kan. 2013), in which an officer went to the suspect's apartment intending to investigate a noise complaint. Approaching the apartment, the officer detected the odor of burnt marijuana. As described by the court, the officer "affirmatively chose to conceal his identity by covering the peephole and positioning himself to block the occupant's ability to determine who was standing at the door — essentially forcing the occupant of the apartment to make an *uninformed* decision." When the door was partially opened, the officer observed a handgun in the suspect's hand and forcibly entered. Ultimately, he was charged with several narcotics offenses and criminal possession of a firearm. The court held, "[p]ursuant to *King*, because [the officer] acted unreasonably by exceeding the scope of a knock and talk, he engaged in conduct that violated the Fourth Amendment."

PROBLEM S
THE CHRISTMAS OPEN HOUSE

At approximately 3:30 p.m. on December 25, 1996, Officers Tan and Cary received the following dispatch: "An open door at 4 Park Lane, number 4 Park Lane. PR says that the door has been open all day and it's all a shambles inside. It's unknown if anyone's home but the PR doesn't think so. The PR can be contacted if necessary." Officer Tan arrived at the residence

> approximately five minutes later. He testified, "I was concerned for possibly the life and property of the people inside." Officer Cary arrived about two minutes after Officer Tan. Cary noted the reporting person pointing to the residence in question, though the officers did not speak to him at that time. Tan testified at the superior court suppression hearing that, looking inside, he saw "clothing, paper, strewn on the ground, on the sofa. It was just a real mess inside." His concern was heightened by what he saw: "It appeared that someone might have been inside, a burglary attempt or in the progress, or the welfare of the people inside." Tan testified during the preliminary hearing: "Due to the fact that the contents in the interior of the house was messy, looked like someone had gone through the house." The officers knocked several times, announcing their presence as Richmond police officers. There were no signs of forced entry. However, increasingly concerned for the welfare of possible occupants, the officers entered the residence to conduct a security check. They did not open any interior doors or containers. They found no one inside but did observe a large quantity of suspected cocaine and money in plain view. They left the residence and informed their supervisor. Ultimately, a search warrant was obtained, based upon the officers' observations. Evidence thus acquired led to the current charges.

Do the officers have probable cause to enter the residence? Do they need probable cause? *See People v. Ray*, 64 Cal. App. 4th 868 (Cal. Ct. App. 1998). Would a 911 call from a neighbor reporting a break-in be sufficient to justify a warrantless entry, if the police observe no evidence of forced entry and through the window see an individual seated on a couch? *See People v. Grazier*, 992 P.2d 1149 (Colo. 2000). *Compare United States v. Richardson*, 208 F.3d 626 (7th Cir.), *cert. denied*, 531 U.S. 910 (2000).

Chapter 4

THE RIGHT TO COUNSEL

§ 4.01 RECOGNITION OF THE RIGHT

The Sixth Amendment to the Constitution provides, in material part: "In all criminal prosecutions, the accused shall enjoy the right . . . to have the Assistance of Counsel for his defence." For the past century, judges have expressed little doubt that this provision guaranteed the right of the affluent accused to the assistance of his or her retained lawyer. The Supreme Court in 1932 stated that a hearing "has always included the right to the aid of counsel when desired and provided by the party asserting the right." *Powell v. Alabama*, 287 U.S. 45, 68 (1932). In *Chandler v. Fretag*, 348 U.S. 3, 9 (1954), Chief Justice Warren made clear the distinction between retained and appointed counsel: "Regardless of whether petitioner would have been entitled to the appointment of counsel, his right to be heard through his own counsel was unqualified."

No, the difficulty has not been in applying the Sixth Amendment to the reaches of retained counsel. Rather, the troublesome issue has been the application of the Sixth Amendment to the indigent defendant who wishes to have counsel appointed by the court. The Supreme Court was faced with this issue in the *Powell* case, but avoided deciding it. In *Powell*, the lack of legal representation was determinative, but only on the question of whether the due process rights of the defendants had been infringed, not whether their right to counsel had been violated.[1]

The first Supreme Court decision to hold that there exists a Sixth Amendment right to appointment of counsel in all federal cases was *Johnson v. Zerbst*, 304 U.S. 458 (1938). In strong language, Justice Black established the indigent's right to appointed counsel:

> The purpose of the constitutional guaranty of a right to counsel is to protect an accused from conviction resulting from his own ignorance of his legal and constitutional rights . . .
>
> Since the Sixth Amendment constitutionally entitles one charged with crime to the assistance of counsel, compliance with this constitutional mandate is an essential jurisdictional prerequisite to a federal court's authority to deprive an accused of his life or liberty. . . . If the accused however is not represented by counsel and has not competently and intelligently waived his constitutional right, the Sixth Amendment stands as a jurisdictional bar to a valid conviction and sentence depriving him of his life or his liberty.

---

[1] This section of the *Powell* opinion is quoted at length in *Betts v. Brady*, *infra*.

The question after *Johnson* was whether Justice Black's *per se* rule of the right to counsel, which applied to federal prosecutions, would also be applied to the states. The answer, just four years later, was that it would not.

BETTS v. BRADY

United States Supreme Court
316 U.S. 455 (1942)

MR. JUSTICE ROBERTS delivered the opinion of the Court.

The petitioner was indicted for robbery in the Circuit Court of Carroll County, Maryland. Due to lack of funds, he was unable to employ counsel, and so informed the judge at his arraignment. He requested that counsel be appointed for him. The judge advised him that this could not be done as it was not the practice in Carroll County to appoint counsel for indigent defendants save in prosecutions for murder and rape.

Was the petitioner's conviction and sentence a deprivation of his liberty without due process of law, in violation of the Fourteenth Amendment, because of the court's refusal to appoint counsel at his request?

The Sixth Amendment of the national Constitution applies only to trials in federal courts. The due process clause of the Fourteenth Amendment does not incorporate, as such, the specific guarantees found in the Sixth Amendment although a denial by a state of rights or privileges specifically embodied in that and others of the first eight amendments may, in certain circumstances, or in connection with other elements, operate, in a given case, to deprive a litigant of due process of law in violation of the Fourteenth. Due process of law is secured against invasion by the federal Government by the Fifth Amendment and is safeguarded against state action in identical words by the Fourteenth. The phrase formulates a concept less rigid and more fluid than those envisaged in other specific and particular provisions of the Bill of Rights. Its application is less a matter of rule. Asserted denial is to be tested by an appraisal of the totality of facts in a given case. That which may, in one setting, constitute a denial of fundamental fairness, shocking to the universal sense of justice, may, in other circumstances, and in the light of other considerations, fall short of such denial.

The petitioner, in this instance, asks us, in effect, to apply a rule in the enforcement of the due process clause. He says the rule to be deduced from our former decisions is that, in every case, whatever the circumstances, one charged with crime, who is unable to obtain counsel, must be furnished counsel by the state.

In *Powell v. Alabama*, ignorant and friendless negro youths, strangers in the community, without friends or means to obtain counsel, were hurried to trial for a capital offense without effective appointment of counsel on whom the burden of preparation and trial would rest, and without adequate opportunity to consult even the counsel casually appointed to represent them. This occurred in a State whose statute law required the appointment of counsel for indigent defendants prosecuted for the offense charged. Thus the trial was conducted in disregard of every principle of fairness and in disregard of that which was declared by the law of the State a requisite of a fair trial. This court held the resulting convictions were without due process of law. It said that, in the light of all the facts, the failure of the trial court to afford the defendants reasonable time and opportunity to secure counsel was a clear denial of due process. The court stated further that "under the circumstances . . . the necessity of counsel was so vital and imperative that the failure of the trial court to make an effective appointment of counsel was likewise a denial of due process," but added: "whether this would be so in other criminal prosecutions, or under other circumstances, we need not determine. All that it is necessary now to decide, as we do decide, is that in a capital case, where the defendant is unable to employ counsel, and is incapable adequately of making his own defense because of ignorance, feeble-mindedness, illiteracy, or the like, it is the duty of the court, whether requested or not, to assign counsel for him as a necessary requisite of due process of law. . . . "

The question we are now to decide is whether due process of law demands that in every criminal case, whatever the circumstances, a state must furnish counsel to an indigent defendant. Is the furnishing of counsel in all cases whatever dictated by natural, inherent, and fundamental principles of fairness?

[I]t is evident that the [state] constitutional provisions to the effect that a defendant should be "allowed" counsel or should have a right "to be heard by himself and his counsel," or that he might be heard by "either or both," at his election, were intended to do away with the rules which denied representation, in whole or in part, by counsel in criminal prosecutions, but were not aimed to compel the state to provide counsel for a defendant. At the least, such a construction by state courts and legislators can not be said to lack reasonable basis.

[I]n the great majority of the states, it has been the considered judgment of the people, their representatives and their courts that appointment of counsel is not a fundamental right, essential to a fair trial. On the contrary, the matter has generally been deemed one of legislative policy. In the light of this evidence we are unable to say that the concept of due process incorporated in the Fourteenth Amendment obligates the states, whatever may be their own views, to furnish counsel in every such case. Every court has power, if it deems proper, to appoint counsel where that course seems to be required in the interest of fairness.

In this case there was no question of the commission of a robbery. The State's case consisted of evidence identifying the petitioner as the perpetrator. The defense was an alibi. Petitioner called and examined witnesses to prove that he was at another place at the time of the commission of the offense. The simple issue was the veracity of the testimony for the State and that for the defendant. As Judge Bond says, the accused was not helpless, but was a man forty-three years old, of ordinary intelligence and ability to take care of his own interests on the trial of that narrow issue. He had once before been in a criminal court, pleaded guilty to larceny and served a sentence and was not wholly unfamiliar with criminal procedure.

To deduce from the due process clause a rule binding upon the states in this matter would be to impose upon them, as Judge Bond points out, a requirement without distinction between criminal charges of different magnitude or in respect of courts of varying jurisdiction. As he says: "Charges of small crimes tried before justices of the peace and capital charges tried in the higher courts would equally require the appointment of counsel. Presumably it would be argued that trials in the Traffic Court would require it." And indeed it was said by petitioner's counsel both below and in this court, that as the Fourteenth Amendment extends the protection of due process to property as well as to life and liberty, if we hold with the petitioner logic would require the furnishing of counsel in civil cases involving property.

The Judgment is affirmed.

MR. JUSTICE BLACK, dissenting, with whom MR. JUSTICE DOUGLAS and MR. JUSTICE MURPHY concur.

To hold that the petitioner had a constitutional right to counsel in this case does not require us to say that "no trial for any offense, or in any court, can be fairly conducted and justice accorded a defendant who is not represented by counsel." This case can be determined by resolution of a narrower question: whether in view of the nature of the offense and the circumstances of his trial and conviction, this petitioner was denied the procedural protection which is his right under the federal constitution. I think he was.

The petitioner, a farm hand, out of a job and on relief, was indicted in a Maryland state court on a charge of robbery. He was too poor to hire a lawyer. He so informed the court and requested that counsel be appointed to defend him. His request was denied. Put to trial without a lawyer, he conducted his own defense, was found guilty, and was sentenced to eight years' imprisonment. The court below found that the petitioner had "at least an ordinary amount of intelligence." It is clear from his examination of witnesses that he was a man of little education.

If this case had come to us from a federal court, it is clear we should have to reverse it, because the Sixth Amendment makes the right to counsel in criminal cases inviolable by the federal government. I believe that the Fourteenth Amendment made the Sixth applicable to the states. But this view, although often urged in dissents, has never been accepted by a majority of this Court and is not accepted today.

This Court has just declared that due process of law is denied if a trial is conducted in such manner that it is "shocking to the universal sense of justice" or "offensive to the common and fundamental ideas of fairness and right."

The right to counsel in a criminal proceeding is "fundamental." *Powell v. Alabama.*

It is guarded from invasion by the Sixth Amendment, adopted to raise an effective barrier against arbitrary or unjust deprivation of liberty by the federal government. *Johnson v. Zerbst.*

A practice cannot be reconciled with "common and fundamental ideas of fairness and right," which subjects innocent men to increased dangers of conviction merely because of their poverty. Whether a man is innocent cannot be determined from a trial in which, as here, denial of counsel has made it impossible to conclude, with any satisfactory degree of certainty, that the defendant's case was adequately presented.

Denial to the poor of the request for counsel in proceedings based on charges of serious crime has long been regarded as shocking to the "universal sense of justice" throughout this country.

[M]ost of the other states have shown their agreement by constitutional provisions, statutes, or established practice judicially approved which assure that no man shall be deprived of counsel merely because of his poverty. Any other practice seems to me to defeat the promise of our democratic society to provide equal justice under the law.

NOTES AND QUESTIONS

(1) Apart from their different approaches as to the importance of the right to counsel, Justices Black and Roberts had very different views concerning the incorporation doctrine. These views were sharply contrasted in *Betts*. Justice Roberts: "The due process clause does not incorporate, as such, the specific guarantees found in the Sixth Amendment although a denial may, in certain circumstances, deprive a litigant of due process of law in violation of the Fourteenth." Justice Black: "I believe that the Fourteenth Amendment made the Sixth applicable to the states. But this view, although often urged in dissent, has never been accepted by a majority of this Court and is not accepted today."

(2) In *Powell*, as discussed by the majority in *Betts*, what were the circumstances that dictated a finding of denial of due process when the defendants were denied effective counsel? Was it the fact that it was a capital case? That the defendants were not from the community? That the trial was conducted very soon after the charges were filed? How important are these factors in determining whether the lack of effective counsel was a denial of due process? Would it really have mattered if the defendants in *Powell* had been from that town, the trial had been a slow affair and they could only have been given sentences of thirty years?

(3) Justice Black attempted to decide the case in favor of the defendants by using the majority's own due process analysis. "[U]nder the prevailing view of due process . . . the judgment below should be reversed." Using this test, the majority could not find that the conviction was "lacking in fundamental fairness." How could Justice Black find that it was? Did he really apply the same test?

(4) Can the Court's opinion in *Johnson v. Zerbst* — which requires counsel in all federal cases — be reconciled with its opinion in *Betts*? In *Johnson*, the majority held that a lawyer was required because "[t]hat which is simple, orderly and necessary to the lawyer, to the untrained layman may appear intricate, complex, and mysterious." In light of this statement, and the sweeping language in *Powell*, how could the majority find that the right to counsel was not fundamental?

(5) In deciding that counsel was not fundamental, Justice Roberts looked to the prevailing state view on the right to counsel. Should state practice control the Court's determination?

(6) Betts' lawyer conceded in argument that apart from criminal cases, if his position prevailed, "logic would require the furnishing of counsel in civil cases

involving property." Would logic require such a rule? Was it necessary for counsel to make that argument? Was it wise?

FROM *BETTS* TO *GIDEON*

In the years just after *Betts* was decided, the Court followed closely the holding there, and required strong showings by defendants of the "special circumstances" necessitating appointed counsel. Typical of this approach was *Foster v. Illinois*, 332 U.S. 134 (1947), where the defendant argued that he should have had counsel appointed to assist him in entering a plea of guilty. In language strongly reminiscent of the *Betts* opinion, Justice Frankfurter disagreed:

> We reject such a claim. Most incarcerations are upon pleas of guilty, and probably most such pleas have been made without the felt need of counsel. It is not for us to suggest that it might be desirable to offer to every accused who desires to plead guilty the opportunities for counsel and to enter with formality upon the record the deliberate disclaimer of his need for counsel because of a full appreciation of the meaning of a plea of guilty as expounded by responsible judges. Our duty does not go beyond safeguarding "rights essential to a fair hearing" by the States.

As the composition of the Court changed, however, its view toward *Betts* changed, implicitly if not explicitly. In *Bute v. Illinois*, 333 U.S. 640 (1948), the Court adopted the position that counsel would be required in all capital cases, not simply capital cases involving other special circumstances:

> [T]his Court repeatedly has held that failure to appoint counsel to assist a defendant or to give a fair opportunity to the defendant's counsel to assist him in his defense where charged with a capital crime is a violation of due process of law under the Fourteenth Amendment.

The most striking illustration of the change in attitude toward *Betts* came in 1962 with the decision in *Chewning v. Cunningham*, 368 U.S. 443 (1962). There, the petitioner, raising claims under Virginia's recidivist statute, did not demonstrate that the denial of his request for appointed counsel resulted in unfairness at trial. Indeed, far from showing such unfairness, he merely raised possible arguments which a lawyer might have asserted in his defense. The Court held that the opportunity to develop such arguments was sufficient to warrant the appointment of counsel.

> Double Jeopardy and *ex post facto* application of a law are also questions which . . . may well be considered by an imaginative lawyer, who looks critically at the layer of prior convictions on which the recidivist charge rests. We intimate no opinion on whether any of the problems mentioned would arise on petitioner's trial nor, if so, whether any would have merit. We only conclude that a trial on a charge of being a habitual criminal is such a serious one, the issues presented under Virginia's statute so complex, and the potential prejudice resulting from the absence of counsel so great that the rule we have followed concerning the appointment of counsel in other types of criminal trials is equally applicable here.

As Justice Harlan noted very clearly in his concurrence, the Court's requirement of appointed counsel when mere possibilities of legal arguments had been raised was contradictory to what the Court had required in *Betts*.

> The Court strikes down the enhanced sentence . . . because it holds that various defenses that were available to Chewning under Virginia law could not have been known to or presented by a layman. To me, the bare possibility that any of these improbable claims could have been asserted does not amount to the "exceptional circumstances" which, under existing law, e.g., *Betts v. Brady*, must be present before the Fourteenth Amendment imposes on the State a duty to provide counsel for an indigent accused in a noncapital case.

Because the defendant was simply raising *possible* arguments in *Chewning*, the holding meant that the burden was now seemingly on the state to disprove the claim of unfairness. Thus, the question remaining after *Chewning* was no longer whether *Betts v. Brady* would be overruled but when it would be overruled. It took the Court just one year to find the petitioner and lawyers necessary to make Justice Black's dissent the majority position.

GIDEON v. WAINWRIGHT

United States Supreme Court
372 U.S. 335 (1963)

Mr. Justice Black delivered the opinion of the Court.

Petitioner was charged in a Florida state court with having broken and entered a poolroom with intent to commit a misdemeanor. This offense is a felony under Florida law. Appearing in court without funds and without a lawyer, petitioner asked the court to appoint counsel for him, whereupon the following colloquy took place:

The COURT: Mr. Gideon, I am sorry, but I cannot appoint Counsel to represent you in this case. Under the laws of the State of Florida, the only time the Court can appoint Counsel to represent a Defendant is when that person is charged with a capital offense. I am sorry, but I will have to deny your request to appoint Counsel to defend you in this case.

The DEFENDANT: The United States Supreme Court says I am entitled to be represented by Counsel.

Put to trial before a jury, Gideon conducted his defense about as well as could be expected from a layman. He made an opening statement to the jury, cross-examined the State's witnesses, presented witnesses in his own defense, declined to testify himself, and made a short argument "emphasizing his innocence to the charge contained in the Information filed in this case." The jury returned a verdict of guilty, and petitioner was sentenced to serve five years in the state prison.

Since 1942, when *Betts v. Brady* was decided by a divided Court, the problem of a defendant's federal constitutional right to counsel in a state court has been a continuing source of controversy and litigation in both state and federal courts. To give this problem another review here, we granted certiorari.

Since Gideon was proceeding *in forma pauperis*, we appointed counsel to represent him and requested both sides to discuss in their briefs and oral arguments the following: "Should this Court's holding in *Betts v. Brady*, be reconsidered?"

Upon full reconsideration we conclude that *Betts v. Brady* should be overruled.

The Sixth Amendment provides, "In all criminal prosecutions, the accused shall enjoy the right . . . to have the Assistance of Counsel for his defence." We have construed this to mean that in federal courts counsel must be provided for defendants unable to employ counsel unless the right is competently and intelligently waived.

We think the Court in *Betts* had ample precedent for acknowledging that those guarantees of the Bill of Rights which are fundamental safeguards of liberty immune from federal abridgment are equally protected against state invasion by the Due Process Clause of the Fourteenth Amendment. This same principle was recognized, explained, and applied in *Powell v. Alabama.*

We accept *Betts v. Brady*'s assumption, based as it was on our prior cases, that a provision of the Bill of Rights which is "fundamental and essential to a fair trial" is made obligatory upon the States by the Fourteenth Amendment. We think the Court in *Betts* was wrong, however, in concluding that the Sixth Amendment's guarantee of counsel is not one of these fundamental rights. Ten years before *Betts v. Brady*, this Court, after full consideration of all the historical data examined in *Betts*, had unequivocally declared that "the right to the aid of counsel is of this fundamental character." *Powell v. Alabama.* While the Court at the close of its *Powell* opinion did by its language, as this Court frequently does, limit its holding to the particular facts and circumstances of that case, its conclusions about the fundamental nature of the right to counsel are unmistakable.

The fact is that in deciding as it did — that "appointment of counsel is not a fundamental right, essential to a fair trial" — the Court in *Betts v. Brady* made an abrupt break with its own well-considered precedents. In returning to these old precedents, sounder we believe than the new, we but restore constitutional principles established to achieve a fair system of justice. Not only these precedents but also reason and reflection require us to recognize that in our adversary system of criminal justice, any person haled into court, who is too poor to hire a lawyer, cannot be assured a fair trial unless counsel is provided for him. This seems to us to be an obvious truth. Governments, both state and federal, quite properly spend vast sums of money to establish machinery to try defendants accused of crime. Lawyers to prosecute are everywhere deemed essential to protect the public's interest in an orderly society. Similarly, there are few defendants charged with crime, few indeed, who fail to hire the best lawyers they can get to prepare and present their defenses. That government hires lawyers to prosecute and defendants who have the money hire lawyers to defend are the strongest indications of the widespread belief that lawyers in criminal courts are necessities, not luxuries. The right of one charged with crime to counsel may not be deemed fundamental and essential to fair trials in some countries, but it is in ours. From the very beginning, our state and national constitutions and laws have laid great emphasis on procedural and substantive safeguards designed to assure fair trials before impartial tribunals in which every defendant stands equal before the law. This noble ideal cannot be realized if the poor man charged with crime has to face his accusers without a lawyer to assist him.

The Court in *Betts v. Brady* departed from the sound wisdom upon which the Court's holding in *Powell v. Alabama* rested. Florida, supported by two other States, has asked that *Betts v. Brady* be left intact. Twenty-two States, as friends of the Court, argue that *Betts* was "an anachronism when handed down" and that it should now be overruled. We agree.

MR. JUSTICE DOUGLAS wrote a separate opinion.

MR. JUSTICE CLARK, concurring in the result.

In *Bute v. Illinois*, this Court found no special circumstances requiring the appointment of counsel but stated that "if these charges had been capital charges, the court would have been required, both by the state statute and the decisions of this Court interpreting the Fourteenth Amendment, to take some such steps."

[I]n *Hamilton v. Alabama*, we said that "[w]hen one pleads to a capital charge without benefit of counsel, we do not stop to determine whether prejudice resulted."

That the Sixth Amendment requires appointment of counsel in "all criminal prosecutions" is clear, both from the language of the Amendment and from this Court's interpretation. See *Johnson v. Zerbst.*

It is equally clear from the above cases, all decided after *Betts v. Brady*, that the Fourteenth Amendment requires such appointment in all prosecutions for capital crimes. The Court's decision today, then, does no more than erase a distinction which has no basis in logic and an increasingly eroded basis in authority.

I must conclude here, that the Constitution makes no distinction between capital and noncapital cases. The Fourteenth Amendment requires due process of law for the deprival of "liberty" just as for deprival of "life," and there cannot constitutionally be a difference in the quality of the process based merely upon a supposed difference in the sanction involved. How can the Fourteenth Amendment tolerate a procedure which it condemns in capital cases on the ground that deprival of liberty may be less onerous than deprival of life — a value judgment not universally accepted — or that only the latter deprival is irrevocable? I can find no acceptable rationalization for such a result, and I therefore concur in the judgment of the Court.

MR. JUSTICE HARLAN, concurring.

I agree that *Betts v. Brady* should be overruled, but consider it entitled to a more respectful burial than has been accorded, at least on the part of those of us who were not on the Court when that case was decided.

I cannot subscribe to the view that *Betts v. Brady* represented "an abrupt break with its own well-considered precedents." In 1932 in *Powell v. Alabama*, a capital case, this Court declared that under the particular facts there presented — "the ignorance and illiteracy of the defendants, their youth, the circumstances of public hostility . . . and above all that they stood in deadly peril of their lives" — the state court had a duty to assign counsel for the trial as a necessary requisite of due process of law. It is evident that these limiting facts were not added to the opinion as an afterthought; they were repeatedly emphasized, and were clearly regarded as important to the result.

Thus when this Court, a decade later, decided *Betts v. Brady*, it did no more than to admit of the possible existence of special circumstances in noncapital as well as capital trials, while at the same time insisting that such circumstances be shown in order to establish a denial of due process. The right to appointed counsel had been recognized as being considerably broader in federal prosecutions, see *Johnson v. Zerbst*, but to have imposed these requirements on the States would indeed have been "an abrupt break" with the almost immediate past. The declaration that the right to appointed counsel in state prosecutions, as established in *Powell v. Alabama*, was not limited to capital cases was in truth not a departure from, but an extension of, existing precedent.

The principles declared in *Powell* and in *Betts*, however, have had a troubled journey throughout the years that have followed first the one case and then the other. Even by the time of the *Betts* decision, dictum in at least one of the Court's opinions had indicated that there was an absolute right to the services of counsel in the trial of state capital cases. Such dicta continued to appear in subsequent decisions, and any lingering doubts were finally eliminated by the holding of *Hamilton v. Alabama.*

In noncapital cases, the "special circumstances" rule has continued to exist in form while its substance has been substantially and steadily eroded. In the first decade after *Betts*, there were cases in which the Court found special circumstances to be lacking, but usually by a sharply divided vote. However, no such decision has been cited to us, and I have found none, after 1950. At the same time, there have been not a few cases in which special circumstances were found in little or nothing more than the "complexity" of the legal questions presented, although those questions were often of only routine difficulty. The Court has come to recognize, in other words, that the mere existence of a serious criminal charge constituted in itself special circumstances requiring the services of counsel at trial. In truth the *Betts v. Brady* rule is no longer a reality.

In what is done today I do not understand the Court to depart from the principles laid down in *Palko v. Connecticut*, or to embrace the concept that the Fourteenth Amendment "incorporates" the Sixth Amendment as such.

On these premises I join in the judgment of the Court.

NOTES AND QUESTIONS

(1) An excellent book discussing this case and focusing attention on the work of Gideon's lawyers is *Gideon's Trumpet* by Anthony Lewis. Gideon was represented,

on a pro bono basis, by Abe Fortas, later a Justice of the United States Supreme Court. The dramatic impact of *Gideon* was immediately apparent. In the years since the opinion, however, serious concerns have been raised as to uneven representation at criminal trials. *See* Cole, *No Equal Justice* at 64–65 (1999):

> [*Gideon* is] a great story, with a great lesson, and for that reason taught in American high schools, colleges, and law schools.
>
> What isn't taught, however, is our utter failure to realize the promise represented by Gideon's case. Lewis's book, published in 1964, one year after the *Gideon* decision was handed down, bears the mark of optimistic faith in progress that so characterized the period. But even Lewis predicted that it would be "an enormous social task to bring to life the dream of *Gideon v. Wainwright*, the dream of a vast, diverse country in which every man charged with crime will be capably defended, no matter what his economic circumstances, and in which the lawyer representing him will do so proudly, without resentment at an unfair burden, sure of the support needed to make an adequate defense." Much like Dr. Martin Luther King, Jr.'s dream of the same year, the dream of *Gideon* has not been realized. The most troubling lesson of the more than thirty-five years since *Gideon v. Wainwright* is that neither the Supreme Court nor the public appears to have any interest in making the constitutional right announced in *Gideon* a reality.

The turn in recent years has been heavily toward representation by public defender offices. However, the problem of public defendants with massive caseloads plagues the entire U.S. criminal justice system. Excellent research has been developed on the problem. *See, e.g.*, Drinan, *The National Right to Counsel Act: A Congressional Solution to the Nation's Indigent Defense Crisis*, 47 Harv. J. on Legis. 487 (2010); Uphoff, Symposium: *Broke and Broken: Can We Fix Our State Indigent Defense System?* 75 Mo. L. Rev. 667 (2010). In *In re E.S.*, 171 Cal. App. 4th 1219, 1237 (Cal. Ct. App. 2009), the court wrote of the professional responsibility of defenders in facing crushing numbers of clients.

> The American Bar Association (ABA) has devoted much attention to the obligations of a public defender in the predicament in which Hauschild found himself. On May 13, 2006, the ABA issued its formal opinion [on point] . . . . Noting that, as under the California Rules of Professional Conduct a public defender's office "is considered to be the equivalent of a law firm" and "responsibility for handling [a] case [] . . . falls upon [the] office as [a] whole . . . ," the opinion makes clear that the ethical obligations of public defenders and other publically funded attorneys who represent indigent persons charged with crimes are no different from those of privately retained defense counsel. Under the ABA Opinion, a deputy public defender whose excessive workload obstructs his or her ability to provide effective assistance to a particular client should, with supervisorial approval, attempt to reduce the caseload, as by transferring nonrepresentational responsibilities to others, refusing new cases, and/or transferring cases to another lawyer with a lesser caseload. If the deputy public defender is unable to obtain relief in that manner the ABA Opinion

provides, he or she must "file a motion with the trial court requesting permission to withdraw from a sufficient number of cases to allow the provision of competent and diligent representation to the remaining clients." In support of the motion, counsel "should provide the court with information necessary to justify the withdrawal, while being mindful of the obligations not to disclose confidential information or information as to strategy or other matters that may prejudice the client." If the request to withdraw is denied by the trial court, the attorney should pursue appellate review.

(2) The Missouri Supreme Court decided that a public defender office may refuse new appointments when the office is at its caseload limits. *State ex rel. Missouri Public Defender Comm'n v. Waters*, 370 S.W. 3d 592 (Mo. 2012): "A judge may not appoint counsel when the judge is aware that, for whatever reason, counsel is unable to provide effective representation to a defendant."

(3) The majority concluded that the right to counsel was fundamental. Were the Justices relying on evidence or legal precedent different from that relied upon in 1942? Justice Black stated that "*Betts* was 'an anachronism when handed down.' " Was it? In the words of the majority opinion, was it "an abrupt break with [the Court's] own well-considered precedents," particularly *Powell v. Alabama*? Or, was Justice Harlan correct that *Betts* was decided properly but that it later had to be overruled because of its "troubled journey throughout the years"?

(4) Was the judgment reversed because the right to counsel was a fundamental right, or because the Sixth Amendment right to counsel was incorporated to apply to the states through the Fourteenth Amendment? Does it matter?

(5) Justice Clark argued that the distinction applied after *Betts* between capital and noncapital cases had no basis in the Constitution. Was this view correct, or were capital cases entitled to closer scrutiny under the fundamental fairness analysis of the Court?

(6) In a very unusual move, twenty-two states filed briefs contrary to the position taken by the State of Florida in *Gideon*. Only two states joined with Florida. How important was this move to the Court's decision to overrule *Betts*? What would have happened if those twenty-two states had all joined with the State of Florida?

Just after the second trial of Gideon, *New York Times* columnist Anthony Lewis wrote of the jury taking only one hour to find Gideon not guilty. The key difference, according to Lewis, was that Gideon at the second trial had a lawyer, W. Fred Turner, "a leading criminal lawyer here in Bay County." Turner vigorously cross-examined the principal prosecution witness, and brought forward a surprise defense witness, the neighborhood grocer. Turner emphasized to the jury its obligation to focus on "reasonable doubt . . . this country was not founded on a man having to prove his innocence — we're all thankful for that." The defense lawyer, in his closing argument to the jury, argued that Gideon had not committed the break-in at the pool hall; rather, the culprit was the prosecution witness who testified that he had seen Gideon coming out of the pool hall that fateful morning.

Anthony Lewis, *High Court Ruling Helps Poor Man to Freedom*, N.Y. Times, August 6, 1943, page 21.

[A] The Determination of Indigency

It became apparent soon after the *Gideon* decision that, while the Court had settled the question of whether the right to counsel was fundamental, two more mundane but related questions had gone unanswered. How was a trial judge to determine which defendants were entitled to state-appointed counsel, and to what categories of cases (all felonies, all misdemeanors, only cases involving substantial punishment, etc.) did the right of counsel requirement apply? The latter issue was resolved in the *Argersinger* and *Scott* cases, *infra*. The former question has never been answered by the Supreme Court.

Few states adopted formal standards for determining eligibility in connection with appointed counsel cases. Instead, most jurisdictions required that the defendant applying for counsel give a reason why she did not have a lawyer and set forth her assets. The following application form is typical of those that have been used by state and federal courts:

FORM

Rule ____________ Application Form for the Assignment of Counsel

The applicant ____________ residing at ____________ shows that:

1. I am named a defendant in the above entitled criminal cause of action alleging that I did commit the crime of ____________ at the ____________ of ____________ in the County of ____________ and State of ____________, on the ____________ day of ____________, 20______
2. I am unable to obtain counsel to defend me in this matter for the reason that ____________
3. I am unable to obtain funds from anyone, including my family and associates, by way of compensation for counsel and represent that the answers to the following questions are true to the best of my information and belief:
    a. Do you have any money? If so, how much?
        (1) On the person
        (2) In custody of the Warden
        (3) In the bank
        (4) At home
        (5) Elsewhere
    b. Do you own an automobile?
        (1) Year and make
        (2) Cost
        (3) I owe $ to
        (4) It is now at
    c. Do you own any real estate?

d. Do you own any other property or do you have any other assets? (If answer is "yes" furnish description thereof and specify its present location):

e. Does anyone owe you money? If yes give the person's name and address and the amount he owes you.

f. If married, what is name, age and address of your (wife) (husband)?

(1) When did you last live with your (wife) (husband)?

(2) Does your (wife) (husband) work?

(3) What is name and address of (her) (his) employer?

g. Do you have any children? (Give names, ages, and addresses.)

h. What is your home address?

i. Where did you work last?

j. What is your Social Security Number?

k. What salary or wages were you receiving?

l. What was the total amount of your income during the past 12 months?

m. Is there a job waiting for you? (Specify)

4. I am presently in jail and unable to obtain bail. I am presently released from jail on bail in the amount of $________. The cost of such bail was defrayed and paid by _____________, in the sum of $________

5. I have not previously been represented by an attorney in court except (give name of attorney, name of case in which you were represented and state whether or not your attorney was paid in this case and by whom).

WHEREFORE, petitioner prays: That this Honorable Court assign counsel to represent (him)(her) in the above entitled criminal cause of action without fee or cost to the defendant. COUNTY OF ______________ ss ______________, being duly sworn according to law, upon (his)(her) oath, deposes and says:

1. I am the petitioner in the above entitled action.

2. I have read the foregoing petition and know the contents thereof and the same are true to my own knowledge, except as to matters therein stated to be alleged as to persons other than myself, as to those matters I believe to be true.

3. This affidavit is made to inform the Court as to my status of indigency and to induce the Court to assign counsel to me as an indigent defendant for my defense against the criminal charges that have been made against me.

4. In making this affidavit I am aware that perjury is a felony and that the punishment is a fine of not more than $15,000 or imprisonment for not more than seven years or both.

____

(SIGNATURE OF DEFENDANT)

FORM
FINANCIAL AFFIDAVIT, UNITED STATES DISTRICT COURT

Reset Form

FINANCIAL AFFIDAVIT CJA 23

IN SUPPORT OF REQUEST FOR ATTORNEY, EXPERT OR OTHER COURT SERVICES WITHOUT PAYMENT OF FEE (Rev. 5/98)

IN UNITED STATES ☐ MAGISTRATE ☐ DISTRICT ☐ APPEALS COURT or ☐ OTHER PANEL (Specify below)

IN THE CASE OF ____ vs. ____ FOR ____ AT ____

LOCATION NUMBER

DOCKET NUMBERS: Magistrate / District Court / Court of Appeals

PERSON REPRESENTED (Show your full name)

1 ☐ Defendant - Adult
2 ☐ Defendant - Juvenile
3 ☐ Appellant
4 ☐ Probation Violator
5 ☐ Parole Violator
6 ☐ Habeas Petitioner
7 ☐ 2255 Petitioner
8 ☐ Material Witness
9 ☐ Other (Specify)

CHARGE/OFFENSE (describe if applicable & check box ☐ Felony ☐ Misdemeanor

ANSWERS TO QUESTIONS REGARDING ABILITY TO PAY

ASSETS

EMPLOYMENT

Are you now employed? ☐ Yes ☐ No ☐ Am Self Employed

Name and address of employer: ____

IF YES, how much do you earn per month? $ ____ **IF NO**, give month and year of last employment. How much did you earn per month? $ ____

If married is your Spouse employed? ☐ Yes ☐ No

IF YES, how much does your Spouse earn per month? $ ____ If a minor under age 21, what is your Parents or Guardian's approximate monthly income? $ ____

OTHER INCOME

Have you received within the past 12 months any income from a business, profession or other form of self-employment, or in the form of rent payments, interest, dividends, retirement or annuity payments, or other sources? ☐ Yes ☐ No

IF YES, GIVE THE AMOUNT RECEIVED & IDENTIFY THE SOURCES — RECEIVED $ ____ SOURCES ____

CASH

Have you any cash on hand or money in savings or checking account? ☐ Yes ☐ No **IF YES**, state total amount $ ____

PROPERTY

Do you own any real estate, stocks, bonds, notes, automobiles, or other valuable property (excluding ordinary household furnishings and clothing)? ☐ Yes ☐ No

IF YES, GIVE THE VALUE AND DESCRIBE IT — VALUE $ ____ DESCRIPTION ____

OBLIGATIONS & DEBTS

DEPENDENTS

MARITAL STATUS: ☐ SINGLE ☐ MARRIED ☐ WIDOWED ☐ SEPARATED OR DIVORCED

Total No. Of Dependents ____

List persons you actually support and your relationship to them ____

DEBTS & MONTHLY BILLS (LIST ALL CREDITORS, INCLUDING BANKS, LOAN COMPANIES, CHARGE ACCOUNTS, ETC.)

APARTMENT OR HOME: ____ Creditors ____ Total Debt $ ____ Monthly Payt. $ ____

I certify under penalty of perjury that the foregoing is true and correct. Executed on (date) ____

SIGNATURE OF DEFENDANT (OR PERSON REPRESENTED) ____

Once the necessary information is set out either in writing or through a hearing process it is generally up to the trial judge to determine if the defendant has shown that he is in need of the services of appointed counsel.

One of the few cases to explore in depth the definition of "indigency" is *United States v. Parker*, 439 F.3d 81, 93–94 (2d Cir. 2006):

> Courts have utilized a broad range of considerations in conducting an "appropriate inquiry" into financial eligibility. . . . The task "necessarily varies with the circumstances presented, and no one method or combination of methods is required." "In many cases, the court's inquiry may properly be limited to review of financial information supplied on the standard form financial affidavit. "Investigation of the applicant's assets, liabilities, income and obligations alone may constitute sufficient inquiry."
>
> We have examined a variety of factors relevant to the financial eligibility determination. [We have] highlighted the "economic realities" of the situation including the costs of a criminal defense [and] we focused on the business investments of the defendant. [W]e considered whether the defendant owned or controlled substantial assets and whether the defendant had concealed those assets. We also indicated that "a defendant's own funds must be weighted against the anticipated cost of trial."
>
> We have also considered the defendant's necessities and the "cost of providing for himself and dependents" [and admonished] a construction of the Act that "ignores the realities of a defendant's duties with respect to his family." . . . "[C]ounsel should be provided to persons who are financially unable to obtain adequate representation without substantial hardship." [W]e have emphasized that "the needs of the defendant himself must be considered" and insisted that the district judge should be satisfied that "the defendant will not suffer extreme hardship." . . . In making similar determinations . . . the United States Supreme Court and other Courts of Appeals have also considered such factors as the availability of income to the defendant from other sources, the possibility of reimbursement of legal fees, the liquidity of assets for purposes of paying counsel, the applicant's ability to pay a portion of his counsel's fees, the defendant's failure to authorize a review of his financial records, the defendant's credibility (or lack thereof) in portraying his financial eligibility. Overall . . . a district court should not restrict itself to a particular method of assessing a criminal defendant's eligibility for appointed counsel.

See also *Commonwealth v. Porter*, 971 N.E.2d 291 (Mass. 2012), where the court held that a criminal defendant who wishes to have appointed counsel has the burden of proving indigency by a preponderance of the evidence.

One issue in this area which the Supreme Court has clearly resolved is whether a convicted indigent defendant could be required to repay to the state the costs of having appointed counsel. Oregon passed a statute which required, as a condition of probation, that the convicted defendant pay back to the state the fees of his appointed attorney. The Supreme Court upheld the statute, relying heavily on the statutory exemption for defendants who could show that repayment would impose "manifest hardship." *Fuller v. Oregon*, 417 U.S. 40 (1974).

In some cases, the question has been raised as to a private lawyer's responsibility to represent indigent defendants for little or no fee. The New Jersey Supreme Court was faced with a difficult dilemma in *Madden v. Township of Delran*, 601 A.2d 211 (N.J. 1992). The state had not developed a requirement that each municipality provide a public defender for the municipal courts. As a consequence, a number of the trial courts had been overloaded with criminal prosecutions. These trial courts began to assign private lawyers to represent indigent defendants but did not provide compensation for such representation. The court on appeal rejected the defense counsel arguments regarding equal protection and the taking of property without due process and just compensation. Instead it focused on the dire need for this drastic action by the trial courts. The court directed the municipal court judges to appoint counsel on a purely alphabetical basis (insuring that there would be no unfair impact on any group of lawyers). Moreover, the court would not generally allow the withdrawal of assigned counsel even though there will be "the certainty that some attorneys will be assigned who have no experience either in municipal court or indeed in any court." *Id.* at 219. Private lawyers in Missouri have a professional responsibility to represent indigent defendants if necessary, for they "have an obligation to perform public service." *State v. Pratte*, 298 S.W.3d 870 (Mo. 2009). The Supreme Court in *Mallard v. District Court*, 490 U.S. 296 (1989), looked to the basic issues in deciding an attorney's obligation for appointment under the *in forma pauperis* statute. Ultimately, the Court found that the statute did not mandate such appointment. Still, the language of the three opinions is striking:

Justice Brennan, for the majority:

> We emphasize that our decision today is limited to interpreting § 1915(d). We do not mean to question, let alone denigrate, lawyers' ethical obligation to assist those who are too poor to afford counsel, or to suggest that requests made pursuant to § 1915(d) may be lightly declined because they give rise to no ethical claim. On the contrary, in a time when the need for legal services among the poor is growing and public funding for such services has not kept pace, lawyers' ethical obligation to volunteer their time and skills *pro bono publico* is manifest. Nor do we express an opinion on the question whether the federal courts possess inherent authority to require lawyers to serve.

Justice Kennedy, concurring:

> Our decision today speaks to the interpretation of a statute, to the requirements of the law, and not to the professional responsibility of the lawyer. Lawyers, like all those who practice a profession have obligations to their calling which exceed their obligations to the State. Lawyers also have obligations by virtue of their special status as officers of the court. Accepting a court's request to represent the indigent is one of those traditional obligations. Our judgment here does not suggest otherwise. To the contrary, it is precisely because our duties go beyond what the law demands that ours remains a noble profession.

Justice Stevens, dissenting (joined by Justices Marshall, Blackmun and O'Connor):

> In my opinion his admission to practice implicitly included an obligation to participate in that procedure for the assignment of counsel to indigent litigants, a formal request to a lawyer by the court pursuant to that procedure is tantamount to a command.

PROBLEM A
COUNSEL FEES

(1) The trial judge is convinced that the lawyer has charged the criminal defendant an exorbitant fee — $11,000 — for forty hours of work. The judge finds that a reasonable fee for the services is $2,500. Can the judge order the lawyer to refund the $8,500? No. The matter should be referred to an ethics panel under Canon 3(B)(3) of the Code of Judicial Conduct for United States Judges ["a federal judge should take or initiate appropriate disciplinary measures against a judge or lawyer for unprofessional conduct. . . ."]. *United States v. Vague*, 697 F.2d 805 (7th Cir. 1983). A different panel of the Seventh Circuit reached a different conclusion in *United States v. Strawser*, 800 F.2d 704 (7th Cir. 1986), *cert. denied*, 480 U.S. 906 (1987). There the defense counsel charged a fee of $47,500 for negotiating two fairly simple guilty pleas to drug charges. The court found that the amount over $20,000 could be ordered reimbursed.

(2) The defendant was accused of murdering his father. Trial counsel arranged with the defendant that if he was acquitted, the attorney's fee would include an additional $25,000. Did this arrangement deny the defendant his right to counsel? Held, the arrangement was contrary to the Code of Professional Responsibility, and the lawyer was guilty of unprofessional and unethical conduct for entering into the agreement. Do you agree? *Compare State v. Winkler*, 515 N.Y.S.2d 488 (N.Y. 1987), *cert. denied*, 511 U.S. 1022 (1994), *with Winkler v. Keane*, 7 F.3d 304, 306–07 (2d Cir. 1993). How about the lawyer's conduct in *Commonwealth v. Perkins*, 883 N.E.2d (Mass. 2008)? He arranged with a television producer to wear a wireless microphone during the trial; held to be a conflict of interest, but a conflict which could be waived by the client.

FORM
INSTRUCTIONS TO CLIENTS

1. WHO IS YOUR ATTORNEY — You are being represented by the Office of the Public Defender for ____________________ County. You may be represented by a different attorney than the one you met in court. Your case will be assigned to a specific attorney and you will be notified at that time. This usually occurs a few weeks after your case comes into our office and after we have had an opportunity to talk to you and investigate the facts in your case. Make your appointments with the attorney you met in court until otherwise notified.
2. ABOUT BAIL — You are responsible for posting your own bail to be released from jail. Our staff will advise you on how to post bond, or you can get this information from the jailers. If you cannot post bail in the amount presently set, our staff will attempt to have your bail reduced to an amount you can post. Your cooperation is mandatory.
3. HOW TO FIND OUR OFFICE — We are located at ____________ Office hours are Monday-Friday from 9:00 A.M. to 5:00 P.M. We close on holidays.
4. WITNESSES — Furnish to us immediately the correct names and addresses and telephone numbers of any and all witnesses you know. If you are in jail, you should try to give us the name of someone you know, either

relative or friend, who can assist us in locating and questioning your witnesses.

5. QUESTIONS — Other than asking you to come in for an initial interview, we will probably not contact you until we have something definite to report. It is your responsibility to appear in Court at the date and time you are told by the court. If your case goes to trial, we will need to speak with you frequently. If you are not sure when you are next due in court, call immediately. If you have any specific questions in regard to these instructions or in regard to your case, please feel free to call us or write us. Our phone number is _______.
6. EMERGENCIES — If you are arrested while your case is pending, DO NOT make any statements to the police until you have spoken to your lawyer. We will try to see you as soon as possible, but this may not occur until you are brought to the County Jail.
7. TALK TO NO ONE — Do not talk to anyone about your case except one of the lawyers or investigators/law students in our office. You should always require identification so that you are sure who you are talking to. Don't even talk to your friends or relatives, as our experience indicates that in many cases this information gets into the wrong hands, and is used against you.
8. APPOINTMENTS — If you are free on bond, make an appointment to talk to one of our staff within one week of your appearance in court. If you are in jail, our staff will try to see you within a day or two of our getting notice that we are to represent you. This may be several days after you are arrested. Be patient. We will do all we can to help you. Do not bother the jailers with repeated demands to see your lawyer; one will do. The jailers have been very diligent in referring messages to us from our clients in jail, and we appreciate their help. Don't hassle them. It makes things easier all the way around for you and our staff. If you have specific complaints about your treatment, save them for us.
9. COMPLAINTS — Obviously, we cannot satisfy all our clients' demands all the time. If you have a specific complaint, you can speak to our staff. If you are dissatisfied with the representation you are receiving by our office, you may report this to the chief Public Defender. You are, of course, free to hire your own attorney; any information we have on your case will be made available to him at his or your request. Talk to your lawyer; he wants to know what you want him to do for you.

_________________________, Assistant Public Defender

ARGERSINGER v. HAMLIN

United States Supreme Court
407 U.S. 25 (1972)

Mr. Justice Douglas delivered the opinion of the Court.

Petitioner, an indigent, was charged in Florida with carrying a concealed weapon, an offense punishable by imprisonment up to six months, a $1,000 fine, or both. The trial was to a judge, and petitioner was unrepresented by counsel. He was sentenced to serve 90 days in jail, and brought this habeas corpus action in the

Florida Supreme Court, alleging that, being deprived of his right to counsel, he was unable as an indigent layman properly to raise and present to the trial court good and sufficient defenses to the charge for which he stands convicted. The Florida Supreme Court . . . held that the right to court-appointed counsel extends only to trials "for non-petty offenses punishable by more than six months imprisonment."

The right to trial by jury, also guaranteed by the Sixth Amendment by reason of the Fourteenth, was limited . . . to trials where the potential punishment was imprisonment for six months or more. But, . . . trial by jury has a different genealogy and is brigaded with a system of trial to a judge alone.

While there is historical support for limiting the "deep commitment" to trial by jury to "serious criminal cases," there is no such support for a similar limitation on the right to assistance of counsel.

The Sixth Amendment thus extended the right to counsel beyond its common-law dimensions. But there is nothing in the language of the Amendment, its history, or in the decisions of this Court, to indicate that it was intended to embody a retraction of the right in petty offenses wherein the common law previously did require that counsel be provided.

We reject, therefore, the premise that since prosecutions for crimes punishable by imprisonment for less than six months may be tried without a jury, they may also be tried without a lawyer.

The assistance of counsel is often a requisite to the very existence of a fair trial. In *Gideon v. Wainwright*, we dealt with a felony trial. But we did not so limit the need of the accused for a lawyer. We said:

> [I]n our adversary system of criminal justice, any person haled into court, who is too poor to hire a lawyer, cannot be assured a fair trial unless counsel is provided for him.

Both *Powell* and *Gideon* involved felonies. But their rationale has relevance to any criminal trial, where an accused is deprived of his liberty. *Powell* and *Gideon* suggest that there are certain fundamental rights applicable to all such criminal prosecutions.

The requirement of counsel may well be necessary for a fair trial even in a petty-offense prosecution. We are by no means convinced that legal and constitutional questions involved in a case that actually leads to imprisonment even for a brief period are any less complex than when a person can be sent off for six months or more.

The trial of vagrancy cases is illustrative. While only brief sentences of imprisonment may be imposed, the cases often bristle with thorny constitutional questions.

Beyond the problem of trials and appeals is that of the guilty plea, a problem which looms large in misdemeanor as well as in felony cases. Counsel is needed so that the accused may know precisely what he is doing, so that he is fully aware of the prospect of going to jail or prison, and so that he is treated fairly by the prosecution.

We must conclude, therefore, that the problems associated with misdemeanor and petty offenses often require the presence of counsel to insure the accused a fair trial. Mr. Justice Powell suggests that these problems are raised even in situations where there is no prospect of imprisonment. We need not consider the requirements of the Sixth Amendment as regards the right to counsel where loss of liberty is not involved, however, for here petitioner was in fact sentenced to jail.

We hold, therefore, that absent a knowing and intelligent waiver, no person may be imprisoned for any offense, whether classified as petty, misdemeanor, or felony, unless he was represented by counsel at his trial.

Under the rule we announce today, every judge will know when the trial of a misdemeanor starts that no imprisonment may be imposed, even though local law permits it, unless the accused is represented by counsel. He will have a measure of the seriousness and gravity of the offense and therefore know when to name a lawyer to represent the accused before the trial starts.

The run of misdemeanors will not be affected by today's ruling. But in those that end up in the actual deprivation of a person's liberty, the accused will receive the benefit of "the guiding hand of counsel" so necessary when one's liberty is in jeopardy.

Reversed.

Mr. Chief Justice Burger, concurring in the result.

I agree with much of the analysis in the opinion of the Court and with Mr. Justice Powell's appraisal of the problems. Were I able to confine my focus solely to the burden that the States will have to bear in providing counsel, I would be inclined, at this stage of the development of the constitutional right to counsel, to conclude that there is much to commend drawing the line at penalties in excess of six months' confinement. Yet several cogent factors suggest the infirmities in any approach that allows confinement for any period without the aid of counsel at trial; any deprivation of liberty is a serious matter. The issues that must be dealt with in a trial for a petty offense or a misdemeanor may often be simpler than those involved in a felony trial and yet be beyond the capability of a layman, especially when he is opposed by a law-trained prosecutor. There is little ground, therefore, to assume that a defendant, unaided by counsel, will be any more able adequately to defend himself against the lesser charges that may involve confinement than more serious charges. Appeal from a conviction after an uncounseled trial is not likely to be of much help to a defendant since the die is usually cast when judgment is entered on an uncounseled trial record.

Mr. Justice Powell, with whom Mr. Justice Rehnquist joins, concurring in the result.

I am unable to agree with the Supreme Court of Florida that an indigent defendant, charged with a petty offense, may in every case be afforded a fair trial without the assistance of counsel. Nor can I agree with the new rule of due process, today enunciated by the Court, that "absent a knowing and intelligent waiver, no person may be imprisoned . . . unless he was represented by counsel at his trial." It seems to me that the line should not be drawn with such rigidity.

There is a middle course, between the extremes of Florida's six-month rule and the Court's rule, which comports with the requirements of the Fourteenth Amendment. I would adhere to the principle of due process that requires fundamental fairness in criminal trials, a principle which I believe encompasses the right to counsel in petty cases whenever the assistance of counsel is necessary to assure a fair trial.

I

I am in accord with the Court that an indigent accused's need for the assistance of counsel does not mysteriously evaporate when he is charged with an offense punishable by six months or less. In *Powell v. Alabama* and *Gideon*, both of which involved felony prosecutions, this Court noted that few laymen can present adequately their own cases, much less identify and argue relevant legal questions. Many petty offenses will also present complex legal and factual issues that may not be fairly tried if the defendant is not assisted by counsel. Even in relatively simple cases, some defendants, because of ignorance or some other handicap, will be incapable of defending themselves. The consequences of a misdemeanor conviction, whether they be a brief period served under the sometimes deplorable conditions found in local jails or the effect of a criminal record on employability, are frequently of sufficient magnitude not to be casually dismissed by the label "petty."

Serious consequences also may result from convictions not punishable by imprisonment. Stigma may attach to a drunken-driving conviction or a hit-and-run escapade. Losing one's driver's license is more serious for some individuals than a brief stay in jail.

When the deprivation of property rights and interest is of sufficient consequence, denying the assistance of counsel to indigents who are incapable of defending themselves is a denial of due process.

This is not to say that due process requires the appointment of counsel in all petty cases, or that assessment of the possible consequences of conviction is the sole test for the need for assistance of counsel. The flat six-month rule of the Florida court and the equally inflexible rule of the majority opinion apply to *all* cases within their defined areas regardless of circumstances. It is precisely because of this mechanistic application that I find these alternatives unsatisfactory. Due process, perhaps the most fundamental concept in our law, embodies principles of fairness rather than immutable line drawing as to every aspect of a criminal trial. While counsel is often essential to a fair trial, this is by no means a universal fact. Some petty offense cases are complex; others are exceedingly simple. As a justification for furnishing counsel to indigents accused of felonies, this Court noted, "That government hires lawyers to prosecute and defendants who have the money hire lawyers to defend are the strongest indications of the widespread belief that lawyers in criminal courts are necessities, not luxuries." Yet government often does not hire lawyers to prosecute petty offenses; instead the arresting police officer presents the case. Nor does every defendant who can afford to do so hire lawyers to defend petty charges. Where the possibility of a jail sentence is remote and the probable fine seems small, or where the evidence of guilt is overwhelming, the costs of assistance of counsel may exceed the benefits. It is anomalous that the Court's opinion today will extend the right of appointed counsel to indigent defendants in cases where the right to counsel would rarely be exercised by nonindigent defendants.

Indeed, one of the effects of this ruling will be to favor defendants classified as indigents over those not so classified, yet who are in low-income groups where engaging counsel in a minor petty-offense case would be a luxury the family could not afford. The line between indigency and assumed capacity to pay for counsel is necessarily somewhat arbitrary, drawn differently from State to State and often resulting in serious inequities to accused persons. The Court's new rule will accent the disadvantage of being barely self-sufficient economically.

It is impossible, as well as unwise, to create a precise and detailed set of guidelines for judges to follow in determining whether the appointment of counsel is necessary to assure a fair trial. Certainly three general factors should be weighed. First, the court should consider the complexity of the offense charged.

Second, the court should consider the probable sentence that will follow if a conviction is obtained. The more serious the likely consequences, the greater is the probability that a lawyer should be appointed.

Third, the court should consider the individual factors peculiar to each case. These, of course, would be the most difficult to anticipate. One relevant factor would be the competency of the individual defendant to present his own case. The attitude of the community toward a particular defendant or particular incident would be another consideration. But there might be other reasons why a defendant would have a peculiar need for a lawyer which would compel the appointment of counsel in a case where the court would normally think this unnecessary. Obviously, the sensitivity and diligence of individual judges would be crucial to the operation of a rule of fundamental fairness requiring the consideration of the varying factors in each case.

NOTES AND QUESTIONS

(1) The Chief Justice expressed concern over "the burden that the States will have to bear in providing counsel." Should the Court have given greater consideration to this burden? Should the result change if the burden would be a substantial one?

(2) Justice Douglas noted that there was historical support for the view that the right to a jury trial is limited to "serious criminal offenses," but there was no similar limitation respecting the right to counsel. Would the result in this case have been different if there had been such historical support as to the right to counsel?

(3) Should an attorney be required if the defendant enters a plea of guilty? Would it matter if the Judge had advised the defendant of the potential sentence, the options concerning trial, etc.? Consider Illinois Supreme Court Rule 402:

> In hearings on pleas of guilty, or in any case in which the defense offers to stipulate that the evidence is sufficient to convict, there must be substantial compliance with the following:
>
> (a) Admonitions to Defendant. The court shall not accept a plea of guilty or a stipulation that the evidence is sufficient to convict without first, by addressing the defendant personally in open court, informing him of and determining that he understands the following:
>
> (1) the nature of the charge;
>
> (2) the minimum and maximum sentence prescribed by law, including, when applicable, the penalty to which the defendant may be subjected because of prior convictions or consecutive sentences;
>
> (3) that the defendant has the right to plead not guilty . . . , and
>
> (4) that if he pleads guilty there will not be a trial of any kind, so that by pleading guilty he waives the right to a trial by jury and the right to be confronted with the witnesses against him; or that by stipulating the evidence is sufficient to convict, he waives the right to a trial by jury and the right to be confronted with any witnesses against him who have not testified.
>
> (b) Determining Whether the Plea is Voluntary. The court shall not accept a plea of guilty without first determining that the plea is voluntary. If the tendered plea is the result of a plea agreement, the agreement shall be stated in open court. The court, by questioning the defendant personally in open court, shall confirm the terms of the plea agreement, or that there is no agreement, and shall determine whether any force or threats or any promises, apart from a plea agreement, were used to obtain the plea.
>
> (c) Determining Factual Basis for Plea. The court shall not enter final judgment on a plea of guilty without first determining that there is a factual basis for the plea.

(4) Justice Brennan concurred in the majority opinion but, with Justices Douglas and Stewart, added the following thought:

> Law students as well as practicing attorneys may provide an important source of legal representation for the indigent. [M]ore than 125 of the country's 147 accredited law schools have established clinical programs in which faculty-supervised students aid clients in a variety of civil and criminal matters. These programs supplement practice rules enacted in 38 States authorizing students to practice law under prescribed conditions. Like the American Bar Association's Model Student Practice Rule (1969), most of these regulations permit students to make supervised court appearances as defense counsel in criminal cases. Given the huge increase in law school enrollments over the past few years, I think it plain that law students can be expected to make a significant contribution, quantitatively and qualitatively, to the representation of the poor in many areas, including cases reached by today's decision.

What role should law students have in the representation of indigent defendants?

In *People v. Perez*, 594 P.2d 1 (Cal. 1979), the defendant was convicted of burglary after being represented by a law student participating in a certified law school clinical program under the supervision of an experienced attorney. The trial judge, at the conclusion of the trial, stated that the student "did what I consider for a law student an outstanding job . . . a better job than some I've seen with . . . people who are full-fledged lawyers." The Court of Appeals reversed the conviction, even though the defendant did not claim that he had received inadequate aid: "[E]ven if (the defendant) and all other defendants represented under the Rules receive reasonably competent representation, in contemplation of law participation by one not yet a member of the bar (there) is an abridgement of the right to assistance of counsel." The California Supreme Court reversed:

> The Rules were carefully drafted with a view to assuring that defendants would receive competent legal assistance. The law student must have completed at least three semesters of legal education or equivalent, and be certified as fit to participate in the program by the dean of his school; in criminal cases he appears in court only under the immediate supervision of an experienced attorney, who assumes personal professional responsibility for the student's performance. When, as in the case at bar, a defendant receives competent representation pursuant to a program carefully formulated to assure such competency of representation, we can find no abridgment of the defendant's constitutional right to the assistance of counsel.

But see the dissenting opinion:

> The State Bar describes the problem to be whether the Sixth Amendment right to counsel is impaired "when attorneys are assisted by law students." The bar misconceives its own program: In general it is the law student who is assisted by the attorney, and that is precisely what the record reveals here. The law student conducted the examination of witnesses and presented the entire argument to the jury; the attorney purported to assist him. Perhaps counsel performed some services that are not evident in the record, but the transcript indicates that while counsel was physically present throughout the 3-day trial, he uttered a total of 36 words. That averages out to 12 words per day, little more than required by a polite daily salutation to the judge, hardly enough to suggest any contribution of substance.

(5) Justice Powell was concerned that "one of the effects of this ruling will be to favor defendants classified as indigents over those not so classified. . . ." Why does he think indigents will be favored? Is there any way to avoid this problem?

(6) If the majority was correct in holding that the right to counsel in misdemeanor cases is so important, was not Justice Powell correct that the rule in *Argersinger* should also apply to some cases in which penalties other than imprisonment are imposed?

(7) The actual holding in this case was narrow: the defendant could not be imprisoned unless he was represented by an attorney at trial. The Court left open

the question of whether counsel was required where the defendant was not actually imprisoned, but could have been had the judge chosen to order it. This question was answered in *Scott v. Illinois.*

SCOTT v. ILLINOIS

United States Supreme Court
440 U.S. 367 (1979)

MR. JUSTICE REHNQUIST delivered the opinion of the Court.

We granted certiorari in this case to resolve a conflict among state and lower federal courts regarding the proper application of our decision in *Argersinger v. Hamlin.* Petitioner Scott was convicted of theft and fined $50 after a bench trial in the Circuit Court of Cook County, Ill. Petitioner Scott was convicted of shoplifting merchandise valued at less than $150. The applicable Illinois statute set the maximum penalty for such an offense at a $500 fine or one year in jail, or both. In his petition for certiorari, petitioner referred to the issue in this case as "the question left open in *Argersinger v. Hamlin.*" Whether this question was indeed "left open" in *Argersinger* depends upon whether one considers that opinion to be a point in a moving line or a holding that the States are required to go only so far in furnishing counsel to indigent defendants. The Supreme Court of Illinois clearly viewed the latter as *Argersinger's* holding. Additional support for this proposition may be derived from the concluding paragraph of the opinion in that case: The run of misdemeanors will not be affected by today's ruling. But in those that end up in the actual deprivation of a person's liberty, the accused will receive the benefit of "the guiding hand of counsel" so necessary where one's liberty is in jeopardy.

Petitioner, on the other hand, refers to language in the Court's opinion, responding to the opinion of Mr. Justice Powell, which states that the Court "need not consider the requirements of the Sixth Amendment as regards the right to counsel where loss of liberty is not involved . . . for here petitioner was in fact sentenced to jail."

The number of separate opinions in *Gideon, Duncan, Baldwin,* and *Argersinger,* suggests that constitutional line drawing becomes more difficult as the reach of the Constitution is extended further, and as efforts are made to transpose lines from one area of Sixth Amendment jurisprudence to another. The process of incorporation creates special difficulties, for the state and federal contexts are often different and application of the same principle may have ramifications distinct in degree and kind. The range of human conduct regulated by state criminal laws is much broader than that of the federal criminal laws, particularly on the "petty" offense part of the spectrum. As a matter of constitutional adjudication, we are, therefore, less willing to extrapolate an already extended line when, although the general nature of the principle sought to be applied is clear, its precise limits and their ramifications become less so. We have now in our decided cases departed from the literal meaning of the Sixth Amendment. And we cannot fall back on the common law as it existed prior to the enactment of that Amendment, since it perversely gave less in the way of right to counsel to accused felons than to those accused of misdemeanors.

In *Argersinger* the Court rejected arguments that social cost or a lack of available lawyers militated against its holding, in some part because it thought these arguments were factually incorrect. But they were rejected in much larger part because of the Court's conclusion that incarceration was so severe a sanction that it should not be imposed as a result of a criminal trial unless an indigent defendant had been offered appointed counsel to assist in his defense, regardless of the cost to the States implicit in such a rule. The Court in its opinion repeatedly referred to trials "where an accused is deprived of his liberty," and to "a case that actually leads to imprisonment even for a brief period." The Chief Justice in his opinion concurring in the result also observed that "any deprivation of liberty is a serious matter."

Although the intentions of the *Argersinger* Court are not unmistakably clear from its opinion, we conclude today that *Argersinger* did indeed delimit the constitutional right to appointed counsel in state criminal proceedings. Even were the matter *res nova*, we believe that the central premise of *Argersinger* — that actual imprisonment is a penalty different in kind from fines or the mere threat of imprisonment — is eminently sound and warrants adoption of actual imprisonment as the line defining the constitutional right to appointment of counsel. *Argersinger* has proved reasonably workable, whereas any extension would create confusion and impose unpredictable, but necessarily substantial, costs on 50 quite diverse States. We therefore hold that the Sixth and Fourteenth Amendments to the United States Constitution require only that no indigent criminal defendant be sentenced to a term of imprisonment unless the State has afforded him the right to assistance of appointed counsel in his defense. The judgment of the Supreme Court of Illinois is accordingly

Affirmed.

MR. JUSTICE POWELL, concurring.

For the reasons stated in my opinion in *Argersinger v. Hamlin*, I do not think the rule adopted by the Court in that case is required by the Constitution. Moreover, the drawing of a line based on whether there is imprisonment (even for overnight) can have the practical effect of precluding provision of counsel in other types of cases in which conviction can have more serious consequences. The *Argersinger* rule also tends to impair the proper functioning of the criminal justice system in that trial judges, in advance of hearing any evidence and before knowing anything about the case except the charge, all too often will be compelled to forego the legislatively granted option to impose a sentence of imprisonment upon conviction. Preserving this option by providing counsel often will be impossible or impracticable — particularly in congested urban courts where scores of cases are heard in a single sitting and in small and rural communities where lawyers may not be available.

Despite my continuing reservations about the *Argersinger* rule, it was approved by the Court in the 1972 opinion and four Justices have reaffirmed it today. It is important that this Court provide clear guidance to the hundreds of courts across the country that confront this problem daily. Accordingly, and mindful of *stare decisis*, I join the opinion of the Court. I do so, however, with the hope that in due time a majority will recognize that a more flexible rule is consistent with due process and will better serve the cause of justice.

MR. JUSTICE BRENNAN, with whom MR. JUSTICE MARSHALL and MR. JUSTICE STEVENS join, dissenting.

[T]he Court today retreats to the indefensible position that the *Argersinger* "actual imprisonment" standard is the *only* test for determining the boundary of the Sixth Amendment right to appointed counsel in state misdemeanor cases, thus necessarily deciding that in many cases (such as this one) a defendant will have no right to appointed counsel even when he has a constitutional right to a jury trial. This is simply an intolerable result. Not only is the "actual imprisonment" standard unprecedented as the exclusive test, but the problems inherent in its application demonstrate the superiority of an "authorized imprisonment" standard that would require the appointment of counsel for indigents accused of any offense for which imprisonment for any time is authorized.

First, the "authorized imprisonment" standard more faithfully implements the principles of the Sixth Amendment identified in *Gideon.* The procedural rules established by state statutes are geared to the nature of the potential penalty for an offense, not to the actual penalty imposed in particular cases. The authorized penalty is also a better predictor of the stigma and other collateral consequences that attach to conviction of an offense.

Second, the "authorized imprisonment" test presents no problems of administration. It avoids the necessity for time-consuming consideration of the likely sentence in each individual case before trial and the attendant problems of inaccurate predictions, unequal treatment, and apparent and actual bias.

Finally, the "authorized imprisonment" test ensures that courts will not abrogate legislative judgments concerning the appropriate range of penalties to be considered for each offense.

The apparent reason for the Court's adoption of the "actual imprisonment" standard for all misdemeanors is concern for the economic burden that an "authorized imprisonment" standard might place on the States. But, with all respect, that concern is both irrelevant and speculative.

This Court's role in enforcing constitutional guarantees for criminal defendants cannot be made dependent on the budgetary decisions of state governments.

In any event, the extent of the alleged burden on the States is, as the Court admits, speculative. Although more persons are charged with misdemeanors punishable by incarceration than are charged with felonies, a smaller percentage of persons charged with misdemeanors qualify as indigent, and misdemeanor cases as a rule require far less attorney time.

Furthermore, public defender systems have proved economically feasible, and the establishment of such systems to replace appointment of private attorneys can keep costs at acceptable levels even when the number of cases requiring appointment of counsel increases dramatically.

Perhaps the strongest refutation of respondent's alarmist prophecies that an authorized imprisonment standard would wreak havoc on the States is that the standard has not produced that result in the substantial number of States that already provide counsel in all cases where imprisonment is authorized — States that include a large majority of the country's population and a great diversity of urban and rural environments. Moreover, of those States that do not yet provide counsel in all cases where *any* imprisonment is authorized, many provide counsel when periods of imprisonment longer than 30 days, 3 months, or 6 months are authorized. In fact, Scott would be entitled to appointed counsel under the current laws of at least 33 States.

NOTES AND QUESTIONS

(1) Justice Rehnquist, in refusing to extend *Argersinger*, noted that the Court there was persuaded to require counsel because "incarceration was so severe a sanction." Why is the punishment relevant to the question of whether counsel should have been appointed? Would the result in this case have changed if the defendant had been fined $5000 instead of $50? If he had shown that his license to practice social work had been forfeited due to the conviction?

(2) The Sixth Amendment states in part that "In all criminal prosecutions, the accused shall enjoy the right. . . to have the Assistance of Counsel for his defence." Once the Court decided that appointed counsel was required in *some* cases under the Sixth Amendment, how did the Court reach its result in *Scott* in light of the inclusive language of the counsel clause?

(3) The plurality was concerned with the burden on the states of a contrary ruling. How important should this consideration be? Does it matter that, according to Justice Brennan, "Scott would be entitled to appointed counsel under the current laws of at least 33 States"?

(4) Justice Powell disagreed with the holding in *Argersinger* and apparently disagreed with the holding in *Scott*, yet he was willing to join the plurality so that there would be "clear guidance." If he disagreed with the plurality, should he not have dissented? What is the role of *stare decisis* here?

(5) In *Nichols v. United States*, 511 U.S. 738 (1994), the Court held that later cases could take into account earlier convictions from trials in which the defendant was not represented by counsel. Such earlier convictions could be considered for the purpose of enhancing punishment in the later cases.

[B] Assistance Other than Counsel

AKE v. OKLAHOMA

United States Supreme Court
470 U.S. 68 (1985)

Justice Marshall delivered the opinion of the Court.

The issue in this case is whether the Constitution requires that an indigent defendant have access to the psychiatric examination and assistance necessary to prepare an effective defense based on his mental condition, when his sanity at the time of the offense is seriously in question.

I

Late in 1979, Glen Burton Ake was arrested and charged with murdering a couple and wounding their two children. He was arraigned in the District Court for Canadian County, Okla., in February 1980. His behavior at arraignment, and in other prearraignment incidents at the jail, was so bizarre that the trial judge *sua sponte*, ordered him to be examined by a psychiatrist "for the purpose of advising with the Court as to his impressions of whether the Defendant may need an extended period of mental observation." App. 2. The examining psychiatrist reported: "At times [Ake] appears to be frankly delusional. . . . He claims to be the 'sword of vengeance' of the Lord and that he will sit at the left hand of God in heaven." *Id.*, at 8. He diagnosed Ake as a probable paranoid schizophrenic and recommended a prolonged psychiatric evaluation to determine whether Ake was competent to stand trial.

In March, Ake was committed to a state hospital to be examined with respect to his "present sanity," *i.e.*, his competency to stand trial. On April 10, less than six months after the incidents for which Ake was indicted, the chief forensic psychiatrist at the state hospital informed the court that Ake was not competent to stand trial. The court then held a competency hearing, at which a psychiatrist testified:

> [Ake] is a psychotic . . . his psychiatric diagnosis was that of paranoid schizophrenia — chronic, with exacerbation, that is with current upset, and that in addition . . . he is dangerous. . . . [B]ecause of the severity of his mental illness and because of the intensities of his rage, his poor control, his delusions, he requires a maximum security facility within — I believe — the State Psychiatric Hospital system.

Id. at 11–12. The court found Ake to be a "mentally ill person in need of care and treatment" and incompetent to stand trial, and ordered him committed to the state mental hospital.

Six weeks later, the chief forensic psychiatrist informed the court that Ake had become competent to stand trial. At the time, Ake was receiving 200 milligrams of Thorazine, an anti-psychotic drug, three times daily, and the psychiatrist indicated that, if Ake continued to receive that dosage, his condition would remain stable. The State then resumed proceedings against Ake.

At a pretrial conference in June, Ake's attorney informed the court that his client would raise an insanity defense. To enable him to prepare and present such a defense adequately, the attorney stated, a psychiatrist would have to examine Ake with respect to his mental condition at the time of the offense. During Ake's 3-month stay at the state hospital, no inquiry had been made into his sanity at the time of the offense, and, as an indigent, Ake could not afford to pay for a psychiatrist. Counsel asked the court either to arrange to have a psychiatrist perform the examination, or to provide funds to allow the defense to arrange one. The trial judge rejected counsel's argument that the Federal Constitution requires that an indigent defendant receive the assistance of a psychiatrist when that assistance is necessary to the defense, and he denied the motion for a psychiatric evaluation at state expense on the basis of this Court's decision in *United States ex rel. Smith v. Baldi*, 344 U.S. 561 (1953).

Ake was tried for two counts of murder in the first degree, a crime punishable by death in Oklahoma, and for two counts of shooting with intent to kill. At the guilt phase of trial, his sole defense was insanity. Although defense counsel called to the stand and questioned each of the psychiatrists who had examined Ake at the state hospital, none testified about his mental state at the time of the offense because none had examined him on that point. The prosecution, in turn, asked each of these psychiatrists whether he had performed or seen the results of any examination diagnosing Ake's mental state at the time of the offense, and each doctor replied that he had not. *As a result, there was no expert testimony for either side on Ake's sanity at the time of the offense.* The jurors were then instructed that Ake could be found not guilty by reason of insanity if he did not have the ability to distinguish right from wrong at the time of the alleged offense. They were further told that Ake was to be presumed sane at the time of the crime unless *he* presented evidence sufficient to raise a reasonable doubt about his sanity at that time. If he raised such a doubt in their minds, the jurors were informed, the burden of proof shifted to the State to prove sanity beyond a reasonable doubt. The jury rejected Ake's insanity defense and returned a verdict of guilty on all counts.

III

This Court has long recognized that when a State brings its judicial power to bear on an indigent defendant in a criminal proceeding, it must take steps to assure that the defendant has a fair opportunity to present his defense. This elementary principle, grounded in significant part on the Fourteenth Amendment's due process guarantee of fundamental fairness, derives from the belief that justice cannot be equal where, simply as a result of his poverty, a defendant is denied the opportunity to participate meaningfully in a judicial proceeding in which his liberty is at stake. In recognition of this right, this Court held almost 30 years ago that once a State offers to criminal defendants the opportunity to appeal their cases, it must provide a trial transcript to an indigent defendant if the transcript is necessary to a decision on the merits of the appeal. Since then, this Court has held that an indigent defendant may not be required to pay a fee before filing a notice of appeal of his conviction, that an indigent defendant is entitled to the assistance of counsel at trial, and on his first direct appeal as of right, and that such assistance must be effective.

Meaningful access to justice has been the consistent theme of these cases. We recognized long ago that mere access to the courthouse doors does not by itself assure a proper functioning of the adversary process, and that a criminal trial is fundamentally unfair if the State proceeds against an indigent defendant without making certain that he has access to the raw materials integral to the building of an effective defense. Thus, while the Court has not held that a State must purchase for the indigent defendant all the assistance that his wealthier counterpart might buy, it has often reaffirmed that fundamental fairness entitles indigent defendants to "an adequate opportunity to present their claims fairly within the adversary system." To implement this principle, we have focused on identifying the "basic tools of an adequate defense or appeal," and we have required that such tools be provided to those defendants who cannot afford to pay for them.

To say that these basic tools must be provided is, of course, merely to begin our inquiry. In this case we must decide whether, and under what conditions, the participation of a psychiatrist is important enough to preparation of a defense to require the State to provide an indigent defendant with access to competent psychiatric assistance in preparing the defense. Three factors are relevant to this determination. The first is the private interest that will be affected by the action of the State. The second is the governmental interest that will be affected if the safeguard is to be provided. The third is the probable value of the additional or substitute procedural safeguards that are sought, and the risk of an erroneous deprivation of the affected interest if those safeguards are not provided. We turn, then, to apply this standard to the issue before us.

The private interest in the accuracy of a criminal proceeding that places an individual's life or liberty at risk is almost uniquely compelling. Indeed, the host of safeguards fashioned by this Court over the years to diminish the risk of erroneous conviction stands as a testament to that concern. The interest of the individual in the outcome of the State's effort to overcome the presumption of innocence is obvious and weighs heavily in our analysis.

We consider, next, the interest of the State. Oklahoma asserts that to provide Ake with psychiatric assistance on the record before us would result in a staggering burden to the State. We are unpersuaded by this assertion. Many States, as well as the Federal Government, currently make psychiatric assistance available to indigent defendants, and they have not found the financial burden so great as to preclude this assistance. This is especially so when the obligation of the State is limited to provision of one competent psychiatrist, as it is in many States, and as we limit the right we recognize today. At the same time, it is difficult to identify any interest of the State, other than that in its economy, that weighs against recognition of this right. The State's interest in prevailing at trial — unlike that of a private litigant — is necessarily tempered by its interest in the fair and accurate adjudication of criminal cases. Thus, also unlike a private litigant, a State may not legitimately assert an interest in maintenance of a strategic advantage over the defense, if the result of that advantage is to cast a pall on the accuracy of the verdict obtained. We therefore conclude that the governmental interest in denying Ake the assistance of a psychiatrist is not substantial, in light of the compelling interest of both the State and the individual in accurate dispositions.

Last, we inquire into the probable value of the psychiatric assistance sought, and the risk of error in the proceeding if such assistance is not offered. We begin by considering the pivotal role that psychiatry has come to play in criminal proceedings. More than 40 States, as well as the Federal Government, have decided either through legislation or judicial decision that indigent defendants are entitled, under certain circumstances, to the assistance of a psychiatrist's expertise. For example, in subsection (e) of the Criminal Justice Act, 18 U.S.C. § 3006A, Congress has provided that indigent defendants shall receive the assistance of all experts "necessary for an adequate defense." Numerous state statutes guarantee reimbursement for expert services under a like standard. And in many States that have not assured access to psychiatrists through the legislative process, state courts have interpreted the State or Federal Constitution to require that psychiatric assistance be provided to indigent defendants when necessary for an adequate defense, or when insanity is at issue.

These statutes and court decisions reflect a reality that we recognize today, namely, that when the State has made the defendant's mental condition relevant to his criminal culpability and to the punishment he might suffer, the assistance of a psychiatrist may well be crucial to the defendant's ability to marshal his defense. In this role, psychiatrists gather facts, through professional examination, interviews, and elsewhere, that they will share with the judge or jury; they analyze the information gathered and from it draw plausible conclusions about the defendant's mental condition, and about the effects of any disorder on behavior; and they offer opinions about how the defendant's mental condition might have affected his behavior at the time in question. They know the probative questions to ask of the opposing party's psychiatrists and how to interpret their answers. Unlike lay witnesses, who can merely describe symptoms they believe might be relevant to the defendant's mental state, psychiatrists can identify the "elusive and often deceptive" symptoms of insanity, and tell the jury why their observations are relevant. Further, where permitted by evidentiary rules, psychiatrists can translate a medical diagnosis into language that will assist the trier of fact, and therefore offer evidence in a form that has meaning for the task at hand. Through this process of investigation, interpretation, and testimony, psychiatrists ideally assist lay jurors, who generally have no training in psychiatric matters, to make a sensible and educated determination about the mental condition of the defendant at the time of the offense.

IV

We turn now to apply these standards to the facts of this case. On the record before us, it is clear that Ake's mental state at the time of the offense was a substantial factor in his defense, and that the trial court was on notice of that fact when the request for a court-appointed psychiatrist was made. For one, Ake's sole defense was that of insanity. Second, Ake's behavior at arraignment, just four months after the offense, was so bizarre as to prompt the trial judge, *sua sponte*, to have him examined for competency. Third, a state psychiatrist shortly thereafter found Ake to be incompetent to stand trial, and suggested that he be committed. Fourth, when he was found to be competent six weeks later, it was only on the condition that he be sedated with large doses of Thorazine three times a day, during trial. Fifth, the psychiatrists who examined Ake for competency described to the trial court the severity of Ake's mental illness less than six months after the offense in question, and suggested that this mental illness might have begun many years earlier. Finally, Oklahoma recognizes a defense of insanity, under which the initial burden of producing evidence falls on the defendant. Taken together, these factors make clear that the question of Ake's sanity was likely to be a significant factor in his defense.

Accordingly, we reverse and remand for a new trial.

It is so ordered.

[Chief Justice Burger concurred in the judgment. Justice Rehnquist dissented.]

NOTES AND QUESTIONS

Does the rule in *Ake* apply to other forms of assistance such as private investigators or scientific experts? The courts have consistently extended the rule beyond the narrow setting of *Ake*. Several cases demonstrate the added protection offered by *Ake*. The failure to appoint a forensic expert regarding the quantity of methamphetamine being produced, when no drugs were actually found at the scene, was found to be error in *United States v. Chase*, 499 F.3d 1061 (9th Cir. 2007). There the defendant was charged with production of the drug and the entire case hinged on the quantity. *State v. Moore*, 364 S.E.2d 648 (N.C. 1988), held that the defendant should have been given the services of both a psychiatrist (to rebut a claim of a valid waiver under the Fifth Amendment) and a fingerprint expert (major piece of evidence was fingerprint found at scene of crime). In *Evans v. State*, 109 So. 3d 1044 (Miss. 2013), the court ruled that the trial judge should have allowed the defendant the services of an expert on post-traumatic stress disorder where the defendant, a 14-year-old, claimed he shot his father because his state of mind was affected by PTSD. But see *Yohey v. Collins*, 985 F.2d 222, 227 (5th Cir. 1993), where the defendant requested the appointment of forensic and ballistic experts to assist in the self-defense claim and also to show that the shot which killed the victim had actually been fired by someone else. The court refused the request, noting that the defendant had not made a clear showing as to the need for the experts:

> This Court has held that non-psychiatric experts, such as ballistic experts, should be provided only if the evidence is both "critical to the conviction and subject to varying expert opinion." [T]he government is not required to automatically provide indigent defendants with expert assistance upon demand. An indigent defendant requesting non-psychiatric experts must demonstrate something more than a mere possibility of assistance from a requested expert.

Requests for experts in connection with DNA evidence are confronting many courts throughout the nation. Consider these two different judicial responses. In *Sanchez v. Commonwealth*, 585 S.E.2d 327 (Va. App. 2003), the appeals court reversed the trial judge's denial of a defense request for a DNA expert in a trial for hit-and-run. The trial judge erred because the defense request was particularized, and the DNA evidence was material (blood found on the vehicle). But see *People v. Tanner*, 671 N.W.2d 728 (Mich. 2003), where a similar request was denied at trial and the denial was upheld on appeal. The court found the defense request to be "speculative." It is not enough for the defendant to show a mere possibility of assistance from the required expert. The dissenting judge disagreed, writing that the holding "sets an impossible goal for defense counsel. . . . If counsel fully understands the prosecution's scientific evidence, there would be no need for an expert to explain it. . . ."

§ 4.02 JOINT REPRESENTATION

Joint defendant trials are common throughout the United States. Marcus, *Re-Evaluating Large Multiple Defendant Criminal Prosecutions*, 11 Wm. & Mary Bill of Rts. L.J. 67 (2002). In some of these trials defendants either choose to be represented by the same attorney or are appointed the same attorney. The reasons in both instances are the same: the costs are less and sometimes a single attorney can have a better grasp of all the issues in the case. With both appointed and retained counsel, however, serious conflict of interest problems can arise. Judges and lawyers must be vigilant as to whether a conflict actually exists and what action should be taken to alleviate the potential or actual conflict. The Supreme Court has only addressed these questions a few times. The first occasion was in *Glasser v. United States*, 315 U.S. 60 (1942). Thirty-five years later, the Court in *Holloway v. Arkansas*, 435 U.S. 475 (1978), discussed *Glasser*:

> [T]his Court held that by requiring an attorney to represent two codefendants whose interests were in conflict the District Court had denied one of the defendants his Sixth Amendment right to the effective assistance of counsel. In that case the Government tried five codefendants in a joint trial for conspiracy to defraud the United States. Two of the defendants, Glasser and Kretske, were represented initially by separate counsel. On the second day of trial, however, Kretske became dissatisfied with his attorney and dismissed him. The District Judge thereupon asked Glasser's attorney, Stewart, if he would also represent Kretske. Stewart responded by noting a possible conflict of interests: his representation of both Glasser and Kretske might lead the jury to link the two men together. Glasser also made known that he objected to the proposal. The District Court nevertheless appointed Stewart, who continued as Glasser's retained counsel to represent Kretske. Both men were convicted.
>
> Glasser contended in this Court that Stewart's representation at trial was ineffective because of a conflict between the interests of his two clients. This Court held that "the 'Assistance of Counsel' guaranteed by the Sixth Amendment contemplates that such assistance be untrammeled and unimpaired by a court order requiring that one lawyer shall simultaneously represent conflicting interests." 315 U.S. at 70. The record disclosed that Stewart failed to cross-examine a Government witness whose testimony linked Glasser with the conspiracy and failed to object to the admission of arguably inadmissible evidence. This failure was viewed by the Court as a result of Stewart's desire to protect Kretske's interests, and was thus "indicative of Stewart's struggle to serve two masters. . . ." *Id.*, at 75. After identifying this conflict of interests, the Court declined to inquire whether the prejudice flowing from it was harmless and instead ordered Glasser's conviction reversed. Kretske's conviction, however, was affirmed.

Glasser, on its facts, was an easy decision, with the Court focusing its attention on the attorney's failure to cross-examine a key witness. It was unclear, however, what *Glasser*'s precedential value would be when such a clear conflict could not be shown. In 1978, there was an answer.

HOLLOWAY v. ARKANSAS

United States Supreme Court
435 U.S. 475 (1978)

MR. CHIEF JUSTICE BURGER delivered the opinion of the Court.

On July 29, 1975, the three defendants were each charged with one count of robbery and two counts of rape. On August 5, the trial court appointed Harold Hall, a public defender, to represent all three defendants. Petitioners were then arraigned and pleaded not guilty. Two days later, their cases were set for a consolidated trial to commence September 4. On August 13, Hall moved the court to appoint separate counsel for each petitioner because "the defendants ha[d] stated to him that there is a possibility of a conflict of interest in each of their cases. . . ." After conducting a hearing on this motion, and on petitioners' motions for a severance, the court declined to appoint separate counsel.

Before trial, the same judge who later presided at petitioners' trial conducted a *Jackson v. Denno* hearing to determine the admissibility of a confession purportedly made by petitioner Campbell to two police officers at the time of his arrest. The essence of the confession was that Campbell had entered the restaurant with his codefendants and had remained, armed with a rifle, one flight of stairs above the site of the robbery and rapes (apparently serving as a lookout), but had not taken part in the rapes. The trial judge ruled the confession admissible, but ordered deletion of the references to Campbell's codefendants. At trial one of the arresting officers testified to Campbell's confession.

On September 4, before the jury was empaneled, Hall renewed the motion for appointment of separate counsel "on the grounds that one or two of the defendants may testify and if they do, then I will not be able to cross-examine them because I have received confidential information from them." The court responded, "I don't know why you wouldn't," and again denied the motion.

The prosecution then proceeded to present its case. The manager of the restaurant identified petitioners Holloway and Campbell as two of the robbers. Another male employee identified Holloway and petitioner Welch. A third identified only Holloway. The victim of the single rape identified Holloway and Welch as two of the robbers but was unable to identify the man who raped her. The victim of the double rape identified Holloway as the first rapist. She was unable to identify the second rapist but identified Campbell as one of the robbers.

On the second day of trial, after the prosecution had rested its case, Hall advised the court that, against his recommendation, all three defendants had decided to testify.

He then stated:

> Now, since I have been appointed, I had previously filed a motion asking the Court to appoint a separate attorney for each defendant because of a possible conflict of interest. This conflict will probably be now coming up since each one of them wants to testify.

THE COURT: That's all right; let them testify. There is no conflict of interest. Every time I try more than one person in this court each one blames it on the other one.

MR. HALL: I have talked to each one of these defendants, and I have talked to them individually, not collectively.

THE COURT: Now talk to them collectively.

The court then indicated satisfaction that each petitioner understood the nature and consequences of his right to testify on his own behalf, whereupon Hall observed:

> I am in a position now where I am more or less muzzled as to any cross-examination.

THE COURT: You have no right to cross-examine your own witness.

MR. HALL: Or to examine them.

THE COURT: You have a right to examine them, but have no right to cross-examine them. The prosecuting attorney does that.

MR. HALL: If one [defendant] takes the stand, somebody needs to protect the other two's interest while that one is testifying, and I can't do that since I have talked to each one individually.

THE COURT: Well, you have talked to them, I assume, individually and collectively, too. They all say they want to testify. I think it's perfectly alright for them to testify if they want to, or not. It's their business. Each defendant said he wants to testify, and there will be no cross-examination of these witnesses, just a direct examination by you.

MR. HALL: Your Honor, I can't even put them on direct examination because if I ask them —

THE COURT: (interposing) You can just put them on the stand and tell the Court that you have advised them of their rights and they want to testify; then you tell the man to go ahead and relate what he wants to. That's all you need to do.

Holloway took the stand on his own behalf, testifying that during the time described as the time of the robbery he was at his brother's home. His brother had previously given similar testimony. When Welch took the witness stand, the record shows Hall advised him, as he had Holloway that "I cannot ask you any questions that might tend to incriminate any one of the three of you. . . . Now, the only thing I can say is tell these ladies and gentlemen of the jury what you know about this case. . . ." Welch responded that he did not "have any kind of speech ready for the jury or anything. I thought I was going to be questioned." When Welch denied, from the witness stand, that he was at the restaurant the night of the robbery, Holloway interrupted, asking: Your Honor, are we allowed to make an objection?

THE COURT: No, sir. Your counsel will take care of any objections.

MR. HALL: Your Honor, that is what I am trying to say. I can't cross-examine them.

THE COURT: You proceed like I tell you to, Mr. Hall. You have no right to cross-examine your own witnesses anyhow.

Welch proceeded with his unguided direct testimony, denying any involvement in the crime and stating that he was at his home at the time it occurred. Campbell gave similar testimony when he took the stand. He also denied making any confession to the arresting officers. The jury rejected the versions of events presented by the three defendants and the alibi witness, and returned guilty verdicts on all counts.

One principle applicable here emerges from *Glasser* without ambiguity. Requiring or permitting a single attorney to represent codefendants, often referred to as joint representation, is not *per se* violative of constitutional guarantees of effective assistance of counsel. This principle recognizes that in some cases multiple defendants can appropriately be represented by one attorney; indeed, in some cases, certain advantages might accrue from joint representation.

Since *Glasser* was decided, however, the courts have taken divergent approaches to two issues commonly raised in challenges to joint representation where — unlike this case — trial counsel did nothing to advise the trial court of the actuality or possibility of a conflict between his several clients' interests. First, appellate courts have differed on how strong a showing of conflict must be made, or how certain the reviewing court must be that the asserted conflict existed, before it will conclude that the defendants were deprived of their right to the effective assistance of counsel.

Second, courts have differed with respect to the scope and nature of the affirmative duty of the trial judge to assure that criminal defendants are not deprived of their right to the effective assistance of counsel by joint representation of conflicting interests.

We need not resolve these two issues in this case, however. Here trial counsel, by the pretrial motions of August 13 and September 4 and by his accompanying representations, made as an officer of the court, focused explicitly on the probable risk of a conflict of interest. The judge then failed either to appoint separate counsel or to take adequate steps to ascertain whether the risk was too remote to warrant separate counsel. We hold that the failure, in the face of the representations made by counsel weeks before trial and again before the jury was empaneled, deprived petitioners of the guarantee of "assistance of counsel."

It is arguable, perhaps, that defense counsel might have presented the requests for appointment of separate counsel more vigorously and in greater detail. As to the former, however, the trial court's responses hardly encouraged pursuit of the separate counsel claim; and as to presenting the basis for that claim in more detail, defense counsel was confronted with a risk of violating, by more disclosure, his duty of confidentiality to his clients.

Additionally, since the decision in *Glasser*, most courts have held that an attorney's request for the appointment of separate counsel, based on his representations as an officer of the court regarding a conflict of interests, should be granted.

In so holding, the courts have acknowledged and given effect to several interrelated considerations. An "attorney representing two defendants in a criminal matter is in the best position professionally and ethically to determine when a conflict of interest exists or will probably develop in the course of a trial." Second, defense attorneys have the obligation, upon discovering a conflict of interest, to advise the court at once of the problem. Finally, attorneys are officers of the court, and "when they address the judge solemnly upon a matter before the court, their declarations are virtually made under oath." We find these considerations persuasive.

The issue remains whether the error committed at petitioners' trial requires reversal of their convictions. It has generally been assumed that *Glasser* requires reversal, even in the absence of a showing of specific prejudice to the complaining codefendant, whenever a trial court improperly permits or requires joint representation.

Some courts and commentators have argued, however, that appellate courts should not reverse automatically in such cases but rather should affirm unless the defendant can demonstrate prejudice.

We read the Court's opinion in *Glasser* however, as holding that whenever a trial court improperly requires joint representation over timely objection reversal is automatic.

[T]his Court has concluded that the assistance of counsel is among those "constitutional rights so basic to a fair trial that their infraction can never be treated as harmless error." Accordingly, when a defendant is deprived of the presence and assistance of his attorney, either throughout the prosecution or during a critical stage in, at least, the prosecution of a capital offense, reversal is automatic.

That an attorney representing multiple defendants with conflicting interests is physically present at pretrial proceedings, during trial, and at sentencing does not warrant departure from this general rule. Joint representation of conflicting interests is suspect because of what it tends to prevent the attorney from doing. For example, in this case it may well have precluded defense counsel for Campbell from exploring possible plea negotiations and the possibility of an agreement to testify for the prosecution, provided a lesser charge or a favorable sentencing recommendation would be acceptable. Generally speaking, a conflict may also prevent an attorney from challenging the admission of evidence prejudicial to one client but perhaps favorable to another, or from arguing at the sentencing hearing the relative involvement and culpability of his clients in order to minimize the culpability of one by emphasizing that of another. Examples can be readily multiplied. The mere physical presence of an attorney does not fulfill the Sixth Amendment guarantee when the advocate's conflicting obligations have effectively sealed his lips on crucial matters.

It may be possible in some cases to identify from the record the prejudice resulting from an attorney's failure to undertake certain trial tasks, but even with a record of the sentencing hearing available it would be difficult to judge intelligently the impact of a conflict on the attorney's representation of a client. And to assess the impact of a conflict of interests on the attorney's options, tactics and decisions in plea negotiations would be virtually impossible. Thus, an inquiry into a claim of harmless error here would require, unlike most cases, unguided speculation.

[JUSTICES POWELL, BLACKMUN, and REHNQUIST dissented.]

NOTES AND QUESTIONS

(1) If the evidence against *Holloway* had been overwhelming, would his conviction have been reversed? If the answer is yes, what policy is served by having such a reversal? Why did the Court adopt the "automatic" reversal rule here?

(2) The Court has been reluctant to expand the automatic reversal rule. See, for example, *United States v. Morrison*, 449 U.S. 361 (1981), where agents of the Drug Enforcement Agency met with the defendant after she had been indicted and had retained counsel. She moved to have the indictment dismissed, claiming that the conduct of the agents violated her Sixth Amendment right to counsel. A unanimous Court upheld the denial of the motion:

> [C]ertain violations of the right to counsel may be disregarded as harmless error. Our approach has thus been to identify and then neutralize the taint by tailoring suitable relief appropriate in the circumstances to assure the defendant the effective assistance of counsel and a fair trial. The premise of our prior cases is that the constitutional infringement identified has had or threatens some adverse effect upon the effectiveness of counsel's representation or has produced some other prejudice to the defense. Absent such impact on the criminal proceeding, however, there is no basis for imposing a remedy in that proceeding, which can go forward with full recognition of the defendant's right to counsel and to a fair trial.

(3) In *Cuyler v. Sullivan*, 446 U.S. 335 (1980), the defendant and his two co-defendants "shared" the services at trial of two retained counsel. The trial judge did not inquire into a personal conflict of interest by the attorneys (*see* Note (6), *infra*) and none of the three defendants objected. For the first time on appeal the defendant raised the conflict of interest claim and alleged a possible conflict but could show no actual, prejudicial conflict. Should the Court have ordered the reversal of the defendant's conviction? How could a defendant show that the possible conflict seriously affected the trial? This was the problem raised by Justice Marshall in dissent:

> I dissent from the Court's formulation of the proper standard for determining whether multiple representation has violated the defendant's right to the effective assistance of counsel. The Court holds that in the absence of an objection at trial, the defendant must show "that an actual conflict of interest adversely affected his lawyer's performance." If the Court's holding would require a defendant to demonstrate that his attorney's trial performance differed from what it would have been if the defendant had been the attorney's only client, I believe it is inconsistent with our previous cases. Such a test is not only unduly harsh, but incurably speculative as well. The appropriate question under the Sixth Amendment is whether an actual, relevant conflict of interests existed during the proceedings. If it did, the conviction must be reversed.

Justice Powell, for the majority, disagreed:

> *Holloway* reaffirmed that multiple representation does not violate the Sixth Amendment unless it gives rise to a conflict of interest. Since a possible conflict inheres in almost every instance of multiple representation, a defendant who objects to multiple representation must have the opportunity to show that potential conflicts impermissibly imperil his right to a fair trial. But unless the trial court fails to afford such an opportunity, a reviewing court cannot presume that the possibility for conflict has resulted in ineffective assistance of counsel. Such a presumption would preclude multiple representation even in cases where " '[a] common defense . . . gives strength against a common attack.' "

(4) A striking conflict of interest problem arose in *United States v. Allen*, 831 F.2d 1487 (9th Cir. 1987), *cert. denied*, 487 U.S. 1237. There, the seventeen defendants were charged with conspiracy to sell drugs. A single law firm represented all seventeen and devised a "culpability list" for purposes of plea bargaining. This list ranked each defendant and the sentence requested for that individual (the defendant's requested sentence was higher than that of his boss in the operation). The court on appeal found that this situation triggered a strong requirement on the part of the trial judge to conduct an extensive inquiry into the serious potential for conflict. See also *Tarwater v. State*, 383 S.E.2d 883 (Ga. 1989), where the attorney representing multiple defendants negotiated a plea bargain conditioned upon more than one of the clients pleading guilty. Held, this was "a *per se* showing of ineffectiveness of counsel which rises to the level of an unconstitutional deprivation of the right to counsel."

The conflict in *United States v. Newell*, 315 F.3d 510 (5th Cir. 2002), occurred during the course of the trial. There the judge before the trial discussed with the defendants the general types of conflicts that could arise from joint representation. At trial, however, the judge did not follow up when antagonistic defenses were raised. The court on appeal found error under Rule 44(c), *infra*. When the conflict develops during trial, the trial judge is "required to again inquire and either obtain a knowing waiver, disqualifying counsel and mistry the case, or, if appropriate, grant the severance that was earlier denied, and require separate counsel."

The conflict can also arise after the trial has ended, as in *Reynolds v. Chapman*, 253 F.3d 1337, 1345 (11th Cir. 2001). There the lawyer, representing the two convicted defendants, moved for new trials for both of them. The motions were made after "each of those defendants had spent the entire trial attempting to foist blame on the other." This was, according to the court on appeal, an "untenable position" rendering the representation constitutionally ineffective.

(5) If the attorney talks first with both defendants and then seeks to withdraw from the case of one defendant, could he remain as attorney for the other defendant? Would that create any practical problems? Any ethical ones? The ABA Standards dealing with the defense function in § 3.5(b), suggest that normally an attorney should not represent more than one defendant unless "after careful investigation, it is clear that no conflict is likely to develop. . . ." How would a lawyer determine that there was "no conflict likely to develop"?

(6) It is becoming increasingly common for the trial judge affirmatively to seek out information regarding a potential conflict when two defendants are represented by the same lawyer.

See ABA Standards Relating to the Administration of Criminal Justice 4-3.5(b):

> In determining the presence of consent by the defendants, the trial judge should make appropriate inquiries respecting actual or potential conflicts of interest of counsel and whether the defendants fully comprehend the difficulties that an attorney sometimes encounters in defending multiple clients.

Rule 44(c), Federal Rules of Criminal Procedure, provides:

> (c) *Inquiry Into Joint Representation.*
>
> (1) *Joint Representation.* Joint representation occurs when:
>
> (A) two or more defendants have been charged jointly under Rule 8(b) or have been joined for trial under Rule 13; and
>
> (B) the defendants are represented by the same counsel, or counsel who are associated in law practice.
>
> (2) *Court's Responsibilities in Cases of Joint Representation.* The court must promptly inquire about the propriety of joint representation and must personally advise each defendant of the right to the effective assistance of counsel, including separate representation. Unless there is good cause to believe that no conflict of interest is likely to arise, the court must take appropriate measures to protect each defendant's right to counsel.

* * *

The following was presented at a state judges' conference dealing with conflict-of-interest problems. Would this inquiry "assure that co-defendants' decision to proceed with one attorney is an informed decision"?

INQUIRY IN MULTIPLE REPRESENTATION CASES: PRIVATE OR APPOINTED

1. *Inquiry of Counsel*

- Do you feel there is any conflict of interest between your clients? Have you discussed the possibility with them?

- I don't want you to go into the evidence — do you feel their interests are antagonistic in any way?

2. *Inquiry of Each Defendant*

- Do you understand you have the legal right to be represented by a lawyer who represents only you?

- Do you understand you have the legal right to be represented by a lawyer whose only interest and loyalty would be to you and you alone?

• I don't know what the evidence will be in this case, but you should understand that in every trial a lawyer must make important decisions. For example:

(1) He decides what defense will be offered;

(2) He decides which witnesses to call;

(3) He decides what questions to ask witnesses for the State and for the defense;

(4) He decides what arguments to make to the judge or to the jury, or to both;

(5) He advises his clients on what plea to enter, whether to seek a jury trial and whether his client should testify.

It could happen that a decision made by the lawyer or the advice he gives his client would be in the best interest of one client but not another.

It could be that when a lawyer does his duty for one client, he would not be able to do his best for the other.

I do not say these things will happen in this case. But I want you to be aware of the chances you take when more than one defendant has the same lawyer.

Have you discussed this with your lawyer?

If not, do it now . . . then report back.

Do you understand the possible problems when you and another defendant have the same lawyer? Do you have any questions about any of the things I have said to you?

If not — do you still wish to go ahead with the same lawyer as ____________________________?

In *Cuyler v. Sullivan*, *supra*, the Court held that there was no *per se* Sixth Amendment requirement on the part of "state courts themselves to initiate inquiries into the propriety of multiple representation in every case." The Court went on to note, however, that numerous federal courts did require such inquiries and "we view such an exercise of the supervisory power as a desirable practice." See, for instance, the rule in the Eighth Circuit:

> [T]he trial court must conduct a pretrial inquiry into the propriety of joint representation and advise both defendants of their right to separate representation. This circuit specifically requires:
>
> > The court should address each defendant personally and advise him of the potential danger of dual representation. The defendant should have an opportunity and be at liberty to question the trial court on the nature and consequences of dual representation and the entire procedure should be placed on the record for review.

United States v. Brekke, 152 F.3d 1042, 1045 (8th Cir. 1998).

(7) In *People v. Mroczko*, 672 P.2d 835 (Cal. 1983), the California Supreme Court recognized that a right to conflict-free counsel may normally be waived. The court then went on to require that

> when the court undertakes to appoint counsel, it must initially select separate and independent counsel for each defendant "with an instruction that if counsel concludes, after fully investigating the case and consulting with their clients, that the interests of justice and of the clients will best be served by joint representation, this conclusion with supporting reasons will be communicated to the court for such on-the-record disposition as the court deems appropriate in the circumstances."

The Wyoming Supreme Court went well beyond the federal rule by requiring the trial judge to presume prejudice in all instances of multiple representation of criminal defendants. In all such cases the trial court must separately advise each defendant of the right to individual counsel and the dangers involved with multiple representation. If the defendant wishes to go forward with joint representation, the trial judge must receive a waiver, preferably in writing. The requirement was established under the state constitution. *Shongutsie v. Wyoming*, 827 P.2d 361 (1992).

PROBLEM B
LAWYERS' PERSONAL INTERESTS

The defendant was charged with first-degree murder. Her defense was that she shot her sleeping husband after years of abuse because she was suffering from "post-traumatic stress disorder and battered wife syndrome." The government offered the defendant an opportunity to plead guilty to voluntary manslaughter, a probational offense. Following the strong advice of her lawyer, the defendant went to trial, was found guilty of murder and was sentenced to two consecutive life sentences. The trial lawyer here had believed that the successful presentation of the self-defense theory "would bring him increased clientele and national acclaim." The court found that the defendant's rights had been violated because the lawyer "based his recommendation and tactical decisions upon factors that would further his personal ambitions as opposed to his client's best interests." *Larson v. State*, 766 P.2d 261 (Nev. 1988).

§ 4.03 THE RIGHT TO A *PRO SE* DEFENSE

FARETTA v. CALIFORNIA
United States Supreme Court
422 U.S. 806 (1975)

MR. JUSTICE STEWART delivered the opinion of the Court.

The Sixth and Fourteenth Amendments of our Constitution guarantee that a person brought to trial in any state or federal court must be afforded the right to the assistance of counsel before he can be validly convicted and punished by imprisonment.

The question before us now is whether a defendant in a state criminal trial has a constitutional right to proceed *without* counsel when he voluntarily and intelligently elects to do so. Stated another way, the question is whether a State may constitutionally hale a person into its criminal courts and there force a lawyer upon him, even when he insists that he wants to conduct his own defense. It is not an easy question, but we have concluded that a State may not constitutionally do so.

I

Anthony Faretta was charged with grand theft. . . . At the arraignment, the Superior Court Judge assigned to preside at the trial appointed the public defender to represent Faretta. Well before the date of trial, however, Faretta requested that he be permitted to represent himself. Questioning by the judge revealed that Faretta had once represented himself in a criminal prosecution, that he had a high school education, and that he did not want to be represented by the public defender because he believed that that office was "very loaded down with . . . a heavy case load." The judge responded that he believed Faretta was "making a mistake" and emphasized that in further proceedings Faretta would receive no special favors. Nevertheless, after establishing that Faretta wanted to represent himself and did not want a lawyer, the judge, in a "preliminary ruling," accepted Faretta's waiver of the assistance of counsel. The judge indicated, however, that he might reverse this ruling if it later appeared that Faretta was unable adequately to represent himself.

Several weeks thereafter, but still prior to trial, the judge *sua sponte* held a hearing to inquire into Faretta's ability to conduct his own defense, and questioned him specifically about both the hearsay rule and the state law governing the challenge of potential jurors.[3] After consideration of Faretta's answers, and

---

[3] [3] The colloquy was as follows:

THE COURT: In the Faretta matter, I brought you back down here to do some reconsideration as to whether or not you should continue to represent yourself. How have you been getting along on your research?

THE DEFENDANT: Not bad, your Honor. Last night I put in the mail a 995 motion and it should be with the Clerk within the next day or two.

THE COURT: Have you been preparing yourself for the intricacies of the trial of the matter?

THE DEFENDANT: Well, your Honor, I was hoping that the case could possibly be disposed of on the 995. Mrs. Ayers informed me yesterday that it was the Court's policy to hear the pretrial motions at the time of trial. If possible, your Honor, I would like a date set as soon as the Court deems adequate after they receive the motion, sometime before trial.

THE COURT: Let's see how you have been doing on your research. How many exceptions are there to the hearsay rule?

THE DEFENDANT: Well, the hearsay rule would, I guess, be called the best evidence rule, your Honor. And there are several exceptions in case law, but in actual statutory law, I don't feel there is none.

THE COURT: What are the challenges to the jury for cause?

THE DEFENDANT: Well, there is twelve peremptory challenges.

THE COURT: And how many for cause?

THE DEFENDANT: Well, as many as the Court deems valid.

THE COURT: And what are they? What are the grounds for challenging a juror for cause?

THE DEFENDANT: Well, numerous grounds to challenge a witness-I mean, a juror, your Honor, one

observation of his demeanor, the judge ruled that Faretta had not made an intelligent and knowing waiver of his right to the assistance of counsel, and also ruled that Faretta had no constitutional right to conduct his own defense. The judge, accordingly, reversed his earlier ruling permitting self-representation and again appointed the public defender to represent Faretta. Faretta's subsequent request for leave to act as co-counsel was rejected, as were his efforts to make certain motions on his own behalf. Throughout the subsequent trial, the judge required that Faretta's defense be conducted only through the appointed lawyer from the public defender's office. At the conclusion of the trial, the jury found Faretta guilty as charged, and the judge sentenced him to prison.

II

In the federal courts, the right of self-representation has been protected by statute since the beginnings of our Nation.

With few exceptions, each of the several States also accords a defendant the right

---

being the juror is perhaps suffered, was a victim of the same type of offense, might be prejudiced toward the defendant. Any substantial ground that might make the juror prejudice[d] toward the defendant.

THE COURT: Anything else?

THE DEFENDANT: Well, a relative perhaps of the victim.

THE COURT: Have you taken a look at that code section to see what it is?

THE DEFENDANT: Challenge a juror?

THE COURT: Yes.

THE DEFENDANT: Yes, your Honor. I have done—

THE COURT: What is the code section?

THE DEFENDANT: On voir diring a jury, your Honor?

THE COURT: Yes.

THE DEFENDANT: I am not aware of section right offhand.

THE COURT: What code is it in?

THE DEFENDANT: Well, the research I have done on challenging would be in Witkins Jurisprudence.

THE COURT: Have you looked at any of the codes to see where these various things are taken up?

THE DEFENDANT: No, your Honor, I haven't.

THE COURT: Have you looked in any of the California Codes with reference to trial procedure?

THE DEFENDANT: Yes, your Honor.

THE COURT: What codes?

THE DEFENDANT: I have done extensive research in the Penal Code, your Honor, and the Civil Code.

THE COURT: If you have done extensive research into it, then tell me about it.

THE DEFENDANT: On empaneling a jury, your Honor?

THE COURT: Yes.

THE DEFENDANT: Well, the District Attorney and the defendant, defense counsel, has both the right to 12 peremptory challenges of a jury. These 12 challenges are undisputable. Any reason that the defense or prosecution should feel that a juror would be inadequate to try the case or to rule on a case, they may then discharge that juror.

But if there is a valid challenge due to grounds of prejudice or some other grounds, that these aren't considered in the 12 peremptory challenges. There are numerous and the defendant, the defense, and the prosecution both have the right to make any inquiry to the jury as to their feelings toward the case.

to represent himself in any criminal case. The constitutions of 36 States explicitly confer that right. Moreover, many state courts have expressed the view that the right is also supported by the Constitution of the United States.

III

This consensus is soundly premised. The right of self-representation finds support in the structure of the Sixth Amendment, as well as in the English and colonial jurisprudence from which the Amendment emerged.

A

The Sixth Amendment includes a compact statement of the rights necessary to a full defense:

> In all criminal prosecutions, the accused shall enjoy the right . . . to be informed of the nature and cause of the accusation; to be confronted with the witnesses against him; to have compulsory process for obtaining witnesses in his favor, and to have the Assistance of Counsel for his defence.

Because these rights are basic to our adversary system of criminal justice, they are part of the "due process of law" that is guaranteed by the Fourteenth Amendment to defendants in the criminal courts of the States. The rights to notice, confrontation, and compulsory process, when taken together, guarantee that a criminal charge may be answered in a manner now considered fundamental to the fair administration of American justice — through the calling and interrogation of favorable witnesses, the cross-examination of adverse witnesses, and the orderly introduction of evidence.

The Sixth Amendment does not provide merely that a defense shall be made for the accused; it grants to the accused personally the right to make his defense. It is the accused, not counsel, who must be "informed of the nature and cause of the accusation," who must be "confronted with the witnesses against him," and who must be accorded "compulsory process for obtaining witnesses in his favor." Although not stated in the Amendment in so many words, the right to self-representation — to make one's own defense personally — is thus necessarily implied by the structure of the Amendment. The right to defend is given directly to the accused; for it is he who suffers the consequences if the defense fails.

The counsel provision supplements this design. It speaks of the "assistance" of counsel, and an assistant, however expert, is still an assistant. The language and spirit of the Sixth Amendment contemplate that counsel, like the other defense tools guaranteed by the Amendment, shall be an aid to a willing defendant — not an organ of the State interposed between an unwilling defendant and his right to defend himself personally. To thrust counsel upon the accused, against his considered wish, thus violates the logic of the Amendment.

B

The Sixth Amendment, when naturally read, thus implies a right of self-representation. This reading is reinforced by the Amendment's roots in English legal history.

In the long history of British criminal jurisprudence, there was only one tribunal that ever adopted a practice of forcing counsel upon an unwilling defendant in a criminal proceeding. The tribunal was the Star Chamber.

The common-law rule . . . has evidently always been that "no person charged with a criminal offence can have counsel forced upon him against his will."

In the American Colonies the insistence upon a right of self-representation was, if anything, more fervent than in England.

The right of self-representation was guaranteed in many colonial charters and declarations of rights. These early documents establish that the "right to counsel" meant to the colonists a right to choose between pleading through a lawyer and representing oneself. After the Declaration of Independence, the right of self-representation, along with other rights basic to the making of a defense, entered the new state constitutions in wholesale fashion.

In sum, there is no evidence that the colonists and the Framers ever doubted the right of self-representation, or imagined that this right might be considered inferior to the right of assistance of counsel. To the contrary, the colonists and the Framers, as well as their English ancestors, always conceived of the right to counsel as an "assistance" for the accused, to be used at his option, in defending himself. The Framers selected in the Sixth Amendment a form of words that necessarily implies the right of self-representation. That conclusion is supported by centuries of consistent history.

IV

There can be no blinking the fact that the right of an accused to conduct his own defense seems to cut against the grain of this Court's decisions holding that the Constitution requires that no accused can be convicted and imprisoned unless he has been accorded the right to the assistance of counsel.

For it is surely true that the basic thesis of those decisions is that the help of a lawyer is essential to assure the defendant a fair trial. And a strong argument can surely be made that the whole thrust of those decisions most inevitably lead to the conclusion that a State may constitutionally impose a lawyer upon even an unwilling defendant.

But it is one thing to hold that every defendant, rich or poor, has the right to the assistance of counsel, and quite another to say that a State may compel a defendant to accept a lawyer he does not want. The value of state-appointed counsel was not unappreciated by the Founders, yet the notion of compulsory counsel was utterly foreign to them. And whatever else may be said of those who wrote the Bill of Rights, surely there can be no doubt that they understood the inestimable worth of free choice.

It is undeniable that in most criminal prosecutions defendants could better defend with counsel's guidance than by their own unskilled efforts. But where the defendant will not voluntarily accept representation by counsel, the potential advantage of a lawyer's training and experience can be realized, if at all, only imperfectly. To force a lawyer on a defendant can only lead him to believe that the law contrives against him. Moreover, it is not inconceivable that in some rare instances, the defendant might in fact present his case more effectively by conducting his own defense. Personal liberties are not rooted in the law of averages. The right to defend is personal. The defendant, and not his lawyer or the State, will bear the personal consequences of a conviction. It is the defendant, therefore, who must be free personally to decide whether in his particular case counsel is to his advantage. And although he may conduct his own defense ultimately to his own detriment, his choice must be honored out of "that respect for the individual which is the lifeblood of the law."

V

When an accused manages his own defense, he relinquishes, as a purely factual matter, many of the traditional benefits associated with the right to counsel. For this reason, in order to represent himself, the accused must "knowingly and intelligently" forgo those relinquished benefits. *Johnson v. Zerbst.*

Although a defendant need not himself have the skill and experience of a lawyer in order competently and intelligently to choose self-representation, he should be made aware of the dangers and disadvantages of self-representation, so that the record will establish that "he knows what he is doing and his choice is made with eyes open."

Here, weeks before trial, Faretta clearly and unequivocally declared to the trial judge that he wanted to represent himself and did not want counsel. The record affirmatively shows that Faretta was literate, competent, and understanding, and that he was voluntarily exercising his informed free will. The trial judge had warned Faretta that he thought it was a mistake not to accept the assistance of counsel, and that Faretta would be required to follow all the "ground rules" of trial procedure.

In forcing Faretta, under these circumstances, to accept against his will a state-appointed public defender, the California courts deprived him of his constitutional right to conduct his own defense. Accordingly, the judgment before us is vacated, and the case is remanded for further proceedings not inconsistent with this opinion.

It is so ordered.

Chief Justice Burger and Justices Blackmun and Rehnquist dissented.

NOTES AND QUESTIONS

(1) Did the Court establish a right of self-representation, or simply the traditional right of the defendant to waive his right to counsel? Note that Justice Stewart was very clear in stating that "a defendant has a constitutionally protected

right to represent himself in a criminal trial" which is not "inferior to the right of assistance of counsel."

(2) If there is a right of self-representation, before that right can be exercised the defendant must make "an intentional relinquishment or abandonment of" the right to counsel. *Johnson v. Zerbst*, 304 U.S. 458, 464 (1938). Will there be cases in which the defendant is not competent to waive counsel? Stated another way, will there be situations in which the defendant is not competent to exercise his constitutional right of self-representation? The Court in *Wade v. Mayo*, 334 U.S. 672, 684 (1948), stated: "There are some individuals who, by reason of age, ignorance or mental capacity, are incapable of representing themselves adequately in a prosecution of a relatively simple nature." The difficulty arises here when the defendant is found competent to stand trial, but there is some question as to whether he can waive counsel and effectively represent himself. The Supreme Court held that the standard for waiving the right to counsel is generally no higher than the competency standard for standing trial. *Godinez v. Moran*, 509 U.S. 389 (1993). Hence, it is error for the trial court to hold that the defendant is competent to stand trial, but not capable of self-representation. *Peters v. Gunn*, 33 F.3d 1190 (9th Cir. 1994). However, in a decision answering one long standing question in self-representation cases, the United States Supreme Court, in *Indiana v. Edwards*, 554 U.S. 208 (2008), held that the standards for competency to stand trial and competency to represent oneself are not necessarily always the same. In deciding whether an individual could represent herself, a trial judge may "take realistic account of the particular defendant's mental capacities." In doing so, the court could determine that the strong interest in a fair trial outweighs the usual Sixth Amendment right to self-representation. Following the decision in *Edwards*, the California Supreme Court denied self-representation to a defendant who was found competent to stand trial. Finding the defendant to be suffering from a delusional thought disorder, the court affirmed the trial judge's decision, because the defendant could not "carry out the basic tasks needed to present the defense without the help of counsel." The opinion noted, however, that "[s]elf-representation by defendants who wish it and validly waive counsel remains the norm and may not be denied lightly." *People v. Johnson*, 267 P.3d 1125 (Cal. 2012). As explained in *Holland v. Tucker*, 854 F. Supp. 2d 1229, 1267 (S.D. Fla. 2012):

> [The] correct standard was not whether Mr. Holland was competent to represent himself because of his legal ability or training but rather was *he competent to waive his Sixth Amendment right to counsel and was that waiver knowing and voluntary* having been made aware of the dangers and disadvantages of self-representation, so that the record would establish that Mr. Holland knew what he was doing and his choice was made with eyes open.

(3) Applying the *Faretta* rule has sometimes been difficult. See, for example, *Colon v. State*, 717 S.W.2d 474 (Tex. App. 1986), where the trial judge was very concerned with defendant's inability to represent himself against theft charges. She repeatedly questioned him as to his wishes and finally appointed counsel due to defendant's lack of knowledge and experience. The court on appeal reversed the defendant's conviction:

> Although it is clear that appellant had no experience in conducting a trial, the record reflects that he was at all times respectful and obedient to the trial judge and that his request to represent himself was not made for purposes of delay. To hold that citizens are unduly disruptive merely because they are inexperienced in the practice of law is tantamount to holding that only attorneys enjoy a constitutional right to self-representation. The record does not support the conclusion that appellant's request to represent himself would have disrupted court proceedings to a degree that would have affected the administration of justice.

The court in *United States v. Baker*, 84 F.3d 1263, 1267 (10th Cir. 1996), agreed with this approach. In response to the argument that defendant could not effectively represent himself, the court wrote:

> The district court's reasons for disallowing Mr. Baker to represent himself are contrary to precedent. The district court focused on Mr. Baker's lack of legal knowledge and its concern that without an attorney he would not have his day in court. We have held "that a court determination that an accused lacks expertise or professional capabilities cannot justify denying the right of self-representation." Any prejudice Mr. Baker may have suffered by foregoing his right to legal representation was a risk he knowingly wished to incur. It is also important to note that the district court's concern of Mr. Baker being successful in an appeal on the ground of ineffective assistance of counsel was unfounded as "a defendant who exercises his right to appear *pro se* cannot thereafter complain that the quality of his own defense amounted to a denial of effective assistance of counsel." In this case, Mr. Baker clearly and unequivocally requested the right to represent himself in a timely manner. It is evident from the record that Mr. Baker understood his rights and wished to knowingly waive them. There is no indication that he was incompetent to do so.

A very different view was taken in *State v. Russo*, 530 A.2d 46, 50 (N.J. 1986), where the defendant was convicted of a capital offense. He, too, wished to represent himself. His request was denied.

> The indictment under which this defendant is charged contains nineteen counts of violent crimes, against three victims, alleging capital murder, armed robbery, kidnapping and weapons offenses. It will take skilled, competent counsel to appropriately contest, pre-trial through post-trial, the validity and sufficiency of these charges. Proper motions, timely objections and necessary side bar conferences or recesses are anticipated by the court, and the court should not conduct the case for the defendant if the defendant does not so perform.
>
> The State will produce several expert witnesses. These witnesses should be properly questioned by the defense, but the defendant admitted that he had no experience or training concerning this area. The Court should not be expected to undertake that task.
>
> The trial of a capital case is conducted in two phases, the guilt phase and the penalty phase. Such a trial requires at least two skilled, knowledgeable

> attorneys to properly prepare the case and conduct the defense. The complexities are many and the duties must be shared by the attorneys. Preparation prior to trial, with the demands of discovery, the interview of witnesses and preparations of motions, combined with the conduct of the actual trial and the arrangement for witnesses to testify, the direct and cross-examination of witnesses, the procedural matters involving objections, motions, requests for charge and evaluation of the court's instructions to the jury, would tax the skill and endurance of two lawyers: it would overwhelm the non-lawyer *pro se* defendant.

The California State Supreme Court upheld the right of self-representation in capital cases in *People v. Clark*, 789 P.2d 127 (Cal. 1990). The trial judge in *United States v. Davis*, 150 F. Supp. 2d 918 (E.D. La. 2001), ruled that the self-representation right did not apply to a capital case. On appeal, however, the court disagreed, finding the defendant had a Sixth Amendment right to represent himself, a right which includes the "ability to preserve actual control over the case he chooses to present to the jury." 285 F.3d 378, 385 (5th Cir. 2002).

In *Fields v. Murray*, 49 F.3d 1024 (4th Cir. 1995), the court was faced with a particularly difficult *Faretta* problem. There the defendant was charged with sexual assault against children. He wished to represent himself and conduct cross-examinations of the complaining children. The trial judge adamantly refused his request, stating, "You can forget about my allowing you to cross-examine these young children." Did this ruling violate the defendant's Sixth Amendment rights? Held, over a strong dissent, no violation had occurred. Compare the majority and dissenting opinions.

Majority:

> [T]he purposes of Fields' self-representation right, to allow Fields to affirm his dignity and autonomy and to present what he believes is his best possible defense, would have been "otherwise assured," even though he was prevented from cross-examining personally the girls who were witnesses against him.
>
> Further, the trial court adequately found that preventing this cross-examination was necessary to further the State's important interest in protecting child sexual abuse victims from further trauma.

Dissent:

> There is no doubt that concern for children can, and should, force accommodations of some constitutional rights; but the right with which we deal here is particularly important, not only to the defendant who is denied his right to defend himself personally against the charges brought against him, but also to our system of justice as a whole, which is made less fair by telling some defendants that they may not serve as their own defense counsel.

Which of the opinions more faithfully applies *Faretta*?

FORM

[Here is a standard waiver of counsel form which has been used in various courts.]

(a) **Generally.** The defendant may waive the right to be represented by counsel.

(b) **Proceedings Before an Issuing Authority.** When the defendant seeks to waive the right to counsel in a summary case or for a preliminary hearing in a court case, the issuing authority shall ascertain from the defendant whether this is a knowing, voluntary and intelligent waiver of counsel. In addition, the waiver shall be in writing, signed by the defendant and the issuing authority, be made a part of the record and be in the following form:

WAIVER OF COUNSEL

I, ________________________, (name of defendant) have been told that I have the right to have a lawyer represent me, and the right to have a free lawyer appointed to represent me without cost to me if I cannot afford to pay a lawyer. I give up these rights and I choose to act as my own lawyer at this hearing/trial.

____________, ____________ Date, Defendant

I have determined that the defendant has made a knowing, voluntary and intelligent waiver of his right to counsel.

____

Issuing Authority

(c) **Proceedings Before a Judge.** When the defendant seeks to waive the right to counsel after the preliminary hearing, the judge shall ascertain from the defendant, on the record, whether this is a knowing, voluntary and intelligent waiver of counsel.

(d) **Standby Counsel.** When the defendant's waiver of counsel is accepted, standby counsel may be appointed for the defendant. Standby counsel shall attend the proceedings and shall be available to the defendant for consultation and advice.

NOTES AND QUESTIONS

(1) Related to the problem discussed above is the question of whether the defendant's self-representation will disrupt the court proceedings. There is little doubt that if the defendant is unruly he or she may be removed from the courtroom and the trial continued without his or her presence. *Illinois v. Allen*, 397 U.S. 337, 343 (1970); *see* § 7.03[A], *infra*. But the risk of danger or disruption must be clear before the defendant can be denied the right of self-representation. For an exchange between judges on how clear that risk must be, see *People v. Butler*, 219 P.3d 982 (Cal. 2009) [record of violent conduct and jail restrictions not sufficient.]

(2) Some defendants want to handle part of the trial but also have an attorney handle other parts of it. Many courts take the position that trial judges can properly

refuse the defendant the opportunity to conduct his defense with the assistance of counsel. *Harris v. State*, 687 A.2d 970 (Md. 1997), *cert. denied*, 552 U.S. 1017 ["The (two) rights are 'mutually exclusive' and the defendant cannot assert both simultaneously."] As stated by the Sixth Circuit in *United States v. Gerritsen*, 571 F.3d 1001, 1007 (9th Cir. 2009):

> A defendant therefore has two correlative and mutually exclusive Sixth Amendment rights: the right to have counsel, on one hand, and the right to refuse counsel and represent himself, on the other.

The court in *State v. Martin*, 816 N.E.2d 227 (Ohio 2004), strongly supported this view, emphasizing the ethical issues for defense counsel if the lawyer and the defendant disagree about trial tactics. Are these cases good law under *Faretta? See United States v. Irorere*, 228 F.3d 816, 827 n.2 (7th Cir. 2000): "When a criminal defendant decides to proceed *pro se*, it is generally advisable for the district court to appoint 'shadow counsel' to be available to assist the defendant if needed." See also *State v. Frye*, 617 A.2d 1382 (Conn. 1992), where the defendant was allowed to conduct his own defense and also to use counsel for the purpose of "advising" him during trial.

(3) In *State v. Garcia*, 600 P.2d 1010 (Wa. 1979), the Washington Supreme Court held that there was no obligation on the trial court to advise the defendant of the self-representation right prior to trial.

> In the vast majority of cases it is contrary to the best interests of a defendant to proceed *pro se*. Routinely informing all defendants of that "right" or inquiring whether they wish to exercise it would encourage many to waive the valuable right to be represented by competent counsel. Further, a defendant cannot claim that by having counsel — because he was not informed of his self-representation right or asked if he wished to waive it — he has been denied a fair trial or due process.

Several courts have found that the request for self-representation must be clear; it cannot be equivocal. *See, e.g., United States v. Mendez-Sanchez*, 563 F.3d 935 (9th Cir. 2009):

> [B]ecause the exercise of self-representation cuts off the exercise of the right to counsel, often to individual detriment, we recognize the right only when it is asserted without equivocation . . . . [I]f [the defendant] equivocates, he is presumed to have requested the assistance of counsel.

Are these correct readings of *Faretta*?

(4) Is the trial court obliged to explain the problems of self-representation to the defendant after she has said she wishes to represent herself? Numerous courts had found such an obligation, absent which there could be no knowing and intelligent decision as to self-representation. Indeed, the Iowa Supreme Court determined that such a decision by the defendant would not be valid without advice by the trial judge which indicated that viable defenses might only be seen by a lawyer and that decisions regarding the prosecution (and whether to plead guilty) would be more wisely made with input by counsel. The United States Supreme Court unanimously rejected this view, concluding that no specific formula is

constitutionally required so long as the judge decides that the defendant fully understands her options. *Iowa v. Tovar*, 541 U.S. 77 (2004). The Court went on to remark, though, that the states are permitted to adopt specific rules regarding warnings to be given to defendants, even though such rules would not be mandated by the federal constitution. The Indiana Supreme Court — exercising its supervisory power — now requires trial judges to warn defendants of the dangers of self representation. *Hopper v. State*, 934 N.E.2d 1086 (Ind. 2010).

(5) Should the prosecutor relish the notion of having as an adversary a *pro se* litigant? *See* Frey, *The State v. The Self-Represented: A Florida Prosecutor's Concerns When Litigating Against a Pro Se Defendant in a Criminal Trial*, 29 Stetson L. Rev. 181, 183 (1999):

> At first blush, it would appear that a prosecutor would eagerly greet the opportunity to oppose a *pro se* defendant. After all, trying a case against a presumably untrained, unskilled opponent seems simple, correct? It should be a slam-dunk, right? This is not necessarily the case. In fact, many prosecutors absolutely dread opposing *pro se* litigants. Meeting and opposing the self-represented may involve difficulties that are not present in cases where a defendant is represented by counsel. Most *pro se* defendants are not practiced litigators. Consequently, most have little or no knowledge of or experience with rules of evidence, rules of procedure, or nuances associated with the proper preparation and trial of criminal cases. Because cases do not necessarily begin and end with trial, these concerns range from pretrial matters through closing argument.

For a strong argument in support of the right of self-representation, *see* Hashimoto, *Defending the Right of Self-Representation: An Empirical Look at the Pro Se Felony Defendant*, 85 N.C. L. Rev. 423 (2007).

Does the rule of self-representation apply to appeals as well as to trials? The United States Supreme Court answered this question in the negative in *Martinez v. California*, 528 U.S. 152 (2000) ("Our experience has taught us that (self-representation) is usually a bad defense, particularly when compared to a defense provided by an experienced criminal defense attorney.").

PROBLEM C
STANDBY COUNSEL

After granting the defendant's request to represent himself, the trial court designated two appointed attorneys only as standby counsel to serve "in a purely advisory capacity." One of the lawyers soon began to actively participate, over the defendant's objection. Does such participation violate *Faretta? See McKaskle v. Wiggins*, 465 U.S. 168 (1984):

> *Faretta* affirmed the defendant's constitutional right to appear on stage at his trial. We recognize that a *pro se* defendant may wish to dance a solo, not a *pas de deux.* Standby counsel must generally respect that preference. But counsel need not be excluded altogether, especially when the participation is outside the presence of the jury or is with the defendant's express or tacit

consent. The defendant in this case was allowed to make his own appearance as he saw fit. In our judgment counsel's unsolicited involvement was held within reasonable limits.

In *Hill v. United States*, 959 A.2d 702 (D.C. App. 2008), the defendant objected to having the "stand-by" lawyer physically near him in sight of the jury. Held, no error, for the lawyer took no "kind of excessively intrusive actions which undercut the jury's perception that the self-represented defendant is in actual control of his defense."

§ 4.04 WHEN THE RIGHT APPLIES

While the Court was struggling to define the concept of right to counsel and decide in what sorts of trials that right would apply, it was also attempting to determine at which proceedings the right would attach. *Betts*, *Gideon* and *Argersinger* all involved the question of the services of an attorney *at trial*. There was little doubt, however, that the Sixth Amendment protection went beyond trial, encompassing proceedings both before and after the trial. In perhaps the most famous trio of criminal procedure cases ever decided on one day, the Sixth Amendment counsel right was applied broadly to pretrial identifications.

THE TRILOGY

UNITED STATES v. WADE

United States Supreme Court
388 U.S. 218 (1967)

Mr. Justice Brennan delivered the opinion of the Court.

The question here is whether courtroom identifications of an accused at trial are to be excluded from evidence because the accused was exhibited to the witnesses before trial at a post-indictment lineup conducted for identification purposes without notice to and in the absence of the accused's appointed counsel.

The federally insured bank in Eustace, Texas, was robbed on September 21, 1964. A man with a small strip of tape on each side of his face entered the bank, pointed a pistol at the female cashier and the vice president, the only persons in the bank at the time, and forced them to fill a pillowcase with the bank's money. The man then drove away with an accomplice who had been waiting in a stolen car outside the bank. On March 23, 1965, an indictment was returned against respondent, Wade, and two others for conspiring to rob the bank, and against Wade and the accomplice for the robbery itself. Wade was arrested on April 2, and counsel was appointed to represent him on April 26. Fifteen days later an FBI agent, without notice to Wade's lawyer, arranged to have the two bank employees observe a lineup made up of Wade and five or six other prisoners and conducted in a courtroom of the local county courthouse. Each person in the line wore strips of tape such as allegedly worn by the robber and upon direction each said something like "put the money in the bag," the words allegedly uttered by the robber. Both bank employees identified Wade in the lineup as the bank robber.

At trial the two employees, when asked on direct examination if the robber was in the courtroom, pointed to Wade. The prior lineup identification was then elicited from both employees on cross-examination.

I

Neither the lineup itself nor anything shown by this record that Wade was required to do in the lineup violated his privilege against self-incrimination. We have only recently reaffirmed that the privilege "protects an accused only from being compelled to testify against himself, or otherwise provide the State with evidence of a testimonial or communicative nature. . . ." *Schmerber v. State of California.*

We there held that compelling a suspect to submit to a withdrawal of a sample of his blood for analysis for alcohol content and the admission in evidence of the analysis report were not compulsion to those ends.

We have no doubt that compelling the accused merely to exhibit his person for observation by a prosecution witness prior to trial involves no compulsion of the accused to give evidence having testimonial significance. It is compulsion of the accused to exhibit his physical characteristics, not compulsion to disclose any knowledge he might have. It is no different from compelling Schmerber to provide a blood sample and, is not within the cover of the privilege. Similarly, compelling Wade to speak within hearing distance of the witnesses, even to utter words purportedly uttered by the robber, was not compulsion to utter statements of a "testimonial" nature; he was required to use his voice as an identifying physical characteristic, not to speak his guilt. We held in *Schmerber*, that the distinction to be drawn under the Fifth Amendment privilege against self-incrimination is one between an accused's "communications" in whatever form, vocal or physical, and "compulsion which makes a suspect or accused the source of 'real or physical evidence'."

II

[I]n this case it is urged that the assistance of counsel at the lineup was indispensable to protect Wade's most basic right as a criminal defendant — his right to a fair trial at which the witnesses against him might be meaningfully cross-examined.

When the Bill of Rights was adopted, there were no organized police forces as we know them today. The accused confronted the prosecutor and the witnesses against him, and the evidence was marshalled, largely at the trial itself. In contrast, today's law enforcement machinery involves critical confrontations of the accused by the prosecution at pretrial proceedings where the results might well settle the accused's fate and reduce the trial itself to a mere formality. In recognition of these realities of modern criminal prosecution, our cases have construed the Sixth Amendment guarantee to apply to "critical" stages of the proceedings. The guarantee reads: "In all criminal prosecutions, the accused shall enjoy the right . . . to have the Assistance of Counsel . . . *for his defence.*" (Emphasis supplied.) The plain wording of this guarantee thus encompasses counsel's assistance whenever necessary to assure a meaningful "defence."

As early as *Powell v. State of Alabama*, we recognized that the period from arraignment to trial was "perhaps the most critical period of the proceedings . . . ," during which the accused "requires the guiding hand of counsel. . . ."

That principle has since been applied to require the assistance of counsel at the type of arraignment — for example, that provided by Alabama — where certain rights might be sacrificed or lost: "What happens there may affect the whole trial. Available defenses may be irretrievably lost, if not then and there asserted. . . ." *Hamilton v. State of Alabama.*

[I]n addition to counsel's presence at trial, the accused is guaranteed that he need not stand alone against the State at any stage of the prosecution, formal or informal, in court or out, where counsel's absence might derogate from the accused's right to a fair trial. The security of that right is as much the aim of the right to counsel as it is of the other guarantees of the Sixth Amendment — the right of the accused to a speedy and public trial by an impartial jury, his right to be informed of the nature and cause of the accusation, and his right to be confronted with the witnesses against him and to have compulsory process for obtaining witnesses in his favor. The presence of counsel at such critical confrontations, as at the trial itself, operates to assure that the accused's interests will be protected consistently with our adversary theory of criminal prosecution.

In sum, the principle of *Powell v. Alabama* and succeeding cases requires that we scrutinize *any* pretrial confrontation of the accused to determine whether the presence of his counsel is necessary to preserve the defendant's basic right to a fair trial as affected by his right meaningfully to cross-examine the witnesses against him and to have effective assistance of counsel at the trial itself. It calls upon us to analyze whether potential substantial prejudice to defendant's rights inheres in the particular confrontation and the ability of counsel to help avoid that prejudice.

III

The Government characterizes the lineup as a mere preparatory step in the gathering of the prosecution's evidence, not different — for Sixth Amendment purposes — from various other preparatory steps, such as systematized or scientific analyzing of the accused's fingerprints, blood sample, clothing, hair, and the like. We think there are differences which preclude such stages being characterized as critical stages at which the accused has the right to the presence of his counsel. Knowledge of the techniques of science and technology is sufficiently available, and the variables in techniques few enough, that the accused has the opportunity for a meaningful confrontation of the Government's case at trial through the ordinary processes of cross-examination of the Government's expert witnesses and the presentation of the evidence of his own experts. The denial of a right to have his counsel present at such analyses does not therefore violate the Sixth Amendment; they are not critical stages since there is minimal risk that his counsel's absence at such stages might derogate from his right to a fair trial.

IV

But the confrontation compelled by the State between the accused and the victim or witnesses to a crime to elicit identification evidence is peculiarly riddled with innumerable dangers and variable factors which might seriously, even crucially, derogate from a fair trial. The vagaries of eyewitness identification are well-known; the annals of criminal law are rife with instances of mistaken identification. Mr. Justice Frankfurter once said: "What is the worth of identification testimony even when uncontradicted? The identification of strangers is proverbially untrustworthy. The hazards of such testimony are established by a formidable number of instances in the records of English and American trials. These instances are recent — not due to the brutalities of ancient criminal procedure." *The Case of Sacco and Vanzetti* 30 (1927). A major factor contributing to the high incidence of miscarriage of justice from mistaken identification has been the degree of suggestion inherent in the manner in which the prosecution presents the suspect to witnesses for pretrial identification. A commentator has observed that "[t]he influence of improper suggestion upon identifying witnesses probably accounts for more miscarriages of justice than any other single factor — perhaps it is responsible for more such errors than all other factors combined." Wall, *Eye-Witness Identification in Criminal Cases* 26. Suggestion can be created intentionally or unintentionally in many subtle ways. And the dangers for the suspect are particularly grave when the witness' opportunity for observation was insubstantial, and thus his susceptibility to suggestion the greatest.

Moreover, "[i]t is a matter of common experience that once a witness has picked out the accused at the line-up, he is not likely to go back on his word later on, so that in practice the issue of identity may (in the absence of other relevant evidence) for all practical purposes be determined there and then, before the trial."

The pretrial confrontation for purpose of identification may take the form of a lineup, also known as an "identification parade" or "showup," as in the present case, or presentation of the suspect alone to the witness, as in *Stovall v. Denno.* It is obvious that risks of suggestion attend either form of confrontation and increase the dangers inhering in eyewitness identification. But as is the case with secret interrogations, there is serious difficulty in depicting what transpires at lineups and other forms of identification confrontations.

[T]he defense can seldom reconstruct the manner and mode of lineup identification for judge or jury at trial. Those participating in a lineup with the accused may often be police officers; in any event, the participants' names are rarely recorded or divulged at trial. The impediments to an objective observation are increased when the victim is the witness. Lineups are prevalent in rape and robbery prosecutions and present a particular hazard that a victim's understandable outrage may excite vengeful or spiteful motives. In any event, neither witnesses nor lineup participants are apt to be alert for conditions prejudicial to the suspect. And if they were, it would likely be of scant benefit to the suspect since neither witnesses nor lineup participants are likely to be schooled in the detection of suggestive influences. Improper influences may go undetected by a suspect, guilty or not, who experiences the emotional tension which we might expect in one being confronted with potential accusers. Even when he does observe abuse, if he has a criminal record he may be reluctant to take the stand and open up the admission of prior convictions.

Moreover any protestations by the suspect of the fairness of the lineup made at trial are likely to be in vain; the jury's choice is between the accused's unsupported version and that of the police officers present. In short, the accused's inability effectively to reconstruct at trial any unfairness that occurred at the lineup may deprive him of his only opportunity meaningfully to attack the credibility of the witness' courtroom identification.

The potential for improper influence is illustrated by the circumstances, insofar as they appear, surrounding the prior identifications in the three cases we decide today. In the present case, the testimony of the identifying witnesses elicited on cross-examination revealed that those witnesses were taken to the courthouse and seated in the courtroom to await assembly of the lineup. The courtroom faced on a hallway observable to the witnesses through an open door. The cashier testified that she saw Wade "standing in the hall" within sight of an FBI agent. Five or six other prisoners later appeared in the hall. The vice president testified that he saw a person in the hall in the custody of the agent who "resembled the person that we identified as the one that had entered the bank."

The few cases that have surfaced therefore reveal the existence of a process attended with hazards of serious unfairness to the criminal accused and strongly suggest the plight of the more numerous defendants who are unable to ferret out suggestive influences in the secrecy of the confrontation. We do not assume that these risks are the result of police procedures intentionally designed to prejudice an accused. Rather we assume they derive from the dangers inherent in eyewitness identification and the suggestibility inherent in the context of the pretrial identification.

Insofar as the accused's conviction may rest on a courtroom identification in fact the fruit of a suspect pretrial identification which the accused is helpless to subject to effective scrutiny at trial, the accused is deprived of that right of cross-examination which is an essential safeguard to his right to confront the witnesses against him.

And even though cross-examination is a precious safeguard to a fair trial, it cannot be viewed as an absolute assurance of accuracy and reliability. Thus in the present context, where so many variables and pitfalls exist, the first line of defense must be the prevention of unfairness and the lessening of the hazards of eyewitness identification at the lineup itself. The trial which might determine the accused's fate may well not be that in the courtroom but that at the pretrial confrontation, with the State aligned against the accused, the witness, the sole jury, and the accused unprotected against the overreaching, intentional or unintentional, and with little or no effective appeal from the judgment there rendered by the witness — "that's the man."

Since it appears that there is grave potential for prejudice, intentional or not, in the pretrial lineup, which may not be capable of reconstruction at trial, and since presence of counsel itself can often avert prejudice and assure a meaningful confrontation at trial, there can be little doubt that for Wade the post-indictment lineup was a critical stage of the prosecution at which he was "as much entitled to such aid [of counsel] as at the trial itself."

Thus both Wade and his counsel should have been notified of the impending lineup, and counsel's presence should have been a requisite to conduct of the lineup, absent an "intelligent waiver."

No substantial countervailing policy considerations have been advanced against the requirement of the presence of counsel. Concern is expressed that the requirement will forestall prompt identifications and result in obstruction of the confrontations. As for the first we note that in the two cases in which the right to counsel is today held to apply, counsel had already been appointed and no argument is made in either case that notice to counsel would have prejudicially delayed the confrontations. Moreover, we leave open the question whether the presence of substitute counsel might not suffice where notification and presence of the suspect's own counsel would result in prejudicial delay. And to refuse to recognize the right to counsel for fear that counsel will obstruct the course of justice is contrary to the basic assumptions upon which this Court has operated in Sixth Amendment cases.

In our view counsel can hardly impede legitimate law enforcement; on the contrary, for the reasons expressed, law enforcement may be assisted by preventing the infiltration of taint in the prosecution's identification evidence.[4] That result cannot help the guilty avoid conviction but can only help assure that the right man has been brought to justice.

Legislative or other regulations, such as those of local police departments, which eliminate the risks of abuse and unintentional suggestion at lineup proceedings and the impediments to meaningful confrontation at trial may also remove the basis for regarding the stage as "critical." But neither Congress nor the federal authorities have seen fit to provide a solution. What we hold today "in no way creates a constitutional straitjacket which will handicap sound efforts at reform, nor is it intended to have this effect."

V

We come now to the question whether the denial of Wade's motion to strike the courtroom identification by the bank witnesses at trial because of the absence of his counsel at the lineup required, as the Court of Appeals held, the grant of a new trial at which such evidence is to be excluded. We do not think this disposition can be justified without first giving the Government the opportunity to establish by clear and convincing evidence that the in-court identifications were based upon observations of the suspect other than the lineup identification. Where, as here, the admissibility of evidence of the lineup identification itself is not involved, a *per se* rule of exclusion of courtroom identification would be unjustified. A rule limited solely to the exclusion of testimony concerning identification at the lineup itself, without regard to admissibility of the courtroom identification, would render the

---

4 [28] Concern is also expressed that the presence of counsel will force divulgence of the identity of government witnesses whose identity the Government may want to conceal. To the extent that this is a valid or significant state interest there are police practices commonly used to effect concealment, for example, masking the face.

right to counsel an empty one. The lineup is most often used, as in the present case, to crystallize the witnesses' identification of the defendant for future reference. We have already noted that the lineup identification will have that effect. The State may then rest upon the witnesses' unequivocal courtroom identification, and not mention the pretrial identification as part of the State's case at trial. Counsel is then in the predicament in which Wade's counsel found himself — realizing that possible unfairness at the lineup may be the sole means of attack upon the unequivocal courtroom identification, and having to probe in the dark in an attempt to discover and reveal unfairness, while bolstering the government witness' courtroom identification by bringing out and dwelling upon his prior identification. Since counsel's presence at the lineup would equip him to attack not only the lineup identification but the courtroom identification as well, limiting the impact of violation of the right to counsel to exclusion of evidence only of identification at the lineup itself disregards a critical element of that right.

We think it follows that the proper test to be applied in these situations is that quoted in *Wong Sun v. United States*, " '[W]hether, granting establishment of the primary illegality, the evidence to which instant objection is made has been come at by exploitation of that illegality or instead by means sufficiently distinguishable to be purged of the primary taint.' Maguire, *Evidence of Guilt*, 221 (1959)."

Application of this test in the present context requires consideration of various factors; for example, the prior opportunity to observe the alleged criminal act, the existence of any discrepancy between any pre-lineup description and the defendant's actual description, any identification prior to lineup of another person, the identification by picture of the defendant prior to the lineup, failure to identify the defendant on a prior occasion, and the lapse of time between the alleged act and the lineup identification. It is also relevant to consider those facts which, despite the absence of counsel, are disclosed concerning the conduct of the lineup.[5]

We doubt that the Court of Appeals applied the proper test for exclusion of the in-court identification of the two witnesses. The court stated that "it cannot be said with any certainty that they would have recognized appellant at the time of trial if this intervening lineup had not occurred," and that the testimony of the two witnesses "may well have been colored by the illegal procedure [and] was prejudicial."

Moreover, the court was persuaded, in part, by the "compulsory verbal responses made by Wade at the instance of the Special Agent." This implies the erroneous holding that Wade's privilege against self-incrimination was violated so that the denial of counsel required exclusion.

---

[5] [33] Thus it is not the case that "[i]t matters not how well the witness knows the suspect, whether the witness is the suspect's mother, brother, or long-time associate, and no matter how long or well the witness observed the perpetrator at the scene of the crime." Such factors will have an important bearing upon the true basis of the witness' in-court identification. Moreover, the State's inability to bolster the witness' courtroom identification by introduction of the lineup identification itself, *see Gilbert v. California, supra*, will become less significant the more the evidence of other opportunities of the witness to observe the defendant. Thus where the witness is a "kidnap victim who has lived for days with his abductor" the value to the State of admission of the lineup identification is indeed marginal, and such identification would be a mere formality.

On the record now before us we cannot make the determination whether the in-court identifications had an independent origin. This was not an issue at trial, although there is some evidence relevant to a determination. That inquiry is most properly made in the District Court. We therefore think the appropriate procedure to be followed is to vacate the conviction pending a hearing to determine whether the in-court identifications had an independent source, or whether, in any event, the introduction of the evidence was harmless error, and for the District Court to reinstate the conviction or order a new trial, as may be proper.

Mr. Justice Black, dissenting in part and concurring in part.

I

In rejecting Wade's claim that his privilege against self-incrimination was violated by compelling him to appear in the lineup wearing the tape and uttering the words given him by the police, the Court relies on the recent holding in *Schmerber v. State of California.* In that case the Court held that taking blood from a man's body against his will in order to convict him of a crime did not compel him to be a witness against himself. I dissented from that holding, and still dissent. The Court's reason for its holding was that the sample of Schmerber's blood taken in order to convict him of crime was neither "testimonial" nor "communicative" evidence. I think it was both. It seems quite plain to me that the Fifth Amendment's Self-incrimination Clause was designed to bar the Government from forcing any person to supply proof of his own crime, precisely what Schmerber was forced to do when he was forced to supply his blood. The Government simply took his blood against his will and over his counsel's protest for the purpose of convicting him of crime. So here, having Wade in its custody awaiting trial to see if he could or would be convicted of crime, the Government forced him to stand in a lineup, wear strips on his face, and speak certain words, in order to make it possible for government witnesses to identify him as a criminal. Had Wade been compelled to utter these or any other words in open court, it is plain that he would have been entitled to a new trial because of having been compelled to be a witness against himself. Being forced by the Government to help convict himself and to supply evidence against himself by talking outside the courtroom is equally violative of his constitutional right not to be compelled to be a witness against himself.

III

I would reverse Wade's conviction without further ado had the prosecution at trial made use of his lineup identification either in place of courtroom identification or to bolster in a harmful manner crucial courtroom identification. But the prosecution here did neither of these things. After prosecution witnesses under oath identified Wade in the courtroom, it was the defense, and not the prosecution, which brought out the prior lineup identification. While stating that "a *per se* rule of exclusion of courtroom identification would be unjustified," the Court, nevertheless remands this case for "a hearing to determine whether the in-court identifications had an independent source," or were the tainted fruits of the invalidly conducted lineup. From this holding I dissent.

In the first place, even if this Court has power to establish such a rule of evidence, I think the rule fashioned by the Court is unsound. The "tainted fruit" determination required by the Court involves more than considerable difficulty. I think it is practically impossible. How is a witness capable of probing the recesses of his mind to draw a sharp line between a courtroom identification due exclusively to an earlier lineup and a courtroom identification due to memory not based on the lineup? What kind of "clear and convincing evidence" can the prosecution offer to prove upon what particular events memories resulting in an in-court identification rest? How long will trials be delayed while judges turn psychologists to probe the subconscious minds of witnesses? All these questions are posed but not answered by the Court's opinion. In my view, the Fifth and Sixth Amendments are satisfied if the prosecution is precluded from using lineup identification as either an alternative to or corroboration of courtroom identification.

MR. JUSTICE WHITE, whom MR. JUSTICE HARLAN and MR. JUSTICE STEWART join, dissenting in part and concurring in part.

The Court has again propounded a broad constitutional rule barring the use of a wide spectrum of relevant and probative evidence, solely because a step in its ascertainment or discovery occurs outside the presence of defense counsel.

The Court's opinion is far-reaching. It proceeds first by creating a new *per se* rule of constitutional law: a criminal suspect cannot be subjected to a pretrial identification process in the absence of his counsel without violating the Sixth Amendment. If he is, the State may not buttress a later courtroom identification of the witness by any reference to the previous identification. Furthermore, the courtroom identification is not admissible at all unless the state can establish by clear and convincing proof that the testimony is not the fruit of the earlier identification made in the absence of defendant's counsel — admittedly a heavy burden for the State and probably an impossible one. To all intents and purposes, courtroom identifications are barred if pretrial identifications have occurred without counsel being present.

The rule applies to any lineup, to any other techniques employed to produce an identification and *a fortiori* to a face-to-face encounter between the witness and the suspect alone, regardless of when the identification occurs in time or place, and whether before or after indictment or information. It matters not how well the witness knows the suspect, whether the witness is the suspect's mother, brother, or long-time associate, and no matter how long or well the witness observed the perpetrator at the scene of the crime. The kidnap victim who has lived for days with his abductor is in the same category as the witness who has had only a fleeting glimpse of the criminal. Neither may identify the suspect without defendant's counsel being present. The same strictures apply regardless of the number of other witnesses who positively identify the defendant and regardless of the corroborative evidence showing that it was the defendant who had committed the crime.

The premise for the Court's rule is not the general unreliability of eyewitness identifications nor the difficulties inherent in observation, recall, and recognition. The Court assumes a narrower evil as the basis for its rule — improper police suggestion which contributes to erroneous identifications. The Court apparently believes that improper police procedures are so widespread that a broad prophylactic rule must be laid down, requiring the presence of counsel at all pretrial identifications, in order to detect recurring instances of police misconduct. I do not share this pervasive distrust of all official investigations. None of the materials the Court relies upon supports it. Certainly, I would bow to solid fact, but the Court quite obviously does not have before it any reliable, comprehensive survey of current police practices on which to base its new rule. Until it does, the Court should avoid excluding relevant evidence from state criminal trials.

MR. JUSTICE FORTAS, with whom the CHIEF JUSTICE and MR. JUSTICE DOUGLAS join, concurring in part and dissenting in part.

1. I agree with the Court that the exhibition of the person of the accused at a lineup is not itself a violation of the privilege against self-incrimination. In itself, it is no more subject to constitutional objection than the exhibition of the person of the accused in the courtroom for identification purposes. It is an incident of the State's power to arrest, and a reasonable and justifiable aspect of the State's custody resulting from arrest. It does not require that the accused take affirmative, volitional action, but only that, having been duly arrested he may be seen for identification purposes. It is, however, a "critical stage" in the prosecution, and I agree with the Court that the opportunity to have counsel present must be made available.

2. In my view, however, the accused may not be compelled in a lineup to speak the words uttered by the person who committed the crime. I am confident that it could not be compelled in court. It cannot be compelled in a lineup. It is more than passive, mute assistance to the eyes of the victim or of witnesses. It is the kind of volitional act — the kind of forced cooperation by the accused — which is within the historical perimeter of the privilege against compelled self-incrimination.

Our history and tradition teach and command that an accused may stand mute. The privilege means just that; not less than that. According to the Court, an accused may be jailed — indefinitely — until he is willing to say, for an identifying audience, whatever was said in the course of the commission of the crime. Presumably this would include, "Your money or your life" — or perhaps, words of assault in a rape case. This is intolerable under our constitutional system.

An accused cannot be compelled to utter the words spoken by the criminal in the course of the crime. I thoroughly disagree with the Court's statement that such compulsion does not violate the Fifth Amendment. The Court relies upon *Schmerber v. State of California*, to support this. I dissented in *Schmerber*, but if it were controlling here, I should, of course, acknowledge its binding effect unless we were prepared to overrule it. But *Schmerber*, which authorized the forced extraction of blood from the veins of an unwilling human being, did not compel the person actively to cooperate — to accuse himself by a volitional act which differs only in degree from compelling him to act out the crime, which, I assume, would be rebuffed by the Court. It is the latter feature which places the compelled utterance by the accused squarely within the history and noble purpose of the Fifth Amendment's commandment.

NOTES AND QUESTIONS

(1) The majority stated clearly why counsel was required in the lineup setting: "[T]he accused's inability effectively to reconstruct at trial any unfairness that occurred at the lineup may deprive him of his only opportunity meaningfully to attack the credibility of the witness' courtroom identification." Is this a sufficient reason for making the presence of counsel mandatory? Can a lawyer truly "often avert prejudice and assure a meaningful confrontation at trial. . . ." What is a lawyer supposed to do to assure this confrontation? Participate in the questioning process? Become a witness at trial if there is unfairness? Does this create any practical problems, any ethical problems?

Should the defendant's attorney be allowed to attend the post-lineup conference when the witness is to make the identification? The courts are split on this point. See *Sams v. Walker*, 18 F.3d 167 (2d Cir. 1994), where the court wrote that there is "no case establishing that, as a matter of federal constitutional law, [the accused has] the right to have his attorney observe the oral portion of the witness's post-lineup identification." The court in *People v. White*, 917 N.E.2d 1018 (Ill. App. Ct. 2009), however, found a Sixth Amendment violation when defense counsel was not allowed to observe the moment of identification of the defendant by the witness.

> [A] general police policy of prohibiting counsel from observing the moment of identification, frustrates the second purpose of *Wade* and *Gilbert*, which is to safeguard against the inherent risks of suggestion (intentional or unintentional) that are present in lineups generally. This is especially true in this case, where defense counsel was in all respects prohibited from any contact with the witnesses or those conducting the lineup.

(2) Justice White asserted that the Court should not adopt a stringent counsel rule without hard evidence that there was widespread police misconduct. Was there evidence of such misconduct? Was that evidence necessary?

(3) Counsel argued that the rule in *Wade* had no impact on the situation where the defendant is identified for the first time at trial and where he "is known to be in custody and charged with the commission of a crime." Does *Wade* apply to this situation? Should it?

(4) The majority contended that legislative or police regulations which eliminated the risks of abuse may remove the counsel requirement. Are such regulations possible? Would recording each lineup be sufficient? Having the witnesses sign sworn affidavits?

(5) Justice Black argued that so long as there was no in-court testimony concerning the pretrial identification, no trial rights were violated. Why did the majority of the Court disagree? How is the taint removed from the earlier illegal identification? Consider the following cases: *Butler v. State*, 102 So. 3d 260 (Miss. 2012) (no taint due to clear opportunity to view, plus good lighting at time of crime); *Moore v. State*, 140 S.W.3d 720 (Tex. App. 2004) (no taint, good and accurate description of the defendant); *United States v. Garner*, 439 F.2d 525 (D.C. Cir. 1970), *cert. denied*, 402 U.S. 930 (1971) (sketch made of defendant by witness, a commercial artist, which was strongly similar to the defendant's appearance dissipated the taint); *United States v. Warden*, 535 F.2d 361 (7th Cir. 1976), *cert.*

denied, 429 U.S. 1045 (1977) (no taint where the witnesses, teenage girls, "stated that their attention had been called to the defendant before he entered the store where the crime took place because they thought he was good looking"). Compare these cases with *People v. Taylor*, 414 N.Y.S.2d 700 (N.Y. 1979):

> Maynard's opportunity to view the perpetrator lasted but a few seconds; she saw only the left profile and she did not initially describe him as a black man to the police. . . . At trial, Maynard admitted that she was not sure of defendant's identity as she observed both victim and assailant through the peephole of her door at the time of the crime. Moreover, at the show up conducted seventeen days later, she was unsure of defendant's identity, and . . . could not identify defendant, a person whom she concededly knew, until he assumed a position conforming to the perpetrator's actions at the time of the crime. . . . In our view Maynard's identification was fraught with doubt. On a review of the record, we cannot conclude that it was unaffected by the earlier tainted procedures.

(6) As Justice Brennan discussed, the Court in the *Schmerber* case held that taking blood from an uncooperative defendant did not infringe that defendant's Fifth Amendment self-incrimination rights. In light of that holding, three separate issues can be raised in connection with pretrial identifications. The first is whether requiring the defendant to appear in a lineup is itself a violation of the Fifth Amendment. This position was taken only by Justice Black.[6]

The second Fifth Amendment issue in *Wade* is whether the defendant can be forced to "assist" the government in the identification, by speaking the words of the criminal, making a voice or handwriting sample, or giving his fingerprints. Once again the majority of the Court found this to be valid, for it was not testimonial in nature and thus did not reach the limits of the self-incrimination right. See also *United States v. Dionisio*, 410 U.S. 1 (1973), where grand jury witnesses were forced to produce voice exemplars. On this participation question, however, there was much less support by the Court's members. Justice Fortas, joined by the Chief Justice and Justice Douglas, took the position in *Wade* that requiring participation was violative of the Fifth Amendment because it was "more than passive, mute assistance to the eyes of the victim or of witnesses." Is this distinction sound? Could the defendant be forced to speak at trial? If not, why can she be forced to speak at the lineup?

The third issue involved here is quite different. If the defendant can be compelled to participate in the lineup, can she compel the government to conduct a lineup when there is a question of eyewitness identification? Most courts have not found the compulsion reciprocal and reject the defendant's claim. *Goree v. Terhune*, 2005 WL 1378846 (E.D. Cal. 2005); *Maxwell v. State*, 10 S.W.3d 785 (Tex. App. 2000) *But see Commonwealth v. Wilder*, 337 A.2d 564 (Pa. 1975) (immediate confrontation request with hospitalized witness). In *People v. Abel*, 271 P.3d 1040, 1059 (Cal. 2012), the California Supreme Court recognized that under certain circumstances (weigh-

---

[6] Actually Justice Douglas, too, stated that "compulsory lineup violates the privilege against self-incrimination contained in the Fifth Amendment." Douglas, however, also joined in Justice Fortas' opinion which specifically said that compulsory lineups were proper so long as the defendant was not required to assist in the identification process by speaking.

ing benefits, reasonableness of request, and burden on prosecution) due process may require a pre-trial lineup, at the defendant's request.

PROBLEM D
COMPELLED PARTICIPATION

The defendant was ordered by the court to give a handwriting sample, responding to words spoken. Apparently, the purpose of the procedure was to determine the defendant's spelling as opposed to his penmanship. Did this order violate the Fifth Amendment? See *United States v. Campbell*, 732 F.2d 1017 (1st Cir. 1984), where the court struck down the order. "When he writes a dictated word, the writer is saying, 'This is how I spell it — A testimonial message in addition to a physical display.' "

NOTE

If the defendant can be required to participate in a lineup, can she be punished for failing to do so? The consistent answer has been affirmative, and the punishment normally takes two forms. Pursuant to court order, the defendant can be held in contempt and actually imprisoned. If the defendant does not participate in the lineup, the prosecutor at trial can also comment to the jury on that failure to participate. *Campbell, supra.*

The defendant in *State v. Reddick*, 619 A.2d 453 (Conn. 1993), moved to suppress identification testimony at trial. The defendant requested that he be allowed to waive his right to be present at the hearing on his motion, during the testimony of the witness. He claimed that his presence would result in improper identification, as he raised questions about the reliability of the cross-racial identification and he was the only African-American in the court room. The majority — over a vigorous dissent — required him to be present. In *United States v. Olvera*, 30 F.3d 1195 (9th Cir. 1994) 513 U.S. 1031 — also over a dissent — the court found that making the defendant recite the words which were spoken during the robbery violated the presumption of innocence. "[The] compelled utterance posed an unacceptably high risk of influencing the jury's judgment in a manner that undermined the presumption of innocence." See also *Logan v. Runnels*, 2011 U.S. Dist. LEXIS 40612 (E.D. Cal. Apr. 13, 2011), where the court was concerned with such an in-court requirement, but found no error because the defendant represented himself at trial so that the jury heard his voice throughout the proceedings.

But see *Morgan v. State*, 558 A.2d 1226 (Md. 1989), where the defendant was required to wear an article of clothing in the courtroom so that the jury could see if it fit him. The court rejected the defendant's self-incrimination claim:

> Requiring a defendant to put on an article of clothing, similar in purpose to fingerprinting, albeit not nearly as conclusive, simply does not constitute an act compelling a testimonial or communicative response. The fact that an article of clothing fits may give rise to an inference of ownership, which under the facts of any given case could be incriminating, is no more a communicative response from the defendant than would be the case where fingerprints were matched.

GILBERT v. CALIFORNIA

United States Supreme Court
388 U.S. 263 (1967)

MR. JUSTICE BRENNAN delivered the opinion of the Court.

This case was argued with *United States v. Wade*, and presents the same alleged constitutional error in the admission in evidence of in-court identifications there considered.

Petitioner was convicted of the armed robbery of the Mutual Savings and Loan Association of Alhambra and the murder of a police officer who entered during the course of the robbery. There were separate guilt and penalty stages of the trial before the same jury, which rendered a guilty verdict and imposed the death penalty.

I. THE HANDWRITING EXEMPLARS.

Petitioner was arrested in Philadelphia by an FBI agent and refused to answer questions about the Alhambra robbery without the advice of counsel. He gave the agent the handwriting exemplars.

First. The taking of the exemplars did not violate petitioner's Fifth Amendment privilege against self-incrimination. The privilege reaches only compulsion of "an accused's communications, whatever form they might take, and the compulsion of responses which are also communications, for example, compliance with a subpoena to produce one's papers," and not "compulsion which makes a suspect or accused the source of 'real or physical evidence. . . .' " *Schmerber v. State of California.*

One's voice and handwriting are, of course, means of communication. It by no means follows, however, that every compulsion of an accused to use his voice or write compels a communication within the cover of the privilege. A mere handwriting exemplar, in contrast to the content of what is written, like the voice or body itself, is an identifying physical characteristic outside its protection. *United States v. Wade.*

Second. The taking of the exemplars was not a "critical" stage of the criminal proceedings entitling petitioner to the assistance of counsel. Putting aside the fact that the exemplars were taken before the indictment and appointment of counsel, there is minimal risk that the absence of counsel might derogate from his right to a fair trial. *Cf. United States v. Wade, supra.* If, for some reason, an unrepresentative exemplar is taken, this can be brought out and corrected through the adversary process at trial since the accused can make an unlimited number of additional exemplars for analysis and comparison by government and defense handwriting experts. Thus, "the accused has the opportunity for a meaningful confrontation of the [State's] case at trial through the ordinary processes of cross-examination of the [State's] expert [handwriting] witnesses and the presentation of the evidence of his own [handwriting] experts." *United States v. Wade.*

. . . .

IV. THE IN-COURT AND LINEUP IDENTIFICATIONS.

Three eyewitnesses to the Alhambra crimes who identified Gilbert at the guilt stage of the trial had observed him at a lineup conducted without notice to his counsel in a Los Angeles auditorium 16 days after his indictment and after appointment of counsel. The manager of the apartment house in which incriminating evidence was found, and in which Gilbert allegedly resided, identified Gilbert in the courtroom and also testified, in substance, to her prior lineup identification on examination by the State. Eight witnesses who identified him in the courtroom at the penalty stage were not eyewitnesses to the Alhambra crimes but to other robberies allegedly committed by him. In addition to their in-court identifications, these witnesses also testified that they identified Gilbert at the same lineup.

The line-up was on a stage behind bright lights which prevented those in the line from seeing the audience. Upwards of 100 persons were in the audience, each an eyewitness to one of the several robberies charged to Gilbert. The record is otherwise virtually silent as to what occurred at the lineup.

At the guilt stage, after the first witness, a cashier of the savings and loan association, identified Gilbert in the courtroom, defense counsel moved, out of the presence of the jury, to strike her testimony on the ground that she identified Gilbert at the pretrial lineup conducted in the absence of counsel in violation of the Sixth Amendment made applicable to the States by the Fourteenth Amendment. He requested a hearing outside the presence of the jury to present evidence supporting his claim that her in-court identification was, and others to be elicited by the State from other eyewitnesses would be, "predicated at least in large part upon their identification or purported identification of Mr. Gilbert at the show up. . . ." The trial judge denied the motion as premature. Defense counsel then elicited the fact of the cashier's lineup identification on cross-examination and again moved to strike her identification testimony. Without passing on the merits of the Sixth Amendment claim, the trial judge denied the motion on the ground that, assuming a violation, it would not in any event entitle Gilbert to suppression of the in-court identification. Defense counsel thereafter elicited the fact of lineup identifications from two other eyewitnesses who on direct examination identified Gilbert in the courtroom. Defense counsel unsuccessfully objected at the penalty stage to the testimony of the eight witnesses to the other robberies that they identified Gilbert at the lineup.

The admission of the in-court identifications without first determining that they were not tainted by the illegal lineup but were of independent origin was constitutional error. *United States v. Wade.* We there held that a post-indictment pretrial lineup at which the accused is exhibited to identifying witnesses is a critical stage of the criminal prosecution; that police conduct of such a lineup without notice to and in the absence of his counsel denies the accused his Sixth Amendment right to counsel and calls in question the admissibility at trial of the in-court identifications of the accused by witnesses who attended the lineup. However, as in *Wade*, the record does not permit an informed judgment whether the in-court identifications at the two stages of the trial had an independent source. Gilbert is therefore entitled only to a vacation of his conviction pending the holding of such proceedings as the California Supreme Court may deem appropriate to afford the State the opportunity to establish that the in-court identifications had an independent source, or that their introduction in evidence was in any event harmless error.

Quite different considerations are involved as to the admission of the testimony of the manager of the apartment house at the guilt phase and of the eight witnesses at the penalty stage that they identified Gilbert at the lineup. That testimony is the direct result of the illegal lineup "come at by exploitation of [the primary] illegality." *Wong Sun v. United States.*

The State is therefore not entitled to an opportunity to show that that testimony had an independent source. Only a *per se* exclusionary rule as to such testimony can be an effective sanction to assure that law enforcement authorities will respect the accused's constitutional right to the presence of his counsel at the critical lineup. In the absence of legislative regulations adequate to avoid the hazards to a fair trial which inhere in lineups as presently conducted, the desirability of deterring the constitutionally objectionable practice must prevail over the undesirability of excluding relevant evidence.

That conclusion is buttressed by the consideration that the witness' testimony of his lineup identification will enhance the impact of his in-court identification on the jury and seriously aggravate whatever derogation exists of the accused's right to a fair trial. Therefore, unless the California Supreme Court is "able to declare a belief that it was harmless beyond a reasonable doubt," Gilbert will be entitled on remand to a new trial or, if no prejudicial error is found on the guilt stage but only in the penalty stage, to whatever relief California law affords where the penalty stage must be set aside.

Mr. Justice Black, Mr. Justice Douglas, Mr. Justice White, and Mr. Justice Fortas wrote separate opinions, concurring in part and dissenting in part.

NOTES AND QUESTIONS

(1) The majority held that the taking of the writing samples was not a critical stage because "there is minimal risk that the absence of counsel might derogate from his right to a fair trial." The assumption is that the lawyer could reconstruct the procedure and point out at trial that the sample taken was unrepresentative. Could not this argument also be made in connection with lineups if some minimal requirements such as recordings and sworn affidavits were utilized?

(2) Under the circumstances in *Gilbert* did the Court even have to discuss the Sixth Amendment question? Was not the due process violation, discussed in the next case, clear? The problem of multiple witnesses viewing a single lineup was addressed by the court in *United States v. Allen*, 408 F.2d 1287 (D.C. Cir. 1969):

> A second problem posed by the multi-witness lineup is the increased potential for inter-witness communication which is unfairly suggestive. The Government thus might do well to consider methods of separating witnesses to prevent communication between witnesses or the identification of suspects by one witness in the presence of other witnesses. The promulgation of carefully written and well-enforced regulations which instruct

both witnesses and the police as to appropriate conduct during the lineup would certainly be a helpful step in the right direction.

What would such regulations look like?

STOVALL v. DENNO

United States Supreme Court
388 U.S. 293 (1967)

MR. JUSTICE BRENNAN delivered the opinion of the Court.

This federal habeas corpus proceeding attacks collaterally a state criminal conviction for the same alleged constitutional errors in the admission of allegedly tainted identification evidence that were before us on direct review of the convictions involved in *United States v. Wade*, and *Gilbert v. State of California*. This case therefore provides a vehicle for deciding whether . . . on the facts of the particular confrontation involved in this case, petitioner was denied due process of law.

Dr. Paul Behrendt was stabbed to death in the kitchen of his home in Garden City, Long Island, about midnight August 23, 1961. Dr. Behrendt's wife, also a physician, had followed her husband to the kitchen and jumped at the assailant. He knocked her to the floor and stabbed her 11 times. The police found a shirt on the kitchen floor and keys in a pocket which they traced to petitioner. They arrested him on the afternoon of August 24. An arraignment was promptly held but was postponed until petitioner could retain counsel.

Mrs. Behrendt was hospitalized for major surgery to save her life. The police, without affording petitioner time to retain counsel, arranged with her surgeon to permit them to bring petitioner to her hospital room about noon of August 25, the day after the surgery. Petitioner was handcuffed to one of five police officers who, with two members of the staff of the District Attorney, brought him to the hospital room. Petitioner was the only Negro in the room. Mrs. Behrendt identified him from her hospital bed after being asked by an officer whether he "was the man" and after petitioner repeated at the direction of an officer a "few words for voice identification." None of the witnesses could recall the words that were used. Mrs. Behrendt and the officers testified at the trial to her identification of the petitioner in the hospital room, and she also made an in-court identification of petitioner in the courtroom.

Petitioner was convicted and sentenced to death.

We turn now to the question whether petitioner, although not entitled to the application of *Wade* and *Gilbert* to his case[7] is entitled to relief on his claim that in any event the confrontation conducted in this case was so unnecessarily suggestive and conducive to irreparable mistaken identification that he was denied due process of law. This is a recognized ground of attack upon a conviction independent of any right to counsel claim. The practice of showing suspects singly to persons for the

[7] The Court held that the rule in *Wade* and *Gilbert* would not be applied in retroactive fashion. — Eds.

purpose of identification, and not as part of a lineup, has been widely condemned. However, a claimed violation of due process of law in the conduct of a confrontation depends on the totality of the circumstances surrounding it, and the record in the present case reveals that the showing of Stovall to Mrs. Behrendt in an immediate hospital confrontation was imperative. The Court of Appeals, *en banc*, stated:

> Here was the only person in the world who could possibly exonerate Stovall. Her words, and only her words, "He is not the man" could have resulted in freedom for Stovall. The hospital was not far from the courthouse and jail. No one knew how long Mrs. Behrendt might live. Faced with the responsibility of identifying the attacker, with the need for immediate action and with the knowledge that Mrs. Behrendt could not visit the jail, the police followed the only feasible procedure and took Stovall to the hospital room. Under these circumstances, the usual police station line-up, which Stovall now argues he should have had, was out of the question.

The judgment of the Court of Appeals is affirmed. It is so ordered.

[Justices White, Harlan, and Stewart concurred. Justices Black, Fortas, and Douglas dissented.]

NOTES AND QUESTIONS

(1) The rule in *Wade* did not apply here because the identification procedure took place well before the Court's opinion, and that opinion was held not to apply retroactively. *Stovall* is important because it established that quite apart from any Sixth Amendment counsel questions, the defendant always retains a right to challenge the inherent fairness of the procedure under the Due Process Clause.

(2) Why was the defendant's due process challenge unsuccessful? Was it because the witness was thought to be dying? Was it because a lawyer could not have been appointed quickly enough? Was it because no other black men were available to appear in the lineup? In contrast to the Court's characterization of the facts here, consider the dissenting opinion of Judge Friendly at the circuit court level, 355 F.2d 731, 744–45 (2d Cir. 1966):

> Grievous as Mrs. Behrendt's injuries had been, nothing in the record indicates that her life was any longer considered to be in peril when Stovall was brought before her; the presence of five police officers and prosecutors in her hospital room would argue to the contrary and also tends to negate the suggestion that Stovall had to be brought in alone. If Mrs. Behrendt's condition had been as serious as my brothers suppose, nothing prevented the prosecutor from informing the state district judge at the preliminary hearing that Stovall had to be taken immediately before her, and suggesting that counsel be assigned forthwith for the limited purpose of advising him in that regard rather than standing silent when Stovall told the judge of his desire to have counsel and then carting him off to a confrontation by the victim which counsel might have done something to mitigate.

(3) In *State v. Riley*, 517 N.E.2d 520 (N.Y. 1987), the victim was at the station house when the two suspects were brought in. The victim was told to look into the

interview room; he did and identified the two defendants. The defendants at that time were handcuffed, in civilian clothes, and were accompanied by uniformed officers. The court would not allow the victim's testimony as to this identification unless evidence was offered concerning exigent circumstances requiring such an identification procedure:

> Show up identifications, by their very nature suggestive, are strongly disfavored but are permissible if exigent circumstances require immediate identification, . . . or if the suspects are captured at or near the crime scene and can be viewed by the witness immediately. . . . Generally, a show up identification will be inadmissible when "there was no effort to make the least provision for reliable identification and the combined result of the procedures employed" establish that the show up was unduly suggestive.
>
> Unreliability of the most extreme kind infects show up identifications of arrested persons held at police stations, and the evidence will be inadmissible as a matter of law unless exigency warrants otherwise.
>
> [The] Court [has] referred to the indicia of the precinct show up as the "ideal of suggestibility." The indicia were multiple witnesses, who had been informed that the robbers were in custody, simultaneously viewing at a station house multiple suspects who were physically restrained by uniformed police officers with no other persons dressed in plain clothes present, at a time and place which were not proximate to the crime, when there was no evidence that a lineup would have been unduly burdensome.
>
> Additionally, in both these cases the police explanation for arranging suggestive station house showups is not supportable and they failed to establish that lineups would have been unduly burdensome. In *Riley*, the only proffered reason for failing to conduct a lineup was that the station house was undergoing renovation. In *Rodriguez*, the justification for not conducting a lineup was to minimize the length of detention of suspects who may have been innocent. As a matter of law, neither excuse constitutes "exigency" and they are insufficient to establish that it would have been unduly burdensome to conduct a reasonably reliable lineup identification procedure. . . .

The importance of identification evidence is, of course, self-evident. But then so, too, are the weaknesses and danger of improper identification evidence. Consider also the strong language of the court in *Ex parte Frazier*, 729 So. 2d 253, 255 (Ala. 1998):

> The danger inherent in a one-man showup, where a witness is shown a single suspect and asked, "Is that the man?" is twofold. First, a one-man showup conveys a clear message that "the police suspect *this* man." Second, a one-man showup does not give the witness a choice of identifying any other person as being the perpetrator of the crime charged. Consequently, when a one-man showup is used to identify the perpetrator of a crime, the reliability of the witness's identification is not put to an objective test, such as a live or photographic lineup, in which a single suspect must be chosen from a group of persons possessing similar physical characteristics.

THE RETREAT KIRBY v. ILLINOIS

United States Supreme Court
406 U.S. 682 (1972)

Mr. Justice Stewart announced the judgment of the Court and an opinion in which The Chief Justice, Mr. Justice Blackmun, and Mr. Justice Rehnquist join.

In the present case we are asked to extend the *Wade-Gilbert per se* exclusionary rule to identification testimony based upon a police station showup that took place *before* the defendant had been indicted or otherwise formally charged with any criminal offense.

On February 21, 1968, a man named Willie Shard reported to the Chicago police that the previous day two men had robbed him on a Chicago street of a wallet containing, among other things, traveler's checks and a Social Security card. On February 22, two police officers stopped the petitioner and a companion, Ralph Bean, on West Madison Street in Chicago. When asked for identification, the petitioner produced a wallet that contained three traveler's checks and a Social Security card, all bearing the name of Willie Shard. Papers with Shard's name on them were also found in Bean's possession. When asked to explain his possession of Shard's property, the petitioner first said that the traveler's checks were "play money," and then told the officers that he had won them in a crap game. The officers then arrested the petitioner and Bean and took them to a police station.

Only after arriving at the police station, and checking the records there, did the arresting officers learn of the Shard robbery. A police car was then dispatched to Shard's place of employment, where it picked up Shard and brought him to the police station. Immediately upon entering the room in the police station where the petitioner and Bean were seated at a table, Shard positively identified them as the men who had robbed him two days earlier. No lawyer was present in the room, and neither the petitioner nor Bean had asked for legal assistance, or been advised of any right to the presence of counsel.

More than six weeks later, the petitioner and Bean were indicted for the robbery of Willie Shard. Upon arraignment, counsel was appointed to represent them, and they pleaded not guilty. A pretrial motion to suppress Shard's identification testimony was denied, and at the trial Shard testified as a witness for the prosecution. In his testimony he described his identification of the two men at the police station on February 22, and identified them again in the courtroom as the men who had robbed him on February 20. He was cross-examined at length regarding the circumstances of his identification of the two defendants. The jury found both defendants guilty, and the petitioner's conviction was affirmed on appeal.

I

We note at the outset that the constitutional privilege against compulsory self-incrimination is in no way implicated here. The Court emphatically rejected the claimed applicability of that constitutional guarantee in *Wade* itself.

In a line of constitutional cases in this Court stemming back to the Court's landmark opinion in *Powell v. Alabama*, it has been firmly established that a person's Sixth and Fourteenth Amendment right to counsel attaches only at or after the time that adversary judicial proceedings have been initiated against him.

This is not to say that a defendant in a criminal case has a constitutional right to counsel only at the trial itself. The *Powell* case makes clear that the right attaches at the time of arraignment, and the Court has recently held that it exists also at the time of a preliminary hearing. *Coleman v. Alabama, supra.* But the point is that, while members of the Court have differed as to existence of the right to counsel in the contexts of some of the above cases, *all* of those cases have involved points of time at or after the initiation of adversary judicial criminal proceedings whether by way of formal charge, preliminary hearing, indictment, information, or arraignment.

The initiation of judicial criminal proceedings is far from a mere formalism. It is the starting point of our whole system of adversary criminal justice. For it is only then that the government has committed itself to prosecute, and only then that the adverse positions of government and defendant have solidified. It is then that a defendant finds himself faced with the prosecutorial forces of organized society, and immersed in the intricacies of substantive and procedural criminal law. It is this point, therefore, that marks the commencement of the "criminal prosecutions" to which alone the explicit guarantees of the Sixth Amendment are applicable.

In this case we are asked to import into a routine police investigation an absolute constitutional guarantee historically and rationally applicable only after the onset of formal prosecutorial proceedings. We decline to do so. Less than a year after *Wade* and *Gilbert* were decided, the Court explained the rule of those decisions as follows: "The rationale of those cases was that an accused is entitled to counsel at any 'critical stage of the *prosecution*,' and that a post-indictment lineup is such a 'critical stage.' " *Simmons v. United States.* We decline to depart from that rationale today by imposing a *per se* exclusionary rule upon testimony concerning an identification that took place long before the commencement of any prosecution whatever.

II

What has been said is not to suggest that there may not be occasions during the course of a criminal investigation when the police do abuse identification procedures. Such abuses are not beyond the reach of the Constitution. As the Court pointed out in *Wade* itself, it is always necessary to "scrutinize *any* pretrial confrontation. . . ."

The Due Process Clause of the Fifth and Fourteenth Amendments forbids a lineup that is unnecessarily suggestive and conducive to irreparable mistaken identification.[8]

When a person has not been formally charged with a criminal offense, *Stovall* strikes the appropriate constitutional balance between the right of a suspect to be

[8] [8] In view of our limited grant of certiorari, we do not consider whether there might have been a deprivation of due process in the particularized circumstances of this case. That question remains open for inquiry in a federal habeas corpus proceeding.

protected from prejudicial procedures and the interest of society in the prompt and purposeful investigation of an unsolved crime.

The judgment is affirmed.

MR. CHIEF JUSTICE BURGER, concurring.

I agree that the right to counsel attaches as soon as criminal charges are formally made against an accused and he becomes the subject of a "criminal prosecution." Therefore, I join in the plurality opinion and in the judgment.

MR. JUSTICE POWELL, concurring in the result.

As I would not extend the *Wade-Gilbert per se* exclusionary rule, I concur in the result reached by the Court.

MR. JUSTICE BRENNAN, with whom MR. JUSTICE DOUGLAS and MR. JUSTICE MARSHALL join, dissenting.

In *Wade*, after concluding that the lineup conducted in that case did not violate the accused's right against self-incrimination, the Court addressed the argument "that the assistance of counsel at the lineup was indispensable to protect Wade's most basic right as a criminal defendant — his right to a fair trial at which the witnesses against him might be meaningfully cross-examined." The Court began by emphasizing that the Sixth Amendment guarantee "encompasses counsel's assistance whenever necessary to assure a meaningful 'defence.' "

This analysis led to the Court's formulation of the controlling principle for pretrial confrontations: In sum, the principle of *Powell v. Alabama* and succeeding cases requires that we scrutinize *any* pre-trial confrontation of the accused to determine whether the presence of his counsel is necessary to preserve the defendant's basic right to a fair trial as affected by his right meaningfully to cross-examine the witnesses against him and to have effective assistance of counsel at the trial itself. It calls upon us to analyze whether potential substantial prejudice to defendant's rights inheres in the particular confrontation and the ability of counsel to help avoid that prejudice.

It was that constitutional principle that the Court applied in *Wade* to pretrial confrontations for identification purposes. The Court first met the Government's contention that a confrontation for identification is "a mere preparatory step in the gathering of the prosecution's evidence," much like the scientific examination of fingerprints and blood samples. The Court responded that in the latter instances "the accused has the opportunity for a meaningful confrontation of the Government's case at trial through the ordinary processes of cross-examination of the Government's expert witnesses and the presentation of the evidence of his own experts." The accused thus has no right to have counsel present at such examinations: "they are not critical stages since there is minimal risk that his counsel's absence at such stages might derogate from his right to a fair trial."

In contrast, the Court said, "the confrontation compelled by the State between the accused and the victim or witnesses to a crime to elicit identification evidence is peculiarly riddled with innumerable dangers and variable factors which might seriously, even crucially, derogate from a fair trial."

Most importantly, "the accused's inability effectively to reconstruct at trial any unfairness that occurred at the lineup may deprive him of his only opportunity meaningfully to attack the credibility of the witness' courtroom identification."

While it should go without saying, it appears necessary, in view of the plurality opinion today, to re-emphasize that *Wade* did not require the presence of counsel at pretrial confrontations for identification purposes simply on the basis of an abstract consideration of the words "criminal prosecutions" in the Sixth Amendment. Counsel is required at those confrontations because "the dangers inherent in eyewitness identification and the suggestibility inherent in the context of the pretrial identification," mean that protection must be afforded to the "most basic right [of] a criminal defendant — his right to a fair trial at which the witnesses against him might be meaningfully cross-examined."

Indeed, the Court expressly stated that "[L]egislative or other regulations, such as those of local police departments, which eliminate the risks of abuse and unintentional suggestion at lineup proceedings and the impediments to meaningful confrontation at trial may also remove the basis for regarding the stage as 'critical.' "

Hence, "the initiation of adversary judicial criminal proceedings," is completely irrelevant to whether counsel is necessary at a pretrial confrontation for identification in order to safeguard the accused's constitutional rights to confrontation and the effective assistance of counsel at his trial.

In view of *Wade*, it is plain, and the plurality today does not attempt to dispute it, that there inhere in a confrontation for identification conducted after arrest the identical hazards to a fair trial that inhere in such a confrontation conducted "after the onset of formal prosecutorial proceedings."

The plurality apparently considers an arrest, which for present purposes we must assume to be based upon probable cause, to be nothing more than part of "a routine police investigation," and thus not "the starting point of our whole system of adversary criminal justice." An arrest, according to the plurality, does not face the accused "with the prosecutorial forces of organized society," nor immerse him "in the intricacies of substantive and procedural criminal law." Those consequences ensue, says the plurality, only with "[t]he initiation of judicial criminal proceedings," "[f]or it is only then that the government has committed itself to prosecute, and only then that the adverse positions of government and defendant have solidified." If these propositions do not amount to "mere formalism," it is difficult to know how to characterize them. An arrest evidences the belief of the police that the perpetrator of a crime has been caught. A post-arrest confrontation for identification is not "a mere preparatory step in the gathering of the prosecution's evidence." A primary, and frequently sole, purpose of the confrontation for identification at that stage is to accumulate proof to buttress the conclusion of the police that they have the offender in hand. The plurality offers no reason, and I can think of none, for concluding that a post-arrest confrontation for identification, unlike a post-charge confrontation, is not among those "critical confrontations of the accused by the prosecution at pretrial proceedings where the results might well settle the accused's fate and reduce the trial itself to a mere formality."

Wade and *Gilbert*, of course, happened to involve post-indictment confrontations. Yet even a cursory perusal of the opinions in those cases reveals that nothing at all turned upon that particular circumstance. In short, it is fair to conclude that rather than "declin[ing] to depart from [the] rationale" of *Wade* and *Gilbert*, the plurality today, albeit purporting to be engaged in "principled constitutional adjudication," refuses even to recognize that "rationale." For my part, I do not agree that we "extend" *Wade* and *Gilbert* by holding that the principles of those cases apply to confrontations for identification conducted after arrest.[9] Because Shard testified at trial about his identification of petitioner at the police station showup, the exclusionary rule of *Gilbert* requires reversal.

Mr. Justice White, dissenting.

United States v. Wade and *Gilbert v. California* govern this case and compel reversal of the judgment below.

NOTES AND QUESTIONS

(1) It is true, as Justice Stewart remarked, that the Court's Sixth Amendment opinions all dealt with cases in which the adversary judicial proceeding had already begun. Is it also true that these cases — *Powell, Gideon, Wade* — held that the "right to counsel attaches only at or after the time that adversary judicial proceedings have been initiated"? Did any of these cases discuss in depth the significance of the adversary judicial proceeding? Is that fact determinative?

(2) The plurality argued that pre-indictment lineups do not come within the Sixth Amendment because only after the "initiation of judicial criminal proceedings" is the defendant "faced with the prosecutorial forces of organized society." Is this statement correct? What different forces was Kirby faced with than Wade? Why should the stage of the proceeding be relevant to the question of whether counsel is necessary due to the "dangers inherent in eyewitness identification and the suggestibility inherent in the context of the pretrial identification"?

(3) Justice White in his dissent in *Wade* wrote that "the rule applies to any lineup . . . whether before or after indictment. . . ." This may explain why Justice White dissented in *Kirby*, stating that "*Wade* and *Gilbert* govern this case." How then can one explain why Justice Stewart wrote the plurality opinion in *Kirby* yet joined in Justice White's dissent in *Wade*?

(4) The apparent standard after *Kirby* is that the right to counsel attaches upon

---

[9] [14] The plurality rather surprisingly asserts that "[t]he issue of the applicability of *Wade* and *Gilbert* to pre-indictment confrontation has *severely* divided the courts." As the plurality's citations reveal, there are decisions from five States, including Illinois, that have refused to apply *Wade* and *Gilbert* to preindictment confrontations for identification. Ranged against those five, however, are decisions from at least 13 States. In addition, *every* United States Court of Appeals that has confronted the question has applied *Wade* and *Gilbert* to preindictment confrontations.

"the commencement of any prosecution" or upon the commencement of "adversary judicial proceedings." Does this take place after the defendant had been arrested pursuant to an arrest warrant? *Lattimore v. State*, 958 So. 2d 192 (Miss. 2007), says that it does.

(5) In footnote 8 the majority hinted that the defendant might have a due process claim in light of the identification procedure utilized. On remand then Judge Stevens found no such due process violation, 510 F.2d 397, 404 (7th Cir. 1975), *cert. denied*, 421 U.S. 1016 (1975):

> Shard's identification of Kirby was sufficiently reliable to avoid the due process objection. The crime occurred in daylight and Shard testified unequivocally that he had a good opportunity to view his assailants before, during and after the crime. His description of the criminals made before the showup apparently fit the defendants. There was nothing at all uncertain about Shard's identification of Kirby and Bean. And finally, less than two days had elapsed between the crime and the confrontation.

(6) Some state courts have declined to follow *Kirby* and have, under their own state constitutions, found that *Wade* applies to all lineups. *See, e.g., Blue v. State*, 558 P.2d 636 (Alaska 1977), where the court focused on the "need for counsel to be present in order to evaluate the circumstances and prepare his argument at trial. . . ."

(7) The court in *United States v. Larkin*, 978 F.2d 964, 969–70 (7th Cir. 1992), *cert. denied*, 507 U.S. 935 (1993), recognized that, pre-indictment, there was no constitutional requirement that counsel attend pre-trial identification proceedings. Still, the court strongly encouraged just such a practice.

> Despite our holding, we reiterate our previously stated view that the government, notwithstanding the absence of constitutional compulsion, should make every effort to provide counsel to custodial defendants appearing in pre-indictment lineups. The presence of defense counsel is always preferred, particularly where most or all of the inculpatory evidence consists of eyewitness testimony delivered by witnesses who previously participated in the lineup at issue. It bears repeating that "counsel can hardly impede legitimate law enforcement; on the contrary law enforcement may be assisted by preventing the infiltration of taint."

UNITED STATES v. ASH

United States Supreme Court
413 U.S. 300 (1973)

MR. JUSTICE BLACKMUN delivered the opinion of the Court.

In this case the Court is called upon to decide whether the Sixth Amendment grants an accused the right to have counsel present whenever the Government conducts a post-indictment photographic display, containing a picture of the accused, for the purpose of allowing a witness to attempt an identification of the offender.

Trial [for bank robbery] was finally set for May 1968, almost three years after the crime. In preparing for trial, the prosecutor decided to use a photographic display to determine whether the witnesses he planned to call would be able to make in-court identifications. Shortly before the trial, an FBI agent and the prosecutor showed five color photographs to the four witnesses who previously had tentatively identified the black-and-white photograph of Ash. Three of the witnesses selected the picture of Ash, but one was unable to make any selection.

This post-indictment identification provides the basis for respondent Ash's claim that he was denied the right to counsel at a "critical stage" of the prosecution.

The Court frequently has interpreted the Sixth Amendment to assure that the "guiding hand of counsel" is available to those in need of its assistance.

[T]he core purpose of the counsel guarantee was to assure "Assistance" at trial, when the accused was confronted with both the intricacies of the law and the advocacy of the public prosecutor. Later developments have led this Court to recognize that "Assistance" would be less than meaningful if it were limited to the formal trial itself.

This extension of the right to counsel to events before trial has resulted from changing patterns of criminal procedure and investigation that have tended to generate pretrial events that might appropriately be considered to be parts of the trial itself. At these newly emerging and significant events, the accused was confronted, just as at trial, by the procedural system, or by his expert adversary, or by both.

The Court consistently has applied a historical interpretation of the guarantee, and has expanded the constitutional right to counsel only when new contexts appear presenting the same dangers that gave birth initially to the right itself.

Throughout this expansion of the counsel guarantee to trial-like confrontations, the function of the lawyer has remained essentially the same as his function at trial. In all cases considered by the Court, counsel has continued to act as a spokesman for, or advisor to, the accused. The accused's right to the "Assistance of Counsel" has meant just that, namely, the right of the accused to have counsel acting as his assistant.

The function of counsel in rendering "Assistance" continued at the lineup under consideration in *Wade* and its companion cases. Although the accused was not confronted there with legal questions, the lineup offered opportunities for prosecuting authorities to take advantage of the accused. Counsel was seen by the Court as being more sensitive to, and aware of, suggestive influences than the accused himself, and as better able to reconstruct the events at trial. Counsel present at lineup would be able to remove disabilities of the accused in precisely the same fashion that counsel compensated for the disabilities of the layman at trial. Thus, the Court mentioned that the accused's memory might be dimmed by "emotional tension," that the accused's credibility at trial would be diminished by his status as defendant, and that the accused might be unable to present his version effectively without giving up his privilege against compulsory self-incrimination.

The above discussion of *Wade* has shown that the traditional Sixth Amendment test easily allowed extension of counsel to a lineup. The similarity to trial was apparent, and counsel was needed to render "Assistance" in counterbalancing any "overreaching" by the prosecution.

After the Court in *Wade* held that a lineup constituted a trial-like confrontation requiring counsel, a more difficult issue remained in the case for consideration. The same changes in law enforcement that led to lineups and pretrial hearings also generated other events at which the accused was confronted by the prosecution. The Government had argued in *Wade* that if counsel was required at a lineup, the same forceful considerations would mandate counsel at other preparatory steps in the "gathering of the prosecution's evidence," such as, for particular example, the taking of fingerprints or blood samples.

The Court concluded that there were differences. Rather than distinguishing these situations from the lineup in terms of the need for counsel to assure an equal confrontation at the time, the Court recognized that there were times when the subsequent trial would cure a one-sided confrontation between prosecuting authorities and the uncounseled defendant. In other words, such stages were not "critical."

The structure of *Wade*, viewed in light of the careful limitation of the Court's language to "confrontations," makes it clear that lack of scientific precision and inability to reconstruct an event are not the tests for requiring counsel in the first instance. These are, instead, the tests to determine whether confrontation with counsel at trial can serve as a substitute for counsel at the pretrial confrontation. If accurate reconstruction is possible, the risks inherent in any confrontation still remain, but the opportunity to cure defects at trial causes the confrontation to cease to be "critical."

IV

A substantial departure from the historical test would be necessary if the Sixth Amendment were interpreted to give Ash a right to counsel at the photographic identification in this case. Since the accused himself is not present at the time of the photographic display, and asserts no right to be present, no possibility arises that the accused might be misled by his lack of familiarity with the law or overpowered by his professional adversary. Similarly, the counsel guarantee would not be used to produce equality in a trial-like adversary confrontation. Rather, the guarantee was used by the Court of Appeals to produce confrontation at an event that previously was not analogous to an adversary trial.

We are not persuaded that the risks inherent in the use of photographic displays are so pernicious that an extraordinary system of safeguards is required.

We hold, then, that the Sixth Amendment does not grant the right to counsel at photographic displays conducted by the Government for the purpose of allowing a witness to attempt an identification of the offender.

MR. JUSTICE STEWART, concurring in the judgment.

Preparing witnesses for trial by checking their identification testimony against a photographic display is little different, in my view, from the prosecutor's other interviews with the victim or other witnesses before trial.

While these procedures can be improperly conducted, the possibility of irretrievable prejudice is remote, since any unfairness that does occur can usually be flushed out at trial through cross-examination of the prosecution witnesses. The presence of defense counsel at such pretrial preparatory sessions is neither appropriate nor necessary under our adversary system of justice "to preserve the defendant's basic right to a fair trial as affected by his right meaningfully to cross-examine the witnesses against him and to have effective assistance of counsel at the trial itself."

Mr. Justice Brennan, with whom Mr. Justice Douglas and Mr. Justice Marshall join, dissenting.

In my view, today's decision is wholly unsupportable in terms of such considerations as logic, consistency, and, indeed, fairness. As a result, I must reluctantly conclude that today's decision marks simply another step towards the complete evisceration of the fundamental constitutional principles established by this Court, only six years ago, in *United States v. Wade, Gilbert v. California*, and *Stovall v. Denno*. I dissent.

To the extent that misidentification may be attributable to a witness' faulty memory or perception, or inadequate opportunity for detailed observation during the crime, the risks are obviously as great at a photographic display as at a lineup.

But "[b]ecause of the inherent limitations of photography, which presents its subject in two dimensions rather than the three dimensions of reality, . . . a photographic identification, even when properly obtained, is clearly inferior to a properly obtained corporeal identification." Indeed, noting "the hazards of initial identification by photograph," we have expressly recognized that "a corporeal identification . . . is normally more accurate" than a photographic identification. Thus, in this sense at least, the dangers of misidentification are even greater at a photographic display than at a lineup.

Moreover, as in the lineup situation, the possibilities for impermissible suggestion in the context of a photographic display are manifold. Such suggestion, intentional or unintentional, may derive from three possible sources. First, the photographs themselves might tend to suggest which of the pictures is that of the suspect. Second, impermissible suggestion may inhere in the manner in which the photographs are displayed to the witness. Third, gestures or comments of the prosecutor at the time of the display may lead an otherwise uncertain witness to select the "correct" photograph.

Moreover, as with lineups, the defense can "seldom reconstruct" at trial the mode and manner of photographic identification. It is true, of course, that the photographs used at the pretrial display might be preserved for examination at trial. But "it may also be said that a photograph can preserve the record of a lineup; yet this does not justify a lineup without counsel." Indeed, in reality, preservation of the photographs affords little protection to the unrepresented accused. For, although retention of the photographs may mitigate the dangers of misidentification due to the suggestiveness of the photographs themselves, it cannot in any sense reveal to defense counsel the more subtle, and therefore more dangerous, suggestiveness that might derive from the manner in which the photographs were displayed or any accompanying comments or gestures. Moreover, the accused cannot rely upon the witnesses themselves to expose these latter sources of suggestion, for the witnesses are not "apt to be alert for conditions prejudicial to the suspect. And if they were, it would likely be of scant benefit to the suspect" since the witnesses are hardly "likely to be schooled in the detection of suggestive influences."

Finally, and *unlike* the lineup situation, the accused himself is not even present at the photographic identification, thereby reducing the likelihood that irregularities in the procedures will ever come to light.

Thus, the difficulties of reconstructing at trial an uncounseled photographic display are at least equal to, and possibly greater than, those involved in reconstructing an uncounseled lineup.

As a result, both photographic and corporeal identifications create grave dangers that an innocent defendant might be convicted simply because of his inability to expose a tainted identification. This being so, considerations of logic, consistency, and, indeed, fairness compel the conclusion that a pretrial photographic identification, like a pretrial corporeal identification, is a "critical stage of the prosecution at which [the accused is] 'as much entitled to such aid [of counsel] . . . as at the trial itself.' "

Ironically, the Court does not seriously challenge the proposition that presence of counsel at a pretrial photographic display is essential to preserve the accused's right to a fair trial on the issue of identification. Rather, in what I can only characterize as a triumph of form over substance, the Court seeks to justify its result by engrafting a wholly unprecedented — and wholly unsupportable — limitation on the Sixth Amendment right of "the accused — to have the Assistance of Counsel for his defence." Although apparently conceding that the right to counsel attaches, not only at the trial itself, but at all "critical stages" of the prosecution, the Court holds today that, in order to be deemed "critical," the particular "stage of the prosecution" under consideration must, at the very least, involve the physical "presence of the accused," at a "trial-like confrontation" with the Government, at which the accused requires the "guiding hand of counsel."

The fundamental premise underlying *all* of this Court's decisions holding the right to counsel applicable at "critical" pretrial proceedings, is that a "stage" of the prosecution must be deemed "critical" for the purposes of the Sixth Amendment if it is one at which the presence of counsel is necessary "to protect the fairness of *the trial itself.*"

Moreover, despite the Court's efforts to rewrite *Wade* so as to suggest a precedential basis for its own analysis, the rationale of *Wade* lends no support whatever to today's decision. In *Wade*, after concluding that compelled participation in a lineup does not violate the accused's right against self-incrimination, the Court addressed the argument "that that assistance of counsel at the lineup was indispensable to protect Wade's most basic right as a criminal defendant — his right to a fair trial at which the witnesses against him might be meaningfully cross-examined." The Court then surveyed the history of the Sixth Amendment, and specifically concluded that the Amendment guarantees "counsel's assistance *when-*

ever necessary to assure a meaningful 'defence.' "

Thus, contrary to the suggestion of the Court, the conclusion in *Wade* that a pretrial lineup is a "critical stage" of the prosecution did not in any sense turn on the fact that a lineup involves the physical "presence of the accused" at a "trial-like confrontation" with the Government. And that conclusion most certainly did not turn on the notion that presence of counsel was necessary so that counsel could offer legal advice or "guidance" to the accused at the lineup. On the contrary, *Wade* envisioned counsel's function at the lineup to be primarily that of a trained observer, able to detect the existence of any suggestive influences and capable of understanding the legal implications of the events that transpire. Having witnessed the proceedings, counsel would then be in a position effectively to reconstruct at trial any unfairness that occurred at the lineup, thereby preserving the accused's fundamental right to a fair trial on the issue of identification.

There is something ironic about the Court's conclusion today that a pretrial lineup identification is a "critical stage" of the prosecution because counsel's presence can help to compensate for the accused's deficiencies as an observer, but that a pretrial photographic identification is not a "critical stage" of the prosecution because the accused is not able to observe at all. In my view, there simply is no meaningful difference, in terms of the need for attendance of counsel, between corporeal and photographic identifications. And applying established and well-reasoned Sixth Amendment principles, I can only conclude that a pretrial photographic display, like a pretrial lineup, is a "critical stage" of the prosecution at which the accused is constitutionally entitled to the presence of counsel.

NOTES AND QUESTIONS

(1) Why was the actual confrontation of the witness with the defendant important to the Court's decision here? If the identification procedure was unfair, could trial maneuvers by defense counsel protect the defendant? Was dissenting Justice Brennan correct that, even more so than the lineup, counsel was needed here because the defendant himself was not there to protect his interests?

(2) The Court approved of the photographic display as a valid identification technique, even without the presence of defense counsel. In light of the difficulties with such displays, can a defendant argue that there should still be a preference for lineups? *Compare People v. Jackson*, 217 N.W.2d 22 (Mich. 1974), *overruled on other grounds, McDougall v. Schanz*, 597 N.W.2d 148 (1999) ("Subject to certain exceptions, identification by photograph should not be used where the accused is in custody"), *with United States v. Reid*, 527 F.2d 380 (2d Cir. 1975) ("It is not necessarily a violation of due process to have a witness view photographs even when the defendant is available for a lineup.").

DUE PROCESS CONSIDERATIONS

As the Court held in *Stovall v. Denno*, the Sixth Amendment right to counsel claim was not the only challenge which could be made to pre-trial identification. When allegedly unfair identification procedures are used by the police, the defendant can challenge the identification on due process grounds. Immediately after *Stovall*, however, there was some confusion concerning the proper standard to be applied in the due process context. Some courts, relying heavily on the language in *Stovall*, stressed the unnecessarily suggestive nature of the identification by the particular witness. Other courts looked to the reliability of the identification by the particular witness. The Supreme Court, in the early years after *Stovall*, did not make clear which of the two routes was preferable.

In *Simmons v. United States*, 390 U.S. 377 (1968), FBI agents showed photos of the defendant to five witnesses. The defendant asserted that the use of the photos "was so unduly prejudicial as fatally to taint his conviction." Justice Harlan, writing for the majority, stated that an identification would be found improper on due process grounds "only if the photographic identification procedure was so impermissibly suggestive as to give rise to a very substantial likelihood of irreparable misidentification." Looking to the two separate grounds of attack the Court concluded that no due process violation had taken place. First, it was necessary that the FBI resort to the photo displays, as the criminals were still at large and had just committed a serious felony (armed bank robbery). "The justification for this method of procedure was hardly less compelling than that which we found to justify the 'one-man lineup' in *Stovall v. Denno.*" Second, evaluating the reliability of the identification, there could be little question as to its validity:

> The robbers wore no masks. Five bank employees had been able to see the robber later identified as Simmons for periods ranging up to five minutes. Those witnesses were shown the photographs only a day later, while their memories were still fresh. At least six photographs were displayed to each witness. Apparently, these consisted primarily of group photographs, with Simmons and Andrews each appearing several times in the series. Each witness was alone when he or she saw the photographs. There is no evidence to indicate that the witnesses were told anything about the progress of the investigation, or that the FBI agents in any other way suggested which persons in the pictures were under suspicion.
>
> Under these conditions, all five eyewitnesses identified Simmons as one of the robbers. None identified Andrews, who apparently was as prominent in the photographs as Simmons. These initial identifications were confirmed by all five witnesses in subsequent viewings of photographs and at trial, where each witness identified Simmons in person. Notwithstanding cross-examination, none of the witnesses displayed any doubt about their respective identifications of Simmons. Taken together, these circumstances leave little room for doubt that the identification of Simmons was correct, even though the identification procedure employed may have in some respects fallen short of the ideal.

In *Foster v. California*, 394 U.S. 440 (1969), the defendant presented a compelling case for application of the due process analysis.

> Except for the robbers themselves, the only witness to the crime was Joseph David, the late-night manager of the Western Union office. After Foster had been arrested, David was called to the police station to view a

> lineup. There were three men in the lineup. One was petitioner. He is a tall man — close to six feet in height. The other two men were short — five feet, five or six inches. Petitioner wore a leather jacket which David said was similar to the one he had seen underneath the coveralls worn by the robber. After seeing this lineup, David could not positively identify petitioner as the robber. He "thought" he was the man, but he was not sure. David then asked to speak to petitioner, and petitioner was brought into an office and sat across from David at a table.
>
> Except for prosecuting officials there was no one else in the room. Even after this one-to-one confrontation David still was uncertain whether petitioner was one of the robbers: "truthfully — I was not sure," he testified at trial. A week or 10 days later, the police arranged for David to view a second lineup. Petitioner was the only person in the second lineup who had appeared in the first lineup. This time David was "convinced" petitioner was the man.

Looking to these facts, the Court had little difficulty finding the identification procedure unconstitutional: "The suggestive elements in this identification procedure made it all but inevitable that David would identify petitioner whether or not he was in fact 'the man.' In effect, the police repeatedly said to the witness, '*This* is the man.' "

Neil v. Biggers, 409 U.S. 188 (1972), gave the Court the opportunity to clear up the confusion regarding the proper due process standard. The defendant there had been picked out of a one person show-up by the witness. Unlike *Stovall*, there was no emergency necessitating the show-up, indeed the crime had taken place seven months earlier. The identification was convincing, the defendant matched the witness' earlier "very general description" (as characterized by the district judge) and the witness had a good memory and a fair chance to view the defendant at the time of the crime. The Court began its opinion by noting that "the primary evil to be avoided is a 'very substantial likelihood of irreparable misidentification.' " Concluding that "unnecessary suggestiveness alone [does not require] the exclusion of evidence" the Court found that under those circumstances there was no substantial likelihood of misidentification. If this rule as to unnecessary suggestiveness had been established without question, the lower courts would have been saved considerable trouble. In *Biggers*, though, the show-up had taken place prior to *Wade, Gilbert*, and *Stovall*. The Court would not apply a *per se* rule, as the police had not been on notice as to the conduct required of them. The ground of unnecessary suggestiveness, therefore, remained very much open to question.

MANSON v. BRATHWAITE

United States Supreme Court
432 U.S. 98 (1977)

Mr. Justice Blackmun delivered the opinion of the Court.

This case presents the issue as to whether the Due Process Clause of the Fourteenth Amendment compels the exclusion, in a state criminal trial, apart from

any consideration of reliability, of pretrial identification evidence obtained by a police procedure that was both suggestive and unnecessary.

I

Jimmy D. Glover, a full-time trooper of the Connecticut State Police, in 1970 was assigned to the Narcotics Division in an undercover capacity. On May 5 of that year, about 7:45 p.m., e.d.t., and while there was still daylight, Glover and Henry Alton Brown, an informant, went to an apartment building at 201 Westland, in Hartford, for the purpose of purchasing narcotics from "Dickie Boy" Cicero, a known narcotics dealer. Cicero, it was thought, lived on the third floor of that apartment building. Glover and Brown entered the building, observed by backup Officers D'Onofrio and Gaffey, and proceeded by stairs to the third floor. Glover knocked at the door of one of the two apartments served by the stairway. The area was illuminated by natural light from a window in the third floor hallway.

The door was opened 12 to 18 inches in response to the knock. Glover observed a man standing at the door and, behind him, a woman. Brown identified himself. Glover then asked for "two things" of narcotics. The man at the door held out his hand, and Glover gave him two $10 bills. The door closed. Soon the man returned and handed Glover two glassine bags. While the door was open, Glover stood within two feet of the person from whom he made the purchase and observed his face. Five to seven minutes elapsed from the time the door first opened until it closed the second time.

Glover and Brown then left the building. This was about eight minutes after their arrival. Glover drove to headquarters where he described the seller to D'Onofrio and Gaffey. Glover at that time did not know the identity of the seller. He described him as being "a colored man, approximately five feet eleven inches tall, dark complexion, black hair, short Afro style, and having high cheekbones, and of heavy build. He was wearing at the time blue pants and a plaid shirt." D'Onofrio, suspecting from this description that respondent might be the seller, obtained a photograph of respondent from the Records Division of the Hartford Police Department. He left it at Glover's office. D'Onofrio was not acquainted with respondent personally but did know him by sight and had seen him "[s]everal times" prior to May 5. Glover, when alone, viewed the photograph for the first time upon his return to headquarters on May 7; he identified the person shown as the one from whom he had purchased the narcotics.

No explanation was offered by the prosecution for the failure to utilize a photographic array or to conduct a lineup. The jury found respondent guilty on both counts of the information.

Fourteen months later, respondent filed a petition for habeas corpus in the United States District Court for the District of Connecticut. He alleged that the admission of the identification testimony at his state trial deprived him of due process of law to which he was entitled under the Fourteenth Amendment. The District Court dismissed respondent's petition. On appeal, the United States Court of Appeals for the Second Circuit reversed. [T]he court felt that evidence as to the photograph should have been excluded, regardless of reliability, because the examination of the single photograph was unnecessary and suggestive.

II

Biggers well might be seen to provide an unambiguous answer to the question before us: The admission of testimony concerning a suggestive and unnecessary identification procedure does not violate due process so long as the identification possesses sufficient aspects of reliability. In one passage, however, the Court observed that the challenged procedure occurred pre-*Stovall* and that a strict rule would make little sense with regard to a confrontation that preceded the Court's first indication that a suggestive procedure might lead to the exclusion of evidence.

One perhaps might argue that, by implication, the Court suggested that a different rule could apply post-*Stovall*. The question before us, then, is simply whether the *Biggers* analysis applies to post-*Stovall* confrontations as well to those pre-*Stovall*.. . .

IV

Petitioner at the outset acknowledges that "the procedure in the instant case was suggestive" [because only one photograph was used] "and unnecessary" [because there was no emergency or exigent circumstance]. The respondent, in agreement with the Court of Appeals, proposes a *per se* rule of exclusion that he claims is dictated by the demands of the Fourteenth Amendment's guarantee of due process. He rightly observes that this is the first case in which this Court has had occasion to rule upon strictly post-*Stovall* out-of-court identification evidence of the challenged kind.

Since the decision in *Biggers*, the courts of appeals appear to have developed at least two approaches to such evidence.

The first, or *per se* approach, employed by the Second Circuit in the present case, focuses on the procedures employed and requires exclusion of the out-of-court identification evidence, without regard to reliability, whenever it has been obtained through unnecessarily suggestive confrontation procedures. The justifications advanced are the elimination of evidence of uncertain reliability, deterrence of the police and prosecutors, and the stated "fair assurance against the awful risks of misidentification."

The second, or more lenient, approach is one that continues to rely on the totality of the circumstances. It permits the admission of the confrontation evidence if, despite the suggestive aspect, the out-of-court identification possesses certain features of reliability. Its adherents feel that the *per se* approach is not mandated by the Due Process Clause of the Fourteenth Amendment. This second approach, in contrast to the other, is *ad hoc* and serves to limit the societal costs imposed by a sanction that excludes relevant evidence from consideration and evaluation by the trier of fact.

There are, of course, several interests to be considered and taken into account. The driving force behind *United States v. Wade*, *Gilbert v. California* (right to counsel at a post-indictment lineup), and *Stovall*, all decided on the same day, was the Court's concern with the problems of eyewitness identification. Usually the witness must testify about an encounter with a total stranger under circumstances of emergency or emotional stress. The witness' recollection of the stranger can be distorted easily by the circumstances or by later actions of the police. Thus, *Wade* and its companion cases reflect the concern that the jury not hear eyewitness testimony unless that evidence has aspects of reliability. It must be observed that both approaches before us are responsive to this concern. The *per se* rule, however, goes too far since its application automatically and peremptorily, and without consideration of alleviating factors, keeps evidence from the jury that is reliable and relevant.

The second factor is deterrence. Although the *per se* approach has the more significant deterrent effect, the totality approach also has an influence on police behavior. The police will guard against unnecessarily suggestive procedures under the totality rule, as well as the *per se* one, for fear that their actions will lead to the exclusion of identifications as unreliable.

The third factor is the effect on the administration of justice. Here the *per se* approach suffers serious drawbacks. Since it denies the trier reliable evidence, it may result, on occasion, in the guilty going free. Also, because of its rigidity, the *per se* approach may make error by the trial judge more likely than the totality approach. And in those cases in which the admission of identification evidence is error under the *per se* approach but not under the totality approach — cases in which the identification is reliable despite an unnecessarily suggestive identification procedure — reversal is a Draconian sanction. Certainly, inflexible rules of exclusion that may frustrate rather than promote justice have not been viewed recently by this Court with unlimited enthusiasm.

We therefore conclude that reliability is the linchpin in determining the admissibility of identification testimony for both pre-and post-*Stovall* confrontations. The factors to be considered . . . include the opportunity of the witness to view the criminal at the time of the crime, the witness' degree of attention, the accuracy of his prior description of the criminal, the level of certainty demonstrated at the confrontation, and the time between the crime and the confrontation. Against these factors is to be weighed the corrupting effect of the suggestive identification itself.

V

We turn, then, to the facts of this case and apply the analysis:

1. The opportunity to view. Glover testified that for two to three minutes he stood at the apartment door, within two feet of the respondent. The door opened twice, and each time the man stood at the door. The moments passed, the conversation took place, and payment was made. Glover looked directly at his vendor. It was near sunset, to be sure, but the sun had not yet set, so it was not dark or even dusk or twilight. Natural light from outside entered the hallway through a window. There was natural light, as well, from inside the apartment.

> 2. The degree of attention. Glover was not a casual or passing observer, as is so often the case with eyewitness identification. Trooper Glover was a trained police officer on duty — and specialized in dangerous duty — when he called at the third floor of 201 Westland in Hartford on May 5, 1970. Glover himself was a Negro and unlikely to perceive only general features of "hundreds of Hartford black males," as the Court of Appeals stated. It is true that Glover's duty was that of ferreting out narcotics offenders and that he would be expected in his work to produce results. But it is also true that, as a specially trained, assigned, and experienced officer, he could be expected to pay scrupulous attention to detail, for he knew that subsequently he would have to find and arrest his vendor. In addition, he knew that his claimed observations would be subject later to close scrutiny and examination at any trial.
>
> 3. The accuracy of the description. Glover's description was given to D'Onofrio within minutes after the transaction. It included the vendor's race, his height, his build, the color and style of his hair, and the high cheekbone facial feature. It also included clothing the vendor wore. No claim has been made that respondent did not possess the physical characteristics so described. D'Onofrio reacted positively at once. Two days later, when Glover was alone, he viewed the photograph D'Onofrio produced and identified its subject as the narcotics seller.
>
> 4. The witness' level of certainty. There is no dispute that the photograph in question was that of respondent. Glover, in response to a question whether the photograph was that of the person from whom he made the purchase, testified: "There is no question whatsoever." This positive assurance was repeated.
>
> 5. The time between the crime and the confrontation. Glover's description of his vendor was given to D'Onofrio within minutes of the crime. The photographic identification took place only two days later. We do not have here the passage of weeks or months between the crime and the viewing of the photograph.

These indicators of Glover's ability to make an accurate identification are hardly outweighed by the corrupting effect of the challenged identification itself. Although identifications arising from single-photograph displays may be viewed in general with suspicion, we find in the instant case little pressure on the witness to acquiesce in the suggestion that such a display entails. D'Onofrio had left the photograph at Glover's office and was not present when Glover first viewed it two days after the event. There thus was little urgency and Glover could view the photograph at his leisure. And since Glover examined the photograph alone, there was no coercive pressure to make an identification arising from the presence of another. The identification was made in circumstances allowing care and reflection.

Surely, we cannot say that under all the circumstances of this case there is "a very substantial likelihood of irreparable misidentification." Short of that point, such evidence is for the jury to weigh. We are content to rely upon the good sense and judgment of American juries, for evidence with some element of untrustworthiness is customary grist for the jury mill. Juries are not so susceptible that they cannot measure intelligently the weight of identification testimony that has some questionable feature.

Of course, it would have been better had D'Onofrio presented Glover with a photographic array including "so far as practicable . . . a reasonable number of persons similar to any person then suspected whose likeness is included in the array." Model Code, § 160.2(2). The use of that procedure would have enhanced the force of the identification at trial and would have avoided the risk that the evidence would be excluded as unreliable. But we are not disposed to view D'Onofrio's failure as one of constitutional dimension to be enforced by a rigorous and unbending exclusionary rule. The defect, if there be one, goes to weight and not to substance.

We conclude that the criteria laid down in *Biggers* are to be applied in determining the admissibility of evidence offered by the prosecution concerning a post-*Stovall* identification, and that those criteria are satisfactorily met and complied with here.

The judgment of the Court of Appeals is reversed.

MR. JUSTICE STEVENS concurred.

MR. JUSTICE MARSHALL, with whom MR. JUSTICE BRENNAN joins, dissenting.

Today's decision can come as no surprise to those who have been watching the Court dismantle the protections against mistaken eyewitness testimony erected a decade ago in *United States v. Wade, Gilbert v. California*, and *Stovall v. Denno.* But it is still distressing to see the Court virtually ignore the teaching of experience embodied in those decisions and blindly uphold the conviction of a defendant who may well be innocent.

II

The Court weighs three factors in deciding that the totality approach, which is essentially the test used in *Biggers*, should be applied. In my view, the Court wrongly evaluates the impact of these factors.

First, the Court acknowledges that one of the factors, deterrence of police use of unnecessarily suggestive identification procedures, favors the *per se* rule. Indeed, it does so heavily, for such a rule would make it unquestionably clear to the police they must never use a suggestive procedure when a fairer alternative is available. I have no doubt that conduct would quickly conform to the rule.

Second, the Court gives passing consideration to the dangers of eyewitness identification recognized in the *Wade* trilogy. It concludes, however, that the grave risk of error does not justify adoption of the *per se* approach because that would too often result in exclusion of relevant evidence. In my view, this conclusion totally ignores the lessons of *Wade.* The dangers of mistaken identification are, as *Stovall* held, simply too great to permit unnecessarily suggestive identifications. Neither *Biggers* nor the Court's opinion today point to any contrary empirical evidence. Studies since *Wade* have only reinforced the validity of its assessment of the dangers of identification testimony. While the Court is "content to rely on the good sense and judgment of American juries," the impetus for *Stovall* and *Wade* was repeated miscarriages of justice resulting from juries' willingness to credit inaccurate eyewitness testimony.

Finally, the Court errs in its assessment of the relative impact of the two approaches on the administration of justice. The Court relies most heavily on this factor, finding that "reversal is a Draconian sanction" in cases where the identification is reliable despite an unnecessarily suggestive procedure used to obtain it. Relying on little more than a strong distaste for "inflexible rules of exclusion," the Court rejects the *per se* test. In so doing, the Court disregards two significant distinctions between the *per se* rule advocated in this case and the exclusionary remedies for certain other constitutional violations.

First, the *per se* rule here is not "inflexible." Where evidence is suppressed, for example, as the fruit of an unlawful search, it may well be forever lost to the prosecution. Identification evidence, however, can by its very nature be readily and effectively reproduced. The in-court identification, permitted under *Wade* and *Simmons* if it has a source independent of an uncounseled or suggestive procedure, is one example. Similarly, when a prosecuting attorney learns that there has been a suggestive confrontation, he can easily arrange another lineup conducted under scrupulously fair conditions. Since the same factors are evaluated in applying both the Court's totality test and the *Wade-Simmons* independent source inquiry, any identification which is "reliable" under the Court's test will support admission of evidence concerning such a fairly conducted lineup. The evidence of an additional, properly conducted confrontation will be more persuasive to a jury, thereby increasing the chance of a justified conviction where a reliable identification was tainted by a suggestive confrontation. At the same time, however, the effect of an unnecessarily suggestive identification — which has no value whatsoever in the law enforcement process — will be completely eliminated.

Second, other exclusionary rules have been criticized for preventing jury consideration of relevant and usually reliable evidence in order to serve interests unrelated to guilt or innocence, such as discouraging illegal searches or denial of counsel. Suggestively obtained eyewitness testimony is excluded, in contrast, precisely because of its unreliability and concomitant irrelevance. Its exclusion both protects the integrity of the truth-seeking function of the trial and discourages police use of needlessly inaccurate and ineffective investigatory methods.

For these reasons, I conclude that adoption of the *per se* rule would enhance, rather than detract from, the effective administration of justice. In my view, the Court's totality test will allow seriously unreliable and misleading evidence to be put before juries. Equally important, it will allow dangerous criminals to remain on the streets while citizens assume that police action has given them protection. According to my calculus, all three of the factors upon which the Court relies point to acceptance of the *per se* approach.

III

Despite my strong disagreement with the Court over the proper standards to be applied in this case, I am pleased that its application of the totality test does recognize the continuing vitality of *Stovall*. In assessing the reliability of the identification, the Court mandates weighing "the corrupting effect of the suggestive identification itself" against the "indicators of [a witness'] ability to make an accurate identification." The Court holds that a due process identification inquiry must take account of the suggestiveness of a confrontation and the likelihood that it led to misidentification. Thus, even if a witness did have an otherwise adequate opportunity to view a criminal, the later use of a highly suggestive identification procedure can render his testimony inadmissible. Indeed, it is my view that, assuming applicability of the totality test enunciated by the Court, the facts of the present case require that result.

I consider first the opportunity that Officer Glover had to view the suspect. Careful review of the record shows that he could see the heroin seller only for the time it took to speak three sentences of four or five short words, to hand over some money, and later after the door reopened, to receive the drugs in return.

The entire face-to-face transaction could have taken as little as 15 or 20 seconds. But during this time, Glover's attention was not focused exclusively on the seller's face. He observed that the door was opened 12 to 18 inches, that there was a window in the room behind the door, and, most importantly, that there was a woman standing behind the man. Glover was, of course, also concentrating on the details of the transaction — he must have looked away from the seller's face to hand him the money and receive the drugs. The observation during the conversation thus may have been as brief as 5 or 10 seconds.

Another factor on which the Court relies — the witness' degree of certainty in making the identification — is worthless as an indicator that he is correct. Even if Glover had been unsure initially about his identification of respondent's picture, by the time he was called at trial to present a key piece of evidence for the State that paid his salary, it is impossible to imagine his responding negatively to such questions as "is there any doubt in your mind whatsoever" that the identification was correct.

Next, the Court finds that because the identification procedure took place two days after the crime, its reliability is enhanced. While such temporal proximity makes the identification more reliable than one occurring months later, the fact is that the greatest memory loss occurs within hours after an event. After that, the dropoff continues much more slowly. Thus, the reliability of an identification is increased only if it was made within several hours of the crime. If the time gap is any greater, reliability necessarily decreases.

Finally, the Court makes much of the fact that Glover gave a description of the seller to D'Onofrio shortly after the incident. Despite the Court's assertion that because "Glover himself was a Negro and unlikely to perceive only general features of 'hundreds of Hartford black males,' as the Court of Appeals stated," the description given by Glover was actually no more than a general summary of the seller's appearance. We may discount entirely the seller's clothing, for that was of no significance later in the proceeding. Indeed, to the extent that Glover noticed clothes, his attention was diverted from the seller's face. Otherwise, Glover merely described vaguely the seller's height, skin color, hairstyle, and build. He did say that the seller had "high cheekbones," but there is no other mention of facial features, nor even an estimate of age. Conspicuously absent is any indication that the seller was a native of the West Indies, certainly something which a member of the black community could immediately recognize from both appearance and accent.

From all of this, I must conclude that the evidence of Glover's ability to make an accurate identification is far weaker than the Court finds it. In contrast, the procedure used to identify respondent was both extraordinarily suggestive and strongly conducive to error. In dismissing "the corrupting effect of the suggestive identification" procedure here, the Court virtually grants the police license to convict the innocent.

The use of a single picture (or the display of a single live suspect, for that matter) is a grave error, of course, because it dramatically suggests to the witness that the person shown must be the culprit. Why else would the police choose the person? And it is deeply ingrained in human nature to agree with the expressed opinions of others — particularly others who should be more knowledgeable — when making a difficult decision. In this case, moreover, the pressure was not limited to that inherent in the display of a single photograph. Glover, the identifying witness, was a state police officer on special assignment. He knew that D'Onofrio, an experienced Hartford narcotics detective, presumably familiar with local drug operations, believed respondent to be the seller. There was at work, then, both loyalty to another police officer and deference to a better-informed colleague. Finally, of course, there was Glover's knowledge that without an identification and arrest, government funds used to buy heroin had been wasted.

The Court discounts this overwhelming evidence of suggestiveness, however. It reasons that because D'Onofrio was not present when Glover viewed the photograph, there was "little pressure on the witness to acquiesce in the suggestion."

That conclusion blinks psychological reality. There is no doubt in my mind that even in D'Onofrio's absence, a clear and powerful message was telegraphed to Glover as he looked at respondent's photograph. He was emphatically told that, "*this* is the man," and he responded by identifying respondent then and at trial "whether or not he was in fact 'the man.' "

I must conclude that this record presents compelling evidence that there was "a very substantial likelihood of misidentification" of respondent Brathwaite. The suggestive display of respondent's photograph to the witness Glover likely erased any independent memory that Glover had retained of the seller from his barely adequate opportunity to observe the criminal.

NOTES AND QUESTIONS

(1) One of the major reasons given for the decision in *Wade* was deterrence — the importance of conveying the message to the police that improper identification techniques would not be tolerated. How successful as a deterrent is the approach adopted by the Court? Would the *per se* approach of the dissent be more successful?

(2) Justice Blackmun expressed doubt as to the impact of the *per se* exclusionary rule on the administration of justice. Would this concern apply equally to the use of the exclusionary rule in the Fourth Amendment context? What, then, is the response to Justice Marshall's argument:

> [O]ther exclusionary rules have been criticized for preventing jury consideration of relevant and usually reliable evidence in order to serve interests unrelated to guilt or innocence, such as discouraging illegal searches or denial of counsel. Suggestively obtained eyewitness testimony is excluded, in contrast, precisely because of its unreliability and concomitant irrelevance. Its exclusion both protects the integrity of the truth-seeking function of the trial and discourages police use of needlessly inaccurate and ineffective investigatory methods.

(3) The majority ultimately concluded that "reliability is the linchpin in determining the admissibility of identification testimony. . . ." Was the identification reliable in this case? What about the dissenters' point that the observation may have been as brief as 5 or 10 seconds? That the description by the witness was vague, omitting the fact that the defendant was a native of the West Indies?

The New York state courts, under the state constitution look heavily to suggestibility in making due process determinations. If the procedure used was unnecessarily suggestive, the identification cannot be used. This result occurs even if reliability is shown. *See People v. Marte*, 912 N.E.2d 37 (N.Y. 2009). The Kansas Supreme Court found that if an identification proceeding is unduly suggestive, reliability must be evaluated by looking to the numerous factors laid out in *Manson v. Brathwaite* and also "the consideration of whether the event was an ordinary one in the mind of the observer during the time it was observed and whether the race of the actor was the same as the observer." *State v. Hunt*, 69 P.3d 571 (Kan. 2003).

(4) In *Watkins v. Sowders*, 449 U.S. 341 (1981), the Court asked "whether a state criminal trial court is constitutionally compelled to conduct a hearing outside the presence of the jury whenever a defendant contends that a witness' identification of him was arrived at improperly." The Justices answered in the negative:

> Where identification evidence is at issue . . . no . . . special considerations justify a departure from the presumption that juries will follow instructions. It is the reliability of identification evidence that primarily determines its admissibility, and the proper evaluation of evidence under the instructions of the trial judge is the very task our system must assume juries can perform. Indeed, as the cases before us demonstrate, the *only* duty of a jury in cases in which identification evidence has been admitted will often be to assess the reliability of that evidence. Thus the Court's opinion in *Manson v. Brathwaite* approvingly quoted Judge Leventhal's statement that, [w]hile identification testimony is significant evidence, such testimony is still only evidence, and, unlike the presence of counsel, is not a factor that goes to the very heart — the "integrity" — of the adversary process.
>
> Counsel can both cross-examine the identification witnesses and argue in summation as to factors causing doubts as to the accuracy of the identifi-

> cation including reference to both any suggestibility in the identification procedure and any countervailing testimony such as alibi.

The question in *Perry v. New Hampshire*, 132 S. Ct. 716 (2012) was whether the trial court, on its own, must screen eyewitness observations made under suggestive circumstances not involving undue police procedures. No, said the 8 Justice majority, deciding that other protections existed. "The fallibility of eyewitness evidence does not . . . warrant a due process rule requiring a trial court to screen such evidence for reliability before allowing the jury to assess its creditworthiness."

(5) The court in *Hudson v. Blackburn*, 601 F.2d 785 (5th Cir. 1979), *cert. denied*, 444 U.S. 1086 (1980), set forth the facts regarding the incident:

> In the predawn morning of May 15, 1967, Oscar Meeks, the manager of a New Orleans service station, received a fatal gunshot wound during a robbery attempt at his station. Frank Wilson, Meeks' assistant and the only eyewitness to the shooting, testified that three men approached the station, entered the small, well-lighted office where the two attendants were working, and inquired the price to fix a flat tire. When Meeks replied, the leader of the group, later identified as Hudson, produced a pistol and demanded money. Meeks resisted and, in the ensuing scuffle, was pushed out the station door and shot. At this point Wilson escaped the robbers by fleeing through a side door. He ran a block and a half and immediately returned to the station. When he arrived, two of the robbers had fled and the third was being held at gunpoint by the wounded Meeks. More than six months later, the day before trial, the district attorney showed the witness a photo of the two defendants. The witness picked out the defendant's picture and then made an in-court identification.

Under the facts in that case, should the identification be admissible under *Manson*? The court affirmed a ruling of admissibility, saying "there was no substantial likelihood of misidentification."

In contrast with *Hudson*, see *Harris v. State*, 350 A.2d 768 (Del. 1975), where the two witnesses were teenage girls working at a sandwich shop. The defendant came into the shop late one night, ordered something to eat and then robbed the two girls. The defendant was found about 30–45 minutes later and brought back to the shop. The two girls at that time were visibly agitated, one of them had previously fainted. The defendant was walked in front of them, but they could not identify him. Ten minutes later, after speaking with the police (the contents of that talk were not brought to light) the witness who had fainted identified the defendant as soon as he uttered the words used in the hold-up. Using the *Biggers* analysis the court found there was a substantial likelihood of unreliability in the identification and ordered the defendant's conviction reversed. Is this case still good law after *Manson*?

The lineup identification procedure in *United States v. Garcia-Alvarez*, 541 F.3d 8 (1st Cir. 2008), was improperly suggestive where all those in the lineup repeated the statement made by the thief. Only one participant, the defendant, had a distinctive Dominican accent, as identified by the victim. The court nevertheless found the identification reliable under the circumstances.

(6) The claim of improper identifications continues to be made in many trials. Recent cases show how difficult the problem can be. In *People v. Hickman*, 305 P.3d 161 (Or. Ct. App. 2013), the identification took place two years after the crime with no opportunity for the witness to identify the defendant during that time period. The identification in *Butler v. State*, 102 So. 3d 260 (Miss. 2012), was found to be improper because the other men in the lineup were all 5-6 inches taller than the defendant. The court in *Commonwealth v. Davis*, 17 A.3d 390, 394 (Pa. Super. Ct. 2011), described the situation thusly:

> Here, we agree with Davis that the police used a suggestive photo array when they showed Flournoy just three photos, one of which depicted Davis. The other two pictures consisted of a man named "Victor", whom Flournoy already knew, and a much older, bald man whose appearance differed markedly from both Davis and Flournoy's prior description of the suspect.

Several state supreme courts have reconsidered earlier rulings and have decided that eyewitness identification testimony requires closer scrutiny. See, for example, the following two recent opinions. *State v. Lawson*, 291 P.3d 673 (Or. 2012):

> We believe that it is imperative that law enforcement, the bench, and the bar be informed of the existence of current scientific research and literature regarding the reliability of eyewitness identification because, as an evidentiary matter, the reliability of eyewitness identification is central to a criminal justice system dedicated to the dual principles accountability and fairness . . . . Because of the alterations to memory that suggestiveness can cause, it is incumbent on courts and law enforcement personnel to treat eyewitness memory just as carefully as they would other forms of trace evidence, like DNA, bloodstains, or fingerprints, the evidentiary value of which can be impaired or destroyed by contamination.

State v. Cabagbag, 277 P.3d 1027 (Haw. 2012):

> Jurors should be instructed to consider:
>
> The opportunity of the witness to observe the alleged criminal act and the perpetrator of the act;
>
> The stress, if any, to which the witness was subject at the time of the observation;
>
> The witness' ability, following the observation, to provide a description of the perpetrator of the act;
>
> The extent to which the defendant fits or does not fit the description of the perpetrator previously given by the witness;
>
> The cross-racial or ethnic nature of the identification;
>
> The witness' capacity to make an identification;
>
> Evidence relating to the witness' ability to identify other alleged perpetrators of the criminal act;
>
> Whether the witness was able to identify the alleged perpetrator in a photographic or physical lineup;

The period of time between the alleged criminal act and the witness' identification;

Whether the witness had prior contacts with the alleged perpetrator;

The extent to which the witness is either certain or uncertain of the identification;

Whether the witness identification is in fact the product of his own recollection . . . .

The leading case is *State v. Henderson*, 27 A.3d 872 (2011), where the New Jersey Supreme Court, in an exhaustive opinion reviewed the validity of eyewitness testimony and the current framework for determining admissibility of eyewitness identification. The defendant was convicted of several manslaughter, aggravated assault, and gun charges, based upon such identification. On appeal, the case was remanded for a special hearing on the scientific research on the subject of eyewitness identification to determine the validity of eyewitness testimony and the factors that affect it. The judge in the hearing found that eyewitness identification is "the single greatest cause of wrongful convictions in this country," accounting for "more than 75% of convictions overturned due to DNA evidence" nationwide. In research experiments, eyewitnesses misidentified the target in a photo array 41% of the time, and in arrays without the suspect, witnesses still identified one of the fillers 36% of the time. Furthermore, an eyewitness' confidence in her identification is not necessarily related to the accuracy of her identification, given that in 57% of convictions overturned by DNA evidence eyewitnesses testified at trial that they were positive of their identification, even though they had previously been unsure.

Many factors were found to have significant effects on the accuracy and confidence of eyewitness identifications, broken down into two categories: *system variables* — those factors that are controlled by the justice system (as in the procedures for conducting photo arrays, including: whether administration of the photo array is "double-blind"; the instructions given to witnesses before being shown a photo array; feedback from the officers; and the makeup of a photo array), and *estimator variables* — those factors outside of the control of the justice system (environmental factors — such as lighting during the incident, the witness' level of stress during the incident, and the effects of race and age bias — that make it more difficult for witnesses to correctly identify suspects of a different race or substantially different age). The court also found that, while jurors may understand the effects of common-sense factors like lighting on witness accuracy, they often hold beliefs contrary to other factors like the distorting effect of high levels of stress.

Based on the findings in the special hearing, the court held that its rule was inadequate, as it: "[1] does not offer an adequate measure for reliability; [2] does not sufficiently deter inappropriate police conduct; and [3] overstates the jury's ability to evaluate identification evidence." The court found that three of the five factors considered by courts in the second prong of the *Manson* test (opportunity to view the crime, witness' degree of attention, and level of uncertainty at the time of ID) are based on self-reporting of the witness and can be poor measures of accuracy, especially when tainted by suggestive police practices.

The opinion established a new framework for the treatment of eyewitness identification evidence: A pretrial hearing shall be administered if the defendant shows some evidence of police (or private actor) suggestiveness that could lead to mistaken ID (without reference to estimator variables). The state must then offer proof that the eyewitness testimony is reliable, accounting for system and estimator variables. The ultimate burden then remains on the defendant to prove a very substantial likelihood of irreparable misidentification by cross-examining eyewitnesses and police officials and by presenting witnesses and other evidence relating to relevant estimator and system variables. If the court then finds, from a totality of circumstances, that there is a very substantial likelihood of irreparable misidentification, the evidence must be suppressed. If the evidence is admitted, the trial court should give tailored jury instructions explaining to jurors the effects of the various system variables.

One recurring issue here is the degree to which the eyewitness' level of certainty should be considered by the jury. The Georgia Supreme Court in *Brodes v. State*, 614 S.E.2d 766 (Ga. 2005), rejected a jury instruction informing jurors they could consider the witness' level of certainty in determining the reliability of the identification. "[T]he idea that a witness' certainty in his or her identification of a person as a perpetrator reflected the witness' accuracy has been 'flatly contradicted by well-respected and essentially unchallenged empirical studies.' " The Kansas Supreme Court took the same view in *State v. Mitchell*, 275 P.3d 905 (Kan. 2012), noting that looking to certainty leads jurors to decide that eyewitness identification is more reliable if the witness expresses greater certainty.

THE STATE OF THE LAW

MOORE v. ILLINOIS

United States Supreme Court
434 U.S. 220 (1977)

MR. JUSTICE POWELL delivered the opinion of the Court.

I

The victim of the offenses in question lived in an apartment on the South Side of Chicago. Shortly after noon on December 14, 1967, she awakened from a nap to find a man standing in the doorway to her bedroom holding a knife. The man entered the bedroom, threw her face down on the bed, and choked her until she was quiet. After covering his face with a bandana, the intruder partially undressed the victim, forced her to commit oral sodomy, and raped her. Then he left, taking a guitar and a flute from the apartment.

When the police arrived, the victim gave them a description of her assailant. Although she did not know who he was and had seen his face for only 10 to 15 seconds during the attack, she thought he was the same man who had made offensive remarks to her in a neighborhood bar the night before. She also gave police a notebook she had found next to her bed after the attack.

In the week that followed, police showed the victim two groups of photographs of men. From the first group of 200 she picked about 30 who resembled her assailant in height, weight, and build. From the second group of about 10, she picked two or three. One of these was of petitioner. Police also found a letter in the notebook that the victim had given them. Investigation revealed that it was written by a woman with whom petitioner had been staying. The letter had been taken from the woman's home in her absence, and petitioner appeared to be the only other person who had access to the home.

On the evening of December 20, 1967, police arrested petitioner at his apartment and held him overnight pending a preliminary hearing to determine whether he should be bound over to the grand jury and to set bail. The next morning, a policeman accompanied the victim to the Circuit Court of Cook County for the hearing. The policeman told her she was going to view a suspect and should identify him if she could. He also had her sign a complaint that named petitioner as her assailant. At the hearing, petitioner's name was called and he was led before the bench. The judge told petitioner that he was charged with rape and deviate sexual behavior. The judge then called the victim, who had been in the courtroom waiting for the case to be called, to come before the bench. The State's Attorney stated that police had found evidence linking petitioner with the offenses charged. He asked the victim whether she saw her assailant in the courtroom, and she pointed at petitioner. Petitioner was not represented by counsel at this hearing, and the court did not offer to appoint counsel.

At a subsequent hearing . . . [c]ounsel was appointed, and he moved to suppress the victim's identification of petitioner because it had been elicited at the preliminary hearing through an unnecessarily suggestive procedure at which petitioner was not represented by counsel. After an evidentiary hearing the trial court denied the motion on the ground that the prosecution had shown an independent basis for the victim's identification.

At trial, the victim testified on direct examination by the prosecution that she had identified petitioner as her assailant at the preliminary hearing. She also testified that the defendant on trial was the man who had raped her. The prosecution's other evidence linking petitioner with the crimes was the letter found in the victim's apartment. Defense counsel stipulated that petitioner had taken the letter from his woman friend's home, but he presented evidence that petitioner might have lost the notebook containing the letter at the neighborhood bar the night before the attack. The defense theory was that the victim, who also was in the bar that night, could have picked up the notebook by mistake and taken it home. The defense also called witnesses who testified that petitioner was with them in a college lunchroom in another part of Chicago at the time the attack was committed.

The jury found petitioner guilty on all four counts, thus rejecting his theory and alibi.

II

United States v. Wade held that a pretrial corporeal identification conducted after a suspect has been indicted is a critical stage in a criminal prosecution at which the Sixth Amendment entitles the accused to the presence of counsel. The Court emphasized the dangers inherent in a pretrial identification conducted in the absence of counsel. Persons who conduct the identification procedure may suggest, intentionally or unintentionally, that they expect the witness to identify the accused. Such a suggestion, coming from a police officer or prosecutor, can lead a witness to make a mistaken identification. The witness then will be predisposed to adhere to this identification in subsequent testimony at trial.

III

In the instant case, petitioner argues that the preliminary hearing at which the victim identified him marked the initiation of adversary judicial criminal proceedings against him. Hence, under *Wade*, *Gilbert*, and *Kirby*, he was entitled to the presence of counsel at that confrontation. Moreover, the prosecution introduced evidence of this uncounseled corporeal identification at trial in its case-in-chief. Petitioner contends that under *Gilbert*, this evidence should have been excluded without regard to whether there was an "independent source" for it.

The Court of Appeals took a different view of the case. It read *Kirby* as holding that evidence of a corporeal identification conducted in the absence of defense counsel must be excluded only if the identification is made after the defendant is *indicted.*

Such a reading cannot be squared with *Kirby* itself, which held that an accused's rights under *Wade* and *Gilbert* attach to identification conducted "at or after the initiation of adversary judicial criminal proceedings," including proceedings instituted "by way of formal charge [or] preliminary hearing."

The prosecution in this case was commenced under Illinois law when the victim's complaint was filed in court. The purpose of the preliminary hearing was to determine whether there was probable cause to bind petitioner over to the grand jury and to set bail. Petitioner had the right to oppose the prosecution at that hearing by moving to dismiss the charges and to suppress the evidence against him. He faced counsel for the State, who elicited the victim's identification, summarized the State's other evidence against petitioner, and urged that the State be given more time to marshal its evidence. It is plain that "the government ha[d] committed itself to prosecute," and that petitioner found "himself faced with the prosecutorial forces of organized society, and immersed in the intricacies of substantive and procedural criminal law."

The reasons supporting *Wade*'s holding that a corporeal identification is a critical stage of a criminal prosecution for Sixth Amendment purposes apply with equal force to this identification. It is difficult to imagine a more suggestive manner in which to present a suspect to a witness for their critical first confrontation than was employed in this case. The victim, who had seen her assailant for only 10 to 15 seconds, was asked to make her identification after she was told that she was going to view a suspect, after she was told his name and heard it called as he was led before the bench, and after she heard the prosecutor recite the evidence believed to implicate petitioner. Had petitioner been represented by counsel, some or all of this suggestiveness could have been avoided.[10]

In sum, we are unpersuaded by the reasons advanced by the Court of Appeals for distinguishing the identification procedure in this case from those considered in *Wade* and *Gilbert*. Here, as in those cases, petitioner's Sixth Amendment rights were violated by a corporeal identification conducted after the initiation of adversary judicial criminal proceedings and in the absence of counsel.

Mr. Justice Stevens took no part in consideration or decision of the case.

Mr. Justice Rehnquist, concurring. I believe the time will come when the Court will have to reevaluate and reconsider the *Wade-Gilbert* rule. The rule was established to ensure the accuracy and reliability of pretrial identifications and the Court will have to decide whether a *per se* exclusionary rule should still apply or whether *Wade-Gilbert* violations, like other questions involving the reliability of pretrial identification, should be judged under the totality of the circumstances. *Cf. Manson v. Brathwaite.*

PRELIMINARY EXAMINATION

Rule 5.1 of the Federal Rules of Criminal Procedure provides in part:

> (a) **In general.** If a defendant is charged with an offense other than a petty offense, a magistrate judge must conduct a preliminary hearing unless:
>
> (1) the defendant waives the hearing;
>
> (2) the defendant is indicted;
>
> (3) the government files an information under Rule 7(b) charging the defendant with a felony;
>
> (4) the government files an information charging the defendant with a misdemeanor; or
>
> (5) the defendant is charged with a misdemeanor and consents to trial before a magistrate judge.
>
> . . .
>
> (e) **Hearing and Finding.** At the preliminary hearing, the defendant may cross-examine adverse witnesses and may introduce evidence but may not object to evidence on the ground that it was unlawfully acquired. If the magistrate judge

---

[10] [5] For example, counsel could have requested that the hearing be postponed until a lineup could be arranged at which the victim would view petitioner in a less suggestive setting. Short of that, counsel could have asked that the victim be excused from the courtroom while the charges were read and the evidence against petitioner was recited, and that petitioner be seated with other people in the audience when the victim attempted an identification. Counsel might have sought to cross-examine the victim to test her identification before it hardened. Because it is in the prosecution's interest as well as the accused's that witnesses' identifications remain untainted, we cannot assume that such requests would have been in vain. Such requests ordinarily are addressed to the sound discretion of the court. [W]e express no opinion as to whether the preliminary hearing court would have been required to grant any such request.

finds probable cause to believe an offense has been committed and the defendant committed it, the magistrate judge must promptly require the defendant to appear for further proceedings.

COLEMAN v. ALABAMA

United States Supreme Court
399 U.S. 1 (1970)

MR. JUSTICE BRENNAN announced the judgment of the Court and delivered the following opinion.

Petitioners were convicted in an Alabama Circuit Court of assault with intent to murder. Petitioners argue that the preliminary hearing prior to their indictment was a "critical stage" of the prosecution and that Alabama's failure to provide them with appointed counsel at the hearing therefore unconstitutionally denied them the assistance of counsel.

This Court has held that a person accused of crime "requires the guiding hand of counsel at every step in the proceedings against him," *Powell v. Alabama*, and that that constitutional principle is not limited to the presence of counsel at trial. "It is central to that principle that in addition to counsel's presence at trial, the accused is guaranteed that he need not stand alone against the State at any stage of the prosecution, formal or informal, in court or out, where counsel's absence might derogate from the accused's right to a fair trial." *United States v. Wade*.

Accordingly, "the principle of *Powell v. Alabama* and succeeding cases requires that we scrutinize *any* pretrial confrontation of the accused to determine whether the presence of his counsel is necessary to preserve the defendant's basic right to a fair trial as affected by his right meaningfully to cross-examine the witnesses against him and to have effective assistance of counsel at the trial itself. It calls upon us to analyze whether potential substantial prejudice to defendant's rights inheres in the particular confrontation and the ability of counsel to help avoid that prejudice."

Applying this test, the Court has held that "critical stages" include the pretrial type of arraignment where certain rights may be sacrificed or lost, *Hamilton v. Alabama*.

The preliminary hearing is not a required step in an Alabama prosecution. The prosecutor may seek an indictment directly from the grand jury without a preliminary hearing.

The opinion of the Alabama Court of Appeals in this case instructs us that under Alabama law the sole purposes of a preliminary hearing are to determine whether there is sufficient evidence against the accused to warrant presenting his case to the grand jury and, if so, to fix bail if the offense is bailable.

However, from the fact that in cases where the accused has no lawyer at the hearing the Alabama courts prohibit the State's use at trial of anything that occurred at the hearing, it does not follow that the Alabama preliminary hearing is not a "critical stage" of the State's criminal process. The determination whether the hearing is a "critical stage" requiring the provision of counsel depends, as noted, upon an analysis "whether potential substantial prejudice to defendant's rights inheres . . . in the . . . confrontation and the ability of counsel to help avoid that prejudice." *United States v. Wade.*

Plainly the guiding hand of counsel at the preliminary hearing is essential to protect the indigent accused against an erroneous or improper prosecution. First, the lawyer's skilled examination and cross-examination of witnesses may expose fatal weaknesses in the State's case that may lead the magistrate to refuse to bind the accused over. Second, in any event, the skilled interrogation of witnesses by an experienced lawyer can fashion a vital impeachment tool for use in cross-examination of the State's witnesses at the trial, or preserve testimony favorable to the accused of a witness who does not appear at the trial. Third, trained counsel can more effectively discover the case the State has against his client and make possible the preparation of a proper defense to meet that case at the trial. Fourth, counsel can also be influential at the preliminary hearing in making effective arguments for the accused on such matters as the necessity for an early psychiatric examination or bail.

There remains, then, the question of the relief to which petitioners are entitled. The trial transcript indicates that the prohibition against use by the State at trial of anything that occurred at the preliminary hearing was scrupulously observed. But on the record it cannot be said whether or not petitioners were otherwise prejudiced by the absence of counsel at the preliminary hearing. That inquiry in the first instance should more properly be made by the Alabama courts. The test to be applied is whether the denial of counsel at the preliminary hearing was harmless error.

We accordingly vacate the petitioners' convictions and remand the case to the Alabama courts for such proceedings not inconsistent with this opinion as they may deem appropriate to determine whether such denial of counsel was harmless error, see *Gilbert v. California*, and therefore whether the convictions should be reinstated or a new trial ordered.

Mr. Justice Blackmun took no part in the consideration or decision of the case.

Mr. Justice Black and Mr. Justice Douglas wrote concurring opinions.

Mr. Justice White concurring.

I agree with Mr. Justice Harlan that recent cases furnish ample ground for holding the preliminary hearing a critical event in the progress of a criminal case. I therefore join the prevailing opinion, but with some hesitation since requiring the appointment of counsel may result in fewer preliminary hearings in jurisdictions where the prosecutor is free to avoid them by taking a case directly to a grand jury. Our ruling may also invite eliminating the preliminary hearing system entirely.

MR. JUSTICE HARLAN, concurring in part and dissenting in part.

If I felt free to consider this case upon a clean slate I would have voted to affirm these convictions. But — in light of the lengths to which the right to appointed counsel has been carried in recent decisions of this Court — I consider that course is not open to me with due regard for the way in which the adjudicatory process of this Court, as I conceive it, should work.

I consider the scope of the Court's remand too broad and amorphous. I do not think that reversal of these convictions, for lack of counsel at the preliminary hearing, should follow unless petitioners are able to show on remand that they have been prejudiced in their defense at trial, in that favorable testimony that might otherwise have been preserved was irretrievably lost by virtue of not having counsel to help present an affirmative case at the preliminary hearing.

MR. CHIEF JUSTICE BURGER dissenting.

With deference I am bound to reject categorically MR. JUSTICE HARLAN's thesis that what the Court said lately controls over the Constitution. While our holdings are entitled to deference I will not join in employing recent cases rather than the Constitution, to bootstrap ourselves into a result, even though I agree with the objective of having counsel at preliminary hearings. By placing a premium on "recent cases" rather than the language of the Constitution, the Court makes it dangerously simple for future Courts, using the technique of interpretation, to operate as a "continuing Constitutional convention."

MR. JUSTICE STEWART, with whom the CHIEF JUSTICE joins, dissenting.

If at the trial the prosecution had used any incriminating statements made by the petitioners at the preliminary hearing, the convictions before us would quite properly have to be set aside.

But that did not happen in this case. Or if the prosecution had used the statement of any other witness at the preliminary hearing against the petitioners at their trial, we would likewise quite properly have to set aside these convictions.

But that did not happen in this case either. For, as the prevailing opinion today perforce concedes, "the prohibition against use by the State at trial of anything that occurred at the preliminary hearing was scrupulously observed."

Nevertheless, the Court sets aside the convictions because, it says, counsel should have been provided for the petitioners at the preliminary hearing. None of the cases relied upon in that opinion points to any such result.

But the prevailing opinion holds today that the Constitution required Alabama to provide a lawyer for the petitioners at their preliminary hearing, not so much, it seems, to assure a fair trial as to assure a fair preliminary hearing. A lawyer at the preliminary hearing, the opinion says, might have led the magistrate to "refuse to bind the accused over." Or a lawyer might have made "effective arguments for the accused on such matters as the necessity for an early psychiatric examination or bail."

If *those* are the reasons a lawyer must be provided, then the most elementary logic requires that a new preliminary hearing must now be held, with counsel made available to the petitioners. In order to provide such relief, it would, of course, be necessary not only to set aside these convictions, but also to set aside the grand jury indictments, and the magistrate's orders fixing bail and binding over the petitioners. Since the petitioners have now been found by a jury in a constitutional trial to be guilty beyond a reasonable doubt, the prevailing opinion understandably boggles at these logical consequences of the reasoning therein. It refrains, in short, from now turning back the clock by ordering a new preliminary hearing to determine all over again whether there is sufficient evidence against the accused to present their case to a grand jury. Instead, the Court sets aside these convictions and remands the case for determination "whether the convictions should be reinstated or a new trial ordered," and this action seems to me even more quixotic.

The petitioners have simply not alleged that anything that happened at the preliminary hearing turned out in this case to be critical to the fairness of their *trial.* They have not alleged that they were affirmatively prejudiced at the trial by anything that occurred at the preliminary hearing. They have not pointed to any affirmative advantage they would have enjoyed at the trial if they had had a lawyer at their preliminary hearing.

No record or transcript of any kind was made of the preliminary hearing. Therefore, if the burden on remand is on the petitioners to show that they were prejudiced, it is clear that that burden cannot be met and the remand is a futile gesture. If, on the other hand, the burden is on the State to disprove beyond a reasonable doubt any and all speculative advantages that the petitioners might conceivably have enjoyed if counsel had been present at their preliminary hearing, then obviously that burden cannot be met either, and the Court should simply reverse these convictions. All I can say is that if the Alabama courts can figure out what they are supposed to do with this case now that it has been remanded to them, their perceptiveness will far exceed mine.

The record before us makes clear that no evidence of what occurred at the preliminary hearing was used against the petitioners at their now completed trial. I would hold, therefore, that the absence of counsel at the preliminary hearing deprived the petitioners of no constitutional rights. Accordingly, I would affirm these convictions.

NOTES AND QUESTIONS

(1) The majority determined that the preliminary hearing was a critical stage requiring the assistance of counsel because counsel was needed "to preserve the defendant's basic right to a fair trial." Why was counsel needed in this case? Was Justice Stewart correct that the fair trial right was not affected because under Alabama law statements made by the defendant or by witnesses could not be used at trial?

(2) Justice Brennan set out four reasons why the preliminary hearing was a critical stage under the Sixth Amendment. In light of this opinion, why did the

Court hold that the preindictment lineup in *Kirby* was not a critical stage? Are the two cases distinguishable?

(3) The majority gave little guidance to the state courts on the remand concerning the harmless error issue. On whom does the burden fall — the defendant to prove that the lack of a lawyer prejudiced his case, or the government to prove that it did not prejudice the defendant's case? With no record or transcript of the hearing, could either side sustain its burden? Is Justice Stewart correct that "the remand is a futile gesture"? Consider *Burgett v. Alabama*, 516 F.2d 524 (5th Cir. 1975), in which there was no counsel appointed at the preliminary hearing held in 1972, but there was an attorney at trial. As in *Coleman*, there was no record of the preliminary hearing. The Court of Appeals remanded the case to the District Court to determine whether Sixth Amendment rights had been violated almost four years earlier. If you were the District Judge, how would you make this determination?

(4) Justice White expressed concern that the decision in *Coleman* might discourage the holding of preliminary examinations in states where the prosecutor could use a grand jury proceeding in its place. Why would this result? Would it be desirable?

(5) Are lawyers required at bail hearings? In *State v. LeDoux*, 770 N.W.2d 504 (Minn. 2009), and *State v. Williams*, 210 S.E.2d 298 (S.C. 1974), the courts said no. As stated by the *Williams* court, "He was not required to plead to the charges nor was any occurrence or statement at the hearing used in his subsequent trial." Were these cases properly decided under the rule in *Coleman*? Would the result change if statements at the hearing were used at trial? A strong argument for requiring lawyers at bail hearings is made in Colbert, Paternoster and Bushway, *Do Attorneys Really Matter? The Empirical and Legal Case for the Right of Counsel at Bail*, 23 Cardozo L. Rev. 1719 (2002).

(6) Justice Harlan made very clear that he felt bound to concur in *Coleman* because of the decisions in other cases, such as *Wade*, in which he dissented. Chief Justice Burger expressly repudiated this position and looked to the language of the Constitution rather than the Court's recent opinions. Which of the two Justices more properly reacted to the Court's prior holdings as well as to the principle of *stare decisis*?

GRAND JURY PROCEEDINGS

The grand jury occupies an important and unique role in the American criminal justice system. As indicated in the introductory chapter, grand juries are used widely throughout the country in the investigation of all types of criminal activity. Justice Black, in *Costello v. United States*, 350 U.S. 359 (1956), explained the background of the institution:

> The Fifth Amendment provides that federal prosecutions for capital or otherwise infamous crimes must be instituted by presentments or indictments of grand juries. But neither the Fifth Amendment nor any other constitutional provision prescribes the kind of evidence upon which grand juries must act. The grand jury is an English institution, brought to this

> country by the early colonists and incorporated in the Constitution by the Founders. There is every reason to believe that our constitutional grand jury was intended to operate substantially like its English progenitor. The basic purpose of the English grand jury was to provide a fair method for instituting criminal proceedings against persons believed to have committed crimes. Grand jurors were selected from the body of the people and their work was not hampered by rigid procedural or evidential rules. In fact, grand jurors could act on their own knowledge and were free to make their presentments or indictments on such information as they deemed satisfactory. Despite its broad power to institute criminal proceedings the grand jury grew in popular favor with the years. It acquired an independence in England free from control by the Crown or judges. Its adoption in our Constitution as the sole method for preferring charges in serious criminal cases shows the high place it held as an instrument of justice. And in this country as in England of old the grand jury has convened as a body of laymen, free from technical rules, acting in secret, pledged to indict no one because of prejudice and to free no one because of special favor.

Traditionally witness' counsel were not allowed to appear before the grand jury as such appearance was thought to be inconsistent with the investigative function of the grand jury. This view was reflected in dicta of the Court in *In re Groban*, 352 U.S. 330, 333 (1957): "A witness before a grand jury cannot insist, as a matter of constitutional right, on being represented by his counsel. . . . Obviously . . . evidence obtained may possibly lay a witness open to criminal charges. When such charges are made in a criminal proceeding, he then may demand the presence of his counsel for his defense." While the opinion stated clearly the counsel rule, question was raised as to its precedential value. The case was decided before *Gideon*. Also, there was a vigorous dissent in *Groban*, filed by Justice Black (and joined by Chief Justice Warren and Justices Douglas and Brennan):

> I also firmly believe that the Due Process Clause requires that a person interrogated be allowed to use legal counsel whenever he is compelled to give testimony to law-enforcement officers which may be instrumental in his prosecution and conviction for a criminal offense. This Court has repeatedly held that an accused in a state criminal prosecution has an unqualified right to make use of counsel at every stage of the proceedings against him.

The question after *Gideon*, then, was whether Justice Black would have his way here, as he had in *Gideon*.

UNITED STATES v. MANDUJANO

United States Supreme Court
425 U.S. 564 (1976)

MR. CHIEF JUSTICE BURGER announced the judgment of the Court in an opinion in which MR. JUSTICE WHITE, MR. JUSTICE POWELL, and MR. JUSTICE REHNQUIST join.

During the course of a grand jury investigation into narcotics traffic in San Antonio, Tex., federal prosecutors assigned to the Drug Enforcement Administration Task Force learned of an undercover narcotics officer's encounter with respondent in March 1973. At that time, the agent had received information that respondent, who was employed as a bartender at a local tavern, was dealing in narcotics. At that time, the Government was seeking information on local drug traffic to present to a special grand jury investigating illicit traffic in the area.

Respondent was subpoenaed to testify before the grand jury on May 2, 1973. When called into the grand jury room and after preliminary statements, the following colloquy occurred between the prosecutor and respondent:

Q: Now, you are required to answer all the questions that I ask you except for the ones that you feel would tend to incriminate you. Do you understand that?

A: Do I answer all the questions you ask?

Q: You have to answer all the questions except for those you think will incriminate you in the commission of a crime. Is that clear?

A: Yes, sir. . . .

Q: You don't have to answer questions which would incriminate you. All other questions you have to answer openly and truthfully. And, of course, if you do not answer those [questions] truthfully, in other words if you lie about certain questions, you could possibly be charged with perjury. Do you understand that?

A: Yes, sir.

Q: Have you contacted a lawyer in this matter? . . .

A: I don't have one. I don't have the money to get one.

Q: Well, if you would like to have a lawyer, he cannot be inside this room. He can only be outside. You would be free to consult with him if you so chose. Now, if during the course of this investigation, the questions that we ask you, if you feel like you would like to have a lawyer outside to talk to, let me know.

Following this appearance, respondent was charged by a grand jury on June 13, 1973, in a two-count indictment with attempting to distribute heroin in violation of 21 U.S.C. §§ 841(a)(1), 846, and for willfully and knowingly making a false material declaration to the grand jury in violation of 18 U.S.C. § 1623. The falsity of his statements was conceded: his sole claim was that the testimony before the grand jury should be suppressed.

The grand jury is an integral part of our constitutional heritage which was brought to this country with the common law. The Framers, most of them trained in English law and traditions, accepted the grand jury as a basic guarantee of individual liberty; notwithstanding periodic criticism, much of which is superficial, overlooking relevant history, the grand jury continues to function as a barrier to reckless or unfounded charges. "Its adoption in our Constitution as the sole method for preferring charges in serious criminal cases shows the high place it held as an instrument of justice." *Costello v. United States.*

Its historic office has been to provide a shield against arbitrary or oppressive action, by insuring that serious criminal accusations will be brought only upon the considered judgment of a representative body of citizens acting under oath and under judicial instruction and guidance.

Earlier we noted that the law vests the grand jury with substantial powers, because "[t]he grand jury's investigative power must be broad if its public responsibility is adequately to be discharged."

Respondent was also informed that if he desired he could have the assistance of counsel, but that counsel could not be inside the grand jury room. That statement was plainly a correct recital of the law. No criminal proceedings had been instituted against respondent, hence the Sixth Amendment right to counsel had not come into play. *Kirby v. Illinois.*

A witness "before a grand jury cannot insist, as a matter of constitutional right, on being represented by his counsel. . . ." *In re Groban*, under settled principles the witness may not insist upon the presence of his attorney in the grand jury room.

MR. JUSTICE STEVENS took no part in the consideration or decision of this case.

MR. JUSTICE BRENNAN, with whom MR. JUSTICE MARSHALL joins, concurring in the judgment.

A disturbing facet of the plurality opinion today is its statement that "[n]o criminal proceedings had been instituted against respondent, hence the Sixth Amendment right to counsel had not come into play." It will not do simply to cite, as does the plurality opinion, *Kirby v. Illinois* for this proposition. *Kirby*'s premise, so fundamental that it was "note[d] at the outset," was that "the constitutional privilege against compulsory self-incrimination is in no way implicated here."

In sharp contrast, the privilege against compulsory self-incrimination is inextricably involved in this case since a putative defendant is called and interrogated before a grand jury. Clearly in such a case a defendant is "faced with the prosecutorial forces of organized society, and immersed in the intricacies of substantive and procedural criminal law."

Accepted principles require scrutiny of any situation wherein a right to the assistance of counsel is claimed by "analyz[ing] whether potential substantial prejudice to defendant's rights inheres in the particular confrontation and the ability of counsel to help avoid that prejudice." *United States v. Wade, Coleman v. Alabama.* Given the inherent danger of subversion of the adversary system in the case of a putative defendant called to testify before a grand jury, and the peculiarly critical role of the Fifth Amendment privilege as the bulwark against such abuse, it is plainly obvious that some guidance by counsel is required. This conclusion entertains only the "realistic recognition of the obvious truth that the average [putative] defendant does not have the professional legal skill to protect himself when brought before a tribunal . . . wherein the prosecution is [represented] by experienced and learned counsel." Under such conditions it "would indeed be strange were this Court" to hold that a putative defendant, called before a grand jury and interrogated concerning the substance of the crime for which he is in imminent danger of being criminally charged, is simply to be left to "fend for himself."

There is clearly no argument that a procedure allowing a putative defendant called to testify before a grand jury to consult at will with counsel outside the grand jury room prior to answering any given question would in any way impermissibly "delay and disrupt grand jury proceedings." This is clearly manifested by the plethora of reported instances in which just such procedures have been followed. Nor would such a procedure damage the constitutional "role and functions of the grand jury," for the only effect on its investigative function is to secure a putative defendant's Fifth Amendment privilege and thereby avoid subversion of the adversary system.

It is, of course, unnecessary in this case to define the exact dimensions of the right to counsel since the testimony obtained by the grand jury interrogation was not introduced as evidence at respondent's trial on the charge concerning which he was questioned. I write only to make plain my disagreement with the implication in the plurality opinion that constitutional rights to counsel are not involved in a grand jury proceeding.

MR. JUSTICE STEWART wrote a concurring opinion in which MR. JUSTICE BLACKMUN joined.

NOTES AND QUESTIONS

(1) If the government has focused its investigation on the defendant, and the defendant was charged after appearing before the grand jury, why would there be no right to counsel before the grand jury? Is it correct to say that "no criminal proceedings had been instituted"? Suppose the defendant could later be charged with contempt for failure to testify before the grand jury. Would the defendant then have a right to counsel at the grand jury proceedings? At the contempt proceeding? See *People v. Johnson*, 283 N.W.2d 632 (Mich. 1979), requiring counsel at state expense at the contempt proceeding. Did the plurality in *Mandujano* adequately respond to the dissent's concern that the self-incrimination issue involved in a grand jury proceeding makes that proceeding the Sixth Amendment equivalent of a post-indictment adversary action?

(2) If the government attorney is present during the grand jury proceeding, is there a good policy reason for keeping the witness' counsel away? What function

would defense counsel serve? Would that function be inconsistent with the role of the grand jury?

(3) In most jurisdictions no attorney is allowed for the defendant during the grand jury deliberations. Some states, though, do provide for counsel. *See, e.g.*, Colo. Rev. Stat. § 16-5-204:

> Any witness subpoenaed to appear and testify before a grand jury or to produce books, papers, documents, or other objects before such grand jury shall be entitled to assistance of counsel during any time that such witness is being questioned in the presence of such grand jury, and counsel may be present in the grand jury room with his client during such questioning. However, counsel for the witness shall be permitted only to counsel with the witness and shall not make objections, arguments, or address the grand jury. Such counsel may be retained by the witness or may, for any person financially unable to obtain adequate assistance, be appointed in the same manner as if that person were eligible for appointed counsel. An attorney present in the grand jury room shall take an oath of secrecy. If the court, at an in camera hearing, determines that counsel was disruptive, then the court may order counsel to remain outside the courtroom when advising his client. No attorney shall be permitted to provide counsel in the grand jury room to more than one witness in the same criminal investigation, except with the permission of the grand jury.

There is still no post-*Gideon* holding regarding the right to counsel in grand jury proceedings, as only four Justices joined the plurality opinion in *Mandujano.* Justice Stevens did not participate, Justices Brennan and Marshall dissented from the narrow conclusion, and Justices Stewart and Blackmun would have reversed the judgment "without reaching the other issues explored in the Chief Justice's opinion and in Mr. Justice Brennan's separate opinion."

(4) One well-known commentator, a former prosecutor, strongly criticizes the decision in *Mandujano*:

> Here [we see] an indigent defendant, alone in a room full of citizens expecting answers from the person who is most qualified to provide explanations. The prosecutor, who controls the proceedings and will conduct the interrogation, provides legalistic explanations. . . . [The prosecutor] is a person steeped in the nuances of the privilege against self-incrimination and in the mechanics of grand jury practice. The isolation and secrecy of the grand jury proceeding is ameliorated by the presence of the grand jurors. How much of a palliative the grand jurors provide, however, is questionable, as they are not there to comfort the witness but to get answers from him. It didn't take Mandujano long to figure out who was in control of the grand jury room: the prosecutor, not the grand jurors.

Garcia, *The Fifth Amendment: A Comprehensive Approach*, at 149 (Greenwood Press, 2002).

SENTENCING

MEMPA v. RHAY

United States Supreme Court
389 U.S. 128 (1967)

MR. JUSTICE MARSHALL delivered the opinion of the Court.

These consolidated cases raise the question of the extent of the right to counsel at the time of sentencing where the sentencing has been deferred subject to probation. Petitioner Jerry Douglas Mempa was convicted in the Spokane County Superior Court of the offense of "joyriding," WASH. REV. CODE § 9.54.020. This conviction was based on his plea of guilty entered with the advice of court-appointed counsel. He was then placed on probation for two years on the condition, *inter alia*, that he first spend 30 days in the county jail, and the imposition of sentence was deferred pursuant to WASH. REV. CODE §§ 9.95.200, 9.95.210. About four months later the Spokane County prosecuting attorney moved to have petitioner's probation revoked on the ground that he had been involved in a burglary on September 15, 1959. A hearing was held in the Spokane County Superior Court on October 23, 1959. Petitioner Mempa, who was 17 years old at the time, was accompanied to the hearing by his stepfather. He was not represented by counsel and was not asked whether he wished to have counsel appointed for him. Nor was any inquiry made concerning the appointed counsel who had previously represented him.

At the hearing Mempa was asked if it was true that he had been involved in the alleged burglary and he answered in the affirmative. A probation officer testified without cross-examination that according to his information petitioner had been involved in the burglary and had previously denied participation in it. Without asking petitioner if he had anything to say or any evidence to supply, the court immediately entered an order revoking petitioner's probation and then sentenced him to 10 years in the penitentiary, but stated that it would recommend to the parole board that Mempa be required to serve only a year.[11]

In 1948 this Court held in *Townsend v. Burke* that the absence of counsel during sentencing after a plea of guilty coupled with "assumptions concerning his criminal record which were materially untrue" deprived the defendant in that case of due process. Mr. Justice Jackson there stated in conclusion, "In this case, counsel might not have changed the sentence, but he could have taken steps to see that the conviction and sentence were not predicated on misinformation or misreading of court records. . . ."

There was no occasion in *Gideon* to enumerate the various stages in a criminal proceeding at which counsel was required, but *Townsend*, and *Hamilton*, when the *Betts* requirement of special circumstances is stripped away by *Gideon*, clearly

[11] [2] Under Washington procedure the trial judge is required by statute to impose the maximum sentence provided by law for the offense, Wash. Rev. Code § 9.95.010, but is also required, along with the prosecuting attorney, to make a recommendation to the parole board of the time that the defendant should serve accompanied by a statement of the facts concerning the crime and any other information about the defendant deemed relevant. Wash. Rev. Code § 9.95.030. However, it is the parole board that actually determines the time to be served. Wash. Rev. Code § 9.95.040.

stand for the proposition that appointment of counsel for an indigent is required at every stage of a criminal proceeding where substantial rights of a criminal accused may be affected. In particular, *Townsend v. Burke, supra,* illustrates the critical nature of sentencing in a criminal case and might well be considered to support by itself a holding that the right to counsel applies at sentencing. Many lower courts have concluded that the Sixth Amendment right to counsel extends to sentencing in federal cases.

The State, however, argues that the petitioners were sentenced at the time they were originally placed on probation and that the imposition of sentence following probation revocation is, in effect, a mere formality constituting part of the probation revocation proceeding. It is true that sentencing in Washington offers fewer opportunities for the exercise of judicial discretion than in many other jurisdictions. The applicable statute requires the trial judge in all cases to sentence the convicted person to the maximum term provided by law for the offense of which he was convicted. The actual determination of the length of time to be served is to be made by the Board of Prison Terms and Paroles within six months after the convicted person is admitted to prison.

On the other hand, the sentencing judge is required by statute, together with the prosecutor, to furnish the Board with a recommendation as to the length of time that the person should serve, in addition to supplying it with various information about the circumstances of the crime and the character of the individual. We were informed during oral argument that the Board places considerable weight on these recommendations, although it is in no way bound by them.

Obviously to the extent such recommendations are influential in determining the resulting sentence, the necessity for the aid of counsel in marshaling the facts, introducing evidence of mitigating circumstances and in general aiding and assisting the defendant to present his case as to sentence is apparent.

Even more important in a case such as this is the fact that certain legal rights may be lost if not exercised at this stage. For one, Washington law provides that an appeal in a case involving a plea of guilty followed by probation can only be taken after sentence is imposed following revocation of probation.

Therefore in a case where an accused agreed to plead guilty, although he had a valid defense, because he was offered probation, absence of counsel at the imposition of the deferred sentence might well result in loss of the right to appeal.

Likewise, the Washington statutes provide that a plea of guilty can be withdrawn at any time prior to the imposition of sentence, if the trial judge in his discretion finds that the ends of justice will be served.

Without undertaking to catalog the various situations in which a lawyer could be of substantial assistance to a defendant in such a case, it can be reiterated that a plea of guilty might well be improperly obtained by the promise to have a defendant placed on the very probation the revocation of which furnishes the occasion for desiring to withdraw the plea. An uncounseled defendant might very likely be unaware of this opportunity.

The two foregoing factors assume increased significance when it is considered that the eventual imposition of sentence on the prior plea of guilty is based on the alleged commission of offenses for which the accused is never tried.

In sum, we do not question the authority of the State of Washington to provide for a deferred sentencing procedure coupled with its probation provisions. Indeed, it appears to be an enlightened step forward. All we decide here is that a lawyer must be afforded at this proceeding whether it be labeled a revocation of probation or a deferred sentencing. We assume that counsel appointed for the purpose of the trial or guilty plea would not be unduly burdened by being requested to follow through at the deferred sentencing stage of the proceeding.

NOTES AND QUESTIONS

(1) Justice Marshall stated that the appointment of a lawyer is required, under *Gideon*, "at every stage of a criminal proceeding where substantial rights of a criminal accused may be affected." What rights of Mempa were affected by not having a lawyer present at his sentencing hearing? Was it a right related to the fact that the judge could make recommendations regarding the sentence to be served? What about the facts that the judge was required to sentence the defendant to the maximum under the statute and that the Board of Parole did not have to follow the judge's recommendation?

(2) The Court relied heavily on the *Townsend* case where the sentencing judge had decided on punishment while having misinformation about the defendant's record. Is that case distinguishable from *Mempa*? Should it matter that *Townsend* was decided under the Due Process Clause rather than the Sixth Amendment?

(3) In *People v. Burton*, 205 N.W.2d 873 (Mich. 1973), the defendant, after being convicted of armed robbery, was interviewed by a probation officer. During this interview the defendant admitted that he had committed three other robberies. The defendant's attorney was not allowed to be present during this interview. The judge relied on the interview in imposing sentence. The defendant argued that the presentence interview was a critical stage and he should have had his lawyer present. The court rejected the argument:

> We do not see a need for the presence of counsel at the presentence interview. To so require would impede the function of the probation department during the interview. Further, the presence of counsel could inhibit defendants from answering questions, which in turn could work to their detriment as the judge would be prevented from obtaining as complete a picture of antecedents, character, and circumstances of the defendant. The sentencing procedure itself should continue to be the proper forum for safeguards where counsel, presumably with the benefit of his client's version of the prior interview, can highlight any irregularities in the report.

In deciding this case, the court did not cite *Mempa*. Was the case correctly decided under *Mempa*? *Burton* was overruled in *People v. Wright*, 430 N.W.2d 133 (Mich. 1988), with the court relying heavily on one of the *Miranda* cases, *Estelle v. Smith*. *See* § 5.03, Problem I, *infra*. *Consider United States v. Hone*, 456 F.2d 495 (6th Cir. 1972), where the trial judge had a practice of conferring with his probation staff to discuss sentencing. The United States Attorney was invited to this conference, but the defense attorney was not. The appellate court directed the trial judge to modify the procedure so that counsel for the defendant would be present as well:

> We believe that the presence of United States Attorneys at the presentence conferences, in the absence of defense counsel, fosters a possibility that the defendant's rights will not be adequately protected. The potential prejudice which might result under this practice is vividly revealed in *Townsend v. Burke, supra.* There the Supreme Court reversed a conviction where the defendant had been prejudiced during sentencing either by the prosecutor's submission of misinformation regarding the defendant's past criminal record or by the trial court's misreading of that record. Whereas the requirement that defense counsel be present at the open-court sentencing proceedings now presumably protects against any such misreading of the information on which the trial judge expressly relies in setting the sentence, we believe that the District Court's practice of inviting the United States Attorneys, but not defense counsel, to the pre-sentence conferences affords an unnecessary risk that the prosecutors might supply incorrect and unchallenged information which could influence the sentence.

PROBLEM E
SENTENCING

What role is the defense counsel to play at the sentencing stage? Does she still remain the advocate, seeking to obtain the most favorable disposition for her client? If she is the advocate, in what ways should she support her client? The ABA Standards for Criminal Justice provide in Section 4-8.1:

> (a) Defense counsel should, at the earliest possible time, . . . become familiar with all of the sentencing alternatives available to the court . . . . The consequences of the various dispositions available should be explained fully by defense counsel to the accused.
>
> (b) Defense counsel should present to the court any ground which will assist in reaching a proper disposition favorable to the accused. . . . [Counsel should] be prepared to suggest a program of rehabilitation based on defense counsel's exploration of employment, educational, and other opportunities made available by community services.
>
> (c) Defense counsel should also insure that the accused understands the nature of the presentence investigation process, and in particular the significance of statements made by the accused to probation officers and related personnel. . . .
>
> (d) Defense counsel should alert the accused . . . to the possible dangers of making a statement that might tend to prejudice an appeal.

The Illinois commentary to this section reiterates the concern as to the function of the lawyer:

> Discussion of the role of the defense counsel with reference to the sentencing process disclosed a variety of responses from practitioners.

Some defense attorneys were of the opinion, that unless the sentence question was related to plea negotiations, that their role in relation to sentence following a guilty finding is to, ad hoc, make the most persuasive arguments possible in favor of lenient treatment for the offender. Many lawyers did not see themselves as being responsible for investigation and the development of evidentiary presentations on the offender's background and needs. Other lawyers felt that representation at the sentence hearing was as important, given a conviction, as representation at trial. Some lawyers commented that they have represented clients where no serious question on the issue of guilt could be raised, but that they felt they could be of great service to the client on the question of sentence.

FORM PRESENTENCE REPORT

In connection with sentencing the trial judge will normally direct the probation department to prepare a presentence report. The following model report was prepared for one federal trial court in Florida.

UNITED STATES DISTRICT COURT
FOR THE MIDDLE DISTRICT OF FLORIDA
OCALA DIVISION

UNITED STATES OF AMERICA	)	
	)	**PRESENTENCE INVESTIGATION REPORT**
v.	)	**Docket No. 5:08-Cr-01-Oc-10GRJ**
	)	
David Mali, Jr.	)	
a/k/a "Malman"	)	
a/k/a "Jr."	)	

Prepared For: The Honorable Wm. Terrell Hodges
Senior United States District Judge

Prepared By: John Smith
United States Probation Officer
Ocala, Florida (352) 629-0435, ext. 14

Assistant United States Attorney:

Sam Spade
Post Office Box 600
Jacksonville, Florida 32201
(904) 232-2682

Defense Counsel:

John Doe (Retained)
123 SE 1st Street
Ocala, Florida 34471
(352) 555-5555

Sentencing Date: May 1, 2009, at 9:00 a.m.

Offense of Conviction: **Count One:** Conspiracy to Distribute Cocaine and Cocaine Base [21U.S.C. §§ 846 and 841(b)(1)(A)] 10 years to Life imprisonment / $4,000,000 fine (Class A Felony)

Count Three: False Tax Return [26 U.S. C. § 7206(1)] Three years imprisonment /$250,000 fine (Class E Felony)

Mandatory Minimum Applies: Yes: Count One - 10 years

Plea or Verdict: Pled guilty on February 5, 2009, before United States Magistrate Judge Gary R. Jones, pursuant to a written plea agreement. Adjudicated guilty on March 21, 2009 by the Honorable Wm. Terrell Hodges.

Date of Arrest/Release Status: December 7, 2008; detained.

Identifying Data:

Social Security No.: 123-45-6789
U.S. Marshal No.: 12345-018
FBI No.: 98765XYZ4321
FDLE No.: 3069332
Address: 1001 SR 200
Ocala, FL 34474
(last known)

Date of Birth: December 21, 1971 (Age 37)
Race: White, Hispanic **Sex:** Male
Citizenship: Mexico **Status:** Resident Alien
Alien Registration No.: A012345678
Dependents: Three (Wife and two children)
Education: Some college

Detainers:

United States Immigration and Naturalization Service - hold for possible deportation proceedings

Marion County Circuit Court - warrant issued for violation of probation.

Codefendants:

John Mali - Pled guilty to Conspiracy to Distribute Cocaine. Pending sentencing.

Kenneth Mali - Pending trial.

Related Cases:

5:08-Cr-02-Oc-10GRJ

Ray Swank - Pled guilty to Conspiracy to Distribute Cocaine. Sentenced May 1, 2008, to 120 months custody of Bureau of Prisons followed by 3 years supervised release.

3:08CR-10-001 (Northern District of Florida)

Darryl Coole - Pending trial.

Aliases:

Ricky Martin, Jr.
Willie Nelson, Jr.

RE: Mali, David Jr.

PART A. THE OFFENSE

Charges and Convictions

1. David Mali, Jr., John Mali, and Kenneth Mali are named as defendants in a three-count indictment with forfeiture provisions returned by a grand jury for the Middle District of Florida , Ocala Division, on January 10, 2009. Count One charges that from on or about August 7, 2008, through December 7, 2008, all of the defendants conspired to possess with intent to distribute two kilograms of cocaine and 100 grams of cocaine base, in violation of 21 U.S.C. § 846. Count Two charges that on December 7, 2008, David Mali, Jr., distributed 100 grams of cocaine base, in violation of 21 U.S. C. § 841(a)(1). Count Three charges that on April 15, 2008, David Mali, Jr., filed a false Individual United States Income Tax Return, in violation of 26 U.S.C. § 7206(1).

2. On February 5, 2009, David Mali, Jr., appeared before United States Magistrate Judge Gary R. Jones and, pursuant to a written plea agreement, pled guilty to Counts One and Three of the indictment. In the plea agreement, the government agreed to move for the dismissal of Count Two of the indictment, and the defendant agreed to cooperate with the Internal Revenue Service in paying all taxes, interest, and penalties due for tax year 2006. On March 21, 2009, Senior United States District Judge Wm. Terrell Hodges accepted the defendant's guilty plea and adjudged him guilty of Counts One and Three. Sentencing is scheduled for May 1, 2009.

3. The offenses were concluded on December 7, 2008, and the advisory guidelines in effect at the time of sentencing (November 1, 2008) were applied to the facts of this case.

Offense Conduct

4. The United States Drug Enforcement Administration (DEA) and the Internal Revenue Service (IRS) in Ocala, Florida, investigated the violations presented in this case. Preliminary information revealed that three brothers, David Mali, Jr., Kenneth Mali, and John Mali, were distributing cocaine and cocaine base from their ranch in Ocala, Florida. On various occasions, the brothers sold cocaine and cocaine base to a confidential source acting at the direction of law enforcement agents. David Mali, Jr., failed to report the proceeds of his drug sales as income to the Internal Revenue Service.

5. In 2008 David Mali, Jr., purchased a horse ranch located at 1001 SR 200 in Ocala, Florida. He shared the residence with his wife and children and with his brothers, John and Kenneth Mali. David Mali, Sr., was a resident of Mexico, and local drug agents in Texas learned that he was in the business of distributing cocaine. The agents

believed that he was supplying his sons with large quantities of cocaine for distribution in the Southeastern United States, especially in the State of Florida. A cooperating individual (CI) agreed to attempt to purchase cocaine from the Mali family at the ranch in Ocala.

6. On August 7, 2008, the CI telephoned John Mali and requested to purchase two kilograms of powder cocaine. They arranged to complete the transaction at the rest area near Ocala later that evening. The cooperating individual met David Mali, Jr., at the rest area and purchased 2 kilograms of cocaine for $25,000. DEA agents recorded the transaction.

7. On December 7, 2008, the CI called Kenneth Mali and requested to purchase one-half kilogram of cocaine base. David Mali, Jr., later informed the CI that he could not supply the requested amount of cocaine base, but he agreed to meet the CI at the same rest area and sell him several ounces. David Mali, Jr., sold 100 grams of cocaine base to the CI for $50,000.

8. Undercover agents arrested David Mali, Jr., immediately after the transaction. Agents took Kenneth and John Mali into custody on January 11, 2009, after the indictment was returned. On January 31, 2009, law enforcement officers in Brownsville, Texas, arrested David Mali, Sr., in possession of 10 kilograms of cocaine; he is awaiting trial for possession with intent to distribute cocaine. On January 8, 2009, agents searched the Ocala ranch and discovered an unloaded .22 caliber rifle in a locked closet in the master bedroom. David Mali, Jr., admitted that he owned the rifle and that he used it to shoot or scare away small rodents near his residence. The agents found no further evidence of drug distribution.

9. During debriefings with Kenneth and John Mali, agents learned that David Mali, Jr., recruited them to participate in the conspiracy after they began living on his ranch. Both Kenneth and John Mali confirmed that David Mali, Jr., controlled the quantities of cocaine that they distributed and received a larger share of the proceeds of their drug sales. They further advised that their father, David Mali, Sr., was the final authority on all matters related to the family's drug trafficking activities. The Mali brothers also indicated to agents that they regularly distributed drugs to Ray Swank and Darryl Coole.

10. Further investigation revealed that David Mali, Jr., failed to report $50,000 in income he earned from the sale of cocaine in 2007. On April 15, 2008, he filed a tax return indicating that his gross income was $18,000, even though his actual income was $68,000. David Mali, Jr.'s failure to report additional income resulted in a tax loss of $14,000.

RE: Mali, David Jr.

Custody Status

11. On December 7, 2008, DEA agents in Ocala, Florida, arrested the defendant. On December 8, 2008, he appeared before United States Magistrate Judge Gary R. Jones, who ordered him temporarily detained. Judge Jones held a detention hearing on January 31, 2009, after which he ordered the defendant detained pending trial.

Victim Impact

12. The probation office identified no victims as defined in 18 U.S.C. §§ 3663 or 3663A. The Internal Revenue Service agent reported that, as of July 1, 2008, the defendant owed a total of $30,000 in unpaid taxes, interest and penalties for tax year 2007. Thus far, the defendant has been cooperating with officials in trying to satisfy this debt.

Adjustment for Obstruction

13. The probation officer has no information suggesting that the defendant impeded or obstructed justice.

Adjustment for Acceptance of Responsibility

14. Following the defendant's guilty plea, he admitted his involvement in the offenses. During an interview with the probation officer, David Mali, Jr., advised that he and his brothers were distributing cocaine and cocaine base from his ranch for approximately six months. He further advised that he did not report his drug proceeds as income on his tax return, and he stated that he needed the money to pay for high medical bills incurred by his wife and children. The defendant indicated that he is sorry for his involvement in the offense and that he is afraid that he might not ever see his family again.

Offense Level Computation

15. The probation office used the 2008 edition of the Guidelines Manual. In determining the particular sentence to be imposed, the Court will take into account the advisory guidelines and the factors listed in 18 U.S.C. § 3553(a).

16. Counts One and Three are unrelated offenses because they represent separate harms; therefore, they are treated separately. USSG § 3D1.1(a)(3).

Group One: Count One - Conspiracy to Distribute Cocaine

17. Base Offense Level: The guideline for violations of 21 U.S.C. § 846 is found at USSG §2D1.1. The base offense level is

the level specified in the Drug Quantity Table. Because the offense involves different controlled substances, the combined marihuana equivalency for all substances is used. Two kilograms of cocaine is equivalent to 400 kilograms of marihuana. One hundred grams of cocaine base is equivalent to 2,000 kilograms of marihuana. The combined marihuana equivalency is 2, 400 kilograms. The base offense level for at least 1,000 kilograms but less than 3,000 kilograms of marihuana is 32. USSG §2D1.1(c)(4). 32

18. Specific Offense Characteristics: Agents recovered an unloaded rifle in a locked closet at Mali's ranch. However, the firearm does not appear to be connected to Mali's drug trafficking activities. 0

19. Victim Related Adjustment: None. 0

20. Adjustment for Role in the Offense: David Mali, Jr., directed the activities of his brothers in Florida and was responsible for obtaining cocaine from his father in Mexico. Thus, he was a manger of the criminal activity in this case. The criminal activity also included the participation of other family members and several local cocaine distributors. Therefore, three levels are added pursuant to USSG §3B1.1(b). 3

21. Adjustment for Obstruction of Justice: None 0

22. Adjusted Offense Level: (Subtotal) 35

Group Two: Count Three - Income Tax Evasion

23. Base Offense Level: The guideline for violations of 26 U.S.C. § 7606(1) is found at USSG § 2T1.1. Pursuant to USSG §2T1.1(a)(1), the base offense level is determined by the corresponding tax loss in the Tax Table at USSG §2T4.1. The tax loss is $14,000, which is more than $13,500, but not more than $23,500. Therefore, pursuant to USSG § 2T4.1(F) the base offense level is 11. 11

24. Specific Offense Characteristics: The defendant failed to identify the source of income exceeding $10,000 in one year from criminal activity. Pursuant to USSG §2T1.1(b)(1) two levels are added. 2

25. Victim Related Adjustment: None. 0

26. Adjustment for Role in the Offense: None. 0

27. Adjusted Offense Level: (Subtotal) 13

RE: Mali, David Jr.

28.	Multiple Count Adjustment (See USSG §3D1.4)			
			Units	
29.	Group One/Count One ....Adjusted Offense Level	35	1	
30.	Group Two/Counts Three ....Adjusted Offense Level	13	0	
31.	Total Number of Units		1	
32.	Greater of the Adjusted Offense ....Levels Above	35		
33.	Increase in Offense Level (USSG §3D1.4)	0		
34.	Combined Adjusted Offense Level:			35

35. Adjustment for Acceptance of Responsibility: The defendant has demonstrated a recognition and affirmative acceptance of personal responsibility for his offense conduct resulting in a two level reduction in the offense level. USSG § 3E1.1(a). -2

36. Additionally, the defendant has assisted authorities in the investigation of the offense and has provided timely complete information or timely notification of intent to plead guilty. Therefore, an additional one level reduction is appropriate. USSG § 3E1.1(a) and (b). -1

37. **Total Offense Level** **32**

---

38. **Chapter Four Enhancements:** The defendant is a career offender as defined in USSG §4B1.1. He was age 28 when he committed the criminal activity. One of the offenses of conviction is a controlled substance offense, and the defendant had at least two prior felony convictions of either a crime of violence or a controlled substance offense. These convictions consist of:

a) Sale of Cocaine, Marion County Circuit Court ,Case No. 99-111-CFA, a felony controlled substance offense, sentenced on April 21, 1999, (paragraph 43) and

b) Possession of Cocaine With Intent to Distribute, Marion County Circuit Court, Case No. 06-200-CFA, a felony controlled substance offense, sentenced on July 15, 2006 (paragraph 47).

Since the statutory maximum penalty for Count One is Life, the total offense level becomes 37.

39. **Total Offense Level** **37**

40. **Adjustment for Acceptance of Responsibility** **-3**

41. **Enhanced Offense Level** **34**

PART B. THE DEFENDANT'S CRIMINAL HISTORY

***(NOTE**: It is the policy of the Probation Office to assume that all defendants were represented by effective counsel or knowingly waived counsel, in convictions which occurred any time after 1972.)*

Juvenile Adjudications

	Date of Referral	Charge/Court	Date Sentence Imposed/ Disposition	Guideline	Score
42	12/10/87 (age 15)	Burglary of a Conveyance Marion County Juvenile Court Ocala, Florida 87-200-JU	1/30/88: Adjudicated Delinquent, community control.	4A1.2(e)(3)	0

Juvenile records in Marion County are destroyed after the defendant reaches age 21; therefore, due to the current age of the defendant, circumstances of the offense were no longer available. The defendant stated that he and a group of friends were caught breaking into a car in Ocala, Florida, while attempting to steal a stereo. He also reported that he was placed on community control and that he successfully completed the term of community control without incident.

Criminal Convictions

Date of Arrest	Charge/Court	Date Sentence Imposed/ Disposition	Guideline	Score

RE: Mali, David Jr.

42	02/03/99 (Age 27)	Sale of Cocaine Marion County Circuit Court Ocala, Florida 99-111-CFA	04/21/99: Pled guilty, adjudged guilty sentenced to 60 days jail. 05/01/99: Released from jail.	4A1.1(b)	2

On February 3, 1999, the defendant sold ¼ gram of cocaine base to an undercover police officer in Dunnellon, Florida.

43.	12/29/00 (Age 34)	No Valid Driver's License Marion County Court Ocala, Florida 00-11593-MM	01/11/00: Pled guilty, adjudged guilty, sentenced to 30 days jail suspended, 1 year probation, $130 fine and $119 court costs, obtain valid license. 08/10/01: Probation revoked, 60 days jail. 09/25/01: Released.	4A1.1(b) 4A1.2(c)(1)(A) 4A1.2(k)(1), comment. (n.11)	2

On December 29, 2000, a law enforcement officer in Ocala, Florida, cited the defendant for not having a valid driver's license.

Probation was revoked for failure to pay the fine. Other than the failure to pay toward monetary obligations and failure to obtain a valid drivers license, the defendant had no other problems while on probation.

44.	05/20/02 (Age 30)	No Valid Driver's License Marion County Court Ocala, Florida 02-935-MM	06/11/02: Pled guilty, adjudged guilty, sentenced to 1 year probation. Must obtain valid license in 30 days. 08/10/02: Probation revoked, 60 days jail. 09/25/02: Released.	4A1.1(c) 4A1.2(k)(1), comment. (n.11)	1

On May 20,1995, a law enforcement officer in Belleview, Florida, stopped the defendant for improper lane change. He cited the defendant because the defendant did have a valid driver's license.

45.	10/28/02 (Age 23)	Disorderly Conduct Marion County Court Ocala, Florida 02-11593-MM	11/21/02: Pled *nolo contendere*, adjudication withheld, sentenced to 60 days jail. 01/30/96: Released.	4A1.2(f)	1

RE: Mali, David Jr.

On October 28, 1995, the defendant was involved in a fight at a bar in Ocala, Florida. He was intoxicated when the Ocala Police Department arrested him.

46.	06/22/06 (Age 35)	1) Possession of Cocaine 2) Possession of Cocaine with Intent to Distribute Marion County Circuit Court Ocala, Florida 06-200-CFA	07/15/06: Ct. 1) *Nolle prosequi,* Ct 2) Pled *nolo contendere,* 15 months custody followed by 3 years probation with credit for 24 days jail time. 01/30/07: Released from prison, to begin probation. 02/01/09: Warrant issued for violation of probation.	4A1.1(a)	3

On June 22, 2006, the Florida Highway Patrol in Dunnellon, Florida, stopped the defendant for speeding. A search of his vehicle revealed one kilogram of cocaine concealed in a hidden compartment in the trunk.

Records from the Florida Department of Corrections indicated that the defendant served his sentence at Lowell Correctional Institute without any incidents or infractions. According to the defendant's probation officer, he had only been on probation a short period of time and, except for the failure to pay court costs and costs of supervision, he was complying with his conditions of supervision at the time of his arrest. The probation officer submitted a violation of probation affidavit citing the present federal charges as a new law violation, and the state court issued a warrant on February 1, 2009.

Criminal History Computation

47. The juvenile adjudication and criminal convictions above result in a subtotal criminal history score of 9.

48. When the defendant committed the criminal activity, he was on probation for the sentence of July 15, 2006. Therefore, 2 points are added. USSG §4A1.1(d).

49. The defendant committed the criminal activity less than two years following his release from custody on January 30, 2007, for the sentence of July 15,2006; therefore, 1 point is added.. USSG §4A1.1(e).

50. The total of the criminal history points is 12. According to the sentencing table (Chapter 5, Part A), 10 to 12 criminal history points establish a criminal history category of V.

Criminal History Enhancements

51. According to USSG §4B1.1, a career offender's criminal history category in every case shall be a **criminal history category of VI.**

RE: Mali, David Jr.

Other Criminal Conduct

	Date	Charge	Disposition
52.	02/12/00 (Age 28)	1) Driving While License Suspended or Revoked 2) Carrying a Concealed Firearm Marion County Circuit Court Ocala, Florida 00-532-CF	11/21/00: No Information filed.

On February 12, 2000, a law enforcement officer in Ocala, Florida, stopped the defendant for a traffic violation. After the defendant exited the vehicle, the officer noticed a semi-automatic handgun on the floor under the driver's seat. A subsequent records check revealed that the defendant's driver's license was suspended on January 16, 2000, for failure to pay a fine.

53.	05/25/00 (Age 28)	1) Battery-Domestic Violence 2) Failure to Appear Marion County Court Ocala, Florida 00-2689-MM	10/17/00: *Nolle prosequi*.

According to court records, on January 29, 2000, law enforcement officials responded to the defendant's residence in Ocala, Florida. At that location, Ana Mali advised that her husband, the defendant, returned home intoxicated after a night out drinking with friends. He became enraged and pulled the telephone from the wall, breaking the telephone. Then he pulled her to the ground by her hair at which time he began punching her in the back. Records reflect that the state did not pursue charges because the victim was not cooperative.

Other Arrests

54.	05/25/89 (Age 17)	Burglary of a Dwelling Marion County Circuit Court Ocala, Florida 00-1890-CF	Disposition unknown

The details of the offense are unavailable, and the defendant could not recall any information about this charge.

Pending Charges

55. As noted above, the defendant is facing charges in Marion County Circuit Court in Ocala, Florida, for violation of probation in case number 99-200-CFA. A warrant was issued on February 1, 2009, and is still active. Extradition outside of Florida will be sought if necessary.

56. A United States Border Patrol agent interviewed the defendant at the Marion County Jail in Ocala, Florida, on March 1, 2009. A detainer has been filed for a deportation hearing to be held once the defendant completes his sentence with the Bureau of Prisons.

PART C. OFFENDER CHARACTERISTICS

Personal and Family Data

57. David Mali, Jr., is literate in both English and Spanish; therefore, an interpreter was not necessary during the interview. The defendant's brother, John Mali, and the defendant's wife, Ana Mali, verified the following personal history information.

58. David Mali, Jr., was born on December 21, 1971, in Guerro, Mexico. He is the oldest of three sons born to David Mali, Sr., and Maria Martinez, who raised the defendant and his siblings in a very impoverished neighborhood in Mexico. The defendant was forced to perform fieldwork at a very young age to help support his family. His father was a strict disciplinarian with a history of alcohol abuse. He was physically abusive to the defendant's mother. The defendant resided in Mexico until 1985, at which time he relocated to the United States to pursue better employment opportunities. The defendant resided in Texas for two years before moving to Ocala, Florida.

59. The defendant's father, David Mali, Sr., is 60 years old and is currently incarcerated in McAllen, Texas, on related charges. The defendant's mother, Maria Mali, age 58, resides in Mexico. She has always been a housewife and has been dependent upon her sons and other family members for support during her husband's prolonged periods of absence. Mrs. Mali suffers from numerous medical problems including kidney disease. Over the years, the defendant has provided financial support to his mother.

60. The defendant has two younger brothers, John Mali, age 25, and Kenneth Mali, age 24. Both of them resided with him in Ocala, Florida, prior to their arrests as codefendants in this drug conspiracy. John Mali was employed as a mechanic for a local automobile repair shop. Kenneth Mali was self-employed as a horse trainer. The defendant was

instrumental in bringing both of his brothers to the United States, and he has provided them with a place to live and financial support.

61. On April 17, 1995, David Mali, Jr., married the former Ana Hernandez in Ocala, Florida. The marriage remains intact, and the defendant and his wife have two children, Alexander and Elizabeth, ages five and three, respectively. During an interview with the probation officer, Ana Mali stated that she is an unemployed housewife and that she is in poor health, suffering from severe arthritis. In 1998 she underwent surgery for breast cancer. Although her cancer is in remission, she must see a physician every six months and might have to undergo radiation treatment or chemotherapy in the near future.

62. Ana Mali expressed that she is concerned about her husband and that she hopes the family will soon be reunited. She indicated that her husband is a hard worker who has provided for the financial support of her and her children, as well as for his parents and siblings. In her opinion, he is a decent person who became involved in criminal activity due to the poor example his father set for him. Regarding the charges of domestic abuse, Mrs. Mali attributed her husband's conduct to his excessive use of alcohol. She related additional past instances when the defendant had abused her while he was intoxicated. Ana Mali also revealed that she suffers from mild depression and that she has been seeing a psychologist since the defendant's arrest.

In June 1998 the defendant purchased his current residence, and the probation officer inspected it on February 19, 2009. The residence is a four bedroom home located at 1001 SR 200, Ocala, Florida, on five acres of land in a semi-rural neighborhood. The property also includes a barn and a stall for boarding horses. The probation officer observed a number of horses on the property. No security concerns were noted. The only current residents are the defendant's wife and two children. Other family members and friends will try to help support Ana Mali and her children while the defendant is in custody.

63. A check with the United States Immigration and Naturalization Service shows that the defendant entered the United States at McAllen, Texas, in 1985 and that he is a permanent resident alien. Due to the nature of the present charges, the defendant possibly will face deportation following the completion of his sentence. If the defendant is deported, the defendant's wife and children may relocate to Mexico to be with him.

Physical Condition

64. David Mali, Jr., is five feet, five inches tall and weighs approximately 143 pounds. He has brown eyes and black hair. He has a tattoo of a heart with "Ana" on his left shoulder. According to the defendant, he is in good health at this time, but he has a history of liver problems.

Ana Mali verified the defendant's medical history and reported that her husband suffers from numerous allergies. Medical records obtained from the defendant's physician, Dr. Juan Garcia of Belleview, Florida, show that the defendant is allergic to grass pollen and many other common plant species. He has been treated for these allergies by receiving yearly cortisone injections and by taking over-the-counter antihistamines.

Mental and Emotional Health

65. David Mali, Jr., advised that he has no history of mental or emotional problems.

Substance Abuse

66. The defendant advised that he has never used illicit drugs. He admitted a history of alcohol abuse, stating that he began drinking when he was 15 years old and that he has consumed alcohol on a regular basis since then. Prior to his arrest he was drinking up to two liters of tequila every week.

67. A urinalysis conducted by pretrial services at the time of the defendant's arrest produced negative results for the presence of any illegal substances.

Education and Vocational Skills

68. According to David Mali, Jr., and as verified by John Mali, he completed four years of formal education while in Mexico. He attended classes at Central Florida Community College between 1990-1992, studying business, but he did not complete his education. Transcripts from the college verify that he attended classes there and that he earned a B average in 18 credit hours he completed.

Employment

69. From January 2007 to the date of his arrest of December 7, 2008, David Mali, Jr., was employed as a waiter for the El Toreo restaurant in Ocala, Florida. According to David Mali, Jr., and as confirmed by his wife, he earned approximately $3,000 per month plus tips from this employment. His former employer verified his dates of employment and indicated that he was a hard worker. The defendant would be eligible for rehiring in the future if he is not deported.

70. From June 2006 to January 2007, the defendant was incarcerated and unemployed.

71. From January 1999 to June 2006, the defendant was employed as a car salesman at Jose's Auto Sales in Belleview, Florida. He was paid on a commission basis and earned approximately $2,500 per month. He was

RE: Mali, David Jr.

terminated due to his incarceration as noted above. His former employer indicated that the defendant was a dependable worker who enjoyed his job.

72. From 1994 to 1999, the defendant was employed as a field worker for various employers throughout the State of Florida. He worked primarily as a laborer earning minimum wages. Social Security Administration records show the defendant earned Social Security covered wages of $10,000 to $15,000 per year during this time.

Financial Condition/Ability to Pay

73. The following information was obtained from a financial statement submitted by the defendant and a review of other available financial documentation.

NET WORTH

Cash	
First Union National Bank - Checking Account	$1,000
Florida Credit Union - Savings Account	5,000
Unencumbered Assets	
1995 Ford F-150 pickup truck	$5,000
Equity in Other Assets	
Residence at 1001 SR 200, Ocala, Florida	$15,000
Total Assets	**$26,000**
Unsecured Debts	
American Express Credit Card	$5,000
Munroe Regional Medical Center	10,000
Raul Ramirez, M.D., P.A.	20,000
Total Unsecured Debts	**$35,000**
NET WORTH	**($9,000)**

MONTHLY CASH FLOW

Income	
Net salary and tips (prior to arrest)	$3,000
Financial support from brothers	1,000
Total Income	**$4,000**
Necessary Living Expenses	
Mortgage	$1200
Electricity	250
Telephone	175
Groceries and supplies	500
Clothing	200
Automobile Insurance	150
Life Insurance	100
Transportation (oil, gas and maintenance)	200
Credit card payments	200
Medical expenses	300
Total Necessary Expenses	**$3,275**
NET MONTHLY CASH FLOW	**$725**

RE: Mali, David Jr.

74. The Internal Revenue Service provided the following information:

Year	*Adjusted Gross Income*
2003	$ 10,000
2004	$ 30,000
2005	$ 33,000
2006	$ 15,000
2007	$ 18,000

75. The above information reflects essential living expenses necessary for the continued health and welfare of the defendant's family. Although he has a negative net worth, the defendant possesses some liquid assets with which he could make a lump sum payment. However, due to his pending lengthy period of incarceration and possible deportation, these assets will be necessary to provide support to his family in his absence.

76. The defendant does not presently have the ability to pay a fine or restitution, but could adhere to a payment schedule while in custody or serving a term of supervision.

PART D. SENTENCING OPTIONS

Custody

77. **Statutory Provisions:** As to Count One, the mandatory term of imprisonment is 10 years, and the maximum term is life. 21 U.S.C. § 841(b)(1)(A).

78. **Statutory Provisions:** As to Count Three, the maximum term of imprisonment is 3 years. 26 U.S. C. § 7206(1).

79. **Guideline Provisions:** Based on a total offense level of 34 and a criminal history category of VI, **the guideline imprisonment range is 262-327 months** (21 years, 10 months - 27 year, 3 months).

Impact of the Plea Agreement

80. A conviction on the remaining count of the indictment would not affect the offense level or any other guideline computation.

Supervised Release

81. **Statutory Provisions:** As to Count One, a term of supervised release of at least 5 years must be imposed. 21 U.S.C. § 841(b)(1)(A).

82. **Statutory Provisions:** As to Count Three, the Court may impose a term of supervised release of not more than one year. 18 U.S.C. § 3583(b)(3).

83. **Guideline Provisions:** As to Count One, since the statute requires a term of supervised release of 5 years, the guideline requirement for a term of supervised release is 5 years. USSG §5D1.2(b).

84. **Guideline Provisions:** As to Count Three, since the offense is a Class E felony, the guideline range for a term of supervised release is one year. USSG §5D1.2(a)(3).

Probation

85. **Statutory Provisions:** The defendant is ineligible for probation because it is expressly precluded by statute as to Count One. 21 U.S.C. § 841(b)(1)(A) and 18 U.S.C. § 3561(a)(3).

86. **Guideline Provisions:** The defendant is ineligible for probation because probation has been expressly precluded by statute as to Count One. USSG §5B1.1(b)(2).

Fines

87. **Statutory Provisions:** As to Count One, the maximum fine is $4,000,000. 21 U.S.C. § 841(b)(1)(A).

88. **Statutory Provisions:** As to Count Three, the maximum fine is $250,000. 18 U.S.C. § 3571.

89. **Statutory Provisions:** As to Count Three, costs of prosecution are required by statute. 26 U.S.C. §7206. Because the defendant pled guilty and did not proceed to trial the government has indicated there are no costs to recover.

90. A special assessment of $100 per count of conviction must be imposed for a total of $200. 18 U.S.C. § 3013(a).

91. **Guideline Provisions:** The fine range for this offense is from $17,500 to $4,000,000. USSG §§5E1.2(c)(3) and 5E1.2(c)(4).

In determining whether to impose a fine and the amount of such fine, the Court shall consider, among other factors, the expected costs to the government of any term of probation, or term of imprisonment and term of supervised release imposed. USSG § 5E1.2(d)(7) and 18 U.S.C. § 3572(a)(6). These costs may include drug and alcohol treatment, electronic monitoring, and/or contract confinement costs. The most

RE: Mali, David Jr.

recent advisory from the Administrative Office of the United States Courts, dated May 6, 2008, provides the following monthly cost data:

Federal Prisons Facilities		Community Correction Centers		Supervision	
Daily	$ 68.28	**Daily**	$ 62.66	**Daily**	$ 9.92
Monthly	$ 2,076.83	**Monthly**	$ 1,905.92	**Monthly**	$ 301.80
Annually	$ 24,922.00	**Annually**	$ 22,871.00	**Annually**	$ 3,621.64

Restitution

92. As to Count One, restitution is not applicable. 18 U.S.C. § 3663.

93. As to Count Three, restitution is not applicable to Title 26 convictions, but the defendant may be ordered to cooperate with the IRS to pay back taxes as a condition of supervised release. 18 U.S.C. § 3583(d).

Denial of Benefits

94. The statutory provisions for denial of federal benefits shall not apply to individuals who cooperate or testify with the government in the prosecution of a federal or state offense. 21 U.S.C. § 862(e).

95. **Statutory Provisions:** The defendant, having been convicted on a **third or subsequent** drug **distribution** offense, is **permanently** ineligible for all federal benefits. 21 U.S.C. § 862(a)(1)(C).

96. This section does not apply to any retirement, welfare, Social Security, health, disability, veteran's benefits, public housing, or other similar benefits, or other benefits for which payments or services are required for eligibility. 21 U.S.C. § 862(d)(1)(B).

97. **Guideline Provisions:** The Court, pursuant to 21 U.S.C. § 862(a)(1)(A), may deny the eligibility for certain federal benefits of any individual convicted of distribution or possession of a controlled substance. USSG §5F1.6.

PART E. FACTORS THAT MAY WARRANT DEPARTURE

***(NOTE:** Presentation of information regarding departures in this section does not necessarily constitute a recommendation by the Probation Office for such departures.)*

98. The government has indicated that the defendant may be eligible for a downward departure based on substantial assistance to authorities. USSG §5K1.1.

PART F. FACTORS THAT MAY WARRANT A SENTENCE OUTSIDE THE ADVISORY GUIDELINE SYSTEM

*(**NOTE:** Presentation of information regarding variances in this section does not necessarily constitute a recommendation by the probation office for such variances.)*

99. The applicable statute, 18 U.S.C. §3553(a)(1)-(7), has been reviewed and there are no factors which appear to warrant a sentence outside the advisory guideline system.

Respectfully submitted,

John Smith
United States Probation Officer

Supervisor's Review:

This Presentence Report has been reviewed for accuracy and completeness.

Eric P. Ordeneaux, Supervising
United States Probation Officer

PAROLE/PROBATION REVOCATIONS

Probation and parole decisions involve considerations very different from guilt or sentencing determinations. In particular, the probation decision raises questions of rehabilitation and predictions of future conduct. These questions were central to the probation agreement between Gerald Scarpelli and the State of Wisconsin, signed on July 9, 1965.

FORM PROBATION AGREEMENT

AGREEMENT

In consideration of Probation or Parole being granted me, I agree to the following:

1. I will make a sincere attempt to avoid all acts which are forbidden by law and contrary to public welfare or my own best interests.
2. I will, to the best of my ability, take advantage of the opportunities offered me by probation or parole; I will practice temperance, conduct myself honestly, and assume my obligations as a citizen and as a member of the community in which I live.
3. I will keep the Probation and Parole Agent informed of my whereabouts and activities at all times and I will submit such reports as may be required.
4. I will secure advance approval from the Probation and Parole Agent, in writing if practicable, if at any time I wish to:
   - Purchase or operate a motor vehicle.
   - Incur debts whether by borrowing money or installment buying.
   - Take on additional responsibilities, such as by marrying.
   - Change employment or place of residence.
   - Leave the state.
   - Own or carry firearms or other weapons.
5. If I prove myself unsuited to supervision, I will hold myself ready to be placed in the institution to which I was committed, returned to the court which placed me on probation, or to the institution from which I was paroled.
6. I will be guided by such specific instructions as may be issued by the Probation and Parole Agent with regard to companions, hours, intoxicants, medical attention, family responsibilities and support of self, court obligations, or other special restrictions as follows:

Date: 7-9-65

Signed /s/ Gerald Scarpelli

(Revocation of Probation: Recommendation and Order) Scarpelli's probation was revoked by the State Department of Public Welfare later that year in response to a recommendation submitted by Officer Thomas Meyer.

Action Recommended: . . . REVOCATION OF PROBATION . . . Recommendation submitted for the following reasons: The aforementioned has shown himself unsuitable for probation in that he:

1. Has associated with known criminals, in direct violation of his probation regulations and his supervising agent's instructions;
2. While associating with a known criminal, namely Fred Kleckner, Jr., was involved in, and arrested for, burglary on the evening of 8/5/65 in Deerfield, Illinois.

Date: 8/20/65 Submitted by Thomas L. Meyer Area No. 1107

ORDER REVOKING PROBATION

THE STATE OF WISCONSIN: BEFORE THE STATE DEPARTMENT OF PUBLIC WELFARE

IN THE CASE OF: Gerald H. Scarpelli, Prob. #19635-A

IT APPEARING that GERALD H. SCARPELLI, hereinafter referred to as the aforesaid, was on the 9th day of July, 1965, convicted of the offense of Armed Robbery in violation of Section 943.32(1)(b)(2) of the Statutes of the State of Wisconsin in the County Court, Branch II, of Racine County and sentenced to the Wisconsin State Reformatory for a term of fifteen years and that execution of the sentence in this case was stayed and the aforesaid was placed on probation for a term of seven years under the provisions of Chapter 57 of the Statutes;

IT FURTHER APPEARING in the reports submitted by the Division of Corrections that the aforesaid has not conducted himself in accordance with the rules and regulations of the State Department of Public Welfare with reference to persons placed on probation in that the aforesaid has violated said rules by the following:

1. The aforesaid has associated with known criminals, in direct violation of his probation regulations and his supervising agent's instructions;
2. The aforesaid while associating with a known criminal, namely Fred Kleckner, Jr., was involved in, and arrested for a burglary on the evening of August 5, 1965 in Deerfield, Illinois.

IT IS NOW ORDERED that in accordance with the provisions of Chapter 57 of the Statutes, the probation of the aforesaid be and hereby is revoked with the effective date of violation being August 5, 1965;

IT IS FURTHER ORDERED THAT the aforesaid be taken into custody and conveyed to the Wisconsin State Reformatory and that the Warden of said institution is hereby authorized and directed to receive the aforesaid and there keep him until discharged pursuant to law.

STATE DEPARTMENT OF PUBLIC WELFARE /s/Wilbur J. Schmidt Director Dated: SEP 1–1965

FORM PETITION FOR WRIT OF HABEAS CORPUS

The following Petition for Writ of Habeas Corpus formed the basis for the Supreme Court's decision in Gagnon v. Scarpelli.

UNITED STATES DISTRICT COURT

EASTERN DISTRICT OF WISCONSIN

PETITION FOR WRIT OF HABEAS CORPUS

Filed December 16, 1968

. . .

4. The date upon which sentence was imposed and the terms of the sentence:

(a) July 9, 1965—15 years confinement in the Wisconsin State

(b) Reformatory at Green Bay, said sentence was stayed and I was

(c) placed on seven (7) years probation. . . .

10. State concisely the grounds on which you base your allegation that you are being held in custody unlawfully.

(a) I was not given a hearing of any kind before a judge or magistrate of any kind to this day, to have reasons presented and proven as to why my probation should be revoked.

(b) I was not afforded the right to counsel at any probation hearing.

(c) I was not afforded the rights of probation under the laws of the state of Illinois in which I was residing.

11. State concisely and in the same order the facts which support each of the grounds set out in (10):

(a) Section 1 of the Fourteenth Amendment of the Constitution of the United States: "Nor shall any state deprive any person of life, liberty, or property, without due process of law, nor deny to any person within its jurisdiction the equal protection of the laws."

(b) The Sixth Amendment of the Constitution of the United States: "In all criminal prosecutions, the accused shall enjoy the right to have the assistance of counsel for his defense."

(c) Chapter 57 Wisconsin State Statutes: 57.13(2), "That each receiving state (Ill.) will assume the duties of visitation of and supervision over probationers or parolees or any sending state (Wis.) and in the exercise of those duties will be governed by the same standards that prevail for its own probationers and parolees. Under the probation laws of Illinois, I would have definitely had counsel and a hearing before a judge and confronted with the charges of my probation violation. I was not afforded any such rights, I was arrested at my place of employment in Illinois, and forcibly and bodily carried by Wisconsin authorities across the state line into Wisconsin, directly to prison.

Gerald H. Scarpelli, being first sworn under oath, presents that he has subscribed to the foregoing petition and does state that the information therein is true and correct to the best of his knowledge and belief.

/s/Gerald H. Scarpelli Signature of affiant

GAGNON v. SCARPELLI

United States Supreme Court
411 U.S. 778 (1973)

MR. JUSTICE POWELL delivered the opinion of the Court.

This case presents the related questions whether a previously sentenced probationer is entitled to a hearing when his probation is revoked and, if so, whether he is entitled to be represented by appointed counsel at such a hearing.

I

Respondent, Gerald Scarpelli, pleaded guilty in July 1965, to a charge of armed robbery in Wisconsin. The trial judge sentenced him to 15 years' imprisonment, but suspended the sentence and placed him on probation for seven years in the custody of the Wisconsin Department of Public Welfare (the Department). At that time, he signed an agreement specifying the terms of his probation and a "Travel Permit and Agreement to Return" allowing him to reside in Illinois, with supervision there under an interstate compact. On August 5, 1965, he was accepted for supervision by the Adult Probation Department of Cook County, Illinois.

On August 6, respondent was apprehended by Illinois police, who had surprised him and one Fred Kleckner, Jr., in the course of the burglary of a house. After being apprised of his constitutional rights, respondent admitted that he and Kleckner had broken into the house for the purpose of stealing merchandise or money, although he now asserts that his statement was made under duress and is false. Probation was revoked by the Wisconsin Department on September 1, without a hearing.

II

Two prior decisions set the bounds of our present inquiry. In *Mempa v. Rhay*, the Court held that a probationer is entitled to be represented by appointed counsel at a combined revocation and sentencing hearing. Reasoning that counsel is required "at every stage of a criminal proceeding where substantial rights of a criminal accused may be affected," and that sentencing is one such stage, the Court concluded that counsel must be provided an indigent at sentencing even when it is accomplished as part of a subsequent probation revocation proceeding. But this line of reasoning does not require a hearing or counsel at the time of probation revocation in a case such as the present one, where the probationer was sentenced at the time of trial.

Of greater relevance is our decision last Term in *Morrissey v. Brewer.* There we held that the revocation of parole is not a part of a criminal prosecution.

> Parole arises after the end of the criminal prosecution, including imposition of sentence. . . . Revocation deprives an individual, not of the absolute liberty to which every citizen is entitled, but only of the conditional liberty properly dependent on observance of special parole restrictions.

Even though the revocation of parole is not a part of the criminal prosecution, we held that the loss of liberty entailed is a serious deprivation requiring that the parolee be accorded due process. Specifically, we held that a parolee is entitled to two hearings, one a preliminary hearing at the time of his arrest and detention to determine whether there is probable cause to believe that he has committed a violation of his parole, and the other a somewhat more comprehensive hearing prior to the making of the final revocation decision.

Petitioner does not contend that there is any difference relevant to the guarantee of due process between the revocation of parole and the revocation of probation, nor do we perceive one.[12] Probation revocation, like parole revocation, is not a stage of a criminal prosecution, but does result in a loss of liberty. Accordingly, we hold that a probationer, like a parolee, is entitled to a preliminary and a final revocation hearing, under the conditions specified in *Morrissey v. Brewer, supra.*

III

The second, and more difficult, question posed by this case is whether an indigent probationer or parolee has a due process right to be represented by appointed counsel at these hearings. In answering that question, we draw heavily on the opinion in *Morrissey.* Our first point of reference is the character of probation or parole. As noted in *Morrissey* regarding parole, the "purpose is to help individuals reintegrate into society as constructive individuals as soon as they are able. . . ." The duty and attitude of the probation or parole officer reflect this purpose:

> While the parole or probation officer recognizes his double duty to the welfare of his clients and to the safety of the general community, by and large concern for the client dominates his professional attitude. The parole agent ordinarily defines his role as representing his client's best interests as long as these do not constitute a threat to public safety.

Because the probation or parole officer's function is not so much to compel conformance to a strict code of behavior as to supervise a course of rehabilitation, he has been entrusted traditionally with broad discretion to judge the progress of rehabilitation in individual cases, and has been armed with the power to recommend or even to declare revocation.

In *Morrissey,* we recognized that the revocation decision has two analytically distinct components:

> The first step in a revocation decision thus involves a wholly retrospective factual question: whether the parolee has in fact acted in violation of one or

[12] [3] Despite the undoubted minor differences between probation and parole, the commentators have agreed that revocation of probation where sentence has been imposed previously is constitutionally indistinguishable from the revocation of parole.

more conditions of his parole. Only if it is determined that the parolee did violate the conditions does the second question arise: should the parolee be recommitted to prison or should other steps be taken to protect society and improve chances of rehabilitation?

The parole officer's attitude toward these decisions reflects the rehabilitative rather than punitive focus of the probation/parole system:

> Revocation . . . is, if anything, commonly treated as a failure of supervision. While presumably it would be inappropriate for a field agent *never* to revoke, the whole thrust of the probation-parole movement is to keep men in the community, working with adjustment problems there, and using revocation only as a last resort when treatment has failed or is about to fail.

But an exclusive focus on the benevolent attitudes of those who administer the probation/parole system when it is working successfully obscures the modification in attitude which is likely to take place once the officer has decided to recommend revocation. Even though the officer is not by this recommendation converted into a prosecutor committed to convict, his role as counsellor to the probationer or parolee is then surely compromised.

When the officer's view of the probationer's or parolee's conduct differs in this fundamental way from the latter's own view, due process requires that the difference be resolved before revocation becomes final. Both the probationer or parolee and the State have interests in the accurate finding of fact and the informed use of discretion — the probationer or parolee to insure that his liberty is not unjustifiably taken away and the State to make certain that it is neither unnecessarily interrupting a successful effort at rehabilitation nor imprudently prejudicing the safety of the community.

It was to serve all of these interests that *Morrissey* mandated preliminary and final revocation hearings. At the preliminary hearing, a probationer or parolee is entitled to notice of the alleged violations of probation or parole, an opportunity to appear and to present evidence in his own behalf, a conditional right to confront adverse witnesses, an independent decision-maker, and a written report of the hearing.

The final hearing is a less summary one because the decision under consideration is the ultimate decision to revoke rather than a mere determination of probable cause, but the "minimum requirements of due process" include very similar elements:

> (a) written notice of the claimed violations of [probation or] parole; (b) disclosure to the [probationer or] parolee of evidence against him; (c) opportunity to be heard in person and to present witnesses and documentary evidence; (d) the right to confront and cross-examine adverse witnesses (unless the hearing officer specifically finds good cause for not allowing confrontation); (e) a "neutral and detached" hearing body such as a traditional parole board, members of which need not be judicial officers or lawyers; and (f) a written statement by the fact finders as to the evidence relied on and reasons for revoking [probation or] parole.

These requirements in themselves serve as substantial protection against ill-considered revocation, and petitioner argues that counsel need never be supplied. What this argument overlooks is that the effectiveness of the rights guaranteed by *Morrissey* may in some circumstances depend on the use of skills which the probationer or parolee is unlikely to possess. Despite the informal nature of the proceedings and the absence of technical rules of procedure or evidence, the unskilled or uneducated probationer or parolee may well have difficulty in presenting his version of a disputed set of facts where the presentation requires the examining or cross-examining of witnesses or the offering or dissecting of complex documentary evidence.

By the same token, we think that the Court of Appeals erred in accepting respondent's contention that the State is under a constitutional duty to provide counsel for indigents in all probation or parole revocation cases. While such a rule has the appeal of simplicity, it would impose direct costs and serious collateral disadvantages without regard to the need or the likelihood in a particular case for a constructive contribution by counsel. In most cases, the probationer or parolee has been convicted of committing another crime or has admitted the charges against him. And while in some cases he may have a justifiable excuse for the violation or a convincing reason why revocation is not the appropriate disposition, mitigating evidence of this kind is often not susceptible of proof or is so simple as not to require either investigation or exposition by counsel.

The introduction of counsel into a revocation proceeding will alter significantly the nature of the proceeding. If counsel is provided for the probationer or parolee, the State in turn will normally provide its own counsel; lawyers, by training and disposition, are advocates and bound by professional duty to present all available evidence and arguments in support of their clients' positions and to contest with vigor all adverse evidence and views. The role of the hearing body itself, aptly described in *Morrissey* as being "predictive and discretionary" as well as factfinding, may become more akin to that of a judge at a trial, and less attuned to the rehabilitative needs of the individual probationer or parolee. In the greater self-consciousness of its quasi-judicial role, the hearing body may be less tolerant of marginal deviant behavior and feel more pressure to reincarcerate than to continue nonpunitive rehabilitation. Certainly, the decision-making process will be prolonged, and the financial cost to the State — for appointed counsel, counsel for the State, a longer record, and the possibility of judicial review — will not be insubstantial.

In some cases, these modifications in the nature of the revocation hearing must be endured and the costs borne because, as we have indicated above, the probationer's or parolee's version of a disputed issue can fairly be represented only by a trained advocate. But due process is not so rigid as to require that the significant interests in informality, flexibility, and economy must always be sacrificed.

In so concluding, we are of course aware that the case-by-case approach to the right to counsel in felony prosecutions adopted in *Betts v. Brady* was later rejected in favor of a *per se* rule in *Gideon v. Wainwright.* See also *Argersinger v. Hamlin.* We do not, however, draw from *Gideon* and *Argersinger* the conclusion that a case-by-case approach to furnishing counsel is necessarily inadequate to protect constitutional rights asserted in varying types of proceedings: there are critical differences between criminal trials and probation or parole revocation hearings, and both society and the probationer or parolee have stakes in preserving these differences.

In a criminal trial, the State is represented by a prosecutor; formal rules of evidence are in force; a defendant enjoys a number of procedural rights which may be lost if not timely raised; and, in a jury trial, a defendant must make a presentation understandable to untrained jurors. In short, a criminal trial under our system is an adversary proceeding with its own unique characteristics. In a revocation hearing, on the other hand, the State is represented, not by a prosecutor, but by a parole officer with the orientation described above; formal procedures and rules of evidence are not employed; and the members of the hearing body are familiar with the problems and practice of probation or parole. The need for counsel at revocation hearings derives, not from the invariable attributes of those hearings, but rather from the peculiarities of particular cases.

The differences between a criminal trial and a revocation hearing do not dispose altogether of the argument that under a case-by-case approach there may be cases in which a lawyer would be useful but in which none would be appointed because an arguable defense would be uncovered only by a lawyer. Without denying that there is some force in this argument, we think it a sufficient answer that we deal here, not with the right of an accused to counsel in a criminal prosecution, but with the more limited due process right of one who is a probationer or parolee only because he has been convicted of a crime.

We thus find no justification for a new inflexible constitutional rule with respect to the requirement of counsel. We think, rather, that the decision as to the need for counsel must be made on a case-by-case basis in the exercise of a sound discretion by the state authority charged with responsibility for administering the probation and parole system. Although the presence and participation of counsel will probably be both undesirable and constitutionally unnecessary in most revocation hearings, there will remain certain cases in which fundamental fairness — the touchstone of due process — will require that the State provide at its expense counsel for indigent probationers or parolees.

It is neither possible nor prudent to attempt to formulate a precise and detailed set of guidelines to be followed in determining when the providing of counsel is necessary to meet the applicable due process requirements. The facts and circumstances in preliminary and final hearings are susceptible of almost infinite variation, and a considerable discretion must be allowed the responsible agency in making the decision. Presumptively, it may be said that counsel should be provided in cases where, after being informed of his right to request counsel, the probationer or parolee makes such a request, based on a timely and colorable claim (i) that he has not committed the alleged violation of the conditions upon which he is at liberty; or (ii) that, even if the violation is a matter of public record or is uncontested, there are substantial reasons which justified or mitigated the violation and make revocation inappropriate, and that the reasons are complex or otherwise difficult to develop or present. In passing on a request for the appointment of counsel, the responsible agency also should consider, especially in doubtful cases, whether the probationer appears to be capable of speaking effectively for himself. In every case in which a request for counsel at a preliminary or final hearing is refused, the grounds for refusal should be stated succinctly in the record.

IV

We return to the facts of the present case. Because respondent was not afforded either a preliminary hearing or a final hearing the revocation of his probation did not meet the standards of due process prescribed in *Morrissey*, which we have here held applicable to probation revocations. Accordingly, respondent was entitled to a writ of habeas corpus. On remand, the District Court should allow the State an opportunity to conduct such a hearing. As to whether the State must provide counsel, respondent's admission to having committed another serious crime creates the very sort of situation in which counsel need not ordinarily be provided. But because of respondent's subsequent assertions regarding that admission, we conclude that the failure of the Department to provide respondent with the assistance of counsel should be re-examined in light of this opinion. The general guidelines outlined above should be applied in the first instance by those charged with conducting the revocation hearing.

Affirmed in part, reversed in part, and remanded.

MR. JUSTICE DOUGLAS, dissenting in part.

I believe that due process requires the appointment of counsel in this case because of the claim that respondent's confession of the burglary was made under duress.

NOTES AND QUESTIONS

(1) If the Constitution requires appointed counsel at sentencing hearings, does it also require appointed counsel at probation revocation hearings? From the viewpoint of the defendant, are the two situations distinguishable? Moreover, once Justice Powell conceded that "there may be cases in which a lawyer would be useful but in which none would be appointed because an arguable defense would be uncovered only by a lawyer," would not *Gideon* require the appointment of counsel?

(2) One reason given for not requiring counsel in all probation revocation cases was that "the hearing body may be less tolerant of marginal deviant behavior and feel more pressure to reincarcerate than to continue nonpunitive rehabilitation." Do you agree?

(3) The majority concluded that the determination of appointing counsel under the Due Process Clause required a case-by-case evaluation. With this situation in *Gagnon*, should counsel be appointed? Is the mere fact that the defendant claimed that his confession was made under duress a sufficient basis for the appointment of counsel, or should the Department take further action before appointing a lawyer? What further action would be appropriate?

(4) While the Constitution does not require counsel at all probation revocation proceedings, many jurisdictions mandate the appointment of a lawyer. *See, e.g.*, Federal Rule of Criminal Procedure 32.1:

(b) **Revocation.**

(1) **Preliminary hearing.**

(A) *In General.* If a person is in custody for violating a condition of probation or supervised release, a magistrate judge must promptly conduct a hearing to determine whether there is probable cause to believe that a violation occurred. The person may waive the hearing.

(B) *Requirements.* The hearing must be recorded by a court reporter or by a suitable recording device. The judge must give the person:

(i) notice of the hearing and its purpose, the alleged violation, and the person's right to retain counsel or to request that counsel be appointed if the person cannot obtain counsel;

(ii) an opportunity to appear at the hearing and present evidence; and

(iii) upon a request, an opportunity to question any adverse witness, unless the judge determines that the interest of justice does not require the witness to appear.

(C) *Referral.* If the judge finds probable cause, the judge must conduct a revocation hearing. If the judge does not find probable cause, the judge must dismiss the proceeding.

(2) **Revocation Hearing.** Unless waived by the person, the court must hold the revocation hearing within a reasonable time in the district having jurisdiction. The person is entitled to:

(A) written notice of the alleged violation;

(B) disclosure of the evidence against the person;

(C) an opportunity to appear, present evidence, and question any adverse witness unless the court determines that the interest of justice does not require the witness to appear; and

(D) notice of the person's right to retain counsel or to request that counsel be appointed if the person cannot obtain counsel.

(5) In *Greenholtz v. Inmates of the Nebraska Penal and Correctional Complex*, 442 U.S. 1 (1979), the inmates claimed that certain due process requirements should be imposed at parole release proceedings, when the parole board is deciding whether the defendant should be released from prison. The Court stated that the release procedure required a lesser standard than the revocation procedure: "The fallacy in respondents' position is that parole *release* and parole *revocation* are quite different. There is a crucial distinction between being deprived of a liberty one has, as in parole, and being denied a conditional liberty that one desires." See also the decision in *Young v. Harper*, 520 U.S. 143 (1997). There, Oklahoma operated a "pre-parole" program allowing the discretionary release of inmates before their

scheduled time, due to prison over-crowding. Relying on the parole revocation holding in *Morrissey v. Brewer* (discussed in *Gagnon v. Scarpelli*) the unanimous Court applied traditional due process protections, as the pre-parole program "differed from parole in name only."

(6) In *Wainwright v. Cottle*, 414 U.S. 895 (1973), Justice Douglas, joined by Justice Blackmun, dissented from a remand of the Supreme Court in which an issue undecided in *Gagnon* was raised. In *Cottle*, the state allowed retained counsel to appear in any probation revocation proceeding, but as to appointed counsel the state proceeded on the *Gagnon* case-by-case analysis. Was the state's policy consistent with the holding in *Gagnon*? Note Justice Douglas' remarks:

> [T]he only issue in this case is whether the court below was correct in holding that the Equal Protection Clause requires the right to appointed counsel at parole revocation hearings in cases where, unlike *Gagnon v. Scarpelli, supra*, a solvent parolee has a statutory right to the presence of retained counsel. *Gagnon* is inapposite. The State of Florida has already determined by statute that any interest in flexibility and informality derived from the absence of attorneys will *always* be sacrificed when a parolee of means desires the assistance of counsel. Whether in such cases the Equal Protection Clause demands that indigent parolees be afforded the same representation rights was not answered in *Gagnon*. I would take this case in order to decide it here.

APPEALS

The Supreme Court has consistently stated that there is no constitutional right to an appeal from a conviction. But, the Court has imposed restrictions on the states once such appeals have been established. During the period in which Sixth Amendment rights were being expanded, two cases, in particular, proved most important for defendants. In *Griffin v. Illinois*, 351 U.S. 12 (1956) [discussed in *Ross v. Moffitt, infra*], the state allowed a defendant to appeal to the state supreme court only if he was able to offer to the court a transcript from the trial. Indigent defendants were not provided with transcripts. This rule was struck down under the Fourteenth Amendment. *Douglas v. California*, 372 U.S. 353 (1963) [decided the same day as *Gideon*, also discussed in *Ross v. Moffitt*], required appointment of an attorney as a matter of right for indigent defendants appealing to the intermediate court of appeals. The important question left open after *Griffin* and *Douglas* was whether the rules there would be applied to discretionary appeals before state supreme courts or the United States Supreme Court.

ROSS v. MOFFITT

United States Supreme Court
417 U.S. 600 (1974)

Mr. Justice Rehnquist delivered the opinion of the Court.

We are asked in this case to decide whether *Douglas v. California*, which requires appointment of counsel for indigent state defendants on their first appeal as of right, should be extended to require counsel for discretionary state appeals and for applications for review in this Court.

I

The case now before us has resulted from consolidation of two separate cases, North Carolina criminal prosecutions brought in the respective Superior Courts for the counties of Mecklenburg and Guilford. In both cases respondent pleaded not guilty to charges of forgery and uttering a forged instrument, and because of his indigency was represented at trial by court-appointed counsel. He was convicted and then took separate appeals to the North Carolina Court of Appeals, where he was again represented by court-appointed counsel, and his convictions were affirmed. At this point the procedural histories of the two cases diverge.

Following affirmance of his Mecklenburg County conviction, respondent sought to invoke the discretionary review procedures of the North Carolina Supreme Court. His court-appointed counsel approached the Mecklenburg County Superior Court about possible appointment to represent respondent on this appeal, but counsel was informed that the State was not required to furnish counsel for that petition.

Following affirmance of his conviction on the Guilford County charges, respondent also sought discretionary review in the North Carolina Supreme Court. On this appeal, however, respondent was not denied counsel but rather was represented by the public defender who had been appointed for the trial and respondent's first appeal. The North Carolina Supreme Court denied certiorari. Respondent then unsuccessfully petitioned the Superior Court for Guilford County for court-appointed counsel to prepare a petition for a writ of certiorari to this Court, and also sought post-conviction relief throughout the state courts. After these motions were denied, respondent again sought federal habeas relief.

II

This Court, in the past 20 years, has given extensive consideration to the rights of indigent persons on appeal. In *Griffin v. Illinois*, the first of the pertinent cases, the Court had before it an Illinois rule allowing a convicted criminal defendant to present claims of trial error to the Supreme Court of Illinois only if he procured a transcript of the testimony adduced at his trial. No exception was made for the indigent defendant, and thus one who was unable to pay the cost of obtaining such a transcript was precluded from obtaining appellate review of asserted trial error. Mr. Justice Frankfurter, who cast the deciding vote, said in his concurring opinion: ". . . Illinois has decreed that only defendants who can afford to pay for the stenographic minutes of a trial may have trial errors reviewed on appeal by the Illinois Supreme Court."

The Court in *Griffin* held that this discrimination violated the Fourteenth Amendment.

Succeeding cases invalidated similar financial barriers to the appellate process, at the same time reaffirming the traditional principle that a State is not obliged to provide any appeal at all for criminal defendants. The cases encompassed a variety of circumstances but all had a common theme. For example, *Lane v. Brown*, 372 U.S. 477, involved an Indiana provision declaring that only a public defender could obtain a free transcript of a hearing on a *coram nobis* application. If the public defender declined to request one, the indigent prisoner seeking to appeal had no recourse. In *Draper v. Washington*, 372 U.S. 487, the State permitted an indigent to obtain a free transcript of the trial at which he was convicted only if he satisfied the trial judge that his contentions on appeal would not be frivolous. The appealing defendant was in effect bound by the trial court's conclusions in seeking to review the determination of frivolousness, since no transcript or its equivalent was made available to him. In *Smith v. Bennett*, 365 U.S. 708, Iowa had required a filing fee in order to process a state habeas corpus application by a convicted defendant, and in *Burns v. Ohio*, 360 U.S. 252, the State of Ohio required a $20 filing fee in order to move the Supreme Court of Ohio for leave to appeal from a judgment of the Ohio Court of Appeals affirming a criminal conviction. Each of these state-imposed financial barriers to the adjudication of a criminal defendant's appeal was held to violate the Fourteenth Amendment.

The decisions discussed above stand for the proposition that a State cannot arbitrarily cut off appeal rights for indigents while leaving open avenues of appeal for more affluent persons. In *Douglas v. California*, however, a case decided the same day as *Lane, supra*, and *Draper, supra*, the Court departed somewhat from the limited doctrine of the transcript and fee cases and undertook an examination of whether an indigent's access to the appellate system was adequate. The Court in *Douglas* concluded that a State does not fulfill its responsibility toward indigent defendants merely by waiving its own requirements that a convicted defendant procure a transcript or pay a fee in order to appeal, and held that the State must go further and provide counsel for the indigent on his first appeal as of right. It is this decision we are asked to extend today.

Petitioners in *Douglas*, took appeals as of right to the California District Court of Appeal. Petitioners claimed that they were entitled to court-appointed and state-compensated counsel because they were indigent.

This Court held unconstitutional California's requirement that counsel on appeal would be appointed for an indigent only if the appellate court determined that such appointment would be helpful to the defendant or to the court itself. The Court noted that under this system an indigent's case was initially reviewed on the merits without the benefit of any organization or argument by counsel. By contrast, persons of greater means were not faced with the preliminary "*ex parte* examination of the record," but had their arguments presented to the court in fully briefed form. The Court noted, however, that its decision extended only to initial appeals as of right, and went on to say:

> We need not now decide whether California would have to provide counsel for an indigent seeking a discretionary hearing from the California Supreme Court after the District Court of Appeal had sustained his conviction . . . or whether counsel must be appointed for an indigent seeking review of an appellate affirmance of his conviction in this Court by

appeal as of right or by petition for a writ of certiorari which lies within the Court's discretion.

The precise rationale for the *Griffin* and *Douglas* lines of cases has never been explicitly stated, some support being derived from the Equal Protection Clause of the Fourteenth Amendment, and some from the Due Process Clause of that Amendment. Neither Clause by itself provides an entirely satisfactory basis for the result reached, each depending on a different inquiry which emphasizes different factors. "Due process" emphasizes fairness between the State and the individual dealing with the State, regardless of how other individuals in the same situation may be treated. "Equal protection," on the other hand, emphasizes disparity in treatment by a State between classes of individuals whose situations are arguably indistinguishable. We will address these issues separately in the succeeding sections.

III

Recognition of the due process rationale in *Douglas* is found both in the Court's opinion and in the dissenting opinion of Mr. Justice Harlan.

We do not believe that the Due Process Clause requires North Carolina to provide respondent with counsel on his discretionary appeal to the State Supreme Court. At the trial stage of a criminal proceeding, the right of an indigent defendant to counsel is fundamental and binding upon the States by virtue of the Sixth and Fourteenth Amendments. But there are significant differences between the trial and appellate stages of a criminal proceeding. The purpose of the trial stage from the State's point of view is to convert a criminal defendant from a person presumed innocent to one found guilty beyond a reasonable doubt. To accomplish this purpose, the State employs a prosecuting attorney who presents evidence to the court, challenges any witnesses offered by the defendant, argues rulings of the court, and makes direct arguments to the court and jury seeking to persuade them of the defendant's guilt. Under these circumstances "reason and reflection require us to recognize that in our adversary system of criminal justice, any person haled into court, who is too poor to hire a lawyer, cannot be assured a fair trial unless counsel is provided for him."

By contrast, it is ordinarily the defendant, rather than the State, who initiates the appellate process, seeking not to fend off the efforts of the State's prosecutor but rather to overturn a finding of guilt made by a judge or a jury below. The defendant needs an attorney on appeal not as a shield to protect him against being "haled into court" by the State and stripped of his presumption of innocence, but rather as a sword to upset the prior determination of guilt. This difference is significant for, while no one would agree that the State may simply dispense with the trial stage of proceedings without a criminal defendant's consent, it is clear that the State need not provide any appeal at all.

The fact that an appeal *has* been provided does not automatically mean that a State then acts unfairly by refusing to provide counsel to indigent defendants at every stage of the way.

Unfairness results only if indigents are singled out by the State and denied meaningful access to the appellate system because of their poverty. That question is more profitably considered under an equal protection analysis.

IV

Language invoking equal protection notions is prominent both in *Douglas* and in other cases treating the rights of indigents on appeal.

Despite the tendency of all rights "to declare themselves absolute to their logical extreme," there are obviously limits beyond which the equal protection analysis may not be pressed without doing violence to principles recognized in other decisions of this Court. The Fourteenth Amendment "does not require absolute equality or precisely equal advantages," nor does it require the State to "equalize economic conditions." It does require that the state appellate system be "free of unreasoned distinctions" and that indigents have an adequate opportunity to present their claims fairly within the adversary system. The State cannot adopt procedures which leave an indigent defendant "entirely cut off from any appeal at all," by virtue of his indigency, or extend to such indigent defendants merely a "meaningless ritual" while others in better economic circumstances have a "meaningful appeal." The question is not one of absolutes, but one of degrees. In this case we do not believe that the Equal Protection Clause, when interpreted in the context of these cases, requires North Carolina to provide free counsel for indigent defendants seeking to take discretionary appeals to the North Carolina Supreme Court, or to file petitions for certiorari in this Court.

A. The North Carolina appellate system, as are the appellate systems of almost half the States, is multi-tiered, providing for both an intermediate Court of Appeals and a Supreme Court. In criminal cases, . . . [most] decisions of the Court of Appeals on direct review of criminal cases may be further reviewed in the Supreme Court on a discretionary basis.

[Thus] North Carolina has followed the mandate of *Douglas v. California, supra*, and authorized appointment of counsel for a convicted defendant appealing to the intermediate Court of Appeals, but has not gone beyond *Douglas* to provide for appointment of counsel for a defendant who seeks either discretionary review in the Supreme Court of North Carolina or a writ of certiorari here.

B. The facts show that respondent, in connection with his Mecklenburg County conviction, received the benefit of counsel in examining the record of his trial and in preparing an appellate brief on his behalf for the state Court of Appeals. Thus, prior to his seeking discretionary review in the State Supreme Court, his claims had "once been presented by a lawyer and passed upon by an appellate court."

We do not believe that it can be said, therefore, that a defendant in respondent's circumstances is denied meaningful access to the North Carolina Supreme Court simply because the State does not appoint counsel to aid him in seeking review in that court. At that stage he will have, at the very least, a transcript or other record of trial proceedings, a brief on his behalf in the Court of Appeals setting forth his claims of error, and in many cases an opinion by the Court of Appeals disposing of his case. These materials, supplemented by whatever submission respondent may make *pro se*, would appear to provide the Supreme Court of North Carolina with an adequate basis for its decision to grant or deny review.

This is not to say, of course, that a skilled lawyer, particularly one trained in the somewhat arcane art of preparing petitions for discretionary review, would not prove helpful to any litigant able to employ him. An indigent defendant seeking review in the Supreme Court of North Carolina is therefore somewhat handicapped in comparison with a wealthy defendant who has counsel assisting him in every conceivable manner at every stage in the proceeding. But both the opportunity to have counsel prepare an initial brief in the Court of Appeals and the nature of discretionary review in the Supreme Court of North Carolina make this relative handicap far less than the handicap borne by the indigent defendant denied counsel on his initial appeal as of right in *Douglas*. And the fact that a particular service might be of benefit to an indigent defendant does not mean that the service is constitutionally required. The duty of the State under our cases is not to duplicate the legal arsenal that may be privately retained by a criminal defendant in a continuing effort to reverse his conviction, but only to assure the indigent defendant an adequate opportunity to present his claims fairly in the context of the State's appellate process. We think respondent was given that opportunity under the existing North Carolina system.

V

Much of the discussion in the preceding section is equally relevant to the question of whether a State must provide counsel for a defendant seeking review of his conviction in this Court. North Carolina will have provided counsel for a convicted defendant's only appeal as of right, and the brief prepared by that counsel together with one and perhaps two North Carolina appellate opinions will be available to this Court in order that it may decide whether or not to grant certiorari. This Court's review, much like that of the Supreme Court of North Carolina, is discretionary and depends on numerous factors other than the perceived correctness of the judgment we are asked to review.

The suggestion that a State is responsible for providing counsel to one petitioning this Court simply because it initiated the prosecution which led to the judgment sought to be reviewed is unsupported by either reason or authority. It would be quite as logical under the rationale of *Douglas* and *Griffin*, and indeed perhaps more so, to require that the Federal Government or this Court furnish and compensate counsel for petitioners who seek certiorari here to review state judgments of conviction. Yet this Court has followed a consistent policy of denying applications for appointment of counsel by persons seeking to file jurisdictional statements or petitions for certiorari in this Court. In the light of these authorities, it would be odd, indeed, to read the Fourteenth Amendment to impose such a requirement on the States, and we decline to do so.

MR. JUSTICE DOUGLAS, with whom MR. JUSTICE BRENNAN and MR. JUSTICE MARSHALL concur, dissenting.

In *Douglas v. California*, we considered the necessity for appointed counsel on the first appeal as of right, the only issue before us. We did not deal with the appointment of counsel for later levels of discretionary review, either to the higher state courts or to this Court, but we noted that "there can be no equal justice where the kind of an appeal a man enjoys depends on the amount of money he has."

Chief Judge Haynsworth could find "no logical basis for differentiation between appeals of right and permissive review procedures in the context of the Constitution and the right to counsel." More familiar with the functioning of the North Carolina criminal justice system than are we, he concluded that "in the context of constitutional questions arising in criminal prosecutions, permissive review in the state's highest court may be predictably the most meaningful review the conviction will receive." The North Carolina Court of Appeals, for example, will be constrained in diverging from an earlier opinion of the State Supreme Court, even if subsequent developments have rendered the earlier Supreme Court decision suspect. "[T]he state's highest court remains the ultimate arbiter of the rights of its citizens."

Chief Judge Haynsworth also correctly observed that the indigent defendant proceeding without counsel is at a substantial disadvantage relative to wealthy defendants represented by counsel when he is forced to fend for himself in seeking discretionary review from the State Supreme Court or from this Court. It may well not be enough to allege error in the courts below in layman's terms; a more sophisticated approach may be demanded:

> An indigent defendant is as much in need of the assistance of a lawyer in preparing and filing a petition for certiorari as he is in the handling of an appeal as of right. In many appeals, an articulate defendant could file an effective brief by telling his story in simple language without legalisms, but the technical requirements for applications for writs of certiorari are hazards which one untrained in the law could hardly be expected to negotiate.
>
> Certiorari proceedings constitute a highly specialized aspect of appellate work. The factors which [a court] deems important in connection with deciding whether to grant certiorari are certainly not within the normal knowledge of an indigent appellant.

Furthermore, the lawyer who handled the first appeal in a case would be familiar with the facts and legal issues involved in the case. It would be a relatively easy matter for the attorney to apply his expertise in filing a petition for discretionary review to a higher court, or to advise his client that such a petition would have no chance of succeeding.

Douglas v. California was grounded on concepts of fairness and equality. The right to seek discretionary review is a substantial one, and one where a lawyer can be of significant assistance to an indigent defendant. It was correctly perceived below that the "same concepts of fairness and equality, which require counsel in a first appeal of right, require counsel in other and subsequent discretionary appeals."

NOTES AND QUESTIONS

(1) If there is no constitutional right to an appeal, why did the Court strike down the respective practices of Illinois and California in *Griffin* and *Douglas*?

Recall that the Court in *Douglas* specifically noted that "there can be no equal justice where the kind of an appeal a man enjoys depends on the amount of money he has." If this is true as a matter of constitutional law, why should it matter that *Moffitt* involved a discretionary appeal rather than an automatic appeal? Consider *Blankenship v. Johnson*, 118 F.3d 312 (5th Cir. 1997). There the defendant was entitled to a lawyer on appeal when the appellate court reversed her conviction. The government then sought discretionary review. Held, due process requires appointment of counsel.

In *Halbert v. Michigan*, 545 U.S. 605 (2005), the Court evaluated an unusual system. Ten years earlier, the state voters changed the rules regarding automatic appeals to the intermediate state court of appeals. "In every criminal prosecution, the accused shall have the right . . . to have an appeal as a matter of right, except as provided by law an appeal by an accused who pleads guilty or nolo contendere shall be by leave of the court." MICH. CONST., art. 1, § 20. The defendant entered a plea of nolo contendere and in seeking to appeal was not given counsel. The state argued that an appointment was not mandated because — as in *Ross* — the first appeal here was discretionary. Distinguishing *Ross*, the Justices held that "the Due Process and Equal Protection Clauses require the appointment of counsel for defendants, convicted on their pleas, who seek access to first-tier review in the Michigan Court of Appeals."

> Whether formally categorized as the decision of an appeal or the disposal of a leave application, the Court of Appeals' ruling on a plea-convicted defendant's claims provides the first, and likely the only, direct review the defendant's conviction and sentence will receive. Parties like Halbert, however, are disarmed in their endeavor to gain first-tier review. As the Court in *Ross* emphasized, a defendant seeking State Supreme Court review following a first-tier appeal as of right earlier had the assistance of appellate counsel. The attorney appointed to serve at the intermediate appellate court level will have reviewed the trial court record, researched the legal issues, and prepared a brief reflecting that review and research. The defendant seeking second-tier review may also be armed with an opinion of the intermediate appellate court addressing the issues counsel raised. A first-tier review applicant, forced to act *pro se*, will face a record unreviewed by appellate counsel, and will be equipped with no attorney's brief prepared for, or reasoned opinion by, a court of review.

(2) The majority was concerned with the broad impact of the lower court's ruling both on state and United States Supreme Court practice. If the lower court ruling had been upheld, as argued by the dissenters, would any person who sought review before the Court have a right to appointed counsel? By most estimates, more than eighty percent of criminal defendants receive court-appointed lawyers. Frensky, *Representation of Criminal Defendants Through Criminal Justice Act Panels Breathes Life in the Accused*, 57 Jun. Fed. Law 36 (2010); Stuntz, *The Virtues and Vices of the Exclusionary Rule*, 20 HARV. J. L. & PUB. POL'Y. 443, 452 (1997). Consider the fact also that in the last several years many thousands of petitioners each year sought Supreme Court review, with half of those asking for leave to file *in forma pauperis*. According to the United States Supreme Court

Public Information Office, each year the Court actually hears less than 100 cases on the merits.

(3) In *Evitts v. Lucey*, 469 U.S. 387 (1985), the Supreme Court held that the Due Process Clause guarantees the defendant the *effective* assistance of counsel on the first appeal of right. Contrast the opinions of Justice Brennan for the majority, and Justice Rehnquist, dissenting.

Justice Brennan:

> In bringing an appeal as of right from his conviction, a criminal defendant is attempting to demonstrate that the conviction, with its consequent drastic loss of liberty, is unlawful. To prosecute the appeal, a criminal appellant must face an adversary proceeding that — like a trial — is governed by intricate rules that to a layperson would be hopelessly forbidding. An unrepresented appellant — like an unrepresented defendant at trial — is unable to protect the vital interests at stake. To be sure, respondent did have nominal representation when he brought this appeal. But nominal representation on an appeal as of right — like nominal representation at trial — does not suffice to render the proceedings constitutionally adequate; a party whose counsel is unable to provide effective representation is in no better position than one who has no counsel at all.

Justice Rehnquist:

> Neither the language of the Constitution nor this Court's precedents establish a right to effective assistance of counsel on appeal. The Sixth Amendment provides that: "In all criminal prosecutions, the accused shall enjoy the right . . . to have the Assistance of Counsel for his defense." As the Court observes, this language has been interpreted to confer a right to effective assistance of counsel, and its guarantee has been extended to state criminal prosecutions by incorporation into the Due Process Clause of the Fourteenth Amendment. But the words "prosecution" and "defense" plainly indicate that the Sixth Amendment right to counsel applies only to trial level proceedings. At this stage, the accused needs an attorney "as a shield to protect him against being 'haled into court' by the State and stripped of his presumption of innocence."
>
> An appeal by a convicted criminal is an entirely different matter. He has been found guilty beyond a reasonable doubt and, if sentenced to a term of imprisonment, is subject to immediate deprivation of his liberty without any constitutional requirement of further proceedings. He seeks "to upset the prior determination of guilt" and universally is permitted to retain an attorney to serve "as a sword" in that endeavor.
>
> There is no constitutional requirement that a State provide an appeal at all. "It is wholly within the discretion of the State to allow or not to allow such a review." If a State decides to confer a right of appeal, it is free to do so "upon such terms as in its wisdom may be deemed proper."

(4) North Carolina allows automatic appeals in death penalty cases. If the defendant was convicted of a capital offense in a jurisdiction without automatic appeals in death penalty cases, would the discussion in *Moffitt* have been different? The District Judge in *Carey v. Garrison*, 403 F. Supp. 395, 397 (W.D.N.C. 1975), ordered that counsel be appointed to represent the defendant in his petition for certiorari in the United States Supreme Court when the conviction was for a capital case. "Where a man's life is at stake, I am not prepared to concede that the law in *Moffitt*, the case of a small time forger, should apply."

(5) In *Mayer v. Chicago*, 404 U.S. 189 (1971), the defendant had been convicted of violating an ordinance, an offense punishable only by fine. Nevertheless, the unanimous Court, relying on *Griffin*, required a free transcript to be provided to the defendant. "The size of the defendant's pocketbook bears no more relationship to his guilt or innocence in a nonfelony than in a felony case." If a defendant is entitled to receive a transcript when reviewing a conviction involving a relatively small fine, why would a defendant convicted of armed robbery not be entitled to appointed counsel in a discretionary appeal? Contrast the holding in *Mayer* with that in *United States v. MacCollom*, 426 U.S. 317 (1976). The petitioner there, sentenced to 10 years in prison, asserted that he had an absolute right to a free transcript in a proceeding under 28 U.S.C. § 2255 (motion attacking sentence). The Court, in a plurality opinion by Justice Rehnquist, disagreed:

> Although the statutory conditions established in § 753(f) with respect to furnishing a free transcript to movants in § 2255 proceedings are therefore consistent with the due process requirements of the Fifth Amendment, it is undoubtedly true that they place an indigent in a somewhat less advantageous position than a person of means. But neither the Equal Protection Clause of the Fourteenth Amendment, nor the counterpart equal protection requirement embodied in the Fifth Amendment, guarantees "absolute equality or precisely equal advantages." In the context of a criminal proceeding they require only "an adequate opportunity to present [one's] claims fairly. . . ." *Ross v. Moffitt.*

PROBLEM F
APPEALS

Does the appointed lawyer's failure to file a timely appeal in connection with a discretionary state review constitute ineffective assistance of counsel? See *Wainwright v. Torna*, 455 U.S. 586 (1982), relying on *Ross v. Moffitt*:

> Since respondent had no constitutional right to counsel, he could not be deprived of the effective assistance of counsel by his retained counsel's failure to file the application timely.

But see Justice Marshall's dissent:

> Although respondent's Sixth Amendment right to effective assistance of counsel may not have been infringed, he was denied his right to due process. Respondent's counsel promised him that he would seek review in the Florida Supreme Court. Respondent reasonably relied on that promise.

Counsel nonetheless failed to file a timely application. As a result, respondent was deprived of his right to seek discretionary review by the State's highest court.

§ 4.05 INEFFECTIVE ASSISTANCE OF COUNSEL

Convicted defendants are often quite dissatisfied with the performance of their attorneys. This dissatisfaction is manifested in appeals, or collateral attacks on convictions, in which it is asserted that the defendant was denied Sixth Amendment rights, or due process rights, because she was denied the *effective* assistance of counsel. Three major lines of attack have been made in recent years regarding effective assistance: denial of counsel of the defendant's choosing, incompetent aid by the attorney, insufficient appellate advocacy.

COUNSEL OF THE DEFENDANT'S CHOOSING

The Supreme Court made clear in *Powell v. Alabama*, 287 U.S. 45, 53 S. Ct. 55, 77 L. Ed. 158 (1932), that judges were to distinguish retained counsel from appointed counsel. In particular, this distinction is most important when the defendant seeks to have a designated attorney handle the case. "[A] defendant should be afforded a fair opportunity to secure counsel of his own choice." The opinion in *Powell* has been followed rather scrupulously when questions have been raised as to the ability of the retained counsel to represent the defendant.

Two situations bear special attention: when the attorney may be incompetent, and when the attorney may be ethically barred from representing the defendant. In the former situation, the courts are reluctant to remove the retained lawyer even if there is a clear indication that counsel is ineffective. Most commonly, the trial judge will make this concern clear to the defendant and make the defendant "waive" the right to effective assistance of counsel on the record. See, for instance, *Illinois v. Johnson*, 387 N.E.2d 688 (Ill. 1979), where the trial judge informed the defendant of the very real possibility that counsel was not competent (repeated disruptions, inappropriate questions, failure to keep incriminating information from the jury, etc.). The judge also told the defendant that he could continue the case with the same lawyer, or have a mistrial declared so that a new lawyer could handle the case. The defendant decided to stay with the original lawyer and was (not surprisingly) convicted. On appeal, he raised a claim of ineffective assistance, which was rejected by the Illinois Supreme Court. The court found that he had knowingly and voluntarily waived his right to effective assistance of counsel.

In *Wheat v. United States*, 486 U.S. 153 (1988), the Court decided that trial judges have considerable discretion in dealing with situations in which a criminal defendant seeks to waive the right to a conflict-free attorney. The defendant here expressly agreed to waive any future claims of conflict of interest resulting from the attorney's representation of two defendants in a complicated conspiracy trial. The trial judge refused to accept the waiver and would not allow the defendant to be represented by that particular attorney. The Supreme Court found that trial judges "have an independent interest in ensuring that criminal trials are conducted within the ethical standards of the profession and that legal proceedings appear fair to all who observe them." As a result, the Court held that while it recognized a presumption for the defendant's attorney of choice, that presumption could "be overcome not only by a demonstration of actual conflict but by a showing of a serious potential for conflict."

With appointed counsel the judicial response to requests for a particular attorney to represent the defendant is quite negative. The standard response was given in *People v. Fitzgerald*, 105 Cal. Rptr. 458 (Cal. 1973):

> We do not quarrel with the proposition that the input received by the judge in determining what attorney to appoint can also include a suggestion made by a defendant. In some cases it may be appropriate to follow the suggestion, but the ultimate discretion to make the specific appointment must be vested in the court. A contrary policy could give hostile or disruptive defendants an incentive to make impossible demands upon the court. Such demands could take the form of requests for unavailable lawyers or lawyers unqualified to handle a particular matter. It could result in capping for "popular" attorneys amongst defendants awaiting trial in jail. For sound policy reasons, it has been held that an indigent defendant does not have the right to representation by a particular lawyer.

But see *Magee v. Superior Court*, 506 P.2d 1023 (Cal. 1973), where the defendant and his court-appointed lawyer sought to have former United States Attorney General Ramsey Clark assigned to assist in the defense. The trial court refused the request even though Clark agreed to assist in the defense without compensation. The request was denied because the judge did not personally know Clark and his qualifications. Recognizing that the circumstances were unique (lengthy trial, expertise of Clark), the California Supreme Court ordered that Clark be allowed to participate in the defense. Is *Magee* consistent with the standard rule? What is the rationale for the usual rule?

Should the defendant be able to designate a particular attorney if the public defender's office is ready to take the appointment? See *Maynes v. State*, 495 P.2d 551 (Colo. 1972), where the defendant did not want to be represented by the public defender and complained that at first he was represented by one assistant public defender and then, just a few days before trial, another member of the staff handled the case. The Colorado Supreme Court strongly rejected defendant's claim of ineffective assistance of counsel: "The defendant's right to counsel does not grant the defendant the right to pick the lawyer of his choice." As stated by the court in *Pitts v. State*, 342 So. 2d 40 (Ala. 1976), "It appears to us that indigents should not be too 'choosy' about getting their choice of lawyers and have no just complaint as long as the appointed attorney is competent, diligent and faithful." Why is it that the indigent should not be "choosy" about his lawyer? What if she simply does not like the lawyer and cannot get along with him? Should the defendant have to accept the assignment of that particular lawyer?

If the conflict between the defendant and the attorney is so strained that they truly cannot get along, the trial court — in its discretion — may appoint new counsel. This was done in *Brown v. Craven*, 424 F.2d 1166 (9th Cir. 1970), where the attorney advised the court that his client would no longer speak with him. "[T]o compel one charged with a grievous crime to undergo a trial with the assistance of an attorney with whom he has become embroiled in irreconcilable conflict is to deprive him of the effective assistance of any counsel whatsoever." See also *Legal Aid Society v. Rothwax*, 415 N.Y.S.2d 432 (N.Y. 1979), where the court allowed the appointed attorney to withdraw from the case when:

> the defendant has already assaulted Legal Aid counsel in a previous case and now threatens repetitive misbehavior. Counsel, as one of the officers of the court, is required to be obedient to the lawful orders of the court. The court has the concomitant duty to protect its officers. This duty embraces the obligation not to subject counsel to unnecessary personal risk.

One area where the courts have been completely consistent has been in their refusal to appoint non-lawyers to represent the accused. The courts take the position that the Sixth Amendment right does not encompass non-lawyers. *See, e.g., United States v. Wright*, 568 F.2d 142 (9th Cir. 1978):

> It is the duty of counsel to assist the court, as well as the client. Representation by skilled lawyers is necessary if our complex, highly refined judicial process is to be fair and efficient. The appointment of nonlawyers as a matter of right would obstruct these objectives, not further them. We would not serve the ends of justice either in this case or in the judicial system generally by adopting the frivolous procedural device of permitting laymen to replace counsel as a matter of right. Nothing in the language or the history of the Sixth Amendment to the Constitution would justify that rule. The privilege to dispense with the constitutional right to the assistance of counsel should not be converted into the affirmative right to demand that a layman try the case.

Do you agree with this analysis? If the defendant is charged in a multi-count tax evasion indictment, should she have the right to have an accountant rather than an attorney represent her? Would such representation be disruptive? The trial judge in *United States v. Whitesel*, 543 F.2d 1176 (6th Cir. 1976), *cert. denied*, 431 U.S. 967 (1977), rejected the defendant's claim in just such a situation, allowing the defendant to handle the case himself with the accountant seated at the counsel table to advise him during the trial.

INCOMPETENT COUNSEL

A more serious difficulty in the area of ineffective assistance of counsel is the allegation that the trial counsel did not perform in a competent fashion. A charge of incompetency is extremely difficult to prove, at least to the satisfaction of the court on appeal.

The standard was set in *Strickland v. Washington*, 466 U.S. 668 (1984). It involves a two-part showing:

> [T]he proper standard for attorney performance is that of reasonably effective assistance. When a convicted defendant complains of the ineffectiveness of counsel's assistance, the defendant must show that counsel's representation fell below an objective standard of reasonableness.

> More specific guidelines are not appropriate. The Sixth Amendment refers simply to "counsel," not specifying particular requirements of effective assistance. It relies instead on the legal profession's maintenance of standards sufficient to justify the law's presumption that counsel will fulfill the role in the adversary process that the Amendment envisions. The proper measure of attorney performance remains simply reasonableness under prevailing professional norms.
>
> Representation of a criminal defendant entails certain basic duties. Counsel's function is to assist the defendant, and hence counsel owes the client a duty of loyalty, a duty to avoid conflicts of interest. From counsel's function as assistant to the defendant derive the overarching duty to advocate the defendant's cause and the more particular duties to consult with the defendant on important decisions and to keep the defendant informed of important developments in the course of the prosecution. Counsel also has a duty to bring to bear such skill and knowledge as will render the trial a reliable adversarial testing process.
>
> . . .
>
> An error by counsel, even if professionally unreasonable, does not warrant setting aside the judgment of a criminal proceeding if the error had no effect on the judgment. . . . The purpose of the Sixth Amendment guarantee of counsel is to ensure that a defendant has the assistance necessary to justify reliance on the outcome of the proceeding. Accordingly, any deficiencies in counsel's performance must be prejudicial to the defense in order to constitute ineffective assistance under the Constitution. . . . The defendant must show that there is a reasonable probability that, but for counsel's unprofessional errors, the result of the proceeding would have been different. A reasonable probability is a probability sufficient to undermine confidence in the outcome.

The courts are reluctant to find a denial of Sixth Amendment rights unless there is a clear showing of serious problems at the trial level which likely affected the outcome. For instance, it is not enough to allege that the attorney did not file an appeal, did not adequately question alibi witnesses and did not properly investigate. The mere failure to object to leading questions or to hearsay evidence is generally held to be insufficient to state a Sixth Amendment claim. Why are such claims insufficient?

Judges do sometimes find that lawyers have performed incompetently, requiring the reversal of defendants' convictions, but a strong showing must be made. *Brown v. Sternes*, 304 F.3d 677, 699 (7th Cir. 2002), involved an especially troubling case in which trial counsel failed to investigate the defendant's history of mental illness.

> This case is a striking example of a legal system that processed this defendant as a number rather than as a human being; it signals a breakdown of a process that might very well be in need of review, adjustment, and repair. Brown's psychiatric illness was not given so much as a sideways glance by the parties involved. Not only did Brown's public defender trial attorneys drop the ball; so did the court-appointed mental

> health doctors (a psychologist and a psychiatrist) and probation officer, all of whom failed to conduct even a sufficient inquiry into his family background and extensive medical history. As a result, the state trial court proceeded without any awareness of his condition. We have a record before us that mandates — in the interest of justice — the conclusion that Brown was denied his Sixth Amendment right to effective assistance of counsel.
>
> . . .

In *Lounds v. State*, 670 S.E.2d 646 (S.C. 2008), the lawyer met with the defendant only once, on the morning of trial. Counsel did not seek out witnesses who could testify on behalf of his client. Held, ineffective assistance of counsel.

> We have reconized that when counsel articlulates a valid reason for employing a certain strategy, such conduct generally will not be deemed ineffective assistance of counsel. The validity of counsel's strategy is reviewed under "an objective standard of reasonableness."
>
> In the instant case, however, Newell did not articulate a strategy because he did not testify at the [post conviction relief] hearing. Although Newell did state to the trial court he believed the witnesses would not add much to petitioner's defense, we find this was not objectively reasonable given the defense theory of the case. The only defense Newell presented to the jury was that petitioner and Garrett knew each other through drug dealing. If witnesses other than petitioner were willing to testify to this fact, certainly that would have added significantly to the credibility of petitioner's case. Thus, we find the PCR court erred in finding that Newell offered an objectively valid strategic reason not to call these witnesses.
>
> Furthermore, both the trial transcript and petitioner's PCR testimony inescapably point to the conclusion that Newell simply had not adequately prepared the defense case. Newell himself admitted to the trial court he had only learned of defense witnesses that morning, and therefore they had neither been interviewed nor subpoenaed. Petitioner corroborated this at the PCR hearing when he stated Newell had only spoken to him about the case on the morning of trial.
>
> We hold the evidence clearly shows that Newell inadequately prepared for trial. [At] a minimum, counsel has the duty to interview potential witnesses. This was unreasonable in light of the fact that Newell had several months' notice that petitioner was facing [life without possibility of parole] if convicted. . . .

See also *Canaan v. McBride*, 395 F.3d 376 (7th Cir. 2005), where the defense lawyer failed in a capital case to advise the defendant of the right to testify at the sentencing hearing. Held to be ineffective assistance.

The Supreme Court has had surprisingly little to say about the effective assistance of counsel in non-capital cases. See this discussion in *Strickland*:

> Judicial scrutiny of counsel's performance must be highly deferential. It is all too tempting for a defendant to second-guess counsel's assistance after conviction or adverse sentence, and it is all too easy for a court, examining

counsel's defense after it has proved unsuccessful, to conclude that a particular act or omission of counsel was unreasonable. A fair assessment of attorney performance requires that every effort be made to eliminate the distorting effects of hindsight, to reconstruct the circumstances of counsel's challenged conduct, and to evaluate the conduct from counsel's perspective at the time. Because of the difficulties inherent in making the evaluation, a court must indulge a strong presumption that counsel's conduct falls within the wide range of reasonable professional assistance; that is, the defendant must overcome the presumption that, under the circumstances, the challenged action "might be considered sound trial strategy." There are countless ways to provide effective assistance in any given case. Even the best criminal defense attorneys would not defend a particular client in the same way.

The availability of intrusive post-trial inquiry into attorney performance or of detailed guidelines for its evaluation would encourage the proliferation of ineffectiveness challenges. Criminal trials resolved unfavorably to the defendant would increasingly come to be followed by a second trial, this one of counsel's unsuccessful defense. Counsel's performance and even willingness to serve could be adversely affected. Intensive scrutiny of counsel and rigid requirements for acceptable assistance could dampen the ardor and impair the independence of defense counsel, discourage the acceptance of assigned cases, and undermine the trust between attorney and client.

Thus, a court deciding an actual ineffectiveness claim must judge the reasonableness of counsel's challenged conduct on the facts of the particular case, viewed as of the time of counsel's conduct.

In *Williams v. Taylor*, 529 U.S. 420 (2000), the Supreme Court found ineffective assistance of counsel in a death penalty case:

Counsel failed to introduce available evidence that Williams was "borderline mentally retarded" and did not advance beyond sixth grade in school. They failed to seek prison records recording Williams' commendations for helping to crack a prison drug ring and for returning a guard's missing wallet, or the testimony of prison officials who described Williams as among the inmates "least likely to act in a violent, dangerous or provocative way." Counsel failed even to return the phone call of a certified public accountant who had offered to testify that he had visited Williams frequently when Williams was incarcerated as part of a prison ministry program, that Williams "seemed to thrive in a more regimented and structured environment," and that Williams was proud of the carpentry degree he earned while in prison.

Of course, not all of the additional evidence was favorable to Williams. . . . But . . . to [not] introduce the comparatively voluminous amount of evidence that did speak in Williams' favor was not justified by a tactical decision to focus on Williams' voluntary confession. . . . [T]rial counsel did not fulfill their obligation to conduct a thorough investigation of the defendant's background.

In a set of short, per curiam opinions dealing with capital cases, the Supreme Court laid out some basic principles regarding ineffective assistance and the duty of the defense lawyer to adequately consider mitigating factors at the sentencing stage. *See Bobby v. Van Hook*, 558 U.S. 4 (2009); *Wong v. Belmontes*, 558 U.S. 15 (2009); *Porter v. McCollum*, 558 U.S. 30 (2009). In *Van Hook* the Justices noted that the *ABA Guidelines for the Appointment and Performance of Defense Counsel in Death Penalty Cases* would be helpful to determine competent assistance, but would not be the set standard. *Wong* established that the failure of the defense lawyer to offer evidence that was "merely cumulative" would not lead to a reversal. *Porter* makes clear that the lawyer will have an obligation to adduce mitigation evidence of significance [there relating to lack of education, mental health, and trauma resulting from battlefield service].

In a far more substantive decision, the Court in *Padilla v. Kentucky*, 559 U.S. 356 (2010) applied the Sixth Amendment right to effective assistance of counsel to include a defendant's need to receive accurate advice about the immigration consequences of a possible guilty plea. The Justices emphasized the serious consequences of deportation proceedings: "The severity of deportation 'the equivalent of banishment or exile,' only underscores how critical it is for counsel to inform her noncitizen client that he faces a risk of deportation . . . . The importance of accurate legal advice for noncitizens accused of crimes has never been more important."

The Justices followed up on *Padilla* in two decisions by ruling that the ineffective assistance doctrine would also be applied to plea bargain negotiations. As a result, defense lawyers must inform their clients of plea bargain offers, even if the lawyers would recommend rejecting the offers, and the lawyers will be held to the *Strickland* standard when giving advice regarding plea offers. The cases are *Missouri v. Frye*, 132 S. Ct. 1399 (2012), and *Lafler v. Cooper*, 132 S. Ct. 1376 (2012).

PROBLEM G
CHOICE OF TACTICS

Can the defendant demand that appointed counsel raise particular legal issues on appeal? In *Jones v. Barnes*, 463 U.S. 745 (1983), the defendant's appointed lawyer refused to argue several nonfrivolous points. The Supreme Court concluded there is no constitutional error when the lawyer is left free to exercise professional judgment. Otherwise, counsel "runs the risk of burying good arguments in a verbal mound made up of strong and weak contentions."

PROBLEM H
PERJURED TESTIMONY

The defense lawyer in *Nix v. Whiteside*, 475 U.S. 157 (1986), was faced with a difficult decision. His client, over a period of time, informed him that the client had not seen a gun in the hands of the victim when the shooting occurred (the claim was self-defense). Just before trial, the client advised counsel that he would testify that he saw a gun in the victim's hand and that is why he shot the victim. The lawyer told the client this would be perjury, he would seek to withdraw from the case if the client lied at trial, and that he "would be allowed to attempt to impeach that particular testimony." Did the lawyer act correctly? The United States Supreme Court concluded that no constitutional right of the defendant had been violated and noted that the Iowa court had commended counsel "for the high ethical manner in which this matter was handled." Justice Stevens concurred in the result, but raised some lingering questions:

> As we view this case, it appears perfectly clear that respondent intended to commit perjury, that his lawyer knew it, and that the lawyer had a duty — both to the court and to his client, for perjured testimony can ruin an otherwise meritorious case — to take extreme measures to prevent the perjury from occurring. The lawyer was unsuccessful and, from our unanimous and remote perspective, it is now pellucidly clear that the client suffered no "legally cognizable prejudice."
>
> Nevertheless, beneath the surface of this case there are areas of uncertainty that cannot be resolved today. A lawyer's certainty that a change in his client's recollection is a harbinger of intended perjury — as well as judicial review of such apparent certainty — should be tempered by the realization that, after reflection, the most honest witness may recall (or sincerely believe he recalls) details that he previously overlooked. Similarly, the post-trial review of a lawyer's pretrial threat to expose perjury that had not yet been committed — and, indeed, may have been prevented by the threat — is by no means the same as review of the way in which such a threat may actually have been carried out. Thus, one can be convinced — as I am — that this lawyer's actions were a proper way to provide his client with effective representation without confronting the much more difficult questions of what a lawyer must, should, or may do after his client has given testimony that the lawyer does not believe. The answer to such questions may well be colored by the particular circumstances attending the actual event and its aftermath.

See also *United States v. Litchfield*, 959 F.2d 1514 (10th Cir. 1992), where the defense lawyer initiated an *ex parte* conversation with the trial judge indicating that the lawyer believed the defendant might lie in giving testimony. The trial judge told the lawyer that the testimony should be given, with the jurors evaluating it and reaching their own conclusions. On appeal, the court found no conflict of interest created by the trial lawyer's action and no ethical violation of the duty to his client.

The court in *State v. Johnson*, 72 Cal. Rptr. 2d 805 (Cal. 1998), explored the various alternatives defense counsel has when faced with a client who appears ready to testify falsely. The judges concluded that the best option would be to call the defendant as a witness and simply allow testimony in a narrative fashion:

> Of the various approaches, we believe the narrative approach represents the best accommodation of the competing interests of the defendant's right to testify and the attorney's obligation not to participate in the presentation of perjured testimony since it allows the defendant to tell the jury, in his own words, his version of what occurred, a right which has been described as fundamental, and allows the attorney to play a passive role.

APPEALS: THE *ANDERS* RULE

ANDERS v. CALIFORNIA

United States Supreme Court
386 U.S. 738 (1967)

MR. JUSTICE CLARK delivered the opinion of the Court.

We are here concerned with the extent of the duty of a court-appointed appellate counsel to prosecute a first appeal from a criminal conviction, after that attorney has conscientiously determined that there is no merit to the indigent's appeal.

After he was convicted of the felony of possession of marijuana, petitioner sought to appeal and moved that the California District Court of Appeal appoint counsel for him. Such motion was granted; however, after a study of the record and consultation with petitioner, the appointed counsel concluded that there was no merit to the appeal. He so advised the court by letter and, at the same time, informed the court that petitioner wished to file a brief in his own behalf. At this juncture, petitioner requested the appointment of another attorney. This request was denied and petitioner proceeded to file his own brief *pro se*. The State responded and petitioner filed a reply brief. [T]he District Court of Appeal unanimously affirmed the conviction.

We have concluded that California's action does not comport with fair procedure and lacks that equality that is required by the Fourteenth Amendment.

I

For a decade or more, a continuing line of cases has reached this Court concerning discrimination against the indigent defendant on his first appeal. Beginning with *Griffin v. Illinois*, where it was held that equal justice was not afforded an indigent appellant where the nature of the review "depends on the amount of money he has," and continuing through *Douglas v. California*, this Court has consistently held invalid those procedures "where the rich man, who appeals as of right, enjoys the benefit of counsel's examination into the record, research of the law, and marshalling of arguments on his behalf, while the indigent, already burdened by a preliminary determination that his case is without merit, is forced to shift for himself."

In *Gideon v. Wainwright*, the Sixth Amendment's requirement that "the accused shall enjoy the right . . . to have the Assistance of Counsel for his defence" was made obligatory on the States by the Fourteenth Amendment, the Court holding that "in our adversary system of criminal justice, any person haled into court, who is too poor to hire a lawyer, cannot be assured a fair trial unless counsel is provided for him." We continue to adhere to these principles.

II

In petitioner's case, his appointed counsel wrote the District Court of Appeal, stating:

> I will not file a brief on appeal as I am of the opinion that there is no merit to the appeal. I have visited and communicated with Mr. Anders and have explained my views and opinions to him. . . .[H]e wishes to file a brief in this matter on his own behalf.

The District Court of Appeal, after having examined the record, affirmed the conviction. We believe that counsel's bare conclusion, as evidenced by his letter, was not enough.

Here the court-appointed counsel had the transcript but refused to proceed with the appeal because he found no merit in it. He filed a no-merit letter with the District Court of Appeal whereupon the court examined the record itself and affirmed the judgment.

III

The constitutional requirement of substantial equality and fair process can only be attained where counsel acts in the role of an active advocate in behalf of his client, as opposed to that of *amicus curiae*. The no-merit letter and the procedure it triggers do not reach that dignity. Counsel should, and can with honor and without conflict, be of more assistance to his client and to the court. His role as advocate requires that he support his client's appeal to the best of his ability. Of course, if counsel finds his case to be wholly frivolous, after a conscientious examination of it, he should so advise the court and request permission to withdraw. That request must, however, be accompanied by a brief referring to anything in the record that might arguably support the appeal. A copy of counsel's brief should be furnished the indigent and time allowed him to raise any points that he chooses; the court — not counsel — then proceeds, after a full examination of all the proceedings, to decide whether the case is wholly frivolous. If it so finds it may grant counsel's request to withdraw and dismiss the appeal insofar as federal requirements are concerned, or proceed to a decision on the merits, if state law so requires. On the other hand, if it finds any of the legal points arguable on their merits (and therefore not frivolous) it must, prior to decision, afford the indigent the assistance of counsel to argue the appeal.

This requirement would not force appointed counsel to brief his case against his client but would merely afford the latter that advocacy which a nonindigent defendant is able to obtain. It would also induce the court to pursue all the more vigorously its own review because of the ready references not only to the record, but also to the legal authorities as furnished it by counsel. The no-merit letter, on the other hand, affords neither the client nor the court any aid. The former must shift entirely for himself while the court has only the cold record which it must review without the help of an advocate. Moreover, such handling would tend to protect counsel from the constantly increasing charge that he was ineffective and had not handled the case with that diligence to which an indigent defendant is entitled. This procedure will assure penniless defendants the same rights and opportunities on appeal — as nearly as is practicable — as are enjoyed by those persons who are in a similar situation but who are able to afford the retention of private counsel.

Judgment reversed and case remanded.

MR. JUSTICE STEWART, whom MR. JUSTICE BLACK and MR. JUSTICE HARLAN join, dissenting.

The Court today imposes upon appointed counsel who wishes to withdraw from a case he deems "wholly frivolous" the requirement of filing "a brief referring to anything in the record that might arguably support the appeal." But if the record did present any such "arguable" issues, the appeal would not be frivolous and counsel would not have filed a "no-merit" letter in the first place.

The quixotic requirement imposed by the Court can be explained, I think, only upon the cynical assumption that an appointed lawyer's professional representation to an appellate court in a "no-merit" letter is not to be trusted. That is an assumption to which I cannot subscribe.

PROBLEM I
APPEALS

The correspondence of the attorney for the accused and the clerk of the court in *Anders* follows:

Appeals

IN THE DISTRICT COURT OF APPEAL OF THE STATE OF CALIFORNIA

IN AND FOR THE THIRD APPELLATE DISTRICT

PATRICK R. MURPHY
Attorney at Law 503
Nicolaus Building
Sacramento, California Gilbert
3-6508
August 1, 1958

3 Crim. 2880 FILED
Aug. 4, 1958 Dist.
Court of Appeal-Third Dist.

L. A. ENDRES, Clerk By
/s/ Kramer, Deputy

Hon. B.F. Van Dyke, Presiding Justice
Third Appellate District 119 Library &
Courts Building Sacramento 14,
California

Dear Judge Van Dyke:

This is to advise you that I have received and examined the trial transcript of CHARLIE ANDERS as it relates to his conviction of the crime of possession of narcotics.

I will not file a brief on appeal as I am of the opinion that there is no merit to the appeal. I have visited and communicated with Mr. Anders and have explained my views and opinions to him as they relate to his appeal.

Mr. Anders has advised me that he wishes to file a brief in this matter.

Appeals

IN THE DISTRICT COURT OF APPEAL OF THE STATE OF CALIFORNIA

IN AND FOR THE THIRD APPELLATE DISTRICT

August 4, 1958

CHARLIE
ANDERS BOX
A-42880 Represa
California

Re: PEOPLE v. CHARLIE ANDERS 3 Crim. 2880

We have been advised by your court-appointed attorney that after examination of the record he can find no merit to your appeal.

This court will not appoint a new attorney to represent you. If you wish, you may file a brief yourself. If we do not hear from you within 30 days, the record will be given to the court for review and decision.

Very truly yours,
L.A. ENDRES, Clerk

by: /s/ Kramer
Deputy Clerk

NOTES AND QUESTIONS

(1) If the attorney is convinced there are no non-frivolous issues to be argued, how can that attorney prepare a "brief referring to anything in the record that might arguably support the appeal"? Justice Stewart argued that central to the Court's opinion was the view that the lawyer, in sending out a no-merit letter, was not to be trusted. Was this the basis for Justice Clark's opinion? Consider the statement made by Chief Justice Day of the Ohio Court of Appeals at the National Judicial Conference on Standards for the Administration of Criminal Justice, 57 F.R.D. 229, 309 (1972):

> [W]e are all aware of what the court has said in *Anders* and other cases about counsel. If a lawyer finally decides that the case is frivolous, that it has no merit whatever, it probably is appropriate for him to get out, and yet I can never remember a case, really never, in a long life at the Bar, I can never remember a case where if the money was there the appeal was so frivolous that the lawyer couldn't make it. I'm not suggesting nobody ever stood up and said grandly, "Take away that $10,000; there's nothing to this case; I will not appeal it." Maybe that happened, but maybe there are angels in the balcony, too. It just doesn't happen often, and therefore I suggest that the times when it is appropriate to let a lawyer out on the

ground that an appeal is frivolous are rare. Moreover, there is always the probability that unless there's an excellent reason, beyond being busy, the lawyer at least ought to be told that he might try to present what the client wanted. He doesn't have to argue as his own points matters that are stupid or ridiculous, but at least there ought to be some effort made to present the point the client believes important. And if he finds that not even that is proper then perhaps it's time to appoint other counsel. But gentlemen, there is nothing we can do in the interest of the administration of criminal justice that would do more for it than to insure the service of competent counsel all along the line.

(2) If a lawyer files an *Anders* brief, has he violated any ethical obligation? See the statement of the Supreme Court of Tennessee in *State v. Williams*, 529 S.W.2d 714, 716 (Tenn. 1975):

> It is unethical for a lawyer to take a frivolous legal position in the courts of this State.
>
> We take judicial notice that some indigent defendants have pursued six (6) or more post-conviction petitions, initiated *pro se* but thereafter mandatorily pursued to this Court, with state paid lawyer assistance because of the requirements of the post-conviction statutes.
>
> We abhor any law that forces a member of the bar to involuntarily commit a breach of ethics. Neither the Constitutions of our State or Nation nor the pursuit of equal justice under the law requires that taxpayers bear the expense of lawyer-prepared frivolous appeals, under the guise of matching the rich man's legal arsenal. The frivolous appeal of the wealthy defendant is as useless and meaningless as the frivolous appeal of the indigent.

Is this statement essentially a critique of *Anders*? Do you agree with it? Contrast it with the ABA Standards for Criminal Justice: The Defense Function.

Standard 4-8.3(a). Counsel on appeal

> Appellate counsel should not seek to withdraw from a case solely on the basis of his or her own determination that the appeal lacks merit.

Standard 5-6.2. Duration of representation

> Counsel should be provided at every stage of the proceedings, including sentencing, appeal, certiorari, and postconviction review. In capital cases, counsel also should be provided in clemency proceedings. Counsel initially provided should continue to represent the defendant throughout the trial court proceedings and should preserve the defendant's right to appeal, if necessary.

See also *Killingsworth v. State*, 490 So. 2d 849, 852 (Miss. 1986), where the court decided to go beyond the "minimum federal requirements of *Anders*." Held, under the state constitution, counsel may not withdraw simply due to a belief that the appeal is without merit:

> No doubt the process we order today will to many lawyers be regarded as a burden. It is a burden each assumed upon acceptance of a license to

practice law. However passe it may be in some circles, we regard as noble the lawyer who gives his all in behalf of the seemingly hopeless cause of his client.

The New Hampshire Supreme Court created an exception to its rules of professional conduct to excuse the filing of frivolous claims. The court would not allow counsel to withdraw simply because of a belief that the appeal would be frivolous. Still, the justices felt that truly frivolous claims would be "extremely rare," as it would not be frivolous to make arguments for the rejection, alteration, or extension of existing law. *State v. Cigic*, 639 A.2d 251 (N.H. 1994). The lawyer has an obligation not to mislead the court, but also has a duty to not simply represent "that the case is frivolous . . . . [The court must] be confident that [the lawyer] conducted a thorough examination of the entire record with an eye to *all* potential appellate issues." *United States v. Palmer*, 600 F.3d 897, 899 (7th Cir. 2010).

Waiver of Appeal

One obvious way of avoiding the result in *Anders* is to have the defendant dismiss his own appeal. This form is a typical one used for this purpose.

Case No._______

____

v.

____

To: Clerk of the Court United States Court of Appeals

I have been informed by my attorney of his intention to move to dismiss my appeal.

I concur in his decision and hereby waive all rights to object or raise any points on appeal.

____
(Name)

____
(Street Address or Prison Box)

____
(City, State, Zip Code)

If the court of appeals received such a form signed by the defendant, would that be a sufficient waiver? Would it be sufficient for waiver of trial counsel?

NOTES AND QUESTIONS

(1) In *Smith v. Robbins*, 528 U.S. 259 (2000), the Court approved a state process which differed from that laid out in *Anders*. California allowed the appeals lawyer to withdraw if she filed a brief with the appeals court that summarized the history of the case, affirmed that she had reviewed the record and discussed her evaluation of the case with the client. In addition, the appeals court was then required to

conduct a review of the entire record. At no point did the lawyer indicate to the court her view of the merits of the case. The Supreme Court found that the state procedure was consistent with the constitutional mandate, as the *Anders* procedure "is a prophylactic one; the States are free to adopt different procedures, so long as those procedures adequately safeguard a defendant's right to appellate counsel."

(2) South Dakota adopted still another alternative to the *Anders* procedure. There, when an appointed attorney believes the criminal appeal to be without merit, she is to file a two part brief. The first is to lay out a statement of the case, the second part of the brief is to discuss issues the client wishes the lawyer to argue. The defense counsel will not then be permitted to withdraw from representation. This process "strikes a balance between protecting a defendant's Sixth Amendment right to appellate counsel, protecting Fourteenth Amendment due process and equal protection rights, and upholding the ethical rules by which attorneys must abide." *State v. Korth*, 650 N.W.2d 528 (S.D. 2002). Do you agree?

(3) In *McCoy v. Court of Appeals*, 486 U.S. 429 (1988), the Wisconsin Supreme Court adopted a rule that required the *Anders* brief to mention any item arguably supporting the appeal and also to include "a discussion of why the issue lacks merit." Such an appeals process resulted in a brief which was characterized by the Court as being "schizophrenic." Did the Wisconsin rule violate the constitution as set out in *Anders*? A majority of the United States Supreme Court affirmed the Wisconsin rule finding that it simply followed the basic ethical obligations of appeals lawyers not to mislead courts or engage in frivolous appeals. Does *McCoy* correctly apply *Anders*?

(4) The appellate counsel in *Penson v. Ohio*, 488 U.S. 75 (1988), violated the *Anders* rule by simply advising the appellate court of his view that the appeal lacked merit ("Certification of Meritless Appeal and Motion"). The court granted his motion to withdraw, considered the appeal without defense counsel and affirmed part of the conviction. The Supreme Court found a clear violation of *Anders* but was presented with two other issues. Should a defendant under *Anders* have to show prejudice, and does the harmless error rule apply to *Anders* violations? In an 8-1 decision, the Court answered "no" to both questions, for any other result "would render meaningless the protections afforded by . . . *Anders*."

Chapter 5

CONFESSIONS AND OTHER INCRIMINATING STATEMENTS

Judges always have struggled with challenges made by defendants to the use of confessions at trial. These challenges fall roughly within three categories: the due process assertion under the Fifth and Fourteenth Amendments, the right to counsel question under the Sixth Amendment, and the self-incrimination issue under the Fifth Amendment. This chapter will deal with these challenges under these various approaches.

§ 5.01 THE DUE PROCESS APPROACH

The use of confessions against defendants has been a major part of the prosecution's case throughout this country. The mere use has never been particularly troublesome; instead the question often has been the manner in which the confessions were elicited. With improper police actions the statements may not have met the traditional constitutional standard:

> The ultimate test remains that which has been the only clearly established test in Anglo-American courts for two hundred years: the test of voluntariness. Is the confession the product of an essentially free and unconstrained choice by its maker? If it is, if he has willed to confess, it may be used against him. If it is not, if his will has been overborne and his capacity for self-determination critically impaired, the use of his confession offends due process. The line of distinction is that at which governing self-direction is lost and compulsion, of whatever nature or however infused, propels or helps to propel the confession.

Culombe v. Connecticut, 367 U.S. 568 (1961). The courts have seen a remarkable variety of techniques utilized by police officers to secure confessions. The Supreme Court catalogued some of these in *Culombe*:

> [There are] cases involving physical brutality, threats of physical brutality, and such convincingly terror-arousing, and otherwise unexplainable, incidents of interrogation as the removal of prisoners from jail at night for questioning in secluded places, the shuttling of prisoners from jail to jail, at distances from their homes, for questioning, the keeping of prisoners unclothed or standing on their feet for long periods during questioning . . . cases where deprivation of sleep has been used to sap a prisoner's strength and drug him or where bald disregard of his rudimentary need for food is a factor that adds to enfeeblement.

As the Court properly noted there, these techniques required the exclusion of the resulting confessions, as the statements were coerced and thus violated the Due Process Clause. Perhaps the most famous of the due process confession cases is *Brown v. Mississippi*, 297 U.S. 278 (1936). The techniques used there were described in graphic detail by Chief Justice Hughes:

> The crime with which these defendants, all ignorant negroes, are charged, was discovered about 1 o'clock p.m. on Friday, March 30, 1934. On that night one Dial, a deputy sheriff, accompanied by others, came to the home of Ellington, one of the defendants, and requested him to accompany them to the house of the deceased, and there a number of white men were gathered, who began to accuse the defendant of the crime. Upon his denial they seized him, and with the participation of the deputy they hanged him by a rope to the limb of a tree, and, having let him down, they hung him again, and when he was let down the second time, and he still protested his innocence, he was tied to a tree and whipped, and, still declining to accede to the demands that he confess, he was finally released, and he returned with some difficulty to his home, suffering intense pain and agony. The record of the testimony shows that the signs of the rope on his neck were plainly visible during the so-called trial. A day or two thereafter the said deputy, accompanied by another, returned to the home of the said defendant and arrested him, and departed with the prisoner towards the jail in an adjoining county, but went by a route which led into the state of Alabama; and while on the way, in that state, the deputy stopped and again severely whipped the defendant, declaring that he would continue the whipping until he confessed, and the defendant then agreed to confess to such a statement as the deputy would dictate, and he did so, after which he was delivered to jail.
>
> The other two defendants, Ed Brown and Henry Shields, were also arrested and taken to the same jail. On Sunday night, April 1, 1934, the same deputy, accompanied by a number of white men, one of whom was also an officer, and by the jailer, came to the jail, and the two last named defendants were made to strip and they were laid over chairs and their backs were cut to pieces with a leather strap with buckles on it, and they were likewise made by the said deputy definitely to understand that the whipping would be continued unless and until they confessed, and not only confessed, but confessed in every matter of detail as demanded by those present; and in this manner the defendants confessed the crime, and as the whippings progressed and were repeated, they changed or adjusted their confession in all particulars of detail so as to conform to the demands of their torturers. When the confessions had been obtained in the exact form and contents as desired by the mob, they left with the parting admonition and warning that, if the defendants changed their story at any time in any respect from that last stated, the perpetrators of the outrage would administer the same or equally effective treatment.

A unanimous Court held that these confessions were not admissible, as the Due Process Clause requires "that state action, whether through one agency or another, shall be consistent with the fundamental principles of liberty and justice which lie at the base of all our civil and political institutions."

Of course, such a ruling was relatively easy in *Brown*, where the police conduct was shocking and where a serious question was raised as to whether the conduct "breaks the will to conceal or lie, [or] even break[s] the will to stand by the truth." *Watts v. Indiana*, 338 U.S. 49 (1949) (dissenting opinion of Justice Jackson). What would happen when the state conduct was not so brutal and shocking, or where the truthfulness of the confession was verified, was another question.

BROOKS v. FLORIDA

United States Supreme Court
389 U.S. 413 (1967)

PER CURIAM.

Petitioner, Bennie Brooks, was convicted of participating in a riot in the Florida prison where he was an inmate.

The disturbance in the prison occurred on May 27, 1965. The same day Brooks was ordered confined in a punishment cell for 35 days with two other prisoners also accused of the rioting. Brooks says the cell was 7 feet long and 6-1/2 feet wide; a witness for the State testified it was 6 feet longer. This minor difference aside, the parties agree that the punishment cell had no external window, that it contained no bed or other furnishings or facilities except a hole flush with the floor which served as a commode, and that during the first 14 days he lived in this cell Brooks' only contact with the outside was an unspecified number of interviews with the prison's investigating officer. It is also agreed that while so confined Brooks was fed a "restricted diet" consisting, according to the testimony of the investigating officer, of "peas and carrots in a soup form" three times daily. Brooks' more detailed description of this concoction — "They fed us four ounces of soup three times a day and eight ounces of water" — was not controverted, nor was his testimony that he was stripped naked before being thrown into the cell. On the 15th day of confinement under these conditions, Brooks was taken from the punishment cell and again brought directly to the investigating officer. This time, shortly after questioning began, Brooks confessed and dictated his statement into a tape recorder. The recording was introduced at trial. Brooks says that he was brutally beaten by one officer while the other was taking his statement. However, we do not consider this claim because the officer denied it and the judge disbelieved Brooks' testimony. The judge also concluded that the confession was voluntary. We disagree.

Putting to one side quibbles over the dimensions of the windowless sweatbox into which Brooks was thrown naked with two other men, we cannot accept his statement as the voluntary expression of an uncoerced will. For two weeks this man's home was a barren cage fitted only with a hole in one corner into which he and his cell mates could defecate. For two weeks he subsisted on a daily fare of 12 ounces of thin soup and eight ounces of water. For two full weeks he saw not one friendly face from outside the prison, but was completely under the control and domination of his jailers. These stark facts belie any contention that the confession extracted from him within minutes after he was brought from the cell was not tainted by the 14 days he spent in such an oppressive hole. In a long line of cases beginning with *Brown v. Mississippi*, we have held that the Constitution does not permit prosecutorial use of an involuntary confession. We have also asserted repeatedly that, in adjudicating the question of voluntariness, "we cannot escape the responsibility of making our own examination of the record."

The record in this case documents a shocking display of barbarism which should not escape the remedial action of this Court. Accordingly, we reverse the judgment below.

MR. JUSTICE BLACK concurs in the result.

NOTES AND QUESTIONS

(1) Why was the confession found to be involuntary in *Brooks*? Was it the fact that the defendant saw no outsiders during the period? Why did the Court reverse the findings by the trial judge that the statement was voluntary; is the Court in a position generally to make determinations regarding questions of compulsion and voluntariness? See also *Knight v. State*, 518 So. 2d 799 (Ala. Crim. App. 1987), where the confession was held to be involuntary. The evidence there showed that the defendant was handcuffed to a chair for almost the entire six hour interrogation; his request for food was denied; he claimed he had been threatened with whipping; the confession was written in answer to specific questions.

(2) In *Lynumn v. Illinois*, 372 U.S. 528 (1963), the defendant was convicted of sale of marijuana after her confession was admitted against her at trial. The defendant testified as follows:

> I told him (Officer Sims) I hadn't sold Zeno; I didn't know anything about narcotics and I had no source of supply. He kept insisting I had a source of supply and had been dealing in narcotics. I kept telling him I did not and that I knew nothing about it. Then he started telling me I could get 10 years and the children could be taken away, and after I got out they would be taken away and strangers would have them, and if I could cooperate he would see they weren't; and he would recommend leniency and I had better do what they told me if I wanted to see my kids again. The two children are three and four years old. Their father is dead; they live with me. I love my children very much. I have never been arrested for anything in my whole life before. I did not know how much power a policeman had in a recommendation to the State's Attorney or to the Court. I did not know that a Court and a State's Attorney are not bound by a police officer's recommendations. I did not know anything about it. All the officers talked to me about my children and the time I could get for not cooperating. All three officers did. After that conversation I believed that if I cooperated with them and answered the questions the way they wanted me to answer, I believed that I would not be prosecuted. They had said I had better say what they wanted me to, or I would lose the kids. I said I would say anything they wanted me to say. I asked what I was to say. I was told to say "You must admit you gave Zeno the package" so I said, "Yes, I gave it to him."

> The only reason I had for admitting it to the police was the hope of saving myself from going to jail and being taken away from my children. The statement I made to the police after they promised that they would intercede for me, the statements admitting the crime, were false.
>
> My statement to the police officers that I sold the marijuana to Zeno was false. I lied to the police at that time. I lied because the police told me they were going to send me to jail for 10 years and take my children, and I would never see them again; so I agreed to say whatever they wanted me to say.

The officers did not refute the defendant's remarks. Was the defendant's confession voluntary or coerced? A unanimous Court held that it was "clear" that the statement had been coerced. In contrast to *Lynumn*, see *McCalvin v. Yukins*, 444 F.3d 713 (6th Cir. 2006), where the criminal defendant confessed after interrogators told her that, if she were convicted of murder, she would not be able to see her children. Unlike *Lynumn*, the court wrote, this defendant received *Miranda* warnings, was not told her children would lose government financial support, and was not promised leniency if she confessed; thus, her confession was voluntary. But see *People v. Medina*, 25 P.3d 1216 (Colo. 2001), where the defendant's statement was found to be involuntary. There the detective told the defendant — accused of child abuse — that if the defendant did not confess, the detective "would cause the child to lose his mother and the mother, her child; and if he did confess, mother and child would be together" ["the deliberate exploitation of a person's weaknesses by psychological intimidation" can render a statement involuntary.].

Promises and threats, both explicit and implicit pose difficult problems. Consider these cases. The defendant in *Collazo v. Estelle*, 940 F.2d 411 (9th Cir. 1991), *cert. denied*, 502 U.S. 1031, asked to see his lawyer. The police officer advised him that this would be his last chance to cooperate and that it would "go worse" for him if he spoke with an attorney. The court found the action of the police to be coercive and the defendant's resulting statement to be violative of the traditional voluntariness test. *See also United States v. Rivera*, 797 F. Supp. 78, 79–80 (D. Puerto Rico 1992) (confession not voluntary where defendant was told "his wife of ten years and their children . . . would be endangered" if he did not cooperate). Officers interrogating the accused did not inform him that he was a capital murder suspect. Held, the resulting confession was voluntary. *Barnes v. Johnson*, 160 F.3d 218, 223 (5th Cir. 1998). The standard rule was stated in *State v. Wiley*, 61 A.3d 750 (Me. 2013). A confession is not voluntary "where an interrogating officer, with no more than apparent authority, leads a suspect to believe that a confession will secure a favorable, concrete sentence, and that belief motivates the suspect to confess." But see the dissenting view in that case:

> Promises of leniency in return for cooperation and confession, and even some deception and cajoling, may be part of acceptable investigatory techniques.

(3) If the statements in *Brooks* and *Lynumn* had been verified, should they have been inadmissible? If the only consideration was that the truth be set out for the trier of fact, it seems clear that the verified statements should be admissible. That, however, is not the only consideration involved in these cases. "The use of

coerced confessions, whether true or false, is forbidden because the method used to extract them offends constitutional principles." *Lego v. Twomey*, 404 U.S. 477, 485 (1972). *See also United States v. Bernett*, 495 F.2d 943, 951–52 (D.C. Cir. 1974):

> [O]ne can enumerate interests protected by exclusion of involuntary confessions from use in criminal prosecutions. One is the interest in trustworthy evidence. Another is preservation of individual "freedom of will" and "rational choice." Still another is deterrence of unlawful police conduct. And last, but hardly least, is the integrity of a criminal justice process which should not stoop to take advantage of a person whose volitional power is seriously impaired. . . .

(4) The court in *United States v. Brooks*, 125 F.3d 484, 492 (7th Cir. 1997), explained the process for determining the voluntariness of a confession:

> Traditionally we have assessed the voluntariness of a statement by considering whether, in light of the totality of the circumstances, the statement was the product of a rational intellect and free will, or whether it was obtained by the authorities through coercive means. "The issue of coercion is determined from the perspective of a reasonable person in the position of the suspect." In making that determination, we consider such personal factors as the defendant's age, education, intelligence level and mental state; we also take into account the length of his detention, the nature of his interrogations, the inclusion of advice about constitutional rights, and the use of physical punishment, including deprivation of food or sleep. Such influences as narcotics, alcohol and fatigue also may be factors to be considered in a particular case. However, the test for voluntariness of the statement is whether the claimed impairments caused the defendant's will to be overborne.

Such an approach, of course, places great emphasis on the review of precise facts and circumstances. As one commentator wrote,

> The pre-*Miranda* "voluntariness" test was too mushy, subjective, and unruly to provide suspects with adequate protection. And it was too time-consuming to administer. As Justice Hugo Black expressed it during the oral arguments in *Miranda*: "If you are going to determine the admissibility of a confession each time on the circumstances . . . if the Court will take them one by one . . . it is more than we are capable of doing."

Kamisar, *Confessions, Search and Seizure, and the Rehnquist Court*, 34 Tulsa L.J. 465, 471–72 (1999).

(5) In *Colorado v. Connelly*, 479 U.S. 157 (1986), the defendant was several times advised of his right to remain silent. He then confessed to a murder. Thereafter it was determined that he was mentally incompetent, suffering from chronic schizophrenia. The expert testimony indicated that defendant suffered from "command hallucinations" which interfered with defendant's "volitional abilities," his ability to make free and rational choices. The trial court suppressed the confession finding it "involuntary."

> The court ruled that a confession is admissible only if it is a product of the defendant's rational intellect and "free will." Although the court found that the police had done nothing wrong or coercive in securing respondent's confession, Connelly's illness destroyed his volition and compelled him to confess.

The United States Supreme Court disagreed, holding that the major basis of the due process confession cases was a "conclusion that police conduct was oppressive . . . [containing] a substantial element of coercive police conduct." For the Court, "coercive police activity is a necessary predicate to the finding that a confession is not 'voluntary' within the meaning of the Due Process Clause."

Under its state constitution, the Hawaii Supreme Court rejected the view in *Connelly* and held that an involuntary confession would be suppressed even if the coercion did not result from governmental misconduct. *State v. Bowe*, 881 P.2d 538 (Haw. 1994).

BEECHER v. ALABAMA

United States Supreme Court
389 U.S. 35 (1967)

Per Curiam.

On the morning of June 15, 1964, the petitioner, a Negro convict in a state prison, escaped from a road gang in Camp Scottsboro, Alabama. On June 16, a woman's lifeless body was found not more than a mile from the prison camp. The next day, the petitioner was captured in Tennessee; he was then returned to Jackson County, Alabama, where he was indicted, tried, and convicted on a charge of first degree murder. The jury fixed his punishment at death.

The uncontradicted facts of record are these. Tennessee police officers saw the petitioner as he fled into an open field and fired a bullet into his right leg. He fell, and the local Chief of Police pressed a loaded gun to his face while another officer pointed a rifle against the side of his head. The Police Chief asked him whether he had raped and killed a white woman. When he said that he had not, the Chief called him a liar and said, "If you don't tell the truth I am going to kill you." The other officer then fired his rifle next to the petitioner's ear, and the petitioner immediately confessed. Later the same day he received an injection to ease the pain in his leg. He signed something the Chief of Police described as "extradition papers" after the officers told him that "it would be best . . . to sign the papers before the gang of people came there and killed" him. He was then taken by ambulance from Tennessee to Kilby Prison in Montgomery, Alabama. By June 22, the petitioner's right leg, which was later amputated, had become so swollen and his wound so painful that he required an injection of morphine every four hours. Less than an hour after one of these injections, two Alabama investigators visited him in the prison hospital. The medical assistant in charge told the petitioner to "cooperate" and, in the petitioner's presence, he asked the investigators to inform him if the petitioner did not "tell them what they wanted to know." The medical assistant then left the petitioner alone with the State's investigators. In the course of a 90-minute "conversation," the investigators prepared two detailed statements similar to the confession the petitioner had given five days earlier at gunpoint in Tennessee.

Still in a "kind of slumber" from his last morphine injection, feverish, and in intense pain, the petitioner signed the written confessions thus prepared for him.

These confessions were admitted in evidence over the petitioner's objection. Although there is some dispute as to precisely what occurred in the petitioner's room at the prison hospital, we need not resolve this evidentiary conflict, for even if we accept as accurate the State's version of what transpired there, the uncontradicted facts set forth above lead to the inescapable conclusion that the petitioner's confessions were involuntary.

The petitioner, already wounded by the police, was ordered at gunpoint to speak his guilt or be killed. From that time until he was directed five days later to tell Alabama investigators "what they wanted to know," there was "no break in the stream of events." For he was then still in pain, under the influence of drugs, and at the complete mercy of the prison hospital authorities.

The State says that the facts in this case differ in some respects from those in previous cases where we have held confessions to be involuntary. But constitutional inquiry into the issue of voluntariness "requires more than a mere color-matching of cases."

A realistic appraisal of the circumstances of *this* case compels the conclusion that this petitioner's confessions were the product of gross coercion. Under the Due Process Clause of the Fourteenth Amendment, no conviction tainted by a confession so obtained can stand.

MR. JUSTICE BLACK concurs.

MR. JUSTICE BRENNAN, whom THE CHIEF JUSTICE and MR. JUSTICE DOUGLAS join [concurring].

BEECHER v. ALABAMA

United States Supreme Court

408 U.S. 234 (1972)

PER CURIAM.

Only three months after this Court's decision, the petitioner was reindicted and retried for the same crime. Again, a confession was introduced in evidence. Again, it was a confession made by the petitioner shortly after he had been shot and arrested and shortly after he had been given a large dose of morphine. Again, the petitioner was convicted and sentenced to death.

The confession used at the second trial was not exactly the same as the ones that had been used against the petitioner at his first trial. It was not one of the written confessions made by the petitioner in an Alabama hospital five days after his arrest. Instead, it was an oral confession that the petitioner had made in a Tennessee hospital only one hour after his arrest.

One hour after the arrest, in extreme pain from the gunshot that had blown most of the bone out of one leg, the petitioner was brought by police to a Tennessee hospital. There, a doctor gave him two large injections of morphine. The petitioner testified that the morphine "kinda made me feel like I wanted to love somebody: took the pain away; made me feel relaxed." From then on, the petitioner said, he could remember nothing. But the doctor testified at trial that he had asked the petitioner "why he did it [the crime]." According to the doctor, the petitioner then made an oral confession. Although police were in the area guarding the petitioner, the confession was made only to the doctor.

The Alabama Supreme Court held that this oral confession was made voluntarily and was admissible in evidence against the petitioner. We do not agree. We held five years ago that the confession elicited from the petitioner at the scene of his arrest was plainly involuntary. We also held that his written confessions five days later, while in custody and under the influence of morphine, were part of the "stream of events" beginning with the arrest and were infected with "gross coercion." The oral confession, made only an hour after the arrest and upon which the State now relies, was surely a part of the same "stream of events."

NOTES AND QUESTIONS

(1) Was the issue in *Beecher* whether the conduct of the police was shocking or was the issue whether the confessions had been freely given by the defendant? Suppose that the defendant had not been given a drug, had not been in pain, would the result in both cases have been the same? Justice Brennan, concurring in the first case, stated:

> [T]he constitutional inquiry is not whether the conduct of state officers in obtaining the confession was shocking, but whether the confession was "free and voluntary: that is, [it] must not be extracted by any sort of threats or violence, nor obtained by any direct or implied promises, however slight, nor by the exertion of any improper influence."

(2) Can a confession given while the defendant is under the influence of drugs ever be voluntary? In *United States v. Reynolds*, 367 F.3d 294 (5th Cir. 2004), the defendant contended that his confession was involuntary because an hour before he was arrested he had taken methamphetamine and had not slept for three days; the court held that the confession had been voluntarily given that the defendant was cooperative, listened to questions, and gave coherent responses, suggesting that he knew fully what he was doing and saying. But see *State v. Mikulewicz*, 462 A.2d 497, 500 (Me. 1983), where the suspect, during a seven hour interrogation, was permitted by law enforcement officers to drink himself into a state of intoxication:

> [B]ecause the officers involved permitted the Defendant to drink himself to a state of inebriation during the interrogation, expecting that this would "loosen his tongue," the Defendant's statements were not voluntary.

(3) In *Mincey v. Arizona*, 437 U.S. 385 (1978), Justices Stewart and Rehnquist disagreed as to the confession which was given by the defendant. For the majority, Justice Stewart wrote:

> It is hard to imagine a situation less conducive to the exercise of "a rational intellect and a free will" than Mincey's. He had been seriously wounded just a few hours earlier, and had arrived at the hospital "depressed almost to the point of coma," according to his attending physician. Although he had received some treatment, his condition at the time of Hust's interrogation was still sufficiently serious that he was in the intensive care unit. He complained to Hust that the pain in his leg was "unbearable." He was evidently confused and unable to think clearly about either the events of that afternoon or the circumstances of his interrogation, since some of his written answers were on their face not entirely coherent. Finally, while Mincey was being questioned he was lying on his back on a hospital bed, encumbered by tubes, needles, and breathing apparatus. He was, in short, "at the complete mercy" of Detective Hust, unable to escape or resist the thrust of Hust's interrogation. *Beecher v. Alabama.*
>
> In this debilitated and helpless condition, Mincey clearly expressed his wish not to be interrogated. As soon as Hust's questions turned to the details of the afternoon's events, Mincey wrote: "This is all I can say without a lawyer." Hust nonetheless continued to question him, and a nurse who was present suggested it would be best if Mincey answered. Mincey gave unresponsive or uninformative answers to several more questions, and then said again that he did not want to talk without a lawyer. Hust ignored that request and another made immediately thereafter.

The majority view should be contrasted with Justice Rehnquist's dissenting opinion:

> The Court in this case, however, ignores entirely some evidence of voluntariness and distinguishes away yet other testimony. There can be no discounting that Mincey was seriously wounded and laden down with medical equipment. Mincey was certainly not able to move about and, because of the breathing tube in his mouth, had to answer Detective Hust's questions on paper. But the trial court was certainly not required to find, as the Court would imply, that Mincey was "a seriously and painfully wounded man on the edge of consciousness." Nor is it accurate to conclude that Detective Hust "ceased the interrogation only during intervals when Mincey lost consciousness or received medical treatment, and after each such interruption returned relentlessly to his task."
>
> As the Arizona Supreme Court observed in affirming the trial court's finding of voluntariness, Mincey's nurse "testified that she had not given [Mincey] any medication and that [he] was alert and able to understand the officer's questions. . . . She said that [Mincey] was in moderate pain but was very cooperative with everyone. The interrogating officer also testified that [Mincey] did not appear to be under the influence of drugs and that [his] answers were generally responsive to the questions."
>
> The uncontradicted testimony of Detective Hust also reveals a questioning that was far from "relentless." While the interviews took place over a three-hour time span, the interviews were not "very long; probably no more than an hour total for everything." Hust would leave the room whenever

> Mincey received medical treatment "or if it looked like he was getting a little bit exhausted." According to Detective Hust, Mincey never "lost consciousness at any time."
>
> As the Court openly concedes, there were in this case none of the "gross abuses that have led the Court in other cases to find confessions involuntary, such as beatings . . . or 'truth serums.' "
>
> Neither is this a case, however, where the defendant's will was "simply overborne" by "mental coercion."
>
> As the Supreme Court of Arizona observed, it was the testimony of both Detective Hust and Nurse Graham "that neither mental nor physical force nor abuse was used on [Mincey]. . . . Nor were any promises made."
>
> According to Mincey's own testimony, he wanted to help Hust "the best I could."

(4) In *Haynes v. Washington*, 373 U.S. 503 (1963), the Court refused to admit a confession which had been given during a 16-hour period in which the defendant asked to talk with both his lawyer and his wife but was simply told that he could not unless he "cooperated" with the police. The Court chastised the police for such conduct:

> This case illustrates a particular facet of police utilization of improper methods. While history amply shows that confessions have often been extorted to save law enforcement officials the trouble and effort of obtaining valid and independent evidence, the coercive devices used here were designed to obtain admissions which would incontrovertibly complete a case in which there had already been obtained, by proper investigative efforts, competent evidence sufficient to sustain a conviction. The procedures here are no less constitutionally impermissible, and perhaps more unwarranted because so unnecessary. There is no reasonable or rational basis for claiming that the oppressive and unfair methods utilized were in any way essential to the detection or solution of the crime or to the protection of the public. The claim, so often made in the context of coerced confession cases, that the devices employed by the authorities were requisite to solution of the crime and successful prosecution of the guilty party cannot here be made.
>
> Official overzealousness of the type which vitiates the petitioner's conviction below has only deleterious effects. Here it has put the State to the substantial additional expense of prosecuting the case through the appellate courts and now, will require even a greater expenditure in the event of retrial, as is likely. But it is the deprivation of the protected rights themselves which is fundamental and the most regrettable, not only because of the effect on the individual defendant, but because of the effect on our system of law and justice. Whether there is involved the brutal "third degree," or the more subtle, but no less offensive, methods here obtaining, official misconduct cannot but breed disrespect for law, as well as for those charged with its enforcement.

The four dissenters in *Haynes* (Justices Clark, Harlan, Stewart and White) did not think there was a due process violation and did not understand, in particular, how the holding there was consistent with the holding in *Crooker v. California*, 357 U.S. 433 (1958). In *Crooker*, the defendant — a law student — repeatedly requested the assistance of counsel. The requests were denied but the Court still found that the confession was voluntary. "[C]oercion seems more likely to result from state denial of a specific request for opportunity to engage counsel. . . . It is negated here by petitioner's age, intelligence, and education." Is *Haynes* consistent with *Crooker*? Note that in *Crooker* the Court specifically referred to the defendant's law education. "While in law school he had studied criminal law; indeed when asked to take the lie detector test, he informed the operator that the results of such a test would not be admissible at trial absent a stipulation by the parties." Should the fact that the defendant was a law student have affected the result in *Crooker*? For a good discussion of many of the earlier Supreme Court decisions in the area, see Hancock, *Due Process Before* Miranda, 70 Tul. L. Rev. 2195 (1996).

PROBLEM A
COERCED CONFESSION

Is a statement resulting from being held in the interrogation room for a lengthy period of time necessarily coercive? No, said the court in *Commonwealth v. Tolan*, 904 N.E.2d 397 (Mass. 2009), for there the officers repeatedly offered the suspect food, drinks, and the use of the restroom; plus, the interrogation was not continuous for the entire 11-hour period. But see *Crowe v. County of San Diego*, 608 F.3d 406 (9th Cir. 2010), where the interrogation process was found to be "shock[ing] to the conscience. The "[suspects] — 14 and 15 years old, respectively — were isolated and subjected to hours and hours of interrogation during which they were cajoled, threatened, lied to, and relentlessly pressured by teams of police officers. 'Psychological torture' is not an inapt description." The age of the suspect — 16 years old — was also of paramount concern in *Moore v. State*, 30 A.3d 945 (Md. Ct. App. 2011), where during the lengthy interrogation, the suspect made 13 requests to speak with his mother. His incriminating statement was held to be involuntary, as youth is "a crucial factor in determining, in the totality of the circumstances, whether the . . . confession was voluntary." But see *Carter v. Thompson*, 690 F.3d 837 (7th Cir. 2012), where the 16-year-old spent 55 hours in a police station. The resulting confession was held to be voluntary as the suspect had access to her father, was allowed to move freely about the station, and the statement was not in response to a question.

SPANO v. NEW YORK

United States Supreme Court
360 U.S. 315 (1959)

MR. CHIEF JUSTICE WARREN delivered the opinion of the Court.

This is another in the long line of cases presenting the question whether a confession was properly admitted into evidence under the Fourteenth Amendment. As in all such cases, we are forced to resolve a conflict between two fundamental interests of society; its interest in prompt and efficient law enforcement, and its interest in preventing the rights of its individual members from being abridged by unconstitutional methods of law enforcement. Because of the delicate nature of the constitutional determination which we must make, we cannot escape the responsibility of making our own examination of the record.

The State's evidence reveals the following: Petitioner Vincent Joseph Spano is a derivative citizen of this country, having been born in Messina, Italy. He was 25 years old at the time of the shooting in question and had graduated from junior high school. He had a record of regular employment. The shooting took place on January 22, 1957.

On that day, petitioner was drinking in a bar. The decedent, a former professional boxer weighing almost 200 pounds who had fought in Madison Square Garden, took some of petitioner's money from the bar. Petitioner followed him out of the bar to recover it. A fight ensued, with the decedent knocking petitioner down and then kicking him in the head three or four times. Shock from the force of these blows caused petitioner to vomit. After the bartender applied some ice to his head, petitioner left the bar, walked to his apartment, secured a gun, and walked eight or nine blocks to a candy store where the decedent was frequently to be found. He entered the store in which decedent, three friends of decedent, at least two of whom were ex-convicts, and a boy who was supervising the store were present. He fired five shots, two of which entered the decedent's body, causing his death. The boy was the only eyewitness; the three friends of decedent did not see the person who fired the shot. Petitioner then disappeared for the next week or so.

On February 1, 1957, the Bronx County Grand Jury returned an indictment for first-degree murder against petitioner. Accordingly, a bench warrant was issued for his arrest, commanding that he be forthwith brought before the court to answer the indictment, or, if the court had adjourned for the term, that he be delivered into the custody of the Sheriff of Bronx County.

On February 3, 1957, petitioner called one Gaspar Bruno, a close friend of 8 or 10 years' standing who had attended school with him. Bruno was a fledgling police officer, having at that time not yet finished attending police academy. According to Bruno's testimony, petitioner told him "that he took a terrific beating, that the deceased hurt him real bad and he dropped him a couple of times and he was dazed; he didn't know what he was doing and that he went and shot at him." Petitioner told Bruno that he intended to get a lawyer and give himself up. Bruno relayed this information to his superiors.

The following day, February 4, at 7:10 p.m., petitioner, accompanied by counsel, surrendered himself to the authorities in front of the Bronx County Building, where both the office of the Assistant District Attorney who ultimately prosecuted his case and the courtroom in which he was ultimately tried were located. His attorney had cautioned him to answer no questions, and left him in the custody of the officers. He was promptly taken to the office of the Assistant District Attorney and at 7:15 p.m. the questioning began, being conducted by Assistant District Attorney Goldsmith, Lt. Gannon, Detectives Farrell, Lehrer and Motta, and Sgt. Clarke. The record reveals that the questioning was both persistent and continuous. Petitioner, in accordance with his attorney's instructions, steadfastly refused to answer. Detective

Motta testified: "He refused to talk to me." "He just looked up to the ceiling and refused to talk to me." Detective Farrell testified:

Q: And you started to interrogate him?

A: That is right. . . .

Q: What did he say?

A: He said "you would have to see my attorney. I tell you nothing but my name." . . .

Q: Did you continue to examine him?

A: Verbally, yes, sir.

He asked one officer, Detective Ciccone, if he could speak to his attorney, but that request was denied. Detective Ciccone testified that he could not find the attorney's name in the telephone book. He was given two sandwiches, coffee and cake at 11 p.m. At 12:15 a.m. on the morning of February 5, after five hours of questioning in which it became evident that petitioner was following his attorney's instructions, on the Assistant District Attorney's orders petitioner was transferred to the 46th Squad, Ryer Avenue Police Station. The Assistant District Attorney also went to the police station and to some extent continued to participate in the interrogation. Petitioner arrived at 12:30 and questioning was resumed at 12:40. The character of the questioning is revealed by the testimony of Detective Farrell:

Q: Who did you leave him in the room with?

A: With Detective Lehrer and Sergeant Clarke came in and Mr. Goldsmith came in or Inspector Halk came in. It was back and forth. People just came in, spoke a few words to the defendant or they listened a few minutes and they left.

But petitioner persisted in his refusal to answer, and again requested permission to see his attorney, this time from Detective Lehrer. His request was again denied.

It was then that those in charge of the investigation decided that petitioner's close friend, Bruno, could be of use. He had been called out on the case around 10 or 11 p.m., although he was not connected with the 46th Squad or Precinct in any way. Although, in fact, his job was in no way threatened, Bruno was told to tell petitioner that petitioner's telephone call had gotten him "in a lot of trouble," and that he should seek to extract sympathy from petitioner for Bruno's pregnant wife and three children. Bruno developed this theme with petitioner without success, and petitioner, also without success, again sought to see his attorney, a request which Bruno relayed unavailingly to his superiors. After this first session with petitioner, Bruno was again directed by Lt. Gannon to play on petitioner's sympathies, but again no confession was forthcoming. But the Lieutenant a third time ordered Bruno falsely to importune his friend to confess but again petitioner clung to his attorney's advice. Inevitably, in the fourth such session directed by the Lieutenant, lasting a full hour, petitioner succumbed to his friend's prevarications and agreed to make a statement. Accordingly, at 3:25 a.m. the Assistant District Attorney, a stenographer, and several other law enforcement officials entered the room where petitioner was being questioned, and took his statement in question and answer form with the Assistant District Attorney asking the questions. The statement was completed at 4:05 a.m.

But this was not the end. At 4:30 a.m. three detectives took petitioner to Police Headquarters in Manhattan. On the way they attempted to find the bridge from which petitioner said he had thrown the murder weapon. They crossed the Triborough Bridge into Manhattan, arriving at Police Headquarters at 5 a.m., and left Manhattan for the Bronx at 5:40 a.m. via the Willis Avenue Bridge. When petitioner recognized neither bridge as the one from which he had thrown the weapon, they re-entered Manhattan via the Third Avenue Bridge, which petitioner stated was the right one, and then returned to the Bronx well after 6 a.m. During that trip the officers also elicited a statement from petitioner that the deceased was always "on [his] back," "always pushing" him and that he was "not sorry" he had shot the deceased. All three detectives testified to that statement at the trial.

At the trial, the confession was introduced in evidence over appropriate objections. The jury was instructed that it could rely on it only if it was found to be voluntary. The jury returned a guilty verdict and petitioner was sentenced to death.

The abhorrence of society to the use of involuntary confessions does not turn alone on their inherent untrustworthiness. It also turns on the deep-rooted feeling that the police must obey the law while enforcing the law; that in the end life and liberty can be as much endangered from illegal methods used to convict those thought to be criminals as from the actual criminals themselves. Accordingly, the actions of police in obtaining confessions have come under scrutiny in a long series of cases. Those cases suggest that in recent years law enforcement officials have become increasingly aware of the burden which they share, along with our courts, in protecting fundamental rights of our citizenry, including that portion of our citizenry suspected of crime. The facts of no case recently in this Court have quite approached the brutal beatings in *Brown v. Mississippi*, or the 36 consecutive hours of questioning present in *Ashcraft v. Tennessee.*

But as law enforcement officers become more responsible, and the methods used to extract confessions more sophisticated, our duty to enforce federal constitutional protections does not cease. It only becomes more difficult because of the more delicate judgments to be made. Our judgment here is that, on all the facts, this conviction cannot stand.

Petitioner was a foreign-born young man of 25 with no past history of law violation or of subjection to official interrogation, at least insofar as the record shows. He had progressed only one-half year into high school and the record indicates that he had a history of emotional instability. He did not make a narrative statement, but was subject to the leading questions of a skillful prosecutor in a question and answer confession.

[T]he effect of such massive official interrogation must have been felt. Petitioner was questioned for virtually eight straight hours before he confessed, with his only respite being a transfer to an arena presumably considered more appropriate by the police for the task at hand. Nor was the questioning conducted during normal business hours, but began in early evening, continued into the night, and did not bear fruition until the not-too-early morning. The drama was not played out, with the final admissions obtained, until almost sunrise. In such circumstances slowly mounting fatigue does, and is calculated to, play its part. The questioners persisted in the face of his repeated refusals to answer on the advice of his attorney, and they ignored his reasonable requests to contact the local attorney whom he had already retained and who had personally delivered him into the custody of these officers in obedience to the bench warrant.

The use of Bruno, characterized in this Court by counsel for the State as a "childhood friend" of petitioner's, is another factor which deserves mention in the totality of the situation. Bruno's was the one face visible to petitioner in which he could put some trust. There was a bond of friendship between them going back a decade into adolescence. It was with this material that the officers felt that they could overcome petitioner's will. They instructed Bruno falsely to state that petitioner's telephone call had gotten him into trouble, that his job was in jeopardy, and that loss of his job would be disastrous to his three children, his wife and his unborn child. And Bruno played this part of a worried father, harried by his superiors, in not one, but four different acts, the final one lasting an hour.

Petitioner was apparently unaware of John Gay's famous couplet:

An open foe may prove a curse,

But a pretended friend is worse,

and he yielded to his false friend's entreaties.

We conclude that petitioner's will was overborne by official pressure, fatigue and sympathy falsely aroused, after considering all the facts in their post-indictment setting. Here a grand jury had already found sufficient cause to require petitioner to face trial on a charge of first-degree murder, and the police had an eyewitness to the shooting. The police were not therefore merely trying to solve a crime, or even to absolve a suspect.

They were rather concerned primarily with securing a statement from defendant on which they could convict him. The undeviating intent of the officers to extract a confession from petitioner is therefore patent. When such an intent is shown, this Court has held that the confession obtained must be examined with the most careful scrutiny, and has reversed a conviction on facts less compelling than these.

The State suggests, however, that we are not free to reverse this conviction, since there is sufficient other evidence in the record from which the jury might have found guilt.

[We] did not hold that a conviction may be sustained on the basis of other evidence if a confession found to be involuntary by this Court was used, even though limiting instructions were given.

[We] held only that when a confession is not found by this Court to be involuntary, this Court will not reverse on the ground that the jury might have found it involuntary and might have relied on it. The judgment must be reversed.

[MR. JUSTICE DOUGLAS with whom MR. JUSTICE BLACK and MR. JUSTICE BRENNAN join, concurred.]

NOTES AND QUESTIONS

(1) What conduct of the police rendered the confession in *Spano* involuntary? Was it that the defendant was not well aware of his rights? Would the result have been different if Spano, as Crooker, had been a law student? How important was it that the statement was not in narrative form? Would it have been voluntary if the statement had been in the defendant's own words? The Court made much over the use of Spano's "false" friend. Is it improper for the police to have questioning handled by a "friend" of the accused? Why does that practice raise due process concerns? See *Abram v. State*, 606 So. 2d 1015 (Miss. 1992), where the defendant was kept in isolation for three days, was refused visitors generally, but was then urged to confess by a minister at the behest of the police. The interrogators admitted that the defendant might have been given the impression that his co-defendant was in bigger trouble and that the defendant's confession would work to his advantage. The defendant confessed and he was convicted of murder. Held, the confession was involuntary. In *Bailey v. Commonwealth*, 194 S.W.3d 296 (Ky. 2006) the court found the confession to be involuntary. There the defendant had an IQ of 50 and the officers knew he was mentally deficient. In addition, they isolated him for seven hours and they repeatedly accused him of lying. The defendant in *United States v. Pacheco*, 819 F. Supp. 2d 1239 (D. Utah 2011), "submitted evidence to show that his personality makes him more susceptible to coercion when threats are made against his family." Resulting confession held to be involuntary.

(2) In *Hutto v. Ross*, 429 U.S. 28 (1976), the Supreme Court held that a "confession is [not] *per se* inadmissible in a criminal trial because it was made subsequent to an agreed upon plea bargain that did not call for such a confession." The question, as always, was whether the confession was voluntary, was it "extracted by any sort of threats or violence, or obtained by any direct or implied promises, however slight, or by the exertion of any improper influence." Even though the plea bargain was later withdrawn the confession was not coerced. In *Gunsby v. Wainwright*, 596 F.2d 654 (5th Cir. 1979), *cert. denied*, 444 U.S. 946 (1979), the court, in applying the rule in *Hutto*, struck down the confession. In *Gunsby* the statement was part of the plea bargain and the defendant was not "advised, as in *Hutto*, that he need not testify in order to retain the benefits of the plea bargain should the court refuse to nullify it. . . ." When the plea bargain in *Gunsby* was later withdrawn, the court found the statement to be involuntary.

(3) At the trial level, who decides if a statement is voluntary, the judge or the jury? " *Jackson v. Denno*, 378 U.S. 368 (1964), held that a defendant's constitutional rights are violated when his challenged confession is introduced without a determination by the trial judge of its voluntariness after an adequate hearing. A confession by the defendant found to be involuntary by the trial judge is not to be heard by the jury which determines his guilt or innocence." *Pinto v. Pierce*, 389 U.S. 31, 88 S. Ct. 192, 19 L. Ed. 2d 31 (1967). Those jurisdictions which do not allow the jury to consider the voluntariness of the confession after the judge has found it to be valid do allow the jury to consider the circumstances surrounding the making of the statement in deciding how much weight to give to the confession. *See, e.g.*, 18 U.S.C. § 3501(a):

> In any criminal prosecution brought by the United States or by the District of Columbia, a confession, as defined in subsection (e) hereof, shall be admissible in evidence if it is voluntarily given. Before such confession is received in evidence, the trial judge shall, out of the presence of the jury determine any issue as to voluntariness. If the trial judge determines that the confession was voluntarily made it shall be admitted in evidence and the trial judge shall permit the jury to hear relevant evidence on the issue of voluntariness and shall instruct the jury to give such weight to the confession as the jury feels it deserves under all the circumstances.

The trial judge in *Crane v. Kentucky*, 476 U.S. 683 (1986), ruled that the defendant's confession was voluntary. Thereafter, he refused to allow the defense to introduce testimony "about the physical and psychological environment in which the confession was obtained." Held, this ruling violated the defendant's constitutional rights. Justice O'Connor wrote for a unanimous Court:

> The manner in which a statement was extracted is, of course, relevant to the purely legal question of its voluntariness, a question most, but not all, States assign to the trial judge alone to resolve. But the physical and psychological environment that yielded the confession can also be of substantial relevance to the ultimate factual issue of the defendant's guilt or innocence. Confessions, even those that have been found to be voluntary, are not conclusive of guilt. And, as with other parts of the prosecutor's case, a confession may be shown to be "insufficiently corroborated or otherwise . . . unworthy of belief." Indeed, stripped of the power to describe to the jury the circumstances that prompted his confession, the defendant is effectively disabled from answering the one question every rational juror needs answered: If the defendant is innocent, why did he previously admit his guilt? Accordingly, regardless of whether the defendant marshaled the same evidence earlier in support of an unsuccessful motion to suppress, and entirely independent of any question of voluntariness, a defendant's case may stand or fall on his ability to convince the jury that the manner in which the confession was obtained casts doubt on its credibility.

(4) In deciding whether a confession is voluntary the admissibility of the statement need not be shown beyond a reasonable doubt — a preponderance of the evidence standard is sufficient. *Lego v. Twomey*, 404 U.S. 477 (1972). As a matter of policy, should the state have to prove voluntariness beyond a reasonable doubt? Justice White, for the majority, said no, "since the purpose that a voluntariness hearing is designed to serve has nothing whatever to do with improving the reliability of jury verdicts. . . ."

Justice Brennan sharply disagreed:

> [U]se of the reasonable-doubt standard is indispensable to command the respect and confidence of the community in applications of the criminal law. It is critical that the moral force of the criminal law not be diluted by a standard of proof that leaves people in doubt whether innocent men are being condemned.

I believe that it is just as critical to our system of criminal justice that when a person's words are used against him, no reasonable doubt remains that he spoke of his own free will.

(5) The so-called *McNabb-Mallory* rule — so named for the cases of *McNabb v. United States*, 318 U.S. 332 (1943), and *Mallory v. United States*, 354 U.S. 449 (1957) — requires an arrested person to be brought before a judicial officer "as soon as possible." If the rule is not complied with, any statements obtained from the accused during the delay must be suppressed. *McNabb-Mallory* was based upon Rule 5 of the Federal Rules of Criminal Procedure which now states that the officer "must take the defendant without unnecessary delay before a magistrate judge, or before a state or local judicial officer. . . ." Nothing in Rule 5, however, has ever provided for a sanction of suppressing the confession if the rule were violated. As a consequence, Congress in part (c) of 18 U.S.C. § 3501 seemingly sought to eliminate *McNabb-Mallory*:

> (c) In any criminal prosecution by the United States or by the District of Columbia, a confession made or given by a person who is a defendant therein, while such person was under arrest or other detention in the custody of any law-enforcement officer or law-enforcement agency, shall not be inadmissible solely because of delay in bringing such person before a magistrate judge or other officer empowered to commit persons charged with offenses against the laws of the United States or of the District of Columbia if such confession is found by the trial judge to have been made voluntarily and if the weight to be given the confession is left to the jury and if such confession was made or given by such person within six hours immediately following his arrest or other detention: Provided, That the time limitation contained in this subsection shall not apply in any case in which the delay in bringing such person before such magistrate or other officer beyond such six-hour period is found by the trial judge to be reasonable considering the means of transportation and the distance to be traveled to the nearest available such magistrate or other officer.

While the Court in both *McNabb* and *Mallory* was careful to note that it was finding the sanction in the purpose of Rule 5, could one argue that under cases like *Spano* and *Brooks* there is a constitutional basis for the sanction? Stated another way, is part (c) constitutional if it overrides *McNabb-Mallory*? Does it? In *Corley v. United States*, 556 U.S. 303 (2009), the Court strongly reaffirmed the doctrine and narrowly construed Congressional intent.

> In a world without *McNabb-Mallory*, federal agents would be free to question suspects for extended periods before bringing them out in the open, and we have always known what custodial secrecy leads to.
>
> No one with any smattering of the history of 20th-century dictatorships needs a lecture on the subject, and we understand the need even within our own system to take care against going too far. "[C]ustodial police interrogation, by its very nature, isolates and pressures the individual," and there is mounting empirical evidence that these pressures can induce a frighteningly high percentage of people to confess to crimes they never committed.

Justice Frankfurter's point in *McNabb* is as fresh as ever: "The history of liberty has largely been the history of observance of procedural safeguards." *McNabb-Mallory* is one of them, and neither the text nor the history of § 3501 makes out a case that Congress meant to do away with it.

PROBLEM B
DECEITFUL INTERROGATION

In all of these cases the defendants were given untrue information by the police and then confessed. Are the confessions admissible: *State v. Manning*, 506 So. 2d 1094 (Fla. 1987) (defendant was told medical records showed his molestation of victim; confession admissible, as "use of tricks or factual misstatements in and of itself does not render a confession involuntary. . . . There must be coercion involved. . . ."); *Ledbetter v. Edwards*, 35 F.3d 1062 (6th Cir. 1994), *cert. denied*, 515 U.S. 1145 (1995), and *State v. Randle*, 366 S.E.2d 750 (W. Va. 1988) (defendants were both told fingerprints were found at scene of crime; statement in *Randle* was involuntary, the evidence "was blatantly misrepresented"; the statement in *Ledbetter* was deemed voluntary); *Sandifer v. State*, 517 So. 2d 646 (Ala. 1987) (police told defendant his co-defendant had implicated him; confession admissible). While courts routinely allow deceptions by the police as to evidence against the accused, does that change if the officers lie about an official document which is supposed to contain the incriminating evidence? *Compare People v. Mays*, 95 Cal. Rptr. 3d 219 (Cal. App. 2009) (interrogation still allowed, trickery was not coercive), *with Wilson v. State*, 2010 WL 1905000 (Tex. 2010) (it is a state crime to present false document for purpose of affecting an investigation). The statement in *United States v. Lall*, 607 F.3d 1277 (11th Cir. 2010), was not allowed because the officers advised the defendant it would not be used against him. But, in *United States v. Brenton-Farley*, 607 F.3d 1294 (11th Cir. 2010), the statement was allowed, even though the court noted that "some police tricks may be 'objectionable as a matter of ethics'." The interrogating officer there tricked the suspect into believing the investigation was about terrorism. "[However], there is no evidence they made any promise that questioning would be limited to that subject, or gave him any assurance that statements relating to other crimes would not be used against him." The court in *Aleman v. Village of Hanover Park*, 662 F.3d 897 (7th Cir. 2011), found the defendant's statement to be coerced. The police there lied to the defendant as to the likely cause of death (suspect arrested in shaken baby prosecution). The officer's remarks "destroy[ed] the information required for a rational choice [by the defendant.]" For an excellent treatment of the area, see Wilson, *An Exclusionary Rule for Police Lies*, 47 Am. Crim. L. Rev. 1 (2010).

The Hawaii Supreme Court in *State v. Kelekolio*, 849 P.2d 58 (Haw. 1993), attempted to formulate rules in the area by distinguishing between intrinsic (*e.g.*, strength of the evidence, witnesses) and extrinsic falsehoods (promises of favorable treatment, lies concerning the legal process). As to an intrinsic falsehood, the courts will view it "as one of the totality of circumstances surrounding the confession." For an extrinsic falsehood, however, the rule is quite different, for such a falsehood "will be regarded as coercive *per se*, thus obviating the need for a 'totality of circumstances' analysis of voluntariness." In light of *Kelekolio*, consider these two recent decisions. *United States v. Boskic*, 545 F.3d 69 (1st Cir. 2008), involved federal agents lying to the defendant by explaining to him that he was not the target of the investigation. In *State v. Morton*, 186 P.3d 785 (Kan. 2008), the defendant was under criminal investigation. She was told the interview was to be informal and she would not need a lawyer there. In both cases the defendants made incriminating statements. The *Boskic* court allowed the statement in evidence, while the *Morton* court ordered it excluded. Are these two cases distinguishable? How about these three:

- *People v. Aveni*, 953 N.Y.S.2d 55 (2012) (police lies about girlfriend being alive and requiring his confession to keep her alive, along with threats to charge defendant with homicide, made confession involuntary);
- *Commonwealth v. Tremblay*, 931 N.E.2d 54, 59 (Mass. Ct. App. 2010), *superseded by*, 950 N.E.2d 421 (Mass. 2011) (confession voluntary, even though police told defendant his statements would be "off the record"); and
- *Daniel v. State*, 677 S.E.2d 120, 125 (Ga. 2009) (police statements that defendant was not a suspect in murder investigation did not make confession involuntary).

§ 5.02 THE RIGHT TO COUNSEL APPROACH

MASSIAH v. UNITED STATES

United States Supreme Court
377 U.S. 201 (1964)

Mr. Justice Stewart delivered the opinion of the Court.

The petitioner was indicted for violating the federal narcotics laws. He retained a lawyer, pleaded not guilty, and was released on bail. While he was free on bail a federal agent succeeded by surreptitious means in listening to incriminating statements made by him. Evidence of these statements was introduced against the petitioner at his trial over his objection. He was convicted, and the Court of Appeals affirmed. We granted certiorari to consider whether, under the circumstances here presented, the prosecution's use at the trial of evidence of the petitioner's own incriminating statements deprived him of any right secured to him under the Federal Constitution.

The petitioner, a merchant seaman, was in 1958 a member of the crew of the *S.S. Santa Maria.* In April of that year federal customs officials in New York received information that he was going to transport a quantity of narcotics aboard that ship from South America to the United States. As a result of this and other information, the agents searched the *Santa Maria* upon its arrival in New York and found in the afterpeak of the vessel five packages containing about three and a half pounds of cocaine. They also learned of circumstances, not here relevant, tending to connect the petitioner with the cocaine. He was arrested, promptly arraigned, and subsequently indicted for possession of narcotics aboard a United States vessel. In July a superseding indictment was returned, charging the petitioner and a man named Colson with the same substantive offense, and in separate counts charging the petitioner, Colson, and others with having conspired to possess narcotics aboard a United States vessel, and to import, conceal, and facilitate the sale of narcotics. The petitioner, who had retained a lawyer, pleaded not guilty and was released on bail, along with Colson.

A few days later, and quite without the petitioner's knowledge, Colson decided to cooperate with the government agents in their continuing investigation of the narcotics activities in which the petitioner, Colson, and others had allegedly been engaged. Colson permitted an agent named Murphy to install a Schmidt radio transmitter under the front seat of Colson's automobile, by means of which Murphy, equipped with an appropriate receiving device, could overhear from some distance away conversations carried on in Colson's car.

On the evening of November 19, 1959, Colson and the petitioner held a lengthy conversation while sitting in Colson's automobile, parked on a New York street. By prearrangement with Colson, and totally unbeknown to the petitioner, the agent Murphy sat in a car parked out of sight down the street and listened over the radio to the entire conversation. The petitioner made several incriminating statements during the course of this conversation. At the petitioner's trial these incriminating statements were brought before the jury through Murphy's testimony, despite the insistent objection of defense counsel. The jury convicted the petitioner of several related narcotics offenses, and the convictions were affirmed by the Court of Appeals.

[The petitioner argues] that the petitioner's Fifth and Sixth Amendment rights were violated by the use in evidence against him of incriminating statements which government agents had deliberately elicited from him after he had been indicted and in the absence of his retained counsel.

In *Spano v. New York*, this Court reversed a state criminal conviction because a confession had been wrongly admitted into evidence against the defendant at his trial. In that case the defendant had already been indicted for first-degree murder at the time he confessed. The Court held that the defendant's conviction could not stand under the Fourteenth Amendment. While the Court's opinion relied upon the totality of the circumstances under which the confession had been obtained, four concurring Justices pointed out that the Constitution required reversal of the conviction upon the sole and specific ground that the confession had been deliberately elicited by the police after the defendant had been indicted, and therefore at a time when he was clearly entitled to a lawyer's help. It was pointed out that under our system of justice the most elemental concepts of due process of law contemplate that an indictment be followed by a trial, "in an orderly courtroom, presided over by a judge, open to the public, and protected by all the procedural safeguards of the law." It was said that a Constitution which guarantees a defendant the aid of counsel at such a trial could surely vouchsafe no less to an indicted defendant under interrogation by the police in a completely extrajudicial proceeding. Anything less, it was said, might deny a defendant "effective representation by counsel at the only stage when legal aid and advice would help him."

Ever since this Court's decision in the *Spano* case, the New York courts have unequivocally followed this constitutional rule. "Any secret interrogation of the defendant, from and after the finding of the indictment, without the protection afforded by the presence of counsel, contravenes the basic dictates of fairness in the conduct of criminal causes and the fundamental rights of persons charged with crime."

This view no more than reflects a constitutional principle established as long ago as *Powell v. Alabama*, where the Court noted that ". . . during perhaps the most critical period of the proceedings . . . that is to say, from the time of their arraignment until the beginning of their trial, when consultation, thorough-going investigation and preparation [are] vitally important, the defendants . . . [are] as much entitled to such aid [of counsel] during that period as at the trial itself."

Here we deal not with a state court conviction, but with a federal case, where the specific guarantee of the Sixth Amendment directly applies.

We hold that the petitioner was denied the basic protections of that guarantee when there was used against him at his trial evidence of his own incriminating words, which federal agents had deliberately elicited from him after he had been indicted and in the absence of his counsel. It is true that in the *Spano* case the defendant was interrogated in a police station, while here the damaging testimony was elicited from the defendant without his knowledge while he was free on bail. But, as Judge Hays pointed out in his dissent in the Court of Appeals, "if such a rule is to have any efficacy it must apply to indirect and surreptitious interrogations as well as those conducted in the jailhouse. In this case, Massiah was more seriously imposed upon . . . because he did not even know that he was under interrogation by a government agent."

Reversed.

Mr. Justice White, with whom Mr. Justice Clark and Mr. Justice Harlan join, dissenting.

[T]oday's rule promises to have wide application well beyond the facts of this case. The reason given for the result here — the admissions were obtained in the absence of counsel — would seem equally pertinent to statements obtained at any time after the right to counsel attaches, whether there has been an indictment or not; to admissions made prior to arraignment, at least where the defendant has counsel or asks for it; to the fruits of admissions improperly obtained under the new rule; to criminal proceedings in state courts; and to defendants long since convicted upon evidence including such admissions. The new rule will immediately do service in a great many cases.

Whatever the content or scope of the rule may prove to be, I am unable to see how this case presents an unconstitutional interference with Massiah's right to counsel. Massiah was not prevented from consulting with counsel as often as he wished. No meetings with counsel were disturbed or spied upon. Preparation for trial was in no way obstructed. It is only a sterile syllogism — an unsound one, besides — to say that because Massiah had a right to counsel's aid before and during the trial, his out-of-court conversations and admissions must be excluded if obtained without counsel's consent or presence.

NOTES AND QUESTIONS

(1) Justice White could see no way in which the "case presents an unconstitutional interference with Massiah's right to counsel." Considering that Massiah was not in custody when the statements were made, and he could have talked at any time with counsel, how were his Sixth Amendment rights violated?

The Supreme Court in *Texas v. Cobb*, 532 U.S. 162 (2001), stated that the right to counsel approach is "charge specific." That is, the Sixth Amendment can only be utilized for the offense with which a formal charge has occurred, and no others. Cobb had been indicted for burglary but was later interrogated while in custody regarding a double murder arising out of the same incident. Although he had waived his *Miranda* rights, he contended that his Sixth Amendment right to counsel has been violated, because the charges for the two crimes were "factually related." The Court held that for this purpose the protection of the Sixth Amendment would extend only to the crime formally charged, the burglary, and not the uncharged crime, the murder. The Indiana Supreme Court, relying on its state constitution, rejected *Cobb* and held that police cannot question a suspect about an uncharged offense that is "inextricably intertwined" with the charged offense. *Jewell v. State*, 957 N.E.2d 625 (Ind. 2011).

(2) The Court was careful to find that the defendant raised a federal claim under the Sixth Amendment. Was Justice White correct that the holding would also apply to criminal proceedings in state courts? In *McLeod v. Ohio*, 378 U.S. 582 (1964), the Court vacated the judgment making specific reference to *Massiah. McLeod* is an interesting case involving judicial construction of Supreme Court decisions. The defendant there was indicted for murder. One week later, before he had retained or requested counsel, or had been advised of his right to do so, he made a confession to the sheriff while riding in the sheriff's car searching for the gun used in the holdup. In affirming the defendant's conviction, neither the court of appeals nor the supreme court issued any opinion, stating only that the appeal was dismissed because "no debatable constitutional question is involved." After the case was remanded by the United States Supreme Court, the State Supreme Court reaffirmed its earlier position, stating that "[t]he circumstances here [were] different as to the manner in which the statements were obtained in the *Massiah* case. . . ." In a vigorous dissent it was pointed out that the key in *Massiah* was "that the Constitution prohibits the use of statements against interest by a defendant who has not even been advised of his right to counsel." Which opinion correctly applied *Massiah*? Less than six months later the United States Supreme Court unanimously reversed the judgment, simply making reference to *Massiah.* 381 U.S. 356 (1965).

(3) If, in the above situation, the prosecutor visits the accused and convinces him voluntarily and knowingly to waive the right to counsel without defense counsel being present, has the prosecutor violated any ethical standard? See *People v. Hobson*, 348 N.E.2d 894 (N.Y. 1976), where the court stated that "an attempt to secure a waiver of the right of counsel in a criminal proceeding in the absence of a lawyer, already retained or assigned, would constitute a breach of professional ethics. . . ." What is the unethical conduct of the prosecutor? Would it matter if it were police officers rather than the prosecutor who spoke with the defendant and

received his waiver of counsel? See then-Judge Stevens' dissenting opinion in *United States v. Springer*, 460 F.2d 1344, 1354–55 (7th Cir.), *cert. denied*, 409 U.S. 873 (1972):

> After counsel had been appointed to represent him, and while he was in custody, the defendant was visited by two agents of the prosecutor. Defense counsel was not present and received no advance notice of their proposed visit. The sole purpose of the visit was to obtain evidence for use at the trial. Accepting the prosecutor's evidence as true, defendant's participation in the crime had already been established and, therefore, no further investigation was necessary. The work of the agents was trial preparation, pure and simple.
>
> In a civil context I would consider this behavior unethical and unfair. In a criminal context I regard it as such a departure from "procedural regularity" as to violate the Due Process Clause of the Fifth Amendment. If the evidence of guilt is as strong as the prosecutor contends, such direct communication is all the more offensive because it was unnecessary. If there is doubt about defendant's guilt, it should not be overcome by a procedure such as this.

(4) Justice White, in his dissenting opinion, remarked that the rule in *Massiah* "would seem equally pertinent to statements obtained at any time after the right to counsel attaches, whether there has been an indictment or not. . . ." Would it?

(5) Does *Massiah* apply to questioning after the suspect has retained counsel and has "been served with a target letter" but before he has been indicted? The court in *United States v. Hayes*, 231 F.3d 663, 673-74 (9th Cir. 2000), thought not:

> [W]e believe the Supreme Court meant what it said in *Ash*, that *Kirby* "forecloses application of the Sixth Amendment to events before the initiation of adversary criminal proceedings." Beyond this, the fact that pre-indictment deposition testimony may have consequences at trial is insufficient to cause the right to counsel to attach. Although *post-indictment* Rule 15 depositions might constitute a "critical stage" in a prosecution-requiring the presence of counsel-because of the potential consequences of such depositions at trial, that fact does not inform our analysis of whether a *pre-indictment* motion to take such depositions constitutes the initiation of formal charges. Being a *target* is not enough, either. As the Court has emphasized, the Sixth Amendment "attaches only at or after the initiation of adversary judicial proceedings *against the defendant.*" While adversary judicial proceedings had been initated against the witnesses, none had been initated against Hayes. And we cannot say that the government was formally charging Hayes (or any of the other targets) or was committing to do so when it sought to take the depositions of departing students, because the depositions served only to preserve their testimony for trial if there were a trial and the students did not return.

Does this ruling faithfully apply *Massiah* and the identification cases in Chapter 4, *supra*?

PROBLEM C
RIGHT TO COUNSEL

Consider *Hoffa v. United States*, 385 U.S. 293 (1966) [the Fourth Amendment issues are discussed in Chapter 3]. In 1962, union leader Jimmy Hoffa was charged with violating the Taft-Hartley Act. Hoffa was later convicted of attempting to bribe members of the jury during the course of that trial (generally known as the Test Fleet trial). The pertinent facts were described in the opinion:

> The Test Fleet trial, in which James Hoffa was the sole individual defendant, was in progress between October 22 and December 23, 1962, in Nashville, Tennessee. James Hoffa was president of the International Brotherhood of Teamsters. During the course of the trial he occupied a three-room suite in the Andrew Jackson Hotel in Nashville. One of his constant companions throughout the trial was the petitioner King, president of the Nashville local of the Teamsters Union. Edward Partin, a resident of Baton Rouge, Louisiana, and a local Teamsters Union official there, made repeated visits to Nashville during the period of the trial. On these visits he frequented the Hoffa hotel suite, and was continually in the company of Hoffa and his associates, including King, in and around the hotel suite, the hotel lobby, the courthouse, and elsewhere in Nashville. During this period Partin made frequent reports to a federal agent named Sheridan concerning conversations he said Hoffa and King had had with him and with each other, disclosing endeavors to bribe members of the Test Fleet jury. Partin's reports and his subsequent testimony at the petitioners' trial unquestionably contributed, directly or indirectly, to the convictions of all four of the petitioners.

Hoffa made a narrow *Massiah* claim. He argued that as soon as the government knew that he attempted to bribe the jurors it should have charged him, and that any statements made after that time violated his right to counsel under *Massiah.* The Court refused to accept this argument finding that there is no constitutional obligation on the police "to guess at their peril the precise moment at which they have probable cause." Could Hoffa have made a broader argument under *Massiah*? What would that argument have been? Would it have been successful?

NOTE

In *United States v. Henry*, 447 U.S. 264 (1980), the defendant was arrested, indicted and jailed pending trial. Government agents contacted another inmate at the jail and "told him to be alert to any statements made by [the defendant], but not to initiate any conversations with or question [the defendant] regarding the bank robbery." Statements regarding the robbery were made to the informant by the defendant and these statements were used at trial against him. A majority of the Court held that this violated defendant's right to counsel under *Massiah*:

> Nichols deliberately used his position to secure incriminating information from Henry when counsel was not present and [this] conduct [was] attributable to the Government . . . Even if the agent's statement that he

> did not intend that Nichols would take affirmative steps to secure incriminating information is accepted, he must have known that such propinquity likely would lead to that result.

Justice Powell concurred: "I understand that the decision today rests on a conclusion that this informant deliberately elicited incriminating information by such conduct. . . ." But see the dissenting opinion of Justice Blackmun:

> [W]hile claiming to retain the "deliberately elicited" test, the Court really forges a new test that saps the word "deliberately" of all significance. The Court's extension of *Massiah* would cover even a "negligent" triggering of events resulting in reception of disclosures.

Henry was reaffirmed and expanded in *Maine v. Moulton*, 474 U.S. 159 (1985). The facts there were fairly similar to *Henry* except that the government did not initiate the contact with the defendant; in *Moulton* it was the defendant who affirmatively came to his co-defendant (a government agent) to discuss a defense for trial and the agent then received approval from his superiors to tape record further conversations for possible use in prosecutions. For the dissenters, these distinctions were crucial:

> The Court's opinion seems to rest on the notion that the evidence here is excludable because "the State 'must have known' that its agent was likely to obtain incriminating statements from the accused," with respect to the crimes for which he was already indicted. But the inquiry mandated by our holdings is whether the State recorded the statements not merely *in spite of*, but *because of* that consequence. If the State is not seeking to elicit information with respect to the crime for which the defendant is already indicted, it cannot rationally be said that the State has "planned an impermissible interference with the right to the assistance of counsel."

The majority, in an opinion by Justice Brennan, believed this argument "fundamentally misunderstands the nature of the [Sixth Amendment] right we recognized in . . . [*Massiah* and *Henry*]":

> The Sixth Amendment guarantees the accused, at least after the initiation of the formal charges, the right to rely on counsel as a "medium" between him and the State. . . . [T]his guarantee includes the State's affirmative obligation not to act in a manner that circumvents the protections accorded the accused by invoking this right. The determination whether particular action by state agents violates the accused's right to the assistance of counsel must be made in light of this obligation. Thus, the Sixth Amendment is not violated whenever — by luck or happenstance — the State obtains incriminating statements from the accused after the right to counsel has attached. See *Henry* . . . (Powell, J., concurring). However, knowing exploitation by the State of an opportunity to confront the accused without counsel being present is as much a breach of the State's obligation not to circumvent the right to the assistance of counsel as is the intentional creation of such an opportunity.

But see *Kuhlmann v. Wilson*, 477 U.S. 436 (1986), where the Court allowed testimony regarding the defendant's admissions. Here no showing was made that the jailhouse informant had made any effort to elicit such admissions.

> A defendant does not make out a violation of that right simply by showing that an informant, either through prior arrangement or voluntarily, reported his incriminating statements to the police. Rather, the defendant must demonstrate that the police and their informant took some action, beyond merely listening, that was designed deliberately to elicit incriminating remarks.

BREWER v. WILLIAMS

United States Supreme Court
430 U.S. 387 (1977)

MR. JUSTICE STEWART delivered the opinion of the Court.

An Iowa trial jury found the respondent, Robert Williams, guilty of murder. The judgment of conviction was affirmed in the Iowa Supreme Court by a closely divided vote. In a subsequent habeas corpus proceeding a Federal District Court ruled that under the United States Constitution Williams is entitled to a new trial, and a divided Court of Appeals for the Eighth Circuit agreed. The question before us is whether the District Court and the Court of Appeals were wrong.

I

On the afternoon of December 24, 1968, a 10-year-old girl named Pamela Powers went with her family to the YMCA in Des Moines, Iowa, to watch a wrestling tournament in which her brother was participating. When she failed to return from a trip to the washroom, a search for her began. The search was unsuccessful.

Robert Williams, who had recently escaped from a mental hospital, was a resident of the YMCA. Soon after the girl's disappearance Williams was seen in the YMCA lobby carrying some clothing and a large bundle wrapped in a blanket. He obtained help from a 14-year-old boy in opening the street door of the YMCA and the door to his automobile parked outside. When Williams placed the bundle in the front seat of his car the boy "saw two legs in it and they were skinny and white." Before anyone could see what was in the bundle Williams drove away. His abandoned car was found the following day in Davenport, Iowa, roughly 160 miles east of Des Moines. A warrant was then issued in Des Moines for his arrest on a charge of abduction.

On the morning of December 26, a Des Moines lawyer named Henry McKnight went to the Des Moines police station and informed the officers present that he had just received a long distance call from Williams, and that he had advised Williams to turn himself in to the Davenport police. Williams did surrender that morning to the police in Davenport, and they booked him on the charge specified in the arrest warrant and gave him the warnings required by *Miranda v. Arizona.*

The Davenport police then telephoned their counterparts in Des Moines to inform them that Williams had surrendered. McKnight, the lawyer, was still at the Des Moines police headquarters, and Williams conversed with McKnight on the telephone. In the presence of the Des Moines chief of police and a police detective named Leaming, McKnight advised Williams that Des Moines police officers would be driving to Davenport to pick him up, that the officers would not interrogate him or mistreat him, and that Williams was not to talk to the officers about Pamela Powers until after consulting with McKnight upon his return to Des Moines. As a result of these conversations, it was agreed between McKnight and the Des Moines police officials that Detective Leaming and a fellow officer would drive to Davenport to pick up Williams, that they would bring him directly back to Des Moines, and that they would not question him during the trip.

In the meantime Williams was arraigned before a judge in Davenport on the outstanding arrest warrant. The judge advised him of his *Miranda* rights and committed him to jail. Before leaving the courtroom, Williams conferred with a lawyer named Kelly, who advised him not to make any statements until consulting with McKnight back in Des Moines.

Detective Leaming and his fellow officer arrived in Davenport about noon to pick up Williams and return him to Des Moines. Soon after their arrival they met with Williams and Kelly, who, they understood, was acting as Williams' lawyer. Detective Leaming repeated the *Miranda* warnings, and told Williams:

> . . . [w]e both know that you're being represented here by Mr. Kelly and you're being represented by Mr. McKnight in Des Moines, and . . . I want you to remember this because we'll be visiting between here and Des Moines.

Williams then conferred again with Kelly alone, and after this conference Kelly reiterated to Detective Leaming that Williams was not to be questioned about the disappearance of Pamela Powers until after he had consulted with McKnight back in Des Moines. When Leaming expressed some reservations, Kelly firmly stated that the agreement with McKnight was to be carried out — that there was to be no interrogation of Williams during the automobile journey to Des Moines. Kelly was denied permission to ride in the police car back to Des Moines with Williams and the two officers.

The two detectives, with Williams in their charge, then set out on the 160-mile drive. At no time during the trip did Williams express a willingness to be interrogated in the absence of an attorney. Instead, he stated several times that "[w]hen I get to Des Moines and see Mr. McKnight, I am going to tell you the whole story." Detective Leaming knew that Williams was a former mental patient, and knew also that he was deeply religious.

The Detective and his prisoner soon embarked on a wide-ranging conversation covering a variety of topics, including the subject of religion. Then, not long after leaving Davenport and reaching the interstate highway, Detective Leaming delivered what has been referred to in the briefs and oral arguments as the "Christian burial speech." Addressing Williams as "Reverend," the detective said:

> I want to give you something to think about while we're traveling down the road. . . . Number one, I want you to observe the weather conditions, it's raining, it's sleeting, it's freezing, driving is very treacherous, visibility is poor, it's going to be dark early this evening. They are predicting several

> inches of snow for tonight, and I feel that you yourself are the only person that knows where this little girl's body is, that you yourself have only been there once, and if you get a snow on top of it you yourself may be unable to find it. And, since we will be going right past the area on the way into Des Moines, I feel that we could stop and locate the body, that the parents of this little girl should be entitled to a Christian burial for the little girl who was snatched away from them on Christmas [E]ve and murdered. And I feel we should stop and locate it on the way in rather than waiting until morning and trying to come back out after a snow storm and possibly not being able to find it at all.

Williams asked Detective Leaming why he thought their route to Des Moines would be taking them past the girl's body, and Leaming responded that he knew the body was in the area of Mitchellville — a town they would be passing on the way to Des Moines.[1] Leaming then stated: "I do not want you to answer me. I don't want to discuss it any further. Just think about it as we're riding down the road."

As the car approached Grinnell, a town approximately 100 miles west of Davenport, Williams asked whether the police had found the victim's shoes. When Detective Leaming replied that he was unsure, Williams directed the officers to a service station where he said he had left the shoes; a search for them proved unsuccessful. As they continued towards Des Moines, Williams asked whether the police had found the blanket, and directed the officers to a rest area where he said he had disposed of the blanket. Nothing was found. The car continued towards Des Moines, and as it approached Mitchellville, Williams said that he would show the officers where the body was. He then directed the police to the body of Pamela Powers.

The jury found Williams guilty of murder, and the judgment of conviction was affirmed by the Iowa Supreme Court, a bare majority of whose members agreed with the trial court that Williams had "waived his right to the presence of his counsel" on the automobile ride from Davenport to Des Moines. The four dissenting justices expressed the view that "when counsel and police have agreed defendant is not to be questioned until counsel is present and defendant has been advised not to talk and repeatedly has stated he will tell the whole story after he talks with counsel, the state should be required to make a stronger showing of intentional voluntary waiver than was made here."

Williams then petitioned for a writ of habeas corpus in the United States District Court for the Southern District of Iowa.

The District Court . . . concluded as a matter of law that the evidence in question had been wrongly admitted at Williams' trial. This conclusion was based on . . . [the] ground[] that Williams had been denied his constitutional right to the assistance of counsel.

The Court of Appeals for the Eighth Circuit, with one judge dissenting, affirmed this judgment.

---

[1] [1] The fact of the matter, of course, was that Detective Leaming possessed no such knowledge.

II

B

[I]t is clear that the judgment before us must in any event be affirmed upon the ground that Williams was deprived . . . [of] the right to the assistance of counsel.

This right, guaranteed by the Sixth and Fourteenth Amendments, is indispensable to the fair administration of our adversary system of criminal justice.

There has occasionally been a difference of opinion within the Court as to the peripheral scope of this constitutional right, see *Kirby v. Illinois; Coleman v. Alabama*, but its basic contours, which are identical in state and federal contexts, *Gideon v. Wainwright, Argersinger v. Hamlin*, are too well established to require extensive elaboration here. Whatever else it may mean, the right to counsel granted by the Sixth and Fourteenth Amendments means at least that a person is entitled to the help of a lawyer at or after the time that judicial proceedings have been initiated against him — "whether by way of formal charge, preliminary hearing, indictment, information, or arraignment."

There can be no doubt in the present case that judicial proceedings had been initiated against Williams before the start of the automobile ride from Davenport to Des Moines. A warrant had been issued for his arrest, he had been arraigned on that warrant before a judge in a Davenport courtroom, and he had been committed by the court to confinement in jail. The State does not contend otherwise.

There can be no serious doubt, either, that Detective Leaming deliberately and designedly set out to elicit information from Williams just as surely as — and perhaps more effectively than — if he had formally interrogated him. Detective Leaming was fully aware before departing for Des Moines that Williams was being represented in Davenport by Kelly and in Des Moines by McKnight. Yet he purposely sought during Williams' isolation from his lawyers to obtain as much incriminating information as possible. Indeed, Detective Leaming conceded as much when he testified at Williams' trial:

Q: In fact, Captain, whether he was a mental patient or not, you were trying to get all the information you could before he got to his lawyer, weren't you?

A: I was sure hoping to find out where that little girl was, yes, sir. . . .

Q: Well, I'll put it this way: You was [sic] hoping to get all the information you could before Williams got back to McKnight, weren't you?

A: Yes, sir.[2]

[2] [6] Counsel for petitioner, in the course of oral argument in this Court, acknowledged that the "Christian burial speech" was tantamount to interrogation:

Q. But isn't the point, really, Mr. Attorney General, what you indicated earlier, and that is that the officer wanted to elicit information from Williams —

A. Yes, sir.

The state courts clearly proceeded upon the hypothesis that Detective Leaming's "Christian burial speech" had been tantamount to interrogation. Both courts recognized that Williams had been entitled to the assistance of counsel at the time he made the incriminating statements. Yet no such constitutional protection would have come into play if there had been no interrogation. The circumstances of this case are thus constitutionally indistinguishable from those presented in *Massiah v. United States.* That the incriminating statements were elicited surreptitiously in the *Massiah* case, and otherwise here, is constitutionally irrelevant. Rather, the clear rule of *Massiah* is that once adversary proceedings have commenced against an individual, he has a right to legal representation when the government interrogates him. It thus requires no wooden or technical application of the *Massiah* doctrine to conclude that Williams was entitled to the assistance of counsel guaranteed to him by the Sixth and Fourteenth Amendments.

III

The District Court and the Court of Appeals were . . . correct in their understanding of the proper standard to be applied in determining the question of waiver as a matter of federal constitutional law — that it was incumbent upon the State to prove "an intentional relinquishment or abandonment of a known right or privilege."

That standard has been reiterated in many cases. We have said that the right to counsel does not depend upon a request by the defendant, and that courts indulge in every reasonable presumption against waiver. This strict standard applies equally to an alleged waiver of the right to counsel whether at trial or at a critical stage of pretrial proceedings.

We conclude, finally that the Court of Appeals was correct in holding that, judged by these standards, the record in this case falls far short of sustaining petitioner's burden. It is true that Williams had been informed of and appeared to understand his right to counsel. But waiver requires not merely comprehension but relinquishment, and Williams' consistent reliance upon the advice of counsel in dealing with the authorities refutes any suggestion that he waived that right. He consulted McKnight by long-distance telephone before turning himself in. He spoke with McKnight by telephone again shortly after being booked. After he was arraigned, Williams sought out and obtained legal advice from Kelly. Williams again consulted with Kelly after Detective Leaming and his fellow officer arrived in Davenport. Throughout, Williams was advised not to make any statements before seeing McKnight in Des Moines, and was assured that the police had agreed not to question him. His statements while in the car that he would tell the whole story *after* seeing McKnight in Des Moines were the clearest expressions by Williams himself that he desired the presence of an attorney before any interrogation took place. But even before making these statements, Williams had effectively asserted his right to counsel by having secured attorneys at both ends of the automobile trip,

---

Q. — by whatever techniques he used, I would suppose a lawyer would consider that he were pursuing interrogation.

A. It is, but it was very brief.

both of whom, acting as his agents, had made clear to the police that no interrogation was to occur during the journey. Williams knew of that agreement and, particularly in view of his consistent reliance on counsel, there is no basis for concluding that he disavowed it.

Despite Williams' express and implicit assertions of his right to counsel, Detective Leaming proceeded to elicit incriminating statements from Williams. Leaming did not preface this effort by telling Williams that he had a right to the presence of a lawyer, and made no effort at all to ascertain whether Williams wished to relinquish that right. The circumstances of record in this case thus provide no reasonable basis for finding that Williams waived his right to the assistance of counsel.

The Court of Appeals did not hold, nor do we, that under the circumstances of this case Williams *could not*, without notice to counsel, have waived his rights under the Sixth and Fourteenth Amendments. It only held, as do we, that he did not.

IV

The crime of which Williams was convicted was senseless and brutal, calling for swift and energetic action by the police to apprehend the perpetrator and gather evidence with which he could be convicted. No mission of law enforcement officials is more important. Yet "[d]isinterested zeal for the public good does not assure either wisdom or right in the methods it pursues."

Although we do not lightly affirm the issuance of a writ of habeas corpus in this case, so clear a violation of the Sixth and Fourteenth Amendments as here occurred cannot be condoned. The pressures on state executive and judicial officers charged with the administration of the criminal law are great, especially when the crime is murder and the victim a small child. But it is precisely the predictability of those pressures that makes imperative a resolute loyalty to the guarantees that the Constitution extends to us all.

The judgment of the Court of Appeals is affirmed.[3]

It is so ordered.

[3] [12] The District Court stated that its decision "does not touch upon the issue of what evidence, if any, beyond the incriminating statements themselves must be excluded as 'fruit of the poisonous tree.' " 375 F. Supp. at 185. We, too, have no occasion to address this issue, and in the present posture of the case there is no basis for the view of our dissenting Brethren (White, J., [dissenting]) (Blackmun, J., [dissenting]), that any attempt to retry the respondent would probably be futile. While neither Williams' incriminating statements themselves nor any testimony describing his having led the police to the victim's body can constitutionally be admitted into evidence, evidence of where the body was found and of its condition might well be admissible on the theory that the body would have been discovered in any event, even had incriminating statements not been elicited from Williams. In the event that a retrial is instituted, it will be for the state courts in the first instance to determine whether particular items of evidence may be admitted.

MR. JUSTICE MARSHALL, concurring.

I concur wholeheartedly in my Brother Stewart's opinion for the Court, but add these words in light of the dissenting opinions filed today. The dissenters have, I believe, lost sight of the fundamental constitutional backbone of our criminal law. They seem to think that Detective Leaming's actions were perfectly proper, indeed laudable, examples of "good police work." In my view, good police work is something far different from catching the criminal at any price. It is equally important that the police, as guardians of the law, fulfill their responsibility to obey its commands scrupulously. For "in the end life and liberty can be as much endangered from illegal methods used to convict those thought to be criminals as from the actual criminals themselves."

In this case, there can be no doubt that Detective Leaming consciously and knowingly set out to violate Williams' Sixth Amendment right to counsel and his Fifth Amendment privilege against self-incrimination, as Leaming himself understood those rights. Leaming knew that Williams had been advised by two lawyers not to make any statements to police until he conferred in Des Moines with his attorney there, Mr. McKnight. Leaming surely understood, because he had overheard McKnight tell Williams as much, that the location of the body would be revealed to police. Undoubtedly Leaming realized the way in which that information would be conveyed to the police: McKnight would learn it from his client and then he would lead police to the body. Williams would thereby be protected by the attorney-client privilege from incriminating himself by directly demonstrating his knowledge of the body's location, and the unfortunate Powers child could be given a "Christian burial."

Of course, this scenario would accomplish all that Leaming sought from his investigation except that it would not produce incriminating statements or actions from Williams. Accordingly, Leaming undertook his charade to pry such evidence from Williams. After invoking the no-passengers rule to prevent attorney Kelly from accompanying the prisoner, Leaming had Williams at his mercy: during the three-or four-hour trip he could do anything he wished to elicit a confession. The detective demonstrated once again "that the efficiency of the rack and the thumbscrew can be matched, given the proper subject by more sophisticated modes of 'persuasion.' "

Leaming knowingly isolated Williams from the protection of his lawyers and during that period he intentionally "persuaded" him to give incriminating evidence. It is this intentional police misconduct — not good police practice — that the Court rightly condemns. The heinous nature of the crime is no excuse, as the dissenters would have it, for condoning knowing and intentional police transgression of the constitutional rights of a defendant. If Williams is to go free — and given the ingenuity of Iowa prosecutors on retrial or in a civil commitment proceeding, I doubt very much that there is any chance a dangerous criminal will be loosed on the streets, the blood-curdling cries of the dissents notwithstanding — it will hardly be because he deserves it. It will be because Detective Leaming, knowing full well that he risked reversal of Williams' conviction, intentionally denied Williams the right of every American under the Sixth Amendment to have the protective shield of a lawyer between himself and the awesome power of the State.

I think it appropriate here to recall not Mr. Justice Cardozo's opinion in *People v. Defore*, see opinion of The Chief Justice, but rather the closing words of Mr. Justice Brandeis' great dissent in *Olmstead v. United States*: In a government of laws, existence of the government will be imperiled if it fails to observe the law scrupulously. Our Government is the potent, the omnipresent teacher. For good or for ill, it teaches the whole people by its example. Crime is contagious. If the Government becomes a lawbreaker, it breeds contempt for law; it invites every man to become a law unto himself; it invites anarchy. To declare that in the administration of the criminal law the end justifies the means — to declare that the Government may commit crimes in order to secure the conviction of a private criminal — would bring terrible retribution. Against that pernicious doctrine this Court should resolutely set its face.

Mr. Justice Powell, concurring.

The dissenting opinion of The Chief Justice states that the Court's holding today "conclusively presumes a suspect is legally incompetent to change his mind and tell the truth until an attorney is present." I find no justification for this view. On the contrary, the opinion of the Court is explicitly clear that the right to assistance of counsel may be waived, after it has attached, without notice to or consultation with counsel. We would have such a case here if petitioner had proved that the police officers refrained from coercion and interrogation, as they had agreed, and that Williams freely on his own initiative had confessed the crime.

Mr. Justice Stevens, concurring.

Mr. Justice Stewart, in his opinion for the Court which I join, Mr. Justice Powell, and Mr. Justice Marshall have accurately explained the reasons why the law requires the result we reach today. Nevertheless, the strong language in the dissenting opinions prompts me to add this brief comment about the Court's function in a case such as this.

Nothing that we write, no matter how well reasoned or forcefully expressed, can bring back the victim of this tragedy or undo the consequences of the official neglect which led to the respondent's escape from a state mental institution. The emotional aspects of the case make it difficult to decide dispassionately, but do not qualify our obligation to apply the law with an eye to the future as well as with concern for the result in the particular case before us.

Underlying the surface issues in this case is the question whether a fugitive from justice can rely on his lawyer's advice given in connection with a decision to surrender voluntarily. The defendant placed his trust in an experienced Iowa trial lawyer who in turn trusted the Iowa law enforcement authorities to honor a commitment made during negotiations which led to the apprehension of a potentially dangerous person. Under any analysis, this was a critical stage of the proceeding in which the participation of an independent professional was of vital importance to the accused and to society. At this stage — as in countless others in which the law profoundly affects the life of the individual — the lawyer is the essential medium through which the demands and commitments of the sovereign are communicated to the citizen. If, in the long run, we are seriously concerned about the individual's effective representation by counsel, the State cannot be permitted to dishonor its promise to this lawyer.[4]

MR. CHIEF JUSTICE BURGER, dissenting.

The result in this case ought to be intolerable in any society which purports to call itself an organized society. It continues the Court — by the narrowest margin — on the much-criticized course of punishing the public for the mistakes and misdeeds of law enforcement officers, instead of punishing the officer directly, if in fact he is guilty of wrongdoing. It mechanically and blindly keeps reliable evidence from juries whether the claimed constitutional violation involves gross police misconduct or honest human error.

Williams is guilty of the savage murder of a small child; no member of the Court contends he is not. While in custody, and after no fewer than *five* warnings of his rights to silence and to counsel, he led police to the concealed body of his victim. The Court concedes Williams was not threatened or coerced and that he spoke and acted voluntarily and with full awareness of his constitutional rights. In the face of all this, the Court now holds that because Williams was prompted by the detective's statement — not interrogation but a statement — the jury must not be told how the police found the body.

Today's holding fulfills Judge (later Mr. Justice) Cardozo's grim prophecy that someday some court might carry the exclusionary rule to the absurd extent that its operative effect would exclude evidence relating to the body of a murder victim because of the means by which it was found.[5] In so ruling the Court regresses to playing a grisly game of "hide and seek," once more exalting the sporting theory of criminal justice which has been experiencing a decline in our jurisprudence. With JUSTICES WHITE, BLACKMUN, and REHNQUIST, I categorically reject the remarkable notion that the police in this case were guilty of unconstitutional misconduct, or any conduct justifying the bizarre result reached by the Court.

---

[4] [*] The importance of this point is emphasized by the State's refusal to permit counsel to accompany his client on the trip from Davenport to Des Moines.

[5] [1] "The criminal is to go free because the constable has blundered. . . . A room is searched against the law, and the body of a murdered man is found. . . . The privacy of the home has been infringed, and the murderer goes free." People v. Defore, 242 N.Y. 13, 21, 23–24, 150 N.E. 585, 587, 588 (1926).

The Court protests that its holding excludes only "Williams' incriminating statements themselves [as well as] any testimony describing his having led the police to the victim's body," thus hinting that successful retrial of this palpably guilty felon is realistically possible. Even if this were all, and the *corpus delicti* could be used to establish the fact and manner of the victim's death, the Court's holding clearly bars all efforts to let the jury know how the police found the body. But the Court's further — and remarkable — statement that "evidence of where the body was found and of its condition" could be admitted *only* "on the theory that the body would have been discovered in any event" makes clear that the Court is determined to keep the truth from the jurors pledged to find the truth. If all use of the *corpus delicti* is to be barred by the Court as "fruit of the poisonous tree" under *Wong Sun v. United States*, 371 U.S. 471, 83 S. Ct. 407, 9 L. Ed. 2d 441 (1963), except on the unlikely theory suggested by the Court, the Court renders the prospects of doing justice in this case exceedingly remote.

Mr. Justice White, with whom Mr. Justice Blackmun and Mr. Justice Rehnquist join, dissenting.

The majority recognizes that even after this "assertion" of his right to counsel, it would have found that respondent waived his right not to talk in counsel's absence if his waiver had been express — *i.e.*, if the officers had asked him in the car whether he would be willing to answer questions in counsel's absence and if he had answered "yes." But waiver is not a formalistic concept. Waiver is shown whenever the facts establish that an accused knew of a right and intended to relinquish it. Such waiver, even if not express, was plainly shown here. The only other conceivable basis for the majority's holding is the implicit suggestion that the right involved in *Massiah v. United States*, as distinguished from the right involved in *Miranda v. Arizona*, is a right not to be asked any questions in counsel's absence rather than a right not to answer any questions in counsel's absence, and that the right not to be asked questions must be waived before the questions are asked. Such wafer-thin distinctions cannot determine whether a guilty murderer should go free. The only conceivable purpose for the presence of counsel during questioning is to protect an accused from making incriminating answers. Questions, unanswered, have no significance at all. Absent coercion — no matter how the right involved is defined — an accused is amply protected by a rule requiring waiver before or simultaneously with the giving by him of an answer or the making by him of a statement.

Mr. Justice Blackmun, with whom Mr. Justice White and Mr. Justice Rehnquist join, dissenting.

[I]t seems to me that the Court is holding that *Massiah* is violated whenever police engage in any conduct, in the absence of counsel, with the subjective desire to obtain information from a suspect after arraignment. Such a rule is far too broad. Persons in custody frequently volunteer statements in response to stimuli other than interrogation. *See, e.g., United States v. Cook*, 530 F.2d 145, 152–153 (C.A.7), *cert. denied*, 426 U.S. 909, 96 S. Ct. 2234, 48 L. Ed. 2d 835 (1976) (defendant engaged officers in conversation while being transported to magistrate); *United States v. Martin*, 511 F.2d 148, 150–151 (C.A.8 1975) (agent initiated conversation with suspect, provoking damaging admission); *United States v. Menichino*, 497 F.2d 935, 939–941 (C.A.5,1974) (incriminating statements volunteered during booking process); *Haire v. Sarver*, 437 F.2d 1262 (C.A.8), *cert. denied*, 404 U.S. 910, 92 S. Ct. 235, 30 L. Ed. 2d 182 (1971) (statements volunteered in response to questioning of defendant's wife). When there is no interrogation, such statements should be admissible as long as they are truly voluntary.[6]

[6] [3] With all deference to the Court, I do not agree that *Massiah* regarded it as "constitutionally irrelevant" that the statements in that case were surreptitiously obtained. The *Massiah* opinion quoted with approval the dissenting Circuit Judge's statement that "*Massiah* was more seriously imposed upon . . . because he did not even know that he was under interrogation by a government agent."

NOTES AND QUESTIONS

(1) This case proved to be one of the most controversial criminal decisions by the Court. The tone of the opinions is illustrated by the beginning comments made by Justice Marshall and Chief Justice Burger.

Justice Marshall:

> The dissenters have, I believe, lost sight of the fundamental constitutional backbone of our criminal law. They seem to think that Detective Leaming's actions were perfectly proper, indeed laudable, examples of "good police work." In my view, good police work is something far different from catching the criminal at any price. It is equally important that the police, as guardians of the law, fulfill their responsibility to obey its commands scrupulously. For "in the end life and liberty can be as much endangered from illegal methods used to convict those thought to be criminals as from the actual criminals themselves."

The Chief Justice:

> The result in this case ought to be intolerable in any society which purports to call itself an organized society. It continues the Court — by the narrowest margin — on the much-criticized course of punishing the public for the mistakes and misdeeds of law enforcement officers, instead of punishing the officer directly, if in fact he is guilty of wrongdoing. It mechanically and blindly keeps reliable evidence from juries whether the claimed constitutional violation involves gross police misconduct or honest human error.

At the session of the Court announcing the judgment the Chief Justice took the unusual step of reading his own dissenting opinion, denouncing, in the words of the New York Times, the majority for its

> . . . "weird," "intolerable," "bizarre" decision. . . . Eruptions of judicial temper are to be expected in this country, where decisions of the courts may have such profound effects. Chief Justice Burger's passion related to a real problem: How to enforce fairness in police conduct. . . .
>
> [Chief Justice Burger asserted that the decision punished] the public to exclude good evidence because one of the policemen made a mistake.

The Doors of Justice, New York Times, March 28, 1977, p. 29.

(2) Can the right to counsel be waived after an attorney has entered the case, without notice to the lawyer? The majority position on this point was not entirely clear: "The Court of Appeals did not hold, nor do we, that under the circumstances of this case Williams *could not*, without notice to counsel, have waived his rights under the Sixth and Fourteenth Amendments. It only held, as do we, that he did not." Assuming that Williams could waive his right to counsel, why was that waiver not accomplished here? As the Chief Justice pointed out, the defendant was given his *Miranda* warnings (including statements that he did not have to answer questions and could have the assistance of counsel) five times and spoke with two attorneys.

The defendant in *Holloway v. State*, 780 S.W.2d 787 (Tex. 1989), was indicted for murder and given appointed counsel. His lawyer advised the defendant not to submit to questioning. The next day, without counsel present, the police advised the defendant of his rights and he stated that he did not want to have his lawyer present. He then made an incriminating statement. Held, the statement was inadmissible under the Sixth Amendment. The court wrote that the police can only interrogate an indicted and represented defendant if notice is given to defense counsel. Is this holding consistent with the Court's opinion in *Brewer v. Williams*? What about *State v. Burdo*, 690 N.E.2d 854 (N.Y. 1997), where the court reaffirmed an earlier holding that under its state constitution once an attorney has been appointed, a defendant "could not be interrogated in the absence of counsel on any matter, whether related or unrelated to the subject of the representation."

(3) In this case there was an explicit agreement between the attorneys and the government that the defendant would not be questioned during the automobile ride. How important was that agreement to the outcome of the case? Would there have been a denial of the right to counsel if there had been no agreement?

(4) The Code of Professional Responsibility provides as follows:

> During the course of his representation of a client a lawyer shall not:
>
> (1) Communicate or cause another to communicate on the subject of the representation with a party he knows to be represented by a lawyer in that matter unless he has the prior consent of the lawyer representing such other party or is authorized by law to do so.

The prosecuting attorney violated this provision by asking the defendant questions after the defendant had retained counsel. The prosecuting attorney had not communicated with the defendant's attorney regarding the questioning. The statement of the defendant was voluntarily given after receiving his *Miranda* warnings. Should the statement have been suppressed at trial? Compare the various opinions in *People v. Green*, 274 N.W.2d 448 (Mich. 1979):

Justice Coleman:

> The facts in the case at bar provide a good example why a violation of DR 7-104(A)(1) standing alone should be dealt with by bar disciplinary action rather than by withholding relevant and material evidence from the jury.
>
> The defendant had a story he wanted to tell to the authorities, presumably to clear himself of the murder charge lodged against him. He sent word to the authorities and asked to speak with them. He waived his *Miranda* rights with full knowledge of what he was doing. He specifically stated that he wanted to talk without his attorney present. The assistant prosecuting attorney and the detective did little except listen to what the defendant had to say and take notes. The defendant's statements were completely voluntary and there was no overreaching of any kind. When asked if he was telling the whole truth, defendant said that he was.
>
> Reversal of the conviction and grant of a new trial (if in fact the witnesses and evidence presented in 1975 could be obtained for a second trial) solely

because of this less than consequential violation of DR 7-104(A)(1) would constitute reprehensible "overkill."

Justice Williams:

[W]hile I agree that the assistant prosecuting attorney's action did not rise to the level of a violation of due process of law, I disagree that his action was "innocuous." I would affirm but order the Clerk to report this matter to bar grievance authorities for appropriate action.

The "prophylactic exclusionary rule" is an indirect method to deter wrongful police action. Since the courts have no effective direct method of disciplining police officers, this indirect method, which costs the public a retrial, has been justified.

However, with respect to attorneys, including prosecuting attorneys, the courts do have a direct method of discipline to deter their wrongful action. Attorneys can be disciplined by the bar grievance authorities, and the courts can refer attorneys to them for appropriate action.

Therefore, to deter future action as here committed, without burdening the public criminal justice system with a retrial, and to directly reach the alleged wrongdoer, I would order the Clerk to report the assistant prosecuting attorney's action in this matter to the grievance authorities for appropriate action.

Justice Kavanagh:

Here the evidence sought to be introduced was obtained in violation of one of this Court's established rules of practice.

This action by the prosecutor is an affront to the whole profession for it diminishes the effectiveness of the attorney-client relationship, and enfeebles defendant's Fifth and Sixth Amendment rights.

But we should not here be diverted by consideration of any violation of defendant's rights. We should treat the affront to this Court and the procedure it has established. I would apply the exclusionary rule for the purpose of deterring unacceptable practice of the type involved in this case.

The evidence should be suppressed to give unmistakable notice that, in addition to exposure to disciplinary action, disregard of our rules will in no way assist an attorney in the performance of professional duty.

Justice Moody:

The prosecutor was a direct participant in the preparation for and the conducting of this interview. The influence of the prosecutor's presence upon the defendant is immeasurable. Defense counsel's presence could have substantially altered the interrogation. Furthermore, the prosecutor twice accompanied the detective to interrogate Green without notification to defense counsel.

The general rule should be that a prosecutor must be prohibited from interviewing a defendant without first obtaining the consent of defense

> counsel or the affirmation of defense counsel that he has advised the defendant of his rights and, following this advice, the defendant still wishes to be interviewed without him. Failure to do so should result in the suppression of any resulting evidence.

Justice Levin:

> DR 7-104(A)(1) was violated in this case. As a result, the prosecutor who violated the rule obtained statements he might not otherwise have obtained which were used against Green. DR 7-104(A)(1) is designed to protect people, not abstractions. This Court should effectuate that protection in the only way which would be meaningful in this case — by reversing Green's conviction and ordering a new trial at which his statement would be suppressed.

In another case remarkably similar to *Green*, the court refused to suppress the defendant's statements:

> In the absence of constitutional grounds for suppression, the only possible basis for suppression would be to discourage violation of DR 7-104(A)(1). Suppression of the statements would therefore be in the same posture as exclusion of evidence under the exclusionary rule. The exclusionary rule exists "to deter — to compel respect for the constitutional guarantee [against illegal search and seizure] in the only effectively available way — by removing the incentive to disregard it." The exclusionary rule thus exists because it is the only effective way to deter violations of a constitutional right. However, we have another effective way to deter violation of an ethical rule. Bar discipline can be initiated by the Florida Bar. . . . The goal of deterrence is therefore achieved without the "overkill" of suppression and reversal.

Suarez v. State, 481 So. 2d 1201, 1207, *cert. denied*, 476 U.S. 1178 (Fla. 1985). *But see State v. Lefthand*, 488 N.W.2d 799, 801–02 (Minn. 1992):

> Long ago we gave notice of our "strong[] disapproval of in-custody interrogations if the defendant is represented by counsel and counsel has not had an opportunity to be present at the questioning." Subsequently, we have reiterated our disapproval of the practice "in the strongest of terms". . . . It is incomprehensible that the attorney-client relationship in the context of a criminal proceeding would be so cavalierly disregarded. . . . Statements obtained without notice to or the presence of counsel are subject to exclusion at trial. We are mindful this requirement may cause some delay in the interrogation process; but the importance of the attorney-client relationship makes it necessary.

(5) On retrial, will there be sufficient evidence to convict Williams? Compare the statements made by several members of the Court. Justice Stewart: "[E]vidence of where the body was found and of its condition might well be admissible on the theory that the body would have been discovered in any event, even had incriminating statements not been elicited from Williams." Justice Marshall: "[G]iven the ingenuity of Iowa prosecutors on retrial or in a civil commitment proceeding, I doubt very much that there is any chance a dangerous criminal will be loosed on the

streets, the bloodcurdling cries of the dissents notwithstanding. . . ." Chief Justice Burger: "If all use of the *corpus delicti* is to be barred by the Court as 'fruit of the poisonous tree' under *Wong Sun v. United States*, except on the unlikely theory suggested by the Court, the Court renders the prospects of doing justice in this case exceedingly remote." On retrial, Williams was convicted, and the conviction was affirmed by the Iowa Supreme Court which expressly held that the evidence of the body of the victim was properly admitted into evidence.

> The Court concludes that the searchers would have arrived at the site of the body within a short time of its actual finding, had they continued the search after dark. The culvert in question was itself uncovered and readily visible and in getting down to look into it, as the searchers were doing, the depressions on either side of it would have been obvious — the body was in one of these depressions. Had the searchers stopped due to the snow and the dark, the next day was a Friday and a weekend was upcoming — the search would clearly have been taken up again where it left off, given the extreme circumstances of this case, and the body would have been found in short order.

State v. Williams, 285 N.W.2d 248, 262 (Iowa 1979). The Federal District Court then denied habeas corpus relief. The Court of Appeals reversed, but the Supreme Court reinstated the District Court's ruling. See the discussion in Chapter 6, *infra*.

§ 5.03 THE SELF-INCRIMINATION APPROACH

The next case is not a self-incrimination case at all. In order to understand the cases which established the broad self-incrimination principle, though, it is important to analyze the holding in, and the cases which follow, *Escobedo v. Illinois*.

ESCOBEDO v. ILLINOIS

United States Supreme Court
378 U.S. 478 (1964)

MR. JUSTICE GOLDBERG delivered the opinion of the Court.

The critical question in this case is whether, under the circumstances, the refusal by the police to honor petitioner's request to consult with his lawyer during the course of an interrogation constitutes a denial of "the Assistance of Counsel" in violation of the Sixth Amendment to the Constitution as "made obligatory upon the States by the Fourteenth Amendment," *Gideon v. Wainwright*, and thereby renders inadmissible in a state criminal trial any incriminating statement elicited by the police during the interrogation.

On the night of January 19, 1960, petitioner's brother-in-law was fatally shot. In the early hours of the next morning, at 2:30 a.m., petitioner was arrested without a warrant and interrogated. Petitioner made no statement to the police and was released at 5 that afternoon pursuant to a state court writ of habeas corpus obtained by Mr. Warren Wolfson, a lawyer who had been retained by petitioner.

On January 30, Benedict DiGerlando, who was then in police custody and who was later indicted for the murder along with petitioner, told the police that petitioner had fired the fatal shots. Between 8 and 9 that evening, petitioner and his sister, the widow of the deceased, were arrested and taken to police headquarters. En route to the police station, the police "had handcuffed the defendant behind his back," and "one of the arresting officers told defendant that DiGerlando had named him as the one who shot" the deceased. Petitioner testified, without contradiction, that the "detectives said they had us pretty well, up pretty tight, and we might as well admit to this crime," and that he replied, "I am sorry but I would like to have advice from my lawyer." A police officer testified that although petitioner was not formally charged "he was in custody" and "couldn't walk out the door."

Shortly after petitioner reached police headquarters, his retained lawyer arrived. The lawyer described the ensuing events in the following terms:

> On that day I received a phone call [from the mother of another defendant] and pursuant to that phone call I went to the Detective Bureau at 11th and State. The first person I talked to was the Sergeant on duty at the Bureau Desk, Sergeant Pidgeon. I asked Sergeant Pidgeon for permission to speak to my client, Danny Escobedo. . . . Sergeant Pidgeon made a call to the Bureau lockup and informed me that the boy had been taken from the lockup to the Homicide Bureau. This was between 9:30 and 10:00 in the evening. Before I went anywhere, he called the Homicide Bureau and told them there was an attorney waiting to see Escobedo. He told me I could not see him. Then I went upstairs to the Homicide Bureau. There were several Homicide Detectives around and I talked to them. I identified myself as Escobedo's attorney and asked permission to see him. They said I could not. . . . The police officer told me to see Chief Flynn who was on duty. I identified myself to Chief Flynn and asked permission to see my client. He said I could not. . . . I think it was approximately 11:00 o'clock. He said I couldn't see him because they hadn't completed questioning. . . . [F]or a second or two I spotted him in an office in the Homicide Bureau. The door was open and I could see through the office. . . . I waved to him and he waved back and then the door was closed, by one of the officers at Homicide.[7] There were four or five officers milling around the Homicide Detail that night. As to whether I talked to Captain Flynn any later that day, I waited around for another hour or two and went back again and renewed by [*sic*] request to see my client. He again told me I could not. . . . I filed an official complaint with Commissioner Phelan of the Chicago Police Department. I had a conversation with every police officer I could find. I was told at Homicide that I couldn't see him and I would have to get a writ of habeas corpus. I left the Homicide Bureau and from the Detective Bureau at 11th and State at approximately 1:00 A.M. [Sunday morning]. I had no opportunity to talk to my client that night. I quoted to Captain

[7] [1] Petitioner testified that this ambiguous gesture "could have meant most anything," but that he "took it upon [his] own to think that [the lawyer was telling him] not to say anything," and that the lawyer "wanted to talk" to him.

Flynn the Section of the Criminal Code which allows an attorney the right to see his client.[8]

Petitioner testified that during the course of the interrogation he repeatedly asked to speak to his lawyer and that the police said that his lawyer "didn't want to see" him. The testimony of the police officers confirmed these accounts in substantial detail.

Notwithstanding repeated requests by each, petitioner and his retained lawyer were afforded no opportunity to consult during the course of the entire interrogation. At one point, as previously noted, petitioner and his attorney came into each other's view for a few moments but the attorney was quickly ushered away. Petitioner testified "that he heard a detective telling the attorney the latter would not be allowed to talk to [him] 'until they were done' " and that he heard the attorney being refused permission to remain in the adjoining room. A police officer testified that he had told the lawyer that he could not see petitioner until "we were through interrogating" him.

There is testimony by the police that during the interrogation, petitioner, a 22-year-old of Mexican extraction with no record of previous experience with the police, "was handcuffed"[9] in a standing position and that he "was nervous, he had circles under his eyes and he was upset" and was "agitated" because "he had not slept well in over a week."

It is undisputed that during the course of the interrogation Officer Montejano, who "grew up" in petitioner's neighborhood, who knew his family, and who uses "Spanish language in [his] police work," conferred alone with petitioner "for about a quarter of an hour. . . ." Petitioner testified that the officer said to him "in Spanish that my sister and I could go home if I pinned it on Benedict DiGerlando," that "he would see to it that we would go home and be held only as witnesses, if anything, if we had made a statement against DiGerlando . . . , that we would be able to go home that night." Petitioner testified that he made the statement in issue because of this assurance. Officer Montejano denied offering any such assurance.

A police officer testified that during the interrogation the following occurred:

> I informed him of what DiGerlando told me and when I did, he told me that DiGerlando was [lying] and I said, Would you care to tell DiGerlando that? and he said, Yes, I will. So, I brought . . . Escobedo in and he confronted DiGerlando and he told him that he was lying and said, "I didn't shoot Manuel, you did it."

In this way, petitioner, for the first time admitted to some knowledge of the crime. After that he made additional statements further implicating himself in the murder plot. At this point an Assistant State's Attorney, Theodore J. Cooper, was summoned "to take" a statement. Mr. Cooper, an experienced lawyer who was

---

[8] [2] The statute then in effect provided in pertinent part that: "All public officers . . . having the custody of any person . . . restrained of his liberty for any alleged cause whatever, shall, except in cases of imminent danger of escape, admit any practicing attorney . . . whom such person . . . may desire to see or consult. . . ."

[9] [3] The trial judge justified the handcuffing on the ground that it "is ordinary police procedure."

assigned to the Homicide Division to take "statements from some defendants and some prisoners that they had in custody," "took" petitioner's statement by asking carefully framed questions apparently designed to assure the admissibility into evidence of the resulting answers. Mr. Cooper testified that he did not advise petitioner of his constitutional rights, and it is undisputed that no one during the course of the interrogation so advised him.

Petitioner moved both before and during trial to suppress the incriminating statement, but the motions were denied. Petitioner was convicted of murder and he appealed the conviction.

In *Massiah v. United States*, this Court observed that "a Constitution which guarantees a defendant the aid of counsel at . . . trial could surely vouchsafe no less to an indicted defendant under interrogation by the police in a completely extra-judicial proceeding. Anything less . . . might deny a defendant 'effective representation by counsel at the only stage when legal aid and advice would help him.' "

The interrogation here was conducted before petitioner was formally indicted. But in the context of this case, that fact should make no difference. When petitioner requested, and was denied, an opportunity to consult with his lawyer, the investigation had ceased to be a general investigation of "an unsolved crime."

Petitioner had become the accused, and the purpose of the interrogation was to "get him" to confess his guilt despite his constitutional right not to do so. At the time of his arrest and throughout the course of the interrogation, the police told petitioner that they had convincing evidence that he had fired the fatal shots. Without informing him of his absolute right to remain silent in the face of this accusation, the police urged him to make a statement.[10] Petitioner, a layman, was undoubtedly unaware that under Illinois law an admission of "mere" complicity in the murder plot was legally as damaging as an admission of firing of the fatal shots.

The "guiding hand of counsel" was essential to advise petitioner of his rights in this delicate situation. This was the "stage when legal aid and advice" were most critical to petitioner. It was a stage surely as critical as was the arraignment in *Hamilton v. Alabama*, and the preliminary hearing in *White v. Maryland*.

What happened at this interrogation could certainly "affect the whole trial," *Hamilton v. Alabama*, since rights "may be as irretrievably lost, if not then and there asserted, as they are when an accused represented by counsel waives a right for strategic purposes." *Ibid.* It would exalt form over substance to make the right to counsel, under these circumstances, depend on whether at the time of the interrogation, the authorities had secured a formal indictment. Petitioner had, for all practical purposes, already been charged with murder.

[I]t "would be highly incongruous if our system of justice permitted the district attorney, the lawyer representing the State, to extract a confession from the

---

[10] [5] Although there is testimony in the record that petitioner and his lawyer had previously discussed what petitioner should do in the event of interrogation, there is no evidence that they discussed what petitioner should or could do in the face of a false accusation that he had fired the fatal bullets.

accused while his own lawyer, seeking to speak with him was kept from him by the police."[11]

In *Gideon v. Wainwright*, we held that every person accused of a crime, whether state or federal, is entitled to a lawyer at trial. The rule sought by the State here, however, would make the trial no more than an appeal from the interrogation; and the "right to use counsel at the formal trial [would be] a very hollow thing [if], for all practical purposes, the conviction is already assured by pretrial examination."

"One can imagine a cynical prosecutor saying: 'Let them have the most illustrious counsel, now. They can't escape the noose. There is nothing that counsel can do for them at the trial.' "

It is argued that if the right to counsel is afforded prior to indictment, the number of confessions obtained by the police will diminish significantly, because most confessions are obtained during the period between arrest and indictment, and "any lawyer worth his salt will tell the suspect in no uncertain terms to make no statement to police under any circumstances." This argument, of course, cuts two ways. The fact that many confessions are obtained during this period points up its critical nature as a "stage when legal aid and advice" are surely needed.

The right to counsel would indeed be hollow if it began at a period when few confessions were obtained. There is necessarily a direct relationship between the importance of a stage to the police in their quest for a confession and the criticalness of that stage to the accused in his need for legal advice. Our Constitution, unlike some others, strikes the balance in favor of the right of the accused to be advised by his lawyer of his privilege against self-incrimination.

We have learned the lesson of history, ancient and modern, that a system of criminal law enforcement which comes to depend on the "confession" will, in the long run, be less reliable and more subject to abuses than a system which depends on extrinsic evidence independently secured through skillful investigation. As Dean Wigmore so wisely said:

> *[A]ny system of administration which permits the prosecution to trust habitually to compulsory self-disclosure as a source of proof must itself suffer morally thereby.* The inclination develops to rely mainly upon such evidence, and to be satisfied with an incomplete investigation of the other sources. The exercise of the power to extract answers begets a forgetfulness of the just limitations of that power. The simple and peaceful process of questioning breeds a readiness to resort to bullying and to physical force and torture. If there is a right to an answer, there soon seems to be a right to the expected answer, — that is, to a confession of guilt. Thus the legitimate use grows into the unjust abuse; ultimately, the innocent are

---

[11] [7] Canon 9 of the American Bar Association's Canons of Professional Ethics provides that:

> A lawyer should not in any way communicate upon the subject of controversy with a party represented by counsel; much less should he undertake to negotiate or compromise the matter with him, but should deal only with his counsel. It is incumbent upon the lawyer most particularly to avoid everything that may tend to mislead a party not represented by counsel, and he should not undertake to advise him as to the law.

> jeopardized by the encroachment of a bad system. Such seems to have been the course of experience in those legal systems where the privilege was not recognized.

This Court also has recognized that "history amply shows that confessions have often been extorted to save law enforcement officials the trouble and effort of obtaining valid and independent evidence. . . ."

We have also learned the companion lesson of history that no system of criminal justice can, or should, survive if it comes to depend for its continued effectiveness on the citizens' abdication through unawareness of their constitutional rights. No system worth preserving should have to *fear* that if an accused is permitted to consult with a lawyer, he will become aware of, and exercise, these rights. If the exercise of constitutional rights will thwart the effectiveness of a system of law enforcement, then there is something very wrong with that system.

We hold, therefore, that where, as here, the investigation is no longer a general inquiry into an unsolved crime but has begun to focus on a particular suspect, the suspect has been taken into police custody, the police carry out a process of interrogations that lends itself to eliciting incriminating statements, the suspect has requested and been denied an opportunity to consult with his lawyer, and the police have not effectively warned him of his absolute constitutional right to remain silent, the accused has been denied "the Assistance of Counsel" in violation of the Sixth Amendment to the Constitution as "made obligatory upon the States by the Fourteenth Amendment," and that no statement elicited by the police during the interrogation may be used against him at a criminal trial.

We hold only that when the process shifts from investigatory to accusatory — when its focus is on the accused and its purpose is to elicit a confession — our adversary system begins to operate, and, under the circumstances here, the accused must be permitted to consult with his lawyer.

Reversed and remanded.

MR. JUSTICE HARLAN, dissenting.

Like my Brother White, I think the rule announced today is most ill-conceived and that it seriously and unjustifiably fetters perfectly legitimate methods of criminal law enforcement.

MR. JUSTICE STEWART, dissenting.

We held that the use of these statements against [Massiah] at his trial denied him the basic protections of the Sixth Amendment guarantee.

[T]he vital fact remains that this case does not involve the deliberate interrogation of a defendant after the initiation of judicial proceedings against him. The Court disregards this basic difference between the present case and Massiah's, with the bland assertion that "that fact should make no difference."

It is "that fact," I submit, which makes all the difference. Under our system of criminal justice the institution of formal, meaningful judicial proceedings, by way of indictment, information, or arraignment, marks the point at which a criminal investigation has ended and adversary proceedings have commenced.

It is at this point that the constitutional guarantees attach which pertain to a criminal trial. Among those guarantees are the right to a speedy trial, the right of confrontation, and the right to trial by jury. Another is the guarantee of the assistance of counsel.

MR. JUSTICE WHITE, with whom MR. JUSTICE CLARK and MR. JUSTICE STEWART join, dissenting.

In *Massiah v. United States*, the Court held that as of the date of the indictment the prosecution is disentitled to secure admissions from the accused. The Court now moves that date back to the time when the prosecution begins to "focus" on the accused.

At the very least the Court holds that once the accused becomes a suspect and, presumably, is arrested, any admission made to the police thereafter is inadmissible in evidence unless the accused has waived his right to counsel. The decision is thus another major step in the direction of the goal which the Court seemingly has in mind — to bar from evidence all admissions obtained from an individual suspected of crime, whether involuntarily made or not.

I reject this step and the invitation to go farther which the Court has now issued.

By abandoning the voluntary-involuntary test for admissibility of confessions, the Court seems driven by the notion that it is uncivilized law enforcement to use an accused's own admissions against him at his trial. It attempts to find a home for this new and nebulous rule of due process by attaching it to the right to counsel guaranteed in the federal system by the Sixth Amendment and binding upon the States by virtue of the due process guarantee of the Fourteenth Amendment. *Gideon v. Wainwright.* The right to counsel now not only entitles the accused to counsel's advice and aid in preparing for trial but stands as an impenetrable barrier to any interrogation once the accused has become a suspect. From that very moment apparently his right to counsel attaches, a rule wholly unworkable and impossible to administer unless police cars are equipped with public defenders and undercover agents and police informants have defense counsel at their side. I would not abandon the Court's prior cases defining with some care and analysis the circumstances requiring the presence or aid of counsel and substitute the amorphous and wholly unworkable principle that counsel is constitutionally required whenever he would or could be helpful.

These cases dealt with the requirement of counsel at proceedings in which definable rights could be won or lost, not with stages where probative evidence might be obtained. Under this new approach one might just as well argue that a potential defendant is constitutionally entitled to a lawyer before, not after, he commits a crime, since it is then that crucial incriminating evidence is put within the reach of the Government by the would-be accused. Until now there simply has been no right guaranteed by the Federal Constitution to be free from the use at trial of a voluntary admission made prior to indictment.

It is incongruous to assume that the provision for counsel in the Sixth Amendment was meant to amend or supersede the self-incrimination provision of the Fifth Amendment, which is now applicable to the States. *Malloy v. Hogan.*

That amendment addresses itself to the very issue of incriminating admissions of an accused and resolves it by proscribing only compelled statements. Neither the Framers, the constitutional language, a century of decisions of this Court nor Professor Wigmore provides an iota of support for the idea that an accused has an absolute constitutional right not to answer even in the absence of compulsion — the constitutional right not to incriminate himself by making voluntary disclosures.

NOTES AND QUESTIONS

(1) Until the very end of the opinion, Justice Goldberg painted with a broad brush in describing the difficulties with confessions. See, for instance, the following statements:

> We have learned the lesson of history, ancient and modern, that a system of criminal law enforcement which comes to depend on the "confession" will, in the long run, be less reliable and more subject to abuses than a system which depends on extrinsic evidence independently secured through skillful investigation.
>
> We have also learned the companion lesson of history that no system of criminal justice can, or should, survive if it comes to depend for its continued effectiveness on the citizens' abdication through unawareness of their constitutional rights. No system worth preserving should have to *fear* that if an accused is permitted to consult with a lawyer, he will become aware of, and exercise, these rights.

Justice White, in his dissent, viewed *Escobedo* as establishing a very sweeping rule indeed.

> At the very least the Court holds that once the accused becomes a suspect and, presumably, is arrested, any admission made to the police thereafter is inadmissible in evidence unless the accused has waived his right to counsel. The decision is thus another major step in the direction of the goal which the Court seemingly has in mind — to bar from evidence all admissions obtained from an individual suspected of crime, whether involuntarily made or not.

What *was* the actual holding in *Escobedo*? Consider the last several paragraphs in the edited majority opinion; how much precedential value did *Escobedo* have?

(2) Why was Escobedo denied his right to counsel? Several times he stated that he understood that his lawyer did not want him to talk so why did the failure to consult with the attorney prior to giving his confession raise Sixth Amendment issues?

(3) Justices Goldberg and Stewart differed sharply on the impact of the confession having been made prior to the indictment of the defendant. How important is the fact of indictment? Recall that Justice Stewart wrote the opinion

for the Court in *Kirby v. Illinois* (Chapter 4, *supra*) holding that the Sixth Amendment does not attach to an identification procedure until there has been some sort of adversary judicial proceeding.

(4) In *Malloy v. Hogan*, 378 U.S. 1 (1964), the Court held that the self-incrimination provision of the Fifth Amendment was applicable to the States. Why was the Court's opinion in *Escobedo* written in Sixth Amendment terms rather than the Fifth Amendment terms it had used a mere one week earlier in *Malloy*? Does the Fifth Amendment approach make more sense?

(5) In one footnote of the opinion, Justice Goldberg seems to raise some question as to the ethical conduct of the government attorney who took the incriminating statement from Escobedo. Under Canon 9, as set out in the footnote, did the lawyer breach his professional responsibility? Apart from the Canons, did the lawyer act in an unethical fashion? In 1999, Congress addressed the question of whether federal attorneys were bound by state ethics rules forbidding contact with represented defendants. Over strong opposition from the United States Justice Department, § 530B, of Title 28 of the U.S. Code was added:

> § 530B. Ethical standards for attorneys for the Government
>
> (a) An attorney for the Government shall be subject to State laws and rules, and local Federal court rules, governing attorneys in each State where such attorney engages in that attorney's duties, to the same extent and in the same manner as other attorneys in that State.

(6) In order for the holding in *Escobedo* to apply, does the defendant have to make a request that he see his attorney, or that he be appointed an attorney? *Contrast State v. Cummings*, 423 P.2d 438 (Haw. 1967) (the court limited "*Escobedo* to its facts making it mandatory for the suspect to request assistance of counsel, if the statement is to be excluded"), *with State v. Neely*, 398 P.2d 482 (Ore. 1965) ("We hold that the Sixth Amendment as made obligatory by the Fourteenth Amendment requires that before law enforcement officials can interrogate a person who is the focal suspect of a crime, such person must effectively be informed of his right to assistance of counsel as well as his right to remain silent.").

(7) If Escobedo could not have afforded an attorney, would the result in the case have been the same? Consider the facts in *Faulkner v. United States*, 368 F.2d 528 (4th Cir. 1966), where the defendant had been advised during an FBI investigation that he had a right to consult with a lawyer, but was not advised that, as an indigent, the state would provide him with counsel. The court found that *Escobedo* did not require "that a person being interviewed in connection with an investigatory inquiry must be informed of an indigent defendant's right to court-appointed counsel." Would the result in *Faulkner* have been different if the defendant had already been arrested or indicted?

(8) *Moran v. Burbine*, 475 U.S. 412 (1986), involved a variation of *Escobedo*. Here the defendant was not aware that his attorney was trying to see him during the course of questioning. During this period, however, he received his full *Miranda* warnings and appeared to understand that he could remain silent and confer with an attorney. The Supreme Court held that he had validly waived his rights and had freely confessed to the crime.

Justice O'Connor wrote for the majority:

> [W]e have no doubt that respondent validly waived his right to remain silent and to the presence of counsel. The voluntariness of the waiver is not at issue. As the Court of Appeals correctly acknowledged, the record is devoid of any suggestion that police resorted to physical or psychological pressure to elicit the statements. Indeed it appears that it was respondent, and not the police, who spontaneously initiated the conversation that led to the first and most damaging confession. Nor is there any question about respondent's comprehension of the full panoply of rights set out in the *Miranda* warnings and of the potential consequences of a decision to relinquish them. Events occurring outside of the presence of the suspect and entirely unknown to him surely can have no bearing on the capacity to comprehend and knowingly relinquish a constitutional right.

Justice Stevens, in dissent, strongly disagreed with the Court's holding:

> The Court concludes that the police may deceive an attorney by giving her false information about whether her client will be questioned, and that the police may deceive a suspect by failing to inform him of his attorney's communications and efforts to represent him. For the majority, this conclusion, though "distaste[ful]," is not even debatable. The deception of the attorney is irrelevant because the attorney has no right to information, accuracy, honesty, or fairness in the police response to her questions about her client. The deception of the client is acceptable, because, although the information would affect the client's assertion of his rights, the client's actions in ignorance of the availability of his attorney are voluntary, knowing, and intelligent; additionally, society's interest in apprehending, prosecuting, and punishing criminals outweighs the suspect's interest in information regarding his attorney's efforts to communicate with him.

MIRANDA v. ARIZONA

United States Supreme Court
384 U.S. 436 (1966)

Mr. Chief Justice Warren delivered the opinion of the Court.

The cases before us raise questions which go to the roots of our concepts of American criminal jurisprudence: the restraints society must observe consistent with the Federal Constitution in prosecuting individuals for crime. More specifically, we deal with the admissibility of statements obtained from an individual who is subjected to custodial police interrogation and the necessity for procedures which assure that the individual is accorded his privilege under the Fifth Amendment to the Constitution not to be compelled to incriminate himself.

We dealt with certain phases of this problem recently in *Escobedo v. State of Illinois.*

This case has been the subject of judicial interpretation and spirited legal debate since it was decided two years ago. Both state and federal courts, in assessing its implications, have arrived at varying conclusions. A wealth of scholarly material has been written tracing its ramifications and underpinnings. Police and prosecutor have speculated on its range and desirability.[12] We granted certiorari in these cases in order further to explore some facets of the problems, thus exposed, of applying the privilege against self-incrimination to in-custody interrogation, and to give concrete constitutional guidelines for law enforcement agencies and courts to follow.

We start here, as we did in *Escobedo*, with the premise that our holding is not an innovation in our jurisprudence, but is an application of principles long recognized and applied in other settings. We have undertaken a thorough reexamination of the *Escobedo* decision and the principles it announced, and we reaffirm it. That case was but an explication of basic rights that are enshrined in our Constitution — that "No person . . . shall be compelled in any criminal case to be a witness against himself," and that "the accused shall . . . have the Assistance of Counsel" — rights which were put in jeopardy in that case through official overbearing.

Our holding will be spelled out with some specificity in the pages which follow but briefly stated it is this: the prosecution may not use statements, whether exculpatory or inculpatory, stemming from custodial interrogation of the defendant unless it demonstrates the use of procedural safeguards effective to secure the privilege against self-incrimination. By custodial interrogation, we mean questioning initiated by law enforcement officers after a person has been taken into custody or otherwise deprived of his freedom of action in any significant way.[13] As for the procedural safeguards to be employed, unless other fully effective means are devised to inform accused persons of their right of silence and to assure a continuous opportunity to exercise it, the following measures are required. Prior to any questioning, the person must be warned that he has a right to remain silent, that any statement he does make may be used as evidence against him, and that he has a right to the presence of an attorney, either retained or appointed. The defendant may waive effectuation of these rights, provided the waiver is made voluntarily, knowingly and intelligently. If, however, he indicates in any manner and at any stage of the process that he wishes to consult with an attorney before

[12] [3] For example, the Los Angeles Police Chief stated that "If the police are required . . . to . . . establish that the defendant was apprised of his constitutional guarantees of silence and legal counsel prior to the uttering of any admission or confession, and that he intelligently waived these guarantees . . . a whole Pandora's box is opened as to under what circumstances . . . can a defendant intelligently waive these rights. . . . Allegations that modern criminal investigation can compensate for the lack of a confession or admission in every criminal case is totally absurd!" Parker, 40 L.A. Bar Bull. 603, 607, 642 (1965). His prosecutorial counterpart, District Attorney Younger, stated that "[I]t begins to appear that many of these seemingly restrictive decisions are going to contribute directly to a more effective, efficient and professional level of law enforcement." L.A. Times, Oct. 2, 1965, p. 1. The former Police Commissioner of New York, Michael J. Murphy, stated of *Escobedo*: "What the Court is doing is akin to requiring one boxer to fight by Marquis of Queensbury rules while permitting the other to butt, gouge and bite." N.Y. Times, May 14, 1965, p. 39. The former United States Attorney for the District of Columbia, David C. Acheson, who is presently Special Assistant to the Secretary of the Treasury (for Enforcement), and directly in charge of the Secret Service and the Bureau of Narcotics, observed that "Prosecution procedure has, at most, only the most remote causal connection with crime. Changes in court decisions and prosecution procedure would have about the same effect on the crime rate as an aspirin would have on a tumor of the brain."

[13] [4] This is what we meant in *Escobedo* when we spoke of an investigation which had focused on an accused.

speaking there can be no questioning. Likewise, if the individual is alone and indicates in any manner that he does not wish to be interrogated, the police may not question him. The mere fact that he may have answered some questions or volunteered some statements on his own does not deprive him of the right to refrain from answering any further inquiries until he has consulted with an attorney and thereafter consents to be questioned.

I

The constitutional issue we decide in each of these cases is the admissibility of statements obtained from a defendant questioned while in custody or otherwise deprived of his freedom of action in any significant way. In each, the defendant was questioned by police officers, detectives, or a prosecuting attorney in a room in which he was cut off from the outside world. In none of these cases was the defendant given a full and effective warning of his rights at the outset of the interrogation process. In all the cases, the questioning elicited oral admissions, and in three of them, signed statements as well which were admitted at their trials. They all thus share salient features — incommunicado interrogation of individuals in a police-dominated atmosphere, resulting in self-incriminating statements without full warnings of constitutional rights.

An understanding of the nature and setting of this in-custody interrogation is essential to our decisions today. The difficulty in depicting what transpires at such interrogations stems from the fact that in this country they have largely taken place incommunicado. From extensive factual studies undertaken in the early 1930's, including the famous Wickersham Report to Congress by a Presidential Commission, it is clear that police violence and the "third degree" flourished at that time.

In a series of cases decided by this Court long after these studies, the police resorted to physical brutality — beatings, hanging, whipping — and to sustained and protracted questioning incommunicado in order to extort confessions. The Commission on Civil Rights in 1961 found much evidence to indicate that "some policemen still resort to physical force to obtain confessions," 1961 Comm'n on Civil Rights Rep., Justice, pt. 5, 17. The use of physical brutality and violence is not, unfortunately, relegated to the past or to any part of the country. Only recently in Kings County, New York, the police brutally beat, kicked and placed lighted cigarette butts on the back of a potential witness under interrogation for the purpose of securing a statement incriminating a third party. *People v. Portelli*, 15 N.Y.2d 235, 257 N.Y.S.2d 931, 205 N.E.2d 857 (1965).[14]

---

[14] [7] In addition, *see* People v. Wakat, 415 Ill. 610, 114 N.E.2d 706 (1953); Wakat v. Harlib, 253 F.2d 59 (C.A. 7th Cir. 1958) (defendant suffering from broken bones, multiple bruises and injuries sufficiently serious to require eight months' medical treatment after being manhandled by five policemen); Kier v. State, 213 Md. 556, 132 A.2d 494 (1957) (police doctor told accused, who was strapped to a chair completely nude, that he proposed to take hair and skin scrapings from anything that looked like blood or sperm from various parts of his body); Bruner v. People, 113 Colo. 194, 156 P.2d 111 (1945) (defendant held in custody over two months, deprived of food for 15 hours, forced to submit to a lie detector test when he wanted to go to the toilet); People v. Matlock, 51 Cal. 2d 682, 336 P.2d 505 (1959) (defendant questioned incessantly over an evening's time, made to lie on cold board and to answer questions whenever it appeared he was getting sleepy).

The examples given above are undoubtedly the exception now, but they are sufficiently widespread to be the object of concern. Unless a proper limitation upon custodial interrogation is achieved — such as these decisions will advance — there can be no assurance that practices of this nature will be eradicated in the foreseeable future.

Again we stress that the modern practice of in-custody interrogation is psychologically rather than physically oriented. . . . "[T]his Court has recognized that coercion can be mental as well as physical, and that the blood of the accused is not the only hallmark of an unconstitutional inquisition." Interrogation still take s place in privacy. Privacy results in secrecy and this in turn results in a gap in our knowledge as to what in fact goes on in the interrogation rooms. A valuable source of information about present police practices, however, may be found in various police manuals and texts which document procedures employed with success in the past and which recommend various other effective tactics. These texts are used by law enforcement agencies themselves as guides.[15]

It should be noted that these texts professedly present the most enlightened and effective means presently used to obtain statements through custodial interrogation. By considering these texts and other data, it is possible to describe procedures observed and noted around the country.

The officers are told by the manuals that the "principal psychological factor contributing to a successful interrogation is privacy — being alone with the person under interrogation." The efficacy of this tactic has been explained as follows:

> If at all practicable, the interrogation should take place in the investigator's office or at least in a room of his own choice. The subject should be deprived of every psychological advantage. In his own home he may be confident, indignant, or recalcitrant. He is more keenly aware of his rights and more reluctant to tell of his indiscretions or criminal behavior within the walls of his home. Moreover his family and other friends are nearby, their presence lending moral support. In his office, the investigator possesses all the advantages. The atmosphere suggests the invincibility of the forces of the law.

To highlight the isolation and unfamiliar surroundings, the manuals instruct the police to display an air of confidence in the suspect's guilt and from outward appearance to maintain only an interest in confirming certain details. The guilt of the subject is to be posited as a fact. The interrogator should direct his comments

---

[15] [9] The methods described in Inbau & Reid Criminal Interrogation and Confessions (1962), are a revision and enlargement of material presented in three prior editions of a predecessor text, Lie Detection and Criminal Interrogation (3d ed. 1953). The authors and their associates are officers of the Chicago Police Scientific Crime Detection Laboratory and have had extensive experience in writing, lecturing and speaking to law enforcement authorities over a 20-year period. They say that the techniques portrayed in their manuals reflect their experiences and are the most effective psychological stratagems to employ during interrogations. Similarly, the techniques described in O'Hara, Fundamentals of Criminal Investigation (1956), were gleaned from long service as observer, lecturer in police science, and work as a federal criminal investigator. All these texts have had rather extensive use among law enforcement agencies and among students of police science with total sales and circulation of over 44,000.

toward the reasons why the subject committed the act, rather than court failure by asking the subject whether he did it. Like other men, perhaps the subject has had a bad family life, had an unhappy childhood, had too much to drink, had an unrequited desire for women. The officers are instructed to minimize the moral seriousness of the offense, to cast blame on the victim or on society. These tactics are designed to put the subject in a psychological state where his story is but an elaboration of what the police purport to know already — that he is guilty. Explanations to the contrary are dismissed and discouraged.

. . .

The manuals suggest that the suspect be offered legal excuses for his actions in order to obtain an initial admission of guilt. Where there is a suspected revenge-killing, for example, the interrogator may say:

> Joe, you probably didn't go out looking for this fellow with the purpose of shooting him. My guess is, however, that you expected something from him and that's why you carried a gun — for your own protection. You knew him for what he was, no good. Then when you met him he probably started using foul, abusive language and he gave some indication that he was about to pull a gun on you, and that's when you had to act to save your own life. That's about it, isn't it, Joe?

Having then obtained the admission of shooting, the interrogator is advised to refer to circumstantial evidence which negates the self-defense explanation. This should enable him to secure the entire story. One text notes that "Even if he fails to do so, the inconsistency between the subject's original denial of the shooting and his present admission of at least doing the shooting will serve to deprive him of a self-defense 'out' at the time of trial."

When the techniques described above prove unavailing, the texts recommend they be alternated with a show of some hostility. One ploy often used has been termed the "friendly-unfriendly" or the "Mutt and Jeff" act:

> . . . In this technique, two agents are employed. Mutt, the relentless investigator, who knows the subject is guilty and is not going to waste any time. He's sent a dozen men away for this crime and he's going to send the subject away for the full term. Jeff, on the other hand, is obviously a kindhearted man. He has a family himself. He has a brother who was involved in a little scrape like this. He disapproves of Mutt and his tactics and will arrange to get him off the case if the subject will cooperate. He can't hold Mutt off for very long. The subject would be wise to make a quick decision. The technique is applied by having both investigators present while Mutt acts out his role. Jeff may stand by quietly and demur at some of Mutt's tactics. When Jeff makes his plea for cooperation, Mutt is not present in the room.

The interrogators sometimes are instructed to induce a confession out of trickery. The technique here is quite effective in crimes which require identification or which run in series. In the identification situation, the interrogator may take a break in his questioning to place the subject among a group of men in a line-up. "The witness or complainant (previously coached, if necessary) studies the line-up and confidently points out the subject as the guilty party." Then the question resumes "as though there were now no doubt about the guilt of the subject." A variation on this technique is called the "reverse line-up":

> The accused is placed in a line-up, but this time he is identified by several fictitious witnesses or victims who associated him with different offenses. It is expected that the subject will become desperate and confess to the offense under investigation in order to escape from the false accusations.

The manuals also contain instructions for police on how to handle the individual who refuses to discuss the matter entirely, or who asks for an attorney or relatives. The examiner is to concede him the right to remain silent. "This usually has a very undermining effect. First of all, he is disappointed in his expectation of an unfavorable reaction on the part of the interrogator. Secondly, a concession of this right to remain silent impresses the subject with the apparent fairness of his interrogator." After this psychological conditioning, however, the officer is told to point out the incriminating significance of the suspect's refusal to talk:

> Joe, you have a right to remain silent. That's your privilege and I'm the last person in the world who'll try to take it away from you. If that's the way you want to leave this, O.K. But let me ask you this. Suppose you were in my shoes and I were in yours and you called me in to ask me about this and I told you, "I don't want to answer any of your questions." You'd think I had something to hide, and you'd probably be right in thinking that. That's exactly what I'll have to think about you, and so will everybody else. So let's sit here and talk this whole thing over.

Few will persist in their initial refusal to talk, it is said, if this monologue is employed correctly. In the event that the subject wishes to speak to a relative or an attorney, the following advice is tendered: [T]he interrogator should respond by suggesting that the subject first tell the truth to the interrogator himself rather than get anyone else involved in the matter. If the request is for an attorney, the interrogator may suggest that the subject save himself or his family the expense of any such professional service, particularly if he is innocent of the offenses under investigation. The interrogator may also add, "Joe, I'm only looking for the truth, and if you're telling the truth, that's it. You can handle this by yourself."

From these representative samples of interrogation techniques, the setting prescribed by the manuals and observed in practice becomes clear. In essence, it is this: To be alone with the subject is essential to prevent distraction and to deprive him of any outside support. The aura of confidence in his guilt undermines his will to resist. He merely confirms the preconceived story the police seek to have him describe. Patience and persistence, at times relentless questioning, are employed. To obtain a confession, the interrogator must "patiently maneuver himself or his quarry into a position from which the desired objective may be attained." When normal procedures fail to produce the needed result, the police may resort to deceptive stratagems such as giving false legal advice. It is important to keep the subject off balance, for example, by trading on his insecurity about himself or his surroundings. The police then persuade, trick, or cajole him out of exercising his constitutional rights.

Even without employing brutality, the "third degree" or the specific stratagems described above, the very fact of custodial interrogation exacts a heavy toll on individual liberty and trades on the weakness of individuals.

. . . In the cases before us today, given this background, we concern ourselves primarily with this interrogation atmosphere and the evils it can bring. In No. 759, *Miranda v. Arizona*, the police arrested the defendant and took him to a special interrogation room where they secured a confession. In No. 760, *Vignera v. New York*, the defendant made oral admissions to the police after interrogation in the afternoon, and then signed an inculpatory statement upon being questioned by an assistant district attorney later the same evening. In No. 761, *Westover v. United States*, the defendant was handed over to the Federal Bureau of Investigation by local authorities after they had detained and interrogated him for a lengthy period, both at night and the following morning. After some two hours of questioning, the federal officers had obtained signed statements from the defendant. Lastly, in No. 584, *California v. Stewart*, the local police held the defendant five days in the station and interrogated him on nine separate occasions before they secured his inculpatory statement.

In these cases, we might not find the defendants statements to have been involuntary in traditional terms. Our concern for adequate safeguards to protect precious Fifth Amendment rights is, of course, not lessened in the slightest. In each of the cases, the defendant was thrust into an unfamiliar atmosphere and run through menacing police interrogation procedures. The potentiality for compulsion is forcefully apparent, for example, in *Miranda*, where the indigent Mexican defendant was a seriously disturbed individual with pronounced sexual fantasies, and in *Stewart*, in which the defendant was an indigent Los Angeles Negro who had dropped out of school in the sixth grade. To be sure, the records do not evince overt physical coercion or patent psychological ploys. The fact remains that in none of these cases did the officers undertake to afford appropriate safeguards at the outset of the interrogation to insure that the statements were truly the product of free choice.

It is obvious that such an interrogation environment is created for no purpose other than to subjugate the individual to the will of his examiner. This atmosphere carries its own badge of intimidation. To be sure, this is not physical intimidation, but it is equally destructive of human dignity.[16] The current practice of incommu-

[16] [26] The absurdity of denying that a confession obtained under these circumstances is compelled is aptly portrayed by an example in Professor Sutherland's recent article, *Crime and Confession*, 79 Harv. L. Rev. 21, 37 (1965):

> Suppose a well-to-do testatrix says she intends to will her property to Elizabeth. John and James want her to bequeath it to them instead. They capture the testatrix, put her in a carefully designed room, out of touch with everyone but themselves and their convenient "witnesses," keep her secluded there for hours while they make insistent demands, weary her with contradictions of her assertions that she wants to leave her money to Elizabeth, and finally induce her to execute the will in their favor. Assume that John and James are deeply and correctly convinced that Elizabeth is unworthy and will make base use of the property if she gets her hands on it, whereas John and James have the noblest and most righteous intentions. Would any judge of probate accept the will so procured as the "voluntary" act of the testatrix?

nicado interrogation is at odds with one of our Nation's most cherished principles — that the individual may not be compelled to incriminate himself. Unless adequate protective devices are employed to dispel the compulsion inherent in custodial surroundings, no statement obtained from the defendant can truly be the product of his free choice.

From the foregoing, we can readily perceive an intimate connection between the privilege against self-incrimination and police custodial questioning.

II

. . .

Because of the adoption by Congress of Rule 5(a) of the Federal Rules of Criminal Procedure, and the Court's effectuation of that Rule in *McNabb v. United States*, and *Mallory v. United States*, we have had little occasion in the past quarter century to reach the constitutional issues in dealing with federal interrogations. These supervisory rules, requiring production of an arrested person before a commissioner "without unnecessary delay" and excluding evidence obtained in default of that statutory obligation, were nonetheless responsive to the same considerations of Fifth Amendment policy that unavoidably face us now as to the States. In *McNabb*, and in *Mallory*, we recognized both the dangers of interrogation and the appropriateness of prophylaxis stemming from the very fact of interrogation itself.[17]

Our decision in *Malloy v. Hogan* necessitates an examination of the scope of the privilege in state cases as well. In *Malloy*, we squarely held the privilege applicable to the States, and held that the substantive standards underlying the privilege applied with full force to state court proceedings. There, we applied the existing Fifth Amendment standards to the case before us. Aside from the holding itself, the reasoning in *Malloy* made clear what had already become apparent — that the substantive and procedural safeguards surrounding admissibility of confessions in state cases had become exceedingly exacting, reflecting all the policies embedded in the privilege. The voluntariness doctrine in the state cases, as *Malloy* indicates, encompasses all interrogation practices which are likely to exert such pressure upon an individual as to disable him from making a free and rational choice. The implications of this proposition were elaborated in our decision in *Escobedo v. State of Illinois*, decided one week after *Malloy* applied the privilege to the States.

Our holding there stressed the fact that the police had not advised the defendant of his constitutional privilege to remain silent at the outset of the interrogation, and we drew attention to that fact at several points in the decision.

This was no isolated factor, but an essential ingredient in our decision. The entire thrust of police interrogation there, as in all the cases today, was to put the defendant in such an emotional state as to impair his capacity for rational judgment. The abdication of the constitutional privilege — the choice on his part to speak to

---

[17] [32] Our decision today does not indicate in any manner, of course, that these rules can be disregarded. When federal officials arrest an individual, they must as always comply with the dictates of the congressional legislation and cases thereunder.

the police — was not made knowingly or competently because of the failure to apprise him of his rights; the compelling atmosphere of the in-custody interrogation, and not an independent decision on his part, caused the defendant to speak.

A different phase of the *Escobedo* decision was significant in its attention to the absence of counsel during the questioning. There, as in the cases today, we sought a protective device to dispel the compelling atmosphere of the interrogation. In *Escobedo*, however, the police did not relieve the defendant of the anxieties which they had created in the interrogation rooms. Rather, they denied his request for the assistance of counsel. This heightened his dilemma, and made his later statements the product of this compulsion.

The denial of the defendant's request for his attorney thus undermined his ability to exercise the privilege — to remain silent if he chose or to speak without any intimidation, blatant or subtle. The presence of counsel, in all the cases before us today, would be the adequate protective device necessary to make the process of police interrogation conform to the dictates of the privilege. His presence would insure that statements made in the government-established atmosphere are not the product of compulsion.

It was in this manner that *Escobedo* explicated another facet of the pre-trial privilege, noted in many of the Court's prior decisions: the protection of rights at trial. That counsel is present when statements are taken from an individual during interrogation obviously enhances the integrity of the fact-finding processes in court. The presence of an attorney, and the warnings delivered to the individual, enable the defendant under otherwise compelling circumstances to tell his story without fear, effectively, and in a way that eliminates the evils in the interrogation process. Without the protections flowing from adequate warning and the rights of counsel, "all the careful safeguards erected around the giving of testimony, whether by an accused or any other witness, would become empty formalities in a procedure where the most compelling possible evidence of guilt, a confession, would have already been obtained at the unsupervised pleasure of the police."

III

Today, then, there can be no doubt that the Fifth Amendment privilege is available outside of criminal court proceedings and serves to protect persons in all settings in which their freedom of action is curtailed in any significant way from being compelled to incriminate themselves. We have concluded that without proper safeguards the process of in-custody interrogation of persons suspected or accused of crime contains inherently compelling pressures which work to undermine the individual's will to resist and to compel him to speak where he would not otherwise do so freely. In order to combat these pressures and to permit a full opportunity to exercise the privilege against self-incrimination, the accused must be adequately and effectively apprised of his rights and the exercise of those rights must be fully honored.

It is impossible for us to foresee the potential alternatives for protecting the privilege which might be devised by Congress or the States in the exercise of their creative rule-making capacities. Therefore we cannot say that the Constitution necessarily requires adherence to any particular solution for the inherent compulsions of the interrogation process as it is presently conducted. Our decision in no way creates a constitutional straitjacket which will handicap sound efforts at reform, nor is it intended to have this effect. We encourage Congress and the States to continue their laudable search for increasingly effective ways of protecting the rights of the individual while promoting efficient enforcement of our criminal laws. However, unless we are shown other procedures which are at least as effective in apprising accused persons of their right of silence and in assuring a continuous opportunity to exercise it, the following safeguards must be observed.

At the outset, if a person in custody is to be subjected to interrogation, he must first be informed in clear and unequivocal terms that he has the right to remain silent. For those unaware of the privilege, the warning is needed simply to make them aware of it — the threshold requirement for an intelligent decision as to its exercise. More important, such a warning is an absolute prerequisite in overcoming the inherent pressures of the interrogation atmosphere. It is not just the subnormal or woefully ignorant who succumb to an interrogator's imprecations, whether implied or expressly stated, that the interrogation will continue until a confession is obtained or that silence in the face of accusation is itself damning and will bode ill when presented to a jury.[18] Further, the warning will show the individual that his interrogators are prepared to recognize his privilege should he choose to exercise it.

The Fifth Amendment privilege is so fundamental to our system of constitutional rule and the expedient of giving an adequate warning as to the availability of the privilege so simple, we will not pause to inquire in individual cases whether the defendant was aware of his rights without a warning being given. Assessments of the knowledge the defendant possessed, based on information as to his age, education, intelligence, or prior contact with authorities, can never be more than speculation; a warning is a clearcut fact. More important, whatever the background of the person interrogated, a warning at the time of the interrogation is indispensable to overcome its pressures and to insure that the individual knows he is free to exercise the privilege at that point in time.

The warning of the right to remain silent must be accompanied by the explanation that anything said can and will be used against the individual in court. This warning is needed in order to make him aware not only of the privilege, but also of the consequences of forgoing it. It is only through an awareness of these consequences that there can be any assurance of real understanding and intelligent exercise of the privilege. Moreover, this warning may serve to make the individual more acutely aware that he is faced with a phase of the adversary system — that he is not in the presence of persons acting solely in his interest.

[18] [37] Lord Devlin has commented: "It is probable that even today, when there is much less ignorance about these matters than formerly, there is still a general belief that you must answer all questions put to you by a policeman, or at least that it will be the worse for you if you do not." Devlin, The Criminal Prosecution in England 32 (1958).

In accord with our decision today, it is impermissible to penalize an individual for exercising his Fifth Amendment privilege when he is under police custodial interrogation. The prosecution may not, therefore, use at trial the fact that he stood mute or claimed his privilege in the face of accusation.

The circumstances surrounding in-custody interrogation can operate very quickly to overbear the will of one merely made aware of his privilege by his interrogators. Therefore, the right to have counsel present at the interrogation is indispensable to the protection of the Fifth Amendment privilege under the system we delineate today. Our aim is to assure that the individual's right to choose between silence and speech remains unfettered throughout the interrogation process. A once-stated warning, delivered by those who will conduct the interrogation, cannot itself suffice to that end among those who most require knowledge of their rights. A mere warning given by the interrogators is not alone sufficient to accomplish that end. Prosecutors themselves claim that the admonishment of the right to remain silent without more "will benefit only the recidivist and the professional."

Even preliminary advice given to the accused by his own attorney can be swiftly overcome by the secret interrogation process. Thus, the need for counsel to protect the Fifth Amendment privilege comprehends not merely a right to consult with counsel prior to questioning, but also to have counsel present during any questioning if the defendant so desires.

The presence of counsel at the interrogation may serve several significant subsidiary functions as well. If the accused decides to talk to his interrogators, the assistance of counsel can mitigate the dangers of untrustworthiness. With a lawyer present the likelihood that the police will practice coercion is reduced, and if coercion is nevertheless exercised the lawyer can testify to it in court. The presence of a lawyer can also help to guarantee that the accused gives a fully accurate statement to the police and that the statement is rightly reported by the prosecution at trial.

An individual need not make a pre-interrogation request for a lawyer. While such request affirmatively secures his right to have one, his failure to ask for a lawyer does not constitute a waiver. No effective waiver of the right to counsel during interrogation can be recognized unless specifically made after the warnings we here delineate have been given. The accused who does not know his rights and therefore does not make a request may be the person who most needs counsel.

Accordingly we hold that an individual held for interrogation must be clearly informed that he has the right to consult with a lawyer and to have the lawyer with him during interrogation under the system for protecting the privilege we delineate today. As with the warnings of the right to remain silent and that anything stated can be used in evidence against him, this warning is an absolute prerequisite to interrogation. No amount of circumstantial evidence that the person may have been aware of this right will suffice to stand in its stead. Only through such a warning is there ascertainable assurance that the accused was aware of this right.

If an individual indicates that he wishes the assistance of counsel before any interrogation occurs, the authorities cannot rationally ignore or deny his request on the basis that the individual does not have or cannot afford a retained attorney. The financial ability of the individual has no relationship to the scope of the rights involved here. The privilege against self-incrimination secured by the Constitution applies to all individuals. The need for counsel in order to protect the privilege exists for the indigent as well as the affluent. In fact, were we to limit these constitutional rights to those who can retain an attorney, our decisions today would be of little significance. The cases before us as well as the vast majority of confession cases with which we have dealt in the past involve those unable to retain counsel.[19] While authorities are not required to relieve the accused of his poverty, they have the obligation not to take advantage of indigence in the administration of justice. Denial of counsel to the indigent at the time of interrogation while allowing an attorney to those who can afford one would be no more supportable by reason or logic than the similar situation at trial and on appeal struck down in *Gideon v. Wainwright.*

In order fully to apprise a person interrogated of the extent of his rights under this system then, it is necessary to warn him not only that he has the right to consult with an attorney, but also that if he is indigent a lawyer will be appointed to represent him. Without this additional warning, the admonition of the right to consult with counsel would often be understood as meaning only that he can consult with a lawyer if he has one or has the funds to obtain one. The warning of a right to counsel would be hollow if not couched in terms that would convey to the indigent — the person most often subjected to interrogation — the knowledge that he too has a right to have counsel present. As with the warnings of the right to remain silent and of the general right to counsel, only by effective and express explanation to the indigent of this right can there be assurance that he was truly in a position to exercise it.[20]

Once warnings have been given, the subsequent procedure is clear. If the individual indicates in any manner, at any time prior to or during questioning, that he wishes to remain silent, the interrogation must cease. At this point he has shown that he intends to exercise his Fifth Amendment privilege; any statement taken after the person invokes his privilege cannot be other than the product of compulsion, subtle or otherwise. Without the right to cut off questioning, the setting of in-custody interrogation operates on the individual to overcome free choice in producing a statement after the privilege has been once invoked. If the individual states that he wants an attorney, the interrogation must cease until an attorney is present. At that time, the individual must have an opportunity to confer with the attorney and to have him present during any subsequent questioning. If the individual cannot obtain an attorney and he indicates that he wants one before speaking to police, they must respect his decision to remain silent.

This does not mean, as some have suggested, that each police station must have a "station house lawyer" present at all times to advise prisoners. It does mean, however, that if police propose to interrogate a person they must make known to him that he is entitled to a lawyer and that if he cannot afford one, a lawyer will be provided for him prior to any interrogation. If authorities conclude that they will not provide counsel during a reasonable period of time in which investigation in the field is carried out, they may refrain from doing so without violating the person's Fifth Amendment privilege so long as they do not question him during that time.

---

[19] [40] Estimates of 50–90% indigency among felony defendants have been reported.

[20] [43] While a warning that the indigent may have counsel appointed need not be given to the person who is known to have an attorney or is known to have ample funds to secure one, the expedient of giving a warning is too simple and the rights involved too important to engage in *ex post facto* inquiries into financial ability when there is any doubt at all on that score.

If the interrogation continues without the presence of an attorney and a statement is taken, a heavy burden rests on the government to demonstrate that the defendant knowingly and intelligently waived his privilege against self-incrimination and his right to retained or appointed counsel. This Court has always set high standards of proof for the waiver of constitutional rights, *Johnson v. Zerbst*, and we reassert these standards as applied to in-custody interrogation. Since the State is responsible for establishing the isolated circumstances under which the interrogation takes place and has the only means of making available corroborated evidence of warnings given during incommunicado interrogation, the burden is rightly on its shoulders.

An express statement that the individual is willing to make a statement and does not want an attorney followed closely by a statement could constitute a waiver. But a valid waiver will not be presumed simply from the silence of the accused after warnings are given or simply from the fact that a confession was in fact eventually obtained. Moreover, where in-custody interrogation is involved, there is room for the contention that the privilege is waived if the individual answers some questions or gives some information on his own prior to invoking his right to remain silent when interrogated.

Whatever the testimony of the authorities as to waiver of rights by an accused, the fact of lengthy interrogation or incommunicado incarceration before a statement is made is strong evidence that the accused did not validly waive his rights. In these circumstances the fact that the individual eventually made a statement is consistent with the conclusion that the compelling influence of the interrogation finally forced him to do so. It is inconsistent with any notion of a voluntary relinquishment of the privilege. Moreover, any evidence that the accused was threatened, tricked, or cajoled into a waiver will, of course, show that the defendant did not voluntarily waive his privilege. The requirement of warnings and waiver of rights is a fundamental with respect to the Fifth Amendment privilege and not simply a preliminary ritual to existing methods of interrogation.

The warnings required and the waiver necessary in accordance with our opinion today are, in the absence of a fully effective equivalent, prerequisites to the admissibility of any statement made by a defendant. No distinction can be drawn between statements which are direct confessions and statements which amount to "admissions" of part or all of an offense. The privilege against self-incrimination protects the individual from being compelled to incriminate himself in any manner; it does not distinguish degrees of incrimination. Similarly, for precisely the same reason, no distinction may be drawn between inculpatory statements and statements alleged to be merely "exculpatory." If a statement made were in fact truly exculpatory it would, of course, never be used by the prosecution. In fact, statements merely intended to be exculpatory by the defendant are often used to impeach his testimony at trial or to demonstrate untruths in the statement given under interrogation and thus to prove guilt by implication. These statements are incriminating in any meaningful sense of the word and may not be used without the full warnings and effective waiver required for any other statement. In *Escobedo* itself, the defendant fully intended his accusation of another as the slayer to be exculpatory as to himself.

The principles announced today deal with the protection which must be given to the privilege against self-incrimination when the individual is first subjected to police interrogation while in custody at the station or otherwise deprived of his freedom of action in any significant way. It is at this point that our adversary system of criminal proceedings commences, distinguishing itself at the outset from the inquisitorial system recognized in some countries. Under the system of warnings we delineate today or under any other system which may be devised and found effective, the safeguards to be erected about the privilege must come into play at this point.

V

Because of the nature of the problem and because of its recurrent significance in numerous cases, we have to this point discussed the relationship of the Fifth Amendment privilege to police interrogation without specific concentration on the facts of the cases before us. We turn now to these facts to consider the application to these cases of the constitutional principles discussed above. In each instance, we have concluded that statements were obtained from the defendant under circumstances that did not meet constitutional standards for protection of the privilege.

No. 759. *Miranda v. Arizona.*

On March 13, 1963, petitioner, Ernesto Miranda, was arrested at his home and taken in custody to a Phoenix police station. He was there identified by the complaining witness. The police then took him to "Interrogation Room No. 2" of the detective bureau. There he was questioned by two police officers. The officers admitted at trial that Miranda was not advised that he had a right to have an attorney present. Two hours later, the officers emerged from the interrogation room with a written confession signed by Miranda. At the top of the statement was a typed paragraph stating that the confession was made voluntarily, without threats or promises of immunity and "with full knowledge of my legal rights, understanding any statement I make may be used against me."

At his trial before a jury, the written confession was admitted into evidence over the objection of defense counsel, and the officers testified to the prior oral confession made by Miranda during the interrogation. Miranda was found guilty of kidnapping and rape. He was sentenced to 20 to 30 years' imprisonment on each count, the sentences to run concurrently. On appeal, the Supreme Court of Arizona held that Miranda's constitutional rights were not violated in obtaining the confession and affirmed the conviction. In reaching its decision, the court emphasized heavily the fact that Miranda did not specifically request counsel.

We reverse. From the testimony of the officers and by the admission of respondent, it is clear that Miranda was not in any way apprised of his right to consult with an attorney and to have one present during the interrogation, nor was his right not to be compelled to incriminate himself effectively protected in any other manner. Without these warnings the statements were inadmissible. The mere fact that he signed a statement which contained a typed-in clause stating that he had "full knowledge" of his "legal rights" does not approach the knowing and intelligent waiver required to relinquish constitutional rights.

No. 760. *Vignera v. New York.* 

Petitioner, Michael Vignera, was picked up by New York police on October 14, 1960, in connection with the robbery three days earlier of a Brooklyn dress shop. They took him to the 17th Detective Squad headquarters in Manhattan. Sometime thereafter he was taken to the 66th Detective Squad. There a detective questioned Vignera with respect to the robbery. Vignera orally admitted the robbery to the detective. The detective was asked on cross-examination at trial by defense counsel whether Vignera was warned of his right to counsel before being interrogated. The prosecution objected to the question and the trial judge sustained the objection. Thus, the defense was precluded from making any showing that warnings had not been given. While at the 66th Detective Squad, Vignera was identified by the store owner and a saleslady as the man who robbed the dress shop. At about 3 p.m. he was formally arrested. The police then transported him to still another station, the 70th Precinct in Brooklyn, "for detention." At 11 p.m. Vignera was questioned by an assistant district attorney in the presence of a hearing reporter who transcribed the questions and Vignera's answers. This verbatim account of these proceedings contains no statement of any warnings given by the assistant district attorney. At Vignera's trial on a charge of first degree robbery, the detective testified as to the oral confession. The transcription of the statement taken was also introduced in evidence. At the conclusion of the testimony, the trial judge charged the jury in part as follows:

> The law doesn't say that the confession is void or invalidated because the police officer didn't advise the defendant as to his rights. Did you hear what I said? I am telling you what the law of the State of New York is.

Vignera was found guilty of first degree robbery. He was subsequently adjudged a third-felony offender and sentenced to 30 to 60 years' imprisonment.

We reverse. The foregoing indicates that Vignera was not warned of any of his rights before the questioning by the detective and by the assistant district attorney. No other steps were taken to protect these rights. Thus he was not effectively apprised of his Fifth Amendment privilege or of his right to have counsel present and his statements are inadmissible.

No. 761. *Westover v. United States.*

At approximately 9:45 p.m. on March 20, 1963, petitioner, Carl Calvin Westover, was arrested by local police in Kansas City as a suspect in two Kansas City robberies. A report was also received from the FBI that he was wanted on a felony charge in California. The local authorities took him to a police station and placed him in a line-up on the local charges, and at about 11:45 p.m. he was booked. Kansas City police interrogated Westover on the night of his arrest. He denied any knowledge of criminal activities. The next day local officers interrogated him again throughout the morning. Shortly before noon they informed the FBI that they were through interrogating Westover and that the FBI could proceed to interrogate him. There is nothing in the record to indicate that Westover was ever given any warning as to his rights by local police. At noon, three special agents of the FBI continued the interrogation in a private interview room of the Kansas City Police Department, this time with respect to the robbery of a savings and loan association and a bank in Sacramento, California. After two or two and one-half hours, Westover signed separate confessions to each of these two robberies which had been prepared by one of the agents during the interrogation. At trial one of the agents testified, and a paragraph on each of the statements states, that the agents advised Westover that he did not have to make a statement, that any statement he made could be used against him, and that he had the right to see an attorney.

Westover was tried by a jury in federal court and convicted of the California robberies. His statements were introduced at trial. He was sentenced to 15 years' imprisonment on each count, the sentences to run consecutively.

We reverse. On the facts of this case we cannot find that Westover knowingly and intelligently waived his right to remain silent and his right to consult with counsel prior to the time he made the statement. At the time the FBI agents began questioning Westover, he had been in custody for over 14 hours and had been interrogated at length during that period. The FBI interrogation began immediately upon the conclusion of the interrogation by Kansas City police and was conducted in local police headquarters. Although the two law enforcement authorities are legally distinct and the crimes for which they interrogated Westover were different, the impact on him was that of a continuous period of questioning. There is no evidence of any warning given prior to the FBI interrogation nor is there any evidence of an articulated waiver of rights after the FBI commenced its interrogation. The record simply shows that the defendant did in fact confess a short time after being turned over to the FBI following interrogation by local police. Despite the fact that the FBI agents gave warnings at the outset of their interview, from Westover's point of view the warnings came at the end of the interrogation process. In these circumstances an intelligent waiver of constitutional rights cannot be assumed.

We do not suggest that law enforcement authorities are precluded from questioning any individual who has been held for a period of time by other authorities and interrogated by them without appropriate warnings. A different case would be presented if an accused were taken into custody by the second authority, removed both in time and place from his original surroundings, and then adequately advised of his rights and given an opportunity to exercise them. But here the FBI interrogation was conducted immediately following the state interrogation in the same police station — in the same compelling surroundings. Thus, in obtaining a confession from Westover the federal authorities were the beneficiaries of the pressure applied by the local in-custody interrogation. In these circumstances the giving of warnings alone was not sufficient to protect the privilege.

No. 584. *California v. Stewart.*

In the course of investigating a series of purse-snatch robberies in which one of the victims had died of injuries inflicted by her assailant, respondent, Roy Allen Stewart, was pointed out to Los Angeles police as the endorser of dividend checks taken in one of the robberies. At about 7:15 p.m., January 31, 1963, police officers went to Stewart's house and arrested him. One of the officers asked Stewart if they could search the house, to which he replied, "Go ahead." The search turned up various items taken from the five robbery victims. At the time of Stewart's arrest, police also arrested Stewart's wife and three other persons who were visiting him. These four were jailed along with Stewart and were interrogated. Stewart was taken to the University Station of the Los Angeles Police Department where he was placed in a cell. During the next five days, police interrogated Stewart on nine different occasions. Except during the first interrogation session, when he was confronted with an accusing witness, Stewart was isolated with his interrogators.

During the ninth interrogation session, Stewart admitted that he had robbed the deceased and stated that he had not meant to hurt her. Police then brought Stewart before a magistrate for the first time. Since there was no evidence to connect them with any crime, the police then released the other four persons arrested with him.

Nothing in the record specifically indicates whether Stewart was or was not advised of his right to remain silent or his right to counsel. In a number of instances, however, the interrogating officers were asked to recount everything that was said during the interrogations. None indicated that Stewart was ever advised of his rights.

Stewart was charged with kidnapping to commit robbery, rape, and murder. At his trial, transcripts of the first interrogation and the confession at the last interrogation were introduced in evidence. The jury found Stewart guilty of robbery and first degree murder and fixed the penalty as death. On appeal, the Supreme Court of California reversed.

It held that under this Court's decision in *Escobedo*, Stewart should have been advised of his right to remain silent and of his right to counsel and that it would not presume in the face of a silent record that the police advised Stewart of his rights.

We affirm. In dealing with custodial interrogation, we will not presume that a defendant has been effectively apprised of his rights and that his privilege against self-incrimination has been adequately safeguarded on a record that does not show that any warnings have been given or that any effective alternative has been employed. Nor can a knowing and intelligent waiver of these rights be assumed on a silent record. Furthermore, Stewart's steadfast denial of the alleged offenses through eight of the nine interrogations over a period of five days is subject to no other construction than that he was compelled by persistent interrogation to forgo his Fifth Amendment privilege.

Mr. Justice Clark, dissenting in Nos. 759, 760, and 761, and concurring in the result in No. 584.

It is with regret that I find it necessary to write in these cases. However, I am unable to join the majority because its opinion goes too far on too little, while my dissenting brethren do not go quite far enough. Nor can I join in the Court's criticism of the present practices of police and investigatory agencies as to custodial interrogation. The materials it refers to as "police manuals" are, as I read them, merely writings in this field by professors and some police officers. Not one is shown by the record here to be the official manual of any police department, much less in universal use in crime detection. Moreover, the examples of police brutality mentioned by the Court are rare exceptions to the thousands of cases that appear every year in the law reports. The police agencies — all the way from municipal and state forces to the federal bureaus — are responsible for law enforcement and public safety in this country. I am proud of their efforts, which in my view are not fairly characterized by the Court's opinion.

I

The *ipse dixit* of the majority has no support in our cases. Indeed, the Court admits that "we might not find the defendants' statements [here] to have been involuntary in traditional terms."

In short, the Court has added more to the requirements that the accused is entitled to consult with his lawyer and that he must be given the traditional warning that he may remain silent and that anything that he says may be used against him. Now, the Court fashions a constitutional rule that the police may engage in no custodial interrogation without additionally advising the accused that he has a right under the Fifth Amendment to the presence of counsel during interrogation and that, if he is without funds, counsel will be furnished him. When at any point during an interrogation the accused seeks affirmatively or impliedly to invoke his rights to silence or counsel, interrogation must be forgone or postponed. The Court further holds that failure to follow the new procedures requires inexorably the exclusion of any statement by the accused, as well as the fruits thereof. Such a strict constitutional specific inserted at the nerve center of crime detection may well kill the patient.

Since there is at this time a paucity of information and an almost total lack of empirical knowledge on the practical operation of requirements truly comparable to those announced by the majority, I would be more restrained lest we go too far too fast.

III

. . . I would consider in each case whether the police officer prior to custodial interrogation added the warning that the suspect might have counsel present at the interrogation and, further, that a court would appoint one at his request if he was too poor to employ counsel. In the absence of warnings, the burden would be on the State to prove that counsel was knowingly and intelligently waived or that in the totality of the circumstances, including the failure to give the necessary warnings, the confession was clearly voluntary.

MR. JUSTICE HARLAN, whom MR. JUSTICE STEWART and MR. JUSTICE WHITE join, dissenting.

I believe the decision of the Court represents poor constitutional law and entails harmful consequences for the country at large. How serious these consequences may prove to be only time can tell. But the basic flaws in the Court's justification seem to me readily apparent now once all sides of the problem are considered.

I. INTRODUCTION

At the outset, it is well to note exactly what is required by the Court's new constitutional code of rules for confessions. The foremost requirement, upon which later admissibility of a confession depends, is that a fourfold warning be given to a person in custody before he is questioned. . . .

While the fine points of this scheme are far less clear than the Court admits, the tenor is quite apparent. The new rules are not designed to guard against police brutality or other unmistakably banned forms of coercion. Those who use third-degree tactics and deny them in court are equally able and destined to lie as skillfully about warnings and waivers. Rather, the thrust of the new rules is to negate all pressures, to reinforce the nervous or ignorant suspect, and ultimately to discourage any confession at all. The aim in short is toward "voluntariness" in a utopian sense, or to view it from a different angle, voluntariness with a vengeance.

II. CONSTITUTIONAL PREMISES

It is most fitting to begin an inquiry into the constitutional precedents by surveying the limits on confessions the Court has evolved under the Due Process Clause of the Fourteenth Amendment. This is so because these cases show that there exists a workable and effective means of dealing with confessions in a judicial manner; because the cases are the baseline from which the Court now departs and so serve to measure the actual as opposed to the professed distance it travels; and because examination of them helps reveal how the Court has coasted into its present position.

There are several relevant lessons to be drawn from this constitutional history. The first is that with over 25 years of precedent the Court has developed an elaborate, sophisticated, and sensitive approach to admissibility of confessions. It is "judicial" in its treatment of one case at a time, flexible in its ability to respond to the endless mutations of fact presented, and ever more familiar to the lower courts.

Of course, strict certainty is not obtained in this developing process, but this is often so with constitutional principles, and disagreement is usually confined to that borderland of close cases where it matters least.

The second point is that in practice and from time to time in principle, the Court has given ample recognition to society's interest in suspect questioning as an instrument of law enforcement. Cases countenancing quite significant pressures can be cited without difficulty and the lower courts may often have been yet more tolerant. Of course the limitations imposed today were rejected by necessary implication in case after case, the right to warnings having been explicitly rebuffed in this Court many years ago.

I turn now to the Court's asserted reliance on the Fifth Amendment, an approach which I frankly regard as a *trompe l'oeil*. The Court's opinion in my view reveals no adequate basis for extending the Fifth Amendment's privilege against self-incrimination to the police station. Far more important, it fails to show that the Court's new rules are well supported, let alone compelled, by Fifth Amendment precedents. Instead, the new rules actually derive from quotation and analogy drawn from precedents under the Sixth Amendment, which should properly have no bearing on police interrogation.

The Court's opening contention, that the Fifth Amendment governs police station confessions, is perhaps not an impermissible extension of the law but it has little to commend itself in the present circumstances. Historically, the privilege against self-incrimination did not bear at all on the use of extra-legal confessions, for which distinct standards evolved; indeed, "the *history* of the two principles is wide apart, differing by one hundred years in origin, and derived through separate lines of precedents. . . ."

Practice under the two doctrines has also differed in a number of important respects.

Even those who would readily enlarge the privilege must concede some linguistic difficulties since the Fifth Amendment in terms proscribes only compelling any person "in any criminal case to be a witness against himself."

Having decided that the Fifth Amendment privilege does apply in the police station, the Court reveals that the privilege imposes more exacting restrictions than does the Fourteenth Amendment's voluntariness test.

It then emerges from a discussion of *Escobedo* that the Fifth Amendment requires for an admissible confession that it be given by one distinctly aware of his right not to speak and shielded from "the compelling atmosphere" of interrogation.

From these key premises, the Court finally develops the safeguards of warning, counsel, and so forth. I do not believe these premises are sustained by precedents under the Fifth Amendment.[21]

III. POLICY CONSIDERATIONS

Without at all subscribing to the generally black picture of police conduct painted by the Court, I think it must be frankly recognized at the outset that police questioning allowable under due process precedents may inherently entail some pressure on the suspect and may seek advantage in his ignorance or weaknesses. The atmosphere and questioning techniques, proper and fair though they be, can in themselves exert a tug on the suspect to confess, and in this light "[t]o speak of any confessions of crime made after arrest as being 'voluntary' or 'uncoerced' is somewhat inaccurate, although traditional. A confession is wholly and incontestably voluntary only if a guilty person gives himself up to the law and becomes his own accuser."

Until today, the role of the Constitution has been only to sift out *undue* pressure, not to assure spontaneous confessions.

The Court's new rules aim to offset these minor pressures and disadvantages intrinsic to any kind of police interrogation. The rules do not serve due process

[21] [9] I lay aside *Escobedo* itself; it contains no reasoning or even general conclusions addressed to the Fifth Amendment and indeed its citation in this regard seems surprising in view of *Escobedo*'s primary reliance on the Sixth Amendment.

interests in preventing blatant coercion since, as I noted earlier, they do nothing to contain the policeman who is prepared to lie from the start. The rules work for reliability in confessions almost only in the Pickwickian sense that they can prevent some from being given at all.[22] In short, the benefit of this new regime is simply to lessen or wipe out the inherent compulsion and inequalities to which the Court devotes some nine pages of description.

What the Court largely ignores is that its rules impair, if they will not eventually serve wholly to frustrate, an instrument of law enforcement that has long and quite reasonably been thought worth the price paid for it.[23] There can be little doubt that the Court's new code would markedly decrease the number of confessions. To warn the suspect that he may remain silent and remind him that his confession may be used in court are minor obstructions. To require also an express waiver by the suspect and an end to questioning whenever he demurs must heavily handicap questioning. And to suggest or provide counsel for the suspect simply invites the end of the interrogation.

MR. JUSTICE WHITE, with whom MR. JUSTICE HARLAN and MR. JUSTICE STEWART join, dissenting.

Even if one were to postulate that the Court's concern is not that all confessions induced by police interrogation are coerced but rather that some such confessions are coerced and present judicial procedures are believed to be inadequate to identify the confessions that are coerced and those that are not, it would still not be essential to impose the rule that the Court has now fashioned. Transcripts or observers could be required, specific time limits, tailored to fit the cause, could be imposed, or other devices could be utilized to reduce the chances that otherwise indiscernible coercion will produce an inadmissible confession.

NOTES AND QUESTIONS: THE MEANING OF THE OPINIONS

(1) *Miranda* precipitated more prolonged criticism than any other criminal law ruling of the Supreme Court. Not only were the narrow holdings in the cases questioned, but the broad rules created were also challenged. Were these rules necessary? Justice Clark argued for a case-by-case approach with some emphasis placed on the failure of the officers to warn the suspect. Justice Harlan asserted that the Court's "elaborate, sophisticated, and sensitive approach to admissibility of confessions," as developed over decades, was sufficient to handle the questions

[22] [12] The court's vision of a lawyer "mitigat[ing] the dangers of untrustworthiness" by witnessing coercion and assisting accuracy in the confession is largely a fancy; for if counsel arrives, there is rarely going to be a police station confession. Watts v. State of Indiana (separate opinion of Jackson, J.): "[A]ny lawyer worth his salt will tell the suspect in no uncertain terms to make no statement to police under any circumstances."

[23] [13] This need is, of course, what makes so misleading the Court's comparison of a probate judge readily setting aside as involuntary the will of an old lady badgered and beleaguered by the new heirs. With wills, there is no public interest save in a totally free choice; with confessions, the solution of crime is a countervailing gain, however the balance is resolved.

raised in *Miranda*. Why did a majority of the Court reject these two approaches? Are the broad based rules of the Court preferable?

The debate over *Miranda* has become far more muted in light of the Court's holding in *Dickerson v. United States*, 530 U.S. 428 (2000). The Court there faced a direct challenge to the *Miranda* holding. In a 7-2 decision, the Chief Justice ruled that the Court would not overrule *Miranda*, and further that the Court's landmark opinion was indeed constitutionally grounded in the Fifth Amendment privilege against self-incrimination.

> [W]e have repeatedly referred to the *Miranda* warnings as "prophylactic," and "not themselves rights protected by the Constitution," [so] the Court of Appeals concluded that the protections announced in *Miranda* are not constitutionally required.
>
> We disagree with the Court of Appeals' conclusion, although we concede that there is language in some of our opinions that supports the view taken by that court. But first and foremost of the factors on the other side — that *Miranda* is a constitutional decision — is that both *Miranda* and two of its companion cases applied the rule to proceedings in state courts — to wit, Arizona, California, and New York. Since that time, we have consistently applied *Miranda's* rule to prosecutions arising in state courts. It is beyond dispute that we do not hold a supervisory power over the courts of the several States. ("Federal courts hold no supervisory authority over state judicial proceedings and may intervene only to correct wrongs of constitutional dimension.") With respect to proceedings in state courts, our "authority is limited to enforcing the commands of the United States Constitution." "Federal judges may not require the observance of any special procedures" in state courts "except when necessary to assure compliance with the dictates of the Federal Constitution."
>
> The *Miranda* opinion itself begins by stating that the Court granted certiorari "to explore some facets of the problems . . . of applying the privilege against self-incrimination to in-custody interrogation, *and to give concrete constitutional guidelines for law enforcement agencies and courts to follow.*" In fact, the majority opinion is replete with statements indicating that the majority thought it was announcing a constitutional rule. Indeed, the Court's ultimate conclusion was that the unwarned confessions obtained in the four cases before the Court in *Miranda* "were obtained from the defendant under circumstances that did not meet constitutional standards for protection of the privilege."
>
> Additional support for our conclusion that *Miranda* is constitutionally based is found in the *Miranda* Court's invitation for legislative action to protect the constitutional right against coerced self-incrimination. After discussing the "compelling pressures" inherent in custodial police interrogation, the *Miranda* Court concluded that, "in order to combat these pressures and to permit a full opportunity to exercise the privilege against self-incrimination, the accused must be adequately and effectively appraised of his rights and the exercise of those rights must be fully honored." However, the Court emphasized that it could not foresee "the potential

alternatives for protecting the privilege which might be devised by Congress or the States," and it accordingly opined that the Constitution would not preclude legislative solutions that differed from the prescribed *Miranda* warnings but which were "at least as effective. . . ."

(2) The Chief Justice placed heavy reliance on the Court's opinion in *Escobedo*, characterizing the decision there as an "explication" of both the right to counsel and the privilege against self-incrimination. Was such reliance proper? Was *Escobedo* a case involving the self-incrimination clause of the Fifth Amendment? A footnote in Justice Harlan's opinion responds to this point:

> I lay aside *Escobedo* itself; it contains no reasoning or even general conclusions addressed to the Fifth Amendment and indeed its citation in this regard seems surprising in view of *Escobedo*'s primary reliance on the Sixth Amendment.

(3) At several points in the majority opinion the Court wrote that it did not intend to limit legislative reforms in this area. Are there legislative approaches which would be "fully effective means . . . devised to inform accused persons of their right of silence and to assure a continuous opportunity to exercise it. . . ."? Would the alternatives suggested by Justice White (e.g., observers, time limits for questioning) be effective? The actual legislative response to *Miranda* has been something short of enthusiastic. 18 U.S.C. § 3501, the subject of the *Dickerson* opinion, provides:

> (a) In any criminal prosecution brought by the United States or by the District of Columbia, a confession . . . shall be admissible in evidence if it is voluntarily given. . . .
>
> (b) The trial judge in determining the issue of voluntariness shall take into consideration all the circumstances surrounding the giving of the confession, including: (1) the time elapsing between arrest and arraignment of the defendant making the confessions, if it was made after arrest and before arraignment, (2) whether such defendant knew the nature of the offense with which he was charged or of which he was suspected at the time of making the confession, (3) whether or not such defendant was advised or knew that he was not required to make any statement and that any such statement could be used against him, (4) whether or not such defendant had been advised prior to questioning of his right to the assistance of counsel, and (5) whether or not such defendant was without the assistance of counsel when questioned and when giving such confession.
>
> The presence or absence of any of the above-mentioned factors to be taken into consideration by the judge need not be conclusive on the issue of voluntariness of the confession.

Is § 3501 consistent with *Miranda*? Is it constitutional under *Miranda*? In a striking development, the United States Court of Appeals for the Fourth Circuit — over a vigorous dissent — held that § 3501, not *Miranda*, governs confessions in the federal courts. The decision was especially unusual because neither of the parties raised the § 3501 claim. *Dickerson,* of course, struck down the Fourth Circuit decision. The Supreme Court made two key findings. First, "Congress intended by its enactment to overrule *Miranda.*" Second, "Congress may not legislatively supersede our decisions interpreting and applying the Constitution." Because *Miranda* "announced a constitutional rule, [and did not] merely exercise its supervisory authority to regulate evidence," § 3501 was invalidated.

(4) Does *Miranda* apply in all criminal cases? In *Berkemer v. McCarty*, 468 U.S. 420 (1984), the Supreme Court ruled unanimously that *Miranda* does not apply to routine traffic stops. In that case the driver was pulled over and he then admitted to being under the influence of alcohol.

> The vast majority of roadside detentions last only a few minutes. A motorist's expectations, when he sees a policeman's light flashing behind him, are that he will be obliged to spend a short period of time answering questions and waiting while the officer checks his license and registration, that he may be given a citation, but that in the end he most likely will be allowed to continue on his way.

The Court went on, however, to find that the warnings must be given whenever a suspect is in police custody, whether that person is being held for a serious crime or for a minor offense.

(5) The holding in *Miranda*, though extremely clear in some ways, gave rise to a number of questions, which will be explored in the sections which follow. One of them was resolved in *Chavez v. Martinez*, 538 U.S. 760 (2003). There the Court held that the Fifth Amendment is not implicated unless the resulting confession — in violation of *Miranda* — is actually offered in evidence against the individual at a criminal trial. In that case the officer engaged in harsh questioning which was arguably improper under both *Miranda* and the Due Process Clause. The individual was not, however, charged with a criminal offense. He then brought a civil suit for damages due to the *Miranda* claim.

(6) Are the warnings still required if a state takes steps to insure a voluntary response by the accused? Recall that portion of the lead opinion which discussed alternatives:

> It is impossible for us to foresee the potential alternatives for protecting the privilege which might be devised by Congress or the States in the exercise of their creative rule-making capacities. Therefore we cannot say that the Constitution necessarily requires adherence to any particular solution for the inherent compulsions of the interrogation process as it is presently conducted. Our decision in no way creates a constitutional straitjacket which will handicap sound efforts at reform, nor is it intended to have this effect. We encourage Congress and the States to continue their laudable search for increasingly effective ways of protecting the rights of the individual while promoting efficient enforcement of our criminal laws.

Several states require electronic recording of stationhouse confessions as a condition of trial admissibility. Section 103-2.1 of ILL. STAT. ANN. 725 ILCS 5/103-2.1 provides:

> (b) An oral, written, or sign language statement of an accused made as a result of a custodial interrogation at a police station or other place of

> detention shall be presumed to be inadmissible as evidence against the accused in any criminal proceeding . . . of the Criminal Code of 1961 . . . unless:
>
> (1) an electronic recording is made of the custodial interrogation; and
>
> (2) the recording is substantially accurate and not intentionally altered.
>
> (c) Every electronic recording required under this Section must be preserved until such time as the defendant's conviction for any offense relating to the statements is final and all direct and habeas corpus appeals are exhausted, or the prosecution of such offenses is barred by law.
>
> (d) If the court finds, by a preponderance of the evidence, that the defendant was subjected to a custodial interrogation in violation of this Section, then any statements made by the defendant during or following that non-recorded custodial interrogation, even if otherwise in compliance with this Section, are presumed to be inadmissible in any criminal proceeding against the defendant except for the purposes of impeachment.

The New Jersey Supreme Court exercised its supervisory authority over the administration of the state criminal court system and promulgated a rule which requires electronic recordation of "custodial interrogations conducted in a place of detention" in virtually all serious criminal offenses. *State v. Cook*, 847 A.2d 530 (N.J. 2004).

PROBLEM D
TESTIMONIAL RESPONSES

In *Pennsylvania v. Muniz*, 496 U.S. 582 (1990), the Supreme Court refined the *Miranda* requirements by focusing on the element of "testimonial responses" to custodial interrogation. The Court held that conduct displayed by the defendant during sobriety tests (slurred speech, answers to routine booking questions, etc.) was not "testimonial" and thus *Miranda* did not apply. The Court did find, however, that answers given in response to questions requiring substantive content ("When you turned six years old, do you remember what the date was?") were testimonial. The correct test was whether "the suspect confronts the 'trilemma' of truth, falsity, or silence."

PROBLEM E
PUBLIC SAFETY

The defendant in *New York v. Quarles*, 467 U.S. 649 (1984), was suspected of having committed the crime of rape. He was cornered in a supermarket and was immediately asked where his gun was. He gave an incriminating answer to the question. No *Miranda* warnings were given. Could the statement be used against him? Held, it was admissible. Then-Justice Rehnquist explained:

> We conclude that the need for answers to questions in a situation posing a threat to the public safety outweighs the need for the prophylactic rule protecting the Fifth Amendment's privilege against self-incrimination. We decline to place officers in the untenable position of having to consider,

often in a matter of seconds, whether it best serves society for them to ask the necessary questions without the *Miranda* warnings and render whatever probative evidence they uncover inadmissible, or for them to give the warnings in order to preserve the admissibility of evidence they might uncover but possibly damage or destroy their ability to obtain that evidence and neutralize the volatile situation confronting them.

Justice O'Connor dissented.

> In my view, a "public safety" exception unnecessarily blurs the edges of the clear line heretofore established and makes *Miranda*'s requirements more difficult to understand. In some cases, police will benefit because a reviewing court will find that an exigency excused their failure to administer the required warnings. But in other cases, police will suffer because, though they thought an exigency excused their noncompliance, a reviewing court will view the "objective" circumstances differently and require exclusion of admissions thereby obtained.

Justice Marshall (joined by Justices Brennan and Stevens) was even stronger in his dissent.

> The policies underlying the Fifth Amendment's privilege against self-incrimination are not diminished simply because testimony is compelled to protect the public's safety. The majority should not be permitted to elude the Amendment's absolute prohibition simply by calculating special costs that arise when the public's safety is at issue. Indeed, were constitutional adjudication always conducted in such an *ad hoc* manner, the Bill of Rights would be a most unreliable protector of individual liberties.

Some courts have added to the "public safety exception" by establishing a "rescue exception." Non-compliance with *Miranda* will be excused where no other action is possible and where the saving of a human life is the primary motive behind the questioning. *See People v. Panah*, 107 P.3d 790 (Cal. 2005); *State v. Provost*, 490 N.W.2d 93 (Minn. 1992), *cert. denied*, 507 U.S. 929 (1993). Still, the government cannot simply allege an "immediate need," it must demonstrate why *Miranda* should not be applied under the circumstances. *See United States v. Mobley*, 40 F.3d 688 (4th Cir. 1994), *cert. denied*, 514 U.S. 1129 (1995). *Quarles* is also discussed in Chapter 6, *infra.*

NOTES AND QUESTIONS
THE WARNINGS

(1) In *Colorado v. Spring*, 479 U.S. 564 (1987), the defendant was suspected of illegal arms sales and murder. He was arrested at the scene of an undercover firearms operation and given his *Miranda* warnings. Thereafter he confessed to the murder. He argued that the confession should be inadmissible because he was unaware he would be questioned about the murder when he waived his right to remain silent. Held, the confession is admissible:

> There is no doubt that Spring's decision to waive his Fifth Amendment privilege was voluntary. He alleges no "coercion of a confession by physical

> violence or other deliberate means calculated to break [his] will," and the trial court found none. His allegation that the police failed to supply him with certain information does not relate to any of the traditional indicia of coercion: "the duration and conditions of detention . . . , the manifest attitude of the police toward him, his physical and mental state, the diverse pressures which sap or sustain his powers of resistance and self-control."
>
> Absent evidence that Spring's "will [was] overborne and his capacity for self-determination critically impaired" because of coercive police conduct, his waiver of his Fifth Amendment privilege was voluntary under this Court's decision in *Miranda*.
>
> There also is no doubt that Spring's waiver of his Fifth Amendment privilege was knowingly and intelligently made: that is, that Spring understood that he had the right to remain silent and that anything he said could be used as evidence against him. The Constitution does not require that a criminal suspect know and understand every possible consequence of a waiver of the Fifth Amendment privilege. The Fifth Amendment's guarantee is both simpler and more fundamental: A defendant may not be compelled to be a witness against himself in any respect. The *Miranda* warnings protect this privilege by ensuring that a suspect knows that he may choose not to talk to law enforcement officers, to talk only with counsel present, or to discontinue talking at any time. The *Miranda* warnings ensure that a waiver of these rights is knowing and intelligent by requiring that the suspect be fully advised of this constitutional privilege, including the critical advice that whatever he chooses to say may be used as evidence against him.

(2) Do the police officers have to give the defendant the *Miranda* warnings if the defendant tells them that he knows his rights and wants to talk? The defendant in *State v. Ross*, 157 N.W.2d 860 (Neb. 1968), told the police that "he knew his rights better than the officer." Held, the failure to give the *Miranda* warnings was error, "can anyone be sure that he was fully informed of those rights unless the full *Miranda* warning was given?" See also *State v. Avila*, 527 P.2d 1221 (1974), where the defendant was advised as follows:

> . . . Now, Jake, you know what your rights are. And, the best thing you can do now is to not make any statement, because I'll have to repeat it in Court. We have been over this before, you know what your rights are. Anything you don't want me to repeat, don't even tell me. . . .

In response the defendant said: ". . . No, you have shot square with me so far, never hassled me or anything." He said, "That's the way it is, I've got to have it. I've got to have some relief. . . ." The court held that the warnings given were not in compliance with *Miranda* and constituted error even though the defendant might have generally known, as stated by the police, what his rights were. Do the rulings in *Ross* and *Avila* make sense? Why do the officers have to give the warnings after the defendant has indicated that she understands her rights? Would the warnings be required if the defendant were a police officer who clearly knew the rights? Yes, said the court in *United States v. Street*, 472 F.3d 1298 (11th Cir. 2006).

CALIFORNIA v. PRYSOCK

United States Supreme Court
453 U.S. 355 (1981)

PER CURIAM.

This case presents the question whether the warnings given to respondent prior to a recorded conversation with a police officer satisfied the requirements of *Miranda v. Arizona.* Although ordinarily this Court would not be inclined to review a case involving application of that precedent to a particular set of facts, the opinion of the California Court of Appeal essentially laid down a flat rule requiring that the content of *Miranda* warnings be a virtual incantation of the precise language contained in the *Miranda* opinion. Because such a rigid rule was not mandated by *Miranda* or any other decision of this Court, and is not required to serve the purposes of *Miranda*, we grant the motion of respondent for leave to proceed *in forma pauperis* and the petition for certiorari and reverse.

On January 30, 1978, Mrs. Donna Iris Erickson was brutally murdered. Later that evening respondent and a codefendant were apprehended for commission of the offense. Respondent was brought to a substation of the Tulare County Sheriff's Department and advised of his *Miranda* rights. He declined to talk and, since he was a minor, his parents were notified. Respondent's parents arrived and after meeting with them respondent decided to answer police questions. An officer questioned respondent, on tape, with respondent's parents present. The tape reflects that the following warnings were given prior to any questioning:

Sgt. Byrd: . . . Mr. Randall James Prysock, earlier today I advised you of your legal rights and at that time you advised me you did not wish to talk to me, is that correct?

Randall P.: Yeh.

Sgt. Byrd: And, uh, during, at the first interview your folks were not present, they are now present. I want to go through your legal rights again with you and after each legal right I would like for you to answer whether you understand it or not. . . . Your legal rights, Mr. Prysock, is [sic] follows: Number One, you have the right to remain silent. This means you don't have to talk to me at all unless you so desire. Do you understand this?

Randall P.: Yeh.

Sgt. Byrd: If you give up your right to remain silent, anything you say can and will be used as evidence against you in a court of law. Do you understand this?

Randall P.: Yes.

Sgt. Byrd: You have the right to talk to a lawyer before you are questioned, have him present with you while you are being questioned, and all during the questioning. Do you understand this?

Randall P.: Yes.

Sgt. Byrd: You also, being a juvenile, you have the right to have your parents present, which they are. Do you understand this?

Randall P.: Yes.

Sgt. Byrd: Even if they weren't here, you'd have this right. Do you understand this?

Randall P.: Yes.

Sgt. Byrd: You all, uh — if, — you have the right to have a lawyer appointed to represent you at no cost to yourself. Do you understand this?

Randall P.: Yes.

Sgt. Byrd: Now, having all these legal rights in mind, do you wish to talk to me at this time?

Randall P.: Yes.

At this point, at the request of Mrs. Prysock, a conversation took place with the tape recorder turned off. According to Sgt. Byrd, Mrs. Prysock asked if respondent could still have an attorney at a later time if he gave a statement now without one. Sgt. Byrd assured Mrs. Prysock that respondent would have an attorney when he went to court and that "he could have one at this time if he wished one."[24]

At trial in the Superior Court of Tulare County the court denied respondent's motion to suppress the taped statement. Respondent was convicted by a jury of first-degree murder with two special circumstances — torture and robbery. He was also convicted of robbery with the use of a dangerous weapon, burglary with the use of a deadly weapon, automobile theft, escape from a youth facility, and destruction

---

[24] [1] The tape reflects the following concerning the off-the-record discussion:

Sgt. Byrd: . . . Okay, Mrs. Prysock, you asked to get off the tape. . . . During that time you asked, decided you wanted some time to think about getting, whether to hire a lawyer or not.

Mrs. P.: 'Cause I didn't understand it.

Sgt. Byrd: And you have decided now that you want to go ahead and you do not wish a lawyer present at this time?

Mrs. P.: That's right.

Sgt. Byrd: And I have not persuaded you in any way, is that correct?

Mrs. P.: No, you have not.

Sgt. Byrd: And, Mr. Prysock is that correct that I have done nothing to persuade you not to, to hire a lawyer or to go on with this?

Mr. P.: That's right.

Sgt. Byrd: Okay, everything we're doing here is strictly in accordance with Randall and yourselves, is that correct?

Mr. P.: That is correct.

Sgt. Byrd: Okay, uh, all right. Randy, I can't remember where I left off, I think I asked you, uh, with your legal rights in mind, do you wish to talk to me at this time? This is with everything I told you, all your legal rights, your right to an attorney, your right, and your right to remain silent, and all these, I mean do you wish to talk to me at this time about the case?

Randall P.: Yes.

of evidence.

The Court of Appeal for the Fifth Appellate District reversed respondent's convictions and ordered a new trial because of what it thought to be error under *Miranda*. The Court of Appeal ruled that respondent's recorded incriminating statements, given with his parents present, had to be excluded from consideration by the jury because respondent was not properly advised of his right to the services of a free attorney before and during interrogation. Although respondent was indisputably informed that he had "the right to talk to a lawyer before you are questioned, have him present with you while you are being questioned, and all during the questioning," and further informed that he had "the right to have a lawyer appointed to represent you at no cost to yourself," the Court of Appeal ruled that these warnings were inadequate because respondent was not explicitly informed of his right to have an attorney appointed before further questioning. The Court of Appeal stated that "[O]ne of [*Miranda*'s] virtues is its precise requirements, which are so easily met." "The rigidity of the *Miranda* rules and the way in which they are to be applied was conceived of and continues to be recognized as the decision's greatest strength." . . . [T]he court ruled that the requirements of *Miranda* were not met in this case.

This Court has never indicated that the "rigidity" of *Miranda* extends to the precise formulation of the warnings given a criminal defendant. This Court and others *have* stressed as one virtue of *Miranda* the fact that the giving of the warnings obviates the need for a case-by-case inquiry into the actual voluntariness of the admissions of the accused. Nothing in these observations suggests any desirable rigidity in the *form* of the required warnings.

Quite the contrary, *Miranda* itself indicated that no talismanic incantation was required to satisfy its strictures. The Court in that case stated that "[t]he warnings required and the waiver necessary in accordance with our opinion today are, *in the absence of a fully effective equivalent*, prerequisites to the admissibility of any statement made by a defendant." Just last Term in considering when *Miranda* applied we noted that that decision announced procedural safeguards including "the now-familiar *Miranda* warnings . . . *or their equivalent*." *Rhode Island v. Innis*, 446 U.S. 291, 297, 100 S. Ct. 1682, 1688, 64 L. Ed. 2d 297 (1980) (emphasis supplied).

Other courts considering the precise question presented by this case — whether a criminal defendant was adequately informed of his right to the presence of appointed counsel prior to and during interrogation — have not required a verbatim recital of the words of the *Miranda* opinion but rather have examined the warnings given to determine if the reference to the right to appointed counsel was linked with some future point in time after the police interrogation. In *United States v. Garcia*, 431 F.2d 134 (CA9 1970) (*per curiam*), for example, the court found inadequate advice to the defendant that she could "have an attorney appointed to represent you when you first appear before the U.S. Commissioner or the Court." *People v. Bolinski* relied upon by the court below, is a case of this type. Two separate sets of warnings were ruled inadequate. In the first, the defendant was advised that "*if he was charged* . . . he would be appointed counsel." 260 Cal. App. 2d at 718 (emphasis supplied). In the second the defendant, then in Illinois and about to be moved to California, was advised that "the court would appoint [an attorney] *in Riverside*

County [California]." *Id.*, at 723 (emphasis supplied). In both instances the reference to appointed counsel was linked to a future point in time after police interrogation, and therefore did not fully advise the suspect of his right to appointed counsel before such interrogation.

Here, in contrast, nothing in the warnings given respondent suggested any limitation on the right to the presence of appointed counsel different from the clearly conveyed rights to a lawyer in general, including the right "to a lawyer before you are questioned, . . . while you are being questioned, and all during the questioning." Like *United States v. Noa*, 443 F.2d 144 (CA9 1971), where the warnings given were substantially similar to those given here and defendant's argument was the same as that adopted by the Court of Appeal, "[T]his is not a case in which the defendant was not informed of his right to the presence of an attorney during questioning . . . or in which the offer of an appointed attorney was associated with a future time in court. . . ."

It is clear that the police in this case fully conveyed to respondent his rights as required by *Miranda*. He was told of his right to have a lawyer present prior to and during interrogation, and his right to have a lawyer appointed at no cost if he could not afford one. These warnings conveyed to respondent his right to have a lawyer appointed if he could not afford one prior to and during interrogation. The Court of Appeal erred in holding that the warnings were inadequate simply because of the order in which they were given.[25]

Because respondent was given the warnings required by *Miranda*, the decision of the California Court of Appeal to the contrary is reversed, and the case is remanded for further proceedings not inconsistent with this opinion.

It is so ordered.

Justice Stevens, with whom Justice Brennan and Justice Marshall join, dissenting.

A juvenile informed by police that he has a right to counsel may understand that right to include one or more of three options: (1) that he has a right to have a lawyer represent him if he or his parents are able and willing to hire one; (2) that, if he cannot afford to hire an attorney, he has a right to have a lawyer represent him without charge *at trial*, even if his parents are unwilling to spend money on his

[25] [3] The dissent, arguing that the Court of Appeal opinion is unfairly criticized as requiring mimicking of *Miranda* ignores substantial portions of the opinion below and substitutes arguments of its own for those articulated by the Court of Appeals. For example, the dissent makes no mention of the lower court's stress on the "precise requirements" of *Miranda* or its "rigidity" in this area, and ignores the portion of the opinion in which the court quotes from *Miranda* and then criticizes the officer for not repeating the exact language in advising respondent of his rights.

The Court of Appeal did conclude that respondent was not advised of his right to appointed counsel prior to and during interrogation, but this was *because* the officer did not parrot the language of *Miranda*. The more substantive reasons suggested by the dissent are implausible. The reference to "appointed" counsel has never been considered as suggesting that the availability of counsel was postponed, and Mrs. Prysock's off-the-record conversation was occasioned by her fear that waiving the right to counsel at interrogation would occasion a waiver of the right to counsel later in court, clearly indicating that the officer conveyed the right to counsel at interrogation.

behalf; or (3) that, if he is unable to afford an attorney, he has a right to consult a lawyer without charge before he decides whether to talk to the police, even if his parents decline to pay for such legal representation.[26] All three of these options are encompassed within the right to counsel possessed by a juvenile charged with a crime. In this case, the first two options were explained to respondent, but the third was not.

In *Miranda v. Arizona*, this Court held that in order to protect an accused's privilege against self-incrimination, certain procedural safeguards must be employed. In particular, an individual taken into police custody and subjected to questioning must be given the *Miranda* warnings:

> He must be warned prior to any questioning that he has the right to remain silent, that anything he says can be used against him in a court of law, that he has the right to the presence of an attorney, and that if he cannot afford an attorney one will be appointed for him prior to any questioning if he so desires.

This formulation makes it clear beyond any doubt that an indigent accused has the right to the presence of an attorney and the right to have that attorney appointed to represent him prior to any questioning. While it is certainly true, as the Court emphasizes today, that the Federal Constitution does not require a "talismanic incantation" of the language of the *Miranda* opinion, it is also indisputable that it requires that an accused be adequately informed of his right to have counsel appointed prior to any police questioning.

The warning recited by the police sergeant is sufficiently ambiguous on its face to provide adequate support for the California court's finding. That court's conclusion is at least reasonable, and is clearly not so patently erroneous as to warrant summary reversal. The ambiguity in the warning given respondent is further demonstrated by the colloquy between the police sergeant and respondent's parents that occurred *after* respondent was told that he had the "right to have a lawyer appointed to represent you at no cost to yourself." Because lawyers are normally "appointed" by judges, and not by law enforcement officers, the reference to appointed counsel could reasonably have been understood to refer to trial counsel.[27] That is what respondent's parents must have assumed, because their ensuing colloquy with the sergeant related to their option "to *hire* a lawyer."

The judges on the California Court of Appeal and on the California Supreme Court, all of whom are presumably more familiar with the procedures followed by

---

26 [1] In his dissenting opinion in *Miranda v. Arizona*, 384 U.S. 436, 504, Justice Harlan accurately summarized the four essential elements of the warning that must be given a person in custody before he is questioned, "namely, that he has a right to remain silent, that anything he says may be used against him, that he has a right to have present an attorney during the questioning, and that if indigent he has a right to a lawyer without charge."

27 [3] The fact that the reference also might have been understood to refer to the appointment of counsel prior to questioning does not undercut the Court of Appeal's conclusion. *Miranda* requires "meaningful advice to the unlettered and unlearned in language which he can comprehend and on which he can knowingly act." Such meaningful advice is not provided by a warning which requires that an accused choose among several reasonable interpretations of the language employed by a police officer in a custodial situation.

California police officers than we are, concluded that respondent was not adequately informed of his right to have a lawyer present without charge during the questioning. This Court is not at all fair to those judges when it construes their conscientious appraisal of a somewhat ambiguous record as requiring "a virtual incantation of the precise language contained in the *Miranda* opinion." It seems clear to me that it is this Court, rather than the state courts, that is guilty of attaching greater importance to the form of the *Miranda* ritual than to the substance of the message it is intended to convey.

I respectfully dissent.

QUESTION

Were the warnings given in *Prysock* "the equivalent" of those discussed in *Miranda*? How about those given in *Florida v. Powell*, 559 U.S. 50 (2010)? There the arresting officer read the defendant this statement of rights:

> You have the right to remain silent. If you give up the right to remain silent, anything you say can be used against you in court. You have the right to talk to a lawyer before answering any of our questions. If you cannot afford to hire a lawyer, one will be appointed for you without cost and before any questioning. You have the right to use any of these rights at any time you want during this interview.

The state court reversed the conviction because the suspect had not been "clearly informed of his right to have counsel present during questioning." The Supreme Court disagreed.

> The Tampa officers did not "entirely omi[t]," any information *Miranda* required them to impart. They informed Powell that he had "the right to talk to a lawyer before answering any of [their] questions" and "the right to use any of [his] rights at any time [he] want[ed] during th[e] interview." The first statement communicated that Powell could consult with a lawyer before answering any particular question, and the second statement confirmed that he could exercise that right while the interrogation was underway. In combination, the two warnings reasonably conveyed Powell's right to have an attorney present, not only at the outset of interrogation, but at all times. . . . Although the warnings were not the *clearest possible* formulation of *Miranda*'s right-to-counsel advisement, they were sufficiently comprehensive and comprehensible when given a commonsense reading.

See also *Duckworth v. Eagan*, 492 U.S. 195 (1989), where the suspect was told that the police had no way of giving him a lawyer, but "one will be appointed for you, if you wish, if and when you go to court." The lower court found that this warning erroneously suggested that "only those accused who can afford an attorney have the right to have one present before answering any questions. . . ." The Supreme Court disagreed, in a 5-4 decision. Chief Justice Rehnquist wrote that the warnings here "touched all of the bases required by *Miranda*" as they did not indicate that the defendant could not have counsel present if he chose to answer questions.

While recognizing that the Supreme Court does not require strict reliance on the precise words in *Miranda*, some judges find that officers' embellishment of the mandate violates the Fifth Amendment. In *People v. Dunbar*, 104 A.D.3d 198 (N.Y. App. Div. 2013), the officers told the suspect — in a "preamble" to the *Miranda* warnings — that he would lose the chance to tell his side of the story unless he spoke immediately. The court was not pleased. "Simply put, suspects cannot knowingly and intelligently waive their rights if they are not effectively advised as to what those rights are, and the consequences of foregoing them. . . ." See also *United States v. Wysinger*, 683 F.3d 784 (7th Cir. 2012), where the defendant was told he could speak with a lawyer before questioning or during questioning. Held, the resulting statement was inadmissible, the officer's statement gave the defendant a "false choice."

For a sobering discussion of the understanding of the rights, see Rogers et al., *"Everyone Knows Their Miranda Rights": Implicit Assumptions and Countervailing Evidence*, 16 Psych. Pub. Pol. & L. 300 (2010).

CUSTODIAL INTERROGATIONS

To avoid problems with the wording of the warnings, and the circumstances when the warnings must be given, many metropolitan areas have developed specific guidelines and procedures regulating the giving of the warnings. The following form is typical of such efforts.

WARNING TO BE GIVEN BEFORE TAKING ANY ORAL OR WRITTEN CONFESSION

I. PURPOSE

This order:

A. defines custodial interrogation.

B. establishes guidelines for custodial interrogations to ensure conformance with the United States Supreme Court decision in *Miranda v. Arizona*, 384 U.S. 436 (1966).

II. DEFINITION

Custodial interrogation has been interpreted by the United States Supreme Court as "questioning initiated by law enforcement officers after a person has been taken into custody or has otherwise been deprived of his freedom of action [by the authorities] in any significant way."

III. ADVISING THE INDIVIDUAL OF HIS RIGHTS

A. Before interrogation of an individual who is in custody anywhere or who is in any way being deprived of his freedom of movement and action, the person must be expressly warned of his constitutional rights in clear and unequivocal words as follows:

1. YOU HAVE A RIGHT TO REMAIN SILENT.
2. IF YOU CHOOSE NOT TO REMAIN SILENT ANYTHING YOU SAY OR WRITE CAN AND WILL BE USED AGAINST YOU IN A COURT OF LAW.
3. YOU HAVE A RIGHT TO CONSULT A LAWYER BEFORE ANY QUESTIONING AND YOU HAVE A RIGHT TO HAVE THE LAWYER PRESENT WITH YOU DURING ANY QUESTIONING.
4. YOU NOT ONLY HAVE A RIGHT TO CONSULT WITH A LAWYER BEFORE ANY QUESTIONING BUT, IF YOU LACK THE FINANCIAL ABILITY TO RETAIN A LAWYER, A LAWYER WILL BE APPOINTED TO REPRESENT YOU BEFORE ANY QUESTIONING, AND YOU MAY HAVE THE APPOINTED LAWYER PRESENT WITH YOU DURING ANY QUESTIONING.
5. IF YOU CHOOSE NOT TO REMAIN SILENT AND DO NOT WISH TO CONSULT WITH A LAWYER OR HAVE THE LAWYER PRESENT, YOU STILL HAVE THE RIGHT TO REMAIN SILENT AND THE RIGHT TO CONSULT WITH A LAWYER AT ANY TIME DURING THE QUESTIONING.

B. These warnings must be stated orally by the police officer and not merely be read by the person to be questioned.

C. If a question answer statement is being typed, *EACH* of the warnings and the response of the person to *EACH* warning must also be included in that statement.

D. After ALL of the warnings have been orally recited, an EXPRESS STATEMENT by the person to be questioned that he UNDERSTANDS THE MEANING of what has been said and that he nonetheless WISHES TO ANSWER questions without speaking to a lawyer and without having a lawyer present also is ABSOLUTELY REQUIRED.

E. The warnings must be expressed prior to any questioning by law enforcement personnel, whether or not the answers by the person to be questioned are incriminating.

F. In addition to the above warnings, before accepting any admission or statement of a juvenile, the juvenile will be advised that he might be certified as an adult and be subjected to prosecution in Criminal Court. An EXPRESS STATEMENT by the juvenile that he UNDERSTANDS THE MEANING of this advice is REQUIRED. A JUVENILE SHOULD BE WARNED AND QUESTIONED ONLY IN THE PRESENCE OF AN ADULT (parent, other relative, or friend) IF SUCH AN ADULT CAN BE LOCATED.

G. It is not enough that the person to be questioned is warned and decides nonetheless to answer questions. Any circumstances of lengthy incommunicado custody, deception, promises or suggestions of benefits, or other forms of psychological pressure will invalidate the acceptability of anything the person questioned states or writes.

H. If the person requests advice as to whether or not he should decide to answer questions, a police officer is not permitted to advise the person.

IV. WAIVER OF RIGHTS

A. An individual may waive these rights, provided the waiver is made voluntarily, knowingly and intelligently. In order to show such waiver, establish and incorporate in the statement the individual's age, education, employment, and the fact that he understands the English language.

B. A waiver is not to be presumed from the fact that the individual remains silent after having been given the warnings, nor is it to be presumed from the fact that the individual confessed after having heard the warnings. An express statement by the individual, after hearing the warnings, that he is willing to make a statement and that he does not want an attorney, followed closely by a confession, should constitute a waiver.

C. Any indication that the person was tricked, threatened or cajoled into a waiver of these rights will establish that the waiver was not voluntary.

V. INTERROGATION PROCEDURE

A. Warning of the individual's rights must be given before *any* in-custody interrogation can commence. If the individual indicates in any manner that he does not wish to be interrogated, he will not be interrogated.

B. An individual who wishes to consult an attorney will not be interrogated until he has had an opportunity to do so.

C. If at any time a lawyer appears, or a parent in cases involving a juvenile, the person to be questioned will have an opportunity to confer privately with the lawyer or parent before the questioning is continued; and the person to be questioned shall have an opportunity to have the lawyer or parent present during any subsequent questioning.

D. If the person to be questioned states or in any manner indicates that he wishes to remain silent, *but has a lawyer present*, the police officer may *state questions* as long as there is no form of physical or psychological pressure exerted on the individual.

E. If the person to be questioned at first states that he understands the meaning of the warnings and that he nonetheless wishes to answer questions without speaking to a lawyer and without having a lawyer present, and later changes his mind, the questioning will immediately cease.

VI. WHEN WARNINGS ARE NOT REQUIRED

A. The warnings need not be given to any person who spontaneously volunteers information without any questioning by anyone.

B. There is no requirement that the police stop and warn a person who enters a police facility and states that he wishes to confess to a crime, nor that they stop and warn a person who telephones the police or approaches any police officer on duty to offer a confession or any statement about some crime and his part in it.

C. A person need not be advised of his rights if the police are engaged in general on-the-scene questioning about a crime or other general questioning of witnesses in the fact-finding process, as long as the questioned person has not been taken into custody and is not in any way restrained from exercising full freedom of movement and action, such as a person who can leave the scene at any time he so desires.

CUSTODY

In *Escobedo* some confusion had been created by the Court's emphasis on the investigation of the police *focusing* on the accused. The holding in *Miranda* made clear, however, that the Fifth Amendment mandate did not begin until the defendant had been taken into custody:

> By custodial interrogation, we mean questioning initiated by law enforcement officers after a person has been taken into custody or otherwise deprived of his freedom in any significant way.
>
> This is what we meant in *Escobedo* when we spoke of an investigation which had focused on the accused.

Merely setting up this threshold standard, though, did not eliminate the difficulties in applying the *Miranda* rules, as the Justices soon realized. It is one thing to speak in terms of being "deprived of freedom"; it is quite another to utilize that test in the multitude of cases throughout the country.

OROZCO v. TEXAS

United States Supreme Court
394 U.S. 324 (1969)

Mr. Justice Black delivered the opinion of the Court.

The petitioner, Reyes Arias Orozco, was convicted in the Criminal District Court of Dallas County, Texas, of murder without malice and was sentenced to serve in the state prison not less than two nor more than 10 years.

The evidence introduced at trial showed that petitioner and the deceased had quarreled outside the El Farleto Cafe in Dallas shortly before midnight on the date of the shooting. The deceased had apparently spoken to petitioner's female companion inside the restaurant. In the heat of the quarrel outside, the deceased is said to have beaten petitioner about the face and called him "Mexican Grease." A shot was fired killing the deceased. Petitioner left the scene and returned to his boardinghouse to sleep. At about 4 a.m. four police officers arrived at petitioner's boardinghouse, were admitted by an unidentified woman, and were told that petitioner was asleep in the bedroom. All four officers entered the bedroom and began to question petitioner. From the moment he gave his name, according to the testimony of one of the officers, petitioner was not free to go where he pleased but was "under arrest." The officers asked him if he had been to the El Farleto restaurant that night and when he answered "yes" he was asked if he owned a pistol. Petitioner admitted owning one. After being asked a second time where the pistol was located, he admitted that it was in the washing machine in a backroom of the boardinghouse. Ballistics tests indicated that the gun found in the washing machine was the gun that fired the fatal shot. At petitioner's trial, held after the effective date of this Court's decision in *Miranda v. Arizona*, the trial court allowed one of the officers, over the objection of petitioner's lawyer, to relate the statements made by petitioner concerning the gun and petitioner's presence at the scene of the shooting. The trial testimony clearly shows that the officers questioned petitioner about incriminating facts without first informing him of his right to remain silent, his right to have the advice of a lawyer before making any statement, and his right to have a lawyer appointed to assist him if he could not afford to hire one. We . . . hold that the use of these admissions obtained in the absence of the required warnings was a flat violation of the Self-Incrimination Clause of the Fifth Amendment as construed in *Miranda*.

The State has argued here that since petitioner was interrogated on his own bed, in familiar surroundings, our *Miranda* holding should not apply. It is true that the Court did say in *Miranda* that "compulsion to speak in the isolated setting of the police station may well be greater than in courts or other official investigations, where there are often impartial observers to guard against intimidation or trickery." But the opinion iterated and reiterated the absolute necessity for officers interrogating people "in custody" to give the described warnings.

According to the officer's testimony, petitioner was under arrest and not free to leave when he was questioned in his bedroom in the early hours of the morning. The *Miranda* opinion declared that the warnings were required when the person being interrogated was "in custody at the station *or otherwise deprived of his freedom of action in any significant way.*" The decision of this Court in *Miranda* was reached after careful consideration and lengthy opinions were announced by both the majority and dissenting Justices. There is no need to canvass those arguments again. We do not, as the dissent implies, expand or extend to the slightest extent our *Miranda* decision. We do adhere to our well-considered holding in that case and therefore reverse the conviction below.

Reversed.

MR. JUSTICE FORTAS took no part in the consideration or decision of this case.

MR. JUSTICE HARLAN concurring.

MR. JUSTICE WHITE, with whom MR. JUSTICE STEWART joins, dissenting.

The opinion of the Court in *Miranda* was devoted in large part to an elaborate discussion of the subtle forms of psychological pressure which could be brought to bear when an accused person is interrogated at length in unfamiliar surroundings. The "salient features" of the cases decided in *Miranda* were "incommunicado interrogation of individuals in a police-dominated atmosphere." The danger was that in such circumstances the confidence of the prisoner could be eroded by techniques such as successive interrogations by police acting out friendly or unfriendly roles. These techniques are best developed in "isolation and unfamiliar surroundings." And they take time: "the major qualities an interrogator should possess are patience and perseverance." The techniques of an extended period of isolation, repeated interrogation, cajolery, and trickery often enough produced admissions which were actually coerced in the traditional sense so that new safeguards were deemed essential.

It is difficult to believe that the requirements there laid down were essential to prevent compulsion in every conceivable case of station house interrogation. Where the defendant himself as a lawyer, policeman, professional criminal, or otherwise has become aware of what his right to silence is, it is sheer fancy to assert that his answer to every question asked him is compelled unless he is advised of those rights with which he is already intimately familiar. If there is any warrant to *Miranda* at all, it rests on the likelihood that in a sufficient number of cases exposure to station house practices will result in compelled confessions and that additional safeguards should be imposed in all cases to prevent possible erosion of Fifth Amendment values. Hence, the detailed ritual which *Miranda* fashioned.

The Court now extends the same rules to all instances of in-custody questioning outside the station house. Once arrest occurs, the application of *Miranda* is automatic. The rule is simple but it ignores the purpose of *Miranda* to guard against what was thought to be the corrosive influence of practices which station house interrogation makes feasible. The Court wholly ignores the question whether similar hazards exist or even are possible when police arrest and interrogate on the spot, whether it be on the street corner or in the home, as in this case.

NOTES AND QUESTIONS

(1) Was *Miranda* designed, as suggested by Justice White, "to guard against what was thought to be the corrosive influence of practices which station house interrogation makes feasible"? If he was correct, how can the majority say that it did not "expand or extend to the slightest extent our *Miranda* decision"?

(2) The custody issue continues to be difficult. *See, e.g.*, *State v. Nightingale*, 58 A.3d 1057 (Me. 2012) (no custody even though police interview took nine hours); *People v. Baez*, 975 N.E.2d 916 (N.Y. 2012) (threat to arrest occupants of stopped car unless someone took responsibility for weapon resulted in detention being custody); *United States v. Savoy*, 889 F. Supp. 2d 78 (D.D.C. 2012) (though at home, defendant was in custody when 16 agents had broken through the doors at 6 a.m.); *United States v. Robinson*, 833 F. Supp. 2d 406 (D. Vt. 2011) (custody found; even though defendant was at her apartment complex, she was questioned in a small room with the door closed and she was not permitted to go to the bathroom); *United States v. Slaight*, 620 F.3d 816, 817 (7th Cir. 2010) (". . . officers . . . made ingenious, pertinacious, but ultimately (as it seems to us) transparent efforts to disguise a custodial interrogation as a noncustodial . . . interviewed suspect at

police station, he did not have car; two large officers and suspect, pretty much filled up the room"); *United States v. Hargrove*, 625 F.3d 170, 179 (4th Cir. 2010) (no custody, even though officers were armed upon entry of defendant's home and conducted pat down — no substantial level of control over defendant); *United States v. Bassignani*, 560 F.3d 989 (9th Cir. 2009) (because defendant was interviewed — for 2.5 hours — in a familiar place, a conference room at his workplace, he was not in custody — he was also told he was not under arrest); *State v. James*, 225 P.3d 1169 (Idaho 2010) (even though officer threatened to arrest all occupants of the car unless one confessed, "the threat of lawful arrest alone does not transform non-custodial questioning into the functional equivalent of arrest"); *United States v. Harrold*, 679 F. Supp. 2d 1336 (N.D. Ga. 2009) (suspect was in custody despite having gone to the police station voluntarily; her wallet and identification were taken from her, she was put in a locked room, and she was never told she could leave).

See also United States v. Craighead, 539 F.3d 1073 (9th Cir. 2008), where custody was found with the defendant in his own home. Even though the officers told him he was free to leave, such a statement did not remove the coercive atmosphere. The court explained:

> If a reasonable person is interrogated inside his own home and is told he is "free to leave," where will he go? The library? The police station? He is already in the most constitutionally protected place on earth. To be "free" to leave is a hollow right if the one place the suspect cannot go is his own home.

FIELD INVESTIGATIONS

To deal with the on-the-scene encounter problem, police departments developed guidelines for their officers. Consider whether the following form provides sufficient assistance for an officer.

II. DEFINITION

A field interrogation is general on-the-scene questioning of a person about a crime or other general questioning of witnesses in the fact-finding process, provided that the person being questioned has not been taken into custody nor has been deprived of his freedom of action in any significant way.

V. GUIDELINES FOR FIELD INTERROGATIONS

> A. Miranda warnings are not necessary when police conduct general, on-the-scene questioning regarding facts of a crime.
>
> B. Confronted with suspicious circumstances, a police officer is permitted to make inquiries of an investigative nature without first giving the Miranda warnings.
>
> C. A police officer may, in appropriate circumstances and in an appropriate manner, approach a person for purposes of investigating possible criminal behavior even though there is no probable cause to make an arrest.

D. On grounds short of arrest, a police officer may "stop" a person under suspicious circumstances and ask the person's name and reason for being in the area. If the person refuses to answer, the police officer must evaluate whether or not valid grounds for arrest exist and proceed accordingly.

E. The person stopped is not obliged to answer; answers may not be compelled, and a refusal to answer furnishes no basis for arrest, although it may alert the police officer to the need for continued observation or additional investigation of the person.

VII. LIMITED SCOPE OF SEARCH OF A PERSON

A. Police officers will exercise extreme propriety when patting down pockets of outer garments of persons of the opposite sex. Any necessary further search of such person will be conducted by a police officer of the same sex as the person being searched.

B. Purses of females, attache cases, etc., may be given a very careful, limited examination solely to discover weapons.

MATHIS v. UNITED STATES

United States Supreme Court
391 U.S. 1 (1968)

Mr. Justice Black delivered the opinion of the Court.

Petitioner was convicted by a jury in a United States District Court on two counts charging that he knowingly filed false claims against the Government in violation of 18 U.S.C. § 287. A part of the evidence on which the conviction rested consisted of documents and oral statements obtained from petitioner by a government agent while petitioner was in prison serving a state sentence. Before eliciting this information, the government agent did not warn petitioner that any evidence he gave the Government could be used against him, and that he had a right to remain silent if he desired as well as a right to the presence of counsel and that if he was unable to afford counsel one would be appointed for him. We granted certiorari to decide whether the *Miranda* case calls for reversal. We hold that it does.

There can be no doubt that the documents and oral statements given by petitioner to the government agent and used against him were strongly incriminating. In the *Miranda* case this Court's opinion stated at some length the constitutional reasons why one in custody who is interrogated by officers about matters that might tend to incriminate him is entitled to be warned "that he has the right to remain silent, that anything he says can be used against him in a court of law, that he has the right to the presence of an attorney, and that if he cannot afford an attorney one will be appointed for him prior to any questioning, if he so desires."

The Government here seeks to escape application of the *Miranda* warnings on two arguments: (1) that these questions were asked as a part of a routine tax investigation where no criminal proceedings might even be brought, and (2) that the petitioner had not been put in jail by the officers questioning him, but was there for an entirely separate offense. These differences are too minor and shadowy to justify a departure from the well-considered conclusions of *Miranda* with reference to warnings to be given to a person held in custody.

It is true that a "routine tax investigation" may be initiated for the purpose of a civil action rather than criminal prosecution. To this extent tax investigations differ from investigations of murder, robbery, and other crimes. But tax investigations frequently lead to criminal prosecutions, just as the one here did. In fact, the last visit of the revenue agent to the jail to question petitioner took place only eight days before the full-fledged criminal investigation concededly began. And, as the investigating revenue agent was compelled to admit, there was always the possibility during his investigation that his work would end up in a criminal prosecution. We reject the contention that tax investigations are immune from the *Miranda* requirements for warnings to be given a person in custody.

The Government also seeks to narrow the scope of the *Miranda* holding by making it applicable only to questioning one who is "in custody" in connection with the very case under investigation. There is no substance to such a distinction, and in effect it goes against the whole purpose of the *Miranda* decision which was designed to give meaningful protection to Fifth Amendments rights. We find nothing in the *Miranda* opinion which calls for a curtailment of the warnings to be given persons under interrogation by officers based on the reason why the person is in custody. In speaking of "custody" the language of the *Miranda* opinion is clear and unequivocal:

> To summarize, we hold that when an individual is taken into custody or otherwise deprived of his freedom by the authorities in any significant way and is subjected to questioning, the privilege against self-incrimination is jeopardized.

And the opinion goes on to say that the person so held must be given the warnings about his right to be silent and his right to have a lawyer.

Thus, the courts below were wrong in permitting the introduction of petitioner's self-incriminating evidence given without warning of his right to be silent and right to counsel. The cause is reversed and remanded for further proceedings consistent with this opinion.

It is so ordered.

MR. JUSTICE MARSHALL took no part in the consideration or decision of this case.

MR. JUSTICE WHITE, with whom MR. JUSTICE HARLAN and MR. JUSTICE STEWART join, dissenting.

Although petitioner was confined, he was at the time of interrogation in familiar surroundings. Neither the record nor the Court suggests reasons why petitioner was "coerced" into answering Lawless' questions any more than is the citizen interviewed at home by a revenue agent or interviewed in a Revenue Service office to which citizens are requested to come for interviews. The rationale of *Miranda* has no relevance to inquiries conducted outside the allegedly hostile and forbidding atmosphere surrounding police station interrogation of a criminal suspect. The Court's willingness to reverse without explaining why the reasons given for the *Miranda* decision have any relevance to the facts of this case is deeply troubling.

NOTES AND QUESTIONS

(1) Does *Mathis* mean that any investigation which would "frequently lead to criminal prosecutions" would be the equivalent of custody for purposes of *Miranda*? To state the question another way, would the result in *Mathis* have been different if the defendant had not been in prison when he was questioned?

In *Beckwith v. United States*, 425 U.S. 341 (1976), the defendant did not receive warnings by Intelligence Special Agents of the IRS during the course of an investigation conducted at a private home where the defendant occasionally stayed. The defendant had been suspected of possible criminal income tax violations and the statements made by him during the investigation were used to convict him. These facts were not sufficient to invoke the protections of *Miranda*:

> Petitioner's argument that he was placed in the functional and, therefore, legal equivalent of the *Miranda* situation asks us now to ignore completely that *Miranda* was grounded squarely in the Court's explicit and detailed assessment of the peculiar "nature and setting of . . . in-custody interrogation," *Mathis v. United States, supra*, directly supports this conclusion in holding that the *Miranda* requirements are applicable to interviews with Internal Revenue agents concerning tax liability, *when the subject is in custody*; the Court thus squarely grounded its holding on the custodial aspects of the situation, not the subject matter of the interview.
>
> An interview with government agents in a situation such as the one shown by this record simply does not present the elements which the *Miranda* Court found so inherently coercive as to require its holding. Although the "focus" of an investigation may indeed have been on Beckwith at the time of the interview in the sense that it was his tax liability which was under scrutiny, he hardly found himself in the custodial situation described by the *Miranda* Court as the basis for its holding. *Miranda* implicitly defined "focus," for its purposes, as "questioning initiated by law enforcement officers *after* a person has been taken into custody or otherwise deprived of his freedom of action in any significant way."

Was the Court's view of *Mathis* and *Miranda* correct?

The Internal Revenue Service routinely gives *Miranda* warnings in connection with criminal investigations, even when the taxpayer is not in custody. See the I.R.S. Handbook, Investigative Techniques, found at http://www.irs.gov/irm/part9/ch04s08.html#d0e19715. It provides in material part:

> **Subject of Investigation**
>
> 1. At the start of the initial interview with the subject of an investigation, a special agent(s) should do the following:

A. Identify himself/herself as a special agent of the IRS, Criminal Investigation and provide his/her last name along with an introduction by title and last name of any other officials present.

B. Display authorized credentials and badge of authority to the subject for visual examination, (always maintain physical control of the badge and credentials and never allow anyone to duplicate, photograph or make an impression of your identification).

C. Provide the subject of the investigation with the special agent(s) unique Identification Number (see IRM 1.2.4, Use of Pseudonyms by Internal Revenue Service) and phone number, either verbally or in writing as required by RRA 98, Section 3705 (a).

Note: Special agents are required to provide the subject and the subject's representative with his/her unique Identification Number and phone number at the initial contact.

D. The special agent will advise the subject, "As a special agent, one of my functions is to investigate the possibility of criminal violations of the Internal Revenue laws and related offenses."

2. Advise the subject of the investigation as follows: "In connection with my investigation of your tax liability (or other matter), I would like to ask you some questions. However, first I advise you that under the Fifth Amendment to the Constitution of the United States, I cannot compel you to answer any questions or to submit any information if such answers or information might tend to incriminate you in any way. I also advise you that anything which you say and any documents which you submit may be used against you in any criminal proceeding which may be undertaken. I advise you further that you may, if you wish, seek the assistance of an attorney before responding. Do you understand these rights?"

3. If the subject requests clarification, either as to his/her rights or the purpose of the investigation, the special agent will give such explanation as is necessary to clarify the matter for the subject.

4. The special agent will immediately terminate the interview if at any stage of an interview the subject indicates the wish to exercise rights to either withhold testimony or records, or to consult with an attorney.

5. The special agent will write a contemporaneous memorandum stating the following:

A. the manner in which the special agent identified himself/herself, including providing the subject with the special agent's unique Identification Number and phone number

B. when and where the subject was advised of constitutional rights

C. what additional explanation, if any, was made

D. how the subject responded

E. who was present at the time

6. During subsequent contacts with the subject, the subject should be advised of his/her constitutional rights before questioning.

7. All contacts with the subject and/or their representative are to be documented in accordance with established policy and procedures.

The interrogation in *United States v. Bencs*, 28 F.3d 555 (6th Cir. 1994), *cert. denied*, 513 U.S. 1117 (1995), violated the internal I.R.S. regulations, as the defendant was being interviewed by government agents. Held, his statement would not be suppressed, for the I.R.S. regulations did not establish any remedy for violation and *Miranda* did not apply because the defendant was not in custody during the interrogation.

(2) Does *Mathis*, taken with *Beckwith*, mean that whenever someone is in custody, for whatever crime, *Miranda* applies? Compare several cases dealing with this point. In *People v. Faulkner*, 282 N.W.2d 377 (Mich. App. 1979), the defendant resided in a halfway house, but was still legally considered an inmate of the prison. He could not leave the premises without the permission of the director of the residency. The defendant was questioned by the director of residency about the theft of various items, but was not given any *Miranda* warnings. Even though the director was not a police officer he "had substantial control over the movement of the residents. The record strongly suggests that the interrogation of defendant by [the director] was, for all relevant purposes, indistinguishable from a police interrogation." As a consequence, the court held that the answers to the questions were barred by *Mathis*. A similar result was reached in *People v. Diesing*, 384 N.E.2d 575 (Ill. App. 1978), where the defendant was an inmate of a work release center. Contrast the holdings in these cases with that in *State v. Alls*, 629 N.E.2d 1018 (N.Y. 1993), *cert. denied*, 511 U.S. 1090, where the defendant argued that any questioning of a prisoner by an individual known by the defendant to be an officer is "*per se* custodial interrogation." The court disagreed, though recognizing that the defendant, of course, was not free to leave the facility. "[W]e can envisage confrontations between correctional officers and prisoners analogous to the relatively brief, generally public, or otherwise on-the-scene investigatory detentions in non-prison settings found not custodial for *Miranda* purposes." The court stated that custody would be found when "added constraint would lead a prison inmate reasonably to believe that there has been a restriction on that person's freedom over and above that of ordinary confinement in a correctional facility."

PROBLEM F
CUSTODY

The 17-year-old minor defendant in *Yarborough v. Alvarado*, 541 U.S. 652 (2004), was questioned by the police during a two-hour interrogation at the police station but was not given *Miranda* warnings. The government contended that the warnings were not required, as the defendant was not in custody at that time. The question before the Court was whether the defendant's age should have been considered in determining if custody was present. Four Justices decided that age is simply not a relevant factor. Four other Justices thought that the age of the minor defendant is important. The key vote came from Justice O'Connor who wrote that under the facts in this case — the defendant was almost 18 years old — his youth was not a factor to be weighed, but "there may be cases in which a suspect's age will be relevant to the *Miranda* 'custody' inquiry." The Supreme Court followed Justice O'Connor's lead in *J.D.B. v. North Carolina*, 131 S. Ct. 2394 (2011). There the Justices split sharply, in a 5-4 decision with the majority holding that a trial court must take into consideration the age of a minor defendant in determining whether the custody element for *Miranda* is present.

Justice Alito, in the dissenting opinion, condemned what he saw as the majority using the case "to run *Miranda* off the rails . . . [resulting in] the extreme makeover of *Miranda*." For the dissenters the holding was both harmful and unnecessary:

> First, many minors subjected to police interrogation are near the age of majority, and for these suspects the one-size-fits-all *Miranda* custody rule may not be a bad fit. Second, many of the difficulties in applying the *Miranda* custody rule to minors arise because of the unique circumstances present when the police conduct interrogations at school. The *Miranda* custody rule has always taken into account the setting in which questioning occurs, and accounting for the school setting in such cases will address many of these problems. Third, in cases like the one now before us, where the suspect is especially young, courts applying the constitutional voluntariness standard can take special care to ensure that incriminating statements were not obtained through coercion.

The majority, in an opinion by Justice Sotomayor, strongly disagreed, "[s]eeing no reason for police officers or courts to blind themselves to [the] commonsense reality . . . that a child's age properly informs the *Miranda* custody analysis." She explained further:

> [A] reasonable child subjected to police questioning will sometimes feel pressured to submit when a reasonable adult would fee free to go. We think it clear that courts can account for that reality without doing any damage to the objective nature of the custody analysis. . . . .
>
> [C]hildren "generally are less mature and responsible than adults," . . . they "often lack the experience, perspective, and judgment to recognize and avoid choices that could be detrimental to them, . . . they "are more vulnerable or susceptible to . . . outside pressures" than adults. . . . [E]vents that "would leave a man cold and unimpressed can overawe and overwhelm a lad in his early teens.". . .
>
> "Our history is replete with laws and judicial recognition" that children cannot be viewed simply as miniature adults. . . . So long as the child's age was known to the officer at the time of the interview, or would have been objectively apparent to any reasonable officer, including age as part of the custody analysis requires officers neither to consider circumstances "unknowable" to them, nor to "anticipat[e] the frailties or idiosyncrasies" of the particular suspect whom they question. . . .

HOWES v. FIELDS

United States Supreme Court
132 S. Ct. 1181 (2012)

Justice Alito delivered the opinion of the Court.

The United States Court of Appeals for the Sixth Circuit held that our precedents clearly establish that a prisoner is in custody within the meaning of *Miranda v. Arizona*, if the prisoner is taken aside and questioned about events that occurred outside the prison walls. Our decisions, however, do not clearly establish such a rule, and therefore the Court of Appeals erred in holding that this rule provides a permissible basis for federal habeas relief. Indeed, the rule applied by the court below does not represent a correct interpretation of our *Miranda* case law. We therefore reverse.

I

While serving a sentence in a Michigan jail, Randall Fields was escorted by a corrections officer to a conference room where two sheriff's deputies questioned him about allegations that, before he came to prison, he had engaged in sexual conduct with a 12-year-old boy. In order to get to the conference room, Fields had to go down one floor and pass through a locked door that separated two sections of the facility. Fields arrived at the conference room between 7 p.m. and 9 p.m. and was questioned for between five and seven hours.

At the beginning of the interview, Fields was told that he was free to leave and return to his cell. Later, he was again told that he could leave whenever he wanted. The two interviewing deputies were armed during the interview, but Fields remained free of handcuffs and other restraints. The door to the conference room was sometimes open and sometimes shut.

About halfway through the interview, after Fields had been confronted with the allegations of abuse, he became agitated and began to yell. Fields testified that one of the deputies, using an expletive, told him to sit down and said that "if [he] didn't want to cooperate, [he] could leave." Fields eventually confessed to engaging in sex acts with the boy. According to Fields' testimony at a suppression hearing, he said several times during the interview that he no longer wanted to talk to the deputies, but he did not ask to go back to his cell prior to the end of the interview.

When he was eventually ready to leave, he had to wait an additional 20 minutes or so because a corrections officer had to be summoned to escort him back to his cell, and he did not return to his cell until well after the hour when he generally retired. At no time was Fields given *Miranda* warnings or advised that he did not have to speak with the deputies.

The jury convicted Fields of two counts of third-degree criminal sexual conduct, and the judge sentenced him to a term of 10 to 15 years of imprisonment. On direct appeal, the Michigan Court of Appeals affirmed, rejecting Fields' contention that his statements should have been suppressed because he was subjected to custodial interrogation without a *Miranda* warning. The court ruled that Fields had not been in custody for purposes of *Miranda* during the interview, so no *Miranda* warnings were required. The court emphasized that Fields was told that he was free to leave and return to his cell but that he never asked to do so. The Michigan Supreme Court denied discretionary review.

Fields then filed a petition for a writ of habeas corpus in Federal District Court, and the court granted relief. The Sixth Circuit affirmed, holding that the interview in the conference room was a "custodial interrogation" within the meaning of *Miranda* because isolation from the general prison population combined with questioning about conduct occurring outside the prison makes any such interrogation custodial *per se.* The Court of Appeals reasoned that this Court clearly established in *Mathis v. United States*, that "*Miranda* warnings must be administered when law enforcement officers remove an inmate from the general prison population and interrogate him regarding criminal conduct that took place outside the jail or prison." Because Fields was isolated from the general prison population and interrogated about conduct occurring in the outside world, the Court of Appeals found that the state court's decision was contrary to clearly established federal law as determined by this Court in *Mathis.*

II

Under AEDPA, a federal court may grant a state prisoner's application for a writ of habeas corpus if the state-court adjudication pursuant to which the prisoner is held "resulted in a decision that was contrary to, or involved an unreasonable application of, clearly established Federal law, as determined by the Supreme Court of the United States." In this context, "clearly established law" signifies "the holdings, as opposed to the dicta, of this Court's decisions."

In this case, it is abundantly clear that our precedents do not clearly establish the categorical rule on which the Court of Appeals relied, *i.e.*, that the questioning of a prisoner is always custodial when the prisoner is removed from the general prison population and questioned about events that occurred outside the prison. On the contrary, we have repeatedly declined to adopt any categorical rule with respect to whether the questioning of a prison inmate is custodial.

In concluding that our precedents establish a categorical rule, the Court of Appeals placed great weight on the decision in *Mathis*, but the Court of Appeals misread the holding in that case. In *Mathis*, an inmate in a state prison was questioned by an Internal Revenue agent and was subsequently convicted for federal offenses. The Court of Appeals held that *Miranda* did not apply to this interview for two reasons: A criminal investigation had not been commenced at the time of the interview, and the prisoner was incarcerated for an "unconnected offense." This Court rejected both of those grounds for distinguishing *Miranda*, and thus the holding in *Mathis* is simply that a prisoner who otherwise meets the requirements for *Miranda* custody is not taken outside the scope of *Miranda* by either of the two factors on which the Court of Appeals had relied. *Mathis* did not hold that imprisonment, in and of itself, is enough to constitute *Miranda* custody.

Miranda itself did not clearly establish the rule applied by the Court of Appeals. *Miranda* adopted a "set of prophylactic measures" designed to ward off the

" 'inherently compelling pressures' of custodial interrogation," but *Miranda* did not hold that such pressures are always present when a prisoner is taken aside and questioned about events outside the prison walls. Indeed, *Miranda* did not even establish that police questioning of a suspect at the station house is always custodial.

In sum, our decisions do not clearly establish that a prisoner is always in custody for purposes of *Miranda* whenever a prisoner is isolated from the general prison population and questioned about conduct outside the prison.

III

Not only does the categorical rule applied below go well beyond anything that is clearly established in our prior decisions, it is simply wrong. The three elements of that rule — (1) imprisonment, (2) questioning in private, and (3) questioning about events in the outside world — are not necessarily enough to create a custodial situation for *Miranda* purposes.

A

As used in our *Miranda* case law, "custody" is a term of art that specifies circumstances that are thought generally to present a serious danger of coercion. In determining whether a person is in custody in this sense, the initial step is to ascertain whether, in light of "the objective circumstances of the interrogation," a "reasonable person [would] have felt he or she was not at liberty to terminate the interrogation and leave." And in order to determine how a suspect would have "gauge[d]" his "freedom of movement," courts must examine "all of the circumstances surrounding the interrogation." Relevant factors include the location of the questioning, its duration, statements made during the interview, the presence or absence of physical restraints during the questioning, and the release of the interviewee at the end of the questioning.

Determining whether an individual's freedom of movement was curtailed, however, is simply the first step in the analysis, not the last. Not all restraints on freedom of movement amount to custody for purposes of *Miranda*. We have "decline[d] to accord talismanic power" to the freedom-of-movement inquiry, and have instead asked the additional question whether the relevant environment presents the same inherently coercive pressures as the type of station house questioning at issue in *Miranda*. "Our cases make clear . . . that the freedom-of-movement test identifies only a necessary and not a sufficient condition for *Miranda* custody." Imprisonment alone is not enough to create a custodial situation within the meaning of *Miranda*.

There are at least three strong grounds for this conclusion. First, questioning a person who is already serving a prison term does not generally involve the shock that very often accompanies arrest. In the paradigmatic *Miranda* situation — a person is arrested in his home or on the street and whisked to a police station for questioning — detention represents a sharp and ominous change, and the shock may give rise to coercive pressures. A person who is "cut off from his normal life and companions," and abruptly transported from the street into a "police-dominated atmosphere," may feel coerced into answering questions.

By contrast, when a person who is already serving a term of imprisonment is questioned, there is usually no such change. "Interrogated suspects who have previously been convicted of crime live in prison." For a person serving a term of incarceration, the ordinary restrictions of prison life, while no doubt unpleasant, are expected and familiar and thus do not involve the same "inherently compelling pressures" that are often present when a suspect is yanked from familiar surroundings in the outside world and subjected to interrogation in a police station.

Second, a prisoner, unlike a person who has not been sentenced to a term of incarceration, is unlikely to be lured into speaking by a longing for prompt release. When a person is arrested and taken to a station house for interrogation, the person who is questioned may be pressured to speak by the hope that, after doing so, he will be allowed to leave and go home. On the other hand, when a prisoner is questioned, he knows that when the questioning ceases, he will remain under confinement.

Third, a prisoner, unlike a person who has not been convicted and sentenced, knows that the law enforcement officers who question him probably lack the authority to affect the duration of his sentence. And "where the possibility of parole exists," the interrogating officers probably also lack the power to bring about an early release. "When the suspect has no reason to think that the listeners have official power over him, it should not be assumed that his words are motivated by the reaction he expects from his listeners." Under such circumstances, there is little "basis for the assumption that a suspect . . . will feel compelled to speak by the fear of reprisal for remaining silent or in the hope of [a] more lenient treatment should he confess."

In short, standard conditions of confinement and associated restrictions on freedom will not necessarily implicate the same interests that the Court sought to protect when it afforded special safeguards to persons subjected to custodial interrogation. Thus, service of a term of imprisonment, without more, is not enough to constitute *Miranda* custody.

IV

A

When a prisoner is questioned, the determination of custody should focus on all of the features of the interrogation. These include the language that is used in summoning the prisoner to the interview and the manner in which the interrogation is conducted. An inmate who is removed from the general prison population for questioning and is "thereafter . . . subjected to treatment" in connection with the interrogation "that renders him 'in custody' for practical purposes . . . will be entitled to the full panoply of protections prescribed by *Miranda*."

"Fidelity to the doctrine announced in *Miranda* requires that it be enforced strictly, but only in those types of situations in which the concerns that powered the decision are implicated." Confessions voluntarily made by prisoners in other situations should not be suppressed. "Voluntary confessions are not merely a proper element in law enforcement, they are an unmitigated good, essential to society's compelling interest in finding, convicting, and punishing those who violate the law."

B

The record in this case reveals that respondent was not taken into custody for purposes of *Miranda*. To be sure, respondent did not invite the interview or consent to it in advance, and he was not advised that he was free to decline to speak with the deputies. The following facts also lend some support to respondent's argument that *Miranda*'s custody requirement was met: The interview lasted for between five and seven hours in the evening and continued well past the hour when respondent generally went to bed; the deputies who questioned respondent were armed; and one of the deputies, according to respondent, "[u]sed a very sharp tone," on one occasion, profanity.

These circumstances, however, were offset by others. Most important, respondent was told at the outset of the interrogation, and was reminded again thereafter, that he could leave and go back to his cell whenever he wanted. Moreover, respondent was not physically restrained or threatened and was interviewed in a well-lit, average-sized conference room, where he was "not uncomfortable." He was offered food and water, and the door to the conference room was sometimes left open. "All of these objective facts are consistent with an interrogation environment in which a reasonable person would have felt free to terminate the interview and leave."

Taking into account all of the circumstances of the questioning — including especially the undisputed fact that respondent was told that he was free to end the questioning and to return to his cell — we hold that respondent was not in custody within the meaning of *Miranda*.

The judgment of the Court of Appeals is

Reversed.

Justice GINSBURG, with whom Justice BREYER and Justice SOTOMAYOR join, concurring in part and dissenting in part.

Given this Court's controlling decisions on what counts as "custody" for *Miranda* purposes, I agree that the law is not "clearly established" in respondent Fields's favor. But I disagree with the Court's further determination that Fields was not in custody under *Miranda*. Were the case here on direct review, I would vote to hold that *Miranda* precludes the State's introduction of Fields's confession as evidence against him.

Miranda v. Arizona, reacted to police interrogation tactics that eroded the Fifth Amendment's ban on compulsory self-incrimination. The opinion did so by requiring interrogators to convey to suspects the now-familiar warnings: The suspect is to be informed, prior to interrogation, that he "has a right to remain silent, that any statement he does make may be used as evidence against him, and that he has a right to the presence of an attorney, either retained or appointed."

Under what circumstances are *Miranda* warnings required? *Miranda* tells us "in all settings in which [a person's] freedom of action is curtailed in any significant way." Given the reality that police interrogators "trad[e] on the weakness of individuals," i.e., their "insecurity about [themselves] or [their] surroundings," the Court found the preinterrogation warnings set out in the opinion "indispensable." Those warnings, the Court elaborated, are "an absolute prerequisite in overcoming the inherent pressures of the interrogation atmosphere," they "insure" that the suspect is timely told of his Fifth Amendment privilege, and his freedom to exercise it.

Fields, serving time for disorderly conduct, was, of course, "i[n] custody," but not "for purposes of *Miranda*," the Court concludes. I would not train, as the Court does, on the question whether there can be custody within custody. Instead, I would ask, as *Miranda* put it, whether Fields was subjected to "incommunicado interrogation . . . in a police-dominated atmosphere," whether he was placed, against his will, in an inherently stressful situation, and whether his "freedom of action [was] curtailed in any significant way." Those should be the key questions, and to each I would answer "Yes."

As the Court acknowledges, Fields did not invite or consent to the interview. He was removed from his cell in the evening, taken to a conference room in the sheriff's quarters, and questioned by two armed deputies long into the night and early morning. He was not told at the outset that he had the right to decline to speak with the deputies. Shut in with the armed officers, Fields felt "trapped." Although told he could return to his cell if he did not want to cooperate, Fields believed the deputies "would not have allowed [him] to leave the room," And with good reason. More than once, "he told the officers . . . he did not want to speak with them anymore." He was given water, but not his evening medications. Yet the Court concludes that Fields was in "an interrogation environment in which a reasonable person would have felt free to terminate the interview and leave."

Critical to the Court's judgment is "the undisputed fact that [Fields] was told that he was free to end the questioning and to return to his cell." Never mind the facts suggesting that Fields's submission to the overnight interview was anything but voluntary. Was Fields "held for interrogation"? Brought to, and left alone with, the gun-bearing deputies, he surely was in my judgment.

Miranda instructed that such a person "must be clearly informed that he has the right to consult with a lawyer and to have the lawyer with him during interrogation." Those warnings, along with "warnings of the right to remain silent and that anything stated can be used in evidence against [the speaker]," *Miranda* explained, are necessary "prerequisite[s] to [an] interrogation" compatible with the Fifth Amendment. Today, for people already in prison, the Court finds it adequate for the police to say: "You are free to terminate this interrogation and return to your cell." Such a statement is no substitute for one ensuring that an individual is aware of his rights.

NOTES AND QUESTIONS

(1) Does the decision here effectively overrule *Mathis v. United States*? Note this language from the majority opinion:

> In concluding that our precedents establish a categorical rule, the Court of Appeals placed great weight on the decision in *Mathis*, but the Court of Appeals misread the holding in that case. In *Mathis*, an inmate in a state prison was questioned by an Internal Revenue agent and was subsequently convicted for federal offenses. The Court of Appeals held that *Miranda* did not apply to this interview for two reasons: A criminal investigation had not been commenced at the time of the interview, and the prisoner was incarcerated for an "unconnected offense." This Court rejected both of those grounds for distinguishing *Miranda*, and thus the holding in *Mathis* is simply that a prisoner who otherwise meets the requirements for *Miranda* custody is not taken outside the scope of *Miranda* by either of the two factors on which the Court of Appeals had relied. *Mathis* did not hold that imprisonment, in and of itself, is enough to constitute *Miranda* custody.

Howes v. Fields, 132 S. Ct. at 1188.

(2) The majority rejects the application of *Miranda* because the Justices look to the "question of whether there can be custody within custody." The dissent focuses on whether the suspect was subject to "incommunicado interrogation . . . in a police dominated atmosphere." Looking to the majority opinion in *Miranda*, which of the two sides gets the better of the argument?

(3) Under the facts here, would "a reasonable person" have felt he or she was at liberty to terminate the interrogation and leave? What result if he had not been told he could return to his cell? What is the rule now for prison or jail interrogations as to the application of *Miranda*?

(4) In *State v. Butt*, 284 P.3d 605 (Utah 2012), the defendant/prisoner was questioned in his cell. Custody? No, said the court even though "*no* defendant being interviewed in his prison cell would ever 'feel free to leave.' " The court explained its holding: "Despite our misgivings that a defendant being interviewed in his cell could feel free to leave, we conclude that the balance tips against requiring *Miranda* warnings in this case . . . he was not restrained beyond his usual status as a jail inmate."

OREGON v. MATHIASON

United States Supreme Court
429 U.S. 492 (1977)

Per Curiam.

Respondent Carl Mathiason was convicted of first-degree burglary after a bench trial in which his confession was critical to the State's case. At trial he moved to suppress the confession as the fruit of questioning by the police not preceded by the warnings required in *Miranda v. Arizona*. The trial court refused to exclude the confession because it found that Mathiason was not in custody at the time of the confession.

The Supreme Court of Oregon described the factual situation surrounding the confession as follows:

> An officer of the State Police investigated a theft at a residence near Pendleton. He asked the lady of the house which had been burglarized if she suspected anyone. She replied that the defendant was the only one she could think of. The defendant was a parolee and a "close associate" of her son. The officer tried to contact defendant on three or four occasions with no success.
>
> Finally, about 25 days after the burglary, the officer left his card at defendant's apartment with a note asking him to call because "I'd like to discuss something with you." The next afternoon the defendant did call. The officer asked where it would be convenient to meet. The defendant had no preference; so the officer asked if the defendant could meet him at the state patrol office in about an hour and a half, about 5:00 p.m. The patrol office was about two blocks from defendant's apartment. The building housed several state agencies.
>
> The officer met defendant in the hallway, shook hands and took him into an office. The defendant was told he was not under arrest. The door was closed. The two sat across a desk. The police radio in another room could be heard. The officer told defendant he wanted to talk to him about a burglary and that his truthfulness would possibly be considered by the district attorney or judge. The officer further advised that the police believed defendant was involved in the burglary and [falsely stated that] defendant's fingerprints were found at the scene. The defendant sat for a few minutes and then said he had taken the property. This occurred within five minutes after defendant had come to the office. The officer then advised defendant of his *Miranda* rights and took a taped confession.
>
> At the end of the taped conversation the officer told defendant he was not arresting him at this time; he was released to go about his job and return to his family. The officer said he was referring the case to the district attorney for him to determine whether criminal charges would be brought. It was 5:30 p.m. when the defendant left the office. The officer gave all the testimony relevant to this issue. The defendant did not take the stand either at the hearing on the motion to suppress or at the trial.

The Supreme Court of Oregon reasoned from these facts that:

> We hold the interrogation took place in a "coercive environment." The parties were in the offices of the State Police; they were alone behind closed doors; the officer informed the defendant he was a suspect in a theft and the authorities had evidence incriminating him in the crime; and the defendant was a parolee under supervision. We are of the opinion that this evidence is not overcome by the evidence that the defendant came to the office in response to a request and was told he was not under arrest.

Our decision in *Miranda* set forth rules of police procedure applicable to "custodial interrogation." "By custodial interrogation, we mean questioning initiated by law enforcement officers after a person has been taken into custody or otherwise deprived of his freedom of action in any significant way."

Subsequently we have found the *Miranda* principle applicable to questioning which takes place in a prison setting during a suspect's term of imprisonment on a separate offense, *Mathis v. United States*, and to questioning taking place in a suspect's home, after he has been arrested and is no longer free to go where he pleases, *Orozco v. Texas*.

In the present case, however, there is no indication that the questioning took place in a context where respondent's freedom to depart was restricted in any way. He came voluntarily to the police station, where he was immediately informed that he was not under arrest. At the close of a 1/2 hour interview respondent did in fact leave the police station without hindrance. It is clear from these facts that Mathiason was not in custody "or otherwise deprived of his freedom of action in any significant way."

Such a noncustodial situation is not converted to one in which *Miranda* applies simply because a reviewing court concludes that, even in the absence of any formal arrest or restraint on freedom of movement, the questioning took place in a "coercive environment." Any interview of one suspected of a crime by a police officer will have coercive aspects to it, simply by virtue of the fact that the police officer is part of a law enforcement system which may ultimately cause the suspect to be charged with a crime. But police officers are not required to administer *Miranda* warnings to everyone whom they question. Nor is the requirement of warnings to be imposed simply because the questioning takes place in the station house, or because the questioned person is one whom the police suspect. *Miranda* warnings are required only where there has been such a restriction on a person's freedom as to render him "in custody." It was *that* sort of coercive environment to which *Miranda* by its terms was made applicable, and to which it is limited.

The officer's false statement about having discovered Mathiason's fingerprints at the scene was found by the Supreme Court of Oregon to be another circumstance contributing to the coercive environment which makes the *Miranda* rationale applicable. Whatever relevance this fact may have to other issues in the case, it has nothing to do with whether respondent was in custody for purposes of the *Miranda* rule.

The petition for certiorari is granted, the judgment of the Oregon Supreme Court is reversed, and the case is remanded for proceedings not inconsistent with this opinion.

Mr. Justice Brennan would grant the writ but dissents from the summary disposition and would set the case for oral argument.

Mr. Justice Marshall, dissenting.

The respondent in this case was interrogated behind closed doors at police headquarters in connection with a burglary investigation. He had been named by the victim of the burglary as a suspect, and was told by the police that they believed he was involved. He was falsely informed that his fingerprints had been found at the scene, and in effect was advised that by cooperating with the police he could help himself. Not until after he had confessed was he given the warnings set forth in *Miranda v. Arizona.*

The Court today holds that for constitutional purposes all this is irrelevant because respondent had not " 'been taken into custody or otherwise deprived of his freedom of action in any significant way.' "

I do not believe that such a determination is possible on the record before us. It is true that respondent was not formally placed under arrest, but surely formalities alone cannot control. At the very least, if respondent entertained an objectively reasonable belief that he was not free to leave during the questioning, then he was "deprived of his freedom of action in a significant way." Plainly the respondent could have so believed, after being told by the police that they thought he was involved in a burglary and that his fingerprints had been found at the scene. Yet the majority is content to note that "there is no indication that . . . respondent's freedom to depart was restricted in any way," as if a silent record (and no state-court findings) means that the State has sustained its burden of demonstrating that respondent received his constitutional due.

More fundamentally, however, I cannot agree with the Court's conclusion that if respondent were not in custody no warnings were required. I recognize that *Miranda* is limited to custodial interrogations, but that is because, as we noted last Term, the facts in the *Miranda* cases raised only this "narrow issue."

The rationale of *Miranda*, however, is not so easily cabined.

Miranda requires warnings to "combat" a situation in which there are "inherently compelling pressures which work to undermine the individual's will to resist and to compel him to speak where he would not otherwise do so freely."

It is of course true, as the Court notes, that "[a]ny interview of one suspected of a crime by a police officer will have coercive aspects to it." But it does not follow that because police "are not required to administer *Miranda* warnings to everyone whom they question," that they need not administer warnings to *anyone*, unless the factual setting of the *Miranda* cases is replicated. Rather, faithfulness to *Miranda* requires us to distinguish situations that resemble the "coercive aspects" of custodial interrogation from those that more nearly resemble "[g]eneral on-the-scene questioning . . . or other general questioning of citizens in the fact-finding process" which *Miranda* states usually can take place without warnings. In my view, even if respondent were not in custody, the coercive elements in the instant case were so pervasive as to require *Miranda*-type warnings. Respondent was interrogated in "privacy" and in "unfamiliar surroundings," factors on which *Miranda* places great stress. The investigations had focused on respondent. And respondent was subjected to some of the "deceptive stratagems," *Miranda v. Arizona*, which called forth the *Miranda* decision. I therefore agree with the Oregon Supreme Court that to excuse the absence of warnings given these facts is "contrary to the rationale expressed in *Miranda.*"

I respectfully dissent.

Mr. Justice Stevens, dissenting.

In my opinion the issues presented by this case are too important to be decided summarily. Of particular importance is the fact that the respondent was on parole at the time of his interrogation in the police station. This fact lends support to inconsistent conclusions.

On the one hand, the State surely has greater power to question a parolee about his activities than to question someone else. Moreover, as a practical matter, it seems unlikely that a *Miranda* warning would have much effect on a parolee's choice between silence and responding to police interrogation. Arguably, therefore, *Miranda* warnings are entirely inappropriate in the parole context.

On the other hand, a parolee is technically in legal custody continuously until his sentence has been served. Therefore, if a formalistic analysis of the custody question is to determine when the *Miranda* warning is necessary, a parolee should always be warned. Moreover, *Miranda* teaches that even if a suspect is not in custody, warnings are necessary if he is "otherwise deprived of his freedom of action in any significant way." If a parolee being questioned in a police station is not described by that language, today's decision qualifies that part of *Miranda* to some extent. I believe we would have a better understanding of the extent of that qualification, and therefore of the situations in which warnings must be given to a suspect who is not technically in custody, if we had the benefit of full argument and plenary consideration.

I therefore respectfully dissent from the Court's summary disposition.

NOTES AND QUESTIONS

(1) In his dissent in *Orozco*, Justice White asserted that *Miranda* was designed "to guard against what was thought to be the corrosive influence of practices which station house interrogation makes feasible." If this truly were the purpose of *Miranda*, how could he join the Court in finding that *Miranda* did not apply to the station house interrogation in *Mathiason*? In what way would the defendant's liberty have to be restrained before *Miranda* would apply to this fact situation? Would the result here change if it were shown that the defendant honestly believed that he could not leave the station house?

The United States Supreme Court reaffirmed the *Mathiason* decision in *California v. Beheler*, 463 U.S. 1121 (1983), finding *Miranda* did not apply "if the suspect is not placed under arrest, voluntarily comes to the police station, and is allowed to leave unhindered by police after a brief interview."

(2) How important is it if the defendant is not told he is not under arrest or is free to leave? Very important, held the majority of the Colorado Supreme Court in *People v. Elmarr*, 181 P.3d 1157 (Colo. 2008). The police there asked the defendant if he would mind accompanying them to the police department for questioning; the defendant agreed. The detectives drove him to the station in the back of their

unmarked police car. Once there, the vehicle was parked in a garage in the basement. The defendant was brought to an area of the building that was not open to the public. He was subjected to a pat-down search upon arrival and placed in a closed interview room measuring 7 by 10 feet. The defendant was not handcuffed. For those justices this was a custodial atmosphere without advising the defendant he could depart. The dissenters sharply disagreed, emphasizing that the defendant was not required to go with the officers.

(3) Two early cases from the state of Tennessee demonstrate the difficulties the courts have had with the custody rule of *Miranda*, in spite of the opinion in *Mathiason*. The defendant in *Childs v. State*, 584 S.W.2d 783 (Tenn. 1979), was considered a possible witness, "but not yet a suspect." The police visited him at his home and asked him to come into their car to answer some questions. After talking with him for 15–20 minutes the officers asked him to come with them to the station house. On arrival at the station, further questions were asked of him, and answers to these questions were given. Immediately thereafter the defendant was given the *Miranda* warnings. The Tennessee Supreme Court held this questioning to be noncustodial. "The only evidence is that the defendant cooperated readily with the police and voluntarily accompanied them to the station." Contrast the holding in *Childs* with that in *Underwood v. State*, 465 S.W.2d 884 (Tenn. 1970), where the Juvenile Judge questioned the defendant's daughter in connection with a call from a clergyman that the daughter and the defendant had been having sexual relations. The defendant came down to the court house and stayed in an outer office while the daughter was being interviewed. The judge then called the defendant into his chambers and asked him about the allegations. The defendant made incriminating statements. The court held that the statements were made in response to custodial interrogation. Are these two cases consistent? If not, which is a more faithful application of *Miranda* and *Mathiason*?

"The test is objective: the actual, subjective beliefs of the defendant and the interviewing officer on whether the defendant was free to leave are irrelevant." *United States v. Lall*, 607 F.3d 1277, 1284 (11th Cir. 2010). One court identified five key factors to consider in the determination:

> (1) [W]hether the officers told the suspect he was under arrest or free to leave; (2) the location or physical surrounding of the interrogation; (3) the length of the interrogation; (4) whether the officers used coercive tactics such as hostile tones of voice, the display of weapons, or physical restraint of the suspect's movement; and (5) whether the suspect voluntarily submitted to questioning.

United States v. King, 604 F.3d 125, 138 (3d Cir. 2010).

(4) How important was the fact that the defendant in *Mathiason* was on parole? For Justice Stevens this was quite significant; should the majority have set the case for full argument on this point?

See also *Minnesota v. Murphy*, 465 U.S. 420 (1984), where the Court refused to apply *Miranda* to a probationer who made incriminating statements to his probation officer. The majority concluded that the probationer simply was not in custody because there was no "formal arrest or restraint on freedom of movement of the degree associated with a formal arrest."

PROBLEM G
CUSTODIAL INTERROGATION

An undercover government agent was placed in the cell of the defendant who was in jail on charges unrelated to the subject of the agent's involvement. The agent was instructed to engage the defendant in "casual conversation" and report back any incriminating statement to the police. The following exchange took place between the agent and the defendant.

Agent: You ever do anyone?

Perkins: Yeah, once in East St. Louis, in a rich white neighborhood.

Agent: I didn't know they had any rich white neighborhoods in East St. Louis.

Perkins: It wasn't in East St. Louis, it was by a race track in Fairview Heights. . . .

Agent: You did a guy in Fairview Heights?

Perkins: Yeah in a rich white section where most of the houses look the same.

Agent: If all the houses look the same, how did you know you had the right house?

Perkins: Me and two guys cased the house for about a week. I knew exactly which house, the second house on the left from the corner.

Agent: How long ago did this happen?

Perkins: Approximately about two years ago. I got paid $5,000 for that job.

Agent: How did it go down?

Perkins: I walked up to . . . this guy['s] house with a sawed-off under my trench coat.

Agent: What type gun[?]

Perkins: A 12 gauge Remmington [*sic*] Automatic Model 1100 sawed-off.

Were these incriminating statements admissible under *Miranda*? The Court, in an 8-1 decision found no violation. *Illinois v. Perkins*, 496 U.S. 292 (1990).

> Conversations between suspects and undercover agents do not implicate the concerns underlying *Miranda*. The essential ingredients of a "police-dominated atmosphere" and compulsion are not present when an incarcerated person speaks freely to someone that he believes to be a fellow inmate. Coercion is determined from the perspective of the suspect. When a suspect considers himself in the company of cellmates and not officers, the coercive atmosphere is lacking.

The opinion by Justice Kennedy, however, was careful to distinguish cases previously decided involving undercover interrogation *after* the defendant had been indicted.

> The Court's Sixth Amendment decisions in *Massiah v. United States*, 377 U.S. 201 (1964), *United States v. Henry*, 447 U.S. 264 (1980), and *Maine v. Moulton*, 474 U.S. 159 (1985), also do not avail respondent. We held in those cases that the government may not use an undercover agent to circumvent the Sixth Amendment right to counsel once a suspect has been charged with the crime. After charges have been filed, the Sixth Amendment prevents the government from interfering with the accused's right to counsel. In the instant case no charges had been filed on the subject of the interrogation, and our Sixth Amendment precedents are not applicable.

See also *Nelson v. Fulcomer*, 911 F.2d 928, 937–38 (3d Cir. 1990), where the court found that *Perkins* was a very different situation:

> At the time Moore confronted Nelson, the police had recently attempted to question Nelson about the rape and murder and had read him *Miranda* warnings. Nelson had refused to speak with the police, invoking his right to cut off questioning, but he remained in the interrogation room and it was the police who brought Moore to that room for the confrontation. Thus, when Nelson made his incriminating remark, he remained the subject of a custodial interrogatory process controlled by the police. The Court in *Perkins* stressed that *Miranda* "was meant to preserve the privilege during 'incommunicado interrogation of individuals in a *police-dominated atmosphere*.'" (emphasis added). While the atmosphere of the cell-block in which Perkins boasted of his exploits to an undercover officer was, from his perspective at least, devoid of police "domination," the interrogation room where Nelson was confronted with Moore was saturated with it.

INTERROGATION

The Court in *Miranda* did not hold that all statements taken from an accused who happened to be in custody were inadmissible. The Fifth Amendment restrictions applied only to statements of the accused responding to interrogation by police officers.

> By custodial interrogation, we mean questioning *initiated* by law enforcement officers after a person has been taken into custody or otherwise deprived of his freedom of action in any significant way.

The comments which follow consider three aspects of the interrogation requirement. First, the issues involved in determining whether a statement is voluntary so that *Miranda* does not apply. Second, questions as to methods used by the police which, though subtle may nevertheless constitute interrogation. Third, the problem of interrogation being initiated, stopped, and then resumed.

VOLUNTEERED STATEMENTS

(1) Defendant in custody was shown a video of him committing a crime. Is this interrogation? Yes, decided the court in *United States v. Green*, 541 F.3d 176 (3d Cir. 2008). The judges there could "hardly imagine a more prototypical example of his 'functional equivalent' of interrogation. . . ." Was the defendant in *People v. White*,

828 N.W.2d 329 (Mich. 2013) interrogated? He was in custody when an officer spoke with him and said, "The only thing that I can tell you is this, and I'm not asking you questions I'm just telling you. I hope that the gun is in a place where nobody can get a hold of it and nobody else can get hurt by it, okay, all right." No interrogation, decided three judges: "[The officer's comment] was not a question because it did not ask for an answer or invite a response. It was a mere expression of hope and concern." Interrogation, decided one judge: "[The officer's] comments were made in a police interrogation room and were expressly directed to the defendant, who was the only other person present when the statements were made." The fifth judge focused on the suspect's youth: "Because juveniles often lack the wherewithal to resist police pressures, they thus become uniquely susceptible to police interrogation efforts including subtly compulsive techniques, and should be expected to respond to those efforts." Do these cases correctly apply *Miranda*?

(2) The interrogation standard may be met even without a particular statement or question being the subject of the analysis. For instance, in *United States v. Jackson*, 544 F.3d 351 (1st Cir. 2008), the police arrived to search the defendant's home. Before doing so, however, the officer urged the defendant to cooperate in the investigation. The officer then told the defendant that another occupant had given them permission to conduct the search. Hearing that, the defendant confessed. The trial court allowed the confession in evidence finding that it was voluntary and spontaneous. The court on appeal disagreed, relying heavily on the facts that the officer asked the defendant some questions before getting permission to search, the officer told the defendant that the officer thought the defendant was involved in the criminal act, there was little time between the initial questioning and the defendant's statement, and "the officer's obvious purpose in the earlier questioning was to secure an incriminating statement from [the defendant]."

(3) The facts in *Haire v. Sarver*, 437 F.2d 1262, 1263 (8th Cir. 1971), *cert. denied*, 404 U.S. 910 (1971), created a unique problem for the court. The chief focus of the investigation was not the defendant at all, but his wife:

> While she was being questioned, defendant appeared voluntarily at the jail and was arrested. Defendant's wife told the officers that the body was in a wheat field on the right side of a county road. She was taken to the area where a search was conducted without success. Defendant was also taken to the scene and when his wife was asked whether she had not told the officers that the body was on the right hand side of the road, defendant, without waiting for her reply, stated, "no, Honey, on the left side." The wife was then asked where the gun was hidden and she replied that it was under the bed at her home. Again, defendant corrected her and stated that the gun was hidden in the fireplace. Defendant had not been given the *Miranda* warnings and was not interrogated.

The defendant argued that his responses were the product of interrogation and should have been excluded under *Miranda*. The court disagreed, finding that he had voluntarily come to the station house, and there was "no evidence of any semblance of pressure or coercion or lack of voluntariness of the statements." Was the court's holding proper? Should the court have placed more weight on the fact that the defendant was formally under arrest during this period and was taken by the police to the spot where the body was found?

(4) *Miranda* only applies to responses to custodial interrogation. If a person appears before a grand jury and gives incriminating answers, does *Miranda* apply? *See United States v. Mandujano*, 425 U.S. 564 (1976):

> In this case, the Court of Appeals required the suppression of perjured testimony given by respondent, as a witness under oath, lawfully summoned before an investigative grand jury and questioned about matters directly related to the grand jury's inquiry. The court reached this result because the prosecutor failed to give *Miranda* warnings at the outset of Mandujano's interrogation. Those warnings were required, in the Court of Appeals' view, because Mandujano was a "virtual" or "putative" defendant — that is, the prosecutor had specific information concerning Mandujano's participation in an attempted sale of heroin and the focus of the grand jury interrogation, as evidenced by the prosecutor's questions, centered on Mandujano's involvement in narcotics traffic. The fundamental error of the prosecutor, in the court's view, was to treat respondent in such a way as to "smack of entrapment"; as a consequence, the court concluded that "elemental fairness" required the perjured testimony to be suppressed. The court's analysis, premised upon the prosecutor's failure to give *Miranda* warnings, erroneously applied the standards fashioned by this Court in *Miranda*. Those warnings were aimed at the evils seen by the Court as endemic to police interrogation of a person in custody. *Miranda* addressed extra-judicial confessions or admissions procured in a hostile, unfamiliar environment which lacked procedural safeguards. The decision expressly rested on the privilege against compulsory self-incrimination; the prescribed warnings sought to negate the "compulsion" thought to be inherent in police station interrogation. But the *Miranda* Court simply did not perceive judicial inquiries and custodial interrogation as equivalents: ". . . the compulsion to speak in the isolated setting of the police station may well be greater than in courts or other official investigations, where there are often impartial observers to guard against intimidation or trickery."
>
> The Court thus recognized that many official investigations, such as grand jury questioning, take place in a setting wholly different from custodial police interrogation. Indeed, the Court's opinion in *Miranda* reveals a focus on what was seen by the Court as police "coercion" derived from "factual studies [relating to] police violence and the third degree . . . physical brutality — beating, hanging, whipping — and to sustained and protracted questioning incommunicado in order to extort confessions. . . ." To extend these concepts to questioning before a grand jury inquiring into criminal activity under the guidance of a judge is an extravagant expansion never remotely contemplated by this Court in *Miranda*, the dynamics of constitutional interpretation do not compel constant extension of every doctrine announced by the Court.

> The marked contrasts between a grand jury investigation and custodial interrogation have been commented on by the Court from time to time. Mr. Justice Marshall observed that the broad coercive powers of a grand jury are justified, because ". . . in contrast to the police it is not likely that [the grand jury] will abuse those powers."

Would *Miranda* have been distorted if applied to the grand jury setting? As a practical matter, what would the impact of such a holding be?

FORMS OF INTERROGATION

Attention to this point has been on the situation of statements which were allegedly volunteered. In other cases, however, defendants argue that seemingly innocuous actions by the police were calculated interrogations which resulted in responses barred by *Miranda.*

In numerous cases, the most innocuous action of all is used — no communication by the police. Here the officers arrest the defendants and place them in a holding room or in the back of the police car. Unknown to the suspects, the officers are secretly listening in on incriminating conversations. If the action of placing the defendants in such situations and leaving them unsupervised is designed to elicit statements, does that constitute interrogation? Not according to the courts in *Napper v. United States*, 22 A.3d 758 (D.C. App. 2011), and *State v. Rollins*, 675 S.E.2d 334 (N.C. 2009). The only exception — as explained in *Cuomo v. State*, 918 So. 3d 1275, 1281 (Fla. App. 2012), occurs "when law enforcement deliberately fosters an expectation of privacy, especially — for the purpose of circumventing a defendant's right to counsel, [then] subsequent jailhouse conversations and confessions are inadmissible."

PROBLEM H
INTERROGATION

Was the defendant in *Drury v. State*, 793 A.2d 567 (Md. App. 2002), *cert. denied,* 537 U.S. 942, interrogated? He was brought to the police station and shown stolen property; officers told him the items would be examined for fingerprints. Held, interrogation had occurred:

> It appears to us that the only reasonable conclusion that can be drawn from the foregoing facts is that the officer should have known, in light of his having told petitioner that he was being brought in for questioning, that putting the evidence before petitioner and telling him that the items were going to be fingerprinted was reasonably likely to evoke an incriminating response from him. The only plausible explanation for the officer's conduct is that he expected to elicit a statement from petitioner.

RHODE ISLAND v. INNIS

United States Supreme Court
446 U.S. 291 (1980)

MR. JUSTICE STEWART delivered the opinion of the Court.

In *Miranda v. Arizona*, 384 U.S. 436, 474, the Court held that, once a defendant in custody asks to speak with a lawyer, all interrogation must cease until a lawyer is present. The issue in this case is whether the respondent was "interrogated" in violation of the standards promulgated in the *Miranda* opinion.

I

On the night of January 12, 1975, John Mulvaney, a Providence, R.I., taxicab driver, disappeared after being dispatched to pick up a customer. His body was discovered four days later buried in a shallow grave in Coventry, R.I. He had died from a shotgun blast aimed at the back of his head.

On January 17, 1975, shortly after midnight, the Providence police received a telephone call from Gerald Aubin, also a taxicab driver, who reported that he had just been robbed by a man wielding a sawed-off shotgun. Aubin further reported that he had dropped off his assailant near Rhode Island College in a section of Providence known as Mount Pleasant. While at the Providence police station waiting to give a statement, Aubin noticed a picture of his assailant on a bulletin board. Aubin so informed one of the police officers present. The officer prepared a photo array, and again Aubin identified a picture of the same person. That person was the respondent. Shortly thereafter, the Providence police began a search of the Mount Pleasant area.

At approximately 4:30 a.m. on the same date, Patrolman Lovell, while cruising the streets of Mount Pleasant in a patrol car, spotted the respondent standing in the street facing him. When Patrolman Lovell stopped his car, the respondent walked towards it. Patrolman Lovell then arrested the respondent, who was unarmed, and advised him of his so-called *Miranda* rights. While the two men waited in the patrol car for other police officers to arrive, Patrolman Lovell did not converse with the respondent other than to respond to the latter's request for a cigarette.

Within minutes, Sergeant Sears arrived at the scene of the arrest, and he also gave the respondent the *Miranda* warnings. Immediately thereafter, Captain Leyden and other police officers arrived. Captain Leyden advised the respondent of his *Miranda* rights. The respondent stated that he understood those rights and wanted to speak with a lawyer. Captain Leyden then directed that the respondent be placed in a "caged wagon," a four-door police car with a wire screen mesh between the front and rear seats, and be driven to the central police station. Three officers, Patrolmen Gleckman, Williams and McKenna, were assigned to accompany the respondent to the central station. They placed the respondent in the vehicle and shut the doors. Captain Leyden then instructed the officers not to question the respondent or intimidate or coerce him in any way. The three officers then entered the vehicle, and it departed.

While en route to the central station, Patrolman Gleckman initiated a conversation with Patrolman McKenna concerning the missing shotgun.[28] As Patrolman Gleckman later testified:

> A. At this point, I was talking back and forth with Patrolman McKenna stating that I frequent this area while on patrol and [that because a school for handicapped children is located nearby,] there's a lot of handicapped children running around in this area, and God forbid one of them might find a weapon with shells and they might hurt themselves. App., at 43–44.

Patrolman McKenna apparently shared his fellow officer's concern: "A. I more or less concurred with him [Gleckman] that it was a safety factor and that we should, you know, continue to search for the weapon and try to find it." *Id.*, at 53.

While Patrolman Williams said nothing, he overheard the conversation between the two officers: "A. He [Gleckman] said it would be too bad if the little — I believe he said girl — would pick up the gun, maybe kill herself." *Id.*, at 59.

The respondent then interrupted the conversation, stating that the officers should turn the car around so he could show them where the gun was located. At this point, Patrolman McKenna radioed back to Captain Leyden that they were returning to the scene of the arrest, and that the respondent would inform them of the location of the gun. At the time the respondent indicated that the officers should turn back, they had traveled no more than a mile, a trip encompassing only a few minutes.

The police vehicle then returned to the scene of the arrest where a search for the shotgun was in progress. There, Captain Leyden again advised the respondent of his *Miranda* rights. The respondent replied that he understood those rights but that he "wanted to get the gun out of the way because of the kids in the area in the school." The respondent then led the police to a nearby field, where he pointed out the shotgun under some rocks by the side of the road.

[W]ithout passing on whether the police officers had in fact "interrogated" the respondent, the trial court sustained the admissibility of the shotgun and testimony related to its discovery. That evidence was later introduced at the respondent's trial, and the jury returned a verdict of guilty on all counts.

II

The issue, therefore, is whether the respondent was "interrogated" by the police officers in violation of the respondent's undisputed right under *Miranda* to remain silent until he had consulted with a lawyer. In resolving this issue, we first define the term "interrogation" under *Miranda* before turning to a consideration of the facts of this case.

[28] [1] Although there was conflicting testimony about the exact seating arrangements, it is clear that everyone in the vehicle heard the conversation.

A

The starting point for defining "interrogation" in this context is, of course, the Court's *Miranda* opinion. There the Court observed that "[by] custodial interrogation, we mean *questioning* initiated by law enforcement officers after a person has been taken into custody or otherwise deprived of his freedom of action in any significant way."

This passage and other references throughout the opinion to "questioning" might suggest that the *Miranda* rules were to apply only to those police interrogation practices that involve express questioning of a defendant while in custody.

We do not, however, construe the *Miranda* opinion so narrowly. The concern of the Court in *Miranda* was that the "interrogation environment" created by the interplay of interrogation and custody would "subjugate the individual to the will of his examiner" and thereby undermine the privilege against compulsory self-incrimination. The police practices that evoked this concern included several that did not involve express questioning. For example, one of the practices discussed in *Miranda* was the use of lineups in which a coached witness would pick the defendant as the perpetrator. This was designed to establish that the defendant was in fact guilty as a predicate for further interrogation. A variation on this theme discussed in *Miranda* was the so-called "reverse line-up" in which a defendant would be identified by coached witnesses as the perpetrator of a fictitious crime, with the object of inducing him to confess to the actual crime of which he was suspected in order to escape the false prosecution. The Court in *Miranda* also included in its survey of interrogation practices the use of psychological ploys, such as to "[posit]" "the guilt of the subject," to "minimize the moral seriousness of the offense," and to "cast blame on the victim or on society." It is clear that these techniques of persuasion, no less than express questioning, were thought, in a custodial setting, to amount to interrogation.[29]

This is not to say, however, that all statements obtained by the police after a person has been taken into custody are to be considered the product of interrogation.

It is clear therefore that the special procedural safeguards outlined in *Miranda* are required not where a suspect is simply taken into custody, but rather where a suspect in custody is subjected to interrogation. "Interrogation," as conceptualized in the *Miranda* opinion, must reflect a measure of compulsion above and beyond that inherent in custody itself.

We conclude that the *Miranda* safeguards come into play whenever a person in custody is subjected to either express questioning or its functional equivalent. That is to say, the term "interrogation" under *Miranda* refers not only to express questioning, but also to any words or actions on the part of the police (other than those normally attendant to arrest and custody) that the police should know are

[29] [3] To limit the ambit of *Miranda* to express questioning would "place a premium on the ingenuity of the police to devise methods of indirect interrogation, rather than to implement the plain mandate of *Miranda*."

reasonably likely to elicit an incriminating response from the suspect.[30] The latter portion of this definition focuses primarily upon the perceptions of the suspect, rather than the intent of the police. This focus reflects the fact that the *Miranda* safeguards were designed to vest a suspect in custody with an added measure of protection against coercive police practices, without regard to objective proof of the underlying intent of the police. A practice that the police should know is reasonably likely to evoke an incriminating response from a suspect thus amounts to interrogation. But, since the police surely cannot be held accountable for the unforeseeable results of their words or actions, the definition of interrogation can extend only to words or actions on the part of police officers that they *should have known* were reasonably likely to elicit an incriminating response.

B

Turning to the facts of the present case, we conclude that the respondent was not "interrogated" within the meaning of *Miranda*. It is undisputed that the first prong of the definition of "interrogation" was not satisfied, for the conversation between Patrolmen Gleckman and McKenna included no express questioning of the respondent. Rather, that conversation was, at least in form, nothing more than a dialogue between the two officers to which no response from the respondent was invited.

Moreover, it cannot be fairly concluded that the respondent was subjected to the "functional equivalent" of questioning. It cannot be said, in short, that Patrolmen Gleckman and McKenna should have known that their conversation was reasonably likely to elicit an incriminating response from the respondent. There is nothing in the record to suggest that the officers were aware that the respondent was peculiarly susceptible to an appeal to his conscience concerning the safety of handicapped children. Nor is there anything in the record to suggest that the police knew that the respondent was unusually disoriented or upset at the time of his arrest.[31]

The case thus boils down to whether, in the context of a brief conversation, the officers should have known that the respondent would suddenly be moved to make a self-incriminating response. Given the fact that the entire conversation appears to have consisted of no more than a few off hand remarks, we cannot say that the officers should have known that it was reasonably likely that Innis would so respond. This is not a case where the police carried on a lengthy harangue in the presence of the suspect. Nor does the record support the respondent's contention that, under the circumstances, the officers' comments were particularly "evocative." It is our view, therefore, that the respondent was not subjected by the police to words or actions that the police should have known were reasonably likely to elicit an incriminating response from him.

---

[30] [5] One of the dissenting opinions seems totally to misapprehend this definition in suggesting that it "will almost certainly exclude every statement [of the police] that is not punctuated with a question mark."

[31] [9] The record in no way suggests that the officers' remarks were *designed* to elicit a response. It is significant that the trial judge, after hearing the officers' testimony, concluded that it was "entirely understandable that [the officers] would voice their concern [for the safety of the handicapped children] to each other."

The Rhode Island Supreme Court erred, in short, in equating "subtle compulsion" with interrogation. That the officers' comments struck a responsive cord is readily apparent. Thus, it may be said, as the Rhode Island Supreme Court did say, that the respondent was subjected to "subtle compulsion." But that is not the end of the inquiry. It must also be established that a suspect's incriminating response was the product of words or actions on the part of the police that they should have known were reasonably likely to elicit an incriminating response.[32] This was not established in the present case.

For the reasons stated, the judgment of the Supreme Court of Rhode Island is vacated, and the case is remanded to that court for further proceedings not inconsistent with this opinion.

It is so ordered.

MR. JUSTICE WHITE concurred.

MR. CHIEF JUSTICE BURGER, concurring in the judgment.

Since the result is not inconsistent with *Miranda v. Arizona*, I concur in the judgment.

The meaning of *Miranda* has become reasonably clear and law enforcement practices have adjusted to its strictures; I would neither overrule *Miranda*, disparage it, nor extend it at this late date. I fear, however, that the rationale in Parts II-A and II-B, of the Court's opinion will not clarify the tension between this holding and *Brewer v. Williams* and our other cases. It may introduce new elements of uncertainty; under the Court's test, a police officer in the brief time available, apparently must evaluate the suggestibility and susceptibility of an accused. Few, if any, police officers are competent to make the kind of evaluation seemingly contemplated; even a psychiatrist asked to express an expert opinion on these aspects of a suspect in custody would very likely employ extensive questioning and observation to make the judgment now charged to police officers.

Trial judges have enough difficulty discerning the boundaries and nuances flowing from post-*Miranda* opinions, and we do not clarify that situation today.

MR. JUSTICE MARSHALL, with whom MR. JUSTICE BRENNAN joins, dissenting.

I am utterly at a loss, however, to understand how this objective standard as applied to the facts before us can rationally lead to the conclusion that there was no interrogation. Innis was arrested at 4:30 a.m., handcuffed, searched, advised of his rights, and placed in the back seat of a patrol car. Within a short time he had been twice more advised of his rights and driven away in a four door sedan with three

[32] [10] By way of example, if the police had done no more than to drive past the site of the concealed weapon while taking the most direct route to the police station, and if the respondent, upon noticing for the first time the proximity of the school for handicapped children, had blurted out that he would show the officers where the gun was located, it could not seriously be argued that this "subtle compulsion" would have constituted "interrogation" within the meaning of the *Miranda* opinion.

police officers. Two officers sat in the front seat and one sat beside Innis in the back seat. Since the car traveled no more than a mile before Innis agreed to point out the location of the murder weapon, Officer Gleckman must have begun almost immediately to talk about the search for the shotgun.

The Court attempts to characterize Gleckman's statements as "no more than a few offhand remarks" which could not reasonably have been expected to elicit a response. If the statements had been addressed to respondent, it would be impossible to draw such a conclusion. The simple message of the "talking back and forth" between Gleckman and McKenna was that they had to find the shotgun to avert a child's death.

One can scarcely imagine a stronger appeal to the conscience of a suspect — *any* suspect — than the assertion that if the weapon is not found an innocent person will be hurt or killed. And not just any innocent person, but an innocent child — a little girl — a helpless, handicapped little girl on her way to school. The notion that such an appeal could not be expected to have any effect unless the suspect were known to have some special interest in handicapped children verges on the ludicrous. As a matter of fact, the appeal to a suspect to confess for the sake of others, to "display some evidence of decency and honor," is a classic interrogation technique.

Gleckman's remarks would obviously have constituted interrogation if they had been explicitly directed to respondent, and the result should not be different because they were nominally addressed to McKenna. This is not a case where police officers speaking among themselves are accidentally overheard by a suspect. These officers were "talking back and forth" in close quarters with the handcuffed suspect, traveling past the very place where they believed the weapon was located. They knew respondent would hear and attend to their conversation, and they are chargeable with knowledge of and responsibility for the pressures to speak which they created.

I firmly believe that this case is simply an aberration, and that in future cases the Court will apply the standard adopted today in accordance with its plain meaning.

Mr. Justice Stevens, dissenting.

In my view any statement that would normally be understood by the average listener as calling for a response is the functional equivalent of a direct question, whether or not it is punctuated by a question mark. The Court, however, takes a much narrower view. It holds that police conduct is not the "functional equivalent" of direct questioning unless the police should have known that what they were saying or doing was likely to elicit an incriminating response from the suspect. This holding represents a plain departure from the principles set forth in *Miranda.*

In *Miranda* the Court required the now-familiar warnings to be given to suspects prior to custodial interrogation in order to dispel the atmosphere of coercion that necessarily accompanies such interrogations. In order to perform that function effectively, the warnings must be viewed by both the police and the suspect as a correct and binding statement of their respective rights. Thus, if, after being told that he has a right to have an attorney present during interrogation, a suspect chooses to cut off questioning until counsel can be obtained, his choice must be "scrupulously honored" by the police. At the least this must mean that the police are prohibited from making deliberate attempts to elicit statements from the suspect. Yet the Court is unwilling to characterize all such attempts as "interrogation," noting only that "where a police practice is designed to elicit an incriminating response from the accused, it is unlikely that the practice will not also be one which the police should have known was reasonably likely to have that effect."

From the suspect's point of view, the effectiveness of the warnings depends on whether it appears that the police are scrupulously honoring his rights. Apparent attempts to elicit information from a suspect after he has invoked his right to cut off questioning necessarily demean that right and tend to reinstate the imbalance between police and suspect that the *Miranda* warnings are designed to correct. Thus, if the rationale for requiring those warnings in the first place is to be respected, any police conduct or statements that would appear to a reasonable person in the suspect's position to call for a response must be considered "interrogation."

In short, in order to give full protection to a suspect's right to be free from any interrogation at all, the definition of "interrogation" must include any police statement or conduct that has the same purpose or effect as a direct question. Statements that appear to call for a response from the suspect, as well as those that are designed to do so, should be considered interrogation. By prohibiting only those relatively few statements or actions that a police officer should know are likely to elicit an incriminating response, the Court today accords a suspect considerably less protection. Indeed, since I suppose most suspects are unlikely to incriminate themselves even when questioned directly, this new definition will almost certainly exclude every statement that is not punctuated with a question mark from the concept of "interrogation."

NOTES AND QUESTIONS

(1) Justice Stewart stated that, "the term 'interrogation' under *Miranda* refers not only to express questioning, but also to any words or actions on the part of the police . . . that the police should know are reasonably likely to elicit an incriminating response from the suspect." With that as the holding, why did the Court vacate the judgment of the Rhode Island Supreme Court? Did the majority answer the statement of Justice Marshall?

> Gleckman's remarks would obviously have constituted interrogation if they had been explicitly directed to petitioner, and the result should not be different because they were nominally addressed to McKenna. This is not a case where police officers speaking among themselves are accidentally overheard by a suspect. These officers were "talking back and forth" in close quarters with the hand-cuffed suspect, traveling past the very place where they believed the weapon was located. They knew petitioner would hear and attend to their conversation, and they are chargeable with knowledge of and responsibility for the pressures to speak which they created.

The trial court never passed on whether the officers had interrogated the defendant. Should the majority have taken its position without such a review by the state court?

Courts here are supposed to look to an objective standard, i.e., were the officer's actions reasonably likely to elicit an incriminating response? Still, the subjective standard continues to creep into the analysis. *See Rodriguez v. State*, 991 A.2d 100 (Md. Ct. Spec. App. 2010) (Officer "testified that she had no intention of interrogating the appellant during the transport for investigative purposes. . . ."); *Shaneberger v. Jones*, 615 F.3d 448 (6th Cir. 2010) ("While we do not focus on the intent of the police, a practice that is subjectively intended to elicit an incriminating response will very likely produce a finding that the police should have known that such a result would occur.")

(2) Justice Stevens argued strongly that the position of the majority offers the defendant considerably less protection than the position he put forth.

> In short, in order to give full protection to a suspect's right to be free from any interrogation at all, the definition of "interrogation" must include any police statement or conduct that has the same purpose or effect as a direct question. Statements that appear to call for a response from the suspect, as well as those that are designed to do so, should be considered interrogation. By prohibiting only those relatively few statements or actions that a police officer should know are likely to elicit an incriminating response, the Court today accords a suspect considerably less protection. Indeed, since I suppose most suspects are unlikely to incriminate themselves even when questioned directly, this new definition will almost certainly exclude every statement that is not punctuated with a question mark from the concept of "interrogation."

Do you agree with Justice Stevens? In what cases would the difference in the formulation of the rule be significant?

(3) In one footnote the Court discussed the non-interrogation situation in which the police drove past the site of the concealed weapon "while taking the most direct route to the police station. . . ." Suppose the police drove past the site of the concealed weapon while taking a circuitous route to the station. Would this be interrogation? Would driving the suspect be action the "police should know [is] reasonably likely to elicit an incriminating response"?

The Supreme Court denied the petition for a writ of certiorari in *Lewis v. Florida*, 486 U.S. 1036 (1988). Justice White dissented:

> [P]etitioner, once in custody, was given *Miranda* warnings and immediately invoked his right to remain silent. The police did not try to question him, but instead took him to a room where he was shown a videotape of the robbery, which also included footage of the shooting of the attendant. While viewing the videotape, petitioner made several incriminating statements to an officer. Petitioner argued that being confronted with evidence of this nature is the "functional equivalent" of express questioning, which is impermissible once a person in custody has invoked his right to remain silent. . . .

We have stated that "interrogation" under *Miranda* does include conditions that are its "functional equivalent," this is, "any words or actions on the part of the police (other than those normally attendant to arrest and custody) that the police should know are reasonably likely to elicit an incriminating response from the suspect. The latter portion of this definition focuses primarily upon the perceptions of the suspect, rather than the intent of the police." *Rhode Island v. Innis.* We also have observed that a "psychological ploy" of any significance would also be treated as the "functional equivalent" of interrogation.

Whether police may confront a suspect with evidence against him, outside the range of normal arrest and charging procedures, without engaging in the "functional equivalent" of interrogation is a substantial question in light of *Innis.* In addition, the federal and state courts disagree over the issue. I would grant certiorari to consider the construction of *Innis* to resolve the significant disagreement on this general issue among the state and federal courts, which has led those courts both to handicap the police in pursuing some apparently legitimate law-enforcement practices and to approve the use of other ploys that have nothing to do with the usual and accepted procedures for arresting and charging a suspect.

(4) Do you agree with the following editorial?

In his majority opinion [in *Innis*], Justice Stewart distinguishes between the apparently casual chatter about the danger of the hidden shotgun and actual "interrogation." The difference, he says in effect, is one of degree. . . ." The definition of interrogation," says the Court, "can extend only to words or actions that (the police) should have known were reasonably likely to elicit an incriminating response." The practical message for arresting officers — except for a vague sense that some over-refinements of the *Miranda* rules are being somewhat relaxed — is a bit hazy. . . .

It seems to be one of those occasional instances in which the Supreme Court sought clarity but found further confusion.

Figuring Out the "Miranda Rules," The Washington Star, May 16, 1980.

(5) In *Arizona v. Mauro*, 481 U.S. 520 (1987), the defendant was arrested and charged with murder. He received his warnings and told the police he did not want to make any statement without having an attorney present. At this time defendant's wife was also to be questioned at the police station. She indicated she wanted to talk with defendant. She was allowed to sit with him in a room along with an officer who attempted (unsuccessfully) to tape record the conversation. Were defendant's comments, as repeated by the officer, admissible against him? Compare the majority and dissenting opinions:

Majority (Justice Powell):

The officers gave Mauro the warnings required by *Miranda.* Mauro indicated that he did not wish to be questioned further without a lawyer present. Mauro never waived his right to have a lawyer present. The sole issue, then, is whether the officers' subsequent actions rose to the level of interrogation — that is, in the language of *Innis*, whether they were the "functional equivalent" of police interrogation. We think it is clear under both *Miranda* and *Innis* that Mauro was not interrogated. The tape recording of the conversation between Mauro and his wife shows that Detective Manson asked Mauro no questions about the crime or his conduct. Nor is it suggested — or supported by any evidence — that Sergeant Allen's decision to allow Mauro's wife to see him was the kind of psychological ploy that properly could be treated as the functional equivalent of interrogation.

Dissent (Justice Stevens):

It is undisputed that a police decision to place two suspects in the same room and then to listen to or record their conversation may constitute a form of interrogation even if no questions are asked by any police officers. That is exactly what happened here. The police placed respondent and his wife, who was also in police custody, in the same small area. Mr. and Mrs. Mauro were suspects in the murder of their son. Each of them had been interrogated separately before the officers decided to allow them to converse, an act that surely did not require a tape recorder or the presence of a police officer within hearing range. Under the circumstances, the police knew or should have known that Mrs. Mauro's encounter with respondent was reasonably likely to produce an incriminating response. Indeed, Officer Allen's supervisor testified that the police had a reasonable expectation that the spousal conversation would provide information on the murder investigation.

(6) Did these cases correctly apply the rule in *Innis*? *People v. Madrid*, 179 P.3d 1010 (Colo. 2008) (*Innis* not violated when officer explained to the in-custody suspect that officers thought shooting might have been a mistake and officers needed to figure out the reasons for the shooting); *Enoch v. Gramley*, 861 F. Supp. 718 (C.D. Ill. 1994), *cert. denied*, 519 U.S. 829 (1996) (*Innis* violated where officer told defendant he would go to jail for murder, and that the officer thought the defendant was involved in the murder and had heard of the involvement from another witness); *United States v. Moreno-Flores*, 33 F.3d 1164, 1169 (9th Cir. 1994) (no Fifth Amendment issue, agents told defendant that he was in serious trouble because they had seized drugs belonging to him). What about *United States v. Blake*, 571 F.3d 331 (4th Cir. 2009)? There the police officer "taunted" the 17-year-old suspect by showing him a charging sheet with a possible death sentence, and saying, "I bet you want to talk now." Held, not interrogation.

The taunt at most contained an implicit suggestion that Blake would be wise to cooperate in light of the information contained in the statement of charges. In the absence of any explanation of why cooperating, rather than conferring with a lawyer, would be the best choice for Blake, [Officer] Reese could not have reasonably anticipated that his taunt would convince Blake to change his mind. Thus, we conclude that any marginal coercive effect that Reese reasonably would have expected the remark to have was even more subtle than that of the conversation at issue in Innis.

Id. at 342.

The issue here is not whether a statement is "made in response to a particular question. The entire course of conduct of the officers must be examined to determine whether the statement was in response to unlawful questioning under *Miranda*." *United States v. Jackson*, 544 F.3d 351, 357 (1st Cir. 2008).

PROBLEM I
PSYCHIATRIC EXAMINATION

In *Estelle v. Smith*, 451 U.S. 454 (1981), the defendant was indicted for murder. The trial judge arranged a psychiatric examination of the defendant by Dr. Grigson to determine the defendant's competency to stand trial. At the sentencing hearing before a jury (bifurcated death penalty proceedings), the government called Dr. Grigson as a witness. Could he testify as to the defendant's statements during the psychiatric examination? Held, the testimony was improper because the defendant had not been advised of his right to remain silent at the psychiatric examination.

> A criminal defendant, who neither initiates a psychiatric evaluation nor attempts to introduce any psychiatric evidence, may not be compelled to respond to a psychiatrist if his statements can be used against him at a capital sentencing proceeding. Because respondent did not voluntarily consent to the pretrial psychiatric examination after being informed of his right to remain silent and the possible use of his statements, the State could not rely on what he said to Dr. Grigson to establish his future dangerousness.

THE RESUMPTION OF QUESTIONING

MICHIGAN v. MOSLEY
United States Supreme Court
423 U.S. 96 (1975)

MR. JUSTICE STEWART delivered the opinion of the Court.

The respondent, Richard Bert Mosley, was arrested in Detroit, Mich., in the early afternoon of April 8, 1971, in connection with robberies that had recently occurred at the Blue Goose Bar and the White Tower Restaurant on that city's lower east side. The arresting officer, Detective James Cowie of the Armed Robbery Section of the Detroit Police Department, was acting on a tip implicating Mosley and three other men in the robberies. After effecting the arrest, Detective Cowie brought Mosley to the Robbery, Breaking and Entering Bureau of the Police Department, located on the fourth floor of the departmental headquarters building. The officer advised Mosley of his rights under this Court's decision in *Miranda v. Arizona*, and had him read and sign the department's constitutional rights notification certificate. After filling out the necessary arrest papers, Cowie began questioning Mosley about the robbery of the White Tower Restaurant. When Mosley said he did not want to answer any questions about the robberies, Cowie promptly ceased the interrogation. The completion of the arrest papers and the questioning of Mosley together took approximately 20 minutes. At no time during the questioning did Mosley indicate a desire to consult with a lawyer, and there is no claim that the procedures followed to this point did not fully comply with the strictures of the *Miranda* opinion. Mosley was then taken to a ninth-floor cell block.

Shortly after 6 P.M., Detective Hill of the Detroit Police Department Homicide Bureau brought Mosley from the cell block to the fifth-floor office of the Homicide Bureau for questioning about the fatal shooting of a man named Leroy Williams. Williams had been killed on January 9, 1971, during a holdup attempt outside the 101 Ranch Bar in Detroit. Mosley had not been arrested on this charge nor interrogated about it by Detective Cowie. Before questioning Mosley about this homicide, Detective Hill carefully advised him of his "*Miranda* rights." Mosley read the notification form both silently and aloud, and Detective Hill then read and explained the warning to him and had him sign the form. Mosley at first denied any involvement in the Williams murder, but after the officer told him that Anthony Smith had confessed to participating in the slaying and had named him as the "shooter," Mosley made a statement implicating himself in the homicide. The interrogation by Detective Hill lasted approximately 15 minutes, and at no time during its course did Mosley ask to consult with a lawyer or indicate that he did not want to discuss the homicide. In short, there is no claim that the procedures followed during Detective Hill's interrogation of Mosley, standing alone, did not fully comply with the strictures of the *Miranda* opinion.

Mosley was subsequently charged in a one-count information with first-degree murder. Before the trial he moved to suppress his incriminating statement on a number of grounds, among them the claim that under the doctrine of the *Miranda* case it was constitutionally impermissible for Detective Hill to question him about the Williams murder after he had told Detective Cowie that he did not want to answer any questions about the robberies.

Neither party in the present case challenges the continuing validity of the *Miranda* decision, or any of the so-called guidelines it established to protect what the Court there said was a person's constitutional privilege against compulsory self-incrimination. The issue in this case, rather, is whether the conduct of the Detroit police that led to Mosley's incriminating statement did in fact violate the *Miranda* "guidelines," so as to render the statement inadmissible in evidence against Mosley at his trial. Resolution of the question turns almost entirely on the interpretation of a single passage in the *Miranda* opinion, upon which the Michigan appellate court relied in finding a *per se* violation of *Miranda*:

> Once warnings have been given, the subsequent procedure is clear. If the individual indicates in any manner, at any time prior to or during questioning, that he wishes to remain silent, the interrogation must cease. At this point he has shown that he intends to exercise his Fifth Amendment privilege; any statement taken after the person invokes his privilege cannot be other than the product of compulsion, subtle or otherwise. Without the right to cut off questioning, the setting of in-custody interrogation operates on the individual to overcome free choice in producing a statement after the privilege has been once invoked.[33]

This passage states that "the interrogation must cease" when the person in

[33] [7] The present case does not involve the procedures to be followed if the person in custody asks

custody indicates that "he wishes to remain silent." It does not state under what circumstances, if any, a resumption of questioning is permissible. The passage could be literally read to mean that a person who has invoked his "right to silence" can never again be subjected to custodial interrogation by any police officer at any time or place on any subject. Another possible construction of the passage would characterize "any statement taken after the person invokes his privilege" as "the product of compulsion" and would therefore mandate its exclusion from evidence, even if it were volunteered by the person in custody without any further interrogation whatever. Or the passage could be interpreted to require only the immediate cessation of questioning, and to permit a resumption of interrogation after a momentary respite.

It is evident that any of these possible literal interpretations would lead to absurd and unintended results. To permit the continuation of custodial interrogation after a momentary cessation would clearly frustrate the purposes of *Miranda* by allowing repeated rounds of questioning to undermine the will of the person being questioned. At the other extreme, a blanket prohibition against the taking of voluntary statements or a permanent immunity from further interrogation, regardless of the circumstances, would transform the *Miranda* safeguards into wholly irrational obstacles to legitimate police investigative activity, and deprive suspects of an opportunity to make informed and intelligent assessments of their interests. Clearly, therefore, neither this passage nor any other passage in the *Miranda* opinion can sensibly be read to create a *per se* proscription of indefinite duration upon any further questioning by any police officer on any subject, once the person in custody has indicated a desire to remain silent.

A reasonable and faithful interpretation of the *Miranda* opinion must rest on the intention of the Court in that case to adopt "fully effective means . . . to notify the person of his right of silence and to assure that the exercise of the right will be scrupulously honored. . . ." The critical safeguard identified in the passage at issue is a person's "right to cut off questioning." Through the exercise of his option to terminate questioning he can control the time at which questioning occurs, the subjects discussed, and the duration of the interrogation. The requirement that law enforcement authorities must respect a person's exercise of that option counteracts the coercive pressures of the custodial setting. We therefore conclude that the admissibility of statements obtained after the person in custody has decided to remain silent depends under *Miranda* on whether his "right to cut off questioning" was "scrupulously honored."[34]

---

to consult with a lawyer, since Mosley made no such request at any time. Those procedures are detailed in the *Miranda* opinion as follows:

> If the individual states that he wants an attorney, the interrogation must cease until an attorney is present. At that time, the individual must have an opportunity to confer with the attorney and to have him present during any subsequent questioning. If the individual cannot obtain an attorney and he indicates that he wants one before speaking to the police, they must respect his decision to remain silent.

[34] [10] The dissenting opinion asserts that *Miranda* established a requirement that once a person has indicated a desire to remain silent, questioning may be resumed only when counsel is present. But clearly the Court in *Miranda* imposed no such requirement, for it distinguished between the procedural safeguards triggered by a request to remain silent and a request for an attorney and directed that "the

A review of the circumstances leading to Mosley's confession reveals that his "right to cut off questioning" was fully respected in this case. Before his initial interrogation, Mosley was carefully advised that he was under no obligation to answer any questions and could remain silent if he wished. He orally acknowledged that he understood the *Miranda* warnings and then signed a printed notification of rights form. When Mosley stated that he did not want to discuss the robberies, Detective Cowie immediately ceased the interrogation and did not try either to resume the questioning or in any way to persuade Mosley to reconsider his position. After an interval of more than two hours, Mosley was questioned by another police officer at another location about an unrelated holdup murder. He was given full and complete *Miranda* warnings at the outset of the second interrogation. He was thus reminded again that he could remain silent and could consult with a lawyer, and was carefully given a full and fair opportunity to exercise these options. The subsequent questioning did not undercut Mosley's previous decision not to answer Detective Cowie's inquiries. Detective Hill did not resume the interrogation about the White Tower Restaurant robbery or inquire about the Blue Goose Bar robbery, but instead focused exclusively on the Leroy Williams homicide, a crime different in nature and in time and place of occurrence from the robberies for which Mosley had been arrested and interrogated by Detective Cowie. Although it is not clear from the record how much Detective Hill knew about the earlier interrogation, his questioning of Mosley about an unrelated homicide was quite consistent with a reasonable interpretation of Mosley's earlier refusal to answer any questions about the robberies.

This is not a case, therefore, where the police failed to honor a decision of a person in custody to cut off questioning, either by refusing to discontinue the interrogation upon request or by persisting in repeated efforts to wear down his resistance and make him change his mind. In contrast to such practices, the police here immediately ceased the interrogation, resumed questioning only after the passage of a significant period of time and the provision of a fresh set of warnings, and restricted the second interrogation to a crime that had not been a subject of the earlier interrogation.

For these reasons, we conclude that the admission in evidence of Mosley's incriminating statement did not violate the principles of *Miranda v. Arizona*.

Mr. Justice White, concurring in the result.

I concur in the result and in much of the majority's reasoning. However, it appears to me that in an effort to make only a limited holding in this case, the majority has implied that some custodial confessions will be suppressed even though they follow an informed and voluntary waiver of the defendant's rights. The majority seems to say that a statement obtained within some unspecified time after an assertion by an individual of his "right to silence" is always inadmissible, even if it was the result of an informed and voluntary decision — following, for example, a disclosure to such an individual of a piece of information bearing on his waiver

---

interrogation must cease until an attorney is present" only "[i]f the individual states that he wants an attorney."

decision which the police had failed to give him prior to his assertion of the privilege but which they gave him immediately thereafter. Indeed, the majority characterizes as "absurd" any contrary rule. I disagree. I do not think the majority's conclusion is compelled by *Miranda v. Arizona*, and I suspect that in the final analysis the majority will adopt voluntariness as the standard by which to judge the waiver of the right to silence by a properly informed defendant. I think the Court should say so now.

MR. JUSTICE BRENNAN, with whom MR. JUSTICE MARSHALL joins, dissenting.

Today's distortion of *Miranda*'s constitutional principles can be viewed only as yet another step in the erosion and, I suppose, ultimate overruling of *Miranda*'s enforcement of the privilege against self-incrimination.

The task that confronts the Court in this case is to satisfy the *Miranda* approach by establishing "concrete constitutional guidelines" governing the resumption of questioning a suspect who, while in custody, has once clearly and unequivocally "indicate[d] . . . that he wishes to remain silent. . . ." As the Court today continues to recognize, under *Miranda*, the cost of assuring voluntariness by procedural tests, independent of any actual inquiry into voluntariness, is that some voluntary statements will be excluded. Thus the consideration in the task confronting the Court is not whether voluntary statements will be excluded, but whether the procedures approved will be sufficient to assure with reasonable certainty that a confession is not obtained under the influence of the compulsion inherent in interrogation and detention. The procedures approved by the Court today fail to provide that assurance.

Observing that the suspect can control the circumstances of interrogation "[t]hrough the exercise of his option to terminate questioning," the Court concludes "that the admissibility of statements obtained after the person in custody has decided to remain silent depends . . . on whether his 'right to cut off questioning' was 'scrupulously honored.' " But scrupulously honoring exercises of the right to cut off questioning is only meaningful insofar as the suspect's will to exercise that right remains wholly unfettered. The Court's formulation thus assumes the very matter at issue here: whether renewed questioning following a lengthy period of detention acts to overbear the suspect's will, irrespective of giving the *Miranda* warnings a second time (and scrupulously honoring them), thereby rendering inconsequential any failure to exercise the right to remain silent. For the Court it is enough conclusorily to assert that "[t]he subsequent questioning did not undercut Mosley's previous decision not to answer Detective Cowie's inquiries." Under *Miranda*, however, Mosley's failure to exercise the right upon renewed questioning is presumptively the consequence of an overbearing in which detention and that subsequent questioning played central roles.

NOTES AND QUESTIONS

(1) Justices Brennan and Marshall were quite concerned that this case was "yet another step toward the erosion and . . . ultimate overruling of *Miranda*'s enforcement of the privilege against self-incrimination." Many other judges read

the majority opinion in much the same way. Was this a correct reading? See especially the Court's later affirmation of *Miranda* in the *Dickerson* case, discussed *supra.* Like the words of the Court in *Escobedo*, the language here may be fairly sweeping, but the actual holding seems narrow. Justice Stewart was careful to limit the precedential impact of the case:

> This is not a case, therefore, where the police failed to honor a decision of a person in custody to cut off questioning, either by refusing to discontinue the interrogation upon request or by persisting in repeated efforts to wear down his resistance and make him change his mind. In contrast to such practices, the police here immediately ceased the interrogation, resumed questioning only after the passage of a significant period of time and the provision of a fresh set of warnings, and restricted the second interrogation to a crime that had not been a subject of the earlier interrogation.

(2) The difficulties the state and lower federal courts have had in construing *Mosley* have arisen in determining whether all of the elements mentioned in Note 1 must be present before questioning can be resumed. Recall that in Justice White's concurring opinion, for instance, he strenuously argued that the passage of a significant period of time was not necessary:

> The majority seems to say that a statement obtained within some unspecified time after an assertion by an individual of his "right to silence" is always inadmissible, even if it was the result of an informed and voluntary decision — following, for example, a disclosure to such an individual of a piece of information bearing on his waiver decision which the police had failed to give him prior to his assertion of the privilege but which they gave him immediately thereafter. Indeed, the majority characterizes as "absurd" any contrary rule. I disagree, I don't think the majority's conclusion is compelled by *Miranda v. Arizona*, and I suspect that in the final analysis the majority will adopt voluntariness as the standard by which to judge the waiver of the right to silence. . . .

After *Mosley*, could the police immediately state to the defendant — after he said he wished to remain silent — "your brother just confessed and named you as the gunman." Would the police have to wait for a period of time? How long would that period have to be?

(3) A related problem concerns the fact that in *Mosley*, as the Court noted, the resumption of questioning was connected to a crime that was not the subject of the first interrogation.

The Nevada Supreme Court in *Dewey v. State*, 169 P.3d 1149 (Nev. 2007), held that for purposes of the *Mosley* doctrine, the officers in the second interrogation could question the suspect about the same subject as in the first interrogation.

> In this case, once Dewey invoked her right to remain silent in the first interview, the detective ended the interview. The police waited two hours before they initiated the next interview. The fact that the second interview concerned the same crime is not of great significance under these facts, since Dewey was provided with a fresh set of *Miranda* warnings at the beginning of the second interview. Thereafter, Dewey read and signed a

> waiver form, and the police repeatedly reminded her of her right to stop the interview at any time. Looking at all the relevant circumstances, the immediate cessation of questioning upon Dewey's initial invocation of the right to remain silent, the two-hour time lapse between the interviews, and the careful and repeated *Miranda* warnings, we conclude that the police "scrupulously honored" Dewey's right to remain silent.

Contrast with *United States v. Cody*, 114 F.3d 772, 775 (8th Cir. 1997):

> Once the right is invoked, the police must immediately cease questioning, allow a "significant amount of time" to pass before questioning begins again, re-advise the detainee of her *Miranda* rights, and limit the ensuing interrogation to questions regarding a separate crime not the subject of the first questioning session.

On this point, what is the holding in *Mosley*?

EDWARDS v. ARIZONA

United States Supreme Court
451 U.S. 477 (1981)

JUSTICE WHITE delivered the opinion of the Court.

We granted certiorari in this case, limited to Question 1 presented in the petition, which in relevant part was "whether the Fifth, Sixth, and Fourteenth Amendments require suppression of a post-arrest confession, which was obtained after Edwards had invoked his right to consult counsel before further interrogation. . . ."

I

On January 19, 1976, a sworn complaint was filed against Edwards in Arizona state court charging him with robbery, burglary, and first-degree murder. An arrest warrant was issued pursuant to the complaint, and Edwards was arrested at his home later that same day. At the police station, he was informed of his rights as required by *Miranda v. Arizona*. Petitioner stated that he understood his rights, and was willing to submit to questioning. After being told that another suspect already in custody had implicated him in the crime, Edwards denied involvement and gave a taped statement presenting an alibi defense. He then sought to "make a deal." The interrogating officer told him that he wanted a statement, but that he did not have the authority to negotiate a deal. The officer provided Edwards with the telephone number of a county attorney. Petitioner made the call, but hung up after a few moments. Edwards then said: "I want an attorney before making a deal." At that point, questioning ceased and Edwards was taken to county jail.

At 9:15 the next morning, two detectives, colleagues of the officer who had interrogated Edwards the previous night, came to the jail and asked to see Edwards. When the detention officer informed Edwards that the detectives wished to speak with him, he replied that he did not want to talk to anyone. The guard told him that "he had" to talk and then took him to meet with the detectives. The officers identified themselves, stated they wanted to talk to him, and informed him of his

Miranda rights. Edwards was willing to talk, but he first wanted to hear the taped statement of the alleged accomplice who had implicated him. After listening to the tape for several minutes, petitioner said that he would make a statement so long as it was not tape recorded. The detectives informed him that the recording was irrelevant since they could testify in court concerning whatever he said. Edwards replied: "I'll tell you anything you want to know, but I don't want it on tape." He thereupon implicated himself in the crime.

Prior to trial, Edwards moved to suppress his confession on the ground that his *Miranda* rights had been violated when the officers returned to question him after he had invoked his right to counsel. The trial court initially granted the motion to suppress, but reversed its ruling when presented with a supposedly controlling decision of a higher Arizona court. The court stated without explanation that it found Edwards' statement to be voluntary. Edwards was tried twice and convicted. Evidence concerning his confession was admitted at both trials.

On appeal, the Arizona Supreme Court held that Edwards had invoked both his right to remain silent and his right to counsel during the interrogation conducted on the night of January 19. The court then went on to determine, however, that Edwards had waived both rights during the January 20 meeting when he voluntarily gave his statement to the detectives after again being informed that he need not answer questions and that he need not answer without the advice of counsel: "The trial court's finding that the waiver and confession were voluntarily and knowingly made is upheld."

Because the use of Edwards' confession against him at his trial violated his rights under the Fifth and Fourteenth Amendments as construed in *Miranda v. Arizona*, *supra*, we reverse the judgment of the Arizona Supreme Court.

II

In *Miranda v. Arizona*, the Court determined that the Fifth and Fourteenth Amendments' prohibition against compelled self-incrimination required that custodial interrogation be preceded by advice to the putative defendant that he has the right to remain silent and also the right to the presence of an attorney. The Court also indicated the procedures to be followed subsequent to the warnings. If the accused indicates that he wishes to remain silent, "the interrogation must cease." If he requests counsel, "the interrogation must cease until an attorney is present."

Miranda thus declared that an accused has a Fifth and Fourteenth Amendment right to have counsel present during custodial interrogation. Here, the critical facts as found by the Arizona Supreme Court are that Edwards asserted his right to counsel and his right to remain silent on January 19, but that the police, without furnishing him counsel, returned the next morning to confront him and as a result of the meeting secured incriminating oral admissions. Contrary to the holdings of the state courts, Edwards insists that having exercised his right on the 19th to have counsel present during interrogation, he did not validly waive that right on the 20th. For the following reasons, we agree.

First, the Arizona Supreme Court applied an erroneous standard for determining waiver where the accused has specifically invoked his right to counsel. It is reasonably clear under our cases that waivers of counsel must not only be voluntary, but must also constitute a knowing and intelligent relinquishment or abandonment of a known right or privilege, a matter which depends in each case "upon the particular facts and circumstances surrounding that case, including the background, experience and conduct of the accused."

Considering the proceedings in the state courts in the light of this standard, we note that in denying petitioner's motion to suppress, the trial court found the admission to have been "voluntary," without separately focusing on whether Edwards had knowingly and intelligently relinquished his right to counsel. The Arizona Supreme Court, in a section of its opinion entitled "Voluntariness of Waiver," stated that in Arizona, confessions are prima facie involuntary and that the State had the burden of showing by a preponderance of the evidence that the confession was freely and voluntarily made. The court stated that the issue of voluntariness should be determined based on the totality of the circumstances as it related to whether an accused's action was "knowing and intelligent and whether his will [was] overborne." Once the trial court determines that "the confession is voluntary, the finding will not be upset on appeal absent clear and manifest error." The court then upheld the trial court's finding that the "waiver and confession were voluntarily and knowingly made."

Here, however sound the conclusion of the state courts as to the voluntariness of Edwards' admission may be, neither the trial court nor the Arizona Supreme Court undertook to focus on whether Edwards understood his right to counsel and intelligently and knowingly relinquished it. It is thus apparent that the decision below misunderstood the requirement for finding a valid waiver of the right to counsel, once invoked.

Second, although we have held that after initially being advised of his *Miranda* rights, the accused may himself validly waive his rights and respond to interrogation, see *North Carolina v. Butler* [excerpted *infra*], the Court has strongly indicated that additional safeguards are necessary when the accused asks for counsel; and we now hold that when an accused has invoked his right to have counsel present during custodial interrogation, a valid waiver of that right cannot be established by showing only that he responded to further police-initiated custodial interrogation even if he has been advised of his rights. We further hold that an accused, such as Edwards, having expressed his desire to deal with the police only through counsel, is not subject to further interrogation by the authorities until counsel has been made available to him, unless the accused himself initiates further communication, exchanges or conversations with the police.

Miranda itself indicated that the assertion of the right to counsel was a significant event and that once exercised by the accused, "the interrogation must cease until an attorney is present." Our later cases have not abandoned that view. In *Michigan v. Mosley*, the Court noted that *Miranda* had distinguished between the procedural safeguards triggered by a request to remain silent and a request for an attorney and had required that interrogation cease until an attorney was present only if the individual stated that he wanted counsel. In *Fare v. Michael C.* [excerpted *supra*], the Court referred to *Miranda*'s "rigid rule that an accused's request for an attorney is *per se* an invocation of his Fifth Amendment rights, requiring that all interrogation cease." And just last Term, in a case where a suspect in custody had invoked his *Miranda* right to counsel, the Court again referred to the "undisputed right" under *Miranda* to remain silent and to be free of interrogation "until he had consulted with a lawyer." *Rhode Island v. Innis.* We reconfirm these views and, to lend them substance, emphasize that it is inconsistent with *Miranda* and its progeny for the authorities, at their instance, to reinterrogate an accused in custody if he has clearly asserted his right to counsel.

In concluding that the fruits of the interrogation initiated by the police on January 20 could not be used against Edwards, we do not hold or imply that Edwards was powerless to countermand his election or that the authorities could in no event use any incriminating statements made by Edwards prior to his having access to counsel. Had Edwards initiated the meeting on January 20, nothing in the Fifth and Fourteenth Amendments would prohibit the police from merely listening to his voluntary, volunteered statements and using them against him at the trial. The Fifth Amendment right identified in *Miranda* is the right to have counsel present at any custodial interrogation. Absent such interrogation, there would have been no infringement of the right that Edwards invoked and there would be no occasion to determine whether there has been a valid waiver. *Rhode Island v. Innis, supra,* makes this sufficiently clear.

But this is not what the facts of this case show. Here, the officers conducting the interrogation on the evening of January 19, ceased interrogation when Edwards requested counsel as he had been advised he had the right to do. The Arizona Supreme Court was of the opinion that this was a sufficient invocation of his *Miranda* rights, and we are in accord. It is also clear that without making counsel available to Edwards, the police returned to him the next day. This was not at his suggestion or request. Indeed, Edwards informed the detention officer that he did not want to talk to anyone. At the meeting, the detectives told Edwards that they wanted to talk to him and again advised him of his *Miranda* rights. Edwards stated that he would talk, but what prompted this action does not appear. He listened at his own request to part of the taped statement made by one of his alleged accomplices and then made an incriminating statement, which was used against him at his trial. We think it is clear that Edwards was subjected to custodial interrogation on January 20 within the meaning of *Rhode Island v. Innis, supra,* and that this occurred at the instance of the authorities. His statement, made without having had access to counsel, did not amount to a valid waiver and hence was inadmissible.

Accordingly, the holding of the Arizona Supreme Court that Edwards had waived his right to counsel was infirm, and the judgment of that court is reversed.

So ordered.

Chief Justice Burger, concurring in the judgment.

I concur only in the judgment because I do not agree that either any constitutional standard or the holding of *Miranda v. Arizona* — as distinguished from its dicta — calls for a special rule as to how an accused in custody may waive the right to be free from interrogation. The extraordinary protections afforded a person in custody suspected of criminal conduct are not without a valid basis, but as with all "good" things they can be carried too far. The notion that any "prompting" of a person in custody is somehow evil *per se* has been rejected. For me, the inquiry in this setting is whether resumption of interrogation is a result of a voluntary waiver, and that inquiry should be resolved under the traditional standards established in *Johnson v. Zerbst*:

> A waiver is ordinarily an intentional relinquishment or abandonment of a known right or privilege. The determination of whether there has been an intelligent waiver . . . must depend, in each case, upon the particular facts and circumstances surrounding that case, including the background, experience, and conduct of the accused.

In this case, the Supreme Court of Arizona described the situation as follows:

> When the detention officer told Edwards the detectives were there to see him, he told the officer he did not wish to speak to anyone. The officer told him *that he had to.*

This is enough for me, and on this record the Supreme Court of Arizona erred in holding that the resumption of interrogation was the product of a voluntary waiver, such as I found to be the situation in both *Innis*, and *Brewer v. Williams.*

JUSTICE POWELL, with whom JUSTICE REHNQUIST joins, concurring in the result.

Although I agree that the judgment of the Arizona Supreme Court must be reversed, I do not join the Court's opinion because I am not sure what it means.

I can agree with much of the opinion. It states the settled rule:

> It is reasonably clear under our cases that waivers of counsel must not only be voluntary, but must also constitute a knowing and intelligent relinquishment or abandonment of a known right or privilege, a matter which depends in each case "upon the particular facts and circumstances surrounding that case, including the background, experience and conduct of the accused."

I have thought it settled law, as these cases tell us, that one accused of crime may waive *any* of the constitutional safeguards — including the right to remain silent, to jury trial, to call witnesses, to cross-examine one's accusers, to testify in one's behalf, and — of course — to have counsel. Whatever the right, the standard for waiver is whether the actor fully understands the right in question and voluntarily intends to relinquish it.

In its opinion today, however, the Court — after reiterating the familiar principles of waiver — goes on to say:

> We further hold that an accused, such as Edwards, having expressed his desire to deal with the police only through counsel, is not subject to further interrogation by the authorities until counsel has been made available to him, *unless the accused [has] himself initiate[d] further communication, exchanges, or conversations with the police.*

In view of the emphasis placed on "initiation," I find the Court's opinion unclear.

If read to create a new *per se* rule, requiring a threshold inquiry as to precisely who opened any conversation between an accused and state officials, I cannot agree. I would not superimpose a new element of proof on the established doctrine of waiver of counsel.

Perhaps the Court's opinion can be read as not departing from established doctrine. Accepting the formulation quoted above, two questions are identifiable: (i) was there in fact "interrogation," and (ii) did the police "initiate" it? Each of these questions is, of course, relevant to the admissibility of a confession. In this case, for example, it is clear that Edwards was taken from his cell against his will and subjected to renewed interrogation. Whether this is described as police-"initiated" interrogation or in some other way, it clearly was questioning under circumstances incompatible with a voluntary waiver of the fundamental right to counsel.

NOTES AND QUESTIONS

(1) The criminal defendant in *Wyrick v. Fields*, 459 U.S. 42 (1982), conferred with his attorney after being charged with rape. He and his attorney agreed that he should take a polygraph examination. He informed the police of this, and further stated his desire to take the test without counsel present. After the examination, the officers asked him about some of his answers, and he made a damaging admission. Held, under *Edwards* the statement was admissible in evidence.

> Fields did not merely initiate a "meeting." By requesting a polygraph examination, he initiated interrogation. That is, Fields waived not only his right to be free of contact with the authorities in the absence of an attorney, but also his right to be free of interrogation about the crime of which he was suspected. Fields validly waived his right to have counsel present at "post-test" questioning, unless the circumstances changed so seriously that his answers no longer were voluntary, or unless he no longer was making a "knowing and intelligent relinquishment or abandonment" of his rights.

In *Davis v. United States*, 512 U.S. 452 (1994), the defendant was arrested and given his warnings. The police then started the interrogation process. During the questioning, the defendant said, "Maybe I should talk to a lawyer." Held, this statement was not sufficient to trigger *Edwards*. For a 5-4 majority, Justice O'Connor wrote:

> [A suspect] must articulate his desire to have counsel present sufficiently clearly that a reasonable police officer in the circumstances would understand the statement to be a request for an attorney [or the result would be to] transform the *Miranda* safeguards into wholly irrational obstacles to legitimate police investigative activity.

The courts have seen much litigation concerning requests for counsel or silence during the interrogation process. Are the following requests for silence or a lawyer unambiguous, as required by *Davis*?

- *United States v. Plugh*, 576 F.3d 135 (2d Cir. 2009): defendant refused to sign waiver form and said, "I don't know if I need a lawyer" [unambiguous, officers should construe those words and refusal to sign as a negative answer to question of whether he was willing to talk];

- *United States v. DeLaurentiis*, 629 F. Supp. 2d 68 (D. Me. 2009): defendant asked to speak with her uncle whom she identified as a lawyer [clear request for a lawyer, she told the police she wanted to "call my Uncle Steve who is an attorney, and they wouldn't let me do it"];
- *State v. Schroeder*, 777 N.W.2d 793 (Neb. 2010): suspect said, "That's the end of this conversation, I'm done" [ambiguous, not "sufficient clarity"];
- *State v. Saylor*, 117 S.W.3d 239, 243 (Tenn. 2003), *cert. denied*, 540 U.S. 1208 (2004): "I guess it don't matter until I get a lawyer present . . . I'm suppose to have a lawyer. . . ." [ambiguous];
- *Taylor v. State*, 553 S.E.2d 598, 601 (Ga. 2001): "[could I] have a lawyer present when I [tell my story]?" [unambiguous];
- *Mueller v. Angelone*, 181 F.3d 557, 573–74 (4th Cir.), *cert. denied*, 527 U.S. 1065 (1999): "Do you think I need an attorney here?" [ambiguous];
- *Alvarez v. Gomez*, 185 F.3d 995, 996–97 (9th Cir. 1999): "Can I get an attorney right now. . . . Well, like right now you got one?" [unambiguous];
- *Mitchell v. Commonwealth*, 518 S.E.2d 330, 331 (Va. 1999): "I ain't got shit to say to y'all." [ambiguous].

The rule applies even as to juveniles. *See People v. Nelson*, 266 P.3d 1008 (Cal. 2012) (the request by the 15-year-old defendant was not unequivocal and unambiguous). In *State v. Hoey*, 881 P.2d 504 (Haw. 1994), the court, under its state constitution, found that an ambiguous request for counsel required interrogation to cease or to be delayed pending clarification of the apparent request. It is one of the few courts to so find.

(2) The defendant in *Sapp v. State*, 690 So. 2d 581 (Fla. 1997), *cert. denied*, 522 U.S. 840 (1997), was formally arrested. At that time he signed a "Claim of Rights Form" asserting his right to remain silent and to have his attorney present during questioning. A week after the form was signed the defendant was given his warnings, he signed a waiver, and he made an incriminating statement in response to police questioning. Over a vigorous dissent, the court found *Miranda* had been satisfied.

> *Miranda*'s safeguards were intended to protect the Fifth Amendment right against self-incrimination by countering the compulsion that inheres in custodial interrogation. . . . [T]he presence of both a custodial setting and official interrogation is required to trigger the *Miranda* right-to-counsel prophylactic. . . . [A]bsent one or the other, *Miranda* is not implicated. . . .
>
> Accordingly, we conclude that the claim of rights form was not effective under federal law to invoke Sapp's *Miranda* right to counsel under these circumstances.

Was the holding in *Sapp* a correct application of *Miranda*?

(3) The defendant in *Connecticut v. Barrett*, 479 U.S. 523 (1987), was arrested and given his *Miranda* warnings. He stated that "he would not give the police any

written statement [without his lawyer present] but he had no problem in talking about the incident." The police questioned the defendant and he made an incriminating admission. The state court held that the admission had to be excluded, relying on *Edwards*:

> The fact that the defendant attached his request for counsel to the making of a written statement does not affect the outcome of . . . our inquiry. No particular form of words has ever been required to trigger an individual's Fifth Amendment protections; nor have requests for counsel been narrowly construed. The defendant's refusal to give a written statement without his attorney present was a clear request for the assistance of counsel to protect his rights in his dealings with the police. Such a request continues to be constitutionally effective despite the defendant's willingness to make oral statements.

The Supreme Court disagreed and reversed.

> Barrett made clear to police his willingness to talk about the crime for which he was a suspect. The trial court found that this decision was a voluntary waiver of his rights, and there is no evidence that Barrett was "threatened, tricked, or cajoled" into this waiver. Nothing in our decisions, however, or in the rationale of *Miranda*, requires authorities to ignore the tenor or sense of a defendant's response to these warnings.
>
> The fundamental purpose of the Court's decision in *Miranda* was "to assure that *the individual's right to choose* between speech and silence remains unfettered throughout the interrogation process."

(4) Once a suspect requests counsel, does that request stay in force forever? No, said the Supreme Court in *Maryland v. Shatzer*, 559 U.S. 98 (2010). The suspect there was interrogated and asked for a lawyer. Thereafter, he was released from custody and then confessed — in response to police questioning — three years later. The Court found such a request for counsel would not last for all time. And, the Justices concluded, it would be "impractical" to let lower courts decide on a case-by-case basis the appropriate time period for such a request. So, they set a quite specific limit: "In our judgment, 14 days will provide plenty of time for the suspect to get reacclimated to his normal life, to consult with friends and counsel and to shake off any residual coercive effects of his prior custody."

(5) Does the protection under *Edwards* cease once the suspect has spoken with an attorney? In *Minnick v. Mississippi*, 498 U.S. 146 (1990), the defendant asked to speak with his lawyer. After talking with the lawyer, he was questioned again by the police. The Supreme Court held that the *Miranda* protections detailed in *Edwards* are "not terminated or suspended by consultation with counsel."

PROBLEM J
DEFENDANT INITIATES CONVERSATION

Does *Edwards* apply if the suspect first asked for a lawyer but then said to the officer, "Well, what is going to happen to me now?" Four members of the Court found that the suspect had "initiated" the conversation because he had begun "a generalized discussion about the investigation." Four other Justices disagreed because the defendant had not offered to discuss "the subject matter of the criminal investigation." The ninth vote was Justice Powell's. He thought the best approach would be to analyze "all relevant facts and circumstances" to determine whether the suspect had agreed to speak. See *Oregon v. Bradshaw*, 459 U.S. 966 (1982), where the Court reinstated the defendant's conviction.

The defendant, after receiving *Miranda* warnings, indicated that he wished to speak with counsel before being interrogated. After a break in time of three days, while still in custody, he was questioned by a different police officer about a different burglary. This second time, the defendant did not indicate he wanted a lawyer and he made an incriminating statement. The Supreme Court, in a 6-2 decision, *Arizona v. Roberson*, 486 U.S. 675 (1988), barred the use of the statement, finding that *Edwards v. Arizona* indicated that all interrogation must cease as soon as the suspect has invoked his right to counsel — the rule applied even as to unrelated interrogation.

WAIVER

The Supreme Court stated that the *Miranda* warnings would have to be given or there could be no use made in the prosecution's case in chief[35] of statements given in response to custodial interrogation. This *per se* rule did not mean, however, that once the warnings were given the defendant could not decide to talk or decide that he did not wish to speak with counsel before talking. But, according to the Court in *Miranda*, if the defendant does speak without consulting counsel, "a heavy burden rests on the government to demonstrate that the defendant knowingly and intelligently waived his privilege against self-incrimination and his right to retained or court appointed counsel."

The Second Circuit in *United States v. Murphy*, 703 F.3d 182, 193 (2d Cir. 2012), discussed the concept of waiver of *Miranda* rights:

> The purpose of the *Miranda* warning is to ensure that the person in custody has sufficient knowledge of his or her constitutional rights relating to the interrogation and that any waiver of such rights is knowing, intelligent, and voluntary." The Government bears the burden of proving by a preponderance of evidence that a valid waiver occurred. The waiver inquiry has two components: the accused's relinquishment of his rights must have been (1) " 'knowing,' which is to say that 'the waiver must have been made with a full awareness of both the nature of the right being abandoned and the consequences of the decision to abandon it,' " and (2 " 'voluntary,' which is to say 'that it was the product of a free and deliberate choice rather than intimidation, coercion, or deception," [B]oth knowledge and voluntariness are necessary for waiver, . . . "a waiver of rights could not be found unless the suspect knew what they were. . . .
>
> The Supreme Court has made it clear that an accused person in custody has the absolute right to remain silent and to have an attorney present during any questioning. These rights, and others, are necessary to protect the

[35] For impeachment use, see *Harris v. New York*, *infra*, Chapter 6.

> accused's Fifth Amendment privilege against self-incrimination. The *Miranda* Court decided that any custodial interrogation was inherently coercive and that, therefore, careful procedures were needed to protect the accused. Merely giving warnings to an accused does not satisfy the duties of an interrogating officer or make any statement the accused might then make admissible. "The requirement of warnings *and* waiver of rights is a fundamental with respect to the Fifth Amendment privilege and not simply a preliminary ritual to existing methods of interrogation." The warnings guarantee that the accused knows what his rights are. But *Miranda* requires the interrogating officer to go further and make sure that the accused, knowing his rights, voluntarily relinquishes them. The accused's "freedom to decide whether to assist the state in securing his conviction" cannot otherwise be protected fully. "[U]nless and until such warnings and waiver are demonstrated by the prosecution at trial, no evidence obtained as a result of interrogation can be used against him."

Since *Miranda*, there have been few occasions where the Supreme Court has defined the waiver requirements in these situations. Most state and lower federal courts have relied heavily in this area on the Court's waiver language in *Johnson v. Zerbst*, 304 U.S. 458 (1938):

> It has been pointed out that "courts indulge every reasonable presumption against waiver" of fundamental constitutional rights and that we "do not presume acquiescence in the loss of fundamental rights." A waiver is ordinarily an intentional relinquishment or abandonment of a known right or privilege. The determination of whether there has been an intelligent waiver of right to counsel must depend, in each case, upon the particular facts and circumstances surrounding that case, including the background, experience, and conduct of the accused.

In two cases, however, the waiver problem has been considered carefully by the Court.

NORTH CAROLINA v. BUTLER

United States Supreme Court
441 U.S. 369 (1979)

MR. JUSTICE STEWART delivered the opinion of the Court.

In evident conflict with the present view of every other court that has considered the issue, the North Carolina Supreme Court has held that *Miranda v. Arizona* requires that no statement of a person under custodial interrogation may be admitted in evidence against him unless, at the time the statement was made, he explicitly waived the right to the presence of a lawyer. We granted certiorari to consider whether this *per se* rule reflects a proper understanding of the *Miranda* decision.

The respondent was convicted in a North Carolina trial court of kidnapping, armed robbery, and felonious assault. The evidence at his trial showed that he and a man named Elmer Lee had robbed a gas station in Goldsboro, N.C., in December

1976, and had shot the station attendant as he was attempting to escape. The attendant was paralyzed, but survived to testify against the respondent.

The prosecution also produced evidence of incriminating statements made by the respondent shortly after his arrest by Federal Bureau of Investigation agents in the Bronx, N.Y., on the basis of a North Carolina fugitive warrant. Outside the presence of the jury, FBI agent Martinez testified that at the time of the arrest he fully advised the respondent of the rights delineated in the *Miranda* case. According to the uncontroverted testimony of Martinez, the agents then took the respondent to the FBI office in nearby New Rochelle, N.Y. There, after the agents determined that the respondent had an 11th grade education and was literate, he was given the Bureau's "Advice of Rights" form which he read. When asked if he understood his rights, he replied that he did. The respondent refused to sign the waiver at the bottom of the form. He was told that he need neither speak nor sign the form, but that the agents would like him to talk to them. The respondent replied: "I will talk to you but I am not signing any form." He then made inculpatory statements. Agent Martinez testified that the respondent said nothing when advised of his right to the assistance of a lawyer. At no time did the respondent request counsel or attempt to terminate the agents' questioning.

At the conclusion of this testimony the respondent moved to suppress the evidence of his incriminating statements on the ground that he had not waived his right to the assistance of counsel at the time the statements were made. The court denied the motion, finding that

> the statement made by the defendant, William Thomas Butler, to Agent David C. Martinez, was made freely and voluntarily to said agent after having been advised of his rights as required by the Miranda ruling, including his right to an attorney being present at the time of the inquiry and that the defendant, Butler, understood his rights; [and] that he effectively waived his rights, including the right to have an attorney present during the questioning by his indication that he was willing to answer questions, having read the rights form together with the Waiver of Rights. . . .

The respondent's statements were then admitted into evidence, and the jury ultimately found the respondent guilty of each offense charged.

On appeal, the North Carolina Supreme Court reversed the convictions and ordered a new trial. It found that the statements had been admitted in violation of the requirements of the *Miranda* decision, noting that the respondent had refused to waive in writing his right to have counsel present and that there had not been a *specific* oral waiver. As it had in at least two earlier cases, the court read the *Miranda* opinion as "provid[ing] in plain language that waiver of the right to counsel during interrogation will not be recognized unless such waiver is 'specifically made' after the *Miranda* warnings have been given."

We conclude that the North Carolina Supreme Court erred in its reading of the *Miranda* opinion. There, this Court said:

> If the interrogation continues without the presence of an attorney and a statement is taken, a heavy burden rests on the government to demonstrate

> that the defendant knowingly and intelligently waived his privilege against self-incrimination and his right to retained or appointed counsel.

The Court's opinion went on to say:

> An express statement that the individual is willing to make a statement and does not want an attorney followed closely by a statement could constitute a waiver. But a valid waiver will not be presumed simply from the silence of the accused after warnings are given or simply from the fact that a confession was in fact eventually obtained.

Thus, the Court held that an express statement can constitute a waiver, and that silence alone after such warnings cannot do so. But the Court did not hold that such an express statement is indispensable to a finding of waiver.

An express written or oral statement of waiver of the right to remain silent or of the right to counsel is usually strong proof of the validity of that waiver, but is not inevitably either necessary or sufficient to establish waiver. The question is not one of form, but rather whether the defendant in fact knowingly and voluntarily waived the rights delineated in the *Miranda* case. As was unequivocally said in *Miranda*, mere silence is not enough. That does not mean that the defendant's silence, coupled with an understanding of his rights and a course of conduct indicating waiver, may never support a conclusion that a defendant has waived his rights. The courts must presume that a defendant did not waive his rights; the prosecution's burden is great; but in at least some cases waiver can be clearly inferred from the actions and words of the person interrogated.

The Court's opinion in *Miranda* explained the reasons for the prophylactic rules it created:

> We have concluded that without proper safeguards the process of in-custody interrogation of persons suspected or accused of crime contains inherently compelling pressures which work to undermine the individual's will to resist and to compel him to speak where he would not otherwise do so freely. In order to combat these pressures and to permit a full opportunity to exercise the privilege against self-incrimination, the accused must be adequately and effectively apprised of his rights and the exercise of those rights must be fully honored.

The *per se* rule that the North Carolina Supreme Court has found in *Miranda* does not speak to these concerns. There is no doubt that this respondent was adequately and effectively apprised of his rights. The only question is whether he waived the exercise of one of those rights, the right to the presence of a lawyer. Neither the state court, nor the respondent has offered any reason why there must be a negative answer to that question in the absence of an *express* waiver. This is not the first criminal case to question whether a defendant waived his constitutional rights. It is an issue with which courts must repeatedly deal. Even when a right so fundamental as that to counsel at trial is involved, the question of waiver must be determined on "the particular facts and circumstances surrounding that case, including the background, experience, and conduct of the accused." *Johnson v. Zerbst*.

MR. JUSTICE POWELL took no part in the consideration or decision of this case.

MR. JUSTICE BLACKMUN concurred.

MR. JUSTICE BRENNAN, with whom MR. JUSTICE MARSHALL and MR. JUSTICE STEVENS join, dissenting.

The instant case presents a clear example of the need for an express waiver requirement. As the Court acknowledges, there is a disagreement over whether respondent was orally advised of his rights at the time he made his statement. The fact that Butler received a written copy of his rights is deemed by the Court to be sufficient basis to resolve the disagreement. But, unfortunately, there is also a dispute over whether Butler could read. And, obviously, if Butler did not have his rights read to him, and could not read them himself, there could be no basis upon which to conclude that he knowingly waived them. Indeed, even if Butler could read there is no reason to believe that his oral statements, which followed a refusal to sign a written waiver form, were intended to signify relinquishment of his rights.

Faced with "actions and words" of uncertain meaning, some judges may find waivers where none occurred. Others may fail to find them where they did. In the former case, the defendant's rights will have been violated; in the latter, society's interest in effective law enforcement will have been frustrated. A simple prophylactic rule requiring the police to obtain an express waiver of the right to counsel before proceeding with interrogation eliminates these difficulties. And since the Court agrees that *Miranda* requires the police to obtain some kind of waiver — whether express or implied — the requirement of an express waiver would impose no burden on the police not imposed by the Court's interpretation. It would merely make that burden explicit. Had Agent Martinez simply elicited a clear answer from Willie Butler to the question, "Do you waive your right to a lawyer?" this journey through three courts would not have been necessary.

NOTES AND QUESTIONS

(1) The majority stated that the question was "whether the defendant in fact knowingly and voluntarily waived the rights delineated in the *Miranda* case." If that is the question, what would the answer be in a situation in which there is no outward sign of a waiver? How is the trial judge to resolve such a problem? What are the problems in having a "simple prophylactic rule requiring the police to obtain an express waiver of the right to counsel before proceeding with interrogation . . ."?

(2) If the defendant is warned of the *Miranda* rights and agrees to waive them and is then interrogated after a break of 31 days, is such a waiver valid? 12 hours? The courts in *Commonwealth v. Cohen*, 53 A.3d 882 (Pa. Super. Ct. 2012), and *Commonwealth v. Wideman*, 334 A.2d 594, 598 (Penn. 1975), held the waivers to be invalid applying the following factors:

> [T]he length of time between the warnings and the challenged interrogation, whether the interrogation was conducted at the same place where the warnings were given, whether the officer who gave the warnings also

> conducted the questioning, and whether the statements obtained are materially different from other statements that may have been made at the time of the warnings.

Cohen, 53 A.3d at 888.

(3) In *Tague v. Louisiana*, 444 U.S. 469 (1980), the arresting officer at the suppression hearing

> testified that he read petitioner his *Miranda* rights from a card, that he could not presently remember what those rights were, that he could not recall whether he asked petitioner whether he understood the rights as read to him, and that he couldn't say yes or no whether he rendered any tests to determine whether petitioner was literate or otherwise capable of understanding his rights.

The state supreme court held that the officer was not required to give "an intelligence test to a person who has been advised of his rights to determine if he understands them. . . . Absent a clear and readily apparent lack thereof, it can be presumed that a person has capacity to understand, and the burden is on the one claiming a lack of capacity to show that lack."

Was this holding proper under *Butler*? The Court, in a summary proceeding, reversed, quoting *Butler* for the proposition that "the courts must presume that a defendant did not waive his rights; the prosecution's burden is great."

(4) Can a defendant knowingly and voluntarily waive the rights where, because of mental problems, he does not appreciate that he could be sent to prison? Yes, said the majority in *Garner v. Mitchell*, 557 F.3d 257 (6th Cir. 2009) (en banc) because the criminal defendant "appeared 'perfectly normal' and 'very coherent' at the time that he waived his rights and confessed to his crimes." The key question for these judges related to the view of the interrogating officers: "[The] police officers had no indication that Garner's 'age, experience, education, background, and intelligence' may have prevented him from understanding the *Miranda* warnings . . . the original purpose underlying the *Miranda* decision [was] to 'reduce the likelihood that the suspects would fall victim to constitutionally impermissible practices of police interrogation.' " Other judges in the case disagreed. One wrote that the "primary focus" should not be "the conduct of the interrogating officers." Another concluded that the majority decision to look to "the conduct and knowledge of police officers is at odds with the Supreme Court's repeated pronouncements that the proper inquiry is whether the defendant had the maturity, intelligence, and competency to make a knowing and intelligent waiver." Which judge correctly applied the *Miranda* doctrine?

(5) As with other rulings of the Supreme Court, the state courts are free to impose a stricter standard for the police under their state constitutions. In *Commonwealth v. Bussey*, 404 A.2d 1309, 1314–15 (Penn. 1979), the Pennsylvania Supreme Court rejected the *Butler* rule and required "an outward manifestation of a waiver such as an oral, written or physical manifestation":

> Our ruling, unlike *North Carolina v. Butler*, will promote certainty in knowing an accused has waived his rights and will avoid a mountain of

litigation which might otherwise result from trying to determine what "implicitly" went on in an accused's mind. (In addition to warnings, an expression of understanding, and the giving of a statement, a multitude of manifestations by an accused can occur between an expression of understanding and a giving of a statement. Our ruling will not eliminate consideration of such manifestations, but, by requiring an express waiver, we can limit the number of cases in which the multitude of manifestations may affect the ultimate finding of a waiver.) Our ruling will also serve to impress on an accused the importance of his decision. Furthermore, assuming *North Carolina v. Butler* was concerned with additional burdens being placed on law enforcement officials, given *Miranda*, we cannot agree our ruling creates any such burden. Surely if the rights must be explained, merely asking for an answer to a question is no great burden, and, even if it is a burden, it will promote certainty in the law and, thereby, eliminate a greater burden resulting from allowing implicit waivers.

BERGHUIS v. THOMPKINS

United States Supreme Court
560 U.S. 370 (2010)

JUSTICE KENNEDY delivered the opinion of the Court.

I

A

On January 10, 2000, a shooting occurred outside a mall in Southfield, Michigan. Among the victims was Samuel Morris, who died from multiple gunshot wounds. The other victim, Frederick France, recovered from his injuries and later testified. Thompkins, who was a suspect, fled. About one year later he was found in Ohio and arrested there.

Two Southfield police officers traveled to Ohio to interrogate Thompkins, then awaiting transfer to Michigan. The interrogation began around 1:30 p.m. and lasted about three hours. The interrogation was conducted in a room that was 8 by 10 feet, and Thompkins sat in a chair that resembled a school desk (it had an arm on it that swings around to provide a surface to write on). At the beginning of the interrogation, one of the officers, Detective Helgert, presented Thompkins with a form derived from the *Miranda* rule. It stated:

"NOTIFICATION OF CONSTITUTIONAL RIGHTS AND STATEMENT

"1. You have the right to remain silent.

"2. Anything you say can and will be used against you in a court of law.

"3. You have a right to talk to a lawyer before answering any questions and you have the right to have a lawyer present with you while you are answering any questions.

"4. If you cannot afford to hire a lawyer, one will be appointed to represent you before any questioning, if you wish one.

"5. You have the right to decide at any time before or during questioning to use your right to remain silent and your right to talk with a lawyer while you are being questioned."

Helgert asked Thompkins to read the fifth warning out loud. Thompkins complied. Helgert later said this was to ensure that Thompkins could read, and Helgert concluded that Thompkins understood English. Helgert then read the other four *Miranda* warnings out loud and asked Thompkins to sign the form to demonstrate that he understood his rights. Thompkins declined to sign the form. The record contains conflicting evidence about whether Thompkins then verbally confirmed that he understood the rights listed on the form.

Officers began an interrogation. At no point during the interrogation did Thompkins say that he wanted to remain silent, that he did not want to talk with the police, or that he wanted an attorney. Thompkins was "[l]argely" silent during the interrogation, which lasted about three hours. He did give a few limited verbal responses, however, such as "yeah," "no," or "I don't know." And on occasion he communicated by nodding his head. Thompkins also said that he "didn't want a peppermint" that was offered to him by the police and that the chair he was "sitting in was hard."

About 2 hours and 45 minutes into the interrogation, Helgert asked Thompkins, "Do you believe in God?" Thompkins made eye contact with Helgert and said "Yes," as his eyes "well[ed] up with tears." Helgert asked, "Do you pray to God?" Thompkins said "Yes." Helgert asked, "Do you pray to God to forgive you for shooting that boy down?" Thompkins answered "Yes" and looked away. Thompkins refused to make a written confession, and the interrogation ended about 15 minutes later.

Thompkins was charged with first-degree murder, assault with intent to commit murder, and certain firearms-related offenses. He moved to suppress the statements made during the interrogation. He argued that he had invoked his Fifth Amendment right to remain silent, requiring police to end the interrogation at once. . . .

III

The *Miranda* Court formulated a warning that must be given to suspects before they can be subjected to custodial interrogation. The substance of the warning still must be given to suspects today. A suspect in custody must be advised as follows:

He must be warned prior to any questioning that he has the right to remain silent, that anything he says can be used against him in a court of law, that he has the right to the presence of an attorney, and that if he cannot afford an attorney one will be appointed for him prior to any questioning if he so desires.

All concede that the warning given in this case was in full compliance with these requirements. The dispute centers on the response — or nonresponse — from the suspect.

A

Thompkins makes various arguments that his answers to questions from the detectives were inadmissible. He first contends that he "invoke[d] his privilege" to remain silent by not saying anything for a sufficient period of time, so the interrogation should have "cease[d]" before he made his inculpatory statements.

This argument is unpersuasive. In the context of invoking the *Miranda* right to counsel, the Court in *Davis v. United States*, 512 U. S. 452, 459 (1994), held that a suspect must do so "unambiguously." If an accused makes a statement concerning the right to counsel "that is ambiguous or equivocal" or makes no statement, the police are not required to end the interrogation, or ask questions to clarify whether the accused wants to invoke his or her *Miranda* rights.

The Court has not yet stated whether an invocation of the right to remain silent can be ambiguous or equivocal, but there is no principled reason to adopt different standards for determining when an accused has invoked the *Miranda* right to remain silent and the *Miranda* right to counsel at issue in Davis. Both protect the privilege against compulsory self-incrimination, by requiring an interrogation to cease when either right is invoked

There is good reason to require an accused who wants to invoke his or her right to remain silent to do so unambiguously. A requirement of an unambiguous invocation of *Miranda* rights results in an objective inquiry that "avoid[s] difficulties of proof and . . . provide[s] guidance to officers" on how to proceed in the face of ambiguity. If an ambiguous act, omission, or statement could require police to end the interrogation, police would be required to make difficult decisions about an accused's unclear intent and face the consequence of suppression "if they guess wrong." Suppression of a voluntary confession in these circumstances would place a significant burden on society's interest in prosecuting criminal activity. Treating an ambiguous or equivocal act, omission, or statement as an invocation of *Miranda* rights "might add marginally to *Miranda*'s goal of dispelling the compulsion inherent in custodial interrogation." But "as *Miranda* holds, full comprehension of the rights to remain silent and request an attorney are sufficient to dispel whatever coercion is inherent in the interrogation process."

Thompkins did not say that he wanted to remain silent or that he did not want to talk with the police. Had he made either of these simple, unambiguous statements, he would have invoked his " 'right to cut off questioning.' " Here he did neither, so he did not invoke his right to remain silent.

B

We next consider whether Thompkins waived his right to remain silent. Even absent the accused's invocation of the right to remain silent, the accused's statement during a custodial interrogation is inadmissible at trial unless the prosecution can establish that the accused "in fact knowingly and voluntarily waived *[Miranda]* rights" when making the statement. The waiver inquiry "has two distinct dimensions": waiver must be "voluntary in the sense that it was the product of a free and deliberate choice rather than intimidation, coercion, or deception," and "made with a full awareness of both the nature of the right being abandoned and the consequences of the decision to abandon it."

Some language in *Miranda* could be read to indicate that waivers are difficult to establish absent an explicit written waiver or a formal, express oral statement. *Miranda* said "a valid waiver will not be presumed simply from the silence of the accused after warnings are given or simply from the fact that a confession was in fact eventually obtained.". . .

The course of decisions since *Miranda*, informed by the application of *Miranda* warnings in the whole course of law enforcement, demonstrates that waivers can be established even absent formal or express statements of waiver that would be expected in, say, a judicial hearing to determine if a guilty plea has been properly entered. The main purpose of *Miranda* is to ensure that an accused is advised of and understands the right to remain silent and the right to counsel. . . .

One of the first cases to decide the meaning and import of *Miranda* with respect to the question of waiver was *North Carolina v. Butler.* The *Butler* Court, after discussing some of the problems created by the language in *Miranda*, established certain important propositions. Butler interpreted the *Miranda* language concerning the "heavy burden" to show waiver, in accord with usual principles of determining waiver, which can include waiver implied from all the circumstances. And in a later case, the Court stated that this "heavy burden" is not more than the burden to establish waiver by a preponderance of the evidence.

The prosecution therefore does not need to show that a waiver of *Miranda* rights was express. An "implicit waiver" of the "right to remain silent" is sufficient to admit a suspect's statement into evidence. *Butler* made clear that a waiver of *Miranda* rights may be implied through "the defendant's silence, coupled with an understanding of his rights and a course of conduct indicating waiver." The Court in *Butler* therefore "retreated" from the "language and tenor of the *Miranda* opinion," which "suggested that the Court would require that a waiver . . . be 'specifically made.' "

If the State establishes that a *Miranda* warning was given and the accused made an uncoerced statement, this showing, standing alone, is insufficient to demonstrate "a valid waiver" of *Miranda* rights. The prosecution must make the additional showing that the accused understood these rights. . . . Where the prosecution shows that a *Miranda* warning was given and that it was understood by the accused, an accused's uncoerced statement establishes an implied waiver of the right to remain silent.

. . .

The record in this case shows that Thompkins waived his right to remain silent. There is no basis in this case to conclude that he did not understand his rights; and on these facts it follows that he chose not to invoke or rely on those rights when he did speak.

. . .

In order for an accused's statement to be admissible at trial, police must have given the accused a *Miranda* warning. If that condition is established, the court can proceed to consider whether there has been an express or implied waiver of *Miranda* rights. In making its ruling on the admissibility of a statement made during custodial questioning, the trial court, of course, considers whether there is evidence to support the conclusion that, from the whole course of questioning, an express or implied waiver has been established. Thus, after giving a *Miranda* warning, police may interrogate a suspect who has neither invoked nor waived his or her *Miranda* rights. On these premises, it follows the police were not required to obtain a waiver of Thompkins's *Miranda* rights before commencing the interrogation.

D

In sum, a suspect who has received and understood the *Miranda* warnings, and has not invoked his *Miranda* rights, waives the right to remain silent by making an uncoerced statement to the police. Thompkins did not invoke his right to remain silent and stop the questioning. Understanding his rights in full, he waived his right to remain silent by making a voluntary statement to the police. The police, moreover, were not required to obtain a waiver of Thompkins's right to remain silent before interrogating him.

. . .

The judgment of the Court of Appeals is reversed, and the case is remanded with instructions to deny the petition.

It is so ordered.

JUSTICE SOTOMAYOR, with whom JUSTICE STEVENS, JUSTICE GINSBURG, and JUSTICE BREYER join, dissenting.

The Court concludes today that a criminal suspect waives his right to remain silent if, after sitting tacit and uncommunicative through nearly three hours of police interrogation, he utters a few one-word responses. The Court also concludes that a suspect who wishes to guard his right to remain silent against such a finding of "waiver" must, counter intuitively, speak — and must do so with sufficient precision to satisfy a clear-statement rule that construes ambiguity in favor of the police. Both propositions mark a substantial retreat from the protection against compelled self-incrimination that *Miranda v. Arizona* has long provided during custodial interrogation. . . .

The strength of Thompkins' *Miranda* claims depends in large part on the circumstances of the 3-hour interrogation, at the end of which he made inculpatory statements later introduced at trial. The Court's opinion downplays record evidence that Thompkins remained almost completely silent and unresponsive throughout that session. One of the interrogating officers, Detective Helgert, testified that although Thompkins was administered Miranda warnings, the last of which he read aloud, Thompkins expressly declined to sign a written acknowledgment that he had been advised of and understood his rights. There is conflicting evidence in the record about whether Thompkins ever verbally confirmed understanding his rights. The record contains no indication that the officers sought or obtained an express waiver.

As to the interrogation itself, Helgert candidly characterized it as "very, very one-sided" and "nearly a monologue." Thompkins was "[p]eculiar," "[s]ullen," and "[g]enerally quiet." Helgert and his partner "did most of the talking," as Thompkins was "not verbally communicative" and "[l]argely" remained silent. To the extent Thompkins gave any response, his answers consisted of "a word or two. A 'yeah,' or a 'no,' or 'I don't know.' . . . And sometimes . . . he simply sat down . . . with [his] head in[his] hands looking down. Sometimes . . . he would look up and make eye-contact would be the only response." After proceeding in this fashion for approximately 2 hours and 45 minutes, Helgert asked Thompkins three questions relating to his faith in God. The prosecution relied at trial on Thompkins' one-word answers of "yes."

Thompkins' nonresponsiveness is particularly striking in the context of the officers' interview strategy, later explained as conveying to Thompkins that "this was his opportunity to explain his side [of the story]" because"[e]verybody else, including [his] co-[d]efendants, had given their version," and asking him "[w]ho is going to speak up for you if you don't speak up for yourself?" Yet, Helgert confirmed that the "*only* thing [Thompkins said] relative to his involvement [in the shooting]" occurred near the end of the interview — *i.e.*, in response to the questions about God. The only other responses Helgert could remember Thompkins giving were that " '[h]e didn't want a peppermint' " and " 'the chair that he was sitting in was hard." ' Nevertheless, the Michigan court concluded on this record that Thompkins had not invoked his right to remain silent because "he continued to talk with the officer, albeit sporadically," and that he voluntarily waived that right.

. . .

Even when warnings have been administered and a suspect has not affirmatively invoked his rights, statements made in custodial interrogation may not be admitted as part of the prosecution's case in chief "unless and until" the prosecution demonstrates that an individual "knowingly and intelligently waive[d] [his] rights." "[A] heavy burden rests on the government to demonstrate that the defendant knowingly and intelligently waived his privilege against self incrimination and his right to retained or appointed counsel."

It is undisputed here that Thompkins never expressly waived his right to remain silent. His refusal to sign even an acknowledgment that he understood his *Miranda* rights evinces, if anything, an intent not to waive those rights. . . . That Thompkins did not make the inculpatory statements at issue until after approximately 2 hours and 45 minutes of interrogation serves as "strong evidence" against waiver.

Miranda and *Butler* expressly preclude the possibility that the inculpatory statements themselves are sufficient to establish waiver.

In these circumstances, Thompkins' "actions and words" preceding the inculpatory statements simply do not evidence a "course of conduct indicating waiver" sufficient to carry the prosecution's burden. . . . I believe it is objectively unreasonable under our clearly established precedents to conclude the prosecution met its "heavy burden" of proof on a record consisting of three one word answers, following 2 hours and 45 minutes of silence punctuated by a few largely nonverbal responses to unidentified questions.

. . .

The Court concludes that when *Miranda* warnings have been given and understood, "an accused's uncoerced statement establishes an implied waiver of the right to remain silent." More broadly still, the Court states that, "[a]s a general proposition, the law can presume that an individual who, with a full understanding of his or her rights, acts in a manner inconsistent with their exercise has made a deliberate choice to relinquish the protection those rights afford."

These principles flatly contradict our long standing views that "a valid waiver will not be presumed . . . simply from the fact that a confession was in fact eventually obtained," *Miranda*, and that "[t]he courts must presume that a defendant did not waive his rights". Indeed, we have in the past summarily reversed a state-court decision that inverted *Miranda*'s antiwaiver presumption, characterizing the error as "readily apparent." At best, the Court today creates an unworkable and conflicting set of presumptions that will undermine *Miranda*'s goal of providing "concrete constitutional guidelines for law enforcement agencies and courts to follow,". At worst, it overrules sub silentio an essential aspect of the protections *Miranda* has long provided for the constitutional guarantee against self-incrimination.

. . .

Davis' clear-statement rule is also a poor fit for the right to silence. Advising a suspect that he has a "right to remain silent" is unlikely to convey that he must speak (and must do so in some particular fashion) to ensure the right will be protected. "What in the world must an individual do to exercise his constitutional right to remain silent beyond actually, in fact, remaining silent?" By contrast, telling a suspect "he has the right to the presence of an attorney, and that if he cannot afford an attorney one will be appointed for him prior to any questioning if he so desires," *Davis*' requirement that a suspect must "clearly reques[t] an attorney" to terminate questioning thus aligns with a suspect's likely understanding of the *Miranda* warnings in a way today's rule does not. The Court suggests Thompkins could have employed the "simple, unambiguous" means of saying "he wanted to remain silent" or "did not want to talk with the police." But the *Miranda* warnings give no hint that a suspect should use those magic words, and there is little reason to believe police — who have ample incentives to avoid invocation — will provide such guidance.

Conversely, the Court's concern that police will face "difficult decisions about an accused's unclear intent" and suffer the consequences of " 'guess[ing] wrong,' " is misplaced. If a suspect makes an ambiguous statement or engages in conduct that creates uncertainty about his intent to invoke his right, police can simply ask for clarification. . . .

The Court asserts in passing that treating ambiguous statements or acts as an invocation of the right to silence will only " 'marginally' " serve *Miranda*'s goals. Experience suggests the contrary. In the 16 years since *Davis* was decided, ample evidence has accrued that criminal suspects often use equivocal or colloquial language in attempting to invoke their right to silence. A number of lower courts that have (erroneously, in my view) imposed a clear-statement requirement for invocation of the right to silence have rejected as ambiguous an array of statements whose meaning might otherwise be thought plain. At a minimum, these decisions suggest that differentiating "clear" from "ambiguous" statements is often a subjective inquiry. . . .

Today's decision turns *Miranda* upside down. Criminal suspects must now unambiguously invoke their right to remain silent — which, counter intuitively, requires them to speak. At the same time, suspects will be legally presumed to have waived their rights even if they have given no clear expression of their intent to do so. Those results, in my view, find no basis in *Miranda* or our subsequent cases and are inconsistent with the fair-trial principles on which those precedents are grounded. Today's broad new rules are all the more unfortunate because they are unnecessary to the disposition of the case before us. I respectfully dissent.

NOTES AND QUESTIONS

(1) Does the government still retain the burden of proving a knowing and willing waiver of *Miranda* rights? Did the government here sustain that burden? *Butler* and *Thompkins* taken together establish that the test for waiver in the *Miranda* area is the totality of circumstances approach, focusing on many factors such as the defendant's words, the officer's conduct, the setting, and so forth.

(2) Are the dissenting Justices correct that the decision "turns *Miranda* upside down"? Or is the majority right in noting that Thompkins "waive[d] the right to remain silent by making an uncoerced statement to the police"?

(3) How does the decision here deal with earlier opinions which indicated that the trial judge should not presume a valid waiver simply because the defendant spoke to the police?

(4) Should the principle put forth in *Thompkins* be applied to *Salinas v. Texas*, 133 S. Ct. 2174 (2013)? There the defendant was being questioned before he was placed in custody (he had voluntarily gone to the police station so that *Miranda* was not yet engaged). He spoke for a time and then refused to answer a key question. The prosecutor relied on this refusal and silence, arguing to the jury that it was a very important piece of evidence. Violation of the Fifth Amendment? No, held the majority Justices, as the defendant "did not expressly invoke the privilege against self-incrimination."

(5) Is there a special rule here for minors? In *People v. Lessie*, 223 P.3d 3 (Cal. 2010), the minor defendant requested that he see a parent. Earlier caselaw in

California indicated that such a request constituted an invocation of rights under the Fifth Amendment. This caselaw, the court held, was no longer valid. Instead, the analysis in each case should be a totality of the circumstances approach looking to the many factors present in each case, including the suspect's age. This decision is consistent with the decision in *Fare v. Michael C.*, 442 U.S. 707 (1979). There the Supreme Court held that a juvenile's request during custodial interrogation for his probation officer did not — *per se* — constitute an invocation of his fifth amendment rights.

> The transcript of the interrogation reveals that the police officers conducting the interrogation took care to ensure that respondent understood his rights. They fully explained to respondent that he was being questioned in connection with a murder. They then informed him of all the rights delineated in *Miranda*, and ascertained that respondent understood those rights. There is no indication in the record that respondent failed to understand what the officers told him. Moreover, after his request to see his probation officer had been denied, and after the police officer once more had explained his rights to him, respondent clearly expressed his willingness to waive his rights and continue the interrogation.
>
> Further, no special factors indicate that respondent was unable to understand the nature of his actions. He was a 16 1/2-year-old juvenile with considerable experience with the police. He had a record of several arrests. He had served time in a youth camp, and he had been on probation for several years. He was under the full-time supervision of probation authorities. There is no indication that he was of insufficient intelligence to understand the rights he was waiving, or what the consequences of that waiver would be. He was not worn down by improper interrogation tactics or lengthy questioning or by trickery or deceit.

Id. at 726–27.

Especially difficult problems continue to be presented with *Miranda* waivers when the suspect is a minor. Consider these two cases. In *Doody v. Schriro*, 548 F.3d 847 (9th Cir. 2008), the 17-year-old defendant was questioned over a 10-hour period and the investigators acted in a very harsh manner. The *Miranda* waiver was held to be inadequate and the resulting confession was deemed to be involuntary. The 16-year-old defendant in *In re H.V*, 252 S.W. 3d 319 (Tex. 2008), received his warnings and then he said he wanted his mother to ask for a lawyer. This statement was held to be "an expression of a desire for the assistance of an attorney" so that the later confession was not allowed.

Chapter 6

VINDICATING CONSTITUTIONAL VIOLATIONS

This Chapter considers who can complain and what remedies are available in criminal cases when the government has violated the Fourth Amendment's protection against unreasonable searches and seizures, Due Process rights (Fifth and Fourteenth Amendments), the protection against compelled self-incrimination (Fifth Amendment), the right to counsel (Sixth Amendment), and the rights provided by *Miranda v. Arizona*, 384 U.S. 436 (1966).

§ 6.01 STANDING

Not everyone is empowered to seek relief even if the government unquestionably violates the Constitution. This section considers who has the legal right to complain. Because issues of "standing" usually arise in cases asserting Fourth Amendment challenges, the bulk of this section explores Fourth Amendment cases. But the limits of standing apply also to the violation of other constitutional rights. Standing in non-Fourth Amendment contexts is, therefore, discussed at the end of the section.

[A] Standing in the Fourth Amendment Context

The rights protected by the Fourth Amendment are personal rights. Therefore, to object to the admission of illegally-seized evidence, the accused was traditionally required to show that she had some interest in the property seized or the premises searched or, at least, that her right of privacy had been invaded.

In *Jones v. United States*, 362 U.S. 257 (1960), the Court declared two significant points, making it easier to establish standing. First, to establish standing respecting the premises searched, the Court said that a property interest was not required. The petitioner in *Jones*, who was an invitee of an apartment tenant, was permitted to object to a search of the apartment. The Court held that "anyone legitimately on premises where a search occurs may challenge its legality." Second, the Court indicated that when the crime charged is possession of the evidence seized, the accused will be granted automatic standing to object to admissibility of the evidence. The Court reasoned that to hold otherwise "would be to permit the Government to have the advantage of contradictory positions." The Court considered an accused in such circumstances to be placed on the horns of a dilemma: By claiming a possessory interest in the property, he would be confessing to the crime charged; by declining to testify, he would effectively assert the privilege against self-incrimination, but necessarily waive the protection of the Fourth Amendment.

The Court's concern with the dilemma of the accused was resolved in a different fashion in *Simmons v. United States*, 390 U.S. 377 (1968). There, the accused did not qualify for automatic standing, but his testimony at a suppression hearing was later introduced against him at his trial. To avoid forcing the accused to choose between Fourth and Fifth Amendment rights, the Court held that testimony given at a suppression hearing would be inadmissible later at trial on the issue of guilt. Because the *Simmons* holding eliminated the need for the automatic standing rule established in *Jones*, many critics and courts suggested that this aspect of the *Jones* decision should be abandoned.

The Supreme Court finally came around to this view, overruling the automatic standing rule of *Jones*, in *United States v. Salvucci*, 448 U.S. 83 (1980). In *Salvucci*, the defendants, who were charged with the unlawful possession of stolen mail, sought to suppress evidence seized from the apartment of one of the defendants' mother. Because the accused had been charged with the possession of the evidence seized, the courts below had given each defendant automatic standing to object to its admissibility. The Supreme Court reversed, holding that defendants charged with crimes of possession may claim standing only if their own Fourth Amendment rights are violated. Such defendants no longer benefitted from automatic standing.

The significance of the standing issue (or non-issue, as the Court would have us believe) is dramatically illustrated in *Rakas v. Illinois.*

RAKAS v. ILLINOIS

United States Supreme Court
439 U.S. 128 (1978)

JUSTICE REHNQUIST delivered the opinion of the Court.

Petitioners were convicted of armed robbery in the Circuit Court of Kankakee County, Ill., and their convictions were affirmed on appeal. At their trial, the prosecution offered into evidence a sawed-off rifle and rifle shells that had been seized by police during a search of an automobile in which petitioners had been passengers. Neither petitioner is the owner of the automobile and neither has ever asserted that he owned the rifle or shells seized. The Illinois Appellate Court held that petitioners lacked standing to object to the allegedly unlawful search and seizure and denied their motion to suppress the evidence. We granted certiorari in light of the obvious importance of the issues raised to the administration of criminal justice and now affirm.

I

Because we are not here concerned with the issue of probable cause, a brief description of the events leading to the search of the automobile will suffice. A police officer on a routine patrol received a radio call notifying him of a robbery of a clothing store in Bourbonnais, Ill., and describing the getaway car. Shortly thereafter, the officer spotted an automobile which he thought might be the getaway car. After following the car for some time and after the arrival of assistance, he and several other officers stopped the vehicle. The occupants of the automobile, petitioners and two female companions, were ordered out of the car and, after the occupants had left the car, two officers searched the interior of the vehicle. They discovered a box of rifle shells in the glove compartment, which had been locked, and a sawed-off rifle under the front passenger seat. After discovering the rifle and the shells, the officers took petitioners to the station and placed them under arrest.

Before trial petitioners moved to suppress the rifle and shells seized from the car on the ground that the search violated the Fourth and Fourteenth Amendments. They conceded that they did not own the automobile and were simply passengers; the owner of the car had been the driver of the vehicle at the time of the search. Nor did they assert that they owned the rifle or the shells seized. The prosecutor challenged petitioners' standing to object to the lawfulness of the search of the car because neither the car, the shells nor the rifle belonged to them. The trial court agreed that petitioners lacked standing and denied the motion to suppress the evidence. In view of this holding, the court did not determine whether there was probable cause for the search and seizure. On appeal after petitioners' conviction, the Appellate Court of Illinois, Third Judicial District, affirmed the trial court's denial of petitioners' motion to suppress because it held that "without a proprietary or other similar interest in an automobile, a mere passenger therein lacks standing to challenge the legality of the search of the vehicle." . . . The court stated:

> We believe that defendants failed to establish any prejudice to their own constitutional rights because they were not persons aggrieved by the unlawful search and seizure. . . . They wrongly seek to establish prejudice only through the use of evidence gathered as a consequence of a search and seizure directed at someone else and fail to prove an invasion of their own privacy. *Alderman v. United States*, 394 U.S. 165 (1969).

The Illinois Supreme Court denied petitioners leave to appeal.

II

Petitioners first urge us to relax or broaden the rule of standing enunciated in *Jones v. United States*, . . . so that any criminal defendant at whom a search was "directed" would have standing to contest the legality of that search and object to the admission at trial of evidence obtained as a result of the search. Alternatively, petitioners argue that they have standing to object to the search under *Jones* because they were "legitimately on [the] premises" at the time of the search.

The concept of standing discussed in *Jones* focuses on whether the person seeking to challenge the legality of a search as a basis for suppressing evidence was himself the "victim" of the search or seizure. Adoption of the so-called "target" theory advanced by petitioners would in effect permit a defendant to assert that a violation of the Fourth Amendment rights of a third party entitled him to have evidence suppressed at his trial. If we reject petitioners' request for a broadened rule of standing such as this, and reaffirm the holding of *Jones* and other cases that Fourth Amendment rights are personal rights that may not be asserted vicariously, we will have occasion to re-examine the "standing" terminology emphasized in *Jones*. For we are not at all sure that the determination of a motion to suppress is materially aided by labeling the inquiry identified in *Jones* as one of standing, rather than simply recognizing it as one involving the substantive question of whether or not the proponent of the motion to suppress has had his own Fourth Amendment rights infringed by the search and seizure which he seeks to challenge. We shall therefore consider in turn petitioners' target theory, the necessity for continued adherence to the notion of standing discussed in *Jones* as a concept that is theoretically distinct from the merits of a defendant's Fourth Amendment claim, and, finally, the proper disposition of petitioners' ultimate claim in this case.

A

We decline to extend the rule of standing in Fourth Amendment cases in the manner suggested by petitioners. A person who is aggrieved by an illegal search and seizure only through the introduction of damaging evidence secured by a search of a third person's premises or property has not had any of his Fourth Amendment rights infringed.

In support of their target theory, petitioners rely on the following quotation from *Jones*:

> In order to qualify as a "person aggrieved by an unlawful search and seizure" *one must have been a victim of a search or seizure, one against whom the search was directed*, as distinguished from one who claims prejudice only through the use of evidence gathered as a consequence of a search or seizure directed at someone else.

362 U.S. at 261 (emphasis added).

The above-quoted statement from *Jones* suggests that the italicized language was meant merely as a parenthetical equivalent of the previous phrase "a victim of a search or seizure." To the extent that the language might be read more broadly, it is dictum which was impliedly repudiated in *Alderman v. United States* and which we now expressly reject.

. . . [T]he question is whether the challenged search or seizure violated the Fourth Amendment rights of a criminal defendant who seeks to exclude the evidence obtained during it. That inquiry in turn requires a determination of whether the disputed search and seizure has infringed an interest of the defendant which the Fourth Amendment was designed to protect. We are under no illusion that by dispensing with the rubric of standing used in *Jones* we have rendered any simpler the determination of whether the proponent of a motion to suppress is entitled to contest the legality of a search and seizure. But by frankly recognizing that this aspect of the analysis belongs more properly under the heading of substantive Fourth Amendment doctrine than under the heading of standing, we think the decision of this issue will rest on sounder logical footing.

. . .

C

Here petitioners, who were passengers occupying a car which they neither owned nor leased, seek to analogize their position to that of the defendant in *Jones v. United States*. In *Jones*, petitioner was present at the time of the search of an apartment which was owned by a friend. The friend had given Jones permission to use the apartment and a key to it, with which Jones had admitted himself on the day of the search. He had a suit and shirt at the apartment and had slept there "maybe a night," but his home was elsewhere. At the time of the search, Jones was the only occupant of the apartment because the lessee was away for a period of several days. . . . Under these circumstances, this Court stated that while one wrongfully on the premises could not move to suppress evidence obtained as a result of searching them, "anyone legitimately on premises where a search occurs may challenge its legality." . . . Petitioners argue that their occupancy of the automobile in question was comparable to that of Jones in the apartment and that they therefore have standing to contest the legality of the search — or as we have rephrased the inquiry, that they, like Jones, had their Fourth Amendment rights violated by the search.

We do not question the conclusion in *Jones* that the defendant in that case suffered a violation of his personal Fourth Amendment rights if the search in question was unlawful. Nonetheless, we believe that the phrase "legitimately on premises" coined in *Jones* creates too broad a gauge for measurement of Fourth Amendment rights. For example, applied literally, this statement would permit a casual visitor who has never seen, or been permitted to visit the basement of another's house to object to a search of the basement if the visitor happened to be in the kitchen of the house at the time of the search. Likewise, a casual visitor who walks into a house one minute before a search of the house commences and leaves one minute after the search ends would be able to contest the legality of the search. The first visitor would have absolutely no interest or legitimate expectation of privacy in the basement, the second would have none in the house, and it advances no purpose served by the Fourth Amendment to permit either of them to object to the lawfulness of the search.

We think that *Jones* on its facts merely stands for the unremarkable proposition that a person can have a legally sufficient interest in a place other than his own home so that the Fourth Amendment protects him from unreasonable governmental intrusion into that place. . . . In defining the scope of that interest, we adhere to the view expressed in *Jones* and echoed in later cases that arcane distinctions developed in property and tort law between guests, licensees, invitees, and the like, ought not to control. But the *Jones* statement that a person need only be "legitimately on premises" in order to challenge the validity of the search of a dwelling place cannot be taken in its full sweep beyond the facts of that case.

Katz v. United States, 389 U.S. 347 (1967), provides guidance in defining the scope of the interest protected by the Fourth Amendment. In the course of repudiating the doctrine derived from *Olmstead v. United States*, 277 U.S. 438 (1928), and *Goldman v. United States*, 316 U.S. 129 (1942), that if police officers had not been guilty of a common-law trespass they were not prohibited by the Fourth Amendment from eavesdropping, the Court in *Katz* held that capacity to claim the protection of the Fourth Amendment depends not upon a property right in the invaded place but upon whether the person who claims the protection of the Amendment has a legitimate expectation of privacy in the invaded place. Viewed in this manner, the holding in *Jones* can best be explained by the fact that Jones had a legitimate expectation of privacy in the premises he was using and therefore could claim the protection of the Fourth Amendment with respect to a governmental invasion of those premises, even though his "interest" in those premises might not have been a recognized property interest at common law.

Our Brother White in dissent expresses the view that by rejecting the phrase "legitimately on [the] premises" as the appropriate measure of Fourth Amendment rights, we are abandoning a thoroughly workable, "bright line" test in favor of a less certain analysis of whether the facts of a particular case give rise to a legitimate expectation of privacy. If "legitimately on premises" were the successful litmus test of Fourth Amendment rights that he assumes it is, his approach would have at least the merit of easy application, whatever it lacked in fidelity to the history and purposes of the Fourth Amendment. But a reading of lower court cases that have applied the phrase "legitimately on premises," and of the dissent itself, reveals that this expression is not a shorthand summary for a bright-line rule which somehow encapsulates the "core" of the Fourth Amendment's protections.

The dissent itself shows that the facile consistency it is striving for is illusory. The dissenters concede that "there comes a point when use of an area is shared with so many that one simply cannot reasonably expect seclusion." But surely the "point" referred to is not one demarcating a line which is black on one side and white on another; it is inevitably a point which separates one shade of gray from another. We are likewise told by the dissent that a person "legitimately on *private* premises — though his privacy is *not absolute*, is entitled to expect that he is sharing it only with those persons [allowed there] and that governmental officials will intrude only with *consent* or by complying with the Fourth Amendment." [Emphasis added.] This single sentence describing the contours of the supposedly easily applied rule virtually abounds with unanswered questions: What are "private" premises? Indeed, what are the "premises?" It may be easy to describe the "premises" when one is confronted with a 1-room apartment, but what of the case of a 10-room house, or of a house with an attached garage that is searched? Also, if one's privacy is not absolute, how is it bounded? If he risks governmental intrusion "with consent," who may give that consent?

Again, we are told by the dissent that the Fourth Amendment assures that "*some* expectations of privacy are justified and will be protected from official intrusion." [Emphasis added.] But we are not told which of many possible expectations of privacy are embraced within this sentence. And our dissenting Brethren concede that "perhaps the Constitution provides some degree less protection for the personal freedom from unreasonable governmental intrusion when one does not have a possessory interest in the invaded private place." But how much "less" protection is available when one does not have such a possessory interest?

Our disagreement with the dissent is not that it leaves these questions unanswered, or that the questions are necessarily irrelevant in the context of the analysis contained in this opinion. Our disagreement is rather with the dissent's bland and self-refuting assumption that there will not be fine lines to be drawn in Fourth Amendment cases as in other areas of the law, and that its rubric, rather than a meaningful exegesis of Fourth Amendment doctrine, is more desirable or more easily resolves Fourth Amendment cases. In abandoning "legitimately on premises" for the doctrine that we announce today, we are not forsaking a time-tested and workable rule, which has produced consistent results when applied, solely for the sake of fidelity to the values underlying the Fourth Amendment. Rather, we are rejecting blind adherence to a phrase which at most has superficial clarity and which conceals underneath that thin veneer all of the problems of line drawing which must be faced in any conscientious effort to apply the Fourth Amendment. Where the factual premises for a rule are so generally prevalent that little would be lost and much would be gained by abandoning case-by-case analysis, we have not hesitated to do so. But the phrase "legitimately on premises" has not been shown to be an easily applicable measure of Fourth Amendment rights so much as it has proved to be simply a label placed by the courts on results which have not been subjected to careful analysis. We would not wish to be understood as saying that legitimate presence on the premises is irrelevant to one's expectation of privacy, but it cannot be deemed controlling.

D

Judged by the foregoing analysis, petitioners' claims must fail. They asserted neither a property nor a possessory interest in the automobile, nor an interest in the property seized. And as we have previously indicated, the fact that they were "legitimately on [the] premises" in the sense that they were in the car with the permission of its owner is not determinative of whether they had a legitimate expectation of privacy in the particular areas of the automobile searched. It is unnecessary for us to decide here whether the same expectations of privacy are warranted in a car as would be justified in a dwelling place in analogous circumstances. We have on numerous occasions pointed out that cars are not to be treated identically with houses or apartments for Fourth Amendment purposes. But here petitioners' claim is one which would fail even in an analogous situation in a dwelling place, since they made no showing that they had any legitimate expectation of privacy in the glove compartment or area under the seat of the car in which they were merely passengers. Like the trunk of an automobile, these are areas in which a passenger *qua* passenger simply would not normally have a legitimate expectation of privacy.

Jones and *Katz* involved significantly different factual circumstances. Jones not only had permission to use the apartment of his friend, but had a key to the apartment with which he admitted himself on the day of the search and kept possessions in the apartment. Except with respect to his friend, Jones had complete dominion and control over the apartment and could exclude others from it. Likewise in *Katz*, the defendant occupied the telephone booth, shut the door behind him to exclude all others and paid the toll, which "entitled [him] to assume that the words he utter[ed] into the mouthpiece [would] not be broadcast to the world." Katz and Jones could legitimately expect privacy in the areas which were the subject of the search and seizure each sought to contest. No such showing was made by these petitioners with respect to those portions of the automobile which were searched and from which incriminating evidence was seized.

III

The Illinois courts were therefore correct in concluding that it was unnecessary to decide whether the search of the car might have violated the rights secured to someone else by the Fourth and Fourteenth Amendments to the United States Constitution. Since it did not violate any rights of these petitioners, their judgment of conviction is *Affirmed.*

[JUSTICE POWELL, joined by the CHIEF JUSTICE, BURGER, wrote a separate concurring opinion.]

JUSTICE WHITE, with whom JUSTICE BRENNAN, JUSTICE MARSHALL, and JUSTICE STEVENS join, dissenting.

The Court today holds that the Fourth Amendment protects property, not people, and specifically that a legitimate occupant of an automobile may not invoke the exclusionary rule and challenge a search of that vehicle unless he happens to own or have a possessory interest in it. Though professing to acknowledge that the primary purpose of the Fourth Amendment's prohibition of unreasonable searches is the protection of privacy — not property — the Court nonetheless effectively ties the application of the Fourth Amendment and the exclusionary rule in this situation to property law concepts. Insofar as passengers are concerned, the Court's opinion today declares an "open season" on automobiles. However unlawful stopping and searching a car may be, absent a possessory or ownership interest, no "mere" passenger may object, regardless of his relationship to the owner. Because the majority's conclusion has no support in the Court's controlling decisions, in the logic of the Fourth Amendment, or in common sense, I must respectfully dissent. If the Court is troubled by the practical impact of the exclusionary rule, it should face the issue of that rule's continued validity squarely instead of distorting other doctrines in an attempt to reach what are perceived as the correct results in specific cases.

. . .

It is true that the Court asserts that it is not limiting the Fourth Amendment bar against unreasonable searches to the protection of property rights, but in reality it is doing exactly that. Petitioners were in a private place with the permission of the owner, but the Court states that that is not sufficient to establish entitlement to a legitimate expectation of privacy. But if that is not sufficient, what would be? We are not told, and it is hard to imagine anything short of a property interest that would satisfy the majority. Insofar as the Court's rationale is concerned, no passenger in an automobile, without an ownership or possessory interest and regardless of his relationship to the owner, may claim Fourth Amendment protection against illegal stops and searches of the automobile in which he is rightfully present. The Court approves the result in *Jones*, but it fails to give any explanation why the facts in *Jones* differ, in a fashion material to the Fourth Amendment, from the facts here. More importantly, how is the Court able to avoid answering the question why presence in a private place with the owner's permission is insufficient? If it is "tautological to fall back on the notion that those expectations of privacy which are legitimate depend primarily on cases deciding exclusionary-rule issues in criminal cases," then it surely must be tautological to decide that issue simply by unadorned fiat.

As a control on governmental power, the Fourth Amendment assures that some expectations of privacy are justified and will be protected from official intrusion. That should be true in this instance, for if protected zones of privacy can only be purchased or obtained by possession of property, then much of our daily lives will be unshielded from unreasonable governmental prying, and the reach of the Fourth Amendment will have been narrowed to protect chiefly those with possessory interests in real or personal property. I had thought that *Katz* firmly established that the Fourth Amendment was intended as more than simply a trespass law applicable to the government. Katz had no possessory interest in the public telephone booth, at least no more than petitioners had in their friend's car; Katz was simply legitimately present. And the decision in *Katz* was based not on property rights, but on the theory that it was essential to securing "conditions favorable to the pursuit of happiness" that the expectation of privacy in question be recognized.

At most, one could say that perhaps the Constitution provides some degree less protection for the personal freedom from unreasonable governmental intrusion when one does not have a possessory interest in the invaded private place. But that would only change the extent of the protection; it would not free police to do the unreasonable, as does the decision today. And since the accused should be entitled to litigate the application of the Fourth Amendment where his privacy interest is merely arguable, the failure to allow such litigation here is the more incomprehensible.

IV

The Court's holding is contrary not only to our past decisions and the logic of the Fourth Amendment but also to the everyday expectations of privacy that we all share. Because of that, it is unworkable in all the various situations that arise in real life. If the owner of the car had not only invited petitioners to join her but had said to them, "I give you a temporary possessory interest in my vehicle so that you will share the right to privacy that the Supreme Court says that I own," then apparently the majority would reverse. But people seldom say such things, though they may mean their invitation to encompass them if only they had thought of the problem. If the nonowner were the spouse or child of the owner, would the Court recognize a sufficient interest? If so, would distant relatives somehow have more of an expectation of privacy than close friends? What if the nonowner were driving with the owner's permission? Would nonowning drivers have more of an expectation of privacy than mere passengers? What about a passenger in a taxicab? *Katz* expressly recognized protection for such passengers. Why should Fourth Amendment rights be present when one pays a cabdriver for a ride but be absent when one is given a ride by a friend?

The distinctions the Court would draw are based on relationships between private parties, but the Fourth Amendment is concerned with the relationship of one of those parties to the government. Divorced as it is from the purpose of the Fourth Amendment, the Court's essentially property-based rationale can satisfactorily answer none of the questions posed above. That is reason enough to reject it.

The *Jones* rule is relatively easily applied by police and courts; the rule announced today will not provide law enforcement officials with a bright line between the protected and the unprotected. Only rarely will police know whether one private party has or has not been granted a sufficient possessory or other interest by another private party. Surely in this case the officers had no such knowledge. The Court's rule will ensnare defendants and police in needless litigation over factors that should not be determinative of Fourth Amendment rights.

More importantly, the ruling today undercuts the force of the exclusionary rule in the one area in which its use is most certainly justified — the deterrence of bad-faith violations of the Fourth Amendment. This decision invites police to engage in patently unreasonable searches every time an automobile contains more than one occupant. Should something be found, only the owner of the vehicle, or of the item, will have standing to seek suppression, and the evidence will presumably be usable against the other occupants. The danger of such bad faith is especially high in cases such as this one where the officers are only after the passengers and can usually infer accurately that the driver is the owner. The suppression remedy for those owners in whose vehicles something is found and who are charged with crime is small consolation for all those owners *and* occupants whose privacy will be needlessly invaded by officers following mistaken hunches not rising to the level of probable cause but operated on in the knowledge that someone in a crowded car will probably be unprotected if contraband or incriminating evidence happens to be found. After this decision, police will have little to lose by unreasonably searching vehicles occupied by more than one person.

Of course, most police officers will decline the Court's invitation and will continue to do their jobs as best they can in accord with the Fourth Amendment. But the very purpose of the Bill of Rights was to answer the justified fear that governmental agents cannot be left totally to their own devices, and the Bill of Rights is enforceable in the courts because human experience teaches that not all such officials will otherwise adhere to the stated precepts. Some policemen simply do act in bad faith, even if for understandable ends, and some deterrent is needed. In the rush to limit the applicability of the exclusionary rule somewhere, anywhere, the Court ignores precedent, logic, and common sense to exclude the rule's operation from situations in which, paradoxically, it is justified and needed.

NOTES AND QUESTIONS

(1) If the government has failed to comply with the Constitution, why should it make any difference *whose* right was violated? Isn't adherence to the Constitution best secured by simply holding that evidence illegally obtained is inadmissible? Is there any constitutional reason for the Supreme Court not so holding?

(2) After *Rakas*, Fourth Amendment "standing" is analytically aligned with substantive Fourth Amendment law. *United States v. Ewing*, 638 F.3d 1226, 1230 (9th Cir. 2011). Because standing is determined by asking the substantive question — whether the disputed search or seizure infringed an interest that the Fourth Amendment was designed to protect — "standing" is not jurisdictional and may be waived by the government if not asserted. *Id.* Nevertheless, the defendant, rather

than the government, bears the burden of proof to establish "standing." *Minnesota v. Carter*, 525 U.S. 83, 88 (1998).

(3) Is it possible to fully agree with Justice Rehnquist on the superfluity of the standing doctrine, yet disagree with the outcome of the case? Accepting as the issue whether Rakas had a reasonable expectation of privacy in the glove compartment and under the seat of the automobile in which he was riding, does the Court offer any explanation for its conclusion?

(4) In *United States v. Padilla*, 508 U.S. 77 (1993), the Supreme Court rejected a "co-conspirator exception" to the standing requirement which had been adopted by the Court of Appeals for the Ninth Circuit. The exception provided that "a co-conspirator obtains a legitimate expectation of privacy for Fourth Amendment purposes if he has either a supervisory role in the conspiracy or joint control over the place or property involved in the search and seizure." *Id.* at 78. Finding that this reasoning "squarely contradicts the controlling case [*Rakas*] from this Court," the Court unanimously reversed the judgment of the Ninth Circuit.

(5) Two years after *Rakas*, in *Rawlings v. Kentucky*, 448 U.S. 98 (1980), Justice Rehnquist, speaking for the Court, applied the analysis prescribed by *Rakas* to hold that the defendant could not object to the seizure of narcotics found in his companion's purse, notwithstanding the fact that he claimed ownership of the purse's contents. When police conducted a search of a house, where defendant and his companion were visiting, defendant and his companion sat on a couch with her purse resting between them. Police ordered defendant's companion to empty the purse. When she did, illegal drugs poured out. Defendant immediately claimed ownership of the drugs. In deciding that the appellate record supported the Supreme Court of Kentucky's conclusion that the defendant lacked a reasonable expectation of privacy in his companion's purse, the Court noted that defendant had known his companion only a few days; had never received access to the purse before dumping his drugs in it; and did not have any right to exclude other persons from the purse. Thus, concluded the Court, there was no basis to reject the Kentucky court's conclusion that defendant lacked a legitimate expectation of privacy in the purse at the time it was searched.

For years after *Rakas*, the Court talked principally in terms of whether a person claiming a Fourth Amendment violation enjoyed "a legitimate expectation of privacy in the invaded place." But recently in *United States v. Jones*, 132 S. Ct. 945 (2012), a majority of the Court indicated that the reasonable expectation of privacy test "did not 'snuf[f] out' the previously recognized protection for property" and "did not erode the principle 'that, when the Government does engage in physical intrusion of a constitutionally protected area in order to obtain information, that intrusion may constitute a violation of the Fourth Amendment.' " In other words, the Court reiterated that real and personal property rights can provide a foundation for a "reasonable expectation of privacy." *Id.* at 951. The police in Jones attached a GPS tracking device to the undercarriage of a Jeep driven by a suspected drug dealer. Over a period of 28 days, the government tracked all of the vehicle's movements. On certiorari, the Court considered whether the tracking device and subsequent use to monitor the defendant's movements on public streets constituted a search or seizure implicating the Fourth Amendment. *Id.* at 948. Held: Yes; police engaged in a "search" implicating Fourth Amendment protection. *Id.* at 949.

(6) Although in *Rakas* a majority of the Supreme Court rejected the passengers' standing to complain about the search of the car, more recently, in *Brendlin v. California*, 551 U.S. 249 (2007), the Court unanimously recognized that such a passenger does have standing to challenge an unconstitutional seizure of the car. Does this mean that the same passenger could have standing to complain about an unconstitutional traffic stop yet lack standing to suppress evidence uncovered during a search of the car?

In *Brendlin*, an officer decided to subject a Buick to a traffic stop because the car displayed a temporary operating permit. The officer admitted that "there was nothing unusual about the permit or the way it was affixed." Once the car was stopped, the officer noticed "one of the Brendlin brothers" in the front passenger seat. One of the brothers had "dropped out of parole supervision." The officer used his radio to confirm that Brendlin was, indeed, in violation of parole and arrested him. In a search incident to Brendlin's arrest, the officer found drugs and drug paraphernalia on Brendlin's person and in the car.

Once formally charged, Brendlin moved to suppress, arguing that the evidence obtained in the searches of his person and the car were "fruits of an unconstitutional seizure" because the officer "lacked probable cause or reasonable suspicion to make the traffic stop." Brendlin did not assert that his Fourth Amendment rights were violated by the search of another's vehicle. He "claimed only that the traffic stop was an unlawful seizure of his person." The Supreme Court agreed. It held that not only is the driver of a car seized when his car is subjected to a traffic stop, but also "a passenger is seized as well and so may challenge the constitutionality of the stop."

MINNESOTA v. CARTER

United States Supreme Court

525 U.S. 83 (1998)

CHIEF JUSTICE REHNQUIST delivered the opinion of the Court.

Respondents and the lessee of an apartment were sitting in one of its rooms, bagging cocaine. While so engaged they were observed by a police officer, who looked through a drawn window blind. The Supreme Court of Minnesota held that the officer's viewing was a search which violated respondents' Fourth Amendment rights. We hold that no such violation occurred.

James Thielen, a police officer in the Twin Cities' suburb of Eagan, Minnesota, went to an apartment building to investigate a tip from a confidential informant. The informant said that he had walked by the window of a ground-floor apartment and had seen people putting a white powder into bags. The officer looked in the same window through a gap in the closed blind and observed the bagging operation for several minutes. He then notified headquarters, which began preparing affidavits for a search warrant while he returned to the apartment building. When two men left the building in a previously identified Cadillac, the police stopped the car. Inside were respondents Carter and Johns. As the police opened the door of the car to let Johns out, they observed a black zippered pouch and a handgun, later determined to be loaded, on the vehicle's floor. Carter and Johns were arrested, and a later police search of the vehicle the next day discovered pagers, a scale, and 47 grams of cocaine in plastic sandwich bags.

After seizing the car, the police returned to Apartment 103 and arrested the occupant, Kimberly Thompson, who is not a party to this appeal. A search of the apartment pursuant to a warrant revealed cocaine residue on the kitchen table and plastic baggies similar to those found in the Cadillac. Thielen identified Carter, Johns, and Thompson as the three people he had observed placing the powder into baggies. The police later learned that while Thompson was the lessee of the apartment, Carter and Johns lived in Chicago and had come to the apartment for the sole purpose of packaging the cocaine. Carter and Johns had never been to the apartment before and were only in the apartment for approximately 2 1/2 hours. In return for the use of the apartment, Carter and Johns had given Thompson one-eighth of an ounce of the cocaine.

Carter and Johns were charged with conspiracy to commit a controlled substance crime in the first degree and aiding and abetting in a controlled substance crime in the first degree. . . . They moved to suppress all evidence obtained from the apartment and the Cadillac, as well as to suppress several post-arrest incriminating statements they had made. They argued that Thielen's initial observation of their drug packaging activities was an unreasonable search in violation of the Fourth Amendment and that all evidence obtained as a result of this unreasonable search was inadmissible as fruit of the poisonous tree. The Minnesota trial court held that since, unlike the defendant in *Minnesota v. Olson*, 495 U.S. 91 (1990), Carter and Johns were not overnight social guests but temporary out-of-state visitors, they were not entitled to claim the protection of the Fourth Amendment against the government intrusion into the apartment. The trial court also concluded that Thielen's observation was not a search within the meaning of the Fourth Amendment. After a trial, Carter and Johns were each convicted of both offenses. The Minnesota Court of Appeals held that the respondent Carter did not have "standing" to object to Thielen's actions because his claim that he was predominantly a social guest was "inconsistent with the only evidence concerning his stay in the apartment, which indicated that he used it for a business purpose — to package drugs." . . . In a separate appeal, the Court of Appeals also affirmed Johns' conviction, without addressing what it termed the "standing" issue.

A divided Minnesota Supreme Court reversed, holding that respondents had "standing" to claim the protection of the Fourth Amendment because they had " 'a legitimate expectation of privacy in the invaded place.' " The court noted that even though "society does not recognize as valuable the task of bagging cocaine, we conclude that society does recognize as valuable the right of property owners or leaseholders to invite persons into the privacy of their homes to conduct a common task, be it legal or illegal activity. We, therefore, hold that [respondents] had standing to bring [their] motion to suppress the evidence gathered as a result of Thielen's observations." . . . Based upon its conclusion that the respondents had "standing" to raise their Fourth Amendment claims, the court went on to hold that Thielen's observation constituted a search of the apartment under the Fourth Amendment, and that the search was unreasonable. We granted certiorari and now reverse.

The Minnesota courts analyzed whether respondents had a legitimate expectation of privacy under the rubric of "standing" doctrine, an analysis that this Court expressly rejected 20 years ago in *Rakas*.

The text of the Amendment suggests that its protections extend only to people in "their" houses. But we have held that in some circumstances a person may have a legitimate expectation of privacy in the house of someone else. In *Minnesota v. Olson*, for example, we decided that an overnight guest in a house had the sort of expectation of privacy that the Fourth Amendment protects.

Respondents here were obviously not overnight guests, but were essentially present for a business transaction and were only in the home a matter of hours. There is no suggestion that they had a previous relationship with Thompson, or that there was any other purpose to their visit. Nor was there anything similar to the overnight guest relationship in *Olson* to suggest a degree of acceptance into the household. While the apartment was a dwelling place for Thompson, it was for these respondents simply a place to do business.

Property used for commercial purposes is treated differently for Fourth Amendment purposes than residential property. "An expectation of privacy in commercial premises, however, is different from, and indeed less than, a similar expectation in an individual's home." And while it was a "home" in which respondents were present, it was not their home. Similarly, the Court has held that in some circumstances a worker can claim Fourth Amendment protection over his own workplace. *See, e.g., O'Connor v. Ortega*, 480 U.S. 709 (1987). But there is no indication that respondents in this case had nearly as significant a connection to Thompson's apartment as the worker in *O'Connor* had to his own private office.

If we regard the overnight guest in *Minnesota v. Olson* as typifying those who may claim the protection of the Fourth Amendment in the home of another, and one merely "legitimately on the premises" as typifying those who may not do so, the present case is obviously somewhere in between. But the purely commercial nature of the transaction engaged in here, the relatively short period of time on the premises, and the lack of any previous connection between respondents and the householder, all lead us to conclude that respondents' situation is closer to that of one simply permitted on the premises. We therefore hold that any search which may have occurred did not violate their Fourth Amendment rights.

Because we conclude that respondents had no legitimate expectation of privacy in the apartment, we need not decide whether the police officer's observation constituted a "search." The judgment of the Supreme Court of Minnesota is accordingly reversed, and the cause is remanded for proceedings not inconsistent with this opinion.

JUSTICE SCALIA, with whom JUSTICE THOMAS joins, concurring.

I join the opinion of the Court because I believe it accurately applies our recent case law, including *Minnesota v. Olson*. I write separately to express my view that that case law — like the submissions of the parties in this case — gives short shrift to the text of the Fourth Amendment, and to the well and long understood meaning of that text. Specifically, it leaps to apply the fuzzy standard of "legitimate expectation of privacy" — a consideration that is often relevant to whether a search or seizure covered by the Fourth Amendment is "unreasonable" — to the threshold question whether a search or seizure covered by the Fourth Amendment *has occurred.* If that latter question is addressed first and analyzed under the text of the Constitution as traditionally understood, the present case is not remotely difficult.

The Fourth Amendment protects "[t]he right of the people to be secure in *their* persons, houses, papers, and effects, against unreasonable searches and seizures. . . ." U.S. Const., amend. IV (emphasis added). It must be acknowledged that the phrase "their . . . houses" in this provision is, in isolation, ambiguous. It could mean "their respective houses," so that the protection extends to each person only in his *own* house. But it could also mean "their respective and each other's houses," so that each person would be protected even when visiting the house of someone else. As today's opinion for the Court suggests, however, it is not linguistically possible to give the provision the latter, expansive interpretation with respect to "houses" without giving it the same interpretation with respect to the nouns that are parallel to "houses" — "persons, . . . papers, and effects" — which would give me a constitutional right not to have your person unreasonably searched. This is so absurd that it has to my knowledge never been contemplated. The obvious meaning of the provision is that *each* person has the right to be secure against unreasonable searches and seizures in *his own* person, house, papers, and effects. . . .

The dissent believes that "[o]ur obligation to produce coherent results" requires that we ignore this clear text and four-century-old tradition, and apply instead the notoriously unhelpful test, adopted in a "benchmar[k]" decision that is 31 years old. In my view, the only thing the past three decades have established about the *Katz* test (which has come to mean the test enunciated by Justice Harlan's separate concurrence in *Katz*) is that, unsurprisingly, those "actual (subjective) expectation[s] of privacy" "that society is prepared to recognize as 'reasonable,' " . . . bear an uncanny resemblance to those expectations of privacy that this Court considers reasonable. When that self-indulgent test is employed (as the dissent would employ it here) to determine whether a "search or seizure" within the meaning of the Constitution has *occurred* (as opposed to whether that "search or seizure" is an "unreasonable" one), it has no plausible foundation in the text of the Fourth Amendment. The provision did not guarantee some generalized "right of privacy" and leave it to this Court to determine which particular manifestations of the value of privacy "society is prepared to recognize as 'reasonable.' " Rather, it enumerated ("persons, houses, papers, and effects") the objects of privacy protection to which the *Constitution* would extend, leaving further expansion to the good judgment, not of this Court, but of the people through their representatives in the legislature.[1]

---

1 [3] The dissent asserts that I "undervalu[e]" the *Katz* Court's observation that "the Fourth Amendment protects people, not places." That catchy slogan would be a devastating response to someone who maintained that *a location* could claim protection of the Fourth Amendment — someone who asserted, perhaps, that "primeval forests have rights, too." Cf. Stone, *Should Trees Have Standing? — Toward Legal Rights For Natural Objects*, 45 S. Cal. L. Rev. 450 (1972). The issue here, however, is the less druidical one of whether respondents (who are people) have suffered a violation of *their* right "to be secure in their persons, houses, papers, and effects, against unreasonable searches and seizures." U.S. Const., amend. IV. That the Fourth Amendment does not protect places is simply unresponsive to the question of whether the Fourth Amendment protects people in other people's homes. In saying this, I do

The dissent may be correct that a person invited into someone else's house to engage in a common business (even common monkey-business, so to speak) *ought* to be protected against government searches of the room in which that business is conducted; and that persons invited in to deliver milk or pizza (whom the dissent dismisses as "classroom hypotheticals," as opposed, presumably, to flesh-and-blood hypotheticals) ought *not* to be protected against government searches of the rooms that they occupy. I am not sure of the answer to those policy questions. But I am sure that the answer is not remotely contained in the Constitution, which means that it is left — as *many*, indeed *most*, important questions are left — to the judgment of state and federal legislators. We go beyond our proper role as judges in a democratic society when we restrict the people's power to govern themselves over the full range of policy choices that the Constitution has left available to them.

JUSTICE KENNEDY, concurring.

I join the Court's opinion, for its reasoning is consistent with my view that almost all social guests have a legitimate expectation of privacy, and hence protection against unreasonable searches, in their host's home.

The dissent, as I interpret it, does not question *Rakas* or the principle that not all persons in the company of the property owner have the owner's right to assert the special protection. *Rakas*, it is true, involved automobiles, where the necessities of law enforcement permit more latitude to the police than ought to be extended to houses. The analysis in *Rakas* was not conceived, however, as a utilitarian exception to accommodate the needs of law enforcement. The Court's premise was a more fundamental one. Fourth Amendment rights are personal, and when a person objects to the search of a place and invokes the exclusionary rule, he or she must have the requisite connection to that place. The analysis in *Rakas* must be respected with reference to dwellings unless that precedent is to be overruled or so limited to its facts that its underlying principle is, in the end, repudiated.

In this case respondents have established nothing more than a fleeting and insubstantial connection with Thompson's home. For all that appears in the record, respondents used Thompson's house simply as a convenient processing station, their purpose involving nothing more than the mechanical act of chopping and packing a substance for distribution. There is no suggestion that respondents engaged in confidential communications with Thompson about their transaction. Respondents had not been to Thompson's apartment before, and they left it even before their arrest.

If respondents here had been visiting twenty homes, each for a minute or two, to drop off a bag of cocaine and were apprehended by a policeman wrongfully present in the nineteenth home; or if they had left the goods at a home where they were not staying and the police had seized the goods in their absence, we would have said that

not, as the dissent claims, clash with "the *leitmotif* of Justice Harlan's concurring opinion" in *Katz; au contraire* (or, to be more Wagnerian, *im Gegenteil*), in this regard I am entirely in harmony with that opinion, and it is the dissent that sings from another opera. *See* 389 U.S. at 361, 88 S. Ct. 507 (Harlan, J., concurring): "As the Court's opinion states, 'the Fourth Amendment protects people, not places.' The question, however, is what protection it affords to those people. Generally, as here, the answer to that question requires reference to a 'place.'"

Rakas compels rejection of any privacy interest respondents might assert. So it does here, given that respondents have established no meaningful tie or connection to the owner, the owner's home, or the owner's expectation of privacy.

We cannot remain faithful to the underlying principle in *Rakas* without reversing in this case, and I am not persuaded that we need depart from it to protect the homeowner's own privacy interests. Respondents have made no persuasive argument that we need to fashion a *per se* rule of home protection, with an automatic right for all in the home to invoke the exclusionary rule, in order to protect homeowners and their guests from unlawful police intrusion. With these observations, I join the Court's opinion.

JUSTICE BREYER, concurring in the judgment.

I agree with Justice Ginsburg that respondents can claim the Fourth Amendment's protection. Petitioner, however, raises a second question, whether under the circumstances Officer Thielen's observation made "from a public area outside the curtilage of the residence" violated respondents' Fourth Amendment rights. In my view, it did not.

I would answer the question on the basis of the following factual assumptions, derived from the evidentiary record presented here: (1) On the evening of May 15, 1994, an anonymous individual approached Officer Thielen, telling him that he had just walked by a nearby apartment window through which he had seen some people bagging drugs; (2) the apartment in question was a garden apartment that was partly below ground level; (3) families frequently used the grassy area just outside the apartment's window for walking or for playing; (4) members of the public also used the area just outside the apartment's window to store bicycles; (5) in an effort to verify the tipster's information, Officer Thielen walked to a position about 1 to 1 1/2 feet in front of the window; (6) Officer Thielen stood there for about 15 minutes looking down through a set of Venetian blinds; (7) what he saw [sic], namely, people putting white powder in bags, verified the account he had heard; and (8) he then used that information to help obtain a search warrant. . . .

Officer Thielen, then, stood at a place used by the public and from which one could see through the window into the kitchen. The precautions that the apartment's dwellers took to maintain their privacy would have failed in respect to an ordinary passerby standing in that place. Given this Court's well-established case law, I cannot say that the officer engaged in what the Constitution forbids, namely, an "unreasonable search."

The Minnesota Supreme Court reached a different conclusion in part because it believed that Officer Thielen had engaged in unusual activity, that he "climbed over some bushes, crouched down and placed his face 12 to 18 inches from the window," and in part because he saw into the apartment through "a small gap" in the blinds that were drawn. But I would not here determine whether the crouching and climbing or "plac[ing] his face" makes a constitutional difference because the record before us does not contain support for those factual conclusions. That record indicates that Officer Thielen would not have needed to, and did not, climb over bushes or crouch. And even though the primary evidence consists of Officer

Thielen's own testimony, who else could have known? Given the importance of factual nuance in this area of constitutional law, I would not determine the constitutional significance of factual assertions that the record denies.

Neither can the matter turn upon "gaps" in drawn blinds. Whether there were holes in the blinds or they were simply pulled the "wrong way" makes no difference. One who lives in a basement apartment that fronts a publicly traveled street, or similar space, ordinarily understands the need for care lest a member of the public simply direct his gaze downward.

Putting the specific facts of this case aside, there is a benefit to an officer's decision to confirm an informant's tip by observing the allegedly illegal activity from a public vantage point. Indeed, there are reasons why Officer Thielen stood in a public place and looked through the apartment window. He had already received information that a crime was taking place in the apartment. He intended to apply for a warrant. He needed to verify the tipster's credibility. He might have done so in other ways, say, by seeking general information about the tipster's reputation and then obtaining a warrant and searching the apartment. But his chosen method — observing the apartment from a public vantage point — would more likely have saved an innocent apartment dweller from a physically intrusive, though warrant-based, search if the constitutionally permissible observation revealed no illegal activity.

For these reasons, while agreeing with Justice Ginsburg, I also concur in the Court's judgment reversing the Minnesota Supreme Court.

JUSTICE GINSBURG, with whom JUSTICE STEVENS and JUSTICE SOUTER join, dissenting.

The Court's decision undermines not only the security of short-term guests, but also the security of the home resident herself. In my view, when a homeowner or lessor personally invites a guest into her home to share in a common endeavor, whether it be for conversation, to engage in leisure activities, or for business purposes licit or illicit, that guest should share his host's shelter against unreasonable searches and seizures.

I do not here propose restoration of the "legitimately on the premises" criterion stated in *Jones v. United States* for the Court rejected that formulation in *Rakas v. Illinois*, as it did the "automatic standing rule" in *United States v. Salvucci.* First, the disposition I would reach in this case responds to the unique importance of the home — the most essential bastion of privacy recognized by the law. Second, even within the home itself, the position to which I would adhere would not permit "a casual visitor who has never seen, or been permitted to visit, the basement of another's house to object to a search of the basement if the visitor happened to be in the kitchen of the house at the time of the search." *Rakas.* Further, I would here decide only the case of the homeowner who chooses to share the privacy of her home and her company with a guest, and would not reach classroom hypotheticals like the milkman or pizza deliverer.

My concern centers on an individual's choice to share her home and her associations there with persons she selects. Our decisions indicate that people have a reasonable expectation of privacy in their homes in part because they have the prerogative to exclude others. The power to exclude implies the power to include. Our Fourth Amendment decisions should reflect these complementary prerogatives.

A home dweller places her own privacy at risk, the Court's approach indicates, when she opens her home to others, uncertain whether the duration of their stay, their purpose, and their "acceptance into the household" will earn protection. It remains textbook law that "[s]earches and seizures inside a home without a warrant are presumptively unreasonable absent exigent circumstances." The law in practice is less secure. Human frailty suggests that today's decision will tempt police to pry into private dwellings without warrant, to find evidence incriminating guests who do not rest there through the night.

Our leading decision in *Katz* is key to my view of this case. Our obligation to produce coherent results in this often visited area of the law requires us to inform our current expositions by benchmarks already established. The Court's decision in this case veers sharply from the path marked in *Katz.* I do not agree that we have a more reasonable expectation of privacy when we place a business call to a person's home from a public telephone booth on the side of the street, *see Katz*, than when we actually enter that person's premises to engage in a common endeavor.[2]

NOTES AND QUESTIONS

(1) Is it possible to discern from these several opinions whether Chief Justice Rehnquist succeeded in his seemingly one-man campaign to eliminate the concept of standing from Fourth Amendment analysis? Is Justice Scalia contending that the Chief Justice is right for the wrong reason? Is Justice Ginsburg claiming that he is wrong for the right reason? If the defendant in this case had been the resident of the apartment, can you tell what the outcome would have been?

(2) Similar issues to those in *Carter* sometimes arise from searches of motel rooms. An overnight guest and a joint occupant of a motel may enjoy a reasonable expectation of privacy that a short-term visitor to the motel does not. *See United States v. Sherrill*, 2011 U.S. Dist. LEXIS 132547 (D. Kan. Nov. 16, 2011).

---

[2] [3] Justice Scalia's lively concurring opinion deplores our adherence to *Katz.* In suggesting that we have elevated Justice Harlan's concurring opinion in *Katz* to first place, Justice Scalia undervalues the clear opinion of the Court that "the Fourth Amendment protects people, not places." That core understanding is the *leitmotif* of Justice Harlan's concurring opinion. One cannot avoid a strong sense of *deja vu* on reading Justice Scalia's elaboration. It so vividly recalls the opinion of Justice Black *in dissent* in *Katz.* See 389 U.S., at 365 (Black, J., dissenting) ("While I realize that an argument based on the meaning of words lacks the scope, and no doubt the appeal, of broad policy discussions and philosophical discourses . . . for me the language of the Amendment is the crucial place to look."); *id.* at 373 ("[B]y arbitrarily substituting the Court's language . . . for the Constitution's language . . . the Court has made the Fourth Amendment its vehicle for holding all laws violative of the Constitution which offend the Court's broadest concept of privacy."); *ibid.* ("I will not distort the words of the Amendment in order to 'keep the Constitution up to date' or 'to bring it into harmony with the times.' "). Justice Scalia relies on what he deems "clear text," . . . to argue that the Fourth Amendment protects people from searches only in the places where they live. . . . Again, as Justice Stewart emphasized in the majority opinion in *Katz,* which *stare decisis* and reason require us to follow, "the Fourth Amendment protects people, not places."

(3) In *United States v. Payner*, 447 U.S. 727 (1980), the Supreme Court considered whether a defendant's lack of standing protects the government against a Fourth Amendment challenge that rests on the government's "knowingly and willfully participated in" unlawful seizure of evidence. The district court in *Payner* found that the government had counseled agents of the Internal Revenue Service that principles of Fourth Amendment standing would permit them to "purposefully conduct an unconstitutional search and seizure of one individual in order to obtain evidence against third parties." *Id.* at 730. Based on this understanding, the agents surreptitiously obtained and copied documents carried in the briefcase of a Bahamian bank officer. The documents were later used as evidence against Defendant Payner, who was charged with falsifying his federal income tax return by falsely claiming that he had no foreign bank accounts. In rejecting Payner's argument that the documents were subject to Fourth Amendment suppression, the Court reasoned: "Our cases have consistently recognized that unbending application of the exclusionary sanction to enforce ideals of governmental rectitude would impede unacceptably the truth-finding functions of judge and jury." *Id.* at 733. The Court concluded: "[T]he supervisory power does not authorize a federal court to suppress otherwise admissible evidence on the ground that it was seized unlawfully from a third party not before the court." *Id.* at 735.

[B] Beyond the Fourth Amendment

In addition to issues of "standing" that regularly arise in Fourth Amendment cases, such issues presumably can occur in cases asserting violations of the Fifth and Fourteenth Amendments, violations of the Sixth Amendment, and in cases in which the accused claims a breach of the protections established in *Miranda*. For instance, if a suspect is coerced into confessing to a crime in violation of his Fifth and Fourteenth Amendment rights, or he confesses although he was subjected to custodial interrogation without the warnings required by *Miranda*, and, in doing so, he implicates a codefendant, can the codefendant successfully exclude the statement from his or her trial? The Supreme Court has not decided. But it is likely that the Court would find that the codefendant lacks standing to assert a violation of another's constitutional right. *See, e.g.*, *Bellis v. United States*, 417 U.S. 85, 90 (1974) (noting, in the context of a dispute over whether a partner in a small firm could invoke his personal privilege against self-incrimination and refuse to comply with a subpoena directed to the partnership, that "the Fifth Amendment privilege is a purely personal one"); *United States v. Escobar*, 50 F.3d 1414, 1422 (8th Cir. 1995) (refusing to allow two defendants to challenge the admission of a third codefendant's statement as taken in violation of *Miranda*, explaining that the codefendant's "*Miranda* rights are personal to him, and [the other defendants] have no standing to assert this alleged violation."). The same is probably true of violations of a defendant's Sixth Amendment right to counsel, which is presumably a personal right. *See United States v. Peterson*, 698 F.2d 921, 924 (8th Cir. 1982) (citing *United States v. Payner*, 447 U.S. 727 (1980), and expressing "doubt" that a defendant has standing to assert a codefendant's Sixth Amendment right to counsel).

At a minimum, we know that in recent years, the Supreme Court has applied the exclusionary rule more and more sparingly, describing the rule as one that "generates 'substantial social costs' . . . which sometimes include setting the guilty free and the dangerous at large." *See, e.g., Hudson v. Michigan*, 547 U.S. 586, 591 (2006), discussed *infra* § 6.02[B]. Because of the policies underlying the standing doctrine and the Court's concern with the social costs exacted by the exclusionary rule, the Court is likely to continue to exclude evidence only when someone demonstrates a sufficient nexus between the constitutional violation and his or her own person, property, or interests.

§ 6.02 THE EXCLUSIONARY RULE(S)

[A] The Fourth Amendment's Exclusionary Rule

MAPP v. OHIO
United States Supreme Court
367 U.S. 643 (1961)

Justice Clark delivered the opinion of the Court.

Appellant stands convicted of knowingly having had in her possession and under her control certain lewd and lascivious books, pictures, and photographs in violation of § 2905.34 of Ohio's Revised Code. As officially stated in the syllabus to its opinion, the Supreme Court of Ohio found that her conviction was valid though "based primarily upon the introduction in evidence of lewd and lascivious books and pictures unlawfully seized during an unlawful search of defendant's home. . . ."

On May 23, 1957, three Cleveland police officers arrived at appellant's residence in that city pursuant to information that "a person [was] hiding out in the home, who was wanted for questioning in connection with a recent bombing, and that there was a large amount of policy paraphernalia being hidden in the home." Miss Mapp and her daughter by a former marriage lived on the top floor of the two-family dwelling. Upon their arrival at that house, the officers knocked on the door and demanded entrance but appellant, after telephoning her attorney, refused to admit them without a search warrant. They advised their headquarters of the situation and undertook a surveillance of the house.

The officers again sought entrance some three hours later when four or more additional officers arrived on the scene. When Miss Mapp did not come to the door immediately, at least one of the several doors to the house was forcibly opened and the policemen gained admittance. Meanwhile Miss Mapp's attorney arrived, but the officers, having secured their own entry, and continuing in their defiance of the law, would permit him neither to see Miss Mapp nor to enter her house. It appears that Miss Mapp was halfway down the stairs from the upper floor to the front door when the officers, in this highhanded manner, broke into the hall. She demanded to see the search warrant. A paper, claimed to be a warrant, was held up by one of the officers. She grabbed the "warrant" and placed it in her bosom. A struggle ensued in which the officers recovered the piece of paper and as a result of which they handcuffed appellant because she had been "belligerent" in resisting their official rescue of the "warrant" from her person.

Running roughshod over appellant, a policeman "grabbed" her, "twisted [her] hand," and she "yelled [and] pleaded with him" because "it was hurting." Appellant, in handcuffs, was then forcibly taken upstairs to her bedroom where the officers searched a dresser, a chest of drawers, a closet and some suitcases. They also looked into a photo album and through personal papers belonging to the appellant. The search spread to the rest of the second floor including the child's bedroom, the living room, the kitchen and a dinette. The basement of the building and a trunk found therein were also searched. The obscene materials for possession of which she was ultimately convicted were discovered in the course of that widespread search.

At the trial no search warrant was produced by the prosecution, nor was the failure to produce one explained or accounted for. At best, "There is, in the record, considerable doubt as to whether there ever was any warrant for the search of defendant's home." The Ohio Supreme Court believed a "reasonable argument" could be made that the conviction should be reversed "because the 'methods' employed to obtain the [evidence] were such as to offend "a sense of justice, but the court found determinative the fact that the evidence had not been taken "from defendant's person by the use of brutal or offensive physical force against defendant. "

The State says that even if the search were made without authority, or otherwise unreasonably, it is not prevented from using the unconstitutionally seized evidence at trial, citing *Wolf v. Colorado*, 338 U.S. 25 (1949), in which this Court did indeed hold "that in a prosecution in a State court for a State crime the Fourteenth Amendment does not forbid the admission of evidence obtained by an unreasonable search and seizure."

I

Seventy-five years ago, in *Boyd v. United States*, 116 U.S. 616, 630 (1886), considering the Fourth and Fifth Amendments as running "almost into each other" on the facts before it, this Court held that the doctrines of those Amendments

> apply to all invasions on the part of the government and its employees of the sanctity of a man's home and the privacies of life. It is not the breaking of his doors, and the rummaging of his drawers, that constitutes the essence of the offence; but it is the invasion of his indefeasible right of personal security, personal liberty and private property. . . . Breaking into a house and opening boxes and drawers are circumstances of aggravation; but any forcible and compulsory extortion of a man's own testimony or of his private papers to be used as evidence to convict him of crime or to forfeit his goods, is within the condemnation . . . [of those Amendments].

The Court noted that "constitutional provisions for the security of person and property should be liberally construed. . . . It is the duty of courts to be watchful for the constitutional rights of the citizen, and against any stealthy encroachments thereon." In this jealous regard for maintaining the integrity of individual rights, the Court gave life to Madison's prediction that "independent tribunals of justice . . . will be naturally led to resist every encroachment upon rights expressly stipulated for in the Constitution by the declaration of rights." I Annals of Cong. 439

(1789). Concluding, the Court specifically referred to the use of the evidence there seized as "unconstitutional."

Less than 30 years after *Boyd*, this Court, in *Weeks v. United States*, 232 U.S. 383 (1914), stated that

> the Fourth Amendment . . . put the courts of the United States and Federal officials, in the exercise of their power and authority, under limitations and restraints [and] . . . forever secure[d] the people, their persons, houses, papers and effects against all unreasonable searches and seizures under the guise of law . . . and the duty of giving to it force and effect is obligatory upon all entrusted under our Federal system with the enforcement of the laws.

Specifically dealing with the use of the evidence unconstitutionally seized, the Court concluded:

> If letters and private documents can thus be seized and held and used in evidence against a citizen accused of an offense, the protection of the Fourth Amendment declaring his right to be secure against such searches and seizures is of no value, and, so far as those thus placed are concerned, might as well be stricken from the Constitution. The efforts of the courts and their officials to bring the guilty to punishment, praiseworthy as they are, are not to be aided by the sacrifice of those great principles established by years of endeavor and suffering which have resulted in their embodiment in the fundamental law of the land.

Finally, the Court in that case clearly stated that use of the seized evidence involved "a denial of the constitutional rights of the accused." Thus, in the year 1914, in the *Weeks* case, this Court "for the first time" held that "in a federal prosecution the Fourth Amendment barred the use of evidence secured through an illegal search and seizure." *Wolf v. Colorado*. This Court has ever since required of federal law officers a strict adherence to that command which this Court has held to be a clear, specific, and constitutionally required — even if judicially implied — deterrent safeguard without insistence upon which the Fourth Amendment would have been reduced to "a form of words." Holmes, J., *Silverthorne Lumber Co. v. United States*. It meant, quite simply, that "conviction by means of unlawful seizures and forced confessions . . . should find no sanction in the judgments of the courts," . . . *Weeks v. United States*, . . . and that such evidence "shall not be used at all." *Silverthorne Lumber Co.*

There are in the cases of this Court some passing references to the *Weeks* rule as being one of evidence. But the plain and unequivocal language of *Weeks* — and its later paraphrase in *Wolf* — to the effect that the *Weeks* rule is of constitutional origin, remains entirely undisturbed. . . .

> The striking outcome of the *Weeks* case and those which followed it was the sweeping declaration that the Fourth Amendment, although not referring to or limiting the use of evidence in court, really forbade its introduction if obtained by government officers through a violation of the amendment.

II

In 1949, 35 years after *Weeks* was announced, this Court, in *Wolf*, again for the first time, discussed the effect of the Fourth Amendment upon the States through the operation of the Due Process Clause of the Fourteenth Amendment. It said:

> [W]e have no hesitation in saying that were a State affirmatively to sanction such police incursion into privacy it would run counter to the guaranty of the Fourteenth Amendment.

Nevertheless, after declaring that the "security of one's privacy against arbitrary intrusion by the police" is "implicit in 'the concept of ordered liberty' and as such enforceable against the States through the Due Process Clause," and announcing that it "stoutly adhere[d]" to the *Weeks* decision, the Court decided that the *Weeks* exclusionary rule would not then be imposed upon the States as "an essential ingredient of the right." The Court's reasons for not considering essential to the right to privacy, as a curb imposed upon the States by the Due Process Clause, that which decades before had been posited as part and parcel of the Fourth Amendment's limitation upon federal encroachment of individual privacy, were bottomed on factual considerations.

[W]e will consider the current validity of the factual grounds upon which *Wolf* was based. The Court in *Wolf* first stated that "[t]he contrariety of views of the States" on the adoption of the exclusionary rule of *Weeks* was "particularly impressive" and, in this connection, that it could not "brush aside the experience of States which deem the incidence of such conduct by the police too slight to call for a deterrent remedy . . . by overriding the [States'] relevant rules of evidence." While in 1949, prior to the *Wolf* case, almost two-thirds of the States were opposed to the use of the exclusionary rule, now, despite the *Wolf* case, more than half of those since passing upon it, by their own legislative or judicial decision, have wholly or partly adopted or adhered to the *Weeks* rule.

III

Some five years after *Wolf*, in answer to a plea made here Term after Term that we overturn its doctrine on applicability of the *Weeks* exclusionary rule, this Court indicated that such should not be done until the States had "adequate opportunity to adopt or reject the [*Weeks*] rule." There again it was said:

> Never until June of 1949 did this Court hold the basic search-and-seizure prohibition in any way applicable to the states under the Fourteenth Amendment.

. . . And only last Term, after again carefully re-examining the *Wolf* doctrine in *Elkins v. United States*, the Court pointed out that "the controlling principles" as to search and seizure and the problem of admissibility "seemed clear" . . . until the announcement in *Wolf* "that the Due Process Clause of the Fourteenth Amendment does not itself require state courts to adopt the exclusionary rule" of the *Weeks* case. At the same time, the Court pointed out, "the underlying constitutional doctrine which *Wolf* established . . . that the Federal Constitution . . . prohibits unreasonable searches and seizures by state officers" had undermined the "foundation upon which the admissibility of state-seized evidence in a federal trial originally rested." The Court concluded that it was therefore obliged to hold, although it chose the narrower ground on which to do so, that all evidence obtained by an unconstitutional search and seizure was inadmissible in a federal court regardless of its source. Today we once again examine *Wolf*'s constitutional documentation of the right to privacy free from unreasonable state intrusion, and, after its dozen years on our books, are led by it to close the only courtroom door remaining open to evidence secured by official lawlessness in flagrant abuse of that basic right, reserved to all persons as a specific guarantee against that very same unlawful conduct. We hold that all evidence obtained by searches and seizures in violation of the Constitution is, by that same authority, inadmissible in a state court.

IV

Since the Fourth Amendment's right of privacy has been declared enforceable against the States through the Due Process Clause of the Fourteenth, it is enforceable against them by the same sanction of exclusion as is used against the Federal Government. Were it otherwise, then just as without the *Weeks* rule the assurance against unreasonable federal searches and seizures would be "a form of words," valueless and undeserving of mention in a perpetual charter of inestimable human liberties, so too, without that rule the freedom from state invasions of privacy would be so epemeral and so neatly severed from its conceptual nexus with the freedom from all brutish means of coercing evidence as not to merit this Court's high regard as a freedom "implicit in 'the concept of ordered liberty.' "

. . .

In extending the substantive protections of due process to all constitutionally unreasonable searches — state or federal — it was logically and constitutionally necessary that the exclusion doctrine — an essential part of the right to privacy — be also insisted upon as an essential ingredient of the right newly recognized by the *Wolf* case. In short, the admission of the new constitutional right by *Wolf* could not consistently tolerate denial of its most important constitutional privilege, namely, the exclusion of the evidence which an accused had been forced to give by reason of the unlawful seizure. To hold otherwise is to grant the right but in reality to withhold its privilege and enjoyment. Only last year the Court itself recognized that the purpose of the exclusionary rule "is to deter — to compel respect for the constitutional guaranty in the only effectively available way — by removing the incentive to disregard it."

V

The ignoble shortcut to conviction left open to the State tends to destroy the entire system of constitutional restraints on which the liberties of the people rest. Having once recognized that the right to privacy embodied in the Fourth Amendment is enforceable against the States, and that the right to be secure against rude invasions of privacy by state officers is, therefore, constitutional in origin, we can no longer permit that right to remain an empty promise. Because it is enforceable in the same manner and to like effect as other basic rights secured by the Due Process

Clause, we can no longer permit it to be revocable at the whim of any police officer who, in the name of law enforcement itself, chooses to suspend its enjoyment. Our decision, founded on reason and truth, gives to the individual no more than that which the Constitution guarantees him, to the police officer no less than that to which honest law enforcement is entitled, and, to the courts, that judicial integrity so necessary in the true administration of justice.

JUSTICE BLACK, concurring.

For nearly fifty years, since the decision of this Court in *Weeks*, federal courts have refused to permit the introduction into evidence against an accused of his papers and effects obtained by "unreasonable searches and seizures" in violation of the Fourth Amendment. In *Wolf*, decided in 1948, however, this Court held that "in a prosecution in a State court for a State crime the Fourteenth Amendment does not forbid the admission of evidence obtained by an 'unreasonable search and seizure.' " I concurred in that holding on these grounds:

> For reasons stated in my dissenting opinion in *Adamson v. California*, I agree with the conclusion of the Court that the Fourth Amendment's prohibition of "unreasonable searches and seizures" is enforceable against the states. Consequently, I should be for reversal of this case if I thought the Fourth Amendment not only prohibited "unreasonable searches and seizures," but also, of itself, barred the use of evidence so unlawfully obtained. But I agree with what appears to be a plain implication of the Court's opinion that the federal exclusionary rule is not a command of the Fourth Amendment but is a judicially created rule of evidence which Congress might negate.

I am still not persuaded that the Fourth Amendment, standing alone, would be enough to bar the introduction into evidence against an accused of papers and effects seized from him in violation of its commands. For the Fourth Amendment does not in itself contain any provision expressly precluding the use of such evidence, and I am extremely doubtful that such a provision could properly be inferred from nothing more than the basic command against unreasonable searches and seizures. Reflection on the problem, however, in the light of cases coming before the Court since *Wolf*, has led me to conclude that when the Fourth Amendment's ban against unreasonable searches and seizures is considered together with the Fifth Amendment's ban against compelled self-incrimination, a constitutional basis emerges which not only justifies but actually requires the exclusionary rule.

The close interrelationship between the Fourth and Fifth Amendments, as they apply to this problem, has long been recognized and, indeed, has expressly made the ground for this Court's holding in *Boyd v. United States*. There the Court fully discussed this relationship and declared itself "unable to perceive that the seizure of a man's private books and papers to be used in evidence against him is substantially different from compelling him to be a witness against himself." It was upon this ground that Mr. Justice Rutledge largely relied in his dissenting opinion in the *Wolf* case. And, although I rejected the argument at that time, its force has, for me at least, become compelling with the more thorough understanding of the problem brought on by recent cases.

Justice Harlan, whom Justice Frankfurter and Justice Whittaker join, dissenting.

In overruling the *Wolf* case the Court, in my opinion, has forgotten the sense of judicial restraint which, with due regard for *stare decisis*, is one element that should enter into deciding whether a past decision of this Court should be overruled. Apart from that I also believe that the *Wolf* rule represents sounder Constitutional doctrine than the new rule which now replaces it.

II

Essential to the majority's argument against *Wolf* is the proposition that the rule of *Weeks v. United States* excluding in federal criminal trials the use of evidence obtained in violation of the Fourth Amendment, derives not from the "supervisory power" of this Court over the federal judicial system, but from Constitutional requirement. This is so because no one, I suppose, would suggest that this Court possesses any general supervisory power over the state courts. Although I entertain considerable doubt as to the soundness of this foundational proposition of the majority, I shall assume, for present purposes, that the *Weeks* rule "is of constitutional origin."

At the heart of the majority's opinion in this case is the following syllogism: (1) the rule excluding in federal criminal trials evidence which is the product of an illegal search and seizure is "part and parcel" of the Fourth Amendment; (2) *Wolf* held that the "privacy" assured against federal action by the Fourth Amendment is also protected against state action by the Fourteenth Amendment; and (3) it is therefore "logically and constitutionally necessary" that the *Weeks* exclusionary rule should also be enforced against the States.

This reasoning ultimately rests on the unsound premise that because *Wolf* carried into the States, as part of "the concept of ordered liberty" embodied in the Fourteenth Amendment, the principle of "privacy" underlying the Fourth Amendment, it must follow that whatever configurations of the Fourth Amendment have been developed in the particularizing federal precedents are likewise to be deemed a part of "ordered liberty," and as such are enforceable against the States. For me, this does not follow at all.

It cannot be too much emphasized that what was recognized in *Wolf* was not that the Fourth Amendment *as such* is enforceable against the States as a facet of due process, a view of the Fourteenth Amendment which, as *Wolf* itself pointed out, has long since been discredited, but the principle of privacy "which is at the core of the Fourth Amendment." It would not be proper to expect or impose any precise equivalence, either as regards the scope of the right or the means of its implementation, between the requirements of the Fourth and Fourteenth Amendments. For the Fourth, unlike what was said in *Wolf* of the Fourteenth, does not state a general principle only; it is a particular command, having its setting in a pre-existing legal context on which both interpreting decisions and enabling statutes must at least build.

Thus, even in a case which presented simply the question of whether a particular search and seizure was constitutionally "unreasonable" — say in a tort action against state officers — we would not be true to the Fourteenth Amendment were we merely to stretch the general principle of individual privacy on a Procrustean bed of federal precedents under the Fourth Amendment. But in this instance more than that is involved, for here we are reviewing not a determination that what the state police did was Constitutionally permissible (since the state court quite evidently assumed that it was not), but a determination that appellant was properly found guilty of conduct which, for present purposes, it is to be assumed the State could Constitutionally punish. Since there is not the slightest suggestion that Ohio's policy is "affirmatively to sanction . . . police incursion into privacy" . . . what the Court is now doing is to impose upon the States not only federal substantive standards of "search and seizure" but also the basic federal remedy for violation of those standards. For I think it entirely clear that the *Weeks* exclusionary rule is but a remedy which, by penalizing past official misconduct, is aimed at deterring such conduct in the future.

I would not impose upon the States this federal exclusionary remedy. The reasons given by the majority for now suddenly turning its back on *Wolf* seem to me notably unconvincing.

. . .

A state conviction comes to us as the complete product of a sovereign judicial system. Typically a case will have been tried in a trial court, tested in some final appellate court, and will go no further. In the comparatively rare instance when a conviction is reviewed by us on due process grounds we deal then with a finished product in the creation of which we are allowed no hand, and our task, far from being one of over-all supervision, is, speaking generally, restricted to a determination of whether the prosecution was Constitutionally fair. The specifics of trial procedure, which in every mature legal system will vary greatly in detail, are within the sole competence of the States. I do not see how it can be said that a trial becomes unfair simply because a State determines that evidence may be considered by the trier of fact, regardless of how it was obtained, if it is relevant to the one issue with which the trial is concerned, the guilt or innocence of the accused. Of course, a court may use its procedures as an incidental means of pursuing other ends than the correct resolution of the controversies before it. Such indeed is the *Weeks* rule, but if a State does not choose to use its courts in this way, I do not believe that this Court is empowered to impose this much-debated procedure on local courts, however efficacious we may consider the *Weeks* rule to be as a means of securing Constitutional rights.

[B] Justifications for the Exclusion of Evidence

In *Mapp v. Ohio*, 367 U.S. 643 (1961), four justices (Warren, Douglas, Clark, and Brennan) ascribed constitutional origins to the Fourth Amendment exclusionary rule. A fifth, Justice Black, asserted that the Fourth Amendment read in conjunction with the Fifth Amendment required the conclusion that the exclusionary rule was constitutionally required.

In all, five justices believed that the Constitution mandated the exclusion of evidence obtained in violation of the Fourth Amendment, and four suggested that the exclusionary rule was necessary to protect judicial integrity and as recognition that law breakers cannot effectively enforce laws. On this point, Justice Clark reasoned:

> There are those who say, as did Justice (then Judge) Cardozo, that under our constitutional exclusionary doctrine "[t]he criminal is to go free because the constable has blundered." In some cases this will undoubtedly be the result. But, as was said in *Elkins v. United States*, 364 U.S. 206, 222 (1960), "there is another consideration — the imperative of judicial integrity." The criminal goes free, if he must, but it is the law that sets him free. Nothing can destroy a government more quickly than its failure to observe its own laws, or worse, its disregard of the charter of its own existence. As Mr. Justice Brandeis, dissenting, said in *Olmstead v. United States*, 277 U.S. 438, 485 (1928): "Our government is the potent, the omnipresent teacher. For good or for ill, it teaches the whole people by its example. . . . If the government becomes a lawbreaker, it breeds contempt for law; it invites every man to become a law unto himself; it invites anarchy." . . .
>
> . . . Having once recognized that the right to privacy embodied in the Fourth Amendment is enforceable against the States, and that the right to be secure against rude invasions of privacy by state officers is, therefore, constitutional in origin, we can no longer permit that right to remain an empty promise. . . . Our decision, founded on reason and truth, gives to the individual no more than that which the Constitution guarantees him, to the police officer no less than that to which honest law enforcement is entitled, and, to the courts, that judicial integrity so necessary in the true administration of justice.

Mapp, 367 U.S. at 659–60.

Since *Mapp*, the Supreme Court has retreated from its robust declaration that application of the Fourth Amendment's protections requires exclusion of evidence obtained in violation of its dictates. In *United States v. Calandra*, 414 U.S. 338, 347 (1974), for example, the Court emphasized the deterrence rationale above all others, reiterating that the exclusionary rule "is calculated to prevent, not to repair." According to the majority in *Calandra*, the purpose of the Fourth Amendment's exclusionary rule is "to deter — to compel respect for the constitutional guaranty in the only effectively available way — by removing the incentive to disregard it." *Id.* at 347. The Court in *Calandra* added that the exclusionary rule was simply a "judicially created remedy designed to safeguard Fourth Amendment rights generally through its deterrent effect, rather than a personal constitutional right of the party aggrieved." *Id.* Likewise, the Court said that the exclusionary rule is not always required. "Despite its broad deterrent purpose, the exclusionary rule has never been interpreted to proscribe the use of illegally seized evidence in all proceedings or against all persons." *Id.*

In *Hudson v. Michigan*, below, the Court applied a balancing, cost-benefit analysis when deciding whether the exclusionary rule precluded the use of evidence obtained in violation of the Fourth Amendment's knock and announce rule.

HUDSON v. MICHIGAN

United States Supreme Court
547 U.S. 586 (2006)

JUSTICE SCALIA delivered the opinion of the Court, except as to Part IV.

We decide whether violation of the "knock-and-announce" rule requires the suppression of all evidence found in the search.

I

Police obtained a warrant authorizing a search for drugs and firearms at the home of petitioner Booker Hudson. They discovered both. Large quantities of drugs were found, including cocaine rocks in Hudson's pocket. A loaded gun was lodged between the cushion and armrest of the chair in which he was sitting. Hudson was charged under Michigan law with unlawful drug and firearm possession.

This case is before us only because of the method of entry into the house. When the police arrived to execute the warrant, they announced their presence, but waited only a short time — perhaps "three to five seconds," before turning the knob of the unlocked front door and entering Hudson's home. Hudson moved to suppress all the inculpatory evidence, arguing that the premature entry violated his Fourth Amendment rights.

The Michigan trial court granted his motion. On interlocutory review, the Michigan Court of Appeals reversed, relying on Michigan Supreme Court cases holding that suppression is inappropriate when entry is made pursuant to warrant but without proper "knock and announce." The Michigan Supreme Court denied leave to appeal. Hudson was convicted of drug possession. He renewed his Fourth Amendment claim on appeal, but the Court of Appeals rejected it and affirmed the conviction. The Michigan Supreme Court again declined review. We granted certiorari.

. . .

III

A

In *Weeks*, we adopted the federal exclusionary rule for evidence that was unlawfully seized from a home without a warrant in violation of the Fourth Amendment. We began applying the same rule to the States, through the Fourteenth Amendment, in *Mapp v. Ohio.*

Suppression of evidence, however, has always been our last resort, not our first impulse. The exclusionary rule generates "substantial social costs," *United States v. Leon*, 468 U.S. 897 (1984), which sometimes include setting the guilty free and the dangerous at large. We have therefore been "cautio[us] against expanding" it . . . and "have repeatedly emphasized that the rule's 'costly toll' upon truth-seeking and law enforcement objectives presents a high obstacle for those urging [its] application." We have rejected "[i]ndiscriminate application" of the rule and have held it to be applicable only "where its remedial objectives are thought most efficaciously served," *United States v. Calandra*, 414 U.S. 338 (1974) — that is, "where its deterrence benefits outweigh its 'substantial social costs.'"

We did not always speak so guardedly. Expansive dicta in *Mapp*, for example, suggested wide scope for the exclusionary rule. *See, e.g.*, 367 U.S. at 655 ("[A]ll evidence obtained by searches and seizures in violation of the Constitution is, by that same authority, inadmissible in a state court"). But we have long since rejected that approach. "[Once] the Court treated identification of a Fourth Amendment violation as synonymous with application of the exclusionary rule to evidence secured incident to that violation. Subsequent case law has rejected this reflexive application of the exclusionary rule." We had said as much in *Leon* when we explained that "[w]hether the exclusionary sanction is appropriately imposed in a particular case, . . . is 'an issue separate from the question whether the Fourth Amendment rights of the party seeking to invoke the rule were violated by police conduct.'"

In other words, exclusion may not be premised on the mere fact that a constitutional violation was a "but-for" cause of obtaining evidence. Our cases show that but-for causality is only a necessary, not a sufficient, condition for suppression. In this case, of course, the constitutional violation of an illegal *manner* of entry was *not* a but-for cause of obtaining the evidence. Whether that preliminary misstep had occurred or *not*, the police would have executed the warrant they had obtained, and would have discovered the gun and drugs inside the house. But even if the illegal entry here could be characterized as a but-for cause of discovering what was inside, we have "never held that evidence is 'fruit of the poisonous tree' simply because 'it would not have come to light but for the illegal actions of the police.'" *Segura v. United States.*

. . .

B

Quite apart from the requirement of unattenuated causation, the exclusionary rule has never been applied except "where its deterrence benefits outweigh its 'substantial social costs.'" The costs here are considerable. In addition to the grave adverse consequence that exclusion of relevant incriminating evidence always entails (viz., the risk of releasing dangerous criminals into society), imposing that massive remedy for a knock-and-announce violation would generate a constant flood of alleged failures to observe the rule. . . . The cost of entering this lottery would be small, but the jackpot enormous: suppression of all evidence, amounting in many cases to a get-out-of-jail-free card.

Another consequence of the incongruent remedy Hudson proposes would be police officers' refraining from timely entry after knocking and announcing. As we have observed, the amount of time they must wait is necessarily uncertain. If the consequences of running afoul of the rule were so massive, officers would be inclined to wait longer than the law requires — producing preventable violence against officers in some cases, and the destruction of evidence in many others.

Next to these "substantial social costs" we must consider the deterrence benefits, existence of which is a necessary condition for exclusion. (It is not, of course, a sufficient condition: "[I]t does not follow that the Fourth Amendment requires adoption of every proposal that might deter police misconduct."). To begin with, the value of deterrence depends upon the strength of the incentive to commit the forbidden act. Viewed from this perspective, deterrence of knock-and-announce violations is not worth a lot. Violation of the warrant requirement sometimes produces incriminating evidence that could not otherwise be obtained. But ignoring knock-and-announce can realistically be expected to achieve absolutely nothing except the prevention of destruction of evidence and the avoidance of life-threatening resistance by occupants of the premises — dangers which, if there is even "reasonable suspicion" of their existence, *suspend the knock-and-announce requirement anyway.* Massive deterrence is hardly required.

. . .

We cannot assume that exclusion in this context is necessary deterrence simply because we found that it was necessary deterrence in different contexts and long ago.

. . .

In sum, the social costs of applying the exclusionary rule to knock-and-announce violations are considerable; the incentive to such violations is minimal to begin with, and the extant deterrences against them are substantial — incomparably greater than the factors deterring warrantless entries when *Mapp* was decided. Resort to the massive remedy of suppressing evidence of guilt is unjustified.

. . .

For the foregoing reasons we affirm the judgment of the Michigan Court of Appeals.

JUSTICE KENNEDY, concurring in part and concurring in the judgment.

Two points should be underscored with respect to today's decision. First, the knock and-announce requirement protects rights and expectations linked to ancient principles in our constitutional order. The Court's decision should not be interpreted as suggesting that violations of the requirement are trivial or beyond the law's concern. Second, the continued operation of the exclusionary rule, as settled and defined by our precedents, is not in doubt. Today's decision determines only that in the specific context of the knock-and-announce requirement, a violation is not sufficiently related to the later discovery of evidence to justify suppression.

JUSTICE BREYER, with whom JUSTICE STEVENS, JUSTICE SOUTER, and JUSTICE GINSBURG join, dissenting.

In *Wilson v. Arkansas*, a unanimous Court held that the Fourth Amendment normally requires law enforcement officers to knock and announce their presence before entering a dwelling. Today's opinion holds that evidence seized from a home following a violation of this requirement need not be suppressed.

As a result, the Court destroys the strongest legal incentive to comply with the Constitution's knock-and-announce requirement. And the Court does so without significant support in precedent. At least I can find no such support in the many Fourth Amendment cases the Court has decided in the near century since it first set forth the exclusionary principle in *Weeks*.

. . .

II

[T]he driving legal purpose underlying the exclusionary rule, namely, the deterrence of unlawful government behavior, argues strongly for suppression. In *Weeks*, *Siverthorne*, and *Mapp*, the Court based its holdings requiring suppression of unlawfully obtained evidence upon the recognition that admission of that evidence would seriously undermine the Fourth Amendment's promise. All three cases recognized that failure to apply the exclusionary rule would make that promise a hollow one, reducing it to "a form of words," "of no value" to those whom it seeks to protect. Indeed, this Court in *Mapp* held that the exclusionary rule applies to the States in large part due to its belief that alternative state mechanisms for enforcing the Fourth Amendment's guarantees had proved "worthless and futile."

Why is application of the exclusionary rule any the less necessary here? Without such a rule, as in *Mapp*, police know that they can ignore the Constitution's requirements without risking suppression of evidence discovered after an unreasonable entry. As in *Mapp*, some government officers will find it easier, or believe it less risky, to proceed with what they consider a necessary search immediately and without the requisite constitutional (say, warrant or knock-and-announce) compliance.

Of course, the State or the Federal Government may provide alternative remedies for knock-and-announce violations. But that circumstance was true of *Mapp* as well. What reason is there to believe that those remedies (such as private damages actions under 42 U.S.C. § 1983), which the Court found inadequate in *Mapp*, can adequately deter unconstitutional police behavior here?

The cases reporting knock-and-announce violations are legion. Yet the majority, like Michigan and the United States, has failed to cite a single reported case in which a plaintiff has collected more than nominal damages solely as a result of a knock-and-announce violation. Even Michigan concedes that, "in cases like the present one . . . , damages may be virtually non-existent." And Michigan's *amici* further concede that civil immunities prevent tort law from being an effective substitute for the exclusionary rule at this time.

As Justice Stewart, the author of a number of significant Fourth Amendment opinions, explained, the deterrent effect of damage actions "can hardly be said to be great," as such actions are "expensive, time-consuming, not readily available, and rarely successful." Stewart, *The Road to* Mapp v. Ohio *and Beyond: The Origins, Development and Future of the Exclusionary Rule in Search-and-Seizure Cases*,

83 Colum. L. Rev. 1365, 1388 (1983). The upshot is that the need for deterrence — the critical factor driving this Court's Fourth Amendment cases for close to a century — argues with at least comparable strength for evidentiary exclusion here.

To argue, as the majority does, that new remedies, such as 42 U.S.C. § 1983 actions or better trained police, make suppression unnecessary is to argue that *Wolf*, not *Mapp*, is now the law.

. . .

I can find no precedent that might offer the majority support for its contrary conclusion. The Court has, of course, recognized that not every Fourth Amendment violation necessarily triggers the exclusionary rule. . . . But the class of Fourth Amendment violations that do not result in suppression of evidence seized, however, is limited.

The Court has declined to apply the exclusionary rule only:

(1) where there is a specific reason to believe that application of the rule would "not result in appreciable deterrence," . . . or

(2) where admissibility in proceedings other than criminal trials was at issue. . . .

Neither of these two exceptions applies here. . . .

I am aware of no other basis for an exception. The Court has decided more than 300 Fourth Amendment cases since *Weeks*. The Court has found constitutional violations in nearly a third of them. . . . The nature of the constitutional violation varies. In most instances officers lacked a warrant; in others, officers possessed a warrant based on false affidavits; in still others, the officers executed the search in an unconstitutional manner. But in every case involving evidence seized during an illegal search of a home (federally since *Weeks*, nationally since *Mapp*), the Court, with the exceptions mentioned, has either explicitly or implicitly upheld (or required) the suppression of the evidence at trial. In not one of those cases did the Court "question[n], in the absence of a more efficacious sanction, the continued application of the [exclusionary] rule to suppress evidence from the State's case" in a criminal trial. *Franks v. Delaware*.

I can find nothing persuasive in the majority's opinion that could justify its refusal to apply the rule.

. . .

The majority's "substantial social costs" argument is an argument against the Fourth Amendment's exclusionary principle itself. And it is an argument that this Court, until now, has consistently rejected.

NOTE

In *United States v. Farias-Gonzalez*, 556 F.3d 1181 (11th Cir. 2009), the Eleventh Circuit Court of Appeals applied the balancing-of-interest approach of *Hudson* and concluded that a defendant's identity, even when discovered through an illegal search, does not require suppression in a criminal case if offered to prove "who the defendant is." There, federal immigration agents were patrolling in-town Atlanta apartment complexes for gang activity when they saw the defendant working on his car. Based on his appearance, they suspected that the defendant might be a gang member. Agents stopped him, asked him questions, lifted his shirt sleeve to expose tattoos, which they thought might be evidence of gang membership, and eventually fingerprinted him to obtain his identity. The Eleventh Circuit assumed, without deciding, that the Fourth Amendment was violated by the agents' conduct but applied the *Hudson* cost-benefit balancing test to conclude that the cost of excluding the fingerprint evidence was too great and the deterrence benefits too small to justify exclusion from defendant's subsequent criminal trial.

[C] The Other Exclusionary Rules

As you have seen in prior chapters, the exclusion of illegally-obtained evidence extends beyond the Fourth Amendment. For instance, a statement obtained from a suspect through coercion is subject to exclusion and may not be used by the government in the accused's subsequent criminal trial. Because the Fifth Amendment protects a person from being "compelled in any criminal case to be a witness against himself," a statement obtained in violation of the Fifth Amendment privilege may not be introduced by the prosecution in its case-in-chief or for any other purpose. *See New Jersey v. Portash*, 440 U.S. 450, 459 (1979) ("a defendant's compelled statements . . . may not be put to any testimonial use whatever against him in a criminal trial.").

In addition to the Fifth Amendment self-incrimination clause, the Fifth and Fourteenth Amendments prohibit coercive police conduct on due process grounds. According to the Fifth Amendment, "No person shall be . . . deprived of life, liberty, or property, without due process of law[.]" *See also* Amendment XIV ("No state shall . . . deprive any person of life, liberty, or property without due process of law[.]"). Therefore, coercive statements obtained in violation of these provisions are excluded because *any use* against a defendant in a criminal trial of his involuntary statement is "a denial of due process of law." *Mincey v. Arizona*, 437 U.S. 385, 398 (1978).

Statements obtained by the government in violation of the right to counsel (Sixth Amendment) are similarly subject to exclusion from use by the government in its case-in-chief. *See Massiah v. United States*, *supra* at § 5.02 (recognizing that a defendant is denied the basic protections of the Sixth Amendment right to counsel when the prosecutor "use[s] against him at his trial evidence of his own incriminating words, which federal agents had deliberately elicited from him" after he was indicted and invoked his right to counsel). *But see Kansas v. Ventris*, 556 U.S. 586 (2009) (holding that a defendant's statements elicited in violation of the Sixth Amendment may be used by the prosecution to impeach the defendant's inconsistent trial testimony).

Finally, violations of the rules established by the Court in *Miranda v. Arizona*, *supra* § 5.03, also lead to the exclusion of some evidence for some purposes at a suspect's criminal trial. In other words, there is an exclusionary rule that applies when *Miranda* is breached, but it operates in a more limited way. See the discussion of *Miranda*, *supra* § 5.03, and discussion of Fruit of the Poisonous Tree, *infra* § 6.03.

[D] The Limits to the Exclusionary Rules

[1] The Application of the Exclusionary Rule in Contexts Other than Criminal Trials

The general rule — that evidence obtained in violation of the Constitution should be excluded from use during criminal trials — is now well established. Does the same rule apply in other contexts and other proceedings? Not necessarily. In *United States v. Calandra*, 414 U.S. 338, 350 (1974), the Court refused to apply the Fourth Amendment exclusionary rule in a grand jury proceeding, reasoning that "allowing a grand jury witness to invoke the exclusionary rule would unduly interfere with the effective and expeditious discharge of the grand jury's duties." The Court has refused to apply the Fourth Amendment exclusionary rule in a federal, civil tax proceeding even though evidence was unlawfully seized by a state criminal law enforcement officer. *United States v. Janis*, 428 U.S. 433, 454 (1976). In *Pennsylvania Bd. of Probation and Parole v. Scott*, 524 U.S. 357 (1998), the Court declined to extend the Fourth Amendment exclusionary rule to parole revocation proceedings. Lower courts have also held the exclusionary rule inapplicable to sentencing proceedings. *See, e.g., United States v. Brimah*, 214 F.3d 854 (7th Cir. 2000); *United States v. Kim*, 25 F.3d 1426 (9th Cir. 1994); *United States v. Montoya-Ortiz*, 7 F.3d 1171 (5th Cir. 1993). In addition to barring application of the exclusionary rule altogether in some contexts, the Court has imposed limits on the rule in others.

[2] The Good-Faith Exception to the Fourth Amendment Exclusionary Rule

If deterrence of police misconduct is now the primary, if not sole, purpose of the exclusionary rule, what if the police act in good faith when they violate the Constitution? In *Leon*, presented below, the Court considered officers' good-faith reliance on a search warrant.

UNITED STATES v. LEON

United States Supreme Court
468 U.S. 897 (1984)

JUSTICE WHITE delivered the opinion of the Court.

This case presents the question whether the Fourth Amendment exclusionary rule should be modified so as not to bar the use in the prosecution's case-in-chief of evidence obtained by officers acting in reasonable reliance on a search warrant issued by a detached and neutral magistrate but ultimately found to be unsupported by probable cause. To resolve this question, we must consider once again the tension between the sometimes competing goals of, on the one hand, deterring official misconduct and removing inducements to unreasonable invasions of privacy and, on the other, establishing procedures under which criminal defendants are "acquitted or convicted on the basis of all the evidence which exposes the truth."

I

In August 1981, a confidential informant of unproven reliability informed an officer of the Burbank Police Department that two persons known to him as "Armando" and "Patsy" were selling large quantities of cocaine and methaqualone from their residence at 620 Price Drive in Burbank, Cal. The informant also indicated that he had witnessed a sale of methaqualone by "Patsy" at the residence approximately five months earlier and had observed at that time a shoebox containing a large amount of cash that belonged to "Patsy." He further declared that "Armando" and "Patsy" generally kept only small quantities of drugs at their residence and stored the remainder at another location in Burbank.

On the basis of this information, the Burbank police initiated an extensive investigation focusing first on the Price Drive residence and later on two other residences as well. Cars parked at the Price Drive residence were determined to belong to respondents Armando Sanchez, who had previously been arrested for possession of marihuana, and Patsy Stewart, who had no criminal record. During the course of the investigation, officers observed an automobile belonging to respondent Ricardo Del Castillo, who had previously been arrested for possession of 50 pounds of marihuana, arrive at the Price Drive residence. The driver of that car entered the house, exited shortly thereafter carrying a small paper sack, and drove away. A check of Del Castillo's probation records led the officers to respondent Alberto Leon, whose telephone number Del Castillo had listed as his employer's. Leon had been arrested in 1980 on drug charges, and a companion had informed the police at that time that Leon was heavily involved in the importation of drugs into this country. Before the current investigation began, the Burbank officers had learned that an informant had told a Glendale police officer that Leon stored a large quantity of methaqualone at his residence in Glendale. During the course of this investigation, the Burbank officers learned that Leon was living at 716 South Sunset Canyon in Burbank.

Subsequently, the officers observed several persons, at least one of whom had prior drug involvement, arriving at the Price Drive residence and leaving with small packages; observed a variety of other material activity at the two residences as well as at a condominium at 7902 Via Magdalena; and witnessed a variety of relevant activity involving respondents' automobiles. The officers also observed respondents Sanchez and Stewart board separate flights for Miami. The pair later returned to Los Angeles together, consented to a search of their luggage that revealed only a small amount of marihuana, and left the airport. Based on these and other observations summarized in the affidavit, Officer Cyril Rombach of the Burbank Police Department, an experienced and well-trained narcotics investigator, prepared an application for a warrant to search 620 Price Drive, 716 South Sunset Canyon, 7902 Via Magdalena, and automobiles registered to each of the respondents for an extensive list of items believed to be related to respondents' drug-trafficking activities. Officer Rombach's extensive application was reviewed by several Deputy District Attorneys.

A facially valid search warrant was issued in September 1981 by a state superior court judge. The ensuing searches produced large quantities of drugs at the Via Magdalena and Sunset Canyon addresses and a small quantity at the Price Drive residence. Other evidence was discovered at each of the residences and in Stewart's and Del Castillo's automobiles. Respondents were indicted by a grand jury in the District Court for the Central District of California and charged with conspiracy to possess and distribute cocaine and a variety of substantive counts.

The respondents then filed motions to suppress the evidence seized pursuant to the warrant. The District Court held an evidentiary hearing and, while recognizing that the case was a close one, granted the motions to suppress in part. It concluded that the affidavit was insufficient to establish probable cause, but did not suppress all of the evidence as to all of the respondents because none of the respondents had standing to challenge all of the searches. In response to a request from the Government, the court made clear that Officer Rombach had acted in good faith, but it rejected the Government's suggestion that the Fourth Amendment exclusionary rule should not apply where evidence is seized in reasonable, good-faith reliance on a search warrant.

The District Court denied the Government's motion for reconsideration, and a divided panel of the Court of Appeals for the Ninth Circuit affirmed. The Court of Appeals first concluded that Officer Rombach's affidavit could not establish probable cause to search the Price Drive residence. To the extent that the affidavit set forth facts demonstrating the basis of the informant's knowledge of criminal activity, the information included was fatally stale. The affidavit, moreover, failed to establish the informant's credibility. Accordingly, the Court of Appeals concluded that the information provided by the informant was inadequate under both prongs of the two-part test established in *Aguilar v. Texas* . . . and *Spinelli v. United States*. . . . The officers' independent investigation neither cured the staleness nor corroborated the details of the informant's declarations. The Court of Appeals then considered whether the affidavit formed a proper basis for the search of the Sunset Canyon residence. In its view, the affidavit included no facts indicating the basis for the informants' statements concerning respondent Leon's criminal activities and was devoid of information establishing the informants' reliability. Because these deficiencies had not been cured by the police investigation, the District Court properly suppressed the fruits of the search. The Court of Appeals refused the Government's invitation to recognize a good-faith exception to the Fourth Amendment exclusionary rule. . . .

The Government's petition for certiorari expressly declined to seek review of the lower courts' determinations that the search warrant was unsupported by probable cause and presented only the question "[w]hether the Fourth Amendment exclusionary rule should be modified so as not to bar the admission of evidence seized in reasonable, good-faith reliance on a search warrant that is subsequently held to be defective." . . .

We have concluded that, in the Fourth Amendment context, the exclusionary rule can be modified somewhat without jeopardizing its ability to perform its intended functions. Accordingly, we reverse the judgment of the Court of Appeals.

II

Language in opinions of this Court and of individual Justices has sometimes implied that the exclusionary rule is a necessary corollary of the Fourth Amendment, . . . or that the rule is required by the conjunction of the Fourth and Fifth Amendments. *Mapp v. Ohio, supra,* (Black, J., concurring). These implications need not detain us long. The Fifth Amendment theory has not withstood critical analysis or the test of time, see *Andresen v. Maryland,* 427 U.S. 463 (1976), and the Fourth Amendment "has never been interpreted to proscribe the introduction of illegally seized evidence in all proceedings or against all persons." *Stone v. Powell,* 428 U.S. 465 (1976).

A

The Fourth Amendment contains no provision expressly precluding the use of evidence obtained in violation of its commands, and an examination of its origin and purposes makes clear that the use of fruits of a past unlawful search or seizure "work[s] no new Fourth Amendment wrong." *United States v. Calandra.* The wrong condemned by the Amendment is "fully accomplished" by the unlawful search or seizure itself, and the exclusionary rule is neither intended nor able to "cure the invasion of the defendant's rights which he has already suffered." The rule thus operates as "a judicially created remedy designed to safeguard Fourth Amendment rights generally through its deterrent effect, rather than a personal constitutional right of the party aggrieved."

Whether the exclusionary sanction is appropriately imposed in a particular case, our decisions make clear, is "an issue separate from the question whether the Fourth Amendment rights of the party seeking to invoke the rule were violated by police conduct." Only the former question is currently before us, and it must be resolved by weighing the costs and benefits of preventing the use in the prosecution's case in chief of inherently trustworthy tangible evidence obtained in reliance on a search warrant issued by a detached and neutral magistrate that ultimately is found to be defective.

The substantial social costs exacted by the exclusionary rule for the vindication of Fourth Amendment rights have long been a source of concern. "Our cases have consistently recognized that unbending application of the exclusionary sanction to enforce ideals of governmental rectitude would impede unacceptably the truth-finding functions of judge and jury." An objectionable collateral consequence of this interference with the criminal justice system's truth-finding function is that some guilty defendants may go free or receive reduced sentences as a result of favorable plea bargains. Particularly when law enforcement officers have acted in objective good faith or their transgressions have been minor, the magnitude of the benefit conferred on such guilty defendants offends basic concepts of the criminal justice system. Indiscriminate application of the exclusionary rule, therefore, may well "generat[e] disrespect for the law and administration of justice." Accordingly, "[a]s with any remedial device, the application of the rule has been restricted to those areas where its remedial objectives are thought most efficaciously served."

. . .

III

A

Because a search warrant "provides the detached scrutiny of a neutral magistrate, which is a more reliable safeguard against improper searches than the hurried judgment of a law enforcement officer engaged in the often competitive enterprise of ferreting out crime," we have expressed a strong preference for warrants and declared that "in a doubtful or marginal case a search under a warrant may be sustainable where without one it would fall." Reasonable minds frequently may differ on the question whether a particular affidavit establishes probable cause, and we have thus concluded that the preference for warrants is most appropriately effectuated by according "great deference" to a magistrate's determination.

Deference to the magistrate, however, is not boundless. It is clear, first, that the deference accorded to a magistrate's finding of probable cause does not preclude inquiry into the knowing or reckless falsity of the affidavit on which that determination was based. *Franks v. Delaware*. . . . Second, the courts must also insist that the magistrate purport to "perform his "neutral and detached" function and not serve merely as a rubber stamp for the police." *Aguilar v. Texas*. . . . See *Illinois v. Gates*. . . . A magistrate failing to "manifest that neutrality and detachment demanded of a judicial officer when presented with a warrant application" and who acts instead as "an adjunct law enforcement officer" cannot provide valid authorization for an otherwise unconstitutional search. . . .

Third, reviewing courts will not defer to a warrant based on an affidavit that does not "provide the magistrate with a substantial basis for determining the existence of probable cause." *Illinois v. Gates*. . . . "Sufficient information must be presented to the magistrate to allow that official to determine probable cause; his action cannot be a mere ratification of the bare conclusions of others." . . . Even if the warrant application was supported by more than a "bare bones" affidavit, a reviewing court may properly conclude that, notwithstanding the deference that magistrates deserve, the warrant was invalid because the magistrate's probable-cause determination reflected an improper analysis of the totality of the circumstances, . . . or because the form of the warrant was improper in some respect.

Only in the first of these three situations, however, has the Court set forth a rationale for suppressing evidence obtained pursuant to a search warrant; in the other areas, it has simply excluded such evidence without considering whether Fourth Amendment interests will be advanced. To the extent that proponents of exclusion rely on its behavioral effects on judges and magistrates in these areas, their reliance is misplaced. First, the exclusionary rule is designed to deter police misconduct rather than to punish the errors of judges and magistrates. Second, there exists no evidence suggesting that judges and magistrates are inclined to ignore or subvert the Fourth Amendment or that lawlessness among these actors requires application of the extreme sanction of exclusion.

Third, and most important, we discern no basis, and are offered none, for believing that exclusion of evidence seized pursuant to a warrant will have a significant deterrent effect on the issuing judge or magistrate. Many of the factors that indicate that the exclusionary rule cannot provide an effective "special" or "general" deterrent for individual offending law enforcement officers apply as well to judges or magistrates. And, to the extent that the rule is thought to operate as a "systemic" deterrent on a wider audience, it clearly can have no such effect on individuals empowered to issue search warrants. Judges and magistrates are not adjuncts to the law enforcement team; as neutral judicial officers, they have no stake in the outcome of particular criminal prosecutions. The threat of exclusion thus cannot be expected significantly to deter them. Imposition of the exclusionary sanction is not necessary meaningfully to inform judicial officers of their errors, and we cannot conclude that admitting evidence obtained pursuant to a warrant while at the same time declaring that the warrant was somehow defective will in any way reduce judicial officers' professional incentives to comply with the Fourth Amendment, encourage them to repeat their mistakes, or lead to the granting of all colorable warrant requests.

B

If exclusion of evidence obtained pursuant to a subsequently invalidated warrant is to have any deterrent effect, therefore, it must alter the behavior of individual law enforcement officers or the policies of their departments. One could argue that applying the exclusionary rule in cases where the police failed to demonstrate probable cause in the warrant application deters future inadequate presentations or "magistrate shopping" and thus promotes the ends of the Fourth Amendment. Suppressing evidence obtained pursuant to a technically defective warrant supported by probable cause also might encourage officers to scrutinize more closely the form of the warrant and to point out suspected judicial errors. We find such arguments speculative and conclude that suppression of evidence obtained pursuant to a warrant should be ordered only on a case-by-case basis and only in those unusual cases in which exclusion will further the purposes of the exclusionary rule.

We have frequently questioned whether the exclusionary rule can have any deterrent effect when the offending officers acted in the objectively reasonable belief that their conduct did not violate the Fourth Amendment. "No empirical researcher, proponent or opponent of the rule, has yet been able to establish with any assurance whether the rule has a deterrent effect. . . ." *United States v. Janis*, 428 U.S., at 452, n. 22. But even assuming that the rule effectively deters some police misconduct and provides incentives for the law enforcement profession as a whole to conduct itself in accord with the Fourth Amendment, it cannot be expected, and should not be applied, to deter objectively reasonable law enforcement activity.

This is particularly true, we believe, when an officer acting with objective good faith has obtained a search warrant from a judge or magistrate and acted within its scope. In most such cases, there is no police illegality and thus nothing to deter. It is the magistrate's responsibility to determine whether the officer's allegations establish probable cause and, if so, to issue a warrant comporting in form with the requirements of the Fourth Amendment. In the ordinary case, an officer cannot be expected to question the magistrate's probable-cause determination or his judgment that the form of the warrant is technically sufficient. "[O]nce the warrant issues, there is literally nothing more the policeman can do in seeking to comply with this law." *Stone v. Powell*, at 498 (Burger, C.J. concurring). Penalizing the officer for the magistrate's error, rather than his own, cannot logically contribute to the deterrence of Fourth Amendment violations.

C

We conclude that the marginal or nonexistent benefits produced by suppressing evidence obtained in objectively reasonable reliance on a subsequently invalidated search warrant cannot justify the substantial costs of exclusion. We do not suggest, however, that exclusion is always inappropriate in cases where an officer has obtained a warrant and abided by its terms. "[S]earches pursuant to a warrant will rarely require any deep inquiry into reasonableness" . . . for "a warrant issued by a magistrate normally suffices to establish" that a law enforcement officer has "acted in good faith in conducting the search." . . . Nevertheless, the officer's reliance on the magistrate's probable-cause determination and on the technical sufficiency of the warrant he issues must be objectively reasonable, . . . and it is clear that in some circumstances the officer will have no reasonable grounds for believing that the warrant was properly issued.

Suppression therefore remains an appropriate remedy if the magistrate or judge in issuing a warrant was misled by information in an affidavit that the affiant knew was false or would have known was false except for his reckless disregard of the truth. *Franks v. Delaware.* The exception we recognize today will also not apply in cases where the issuing magistrate wholly abandoned his judicial role in the manner condemned in *Lo-Ji Sales, Inc. v. New York*, 442 U.S. 319 (1979); in such circumstances, no reasonably well trained officer should rely on the warrant. Nor would an officer manifest objective good faith in relying on a warrant based on an affidavit "so lacking in indicia of probable cause as to render official belief in its existence entirely unreasonable." Finally, depending on the circumstances of the particular case, a warrant may be so facially deficient — i.e., in failing to particularize the place to be searched or the things to be seized that the executing officers cannot reasonably presume it to be valid.

In so limiting the suppression remedy, we leave untouched the probable-cause standard and the various requirements for a valid warrant. Other objections to the modification of the Fourth Amendment exclusionary rule we consider to be insubstantial. The good-faith exception for searches conducted pursuant to warrants is not intended to signal our unwillingness strictly to enforce the requirements of the Fourth Amendment, and we do not believe that it will have this effect. As we have already suggested, the good-faith exception, turning as it does on objective reasonableness, should not be difficult to apply in practice. When officers have acted pursuant to a warrant, the prosecution should ordinarily be able to establish objective good faith without a substantial expenditure of judicial time.

Nor are we persuaded that application of a good-faith exception to searches conducted pursuant to warrants will preclude review of the constitutionality of the search and seizure, deny needed guidance from the courts, or freeze Fourth Amendment law in its present state. There is no need for courts to adopt the inflexible practice of always deciding whether the officers' conduct manifested objective good faith before turning to the question whether Fourth Amendment has been violated.

IV

When the principles we have enunciated today are applied to the facts of this case, it is apparent that the judgment of the Court of Appeals cannot stand. The Court of Appeals applied the prevailing legal standards to Officer Rombach's warrant application and concluded that the application could not support the magistrate's probable-cause determination. In so doing, the court clearly informed the magistrate that he had erred in issuing the challenged warrant. This aspect of the court's judgment is not under attack in this proceeding.

Having determined that the warrant should not have issued, the Court of Appeals understandably declined to adopt a modification of the Fourth Amendment exclusionary rule that this Court had not previously sanctioned. Although the modification finds strong support in our previous cases, the Court of Appeals' commendable self-restraint is not to be criticized. We have now re-examined the purposes of the exclusionary rule and the propriety of its application in cases where officers have relied on a subsequently invalidated search warrant. Our conclusion is that the rule's purposes will only rarely be served by applying it in such circumstances.

In the absence of an allegation that the magistrate abandoned his detached and neutral role, suppression is appropriate only if the officers were dishonest or reckless in preparing their affidavit or could not have harbored an objectively reasonable belief in the existence of probable cause. Only respondent Leon has contended that no reasonably well-trained police officer could have believed that there existed probable cause to search his house; significantly, the other respondents advance no comparable argument. Officer Rombach's application for a warrant clearly was supported by much more than a "bare bones" affidavit. The affidavit related the results of an extensive investigation and, as the opinions of the divided panel of the Court of Appeals make clear, provided evidence sufficient to create disagreement among thoughtful and competent judges as to the existence of probable cause. Under these circumstances, the officers' reliance on the magistrate's determination of probable cause was objectively reasonable, and application of the extreme sanction of exclusion is inappropriate.

Accordingly, the judgment of the Court of Appeals is *Reversed.*

Justice Blackmun, concurring.

As the Court's opinion in this case makes clear, the Court has narrowed the scope of the exclusionary rule because of an empirical judgment that the rule has little appreciable effect in cases where officers act in objectively reasonable reliance on search warrants.

What must be stressed, however, is that any empirical judgment about the effect of the exclusionary rule in a particular class of cases necessarily is a provisional one. By their very nature, the assumptions on which we proceed today cannot be cast in stone. To the contrary, they now will be tested in the real world of state and federal law enforcement, and this Court will attend to the results. If it should emerge from experience that, contrary to our expectations, the good faith exception to the exclusionary rule results in a material change in police compliance with the Fourth Amendment, we shall have to reconsider what we have undertaken here. The logic of a decision that rests on untested predictions about police conduct demands no less.

If a single principle may be drawn from this Court's exclusionary rule decisions, from *Weeks* through *Mapp*, to the decisions handed down today, it is that the scope of the exclusionary rule is subject to change in light of changing judicial understanding about the effects of the rule outside the confines of the courtroom. It is incumbent on the Nation's law enforcement officers, who must continue to observe the Fourth Amendment in the wake of today's decisions, to recognize the double-edged nature of that principle.

JUSTICE BRENNAN, with whom JUSTICE MARSHALL joins, dissenting.

Ten years ago in *Calandra*, I expressed the fear that the Court's decision "may signal that a majority of my colleagues have positioned themselves to reopen the door [to evidence secured by official lawlessness] still further and abandon altogether the exclusionary rule in search-and-seizure cases." *Id.*, at 365 (Brennan, J., dissenting). Since then, in case after case, I have witnessed the Court's gradual but determined strangulation of the rule. It now appears that the Court's victory over the Fourth Amendment is complete. That today's decision represents the *piece de resistance* of the Court's past efforts cannot be doubted, for today the Court sanctions the use in the prosecution's case-in-chief of illegally obtained evidence against the individual whose rights have been violated — a result that had previously been thought to be foreclosed.

The Court seeks to justify this result on the ground that the "costs" of adhering to the exclusionary rule in cases like those before us exceed the "benefits." But the language of deterrence and of cost/benefit analysis, if used indiscriminately, can have a narcotic effect. It creates an illusion of technical precision and ineluctability. It suggests that not only constitutional principle but also empirical data supports the majority's result. When the Court's analysis is examined carefully, however, it is clear that we have not been treated to an honest assessment of the merits of the exclusionary rule, but have instead been drawn into a curious world where the "costs" of excluding illegally obtained evidence loom to exaggerated heights and where the "benefits" of such exclusion are made to disappear with a mere wave of the hand.

The majority ignores the fundamental constitutional importance of what is at stake here. While the machinery of law enforcement and indeed the nature of crime itself have changed dramatically since the Fourth Amendment became part of the Nation's fundamental law in 1791, what the Framers understood then remains true today — that the task of combating crime and convicting the guilty will in every era seem of such critical and pressing concern that we may be lured by the temptations of expediency into forsaking our commitment to protecting individual liberty and privacy.

This reading of the Amendment implies that its proscriptions are directed solely at those government agents who may actually invade an individual's constitutionally protected privacy. The courts are not subject to any direct constitutional duty to exclude illegally obtained evidence, because the question of the admissibility of such evidence is not addressed by the Amendment. This view of the scope of the Amendment relegates the judiciary to the periphery. Because the only constitutional cognizable injury has already been "fully accomplished" by the police by the time a case comes before the courts, the Constitution is not itself violated if the judge decides to admit the tainted evidence. Indeed, the most the judge *can* do is wring his hands and hope that perhaps by excluding such evidence he can deter future transgressions by the police.

Such a reading appears plausible, because, as critics of the exclusionary rule never tire of repeating, the Fourth Amendment makes no express provision for the exclusion of evidence secured in violation of its commands. A short answer to this claim, of course, is that many of the Constitution's most vital imperatives are stated in general terms and the task of giving meaning to these precepts is therefore left to subsequent judicial decision-making in the context of concrete cases. The nature of our Constitution, as Chief Justice Marshall long ago explained, "requires that only its great outlines should be marked, its important objects designated, and the minor ingredients which compose those objects be deduced from the nature of the objects themselves." *McCulloch v. Maryland*, 4 Wheat. 316, 407 (1819).

A more direct answer may be supplied by recognizing that the Amendment, like other provisions of the Bill of Rights, restrains the power of the government as a whole; it does not specify only a particular agency and exempt all others. The judiciary is responsible, no less than the executive, for ensuring that constitutional rights are respected.

When that fact is kept in mind, the role of the courts and their possible involvement in the concerns of the Fourth Amendment comes into sharper focus. Because seizures are executed principally to secure evidence, and because such evidence generally has utility in our legal system only in the context of a trial supervised by a judge, it is apparent that the admission of illegally obtained evidence implicates the same constitutional concerns as the initial seizure of that evidence. Indeed, by admitting unlawfully seized evidence, the judiciary becomes a part of what is in fact a single governmental action prohibited by the terms of the Amendment. Once that connection between the evidence-gathering role of the police and the evidence-admitting function of the courts is acknowledged, the plausibility of the Court's interpretation becomes more suspect. Certainly nothing in the language or history of the Fourth Amendment suggests that a recognition of this evidentiary link between the police and the courts was meant to be foreclosed. It is difficult to give any meaning at all to the limitations imposed by the Amendment if they are read to proscribe only certain conduct by the police but to allow other agents of the same government to take advantage of evidence secured by the police in violation of its requirements. The Amendment therefore must be read to condemn not only the initial unconstitutional invasion of privacy — which is done, after all, for the purpose of securing evidence — but also the subsequent use of any evidence so obtained.

III

Even if I were to accept the Court's general approach to the exclusionary rule, I could not agree with today's result.

At the outset, the Court suggests that society has been asked to pay a high price — in terms either of setting guilty persons free or of impeding the proper functioning of trials — as a result of excluding relevant physical evidence in cases where the police, in conducting searches and seizing evidence, have made only an "objectively reasonable" mistake concerning the constitutionality of their actions. But what evidence is there to support such a claim?

Significantly, the Court points to none, and, indeed, as the Court acknowledges, recent studies have demonstrated that the "costs" of the exclusionary rule — calculated in terms of dropped prosecutions and lost convictions — are quite low.

. . .

What then supports the Court's insistence that this evidence be admitted? Apparently, the Court's only answer is that even though the costs of exclusion are not very substantial, the potential deterrent effect in these circumstances is so marginal that exclusion cannot be justified. The key to the Court's conclusion in this respect is its belief that the prospective deterrent effect of the exclusionary rule operates only in those situations in which police officers, when deciding whether to go forward with some particular search, have reason to know that their planned conduct will violate the requirements of the Fourth Amendment.

. . .

At first blush, there is some logic to this position. Undoubtedly, in the situation hypothesized by the Court, the existence of the exclusionary rule cannot be expected to have any deterrent effect on the particular officers at the moment they are deciding whether to go forward with the search. Indeed, the subsequent exclusion of any evidence seized under such circumstances appears somehow "unfair" to the particular officers involved. As the Court suggests, these officers have acted in what they thought was an appropriate and constitutionally authorized manner, but then the fruit of their efforts is nullified by the application of the exclusionary rule.

The flaw in the Court's argument, however, is that its logic captures only one comparatively minor element of the generally acknowledged deterrent purposes of the exclusionary rule. To be sure, the rule operates to some extent to deter future misconduct by individual officers who have had evidence suppressed in their own cases. But what the Court overlooks is that the deterrence rationale for the rule is not designed to be, nor should it be thought of as, a form of "punishment" of individual police officers for their failures to obey the restraints imposed by the Fourth Amendment. Instead, the chief deterrent function of the rule is its tendency to promote institutional compliance with Fourth Amendment requirements on the part of law enforcement agencies generally. Thus, as the Court has previously recognized, "over the long term, [the] demonstration [provided by the exclusionary rule] that our society attaches serious consequences to violation of constitutional rights is thought to encourage those who formulate law enforcement policies, and the officers who implement them, to incorporate Fourth Amendment ideals into their value system."

. . .

After today's decision, however, that institutional incentive will be lost. Indeed, the Court's "reasonable mistake" exception to the exclusionary rule will tend to put a premium on police ignorance of the law. Armed with the assurance provided by today's decision that evidence will always be admissible whenever an officer has "reasonably" relied upon a warrant, police departments will be encouraged to train officers that if a warrant has simply been signed, it is reasonable, without more, to rely on it. Since in close cases there will no longer be any incentive to err on the side of constitutional behavior, police would have every reason to adopt a "let's-wait-until-its-decided" approach in situations in which there is a question about a warrant's validity or the basis for its issuance. . . .

Although the Court brushes these concerns aside, a host of grave consequences can be expected to result from its decision to carve this new exception out of the exclusionary rule. A chief consequence of today's decision will be to convey a clear and unambiguous message to magistrates that their decisions to issue warrants are now insulated from subsequent judicial review. Creation of this new exception for good faith reliance upon a warrant implicitly tells magistrates that they need not take much care in reviewing warrant applications, since their mistakes will from now on have virtually no consequence: If their decision to issue a warrant was correct, the evidence will be admitted; if their decision was incorrect but the police relied in good faith on the warrant, the evidence will also be admitted. Inevitably, the care and attention devoted to such an inconsequential chore will dwindle. Although the Court is correct to note that magistrates do not share the same stake in the outcome of a criminal case as the police, they nevertheless need to appreciate that their role is of some moment in order to continue performing the important task of carefully reviewing warrant applications. Today's decision effectively removes that incentive.

Moreover, the good faith exception will encourage police to provide only the bare minimum of information in future warrant applications. The police will now know that if they can secure a warrant, so long as the circumstances of its issuance are not "entirely unreasonable," all police conduct pursuant to that warrant will be protected from further judicial review. The clear incentive that operated in the past to establish probable cause adequately because reviewing courts would examine the magistrate's judgment carefully, has now been so completely vitiated that the police need only show that it was not "entirely unreasonable" under the circumstances of a particular case for them to believe that the warrant they were issued was valid. The long-run effect unquestionably will be to undermine the integrity of the warrant process.

Finally, even if one were to believe, as the Court apparently does, that police are hobbled by inflexible and hyper-technical warrant procedures, today's decision cannot be justified. This is because, given the relaxed standard for assessing probable cause established just last Term in *Illinois v. Gates*, . . . the Court's newly fashioned good faith exception, when applied in the warrant context, will rarely, if ever, offer any greater flexibility for police than the *Gates* standard already supplies. In *Gates*, the Court held that "the task of an issuing magistrate is simply to make a practical, common-sense decision whether, given all the circumstances set forth in the affidavit before him, . . . there is a fair probability that contraband or evidence of a crime will be found in a particular place." The task of a reviewing court is confined to determining whether "the magistrate had a 'substantial basis' for concluding that probable cause existed." *Ibid.* Given such a relaxed standard, it is virtually inconceivable that a reviewing court, when faced with a defendant's motion to suppress, could first find that a warrant was invalid under the new *Gates* standard, but then, at the same time, find that a police officer's reliance on such an invalid warrant was nevertheless "objectively reasonable" under the test announced today. Because the two standards overlap so completely, it is unlikely that a warrant could be found invalid under *Gates* and yet the police reliance upon it could be seen as objectively reasonable; otherwise, we would have to entertain the mind-boggling concept of objectively reasonable reliance upon an objectively unreasonable warrant.

NOTES AND QUESTIONS

(1) In *Leon*, the Court not only established an exception to the exclusionary rule, it also recognized exceptions to that good-faith exception, including when a police affidavit is "so lacking in indicia of probable cause as to render official belief in its existence entirely unreasonable" and when a warrant is "facially deficient." In *Messerschmidt v. Millender*, a civil action brought under 42 U.S.C. § 1983, occupants of a residence asserted that one of the exceptions to *Leon* applied. There, the occupants claimed officers were personally liable for a search of a home conducted pursuant to a warrant that was unconstitutionally overbroad in authorizing a search for multiple firearms and gang-related materials when the evidence supporting the warrant was limited to use of a very specific weapon — a black sawed-off shotgun with a pistol grip — and there was no evidence that the crime under investigation was gang-related. 132 S. Ct. 1235, 1243 (2012). The Ninth Circuit, sitting *en banc*, had applied one of the exceptions identified in *Leon* to deny qualified immunity to the officers. That court held that a reasonable officer would have "been well aware of th[e] deficiency" in the overly-broad warrant. The Supreme Court reversed the decision of the Ninth Circuit. The Court emphasized that the threshold for recognizing the exception based on an officer's entirely unreasonable reliance on a warrant is "a high one." Citing *Leon*, the Court reiterated that in the ordinary case, an officer "cannot be expected to question the magistrate's probable-cause determination." And, the Court found that if the scope of the warrant was overbroad, under the circumstances, it was not unreasonable for an officer "to conclude that there was a fair probability that the sawed-off shotgun was not the only firearm" the suspect owned. The Court also decided that a reasonable officer could have linked the crime under investigation with the suspect's desire to prevent the victim from disclosing the suspect's gang activity. The Court concluded: "The officers' judgment that the scope of the warrant was supported by probable cause may have been mistaken, but it was not 'plainly incompetent.' "

(2) Should it matter why the warrant is defective? On the same day it decided *Leon*, the Court considered the exclusionary consequences of evidence seized pursuant to a warrant subsequently invalidated because of errors precipitated by

the issuing judge. In *Massachusetts v. Sheppard*, 468 U.S. 981 (1984), officers had uncovered evidence that defendant Sheppard may have killed his girlfriend. A detective drafted an affidavit in support of a search warrant to search Sheppard's home and in support of an arrest warrant for Sheppard. Prosecutors reviewed the affidavit and agreed that it set forth probable cause for the search and the arrest, but officers had difficulty finding a warrant form to accompany their affidavit. Finally, officers found a form previously used for a drug search. Recognizing that the form had to be changed, a detective deleted some information and changed other parts of the form, but the form still contained some information tailored for a drug search. The officer took the affidavit and the inaccurate warrant form to a judge for consideration. When he offered the warrant to the judge, the officer told the judge that the warrant form "dealt with controlled substances." The judge told the officer "that he would make the necessary changes so as to provide a proper search warrant." The judge then took the form, made some changes on it, and dated and signed the warrant. In error, the judge failed to change the portion of the warrant that allowed a search for controlled substances. Similarly, the judge failed to incorporate the officers' affidavit. Nevertheless, after signing the warrant, the judge returned it to the officer, informing him that the warrant was sufficient authority for the search.

The Supreme Court framed the pertinent issue in *Sheppard* as "whether there was an objectively reasonable basis for the officers' mistaken belief" that the defective warrant authorized the search they conducted in good faith. *Id.* at 988. The Court concluded that there was. "[W]e refuse to rule that an officer is required to disbelieve a judge who has just advised him, by word and by action, that the warrant he possesses authorizes him to conduct the search he has requested." *Id.* at 989. The Court added: "[I]t was the judge, not the police officers, who made the critical mistake." *Id.* at 990.

(3) Does *Leon* end the significance of *Illinois v. Gates, supra* § 3.02[D]? Consider the following affidavits:

A. I, Gary Lomenick, a duly sworn Chattanooga Police Officer, hereby apply for a search warrant and make oath as follows:

1. I am a sworn Chattanooga Police Officer with the Narcotics Division, where I have been assigned for over 15 years, and a commissioned Special Deputy for Hamilton County, Tennessee.

2. On the 11th day of October 1995 I, Gary Lomenick, received information from an informant, a responsible and credible citizen of the county and state, who I know to be a responsible and credible citizen because I have known said informant for 5 years and said informant has given me information about individuals involved in criminal activity in the past that has proven to be reliable. Said informant's name whom I have this day disclosed to the Judge to whom this application is made, that [sic] John Doe (Alias) Red Dog who resides in or occupies and is in possession of the following described premises — 910 North Market Street, apartment directly underneath carport located in Chattanooga, Hamilton County Tennessee, unlawfully has in his possession on said premises legend and/or

narcotic drugs including Cocaine in violation of law made and provided in such cases.

3. On the 11th day of October 1995 said informant advised me that said informant was on the premises of the said John Doe (Alias) Red Dog, located at 910 North Market Street, apartment directly underneath carport within seventy-two hours prior to our conversation on October 11th, 1995 and while there saw Cocaine in possession of the said John Doe (Alias) Red Dog[.]

WHEREFORE, as such officer acting in performance of my duty in the premises I pray that the Court issue a warrant authorizing the search of the said John Doe (Alias) Red Dog and the premises located at 910 North Market Street, apartment directly underneath the carport, for said legend and/or narcotic drugs including Cocaine and that such search be made either by day or by night.

Are the contents of the affidavit sufficient to provide probable cause for a warrant? Does it matter after *Leon? See United States v. Allen*, 211 F.3d 970 (6th Cir. 2000) (en banc).

How about the following affidavit, which was comprised of "boilerplate text" with open spaces in which the affiant added information? (The information provided by the affiant is italicized.)

B. Personally appeared before *James W. Buckner*, Judge of the Court of *Gen. Session* for Rutherford County, Tennessee the undersigned *Mickey McCullough*, a lawful officer of said County and State, who makes affidavit that there is probable cause to believe, and that affiant does believe, that *Gary Weaver* is now unlawfully keeping a quantity of *marijuana* for the purpose or with the intention of unlawful possession, sale or transportation thereof, and upon his, her or their person, or in his, her, or their possession, custody or control upon premises used, occupied, possessed or controlled by him, her, or them, and which premises are located and described as follows:

A two story brick dwelling house having a city designated street address of 3031 Hartford Drive. Having a two car attached garage and a detached brick building behind the main house having a concrete driveway and a mailbox erected adjacent to said driveway with the numbers 3031 attached to it. Having a city designated street address of 3031 Harford Drive, M'boro, Ruth. Co. TN.

Affiant further makes affidavit that on the *25* day of *May*, 199 *3*, affiant received information from a reputable and reliable person, whose name and identity have been disclosed to the Judge to whom this application is made, that Affiant verily believes, and accordingly represents to the Court, that the said informer is truthful, reliable and credible, and that the information so given is accurate and reliable, because: (1) the said informer appears to have intelligence and unimpaired physical senses; (2) the said informer appears to affiant to have sufficient personal knowledge or familiarity or experience with the contraband substance herein mentioned to be able to identify the same by sight, smell and other senses, insofar as such identification can usually be made by the human physical senses unaided by laboratory analysis; (3) there has been a previous occasion, or occasions, on which the same informer has given information of violation of law of the state, which information thereafter was found to have been accurate and reliable; (4) that within the last 72 hours said informant was upon the above described premises and while thereon personally observed (*Gary Weaver*) having personal possession and control over a quantity of (*marijuana*) being held expressly for the purpose of unlawful distribution. Affiant knows of no reasons why said informer would falsify or fabricate any of the information given. Consequently, affiant believes that all or some portion of the said (*marijuana*) still remains upon the above described premises.

See United States v. Weaver, 99 F.3d 1372 (6th Cir. 1996).

(4) Compare *Leon* and *Sheppard* with *Groh v. Ramirez*, 540 U.S. 551 (2004) (holding a search unconstitutional in violation of the particularity requirement of the Fourth Amendment because although the law enforcement officer prepared and presented an affidavit particularly describing the place to be searched and the items officers expected to find during the search, the warrant itself, which the judge signed, failed altogether to identify any of the items that were to be seized, and the warrant did not incorporate by reference the itemized list in the warrant application).

(5) What if evidence is seized in violation of the Fourth Amendment by an officer who relies on an inaccurate record indicating the existence of an outstanding arrest warrant? In *Arizona v. Evans*, 514 U.S. 1 (1995), the Court addressed this issue in a case in which an officer stopped a driver for a traffic violation and then checked the driver's name in a computer data bank. The computer search indicated that there was an outstanding misdemeanor warrant for the driver's arrest. When officers arrested the driver, they searched his car and found marijuana. In actuality, the arrest warrant had been quashed seventeen days before the arrest. The driver argued that the marijuana was "fruit of an unlawful arrest." The Supreme Court rejected this argument, applying the reasoning of *Leon*. The evidence in the case suggested that the error was that of a court employee. In applying *Leon*, the Court noted: (1) "If court employees were responsible for the erroneous computer record, the exclusion of evidence at trial would not sufficiently deter future errors"; (2) there was "no evidence that court employees are inclined to ignore or subvert the Fourth Amendment"; and (3) "there is no basis for believing that application of the exclusionary rule in these circumstances will have a significant effect on court employees responsible for informing the police that a warrant has been quashed." *Id.* at 14–15.

What if the computer error involved in *Evans* had been committed by an employee of the police, not a court employee?

HERRING v. UNITED STATES

United States Supreme Court
555 U.S. 135 (2009)

CHIEF JUSTICE ROBERTS delivered the opinion of the Court.

The Fourth Amendment forbids "unreasonable searches and seizures," and this usually requires the police to have probable cause or a warrant before making an arrest. What if an officer reasonably believes there is an outstanding arrest warrant, but that belief turns out to be wrong because of a negligent bookkeeping error by another police employee? The parties here agree that the ensuing arrest is still a violation of the Fourth Amendment, but dispute whether contraband found during a search incident to that arrest must be excluded in a later prosecution.

Our cases establish that such suppression is not an automatic consequence of a Fourth Amendment violation. Instead, the question turns on the culpability of the police and the potential of exclusion to deter wrongful police conduct. Here the error was the result of isolated negligence attenuated from the arrest. We hold that in these circumstances the jury should not be barred from considering all the evidence.

I

On July 7, 2004, Investigator Mark Anderson learned that Bennie Dean Herring had driven to the Coffee County Sheriff's Department to retrieve something from his impounded truck. Herring was no stranger to law enforcement, and Anderson asked the county's warrant clerk, Sandy Pope, to check for any outstanding warrants for Herring's arrest. When she found none, Anderson asked Pope to check with Sharon Morgan, her counterpart in neighboring Dale County. After checking Dale County's computer database, Morgan replied that there was an active arrest warrant for Herring's failure to appear on a felony charge. Pope relayed the information to Anderson and asked Morgan to fax over a copy of the warrant as confirmation. Anderson and a deputy followed Herring as he left the impound lot, pulled him over, and arrested him. A search incident to the arrest revealed methamphetamine in Herring's pocket, and a pistol (which as a felon he could not possess) in his vehicle.

There had, however, been a mistake about the warrant. The Dale County sheriff's computer records are supposed to correspond to actual arrest warrants, which the office also maintains. But when Morgan went to the files to retrieve the actual warrant to fax to Pope, Morgan was unable to find it. She called a court clerk and learned that the warrant had been recalled five months earlier. Normally when a warrant is recalled the court clerk's office or a judge's chambers calls Morgan, who enters the information in the sheriff's computer database and disposes of the physical copy. For whatever reason, the information about the recall of the warrant for Herring did not appear in the database. Morgan immediately called Pope to alert her to the mix-up, and Pope contacted Anderson over a secure radio. This all unfolded in 10 to 15 minutes, but Herring had already been arrested and found with the gun and drugs, just a few hundred yards from the sheriff's office.

Herring was indicted in the District Court for the Middle District of Alabama for illegally possessing the gun and drugs. He moved to suppress the evidence on the ground that his initial arrest had been illegal because the warrant had been rescinded. The Magistrate Judge recommended denying the motion because the arresting officers had acted in a good-faith belief that the warrant was still outstanding. Thus, even if there were a Fourth Amendment violation, there was "no reason to believe that application of the exclusionary rule here would deter the occurrence of any future mistakes." The District Court adopted the Magistrate Judge's recommendation, and the Court of Appeals for the Eleventh Circuit affirmed.

The Eleventh Circuit found that the arresting officers in Coffee County "were entirely innocent of any wrongdoing or carelessness." The court assumed that whoever failed to update the Dale County sheriff's records was also a law enforcement official, but noted that "the conduct in question [wa]s a negligent failure to act, not a deliberate or tactical choice to act." Because the error was merely negligent and attenuated from the arrest, the Eleventh Circuit concluded that the benefit of suppressing the evidence "would be marginal or nonexistent," and the evidence was therefore admissible under the good-faith rule of *United States v. Leon.*

Other courts have required exclusion of evidence obtained through similar police errors, so we granted Herring's petition for certiorari to resolve the conflict. We now affirm the Eleventh Circuit's judgment.

II

When a probable-cause determination was based on reasonable but mistaken assumptions, the person subjected to a search or seizure has not necessarily been the victim of a constitutional violation. The very phrase "probable cause" confirms that the Fourth Amendment does not demand all possible precision. And whether the error can be traced to a mistake by a state actor or some other source may bear on the analysis. For purposes of deciding this case, however, we accept the parties' assumption that there was a Fourth Amendment violation. The issue is whether the exclusionary rule should be applied.

A

The Fourth Amendment protects "[t]he right of the people to be secure in their persons, houses, papers, and effects, against unreasonable searches and seizures," but "contains no provision expressly precluding the use of evidence obtained in violation of its commands," *Arizona v. Evans*, 514 U.S. 1 (1995). Nonetheless, our decisions establish an exclusionary rule that, when applicable, forbids the use of improperly obtained evidence at trial.

In analyzing the applicability of the rule, *Leon* admonished that we must consider the actions of all the police officers involved. The Coffee County officers did nothing improper. Indeed, the error was noticed so quickly because Coffee County requested a faxed confirmation of the warrant.

The Eleventh Circuit concluded, however, that somebody in Dale County should have updated the computer database to reflect the recall of the arrest warrant. The court also concluded that this error was negligent, but did not find it to be reckless or deliberate. That fact is crucial to our holding that this error is not enough by itself to require "the extreme sanction of exclusion."

B

The fact that a Fourth Amendment violation occurred — *i.e.*, that a search or arrest was unreasonable — does not necessarily mean that the exclusionary rule applies. Indeed, exclusion "has always been our last resort, not our first impulse," *Hudson v. Michigan*, and our precedents establish important principles that constrain application of the exclusionary rule.

First, the exclusionary rule is not an individual right and applies only where it "result[s] in appreciable deterrence." We have repeatedly rejected the argument that exclusion is a necessary consequence of a Fourth Amendment violation. Instead we have focused on the efficacy of the rule in deterring Fourth Amendment violations in the future.

In addition, the benefits of deterrence must outweigh the costs. "We have never suggested that the exclusionary rule must apply in every circumstance in which it might provide marginal deterrence."

. . .

[I]n *Evans*, we applied this good-faith rule to police who reasonably relied on mistaken information in a court's database that an arrest warrant was outstanding. We held that a mistake made by a judicial employee could not give rise to exclusion for three reasons: The exclusionary rule was crafted to curb police rather than judicial misconduct; court employees were unlikely to try to subvert the Fourth Amendment; and "most important, there [was] no basis for believing that application of the exclusionary rule in [those] circumstances" would have any significant effect in deterring the errors. *Evans* left unresolved "whether the evidence should be suppressed if police personnel were responsible for the error," an issue not argued by the State in that case, but one that we now confront.

. . .

As we said in *Leon*, "an assessment of the flagrancy of the police misconduct constitutes an important step in the calculus" of applying the exclusionary rule. . . . "[E]vidence should be suppressed only if it can be said that the law enforcement officer had knowledge, or may properly be charged with knowledge, that the search was unconstitutional under the Fourth Amendment."

. . .

Anticipating the good-faith exception to the exclusionary rule, Judge Friendly wrote that "[t]he beneficent aim of the exclusionary rule to deter police misconduct can be sufficiently accomplished by a practice . . . outlawing evidence obtained by flagrant or deliberate violation of rights."

Indeed, the abuses that gave rise to the exclusionary rule featured intentional conduct that was patently unconstitutional. In *Weeks*, a foundational exclusionary rule case, the officers had broken into the defendant's home (using a key shown to them by a neighbor), confiscated incriminating papers, then returned again with a U.S. Marshal to confiscate even more. Not only did they have no search warrant, which the Court held was required, but they could not have gotten one had they tried. They were so lacking in sworn and particularized information that "not even an order of court would have justified such procedure."

Equally flagrant conduct was at issue in *Mapp*, which overruled *Wolf v. Colorado*, and extended the exclusionary rule to the States. Officers forced open a door to Ms. Mapp's house, kept her lawyer from entering, brandished what the court concluded was a false warrant, then forced her into handcuffs and canvassed the house for obscenity. An error that arises from nonrecurring and attenuated negligence is thus far removed from the core concerns that led us to adopt the rule in the first place. And in fact since *Leon*, we have never applied the rule to exclude evidence obtained in violation of the Fourth Amendment, where the police conduct was no more intentional or culpable than this.

To trigger the exclusionary rule, police conduct must be sufficiently deliberate that exclusion can meaningfully deter it, and sufficiently culpable that such deterrence is worth the price paid by the justice system. As laid out in our cases, the exclusionary rule serves to deter deliberate, reckless, or grossly negligent conduct, or in some circumstances recurring or systemic negligence. The error in this case does not rise to that level.

. . .

The pertinent analysis of deterrence and culpability is objective, not an "inquiry into the subjective awareness of arresting officers." We have already held that "our good-faith inquiry is confined to the objectively ascertainable question whether a reasonably well trained officer would have known that the search was illegal" in light of "all of the circumstances." These circumstances frequently include a particular officer's knowledge and experience, but that does not make the test any more subjective than the one for probable cause, which looks to an officer's knowledge and experience.

We do not suggest that all recordkeeping errors by the police are immune from the exclusionary rule. In this case, however, the conduct at issue was not so objectively culpable as to require exclusion. In *Leon* we held that "the marginal or nonexistent benefits produced by suppressing evidence obtained in objectively reasonable reliance on a subsequently invalidated search warrant cannot justify the substantial costs of exclusion." The same is true when evidence is obtained in objectively reasonable reliance on a subsequently recalled warrant.

If the police have been shown to be reckless in maintaining a warrant system, or to have knowingly made false entries to lay the groundwork for future false arrests, exclusion would certainly be justified under our cases should such misconduct cause a Fourth Amendment violation. We said as much in *Leon*, explaining that an officer could not "obtain a warrant on the basis of a 'bare bones' affidavit and then rely on colleagues who are ignorant of the circumstances under which the warrant was obtained to conduct the search." Petitioner's fears that our decision will cause police departments to deliberately keep their officers ignorant are thus unfounded.

[The] dissent also adverts to the possible unreliability of a number of databases not relevant to this case. In a case where systemic errors were demonstrated, it might be reckless for officers to rely on an unreliable warrant system. . . . But there is no evidence that errors in Dale County's system are routine or widespread. Officer Anderson testified that he had never had reason to question information about a Dale County warrant, and both Sandy Pope and Sharon Morgan testified that they could remember no similar miscommunication ever happening on their watch. That is even less error than in the database at issue in Evans, where we also found reliance on the database to be objectively reasonable. Because no such showings were made here, the Eleventh Circuit was correct to affirm the denial of the motion to suppress.

Petitioner's claim that police negligence automatically triggers suppression cannot be squared with the principles underlying the exclusionary rule, as they have been explained in our cases. In light of our repeated holdings that the deterrent effect of suppression must be substantial and outweigh any harm to the justice system, *e.g.*, *Leon*, we conclude that when police mistakes are the result of negligence such as that described here, rather than systemic error or reckless disregard of constitutional requirements, any marginal deterrence does not "pay its way." In such a case, the criminal should not "go free because the constable has blundered."

The judgment of the Court of Appeals for the Eleventh Circuit is affirmed.

JUSTICE GINSBURG, with whom JUSTICE STEVENS, JUSTICE SOUTER, and JUSTICE BREYER join, dissenting.

The exclusionary rule provides redress for Fourth Amendment violations by placing the government in the position it would have been in had there been no unconstitutional arrest and search. The rule thus strongly encourages police compliance with the Fourth Amendment in the future. The Court, however, holds the rule inapplicable because careless recordkeeping by the police — not flagrant or deliberate misconduct — accounts for Herring's arrest.

I would not so constrict the domain of the exclusionary rule and would hold the rule dispositive of this case: "[I]f courts are to have any power to discourage [police] error of [the kind here at issue], it must be through the application of the exclusionary rule." The unlawful search in this case was contested in court because the police found methamphetamine in Herring's pocket and a pistol in his truck. But the "most serious impact" of the Court's holding will be on innocent persons "wrongfully arrested based on erroneous information [carelessly maintained] in a computer data base."

I

A warrant for Herring's arrest was recalled in February 2004, apparently because it had been issued in error. The warrant database for the Dale County Sheriff's Department, however, does not automatically update to reflect such changes. A member of the Dale County Sheriff's Department — whom the parties have not identified — returned the hard copy of the warrant to the County Circuit Clerk's office, but did not correct the Department's database to show that the warrant had been recalled. The erroneous entry for the warrant remained in the database, undetected, for five months.

On a July afternoon in 2004, Herring came to the Coffee County Sheriff's Department to retrieve his belongings from a vehicle impounded in the Department's lot. Investigator Mark Anderson, who was at the Department that day, knew Herring from prior interactions: Herring had told the district attorney, among others, of his suspicion that Anderson had been involved in the killing of a local teenager, and Anderson had pursued Herring to get him to drop the accusations. Informed that Herring was in the impoundment lot, Anderson asked the Coffee County warrant clerk whether there was an outstanding warrant for Herring's arrest. The clerk, Sandy Pope, found no warrant. Anderson then asked Pope to call the neighboring Dale County Sheriff's Department to inquire whether a warrant to arrest Herring was outstanding there. Upon receiving Pope's phone call, Sharon Morgan, the warrant clerk for the Dale County Department, checked her computer database. As just recounted, that Department's database preserved an error. Morgan's check therefore showed — incorrectly — an active warrant for Herring's arrest. Morgan gave the misinformation to Pope, who relayed it to Investigator Anderson. Armed with the report that a warrant existed, Anderson promptly arrested Herring and performed an incident search minutes before detection of the error.

The Court of Appeals concluded, and the Government does not contest, that the "failure to bring the [Dale County Sheriff's Department] records up to date [was] " 'at the very least negligent.' " And it is uncontested here that Herring's arrest violated his Fourth Amendment rights. The sole question presented, therefore, is whether evidence the police obtained through the unlawful search should have been suppressed. The Court holds that suppression was unwarranted because the exclusionary rule's "core concerns" are not raised by an isolated, negligent recordkeeping error attenuated from the arrest. In my view, the Court's opinion underestimates the need for a forceful exclusionary rule and the gravity of recordkeeping errors in law enforcement.

II

A

The Court states that the exclusionary rule is not a defendant's right; rather, it is simply a remedy applicable only when suppression would result in appreciable deterrence that outweighs the cost to the justice system. . . .

B

Others have described "a more majestic conception" of the Fourth Amendment and its adjunct, the exclusionary rule. *Evans* (Stevens, J., dissenting). Protective of the fundamental "right of the people to be secure in their persons, houses, papers, and effects," the Amendment "is a constraint on the power of the sovereign, not merely on some of its agents." I share that vision of the Amendment.

The exclusionary rule is "a remedy necessary to ensure that" the Fourth Amendment's prohibitions "are observed in fact." The rule's service as an essential auxiliary to the Amendment earlier inclined the Court to hold the two inseparable.

Beyond doubt, a main objective of the rule "is to deter — to compel respect for the constitutional guaranty in the only effectively available way — by removing the incentive to disregard it." But the rule also serves other important purposes: It "enabl[es] the judiciary to avoid the taint of partnership in official lawlessness," and it "assur[es] the people — all potential victims of unlawful government conduct — that the government would not profit from its lawless behavior, thus minimizing the risk of seriously undermining popular trust in government."

The exclusionary rule, it bears emphasis, is often the only remedy effective to redress a Fourth Amendment violation. . . .

III

The Court maintains that Herring's case is one in which the exclusionary rule could have scant deterrent effect and therefore would not "pay its way." I disagree.

A

The exclusionary rule, the Court suggests, is capable of only marginal deterrence when the misconduct at issue is merely careless, not intentional or reckless. The suggestion runs counter to a foundational premise of tort law — that liability for negligence, *i.e.*, lack of due care, creates an incentive to act with greater care. The Government so acknowledges. That the mistake here involved the failure to make a computer entry hardly means that application of the exclusionary rule would have minimal value. "Just as the risk of *respondeat superior* liability encourages employers to supervise . . . their employees' conduct [more carefully], so the risk of exclusion of evidence encourages policymakers and systems managers to monitor the performance of the systems they install and the personnel employed to operate those systems." *Evans* (Ginsburg, J., dissenting).

Consider the potential impact of a decision applying the exclusionary rule in this case. As earlier observed, the record indicates that there is no electronic connection between the warrant database of the Dale County Sheriff's Department and that of the County Circuit Clerk's office, which is located in the basement of the same building. When a warrant is recalled, one of the "many different people that have access to th[e] warrants," must find the hard copy of the warrant in the "two or three different places" where the department houses warrants, return it to the Clerk's office, and manually update the Department's database. The record reflects no routine practice of checking the database for accuracy, and the failure to remove the entry for Herring's warrant was not discovered until Investigator Anderson sought to pursue Herring five months later. Is it not altogether obvious that the Department could take further precautions to ensure the integrity of its database? The Sheriff's Department "is in a position to remedy the situation and might well do so if the exclusionary rule is there to remove the incentive to do otherwise."

B

Is the potential deterrence here worth the costs it imposes? In light of the paramount importance of accurate recordkeeping in law enforcement, I would answer yes, and next explain why, as I see it, Herring's motion presents a particularly strong case for suppression.

Electronic databases form the nervous system of contemporary criminal justice operations. In recent years, their breadth and influence have dramatically expanded. Police today can access databases that include not only the updated National Crime Information Center (NCIC), but also terrorist watchlists, the Federal Government's employee eligibility system, and various commercial databases. Moreover, States are actively expanding information sharing between jurisdictions. As a result, law enforcement has an increasing supply of information within its easy electronic reach.

The risk of error stemming from these databases is not slim. Herring's *amici* warn that law enforcement databases are insufficiently monitored and often out of date. Government reports describe, for example, flaws in NCIC databases, terrorist watchlist databases, and databases associated with the Federal Government's employment eligibility verification system.

Inaccuracies in expansive, interconnected collections of electronic information raise grave concerns for individual liberty. "The offense to the dignity of the citizen who is arrested, handcuffed, and searched on a public street simply because some bureaucrat has failed to maintain an accurate computer data base" is evocative of the use of general warrants that so outraged the authors of our Bill of Rights.

C

The Court assures that "exclusion would certainly be justified" if "the police have been shown to be reckless in maintaining a warrant system, or to have knowingly made false entries to lay the groundwork for future false arrests." This concession provides little comfort.

First, by restricting suppression to bookkeeping errors that are deliberate or reckless, the majority leaves Herring, and others like him, with no remedy for violations of their constitutional rights. There can be no serious assertion that relief is available under 42 U.S.C. § 1983. The arresting officer would be sheltered by qualified immunity, see *Harlow v. Fitzgerald*, 457 U.S. 800 (1982), and the police department itself is not liable for the negligent acts of its employees, see *Monell v. New York City Dept. of Social Servs.*, 436 U.S. 658 (1978). Moreover, identifying the department employee who committed the error may be impossible.

Second, I doubt that police forces already possess sufficient incentives to maintain up-to-date records. The Government argues that police have no desire to send officers out on arrests unnecessarily, because arrests consume resources and place officers in danger. The facts of this case do not fit that description of police motivation. Here the officer wanted to arrest Herring and consulted the Department's records to legitimate his predisposition.

Third, even when deliberate or reckless conduct is afoot, the Court's assurance will often be an empty promise: How is an impecunious defendant to make the required showing? If the answer is that a defendant is entitled to discovery (and if necessary, an audit of police databases), then the Court has imposed a considerable administrative burden on courts and law enforcement.

IV

Negligent recordkeeping errors by law enforcement threaten individual liberty, are susceptible to deterrence by the exclusionary rule, and cannot be remedied effectively through other means. Such errors present no occasion to further erode the exclusionary rule. The rule "is needed to make the Fourth Amendment something real; a guarantee that does not carry with it the exclusion of evidence obtained by its violation is a chimera." *Calandra*, 414 U.S. at 361 (Brennan, J., dissenting). In keeping with the rule's "core concerns," suppression should have attended the unconstitutional search in this case.

For the reasons stated, I would reverse the judgment of the Eleventh Circuit.

[JUSTICE BREYER, joined by JUSTICE SOUTER, wrote a separate dissenting opinion.]

NOTE

The Sixth Circuit applied the principles of *Groh v. Ramirez*, *supra* § 6.02[D][2] Note (4), rather than those established in *Herring v. United States*, in holding that patient records seized pursuant to a warrant that did not list the corresponding individual patient names would be suppressed. "As regards records of patients whose names did not appear on a patient list presented to the issuing Magistrate Judge, the facts of this case mirror those in *Groh* and require suppression of those files. This facial deficiency was so evident, moreover, that no officer could reasonably presume the warrants [sic] valid." *United States v. Lazar*, 604 F.3d 230 (6th Cir. 2010).

DAVIS v. UNITED STATES
United States Supreme Court
131 S. Ct. 2419 (2011)

JUSTICE ALITO delivered the opinion of the Court.

The Fourth Amendment protects the right to be free from "unreasonable searches and seizures," but it is silent about how this right is to be enforced. To supplement the bare text, this Court created the exclusionary rule, a deterrent sanction that bars the prosecution from introducing evidence obtained by way of a Fourth Amendment violation. The question here is whether to apply this sanction when the police conduct a search in compliance with binding precedent that is later overruled. Because suppression would do nothing to deter police misconduct in these circumstances, and because it would come at a high cost to both the truth and the public safety, we hold that searches conducted in objectively reasonable reliance on binding appellate precedent are not subject to the exclusionary rule.

I

The question presented arises in this case as a result of a shift in our Fourth Amendment jurisprudence on searches of automobiles incident to arrests of recent occupants.

A

Under this Court's decision in *Chimel v. California*, a police officer who makes a lawful arrest may conduct a warrantless search of the arrestee's person and the area "within his immediate control." This rule "may be stated clearly enough," but in the early going after *Chimel* it proved difficult to apply, particularly in cases that involved searches inside of automobiles after the arrestees were no longer in them. A number of courts upheld the constitutionality of vehicle searches that were "substantially contemporaneous" with occupants' arrests. Other courts disapproved of automobile searches incident to arrests, at least absent some continuing threat that the arrestee might gain access to the vehicle and destroy evidence or grab a weapon. In *New York v. Belton*, this Court granted certiorari to resolve the conflict.

. . .

For years, *Belton* was widely understood to have set down a simple, bright-line rule. Numerous courts read the decision to authorize automobile searches incident to arrests of recent occupants, regardless of whether the arrestee in any particular case was within reaching distance of the vehicle at the time of the search. Even after the arrestee had stepped out of the vehicle and had been subdued by police, the prevailing understanding was that *Belton* still authorized a substantially contemporaneous search of the automobile's passenger compartment. Not every court, however, agreed with this reading of *Belton*. . . . .

This Court granted certiorari in *Gant* [to consider the split in authority]. . . . As a result, the Court adopted a new, two-part rule under which an automobile search incident to a recent occupant's arrest is constitutional (1) if the arrestee is within reaching distance of the vehicle during the search, or (2) if the police have reason to believe that the vehicle contains evidence relevant to the crime of arrest.

. . .

B

The search at issue in this case took place a full two years before this Court announced its new rule in *Gant*. On an April evening in 2007, police officers in Greenville, Alabama, conducted a routine traffic stop that eventually resulted in the arrests of driver Stella Owens and passenger Willie Davis. The police handcuffed both Owens and Davis, and they placed the arrestees in the back of separate patrol cars. The police then searched the passenger compartment of Owens's vehicle and found a revolver inside Davis's jacket pocket.

Davis was indicted on one count of possession of a firearm by a convicted felon. In his motion to suppress the revolver, Davis acknowledged that the officers' search fully complied with "existing Eleventh Circuit precedent." Like most courts, the Eleventh Circuit had long read *Belton* to establish a bright-line rule authorizing substantially contemporaneous vehicle searches incident to arrests of recent occupants. Davis recognized that the District Court was obligated to follow this precedent, but he raised a Fourth Amendment challenge to preserve the issue for review on appeal.

While Davis's appeal was pending, this Court decided *Gant*. The Eleventh Circuit, in the opinion below, applied *Gant'* s new rule and held that the vehicle search incident to Davis's arrest violated his Fourth Amendment rights. As for whether this constitutional violation warranted suppression, the Eleventh Circuit viewed that as a separate issue that turned on the potential of exclusion to deter wrongful police conduct. The court concluded that penalizing the arresting officer for following binding appellate precedent would do nothing to deter Fourth Amendment violations. It therefore declined to apply the exclusionary rule and affirmed Davis's conviction. We granted certiorari.

II

The Fourth Amendment protects the "right of the people to be secure in their persons, houses, papers, and effects, against unreasonable searches and seizures." The Amendment says nothing about suppressing evidence obtained in violation of this command. That rule — the exclusionary rule — is a "prudential" doctrine created by this Court to "compel respect for the constitutional guaranty." Exclusion is not a personal constitutional right, nor is it designed to redress the injury occasioned by an unconstitutional search. The rule's sole purpose, we have repeatedly held, is to deter future Fourth Amendment violations. Our cases have thus limited the rule's operation to situations in which this purpose is thought most efficaciously served.

. . .

The basic insight of the *Leon* line of cases is that the deterrence benefits of exclusion vary with the culpability of the law enforcement conduct at issue. When the police exhibit deliberate, reckless, or grossly negligent disregard for Fourth Amendment rights, the deterrent value of exclusion is strong and tends to outweigh the resulting costs. But when the police act with an objectively reasonable good-faith belief that their conduct is lawful, or when their conduct involves only simple, isolated negligence, the deterrence rationale loses much of its force, and exclusion cannot "pay its way."

. . .

III

The question in this case is whether to apply the exclusionary rule when the police conduct a search in objectively reasonable reliance on binding judicial precedent. At the time of the search at issue here, we had not yet decided *Gant*, and the Eleventh Circuit had interpreted our decision in *Belton* to establish a bright-line rule authorizing the search of a vehicle's passenger compartment incident to a recent occupant's arrest. The search incident to Davis's arrest in this case followed the Eleventh Circuit's precedent to the letter. Although the search turned out to be unconstitutional under *Gant*, all agree that the officers' conduct was in strict compliance with then-binding Circuit law and was not culpable in any way.

Under our exclusionary-rule precedents, this acknowledged absence of police culpability dooms Davis's claim. Police practices trigger the harsh sanction of exclusion only when they are deliberate enough to yield meaningful deterrence, and culpable enough to be worth the price paid by the justice system. The conduct of the officers here was neither of these things. The officers who conducted the search did not violate Davis's Fourth Amendment rights deliberately, recklessly, or with gross negligence. Nor does this case involve any recurring or systemic negligence on the part of law enforcement. The police acted in strict compliance with binding precedent, and their behavior was not wrongful. Unless the exclusionary rule is to become a strict-liability regime, it can have no application in this case.

Indeed, in 27 years of practice under *Leon's* good-faith exception, we have never applied the exclusionary rule to suppress evidence obtained as a result of nonculpable, innocent police conduct. . . .

About all that exclusion would deter in this case is conscientious police work. . . . An officer who conducts a search in reliance on binding appellate precedent does no more than act as a reasonable officer would and should act under the circumstances. The deterrent effect of exclusion in such a case can only be to discourage the officer from doing his duty.

. . .

It is one thing for the criminal "to go free because the constable has blundered." It is quite another to set the criminal free because the constable has scrupulously adhered to governing law. Excluding evidence in such cases deters no police misconduct and imposes substantial social costs. We therefore hold that when the police conduct a search in objectively reasonable reliance on binding appellate precedent, the exclusionary rule does not apply. The judgment of the Court of Appeals for the Eleventh Circuit is *Affirmed.*

Justice Sotomayor, concurring in the judgment.

Under our precedents, the primary purpose of the exclusionary rule is to deter future Fourth Amendment violations. Accordingly, we have held, application of the exclusionary rule is unwarranted when it does not result in appreciable deterrence. In the circumstances of this case, where binding appellate precedent specifically *authorized* a particular police practice — in accord with the holdings of nearly every other court in the country — application of the exclusionary rule cannot reasonably be expected to yield appreciable deterrence. I am thus compelled to conclude that the exclusionary rule does not apply in this case and to agree with the Court's disposition.

This case does not present the markedly different question whether the exclusionary rule applies when the law governing the constitutionality of a particular search is unsettled. . . .

> If, as the Government argues, all rulings resolving unsettled Fourth Amendment questions should be nonretroactive, then, in close cases, law enforcement officials would have little incentive to err on the side of constitutional behavior. Official awareness of the dubious constitutionality of a practice would be counterbalanced by official certainty that, so long as the Fourth Amendment law in the area remained unsettled, evidence obtained through the questionable practice would be excluded only in the one case definitively resolving the unsettled question.

The Court of Appeals recognized as much in limiting its application of the good-faith exception it articulated in this case to situations where its precedent on a given point is unequivocal. Whether exclusion would deter Fourth Amendment violations where appellate precedent does not specifically authorize a certain practice and, if so, whether the benefits of exclusion would outweigh its costs are questions unanswered by our previous decisions. . . . In my view, whether an officer's conduct can be characterized as "culpable" is not itself dispositive. . . . Rather, an officer's culpability is relevant because it may inform the overarching inquiry whether exclusion would result in appreciable deterrence. . . .

As stated, whether exclusion would result in appreciable deterrence in the circumstances of this case is a different question from whether exclusion would appreciably deter Fourth Amendment violations when the governing law is unsettled. The Court's answer to the former question in this case thus does not resolve the latter one.

[JUSTICE BREYER, joined by JUSTICE GINSBURG, dissented on grounds of retroactivity.]

NOTE

After *Davis*, lower courts are left to decide when police action is "objectively reasonable given binding judicial precedent." *See, e.g., United States v. Sparks*, 711 F.3d 58 (1st Cir. 2013) (outlining the opposing views — binding precedent means binding in the circuit, or it means in the absence of directly applicable circuit precedent, precedent from appellate courts outside the circuit). In *Sparks*, the First Circuit held that police complied with authoritative precedent and their acts fit within the good-faith exception when, prior to the GPS decision of *United States v. Jones, supra* § 3.01, police applied a GPS tracking device to defendant's car without a warrant to track his whereabouts. The court concluded that the Supreme Court's earlier decision in *Knotts, see supra* § 3.03[C][2], coupled with its own circuit precedent, fulfilled the requirement that precedent be clear and well-settled.

[3] The Exclusion of Evidence for Some Purposes But Not Others

A majority of the Court now views the Fourth Amendment's exclusionary rule as a judicially-created means of protecting the guarantees of the Fourth Amendment, rather than a constitutionally-mandated remedy required by the Amendment itself.

As a result, the Court can pick and choose when evidence obtained in violation of the Fourth Amendment is and is not excluded from a criminal trial. The Court treats violations of *Miranda* similarly, allowing the prosecution to use evidence obtained in violation of *Miranda* for some purposes but not others. *Harris v. New York*, presented below, illustrates the way in which the Court limits the impact of *Miranda*'s exclusionary rule.

HARRIS v. NEW YORK

United States Supreme Court
401 U.S. 222 (1971)

Chief Justice Burger delivered the opinion of the Court.

We granted the writ in this case to consider petitioner's claim that a statement made by him to police under circumstances rendering it inadmissible to establish the prosecution's case in chief under *Miranda v. Arizona* may not be used to impeach his credibility.

The State of New York charged petitioner in a two-count indictment with twice selling heroin to an undercover police officer. At a subsequent jury trial the officer was the State's chief witness, and he testified as to details of the two sales. A second officer verified collateral details of the sales, and a third offered testimony about the chemical analysis of the heroin.

Petitioner took the stand in his own defense. He admitted knowing the undercover police officer but denied a sale on January 4, 1966. He admitted making a sale of contents of a glassine bag to the officer on January 6 but claimed it was baking powder and part of a scheme to defraud the purchaser.

On cross-examination petitioner was asked seriatim whether he had made specified statements to the police immediately following his arrest on January 7 — statements that partially contradicted petitioner's direct testimony at trial. In response to the cross-examination, petitioner testified that he could not remember virtually any of the questions or answers recited by the prosecutor. At the request of petitioner's counsel the written statement from which the prosecutor had read questions and answers in his impeaching process was placed in the record for possible use on appeal; the statement was not shown to the jury.

The trial judge instructed the jury that the statements attributed to petitioner by the prosecution could be considered only in passing on petitioner's credibility and not as evidence of guilt. In closing summations both counsel argued the substance of the impeaching statements. The jury then found petitioner guilty on the second count of the indictment.

At trial the prosecution made no effort in its case in chief to use the statements allegedly made by petitioner, conceding that they were inadmissible under *Miranda v. Arizona.* The transcript of the interrogation used in the impeachment, but not given to the jury, shows that no warning of a right to appoint counsel was given before questions were put to petitioner when he was taken into custody. Petitioner makes no claim that the statements made to the police were coerced or involuntary.

Some comments in the *Miranda* opinion can indeed be read as indicating a bar to use of uncounseled statement for any purpose, but discussion of that issue was not at all necessary to the Court's holding and cannot be regarded as controlling. *Miranda* barred the prosecution from making its case with statements of an accused made while in custody prior to having or effectively waiving counsel. It does not follow from *Miranda* that evidence inadmissible against an accused in the prosecution's case in chief is barred for all purposes, provided of course that the trustworthiness of the evidence satisfies legal standards.

In *Walder v. United States*, 347 U.S. 62 (1954), the Court permitted physical evidence, inadmissible in the case in chief, to be used for impeachment purposes.

> It is one thing to say that the Government cannot make an affirmative use of evidence unlawfully obtained. It is quite another to say that the defendant can turn the illegal method by which evidence in the Government's possession was obtained to his own advantage, and provide himself with a shield against contradiction of his untruths. Such an extension of the *Weeks* doctrine would be a perversion of the Fourth Amendment.
>
> [T]here is hardly justification for letting the defendant affirmatively resort to perjurious testimony in reliance on the Government's disability to challenge his credibility.

It is true that Walder was impeached as to collateral matters included in his direct examination, whereas petitioner here was impeached as to testimony bearing more directly on the crimes charged. We are not persuaded that there is a difference in principle that warrants a result different from that reached by the Court in *Walder*. Petitioner's testimony in his own behalf concerning the events of January 7 contrasted sharply with what he told the police shortly after his arrest. The impeachment process here undoubtedly provided valuable aid to the jury in assessing petitioner's credibility, and the benefits of this process should not be lost, in our view, because of the speculative possibility that impermissible police conduct will be encouraged thereby. Assuming that the exclusionary rule has a deterrent effect on proscribed police conduct, sufficient deterrence flows when the evidence in question is made unavailable to the prosecution in its case in chief.

Every criminal defendant is privileged to testify in his own defense, or to refuse to do so. But that privilege cannot be construed to include the right to commit perjury. Having voluntarily taken the stand, petitioner was under an obligation to speak truthfully and accurately, and the prosecution here did no more than utilize the traditional truth-testing devices of the adversary process.[3] Had inconsistent statements been made by the accused to some third person, it could hardly be contended that the conflict could not be laid before the jury by way of cross-examination and impeachment.

---

[3] [2] If, for example, an accused confessed fully to a homicide and led the police to the body of the victim under circumstances making his confession inadmissible, the petitioner would have us allow that accused to take the stand and blandly deny every fact disclosed to the police or discovered as a "fruit" of his confession, free from confrontation with his prior statements and acts. The voluntariness of the confession would, on this thesis, be totally irrelevant. We reject such an extravagant extension of the Constitution.

The shield provided by *Miranda* cannot be perverted into a license to use perjury by way of a defense, free from the risk of confrontation with prior inconsistent utterances. We hold, therefore, that petitioner's credibility was appropriately impeached by use of his earlier conflicting statements.

Affirmed.

[Justice Black dissented.]

Justice Brennan, with whom Justice Douglas and Justice Marshall, join, dissenting.

It is conceded that the question-and-answer statement used to impeach petitioner's direct testimony was, under *Miranda v. Arizona*, constitutionally inadmissible as part of the State's direct case against petitioner. I think that the Constitution also denied the State the use of the statement on cross-examination to impeach the credibility of petitioner's testimony given in his own defense.

[T]he accused is denied an "unfettered" choice when the decision whether to take the stand is burdened by the risk that an illegally obtained prior statement may be introduced to impeach his direct testimony denying complicity in the crime charged against him. We settled this proposition in *Miranda* where we said:

> The privilege against self-incrimination protects the individual from being compelled to incriminate himself in any manner. . . . [S]tatements merely intended to be exculpatory by the defendant are often *used to impeach his testimony at trial. . . . These statements are incriminating in any meaningful sense of the word and may not be used without the full warnings and effective waiver required for any other statement.*

[Emphasis added]. This language completely disposes of any distinction between statements used on direct as opposed to cross-examination.

. . .

The objective of deterring improper police conduct is only part of the larger objective of safeguarding the integrity of our adversary system. The "essential mainstay" of that system, *Miranda v. Arizona*, is the privilege against self-incrimination, which for that reason has occupied a central place in our jurisprudence since before the Nation's birth. Moreover, "we may view the historical development of the privilege as one which groped for the proper scope of governmental power over the citizen. . . . All these policies point to one overriding thought: the constitutional foundation underlying the privilege is the respect a government . . . must accord to the dignity and integrity of its citizens." These values are plainly jeopardized if an exception against admission of tainted statements is made for those used for impeachment purposes. Moreover, it is monstrous that courts should aid or abet the law-breaking police officer. It is abiding truth that "[n]othing can destroy a government more quickly than its failure to observe its own laws, or worse, its disregard of the charter of its own existence." *Mapp v. Ohio.*

Thus, even to the extent that *Miranda* was aimed at deterring police practices in disregard of the Constitution, I fear that today's holding will seriously undermine the achievement of that objective. The Court today tells the police that they may freely interrogate an accused incommunicado and without counsel and know that although any statement they obtain in violation of *Miranda* cannot be used on the State's direct case, it may be introduced if the defendant has the temerity to testify in his own defense. This goes far toward undoing much of the progress made in conforming police methods to the Constitution. I dissent.

NOTES AND QUESTIONS

(1) What is the difference between evidence offered to prove the government's case in chief and evidence offered for impeachment purposes? Will jurors be able to understand this difference? When dealing with impeachment evidence, most trial judges give a very basic instruction to the jury. See, for instance, Eleventh Circuit Pattern Jury Instructions (Criminal Cases), 6.1 (2010):

> You should . . . ask yourself whether there was evidence that a witness testified falsely about an important fact. And ask, whether there was evidence that at some other time a witness said or did something, or didn't say or do something, that was different from the testimony the witness gave during the trial.
>
> But keep in mind that a simple mistake doesn't mean a witness wasn't telling the truth as he or she remembers it. People naturally tend to forget some things or remember them inaccurately. So, if a witness misstated something, you must decide whether it was because of an innocent lapse in memory or an intentional deception. The significance of your decision may depend on whether the misstatement is about an important fact or about an unimportant detail.

(2) In *Oregon v. Hass*, 420 U.S. 714 (1975), proper *Miranda* warnings were given to the defendant. The defendant requested a lawyer, but the police ignored his request. Statements by the defendant were then used to impeach the defendant's trial testimony. Do the facts in *Hass* fall within *Harris*? The justices sharply disagreed on the applicability of *Harris*. Justice Blackmun, for the majority, wrote:

> We see no valid distinction to be made in the application of the principles of *Harris* to that case and to Hass' case. Hass' statements were made after the defendant knew [Officer] Osterholme's opposing testimony had been ruled inadmissible for the prosecution's case in chief.
>
> As in *Harris*, it does not follow from *Miranda* that evidence inadmissible against Hass in the prosecutions' case in chief is barred for all purposes, always provided that "the trustworthiness of the evidence satisfied legal standards." Again, the impeaching material would provide valuable aid to the jury in assessing the defendant's credibility; again, "the benefits of this process should not be lost"; and again, making the deterrent-effect assumption, there is sufficient deterrence when the evidence in question is made unavailable to the prosecution in its case in chief. If all this sufficed for the result in *Harris*, it supports and demands a like result in Hass' case. Here, too, the shield provided by *Miranda* is not to be perverted to a license to testify inconsistently, or even perjuriously, free from the risk of

confrontation with prior inconsistent utterances.

We are, after all, always engaged in a search for truth in a criminal case so long as the search is surrounded with the safeguards provided by our Constitution. There is no evidence or suggestion that Hass' statements to Officer Osterholme on the way to Moyina Heights were involuntary or coerced. He properly sensed, to be sure, that he was in "trouble"; but the pressure on him was no greater than that on any person in like custody or under inquiry by any investigating officer.

The only possible factual distinction between *Harris* and this case lies in the fact that the *Miranda* warnings given Hass were proper, whereas those given Harris were defective. The deterrence of the exclusionary rule, of course, lies in the necessity to give the warnings. That these warnings, in a given case, may prove to be incomplete, and therefore defective, as in *Harris*, does not mean that they have not served as a deterrent to the officer who is not then aware of their defect; and to the officer who is aware of the defect the full deterrence remains. The effect of inadmissibility in the *Harris* case and in this case is the same: inadmissibility would pervert the constitutional right into a right to falsify free from the embarrassment of the impeachment evidence from the defendant's own mouth.

One might concede that when proper *Miranda* warnings have been given, and the officer then continues his interrogation after the suspect asks for an attorney, the officer may be said to have little to lose and perhaps something to gain by way of possibly uncovering impeachment material. This speculative possibility, however, is even greater where the warnings are defective and the defect is not known to the officer. In any event, the balance was struck in *Harris*, and we are not disposed to change it now. If, in a given case, the officer's conduct amounts to an abuse, that case, like those involving coercion or duress, may be taken care of when it arises measured by the traditional standards for evaluating voluntariness and trustworthiness.

Id. at 722–23.

Justice Brennan (joined in dissent by Justice Marshall):

The Court's decision today goes beyond *Harris* in undermining *Miranda*. Even after *Harris*, police had some incentive for following *Miranda* by warning an accused of his right to remain silent and his right to counsel. If the warnings were given, the accused might still make a statement which could be used in the prosecution's case in chief. Under today's holding, however, once the warnings are given, police have almost no incentive for following *Miranda*' s requirement that "[i]f the individual states that he wants an attorney, the interrogation must cease until an attorney is present." *Miranda*, 384 U.S. at 474. If the requirement is followed there will almost surely be no statement since the attorney will advise the accused to remain silent. If, however, the requirement is disobeyed, the police may obtain a statement which can be used for impeachment if the accused has the temerity to testify in his own defense. Thus, after today's decision, if an individual states that he wants an attorney, police interrogation will doubtless be vigorously pressed to obtain statements before the attorney arrives.

I am unwilling to join this fundamental erosion of Fifth and Sixth Amendment rights and therefore dissent. *Id.* at 725-26.

(3) In *Michigan v. Harvey*, 494 U.S. 344 (1990), the Court linked *Harris* to the Sixth Amendment case, *Michigan v. Jackson*, 475 U.S. 625 (1986), in which the Court created a presumption of an invalid waiver of the Sixth Amendment right to counsel, provided the accused had requested an attorney. While such a confession could not be used to prove the defendant's guilt, the Court in *Harvey* allowed it to be used to impeach the defendant's in-court statement. *Michigan v. Jackson*, which had held that a request for counsel at an arraignment should be treated as an invocation of the Sixth Amendment at all critical stages of the prosecution and that any subsequent waiver by the accused would not justify police-initiated interrogation, was overruled by *Montejo v. Louisiana*, 556 U.S. 778 (2009). After *Montejo*, there is no distinction between represented and unrepresented defendants who knowingly and voluntarily waive their Sixth Amendment rights. *Miranda* warnings are adequate to inform all of these defendants of their rights. *Montejo*, 556 U.S. at 798–99.

Similarly, in *Kansas v. Ventris*, 556 U.S. 586 (2009), the Supreme Court ruled that statements, even those obtained by the government in violation of *Massiah v. United States*, [*see supra* § 5.02], may be used for impeachment purposes. The majority first decided that a violation of the Sixth Amendment right to counsel under *Massiah* occurs "when the uncounseled interrogation is conducted" not later when the evidence is introduced at the defendant's trial. Then, relying on the same reasoning that appears in *Harris, Hass*, and *Harvey*, the Court concluded that the government may introduce evidence deliberately elicited in violation of the Sixth Amendment to challenge the defendant's inconsistent testimony at trial. In reaching this result, the majority explained:

> This case does not involve . . . the prevention of a constitutional violation, but rather the scope of the remedy for a violation that has already occurred. Our precedents make clear that the game of excluding tainted evidence for impeachment purposes is not worth the candle. The interests safeguarded by such exclusion are "outweighed by the need to prevent perjury and to assure the integrity of the trial process."

Id. at 593. The Court reasoned further, "Once the defendant testifies in a way that contradicts prior statements, denying the prosecution use of 'the traditional truth-testing devices of the adversary process,' *Harris*, is a high price to pay for vindication of the right to counsel at the prior stage." *Id.* Justices Stevens and Ginsburg dissented.

(4) Does *Harris* apply if the defendant testifies and on direct examination simply denies having committed the offense? In *United States v. Havens*, 446 U.S. 620 (1980), the defendant was charged with importing cocaine. Before trial, his luggage had been seized and searched without a warrant in violation of the Fourth Amendment. No drugs were found but t-shirts with altered pockets, which

implicated defendant in the smuggling operation, were found in the luggage. In his defense, Havens took the stand and denied involvement in the drug smuggling operation. On cross-examination, the prosecutor asked Havens whether he had been involved in sewing swatches on t-shirts. When Havens denied that activity, the prosecutor impeached him with evidence illegally seized from the suitcase, rather than by a prior statement.

Still, the Court applied the reasoning of *Harris*:

> Neither *Harris* nor *Hass* involved the impeachment of assertedly false testimony first given on cross-examination, but the reasoning of those cases controls this one. There is no gainsaying that arriving at the truth is a fundamental goal of our legal system. We have repeatedly insisted that when defendants testify, they must testify truthfully or suffer the consequences. This is true even though a defendant is compelled to testify against his will. It is essential, therefore, to the proper functioning of the adversary system that when a defendant takes the stand, the government be permitted proper and effective cross-examination in an attempt to elicit the truth. The defendant's obligation to testify truthfully is fully binding on him when he is cross-examined. His privilege against self-incrimination does not shield him from proper questioning. He would unquestionably be subject to a perjury prosecution if he knowingly lies on cross-examination. In terms of impeaching a defendant's seemingly false statements with his prior inconsistent utterances or with other reliable evidence available to the government, we see no difference of constitutional magnitude between the defendant's statements on direct examination and his answers to questions put to him on cross-examination that are plainly within the scope of the defendant's direct examination. Without this opportunity, the normal function of cross-examination would be severely impeded. *Id.* at 626-27.

(5) As indicated previously, state courts may interpret their own state constitutions to provide more protections to criminal defendants. The *Harris* decision led Hawaii to reject the Supreme Court's position. In *State v. Santiago*, 492 P.2d 657, 664 (Haw. 1971), the court explained:

> We base our decision on our belief that the privilege against self-incrimination bestows on every accused the right to choose whether or not to confess to the commission of a crime. In order to protect that freedom of choice, we believe that every accused, must be informed of the fact that he has certain rights under the Hawaii Constitution. In order to encourage the police to inform persons accused of crimes of their rights, and in order to preserve the integrity of the judicial process, we believe that where the accused is not informed of his rights, any admissions or confessions must be entirely excluded from his trial. Finally, we believe that if the rationale underlying *Miranda* is sufficient to warrant the exclusion of prior statements from the prosecutor's cases in chief, then that same rationale precludes use of those statements for impeachment.

In 1975, the Pennsylvania Supreme Court held that Article 1, Section 9 of the Pennsylvania Constitution prohibited the use of a statement obtained in violation of *Miranda*, even for impeachment. *Commonwealth v. Triplett*, 341 A.2d 62 (Pa. 1975).

But in 1984, the provision was amended to align with the *Harris* decision. *See Commonwealth v. Baxter*, 532 A.2d 1177 (Pa. Super. 1987) (explaining history of amendment).

If you were sitting on a court in a state which had comparable constitutional provisions, would you follow the Court's rule in *Harris*?

(6) Certainly, not every otherwise inadmissible statement falls within the ambit of *Harris*. In fact, in *Mincey v. Arizona*, 437 U.S. 385 (1978), the Court reiterated: "[*A*]*ny* criminal trial use against a defendant of his *involuntary* statements is a denial of due process of law." (emphasis in original). And in *New Jersey v. Portash*, 440 U.S. 450 (1979), the defendant was given immunity and testified before the grand jury. The trial judge ruled that the grand jury testimony could be used at trial for impeachment purposes. Was the trial judge's ruling correct under *Harris*? No, said a majority of the Supreme Court:

> Testimony given in response to a grant of legislative immunity is the essence of coerced testimony. In such cases there is no question whether physical or psychological pressures overrode the defendant's will; the witness is told to talk or face the government's coercive sanctions, notably, a conviction for contempt. The information given in response to a grant of immunity may well be more reliable than information beaten from a helpless defendant, but it is no less compelled. The Fifth and Fourteenth Amendments provide a privilege against *compelled* self-incrimination, not merely against unreliable self-incrimination. Balancing of interests was thought to be necessary in *Harris* and *Hass* when the attempt to deter unlawful police conduct collided with the need to prevent perjury. Here, by contrast, we deal with the constitutional privilege against compulsory self-incrimination in its most pristine form. Balancing, therefore, is not simply unnecessary. It is impermissible. *Id.* at 459.

What about using a defendant's otherwise inadmissible statement to impeach his other witnesses?

JAMES v. ILLINOIS

United States Supreme Court
493 U.S. 307 (1990)

JUSTICE BRENNAN delivered the opinion of the Court.

The impeachment exception to the exclusionary rule permits the prosecution in a criminal proceeding to introduce illegally obtained evidence to impeach the defendant's own testimony. The Illinois Supreme Court extended this exception to permit the prosecution to impeach the testimony of *all* defense witnesses with illegally obtained evidence. Finding this extension inconsistent with the balance of values underlying our previous applications of the exclusionary rule, we reverse.

I

On the night of August 30, 1982, eight young boys returning home from a party were confronted by a trio of other boys who demanded money. When the eight boys refused to comply, one member of the trio produced a gun and fired into the larger group, killing one boy and seriously injuring another. When the police arrived, the remaining members of the larger group provided eyewitness accounts of the event and descriptions of the perpetrators.

The next evening, two detectives of the Chicago Police Department took 15-year-old Darryl James into custody as a suspect in the shooting. James was found at his mother's beauty parlor sitting under a hair dryer; when he emerged, his hair was black and curly. After placing James in their car, the detectives questioned him about his prior hair color. He responded that the previous day his hair had been reddish brown, long, and combed straight back. The detectives questioned James again later at the police station, and he further stated that he had gone to the beauty parlor in order to have his hair "dyed black and curled in order to change his appearance."

The State subsequently indicted James for murder and attempted murder. Prior to trial, James moved to suppress the statements regarding his hair, contending that they were the fruit of a Fourth Amendment violation because the detectives lacked probable cause for his warrantless arrest. After an evidentiary hearing, the trial court sustained this motion and ruled that the statements would be inadmissible at trial.

At trial, five members of the larger group of boys testified for the State, and each made an in-court identification of the defendant. Each testified that the person responsible for the shooting had "reddish" hair, worn shoulder length in a slicked-back "butter" style. Each also recalled having seen James several weeks earlier at a parade, at which time James had the aforementioned hair color and style. At trial, however, his hair was black and worn in a "natural" style. Despite the discrepancy between the witnesses' description and his present appearance, the witnesses stood firm in their conviction that James had been present and had fired the shots.

James did not testify in his own defense. He called as a witness Jewel Henderson, a friend of his family. Henderson testified that on the day of the shooting she had taken James to register for high school and that, at that time, his hair was black. The State then sought, over James' objection, to introduce his illegally obtained statements as a means of impeaching the credibility of Henderson's testimony. After determining that the suppressed statements had been made voluntarily, the trial court overruled James' objection. One of the interrogating detectives then reported James' prior admissions that he had reddish hair the night of the shooting and he dyed and curled his hair the next day in order to change his appearance. James ultimately was convicted of both murder and attempted murder and sentenced to 30 years' imprisonment.

On appeal, the Illinois Appellate Court reversed James' convictions and ordered a new trial. The appellate court held that the exclusionary rule barred admission of James' illegally obtained statements for the purpose of impeaching a defense witness' testimony and that the resulting constitutional error was not harmless. However, the Illinois Supreme Court reversed. The court reasoned that, in order to deter the defendant from engaging in perjury "by proxy," the impeachment exception to the exclusionary rule ought to be expanded to allow the State to introduce illegally obtained evidence to impeach the testimony of defense witnesses other than the defendant himself. The court therefore ordered James' convictions reinstated. We granted certiorari.

II

"There is no gainsaying that arriving at the truth is a fundamental goal of our legal system." But various constitutional rules limit the means by which government may conduct this search for truth in order to promote other values embraced by the Framers and cherished throughout our Nation's history. "Ever since its inception, the rule excluding evidence seized in violation of the Fourth Amendment has been recognized as a principal mode of discouraging lawless police conduct. . . . [W]ithout it the constitutional guarantee against unreasonable searches and seizures would be a mere 'form of words.' " The occasional suppression of illegally obtained yet probative evidence has long been considered a necessary cost of preserving overriding constitutional values: "[T]here is nothing new in the realization that the Constitution sometimes insulates the criminality of a few in order to protect the privacy of us all."

This Court has carved out exceptions to the exclusionary rule, however, where the introduction of reliable and probative evidence would significantly further the truth-seeking function of a criminal trial and the likelihood that admissibility of such evidence would encourage police misconduct is but a "speculative possibility." One exception to the rule permits prosecutors to introduce illegally obtained evidence for the limited purpose of impeaching the credibility of the defendant's own testimony.

. . .

This Court insisted throughout this line of cases that "evidence that has been illegally obtained . . . is inadmissible on the government's direct case, or otherwise, as substantive evidence of guilt." However, because the Court believed that permitting the use of such evidence to impeach defendants' testimony would further the goal of truth-seeking by preventing defendants from perverting the exclusionary rule " 'into a license to use perjury by way of a defense,' " and because the Court further believed that permitting such use would create only a "speculative possibility that impermissible police conduct will be encouraged thereby," the Court concluded that the balance of values underlying the exclusionary rule justified an exception covering impeachment of defendants' testimony.

III

In this case, the Illinois Supreme Court held that our balancing approach in *Walder* and its progeny justifies expanding the scope of the impeachment exception to permit prosecutors to use illegally obtained evidence to impeach the credibility of defense witnesses. We disagree. Expanding the class of impeachable witnesses from the defendant alone to all defense witnesses would create different incentives affecting the behavior of both defendants and law enforcement officers. As a result, this expansion would not promote the truthseeking function to the same extent as did creation of the original exception, and yet it would significantly undermine the deterrent effect of the general exclusionary rule. Hence, we believe that this proposed expansion would frustrate rather than further the purposes underlying the exclusionary rule.

The previously recognized exception penalizes defendants for committing perjury by allowing the prosecution to expose their perjury through impeachment using illegally obtained evidence. Thus defendants are discouraged in the first instance from "affirmatively resort[ing] to perjurious testimony." But the exception leaves defendants free to testify truthfully on their own behalf; they can offer probative and exculpatory evidence to the jury without opening the door to impeachment by carefully avoiding any statements that directly contradict the suppressed evidence. The exception thus generally discourages perjured testimony without discouraging truthful testimony.

In contrast, expanding the impeachment exception to encompass the testimony of all defense witnesses would not have the same beneficial effects. First, the mere threat of a subsequent criminal prosecution for perjury is far more likely to deter a witness from intentionally lying on a defendant's behalf than to deter a defendant, already facing conviction for the underlying offense, from lying on his own behalf. Hence the Illinois Supreme Court's underlying premise that a defendant frustrated by our previous impeachment exception can easily find a witness to engage in "perjury by proxy" is suspect.[4]

More significantly, expanding the impeachment exception to encompass the testimony of all defense witnesses likely would chill some defendants from presenting their best defense and sometimes any defense at all — through the testimony of others. Whenever police obtained evidence illegally, defendants would have to assess prior to trial the likelihood that the evidence would be admitted to impeach the otherwise favorable testimony of any witness they call. Defendants might reasonably fear that one or more of their witnesses, in a position to offer truthful and favorable testimony, would also make some statement in sufficient tension with the tainted evidence to allow the prosecutor to introduce that evidence for impeachment. First, defendants sometimes need to call "reluctant" or "hostile" witnesses to provide reliable and probative exculpatory testimony, and such witnesses likely will not share the defendants' concern for avoiding statements that invite impeachment through contradictory evidence. Moreover, defendants often cannot trust even "friendly" witnesses to testify without subjecting themselves to impeachment, simply due to insufficient care or attentiveness. This concern is magnified in those occasional situations when defendants must call witnesses to testify despite having had only a limited opportunity to consult with or prepare

---

[4] [4] The dissent concedes, as it must, that "of course, false testimony can result from faulty recollection" as opposed to intentional lying. Even assuming that Henderson's testimony in this case (as opposed to the detective's contrary testimony) was indeed false, nothing in the record suggests that Henderson intentionally committed perjury rather than honestly provided her best (even if erroneous) perception and recollection of events.

them in advance. For these reasons, we have recognized in a variety of contexts that a party "cannot be absolutely certain that his witnesses will testify as expected." As a result, an expanded impeachment exception likely would chill some defendants from calling witnesses who would otherwise offer probative evidence.

This realization alters the balance of values underlying the current impeachment exception governing defendants' testimony. Our prior cases make clear that defendants ought not be able to "pervert" the exclusion of illegally obtained evidence into a shield for perjury, but it seems no more appropriate for the State to brandish such evidence as a sword with which to dissuade defendants from presenting a meaningful defense through other witnesses. Given the potential chill created by expanding the impeachment exception, the conceded gains to the truth-seeking process from discouraging or disclosing perjured testimony would be offset to some extent by the concomitant loss of probative witness testimony. Thus, the truth-seeking rationale supporting the impeachment of defendants in *Walder* and its progeny does not apply to other witnesses with equal force.

Moreover, the proposed expansion of the current impeachment exception would significantly weaken the exclusionary rule's deterrent effect on police misconduct. This Court has characterized as a mere "speculative possibility," *Harris v. New York*, the likelihood that permitting prosecutors to impeach defendants with illegally obtained evidence would encourage police misconduct. Law enforcement officers will think it unlikely that the defendant will first decide to testify at trial and will also open the door inadvertently to admission of any illegally obtained evidence. Hence, the officers' incentive to acquire evidence through illegal means is quite weak.

In contrast, expanding the impeachment exception to *all* defense witnesses would significantly enhance the expected value to the prosecution of illegally obtained evidence. First, this expansion would vastly increase the number of occasions on which such evidence could be used. Defense witnesses easily outnumber testifying defendants, both because many defendants do not testify themselves and because many if not most defendants call multiple witnesses on their behalf. Moreover, due to the chilling effect identified above, illegally obtained evidence holds even greater value to the prosecution for each individual witness than for each defendant. The prosecutor's access to impeachment evidence would not just deter perjury; it would also deter defendants from calling witnesses in the first place, thereby keeping from the jury much probative exculpatory evidence. For both of these reasons, police officers and their superiors would recognize that obtaining evidence through illegal means stacks the deck heavily in the prosecution's favor. It is thus far more than a "speculative possibility" that police misconduct will be encouraged by permitting such use of illegally obtained evidence.

The United States argues that this result is constitutionally acceptable because excluding illegally obtained evidence solely from the prosecution's case in chief would still provide a quantum of deterrence sufficient to protect the privacy interests underlying the exclusionary rule. We disagree. Of course, a police officer might in certain situations believe that obtaining particular evidence through illegal means, resulting in its suppression from the case in chief, would prevent the prosecution from establishing a prima facie case to take to a jury. In such situations, the officer likely would be deterred from obtaining the evidence illegally for fear of jeopardizing the entire case. But much if not most of the time, police officers confront opportunities to obtain evidence illegally after they have already legally obtained (or know that they have other means of legally obtaining) sufficient evidence to sustain a prima facie case. In these situations, a rule requiring exclusion of illegally obtained evidence from only the government's case in chief would leave officers with little to lose and much to gain by overstepping constitutional limits on evidence gathering.[5] Narrowing the exclusionary rule in this manner, therefore, would significantly undermine the rule's ability "to compel respect for the constitutional guaranty in the only effectively available way — by removing the incentive to disregard it." So long as we are committed to protecting the people from the disregard of their constitutional rights during the course of criminal investigations, inadmissibility of illegally obtained evidence must remain the rule, not the exception.

IV

The cost to the truth-seeking process of evidentiary exclusion invariably is perceived more tangibly in discrete prosecutions than is the protection of privacy values through deterrence of future police misconduct. When defining the precise scope of the exclusionary rule, however, we must focus on systemic effects of proposed exceptions to ensure that individual liberty from arbitrary or oppressive police conduct does not succumb to the inexorable pressure to introduce all incriminating evidence, no matter how obtained, in each and every criminal case. Our previous recognition of an impeachment exception limited to the testimony of defendants reflects a careful weighing of the competing values. Because expanding the exception to encompass the testimony of all defense witnesses would not further the truth-seeking value with equal force but would appreciably undermine the deterrent effect of the exclusionary rule, we adhere to the line drawn in our previous cases.

Accordingly, we hold that the Illinois Supreme Court erred in affirming James' convictions despite the prosecutor's use of illegally obtained statements to impeach a defense witness' testimony. The court's judgment is reversed, and the case is remanded for further proceedings not inconsistent with this opinion.

It is so ordered.

Justice Stevens, concurring.

While I join the opinion of the Court, certain comments in the dissent prompt this postscript. The dissent answers the wrong question when it states that "[t]he interest in protecting the truth-seeking function of the criminal trial is every bit as strong in this case as in our earlier cases."

---

[5] [8] Indeed, the detectives who unlawfully detained James and elicited his incriminating statements already knew that there were several eyewitnesses to the shooting. Because the detectives likely believed that the exclusion of any statement they obtained from James probably would not have precluded the prosecution from making a prima facie case, an exclusionary rule applicable only to the prosecution's case in chief likely would have provided little deterrent effect in this case.

This is self-evident. The State always has a strong interest in the truth-seeking function. The proper question, however, is whether the admission of the illegally obtained evidence in this case would sufficiently advance the truth-seeking function to overcome the loss to the deterrent value of the exclusionary rule. With respect to this issue, the dissent overestimates the benefit of the exclusionary rule even to the defendant bent on presenting perjured testimony and exaggerates the injury that exclusion of unlawfully obtained evidence causes to the truth-seeking function.

JUSTICE KENNEDY, with whom the CHIEF JUSTICE, JUSTICE O'CONNOR, and JUSTICE SCALIA join, dissenting.

To deprive the prosecution of probative evidence acquired in violation of the law may be a tolerable and necessary cost of the exclusionary rule. Implementation of the rule requires us to draw certain lines to effect its purpose of deterring unlawful conduct. But the line drawn by today's opinion grants the defense side in a criminal case broad immunity to introduce whatever false testimony it can produce from the mouth of a friendly witness. Unless petitioner's conviction is reversed, we are told, police would flout the Fourth Amendment, and as a result, the accused would be unable to offer any defense. This exaggerated view leads to a drastic remedy: The jury cannot learn that defense testimony is inconsistent with probative evidence of undoubted value. A more cautious course is available, one that retains Fourth Amendment protections and yet safeguards the truth-seeking function of the criminal trial.

Our precedents establish that the exclusionary rule does not apply where the interest in pursuing truth or other important values outweighs any deterrence of unlawful conduct that the rule might achieve.

One instance is a defendant's attempt to take advantage by presenting testimony in outright contradiction of excluded facts, secure in the knowledge that the inconsistency will not be revealed to the jury. . . . Under this rationale, our consistent rule has been that a defendant's testimony is subject to rebuttal by contradicting evidence that otherwise would be excluded.

Petitioner argues that the rationale of these cases is confined to "impeachment" of testimony presented by the defendant himself because these cases involve only "impeachment by self-contradiction." The theory, it seems, is that excluded evidence introduced in opposition to the defendant's testimony impeaches by means of the contradiction itself; the substantive truth or falsity of the suppressed evidence is irrelevant. Our cases do not bear this reading.

I agree with the majority that the resolution of this case depends on a balance of values that informs our exclusionary rule jurisprudence. We weigh the " 'likelihood of . . . deterrence against the costs of withholding reliable information from the truth-seeking process.' " The majority adopts a sweeping rule that the testimony of witnesses other than the defendant may never be rebutted with excludable evidence. I cannot draw the line where the majority does.

The interest in protecting the truth-seeking function of the criminal trial is every bit as strong in this case as in our earlier cases that allowed rebuttal with evidence that was inadmissible as part of the prosecution's case in chief. Here a witness who knew the accused well took the stand to testify about the accused's personal appearance. The testimony could be expected to create real doubt in the minds of jurors concerning the eyewitness identifications by persons who did not know the accused. To deprive the jurors of knowledge that statements of the defendant himself revealed the witness' testimony to be false would result in a decision by triers of fact who were not just kept in the dark as to excluded evidence, but positively misled. The potential for harm to the truth-seeking process resulting from the majority's new rule in fact will be greater than if the defendant himself had testified. It is natural for jurors to be skeptical of self-serving testimony by the defendant. Testimony by a witness said to be independent has the greater potential to deceive. And if a defense witness can present false testimony with impunity, the jurors may find the rest of the prosecution's case suspect, for ineffective and artificial cross-examination will be viewed as a real weakness in the state's case.

Jurors will assume that if the prosecution had any proof the statement was false, it would make the proof known. The majority does more than deprive the prosecution of evidence. The state must also suffer the introduction of false testimony and appear to bolster the falsehood by its own silence.

The majority's fear that allowing the jury to know the whole truth will chill defendants from putting on any defense seems to me far too speculative to justify the rule here announced. No restriction on the defense results if rebuttal of testimony by witnesses other than the defendant is confined to the introduction of excludable evidence that is in direct contradiction of the testimony. If mere "tension with the tainted evidence," opened the door to introduction of *all* the evidence subject to suppression, then the majority's fears might be justified. But in this context rebuttal can and should be confined to situations where there is direct conflict, which is to say where, within reason, the witness' testimony and the excluded testimony cannot both be true.

NOTES AND QUESTONS

(1) Is the result in *James* consistent with the Court's holdings in *Harris* and *Walder*?

(2) Does the majority adequately respond to Justice Kennedy's concern that the decision "grants the defense side in a criminal case broad immunity to introduce whatever false testimony it can produce from the mouth of a friendly witness"?

(3) What if the prosecution seeks to impeach the defendant with the fact that he told his exculpatory story for the first time at trial? *Doyle v. Ohio*, below, answers this question.

DOYLE v. OHIO

United States Supreme Court
426 U.S. 610 (1976)

JUSTICE POWELL delivered the opinion of the Court.

The question in these consolidated cases is whether a state prosecutor may seek to impeach a defendant's exculpatory story, told for the first time at trial, by cross-examining the defendant about his failure to have told the story after receiving *Miranda* warnings at the time of his arrest. We conclude that use of the defendant's post-arrest silence in this manner violates due process, and therefore reverse the convictions of both petitioners.

I

Petitioners Doyle and Wood were arrested together and charged with selling 10 pounds of marihuana to a local narcotics bureau informant. They were convicted in the Common Pleas Court of Tuscarawas County, Ohio, in separate trials held about one week apart. The evidence at their trials was identical in all material respects.

Petitioners' explanation of the events presented some difficulty for the prosecution, as it was not entirely implausible and there was little if any direct evidence to contradict it. As part of a wide-ranging cross-examination for impeachment purposes, and in an effort to undercut the explanation, the prosecutor asked each petitioner at his respective trial why he had not told the frameup story to Agent Beamer when he arrested petitioners. In the first trial, that of petitioner Wood, the following colloquy occurred:

Q: [By the prosecutor.] Mr. Beamer did arrive on the scene?

A: [by Wood.] Yes, he did.

Q: And I assume you told him all about what happened to you?

A: No.

Q: You didn't tell Mr. Beamer this guy put $1,300 in your car?

A: No, sir.

Q: And we can't understand any reason why anyone would put money in your car and you were chasing him around town and trying to give it back?

A: I didn't understand that.

Q: You mean you didn't tell him that?

A: Tell him what?

Q: Mr. Wood, if that is all you had to do with this and you are innocent, when Mr. Beamer arrived on the scene why didn't you tell him? . . .

Q: But in any event you didn't bother to tell Mr. Beamer anything about this?

A: No, sir."

Defense counsel's timely objections to the above questions of the prosecutor were overruled. The cross-examination of petitioner Doyle at his trial contained a similar exchange, and again defense counsel's timely objections were overruled.

II

The State pleads necessity as justification for the prosecutor's action in these cases. It argues that the discrepancy between an exculpatory story at trial and silence at time of arrest gives rise to an inference that the story was fabricated somewhere along the way, perhaps to fit within the seams of the State's case as it was developed at pretrial hearings. Noting that the prosecution usually has little else with which to counter such an exculpatory story, the State seeks only the right to cross-examine a defendant as to post-arrest silence for the limited purpose of impeachment. In support of its position the State emphasizes the importance of cross-examination in general, and relies upon those cases in which this Court has permitted use for impeachment purposes of post-arrest statements that were inadmissible as evidence of guilt because of an officer's failure to follow *Miranda*'s dictates. *Harris v. New York, Oregon v. Hass.* Thus, although the State does not suggest petitioners' silence could be used as evidence of guilt, it contends that the need to present to the jury all information relevant to the truth of petitioners' exculpatory story fully justifies the cross-examination that is at issue.

Despite the importance of cross-examination, we have concluded that the *Miranda* decision compels rejection of the State's position. The warnings mandated by that case, as a prophylactic means of safeguarding Fifth Amendment rights, require that a person taken into custody be advised immediately that he has the right to remain silent, that anything he says may be used against him, and that he has a right to retained or appointed counsel before submitting to interrogation. Silence in the wake of these warnings may be nothing more than the arrestee's exercise of these *Miranda* rights. Thus, every post-arrest silence is insolubly ambiguous because of what the State is required to advise the person arrested.

Moreover, while it is true that the *Miranda* warnings contain no express assurance that silence will carry no penalty, such assurance is implicit to any person who receives the warnings. In such circumstances, it would be fundamentally unfair and a deprivation of due process to allow the arrested person's silence to be used to impeach an explanation subsequently offered at trial. Mr. Justice White, concurring in the judgment in *United States v. Hale*, put it very well:

> [W]hen a person under arrest is informed, as *Miranda* requires, that he may remain silent, that anything he says may be used against him, and that he may have an attorney if he wishes, it seems to me that it does not comport with due process to permit the prosecution during the trial to call attention to his silence at the time of arrest and to insist that because he did not speak about the facts of the case at that time, as he was told he need not do, an unfavorable inference might be drawn as to the truth of his trial testimony. . . . Surely Hale was not informed here that his silence, as well

as his words, could be used against him at trial. Indeed, anyone would reasonably conclude from *Miranda* warnings that this would not be the case.

We hold that the use for impeachment purposes of petitioners' silence, at the time of arrest and after receiving *Miranda* warnings, violated the Due Process Clause of the Fourteenth Amendment. The State has not claimed that such use in the circumstances of this case might have been harmless error. Accordingly, petitioners' convictions are reversed and their causes remanded to the state courts for further proceedings not inconsistent with this opinion.

JUSTICE STEVENS, with whom JUSTICE BLACKMUN and JUSTICE REHNQUIST join, dissenting.

I

The Court's due process rationale has some of the characteristics of an estoppel theory. If (a) the defendant is advised that he may remain silent, and (b) he does remain silent, then we (c) presume that his decision was made in reliance on the advice, and (d) conclude that it is unfair in certain cases, though not others, to use his silence to impeach his trial testimony. The key to the Court's analysis is apparently a concern that the *Miranda* warning, which is intended to increase the probability that a person's response to police questioning will be intelligent and voluntary, will actually be deceptive unless we require the State to honor an unstated promise not to use the accused's silence against him.

In my judgment there is nothing deceptive or prejudicial to the defendant in the *Miranda* warning. Nor do I believe that the fact that such advice was given to the defendant lessens the probative value of his silence, or makes the prosecutor's cross-examination about his silence any more unfair than if he had received no such warning.

This is a case in which the defendants' silence at the time of their arrest was graphically inconsistent with their trial testimony that they were the unwitting victims of a "frameup" in which the police did not participate. If defendants had been framed, their failure to mention that fact at the time of their arrest is almost inexplicable; for that reason, under accepted rules of evidence, their silence is tantamount to a prior inconsistent statement and admissible for purposes of impeachment.

Indeed, there is irony in the fact that the *Miranda* warning provides the only plausible explanation for their silence. If it were the true explanation, I should think that they would have responded to the questions on cross-examination about why they had remained silent by stating that they relied on their understanding of the advice given by the arresting officers. Instead, however, they gave quite a different jumble of responses. Those response negate the Court's presumption that their silence was induced by reliance on deceptive advice.

Since the record requires us to put to one side the Court's presumption that the defendants' silence was the product of reliance on the *Miranda* warning, the Court's entire due process rationale collapses. For without reliance on the waiver, the case is no different than if no warning had been given, and nothing in the Court's opinion suggests that there would be any unfairness in using petitioners' prior inconsistent silence for impeachment purposes in such a case.

Indeed, as a general proposition, if we assume the defendant's silence would be admissible for impeachment purposes if no *Miranda* warning had been given, I should think that the warning would have a tendency to salvage the defendant's credibility as a witness. If the defendant is a truthful witness, and if his silence is the consequence of his understanding of the *Miranda* warning, he may explain that fact when he is on the stand. Even if he is untruthful, the availability of that explanation puts him in a better position than if he had received no warning. In my judgment, the risk that a truthful defendant will be deceived by the *Miranda* warning and also will be unable to explain his honest misunderstanding is so much less than the risk that exclusion of the evidence will merely provide a shield for perjury that I cannot accept the Court's due process rationale.

Accordingly, if we assume that the use of a defendant's silence for impeachment purposes would be otherwise unobjectionable, I find no merit in the notion that he is denied due process of law because he received a *Miranda* warning.

NOTES AND QUESTIONS

(1) Justice Stevens asserted that the defendant was not prejudiced by the conduct of the government in *Doyle* because if he were truthful "and if his silence is the consequence of his understanding of the *Miranda* warning, he may explain that fact when he is on the stand. Even if he is untruthful, the availability of that explanation puts him in a better position than if he had received no warning." Is Justice Stevens correct in his analysis? Once *Miranda* warnings are given, why is the government prohibited from using the defendant's silence to impeach?

(2) In *Anderson v. Charles*, 447 U.S. 404 (1980), the Court, in a per curiam opinion, held that *Doyle* is not implicated when a prosecutor's cross-examination "merely inquires into prior inconsistent statements," even if some of the statements contained omissions (or silence) about certain facts. The defendant in *Charles* was arrested while driving a stolen car belonging to a murder victim. Shortly after his arrest, a detective advised the defendant of his *Miranda* rights and then interviewed the defendant about the stolen car. The defendant said that the car was stolen from the vicinity of Washtenaw and Hill streets in Ann Arbor. The defendant was later charged with first-degree murder. He testified at trial and added to the story he previously told the detective. Under oath, the defendant said that he stole the car from a Kelly's Tire Company. When cross-examined, the prosecutor suggested that the defendant had fabricated his testimony, asking: "Don't you think it's rather odd that if it were the truth that you didn't come forward and tell anybody at the time you were arrested, where you got that car?" The jury convicted the defendant of murder, and after his appeals were denied, he sought habeas review, relying on *Doyle*. The U.S. Supreme Court found *Doyle* inapposite, explaining that "a defendant who voluntarily speaks after receiving *Miranda* warnings has not been induced to remain silent. As to the subject matter of his statements, the defendant has not remained silent at all." *Id.* at 408. The Court concluded by finding

that the defendant's "descriptions of events may be said to involve 'silence' insofar as it omits facts included in the other version. But *Doyle* does not require any such formalistic understanding of 'silence[.]' " *Id.* at 409.

(3) In *Jenkins v. Anderson*, 447 U.S. 231 (1980), the defendant was convicted of manslaughter. He unsuccessfully contended at trial that he acted in self-defense. His defense was shaken by a showing at trial that for two weeks after the killing — but before his arrest — he did not tell the police about his involvement and self-defense contention. The district attorney questioned the defendant about his actions.

Q: Did you ever go to a Police Officer or to anyone else?

A: No, I didn't.

Q: As a matter of fact, it was two weeks later, wasn't it?

A: Yes.

Id. at 233. In closing argument to the jury, the prosecutor again referred to the defendant's pre-arrest silence, noting that "petitioner had waited two weeks, according to the testimony — at least two weeks before he did anything about surrendering himself or reporting [the stabbing] to anybody." Did the government's trial tactics violate *Doyle*?

(4) What result if the defendant remained silent after he was arrested but before he received the *Miranda* warnings? *See Fletcher v. Weir*, 455 U.S. 603 (1982). If such post-arrest, pre-*Miranda* silence is available as impeachment material, can the government use the silence in its case-in-chief also? *See United States v. Frazier*, 394 F.3d 612 (8th Cir. 2005); *compare United States v. Velarde-Gomez*, 269 F.3d 1023 (9th Cir. 2001). In *Salinas v. Texas*, 133 S. Ct. 2174 (2013), the Supreme Court held that a prosecutor may use an accused's pre-arrest, pre-*Miranda* silence as evidence of guilt. *See infra* § 7.04. The defendant in *Salinas* answered police questions for about an hour voluntarily before arrest. When questions turned uncomfortable, Salinas went quiet. He shuffled his feet and bit his lip. This silence and accompanying behavior was used at trial as evidence of guilt.

(5) Why does the Court allow the prosecution to use some statements obtained in violation of *Miranda*, when it precludes any use of statements deemed "involuntary" in violation of Due Process or the Fifth Amendment right against compelled self incrimination? Is there a constitutionally-based distinction between these rights? In *Dickerson v. United States*, 530 U.S. 428 (2000), the Court attempted to explain this difference in treatment. There, a defendant was charged with bank robbery and related crimes. He moved to exclude statements he made to FBI agents in the absence of *Miranda* warnings. The government contended that the statements were not excludable because, although admittedly made in violation of *Miranda*, the statements complied with Congressional mandates that the statements merely be voluntary. After the decision in *Miranda*, Congress had passed a statute making a confession admissible, if it were voluntarily given, regardless of the government's compliance with *Miranda*. Writing for the majority, Chief Justice Rehnquist first rejected the Fourth Circuit's reasoning that *Miranda* was not a constitutional holding. He referred to the *Miranda* decision as "constitutionally based" and explained that many cases following *Miranda* recognized

"*Miranda*'s constitutional underpinnings." Then, the majority attempted to explain the Court's previous decisions treating the exclusion of evidence obtained in violation of *Miranda* differently than it treats Fifth Amendment cases.

> The Court of Appeals also relied on the fact that we have, after our *Miranda* decision, made exceptions from its rule in cases such as *New York v. Quarles* and *Harris v. New York.* But we have also broadened the application of the *Miranda* doctrine in cases such as *Doyle v. Ohio* and *Arizona v. Roberson.* These decisions illustrate the principle — not that *Miranda* is not a constitutional rule — but that no constitutional rule is immutable. No court laying down a general rule can possibly foresee the various circumstances in which counsel will seek to apply it, and the sort of modifications represented by these cases are as much a normal part of constitutional law as the original decision.

Dickerson, 530 U.S. at 441. The majority added:

> The Court of Appeals also noted that in *Oregon v. Elstad*, 470 U.S. 298 (1985), we stated that " '[t]he *Miranda* exclusionary rule . . . serves the Fifth Amendment and sweeps more broadly than the Fifth Amendment itself.' " Our decision in that case — refusing to apply the traditional "fruits" doctrine developed in Fourth Amendment cases — does not prove that *Miranda* is a nonconstitutional decision, but simply recognizes the fact that unreasonable searches under the Fourth Amendment are different from unwarned interrogation under the Fifth Amendment.

Id. Was the Court's explanation convincing?

§ 6.03 THE FRUIT OF THE POISONOUS TREE

[A] The Principle

Not only can statements and other evidence obtained by the government's unconstitutional conduct be excluded from use at a defendant's criminal trial, but also secondary evidence derived from such evidence may be excluded as "fruit" of the "poisonous tree."

SILVERTHORNE LUMBER CO. v. UNITED STATES

United States Supreme Court
251 U.S. 385 (1920)

Mr. Justice Holmes delivered the opinion of the court.

The facts are simple. An indictment upon a single specific charge having been brought against the two Silverthornes mentioned, they both were arrested at their homes early in the morning of February 25, 1919, and were detained in custody a number of hours. While they were thus detained representatives of the Department of Justice and the United States Marshall without a shadow of authority went to the office of their company and made a clean sweep of all the books, papers and documents found there. All the employees were taken or directed to go to the office of the District Attorney of the United States to which also the books, etc., were taken at once. An application was made as soon as might be to the District Court for a return of what thus had been taken unlawfully. It was opposed by the District Attorney so far as he had found evidence against the plaintiffs in error, and it was stated that the evidence so obtained was before the grand jury.

Color had been given by the District Attorney to the approach of those concerned in the act by an invalid subpoena for certain documents relating to the charge in the indictment then on file. Thus the case is not that of knowledge acquired through the wrongful act of a stranger, but it must be assumed that the Government planned or at all events ratified the whole performance. Photographs and copies of material papers were made and a new indictment was framed based upon the knowledge thus obtained. The District Court ordered a return of the originals but impounded the photographs and copies. Subpoenas to produce the originals then were served and on the refusal of the plaintiffs in error to produce them the Court made an order that the subpoenas should be complied with, although it had found that all the papers had been seized in violation of the parties' constitutional rights. The refusal to obey this order is the contempt alleged. The Government now, while in form repudiating and condemning the illegal seizure, seeks to maintain its right to avail itself of the knowledge obtained by that means which otherwise it would not have had.

The proposition could not be presented more nakedly. It is that although of course its seizure was an outrage which the Government now regrets, it may study the papers before it returns them, copy them, and then may use the knowledge that it has gained to call upon the owners in a more regular form to produce them; that the protection of the Constitution covers the physical possession but not any advantages that the Government can gain over the object of its pursuit by doing the forbidden act. *Weeks v. United States* to be sure, had established that laying the papers directly before the grand jury was unwarranted, but it is taken to mean only that two steps are required instead of one. In our opinion such is not the law. It reduces the Fourth Amendment to a form of words. . . . The essence of a provision forbidding the acquisition of evidence in a certain way is that not merely evidence so acquired shall not be used before the Court but that it shall not be used at all.

WONG SUN v. UNITED STATES

United States Supreme Court
371 U.S. 471 (1963)

JUSTICE BRENNAN delivered the opinion of the Court.

The petitioners were tried without a jury in the District Court for the Northern District of California under a two-count indictment for violation of the Federal Narcotics Laws, 21 U.S.C. § 174. They were acquitted under the first count which charged a conspiracy, but convicted under the second count which charged the substantive offense of fraudulent and knowing transportation and concealment of illegally imported heroin. The Court of Appeals for the Ninth Circuit, one judge dissenting, affirmed the convictions.

About 2 a.m. on the morning of June 4, 1959, federal narcotics agents in San Francisco, after having had one Hom Way under surveillance for six weeks, arrested him and found heroin in his possession. Hom Way, who had not before been an informant, stated after his arrest that he had bought an ounce of heroin the night before from one known to him only as "Blackie Toy," proprietor of a laundry on Leavenworth Street.

About 6 a.m. that morning six or seven federal agents went to a laundry at 1733 Leavenworth Street. The sign above the door of this establishment said "Oye's Laundry." It was operated by the petitioner James Wah Toy. There is, however, nothing in the record which identifies James Wah Toy and "Blackie Toy" as the same person. The other federal officers remained nearby out of sight while Agent Alton Wong, who was of Chinese ancestry, rang the bell. When petitioner Toy appeared and opened the door, Agent Wong told him that he was calling for laundry and dry cleaning. Toy replied that he didn't open until 8 o'clock and told the agent to come back at that time. Toy started to close the door. Agent Wong thereupon took his badge from his pocket and said, "I am a federal narcotics agent." Toy immediately "slammed the door and started running" down the hallway through the laundry to his living quarters at the back where his wife and child were sleeping in a bedroom. Agent Wong and the other federal officers broke open the door and followed Toy down the hallway to the living quarters and into the bedroom. Toy reached into a nightstand drawer. Agent Wong thereupon drew his pistol, pulled Toy's hand out of the drawer, placed him under arrest and handcuffed him. There was nothing in the drawer and a search of the premises uncovered no narcotics.

One of the agents said to Toy " . . . [Hom Way] says he got narcotics from you." Toy responded, "No. I haven't been selling any narcotics at all. However, I do know somebody who has." When asked who that was, Toy said, "I only know him as Johnny. I don't know his last name." However, Toy described a house on Eleventh Avenue where he said Johnny lived; he also described a bedroom in the house where he said "Johnny kept about a piece" of heroin, and where he and Johnny had smoked some of the drug the night before. The agents left immediately for Eleventh Avenue and located the house. They entered and found one Johnny Yee in the bedroom. After a discussion with the agents, Yee took from a bureau drawer several tubes containing in all just less than one ounce of heroin, and surrendered them. Within the hour Yee and Toy were taken to the Office of the Bureau of Narcotics. Yee there stated that the heroin had been brought to him some four days earlier by petitioner Toy and another Chinese known to him only as "Sea Dog."

Toy was questioned as to the identity of "Sea Dog" and said that "Sea Dog" was Wong Sun. Some agents, including Agent Alton Wong, took Toy to Wong Sun's neighborhood where Toy pointed out a multifamily dwelling where he said Wong Sun lived. Agent Wong rang a downstairs door bell and a buzzer sounded, opening the door. The officer identified himself as a narcotics agent to a woman on the landing and asked "for Mr. Wong." The woman was the wife of petitioner Wong Sun. She said that Wong Sun was "in the back room sleeping." Alton Wong and the same six other officers climbed the stairs and entered the apartment. One of the officers went into the back room and brought petitioner Wong Sun from the bedroom in handcuffs. A thorough search of the apartment followed, but no narcotics were discovered.

Petitioner Toy and Johnny Yee were arraigned before a United States Commissioner on June 4 on a complaint charging a violation of 21 U.S.C. § 174. Later that day, each was released on his own recognizance. Petitioner Wong Sun was arraigned on a similar complaint filed the next day and was also released on his own recognizance. Within a few days, both petitioners and Yee were interrogated at the office of the Narcotics Bureau by Agent William Wong, also of Chinese ancestry. The agent advised each of the three of his right to withhold information which might be used against him, and stated to each that he was entitled to the advice of counsel, though it does not appear that any attorney was present during the questioning of any of the three. The officer also explained to each that no promises or offers of immunity of leniency were being or could be made.

The agent interrogated each of the three separately. After each had been interrogated the agent prepared a statement in English from rough notes. The agent read petitioner Toy's statement to him in English and interpreted certain portions of it for him in Chinese. Toy also read the statement in English aloud to the agent, said there were corrections to be made, and made the corrections in his own hand. Toy would not sign the statement, however; in the agent's words "he wanted to know first if the other persons involved in the case had signed theirs." Wong Sun had considerable difficulty understanding the statement in English and the agent restated its substance in Chinese. Wong Sun refused to sign the statement although he admitted the accuracy of its contents.

Hom Way did not testify at petitioners' trial. The Government offered Johnny Yee as its principal witness but excused him after he invoked the privilege against self-incrimination and flatly repudiated the statement he had given to Agent William Wong. That statement was not offered in evidence nor was any testimony elicited from him identifying either petitioner as the source of the heroin in his possession, or otherwise tending to support the charges against the petitioners.

The statute expressly provides that proof of the accused's possession of the drug will support a conviction under the statute unless the accused satisfactorily explains the possession. The Government's evidence tending to prove the petitioners' possession (the petitioners offered no exculpatory testimony) consisted of four items which the trial court admitted over timely objections that they were inadmissible as "fruits" of unlawful arrests or of attendant searches: (1) the statement made orally by petitioner Toy in his bedroom at the time of his arrest; (2) the heroin surrendered to the agent by Johnny Yee; (3) petitioner Toy's pretrial unsigned statement; and (4) petitioner Wong Sun's similar statement. The dispute below and here has centered around the correctness of the rulings of the trial judge allowing these items in evidence.

I

The Court of Appeals found there were neither reasonable grounds nor probable cause for Toy's arrest. Giving the weight to that finding, we think it is amply justified by the facts clearly shown on this record.

The narcotics agents had no basis in experience for confidence in the reliability of Hom Way's information; he had never before given information. And yet they acted upon his imprecise suggestion that a person described only as "Blackie Toy," the proprietor of a laundry somewhere on Leavenworth Street, had sold one ounce of heroin. We have held that identification of the suspect by a reliable informant may constitute probable cause for arrest where the information given is sufficiently accurate to lead the officers directly to the suspect. *Draper*. That rule does not, however, fit this case. For aught that the record discloses, Hom Way's accusation merely invited the officers to roam the length of Leavenworth Street (some 30 blocks) in search of one "Blackie Toy's" laundry — and whether by chance or other means (the record does not say) they came upon petitioner Toy's laundry, which bore not his name over the door, but the unrevealing label "Oye's." Not the slightest intimation appears on the record, or was made on oral argument, to suggest that the agents had information giving them reason to equate "Blackie" Toy and James Wah Toy — *e.g.*, that they had the criminal record of a Toy, or that they had consulted some other kind of official record or list, or had some information of some kind which had narrowed the scope of their search to this particular Toy.

The Government contends, however, that any defects in the information which somehow took the officers to petitioner Toy's laundry were remedied by events which occurred after they arrived. Specifically, it is urged that Toy's flight down the hall when the supposed customer at the door revealed that he was a narcotics agent adequately corroborates the suspicion generated by Hom Way's accusation. . . . In the instant case, Toy's flight from the door afforded no surer an inference of guilty knowledge. . . . Agent Wong did eventually disclose that he was a narcotics officer. However, he affirmatively misrepresented his mission at the outset, by stating that he had come for laundry and dry cleaning. And before Toy fled, the officer never adequately dispelled the misimpression engendered by his own ruse.

Moreover, he made no effort at that time, nor indeed at any time thereafter, to ascertain whether the man at the door was the "Blackie Toy" named by Hom Way. Therefore, this is not the case we hypothesized in *Miller* [v. United States] when "without an express announcement of purpose, the fact known to officers would justify them in being virtually certain" that the person at the door knows their purpose. Toy's refusal to admit the officers and his flight down the hallway thus signified a guilty knowledge no more clearly than it did a natural desire to repel an apparently unauthorized intrusion. Here, as in *Miller*, the Government claims no extraordinary circumstances such as the imminent destruction of vital evidence, or need to rescue a victim in peril which excused the officer's failure truthfully to state mission before he broke in.

II

It is conceded that Toy's declarations in his bedroom are to be excluded if they are held to be "fruits" of the agents' unlawful action.

The Government argues that Toy's statements to the officers in his bedroom, although closely consequent upon the invasion which we hold unlawful, were nevertheless admissible because they resulted from "an intervening independent act of a free will." This contention, however, takes insufficient account of the circumstances. Six or seven officers had broken the door and followed on Toy's heels into the bedroom where his wife and child were sleeping. He had been almost immediately handcuffed and arrested. Under such circumstances it is unreasonable to infer that Toy's response was sufficiently an act of free will to purge the primary taint of the unlawful invasion.

The Government also contends that Toy's declarations should be admissible because they were ostensibly exculpatory rather than incriminating. There are two answers to this argument. First, the statements soon turned out to be incriminating, for they led directly to the evidence which implicated Toy. Second, when circumstances are shown such as those which induced these declarations, it is immaterial whether the declarations be termed "exculpatory." Thus we find no substantial reason to omit Toy's declarations from the protection of the exclusionary rule.

III

We now consider whether the exclusion of Toy's declarations requires also the exclusion of the narcotics taken from Yee, to which those declarations led the police. The prosecutor candidly told the trial court that "we wouldn't have found those drugs except that Mr. Toy helped us to." Hence this is not the case envisioned by this Court where the exclusionary rule has no application because the Government learned of the evidence "from an independent source," *Silverthorne Lumber Co. v. United States*, . . . nor is this a case in which the connection between the lawless conduct of the police and the discovery of the challenged evidence has "become so attenuated as to dissipate the taint." We need not hold that all evidence is "fruit of the poisonous tree" simply because it would not have come to light but for the illegal actions of the police. Rather, the more apt question in such a case is "whether, granting establishment of the primary illegality, the evidence to which instant objection is made has been come at by exploitation of that illegality or instead by means sufficiently distinguishable to be purged of the primary taint." We think it clear that the narcotics were "come at by the exploitation of that illegality" and hence that they may not be used against Toy.

IV

It remains only to consider Toy's unsigned statement. We need not decide whether, in light of the fact that Toy was free on his own recognizance when he made the statement, that statement was a fruit of the illegal arrest. Since we have concluded that his declarations in the bedroom and the narcotics surrendered by Yee should not have been admitted in evidence against him, the only proofs remaining to sustain his conviction are his and Wong Sun's unsigned statements. Without scrutinizing the contents of Toy's ambiguous recitals, we conclude that no reference to Toy in Wong Sun's statement constitutes admissible evidence corroborating any admission by Toy. We arrive at this conclusion upon two clear lines of decisions which converge to require it. One line of our decisions establishes that criminal confessions and admissions of guilt require extrinsic corroboration; the other line of precedents holds that an out-of-court declaration made after arrest may not be used at trial against one of the declarant's partners in crime.

V

We turn now to the case of the other petitioner, Wong Sun. We have no occasion to disagree with the finding of the Court of Appeals that his arrest, also, was without probable cause or reasonable grounds. At all events no evidentiary consequences turn upon that question. For Wong Sun's unsigned confession was not the fruit of that arrest, and was therefore properly admitted at trial. On the evidence that Wong Sun had been released on his own recognizance after a lawful arraignment, and had returned voluntarily several days later to make the statement, we hold that the connection between the arrest and the statement had "become so attenuated as to dissipate the taint." The fact that the statement was unsigned, whatever bearing this may have upon its weight and credibility does not render it inadmissible; Wong Sun understood and adopted its substance, though he could not comprehend the English words. The petitioner has never suggested any impropriety in the interrogation itself which would require the exclusion of this statement.

We must then consider the admissibility of the narcotics surrendered by Yee. Our holding, *supra*, that this ounce of heroin was inadmissible against Toy does not compel a like result with respect to Wong Sun. The exclusion of the narcotics as to Toy was required solely by their tainted relationship to information unlawfully obtained from Toy, and not by any official impropriety connected with their surrender by Yee. The seizure of this heroin invaded no right of privacy of person or premises which would entitle Wong Sun to object to its use at his trial.

However, for the reasons that Wong Sun's statement was incompetent to corroborate Toy's admissions contained in Toy's own statement, any references to Wong Sun in Toy's statement were incompetent to corroborate Wong Sun's admissions. Thus, the only competent source of corroboration for Wong Sun's statement was the heroin itself. We cannot be certain, however, on this state of the record, that the trial judge may not also have considered the contents of Toy's statements as a source of corroboration. Petitioner raised as one ground of objection to the introduction of the statements the claim that each statement, "even if it were a purported admission or confession or declaration against interest of a defendant . . . would not be binding upon the other defendant." The trial judge, in allowing the statements in, apparently overruled all of petitioners' objections, including this one. Thus we presume that he considered all portions of both statements as bearing upon the guilt of both petitioners.

We intimate no view one way or the other as to whether the trial judge might have found in the narcotics alone sufficient evidence to corroborate Wong Sun's admissions that he delivered heroin to Yee and smoked heroin at Yee's house around the date in question. But because he might, as the factfinder, have found insufficient corroboration from the narcotics alone, we cannot be sure that the scales were not tipped in favor of conviction by reliance upon the inadmissible Toy statement. This is particularly important because of the nature of the offense involved here.

Surely, under the narcotics statute, the discovery of heroin raises a presumption that someone — generally the possessor — violated the law. As to him, once possession alone is proved, the other elements of the offense — transportation and concealment with knowledge of the illegal importation of the drug — need not be separately demonstrated, much less corroborated. Thus particular care ought to be taken in this area, when the crucial element of the accused's possession is proved solely by his own admissions, that the requisite corroboration be found among the evidence which is properly before the trier of facts. We therefore hold that petitioner Wong Sun is also entitled to a new trial.

The judgment of the Court of Appeals is reversed and the case is remanded to the District Court for further proceedings consistent with this opinion.

NOTES AND QUESTIONS

(1) Applying contemporary constitutional standards, could a warrant have been obtained for the arrest of "Blackie Toy"? If not, would a warrantless arrest under the circumstances described have been constitutional?

(2) Suppose Johnny Yee is convicted of the possession of heroin. Can he claim a violation of his Fourth Amendment rights in the seizure of the heroin?

(3) What is the justification for excluding the heroin seized from Yee from the prosecution of Toy but not from the prosecution of Wong Sun?

[B] The "Tree" Matters

The fruit of the poisonous tree principle applies when the government violates the Fourth Amendment, the Due Process Clause, the guarantee against compelled self-incrimination, and for violations of the Sixth Amendment right to counsel. Nevertheless, despite the decision's constitutional status, *see Dickerson v. United States*, 530 U.S. 428 (2000), *supra*, violations of *Miranda* receive less "fruit" protection.

MICHIGAN v. TUCKER

United States Supreme Court
417 U.S. 433 (1974)

JUSTICE REHNQUIST delivered the opinion of the Court.

This case presents the question whether the testimony of a witness in respondent's state court trial for rape must be excluded simply because police had learned the identity of the witness by questioning respondent at a time when he was in custody as a suspect, but had not been advised that counsel would be appointed for him if he was indigent. The questioning took place before this Court's decision in *Miranda*, but respondent's trial, at which he was convicted, took place afterwards. Therefore, *Miranda* is applicable to this case.

I

On the morning of April 19, 1966, a 43-year-old woman in Pontiac, Michigan was found in her home by a friend and coworker, Luther White, in serious condition. At the time she was found the woman was tied, gagged, and partially disrobed, and had been both raped and severely beaten. She was unable to tell White anything about her assault at that time and still remains unable to recollect what happened.

While White was attempting to get medical help for the victim and to call for the police, he observed a dog inside the house. This apparently attracted White's attention for he knew that the woman did not own a dog herself. Later, when talking with police officers, White observed the dog a second time, and police followed the dog to respondent's house. Neighbors further connected the dog with respondent.

The police then arrested respondent and brought him to the police station for questioning. Prior to the actual interrogation the police asked respondent whether he knew for what crime he had been arrested, whether he wanted an attorney, and whether he understood his constitutional rights. Respondent replied that he did understand the crime for which he was arrested, that he did not want an attorney, and that he understood his rights. The police further advised him that any statements he might make could be used against him at a later date in court. The police, however, did not advise respondent that he would be furnished counsel free of charge if he could not pay for such services himself.

The police then questioned respondent about his activities on the night of the rape and assault. Respondent replied that during the general time period at issue he had first been with one Robert Henderson and then later at home, alone, asleep. The police sought to confirm this story by contacting Henderson, but Henderson's story served to discredit rather than to bolster respondent's account. Henderson acknowledged that respondent had been with him on the night of the crime but said that he had left at a relatively early time. Furthermore, Henderson told police that he saw respondent the following day and asked him at that time about scratches on his face — "asked him if he got hold of a wild one or something." Respondent answered: "[S]omething like that." Then, Henderson said, he asked respondent "who it was," and respondent said: "[S]ome woman lived the next block over," adding: "She is a widow woman" or words to that effect.

Prior to trial respondent's appointed counsel made a motion to exclude Henderson's expected testimony because respondent had revealed Henderson's identity without having received full *Miranda* warnings. Although respondent's own statements taken during interrogation were excluded, the trial judge denied the motion to exclude Henderson's testimony. Henderson therefore testified at trial, and respondent was convicted of rape and sentenced to 20 to 40 years' imprisonment. His conviction was affirmed by both the Michigan Court of Appeals and the Michigan Supreme Court.

. . .

II

Although respondent's sole complaint is that the police failed to advise him that he would be given free counsel if unable to afford counsel himself, he did not, and does not now, base his arguments for relief on a right to counsel under the Sixth and Fourteenth Amendments. Nor was the right to counsel, as such, considered to be persuasive by either federal court below.

. . .

Respondent's argument, and the opinions of the District Court and Court of Appeals, instead rely upon the Fifth Amendment right against compulsory self-incrimination and the safeguards designed in *Miranda* to secure that right. In brief, the position urged upon this Court is that proper regard for the privilege against compulsory self-incrimination requires, with limited exceptions not applicable here, that all evidence derived solely from statements made without full *Miranda* warnings be excluded at a subsequent criminal trial. For purposes of analysis in this case we believe that the question thus presented is best examined in two separate parts. We will therefore first consider whether the police conduct complained of directly infringed upon respondent's right against compulsory self-incrimination or whether it instead violated only the prophylactic rules developed to protect that right. We will then consider whether the evidence derived from this interrogation must be excluded.

III

The history of the Fifth Amendment right against compulsory self-incrimination, and the evils against which it was directed, have received considerable attention in the opinions of this Court. At this point in our history virtually every schoolboy is familiar with the concept, if not the language, of the provision that reads: "No person . . . shall be compelled in any criminal case to be a witness against himself. . . ." This Court's decisions have referred to the right as "the mainstay of our adversary system of criminal justice," and as "one of the great landmarks in man's struggle to make himself civilized." It is not surprising that the constitution of virtually every State has a comparable provision.

. . .

A comparison of the facts in this case with the historical circumstances underlying the privilege against compulsory self-incrimination strongly indicates that the police conduct here did not deprive respondent of his privilege against compulsory self-incrimination as such, but rather failed to make available to him the full measure of procedural safeguards associated with that right since *Miranda*. Certainly no one could contend that the interrogation faced by respondent bore any resemblance to the historical practices at which the right against compulsory self-incrimination was aimed. The District Court in this case noted that the police had "warned (respondent) that he had the right to remain silent," and the record in this case clearly shows that respondent was informed that any evidence taken could be used against him. The record is also clear that respondent was asked whether he wanted an attorney and that he replied that he did not. Thus, his statements could hardly be termed involuntary as that term has been defined in the decisions of this Court. Additionally, there were no legal sanctions, such as the threat of contempt, which could have been applied to respondent had he chosen to remain silent. He was simply not exposed to "the cruel trilemma of self-accusation, perjury or contempt."

Our determination that the interrogation in this case involved no compulsion sufficient to breach the right against compulsory self-incrimination does not mean there was not a disregard, albeit an inadvertent disregard, of the procedural rules later established in *Miranda*. The question for decision is how sweeping the judicially imposed consequences of this disregard shall be. This Court said in

Miranda that statements taken in violation of the *Miranda* principles must not be used to prove the prosecution's case at trial. That requirement was fully complied with by the state court here: respondent's statements, claiming that he was with Henderson and then asleep during the time period of the crime were not admitted against him at trial. This Court has also said, in *Wong Sun*, that the "fruits" of police conduct which actually infringed a defendant's Fourth Amendment rights must be suppressed. But we have already concluded that the police conduct at issue here did not abridge respondent's constitutional privilege against compulsory self-incrimination, but departed only from the prophylactic standards later laid down by this Court in *Miranda* to safeguard that privilege. Thus, in deciding whether Henderson's testimony must be excluded, there is no controlling precedent of this Court to guide us. We must therefore examine the matter as a question of principle.

. . .

IV

The statements actually made by respondent to the police, as we have observed, were excluded at trial in accordance with *Johnson v. New Jersey*, 384 U.S. 710 (1966). Whatever deterrent effect on future police conduct the exclusion of those statements may have had, we do not believe it would be significantly augmented by excluding the testimony of the witness Henderson as well.

When involuntary statements or the right against compulsory self-incrimination are involved, a second justification for the exclusionary rule also has been asserted: protection of the courts from reliance on untrustworthy evidence. Cases which involve the Self-Incrimination Clause must, by definition, involve an element of coercion, since the Clause provides only that a person shall not be compelled to give evidence against himself. And cases involving statements often depict severe pressures which may override a particular suspect's insistence on innocence. Fact situations ranging from classical third-degree torture, to prolonged isolation from family or friends in a hostile setting, or to a simple desire on the part of a physically or mentally exhausted suspect to have a seemingly endless interrogation end, all might be sufficient to cause a defendant to accuse himself falsely.

But those situations are a far cry from that presented here. The pressures on respondent to accuse himself were hardly comparable even with the least prejudicial of those pressures which have been dealt within our cases. More important, the respondent did not accuse himself. The evidence which the prosecution successfully sought to introduce was not a confession of guilt by respondent, or indeed even an exculpatory statement by respondent, but rather the testimony of a third party who was subjected to no custodial pressures. There is plainly no reason to believe that Henderson's testimony is untrustworthy simply because respondent was not advised of his right to appointed counsel. Henderson was both available at trial and subject to cross-examination by respondent's counsel, and counsel fully used this opportunity, suggesting in the course of his cross-examination that Henderson's character was less than exemplary and that he had been offered incentives by the police to testify against respondent. Thus the reliability of his testimony was subject to the normal testing process of an adversary trial.

. . .

Here we deal, not with the offer of respondent's own statements in evidence, but only with the testimony of a witness whom the police discovered as a result of respondent's statements. This recourse to respondent's voluntary statements does no violence to such elements of the adversary system as may be embodied in the Fifth, Sixth, and Fourteenth Amendments.

In summary, we do not think that any single reason supporting exclusion of this witness' testimony, or all of them together, are very persuasive. By contrast, we find the arguments in favor of admitting the testimony quite strong. For, when balancing the interests involved, we must weigh the strong interest under any system of justice of making available to the trier of fact all concededly relevant and trustworthy evidence which either party seeks to adduce. In this particular case we also "must consider society's interest in the effective prosecution of criminals in light of the protection our pre-*Miranda* standards afford criminal defendants." These interests may be outweighed by the need to provide an effective sanction to a constitutional right, *Weeks*, but they must in any event be valued. Here respondent's own statement, which might have helped the prosecution show respondent's guilty conscience at trial, had already been excised from the prosecution's case pursuant to this Court's *Johnson* decision. To extend the excision further under the circumstances of this case and exclude relevant testimony of a third-party witness would require far more persuasive arguments than those advanced by respondent.

This Court has already recognized that a failure to give interrogated suspects full *Miranda* warnings does not entitle the suspect to insist that statements made by him be excluded in every conceivable context. *Harris.*

We believe that this reasoning is equally applicable here. Although *Johnson* enabled respondent to block admission of his own statements, we do not believe that it requires the prosecution to refrain from all use of those statements, and we disagree with the courts below that Henderson's testimony should have been excluded in this case.

[Justice Stewart filed a concurring opinion. Justice Brennan filed a concurring opinion in which Justice Marshall joined. Justice White filed a concurring opinion, and Justice Douglas dissented.]

NOTES AND QUESTIONS
CONSECUTIVE CONFESSIONS

(1) In *Oregon v. Elstad*, 470 U.S. 298 (1985), the defendant confessed without receiving *Miranda* warnings. Thereafter, he was given the warnings, and he gave a more detailed confession a second time. The first confession was inadmissible under *Miranda.* What about the second confession? Justice O'Connor explained why it was admissible:

> The relevant inquiry is whether, in fact, the second statement was also voluntarily made. As in any such inquiry, the finder of fact must examine the surrounding circumstances and the entire course of police conduct with

> respect to the suspect in evaluating the voluntariness of his statements. The fact that a suspect chooses to speak after being informed of his rights is, of course, highly probative. We find that the dictates of *Miranda* and the goals of the Fifth Amendment proscription against use of compelled testimony are fully satisfied in the circumstances of this case by barring use of the unwarned statement in the case in chief. No further purpose is served by imputing "taint" to subsequent statements obtained pursuant to a voluntary and knowing waiver. We hold today that a suspect who has once responded to unwarned yet uncoercive questioning is not thereby disabled from waiving his rights and confessing after he has been given the requisite *Miranda* warnings.

Id. at 318.

Does the holding in *Elstad* allow for all consecutive confessions under a voluntariness test? No, said a divided Court in *Missouri v. Seibert*, 542 U.S. 600 (2004). Justice Souter, joined by Justices Stevens, Ginsburg, and Breyer, reasoned:

> The threshold issue when interrogators question first and warn later is thus whether it would be reasonable to find that in these circumstances the warnings could function "effectively" as *Miranda* requires. Could the warnings effectively advise the suspect that he had a real choice about giving an admissible statement at that juncture? Could they reasonably convey that he could choose to stop talking even if he had talked earlier? For unless the warnings could place a suspect who has just been interrogated in a position to make such an informed choice, there is no practical justification for accepting the formal warnings as compliance with *Miranda* or for treating the second stage of interrogation as distinct from the first, unwarned and inadmissible segment.

542 U.S. at 611-12. Then, Justice Souter distinguished *Elstad.*

> Although the *Elstad* Court expressed no explicit conclusion about either officer's state of mind, it is fair to read *Elstad* as treating the living room conversation as a good-faith *Miranda* mistake, not only open to correction by careful warnings before systematic questioning in that particular case, but posing no threat to warn-first practice generally.
>
> The contrast between *Elstad* and this case reveals a series of relevant facts that bear on whether *Miranda* warnings delivered midstream could be effective enough to accomplish their object: the completeness and detail of the questions and answers in the first round of interrogation, the overlapping content of the two statements, the timing and setting of the first and the second, the continuity of police personnel, and the degree to which the interrogator's questions treated the second round as continuous with the first. In *Elstad* it was not unreasonable to see the occasion for questioning at the station house as presenting a markedly different experience from the short conversation at home; since a reasonable person in the suspect's shoes could have seen the station house questioning as a new and distinct experience, the *Miranda* warnings could have made sense as presenting a genuine choice whether to follow up on the earlier admission.

> At the opposite extreme are the facts here, which by any objective measure reveal a police strategy adapted to undermine the *Miranda* warnings. The unwarned interrogation was conducted in the station house, and the questioning was systematic, exhaustive, and managed with psychological skill. When the police were finished there was little, if anything, of incriminating potential left unsaid. The warned phase of questioning proceeded after a pause of only 15 to 20 minutes, in the same place as the unwarned segment. When the same officer who had conducted the first phase recited the *Miranda* warnings, he said nothing to counter the probable misimpression that the advice that anything Seibert said could be used against her also applied to the details of the inculpatory statement previously elicited. In particular, the police did not advise that her prior statement could not be used. Nothing was said or done to dispel the oddity of warning about legal rights to silence and counsel right after the police had led her through a systematic interrogation. . . . These circumstances must be seen as challenging the comprehensibility and efficacy of the *Miranda* warnings to the point that a reasonable person in the suspect's shoes would not have understood them to convey a message that she retained a choice about continuing to talk. . . .
>
> Strategists dedicated to draining the substance out of *Miranda* cannot accomplish by training instructions what *Dickerson* held Congress could not do by statute. Because the question-first tactic effectively threatens to thwart *Miranda*'s purpose of reducing the risk that a coerced confession would be admitted, and because the facts here do not reasonably support a conclusion that the warnings given could have served their purpose, Seibert's postwarning statements are inadmissible.

Id. 615-17.

Justice Kennedy concurred in the judgment but wrote separately:

> The interrogation technique used in this case is designed to circumvent *Miranda*. It undermines the *Miranda* warning and obscures its meaning. The plurality opinion is correct to conclude that statements obtained through the use of this technique are inadmissible. Although I agree with much in the careful and convincing opinion for the plurality, my approach does differ in some respects, requiring this separate statement.
>
> . . .
>
> Evidence is admissible when the central concerns of *Miranda* are not likely to be implicated and when other objectives of the criminal justice system are best served by its introduction. Thus, we have held that statements obtained in violation of the rule can be used for impeachment, so that the truth-finding function of the trial is not distorted by the defense, see *Harris*; that there is an exception to protect countervailing concerns of public safety, see *Quarles*; and that physical evidence obtained in reliance on statements taken in violation of the rule is admissible, *Patane*. These cases, in my view, are correct. They recognize that admission of evidence is proper when it would further important objectives without compromising

> *Miranda*'s central concerns. Under these precedents, the scope of the *Miranda* suppression remedy depends on a consideration of those legitimate interests and on whether admission of the evidence under the circumstances would frustrate *Miranda*'s central concerns and objectives.
>
> . . .
>
> This case presents different considerations. The police used a two-step questioning technique based on a deliberate violation of *Miranda*. The *Miranda* warning was withheld to obscure both the practical and legal significance of the admonition when finally given.

Id. at 618-20.

As shown by *Seibert*, the decision in *Elstad* saves many confessions from exclusion, but it does not allow the admission of all warned statements. The Seventh Circuit has declared that a second, voluntary, and Mirandized statement will be excluded when it follows too closely from an involuntary and non-Mirandized confession. In *United States v. Swanson*, 635 F.3d 995 (7th Cir. 2011), the court deemed the accused's first unwarned statement to be involuntary and distinguished *Elstad*. "We have found that Swanson's initial statements were not voluntary. So in deciding whether Swanson's Mirandized second written statement is insulated from the taint of the first statements we consider whether there has been a sufficient break in the stream of events."

(2) In *Martinez v. State*, 272 S.W. 3d 615 (Tex. Crim. App. 2008), the Court of Criminal Appeals of Texas quoted heavily from Justice Kennedy's concurring opinion in *Seibert*. The court granted the defendant's petition for discretionary review to decide whether the Texas Court of Appeals "misapplied the standards of *Seibert*." The record on appeal revealed: (1) the defendant was arrested for capital murder; (2) the arresting officer did not advise the defendant of his rights under *Miranda* at the time of arrest; (3) two officers, including the arresting officer, questioned the defendant about the murder at the police station shortly after the arrest without giving the required warnings; (4) the defendant was then subjected to a polygraph examination without being told that he was under no obligation to submit to the exam; (5) the identity of the examiner and the content of the polygraph-examination questions were not included in the trial or appellate record; and (6) a magistrate judge read the *Miranda* warnings to the defendant only after both the first round of interrogation and the polygraph examination. *Id.* at 622. The Texas Criminal Appeals court concluded: "Based on these facts, we have determined that 'the two-step interrogation technique was used in a calculated way to undermine the *Miranda* warning. . . .' " *Id.* at 623 (citing *Seibert* (Kennedy, J., concurring)).

In *Bobby v. Dixon*, 132 S. Ct. 26 (2011), the Court found no two-step interrogation technique of the type discussed in *Seibert* although police first interrogated the defendant without *Miranda* warnings, fearing that the defendant would refuse to talk if warned. Defendant Dixon was interrogated three times. The first occurred during a "chance encounter" with police when Dixon was not in custody. He was issued *Miranda* warnings. He refused to answer questions without his lawyer present. Five days later, while in custody after his arrest, Dixon was interrogated a second time without warnings. He admitted to forgery but denied any involvement in murder. Later that same day, Dixon was Mirandized and inculpated himself in a murder. In distinguishing *Seibert*, the per curiam decision stressed that during his first, unwarned interrogation, Dixon claimed to have no involvement in the murder. His contradiction in stories was different than the defendant's situation in *Seibert* in which the "suspect's first, unwarned interrogation left 'little, if anything, of incriminating potential left unsaid,' making it 'unnatural' not to 'repeat at the second stage' " of interrogation. The Court in *Dixon* saw no nexus between the unwarned admission to forgery and the later, warned admission of murder. Unlike *Seibert*, there was also a break in time and circumstances between the unwarned and warned interrogations. And, there was no question in *Dixon* that both the warned and unwarned confessions were voluntary, involving no "actual compulsion."

(3) In *United States v. Patane*, 542 U.S. 630 (2004), a post-*Dickerson* case, a sorely divided Court considered whether an officer's failure to give a suspect *Miranda* warnings requires suppression of physical evidence resulting from the suspect's unwarned, but voluntary statements. Justices Thomas, Rehnquist, and Scalia declared that the *Miranda* rule is merely "a prophylactic employed to protect against violations of the Self-Incrimination Clause" and that self -incrimination is "not implicated" by the admission of "physical fruit of a voluntary statement." *Id.* at 636. Justice Kennedy, joined by Justice O'Connor, wrote a separate concurring opinion, which relied heavily on the precedents of *Elstad*, *Quarles*, and *Harris*. They concluded that the government's case in *Patane* was

> even stronger . . . for admitting the evidence obtained as the result of Patane's unwarned statement. Admission of nontestimonial physical fruits ([a] Glock in this case), even more so than the postwarning statements to the police in *Elstad* and *Tucker*, does not run the risk of admitting into trial an accused's coerced incriminating statements against himself.

Id. at 645. Justice Souter wrote a dissent in which Justices Stevens and Ginsburg joined, contending that the plurality was providing "an evidentiary advantage to those who ignore *Miranda*" and offering "an important inducement for interrogators to ignore the rule in that case." *Id.* In his own dissent, Justice Breyer reiterated his views from *Seibert*, that physical evidence derived from questioning without *Miranda* warnings should be excluded unless officers' failure was made "in good faith." *Id.* at 648.

(4) The defendant in *Fellers v. United States*, 540 U.S. 519 (2004), was arrested after having been indicted. At that point he made incriminating statements and later, at the jail, was told of his *Miranda* rights and made additional and similar incriminating statements. He moved to suppress the statements which had been made after indictment and before the warnings, and also to exclude the later jail-house statements. Fellers contended that the latter statements were "tainted" by the earlier and should be viewed as inadmissible fruits of the poisonous tree. The court of appeals allowed the later statements in evidence, finding that under a Fifth Amendment fruit of the poisonous tree analysis, no constitutional violation had occurred. A unanimous Supreme Court rejected that view. The Court agreed that the earlier statements were inadmissible under the Sixth Amendment, as they had been "deliberately elicited" by the police. As to the later statements, however, the

Court chose not to decide. It held that the court of appeals had applied the wrong standard. "The Court of Appeals did not reach the question whether the Sixth Amendment requires suppression of petitioner's jailhouse statements on the ground that they were the fruits of previous questions conducted in violation of the Sixth Amendment deliberate-elicitation standard." On remand the Eighth Circuit did not require exclusion because "the use of the exclusionary rule in this case would serve neither deterrence nor any other goal of the Sixth Amendment." 397 F.3d 1090, 1095 (8th Cir. 2005).

[C] Limits to the Exclusion of "Fruit"

[1] The Independent Source Exception

SEGURA v. UNITED STATES
United States Supreme Court
468 U.S. 796 (1984)

The Chief Justice delivered the opinion of the Court.

. . .

II

In January 1981, the New York Drug Enforcement Task Force received information indicating that petitioners Andres Segura and Luz Marina Colon probably were trafficking in cocaine from their New York apartment. Acting on this information, Task Force agents maintained continuous surveillance over petitioners until their arrest on February 12, 1981. On February 9, agents observed a meeting between Segura and Enrique Rivudalla-Vidal, during which, as it later developed, the two discussed the possible sale of cocaine by Segura to Rivudalla-Vidal. Three days later, February 12, Segura telephoned Rivudalla-Vidal and agreed to provide him with cocaine. The two agreed that the delivery would be made at 5 p.m. that day at a designated fast-food restaurant in Queens. Rivudalla-Vidal and one Esther Parra, arrived at the restaurant at 5 p.m., as agreed. While Segura and Rivudalla-Vidal visited inside the restaurant, agents observed Luz Marina Colon deliver a bulky package to Parra, who had remained in Rivudalla-Vidal's car in the restaurant parking lot. A short time after the delivery of the package, Rivudalla-Vidal and Parra left the restaurant and proceeded to their apartment. Task Force agents followed. The agents stopped the couple as they were about to enter Rivudalla-Vidal's apartment. Parra was found to possess cocaine; both Rivudalla-Vidal and Parra were immediately arrested.

After Rivudalla-Vidal and Parra were advised of their constitutional rights, Rivudalla-Vidal agreed to cooperate with the agents. He admitted that he had purchased the cocaine from Segura and he confirmed that Colon had made the delivery at the fast-food restaurant earlier that day, as the agents had observed. Rivudalla-Vidal informed the agents that Segura was to call him at approximately

10 o'clock that evening to learn if Rivudalla-Vidal had sold the cocaine, in which case Segura was to deliver additional cocaine.

Between 6:30 and 7 p.m., the same day, Task Force agents sought and received authorization from an Assistant United States Attorney to arrest Segura and Colon. The agents were advised by the Assistant United States Attorney that because of the lateness of the hour, a search warrant for petitioners' apartment probably could not be obtained until the following day, but that the agents should proceed to secure the premises to prevent the destruction of evidence.

At about 7:30 p.m., the agents arrived at petitioners' apartment and established external surveillance. At 11:15 p.m., Segura, alone, entered the lobby of the apartment building where he was immediately arrested by agents. He first claimed he did not reside in the building. The agents took him to his third floor apartment, and when they knocked on the apartment door, a woman later identified as Luz Colon appeared; the agents then entered with Segura, without requesting or receiving permission. There were three persons in the living room of the apartment in addition to Colon. Those present were informed by the agents that Segura was under arrest and that a search warrant for the apartment was being obtained.

Following this brief exchange in the living room, the agents conducted a limited security check of the apartment to ensure that no one else was there who might pose a threat to their safety or destroy evidence. In the process, the agents observed, in a bedroom in plain view, a triple-beam scale, jars of lactose, and numerous small cellophane bags, all accouterments of drug trafficking. None of these items was disturbed by the agents. After this limited security check, Luz Colon was arrested. In the search incident to her arrest, agents found in her purse a loaded revolver and more than $2,000 in cash. Colon, Segura, and the other occupants of the apartment were taken to Drug Enforcement Administration headquarters.

Two Task Force agents remained in petitioners' apartment awaiting the warrant. Because of what is characterized as "administrative delay" the warrant application was not presented to the magistrate until 5 p.m. the next day. The warrant was issued and the search was performed at approximately 6 p.m., some 19 hours after the agents' initial entry into the apartment. In the search pursuant to the warrant, agents discovered almost three pounds of cocaine, 18 rounds of.38-caliber ammunition fitting the revolver agents had found in Luz Colon's possession at the time of her arrest, more than $50,000 cash, and records of narcotics transactions. Agents seized these items, together with those observed during the security check the previous night.

III

[T]he Court of Appeals agreed with the District Court that the initial warrantless entry, and the limited security search were not justified by exigent circumstances and were therefore illegal. No review of that aspect of the case was sought by the Government and no issue concerning items observed during the initial entry is before the Court. The only issue here is whether drugs and the other items not observed during the initial entry and first discovered by the agents the day after the entry, under an admittedly valid search warrant should have been suppressed.

. . .

V

Whether the initial entry was illegal or not is irrelevant to the admissibility of the challenged evidence because there was an independent source for the warrant under which that evidence was seized. Exclusion of evidence as derivative or "fruit of the poisonous tree" is not warranted because of that independent source.

None of the information on which the warrant was secured was derived from or related in any way to the initial entry into petitioners' apartment; the information came from sources wholly unconnected with the entry and was known to the agents well before the initial entry. No information obtained during the initial entry or occupation of the apartment was needed or used by the agents to secure the warrant. It is therefore beyond dispute that the information possessed by the agents before they entered the apartment constituted an independent source for the discovery and seizure of the evidence now challenged. This evidence was discovered the day following the entry, during the search conducted under a valid warrant; it was the product of that search, wholly unrelated to the prior entry. Had the police never entered the apartment, but instead conducted a perimeter stake out to prevent anyone from entering the apartment and destroying evidence, the contraband now challenged would have been discovered and seized precisely as it was here. The legality of the initial entry is, thus, wholly irrelevant under *Wong Sun* and *Silverthorne.*

The dissent contends that the initial entry and securing of the premises are the "but for" causes of the discovery of the evidence in that, had the agents not entered the apartment, but instead secured the premises from the outside, Colon or her friends if alerted, could have removed or destroyed the evidence before the warrant issued. While the dissent embraces this "reasoning," petitioners do not press this argument. The Court of Appeals rejected this argument as "prudentially unsound" and because it rested on "wholly speculative assumptions." Among other things, the Court of Appeals suggested that, had the agents waited to enter the apartment until the warrant issued, they might not have decided to take Segura to the apartment and thereby alert Colon. Or, once alerted by Segura's failure to appear, Colon might have attempted to remove the evidence, rather than destroy it, in which event the agents could have intercepted her and the evidence.

We agree fully with the Court of Appeals that the District Court's suggestion that Colon and her cohorts would have removed or destroyed the evidence was pure speculation. Even more important, however, we decline to extend the exclusionary rule, which already exacts an enormous price from society and our system of justice, to further "protect" criminal activity, as the dissent would have us do.

The essence of the dissent is that there is some "constitutional right" to destroy evidence. This concept defies both logic and common sense.

JUSTICE STEVENS, with whom JUSTICE BRENNAN, JUSTICE MARSHALL and JUSTICE BLACKMUN join, dissenting.

. . .

If Segura had not returned home at all that night, or during the next day, it is probable that the occupants of the apartment would have become concerned and might at least have destroyed the records of their illegal transactions, or removed some of the evidence. If one of the occupants had left the apartment and taken evidence with him or her during the 18-20 hour period prior to the execution of the search warrant, then obviously that evidence would not have been accessible to the agents when the warrant finally was executed. The District Court concluded that there was a possibility that the evidence's availability when the warrant was executed hinged solely on the illegal impoundment. . . .

The majority insists that the idea that access to evidence is a relevant consideration is "unsound" because it would "extend" the exclusionary rule and "further 'protect' criminal activity,". . . . However, this very point is far from novel; it actually has been the long-settled rule. It is implicit in virtually every case in which we have applied the exclusionary rule.

NOTES

(1) *Segura* was cited by the Supreme Court in *Illinois v. McArthur*, 531 U.S. 326 (2001), to sustain officers' refusal to permit the defendant to enter his residence unaccompanied while a search warrant was being obtained. But in *Commonwealth v. DeJesus*, 790 N.E.2d 231, 236 (Mass. 2003), the Supreme Court of Massachusetts held that the authority to secure a dwelling did not allow police officers to enter a dwelling to ascertain whether it was unoccupied. "[T]here is a fundamental difference between securing or controlling the perimeter of a dwelling from the outside and the entry and physical surveillance of a dwelling from the inside."

(2) The question left open in *Segura* (whether evidence observed in plain view at the time of the illegal entry could also be seized under a valid, after-acquired search warrant) was decided favorably to the government by a plurality in *Murray v. United States*, 487 U.S. 533, 537 (1988). Justice Scalia, joined by Chief Justice Rehnquist, and Justices White and Blackmun, agreed with the government that evidence initially discovered during an unlawful search need not be excluded at trial if the same evidence is later "obtained independently from activities untainted by the initial illegality." According to the plurality, the salient question is "whether the search pursuant to warrant was in fact a genuinely independent source of the information and tangible evidence[.]" *Id.* at 542.

(3) A panel of the Sixth Circuit recently decided that the government may use knowledge it obtains in violation of the Fourth Amendment, even if it may not use the physical evidence uncovered by an unconstitutional search. In *United States v. Fofana*, 666 F.3d 985, 986 (6th Cir. 2012), the court held: "Although the actual documentation seized during the search must be suppressed, evidence obtained legally and independently of the search is not suppressible, even if the Government cannot show that it would have discovered its significance without the illegal search." In *Fofana*, law enforcement conducted a concededly illegal search of

Fofana and his belongings at an airport. That search linked Fofana to a bank fraud scheme. The government lawfully obtained banking records, which proved the fraud, but the government would not have understood Fofana's connection to the bank fraud without viewing Fofana's belongings during the unconstitutional airport search. The Sixth Circuit declared:

> There is a difference between evidence that the Government *obtains* because of knowledge illegally acquired, and evidence properly in the Government's possession that it *learns the relevance of* because of knowledge illegally acquired.

Id. at 987. The court did not suggest that such information could always be used, but it concluded that the balance of interests in that case weighed against suppression. First, the bank records reflecting the fraud were obtained entirely through legal means. Second, the illegal airport search was not directed to the crime of bank fraud; therefore, the likelihood of deterrence of police illegality was slight. Third, a more effective deterrent — excluding physical evidence from the airport search — was available. Finally, exclusion of the bank records would "unduly burden[] the truth-seeking function of courts by effectively precluding relevant and legitimately obtained evidence from ever being used."

(4) In *United States v. Liss*, 103 F.3d 617 (7th Cir. 1997), officers had requested and received consent to seize a stolen motorcycle from a barn. Once within the barn, however, the officers continued to search for some four hours, far in excess of the consent granted, in the process discovering marijuana, vials of white powder and silencers, as well as what appeared to be a still. Once advised by a sergeant that their authority for the search was dubious, the officers returned to the accused and, after telling him that they had found some marijuana, induced him to sign a consent form authorizing the seizure of "anything illegal." After they found more marijuana, white powder, and firearms, the accused called a halt to the search. Thereafter, the officers returned with a search warrant, which they had obtained relying in part upon the discoveries made during the preceding searches. The accused contended that the second purported consent was the fruit of the prior illegal search and hence unconstitutional and that the warrant was the fruit of this illegal search and likewise invalid. Relying on *Murray*, the Seventh Circuit sustained the search, finding that the second consent was not tainted by the first, and finding irrelevant the fact that the officers would never have asked for the second consent but for what they had discovered in the prior illegal search.

[2] The Inevitable Discovery Exception

NIX v. WILLIAMS
United States Supreme Court
467 U.S. 431 (1984)

Chief Justice Burger delivered the opinion of the Court.

We granted certiorari to consider whether, at respondent Williams' second murder trial in state court, evidence pertaining to the discovery and condition of the victim's body was properly admitted on the ground that it would ultimately or inevitably have been discovered even if no violation of any constitutional or statutory provision had taken place.

I.A.

On December 24, 1968, 10-year-old Pamela Powers disappeared from a YMCA building in Des Moines, Iowa, where she had accompanied her parents to watch an athletic contest. Shortly after she disappeared, Williams was seen leaving the YMCA carrying a large bundle wrapped in a blanket; a 14-year-old boy who had helped Williams open his car door reported that he had seen "two legs in it and they were skinny and white."

Williams' car was found the next day 160 miles east of Des Moines in Davenport, Iowa. Later several items of clothing belonging to the child, some of Williams' clothing, and an army blanket like the one used to wrap the bundle that Williams carried out of the YMCA were found at a rest stop on Interstate 80 near Grinnell, between Des Moines and Davenport. A warrant was issued for Williams' arrest.

Police surmised that Williams had left Pamela Powers or her body somewhere between Des Moines and the Grinnell rest stop where some of the young girl's clothing had been found. On December 26, the Iowa Bureau of Criminal Investigation initiated a large-scale search. Two hundred volunteers divided into teams began the search 21 miles east of Grinnell, covering an area several miles to the north and south of Interstate 80. They moved westward from Poweshiek County, in which Grinnell was located, into Jasper County. Searchers were instructed to check all roads, abandoned farm buildings, ditches, culverts, and any other place in which the body of a small child could be hidden.

Meanwhile, Williams surrendered to local police in Davenport, where he was promptly arraigned. Williams contacted a Des Moines attorney who arranged for an attorney in Davenport to meet Williams at the Davenport police station. Des Moines police informed counsel they would pick Williams up in Davenport and return him to Des Moines without questioning him. Two Des Moines detectives then drove to Davenport, took Williams into custody, and proceeded to drive him back to Des Moines.

During the return trip, one of the policemen, Detective Leaming, began a conversation with Williams, saying:

> I want to give you something to think about while we're traveling down the road. . . . They are predicting several inches of snow for tonight, and I feel that you yourself are the only person that knows where this little girl's body is . . . and if you get a snow on top of it you yourself may be unable to find it. And since we will be going right past the area where the body is on the way into Des Moines, I feel that we could stop and locate the body, that the parents of this little girl should be entitled to a Christian burial for the little girl who was snatched away from them on Christmas [E]ve and murdered. . . . [A]fter a snow storm [we may not be] able to find it at all.

Leaming told Williams he knew the body was in the area of Mitchellville — a town they would be passing on the way to Des Moines. He concluded the conversation by saying, "I do not want you to answer me. . . . Just think about it. . . ."

Later, as the police car approached Grinnell, Williams asked Leaming whether the police had found the young girl's shoes. After Leaming replied that he was unsure, Williams directed the police to a point near a service station where he said he had left the shoes; they were not found. As they continued the drive to Des Moines, Williams asked whether the blanket had been found and then directed the officers to a rest area in Grinnell where he said he had disposed of the blanket; they did not find the blanket. At this point Leaming and his party were joined by the officers in charge of the search. As they approached Mitchellville, Williams, without any further conversation, agreed to direct the officers to the child's body.

The officers directing the search had called off the search at 3 p.m., when they left the Grinnell Police Department to join Leaming at the rest area. At that time, one search team near the Jasper County-Polk County line was only two and one-half miles from where Williams soon guided Leaming and his party to the body. The child's body was found next to a culvert in a ditch beside a gravel road in Polk County, about two miles south of Interstate 80, and essentially within the area to be searched.

[Williams' first conviction was overturned, the Supreme Court holding that Detective Leaming had obtained incriminating statements from him in violation of his Sixth Amendment right to counsel. *See Brewer v. Williams*, § 5.02, *supra*. The Court noted, however, that while the statements could not be admitted at a retrial, evidence regarding the body "might well be admissible on the theory that the body would have been discovered in any event, even had incriminating statements not been elicited from Williams." At a second trial in accordance with this opinion, Williams was again convicted, and the Supreme Court of Iowa affirmed, relying on the independent source exception to the exclusionary rule.]

C.

In 1980 Williams renewed his attack on the state-court conviction by seeking a writ of habeas corpus in the United States District Court for the Southern District of Iowa. The District Court conducted its own independent review of the evidence and concluded, as had the state courts, that the body would inevitably have been found by the searchers in essentially the same condition it was in when Williams led police to its discovery. The District Court denied Williams' petition.

. . .

The Court of Appeals for the Eighth Circuit reversed. . . . That court assumed, without deciding, that there is an inevitable discovery exception to the Exclusionary Rule and that the Iowa Supreme Court correctly stated that exception to require proof that the police did not act in bad faith and that the evidence would have been discovered absent any constitutional violation. In reversing the District Court's denial of habeas relief, the Court of Appeals stated:

> We hold that the State has not met the first requirement. It is therefore unnecessary to decide whether the state courts' finding that the body would have been discovered anyway is fairly supported by the record. It is also unnecessary to decide whether the State must prove the two elements of the exception by clear and convincing evidence, as defendant argues, or by a preponderance of the evidence, as the state courts held.
>
> The state trial court, in denying the motion to suppress, made no finding one way or the other on the question of bad faith. Its opinion does not even mention the issue and seems to proceed on the assumption — contrary to the rule of law later laid down by the Supreme Court of Iowa — that the State needed to show only that the body would have been discovered in any event. The Iowa Supreme Court did expressly address the issue . . . and a finding by an appellate court of a state is entitled to the same presumption of correctness that attaches to trial-court findings under 28 U.S.C. § 2254(d). . . . We conclude, however, that the state Supreme Court's finding that the police did not act in bad faith is not entitled to the shield of § 2254(d). . . .

We granted the State's petition for certiorari, and we reverse.

II.B.

The requirement that the prosecution must prove the absence of bad faith, imposed here by the Court of Appeals, would place courts in the position of withholding from juries relevant and undoubted truth that would have been available to police absent any unlawful police activity. Of course, that view would put the police in a *worse* position than they would have been in if no unlawful conduct had transpired. And, of equal importance, it wholly fails to take into account the enormous societal cost of excluding truth in the search for truth in the administration of justice. Nothing in this Court's prior holdings supports any such formalistic, pointless, and punitive approach.

The Court of Appeals concluded, without analysis, that if an absence-of-bad-faith requirement were not imposed, "the temptation to risk deliberate violations of the Sixth Amendment would be too great, and the deterrent effect of the Exclusionary Rule reduced too far." . . . We reject that view. A police officer who is faced with the opportunity to obtain evidence illegally will rarely, if ever, be in a position to calculate whether the evidence sought would inevitably be discovered. Cf. *United States v. Ceccolini*, 435 U.S. 268, 283 (1978):

> [The] concept of effective deterrence assumes that the police officer consciously realizes the probable consequences of a presumably impermissible course of conduct.

On the other hand, when an officer is aware that the evidence will inevitably be discovered, he will try to avoid engaging in any questionable practice. In that situation, there will be little to gain from taking any dubious "shortcuts" to obtain the evidence. Significant disincentives to obtaining evidence illegally — including the possibility of departmental discipline and civil liability — also lessen the likelihood that the ultimate or inevitable discovery exception will promote police misconduct. In these circumstances, the societal costs of the Exclusionary Rule far outweigh any possible benefits to deterrence that a good-faith requirement might produce.

Williams contends that because he did not waive his right to the assistance of counsel, the Court may not balance competing values in deciding whether the challenged evidence was properly admitted. He argues that, unlike the Exclusionary Rule in the Fourth Amendment context, the essential purpose of which is to deter police misconduct, the Sixth Amendment Exclusionary Rule is designed to protect the right to a fair trial and the integrity of the factfinding process. Williams contends that, when those interests are at stake, the societal costs of excluding evidence obtained from responses presumed involuntary are irrelevant in determining whether such evidence should be excluded. We disagree.

Exclusion of physical evidence that would inevitably have been discovered adds nothing to either the integrity or fairness of a criminal trial. The Sixth Amendment right to counsel protects against unfairness by preserving the adversary process in which the reliability of proffered evidence may be tested in cross-examination. Here, however, Detective Leaming's conduct did nothing to impugn the reliability of the evidence in question — the body of the child and its condition as it was found, articles of clothing found on the body, and the autopsy. No one would seriously contend that the presence of counsel in the police car when Leaming appealed to Williams' decent human instincts would have had any bearing on the reliability of the body as evidence. Suppression, in these circumstances, would do nothing whatever to promote the integrity of the trial process, but would inflict a wholly unacceptable burden on the administration of criminal justice.

Nor would suppression ensure fairness on the theory that it tends to safeguard the adversary system of justice. To assure the fairness of trial proceedings, this Court has held that assistance of counsel must be available at pretrial confrontations where "the subsequent trial [cannot] cure a[n otherwise] one-sided confrontation between prosecuting authorities and the uncounseled defendant." Fairness can be assured by placing the State and the accused in the same positions they would have been in had the impermissible conduct not taken place. However, if the government can prove that the evidence would have been obtained inevitably and, therefore, would have been admitted regardless of any overreaching by the police, there is no rational basis to keep that evidence from the jury in order to ensure the fairness of the trial proceedings. In that situation, the State has gained no advantage at trial and the defendant has suffered no prejudice. Indeed, suppression of the evidence would operate to undermine the adversary system by putting the State in a *worse* position than it would have occupied without any police misconduct. Williams' argument that inevitable discovery constitutes impermissible balancing of values is without merit.

C.

On this record it is clear that the search parties were approaching the actual location of the body and we are satisfied, along with three courts earlier, that the volunteer search teams would have resumed the search had Williams not earlier led the police to the body and the body inevitably would have been found. The evidence asserted by Williams as newly discovered, *i.e.*, certain photographs of the body and deposition testimony of Agent Ruxlow made in connection with the federal habeas proceeding, does not demonstrate that the material facts were inadequately developed in the suppression hearing in state court or that Williams was denied a full, fair, and adequate opportunity to present all relevant facts at the suppression hearing.

[JUSTICE STEVENS concurred in the judgment.]

JUSTICE BRENNAN, with whom JUSTICE MARSHALL joins, dissenting.

. . .

In its zealous efforts to emasculate the exclusionary rule . . . the Court loses sight of the crucial difference between the "inevitable discovery" doctrine and the "independent source" exception from which it is derived. When properly applied, the "independent source" exception allows the prosecution to use evidence only if it was, in fact, obtained by fully lawful means. It therefore does no violence to the constitutional protections that the exclusionary rule is meant to enforce.

The "inevitable discovery" exception is likewise compatible with the Constitution, though it differs in one key respect from its next of kin: specifically, the evidence sought to be introduced at trial has not actually been obtained from an independent source, but rather would have been discovered as a matter of course if independent investigations were allowed to proceed.

In my view, this distinction should require that the government satisfy a heightened burden of proof before it is allowed to use such evidence. The inevitable discovery exception necessarily implicates a hypothetical finding that differs in kind from the factual finding that precedes application of the independent source rule. To ensure that this hypothetical finding is narrowly confined to circumstances that are functionally equivalent to an independent source, and to protect fully the fundamental rights served by the exclusionary rule, I would require clear and convincing evidence before concluding that the government had met its burden of proof on this issue.

NOTES AND QUESTIONS

(1) What does "inevitable" mean? Can it be said to an absolute certainty that one or more of the two hundred volunteers would have found the body? Does "inevitable" really mean "highly probable"? Would the Court have held for the defendant if, because of bad weather, the large scale search had been abandoned before the defendant directed the officers to the body? Some federal courts of appeal require a strong showing of probability. *See, e.g., United States v. Cunningham*, 413 F.3d 1199, 1203 (10th Cir. 2005) (requiring courts to have "a high level of confidence that the warrant in fact would have issued and that the specific evidence in question would have been obtained by lawful means"); *United States v. Heath*, 455 F.3d 52, 60 (2d Cir. 2006) ("illegally-obtained evidence will be admissible under the inevitable discovery exception . . . only where a court can find, with a high level of confidence, that each of the contingencies necessary to the legal discovery of the

contested evidence would be resolved in the government's favor"). But others use a more lenient standard. *See United States v. Allen*, 713 F.3d 382, 387 (8th Cir. 2013) (requiring a "reasonable probability" that evidence would have been discovered by lawful means and active pursuit of alternative line of investigation); *Jefferson v. Fountain*, 382 F.3d 1286, 1296 (11th Cir. 2004) (requiring that there "be a reasonable probability that the evidence in question would have been discovered by lawful means, and the prosecution must demonstrate that the lawful means which made discovery inevitable were being actively pursued prior to the occurrence of the illegal conduct"). *See also United States v. McManaman*, 673 F.3d 841 (8th Cir. 2012) (explaining that for the inevitable discovery exception to apply, the government must prove by a preponderance of the evidence: "(1) that there was a reasonable probability that the evidence would have been discovered by lawful means in the absence of police misconduct, and (2) that the government was actively pursuing a substantial, alternative line of investigation at the time of the constitutional violation.").

(2) In *United States v. Johnson*, 380 F.3d 1013, 1017 (7th Cir. 2004), the prosecution sought to introduce illegally-seized evidence from the vehicle of the accused on the theory that it would have been inevitably discovered in the course of a search of the passengers. Concededly, the search of the passengers would also have been illegal, but the prosecution argued that the defendant would lack standing to object to such seizures. The court responded that "[t]he fallacious character of the argument is demonstrated by the fact that if the passengers tried to exclude the evidence in their own cases, they would be met by the identical argument." This led to the anomalous result that "the more illegal searches there are, the narrower is the scope of application of the exclusionary rule," which the court found nonsensical.

[3] Attenuation

UNITED STATES v. CECCOLINI

United States Supreme Court
435 U.S. 268 (1978)

Justice Rehnquist delivered the opinion of the Court.

In December 1974, Ronald Biro, a uniformed police officer on assignment to patrol school crossings, entered respondent's place of business, the Sleepy Hollow Flower Shop, in North Tarrytown, N.Y. He went behind the customer counter and, in the words of Ichabod Crane, one of Tarrytown's more illustrious inhabitants of days gone past, "tarried," spending his short break engaged in conversation with his friend Lois Hennessey, an employee of the shop. During the course of conversation he noticed an envelope with money sticking out of it lying on the drawer of the cash register behind the counter. Biro picked up the envelope and, upon examining its contents, discovered that it contained not only money but policy slips. He placed the envelope back on the register and, without telling Hennessey of what he had seen, asked her to whom the envelope belonged. She replied that the envelope belonged to respondent Ceccolini, and that he had instructed her to give it to someone.

The next day, Officer Biro mentioned his discovery to North Tarrytown detectives who in turn told Lance Emory, an FBI agent. This very ordinary incident in the lives of Biro and Hennessey requires us, four years later, to decide whether Hennessey's testimony against respondent Ceccolini should have been suppressed in his trial for perjury. Respondent was charged with that offense because he denied that he knew anything of, or was in any way involved with, gambling operations. Respondent was found guilty after a bench trial in the United States District Court for the Eastern District of New York, but immediately after the finding of guilt the District Court granted respondent's motion to "suppress" the testimony of Hennessey because the court concluded that the testimony was a "fruit of the poisoned tree"; assuming respondent's motion for a directed verdict included a motion to set aside the verdict of guilty, the District Court granted the motion because it concluded that without Hennessey's testimony there was insufficient evidence of respondent's guilt. . . .

I

The Court of Appeals affirmed this ruling on the Government's appeal, reasoning that "the road to Miss Hennessy's [*sic*] testimony from Officer Biro's concededly unconstitutional search is both straight and uninterrupted." . . . The Court of Appeals also concluded that there was support in the record for the District Court's finding that the ongoing investigation would not have inevitably led to the evidence in question even without Biro's discovery of the two policy slips. . . .

II

The "road" to which the Court of Appeals analogized the train of events from Biro's discovery of the policy slips to Hennessey's testimony at respondent's trial for perjury is one of literally thousands of such roads traveled periodically between an original investigative discovery and the ultimate trial of the accused. The constitutional question under the Fourth Amendment was phrased in *Wong Sun v. United States* . . . as whether "the connection between the lawless conduct of the police and the discovery of the challenged evidence has become 'so attenuated as to dissipate the taint.' " . . . The question was in turn derived from the Court's earlier decision in *Nardone v. United States*, 308 U.S. 338, 341 (1939), where Mr. Justice Frankfurter stated for the Court:

> Here, as in the *Silverthorne* case, the facts improperly obtained do not "become sacred and inaccessible. If knowledge of them is gained from an independent source they may be proved like any others, but the knowledge gained by the Government's own wrong cannot be used by it" simply because it is used derivatively. 251 U.S. 385, 392.
>
> In practice this generalized statement may conceal concrete complexities. Sophisticated argument may prove a causal connection between information obtained through illicit wire-tapping and the Government's proof. As a matter of good sense, however, such connection may have become so attenuated as to dissipate the taint.

This, of course, makes it perfectly clear, if indeed ever there was any doubt about the matter, that the question of causal connection in this setting, as in so many other questions with which the law concerns itself, is not to be determined solely through the sort of analysis which would be applicable in the physical sciences. The issue cannot be decided on the basis of causation in the logical sense alone, but necessarily includes other elements as well. And our cases subsequent to *Nardone*, have laid out the fundamental tenets of the exclusionary rule, from which the elements that are relevant to the causal inquiry can be divined.

An examination of these cases leads us to reject the Government's suggestion that we adopt what would in practice amount to a *per se* rule that the testimony of a live witness should not be excluded at trial no matter how close and proximate the connection between it and a violation of the Fourth Amendment. We also reaffirm the holding of *Wong Sun* . . . that "verbal evidence which derives so immediately from unlawful entry and an unauthorized arrest as the officer's action in the present case is no less the 'fruit' of official illegality than the more commonplace tangible fruits of the unwarranted intrusion." We are of the view, however, that cases decided since *Wong Sun* significantly qualify its further observation that "the policies underlying the exclusionary rule do not invite any logical distinction between physical and verbal evidence." . . . Rather, at least in a case such as this, where not only was the alleged "fruit of the poisonous tree" the testimony of a live witness, but unlike *Wong Sun* the witness was not a putative defendant, an examination of our cases persuades us that the Court of Appeals was simply wrong in concluding that if the road were uninterrupted, its length was immaterial. Its length, we hold, is material, as are certain other factors enumerated below to which the court gave insufficient weight.

Even in situations where the exclusionary rule is plainly applicable, we have declined to adopt a "*per se* or 'but for' rule" that would make inadmissible any evidence, whether tangible or live-witness testimony, which somehow came to light through a chain of causation that began with an illegal arrest.

Evaluating the standards for application of the exclusionary rule to live-witness testimony in light of this balance, we are first impelled to conclude that the degree of free will exercised by the witness is not irrelevant in determining the extent to which the basic purpose of the exclusionary rule will be advanced by its application. This is certainly true when the challenged statements are made by a putative defendant after arrest, . . . and *a fortiori* is true in testimony given by nondefendants.

The greater the willingness of the witness to freely testify, the greater the likelihood that he or she will be discovered by legal means and, concomitantly, the smaller the incentive to conduct an illegal search to discover the witness.[6] Witnesses are not like guns or documents which remain hidden from view until one turns over a sofa or opens a filing cabinet. Witnesses can, and often do, come forward and offer evidence entirely of their own volition. And evaluated properly, the degree of free will necessary to dissipate the taint will very likely be found more often in the case of live-witness testimony than other kinds of evidence. The time, place and manner

---

[6] [4] Of course, the analysis might be different where the search was conducted by the police for the specific purpose of discovering potential witnesses.

of the initial questioning of the witness may be such that any statements are truly the product of detached reflection and a desire to be cooperative on the part of the witness. And the illegality which led to the discovery of the witness very often will not play any meaningful part in the witness's willingness to testify.

Another factor which is not only relevant in determining the usefulness of the exclusionary rule in a particular context, but also seems to us to differentiate the testimony of all live witnesses — even putative defendants — from the exclusion of the typical documentary evidence, is that such exclusion would perpetually disable a witness from testifying about relevant and material facts, regardless of how unrelated such testimony might be to the purpose of the originally illegal search or the evidence discovered thereby.

This is not to say, of course, that live-witness testimony is always or even usually more reliable or dependable than inanimate evidence. Indeed, just the opposite may be true. But a determination that the discovery of certain evidence is sufficiently unrelated to or independent of the constitutional violation to permit its introduction at trial is not a determination which rests on the comparative reliability of that evidence. Attenuation analysis, appropriately concerned with the differences between live-witness testimony and inanimate evidence, can consistently focus on the factors enumerated above with respect to the former, but on different factors with respect to the latter.

. . .

III

Viewing this case in the light of the principles just discussed, we hold that the Court of Appeals erred in holding that the degree of attenuation was not sufficient to dissipate the connection between the illegality and the testimony. The evidence indicates overwhelmingly that the testimony given by the witness was an act of her own free will in no way coerced or even induced by official authority as a result of Biro's discovery of the policy slips. Nor were the slips themselves used in questioning Hennessey. Substantial periods of time elapsed between the time of the illegal search and the initial contact with the witness, on the one hand, and between the latter and the testimony at trial on the other. While the particular knowledge to which Hennessey testified at trial can be logically traced back to Biro's discovery of the policy slips, both the identity of Hennessey and her relationship with the respondent was well known to those investigating the case. There is, in addition, not the slightest evidence to suggest that Biro entered the shop or picked up the envelope with the intent of finding tangible evidence bearing on an illicit gambling operation, much less any suggestion that he entered the shop and searched with the intent of finding a willing and knowledgeable witness to testify against respondent. Application of the exclusionary rule in this situation could not have the slightest deterrent effect on the behavior of an officer such as Biro. The cost of permanently silencing Hennessey is too great for an even-handed system of law enforcement to bear in order to secure such a speculative and very likely negligible deterrent effect.

Obviously no mathematical weight can be assigned to any of the factors which we have discussed, but just as obviously they all point to the conclusion that the exclusionary rule should be invoked with much greater reluctance where the claim is based on a causal relationship between a constitutional violation and the discovery of a live witness than when a similar claim is advanced to support suppression of an inanimate object. The judgment of the Court of Appeals is accordingly *Reversed.*

Chief Justice Burger, concurring in the judgment.

I agree with the Court's ultimate conclusion that there is a fundamental difference, for purposes of the exclusionary rule, between live-witness testimony and other types of evidence. I perceive this distinction to be so fundamental, however, that I would not prevent a fact finder from hearing and considering the relevant statements of any witness, except perhaps under the most remarkable of circumstances — although none such have ever been postulated that would lead me to exclude the testimony of a live witness.

In the history of ideas many thinkers have maintained with persuasion that there is no such thing as "free will," in the sense that the term implies the independent ability of an actor to regulate his or her conduct. Others have steadfastly maintained the opposite, arguing that the human personality is one innately free to choose among alternatives. Still a third group would deny that the very term "free will" has coherent meaning. These are only a few of the many perspectives on a subject which lies at the core of our intellectual and religious heritage. While this ancient debate will undoubtedly continue, "society and the law have no choice in the matter. We must proceed on the scientifically unprovable assumption that human beings make choices in the regulation of their conduct and that they are influenced by society's standards as well as by personal standards." *Blocker v. United States*, 288 F.2d 853, 865 (1961) (Burger, J., concurring). . . .

We are nonetheless cognizant to the fact that this assumption must continually confront the inherent practical obstacle of one person being unable to know with certainty the content of another's mind. We cross this barrier daily, of course, in the process of determining criminal culpability. Yet in criminal trials we are willing to bear the risk of error — substantially diminished by the requirement of proof beyond a reasonable doubt — in order to effectuate the common law tradition of imposing punishment only upon those who can be said to be morally responsible for their acts. There is no analogue to this concern, however, in the area of Fourth Amendment exclusion, which has an admitted pragmatic purpose based as I suggested on speculative hypotheses which ought to lead us to apply it with reasoned discrimination, not as an automatic response. In short, the results achieved from current exclusionary rule standards are bizarre enough without steering the analysis in the direction of areas which offer no reasonable hope of a comprehensible framework for inquiry.

NOTES AND QUESTIONS

(1) The search of the envelope in *Ceccolini* would appear to be little more than a case of idle curiosity. At the same time, Justice Rehnquist noted that the analysis "might be different" had the search been conducted "for the specific purpose of discovering potential witnesses." Most cases are likely to fall between these two

extremes — the police know or have reason to know that the search is unconstitutional, but the discovery of witness identities is entirely fortuitous. How should such cases be resolved?

(2) A confession following an illegal arrest can also be so "attenuated" that exclusion of the confession is inappropriate. The Supreme Court has identified five factors to be taken into account in determining whether a confession given following an illegal arrest is to be excluded as a fruit of the illegality. *See Brown v. Illinois*, 422 U.S. 590 (1975) and *Rawlings v. Kentucky*, 448 U.S. 98 (1980). For example, in *Brown*, a suspect was arrested without probable cause or a warrant. He was, however, advised of his rights according to *Miranda*, after which he implicated himself in a murder for which he was later tried in state court. The question before the Court was whether the inculpatory statements were excludable from Brown's trial as fruit of the illegal arrest or, on the other hand, admissible under the theory that the *Miranda* warnings sufficiently purged the taint of the illegal arrest. *Brown*, 422 U.S. at 591-92. The Court concluded that this case, and ones like it, demand a factually-specific inquiry.

> The question whether a confession is the product of a free will under *Wong Sun* must be answered on the facts of each case. No single fact is dispositive. The workings of the human mind are too complex, and the possibilities of misconduct too diverse, to permit protection of the Fourth Amendment to turn on such a talismanic test. The *Miranda* warnings are an important factor, to be sure, in determining whether the confession is obtained by exploitation of an illegal arrest. But they are not the only factor to be considered.

Id. at 603. In short, a careful reading of the Court's cases shows that first, the Court looks to see if the defendant's statements were voluntary. "The voluntariness of the statement is a threshold requirement." *Id.* at 604. Next, the Court considers whether the defendant was given *Miranda* warnings prior to the confession. The Court has emphasized that violations of the Fourth Amendment cannot be neutralized by the simple expedient of *Miranda* warnings. *See, e.g., Taylor v. Alabama*, 457 U.S. 687 (1982) (holding that a confession following an arrest without probable cause should have been suppressed even though *Miranda* warnings were given and the confession was voluntary in the Fifth Amendment sense, because the six hours between the arrest and the confession, a short visit with defendant's girlfriend, and the other facts did not dissipate the taint of the illegal arrest). While not a cure all, the Court, nonetheless, considers *Miranda* warnings an important factor.

Third, the Court considers the "temporal proximity of the arrest and the confession." As *Wong Sun* demonstrated, the longer the passage of time, the greater the likelihood that the taint will have dissipated. Fourth, consideration will be given to any circumstances that intervened between the illegality and the challenged statements. Fifth, "the purpose and flagrancy of the official misconduct" will be taken into account, a consideration that reflects the contemporary Court's preoccupation with the deterrent effect of the exclusionary rule. Except for the presence or absence of *Miranda* warnings, it is clear that the factors are closely related and often overlapping. The decision is reached based on the totality of the circumstances with no single fact (with the exception of voluntariness) dispositive.

(3) The Court takes an entirely different approach in the case of a *Payton* violation — an arrest made with probable cause but within a residence without judicial authorization or exigent circumstances. In *New York v. Harris*, 495 U.S. 14 (1990), the Court held that when the illegality is thus limited to the situs of the arrest, the exclusionary rule is potentially applicable only to events which occur within the residence. Indeed, even if the arrest is illegal, the Court volunteered that once removed from the premises, the suspect could be rearrested without violating any constitutional protections. Any statements made once the suspect has been removed from the premises would not be tainted merely by virtue of the illegal entry.

(4) In *State v. Simmons*, 585 N.W.2d 165 (Wis. App. 1998), a warrant was issued authorizing both a search of the accused's apartment and a strip search of the accused. In support of the request for the strip search, the affidavit stated that when arrested in 1990 (five years prior to the present application for a warrant) the accused "was found to be concealing Cocaine in a plastic bag stuffed between the cheeks of his buttocks completely up to his rectum." *Id.* at 166. The affidavit did not note that the search was found to be unconstitutional and the evidence suppressed. Nothing else contained in the affidavit supported the strip-search aspect of the warrant. The accused contended that evidence discovered by the strip search must be excluded as fruit of the poisonous tree. The court of appeals conceded that the authorization was based on an earlier illegal search but nevertheless concluded that the taint had been dissipated. The court conceded that the passage of five years was itself "of no real significance." Rather, the dispositive factor was that the present investigation had been initiated on the basis of new information received from different sources. Hence the warrant had not been generated through the exploitation of the prior illegality. "Only after the police were tipped off as to Simmons' illegal activity did they comb their files and discover his modus operandi of secreting cocaine between the cheeks of his buttocks. The illegal information merely facilitated the police in their subsequent investigation: it was not the progenitor of the new investigation." *Id.* at 168.

§ 6.04 HARMLESS ERROR

Even if the government violates the Constitution and evidence obtained as a result of that violation is wrongfully introduced at trial against the defendant, there is no guarantee that these breaches of rights will lead to reversal of a conviction. Not uncommonly, the appellate court concludes that the admission of the illegally-seized evidence did not affect the outcome of the trial adversely to the accused. Thus, the error is deemed "harmless."

The harmless error rule appears eminently plausible when the illegally-seized evidence is mere surplusage, as for example, where the accused, charged with the illegal possession of untaxed liquor, correctly maintains that one of the ten cases of whisky introduced in evidence at his trial was illegally seized. The result is far more problematic when the impact upon the fact finder of the improperly-admitted evidence is more uncertain. Suppose, for example, the only tangible evidence introduced at the accused's homicide trial was the illegally-seized murder weapon, but the prosecution also introduced the legally-obtained confession of the accused.

In *Fahy v. Connecticut*, 375 U.S. 85, 86 (1963), the Court said that "[t]he question is whether there is a reasonable possibility that the evidence complained of might have contributed to the conviction." In *Arizona v. Fulminante*, 499 U.S. 279 (1991), a majority of the Court held the harmless-error rule applicable even to an involuntary confession, explaining:

> [T]he doctrine is essential to preserve "the principle that the central purpose of a criminal trial is to decide the factual question of the defendant's guilt or innocence, and promotes public respect for the criminal process by focusing on the underlying fairness of the trial rather than on the virtually inevitable presence of immaterial error."

Id. at 308.

In fact, the harmless error rule has been employed in many contexts. *See, e.g.*, *Pope v. Illinois*, 481 U.S. 497, 501-04 (1987) (applying harmless-error standard to a jury instruction misstating an element of the crime charged); *Crane v. Kentucky*, 476 U.S. 683, 691 (1986) (applying harmless-error analysis to the exclusion of a defendant's testimony regarding the circumstances of his confession); *Rushen v. Spain*, 464 U.S. 114, 117–18 (1983) (applying harmless-error rule to denial of defendant's right to be present at trial); *Chapman v. California*, 386 U.S. 18 (1967) (applying harmless error standard to comment on the failure of the accused to testify); *Harrington v. California*, 395 U.S. 250 (1969) (applying harmless-error rule to denial of confrontation rights by the admission of the confession of a non-testifying codefendant).

Nevertheless, not all constitutional errors are subject to the harmless-error analysis. For instance, in *United States v. Gonzalez-Lopez*, 548 U.S. 140 (2006), Justice Scalia, writing for the majority, held that an erroneous deprivation of a defendant's Sixth Amendment right to his choice of counsel is a "structural error," which requires reversal of a conviction. In other words, structural errors are not subject to a harmless-error assessment.

The Court in *Gonzalez-Lopez* explained further:

> [T]he Sixth Amendment right to counsel of choice . . . commands, not that a trial be fair, but that a particular guarantee of fairness be provided — to wit, that the accused be defended by the counsel he believes to be best. "The Constitution guarantees a fair trial through the Due Process Clauses, but it defines the basic elements of a fair trial largely through the several provisions of the Sixth Amendment, including the Counsel Clause." In sum, the right at stake here is the right to counsel of choice, not the right to a fair trial; and that right was violated because the deprivation of counsel was erroneous. No additional showing of prejudice is required to make the violation "complete." *Id.* at 146.

The Court in *Fulminante* had recognized the significance of structural errors, stating:

> These are structural defects in the constitution of the trial mechanism, which defy analysis by "harmless-error" standards. . . . Each of these

> constitutional deprivations . . . affect[s] the framework within which the trial proceeds, rather than simply an error in the trial process itself. "Without these basic protections, a criminal trial cannot reliably serve its function as a vehicle for determination of guilt or innocence, and no criminal punishment may be regarded as fundamentally fair."

Fulminante, 499 U.S. at 309-10. Examples of other structural errors include the absence of counsel for a criminal defendant and the presence on the bench of a biased judge; *id.*; exclusion from the grand jury of members of the defendant's race; *Vasquez v. Hillery*, 474 U.S. 254 (1986); and the right to a public trial. *Waller v. Georgia*, 467 U.S. 39 (1984).

Chapter 7

PRINCIPLES OF FAIR TRIAL

Various constitutional provisions directly impact a criminal trial. Concerns over the speed with which the accused has been brought to trial, issues regarding the selection of jurors, questions about the specificity of the charges, and difficulties with the objectivity of the trial judge all affect the ability of the accused to have a fair trial during which his or her guilt will be decided. In this chapter, six different, but ultimately related, trial issues will be discussed: the presumption of innocence; the right to trial by jury; the right of the accused to confront witnesses; comments by the prosecution at trial on the defendant's silence; the prosecutor's duty to produce exculpatory evidence; and prosecutorial misconduct.

§ 7.01 THE PRESUMPTION OF INNOCENCE

MULLANEY v. WILBUR

United States Supreme Court
421 U.S. 684 (1975)

Justice Powell delivered the opinion of the Court.

The State of Maine requires a defendant charged with murder to prove that he acted "in the heat of passion on sudden provocation" in order to reduce the homicide to manslaughter. We must decide whether this rule comports with the due process requirement, as defined in *In re Winship*, 397 U.S. 358 (1970), that the prosecution prove beyond a reasonable doubt every fact necessary to constitute the crime charged.

I

In June 1966 a jury found respondent Stillman E. Wilbur, Jr., guilty of murder. The case against him rested on his own pretrial statement and on circumstantial evidence showing that he fatally assaulted Claude Hebert in the latter's hotel room. Respondent's statement, introduced by the prosecution, claimed that he had attacked Hebert in a frenzy provoked by Hebert's homosexual advance. The defense offered no evidence, but argued that the homicide was not unlawful since respondent lacked criminal intent. Alternatively, Wilbur's counsel asserted that at most the homicide was manslaughter rather than murder, since it occurred in the heat of passion provoked by the homosexual assault.

The trial court instructed the jury that Maine law recognizes two kinds of homicide, murder and manslaughter, and that these offenses are not subdivided into different degrees. The common elements of both are that the homicide be unlawful — *i.e.*, neither justifiable nor excusable — and that it be intentional. The prosecution is required to prove these elements by proof beyond a reasonable doubt, and only if they are so proved is the jury to consider the distinction between murder and manslaughter.

In view of the evidence the trial court drew particular attention to the difference between murder and manslaughter. After reading the statutory definitions of both offenses, the court charged that "malice aforethought is an essential and indispensable element of the crime of murder," without which the homicide would be manslaughter. The jury was further instructed, however, that if the prosecution established that the homicide was both intentional and unlawful, malice aforethought was to be conclusively implied unless the defendant proved by a fair preponderance of the evidence that he acted in the heat of passion on sudden provocation. The court emphasized that "malice aforethought and heat of passion on sudden provocation are two inconsistent things"; thus, by proving the latter the defendant would negate the former and reduce the homicide from murder to manslaughter. The court then concluded its charge with elaborate definitions of "heat of passion" and "sudden provocation."

. . .

III

The Maine law of homicide, as it bears on this case, can be stated succinctly: Absent justification or excuse, all intentional or criminally reckless killings are felonious homicides. Felonious homicide is punished as murder — *i.e.*, by life imprisonment — unless the defendant proves by a fair preponderance of the evidence that it was committed in the heat of passion on sudden provocation, in which case it is punished as manslaughter — *i.e.*, by a fine not to exceed $1,000 or by imprisonment not to exceed 20 years. The issue is whether the Maine rule requiring the defendant to prove that he acted in the heat of passion on sudden provocation accords with due process.

. . .

B

Petitioners, the warden of the Maine Prison and the State of Maine, argue that *In re Winship* should not be extended to the present case. They note that as a formal matter the absence of the heat of passion on sudden provocation is not a "fact necessary to constitute the crime" of felonious homicide in Maine. This distinction is relevant, according to petitioners, because in *Winship* the facts at issue were essential to establish criminality in the first instance, whereas the fact in question here does not come into play until the jury already has determined that the defendant is guilty and may be punished at least for manslaughter. In this situation, petitioners maintain, the defendant's critical interests in liberty and reputation are no longer of paramount concern since, irrespective of the presence or absence of the heat of passion on sudden provocation, he is likely to lose his liberty and certain to be stigmatized. In short, petitioners would limit *Winship* to those facts which, if not proved, would wholly exonerate the defendant.

This analysis fails to recognize that the criminal law of Maine, like that of other jurisdictions, is concerned not only with guilt or innocence in the abstract but also with the degree of criminal culpability. Maine has chosen to distinguish those who kill in the heat of passion from those who kill in the absence of this factor. Because the former are less "blameworthy," they are subject to substantially less severe penalties. By drawing this distinction, while refusing to require the prosecution to establish beyond a reasonable doubt the fact upon which it turns, Maine denigrates the interests found critical in *Winship*.

The safeguards of due process are not rendered unavailing simply because a determination may already have been reached that would stigmatize the defendant and that might lead to a significant impairment of personal liberty. The fact remains that the consequences resulting from a verdict of murder, as compared with a verdict of manslaughter, differ significantly. Indeed, when viewed in terms of the potential difference in restrictions of personal liberty attendant to each conviction, the distinction established by Maine between murder and manslaughter may be of greater importance than the difference between guilt or innocence for many lesser crimes.

Moreover, if *Winship* were limited to those facts that constitute a crime as defined by state law, a State could undermine many of the interests that decision sought to protect without effecting any substantive change in its law. It would only be necessary to redefine the elements that constitute different crimes, characterizing them as factors that bear solely on the extent of punishment. . . . *Winship* is concerned with substance rather than this kind of formalism. The rationale of that case requires an analysis that looks to the "operation and effect of the law as applied and enforced by the State," and to the interests of both the State and the defendant as affected by the allocation of the burden of proof.

In *Winship* the Court emphasized the societal interests in the reliability of jury verdicts:

> The requirement of proof beyond a reasonable doubt has (a) vital role in our criminal procedure for cogent reasons. The accused during a criminal prosecution has at stake interests of immense importance, both because of the possibility that he may lose his liberty upon conviction and because of the certainty that he would be stigmatized by the conviction. . . .
>
> Moreover, use of the reasonable-doubt standard is indispensable to command the respect and confidence of the community in applications of the criminal law. It is critical that the moral force of the criminal law not be diluted by a standard of proof that leaves people in doubt whether innocent men are being condemned.

These interests are implicated to a greater degree in this case than they were in *Winship* itself. Petitioner there faced an 18-month sentence, with a maximum possible extension of an additional four and one-half years, whereas respondent here faces a differential in sentencing ranging from a nominal fine to a mandatory life sentence. Both the stigma to the defendant and the community's confidence in the administration of the criminal law are also of greater consequence in this case, since the adjudication of delinquency involved in *Winship* was "benevolent" in intention, seeking to provide "a generously conceived program of compassionate treatment."

Not only are the interests underlying *Winship* implicated to a greater degree in this case, but in one respect the protection afforded those interests is less here. In *Winship* the ultimate burden of persuasion remained with the prosecution, although the standard had been reduced to proof by a fair preponderance of the evidence. In this case, by contrast, the State has affirmatively shifted the burden of proof to the defendant. The result, in a case such as this one where the defendant is required to prove the critical fact in dispute, is to increase further the likelihood of an erroneous murder conviction.

IV

Maine law requires a defendant to establish by a preponderance of the evidence that he acted in the heat of passion on sudden provocation in order to reduce murder to manslaughter. Under this burden of proof a defendant can be given a life sentence when the evidence indicates that it is as likely as not that he deserves a significantly lesser sentence. This is an intolerable result in a society where, to paraphrase Mr. Justice Harlan, it is far worse to sentence one guilty only of manslaughter as a murderer than to sentence a murderer for the lesser crime of manslaughter.

We therefore hold that the Due Process Clause requires the prosecution to prove beyond a reasonable doubt the absence of the heat of passion on sudden provocation when the issue is properly presented in a homicide case. Accordingly, the judgment below is affirmed.

[JUSTICE REHNQUIST, with whom CHIEF JUSTICE BURGER joined, concurred.]

NOTES AND QUESTIONS

(1) In *Patterson v. New York*, 432 U.S. 197 (1977), the New York law required the defendant in a prosecution for second-degree murder to prove — by a preponderance of the evidence — that he acted under the influence of extreme emotional disturbance to reduce the crime to manslaughter. Was this statute violative of the Due Process Clause? For the majority, Justice White wrote that the statute was constitutional even under the analysis in *Mullaney*:

> *Mullaney* surely held that a State must prove every ingredient of an offense beyond a reasonable doubt, and that it may not shift the burden of proof to the defendant by presuming that ingredient upon proof of the other elements of the offense. This is true even though the State's practice, as in Maine, had been traditionally to the contrary. Such shifting of the burden of persuasion with respect to a fact which the State deems so important that it must be either proved or presumed is impermissible under the Due Process Clause.
>
> It was unnecessary to go further in *Mullaney*. The Maine Supreme Court made it clear that malice aforethought, which was mentioned in the

> statutory definition of the crime, was not equivalent to premeditation and that the presumption of malice traditionally arising in intentional homicide cases carried no factual meaning insofar as premeditation was concerned. Even so, a killing became murder in Maine when it resulted from a deliberate, cruel act committed by one person against another, "suddenly without any, or without considerable provocation."
>
> Premeditation was not within the definition of murder; but malice, in the sense of the absence of provocation, was part of the definition of that crime. Yet malice, *i.e.*, lack of provocation, was presumed and could be rebutted by the defendant only by proving by a preponderance of the evidence that he acted with heat of passion upon sudden provocation. In *Mullaney* we held that however traditional this mode of proceeding might have been, it is contrary to the Due Process Clause as construed in *Winship*.
>
> As we have explained, nothing was presumed or implied against Patterson; and his conviction is not invalid under any of our prior cases.

Justice Powell, joined by Justices Brennan and Marshall, dissented, arguing:

> Perhaps the Court's interpretation of *Winship* is consistent with the letter of the holding in that case. But little of the spirit survives. Indeed, the Court scarcely could distinguish this case from *Mullaney* without closing its eyes to the constitutional values for which *Winship* stands. As Mr. Justice Harlan observed in *Winship*, "a standard of proof represents an attempt to instruct the factfinder concerning the degree of confidence our society thinks he should have in the correctness of factual conclusions for a particular type of adjudication."
>
> Explaining *Mullaney*, the Court says today, in effect, that society demands full confidence before a Maine factfinder determines that heat of passion is missing — a demand so insistent that this Court invoked the Constitution to enforce it over the contrary decision by the State. But we are told that society is willing to tolerate far less confidence in New York's factual determination of precisely the same functional issue. One must ask what possibly could explain this difference in societal demands. According to the Court, it is because Maine happened to attach a name "malice aforethought" to the absence of heat of passion, whereas New York refrained from giving a name to the absence of extreme emotional disturbance.
>
> With all respect, this type of constitutional adjudication is indefensibly formalistic. A limited but significant check on possible abuses in the criminal law now becomes an exercise in arid formalities. What *Winship* and *Mullaney* had sought to teach about the limits a free society places on its procedures to safeguard the liberty of its citizens becomes a rather simplistic lesson in statutory draftsmanship. Nothing in the Court's opinion prevents a legislature from applying this new learning to many of the classical elements of the crimes it punishes.

The Court has reiterated that Due Process is not violated even when the accused is burdened with establishing an affirmative defense of withdrawal from a conspiracy by a preponderance of the evidence. *Smith v. United States*, 133 S. Ct. 714, 719

(2013). Although the government is obligated to prove "every fact necessary to constitute the crime," *id.* (quoting *In re Winship*, 397 U.S. at 364), it is not required to disprove an affirmative defense. *Id.* (citing *Patterson*, 432 U.S. at 210). When a defendant joins a criminal conspiracy, her membership in the unlawful group conduct continues until she withdraws from that conspiracy. But when a defendant withdraws, it starts the statute of limitations running and may provide a complete defense from prosecution if the government brings charges too late — after the statute of limitations expires. In *Smith*, the government established beyond a reasonable doubt the existence of a conspiracy, that the accused was a member, and that the conspiracy continued within the applicable statute of limitations. The accused was left to prove his withdrawal from the conspiracy outside of the statute of limitations.

(2) What happens when there is overlap in the elements of the crime charged and the defense asserted in the case? In *Martin v. Ohio*, 480 U.S. 228 (1987), a defendant was charged with aggravated murder and claimed she acted in self defense. To establish aggravated murder, the prosecution was obligated to prove that the defendant caused the death of the victim "purposely, and with prior calculation and design." The Ohio legislature placed the burden of proving self defense on the defendant under a preponderance standard.

The defendant argued that an element of self defense (the requirement that the defendant show that she held an honest belief that she faced an imminent and deadly threat) negated the prosecutor's burden to prove prior calculation and design, an element of aggravated murder. Thus, contended the defendant, the dictates of *Winship* were violated. A majority of the Court rejected this argument.

> We agree with the State and its Supreme Court that this conviction did not violate the Due Process Clause. The State did not exceed its authority in defining the crime of murder as purposely causing the death of another with prior calculation or design. It did not seek to shift to Martin the burden of proving any of those elements, and the jury's verdict reflects that none of her self-defense evidence raised a reasonable doubt about the State's proof that she purposefully killed with prior calculation and design. She nevertheless had the opportunity under state law and the instructions given to justify the killing and show herself to be blameless by proving that she acted in self-defense. The jury thought she had failed to do so, and Ohio is as entitled to punish Martin as one guilty of murder as New York was to punish Patterson.

The United States Supreme Court, in a divided opinion, also rejected a constitutional attack on a Montana statute completely barring defendants from using voluntarily-induced intoxication as a defense to any criminal offense, including to negate mens rea when facing a charge of purposeful murder. *See Montana v. Egelhoff*, 518 U.S. 37 (1996).

(3) How do the principles of *Winship* affect sentencing enhancements? New Jersey enacted a statute which required the prosecution to prove to the jury all elements of a firearm possession charge beyond a reasonable doubt. The statutory penalty could be enhanced substantially, however, if the judge further found, by a preponderance of the evidence, that the crime was committed "with a purpose to

intimidate an individual or group of individuals because of race, color, gender, handicap, religion, sexual orientation or ethnicity." In *Apprendi v. New Jersey*, 530 U.S. 466 (2000), the sentencing judge increased the defendant's term of imprisonment as a result of such a hate-crime finding. Did the statutory scheme violate the Constitution? The four dissenters (O'Connor, Rehnquist, Kennedy, and Breyer) thought not, relying on the established principle that a legislature can define the elements of a crime. "Our court has long recognized that not every fact that bears on a defendant's punishment need be charged in an indictment, submitted to a jury and proved by the government beyond a reasonable doubt." *Id.* at 524. But the majority struck down New Jersey's sentencing procedure, holding that the Due Process Clause requires that the bias finding be made by the jury, beyond a reasonable doubt. The majority explained: "The New Jersey procedure challenged in this case is an unacceptable departure from the jury tradition that is an indispensable part of our criminal justice system." *Id.* at 497.

Apprendi was followed and amplified in *Blakely v. Washington*, 542 U.S. 296 (2004), in which the Supreme Court struck down Washington State's sentencing guideline scheme due to the involvement of the trial judge in the fact-finding process. The Supreme Court explained that the " 'statutory maximum' for *Apprendi* purposes is the maximum sentence a judge may impose *solely on the basis of the facts reflected in the jury verdict or admitted by the defendant.*" *Blakely*, 542 U.S. at 303. The government had argued that the sentence imposed fell within the "statutory maximum" because the maximum sentence permitted by the statute prohibiting crimes of this type was ten years; the defendant was sentenced to only seven and one half years. The Court rejected this argument. "When a judge inflicts punishment that the jury's verdict alone does not allow, the jury has not found all the facts 'which the law makes essential to the punishment,' . . . and the judge exceeds his proper authority." *Id.* at 304.

After *Blakely*, in *United States v. Booker*, 543 U.S. 220 (2005), the Court reaffirmed the rules established in *Apprendi* and *Blakely*, but in a two-part majority opinion, with different Justices joining the different parts, the Court excised portions of the federal sentencing statute in an effort to adhere to the *Apprendi* and *Blakely* rules while, at the same time, saving the United States Federal Sentencing Guidelines from unconstitutionality. The first majority concluded: "[W]e reaffirm our holding in *Apprendi*: Any fact (other than a prior conviction) which is necessary to support a sentence exceeding the maximum authorized by the facts established by a plea of guilty or a jury verdict must be admitted by the defendant or proved to a jury beyond a reasonable doubt." *Id.* at 244. In the second majority opinion, the Court held that the remedy for the constitutional violation was to excise from the federal sentencing statute the provisions that made the Guidelines mandatory.

> Application of these criteria indicates that we must sever and excise two specific statutory provisions: the provision that requires sentencing courts to impose a sentence within the applicable Guidelines range (in the absence of circumstances that justify a departure) . . . and the provision that sets forth standards of review on appeal, including *de novo* review of departures from the applicable Guidelines range . . .). With these two sections excised

> (and statutory cross-references to the two sections consequently invalidated), the remainder of the Act satisfies the Court's constitutional requirements.

Id. at 259. The result of the second opinion was to give the trial judge extensive discretion to sentence between the statutory minimum and maximum for every crime. *See also Gall v. United States*, 552 U.S. 38 (2007) (because the Federal Guidelines are advisory after *Booker*, appellate review consists of deciding whether the sentence imposed is "reasonable," regardless of whether the sentence falls inside or outside the Guidelines range); Ian Weinstein, *The Revenge of* Mullaney v. Wilbur: United States v. Booker *and the Reassertion of Judicial Limits on Legislative Power to Define Crimes*, 84 Or. L. Rev. 393 (2005) (discussing the *Winship* principles as they apply to sentencing).

The rule established in *Apprendi*, which reserves to a jury the finding of any fact (other than the fact of prior conviction) that may increase a defendant's punishment of imprisonment, also applies to criminal fines. *Southern Union Co. v. United States*, 132 S. Ct. 2344 (2012). Moreover, the Court recently declared that because mandatory minimum sentences increase the penalty for a crime, "any fact that increases the mandatory minimum is an 'element' that must be submitted to the jury." *Alleyne v. United States*, 133 S. Ct. 2151, 2155 (2013) (overruling *Harris v. United States*, 536 U.S. 545 (2002)). In *Alleyne* the defendant was charged with multiple offenses, including robbery while using or carrying a firearm. The jury convicted him, and on the verdict form indicated that he had "[u]sed or carried a firearm during and in relation to a crime of violence[.]" *Id.* The presentence report found that defendant had "brandished" a weapon during the crime, not just used one. Brandishing carries a more severe mandatory minimum sentence than use. *See* 18 U.S.C. § 924. Although the defendant objected to this finding in the presentence report, the trial court ruled that brandishing was a sentencing factor, not an element of the crime. Accordingly, finding by a preponderance of the evidence that defendant had, indeed, brandished a weapon, the trial judge increased the defendant's sentence. The Supreme Court held the Sixth Amendment was violated.

Even after *Apprendi*, a sentencing judge has significant power and may consider evidence of a defendant's post-sentencing rehabilitation if the defendant's initial sentence has been set aside on appeal. *See Pepper v. United States*, 131 S. Ct. 1229 (2011). The judge may also impose a sentence below the guideline range to reflect the difference between the high sentencing ranges for crack cocaine and the lower sentencing ranges for powder cocaine. *Kimbrough v. United States*, 552 U.S. 85 (2007). Nevertheless, a sentencing judge may not impose or lengthen a prison term to promote a criminal defendant's rehabilitation. *Tapia v. United States*, 131 S. Ct. 2382, 2386 (2011). In *Tapia*, the sentencing judge determined that the guideline range for the defendant's crime was 41 to 51 months and imposed 51 months, citing the defendant's need for drug treatment and the Bureau of Prison's requirement that a prisoner admitted for drug rehabilitation be incarcerated long enough to complete 500 hours of treatment. The Court found the sentencing court's reasoning flawed, explaining that the sentencing statute limits the factors a judge may consider when imposing incarceration and using statutory interpretation to conclude that "imprisonment is not an appropriate means of promoting correction and rehabilitation."

(4) What must the jury be told about the burden of proof? In *Taylor v. Kentucky*, 436 U.S. 478 (1978), the defendant requested a jury instruction on the presumption of innocence and the indictment's lack of evidentiary value. The trial judge refused the request but did instruct that the government had the burden of proving the defendant's guilt beyond a reasonable doubt. The defendant was convicted of robbery. Did the trial judge commit constitutional error in rejecting the defendant's jury instruction? Stating that the "presumption of innocence, although not articulated in the Constitution, is a basic component of a fair trial under our system of criminal justice," the Court found that the defendant's right to a fair trial under the Due Process Clause had been violated. *Id.* at 479. Compare *Kentucky v. Whorton*, 441 U.S. 786 (1979), where a majority of the Court said that *Taylor* did *not* mean that a presumption-of-innocence instruction was required in *all* criminal trials. The Court explained further in *Whorton*:

> While this Court in *Taylor* reversed a conviction resulting from a trial in which the judge had refused to give a requested instruction on the presumption of innocence, the Court did not there fashion a new rule of constitutional law requiring that such an instruction be given in every criminal case. Rather, the Court's opinion focused on the failure to give the instruction as it related to the overall fairness of the trial considered in its entirety.
>
> In short, the failure to give a requested instruction on the presumption of innocence does not in and of itself violate the Constitution. Under *Taylor*, such a failure must be evaluated in light of the totality of the circumstances — including all the instructions to the jury, the arguments of counsel, whether the weight of the evidence was overwhelming, and other relevant factors — to determine whether the defendant received a constitutionally fair trial.

Id. at 788-89. The three dissenting Justices (Stewart, Brennan, and Marshall) would have fashioned a *per se* rule:

> While an instruction on the presumption of innocence in one sense only serves to remind the jury that the prosecutor has the burden of proof beyond a reasonable doubt, it also has a separate and distinct function. Quite apart from considerations of the burden of proof, the presumption of innocence "cautions the jury to put away from their minds all the suspicion that arises from the arrest, the indictment, and the arraignment, and to reach their conclusion solely from the evidence adduced." . . . And because every defendant, regardless of the totality of the circumstances, is entitled to have his guilt determined only on the basis of the evidence properly introduced against him at trial, I would hold that an instruction on the presumption of innocence is constitutionally required in every case where a timely request has been made.

Id. at 790-91.

(5) In *Sandstrom v. Montana*, 442 U.S. 510 (1979), the defendant was charged with deliberate homicide. He had admitted killing the victim but claimed that "he did not do so 'purposely or knowingly' and was therefore not guilty of 'deliberate

homicide' but of a lesser crime." In response to the defendant's argument, the prosecution asked for, and received, an instruction that "the law presumes that a person intends the ordinary consequences of his voluntary acts." Because the question of whether the crime was committed purposely or knowingly was a fact necessary to constitute the crime of deliberate homicide (indeed it was the only fact needed to be shown), the Court concluded that the instruction was constitutionally impermissible. "[T]he challenged jury instruction had the effect of relieving the State of the burden of proof . . . on the critical question of petitioner's state of mind." In reaching this conclusion Justice Brennan relied upon *Winship, Mullaney,* and *Patterson.* Was this reliance proper? Did not these cases involve very different issues, both in terms of their constitutional dimensions and their trial impact? Another case raising the presumption question is *Francis v. Franklin,* 471 U.S. 307 (1985), in which the Court disapproved of the following instruction:

> The acts of a person of sound mind and discretion are presumed to be the product of the person's will, but the presumption may be rebutted. A person of sound mind and discretion is presumed to intend the natural and probable consequences of his acts but the presumption may be rebutted.

§ 7.02 THE RIGHT TO TRIAL BY JURY

DUNCAN v. LOUISIANA

United States Supreme Court
391 U.S. 145 (1968)

JUSTICE WHITE delivered the opinion of the Court.

Appellant, Gary Duncan, was convicted of simple battery in the Twenty-fifth Judicial District Court of Louisiana. Under Louisiana law simple battery is a misdemeanor, punishable by a maximum of two years' imprisonment and a $300 fine. Appellant sought trial by jury, but because the Louisiana Constitution grants jury trials only in cases in which capital punishment or imprisonment at hard labor may be imposed, the trial judge denied the request. Appellant was convicted and sentenced to serve 60 days in the parish prison and pay a fine of $150. Appellant sought review in the Supreme Court of Louisiana, asserting that the denial of jury trial violated rights guaranteed to him by the United States Constitution. The Supreme Court, finding "(n)o error of law in the ruling complained of," denied appellant a writ of certiorari. Appellant sought review in this Court, alleging that the Sixth and Fourteenth Amendments to the United States Constitution secure the right to jury trial in state criminal prosecutions where a sentence as long as two years may be imposed. We noted probable jurisdiction, and set the case for oral argument.

I

. . . The position of Louisiana is that the Constitution imposes upon the States no duty to give a jury trial in any criminal case, regardless of the seriousness of the crime or the size of the punishment which may be imposed. Because we believe that trial by jury in criminal cases is fundamental to the American scheme of justice, we hold that the Fourteenth Amendment guarantees a right of jury trial in all criminal cases which — were they to be tried in a federal court — would come within the Sixth Amendment's guarantee. Since we consider the appeal before us to be such a case, we hold that the Constitution was violated when appellant's demand for jury trial was refused.

. . .

The guarantees of jury trial in the Federal and State Constitutions reflect a profound judgment about the way in which law should be enforced and justice administered. A right to jury trial is granted to criminal defendants in order to prevent oppression by the Government. Those who wrote our constitutions knew from history and experience that it was necessary to protect against unfounded criminal charges brought to eliminate enemies and against judges too responsive to the voice of higher authority. The framers of the constitutions strove to create an independent judiciary but insisted upon further protection against arbitrary action. Providing an accused with the right to be tried by a jury of his peers gave him an inestimable safeguard against the corrupt or overzealous prosecutor and against the compliant, biased, or eccentric judge. If the defendant preferred the common-sense judgment of a jury to the more tutored but perhaps less sympathetic reaction of the single judge, he was to have it. Beyond this, the jury trial provisions in the Federal and State Constitutions reflect a fundamental decision about the exercise of official power — a reluctance to entrust plenary powers over the life and liberty of the citizen to one judge or to a group of judges. Fear of unchecked power, so typical of our State and Federal Governments in other respects, found expression in the criminal law in this insistence upon community participation in the determination of guilt or innocence. The deep commitment of the Nation to the right of jury trial in serious criminal cases as a defense against arbitrary law enforcement qualifies for protection under the Due Process Clause of the Fourteenth Amendment, and must therefore be respected by the States.

Of course jury trial has "its weaknesses and the potential for misuse." We are aware of the long debate, especially in this century, among those who write about the administration of justice, as to the wisdom of permitting untrained laymen to determine the facts in civil and criminal proceedings. Although the debate has been intense, with powerful voices on either side, most of the controversy has centered on the jury in civil cases. Indeed, some of the severest critics of civil juries acknowledge that the arguments for criminal juries are much stronger. In addition, at the heart of the dispute have been express or implicit assertions that juries are incapable of adequately understanding evidence or determining issues of fact, and that they are unpredictable, quixotic, and little better than a roll of dice. Yet, the most recent and exhaustive study of the jury in criminal cases concluded that juries do understand the evidence and come to sound conclusions in most of the cases presented to them and that when juries differ with the result at which the judge would have arrived, it is usually because they are serving some of the very purposes for which they were created and for which they are now employed.

II

Louisiana's final contention is that even if it must grant jury trials in serious criminal cases, the conviction before us is valid and constitutional because here the petitioner was tried for simple battery and was sentenced to only 60 days in the parish prison. We are not persuaded. It is doubtless true that there is a category of petty crimes or offenses which is not subject to the Sixth Amendment jury trial provision and should not be subject to the Fourteenth Amendment jury trial requirement here applied to the States. Crimes carrying possible penalties up to six months do not require a jury trial if they otherwise qualify as petty offenses. But the penalty authorized for a particular crime is of major relevance in determining whether it is serious or not and may in itself, if severe enough, subject the trial to the mandates of the Sixth Amendment. The penalty authorized by the law of the locality may be taken "as a gauge of its social and ethical judgments" of the crime in question. . . . In the case before us the Legislature of Louisiana has made simple battery a criminal offense punishable by imprisonment for up to two years and a fine. The question, then, is whether a crime carrying such a penalty is an offense which Louisiana may insist on trying without a jury.

We think not. So-called petty offenses were tried without juries both in England and in the Colonies and have always been held to be exempt from the otherwise comprehensive language of the Sixth Amendment's jury trial provisions. There is no substantial evidence that the Framers intended to depart from this established common-law practice, and the possible consequences to defendants from convictions for petty offenses have been thought insufficient to outweigh the benefits to efficient law enforcement and simplified judicial administration resulting from the availability of speedy and inexpensive nonjury adjudications. These same considerations compel the same result under the Fourteenth Amendment. Of course the boundaries of the petty offense category have always been ill-defined, if not ambulatory. In the absence of an explicit constitutional provision, the definitional task necessarily falls on the courts, which must either pass upon the validity of legislative attempts to identify those petty offenses which are exempt from jury trial or, where the legislature has not addressed itself to the problem, themselves face the question in the first instance. In either case it is necessary to draw a line in the spectrum of crime, separating petty from serious infractions. This process, although essential, cannot be wholly satisfactory, for it requires attaching different consequences to events which, when they lie near the line, actually differ very little.

. . .

We need not settle in this case the exact location of the line between petty offenses and serious crimes. It is sufficient for our purposes to hold that a crime punishable by two years in prison is, based on past and contemporary standards in this county, a serious crime and not a petty offense. Consequently, appellant was entitled to a jury trial and it was error to deny it.

The judgment below is reversed and the case is remanded for proceedings not inconsistent with this opinion.

[JUSTICES HARLAN and STEWART dissented. JUSTICE DOUGLAS joined JUSTICE BLACK'S concurring opinion; JUSTICE FORTAS concurred in his own opinion.]

NOTE

Part of the Sixth Amendment's guarantee of trial by jury includes the right to a "public trial." That right is violated when the trial judge precludes the public from the *voir dire* of prospective jurors. *See Presley v. Georgia*, 558 U.S. 209 (2010) (per curiam). In *Presley*, the judge instructed the lone observer in the courtroom, who happened to be the defendant's uncle, to leave the courtroom to allow potential jurors to occupy the space. The trial judge said that the observer could return "once the trial starts." The Supreme Court noted that there are exceptions to the general rule that *voir dire* of jurors be open to the public but wrote that those circumstances would be rare. The Court added that trial courts are obligated to take reasonable measures to accommodate public attendance at criminal trials, including considering alternatives to closure of the proceedings.

In addition to guaranteeing to a criminal defendant a jury to evaluate guilt and a public trial, the Court in *Batson v. Kentucky*, 476 U.S. 79 (1986), held that a defendant's constitutional rights can be violated by purposeful racial discrimination in jury selection. The Court explained: "Purposeful racial discrimination in selection of the [jury] venire violates a defendant's right to equal protection because it denies him the protection that a trial by jury is intended to secure." The Court then held that the government violates the Equal Protection Clause when a prosecutor exercises her peremptory challenges "solely on account of . . . race or on the assumption that black jurors as a group will be unable impartially to consider the State's case against a black defendant." *Id.* at 89. Since *Batson*, the Court has extended these principles to gender, *see J.E.B. v. Alabama ex rel. T.B.*, 511 U.S. 127 (1994) (gender, like race, is an unconstitutional proxy for jury impartiality), and has restricted the discriminatory peremptory strikes of defendants also. *See Georgia v. McCollum*, 505 U.S. 42 (1992).

Neither the prosecution nor the defense may strike a juror based on the juror's race or gender. However, there is no prohibition against using a peremptory challenge because of a prospective juror's "demeanor." When evaluating a lawyer's motives for purportedly striking a juror based on demeanor, "the judge should take into account . . . any observations of the juror that the judge was able to make during the *voir dire*," but the Supreme Court refused the contention that "a demeanor-based explanation must be rejected if the judge did not observe or cannot recall the juror's demeanor." *Thaler v. Haynes*, 559 U.S. 43 (2010) (per curiam).

§ 7.03 THE RIGHT TO CONFRONT WITNESSES

[A] The Presence of the Accused

ILLINOIS v. ALLEN

United States Supreme Court

397 U.S. 337 (1970)

Justice Black delivered the opinion of the Court.

The Confrontation Clause of the Sixth Amendment to the United States Constitution provides that: "In all criminal prosecutions, the accused shall enjoy the right . . . to be confronted with the witnesses against him. . . ." We have held that the Fourteenth Amendment makes the guarantees of this clause obligatory upon the States. *Pointer v. Texas*, 380 U.S. 400 (1965). One of the most basic of the rights guaranteed by the Confrontation Clause is the accused's right to be present in the courtroom at every stage of his trial. *Lewis v. United States*, 146 U.S. 370 (1892).

The question presented in this case is whether an accused can claim the benefit of this constitutional right to remain in the courtroom while at the same time he engages in speech and conduct which is so noisy, disorderly, and disruptive that it is exceedingly difficult or wholly impossible to carry on the trial.

The issue arose in the following way. The respondent, Allen, was convicted by an Illinois jury of armed robbery and was sentenced to serve 10 to 30 years in the Illinois State Penitentiary.

The facts surrounding Allen's expulsion from the courtroom are set out in the Court of Appeals' opinion sustaining Allen's contention:

> After his indictment and during the pretrial stage, the petitioner Allen refused court-appointed counsel and indicated to the trial court on several occasions that he wished to conduct his own defense. After considerable argument by the petitioner, the trial judge told him, "I'll let you be your own lawyer, but I'll ask Mr. Kelly [court-appointed counsel] to sit in and protect the record for you, insofar as possible."
>
> The trial began on September 9, 1957. After the State's Attorney had accepted the first four jurors following their voir dire examination, the petitioner began examining the first juror and continued at great length. Finally, the trial judge interrupted the petitioner, requesting him to confine his questions solely to matters relating to the prospective juror's qualifications. At that point, the petitioner started to argue with the judge in a most abusive and disrespectful manner. At last, and seeming in desperation, the judge asked appointed counsel to proceed with the examination of the jurors. The petitioner continued to talk, proclaiming that the appointed attorney was not going to act as his lawyer. He terminated his remarks by saying, "When I go out for lunchtime, you're [the judge] going to be a corpse here." At that point he tore the file which his attorney had and threw the papers on the floor. The trial judge thereupon stated to the petitioner,

> "One more outbreak of that sort and I'll remove you from the courtroom." This warning had no effect on the petitioner. He continued to talk back to the judge, saying, "There's not going to be no trial, either. I'm going to sit here and you're going to talk and you can bring your shackles out and straight jacket and put them on me and tape my mouth, but it will do no good because there's not going to be no trial." After more abusive remarks by the petitioner, the trial judge ordered the trial to proceed in the petitioner's absence. The petitioner was removed from the courtroom. The voir dire examination then continued and the jury was selected in the absence of the petitioner.
>
> After a noon recess and before the jury was brought into the courtroom, the petitioner, appearing before the judge, complained about the fairness of the trial and his appointed attorney. He also said he wanted to be present in the court during his trial. In reply, the judge said that the petitioner would be permitted to remain in the courtroom if he "behaved [himself] and [did] not interfere with the introduction of the case." The jury was brought in and seated. Counsel for the petitioner then moved to exclude the witnesses from the courtroom. The [petitioner] protested this effort on the part of his attorney, saying: "There is going to be no proceeding. I'm going to start talking and I'm going to keep on talking all through the trial. There's not going to be no trial like this. I want my sister and my friends here in court to testify for me." The trial judge thereupon ordered the petitioner removed from the courtroom.

After this second removal, Allen remained out of the courtroom during the presentation of the State's case-in-chief, except that he was brought in on several occasions for purposes of identification. During one of these latter appearances, Allen responded to one of the judge's questions with vile and abusive language. After the prosecution's case had been presented, the trial judge reiterated his promise to Allen that he could return to the courtroom whenever he agreed to conduct himself properly. Allen gave some assurances of proper conduct and was permitted to be present through the remainder of the trial, principally his defense, which was conducted by his appointed counsel.

. . .

The Court of Appeals felt that the defendant's Sixth Amendment right to be present at his own trial was so "absolute" that, no matter how unruly or disruptive the defendant's conduct might be, he could never be held to have lost that right so long as he continued to insist upon it, as Allen clearly did. Therefore the Court of Appeals concluded that a trial judge could never expel a defendant from his own trial and that the judge's ultimate remedy when faced with an obstreperous defendant like Allen who determines to make his trial impossible is to bind and gag him. We cannot agree that the Sixth Amendment, the cases upon which the Court of Appeals relied, or any other cases of this Court so handicap a trial judge in conducting a criminal trial. . . . We accept instead the statement of Mr. Justice Cardozo who, speaking for the Court in *Snyder v. Massachusetts*, 291 U.S. 97 (1934), said: "No doubt the privilege [of personally confronting witnesses] may be lost by consent or at times even by misconduct." Although mindful that courts must indulge every reasonable presumption against the loss of constitutional rights, we explicitly hold today that a defendant can lose his right to be present at trial if, after he has been warned by the judge that he will be removed if he continues his disruptive behavior, he nevertheless insists on conducting himself in a manner so disorderly, disruptive, and disrespectful of the court that his trial cannot be carried on with him in the courtroom. Once lost, the right to be present can, of course, be reclaimed as soon as the defendant is willing to conduct himself consistently with the decorum and respect inherent in the concept of courts and judicial proceedings.

It is essential to the proper administration of criminal justice that dignity, order, and decorum be the hallmarks of all court proceedings in our country. The flagrant disregard in the courtroom of elementary standards of proper conduct should not and cannot be tolerated. We believe trial judges confronted with disruptive, contumacious, stubbornly defiant defendants must be given sufficient discretion to meet the circumstances of each case. No one formula for maintaining the appropriate courtroom atmosphere will be best in all situations. We think there are at least three constitutionally permissible ways for a trial judge to handle an obstreperous defendant like Allen: (1) bind and gag him, thereby keeping him present; (2) cite him for contempt; (3) take him out of the courtroom until he promises to conduct himself properly.

I

Trying a defendant for a crime while he sits bound and gagged before the judge and jury would to an extent comply with that part of the Sixth Amendment's purposes that accords the defendant an opportunity to confront the witnesses at the trial. But even to contemplate such a technique, much less see it, arouses a feeling that no person should be tried while shackled and gagged except as a last resort. Not only is it possible that the sight of shackles and gags might have a significant effect on the jury's feelings about the defendant, but the use of this technique is itself something of an affront to the very dignity and decorum of judicial proceedings that the judge is seeking to uphold. Moreover, one of the defendant's primary advantages of being present at the trial, his ability to communicate with his counsel, is greatly reduced when the defendant is in a condition of total physical restraint. It is in part because of these inherent disadvantages and limitations in this method of dealing with disorderly defendants that we decline to hold with the Court of Appeals that a defendant cannot under any possible circumstances be deprived of his right to be present at trial. However, in some situations which we need not attempt to foresee, binding and gagging might possibly be the fairest and most reasonable way to handle a defendant who acts as Allen did here.

II

In a footnote the Court of Appeals suggested the possible availability of contempt of court as a remedy to make Allen behave in his robbery trial, and it is true that citing or threatening to cite a contumacious defendant for criminal contempt might in itself be sufficient to make a defendant stop interrupting a trial. If so, the problem would be solved easily, and the defendant could remain in the courtroom. Of course, if the defendant is determined to prevent any trial, then a court in attempting to try the defendant for contempt is still confronted with the identical dilemma that the Illinois court faced in this case. And criminal contempt has obvious limitations as a sanction when the defendant is charged with a crime so serious that a very severe sentence such as death or life imprisonment is likely to be imposed. In such a case the defendant might not be affected by a mere contempt sentence when he ultimately faces a far more serious sanction. Nevertheless, the contempt remedy should be borne in mind by a judge in the circumstances of this case.

Another aspect of the contempt remedy is the judge's power, when exercised consistently with state and federal law, to imprison an unruly defendant such as Allen for civil contempt and discontinue the trial until such time as the defendant promises to behave himself. This procedure is consistent with the defendant's right to be present at trial, and yet it avoids the serious shortcomings of the use of shackles and gags. It must be recognized, however, that a defendant might conceivably, as a matter of calculated strategy, elect to spend a prolonged period in confinement for contempt in the hope that adverse witnesses might be unavailable after a lapse of time. A court must guard against allowing a defendant to profit from his own wrong in this way.

III

The trial court in this case decided under the circumstances to remove the defendant from the courtroom and to continue his trial in his absence until and unless he promised to conduct himself in a manner befitting an American courtroom. As we said earlier, we find nothing unconstitutional about this procedure. Allen's behavior was clearly of such an extreme and aggravated nature as to justify either his removal from the courtroom or his total physical restraint. Prior to his removal he was repeatedly warned by the trial judge that he would be removed from the courtroom if he persisted in his unruly conduct, and, as Judge Hastings observed in his dissenting opinion, the record demonstrates that Allen would not have been at all dissuaded by the trial judge's use of his criminal contempt powers. Allen was constantly informed that he could return to the trial when he would agree to conduct himself in an orderly manner. Under these circumstances we hold that Allen lost his right guaranteed by the Sixth and Fourteenth Amendments to be present throughout his trial.

IV

It is not pleasant to hold that the respondent Allen was properly banished from the court for a part of his own trial. But our courts, palladiums of liberty as they are, cannot be treated disrespectfully with impunity. Nor can the accused be permitted by his disruptive conduct indefinitely to avoid being tried on the charges brought against him. It would degrade our country and our judicial system to permit our courts to be bullied, insulted, and humiliated and their orderly progress thwarted and obstructed by defendants brought before them charged with crimes. As guardians of the public welfare, our state and federal judicial systems strive to administer equal justice to the rich and the poor, the good and the bad, the native and foreign born of every race, nationality and religion. Being manned by humans, the courts are not perfect and are bound to make some errors. But, if our courts are to remain what the Founders intended, the citadels of justice, their proceedings cannot and must not be infected with the sort of scurrilous, abusive language and conduct paraded before the Illinois trial judge in this case. The record shows that the Illinois judge at all times conducted himself with that dignity, decorum, and patience that befit a judge. Even in holding that the trial judge had erred, the Court of Appeals praised his "commendable patience under severe provocation."

We do not hold that removing this defendant from his own trial was the only way the Illinois judge could have constitutionally solved the problem he had. We do hold, however, that there is nothing whatever in this record to show that the judge did not act completely within his discretion. Deplorable as it is to remove a man from his own trial, even for a short time, we hold that the judge did not commit legal error in doing what he did.

The judgment of the Court of Appeals is reversed.

NOTES AND QUESTIONS

(1) According to the Court, the measures discussed could be used if the defendant had been sufficiently warned of the consequences of his behavior. What kind of warning is necessary? In *United States v. Munn*, 507 F.2d 563 (10th Cir. 1974), *cert. denied*, 421 U.S. 968 (1975), the defendant had assaulted three of his lawyers and made abusive comments to the judge during pretrial proceedings. The judge told the defendant that if he created any further disturbance he would be removed from the courtroom. A few weeks later, the defendant "directed exceedingly foul and abusive language at the trial judge and his counsel" and the judge immediately ordered him removed. Did this action violate the defendant's right to be present? Held, no violation; the defendant had been warned previously and "it was not necessary for the trial court to thereafter warn him a second time before taking affirmative action."

Compare the sufficient warnings in *Munn* with the trial court's constitutionally inadequate warning in *Gray v. Moore*, 520 F.3d 616 (6th Cir. 2008). In *Gray*, the defendant, who was charged with the murder of his brother, yelled out repeatedly in the middle of testimony from the deceased brother's girlfriend. Interjecting when the girlfriend tried to discuss the defendant's behavior immediately before and after the killing, the defendant exclaimed: "Why are you lying? You lying. You know it." In response, the judge instructed a deputy to remove the defendant from the courtroom. Hearing the judge's directive to the deputy, the defendant continued his outburst: "She's lying, your Honor . . . Your Honor, she's lying. She knows it. She's lying." *Id.* at 620. The Sixth Circuit found that the trial judge had breached the mandates of *Allen*. "While it is without question that Gray engaged in disorderly and disruptive behavior when he repeatedly yelled, . . . at most this conduct entitled the trial court to *threaten* removal." *Id.* at 623.

(2) What if the defendant is pro se, and the trial judge excludes him for misconduct without appointing replacement counsel in his absence?

In *Davis v. Grant*, 532 F.3d 132 (2d Cir. 2008), the court considered this issue in the context of a habeas petition. The defendant had exercised his right to represent himself on charges of assault, reckless endangerment, and grand larceny. The trial judge appointed standby counsel to assist. Before trial began, the judge warned Davis that if he misbehaved, he would be removed from the courtroom. When trial began, Davis started complaining about his standby counsel's inadequacies and the lawyer's defense strategy. Out of the presence of the jury, the judge removed Davis from the courtroom because Davis refused to stop complaining. Davis was later brought back into the courtroom, but before the prosecutor could call his first witness, Davis yelled: "Ladies and Gentlemen of the jury . . . I don't believe I'm receiving a fair trial because in this courtroom because this judge is prejudice. [sic]" *Id.* at 136. Davis was again removed from the courtroom for a short time. When Davis was returned to the courtroom, he reiterated his complaints about standby counsel and said that he did not want his appointed counsel to sit next to him. The trial judge instructed the lawyer to move to the public seating area. Before the judge could bring the jury back, Davis announced that "I'm going to prejudice the jury." *Id.* at 137. When Davis would not tell the judge what he meant, Davis was again removed from the courtroom, and the judge announced that the case would be tried without the defendant or the assistance of his stand-by counsel. The prosecutor called a police officer as the government's first witness. After the officer's direct testimony, the trial judge took a recess to determine whether Davis could be returned to the trial without further disruption. Despite renewed assurances that he would behave, "as soon as the jury entered the courtroom, Davis started screaming racial epithets." *Id.* Davis was once again removed from the courtroom, and the court told the officer/witness that she would not be subject to cross-examination, even though standby counsel was still in the courtroom. The prosecution called two more law enforcement officers who testified on direct but were spared any cross-examination. Following this testimony, Davis was brought back into the courtroom, and he permitted his appointed counsel to cross-examine the remaining prosecution witnesses. The jury convicted Davis on all charges.

Davis's direct appeals were rejected, so he petitioned for a writ of habeas corpus, contending that his Sixth Amendment rights were violated when he was removed from the courtroom with no standby counsel representing him in his absence. The Second Circuit Court of Appeals indicated that if it were deciding the issue de novo, the court might "conclude that the trial court was constitutionally required to appoint standby counsel for Davis during his involuntary absence from the courtroom." *Id.* at 139-40. But, the court said that it was not convinced that the trial judge's failure to require counsel during the defendant's absence was "an objectively unreasonable application of, or failure to extend, clearly established Supreme Court precedent," as required to satisfy the habeas standard of review. Nevertheless, the court added: "Frankly, more guidance from the Supreme Court would be helpful." *Id.* at 140.

(3) The United States Supreme Court extended the *Allen* principle to sentencing proceedings in capital cases. In *Deck v. Missouri*, 544 U.S. 622 (2005), the trial judge ordered the defendant shackled with handcuffs, leg irons, and a belly chain at a sentencing hearing before a jury. The judge made no findings as to the need for the restraints. The Supreme Court found a constitutional violation. Relying on *Allen*, the Court wrote that the government may only order the defendant shackled "in the presence of a special need . . . [with] a trial court determination . . . [that

the shackles] are justified by a state interest specific to the particular defendant on trial." *Id.* The Court explained further:

> There will be cases, of course, where these perils of shackling are unavoidable. . . . We do not underestimate the need to restrain dangerous defendants to prevent courtroom attacks, or the need to give trial courts latitude in making individualized security determinations. We are mindful of the tragedy that can result if judges are not able to protect themselves and their courtrooms. But given their prejudicial effect, due process does not permit the use of visible restraints if the trial court has not taken account of the circumstances of the particular case.

Id. at 632. The court in *United States v. Baker*, 432 F.3d 1189 (11th Cir. 2005), elaborated on the principles of *Deck*:

> First, the decision to use shackles to restrain a defendant at trial should rarely be employed as a security device. The Supreme Court has observed that "no person should be tried while shackled . . . except as a last resort." Second, the act of shackling a defendant implicates a defendant's right to a fair trial. Among the important interests implicated by shackling are the presumption that a defendant is innocent until proven guilty, the right of the accused to secure a meaningful defense, and the need to maintain a judicial process that is not an affront to the dignity and decorum of the proceeding itself.
>
> Third, if a judge intends to shackle a defendant, he must make a case specific and individualized assessment of each defendant in that particular trial. That assessment may include consideration of, among other things, the criminal history and background of each of the defendants, including whether the defendant has a history of violent acts; the number of defendants being tried together; the nature of the charges pending against the defendants, including whether the charged offenses include violent criminal conduct; any past history of conduct by a defendant that may have disrupted a criminal proceeding; and other circumstances, such as threatening behavior against witnesses or court personnel, that may reasonably bear upon the safety of the courtroom and its occupants or upon the danger of escape.

Baker, 432 F.3d at 1244. The Eleventh Circuit concluded: "*Deck* has made clear that the district court must identify particular security concerns, related to the defendants on trial, that justify shackling." *Id.* at 1245.

(4) The criminal defendant in *Bass v. Scully*, 556 F. Supp. 778 (S.D.N.Y. 1983), interrupted the state trial on several occasions, complaining to judge and jury about the inadequacy of appointed counsel. After repeated warnings, the defendant was handcuffed and gagged in view of the jury. Were the defendant's actions sufficient to warrant the handcuffing and gagging? Yes, held the federal judge.

> It is true, as Bass contends, that his conduct was a far cry from the behavior of the defendant in *Allen*, who threatened to kill the trial judge, or from the defendants in *United States v. Bentvena*, 319 F.2d 916 (2d Cir. 1963)375 U.S. 940 (1963), who threw a chair at the prosecutor and climbed into the

> jury box to assault the jurors. However, Bass' interruptions were sufficiently serious and continuous to make it impossible for the voir dire to proceed. Judge Walsh was faced with the prospect either of restraining Bass and his co-defendant or adjourning the proceedings indefinitely.
>
> . . .
>
> [B]inding and gagging is strenuously discouraged, although, in certain circumstances, it may be the preferable means of restoring order. The circumstances of the instant case are a good example of those in which binding and gagging, as distasteful as it is, was preferable to removing the defendants from the courtroom.
>
> The cause of the disruption was the defendants' dissatisfaction with and distrust of their counsel. If the defendants had been removed from the courtroom, they would not even have had the opportunity to observe counsel's actions. Where a defendant's distrust of his appointed counsel is so great, excluding him from the proceedings would only exacerbate his sense of uneasiness as to his counsel's behavior, and his lack of opportunity to confer with counsel at trial, to instruct him and to be a personal witness to counsel's handling of the case should he wish to pursue his claim of inadequacy of representation.

Id. at 781. *See also Rhoden v. Rowland*, 172 F.3d 633, 636 (9th Cir. 1999) ("Because visible shackling during trial is so likely to cause a defendant prejudice, it is permitted only when justified by an essential state interest specific to each trial. Therefore, due process requires the trial court to engage in an analysis of the security risks posed by the defendant and to consider less restrictive alternatives before permitting a defendant to be restrained."); *State v. Artwell*, 832 A.2d 295 (N.J. 2003) (deciding that requiring defense *witnesses* to appear in shackles or prison garb "presents a risk of unfair prejudice to a defendant" and a trial court may subject a witness to such physical restraints "only when it has reason to believe it is necessary to maintain the security of the courtroom"); *State v. Kuchera*, 969 A.2d 1052 (N.J. 2009) (exercising its "supervisory powers" to extend the principles of *Deck* and *Artwell* to the prosecution's witnesses so that "unless otherwise affirmatively permitted by the trial court in the exercise of its discretion, witnesses in criminal cases — both for the prosecution and for the defense — should not testify in prison garb). Nevertheless, the non-visible shackling of a defendant during trial does not violate due process. *United States v. Jackson*, 2011 U.S. App. LEXIS 8963 (7th Cir. Apr. 6, 2011).

(5) Rule 43 of the Federal Rules of Criminal Procedure expressly addresses a defendant's presence in federal criminal proceedings.

Defendant's Presence

(a) When Required. Unless this Rule, Rule 5, or Rule 10 provides otherwise, the defendant must be present at:

(1) the initial appearance, the initial arraignment, and the plea;

(2) every trial stage, including jury impanelment and the return of the verdict; and

(3) sentencing.

(b) When Not Required. A defendant need not be present under any of the following circumstances:

(1) Organizational Defendant. The defendant is an organization represented by counsel who is present.

(2) Misdemeanor Offense. The offense is punishable by fine or by imprisonment for not more than one year, or both, and with the defendant's written consent, the court permits arraignment, plea, trial, and sentencing to occur in the defendant's absence.

(3) Conference or Hearing on a Legal Question. The proceeding involves only a conference or hearing on a question of law.

(4) Sentence Correction. The proceeding involves the correction or reduction of sentence under Rule 35 or 18 U.S.C. 3582(c).

(c) Waiving Continued Presence.

(1) In General. A defendant who was initially present at trial, or who had pleaded guilty or nolo contendere, waives the right to be present under the following circumstances:

(A) when the defendant is voluntarily absent after the trial has begun, regardless of whether the court informed the defendant of an obligation to remain during trial;

(B) in a noncapital case, when the defendant is voluntarily absent during sentencing; or

(C) when the court warns the defendant that it will remove the defendant from the courtroom for disruptive behavior, but the defendant persists in conduct that justifies removal from the courtroom.

(2) Waiver's Effect. If the defendant waives the right to be present, the trial may proceed to completion, including the verdict's return and sentencing, during the defendant's absence.

In 2002, Rule 43 was amended to make it easier to read and to recognize several exceptions to the requirement that a defendant be present in court for all proceedings. In addition to allowing for some specific exceptions, the Rule references Rules 5 and 10, F. R. Crim. P., permitting video teleconferencing for an initial appearance and waivers of the right to be present for arraignment.

(6) As Rule 43 says, a defendant can lose his right to be present at trial because of his voluntary absence. Nevertheless, the New Jersey Supreme Court has held that under New Jersey's analog to Rule 43, a defendant does not waive his right to be present for charges added after he received the initial trial notice, if he was never arraigned on those charges and did not receive actual notice at a court proceeding.

State v. Grenci, 964 A.2d 776 (N.J. 2009). In *Grenci*, the defendant was initially indicted and arraigned on one count of second degree burglary. He absconded. Later, the indictment was superseded to add six counts of aggravated assault. The defendant was never arraigned on the new charges and was tried in absentia. The New Jersey Supreme Court found error.

[B] Use of Codefendants' Confessions

BRUTON v. UNITED STATES

United States Supreme Court
391 U.S. 123 (1968)

JUSTICE BRENNAN delivered the opinion of the Court.

This case presents the question . . . whether the conviction of a defendant at a joint trial should be set aside although the jury was instructed that a codefendant's confession inculpating the defendant had to be disregarded in determining his guilt or innocence.

A joint trial of petitioner and one Evans in the District Court for the Eastern District of Missouri resulted in the conviction of both by a jury on a federal charge of armed postal robbery. A postal inspector testified that Evans orally confessed to him that Evans and petitioner committed the armed robbery. The postal inspector obtained the oral confession, and another in which Evans admitted he had an accomplice whom he would not name, in the course of two interrogations of Evans at the city jail in St. Louis, Missouri, where Evans was held in custody on state criminal charges. Both petitioner and Evans appealed their convictions to the Court of Appeals for the Eighth Circuit. That court set aside Evans' conviction on the ground that his oral confessions to the postal inspector should not have been received in evidence against him. However, the court . . . affirmed petitioner's conviction because the trial judge instructed the jury that although Evans' confession was competent evidence against Evans it was inadmissible hearsay against petitioner and therefore had to be disregarded in determining petitioner's guilt or innocence.[1]

---

[1] [2] At the close of the Government's direct case, the trial judge cautioned the jury that Evans' admission implicating petitioner "if used, can only be used against the defendant Evans. It is hearsay insofar as the defendant George William Bruton is concerned, and you are not to consider it in any respect to the defendant Bruton, because insofar as he is concerned it is hearsay."

The instructions to the jury included the following:

> A confession made outside of court by one defendant may not be considered as evidence against the other defendant, who was not present and in no way a party to the confession. Therefore, if you find that a confession was in fact voluntarily and intentionally made by the defendant Evans, you should consider it as evidence in the case against Evans, but you must not consider it, and should disregard it, in considering the evidence in the case against the defendant Bruton. . . . It is your duty to give separate, personal consideration to the cause of each individual defendant. When you do so, you should analyze what the evidence shows with respect to that individual, leaving out of consideration entirely any evidence admitted solely against some other defendant. Each defendant is entitled to have his case determined from his

. . .

We hold that, because of the substantial risk that the jury, despite instructions to the contrary, looked to the incriminating extrajudicial statements in determining petitioner's guilt, admission of Evans' confession in this joint trial violated petitioner's right of cross-examination secured by the Confrontation Clause of the Sixth Amendment.

. . .

If it were true that the jury disregarded the reference to the codefendant, no question would arise under the Confrontation Clause, because by hypothesis the case is treated as if the confessor made no statement inculpating the nonconfessor.

[W]e pause to observe that in *Pointer v. State of Texas*, 380 U.S. 400 (1965), we confirmed "that the right of cross-examination is included in the right of an accused in a criminal case to confront the witnesses against him" secured by the Sixth Amendment; "a major reason underlying the constitutional confrontation rule is to give a defendant charged with crime an opportunity to cross-examine the witnesses against him."

Here Evans' oral confessions were in fact testified to, and were therefore actually in evidence. That testimony was legitimate evidence against Evans and to that extent was properly before the jury during its deliberations. Even greater, then, was the likelihood that the jury would believe Evans made the statements and that they were true — not just the self-incriminating portions but those implicating petitioner as well. Plainly, the introduction of Evans' confession added substantial, perhaps even critical, weight to the Government's case in a form not subject to cross-examination, since Evans did not take the stand. Petitioner thus was denied his constitutional right of confrontation.

[We previously] assumed that this encroachment on the right to confrontation could be avoided by the instruction to the jury to disregard the inadmissible hearsay evidence.[2] But, as we have said, that assumption has since been effectively repudiated. . . . [T]he dissenting opinion of Mr. Justice Frankfurter for the four Justices who dissented in *Delli Paoli* challenged the basic premise that a properly instructed jury would ignore the confessor's inculpation of the nonconfessor in determining the latter's guilt. "The fact of the matter is that too often such admonition against misuse is intrinsically ineffective in that the effect of such a nonadmissible declaration cannot be wiped from the brains of the jurors. The admonition therefore becomes a futile collocation of words and fails of its purpose as a legal protection to defendants against whom such a declaration should not tell."

The dissent went on to say, "The government should not have the windfall of having the jury be influenced by evidence against a defendant which, as a matter of

---

own acts and statements and the other evidence in the case which may be applicable to him.

[2] [3] We emphasize that the hearsay statement inculpating petitioner was clearly inadmissible against him under traditional rules of evidence, the problem arising only because the statement was admissible against the declarant Evans. There is not before us, therefore, any recognized exception to the hearsay rule insofar as petitioner is concerned and we intimate no view whatever that such exceptions necessarily raise questions under the Confrontation Clause.

law, they should not consider but which they cannot put out of their minds."

To the same effect . . . is the statement of Mr. Justice Jackson in his concurring opinion in *Krulewitch v. United States*: "The naive assumption that prejudicial effects can be overcome by instructions to the jury . . . all practicing lawyers know to be unmitigated fiction. . . ."[3] In Judge Hand's view the limiting instruction, although not really capable of preventing the jury from considering the prejudicial evidence, does as a matter of form provide a way around the exclusionary rules of evidence that is defensible because it "probably furthers, rather than impedes, the search for truth."

Insofar as this implies the prosecution ought not to be denied the benefit of the confession to prove the confessor's guilt, however, it overlooks alternative ways of achieving that benefit without at the same time infringing the nonconfessor's right of confrontation.[4] Where viable alternatives do exist, it is deceptive to rely on the pursuit of truth to defend a clearly harmful practice.

Another reason cited is the justification for joint trials in general, the argument being that the benefits of joint proceedings should not have to be sacrificed by requiring separate trials in order to use the confession against the declarant. Joint trials do conserve state funds, diminish inconvenience to witnesses and public authorities, and avoid delays in bringing those accused of crime to trial. But the answer to this argument was cogently stated by Judge Lehman of the New York Court of Appeals:

> We still adhere to the rule that an accused is entitled to confrontation of the witnesses against him and the right to cross-examine them. . . . We destroy the age-old rule which in the past has been regarded as a fundamental principle of our jurisprudence by a legalistic formula, required of the judge, that the jury may not consider any admissions against any party who did not join in them. We secure greater speed, economy and convenience in the administration of the law at the price of fundamental principles of constitutional liberty. That price is too high.

Finally, the reason advanced by the majority in *Delli Paoli* was to tie the result to maintenance of the jury system. "Unless we proceed on the basis that the jury will follow the court's instructions where those instructions are clear and the

---

[3] [8] Judge Learned Hand addressed the subject of limiting instructions several times. The limiting instruction, he said, is a "recommendation to the jury of a mental gymnastic which is beyond, not only their powers, but anybody's else." He said that "[n]obody can indeed fail to doubt whether the caution is effective, or whether usually the practical result is not to let in hearsay"[;] "it is indeed very hard to believe that a jury will, or for that matter can, in practice observe the admonition[.]" Judge Hand referred to the instruction as a "placebo," medically defined as "a medicinal lie." Judge Jerome Frank suggested that its legal equivalent "is a kind of 'judicial lie': It undermines a moral relationship between the courts, the jurors, and the public; like any other judicial deception, it damages the decent judicial administration of justice." *Compare* E. Morgan, *Some Problems of Proof Under the Anglo-American System of Litigation* 105 (1956), who suggests that the use of limiting instructions fosters an inconsistent attitude toward juries by "treating them at times as a group of low-grade morons and at other times as men endowed with a superhuman ability to control their emotions and intellects."

[4] [10] Some courts have required deletion of references to codefendants where practicable.

circumstances are such that the jury can reasonably be expected to follow them, the jury system makes little sense."

We agree that there are many circumstances in which this reliance is justified. Not every admission of inadmissible hearsay or other evidence can be considered to be reversible error unavoidable through limiting instructions; instances occur in almost every trial where inadmissible evidence creeps in, usually inadvertently. "A defendant is entitled to a fair trial but not a perfect one."

It is not unreasonable to conclude that in many such cases the jury can and will follow the trial judge's instructions to disregard such information. Nevertheless, there are some contexts in which the risk that the jury will not, or cannot, follow instructions is so great, and the consequences of failure so vital to the defendant, that the practical and human limitations of the jury system cannot be ignored. Such a context is presented here, where the powerfully incriminating extrajudicial statements of a codefendant, who stands accused side-by-side with the defendant, are deliberately spread before the jury in a joint trial. Not only are the incriminations devastating to the defendant but their credibility is inevitably suspect, a fact recognized when accomplices do take the stand and the jury is instructed to weigh their testimony carefully given the recognized motivation to shift blame onto others. The unreliability of such evidence is intolerably compounded when the alleged accomplice, as here, does not testify and cannot be tested by cross-examination. It was against such threats to a fair trial that the Confrontation Clause was directed.

Here the introduction of Evans' confession posed a substantial threat to petitioner's right to confront the witnesses against him, and this is a hazard we cannot ignore. Despite the concededly clear instructions to the jury to disregard Evans' inadmissible hearsay evidence inculpating petitioner, in the context of a joint trial we cannot accept limiting instructions as an adequate substitute for petitioner's constitutional right of cross-examination. The effect is the same as if there had been no instruction at all.

Reversed.

JUSTICE BLACK concurs in the result for the reasons stated in the dissent in *Delli Paoli v. United States.*

JUSTICE MARSHALL took no part in the consideration or decision of this case.

JUSTICE STEWART, concurring.

I think it clear that the underlying rationale of the Sixth Amendment's Confrontation Clause precludes reliance upon cautionary instructions when the highly damaging out-of-court statement of a codefendant, who is not subject to cross-examination, is deliberately placed before the jury at a joint trial. A basic premise of the Confrontation Clause, it seems to me, is that certain kinds of hearsay are at once so damaging, so suspect, and yet so difficult to discount, that jurors cannot be trusted to give such evidence the minimal weight it logically deserves, *whatever* instructions the trial judge might give.

Justice White [joined by Justice Harlan], dissenting.

Whether or not Evans' confession was inadmissible against him, nothing in that confession which was relevant and material to Bruton's case was admissible against Bruton. As to him it was inadmissible hearsay, a presumptively unreliable out-of-court statement of a non-party who was not a witness subject to cross-examination. Admitting Evans' confession against Bruton would require a new trial unless the error was harmless.

The trial judge in this case had no different view. He admitted Evans' confession only against Evans, not against Bruton, and carefully instructed the jury to disregard it in determining Bruton's guilt or innocence.

[T]he Court now holds this instruction insufficient and reverses Bruton's conviction. It would apparently also reverse every other case where a court admits a codefendant's confession implicating a defendant, regardless of cautionary instructions and regardless of the circumstances. I dissent from this excessively rigid rule. There is nothing in this record to suggest that the jury did not follow the trial judge's instructions.

It is a common experience of all men to be informed of "facts" relevant to an issue requiring their judgment, and yet to disregard those "facts" because of sufficient grounds for discrediting their veracity or the reliability of their source. Responsible judgment would be impossible but for the ability of men to focus their attention wholly on reliable and credible evidence, and jurymen are no less capable of exercising this capacity than other men. Because I have no doubt that serious-minded and responsible men are able to shut their minds to unreliable information when exercising their judgment, I reject the assumption of the majority that giving instructions to a jury to disregard a codefendant's confession is an empty gesture.

The rule which the Court announces today will severely limit the circumstances in which defendants may be tried together for a crime which they are both charged with committing. Unquestionably, joint trials are more economical and minimize the burden on witnesses, prosecutors, and courts. They also avoid delays in bringing those accused of crime to trial. This much the Court concedes. It is also worth saying that separate trials are apt to have varying consequences for legally indistinguishable defendants. The unfairness of this is confirmed by the common prosecutorial experience of seeing codefendants who are tried separately strenuously jockeying for position with regard to who should be the first to be tried.

NOTES AND QUESTIONS

(1) The essential question in *Bruton* was whether the jurors could follow the limiting instruction that told them to consider the confession only against the party making it. What basis did the majority have for deciding that the jurors might not follow such an instruction? Is there something particularly unusual about the codefendant confession situation that makes the jury instruction difficult to follow? If the jurors cannot follow the instruction here, can they be trusted to follow the instruction concerning the limited use of the defendant's own confession offered for impeachment purposes as in *Harris v. New York*, 401 U.S. 222 (1971), *supra*

§ 6.02[D][3]? How does *Bruton* affect bench trials; does it apply at all? No, said the Third Circuit Court of Appeals. *See Johnson v. Tennis*, 549 F.3d 296 (3d Cir. 2008) (holding that by its own terms, "*Bruton* applies to jury trials only.").

(2) In *Bruton*, Justice Brennan suggested that one way out of the confrontation dilemma was to have the codefendant's confession purged of references to the defendant. Would such a process of deletion or "redaction" be successful? The Supreme Court has twice dealt with the issue since *Bruton*. In *Richardson v. Marsh*, 481 U.S. 200 (1987), the codefendant's confession was redacted so that all references to the defendant were omitted. The jury was specifically instructed not to use the codefendant's confession against the defendant. The defendant complained about the use of this confession, however, because other evidence clearly implicated her in the crime and indicated to the jury that she was the one whose name had been redacted from the codefendant's confession. The majority rejected the defense's position:

> [E]vidence requiring linkage differs from evidence incriminating on its face in the practical effects which application of the *Bruton* exception would produce. If limited to facially incriminating confessions, *Bruton* can be complied with by redaction — a possibility suggested in that opinion itself. If extended to confessions incriminating by connection, not only is that not possible, but it is not even possible to predict the admissibility of a confession in advance of trial. The "contextual implication" doctrine articulated by the Court of Appeals would presumably require the trial judge to assess at the end of each trial whether, in light of all of the evidence, a nontestifying codefendant's confession has been so "powerfully incriminating" that a new, separate trial is required for the defendant. This obviously lends itself to manipulation by the defense — and even without manipulation will result in numerous mistrials and appeals.
>
> . . . The rule that juries are presumed to follow their instructions is a pragmatic one, rooted less in the absolute certitude that the presumption is true than in the belief that it represents a reasonable practical accommodation of the interests of the state and the defendant in the criminal justice process. On the precise facts of *Bruton*, involving a facially incriminating confession, we found that accommodation inadequate. As our discussion above shows, the calculus changes when confessions that do not name the defendant are at issue. While we continue to apply *Bruton* where we have found that its rationale validly applies, we decline to extend it further. We hold that the Confrontation Clause is not violated by the admission of a nontestifying codefendant's confession with a proper limiting instruction when, as here, the confession is redacted to eliminate not only the defendant's name, but any reference to her existence.

Id. at 208-09, 211.

Richardson v. Marsh was limited in *Gray v. Maryland*, 523 U.S. 185 (1998). In *Gray*, the prosecution, seeking to satisfy *Bruton*, redacted the confession by substituting for the codefendant's name the word "deleted," or a blank space. The majority found that *Bruton* had been violated; it also distinguished *Richardson*. The Court explained that in *Richardson v. Marsh*, the government "had redacted the confession of one defendant, Williams, so as to 'omit all reference' to his codefendant, Marsh — 'indeed, to omit all indication that *anyone* other than . . . Williams' and a third person had 'participated in the crime.' " *Gray*, 523 U.S. at 190-91. The Court reasoned:

> [U]nlike *Richardson*'s redacted confession, this confession refers directly to the "existence" of the nonconfessing defendant. The State has simply replaced the nonconfessing defendant's name with a kind of symbol, namely the word "deleted" or a blank space set off by commas. The redacted confession, for example, responded to the question "Who was in the group that beat Stacey," with the phrase, "Me, and a few other guys." . . . We therefore must decide a question that *Richardson* left open, namely whether redaction that replaces a defendant's name with an obvious indication of deletion, such as a blank space, the word "deleted," or a similar symbol, still falls within *Bruton*'s protection rule. We hold that it does. . . .
>
> Redactions that simply replace a name with an obvious blank space or a word such as "deleted" or a symbol or other similarly obvious indications of alteration, however, leave statements that, considered as a class, so closely resemble *Bruton*'s unredacted statements that, in our view, the law must require the same result.
>
> For one thing, a jury will often react similarly to an unredacted confession and a confession redacted in this way, for the jury will often realize that the confession refers specifically to the defendant. . . .
>
> For another thing, the obvious deletion may well call the jurors' attention specifically to the removed name. By encouraging the jury to speculate about the reference, the redaction may overemphasize the importance of the confession's accusation — once the jurors work out the reference.
>
> Finally, *Bruton*'s protected statements and statements redacted to leave a blank or some other similarly obvious alteration, function the same way grammatically. They are directly accusatory.

Id. at 192-94.

(3) Deciding whether redacted statements fall within the mandates of *Richardson v. Marsh* or, on the other hand, *Gray v. Maryland*, may take a careful case-by-case evaluation. In *Vazquez v. Wilson*, 550 F.3d 270 (10th Cir. 2008), the court found a prejudicial *Bruton* violation. *Vazquez* was a murder case in which three men were present when a shooting occurred. Two of the three, Vazquez and Santiago, were tried together before a jury. Vazquez took the stand and denied shooting the victim. Santiago did not testify, but his prior statement to police was read to the jury. In that statement, Santiago also denied shooting the victim. Defendant Vazquez objected to any use of Santiago's statement, asserting that the statement would identify Vazquez as the shooter. In contrast, Santiago's counsel wanted to use an unredacted version of the statement, urging that it showed Santiago's immediate and full cooperation with police after his arrest.

The trial court allowed a detective to read a redacted version of the statement to the jury, "substituting 'my boy' or 'the other guy' for the names of Vazquez" and the third man present at the killing. *Id.* at 274. In closing argument, Santiago's counsel contended that his client had cooperated with police in identifying the other two men who were present at the killing, and later in the government's closing, the prosecutor inadvertently identified the third man as "George" and argued that Santiago had said that neither he nor "George" had been the shooter. Taking all of the evidence together, the Tenth Circuit concluded that even as redacted, "Santiago's statement assigned th[e] unwanted role [of shooter] to Vazquez as he was the only person left to fill it." *Id.* at 275.

For more analysis of this difficult area, see Bryan M. Shay, Note, *"So I Says To 'the Guy,' I Says . . .": The Constitutionality of Neutral Pronoun Redaction in Multi-Defendant Criminal Trials*, 48 Wm. & Mary L. Rev. 345 (2006).

(4) In a case in which there are several defendants, some of whom initially confessed, and some of whom claimed their innocence, do any of the defendants have a right to have individual rather than joint trials? Rule 14 of the Federal Rules of Criminal Procedure explains the standard discretionary principle. It provides:

> (a) Relief. If the joinder of offenses or defendants in an indictment, an information, or a consolidation for trial appears to prejudice a defendant or the government, the court may order separate trials of counts, sever the defendants' trials, or provide any other relief that justice requires.
>
> (b) Defendant's Statements. Before ruling on a defendant's motion to sever, the court may order an attorney for the government to deliver to the court for in camera inspection any defendant's statement that the government intends to use as evidence.

Would joinder of defendants be prejudicial if the case against one defendant was far stronger than the case against another defendant? The courts consistently find no prejudice. *See, e.g., United States v. Gardiner*, 463 F.3d 445, 473 (6th Cir. 2006) (rejecting a defendant's argument that severance should have been granted because the "overwhelming evidence at trial pertained to [the codefendant's] case"); *United States v. Powell*, 982 F.2d 1422, 1432 (10th Cir. 1992) (rejecting the notion that "spillover effect" is sufficient to warrant severance).

CRUZ v. NEW YORK

United States Supreme Court
481 U.S. 186 (1987)

JUSTICE SCALIA delivered the opinion of the Court.

In *Bruton v. United States*, we held that a defendant is deprived of his rights under the Confrontation Clause when his codefendant's incriminating confession is introduced at their joint trial, even if the jury is instructed to consider that confession only against the codefendant. In *Parker v. Randolph*, 442 U.S. 62 (1979), we considered, but were unable authoritatively to resolve, the question whether *Bruton* applies where the defendant's own confession, corroborating that of his codefendant, is introduced against him. We resolve that question today.

I

Jerry Cruz was murdered on March 15, 1982. That is not the murder for which petitioner was tried and convicted, but the investigation of the one led to the solving of the other. On the day following Jerry Cruz's murder, and on several later occasions, the police talked to Jerry's brother Norberto about the killing. On April 27, Norberto for the first time informed the police of a November 29, 1981, visit by petitioner Eulogio Cruz and his brother Benjamin to the apartment Norberto shared with Jerry. (Eulogio and Benjamin Cruz were longtime friends of Norberto and Jerry Cruz, but the two sets of brothers were not related.) Norberto said that at the time of the visit Eulogio was nervous and was wearing a bloodstained bandage around his arm. According to Norberto, Eulogio confided that he and Benjamin had gone to a Bronx gas station the night before, intending to rob it; that Eulogio and the attendant had struggled; and that, after the attendant had grabbed a gun from behind a counter and shot Eulogio in the arm, Benjamin had killed him. Norberto claimed that Benjamin gave a similar account of the incident.

On May 3, 1982, the police questioned Benjamin about the murder of Jerry Cruz. He strongly denied any connection with that homicide and became frustrated when the police seemed unwilling to believe him. Suddenly, to prove that he would tell the truth about killing someone if he were guilty, Benjamin spontaneously confessed to the murder of the gas station attendant. Later that evening, he gave a detailed videotaped confession to an Assistant District Attorney, in which he admitted that he, Eulogio, Jerry Cruz, and a fourth man had robbed the gas station, and that he had killed the attendant after the attendant shot Eulogio. Benjamin and Eulogio were indicted for felony murder of the station attendant.

The brothers were tried jointly, over Eulogio's objection. Likewise over Eulogio's objection, the trial judge allowed the prosecutor to introduce Benjamin's videotaped confession, warning the jury that the confession was not to be used against Eulogio. The government also called Norberto, who testified about his November 29 conversation with Eulogio and Benjamin. Finally, the government introduced police testimony, forensic evidence, and photographs of the scene of the murder, all of which corroborated Benjamin's videotaped confession and the statements recounted by Norberto. At the trial's end, however, Norberto's testimony stood as the only evidence admissible against Eulogio that directly linked him to the crime. Eulogio's attorney tried to persuade the jury that Norberto had suspected Eulogio and Benjamin of killing his brother Jerry and had fabricated his testimony to gain revenge. Unconvinced, the jury convicted both defendants.

The New York Court of Appeals affirmed Eulogio's conviction, adopting the reasoning of the plurality opinion in *Parker* that *Bruton* did not require the codefendant's confession to be excluded because Eulogio had himself confessed and his confession "interlocked" with Benjamin's. We granted certiorari.

II

The Confrontation Clause of the Sixth Amendment guarantees the right of a criminal defendant "to be confronted with the witnesses against him." We have held that that guarantee includes the right to cross-examine witnesses. Where two or more defendants are tried jointly, therefore, the pretrial confession of one of them that implicates the others is not admissible against the others unless the confessing defendant waives his Fifth Amendment right so as to permit cross-examination.

Ordinarily, a witness is considered to be a witness "against" a defendant for purposes of the Confrontation Clause only if his testimony is part of the body of evidence that the jury may consider in assessing his guilt. Therefore, a witness whose testimony is introduced in a joint trial with the limiting instruction that it be used only to assess the guilt of one of the defendants will not be considered to be a witness "against" the other defendants. In *Bruton*, however, we held that this principle will not be applied to validate, under the Confrontation Clause, introduction of a nontestifying codefendant's confession implicating the defendant, with instructions that the jury should disregard the confession insofar as its consideration of the defendant's guilt is concerned.

. . .

We had occasion to revisit this issue in *Parker*, which resembled *Bruton* in all major respects save one: Each of the jointly tried defendants had himself confessed, his own confession was introduced against him, and his confession recited essentially the same facts as those of his nontestifying codefendants. The plurality of four Justices found no Sixth Amendment violation. It understood *Bruton* to hold that the Confrontation Clause is violated only when introduction of a codefendant's confession is "devastating" to the defendant's case. When the defendant has himself confessed, the plurality reasoned, "[his] case has already been devastated," so that the codefendant's confession "will seldom, if ever, be of the 'devastating' character referred to in *Bruton*," and impeaching that confession on cross-examination "would likely yield small advantage." Thus, the plurality would have held *Bruton* inapplicable to cases involving interlocking confessions. The four remaining Justices participating in the case disagreed, subscribing to the view expressed by Justice Blackmun that introduction of the defendant's own interlocking confession might, in some cases, render the violation of the Confrontation Clause harmless, but could not cause introduction of the nontestifying codefendant's confession not to constitute a violation. We face again today the issue on which the Court was evenly divided in *Parker*.

We adopt the approach espoused by Justice Blackmun. While "devastating" practical effect was one of the factors that *Bruton* considered in assessing whether the Confrontation Clause might sometimes require departure from the general rule that jury instructions suffice to exclude improper testimony, it did not suggest that the existence of such an effect should be assessed on a case-by-case basis. Rather, that factor was one of the justifications for excepting from the general rule the entire category of codefendant confessions that implicate the defendant in the crime. It is impossible to imagine why there should be excluded from that category, as generally not "devastating," codefendant confessions that "interlock" with the defendant's own confession. "[T]he infinite variability of inculpatory statements (whether made by defendants or codefendants), and of their likely effect on juries, makes [the assumption that an interlocking confession will preclude devastation] untenable." In this case, for example, the precise content and even the existence of petitioner's own confession were open to question, since they depended upon acceptance of Norberto's testimony, whereas the incriminating confession of codefendant Benjamin was on videotape.

In fact, it seems to us that "interlocking" bears a positively inverse relationship to devastation. A codefendant's confession will be relatively harmless if the incriminating story it tells is different from that which the defendant himself is alleged to have told, but enormously damaging if it confirms, in all essential respects, the defendant's alleged confession. It might be otherwise if the defendant were *standing by* his confession, in which case it could be said that the codefendant's confession does no more than support the defendant's very own case. But in the real world of criminal litigation, the defendant is seeking to *avoid* his confession — on the ground that it was not accurately reported, or that it was not really true when made. In the present case, for example, the petitioner sought to establish that Norberto had a motive for falsely reporting a confession that never in fact occurred. In such circumstances a codefendant's confession that corroborates the defendant's confession significantly harms the defendant's case, whereas one that is positively incompatible gives credence to the defendant's assertion that his own alleged confession was nonexistent or false. Quite obviously, what the "interlocking" nature of the codefendant's confession pertains to is not its *harmfulness* but rather its *reliability*: If it confirms essentially the same facts as the defendant's own confession it is more likely to be true. Its reliability, however, may be relevant to whether the confession should (despite the lack of opportunity for cross-examination) be *admitted as evidence* against the defendant, but cannot conceivably be relevant to whether, assuming it cannot be admitted, the jury is likely to obey the instruction to disregard it, or the jury's failure to obey is likely to be inconsequential. The law cannot command respect if such an inexplicable exception to a supposed constitutional imperative is adopted. Having decided *Bruton*, we must face the honest consequences of what it holds.

. . .

This case is indistinguishable from *Bruton* with respect to those factors the Court has deemed relevant in this area: the likelihood that the instruction will be disregarded, *Bruton*; the probability that such disregard will have a devastating effect, *Bruton*; and the determinability of these facts in advance of trial, *Richardson v. Marsh*.

We hold that, where a nontestifying codefendant's confession incriminating the defendant is not directly admissible against the defendant, the Confrontation Clause bars its admission at their joint trial, even if the jury is instructed not to consider it against the defendant, and even if the defendant's own confession is admitted against him. Of course, the defendant's confession may be considered at trial in assessing whether his codefendant's statements are supported by sufficient "indicia of reliability" to be directly admissible against him (assuming the "unavailability" of the codefendant) despite the lack of opportunity for cross-examination, and may be considered on appeal in assessing whether any Confrontation Clause violation was harmless.

Because the Court of Appeals analyzed petitioner's Confrontation Clause claim under an approach we have now rejected, we reverse and remand for further proceedings not inconsistent with this opinion.

So ordered.

JUSTICE WHITE, with whom CHIEF JUSTICE REHNQUIST, JUSTICE POWELL, and JUSTICE O'CONNOR join, dissenting.

In *Bruton,* the defendant himself had not confessed. Here, it is otherwise: defendant Cruz had confessed and his confession was properly before the jury. Yet the Court's holding is that the codefendant's confession was inadmissible even if it completely "interlocked" with that of Cruz himself, that is, was substantially the same as and consistent with Cruz's confession with respect to all elements of the crime and did not threaten to incriminate Cruz any more than his own confession.

This makes little sense to me. The defendant's own confession is probably the most probative and damaging evidence that can be admitted against him. Though itself an out-of-court statement, it is admitted as reliable evidence because it is an admission of guilt by the defendant and constitutes direct evidence of the facts to which it relates. Even the testimony of an eyewitness may be less reliable than the defendant's own confession. An observer may not correctly perceive, understand, or remember the acts of another, but the admissions of a defendant come from the actor himself, the most knowledgeable and unimpeachable source of information about his past conduct. *Bruton* held that where the defendant has not himself confessed, there is too great a chance that the jury would rely on the codefendant's confession. But here, Cruz had admitted the crime and this fact was before the jury. I disagree with the Court's proposition that in every interlocking confession case, the jury, with the defendant's confession properly before it, would be tempted to disobey its instructions and fail to understand that presumptively unreliable evidence must not be used against the defendant. Nor is it remotely possible that in every case the admission of an interlocking confession by a codefendant will have the devastating effect referred to in *Bruton.*

. . .

That the error the Court finds may be harmless and the conviction saved will not comfort prosecutors and judges. I doubt that the former will seek joint trials in interlocking confession cases, and if that occurs, the judge is not likely to commit error by admitting the codefendant's confession. Of course, defendants may be tried separately and *Bruton* problems avoided. But joint trials "conserve state funds, diminish inconvenience to witnesses and public authorities, and avoid delays in bringing those accused of crime to trial," *Bruton,* to say nothing of the possibility of inconsistent verdicts and the effect of severance on already overburdened state and federal court systems.

I thus adhere to the views expressed by the plurality in *Parker v. Randolph.*

NOTES AND QUESTIONS

(1) The plurality in *Parker v. Randolph* strongly rejected the defense argument, finding great significance in the presence of the defendant's own confession. Why does Justice Scalia disagree?

(2) If the confessing codefendant took the stand at the defendant's trial and was willing to answer questions about his confession, would any Sixth Amendment argument remain? In *Nelson v. O'Neil*, 402 U.S. 622 (1971), the codefendant testified fully as to his activities during the period in question, but denied that he made the confession and claimed that its substance was false. The Court held that the cooperation of the codefendant at trial (testifying "favorably to the defendant concerning the underlying facts") eliminated the Confrontation Clause concerns expressed in *Bruton*.

(3) Currently, the greatest source of litigation over Sixth Amendment confrontation issues rests not with statements of non-testifying codefendants but, rather, with the rules of evidence allowing the admission of out-of-court statements by victims, laboratory technicians, and others who do not testify at trial. For instance, the Federal Rules of Evidence permit the government to introduce certain out-of-court statements against a defendant, so long as the statements bear adequate indicators of reliability, whether or not the speaker of the statement testifies at trial. Thus, the rules of evidence allow these statements even when the declarant is unavailable for cross-examination. In *Crawford v. Washington*, 541 U.S. 36 (2004), the Court held that to the extent "testimonial statements" are at issue, the Sixth Amendment guarantees confrontation, not reliability, explaining that "[a]dmitting statements deemed reliable by a judge is fundamentally at odds with the right of confrontation." Thus, the Court in *Crawford* established the groundwork to exclude "testimonial" statements pursuant to the Sixth Amendment, regardless of their admissibility under evidentiary rules. Although the reach of *Crawford* is best explored in an evidence course, students should be aware that the *Crawford* decision left numerous confrontation issues unresolved and that the case is a fertile source for development of a defendant's confrontation rights. *See, e.g., Williams v. Illinois*, 132 S. Ct. 2221 (2012) (expert witness allowed to testify at bench trial about DNA test results that identified the defendant as the assailant even though the testifying witness had not personally performed the DNA tests); *Bullcoming v. New Mexico*, 131 S. Ct. 2705 (2011) (introduction at trial of a forensic lab report certifying defendant's blood alcohol level in DWI trial, which was prepared by non-testifying analyst, implicated the Confrontation Clause because it was testimonial); *Michigan v. Bryant*, 131 S. Ct. 1143 (2011) (a statement by a dying witness in response to police questioning which has as its primary purpose to help police meet an ongoing emergency is not testimonial); *Melendez-Diaz v. Massachusetts*, 557 U.S. 305 (2009) (forensic lab report prepared for a criminal trial is testimonial requiring a witness who can testify to the truth of the statements in the report); *Giles v. California*, 554 U.S. 353 (2008); *Davis v. Washington*, 547 U.S. 813 (2006) (doctrine of forfeiture by wrongdoing applies to Confrontation Clause issues but only if the defendant intended to prevent the declarant-witness from testifying at a trial or hearing; general wrongdoing directed at witness is insufficient to trigger a forfeiture).

§ 7.04 COMMENTING ON THE DEFENDANT'S FAILURE TO TESTIFY

GRIFFIN v. CALIFORNIA

United States Supreme Court
380 U.S. 609 (1965)

JUSTICE DOUGLAS delivered the opinion of the Court.

Petitioner was convicted of murder in the first degree after a jury trial in a California court. He did not testify at the trial on the issue of guilt, though he did testify at the separate trial on the issue of penalty. The trial court instructed the jury on the issue of guilt, stating that a defendant has a constitutional right not to testify. But it told the jury:[5]

> As to any evidence or facts against him which the defendant can reasonably be expected to deny or explain because of facts within his knowledge, if he does not testify or if, though he does testify, he fails to deny or explain such evidence, the jury may take that failure into consideration as tending to indicate the truth of such evidence and as indicating that among the inferences that may be reasonably drawn there from those unfavorable to the defendant are the more probable.

It added, however, that no such inference could be drawn as to evidence respecting which he had no knowledge. It stated that failure of a defendant to deny or explain the evidence of which he had knowledge does not create a presumption of guilt nor by itself warrant an inference of guilt nor relieve the prosecution of any of its burden of proof.

Petitioner had been seen with the deceased the evening of her death, the evidence placing him with her in the alley where her body was found. The prosecutor made much of the failure of petitioner to testify:

> The defendant certainly knows whether Essie Mae had this beat up appearance at the time he left her apartment and went down the alley with her.
>
> What kind of a man is it that would want to have sex with a woman that beat up if she was beat up at the time he left?
>
> He would know that. He would know how she got down the alley. He would know how the blood got on the bottom of the concrete steps. He would know how long he was with her in that box. He would know how her wig got off. He would know whether he beat her or mistreated her. He would know whether he walked away from that place cool as a cucumber when he saw

---

[5] [2] Article I § 13, of the California Constitution provides in part: ". . . in any criminal case, whether the defendant testifies or not, his failure to explain or to deny by his testimony any evidence or facts in the case against him may be commented upon by the court and by counsel, and may be considered by the court or the jury."

> Mr. Villasenor because he was conscious of his own guilt and wanted to get away from that damaged or injured woman.
>
> These things he has not seen fit to take the stand and deny or explain.
>
> And in the whole world, if anybody would know, this defendant would know.
>
> Essie Mae is dead, she can't tell you her side of the story. The defendant won't.

The death penalty was imposed and the California Supreme Court affirmed. The case is here on a writ of certiorari which we granted to consider whether comment on the failure to testify violated the Self-Incrimination Clause of the Fifth Amendment which we made applicable to the States by the Fourteenth.

We think it does. It is in substance a rule of evidence that allows the State the privilege of tendering to the jury for its consideration the failure of the accused to testify. No formal offer of proof is made as in other situations; but the prosecutor's comment and the court's acquiescence are the equivalent of an offer of evidence and its acceptance.

[We previously] stated:

> . . . [T]he act was framed with a due regard also to those who might prefer to rely upon the presumption of innocence which the law gives to every one, and not wish to be witnesses. It is not every one who can safely venture on the witness stand though entirely innocent of the charge against him. Excessive timidity, nervousness when facing others and attempting to explain transactions of a suspicious character, and offenses charged against him, will often confuse and embarrass him to such a degree as to increase rather than remove prejudices against him. It is not every one, however honest, who would, therefore willingly be placed on the witness stand. The statute, in tenderness to the weakness of those who from the causes mentioned might refuse to ask to be a witness, particularly when they may have been in some degree compromised by their association with others, declares that the failure of the defendant in a criminal action to request to be a witness shall not create any presumption against him.

If the words " Fifth Amendment" are substituted for "act" and for "statute" the spirit of the Self-Incrimination Clause is reflected. For comment on the refusal to testify is a remnant of the "inquisitorial system of criminal justice," which the Fifth Amendment outlaws. It is a penalty imposed by courts for exercising a constitutional privilege. It cuts down on the privilege by making its assertion costly. It is said, however, that the inference of guilt for failure to testify as to facts peculiarly within the accused's knowledge is in any event natural and irresistible, and that comment on the failure does not magnify that inference into a penalty for asserting a constitutional privilege.

What the jury may infer, given no help from the court, is one thing. What it may infer when the court solemnizes the silence of the accused into evidence against him is quite another.

Reversed.

THE CHIEF JUSTICE took no part in the decision of this case.

JUSTICE HARLAN, concurring.

I agree with the Court that within the federal judicial system the Fifth Amendment bars adverse comment by federal prosecutors and judges on a defendant's failure to take the stand in a criminal trial, a right accorded him by that amendment. And given last Term's decision in *Malloy v. Hogan*, 378 U.S. 1 (1964), that the Fifth Amendment applies to the States in all its refinements, I see no legitimate escape from today's decision and therefore concur in it. I do so, however, with great reluctance, since for me the decision exemplifies the creeping paralysis with which this Court's recent adoption of the "incorporation" doctrine is infecting the operation of the federal system.

JUSTICE STEWART, with whom JUSTICE WHITE joins, dissenting.

We must determine whether the petitioner has been "compelled . . . to be a witness against himself." Compulsion is the focus of the inquiry. Certainly, if any compulsion be detected in the California procedure, it is of a dramatically different and less palpable nature than that involved in the procedures which historically gave rise to the Fifth Amendment guarantee. When a suspect was brought before the Court of High Commission or the Star Chamber, he was commanded to answer whatever was asked of him, and subjected to a far-reaching and deeply probing inquiry in an effort to ferret out some unknown and frequently unsuspected crime. He declined to answer on pain of incarceration, banishment, or mutilation. And if he spoke falsely, he was subject to further punishment. Faced with this formidable array of alternatives, his decision to speak was unquestionably coerced.

Those were the lurid realities which lay behind enactment of the Fifth Amendment, a far cry from the subject matter of the case before us. I think that the Court in this case stretches the concept of compulsion beyond all reasonable bounds, and that whatever compulsion may exist derives from the defendant's choice not to testify, not from any comment by court or counsel. In support of its conclusion that the California procedure does compel the accused to testify, the Court has only this to say: "It is a penalty imposed by courts for exercising a constitutional privilege. It cuts down on the privilege by making its assertion costly." Exactly what the penalty imposed consists of is not clear. It is not, as I understand the problem, that the jury becomes aware that the defendant has chosen not to testify in his own defense, for the jury will, of course, realize this quite evident fact, even though the choice goes unmentioned. Since comment by counsel and the court does not compel testimony by creating such an awareness, the Court must be saying that the California constitutional provision places some other compulsion upon the defendant to incriminate himself, some compulsion which the Court does not describe and which I cannot readily perceive.

It is not at all apparent to me, on any realistic view of the trial process, that a defendant will be at more of a disadvantage under the California practice than he would be in a court which permitted no comment at all on his failure to take the witness stand. How can it be said that the inferences drawn by a jury will be more detrimental to a defendant under the limiting and carefully controlling language of the instruction here involved than would result if the jury were left to roam at large with only its untutored instincts to guide it, to draw from the defendant's silence broad inferences of guilt? The instructions in this case expressly cautioned the jury that the defendant's failure to testify "does not create a presumption of guilt or by itself warrant an inference of guilt"; it was further admonished that such failure does not "relieve the prosecution of its burden of proving every essential element of the crime," and finally the trial judge warned that the prosecution's burden remained that of proof "beyond a reasonable doubt." Whether the same limitations would be observed by a jury without the benefit of protective instructions shielding the defendant is certainly open to real doubt.

NOTES AND QUESTIONS

(1) In what way did the California "comment rule" serve as a penalty to the defendant for remaining silent? The majority stated that the rule "cuts down on the privilege by making its assertion costly." Yet, isn't Justice Stewart's point well taken, that a defendant may be at more of a disadvantage by having the jury "left to roam at large with only its untutored instincts to guide it, to draw from the defendant's silence broad inferences of guilt?" Stated another way, if it is assumed that the jury will in fact consider the defendant's silence, should we not formally instruct the jury as to the way in which it should consider the silence? Should we assume that the jury will consider the defendant's silence?

(2) Under *Griffin*, both direct and indirect comments violate the Fifth Amendment. The Seventh Circuit has explained that improper indirect comments occur "only if (1) the prosecutor manifestly intended to refer to the defendant's silence or (2) a jury would naturally and necessarily take the remark for a comment on the defendant's silence." *United States v. Jackson*, 540 F.3d 578, 597 (7th Cir. 2008).

United States v. Hardy, 37 F.3d 753, 757 (1st Cir. 1994), provides an example of an improper indirect comment on a defendant's silence. There, the prosecutor argued to the jury that the defendant tried to run and hide at the time of the crime, and was "still running and hiding today."

In contrast, the Seventh Circuit in *United States v. Butler*, 71 F.3d 243, 255 (7th Cir. 1995), found that the prosecutor had not indirectly commented on the defendant's right to silence when in closing argument the prosecutor responded to defense counsel's argument that an officer had "planted the gun" on his client and that the officer "should not be believed because he had planted evidence in the past." The prosecutor replied that the officer's past actions were irrelevant, that the defense was "simply attempting to smear the officer[,]" and that "there is nothing preventing [defense counsel] from presenting any evidence in this case. It is a trial. And if he had any evidence that supports his view of the facts he would have submitted it to you." In concluding that the prosecutor's argument was not improper, the court explained:

> We do not find that the prosecutor's remarks were "manifestly intended" to be a comment on Butler's silence, nor do we believe the jury would "naturally and necessarily" take them as such. When viewed in context, the

> prosecutor's statement was a reference to the defense's failure to support their theory that Officer Figueroa lied about finding Butler with the gun. . . . [T]his is proper comment as long as Butler is not the only one who could have supported the theory or rebutted the prosecution's witnesses. There were several police officers and other gang members present when Butler was arrested, any one of whom could have provided the necessary evidence.

Is the prosecutor's reference — in opening statement — to the defendant's refusal to submit to a polygraph test impermissible? Yes, held the court in *State v. Gutierrez*, 162 P.3d 156 (N.M. 2007). The reference is a comment on the defendant's silence.

(3) What about pre-trial silence? The California Court of Appeals considered custodial pre-trial silence in *People v. Cleland*, 134 Cal. Rptr. 2d 479 (Cal. App. 2003). Two defendants were placed in one police car upon arrest. The officers hoped that one (or both) would make an incriminating statement. Neither did. At trial, the defendants did not testify, and the government used the silence of the defendants as evidence of guilt in closing argument to the jury:

> If they hadn't done anything and they are both sitting in the back of a police car, why didn't defendant Rebecca Cleland turn to her cousin and say, "what are you doing here?" And why didn't he say, "what are you doing here?" Why? Because they both knew what they were doing there. That's why there was no conversation. It all fits.

Id. at 489. The court in *Cleland* found this argument to violate *Griffin* and *Miranda*, for the police approach "was simply a technique intended to elicit a statement," and "impermissibly drew attention" to the defendants' decision not to testify at trial.

The District of Columbia Circuit concluded similarly in *United States v. Moore*, 104 F.3d 377 (D.C. Cir. 1997). In *Moore*, the defendant was convicted of drug and gun crimes after police found drugs and guns under the hood of his car. At trial, the prosecutor asked the officer, who found the contraband, "if the defendants said anything when the guns and drugs were found under the hood of the car?" Later, during closing argument, the prosecutor told the jury, "[I]f Moore didn't know the stuff was underneath the hood, he would at least look surprised. He would at least have said, 'Well, I didn't know it was there.' " *Id.* at 384. In concluding that these questions and comments had "unduly burdened" the defendant's Fifth Amendment privilege against compelled self-incrimination, the D.C. Circuit acknowledged that "*Griffin* did not determine the propriety of prosecutorial comment on a defendant's pre-trial silence"; nevertheless, concluded the court:

> [A] prosecutor's comment on a defendant's post-custodial silence unduly burdens that defendant's Fifth Amendment right to remain silent at trial, as it calls a jury's further attention to the fact that he has not arisen to remove whatever taint the pretrial but post-custodial silence may have spread. . . . [T]he prosecution's use of Moore's pre-trial silence in its summation violated his Fifth Amendment rights.

Id. at 385.

Recently, in *Salinas v. Texas*, 133 S. Ct. 2174 (2013), the Supreme Court held that a prosecutor does not violate a defendant's Fifth Amendment right against compelled self-incrimination if she argues at trial that the defendant's pretrial, non-custodial, silence is evidence of guilt. In *Salinas*, the defendant had voluntarily talked with police about a murder. He was not in custody; he was not Mirandized. For most of the interview, he answered the officer's questions. When asked whether his shotgun would match shells found at the scene of the murder, however, the defendant said nothing. Instead, he "shuffled his feet, bit his bottom lip, cl[e]nched his hands in his lap, [and] began to tighten up." *Id.* at 2178. Justices Alito, Roberts, and Kennedy reasoned that "it would have been a simple matter for [the defendant] to say that he was not answering the officer's questions on Fifth Amendment grounds." *Id.* at 2180. Because the defendant had failed to assert this right, there was no violation. Justices Thomas and Scalia, concurring, argued that "the prosecutor's comments regarding his precustodial silence did not compel [the defendant] to give self-incriminating testimony." *Id.* at 2184.

(4) Although *Griffin* prohibits the government from commenting on the defendant's failure to testify at trial, a defendant can "open the door" to a "fair response" by the government, if he suggests that the government has unfairly denied him the opportunity to explain his conduct. *See United States v. Robinson*, 485 U.S. 25, 32 (1988) (explaining that although the prosecutor violates the privilege against compulsory self-incrimination when, on her own initiative, she asks the jury to draw an adverse inference from a defendant's silence, "where . . . the prosecutor's reference to the defendant's opportunity to testify is a fair response to a claim made by defendant or his counsel, we think there is no violation of the privilege.").

(5) Does it violate the Constitution for a codefendant's lawyer — not government counsel — to comment on the defendant's failure to testify? Yes, decided the court in *Payne v. State*, 586 S.E.2d 857 (S.C. 2003). According to the court, the effect of such a comment on the jury may be substantial, regardless of which lawyer makes it. *See also United States v. Mena*, 863 F.2d 1522, 1533 (11th Cir. 1989) (recognizing that comment by a codefendant's lawyer can impair a defendant's Fifth Amendment privilege against self incrimination but distinguishing cases in which a codefendant's counsel "merely comment[s] favorably on his own client's willingness to testify.").

PROBLEM A

In *Lent v. Wells*, 861 F.2d 972 (6th Cir. 1988), *cert. denied*, 489 U.S. 1100 (1989), the defense presented no evidence or testimony. During closing argument the prosecutor made these statements:

> (1) "The evidence in this case is completely, totally uncontradicted. There are not two types of evidence in this case, there's only one, the testimony of the victim from the witness stand."
>
> (2) "Again, did you hear any evidence to the contrary? You heard no other evidence. . . . [The defense attorney] is going to get up here and say well, this could've been, and that could've been. Well, could've been didn't take the stand. The evidence that you have is evidence from the witness stand, and not could've been."

(3) "Did you hear anybody else get up here and testify? Did you hear anybody else get on the witness stand, one of the other people at the bar, and say, well, yeah, Pam. She was pretty blasted. . . . No, there's no other evidence, none."

(4) "The evidence shows, ladies and gentlemen, that about 4:00 a.m. on August 6, 1982 that young man right there raped that young lady right there, and there is no other evidence. It's uncontradicted, it's unrebutted."

Did the prosecutor commit constitutional error?

PROBLEM B

In *Arizona v. Ikirt*, 770 P.2d 1159 (Ariz. 1989), *cert. denied*, 493 U.S. 872 (1989), defense counsel brought out defendant's statements through his mother's testimony. The prosecutor objected on hearsay grounds, noting that the declarant — the defendant — was present in the courtroom.

Did the prosecutor improperly comment on the defendant's right to silence?

LAKESIDE v. OREGON

United States Supreme Court
435 U.S. 333 (1978)

JUSTICE STEWART delivered the opinion of the Court.

The petitioner did not take the witness stand at his trial on a criminal charge in a state court. Over his objection the trial judge instructed the jury not to draw any adverse inference from the petitioner's decision not to testify. The question before us is whether the giving of such an instruction over the defendant's objection violated the Constitution.

I

The petitioner was brought to trial in an Oregon court on a charge of escape in the second degree. The evidence showed that he had been an inmate of the Multnomah County Correctional Institution, a minimum security facility in Multnomah County, Ore. On June 16, 1975, he received a special overnight pass requiring him to return by 10 o'clock the following evening. He did not return. The theory of the defense, supported by the testimony of a psychiatrist and three lay witnesses, was that the petitioner was not criminally responsible for his failure to return to the institution.

At the conclusion of the evidence, the trial judge informed counsel in chambers that he intended to include the following instruction in his charge to the jury:

> Under the laws of this State a defendant has the option to take the witness stand to testify in his or her own behalf. If a defendant chooses not to testify, such a circumstance gives rise to no inference or presumption against the defendant, and this must not be considered by you in determining the question of guilt or innocence.

Defense counsel objected to the giving of that instruction, and, after it was given, the following colloquy took place in chambers:

> DEFENSE COUNSEL: . . . I have one exception.
>
> I made this in Chambers prior to the closing statement. I told the Court that I did not want an instruction to the effect that the defendant doesn't have to take the stand, because I felt that that's like waving a red flag in front of the jury. . . .
>
> THE COURT: The defendant did orally request the Court just prior to instructing that the Court not give the usual instruction to the effect that there are no inferences to be drawn against the defendant for failing to take the stand in his own behalf.
>
> The Court felt that it was necessary to give that instruction in order to properly protect the defendant, and therefore, the defendant may have his exception.

II

A

. . .

In the *Griffin* case, the petitioner argues, the Court said that "comment on the refusal to testify" violates the constitutional privilege against compulsory self-incrimination, and thus the "comment" made by the trial judge over the defendant's objection in the present case was a literal violation of the language of the *Griffin* opinion. Quite apart from this semantic argument, the petitioner contends that it is an invasion of the privilege against compulsory self-incrimination, as that privilege was perceived in the *Griffin* case, for a trial judge to draw the jury's attention in any way to a defendant's failure to testify unless the defendant acquiesces. We cannot accept this argument, either in terms of the language of the *Griffin* opinion or in terms of the basic postulates of the Fifth and Fourteenth Amendments.

It is clear from even a cursory review of the facts and the square holding of the *Griffin* case that the Court was there concerned only with *adverse* comment, whether by the prosecutor or the trial judge — "comment by the prosecution on the accused's silence or instructions by the court that such silence is evidence of guilt." The Court reasoned that such adverse comment amounted to "a penalty imposed by courts for exercising a constitutional privilege. It cuts down on the privilege by making its assertion costly."

By definition, "a necessary element of compulsory self-incrimination is some kind of compulsion." The Court concluded in *Griffin* that unconstitutional compulsion was inherent in a trial where prosecutor and judge were free to ask the jury to draw adverse inferences from a defendant's failure to take the witness stand.[6] But a

---

[6] [9] Compulsion was also found to be present in *Brooks v. Tennessee*, 406 U.S. 605 (1972), where the State required a defendant who chose to testify to take the witness stand ahead of any other defense

judge's instruction that the jury must draw *no* adverse inferences of any kind from the defendant's exercise of his privilege not to testify is "comment" of an entirely different order. Such an instruction cannot provide the pressure on a defendant found impermissible in *Griffin*. On the contrary, its very purpose is to remove from the jury's deliberations any influence of unspoken adverse inferences. It would be strange indeed to conclude that this cautionary instruction violates the very constitutional provision it is intended to protect.

The petitioner maintains, however, that whatever beneficent effect such an instruction may have in most cases, it may in some cases encourage the jury to draw adverse inferences from a defendant's silence, and, therefore, it cannot constitutionally be given in any case when a defendant objects to it. Specifically, the petitioner contends that in a trial such as this one, where the defense was presented through several witnesses, the defendant can reasonably hope that the jury will not notice that he himself did not testify. In such circumstances, the giving of the cautionary instruction, he says, is like "waving a red flag in front of the jury."

The petitioner's argument would require indulgence in two very doubtful assumptions: First, that the jurors have not noticed that the defendant did not testify and will not, therefore, draw adverse inferences on their own; second, that the jurors will totally disregard the instruction, and affirmatively give weight to what they have been told not to consider at all.[7] Federal constitutional law cannot rest on speculative assumptions so dubious as these.

Moreover, even if the petitioner's simile be accepted, it does not follow that the cautionary instruction in these circumstances violates the privilege against compulsory self-incrimination. The very purpose of a jury charge is to flag the jurors' attention to concepts that must not be misunderstood, such as reasonable doubt and burden of proof. To instruct them in the meaning of the privilege against compulsory self-incrimination is no different.

It may be wise for a trial judge not to give such a cautionary instruction over a defendant's objection. And each State is, of course, free to forbid its trial judges from doing so as a matter of state law. We hold only that the giving of such an instruction over the defendant's objection does not violate the privilege against compulsory self-incrimination guaranteed by the Fifth and Fourteenth Amendments.

JUSTICE BRENNAN took no part in the consideration or decision of this case.

JUSTICE STEVENS, dissenting.

Experience teaches us that most people formally charged with crime are guilty; yet we presume innocence until the trial is over. Experience also justifies the inference that most people who remain silent in the face of serious accusation have

---

witnesses. Thus, a defendant was compelled to make his decision — whether or not to testify — at a point in the trial when he could not know if his testimony would be necessary or even helpful to his case.

[7] [11] As this Court has remarked before: "[W]e have not yet attained that certitude about the human mind which would justify us in . . . a dogmatic assumption that jurors, if properly admonished, neither could nor would heed the instructions of the trial court. . . ."

something to hide and are therefore probably guilty; yet we forbid trial judges or juries to draw that inference. The presumption of innocence and the protections afforded by the Due Process Clause impose a significant cost on the prosecutor who must prove the defendant's guilt beyond a reasonable doubt without the aid of his testimony. That cost is justified by the paramount importance of protecting a small minority of accused persons — those who are actually innocent — from wrongful conviction.

The Fifth Amendment itself is predicated on the assumption that there are innocent persons who might be found guilty if they could be compelled to testify at their own trials. Every trial lawyer knows that some truthful denials of guilt may be considered incredible by a jury — either because of their inherent improbability or because their explanation, under cross-examination, will reveal unfavorable facts about the witness or his associates. The Constitution therefore gives the defendant and his lawyer the absolute right to decide that the accused shall not become a witness against himself. Even if the judge is convinced that the defendant's testimony would exonerate him, and even if he is motivated only by a desire to protect the defendant from the risk of an erroneous conviction, the judge has no power to override counsel's judgment about what is in his client's best interests.[8]

The Constitution wisely commits the critical decision of whether the defendant shall take the stand to the defendant and his lawyer, rather than the judge, for at least two reasons. First, they have greater access to information bearing on the decision than the judge can normally have. Second, they are motivated solely by concern for the defendant's interests; the judge inevitably is concerned with society's interest in convicting the guilty as well as protecting the innocent. The choice, therefore, to testify or not to testify is for the defendant and his lawyer, not the judge, to make. The Constitution commands that the decision be made free of any compulsion by the State.

. . . *Griffin* stands for the proposition that the government may not add unnecessarily to the risk taken by a defendant who stands mute. Reasonable men may differ about the wisdom of that holding.[9] But if it is still the law, this conviction should be overturned.

In some trials, the defendant's silence will be like "the sun . . . shining with full blaze on the open eye." But in other trials — perhaps when the whole story has been told by other witnesses or when the prosecutor's case is especially weak — the jury may not focus on the defendant's failure to testify. For the judge or prosecutor to call it to the jury's attention has an undeniably adverse effect on the defendant. Even if jurors try faithfully to obey their instructions, the connection between silence and guilt is often too direct and too natural to be resisted. When the jurors have in fact overlooked it, telling them to ignore the defendant's silence is like telling them not to think of a white bear.

---

[8] [2] Moreover, there are defendants who prefer to risk a finding of guilt rather than being required to incriminate others whom they either love or fear.

[9] [5] The Court today cites the same scholarly materials, prepared in the 1930's and 1940's, that Justice Stewart cited in his dissent in *Griffin*. The list could have been much longer. In fact, the roster of scholars and judges with reservations about expanding the Fifth Amendment privilege reads like an honor roll of the legal profession.

The Court thinks it "would be strange indeed to conclude that this cautionary instruction violates the very constitutional provision it is intended to protect."

Unless the same words mean different things in different mouths, this holding also applies to statements made by the prosecutor in his closing argument. Yet I wonder if the Court would find petitioner's argument as strange if the prosecutor, or even the judge, had given the instruction three or four times, in slightly different form, just to make sure the jury knew that silence, like killing Caesar, is consistent with honor.[10]

It is unrealistic to assume that instructions on the right to silence always have a benign effect. At times the instruction will make the defendant's silence costly indeed. So long as *Griffin* is good law, the State must have a strong reason for ignoring the defendant's request that the instruction not be given. Remarkably, the Court fails to identify any reason for overriding the defendant's choice. Eliminating the instruction on request costs the State nothing, other than the advantage of calling attention to the defendant's silence. A defendant may waive his Fifth Amendment right to silence, and a judge who thinks his decision unwise may not overrule it. The defendant should also be able to waive, without leave of court, his lesser right to an instruction about his Fifth Amendment right to silence. Many state courts have accepted this conclusion by ruling that no self-incrimination instruction should be given over the defendant's objection. An ungrudging application of *Griffin* requires that we do the same.

I respectfully dissent.

---

[10] [6] *Cf.* W. Shakespeare, Julius Caesar, Act III, Sc. II:

> Here, under leave of Brutus and the rest (For Brutus is an honourable man; So are they all, all honourable men) Come I to speak in Caesar's funeral. He was my friend, faithful and just to me: But Brutus says he was ambitious; And Brutus is an honourable man. He hath brought many captives home to Rome, Whose ransoms did the general coffers fill: Did this in Caesar seem ambitious? When that the poor have cried, Caesar hath wept: Ambition should be made of sterner stuff: Yet Brutus says he was ambitious; And Brutus is an honourable man. You all did see that on the Lupercal I thrice presented him a kingly crown, Which he did thrice refuse: was this ambition? Yet Brutus says he was ambitious; And, sure, he is an honourable man.

For the sake of comparison, here is a charge actually given in one reported case: "I recall that the defendant, even though he offered evidence, he did not take the stand and testify in his own behalf. Now, I make mention of that fact for this purpose. I have told you that he had no responsibility to offer any evidence, had a right to but no responsibility to; that he owed you no duty to offer any evidence; that the State had the whole burden and has the whole burden of proof throughout this case. Now that being so, he had an absolute right under the law to try his lawsuit in the fashion that he decided that it ought to be tried. He had a right to offer no evidence. If he offered any, he had a right to remain off the stand. You can't punish any man for exercising a lawful right. So I give emphasis to this fact: The fact that the defendant did not testify does not permit you to speculate about why he did not. I have told you why he did not. He has exercised a lawful right. You may not take the position during your deliberations did he have something he didn't want us to know. He has exercised the lawful right and you may not hold it against him to any extent the fact that he did not testify. You must deal with what you have before you in this evidence and you may not hold against the defendant at all the fact that he did not testify."

Justice Marshall joins this opinion, with the exception of the first paragraph and footnote 5.

NOTES AND QUESTIONS

(1) Is it clear, as stated by Justice Stewart, that the *Griffin* Court "was there concerned only with *adverse* comment"? What of Justice Stevens' statement that in some trials — "perhaps when the whole story has been told by other witnesses or when the prosecutor's case is especially weak — the jury may not focus on the defendant's failure to testify"? That is, was *Griffin* concerned only with focusing in an adverse way on the defendant's silence, or was it concerned with focusing in any way in some cases? Justice Stevens remarked, "I cannot believe that any member of the *Griffin* majority would join today's opinion." Do you agree?

(2) Defendant Lakeside argued that jurors in some cases will "totally disregard the instruction, and affirmatively give weight to what they have been told not to consider at all." The Court rejected this argument, stating that it could not rely on "speculative assumptions so dubious as these." Was the assumption speculative in this case? Could the holding in *Bruton* be used to buttress the defendant's argument?

(3) The trial judge in *Smith v. State*, 370 So. 2d 312 (Ala. Crim. Ct. App. 1979), *cert. denied*, 370 So. 2d 319 (1979), instructed the jury as follows, over the defendant's objection:

> Now, during the course of this trial, the defendant has not testified during the course of this trial. I instruct you that no inference can be drawn from this fact. The defendant has a right under our Constitution not to be compelled to be a witness against himself.

Was this instruction error under *Lakeside*? The court on appeal reversed the conviction:

> [If] the trial court, in the absence of a request of the defendant, charge[s] the jury as to defendant's failure to testify, the charge should give defendant full benefit of the principle that no inference adverse to him should be drawn from his failure to testify. In the trial court's reference in its oral charge to the failure of defendant to testify, there was included the statement, "that no inference can be drawn" from the fact that defendant had not testified, but this, in our opinion, was a de-emphasis of the protective principle that the inference that is not to be drawn is an inference unfavorable to defendant. This is made even clearer by the last statement of the court on the subject, "The defendant has a right under our Constitution not to be compelled to be a witness against himself." The statement as to "no inference" in the instruction is subject to a reasonable construction by the jury, unacquainted with the refinements of the law on the subject, that no inference unfavorable to the State could be drawn from the failure of the State to have defendant testify as to his guilt or innocence. The statement as to defendant's constitutional right could have been reasonably construed as implying that if defendant had testified, he would have testified "against himself."

Smith, 370 So. 2d at 317-18. In sharp disagreement with the decision in *Lakeside*, the Pennsylvania Supreme Court in *Pennsylvania v. Edwards*, 637 A.2d 259 (Pa. 1993), held that it is *per se* reversible error for the trial judge to instruct the jury, over the defendant's objection, about the defendant's failure to testify. According to the Pennsylvania court, a *per se* rule "will avoid time consuming appeals arguing about harmless error and will clearly instruct trial judges as to how to proceed on this question." *Id.* at 580. *See also Bush v. State*, 775 N.E.2d 309, 310 (Ind. 2002) (holding that giving of jury instruction "that highlights a defendant's failure to testify" violates defendant's right against self incrimination provided in the Indiana Constitution, if instruction is given over defendant's objection).

(4) In *Carter v. Kentucky*, 450 U.S. 288 (1981), the trial judge refused a defendant's request for an instruction that the defendant is not compelled to testify and that if he does not, that fact cannot be used to infer guilt and should not prejudice him in any way.

The Supreme Court reversed the defendant's conviction, explaining:

> The freedom of a defendant in a criminal trial to remain silent "unless he chooses to speak in the unfettered exercise of his own free will" is guaranteed by the Fifth Amendment and made applicable to state criminal proceedings through the Fourteenth. And the Constitution further guarantees that no adverse inferences are to be drawn from the exercise of that privilege. Just as adverse comment on a defendant's silence "cuts down on the privilege by making its assertion costly," the failure to limit the jurors' speculation on the meaning of that silence, when the defendant makes a timely request that a prophylactic instruction be given, exacts an impermissible toll on the full and free exercise of the privilege.

Id. at 305.

§ 7.05 THE PROSECUTOR'S DUTY TO PRODUCE EXCULPATORY EVIDENCE

BRADY v. MARYLAND

United States Supreme Court
373 U.S. 83 (1963)

Opinion of the Court by Justice Douglas, announced by Justice Brennan.

Petitioner and a companion, Boblit, were found guilty of murder in the first degree and were sentenced to death, their convictions being affirmed by the Court of Appeals of Maryland. Their trials were separate, petitioner being tried first. At his trial Brady took the stand and admitted his participation in the crime, but he claimed that Boblit did the actual killing. And, in his summation to the jury, Brady's counsel conceded that Brady was guilty of murder in the first degree, asking only that the jury return that verdict "without capital punishment." Prior to the trial petitioner's counsel had requested the prosecution to allow him to examine Boblit's extrajudicial statements. Several of those statements were shown to him; but one dated July 9, 1958, in which Boblit admitted the actual homicide, was withheld by the prosecution and did not come to petitioner's notice until after he had been tried, convicted, and sentenced, and after his conviction had been affirmed.

Petitioner moved the trial court for a new trial based on the newly discovered evidence that had been suppressed by the prosecution. Petitioner's appeal from a denial of that motion was dismissed by the Court of Appeals without prejudice to relief under the Maryland Post Conviction Procedure Act. The petition for post-conviction relief was dismissed by the trial court; and on appeal the Court of Appeals held that suppression of the evidence by the prosecution denied petitioner due process of law and remanded the case for a retrial of the question of punishment, not the question of guilt. The case is here on certiorari.

The crime in question was murder committed in the perpetration of a robbery. Punishment for that crime in Maryland is life imprisonment or death, the jury being empowered to restrict the punishment to life by addition of the words "without capital punishment."

We agree with the Court of Appeals that suppression of this confession was a violation of the Due Process Clause of the Fourteenth Amendment.

In *Pyle v. Kansas*, 317 U.S. 213 (1942), we phrased the rule in broad terms:

> Petitioner's papers are inexpertly drawn, but they do set forth allegations that his imprisonment resulted from perjured testimony, knowingly used by the State authorities to obtain his conviction, and from the deliberate suppression by those same authorities of evidence favorable to him. These allegations sufficiently charge a deprivation of rights guaranteed by the Federal Constitution, and, if proven, would entitle petitioner to release from his present custody.

In *Napue v. Illinois*, 360 U.S. 264 (1959), we extended the test . . . when we said: "The same result obtains when the State, although not soliciting false evidence, allows it to go uncorrected when it appears."

We now hold that the suppression by the prosecution of evidence favorable to an accused upon request violates due process where the evidence is material either to guilt or to punishment, irrespective of the good faith or bad faith of the prosecution.

The principle is not punishment of society for misdeeds of a prosecutor but avoidance of an unfair trial to the accused. Society wins not only when the guilty are convicted but when criminal trials are fair; our system of the administration of justice suffers when any accused is treated unfairly. An inscription on the walls of the Department of Justice states the proposition candidly for the federal domain: "The United States wins its point whenever justice is done its citizens in the courts."[11] A prosecution that withholds evidence on demand of an accused which, if

---

[11] [2] Judge Simon E. Sobeloff when Solicitor General put the idea as follows in an address before the Judicial Conference of the Fourth Circuit on June 29, 1954: "The Solicitor General is not a neutral, he is an advocate; but an advocate for a client whose business is not merely to prevail in the instant case. My client's chief business is not to achieve victory but to establish justice. We are constantly reminded of the now classic words penned by one of my illustrious predecessors, Frederick William Lehmann, that the Government wins its point when justice is done in its courts."

made available, would tend to exculpate him or reduce the penalty helps shape a trial that bears heavily on the defendant. That casts the prosecutor in the role of an architect of a proceeding that does not comport with standards of justice, even though, as in the present case, his action is not "the result of guile," to use the words of the Court of Appeals.

The question remains whether petitioner was denied a constitutional right when the Court of Appeals restricted his new trial to the question of punishment. In justification of that ruling the Court of Appeals stated:

> There is considerable doubt as to how much good Boblit's undisclosed confession would have done Brady if it had been before the jury. It clearly implicated Brady as being the one who wanted to strangle the victim, Brooks. Boblit, according to this statement, also favored killing him, but he wanted to do it by shooting. We cannot put ourselves in the place of the jury and assume what their views would have been as to whether it did or did not matter whether it was Brady's hands or Boblit's hands that twisted the shirt about the victim's neck. . . . (I)t would be "too dogmatic" for us to say that the jury would not have attached any significance to this evidence in considering the punishment of the defendant Brady. Not without some doubt, we conclude that the withholding of this particular confession of Boblit's was prejudicial to the defendant Brady. . . . The appellant's sole claim of prejudice goes to the punishment imposed. If Boblit's withheld confession had been before the jury, nothing in it could have reduced the appellant Brady's offense below murder in the first degree. We, therefore, see no occasion to retry that issue.

. . . We usually walk on treacherous ground when we explore state law, for state courts, state agencies, and state legislatures are its final expositors under our federal regime. But, as we read the Maryland decisions, it is the court, not the jury, that passes on the "admissibility of evidence" pertinent to "the issue of the innocence or guilt of the accused." In the present case a unanimous Court of Appeals has said that nothing in the suppressed confession "could have reduced the appellant Brady's offense below murder in the first degree." We read that statement as a ruling on the admissibility of the confession on the issue of innocence or guilt. A sporting theory of justice might assume that if the suppressed confession had been used at the first trial, the judge's ruling that it was not admissible on the issue of innocence or guilt might have been flouted by the jury just as might have been done if the court had first admitted a confession and then stricken it from the record. But we cannot raise that trial strategy to the dignity of a constitutional right and say that the deprival of this defendant of that sporting chance through the use of a bifurcated trial denies him due process or violates the Equal Protection Clause of the Fourteenth Amendment.

Affirmed.

[Separate opinion of JUSTICE WHITE and dissenting opinion of JUSTICE HARLAN, with whom JUSTICE BLACK joined, are omitted].

NOTES

(1) In *Brady*, the Supreme Court held that it violates due process for a prosecutor to fail to produce evidence favorable and material to the issue of guilt or punishment, if that evidence is in the government's possession and the defendant requests it. What if the defendant fails to request such evidence, or the evidence is in the files of a law enforcement officer, unbeknownst to the prosecutor? In *United States v. Agurs*, 427 U.S. 97 (1976), the Court expressly recognized that "exculpatory information in the possession of the prosecutor may be unknown to defense counsel." Thus, concluded the Court, "[T]here are situations in which evidence is obviously of such substantial value to the defense that elementary fairness requires it to be disclosed even without a specific request."

In addition to its obligation to produce material and exculpatory information in the prosecutor's files, the government has an obligation to search the files of police and others acting on behalf of the prosecution. In *Kyles v. Whitley*, 514 U.S. 419 (1995), the Court explained: "[T]he individual prosecutor has a duty to learn of any favorable evidence known to the others acting on the government's behalf in the case, including the police. But whether the prosecutor succeeds or fails in meeting this obligation . . . the prosecution's responsibility for failing to disclose known, favorable evidence rising to a material level of importance is inescapable." Nevertheless, the state does not violate due process standards when it fails to preserve evidentiary material that might have been useful to a criminal defendant, provided the evidence is not destroyed in bad faith. *Arizona v. Youngblood*, 488 U.S. 51 (1988). Moreover, the government has no duty to obtain or produce evidence not in its possession. "*Brady* prohibits suppression of evidence, it does not require the government to act as a private investigator and valet for the defendant, gathering evidence and delivering it to opposing counsel." *U.S. v. Tadros*, 310 F.3d 999, 1005 (7th Cir. 2002).

(2) Evidence bearing on the credibility of a government witness is a regular source of "*Brady*" material. The Court in *Giglio v. United States*, 405 U.S. 150 (1972), emphasized that issues of witness credibility can fall within the *Brady* disclosure requirements, remarking: "When the 'reliability of a given witness may well be determinative of guilt or innocence,' nondisclosure of evidence affecting credibility falls within this general rule." The Ninth Circuit found such a *Giglio* violation in *United States v. Blanco*, 392 F.3d 382 (9th Cir. 2004). There, a defendant was convicted of drug crimes. He contended, on appeal, that the government violated *Brady* and *Giglio* by failing "to disclose material impeachment evidence" about a confidential informant. The Ninth Circuit agreed. "It is obvious . . . that the government suppressed information that should have been turned over to [the defendant] under *Brady* and *Giglio*. Any competent lawyer would have known that [the confidential informant]'s special immigration treatment by the INS and the DEA was highly relevant impeachment material."

In *Smith v. Cain*, 132 S. Ct. 627 (2012), the Court found a material *Brady* violation in the context of a habeas review after the government failed to produce files in the police investigation that conflicted with the single trial witness's identification of the defendant as the perpetrator of a five-person killing. At trial, the witness claimed he had been "face to face" with the killer. But notes from the police files indicated the witness had previously said that he could not identify the perpetrators other than their race and gender and that he could not identify the perpetrators because he could not see their faces. The court found that the prior inconsistent statements were "material" to a determination of the defendant's guilt because there was sufficient likelihood of a different result, undermining confidence in the outcome of the trial. The witness's testimony "was the *only* evidence linking Smith to the crime" and his statements "directly contradict his testimony." *Id.* at 630.

(3) On April 1, 2009, newly-confirmed United States Attorney General Eric Holder announced that he would move to dismiss the case pending against former U.S. Senator Ted Stevens. Stevens had been convicted by a jury on October 27, 2008, of multiple counts of lying on his Senate disclosure form to conceal gifts from oil industry executives and friends. General Holder decided to move to dismiss the case despite the conviction, explaining: "After careful review, I have concluded that certain information should have been provided to the defense for use at trial[.]" Nina Totenberg, *Justice Department Seeks to Void Stevens' Conviction*, National Public Radio, Apr. 1 2009. In other words, the prosecutors who tried Stevens' case violated their *Brady* obligations.

(4) Even when a prosecutor breaches her *Brady* obligations, it will be difficult for the accused to recover money damages in a subsequent civil rights lawsuit. For example, in *Connick v. Thompson*, 131 S. Ct. 1350 (2011), a district attorney's office conceded that prosecutors violated their *Brady* obligations in prosecuting the defendant for armed robbery. Nevertheless, the Court ruled that the accused was not entitled to damages against the district attorney's office under 42 U.S.C. § 1983 because a single incident of prosecutorial misconduct of this kind did not establish the necessary pattern of a failure to train prosecutors sufficient to show that the district attorney acted with deliberate indifference to the rights of the accused.

§ 7.06 THE PROSECUTOR'S MISCONDUCT

Prosecutors are constrained by the mandates of due process as already discussed in this Chapter. Furthermore, like other lawyers, prosecutors are subject to the ethical standards imposed by the state in which they practice law and to the local court rules where they prosecute. Beyond those obligations, prosecutors are cloaked with an additional responsibility to "seek justice." As Justice Sutherland explained in *Berger v. United States*, 295 U.S. 78, 88 (1935), in describing the responsibilities of the United States Attorney, the chief federal prosecutor in a district:

> The United States Attorney is the representative not of an ordinary party to a controversy, but of a sovereignty whose obligation to govern impartially is as compelling as its obligation to govern at all; and whose interest, therefore, in a criminal prosecution is not that it shall win a case, but that justice shall be done. As such, he is in a peculiar and very definite sense the servant of the law, the twofold aim of which is that guilt shall not escape or innocence suffer. . . . It is as much his duty to refrain from improper methods calculated to produce a wrongful conviction as it is to use every legitimate means to bring about a just one.

The American Bar Association enacted Rule 3.8, Model Rules of Professional Conduct, to identify specific ethical obligations of prosecutors.

Rule 3.8 Special Responsibilities of a Prosecutor

The prosecutor in a criminal case shall:

(a) refrain from prosecuting a charge that the prosecutor knows is not supported by probable cause;

(b) make reasonable efforts to assure that the accused has been advised of the right to, and the procedure for obtaining, counsel and has been given reasonable opportunity to obtain counsel;

(c) not seek to obtain from an unrepresented accused a waiver of important pretrial rights, such as the right to a preliminary hearing;

(d) make timely disclosure to the defense of all evidence or information known to the prosecutor that tends to negate the guilt of the accused or mitigates the offense, . . .

What specific conduct should a prosecutor avoid to ensure compliance with a defendant's due process rights and her obligations to act ethically and professionally?

Beyond the obvious, intentional wrongdoing, such as falsifying evidence, prosecutors must never charge a defendant with a crime that he or she knows is unsupported by probable cause. *See* R. 3.8(a), Model Rules of Prof'l Conduct.

Once the trial begins, a prosecutor should avoid concentrating her opening statement or closing argument on facts and issues that will evoke excessive emotion from the jury. *See United States v. Mooney*, 315 F.3d 54, 59 (1st Cir. 2002) (recognizing the impropriety of a prosecutor's opening statement, which contrasted the jury's sense of community safety with the armed robbery of a hotel, describing the comparison as "having no bearing on the defendant's guilt or innocence and improperly appeal[ing] to the jury to act in ways other than as dispassionate arbiters of the facts."). Prosecutors must avoid indirect comments on the defendant's failure to testify, *see supra* § 7.04, and they should never "vouch for" the truthfulness of a witness. A prosecutor's argument constitutes improper vouching "if the jury could reasonably believe that the prosecutor is indicating a personal belief in the witness' credibility, either through explicit personal assurance of the witness' veracity or by implicitly indicating that information not presented to the jury supports the witness' testimony." *United States v. Franklin-El*, 555 F.3d 1115, 1125 (10th Cir. 2009); *see also United States v. Combs*, 379 F.3d 564 (9th Cir. 2004).

Prosecutors must also be careful not to ask a witness to comment on another witness's credibility. *See United States v. Ramirez*, 537 F.3d 1075 (9th Cir. 2008). And, they must not argue to the jury their personal beliefs about a defendant's guilt. *See United States v. Young*, 470 U.S. 1, 7 (1985) (indicating that the line between acceptable and improper advocacy by prosecutors is not easily drawn and acknowledging that "[p]rosecutors sometimes breach their duty to refrain from overzealous conduct by commenting on a defendant's guilt and offering unsolicited personal views on the evidence."). Such personal comments are improper because they "can leave the impression that the prosecutor is basing his conclusion on evidence not presented to the jury and also may induce the jury to rely on the prosecutor's personal conclusion rather than an independent review of the evidence." *United States v. Meienberg*, 263 F.3d 1177, 1180 (10th Cir. 2001).

Finally, prosecutors should not comment on the courtroom behavior of a non-testifying defendant. The Fourth Circuit reversed a defendant's conviction for such a reference in *United States v. Carroll*, 678 F.2d 1208 (4th Cir. 1982). A jury had convicted Carroll of bank robbery, bank larceny, and assault with a dangerous weapon. A bank had been robbed by two masked men and one unmasked. The government contended that Carroll was the unmasked robber. The question of identity was a central issue in the trial, and the evidence presented was inconclusive and contradictory. Carroll did not testify.

During the government's closing argument, the prosecutor focused on interaction between Carroll and his lawyer during the trial, noting that at one point Carroll and his lawyer had examined bank surveillance photographs introduced as evidence. The prosecutor argued in closing:

> . . . and if you will recall, it was the defendant who was doing most of the pointing. It was the defendant who was explaining to his lawyer what the pictures were all about. It was the defendant who knew more about the pictures than the lawyer did. Now, I submit to you . . . the reason he knew so much about those pictures is because he was in the bank there at the robbery. That's the only reasonable explanation. If there was an explanation, an innocent explanation, as to why he knew more about the pictures than his lawyer did, I honestly don't know what it is.

Id. at 1209. In the court's instructions at the close of the case, the judge told the jury to "disregard the prosecutor's comments on the defendant's examination of the photographs," explaining that Carroll and his lawyer were provided with copies of the photos before trial. The Fourth Circuit, nevertheless, found the prosecutor's comments improper and reversed and remanded the case. The court explained that the prosecutor's comments violated Carroll's Fifth and Sixth Amendment rights. "Defendant had a Fifth Amendment right not to testify, and he elected to exercise that right. He also had a Fifth Amendment right not to be convicted except on the basis of evidence adduced against him." Likewise, the court explained that under the Sixth Amendment, Carroll had "the right to counsel, including the right to assist his counsel in his own defense." At bottom, the court decided that "the prosecutor erred in asking the jury to consider defendant's examination of the photographs as evidence of his participation in the bank robbery."

Chapter 8

GLOSSARY AND THE U.S. CONSTITUTION

A. GLOSSARY

ABANDONED PROPERTY — No warrant is required to seize evidence which has been abandoned. The doctrine may apply when evidentiary items have been discarded as well as when particular premises have been abandoned by the party in interest. The doctrine will not apply if the abandonment is the result of illegal police activity.

ACQUITTAL — A finding of not guilty in a criminal trial. The finding can be made by judge or jury, and the judge can direct an order for acquittal if there is insufficient evidence.

ADVERSARY JUDICIAL PROCEEDINGS — The stage at which the right to counsel attaches (under the 6th and 14th Amendments). This is chiefly important in determining the admissibility of pre-trial identification testimony. Thus, no testimony about a *post*-indictment lineup is admissible unless counsel was present, but testimony about a *pre*-indictment lineup is admissible without counsel being present.

AMICUS CURIAE — A "friend of the court," someone not a party to the action, i.e., not the defendant or the prosecution. Most often seen when filing a brief to argue a particular point.

APPEAL — The process by which a trial order or judgment is reviewed by a higher court. At the first appeal the defendant has an automatic right of review and normally a right to counsel. Thereafter, both are discretionary.

ARRAIGNMENT — The defendant's first official court appearance. At this stage the defendant is informed of the pending charge and enters a plea.

ARREST — The act of depriving an individual of his or her liberty of movement, ostensibly for the purpose of charging some criminal activity. To be constitutionally legitimate, the party making the arrest must have probable cause. An arrest may occur even though the party arrested is not taken into custody.

BURDEN OF PROOF — The jury is instructed that one of the parties has the obligation to demonstrate a particular point. On all elements of the offense the government has the burden of proof.

BRIEF — The written appellate argument filed by counsel for the parties. The defendant normally has the right to have a lawyer prepare a brief on his or her behalf.

CODE OF PROFESSIONAL RESPONSIBILITY — Bar Association statement of ethical considerations for both prosecuting and defense lawyers. The question arises in some cases as to whether a violation of the Code is an enforceable right of the defendant.

COLLATERAL ATTACK — A challenge to the defendant's conviction after all direct appeals have been exhausted. The most common forms are *habeas corpus* and *coram nobis*.

COMMENT ON THE FAILURE

TO TESTIFY — The prosecution may not mention to the jury the defendant's failure to testify at trial.

TO ASSIST IN PRE-TRIAL IDENTIFICATION — The prosecution may inform the jury of the defendant's refusal to participate in a required lineup or voice test.

CONFESSIONS — An inclusive term describing any incriminating statement made by the defendant. Many different legal considerations affect the validity of a confession: due process, right to counsel, self-incrimination.

CONFLICT OF INTEREST — Counsel has an obligation to defend his or her client without any contrary consideration. Therefore, the lawyer who by representing two defendants endangers the defense of one must move to withdraw because of the conflict of interest.

CONFRONTATION — Under the 6th Amendment Confrontation Clause the defendant has the right to physically confront adverse witnesses at trial. This right can be waived by the defendant's own disruptive conduct (*Allen*).

COUNSEL — *Gideon v. Wainwright* established that the 6th Amendment Right to Counsel (incorporated by the 14th Amendment) guaranteed all persons a lawyer at serious trials. Later cases extended the right to non-serious trial (*Argersinger*) and to both pre-and post-trial proceedings (*Coleman, Mempa*).

CRITICAL STAGE — The 6th Amendment Right to Counsel attaches at all pre-trial judicial proceedings (preliminary hearing, arraignment) which are critical, which would affect the outcome of the trial.

CUSTODY — Under *Miranda v. Arizona*, all statements given by the defendant while in custody in response to police interrogation are subject to the 5th Amendment self-incrimination strictures. Custody has been defined as subjecting a defendant to restraings on his freedom of movement comparable to those associated with a formal arrest.

DUE PROCESS CLAUSE — Found in the 5th and 14th Amendments, it has traditionally been used in criminal trials to ensure that the defendant receives a trial which is fundamentally fair. The incorporation doctrine, *infra*, is linked to the due process clause, as is the rule against the use of involuntary confessions and unreliable eyewitness identifications.

EXIGENT CIRCUMSTANCES — An open-ended category of situations in which a warrant will not be required for a search or seizure of evidence. A common case is the police responding to a report that a death or serious injury has occurred on a particular premises.

FELONY — A serious crime, normally defined by a set sentence of at least one year in prison.

FRISK — The superficial pat-down of the outer garments of a suspect for the purpose of determining whether the individual may be armed.

FRUIT OF THE POISONOUS TREE — The doctrine developed to determine if a distant result of an illegal police act will be admissible at trial. Hence, if there is an illegal search the question is whether a witness whose name was found during that search will be allowed to testify. The Supreme Court has stated that the test is whether the end product has the "taint" of the earlier illegality.

GRAND JURY — A group of citizens who receives evidence in closed proceedings and decides whether to issue an indictment against any individuals. In most jurisdictions the defendant has no right to participate in grand jury deliberations.

HABEAS CORPUS — After direct appeals have been exhausted, the defendant may petition the trial court claiming that his or her continued detention is unlawful. If a sufficient basis exists, the government may be called to establish the legality of the detention. A major limitation was imposed in 1976 (*Stone v. Powell*). The Supreme Court said there can be no federal habeas corpus relief if the state provided the defendant an opportunity for full and fair litigation of any search and seizure claim. In more recent legislation, Congress has further restricted the relief, including imposing a one year statute of limitations on such claims.

HABITUAL OFFENDER STATUTES — Many jurisdictions have laws which impose greater sentences on second or third time offenders (habitual offenders). These sentences involving imprisonment cannot be imposed unless the defendant was represented by counsel at both the earlier and present trials.

HARMLESS ERROR — If the defendant on appeal proves that evidence was erroneously admitted at trial the prosecution must then prove, beyond a reasonable doubt, that the error did not affect the outcome of the trial. Two important errors are not subject to this rule and result in an automatic reversal of conviction: violation of the right to a trial lawyer under *Gideon* and conflict of interest problems for counsel at trial.

IDENTIFICATION — Eyewitness identification is often relied on heavily by juries. Testimony as to identification is subject to both the due process clause and the right to counsel. The reliability of eyewitness identification has been heavily disputed.

IMMUNITY — The prosecution can grant a possible defendant immunity, promising not to prosecute her for an offense (or promising not to use a statement against her if she agrees to testify at another's trial).

IMPEACHMENT EVIDENCE — Evidence which is not used to prove the guilt of the defendant but is used to discredit the defendant's trial testimony. Even confessions obtained in violation of *Miranda* may be used to impeach the defendant's own conflicting trial statement (*Harris v. New York*). Many critics claim that juries use impeachment evidence in evaluating the guilt or innocence of the accused.

INCRIMINATION, PRIVILEGE AGAINST SELF — The 5th Amendment privilege (incorporated by the 14th Amendment) was designed to ensure that no one makes a statement against self-interest unless the person freely and intelligently wishes to do so. The *Miranda* decision construed the privilege to require four (4) warnings to have been given the accused if the government, in proving guilt, tries to use at trial statements made by the accused in response to custodial interrogation.

INDICTMENT — Issued by a grand jury, the indictment accuses the defendant of criminal conduct.

INDIGENT — Persons who cannot afford private counsel are entitled, under *Gideon* and *Miranda,* to a lawyer at state expense. Often the state appointed counsel will be a lawyer in a local public defender's office. The defendant need not be wholly destitute to be deemed indigent, but more uniform standards are difficult to articulate.

INEFFECTIVE ASSISTANCE — The defendant is entitled to be represented by a competent lawyer. It is error if the defendant's lawyer behaved in an incompetent fashion.

INEVITABLE DISCOVERY — If the police find evidence through unlawful means, the evidence will be admissible under the Fruit of the Poisonous Tree doctrine if the police would have necessarily found the evidence through lawful means (*Brewer v. Williams*).

INFORMANT — An individual who supplies law enforcement authorities with information relating to criminal activity. Such information received from victims and witnesses of crimes can normally be taken at face value. When information is received from an individual with purported contacts with the criminal milieu, to establish reliability it must be shown either that the individual has an established reputation for supplying authorities with accurate information or that the information has been corroborated.

INFORMATION — Issued by the prosecutor, rather than the grand jury, the information accuses the defendant of criminal conduct.

INTERLOCKING CONFESSIONS — Statements by two or more coconspirators which are essentially the same (are interlocking). These statements are not admissible at trial if the declarant is not available to testify (*Cruz v. New York*).

INTERROGATION — A major 5th Amendment self-incrimination issue is whether the defendant's statement resulted from interrogation. The Supreme Court has defined interrogation as police words or actions reasonably likely to elicit an incriminating response.

JOINDER — Related charges may be joined together against the defendant in a single trial. Defendants who have acted together (often when the charge is conspiracy) may all be joined together in a single trial.

JOINT REPRESENTATION — One lawyer may represent more than one defendant in the same trial. The lawyer is obliged to be sure there is no conflict of interest in such joint representation. Judges often inquire of both defendants and the lawyers concerning the possibility of a conflict.

KNOCK AND ANNOUNCE — Requirement under the Fourth Amendment that officers executing a warrant must, generally, advise occupants of their presence and intent to enter. An exception is available if the government shows that such notice would create a risk of danger or destruction of evidence.

LINEUP — The standard procedure for pretrial witness identification. Typically, five or six persons are brought before the witness. If the lineup is after indictment the defendant is entitled to have a lawyer present during the lineup.

MAGISTRATE — The Constitution requires a neutral magistrate in passing on warrant requests and in determining probable cause at preliminary hearings.

MISDEMEANOR — A less serious crime than a felony, normally defined by a set sentence such as less than one year in county jail.

NON-FRIVOLOUS ISSUES — Appointed counsel on appeal must file on behalf of the defendant a brief which raises all non-frivolous or arguable issues (*Anders*).

PAROLE — After being imprisoned the defendant may be freed prior to the normal release date, conditioned on adherence to certain rules. If any of the rules are broken, the government will move to have the defendant's parole revoked. A revocation hearing will be held where the defendant will be informed of the rules he or she is supposed to have broken and will, in some cases, be represented by counsel (*Morrissey, Gragnon*).

PLAIN VIEW DOCTRINE — Evidence of a crime may be seized by an official without a warrant if discovered in plain view. For the doctrine to apply, the officer must be legitimately on the location from which the evidence is observed or seized. The discovery of the evidence need not be inadvertent.

PLEA BARGAIN — In exchange for the defendant's promise to forego a trial, the government may promise to charge the defendant with a lesser crime or to ask the judge for a lesser sentence. When the "bargain" is reached the defendant pleads guilty and no trial is held.

PRELIMINARY HEARING (EXAMINATION) — A hearing before a magistrate to determine if there is sufficient evidence (probable cause) to justify a trial. This is typically used as an alternative to the grand jury proceeding, but here the defendant is entitled to participate and be represented by counsel.

PREPONDERANCE OF THE EVIDENCE — The normal standard by which civil cases are decided, "more likely than not." Rarely used in the criminal setting where the standard is "guilt beyond a reasonable doubt." The preponderance standard is used by the judge to determine the voluntariness of a confession.

PRESUMPTION OF INNOCENCE — The prosecution has the burden of proving the defendant committed each element of the stated offense(s). Unless this burden is met, beyond a reasonable doubt, the presumption of innocence will not be rebutted and the defendant must be found not guilty.

PROBABLE CAUSE — The constitutional standard for the determination of the sufficiency of the justification for an arrest or search. The concept is defined in *Beck v. Ohio*, 379 U.S. 89, 85 S. Ct. 223, 13 L. Ed. 2d 142 (1964), regarding arrests: "[W]hether at that moment the facts and circumstances within their knowledge and of which they had reasonably trustworthy information were sufficient to warrant a prudent man in believing that the petitioner had committed or was committing an offense."

PROBATION — In lieu of a sentence of imprisonment, the judge can suspend sentence and free the defendant on condition that the defendant adhere to certain rules. If the defendant breaks any of the rules the government will move to revoke probation. A revocation hearing will be held where the defendant will be informed of the rules he or she is supposed to have broken and will, in some cases, be represented by counsel (*Morrissey, Gagnon*).

REASONABLE DOUBT — The standard of proof in criminal cases. Unless the prosecution proves the defendant committed each element of the stated offense(s) beyond a reasonable doubt the defendant must be found not guilty.

RECOUPMENT STATUTES — Schemes devised to have indigents repay the state for the cost of their defense. While the statutes have been criticized as a matter of policy, the Supreme Court declared them constitutional (*Fuller v. Oregon*).

RELIABILITY — The major factor in deciding if eyewitness identification testimony will be admissible, "the linchpin in determining admissibility of identification testimony" (*Manson v. Brathwaite*).

RETROACTIVITY — The Supreme Court has said that the Constitution does not require that a court ruling be given retrospective application; it can simply apply to the named defendant and later defendants. In some cases the Court has given retroactive effect when the ruling concerns practices which affected the fairness of trials.

SELF REPRESENTATION — In the *Faretta* case, it was decided that a defendant has a right independent of the right of counsel to represent himself or herself at trial without the assistance of a lawyer.

SENTENCING — The process by which the judge decides on the punishment to be meted out to the convicted offender. At the sentencing hearing the judge will often rely heavily on a report (presentence, probation report) filed by a probation officer. The defendant has the right to have a lawyer present at the hearing.

SHOW-UP — A procedure for pre-trial witness identification where the suspect alone is brought before the witness. The process is thought to be suggestive, but if the identification is reliable the witness's identification testimony will be admissible at trial.

SPECIAL CIRCUMSTANCES — Prior to *Gideon v. Wainwright*, the Supreme Court would not find a constitutional violation in the failure to appoint trial counsel unless "special circumstances" were present. In the years just before its landmark opinion, the Court was easily convinced that special circumstances were present in many cases.

STANDING — The requirement that an individual be so affected by a purported constitutional violation that he or she will be heard to object to it. For example, an individual normally cannot on constitutional grounds object to the admissibility of a confession or other evidence improperly obtained from a third party, unless the individual can show that the confession or evidence was obtained as a result of the violation of his or her own rights.

SUPERVISORY POWERS — Apart from their power to enforce the Constitution, the federal courts also have the power to generally control the conduct of federal trials. Thus, when courts are required to inquire into the dangers of multiple (joint) representation this requirement is mandated under the court's supervisory power rather than the Constitution.

SUPPRESS — Exclude, delete. In criminal trials defense lawyers often move to suppress evidence claimed to be unlawful under the exclusionary rule.

SUSPENDED SENTENCE — After a term of imprisonment is imposed the judge may direct that the term not be served if certain probationary conditions are satisfied. If they ultimately are not, and probation is revoked, the original sentence is reinstated.

TEMPORARY DETENTION — An interference with freedom of movement, short of arrest. Such detentions require only reasonable suspicion, not probable cause. If the suspect is taken into custody or moved to a different location, a court is more likely to construe the facts as an arrest.

TOTALITY OF CIRCUMSTANCES — In deciding if a waiver of rights was valid the judge is to look to all the facts: what was the defendant told, when/ where did the waiver take place, how long had the defendant been in custody, etc.

UNIFORM CODE OF MILITARY JUSTICE — The statutory rules, Title 10 of the United States Code, which govern military trials for actions which would otherwise be civilian criminal matters.

VENUE — The place (district, county) where a portion of the crime took place and where the trial can be held. Venue can be changed and the trial moved if the judge concludes that a jury drawn from the area could not fairly decide the case.

VOLUNTARINESS — The standard by which the validity of confessions, among other matters, is determined. The judge decides this question of admissibility outside the hearing of the jury; the determination is made by a preponderance of the evidence.

WAIVER — The defendant may wish to give up, waive, his or her rights. For instance, after receiving *Miranda* warnings the defendant may wish to confess without the presence of a lawyer. The State must show that the defendant voluntarily waived the right to have an attorney present.

WARNINGS — In *Miranda v. Arizona*, the Supreme Court construed the 5th Amendment privilege against self-incrimination. Before the defendant's statement will be admissible at trial to prove guilt, if the statement resulted from custodial interrogation, the defendant must have been given four warnings, namely that:

1) He or she has the right to remain silent.

2) Anything he or she says can be used against the accused at trial
3) He or she has a right to have an attorney present during questioning.
4) If he or she cannot afford an attorney, but wishes one present, the State will provide a lawyer.

WARRANT — An order issued by a judicial official authorizing the bearer to arrest a particular individual or search a described place for enumerated items. A warrant is issued upon a showing of probable cause that an individual has committed a described crime or that evidence of criminal activity will be found at a designated location.

B. UNITED STATES CONSTITUTION — SELECTED PROVISIONS

Amendment IV

The right of the people to be secure in their persons, houses, papers, and effects, against unreasonable searches and seizures, shall not be violated, and no Warrants shall issue, but upon probable cause, supported by Oath or affirmation, and particularly describing the place to be searched, and the person or things to be seized.

Amendment V

No person shall be held to answer for a capital, or otherwise infamous crime, unless on a presentment or indictment of a Grand Jury, except in cases arising in the land or naval forces, or in the Militia, when in actual service in time of War or public danger; nor shall any person be subject for the same offense to be twice put in jeopardy of life or limb; nor shall be compelled in any criminal case to be a witness against himself, nor be deprived of life, liberty, or property, without due process of law; nor shall private property be taken for public use, without just compensation.

Amendment VI

In all criminal prosecutions, the accused shall enjoy the right to a speedy and public trial, by an impartial jury of the State and district wherein the crime shall have been committed, which district shall have been previously ascertained by law, and to be informed of the nature and cause of the accusation; to be confronted with the Witnesses against him; to have compulsory process for obtaining witnesses in his favor, and to have the Assistance of Counsel for his defense.

Amendment XIV

Section 1. All persons born or naturalized in the United States, and subject to the jurisdiction thereof, are citizens of the United States and of the State wherein they reside. No State shall make or enforce any law which shall abridge the privileges or immunities of citizens of the United States; nor shall any State deprive any person of life, liberty, or property without due process of law; nor deny to any person within its jurisdiction the equal protection of the laws.

TABLE OF CASES

[References are to pages]

A

B

[References are to pages]

[References are to pages]

C

[References are to pages]

D

[References are to pages]

E

F

G

[References are to pages]

H

[References are to pages]

I

J

[References are to pages]

K

L

[References are to pages]

M

[References are to pages]

[References are to pages]

N

O

P

[References are to pages]

R

[References are to pages]

S

[References are to pages]

T

[References are to pages]

U

V

W

[References are to pages]

Y

Z

INDEX

[References are to sections.]

[References are to sections.]

F

G

H

I

J

M

N

O

P

[References are to sections.]

[References are to sections.]

BILINGUALISM AND LANGUAGE DISABILITY